College Football Encyclopedia

The Authoritative Guide to 124 Years of College Football

Robert Ours

Prima Publishing
P.O. Box 1260BK
Rocklin, CA 95677
(916) 786-0426

Production by Melanie Field, Bookman Productions
Copyediting by Chris Bernard
Typography by Graphic World, Inc.
Interior design by Mike Yazzalino
Cover design by The Dunlavey Studio, Sacramento

Library of Congress Cataloging-in-Publication Data
Ours, Robert M.
   College football encyclopedia : the authoritative guide to 124 years of college football / by Robert M. Ours.
     p.   cm.
  ISBN 1-55958-217-0 pbk
  ISBN 1-55958-411-4
  1. Football—United States—Statistics. 2. National Collegiate Athletic Association—Records.   I. Title.
GV956.8.O87 1993
796.332'63'0973—dc20   92-20124
                                     CIP

94 95 96 97 98 RRD 10 9 8 7 6 5 4 3 2 1
Printed in the United States of America

How to Order:
Single copies may be ordered from Prima Publishing, P.O. Box 1260BK, Rocklin, CA 95677; telephone (916) 786-0426. Quantity discounts are also available. On your letterhead, include information concerning the intended use of the books and the number of books you wish to purchase.

CONTENTS

Preface   vii
Acknowledgments   ix

A BRIEF HISTORY OF COLLEGE FOOTBALL   1
ATLANTIC COAST CONFERENCE   7
    Clemson   12
    Duke   17
    Florida State   21
    Georgia Tech   25
    Maryland   30
    North Carolina   35
    North Carolina State   41
    Virginia   45
    Wake Forest   49

BIG EAST CONFERENCE   52
    Boston College   56
    Miami (Fla.)   60
    Pittsburgh   65
    Rutgers   71
    Syracuse   74
    Temple   79
    Virginia Tech   81
    West Virginia   85

BIG 8 CONFERENCE   93
    Colorado   100
    Iowa State   105
    Kansas   108
    Kansas State   112
    Missouri   114
    Nebraska   119
    Oklahoma   128
    Oklahoma State   136

BIG 10 CONFERENCE   141

Illinois   153
Indiana   156
Iowa   159
Michigan   163
Michigan State   172
Minnesota   176
Northwestern   180
Ohio State   182
Penn State   190
Purdue   202
Wisconsin   205

INDEPENDENTS   209

Army (U.S. Military Academy)   223
Cincinnati   229
East Carolina   232
Louisville   234
Memphis State   236
Navy (U.S. Naval Academy)   238
Notre Dame   243
Southern Mississippi   253
Tulane   256
Tulsa   259
William & Mary   263

PACIFIC-10 CONFERENCE   267

Arizona   274
Arizona State   277
California   282
Oregon   286
Oregon State   290
Southern California   292
Stanford   302
UCLA   306
Washington   313
Washington State   319

SOUTHEASTERN CONFERENCE   323

Alabama   331
Arkansas   340
Auburn   345
Florida   351
Georgia   356
Kentucky   363
Louisiana State   366

Mississippi   372
Mississippi State   378
South Carolina   381
Tennessee   384
Vanderbilt   392

SOUTHWEST CONFERENCE   396
Baylor   403
Houston   407
Rice   411
Southern Methodist   413
Texas   418
Texas A&M   426
Texas Christian University   432
Texas Tech   436

WESTERN ATHLETIC CONFERENCE   440
Air Force (U.S. Air Force Academy)   443
Brigham Young   445
Colorado State   450
Fresno State   452
Hawaii   457
New Mexico   460
San Diego State   463
Texas–El Paso   468
Utah   470
Wyoming   473

APPENDIX A   INDIVIDUAL AWARDS   478
Heisman Trophy Winners   478
Maxwell Award Winners   479
Outland Trophy Winners   479
Lombardi Award Winners   480
Coach of the Year Winners   480

APPENDIX B   TEAM NATIONAL
CHAMPIONS   483

APPENDIX C   ALL-TIME COACHING
RECORDS   485

APPENDIX D   TOP-10 TEAM AND
INDIVIDUAL STATISTICS, AND
MISCELLANEOUS RECORDS   487

Photo Credits   501

PREFACE

Attachments are formed at a young age, and my fascination with college football dates to 1946, the first year after World War II, when such storied players as Felix "Doc" Blanchard and Glenn Davis of Army, Johnny Lujack of Notre Dame, Charley Trippi of Georgia, Charlie "Choo Choo" Justice of North Carolina, and Bobby Layne of Texas were making sports headlines. I had already formed a lifelong attachment to my home-state West Virginia University Mountaineers, but was a fan too of the powerful Army team that had been undefeated national champion in 1944 and 1945.

The sunny autumn afternoon of November 9, 1946, still lives in my memory. That was the day on which Army, once more unbeaten, faced undefeated Notre Dame before more than 74,000 fans in New York's Yankee Stadium in one of those "game of the century" contests that crop up every decade or so. In those pre-television days, millions of fans throughout the nation listened to the game on radio, and I had expected to be one of those eager listeners. However, I spent a good part of the day playing sandlot football, and when I ran home and warmed up the big living room radio set, I found I was in time to hear only the last couple of plays of that classic 0–0 tie. My disappointment was great, but my interest in college football was even more deeply kindled. Over the next four and a half decades I watched thousands of games (live and on TV) on all levels of play, covered a number as a reporter for the Associated Press and several newspapers, read numerous histories of the sport, and immersed myself in statistics.

Many of the questions I had about various teams could not be researched through any one source. To find the answers, I needed to check NCAA tables and guides, individual school media guides, old newspaper accounts, and various books and magazines. Many of these turned out to be unreliable because of typographical or other errors. So I began to collate my own set of statistics and formulate lists, double-checking to make my information as accurate as possible. In the early 1980s I turned these statistical lists into a practical guide to 105 teams representing the majority of NCAA Division I-A schools and some Division I-AA schools (such as Ivy League members) with notable football pasts. In 1984 this was published as the *College Football Almanac*.

Later I expanded the original material to form this book, *College Football Encyclopedia*. Included here are records and highlights of 87 teams (reduced from the original 105 because of length), listing schools by conference affiliation, with a section on independents. The *Encyclopedia* covers all members of the Atlantic Coast, Big East, Big 8, Big 10, Pacific-10, Southeastern, Southwest, and Western Athletic conferences.

Each conference section in the *Encyclopedia* includes an introduction, with information and anecdotes about various members, and a list of annual conference champions. Under the school listings are the following: game results and individual stars for every season in which the team won at least 70 percent of its games or had at least an 8-4 record, including bowl results, or played in the Rose, Sugar, Orange, or Cotton bowls; complete bowl records; conference championships won (with co-championships indicated by an asterisk); final Top 20 rankings in the Associated Press and United Press International polls (the latter replaced by USA Today/Cable News Network in 1991, when the coaches' poll switched from UPI); won-lost-tied records against opponents that were met at least 10 times (records vary in a few instances when the schools disagree on whether some early games were played or whether to count forfeited contests); top coaches' records; and a miscellanea section that includes results of the first game played by each school, longest winning or unbeaten streaks, longest winless or losing strings, highest point totals for and against—all-time and since World War II—and individual honors, including complete lists of consensus All-Americans, Academic All-Americans, and winners of the Heisman Trophy, Maxwell Award, Outland Trophy, and Lombardi Award.

Appendices contain annual winners of the Heisman, Maxwell, Outland, and Lombardi awards; Coach of the Year winners; annual national champions chosen by the Associated Press and by UPI (the latter replaced by the USA Today/CNN poll in 1991); records of coaches who won at least 200 games on the major college level; and tables listing top-10 team and individual leaders in various statistical categories.

Robert Ours
Morgantown, W. Va.

ACKNOWLEDGMENTS

Thousands of individuals in the course of college football history have recorded the statistical information that makes up the bulk of the *College Football Encyclopedia*. I wish to acknowledge those record keepers and express special appreciation to the sports information directors, coaches, athletic directors, and staff personnel at the 87 schools included in the *Encyclopedia*, as well as staffers at the NCAA national headquarters, who provided information to me over the past several years. Particular thanks go to the SIDs who supplied photographs from their schools. I also wish to express my appreciation to the copyeditors and proofreaders who worked on the *Encyclopedia* to help make it as error-free and accurate as possible.

While I cannot list by name every person who aided in this endeavor, I would like to mention specifically:

Melanie Field, my production editor at Bookman Productions, who offered a number of excellent suggestions, kept the project moving efficiently, and was always a pleasure to work with.

Jennifer Basye, my editor at Prima Publishing, who directed the project in its early stages and made several key suggestions for the book's final format.

Andi Reese Brady, Karen Blanco, and Diane Durrett, all of Prima Publishing, who were consistently friendly and helpful.

My agent, Susan P. Urstadt, whose persistence and belief in the project is much appreciated.

My wife Ann, daughters Dorothy and Linda, and sisters Juanita, Evelyn, and Jean, along with some very special friends, also offered constant encouragement over the years it took to compile the *Encyclopedia*.

A BRIEF HISTORY OF COLLEGE FOOTBALL

Football has been an intercollegiate sport for nearly 125 years, but modern fans would scarcely recognize the game as played in the first contest on November 6, 1869, at New Brunswick, New Jersey. On that day Princeton and Rutgers, using a soccer-style round ball, played on a huge field (120 yards long and 75 yards wide) with 25 players on each side—and no officials. Rutgers scored 6 goals to the visitors' 4, after which the teams had dinner together. Princeton issued a challenge for a return match on its field and a week later (using Princeton's slightly different rules) got revenge by blanking Rutgers 8 goals to 0, then entertained the visitors with dinner accompanied by speeches and songs.

The sport grew slowly at first with Columbia, Yale, Harvard, and Stevens Tech fielding teams by 1875. In that year an egg-shaped, leather-covered rugby ball was adopted for play and normal procedure was to have three officials on hand: a judge from each team plus a referee to settle disputes.

In 1876 a crossbar was added to the goal posts at a height of 10 feet (in effect to the present day), and the field was reduced to nearly modern dimensions. At the same time the number of players on each side was lowered to 15.

Still, the sport did not really begin to resemble the modern game until former Yale player Walter Camp revised the rules in the early 1880s. Camp's 1880 revisions limited players to 11 on a side and established a scrimmage system for putting the ball in play. Two years later he instituted a system of downs for advancing the ball, requiring a team to make 5 yards in 3 downs (the current system of 4 downs to make 10 yards was not adopted until 1912). The first-down rule of 1882 required the marking of yard lines on the field and led to the term *gridiron*. It also inspired the first planned play strategy and verbal signals. With these changes the game spread more rapidly, and some 250 colleges were participating by the beginning of the twentieth century.

The nineteenth-century game was primarily one of brute force. There was no such thing as a forward pass, and strategy centered on formations such as the "flying wedge," in which the ball carrier was surrounded by a wedge of teammates (sometimes clasping hands). The best way to break the wedge was for a defensive player to throw himself into the legs of the onrushing foes, a particularly dangerous practice in the days when a stocking cap or heavy thatch of hair was considered adequate head protection.

The first real uniform, devised in 1877 by a Princeton player aptly named L. P. Smock, consisted of a tightly laced canvas jacket (difficult for opponents to get a grip on), along with black knee pants, stockings, and a jersey trimmed in orange. Other than extra cloth padding sometimes added to shoulders and over thighs and knees, there was little in the way of protection for players in the first decades of the game.

A number of deaths and serious injuries marred the game, and in 1894 the flying wedge and similar formations were outlawed. By 1896 only one offensive back could be in motion at the snap of the ball, and he could not be running forward. The rule requiring that at least seven offensive players be on the line of scrimmage at the snap of the ball was experimented with as early as 1895, but was not permanently adopted until 1910.

By 1894 the officiating crew had grown from a single referee (first required in 1885) to a trio: referee, umpire, and linesman. A field judge was added in 1907, the back judge not until 1955. The modern crew also includes a line judge and a side judge as well as a clock operator.

Keeping an eye on all of the players undoubtedly was difficult for the small officiating crews of the nineteenth century, but identifying their gridiron heroes was even more difficult for the fans. Although the first All-America team was named in 1889, numbers to identify individual players were not authorized until 1915, and it wasn't until 1937 that numerals were required on both the front and back of game jerseys. In 1967, this rule was further modified to require numbering according to position, with offensive players ineligible to receive forward passes assigned numbers in the 50–79 range.

Charges of extravagance in football erupted as early as 1878, when Princeton and Yale rented a field for $300 at Hoboken, New Jersey, to play before a crowd of 4,000 (Princeton won 1–0). But the sport really was becoming "big time" by 1903, when Harvard unveiled the first large concrete stadium designed specifically for football.

Despite rapidly growing popularity, college football was in serious trouble in the early twentieth century. The rule changes of the 1890s led to only a brief decrease in the rate of injury and death on the playing field. By 1905 the public outcry against the game's brutality was so great that several colleges (including Columbia, the third school to take up the sport) banned football, and others threatened to do so. Even President Theodore Roosevelt, hardly a pantywaist, demanded that reforms be made. The movement led to the creation of a body that five years later, in 1910, became known as the National Collegiate Athletic Association. The NCAA since has been the major power in formulating rule changes and in setting up and policing the procedures under which members operate their football programs.

The reform movement also brought about many changes in the rules and in player equipment by which the immensely popular modern game was created. By the early 1990s nearly 675 four-year colleges and universities (more than 550 of them members of the NCAA) were fielding teams, with home attendance records reaching more than 30 million a year for Divisions I-A and I-AA, 25 million of the total in the former. Probably the biggest change that opened up the game to more fan interest was the 1906 rule legalizing the forward pass. At first players could pass the ball only under narrow restrictions, and the pass did not become a major offensive tool until rules modifications in 1910 and 1912 allowed more passing flexibility.

Tiny West Virginia Wesleyan College had its first undefeated season in 1912, thanks partly to the pass. The Bobcats upset West Virginia 19–14 behind three touchdown passes (all caught by future college and professional Coach Earle "Greasy" Neale). In six previous games with the Mountaineers, all losses, the Bobcats had come no closer than 36–0. The following year unbeaten Notre Dame, then an excellent but little-known team, called the entire nation's attention to the new weapon when it utilized the pass to shock powerful Army 35–13 at West Point, the only defeat the Cadets suffered in 1913.

Through the 1920s various restrictions continued to discourage some coaches from utilizing a passing attack, but by the 1930s the rules had changed sufficiently (including a slight size modification of the ball to make it easier to grip) to make the pass an important factor in most offensive schemes.

A prolate spheroid had been required for the football's shape as early as 1896, but specific measurements did not go into effect until 1912. Further specifications in the 1920s and 1930s not only led to narrower, more bullet-shaped balls, but allowed the use of white or other-colored balls for night games. Rubber-covered balls were permitted in 1956, and size and composition specifications for the current ball have been in effect since 1982.

Scoring changes in the early twentieth century also helped popularize the game by increasing the value of touchdowns. When the first true football scoring system was devised in 1883 (replacing customary scoring procedures in which one point usually was awarded for advancing the ball across the goal in any fashion), kicking was emphasized. Field goals counted 5 points and conversions after touchdowns counted 4, while the TD itself counted only 2. That was changed the next year, and from 1884 through 1897 a TD counted 4 points and the conversion 2. The field goal remained king at 5 points. Safeties were increased from 1 point to 2 points in 1884 and have remained so since. In 1898 the value of a TD was raised to 5 points and the conversion was reduced to 1. The field goal remained at 5 points until 1904, when it was reduced to 4 points. In 1909 it was further lowered to its modern 3-point value. The touchdown was given its modern 6-point value in 1912.

No further point modifications were made until 1958, when teams were given the option of running or passing the ball across the goal line for 2 points after a TD, while a successful kicked conversion remained worth 1 point. At the same time the scrimmage line for conversion attempts was moved back one yard to the 3-yard line (it had been moved from the 5-yard line to the 2-yard line in 1929). A 1988 rule gave the defensive team 2 points for returning a blocked kick or an intercepted pass to the opponent's end zone during a conversion attempt. In 1992 this was extended to include a fumble return from any spot outside the end zone.

Goal posts, originally placed on the goal line, were moved back 10 yards to the rear of the end zone in 1927 in an effort to avert injuries by ball carriers or other players running into the uprights. That move, of course, increased the distance for field goal tries by 10 yards. In 1959, in a successful attempt to bring the field goal back into college prominence, the distance between the goal posts was increased nearly 5 feet to a width of 23 feet, 4 inches. Because of a proliferation of successful field goals over the next three decades, the rules makers in 1988 disallowed the kicking tee for field goal and conversion attempts, and in 1991 returned the goal post width to 18 feet, 6 inches.

Among the safety factors that have developed during the twentieth century are improvements in padding and headgear. Leather helmets came into use in the 1890s and were common before World War I, although head protectors were not required by the rules until 1939. Plastic helmets came into wide use after World War II. Shoulder pads, knee pads, hip pads, and thigh pads also evolved in the twentieth century, becoming larger and stronger in recent decades. Face masks were made legal in 1951, and mouthpieces became required two decades later.

The modern football gladiator, nearly hidden by his protective equipment, has become largely a specialist playing either offense or defense, or perhaps coming onto the field just to punt or kick field goals and extra points. No substitutions were allowed in the early years of the game until rules in the late 1880s permitted substitutions for injured or disqualified players. Even during a brief period of unlimited substitution in 1898–1905, football was a game for players who participated in all aspects. Two-platoon football was made possible, with minor restrictions, under rule changes in 1941 but was not really put into practice until the last year of World War II. Unlimited substitution was allowed in 1948, but single-platoon football was reestablished under the 1953 rules, and free substitution and two-platoon football did not return to full flower until 1965.

College football's rich heritage and lore are sometimes lost in these days of emphasizing the present and hyping superstars as "the greatest ever" at running, passing, kicking, or whatever. More's the pity, for the sport has thrived for more than a century, and the modern game owes much to the coaches and players who developed it from its early stages of soccer and rugby-style play to the innovative techniques of the decades between the world wars to the highly popular game of the past four decades. Some of the most colorful stories from college football's past involve schools now classified as Division I-AA, Division II, or Division III—or ones that do not field teams at all in the late twentieth century.

Are the players of the present better than those of the past? Statistics can be used to "prove" they are, but are figures alone a fair indication of the relative merits of players from different eras?

Most teams played 8 or 9 games a season in the decades preceding World War II, compared to the 11 or 12 games a season played by modern teams. The game of the 1920s and 1930s averaged 110 plays; the modern game averages more than 150. Also, players in the pre-World War II years played both offense and defense, as did those of 1953 to the mid-1960s, sometimes going entire games with no rest on the bench.

In addition, records are often incomplete for players who performed in the years before the NCAA started keeping official statistics in 1937. In many cases game or even season statistics simply no longer exist. Before 1937, such categories as punt or kickoff-return yardage and pass-reception yardage were often totaled together with rushing yardage to give a player's "offense" for a game; NCAA figures themselves are not totally complete or reliable for those years. NCAA figures since World War II are reliable, but from 1937 through 1969 NCAA season champions were based on totals; since 1970 most categories have been based on per-game average.

Thus, it is difficult to compare accomplishments of players from different eras. And if intangibles are not considered, such comparisons can be even more misleading. How can an offensive lineman be compared with a running back or quarterback in value to a team? What about inspirational qualities not reflected in statistics?

Still, statistics are a starting point for arguing merits of individuals and teams, and the heart of this book is a compilation of facts and figures concerning football histories of 86 schools that make up the bulk of Division I-A members—plus William and Mary, an institution representing schools that used to play at the top level and successfully compete these days at the Division I-AA level while maintaining high academic standards. Because of its special status William and Mary, which begins play in the Yankee Conference in 1993, is listed with the Independents in this book.

ABBREVIATION KEYS

ACC—Atlantic Coast Conference
avg—average
B—back
C—center
DB—defensive back
DE—defensive end
DL—defensive lineman
DT—defensive tackle
E—end
ex pts—extra points
FB—fullback
FG—field goal
FL—flanker
frosh—freshman
G—guard
HB—halfback
int—interceptions
K—kicker
LB—linebacker
MAC—Mid-American Conference
MG—middle guard
MVC—Missouri Valley Conference
NG—nose guard
NT—nose tackle
off—offense
OG—offensive guard
OL—offensive lineman

OT—offensive tackle
P—punter
pass—passing
pass rec—pass receptions
PCAA—Pacific Coast Athletic
    Association
PCC—Pacific Coast Conference
pts—points
QB—quarterback
RB—running back
rush—rushing
S—safety
SC—Southern Conference
SE—split end
SEC—Southeastern Conference
soph—sophomore
SWC—Southwest Conference
T—tackle
TB—tailback
TD—touchdown
TE—tight end
U—unranked
WAC—Western Athletic
    Conference
WB—wingback
WR—wide receiver
yds—yards

Note: For certain players (generally from college football's earlier years), team-position information is not available; these players therefore have no position given to them.

ATLANTIC COAST CONFERENCE

Founded on May 8, 1953, the Atlantic Coast Conference (ACC) was the second league formed from the sprawling Southern Conference (SC) in a 20-year period. In 1932 the 13 members west and south of the Carolinas, Virginia, and Maryland pulled out to begin football play in 1933 as the Southeastern Conference (SEC), leaving 10 schools still in the SC—Clemson, Duke, Maryland, North Carolina, North Carolina State, South Carolina, Virginia, Virginia Military Institute, Virginia Tech, and Washington and Lee. In 1936, however, six new members—The Citadel, Davidson, Furman, Richmond, Wake Forest, and William and Mary—were added to the old conference. Virginia withdrew the following year, but George Washington was admitted in 1941 and West Virginia in 1950. Thus, by mid-century the SC had once again become a motley league of 17 members, making it impossible to play a round-robin schedule for the championship.

Representatives of Clemson, Duke, Maryland, North Carolina, North Carolina State, South Carolina, and Wake Forest, meeting at Sedgefield Inn near Greensboro, North Carolina, agreed in the spring of 1953 to withdraw from the SC and set up a new league to be known as the Atlantic Coast Conference. Competition for the football crown began that fall.

On December 4, 1953, Virginia was admitted as the eighth member, and the league was stable from then until June 30, 1971, when South Carolina withdrew to compete as an independent. The ACC operated as a seven-member conference for several years while considering applications from a number of schools. On April 3, 1978, Georgia Tech, which had withdrawn from the SEC in 1964, was admitted to the ACC effective July 1, 1979, although the Yellow Jackets were not eligible for the football title until 1983.

There was no further change in membership until 1990, when Florida State was admitted, raising the number of ACC schools to nine for the first time. The Seminoles began conference play in 1992 with a league championship in their first year.

FACTS AND ODDITIES ON ACC MEMBERS

The ACC had a national champion in its first year of existence when Jim Tatum's powerful Maryland team went 10–0 and, despite a 7–0 loss to Oklahoma in the Orange Bowl, received most of the votes for the 1953 football title. Danny Ford's 1981 Clemson team finished 11–0 and beat Nebraska 22–15 in the Orange Bowl to earn the second national championship won by an ACC school. In 1990 Bobby Ross directed Georgia Tech to a share of the ACC's third national title, with a 10–0–1 record (the tie was with North Carolina 13–13) topped by a 45–21 win over Nebraska in the Florida Citrus Bowl.

Georgia Tech won two national titles before entering the ACC, winning outright with a 9–0 record in 1917 and earning a share of the crown in 1928 with a 9–0 record followed by a Rose Bowl win over California 8–7.

Although ACC players are well represented in the All-America selections, none has won the Heisman Trophy or the Maxwell Award, given to the nation's top player. Virginia TB Bill Dudley won the Maxwell in 1941, long before the ACC was founded. League members have supplied winners of the other major awards.

The Outland Trophy was won by T Mike McGee of Duke, 1959; DE Randy White of Maryland, 1974; and C Jim Ritcher of North Carolina State, 1979. Ritcher was one of only two centers ever to win the award. In addition, Maryland T Dick Modzelewski won the Outland in 1952, a year before the ACC started competition. Winners of the Lombardi Award were Maryland DE Randy White, 1974; and Florida State LB Marvin Jones, 1992.

ACC coaches who received national Coach of the Year awards were Jim Tatum of Maryland, 1953; Danny Ford of Clemson, 1981; and Bobby Ross of Georgia Tech, 1990. William A. Alexander of Georgia Tech won in 1942, before the ACC was formed.

Florida State coach Bobby Bowden is one of only two active coaches in the nation to enter the 1993 season with more than 200 victories, having compiled a record of 227–77–3 between 1959 and 1992, and is the ACC coach with the current longest tenure. Since taking the head coaching position at Florida State in 1976, Bowden has compiled a record of 154–45–3.

Bowden coached for 18 years at three schools—Samford, West Virginia, and Florida State—before one of his teams played a tie game. That occurred in 1984 when Bowden's Seminoles were tied by Memphis State 17–17. At the end of that season Florida State played another tie game in the Florida Citrus Bowl, tying Georgia by the same 17–17 score. The only other tie game Bowden coached was in 1986, when the Seminoles tied North Carolina 10–10.

Coaches who won at least 100 games at schools now in the ACC were John Heisman, Wallace Wade, Bobby Dodd, and Frank Howard. Heisman was 19–3–2 at Clemson in 1900–1903 and 102–29–6 at Georgia

Tech in 1904–1919. At the latter, he had four unbeaten teams and one national champion. Wade was 110–36–7 at Duke in 1931–1941 and 1946–1950 with six conference titles and two Rose Bowl teams unbeaten in regular season. Dodd was 165–64–8 at Georgia Tech for 1945–1966 with two conference titles, thirteen bowl teams, and two unbeaten teams. Howard was 165–118–12 at Clemson for 1940–1969 with eight conference titles, six bowl teams, and two unbeaten teams.

The first Southern player to make consensus All-America was B Eugene Mayer of future ACC member Virginia in 1915. That year Mayer scored six touchdowns in a 74–0 trouncing of Richmond. As a junior the previous year he had 21 TDs and 142 points. Mayer had 48 TDs and 312 points in his four years on the varsity, 1912–1915.

Maryland is credited with being the first college football team to put players' names on the backs of jerseys. That took place in 1961 under Coach Tom Nugent when the Terps opened the season with a 14–6 win over Southern Methodist.

Two of the most-played football rivalries in the nation involve ACC teams. North Carolina and Virginia have met 97 times since 1892, tying that series for sixth longest in the country. Through the 1992 season the series stood at 53–40–4 in favor of the Tar Heels (although Virginia claims it stands at 52–41–4 because of a 1956 forfeit). Clemson and former ACC member South Carolina have met 90 times since 1896, tying for fifteenth place in the longest series listings. That series stood at 53–33–4 in Clemson's favor through 1992.

Among ACC teams only the Clemson nickname, Tigers, is a common one on the major college football level. Unusual nicknames on the Division I-A level are carried by the Duke Blue Devils, Florida State Seminoles, Georgia Tech Yellow Jackets or Rambling Wreck, Maryland Terrapins or Terps, North Carolina Tar Heels, North Carolina State Wolfpack, Wake Forest Demon Deacons, and Virginia Cavaliers or Wahoos.

Georgia Tech at one time was known as the Golden Tornado and informally as the Engineers, but Yellow Jackets was a long-established nickname at the time of the school's entrance into the ACC. The name apparently was based on colors worn by Georgia Tech fans in the school's early days of football. Maryland teams were first known as Farmers and then as Old Liners before adopting the nickname Terrapins.

North Carolina's nickname, Tar Heels, comes from the state nickname, the Tar Heel state, a term dating either to the Revolutionary War or Civil War periods depending on which legend is followed. North Carolina State had been known as the Red Terrors for a number of years before 1922, when a disgruntled fan complained to State officials that the school never would have a winning record so long as the players behaved on and off the field like a wolfpack. Players and fans liked the simile and adopted it as the official nickname.

Virginia teams usually are referred to by the media as Cavaliers, an emblem dating to 1923, when the winning entry in an alma-mater contest was "The Cavalier Song." The song never caught on, but it inspired the new nickname. Virginia teams previously had been called V-Men or Virginians. The favorite nickname of many students and alumni, however, is Wahoos, derived from a cheer dating to the early 1890s. The term was incorporated into "The Good Old Song," sung since 1893.

Wake Forest has not had many winning seasons in its football history, but in 1923–1925 the team went 19–7–1 under Coach Hank Garrity. Following a win over Duke during that period, the editor of the school newspaper, Mayon Parker, started calling the squad the Demon Deacons, and the name caught on. Previously, Wake Forest teams had been known as the Baptists or simply the Old Gold and Black.

Maryland is unique on the college scene in having two sets of official colors—red and white, and black and gold. This stems from the fact that Maryland uses the colors of the official state flag.

North Carolina's blue and white came from the colors of two literary societies in the late nineteenth century. The light blue is termed Carolina Blue, but also could be termed powder blue, sky blue, or Columbia Blue. North Carolina State's red and white were adopted in 1895 to replace the old standards, pink and blue.

Clemson for years wore uniforms of pale purple and gold, but in the 1930s Coach Jess Neely changed the colors to Northwestern purple and burnt orange in an attempt to find a colorfast uniform that would not fade in the laundry. Orange quickly became a favorite with the fans. Orange had long been popular at Virginia. A mass meeting of students at that university in early spring of 1889, a year after the school's first football team was formed, adopted orange and blue as the school's official colors. Wake Forest's colors of old gold and black date at least to 1895.

ALL-TIME ATLANTIC COAST CONFERENCE CHAMPIONS

Annual Champion	ACC Record	Regular Season and Bowl	
1953 Duke	4–0	7–2–1	
Maryland	3–0	10–0	Orange (L)
1954 Duke	4–0	7–2–1	Orange (W)
1955 Duke	4–0	7–2–1	
Maryland	4–0	10–0	Orange (L)
1956 Clemson	4–0–1	7–1–2	Orange (L)
1957 N.C. State	5–0–1	7–1–2	
1958 Clemson	5–1	8–2	Sugar (L)
1959 Clemson	6–1	8–2	Bluebonnet (W)
1960 Duke	5–1	7–3	Cotton (W)
1961 Duke	5–1	7–3	
1962 Duke	6–0	8–2	
1963 North Carolina	6–1	8–2	Gator (W)
N.C. State	6–1	8–2	Liberty (L)
1964 N.C. State	5–2	5–5	

(continued)

ALL-TIME ATLANTIC COAST
CONFERENCE CHAMPIONS *(continued)*

Annual Champion	ACC Record	Regular Season and Bowl	
1965 Clemson	4–3	5–5	
N.C. State	4–3	6–4	
1966 Clemson	6–1	6–4	
1967 Clemson	6–0	6–4	
1968 N.C. State	6–1	6–4	
1969 South Carolina	6–0	7–3	Peach (L)
1970 Wake Forest	5–1	6–5	
1971 North Carolina	6–0	9–2	Gator (L)
1972 North Carolina	6–0	10–1	Sun (W)
1973 N.C. State	6–0	8–3	Liberty (W)
1974 Maryland	6–0	8–3	Liberty (L)
1975 Maryland	5–0	8–2–1	Gator (W)
1976 Maryland	5–0	11–0	Cotton (L)
1977 North Carolina	5–0–1	8–2–1	Liberty (L)
1978 Clemson	6–0	10–1	Gator (W)
1979 N.C. State	5–1	7–4	
1980 North Carolina	6–0	10–1	Bluebonnet (W)
1981 Clemson	6–0	11–0	Orange (W)
1982 Clemson	6–0	9–1–1	
1983 Maryland	5–0	8–3	Florida Citrus (L)
1984 Maryland	5–0	8–3	Sun (W)
1985 Maryland	6–0	8–3	Cherry (W)
1986 Clemson	5–1–1	7–2–2	Gator (W)
1987 Clemson	6–1	9–2	Florida Citrus (W)
1988 Clemson	6–1	9–2	Florida Citrus (W)
1989 Duke	6–1	8–3	All-American (L)
Virginia	6–1	10–2	Florida Citrus (L)
1990 Georgia Tech	6–0–1	10–0–1	Florida Citrus (W)
1991 Clemson	6–0–1	9–1–1	Florida Citrus (L)
1992 Florida State	8–0	10–1	Orange (W)

CLEMSON *(Tigers; Burnt Orange and Purple)*

NOTABLE TEAMS

1900 (6–0) *Won:* Davidson 64–0, Wofford 21–0, South Carolina 51–0, Georgia 39–5, Virginia Tech 12–5 (1st meeting), Alabama 35–0. *Noteworthy:* had 1st undefeated season in 1st year under John Heisman.

1901 (3–1–1) *Won:* Guilford 122–0, Georgia 29–5, North Carolina 22–10. *Lost:* Virginia Tech 17–11. *Tied:* Tennessee 6–6 (1st meeting).

1902 (6–1) *Won:* N.C. State 11–5, Georgia Tech 44–5, Furman 28–0, Georgia 36–0, Auburn 16–0, Tennessee 11–0. *Lost:* South Carolina 12–6. *Stars:* QB John Maxwell, E Hope Sadler. *Noteworthy:* won Southern Intercollegiate Athletic Association title.

1903 (4–1–1) *Won:* Georgia 29–0, Georgia Tech 73–0, N.C. State 24–0, Davidson 24–0. *Lost:* North Carolina 11–6. *Tied:* Cumberland 11–11. *Stars:* Maxwell, FB Jock Hanvey, frosh G O.L. Derrick, E Vet Sitton. *Noteworthy:* Heisman's last team.

1906 (4–0–3) *Won:* Georgia 6–0, Auburn 6–4, Tennessee 16–0, Georgia Tech 10–0. *Tied:* Virginia Tech 0–0, N.C. State 0–0, Davidson 0–0. *Noteworthy:* 1st year under Bob Williams.

1917 (6–2) *Won:* Presbyterian 13–0, Furman 38–0, South Carolina 21–13, Wofford 27–16, The Citadel 20–0, Florida 55–7. *Lost:* Auburn 7–0, Davidson 21–9. *Star:* C Mutt Gee. *Noteworthy:* 1st year under E.A. Donahue.

1918 (5–2) *Won:* Camp Sevier 65–0, South Carolina 39–0, The Citadel 7–0, Furman 68–7, Davidson 7–0. *Lost:* Georgia Tech 28–0, Camp Hancock 66–13.

1919 (6–2–2) *Won:* Erskine 52–0, Davidson 7–0, Tennessee 14–0, South Carolina 19–6, Presbyterian 19–7, The Citadel 33–0. *Lost:* Georgia Tech 28–0, Auburn 7–0 in successive early games. *Tied:* Furman 7–7, Georgia 0–0. *Stars:* G L.M. Lightsey, T R.C. Potts, QB Stumpy Banks.

1928 (8–3) *Won:* Newberry 30–0, Davidson 6–0, Auburn 6–0, N.C. State 7–0, Erskine 52–0, South Carolina 32–0, Virginia Military Institute (VMI) 12–0, Furman 27–12. *Lost:* Mississippi 26–7, Florida 27–6, The Citadel 12–7. *Stars:* C O.K. Pressley, B O.D. Padgett (7 TDs).

1929 (8–3) *Won:* Newberry 68–0, Davidson 32–

14, Auburn 26–7, N.C. State 26–0, Wofford 30–0, South Carolina 21–14, The Citadel 13–0, Furman 7–6. *Lost:* Kentucky 44–6, VMI 12–0, Florida 13–7 in consecutive late games. *Star:* TB Goat Mc-Millan (9 TDs).

1930 (8–2) *Won:* Presbyterian 28–7, Wofford 32–0, The Citadel 13–7, N.C. State 27–0, Newberry 75–0, South Carolina 20–7, VMI 32–0, Furman 12–7. *Lost:* Tennessee 27–0, Florida 27–0. *Stars:* TB Maxcy Welch (10 TDs), C Red Fordham, E Bob Jones. *Noteworthy:* Josh Cody's last team.

1938 (7–1–1) *Won:* Presbyterian 26–0, Tulane 13–10, South Carolina 34–12, Wake Forest 7–0, George Washington 27–0, Kentucky 14–0, Furman 10–7. *Lost:* unbeaten Tennessee 20–7. *Tied:* VMI 7–7. *Stars:* FB Don Willis, TB Banks McFadden (5 TDs), WB Shad Bryant (5 TDs), E Gus Goins.

1939 (9–1) *Won:* Presbyterian 18–0, N.C. State 25–6, South Carolina 27–0, Navy 15–7, George Washington 13–6, Wake Forest 20–7, Southwestern (Tenn.) 21–6, Furman 14–3. *Lost:* unbeaten Tulane 7–6. *Stars:* McFadden (977 yds and 10 TDs total off, 43.3-yd punting avg), soph FB Charlie Timmons (556 yds rush), Bryant, soph E Joe Blalock (15 pass rec for 322 yds), soph T George Fritts, C Bob Sharpe. *Noteworthy:* Jess Neely's last team. Made 1st bowl appearance, beating Boston College 6–3 in Cotton Bowl behind Timmons (115 yds and a TD rush).

1940 (6–2–1) *Won:* Presbyterian 38–0, Wofford 26–0, N.C. State 26–7, Wake Forest 39–0, South Carolina 21–13, Furman 13–7. *Lost:* Tulane 13–0, Auburn 21–7 in successive late games. *Tied:* Southwestern (Tenn.) 12–12. *Stars:* Blalock (10 pass rec for 211 yds), Fritts, Timmons. *Noteworthy:* won 1st SC title in 1st year under Frank Howard.

1941 (7–2) *Won:* Presbyterian 41–12, VMI 36–7, N.C. State 27–6, Boston College 26–13, George Washington 19–0, Wake Forest 29–0, Furman 34–6. *Lost:* South Carolina 18–14, Auburn 28–7. *Stars:* Timmons (635 yds rush, 9 TDs), Blalock (13 pass rec for 240 yds), Fritts.

1948 (11–0) *Won:* Presbyterian 53–0, N.C. State 6–0, Mississippi St. 21–7, South Carolina 13–7, Boston College 26–19, Furman 41–0, Wake Forest 21–14, Duquesne 42–0, Auburn 7–6, The Citadel 20–0. *Stars:* TB Bobby Gage (799 yds pass), soph WB Ray Mathews (646 yds rush, 13 TDs, 5 int), soph E Oscar Thompson (19 pass rec for 333 yds),

G Frank Gillespie. *Noteworthy:* Nation's most-improved team won 2nd SC title. Edged Missouri 24–23 in Gator Bowl as soph FB Fred Cone scored 2 TDs and Gage passed for 112 yds and a TD.

1950 (9–0–1) *Won:* Presbyterian 55–0, Missouri 34–0, N.C. State 27–0, Wake Forest 13–12, Duquesne 53–20, Boston College 35–14, Furman 57–2 (10th straight over Paladins), Auburn 41–0. *Tied:* South Carolina 14–14. *Stars:* Cone (845 yds rush, 15 TDs), E Glenn Smith (22 pass rec for 498 yds), LB Wyndie Wyndham, DBs Jackie Calvert and soph Fred Knoebel (6 int). *Noteworthy:* edged unbeaten Miami (Fla.) 15–14 in Orange Bowl as DL Sterling Smith tackled Miami runner for safety in last quarter; Cone ran for 81 yds and a TD and soph TB Billy Hair passed for 178 yds and other TD.

1951 (7–3) *Won:* Presbyterian 53–6, Rice 20–14, N.C. State 6–0, Wake Forest 21–6, Boston College 21–2, Furman 34–14, Auburn 34–0. *Lost:* Pacific 21–7, South Carolina 20–0 in successive mid-season games. *Stars:* Hair (1,004 yds pass, 698 rush), Glenn Smith (39 pass rec for 632 yds and 7 TDs), Knoebel (7 int). *Noteworthy:* lost to Miami (Fla.) 14–0 in Gator Bowl; had 3 passes intercepted inside Miami's 20-yd line.

1955 (7–3) *Won:* Presbyterian 33–0, Virginia 20–7 (1st meeting), Georgia 26–7 (1st over Bulldogs in 14 games since 1914), South Carolina 28–14, Wake Forest 19–13, Virginia Tech 21–16, Furman 40–20. *Lost:* Rice 21–7, unbeaten Maryland 25–12, Auburn 21–0. *Stars:* Bs Joel Wells (782 yds rush) and Joe Pagliei (7 TDs, 10 pass rec for 233 yds).

1956 (7–2–2) *Won:* Presbyterian 27–7, N.C. State 13–7, Wake Forest 17–0, South Carolina 7–0, Virginia Tech 21–6, Virginia 7–0, Furman 28–7. *Lost:* Miami (Fla.) 21–0. *Tied:* Florida 20–20, Maryland 6–6. *Stars:* Wells (803 yds rush, 8 TDs), QB Charlie Bussey, G John Grdijan. *Noteworthy:* Won 1st ACC title. Lost to Colorado 27–21 in Orange Bowl as 2nd half rally fell short; Wells ran for 125 yds and 2 TDs (including 58-yd run).

1957 (7–3) *Won:* Presbyterian 66–0, Virginia 20–6, South Carolina 13–0, Rice 20–7, Maryland 26–7, Wake Forest 13–6, Furman 45–6 (15th straight over Paladins). *Lost:* North Carolina 26–0 (1st meeting since 1915), N.C. State 13–7, Duke 7–6 (1st meeting since 1936). *Stars:* soph Harvey White (841 yds pass), Whitey Jordan (12 pass rec for 369 yds), RBs Bob Spooner (5 TDs) and soph Bill Mathis (5 TDs).

1958 (8–3) *Won:* Virginia 20–15, North Carolina 26–21, Maryland 8–0, Vanderbilt 12–7, Wake Forest 14–12, N.C. State 13–6, Boston College 34–12, Furman 36–19. *Lost:* South Carolina 26–6, Georgia Tech 13–0. *Stars:* White (5 TDs rush), C Bill Thomas, T Jim Padgett, E Ray Masneri. *Noteworthy:* Won 2nd ACC crown. Lost to unbeaten national champ Louisiana St. (LSU) 7–0 in Sugar Bowl despite edge in total yds.

1959 (9–2) *Won:* North Carolina 20–18, Virginia 47–0, N.C. State 23–0, South Carolina 27–0, Rice 19–0, Duke 6–0, Wake Forest 33–31, Furman 56–3. *Lost:* Georgia Tech 16–6, Maryland 28–25. *Stars:* White (770 yds pass), FB Doug Cline (482 yds rush), Mathis (11 TDs, 18 pass rec for 319 yds), soph E Gary Barnes, Ts Harold Olson and Lou Cordileone, C Paul Snyder. *Noteworthy:* Repeated as ACC champ. Beat Texas Christian (TCU) 23–7 in inaugural Bluebonnet Bowl; scored 20 pts in last quarter, including TD passes of 68 yds from White to Barnes and 23 yds from QB Lowndes Shingler to soph E Tommy King.

1977 (8–3–1) *Won:* Georgia 7–6, Georgia Tech 31–14, Virginia Tech 31–13 (1st meeting since 1960), Virginia 31–0, Duke 17–11, N.C. State 7–3, Wake Forest 26–0, South Carolina 31–27. *Lost:* Maryland 21–14, national champ Notre Dame 21–17. *Tied:* North Carolina 13–13. *Stars:* QB Steve Fuller (1,655 yds pass), SE Jerry Butler (47 pass rec for 824 yds), TBs Warren Ratchford (616 yds rush) and soph Lester Brown (9 TDs), OG Joe Bostic, OT Larry Brumley, DE Jonathan Brooks, LB Randy Scott, DB Steve Ryan (6 int). *Noteworthy:* 1st year under Charley Pell. Lost to Pittsburgh 34–3 in Gator Bowl; Fuller had 158 yds pass and frosh K Obed Ariri had 49-yd FG.

1978 (11–1) *Won:* The Citadel 58–3, Villanova 31–0, Virginia Tech 38–7, Virginia 30–14, Duke 28–8, N.C. State 33–10, Wake Forest 51–6, North Carolina 13–9, Maryland 28–24, South Carolina 41–23. *Lost:* Georgia 12–0. *Stars:* Fuller (1,515 yds pass), Butler (58 pass rec for 908 yds), Lester Brown (1,022 yds rush and 17 TDs), Bostic, OT Steve Kenney, Brooks, Ryan, LBs Bubba Brown and Scott, DT Jim Stuckey. *Noteworthy:* Took 7th ACC title. Danny Ford coached Tigers to win over Ohio St. 17–15 in Gator Bowl; Fuller passed for 123 yds and ran for a TD, and Ariri had 47-yd FG.

1979 (8–4) *Won:* Furman 21–0 (1st meeting since 1964, 22nd straight over Paladins), Georgia 12–7,

Virginia 17–7, Virginia Tech 21–0, Duke 28–10, Wake Forest 31–0, North Carolina 19–10, Notre Dame 16–10. *Lost:* Maryland 19–0, N.C. State 16–13, South Carolina 13–9. *Stars:* QB Billy Lott (1,184 yds pass), soph FL Perry Tuttle (36 pass rec for 544 yds), FB Marvin Sims (743 yds rush), frosh TB Chuck McSwain (6 TDs rush), Bostic, Ariri (16 FGs), DTs Stuckey and Steve Durham, Bubba Brown, DB Rex Varn, P David Sims (43.9-yd avg). *Noteworthy:* 1st full year under Ford. Lost to Baylor 24–18 in Peach Bowl when late rally fell short; Lott passed for 213 yds, Tuttle caught 8 passes for 108 yds, and Lester Brown ran for 76 yds and a TD.

1981 (12–0) *Won:* Wofford 45–10, Tulane 13–5, Georgia 13–3, Kentucky 21–3, Virginia 27–0, Duke 38–10, N.C. State 17–7, Wake Forest 82–24, North Carolina 10–8, Maryland 21–7, South Carolina 29–13. *Stars:* QB Homer Jordan (1,630 yds pass, 486 yds and 6 TDs rush), Tuttle (52 pass rec for 883 yds and 8 TDs), WRs Jerry Gaillard (19 pass rec for 218 yds) and Frank Magwood (17 pass rec for 345 yds), TB Cliff Austin (824 yds rush, 9 TDs), McSwain (692 yds and 7 TDs rush), FB Jeff McCall (5 TDs), OT Lee Nanney, C Tony Berryhill, LB Jeff Davis, DTs Jeff Bryant and Dan Benish, DB Terry Kinard (6 int), frosh P Dale Hatcher (43.4-yd avg). *Noteworthy:* Nation's most-improved team won 8th ACC title in 1st unbeaten season since 1950. Beat Nebraska 22–15 in Orange Bowl to earn 1st national championship; Jordan passed for 134 yds and a TD (to Tuttle, who caught 5 for 56 yds), Austin ran for a TD, and frosh K Donald Igwebuike had 3 FGs.

1982 (9–1–1) *Won:* Western Carolina 21–10, Kentucky 24–6, Virginia 48–0, Duke 49–14, N.C. State 38–29, North Carolina 16–13, Maryland 24–22, South Carolina 24–6, Wake Forest 21–17 (in Tokyo). *Lost:* unbeaten Georgia 13–7. *Tied:* Boston College 17–17 (1st meeting since 1960). *Stars:* Kinard, Austin (1,064 yds rush, 14 TDs), SE Jeff Stockstill (25 pass rec for 247 yds), LB Johnny Rembert (6 int), soph MG William Perry, DE Andy Headen. *Noteworthy:* Repeated as ACC champ. Ineligible for postseason play, NCAA probation.

1983 (9–1–1) *Won:* Western Carolina 44–10, Georgia Tech 41–14, Virginia 42–21, Duke 38–31, N.C. State 27–17, Wake Forest 24–17, North Carolina 16–3, Maryland 52–27, South Carolina 22–13. *Lost:* Boston College 31–16. *Tied:* Georgia 16–16.

Stars: QB Mike Eppley (1,410 yds and 13 TDs pass), frosh SE Ray Williams (19 pass rec for 342 yds), FB Kevin Mack (862 yds rush), TE K.D. Dunn, OG James Farr, K Bob Pauling (18 FGs, 90 pts), Perry, DE Edgar Pickett, DT James Robinson, DB Rod McSwain, Hatcher (43.6-yd punting avg). *Noteworthy:* Ineligible for both ACC title and postseason play.

1986 (8–2–2) *Won:* Georgia 31–28, Georgia Tech 27–3, The Citadel 24–0, Virginia 31–17, Duke 35–3, Wake Forest 28–20 (10th straight over Deacons), North Carolina 38–10. *Lost:* Virginia Tech 20–14 (1st to Gobblers in 10 games since 1954), N.C. State 27–3. *Tied:* Maryland 17–17, South Carolina 21–21. *Stars:* TB Terrence Flagler (1,176 yds rush, 10 TDs), FL Terrance Roulhac (20 pass rec for 228 yds, nation's leader in kickoff returns with 33-yd avg), QB Rod Williams (1,245 yds pass, 352 yds and 5 TDs rush), WR Ray Williams (20 pass rec for 280 yds), soph FB Tracy Johnson (5 TDs rush), TE Jim Riggs, OG John Phillips, K David Treadwell (10 FGs), DE Terence Mack, DB Delton Hall (5 int). *Noteworthy:* Won 10th ACC title. Beat Stanford 27–21 in Gator Bowl, jumping to 27–0 halftime lead; Rod Williams passed for 135 yds and scored a TD, and Treadwell had 2 FGs (including 46–yarder).

1987 (10–2) *Won:* Western Carolina 43–0, Virginia Tech 22–10, Georgia 21–20, Georgia Tech 33–12, Virginia 38–21, Duke 17–10, Wake Forest 31–17, North Carolina 13–10, Maryland 45–16. *Lost:* N.C. State 30–28, South Carolina 20–7. *Stars:* Phillips, Rod Williams (1,486 yds pass), soph WR Gary Cooper (34 pass rec for 618 yds), FL Keith Jennings (31 pass rec for 475 yds), frosh TB Terry Allen (973 yds and 8 TDs rush), soph TBs Wesley McFadden (781 yds and 6 TDs rush) and Joe Henderson (6 TDs), Johnson (557 yds and 9 TDs rush), OT Jeff Nunamacher, Treadwell (18 FGs, 82 pts), MG Tony Stephens, DT Michael Dean Perry, DB Donnell Woolford (5 int). *Noteworthy:* Again won ACC. Beat Penn St. 35–10 in Florida Citrus Bowl; Johnson ran for 88 yds and 3 TDs, Allen ran for 105 yds and a TD, and Williams passed for 214 yds.

1988 (10–2) *Won:* Virginia Tech 40–7, Furman 23–3, Georgia Tech 30–13, Virginia 10–7, Duke 49–17, Wake Forest 38–21, North Carolina 37–14, Maryland 49–25, South Carolina 29–10. *Lost:* Florida St. 24–21 (1st meeting since 1976), N.C. State 10–3. *Stars:* Allen (1,192 yds rush, 10 TDs),

Williams (1,144 yds pass, 6 TDs rush), Jennings (30 pass rec for 397 yds), Cooper (13 pass rec for 417 yds, 5 TDs), Henderson (538 yds rush), Johnson (8 TDs rush), Nunamacher, MG Mark Drag, frosh LB Ed McDaniel, Woolford. *Noteworthy:* Won 3rd straight ACC crown (12th overall). Beat Oklahoma 13–6 in Florida Citrus Bowl; frosh K Cris Gardocki had 2 FGs (including 46-yarder) and Allen scored winning TD on 4-yd run early in 4th quarter.

1989 (10–2)   *Won:* Furman 30–0, Florida St. 34–23, Virginia Tech 27–7, Maryland 31–7, Virginia 34–20, N.C. State 30–10, Wake Forest 44–10, North Carolina 35–3, South Carolina 45–0.   *Lost:* Duke 21–17, Georgia Tech 30–14.   *Stars:* Allen (613 yds and 10 TDs rush), Henderson (760 yds rush, 8 TDs), FB McFadden (6 TDs), QB Chris Morocco (1,074 yds pass), WR Rodney Fletcher (32 pass rec for 490 yds), Cooper (27 pass rec for 489 yds), OT Stacy Long, C Hank Phillips, DT Vance Hammond, LBs Doug Brewster and soph Levon Kirkland, soph DB Dexter Davis, frosh DB Robert O'Neal (7 int), Gardocki (20 FGs, 98 pts, 42.6-yd punting avg). *Noteworthy:* Ford's last team. Beat West Virginia 27–7 in Gator Bowl; Henderson ran for 92 yds and a TD, McFadden and frosh DT Chester McGlockton scored TDs, and Gardocki kicked 2 FGs.

1990 (10–2)   *Won:* Long Beach St. 59–0, Maryland 18–17, Appalachian St. 48–0, Duke 26–7, Georgia 34–3, N.C. State 24–17, Wake Forest 24–6, North Carolina 20–3, South Carolina 24–15.   *Lost:* Virginia 20–7 (1st to Cavaliers in 30-game series dating to 1955), unbeaten national cochamp Georgia Tech 21–19.   *Stars:* Gardocki (22 FGs, 96 pts, 44.5-yd punting avg), Long, Kirkland, Brewster, Hammond, O'Neal, McDaniel, Davis (6 int), QB

DeChane Cameron (1,185 yds pass, 361 yds rush), frosh WR Terry Smith (34 pass rec for 480 yds), WR Doug Thomas (21 pass rec for 309 yds), frosh TB Ronald Williams (941 yds and 8 TDs rush), OG Eric Harmon, MG Rob Bodine. *Noteworthy:* Led nation in total defense in 1st year under Ken Hatfield. Beat Illinois 30–0 in Hall of Fame Bowl; Cameron passed for 141 yds and 2 TDs and ran for 76 yds, Thomas caught 5 passes for 57 yds and a TD, DB Arlington Nunn scored on 34-yd pass int return, and Gardocki had 3 FGs.

1991 (9–2–1)   *Won:* Appalachian St. 34–0, Temple 37–7, Georgia Tech 9–7, N.C. State 29–19, Wake Forest 28–10 (15th straight over Deacons), North Carolina 21–6, Maryland 40–7, South Carolina 41–24, Duke 33–21 (in Tokyo).   *Lost:* Georgia 27–12.   *Tied:* Virginia 20–20.   *Stars:* Cameron (1,478 yds pass, 392 yds rush), Smith (45 pass rec for 758 yds and 6 TDs), Williams (585 yds rush), WR Larry Ryans (20 pass rec for 273 yds), soph TB Rodney Blunt (706 yds rush), FB Rudy Harris (9 TDs rush), C Mike Brown, OG Jeb Flesch, frosh K Nelson Welch (17 FGs, 81 pts), McGlockton, Bodine, Kirkland, McDaniel, O'Neal. *Noteworthy:* Led nation in rush defense and won 13th ACC title. Lost to California 37–13 in Florida Citrus Bowl (breaking 5-bowl win streak); Cameron passed for 123 yds and scored on 62-yd run, Smith caught 7 passes for 71 yds, and Welch kicked 2 FGs.

BOWL SUMMARY

Bluebonnet 1–0; Cotton 1–0; Florida Citrus 2–1; Gator 4–2; Hall of Fame 1–0; Independence 0–1; Orange 2–1; Peach 0–1; Sugar 0–1.

BOWL RECORD (11–7)

Regular Season	Bowl	Score	Opponent	Record
1939 (8–1)	Cotton	6–3	Boston College	(9–1)
1948 (10–0)	Gator	24–23	Missouri	(8–2)
1950 (8–0–1)	Orange	15–14	Miami (Fla.)	(9–0–1)
1951 (7–2)	Gator	0–14	Miami (Fla.)	(7–3)
1956 (7–1–2)	Orange	21–27	Colorado	(7–2–1)
1958 (8–2)	Sugar	0–7	LSU	(10–0)
1959 (8–2)	Bluebonnet	23–7	TCU	(8–2)
1977 (8–2–1)	Gator	3–34	Pittsburgh	(8–2–1)

(continued)

Regular Season	Bowl	Score	Opponent	Record
1978 (10–1)	Gator	17–15	Ohio State	(7–3–1)
1979 (8–3)	Peach	18–24	Baylor	(7–4)
1981 (11–0)	Orange	22–15	Nebraska	(9–2)
1985 (6–5)	Independence	13–20	Minnesota	(6–5)
1986 (7–2–2)	Gator	27–21	Stanford	(8–3)
1987 (9–2)	Fla. Citrus	35–10	Penn State	(8–3)
1988 (9–2)	Fla. Citrus	13–6	Oklahoma	(9–2)
1989 (9–2)	Gator	27–7	West Virginia	(8–2–1)
1990 (9–2)	Hall of Fame	30–0	Illinois	(8–3)
1991 (9–1–1)	Fla. Citrus	13–37	California	(9–2)

CONFERENCE TITLES

Southern—1940, 1948. **Atlantic Coast**—1956, 1958, 1959, 1965*, 1966, 1967, 1978, 1981, 1982, 1986, 1987, 1988, 1991.

TOP 20 AP AND UPI
(USA TODAY/CNN SINCE 1991) RANKING

1939	12	1957	U–18	1981	1–1	1988	9–8
1948	11	1958	12–13	1982	8–U	1989	12–11
1950	10–12	1959	11–U	1983	11–U	1990	9–9
1951	20–U	1977	19–U	1986	17–19	1991	18–17
1956	19–U	1978	6–7	1987	12–10		

MAJOR RIVALS

Clemson has played at least 10 games with Alabama 3–11, Auburn 11–31–2, Boston College 7–5–2, The Citadel 28–5–1, Davidson 11–5–4, Duke 23–13–1, Florida 3–9–1, Furman 36–10–4, Georgia 17–37–4, Georgia Tech 16–39–2, Kentucky 3–7, Maryland 19–20–2, North Carolina 27–13–1, N.C. State 38–22–1, Presbyterian 32–3–4, South Carolina 53–33–4, Tennessee 5–11–2, Tulane 4–6, Virginia 30–1–1, VMI 5–5–2, Virginia Tech 17–7–1, Wake Forest 45–12–1, Wofford 9–3. Record against ACC member Florida St. is 2–4.

COACHES

Dean of Clemson coaches is Frank Howard with record of 165–118–12 for 1940–69, including 8 conference titles, 6 bowl teams, and 2 unbeaten teams. Other top records for at least 3 years were by John Heisman, 19–3–2 for 1900–03 with 1 unbeaten team; Bob Williams, 21–14–6 for 1906, 1909, and 1913–15 with 1 unbeaten team; Edward A. Donahue, 21–12–3 for 1917–20; Josh Cody, 29–11–1 for 1927–30; Jess Neely, 45–35–7 for 1931–39 with 1 Cotton Bowl champion; Danny Ford (1981 national Coach of Year), 96–29–4 for 1978–89 with 5 ACC titles, 7 bowl teams, and 1 unbeaten national champion; and Ken Hatfield, 24–10–1 for 1990–92 with 1 ACC title and 2 bowl teams.

MISCELLANEA

First game was win over Furman 14–6 in 1896 . . . highest score was over Guilford 122–0 in 1901 . . . highest since W.W. II was over Wake Forest 82–24 in 1981 . . . biggest margin since W.W. II was over Presbyterian 66–0 in 1957 . . . worst defeat was by

Alabama 74–7 in 1931 . . . worst since W.W. II was by Alabama 56–0 in 1975 . . . longest unbeaten string of 16 in 1949–51 ended by Pacific 21–7 . . . 15-game win streak in 1947–49 ended by Rice 33–7 . . . longest losing string of 11 in 1924–25 broken with win over The Citadel 6–0 . . . consensus All-Americans were Harry Olszewski, G, 1967; Bennie Cunningham, TE, 1974; Jim Stuckey, DL, 1979; Jeff Davis, LB, 1981; Terry Kinard, DB, 1981–82; William Perry, DL, 1983; Terrence Flagler, RB, 1986; David Treadwell, K, 1987; Donnell Woolford, DB, 1988; Stacy Long, OL, 1990; and Jeb Flesch, OG, and Levon Kirkland, LB, 1991 . . . Academic All-Americans were Lou Cordileone, T, 1959; and Steve Fuller, QB, 1978.

DUKE *(Blue Devils; Royal Blue and White)*

NOTABLE TEAMS

1920 (4–0–1) *Won:* Guilford 20–7, Emory & Henry 7–0, Lynchburg 13–7, Elon 13–6. *Tied:* Wofford 0–0. *Noteworthy:* Football returned to Trinity (Duke) after being banned 1895–1919.

1921 (6–1–2) *Won:* Lynchburg 14–13, Randolph-Macon 6–0, Emory & Henry 7–0, Guilford 28–0, Wake Forest 17–0, Wofford 68–0. *Lost:* William & Mary 12–0. *Tied:* Elon 0–0, New York U. 7–7.

1922 (7–2–1) *Won:* Guilford 43–0, Hampden-Sydney 27–0, Davidson 12–0, Oglethorpe 7–6, Wake Forest 3–0, Randolph-Macon 25–12, Wofford 26–0. *Lost:* North Carolina 20–0 (1st meeting since 1894), William & Mary 13–7. *Tied:* Presbyterian 6–6.

1930 (8–1–2) *Won:* Virginia 32–0, Davidson 12–0, Navy 18–0, Wofford 14–0, Villanova 12–6, Kentucky 14–7, N.C. State 18–0, Washington & Lee 14–0. *Lost:* South Carolina 22–0 (1st meeting) in opener. *Tied:* Wake Forest 13–13, North Carolina 0–0. *Noteworthy:* James DeHart's last team.

1932 (7–3) *Won:* Davidson 13–0, Virginia Military Institute (VMI) 44–0, Maryland 34–0 (1st meeting), Wake Forest 9–0, Kentucky 13–0, North Carolina 7–0 (1st over Tar Heels in 12 games since 1893), Washington & Lee 13–0. *Lost:* unbeaten Auburn 18–7, unbeaten Tennessee 16–13, N.C. State 6–0. *Star:* T Fred Crawford.

1933 (9–1) *Won:* VMI 37–6, Wake Forest 22–0, Tennessee 10–2 (1st loss for Vols in 3 years),

Davidson 19–7, Kentucky 14–7, Auburn 13–7, Maryland 38–7, North Carolina 21–0, N.C. State 7–0. *Lost:* Georgia Tech 6–0 (1st meeting) in finale. *Stars:* Crawford (1st Duke consensus All-American), E Tom Rogers, FB Robert Cox. *Noteworthy:* won 1st SC title.

1934 (7–2) *Won:* VMI 46–0, Clemson 20–6 (1st meeting), Georgia Tech 20–0, Davidson 20–0, Auburn 13–6, Wake Forest 28–7, N.C. State 32–0. *Lost:* Tennessee 14–6, North Carolina 7–0. *Stars:* soph TB Ace Parker, E Earle Wentz, G Jack Dunlap, T Gus Durner.

1935 (8–2) *Won:* Wake Forest 26–7, South Carolina 47–0, Washington & Lee 26–0, Clemson 38–12, Tennessee 19–6, Davidson 26–7, North Carolina 25–0, N.C. State 7–0. *Lost:* Georgia Tech 6–0, Auburn 7–0 in successive mid-season games. *Stars:* Parker, Durner, G Jim Johnston. *Noteworthy:* won 2nd SC crown.

1936 (9–1) *Won:* Davidson 13–0, Colgate 6–0, South Carolina 21–0, Clemson 25–0, Georgia Tech 19–6, Washington & Lee 51–0, Wake Forest 20–0, North Carolina 27–7, N.C. State 13–0. *Lost:* Tennessee 15–13. *Stars:* Parker, soph HB Eric Tipton (577 yds rush, 6 TDs), QB Elmore Hackney, soph C/LB Dan Hill, Ts Joe Brunansky and Joe Cardwell. *Noteworthy:* won 3rd SC title.

1937 (7–2–1) *Won:* Virginia Tech 25–0, Davidson 34–6, Georgia Tech 20–19, Colgate 13–0, Washington & Lee 43–0, Wake Forest 67–0, N.C. State 20–7. *Lost:* North Carolina 14–6, unbeaten national cochamp Pittsburgh 10–0. *Tied:* Tennessee 0–0. *Stars:* Tipton (594 yds rush, 7 TDs, 40.6-yd punting avg), Hackney, Brunansky, G Woodrow Lipscomb.

1938 (9–1) *Won:* Virginia Tech 18–0, Davidson 27–0, Colgate 7–0, Georgia Tech 6–0, Wake Forest 7–0, North Carolina 14–0, Syracuse 21–0, N.C. State 7–0, Pittsburgh 7–0. *Stars:* Tipton (737 yds total off, 40.3-yd punting avg), FB Bob O'Mara (703 yds rush, 5 TDs), Hill, E Willard Perdue, G Fred Yorke. *Noteworthy:* led nation in scoring defense (0.0 pts per game) in 1st unbeaten season since 1920 and won 4th SC title. Made 1st postseason appearance but lost to Southern California 7–3 in Rose Bowl when tiring Blue Devils gave up 18-yard TD pass with 40 seconds to play; scored earlier in period on 24-yd FG by Tony Ruffa.

1939 (8–1) *Won:* Davidson 26–6, Colgate 37–0,

Syracuse 33–6, Wake Forest 6–0, Georgia Tech 7–6, VMI 20–7, North Carolina 13–3, N.C. State 28–0. *Lost:* Pittsburgh 14–13. *Stars:* HB George McAfee (596 yds rush, 7 TDs, 10 pass rec for 229 yds), FB Roger Robinson (7 TDs), T Frank Ribar, G Allen Johnson. *Noteworthy:* won 5th SC crown.

1940 (7–2) *Won:* VMI 23–0, Colgate 13–0, Wake Forest 23–0, Georgia Tech 41–7, Davidson 46–13, N.C. State 42–6, Pittsburgh 12–7. *Lost:* unbeaten Tennessee 13–0, North Carolina 6–3. *Stars:* Steve Lach (5 TDs, 26 pass rec for 335 yds), Jasper Davis (591 yds rush), Ts Tony Ruffa and Alex Winterson, C Bob Barnett.

1941 (9–1) *Won:* Wake Forest 43–14, Tennessee 19–0, Maryland 50–0, Colgate 27–14, Pittsburgh 27–7, Georgia Tech 14–0, Davidson 56–0 (10th straight over Wildcats), North Carolina 20–0, N.C. State 55–6. *Stars:* frosh Tom Davis (569 yds rush, 506 pass), Lach (22 pass rec for 366 yds), Winston Siegfried (14 TDs), frosh E Bob Gantt, T Mike Karmazin, Barnett. *Noteworthy:* Led nation in total off and took 6th SC title. Upset by Oregon St. 20–16 in Rose Bowl played in Durham because of fears of Japanese attack on West Coast following Pearl Harbor (only Rose Bowl game played outside Pasadena, Calif.); Lach ran for 124 yds and a TD, and Siegfried scored other Blue Devil TD.

1943 (8–1) *Won:* Camp Lejeune 40–0, Richmond 61–0, North Carolina Pre-Flight 42–0, North Carolina 14–7, 27–6, Georgia Tech 14–7, N.C. State 75–0, Virginia 49–0 (1st meeting since 1930). *Lost:* Navy 14–13. *Stars:* Buddy Luper (871 yds total off), Davis, Lamar Blount (6 pass rec for 227 yds), Gantt, G Bill Millner, T Pat Preston. *Noteworthy:* led nation in scoring (37.2-pt avg), total defense, rush defense, and scoring defense (3.8-pt avg) and won 7th SC title.

1944 (6–4) *Won:* Richmond 61–7, Georgia Tech 19–13, Wake Forest 34–0, South Carolina 34–7, North Carolina 33–0. *Lost:* Pennsylvania 18–7, North Carolina Pre-Flight 13–6, Navy 7–0, unbeaten national champ Army 27–7 (1st meeting) in successive early games. *Stars:* George Clark (528 yds rush), Davis (8 TDs), Gordon Carver (13 pass rec for 252 yds). *Noteworthy:* again won SC title. Upset Alabama 29–26 in Sugar Bowl on 20-yd TD run by Clark (123 yds and 2 TDs rush) with 2:15 left; Davis ran for 101 yds and 2 TDs, and Harold Raether kicked 3 ex pts.

1945 (6–2) *Won:* South Carolina 60–0, Bogue Field 76–0, Wake Forest 26–19, Georgia Tech 14–6, N.C. State 26–13, North Carolina 14–7. *Lost:* Navy 21–0, unbeaten national champ Army 48–13. *Stars:* Clark (530 yds rush, 7 TDs), G Ernie Knotts, E Kelley Mote, C Ed Sharkey. *Noteworthy:* wartime coach Eddie Cameron's last team took 3rd straight SC title.

1950 (7–3) *Won:* South Carolina 14–0, Pitt 28–14, N.C. State 7–0, Richmond 41–0, Georgia Tech 30–21, Virginia Tech 47–6, North Carolina 7–0. *Lost:* Tennessee 28–7, Maryland 26–14 (1st in 7-game series dating to 1932), Wake Forest 13–7. *Stars:* TB Billy Cox (1,428 yds pass, 567 yds rush), Corren Youmans (40 pass rec for 446 yds), Tom Powers (9 TDs), E Blaine Earon. *Noteworthy:* Wallace Wade's last team.

1952 (8–2) *Won:* Washington & Lee 34–0, Southern Methodist 14–7, Tennessee 7–0, South Carolina 33–7, N.C. State 57–0, Virginia 21–7, Wake Forest 14–7, North Carolina 34–0. *Lost:* unbeaten Georgia Tech 28–7, Navy 16–6 in successive late games. *Stars:* T Ed Meadows, Howard Pitt (20 pass rec for 277 yds), Red Smith (50 pts on 5 TDs and 20 ex pts), soph B Worth Lutz, G Bobby Burrows. *Noteworthy:* won 10th SC crown in last year in league.

1953 (7–2–1) *Won:* South Carolina 20–7, Wake Forest 19–0, Tennessee 21–7, Purdue 20–14, N.C. State 31–0, Virginia 48–6, North Carolina 35–20. *Lost:* Army 14–13, Georgia Tech 13–10. *Tied:* Navy 0–0. *Stars:* Smith, Pitt, Lloyd Caudle (510 yds rush and 9 TDs), Meadows, Burrows. *Noteworthy:* got share of inaugural ACC title.

1954 (8–2–1) *Won:* Pennsylvania 52–0, Tennessee 7–6, N.C. State 21–7, Georgia Tech 21–20, Wake Forest 28–21, South Carolina 26–7, North Carolina 47–12. *Lost:* Army 28–14, Navy 40–7. *Tied:* Purdue 13–13. *Stars:* Bs Bob Pascal (561 yds rush and 10 TDs) and Jerry Barger, G Ralph Torrance. *Noteworthy:* Took 2nd straight ACC title. Beat Nebraska 34–7 in Orange Bowl, outrushing Cornhuskers by 288–84 yds; Barger passed for 2 TDs and Pascal ran for 91 yds and a TD.

1955 (7–2–1) *Won:* N.C. State 33–7, Tennessee 21–0, William & Mary 47–7, Ohio St. 20–14, South Carolina 41–7, Wake Forest 14–0, North Carolina 6–0. *Lost:* Pitt 26–7, Georgia Tech 27–0. *Tied:* Navy 7–7. *Stars:* QB Sonny Jurgensen, Pascal

(750 yds rush, 8 TDs), E Sonny Sorrell, G Jesse Birchfield. *Noteworthy:* got share of 3rd straight ACC title.

1957 (6–3–2) *Won:* South Carolina 26–14, Virginia 40–0, Maryland 14–0, Rice 7–6, Wake Forest 34–7, Clemson 7–6 (1st meeting since 1936). *Lost:* Georgia Tech 13–0, North Carolina 21–13. *Tied:* N.C. State 14–14, Navy 6–6. *Stars:* T Tom Topping, G Roy Hord, B Wray Carlton (833 yds rush and 10 TDs). *Noteworthy:* lost to Oklahoma 48–21 in Orange Bowl as Sooners converted 6 turnovers into scores and had 27 pts in final quarter; FB Harold McElhaney scored 2 Duke TDs.

1960 (8–3) *Won:* South Carolina 31–0, Maryland 20–7, N.C. State 17–13, Clemson 21–6, Georgia Tech 6–0, Navy 19–10, Wake Forest 34–7. *Lost:* Michigan 31–6, North Carolina 7–6, UCLA 27–6. *Stars:* E Claude "Tee" Moorman (54 pass rec for 476 yds), T Dwight Bumgarner, G Art Browning, soph B Mark Leggett. *Noteworthy:* Won 4th ACC crown. Beat Arkansas 7–6 in Cotton Bowl on TD pass from Don Altman to Moorman (and conversion by Art Browning) with 2:45 left.

1961 (7–3) *Won:* South Carolina 7–6, Virginia 42–0, Wake Forest 23–3 (10th straight over Deacons), N.C. State 17–6, Navy 30–9, North Carolina 6–3, Notre Dame 37–13. *Lost:* Georgia Tech 21–0, Clemson 17–7, Michigan 28–14. *Stars:* soph E Stan Crisson (20 pass rec for 241 yds), T Art Gregory, G Jean Berry, Bs Leggett and Walt Rappold. *Noteworthy:* again won ACC title.

1962 (8–2) *Won:* South Carolina 21–8, Florida 28–21, California 21–7, Clemson 16–0, N.C. State 21–14, Maryland 10–7, Wake Forest 50–0, North Carolina 16–14. *Lost:* unbeaten national champ Southern California 14–7, Georgia Tech 20–9. *Stars:* Berry, Gregory, Rappold, Leggett, B Mike Curtis (8 TDs), Crisson (30 pass rec for 307 yds). *Noteworthy:* won 3rd straight ACC title (6th overall).

1989 (8–4) *Won:* Northwestern 41–31, Clemson 21–17, Army 35–29, Maryland 46–25 (1st over Terps in 16 games since 1972), Georgia Tech 30–19, Wake Forest 52–35, N.C. State 35–26, North Carolina 41–0. *Lost:* South Carolina 27–21, Tennessee 28–6, Virginia 49–28. *Stars:* WR Clarkston Hines (61 pass rec for 1,149 yds and 17 TDs), soph SE Walter Jones (33 pass rec for 520 yds), TE Dave Colonna (35 pass rec for 495 yds), QBs Billy Ray

QB Dave Brown, 1989–1991

(2,035 yds and 15 TDs pass) and soph David Brown (1,479 yds and 14 TDs pass), soph RB Randy Cuthbert (50 pass rec for 470 yds, 1,042 yds and 10 TDs rush), TB Roger Boone (32 pass rec for 223 yds, 522 yds rush), C Carey Metts, OT Chris Port, LB George Edwards, DBs Erwin Sampson and soph Wyatt Smith (6 int, 2 returned for TDs). *Noteworthy:* Steve Spurrier's last team earned share of 7th ACC title (1st since 1962). Made 1st postseason appearance in nearly 30 years but turned over ball 4 times in losing to Texas Tech 49–21 in All-American Bowl; Brown passed for 268 yds and 2 TDs (both to Colonna), and Hines had 6 pass rec for 112 yds.

BOWL SUMMARY

All-American 0–1; Cotton 1–0; Orange 1–1; Rose 0–2; Sugar 1–0.

BOWL RECORD (3–4)

Regular Season	Bowl	Score	Opponent	Record
1938 (9–0)	Rose	3–7	USC	(8–2)
1941 (9–0)	Rose	16–20	Oregon State	(7–2)
1944 (5–4)	Sugar	29–26	Alabama	(5–1–2)
1954 (7–2–1)	Orange	34–7	Nebraska	(6–4)
1957 (6–2–2)	Orange	21–48	Oklahoma	(9–1)
1960 (7–3)	Cotton	7–6	Arkansas	(8–2)
1989 (8–3)	All-American	21–49	Texas Tech	(8–3)

CONFERENCE TITLES

Southern—1933, 1935, 1936, 1938, 1939, 1941, 1943, 1944, 1945, 1952. **Atlantic Coast**—1953*, 1954, 1955*, 1960, 1961, 1962, 1989*.

TOP 20 AP AND UPI RANKING

1936	11	1941	2	1952	16–18	1957	16–14
1937	20	1943	7	1953	18–18	1960	10–11
1938	3	1944	11	1954	14–14	1961	20–14
1939	8	1945	13	1955	U–16	1962	U–14
1940	18	1947	19	1956	U–20		

MAJOR RIVALS

Duke has played at least 10 games with Army 6–8–1, Clemson 13–23–1, Davidson 16–4–1, Georgia Tech 28–31–1, Maryland 16–20, Navy 9–14–5, North Carolina 35–40–4, N.C. State 38–25–5, Pittsburgh 8–9, Richmond 9–1, South Carolina 24–17–3, Tennessee 13–12–2, Virginia 25–19, Virginia Tech 7–4, Wake Forest 48–23–2. Record against ACC member Florida St. is 0–1.

COACHES

Dean of Duke coaches is Wallace Wade with record of 110–36–7 for 1931–41 and 1946–50, including 6 SC titles, 2 Rose Bowl teams, and 2 teams unbeaten in regular season. Other top records for at least 3 years were by James DeHart, 24–23–2 for 1926–30; Eddie Cameron, 25–11–1 for 1942–45 with 3 SC titles and 1 Sugar Bowl champion; Bill Murray, 93–51–9 for 1951–65 with 7 conference titles and 3 bowl teams; and Steve Spurrier, 20– 13–1 for 1987–89 with 1 ACC title and 1 bowl team.

MISCELLANEA

First game was win over North Carolina 16–0 in 1888 . . . highest score was over Furman 96–0 in 1891 . . . highest since 1900 was over Bogue Field 76–0 in 1945 . . . highest since W.W. II was over Richmond 67–0 in 1949 . . . worst defeat was by Notre Dame 64–0 in 1966 . . . longest win streaks of 11, in 1932–33 ended by Georgia Tech 6–0 and in 1940–41 by Oregon St. 20–16 in 1942 Rose Bowl . . . longest losing string of 11 in 1979–80 broken with win over Clemson 34–17 . . . consensus All-Americans were Fred Crawford, T, 1933; Ace Parker, B, 1936; Ernie Jackson, DB, 1971; and Clarkston Hines, WR, 1989 . . . Academic All-Americans were Roger Hayes, DE, 1966; Bob Lasky, DT, 1967; Curt Rawley, DT, 1970; Mike Diminick, DB, 1986–88; and Doug Kley, DL, 1989 . . . Outland Trophy winner was Mike McGee, T, 1959.

FLORIDA STATE *(Seminoles; Garnet and Gold)*

NOTABLE TEAMS

1948 (7–1)   *Won:* Cumberland 30–0, Millsaps 7–6, Stetson 18–7, Mississippi College 26–6, Livingston St. 12–6, Troy St. 20–13, Tampa 33–12 (1st meeting, 1st homecoming). *Lost:* Erskine 14–6. *Star:* T Hugh Adams. *Noteworthy:* 1st year under Don Veller.

1949 (9–1)   *Won:* Whiting Field 74–0, Mississippi College 33–12, Erskine 26–7, Sewanee 6–0, Stetson 33–14, Millsaps 40–0, Tampa 34–7, Troy St. 20–0. *Lost:* Livingston St. 13–6. *Stars:* Adams, Ted Hewitt (6 int). *Noteworthy:* beat Wofford 19–6 in Cigar Bowl as Buddy Strauss ran for 132 yds and Red Parrish scored 2 TDs.

1950 (8–0)   *Won:* Troy St. 26–7, Randolph-Macon 40–7, Howard 20–6, Newberry 24–0, Sewanee 14–8, Stetson 27–7, Mississippi College 33–0, Tampa 35–19. *Star:* T Jerry Morrical. *Noteworthy:* outscored foes 219–54 in 1st unbeaten season.

1951 (6–2)   *Won:* Troy St. 40–0, Delta St. 34–0, Sul Ross St. 35–13, Stetson 13–10, Jacksonville Navy 39–0, Wofford 14–0. *Lost:* Miami (Fla.) 35–13 (1st meeting), Tampa 14–6. *Stars:* G Bill Dawkins, Curt Campbell (8 int).

1954 (8–4)   *Won:* Louisville 47–6, Villanova 52–13, N.C. State 13–7, Virginia Military Institute (VMI) 33–19, Furman 33–14, Stetson 47–6, Mississippi Southern 19–18, Tampa 13–0. *Lost:* Georgia 14–0 (1st meeting), Abilene Christian 13–0, Auburn 33–0 (1st meeting). *Stars:* G Al Makowiecke, Lee Corso (6 int), Tom Feamster (6 int). *Noteworthy:* lost to Texas Western (Texas–El Paso) 47–20 in Sun Bowl, dropping behind 34–7 by halftime.

1958 (7–4)   *Won:* Tennessee Tech 22–7, Furman 42–6, Wake Forest 27–24, Virginia Tech 28–0, Tennessee 10–0, Tampa 43–0, Miami (Fla.) 17–6 (1st in 6-game series begun in 1951). *Lost:* Georgia Tech 17–3, Georgia 28–13, Florida 21–7 (1st meeting). *Stars:* Fred Pickard (615 yds rush), Bobby Renn (7 TDs), Jack Espenship (18 pass rec for 200 yds). *Noteworthy:* Tom Nugent's last team. Lost to Oklahoma St. 15–6 in Bluegrass Bowl in 10-degree weather at Louisville, Ky.; scored on pass from QB Joe Majors to Carl Meyer.

1964 (9–1–1)   *Won:* Miami (Fla.) 14–0, Texas Chris-tian (TCU) 10–0, New Mexico St. 36–0, Kentucky 48–6, Georgia 17–14, Southern Mississippi 34–0, N.C. State 28–6, Florida 16–7 (1st meeting in Tallahassee, 1st win since series began in 1958). *Lost:* Virginia Tech 20–11. *Tied:* Houston 13–13. *Stars:* QB Steve Tensi (1,681 yds and 14 TDs pass), FL Fred Biletnikoff (57 pass rec for 987 yds and 11 TDs; 1st Florida St. consensus All-American), Phil Spooner (516 yds and 5 TDs rush), Winfred Bailey (6 int). *Noteworthy:* beat Oklahoma 36–19 in Gator Bowl; Tensi passed for 303 yds and 5 TDs, and Biletnikoff had 13 pass rec for 192 yds and 4 TDs.

1967 (7–2–2)   *Won:* Texas A&M 19–18, South Carolina 17–0, Texas Tech 28–12, Mississippi St. 24–12, Memphis St. 26–7, Virginia Tech 38–15, Florida 21–16 (1st win at Gainesville). *Lost:* Houston 33–13, N.C. State 20–10. *Tied:* Alabama 37–37. *Stars:* QB Kim Hammond (1,991 yds and 15 TDs pass), FL Ron Sellers (70 pass rec for 1,228 yds and 8 TDs), Bill Moreman (5 TDs). *Noteworthy:* overcame 17–0 halftime deficit to tie Penn St. 17–17 in Gator Bowl; Hammond passed to Sellers for 1 TD and scored another, and soph K Grant Guthrie kicked tying FG with 17 seconds left.

1968 (8–3)   *Won:* Maryland 24–14, Texas A&M 20–14, Memphis St. 20–10, South Carolina 35–28, Mississippi St. 27–14, N.C. State 48–7, Wake Forest 42–24, Houston 40–20. *Lost:* Florida 9–3, Virginia Tech 40–22. *Stars:* Sellers (nation's leader with 86 pass rec for 1,496 yds and 12 TDs), QB Bill Cappleman (2,410 yds and 25 TDs pass), soph RB Tom Bailey (570 yds rush), OT Jack Fenwick, LB Dale McCullers, DB John Crowe. *Noteworthy:* lost to Louisiana St. 31–27 in inaugural Peach Bowl; Cappleman passed for 3 TDs, 2 to Sellers.

1971 (8–4)   *Won:* Southern Mississippi 24–9, Miami (Fla.) 20–17, Kansas 30–7, Virginia Tech 17–3, Mississippi St. 27–9, South Carolina 49–18, Tulsa 45–10, Pittsburgh 31–13. *Lost:* Florida 17–15, Houston 14–7, Georgia Tech 12–6. *Stars:* QB Gary Huff (2,736 yds and 23 TDs pass), WR Rhett Dawson (62 pass rec for 817 yds and 7 TDs), Phil Magalski (516 yds rush), K Frank Fontes (13 FGs), DT Joe Strickler, LB Larry Strickland, DB James Thomas. *Noteworthy:* 1st year under Larry Jones. Lost to Arizona St. 45–38 in inaugural Fiesta Bowl; Huff passed to Dawson for 3 TDs.

1977 (10–2)   *Won:* Southern Mississippi 35–6, Kansas St. 18–10, Oklahoma St. 25–17, Cincinnati

14–0, Auburn 24–3 (1st in 11-game series dating to 1954), North Texas St. 35–14, Virginia Tech 23–21, Memphis St. 30–9, Florida 37–9 (1st over Gators since 1967). *Lost:* Miami (Fla.) 23–17, San Diego St. 41–16. *Stars:* Larry Key (1,117 yds rush), QB Wally Woodham (1,270 yds pass), Roger Overby (38 pass rec for 626 yds and 5 TDs), WR Mike Shumann, OG Wade Johnson, soph K Dave Cappelen (13 FGs), frosh MG Ron Simmons, DE Willie Jones, DB Nat Terry. *Noteworthy:* beat Texas Tech 40–17 in Tangerine Bowl; soph QB Jimmy Jordan and Woodham each threw 2 TD passes and Key scored on 93-yd kickoff return.
1978 (8–3) *Won:* Syracuse 28–0, Oklahoma St. 38–20, Miami (Fla.) 31–21, Cincinnati 26–21, Southern Mississippi 38–16, Virginia Tech 24–14, Navy 38–6, Florida 38–21. *Lost:* Houston 27–21, Mississippi St. 55–27, Pitt 7–3. *Stars:* Jordan (1,427 yds and 14 TDs pass), WR Jackie Flowers (43 pass rec for 757 yds and 7 TDs), soph Sam Platt (7 TDs on pass rec), Homes Johnson (817 yds rush), Mark Lyles (7 TDs), OG Mike Good, Cappelen (60 pts), Simmons, Jones, DE Nate Henderson.
1979 (11–1) *Won:* Southern Mississippi 17–14, Arizona St. 31–3, Miami (Fla.) 40–23, Virginia Tech 17–10, Louisville 27–0, Mississippi St. 17–6, Louisiana St. (LSU) 24–19, Cincinnati 26–21, South Carolina 27–7, Memphis St. 66–17, Florida 27–16. *Stars:* Lyles (1,011 yds rush, 35 pass rec for 211 yds, 9 TDs), Jordan (1,173 yds and 13 TDs pass), Flowers (37 pass rec for 622 yds and 7 TDs), Grady King (23 pass rec for 246 yds), soph Mike Whiting (522 yds rush), Good, C Gil Wesley, Cappelen (14 FGs, 70 pts), Simmons, DE Scott Warren, DBs Monk Bonasorte (8 int) and Bobby Butler (6 int). *Noteworthy:* 1st unbeaten season since 1950. Lost to Oklahoma 24–7 in Orange Bowl after taking early 7–0 lead on short run by Whiting; outgained 447–182 in total yds.
1980 (10–2) *Won:* LSU 16–0, Louisville 52–0, East Carolina 63–7, Nebraska 18–14 (1st meeting), Pitt 36–22, Boston College 41–7, Memphis St. 24–3, Tulsa 45–2, Virginia Tech 31–7, Florida 17–13. *Lost:* Miami (Fla.) 10–9. *Stars:* Simmons, DT Mark Macek, Bonasorte, Butler, LB Reggie Herring, QB Rick Stockstill (1,377 yds and 15 TDs pass), Whiting (25 pass rec for 203 yds), Platt (983 yds rush), soph RB Ricky Williams (6 TDs rush), OT Ken Lanier, OG Greg Futch, K Bill Capece (22 FGs, 104 pts), P Rohn Stark. *Noteworthy:* Led nation in scoring

defense (7.7-pt avg). Lost to Oklahoma 18–17 in Orange Bowl when Sooners scored TD and 2-pt conversion with 1:27 left; Williams scored 1st Seminole TD and Butler recovered errant center snap in Sooner end zone for other TD.
1982 (9–3) *Won:* Cincinnati 38–31, Southern Mississippi 24–17, Ohio St. 34–17, Southern Illinois 59–8, East Carolina 56–17, Miami (Fla.) 24–7, South Carolina 56–26, Louisville 49–14. *Lost:* Pitt 37–17, LSU 55–21, Florida 13–10. *Stars:* soph RB Greg Allen (776 yds rush, 16 pass rec for 233 yds, 1,524 all-purpose yds, nation's leader with 126 pts on 21 TDs), QB Kelly Lowrey (1,671 yds and 11 TDs pass), soph WR Jessie Hester (25 pass rec for 541 yds and 5 TDs), Tony Johnson (30 pass rec for 500 yds), Ricky Williams (857 yds rush), C Tom McCormick, frosh OL Jamie Dukes, DT Alphonso Carreker, frosh DL Isaac Williams, LB Tommy Young, Larry Harris (6 int), DB Harvey Clayton. *Noteworthy:* beat West Virginia 31–12 in Gator Bowl; Allen ran for 138 yds and 2 TDs, and QB Blair Williams passed for 202 yds and a TD.
1985 (9–3) *Won:* Tulane 38–12, Nebraska 17–13, Memphis St. 19–10, Kansas 24–20, Tulsa 76–14, North Carolina 20–10, South Carolina 56–14, Western Carolina 50–10. *Lost:* Auburn 59–27, Miami (Fla.) 35–27, Florida 38–14. *Stars:* Dukes, OT John Ionata, frosh QB Chip Ferguson (11 TDs pass), Hassan Jones (34 pass rec for 738 yds and 5 TDs), Tony Smith (678 yds rush), frosh TB Victor Floyd (619 yds rush), soph K Derek Schmidt (18 FGs, 98 pts), DT Gerald Nichols, soph LB Paul McGowan, soph DB Martin Mayhew, P Louis Berry. *Noteworthy:* beat Oklahoma St. 34–23 in Gator Bowl; Ferguson passed for 338 yds and 2 TDs, soph WR Herb Gainer had 7 pass rec for 148 yds and 2 TDs, and Smith ran for 201 yds.
1987 (11–1) *Won:* Texas Tech 40–16, East Carolina 44–3, Memphis St. 41–24, Michigan St. 31–3, Southern Mississippi 61–10, Louisville 32–9 (10th straight over Cardinals), Tulane 73–14, Auburn 34–6, Furman 41–10, Florida 28–14 (1st over Gators since 1980). *Lost:* unbeaten national champ Miami (Fla.) 26–25. *Stars:* soph TBs Sammie Smith (1,230 yds and 7 TDs rush) and Dexter Carter (679 yds rush, 19 pass rec for 216 yds, 7 TDs), QB Danny McManus (1,964 yds and 14 TDs pass), Gainer (30 pass rec for 478 yds and 6 TDs), soph WR Ronald Lewis (23 pass rec for 418 yds), Dayne Williams (15 TDs), TE Pat Carter, OG Jason Kuipers, OT Pat

Tomberlin, Schmidt (116 pts, nation's leader with 23 FGs), soph MG Odell Haggins, DT Eric Hayes, McGowan, LB Terry Warren, DB Deion Sanders. *Noteworthy:* beat Nebraska 31–28 in Fiesta Bowl; McManus passed for 375 yds and 3 TDs, and Gainer caught 5 for 89 yds and 2 TDs.

1988 (11–1) *Won:* Southern Mississippi 49–13, Clemson 24–21 (1st meeting since 1976), Michigan St. 30–7, Tulane 48–28, Georgia Southern 28–10, East Carolina 45–21, Louisiana Tech 66–3, South Carolina 59–0, Virginia Tech 41–14, Florida 52–17. *Lost:* Miami (Fla.) 31–0 in opener. *Stars:* Ferguson (1,714 yds and 16 TDs pass), WRs Terry Anthony (32 pass rec for 550 yds and 8 TDs), soph Lawrence Dawsey (10 TDs, 18 pass rec for 365 yds and 9 TDs) and Bruce LaSane (22 pass rec for 406 yds), Lewis (27 pass rec for 484 yds), Smith (577 yds rush, 5 TDs), Tomberlin, Kuipers, OT Joey Ionata, K Richie Andrews (72 pts), Haggins, DT Steve Gabbard, soph LB Kelvin Smith, DBs Stan Shiver, Dedrick Dodge (5 int) and Sanders (5 int, nation's punt return leader with 15.2-yd avg). *Noteworthy:* beat Auburn 13–7 in Sugar Bowl; Smith ran for 115 yds and Seminoles intercepted 3 passes, one by Sanders in end zone as game ended.

1989 (10–2) *Won:* LSU 31–21, Tulane 59–9, Syracuse 41–10, Virginia Tech 41–7, Auburn 22–14, national champ Miami (Fla.) 24–10, South Carolina 35–10, Memphis St. 57–20, Florida 24–17. *Lost:* Southern Mississippi 30–26, Clemson 34–23 in 1st 2 games. *Stars:* QB Peter Tom Willis (3,124 yds and 20 TDs pass), Anthony (33 pass rec for 569 yds and 8 TDs), Dawsey (38 pass rec for 683 yds), Lewis (27 pass rec for 535 yds), Carter (684 yds rush, 25 pass rec for 297 yds, 9 TDs), LaSane (22 pass rec for 299 yds), frosh RB Amp Lee (6 TDs, 10 pass rec for 272 yds), C Michael Tanks, DT Eric Hayes, Haggins, soph LB Kirk Carruthers, DB Leroy Butler (7 int). *Noteworthy:* beat Nebraska 41–17 in Fiesta Bowl; Willis passed for 422 yds and 5 TDs, Anthony caught 6 for 88 yds and 2 TDs, Lewis caught 5 for 106 yds, and Carter ran for 72 yds and caught a TD pass.

1990 (10–2) *Won:* East Carolina 45–24, Georgia Southern 48–6, Tulane 31–13, Virginia Tech 39–28, LSU 42–3, South Carolina 41–10, Cincinnati 70–21, Memphis St. 35–3, Florida 45–30. *Lost:* Miami (Fla.) 31–22, Auburn 20–17 in consecutive mid-season games. *Stars:* Dawsey (65 pass rec for 999

yds and 7 TDs), Lee (18 TDs, 825 yds rush, 34 pass rec for 360 yds), QBs Casey Weldon (1,600 yds and 12 TDs pass) and Brad Johnson (1,136 yds and 8 TDs pass), FBs Edgar Bennett (35 pass rec for 395 yds and 4 TDs, 5 TDs rush) and Paul Moore (5 TDs), Andrews (13 FGs, 91 pts), Carruthers, frosh LB Marvin Jones, soph DB Terrell Buckley (6 int). *Noteworthy:* beat Penn St. 24–17 in inaugural Blockbuster Bowl; Weldon passed for 248 yds and ran for a TD, Lee ran for 86 yds and 2 TDs, and Seminoles blocked FG attempt and intercepted 3 passes.

1991 (11–2) *Won:* Brigham Young 44–28, Tulane 38–11, Western Michigan 58–0, Michigan 51–31, Syracuse 46–14, Virginia Tech 33–20, Middle Tennessee St. 39–10, LSU 27–16, Louisville 40–15, South Carolina 38–10. *Lost:* unbeaten national cochamp Miami (Fla.) 17–16, Florida 14–9 in last 2 games. *Stars:* Weldon (2,527 yds and 22 TDs pass), Lee (14 TDs, 977 yds rush, 26 pass rec for 336 yds), WRs Shannon Baker (30 pass rec for 451 yds), Eric Turral (24 pass rec for 324 yds), soph Kevin Knox (22 pass rec for 441 yds) and frosh Kez McCorvey (22 pass rec for 303 yds), Bennett (29 pass rec for 345 yds, 7 TDs), Jones, Carruthers, Buckley (nation's leader with 12 int, 2 returned for TDs), P Scott Player (40.4-yd avg). *Noteworthy:* overcame 4 int to beat Texas A&M 10–2 in rainy, cold Cotton Bowl; soph TB Sean Jackson ran for 119 yds, Weldon scored on 4-yd run, soph K Gerry Thomas had 27-yd FG, and Seminoles recovered 6 Aggie fumbles.

1992 (11–1) *Won:* Duke 48–21 (1st meeting), Clemson 24–20, N.C. State 34–13 (1st meeting since 1969), Wake Forest 35–7 (1st meeting since 1973), North Carolina 36–13 (1st meeting since 1986), Georgia Tech 29–24 (1st meeting since 1975, 1st win in 9-game series dating to 1952), Virginia 13–3 (1st meeting), Maryland 69–21 (1st meeting since 1968), Tulane 70–7, Florida 45–24. *Lost:* unbeaten Miami (Fla.) 19–16. *Stars:* QB Charlie Ward (2,647 yds and 22 TDs pass, 504 yds and 6 TDs rush), frosh WR Tamarick Vanover (42 pass rec for 581 yds; 7 TDs, 2 on kickoff returns), McCorvey (34 pass rec for 521 yds and 6 TDs), Knox (35 pass rec for 396 yds), FL Matt Frier (22 pass rec for 340 yds), Baker (22 pass rec for 297 yds), soph TB Tiger McMillon (579 yds rush), soph FB William Floyd (10 TDs), OT Robert Stevenson, soph OG Patrick McNeil, soph K Dan Mowrey (10 FGs, 81 pts),

Lombardi Award–winner Jones, soph LB Derrick Brooks, soph DBs Corey Sawyer (7 int) and Clifton Abraham. *Noteworthy:* Won ACC title in 1st year in league. Beat Nebraska 27–14 in Orange Bowl (8th straight postseason win) as Ward passed for 187 yds and 2 TDs (to Vanover and McCorvey), Jackson ran for 101 yds and a TD, and Mowrey had 2 FGs.

BOWL SUMMARY

All-American 1–0; Blockbuster 1–0; Bluegrass 0–1; Cotton 1–0; Fiesta 2–1; Florida Citrus 0–0–1; Gator 3–0–1; Orange 1–2; Peach 1–1; Sugar 1–0; Sun 0–2; Tangerine 1–0.

BOWL RECORD (12–7–2)

Regular Season	Bowl	Score	Opponent	Record
1954 (8–3)	Sun	20–47	Texas–El Paso	(7–3)
1958 (7–3)	Bluegrass	6–15	Oklahoma St.	(7–3)
1964 (8–1–1)	Gator	36–19	Oklahoma	(6–3–1)
1966 (6–4)	Sun	20–28	Wyoming	(9–1)
1967 (7–2–1)	Gator	17–17	Penn State	(8–2)
1968 (8–2)	Peach	27–31	LSU	(7–3)
1971 (8–3)	Fiesta	38–45	Arizona St.	(10–1)
1977 (9–2)	Tangerine	40–17	Texas Tech	(7–4)
1979 (11–0)	Orange	7–24	Oklahoma	(10–1)
1980 (11–0)	Orange	17–18	Oklahoma	(9–2)
1982 (8–3)	Gator	31–12	West Virginia	(9–2)
1983 (6–5)	Peach	28–3	North Carolina	(8–3)
1984 (7–3–1)	Fla. Citrus	17–17	Georgia	(7–4)
1985 (8–3)	Gator	34–23	Oklahoma St.	(8–3)
1986 (6–4–1)	All-American	27–13	Indiana	(6–5)
1987 (10–1)	Fiesta	31–28	Nebraska	(10–1)
1988 (10–1)	Sugar	13–7	Auburn	(10–1)
1989 (9–2)	Fiesta	41–17	Nebraska	(10–1)
1990 (9–2)	Blockbuster	24–17	Penn State	(9–2)
1991 (10–2)	Cotton	10–2	Texas A&M	(10–1)
1992 (10–1)	Orange	27–14	Nebraska	(9–2)

CONFERENCE TITLES

Atlantic Coast—1992.

TOP 20 AP AND UPI
(USA TODAY/CNN SINCE 1991) RANKING

1964	U–11	1979	6–8	1986	U–20	1991	4–4
1967	U–15	1980	5–5	1987	2–2	1992	2–2
1968	U–14	1982	13–10	1988	3–3		
1971	U–19	1984	17–19	1989	3–2		
1977	14–11	1985	15–13	1990	4–4		

MAJOR RIVALS

Florida St. has played at least 10 games with Auburn 4–13–1, Florida 11–23–1, Furman 8–2, Georgia 4–5–1, Houston 2–12–2, Louisville 11–1, Memphis St. 10–7–1, Miami (Fla.) 14–22, N.C. State 9–4, South Carolina 15–3, Southern Mississippi 12–8–1, Tampa 9–2, Tulane 10–0, Virginia Tech 18–10–1, Wake Forest 8–2–1. Record against ACC foes met fewer than 10 times is Clemson 4–2, Duke 1–0, Georgia Tech 1–7–1, Maryland 3–0, North Carolina 3–0–1, Virginia 1–0.

COACHES

Dean of Florida State coaches is Bobby Bowden with record of 154–45–3 for 1976–92 with 14 bowl teams (11 winners) and 1 team unbeaten in regular season. Other top records for at least 3 seasons were by Don Veller, 31–12–1 for 1948–52 with 1 unbeaten team and 1 minor bowl team; Tom Nugent, 34–28–1 for 1953–58 with 2 bowl teams; and Bill Peterson, 62–42–11 for 1960–70 with 4 bowl teams.

MISCELLANEA

First game was loss to Stetson 14–6 in 1947 . . . 1st win was over Cumberland 30–0 in 1948 . . . highest score was over Tulsa 76–14 in 1985 . . . biggest margin was over Whiting Field 74–0 in 1949 . . . biggest margin over college foe was over Louisiana Tech 66–3 in 1988 and over Tulane 70–7 in 1992 . . . worst defeat was by Florida 49–0 in 1973 . . . highest against Seminoles was by Auburn 59–27 in 1985 . . . longest win streak of 16 in 1990–91 ended by Miami (Fla.) 17–16 . . . 15-game win streak in 1978–79 ended by Oklahoma 24–7 in 1980 Orange Bowl . . . 13-game win streak in 1949–51 ended by Miami (Fla.) 35–13 . . . longest losing string of 20 in 1972–74 broken with win over Miami (Fla.) 21–14 . . . consensus All-Americans were Fred Biletnikoff, E, 1964; Ron Sellers, E, 1967; Ron Simmons, MG, 1979–80; Greg Allen, RB, 1983; Jamie Dukes, OL, 1985; Deion Sanders, DB, 1987–88; LeRoy Butler, DB, 1989; Terrell Buckley, DB, 1991; and Marvin Jones, LB, 1991–92 . . . Academic All-Americans were Gary Huff, QB,

1972; Phil Williams, WR, 1979; William Keith Jones, DB, 1979–80; and Rohn Stark, P, 1981 . . . Lombardi Award–winner was Marvin Jones, LB, 1992.

GEORGIA TECH (Yellow Jackets, *Rambling Wreck; Old Gold and White*)

NOTABLE TEAMS

1901 (4–0–1) *Won:* Gordon 29–0, Furman 17–0 (1st meeting), Wofford 33–0, South Carolina 13–0 (1st meeting). *Tied:* Furman 5–5. *Noteworthy:* Had 1st unbeaten season under Dr. Cyrus W. Strickler.

1904 (8–1–1) *Won:* Ft. McPherson 11–5, Florida St. (not FSU) 35–0, Mooney School 51–0, Florida 77–0 (1st meeting), Tennessee 2–0, Georgia 23–6 (1st over Bulldogs in 7 games since 1893), Tennessee Meds 59–0, Cumberland 18–0. *Lost:* unbeaten Auburn 12–0. *Tied:* Clemson 11–11. *Stars:* E Craig Day, soph T/E Lob Brown, FB Lewis Clark. *Noteworthy:* 1st year under John Heisman.

1905 (6–0–1) *Won:* Dahlonega 54–0 (1st game on present Grant Field), Clemson 17–10 (1st in 6-game series dating to 1898), Alabama 12–5, Cumberland 15–0, Tennessee 45–0, Georgia 46–0. *Tied:* Sewanee 18–18.

1909 (7–2) *Won:* Gordon 18–6, Mooney 35–0, South Carolina 59–0, Tennessee 29–0, Georgia 12–6, Mercer 35–0, Clemson 29–3. *Lost:* Sewanee 15–0, Auburn 9–0. *Star:* FB J.W. Davis.

1911 (6–2–1) *Won:* 11th Cavalry 22–5, Howard 28–0, Tennessee 24–0, Mercer 17–0, Sewanee 23–0 (1st in 8-game series dating to 1899), Clemson 32–0. *Lost:* Auburn 11–6, Georgia 5–0. *Tied:* Alabama 0–0. *Stars:* T Pat Patterson, E Roy Goree.

1913 (7–2) *Won:* Ft. McPherson 19–0, The Citadel 47–0, Chattanooga 71–6, Mercer 33–0, Florida 13–3, Sewanee 33–0, Clemson 34–0. *Lost:* unbeaten Auburn 20–0, Georgia 14–0 in successive late games.

1914 (6–2) *Won:* South Carolina 20–0, Mercer 105–0, Virginia Military Institute (VMI) 28–7 (1st meeting), Sewanee 20–0, Georgia 7–0, Clemson 26–6. *Lost:* Alabama 13–0, unbeaten Auburn 14–0. *Stars:* soph E Jim Senter, HB K.J. "Wooch" Fielder.

1915 (7–0–1) *Won:* Mercer 52–0, Davidson 27–7, Transylvania 67–0, Louisiana State (LSU) 36–7 (1st meeting), North Carolina 23–3 (1st meeting),

Alabama 21–7, Auburn 7–0 (1st over Tigers since 1906). *Tied:* Georgia 0–0. *Stars:* Fielder, Senter, B D.E. "Froggy" Morrison. *Noteworthy:* 1st unbeaten season since 1905.

1916 (8–0–1) *Won:* Mercer 61–0, Cumberland 222–0 (highest score ever in college football game), Davidson 9–0, North Carolina 10–6, Tulane 45–0 (1st meeting), Alabama 13–0, Georgia 21–0, Auburn 33–7. *Tied:* Washington & Lee 7–7. *Stars:* T Walker Carpenter, G Bob Lang, soph C G.M. "Pup" Phillips, Bs Everett Strupper and Tommy Spence.

1917 (9–0) *Won:* Wake Forest 33–0 (1st meeting), Furman 25–0, Pennsylvania 41–0, Davidson 32–10, Washington & Lee 63–0, Vanderbilt 83–0 (1st in 5-game series dating to 1892), Tulane 48–0, Carlisle Indians 98–0, Auburn 68–7. *Stars:* Strupper (1st Tech consensus All-American), Carpenter, Phillips, Bs Albert Hill (132 pts) and Joe Guyon, Es Bill Fincher and M.F. "Shorty" Guill. *Noteworthy:* Heisman's 3rd straight unbeaten team outscored foes 494–17 and won 1st national championship. Turned down Rose Bowl bid when many players enlisted in service for W.W. I.

1918 (6–1) *Won:* Clemson 28–0, Furman 118–0, Camp Gordon 28–0, 11th Cavalry 119–0, N.C. State 128–0 (1st meeting), Auburn 41–0. *Lost:* national champ Pittsburgh 32–0 (1st meeting). *Stars:* Guyon, Fincher, C Ashel Day.

1919 (7–3) *Won:* 5th Division 48–0, Furman 74–0, Wake Forest 14–0, Clemson 28–0, Vanderbilt 20–0, Davidson 33–0, Georgetown 27–0. *Lost:* Pittsburgh 16–6, Washington & Lee 3–0, Auburn 14–7. *Stars:* Phillips, G Dave LeBey, frosh E Albert Staton, soph Bs J.W. Harlan, A.R. "Buck" Flowers, and D.I. "Red" Barron. *Noteworthy:* Heisman's last team.

1920 (8–1) *Won:* Wake Forest 44–0, Oglethorpe 55–0, Davidson 66–0, Vanderbilt 44–0, Centre 24–0, Clemson 7–0 (10th straight over Tigers), Georgetown 35–6, Auburn 34–0. *Lost:* unbeaten Pittsburgh 10–3. *Stars:* Fincher, Staton, Flowers (47.7-yd punting avg, 6 drop-kicked FGs), Barron, Harlan. *Noteworthy:* 1st year under William A. Alexander.

1921 (8–1) *Won:* Wake Forest 42–0, Oglethorpe 41–0, Davidson 70–0, Furman 69–0, Rutgers 48–14, Clemson 48–7, Georgetown 21–7, Auburn 14–0. *Lost:* unbeaten Penn St. 28–7 (in New York). *Stars:* E/T Staton, Barron, Harlan.

1922 (7–2) *Won:* Oglethorpe 31–6, Davidson 19–0,

Alabama 33–7, Georgetown 19–7, Clemson 21–7, Auburn 14–6, N.C. State 17–0. *Lost:* Navy 13–0 (1st meeting), Notre Dame 13–3 (1st meeting) in successive mid-season games. *Stars:* 5th-year back Barron, 5th–year G Oscar Davis, soph C Claire Frye. *Noteworthy:* won 1st SC title.

1925 (6–2–1) *Won:* Oglethorpe 13–7, VMI 33–0, Penn St. 16–7, Florida 23–7, Vanderbilt 7–0, Georgia 3–0 (1st meeting since 1916). *Lost:* unbeaten Alabama 7–0, Notre Dame 13–0 in successive mid-season games. *Tied:* Auburn 7–7 in finale. *Stars:* B Doug Wycoff, G Walter Godwin, C Owen Poole, T Mack Tharpe.

1927 (8–1–1) *Won:* VMI 7–0, Tulane 13–6, Alabama 13–0, North Carolina 13–0 (1st meeting since 1916), LSU 23–0, Oglethorpe 19–7, Auburn 18–0, Georgia 12–0. *Lost:* Notre Dame 26–7. *Tied:* Vanderbilt 0–0. *Stars:* C Peter Pund, T Frank Speer, E Ed Crowley, soph B J.G. "Stumpy" Thomason. *Noteworthy:* won 2nd SC title.

1928 (10–0–0) *Won:* VMI 13–0, Tulane 12–0, Notre Dame 13–0 (1st in 7-game series dating to 1922), North Carolina 20–7, Oglethorpe 32–7, Vanderbilt 19–7, Alabama 33–13, Auburn 51–0, Georgia 20–6. *Stars:* Pund, Speer, Thomason, B Warner Mizell, soph E Tom Jones, G Raleigh Drennon. *Noteworthy:* Got share of 2nd national crown and won 3rd and last SC title in 1st unbeaten season since 1917. Made 1st postseason appearance, edging California 8–7 in Rose Bowl when Roy Riegels' wrong-way run set up safety on blocked punt by soph T Vance Maree in 2nd quarter; scored TD in 3rd quarter to take 8–0 lead.

1939 (8–2) *Won:* Howard 35–0 (1st meeting since 1911), Vanderbilt 14–6, Alabama 6–0, Kentucky 13–6, Auburn 7–6, Florida 21–7, Georgia 13–0. *Lost:* Notre Dame 17–14 (in opener), Duke 7–6. *Star:* E Rob Ison. *Noteworthy:* Got share of 1st SEC title. Beat Missouri 21–7 in Orange Bowl as Ison broke 7–7 tie with 59-yd TD run in 2nd quarter and Earl Wheby ran 34 yds for clinching TD in 3rd period.

1942 (9–2) *Won:* Auburn 15–0, Notre Dame 13–6 (1st over Irish in 6 games since 1928), Chattanooga 30–6, Davidson 33–0 (1st meeting since 1922), Navy 21–0 (1st meeting since 1922), Duke 26–7, Kentucky 47–7, Alabama 7–0, Florida 20–7. *Lost:* Georgia 34–0 in finale. *Stars:* G Harvey Hardy, B Clint Castleberry. *Noteworthy:* lost to Texas 14–7 in Cotton Bowl when last-ditch effort fell short at

Texas 3-yd line; Yellow Jackets scored earlier on TD by Davey Eldredge on 4th down statue of liberty play.

1943 (8–3) *Won:* North Carolina 20–7, Georgia Navy Pre-Flight 35–7, Ft. Benning 27–0, LSU 42–7 (1st meeting since 1927), Tulane 33–0 (1st over Green Wave in 7 games since 1928), Clemson 41–6, Georgia 48–0. *Lost:* national champ Notre Dame 55–13, Navy 28–14, Duke 14–7. *Stars:* G John Steber, T Bill Chambers, E Phil Tinsley, B Eddie Prokop. *Noteworthy:* Took 2nd SEC title. Beat undefeated Tulsa 20–18 in Sugar Bowl after trailing 18–7 when Ed Scharfschwerdt scored winning TD on 1-yd plunge midway in 4th quarter; Prokop ran for 199 yds, threw a TD pass to Tinsley, and kicked 2 ex pts.

1944 (8–3) *Won:* Clemson 51–0, North Carolina 28–0, Auburn 27–0, Navy 17–15, Georgia Navy Pre-Flight 13–7, Tulane 34–7, LSU 14–6, Georgia 44–0. *Lost:* Duke 19–13, Notre Dame 21–0. *Stars:* Tinsley, B Frank Broyles. *Noteworthy:* Alexander's last team repeated as SEC champ. Lost to Tulsa 26–12 in Orange Bowl; Broyles passed for 304 yds and a TD (51 yds to Johnny McIntosh), and Rumsey Taylor scored on 2-yd run.

1946 (9–2) *Won:* VMI 32–6 (1st meeting since 1928), Mississippi 24–7 (1st meeting), LSU 26–7, Auburn 27–6, Duke 14–0, Navy 28–20, Tulane 35–7, Furman 41–7 (1st meeting since 1921). *Lost:* Tennessee 13–9 (1st meeting since 1911) in opener, unbeaten Georgia 35–7 in finale. *Stars:* T Bobby Davis, C Paul Duke, Broyles (back from military service). *Noteworthy:* beat St. Mary's 41–19 in rainy, muddy Oil Bowl; picked off 8 passes (HB Pat McHugh returned one 73 yds for TD) and scored twice on passes to soph E George Brodnax.

1947 (10–1) *Won:* Tennessee 27–0, Tulane 20–6, VMI 20–0, Auburn 27–7, The Citadel 38–0 (1st meeting since 1913), Duke 7–0, Navy 16–14, Furman 51–0, Georgia 7–0. *Lost:* Alabama 14–7. *Stars:* Davis, G Bill Healy. *Noteworthy:* beat undefeated Kansas 20–14 in Orange Bowl as Rollo Phillips recovered Kansas fumble inches from Tech goal line in closing minutes; QB Jim Still threw 3 TD passes (2 to frosh Jim Patton).

1948 (7–3) *Won:* Vanderbilt 13–0, Tulane 13–7, Washington & Lee 27–0 (1st meeting since 1926), Auburn 27–0, Florida 42–7, Duke 19–7, The Citadel 54–0. *Lost:* Tennessee 13–6, Alabama 14–12, Georgia 21–13. *Stars:* Healy, Brodnax. *Note-*

worthy: led nation in total defense and rush defense.

1949 (7–3) *Won:* Vanderbilt 12–7, Washington & Lee 36–0, Auburn 35–21, Florida 43–14, Tennessee 30–13, South Carolina 13–3 (1st meeting since 1931), Georgia 7–6. *Lost:* Tulane 18–0, Duke 27–14, Alabama 20–7.

1951 (11–0–1) *Won:* Southern Methodist (SMU) 21–7, Florida 27–0, Kentucky 13–7, LSU 25–7, Auburn 27–7 (10th straight over Tigers), Vanderbilt 8–7, VMI 34–7, Alabama 27–7, Davidson 34–7, Georgia 48–6. *Tied:* Duke 14–14 in mid-season. *Stars:* G Ray Beck, DT Lamar Wheat, OT Lum Snyder, QB Darrell Crawford (1,237 yds and 13 TDs pass), WR Buck Martin (9 TDs, 37 pass rec for 506 yds and 8 TDs), soph RB Leon Hardeman (617 yds rush, 8 TDs), soph LB George Morris (6 int). *Noteworthy:* Nation's most-improved team got share of 4th SEC title in 1st unbeaten season since 1928. Beat Baylor 17–14 in Orange Bowl on TD pass from Crawford to Martin and 16-yd FG by soph QB Pepper Rodgers in 4th quarter; Hardeman scored on 3-yd 1st quarter run.

1952 (12–0) *Won:* The Citadel 54–6, Florida 17–14, SMU 20–7, Tulane 14–0, Auburn 33–0, Vanderbilt 30–0, Duke 28–7, Army 45–6, Alabama 7–3, Florida St. 30–0 (1st meeting), Georgia 23–9. *Stars:* OT Hal Miller, C Pete Brown, Rodgers (5 FGs, 60 pts), Hardeman, B Bill Teas (825 yds and 6 TDs rush), Martin (28 pass rec for 398 yds and 6 TDs), DB Bobby Moorhead (7 int, 2 returned for TDs), Morris. *Noteworthy:* Won 5th and last SEC title. Beat undefeated Mississippi 24–7 in Sugar Bowl; Hardeman ran for 76 yds and a TD, Rodgers threw TD pass and kicked FG, and Morris starred on defense.

1953 (9–2–1) *Won:* Davidson 53–0, SMU 6–4, Tulane 27–13, Auburn 36–6, Vanderbilt 43–0, Clemson 20–7, Duke 13–10, Georgia 28–12. *Lost:* unbeaten national cochamp Notre Dame 27–14, Alabama 13–6. *Tied:* Florida 0–0. *Stars:* C/LB Morris, Teas (610 yds rush), B Glen Turner. *Noteworthy:* beat West Virginia 42–19 in Sugar Bowl; Rodgers passed for 195 yds and 3 TDs and kicked FG and 2 ex pts, and Sam Hensley caught 4 passes for 76 yds and TD.

1954 (8–3) *Won:* Tulane 28–0, SMU 10–7, LSU 30–20, Auburn 14–7, Tennessee 28–7, Alabama 20–0, Georgia 7–3. *Lost:* Florida 13–12 (1st to Gators in 8 games since 1941), Kentucky 13–6,

Duke 21–20. *Stars:* Morris, G Franklin Brooks, E Henry Hair (24 pass rec for 270 yds). *Noteworthy:* beat Arkansas 14–6 in Cotton Bowl; George Humphreys ran for 99 yds, and soph Paul Rotenberry and QB Wade Mitchell each scored TDs.

1955 (9–1–1) *Won:* Miami (Fla.) 14–6 (1st meeting), Florida 14–7, SMU 20–7, LSU 7–0, Florida St. 34–0, Duke 27–0, Alabama 26–2, Georgia 21–3. *Lost:* Auburn 14–12 (1st to Tigers in 14 games since 1940). *Tied:* Tennessee 7–7. *Stars:* Brooks, Hair, George Volkert (583 yds rush), Ronald "Toppy" Vann (6 TDs). *Noteworthy:* Led nation in scoring defense (4.6-pt avg). Beat Pittsburgh 7–0 (1st meeting since 1920) in Sugar Bowl on Mitchell's TD in 1st quarter; Brooks starred on defense.

1956 (10–1) *Won:* Kentucky 14–6, SMU 9–7, LSU 39–7, Auburn 28–7, Tulane 40–0, Duke 7–0, Alabama 27–0, Florida 28–0, Georgia 35–0. *Lost:* unbeaten Tennessee 6–0 in mid-season. *Stars:* C/LB Don Stephenson, Vann (5 TDs), B Ken Owen, G Allen Ecker. *Noteworthy:* Again led nation in scoring defense (3.3-pt avg). Beat Pittsburgh 21–14 in Gator Bowl with help of 2 int and 2 fumble recoveries; TDs scored by Owen, E Jerry Nabors (on pass from Volkert), and Rotenberry.

1961 (7–4) *Won:* Southern California 27–7, Rice 24–0, Duke 21–0, Auburn 7–6, Tulane 35–0, Florida 20–0, Georgia 22–7. *Lost:* LSU 10–0, Tennessee 10–6, unbeaten national cochamp Alabama 10–0. *Stars:* G Dave Watson, Billy Williamson (21 pass rec for 221 yds). *Noteworthy:* lost to Penn St. 30–15 (1st meeting since 1925) in Gator Bowl after 68-yd run by soph Joe Auer gave Tech early 9–0 lead; soph QB Billy Lothridge passed for 154 yds.

1962 (7–3–1) *Won:* Clemson 26–9, Florida 17–0, Tennessee 17–0, Tulane 42–12 (10th straight over Green Wave), Duke 20–9, Alabama 7–6, Georgia 37–6. *Lost:* LSU 10–7, Auburn 17–14. *Tied:* Florida St. 14–14. *Stars:* Lothridge (1,006 yds and 6 TDs pass, 478 yds and 9 TDs rush, 5 FGs, 89 pts), E Billy Martin (21 pass rec for 323 yds), Watson, G Rufus Guthrie. *Noteworthy:* lost to Missouri 14–10 in Bluebonnet Bowl; Auer had 62 yds and a TD rush and 57 yds on 3 pass rec.

1963 (7–3) *Won:* Florida 9–0, Clemson 27–0, Tennessee 23–7, Tulane 17–3, Duke 30–6, Florida St. 15–7, Georgia 14–3. *Lost:* LSU 7–6, Auburn 29–21,

Alabama 27–11. *Stars:* Lothridge (1,017 yds and 10 TDs pass, 223 yds and 3 TDs rush, 41-yd punting avg, 69 pts, nation's leader with 12 FGs), Martin (19 pass rec for 221 yds). *Noteworthy:* last year of SEC competition.

1964 (7–3) *Won:* Vanderbilt 14–2, Miami (Fla.) 20–0, Clemson 14–7, Navy 17–0 (1st meeting since 1947), Auburn 7–3, Tulane 7–6, Duke 21–8. *Lost:* Tennessee 22–14, unbeaten national cochamp Alabama 24–7, Georgia 7–0 in last 3 games. *Stars:* DB Gerry Bussell, C Bill Curry, Johnny Gresham (22 pass rec for 290 yds).

1966 (9–2) *Won:* Texas A&M 38–3, Vanderbilt 42–0, Clemson 13–12, Tennessee 6–3, Auburn 17–3, Tulane 35–17, Duke 48–7, Virginia 14–13, Penn St. 21–0. *Lost:* Georgia 23–14 in finale. *Stars:* C Jim Breland, Lenny Snow (761 yds and 12 TDs rush), Steve Almond (24 pass rec for 265 yds), DB Bill Eastman (4 int). *Noteworthy:* Bobby Dodd's last team. Lost to Florida 27–12 in Orange Bowl after early 6–0 lead; Snow ran for 110 yds.

1970 (9–3) *Won:* South Carolina 23–20 (1st meeting since 1950), Florida St. 23–13, Miami (Fla.) 31–21, Clemson 28–7, Tulane 20–6, Duke 24–16, Navy 30–8, Georgia 17–7. *Lost:* Tennessee 17–6, Auburn 31–7, Notre Dame 10–7. *Stars:* DT Rock Perdoni, DBs Jeff Ford and Rick Lewis (6 int, 2 returned for TDs), soph QB Eddie McAshan (1,138 yds pass), Larry Studdard (29 pass rec for 355 yds), Brent Cunningham (740 yds rush, 7 TDs). Beat Texas Tech 17–9 in Sun Bowl; QB Jack Williams passed for 123 yds and Tech scored on TDs by Rob Healy and TB Kevin McNamara, and FG by Jack Moore.

1985 (9–2–1) *Won:* N.C. State 28–18, Clemson 14–3, North Carolina 31–0, Western Carolina 24–17, Duke 9–0, UT-Chattanooga 35–7 (1st meeting since 1942), Wake Forest 41–10, Georgia 20–16. *Lost:* Virginia 24–13 (1st in 8-game series dating to 1965), Auburn 17–14. *Tied:* Tennessee 6–6. *Stars:* QB John Dewberry (1,557 yds pass), B Cory Collier (606 yds rush), Gary Lee (7 TDs, 29 pass rec for 645 yds and 6 TDs), DE Pat Swilling, LB Ted Roof, DB Cleve Pounds. *Noteworthy:* beat Michigan St. 17–14 in All-American Bowl as soph TB Malcolm King (122 yds rush) scored winning TD on 5-yd run with 1:50 left; soph QB Todd Rampley scored other Tech TD and David Bell kicked 40-yd FG.

1990 (11–0–1) *Won:* N.C. State 21–13, UT-Chattanooga 44–9, South Carolina 27–6, Maryland 31–3, Clemson 21–19, Duke 48–31, Virginia 41–38, Virginia Tech 6–3, Wake Forest 42–7, Georgia 40–23. *Tied:* North Carolina 13–13. *Stars:* soph QB Shawn Jones (2,008 yds and 13 TDs pass, 277 yds and 6 TDs rush), FLs Emmett Merchant (29 pass rec for 489 yds), Bobby Rodriguez (27 pass rec for 493 yds) and Greg Lester (16 pass rec for 236 yds), soph RB William Bell (891 yds rush, 7 TDs), FB Stefen Scotton (5 TDs rush), soph K Scott Sisson (15 FGs, 84 pts), LBs Jerrelle Williams, Calvin Tiggle and soph Marco Coleman, DBs Willie Clay and Ken Swilling (5 int). *Noteworthy:* Won 1st ACC title in 1st unbeaten season since 1952. Beat Nebraska 45–21 in Florida Citrus Bowl to earn share of 3rd national championship; Jones passed for 277 yds and 2 TDs and scored another, and Bell ran for 127 yds and 2 TDs (including 57-yd run) and scored on pass rec.

BOWL SUMMARY

All-American 1–0; Aloha 1–0; Bluebonnet 0–1; Cotton 1–1; Florida Citrus 1–0; Gator 2–2; Liberty 1–0; Oil 1–0; Orange 3–2; Peach 0–2; Rose 1–0; Sugar 4–0; Sun 1–0.

BOWL RECORD (17–8)

Regular Season	Bowl	Score	Opponent	Record
1928 (9–0)	Rose	8–7	California	(6–1–2)
1939 (7–2)	Orange	21–7	Missouri	(9–1)
1942 (9–1)	Cotton	7–14	Texas	(8–2)
1943 (7–3)	Sugar	20–18	Tulsa	(6–0–1)
1944 (8–2)	Orange	12–26	Tulsa	(7–2)
1946 (8–2)	Oil	41–19	St. Mary's	(6–2)
1947 (9–1)	Orange	20–14	Kansas	(8–0–2)
1951 (10–0–1)	Orange	17–14	Baylor	(8–1–1)
1952 (11–0)	Sugar	24–7	Mississippi	(8–0–2)
1953 (8–2–1)	Sugar	42–19	West Virginia	(8–1)
1954 (7–3)	Cotton	14–6	Arkansas	(8–2)
1955 (8–1–1)	Sugar	7–0	Pittsburgh	(7–3)
1956 (9–1)	Gator	21–14	Pittsburgh	(7–2–1)
1959 (6–4)	Gator	7–14	Arkansas	(8–2)
1961 (7–3)	Gator	15–30	Penn State	(7–3)
1962 (7–2–1)	Bluebonnet	10–14	Missouri	(7–1–2)
1965 (6–3–1)	Gator	31–21	Texas Tech	(8–2)
1966 (9–1)	Orange	12–27	Florida	(8–2)
1970 (8–3)	Sun	17–9	Texas Tech	(8–3)
1971 (6–5)	Peach	18–41	Mississippi	(9–2)
1972 (6–4–1)	Liberty	31–30	Iowa State	(5–5–1)
1978 (7–4)	Peach	21–41	Purdue	(8–2–1)
1985 (8–2–1)	All-American	17–14	Michigan St.	(7–4)
1990 (10–0–1)	Fla. Citrus	45–21	Nebraska	(9–2)
1991 (7–5)	Aloha	18–17	Stanford	(8–3)

CONFERENCE TITLES

Southern—1922, 1927, 1928. **Southeastern**—1939*, 1943, 1944, 1951*, 1952. **Atlantic Coast**—1990.

TOP 20 AP AND UPI RANKING

1939	16	1947	10	1955	7–7	1970	13–17
1942	5	1951	5–5	1956	4–4	1972	20–U
1943	13	1952	2–2	1961	13–13	1985	19–18
1944	13	1953	8–9	1962	U–11	1990	2–1
1946	11	1954	U–11	1966	8–8		

MAJOR RIVALS

Georgia Tech has played at least 10 games with Alabama 21–28–3, Auburn 39–47–4, Clemson 39–16–2, Davidson 12–2, Duke 31–28–1, Florida 23–9–6, Furman 8–2–3, Georgia 35–47–5, Kentucky 11–7–1, LSU 12–5, Mercer 13–1–1, Navy 13–8, North Carolina 13–12–3, N.C. State 7–5, Notre Dame 4–25–1, Sewanee 5–7–1, South Carolina 12–9, SMU 8–2–1, Tennessee 17–24–2, Tulane 35–13, Vanderbilt 16–15–3, Virginia 9–5–1, VMI 14–1, Wake Forest 11–4. Record against ACC foes met fewer than 10 times is Florida St. 7–1–1, Maryland 4–1.

COACHES

Georgia Tech's coach with most wins is Bobby Dodd with record of 165–64–8 for 1945–66, including 2 SEC titles, 13 bowl teams, and 2 unbeaten teams. Dean of Tech coaches is William A. Alexander (1942 national Coach of Year) with record of 134–95–15 for 1920–44, including 6 conference titles, 5 bowl teams, and 1 unbeaten national champion. Other top records for at least 3 years were by John Heisman, 102–29–7 for 1904–19 with 4 unbeaten teams and 1 national champion; Bud Carson, 27–27 for 1967–71 with 2 bowl teams; Pepper Rodgers, 34–31–2 for 1974–79 with 1 bowl team; Bill Curry, 31–43–4 for 1980–86 with 1 bowl team; and Bobby Ross (1990 national Coach of Year), 31–26–1 for 1987–91 with 1 ACC title, 2 bowl champions, and 1 unbeaten national champion.

MISCELLANEA

First game was loss to Mercer 12–0 in 1892 . . . 1st win was over Georgia 28–6 in 1893 . . . highest score was over Cumberland 222–0 (highest ever in college football) in 1916 . . . highest since W.W. II was over N.C. State 59–21 in 1986 . . . biggest margin since W.W. II was over The Citadel 54–0 in 1948 . . . worst defeat was by Auburn 94–0 in 1894 . . . worst since 1900 was by Clemson 73–0 in 1903 . . . worst since W.W. II was by Notre Dame 69–14 in 1977 . . . longest unbeaten string of 33 in 1914–18 ended by Pittsburgh 32–0 . . . 31-game unbeaten string in 1950–53 ended by Notre Dame 27–14 . . . 16-game unbeaten strings in 1927–29 ended by North Carolina 18–7 and in 1989–90 ended by Penn State 34–22 in 1991 opener . . . longest winless string of 15 in 1896–1901 broken with win over Gordon 29–0 . . . consensus All-Americans were Everett Strupper, B, 1917; Joe Guyon, B, and Ashel Day, C, 1918; Bill Fincher, E, 1918, 1920; Pete Pund, C, 1928; Harvey Hardy, G, 1942; Phil Tinsley, E, 1944; Paul Duke, C, 1946; Bob Davis, T, 1947; Hal Miller, T, 1952; Larry Morris, C, 1953; Maxie Baughan, C, 1959; Jim Breland, C, 1966; Rock Perdoni, DT, 1970; Randy Rhino, DB, 1973; and Ken Swilling, DB, 1990 . . . Academic All-Americans were Ed Gossage, G, Cecil Trainer, E, and George Morris, LB, 1952; Wade Mitchell, B, 1955; Allen Ecker, G, 1956; Jim Breland, C, and W.J. Blaine, LB, 1966; Bill Eastman, DB, 1966–67; Sheldon Fox, LB, 1980; and Stefen Scotton, RB, 1990.

MARYLAND (Terrapins, Terps; Red and White, Black and Gold)

NOTABLE TEAMS

1893 (6–0) *Won:* Eastern H.S. 36–0, Central H.S. 10–0, Baltimore City College 18–0, St. John's College 6–0, Western Maryland 18–10, Orient A.C. 16–6. *Noteworthy:* 1st undefeated season.
1896 (6–2–2) *Won:* Business H.S. 32–0, Central H.S. 10–6, 14–0, Alexandria H.S. 18–0, Bethel Military Academy 20–10, Western Maryland 16–6. *Lost:* Eastern H.S. 6–0, Episcopal H.S. 6–0. *Tied:*

Gallaudet 0–0, U. of Maryland 0–0. *Noteworthy:* resumed competition after 1-year layoff.

1912 (6–1–1) *Won:* Technical H.S. 31–6, Richmond 46–0, U. of Maryland 58–0, Johns Hopkins 13–0 (1st in 9-game series dating to 1892), Gallaudet 13–6, Western Maryland 17–7. *Lost:* St. John's 27–0. *Tied:* Pennsylvania Military College 13–13.

1916 (6–2) *Won:* Dickinson 6–0, Virginia Military Institute (VMI) 15–9, St. John's 31–6, New York U. 10–7, Catholic U. 13–9, Johns Hopkins 54–0. *Lost:* Navy 14–7, Haverford 7–6. *Noteworthy:* 1st year as Maryland State.

1918 (4–1–1) *Won:* VMI 7–6, Western Maryland 19–0, New York U. 6–2, St. John's 19–14. *Lost:* American U. 13–6 in opener. *Tied:* Johns Hopkins 0–0 in finale.

1920 (7–2) *Won:* Randolph-Macon 54–0, Catholic U. 14–0, Washington College 27–0, Virginia Tech 7–0, North Carolina 13–0 (1st meeting since 1899), Syracuse 10–7 (1st meeting), Johns Hopkins 24–7. *Lost:* Rutgers 6–0, unbeaten Princeton 35–0. *Noteworthy:* 1st year as University of Maryland. 9th straight winning season under H.C. Byrd.

1923 (7–2–1) *Won:* Randolph-Macon 53–0, Pennsylvania 3–0, Richmond 23–0, North Carolina 14–0, St. John's 26–0, N.C. State 26–12, Catholic U. 40–6. *Lost:* Virginia Tech 16–7, unbeaten Yale 16–14. *Tied:* Johns Hopkins 6–6. *Star:* soph E Bill Supplee.

1931 (8–1–1) *Won:* Washington College 13–0, Virginia 7–6, Navy 6–0 (1st in 9-game series dating to 1905), VMI 41–20, Virginia Tech 20–0, Washington & Lee 13–7, Johns Hopkins 35–14, Western Maryland 41–6. *Lost:* Vanderbilt 39–12. *Tied:* Kentucky 6–6. *Star:* G Jess Krajcovic.

1934 (7–3) *Won:* St. John's 13–0, Virginia Tech 14–9, Florida 21–0, Virginia 20–0, VMI 23–0, Georgetown 6–0 (1st meeting since 1907), Johns Hopkins 19–0. *Lost:* Washington & Lee 7–0, Navy 16–13, Indiana 17–14. *Stars:* FB Norwood Sothoron, soph HB Bill Guckeyson, soph E Vic Willis, T Ed Minion. *Noteworthy:* Byrd's last team.

1935 (7–2–2) *Won:* St. John's 39–6, Virginia Tech 7–0, VMI 6–0, Florida 20–6, Virginia 14–7, Georgetown 12–6, Western Maryland 22–7. *Lost:* North Carolina 33–0, Indiana 13–7. *Tied:* Washington & Lee 0–0, Syracuse 0–0 (1st meeting since 1921). *Stars:* Guckeyson, Willis. *Noteworthy:* 1st year under Jack Faber.

1937 (8–2) *Won:* St. John's 28–0, Western Maryland 6–0, Virginia 3–0, Syracuse 13–0, Florida 13–7, VMI 9–7, Georgetown 12–2, Washington & Lee 8–0. *Lost:* Pennsylvania 28–21, Penn St. 21–14 (1st meeting since 1917). *Star:* HB Jim Meade. *Noteworthy:* won 1st SC title.

1942 (7–2) *Won:* Connecticut 34–0, Lakehurst Naval Air Station 14–0, Rutgers 27–13, Western Maryland 51–0, Florida 13–0, Virginia 27–12, Washington & Lee 32–28. *Lost:* VMI 29–0, Duke 42–0. *Stars:* Tommy Mont (1,076 yds and 12 TDs pass), C Paul Flick. *Noteworthy:* 1st year under Clark Shaughnessy.

1945 (6–2–1) *Won:* Guilford 60–6, Richmond 21–0, Merchant Marine Academy 22–6, VMI 38–0, Virginia 19–13, South Carolina 19–13 (1st meeting since 1929). *Lost:* Virginia Tech 21–13, William & Mary 33–14. *Tied:* West Virginia 13–13. *Noteworthy:* Paul "Bear" Bryant's only Maryland team (his 1st as college head coach).

1947 (7–2–2) *Won:* South Carolina 19–13, Delaware 43–19 (1st meeting since 1917), Richmond 18–6, Virginia Tech 21–19, West Virginia 27–0 (1st in 5-game series dating to 1919), Duquesne 32–0, Vanderbilt 20–6 (1st meeting since 1932, 1st win in 5-game series dating to 1927). *Lost:* Duke 19–7, North Carolina 19–0. *Tied:* N.C. State 0–0. *Stars:* Lu Gambino (904 yds rush, nation's leader with 96 pts on 16 TDs), C Gene Kinney, frosh John Idzik (5 int). *Noteworthy:* 1st year under Jim Tatum. Made 1st bowl appearance, tying Georgia 20–20 in Gator Bowl; Gambino ran for 165 yds and scored all 3 Terp TDs (one on pass from John Baroni).

1949 (9–1) *Won:* Virginia Tech 34–7, Georgetown 33–7, N.C. State 14–6, South Carolina 44–7, George Washington 40–14, Boston U. 14–13, West Virginia 47–7, Miami (Fla.) 13–0. *Lost:* Michigan St. 14–7. *Stars:* T Ray Krouse, soph FB Ed Modzelewski (589 yds rush), Stan Lavine (7 TDs), Stan Karnash (16 pass rec for 245 yds), Jim Larue (5 int). *Noteworthy:* beat Missouri 20–7 in Gator Bowl; Bob Shemonski ran for 2 TDs and Modzelewski scored once.

1950 (7–2–1) *Won:* Navy 35–21 (1st meeting since 1934), Michigan St. 34–7, Georgetown 25–14, Duke 26–14 (1st in 7-game series dating to 1932), George Washington 23–7, West Virginia 41–0, Virginia Tech 63–7. *Lost:* Georgia 27–7, N.C. State 16–13. *Tied:* North Carolina 7–7. *Stars:* soph QB Jack

Scarbath (715 yds total off), Pete Augsberger (25 pass rec for 422 yds), Modzelewski, Shemonski (560 yds rush, 16 TDs, 97 pts), G Bob Ward.

1951 (10–0) *Won:* Washington & Lee 54–14, George Washington 33–6, Georgia 43–7, North Carolina 14–7 (1st over Tar Heels in 11 games since 1926), Louisiana St. (LSU) 27–0, Missouri 35–0, Navy 40–21, N.C. State 53–0, West Virginia 54–7. *Stars:* Ed Modzelewski (834 yds and 11 TDs rush), Ward (Maryland's 1st consensus All-American), Scarbath (831 yds and 15 TDs total off), C Tom Cosgrove, HB Joe Petruzzo, T Dick Modzelewski (Ed's younger brother), frosh DB Joe Horning (6 int). *Noteworthy:* Led nation in scoring avg (39.2) and got share of 2nd SC title in 1st unbeaten season since 1893. Upset unbeaten national champ Tennessee 28–13 in Sugar Bowl as Ed Fullerton scored on 2-yd run, passed to Shemonski for a TD, and iced game on 46-yd pass int return for TD; Ed Modzelewski ran for 153 yds and Scarbath scored on 1-yd run.

1952 (7–2) *Won:* Missouri 13–10, Auburn 13–7, Clemson 28–0 (1st meeting), Georgia 37–0, Navy 38–7, LSU 34–6, Boston U. 34–7. *Lost:* unbeaten Mississippi 21–14, Alabama 27–7 in last 2 games. *Stars:* Scarbath (1,149 yds and 10 TDs pass, 227 yds and 3 TDs rush), Lloyd Colteryahn (32 pass rec for 593 yds), HB Chet Hanulak (6 TDs), Outland Trophy–winner Dick Modzelewski, Cosgrove, T Stan Jones.

1953 (10–1) *Won:* Missouri 20–6, Washington & Lee 52–0, Clemson 20–0, Georgia 40–13, North Carolina 26–0, Miami (Fla.) 30–0, South Carolina 24–6, George Washington 27–6, Mississippi 38–0, Alabama 21–0. *Stars:* Jones, QB/S Bernie Faloney (9 TDs rush, 6 int), Hanulak (753 yds rush), FB Ralph Felton (558 yds rush), C John Irvine, T Bob Morgan, soph E Bill Walker. *Noteworthy:* Led nation in rush defense and scoring defense (3.1-pt avg) and earned share of inaugural ACC title. Got share of 1st national title but lost to Oklahoma 7–0 in Orange Bowl as Faloney sat out most of game with ankle injury.

1954 (7–2–1) *Won:* Kentucky 20–0, North Carolina 33–0, South Carolina 20–0, N.C. State 42–14, Clemson 16–0, George Washington 48–6, Missouri 74–13. *Lost:* unbeaten national cochamp UCLA 12–7, Miami (Fla.) 9–7. *Tied:* Wake Forest 13–13 (1st meeting since 1944). *Stars:* Walker, Irvine, G

Jack Bowersox, HB Ronnie Waller (592 yds rush), FB Dick Bielski (6 TDs, 54 pts).

1955 (10–1) *Won:* Missouri 13–12, UCLA 7–0, Baylor 20–6, Wake Forest 28–7, North Carolina 25–7, Syracuse 34–13 (1st meeting since 1939), South Carolina 27–0, LSU 13–0, Clemson 25–12, George Washington 19–0. *Stars:* C/LB Bob Pellegrini, E Russell Dennis, T Mike Sandusky, HB Ed Vereb (642 yds rush, 16 TDs), Walker (43.7-yd punting avg), G Jack Davis, QB Frank Tamburello. *Noteworthy:* Tatum's last team led nation in rush defense and won share of 2nd ACC title. Lost national championship game to unbeaten Oklahoma 20–6 in Orange Bowl; Vereb ran for 108 yds and a TD.

1961 (7–3) *Won:* Southern Methodist (SMU) 14–6, Clemson 24–21, Syracuse 22–21, Air Force 21–0, Penn St. 21–17 (1st in 8-game series dating to 1917), N.C. State 10–7, Wake Forest 10–7. *Lost:* North Carolina 14–8, South Carolina 20–10, Virginia 28–16 (1st to Cavaliers in 6 games since 1944). *Stars:* E Gary Collins (30 pass rec for 428 yds), soph QB Dick Shiner, C Bob Hacker, T Roger Shoals, DB Tom Brown (8 int).

1973 (8–4) *Won:* North Carolina 23–3, Villanova 31–3, Syracuse 38–0 (1st over Orange in 9 games since 1961), Wake Forest 37–0, Duke 30–10, Virginia 33–0, Clemson 28–13, Tulane 42–9. *Lost:* West Virginia 20–13, N.C. State 24–22, unbeaten Penn St. 42–22. *Stars:* TB Louis Carter (801 yds and 14 TDs rush), Frank Russell (39 pass rec for 468 yds), Walter White (27 pass rec and 5 TDs), K Steve Mike-Mayer (69 pts), DT Randy White, DL Paul Vallano, LB Harry Walters, DBs Bob Smith and soph Jim Brechbiel (5 int). *Noteworthy:* lost to Georgia 17–16 in Peach Bowl; Carter ran for 126 yds and passed 68 yds to Walter White for only TD and Mike–Mayer kicked 3 FGs.

1974 (8–4) *Won:* North Carolina 24–12, Syracuse 31–0, Clemson 41–0, Wake Forest 47–0, N.C. State 20–10, Villanova 41–0, Duke 56–13, Virginia 10–0. *Lost:* unbeaten Alabama 21–16, Florida 17–10, Penn St. 24–17. *Stars:* QB Bob Avellini (1,648 yds pass), Russell (31 pass rec for 404 yds), Walter White (27 pass rec), Carter (991 yds rush), John Schultz (9 TDs), Mike-Mayer (15 FGs, 79 pts), Outland Trophy– and Lombardi Award–winner Randy White, Smith, Walters, T Stan Rogers. *Noteworthy:* Won 3rd ACC title (1st in 19 years). Lost

to Tennessee 7–3 in Liberty Bowl; Avellini passed for 158 yds and Mike-Mayer kicked 28-yd FG.
1975 (9–2–1) *Won:* Villanova 41–0, North Carolina 34–7, Syracuse 24–7, N.C. State 37–22, Wake Forest 27–0, Cincinnati 21–19, Clemson 22–20, Virginia 62–24. *Lost:* Tennessee 26–8, Penn St. 15–13. *Tied:* Kentucky 10–10. *Stars:* QB Larry Dick (1,190 yds pass), Kim Hoover (38 pass rec for 532 yds and 5 TDs), Schultz (nation's kickoff return leader with 31-yd avg), DE Leroy Hughes, DT Joe Campbell, LB Kevin Benson, Brechbiel, K Mike Sochko (12 FGs). *Noteworthy:* Again won ACC title. Beat Florida 13–0 in Gator Bowl; Steve Atkins ran for 127 yds and Terps scored on 19-yd pass from Dick to Hoover and 2 FGs by Sochko.
1976 (11–1) *Won:* Richmond 31–7 (1st meeting since 1948), West Virginia 24–3, Syracuse 42–28, Villanova 20–9, N.C. State 16–6, Wake Forest 17–15, Duke 30–3, Kentucky 24–14, Cincinnati 21–0, Clemson 20–0, Virginia 28–0. *Stars:* Campbell, LB Brad Carr, DL Larry Seder, DB Ken Roy, QB Mark Manges (1,593 yds total off, 11 TDs pass), Charles White (23 pass rec for 402 yds), soph B Alvin Maddox (678 yds rush), Atkins (621 yds rush), B Tim Wilson (610 yds rush, 7 TDs), G Ed Fulton, T Tom Schick. *Noteworthy:* Won 5th ACC title (3rd straight) in 1st unbeaten season since 1955. Lost to Houston 30–21 in Cotton Bowl; Manges passed for 179 yds and a TD and ran for another, and Wilson scored other Terp TD.
1977 (8–4) *Won:* Clemson 21–14, Syracuse 24–10, Wake Forest 35–7, Duke 31–13, Villanova 19–13, Richmond 27–24, Virginia 28–0. *Lost:* West Virginia 24–16, Penn St. 27–9 (15th straight to Nittany Lions), N.C. State 24–20, North Carolina 16–7. *Stars:* Dick (1,351 yds pass), Vince Kinney (32 pass rec for 505 yds), Atkins (9 TDs), Maddox (9 TDs), George Scott (894 yds rush), Carr, DL Ted Klaube. *Noteworthy:* beat Minnesota 17–7 in Hall of Fame Bowl; Dick passed for 211 yds, White caught 8 for 126 yds, and Scott ran for 75 yds and 2 TDs.
1978 (9–3) *Won:* Tulane 31–7, Louisville 24–17, North Carolina 21–20, Kentucky 20–3, N.C. State 31–7, Syracuse 34–9, Wake Forest 39–0, Duke 27–0, Virginia 17–7. *Lost:* unbeaten Penn St. 27–3, Clemson 28–24. *Stars:* Atkins (1,261 yds and 11 TDs rush), QB Tim O'Hare (1,388 yds pass), Dean Richards (35 pass rec for 575 yds), K Ed Loncar (16 FGs, 73 pts), DT Charles Johnson, DL Bruce Palmer, DB Lloyd Burruss. *Noteworthy:* lost to

Texas 42–0 in Sun Bowl as Terps gained only 34 yds rush and O'Hare (146 yds pass) was intercepted 3 times.
1980 (8–4) *Won:* Villanova 7–3, Vanderbilt 31–6 (1st meeting since 1948), West Virginia 14–11, Wake Forest 11–10, Duke 17–14, N.C. State 24–0, Clemson 34–7, Virginia 31–0. *Lost:* North Carolina 17–3, Pittsburgh 38–9, Penn St. 24–10 in consecutive early games. *Stars:* B Charlie Wysocki (1,359 yds and 11 TDs rush), Chris Havener (29 pass rec for 436 yds), Burruss, DL Martin Van Horn, soph LB Joe Wilkins, K/P Dale Castro (10 FGs, 40.9-yd punting avg). *Noteworthy:* lost to Florida 35–20 in Tangerine Bowl; Wysocki ran for 159 yds and a TD, and Castro kicked 4 FGs.
1982 (8–4) *Won:* N.C. State 23–6, Syracuse 26–3, Indiana St. 38–0, Wake Forest 52–31, Duke 49–22, North Carolina 31–24, Miami (Fla.) 18–17 (1st meeting since 1972), Virginia 45–14. *Lost:* national champ Penn St. 39–31, West Virginia 19–18, Clemson 24–22. *Stars:* QB Boomer Esiason (2,302 yds and 18 TDs pass), TE John Tice (34 pass rec for 396 yds), Russell Davis (27 pass rec for 445 yds and 5 TDs), soph WR Greg Hill (19 pass rec for 331 yds and 7 TDs), Willie Joyner (1,039 yds and 7 TDs rush), frosh FB Rich Badanjek (9 TDs rush), K Jess Atkinson (16 FGs, 87 pts), T Dave Pacella, Wilkins, DB Lendell Jones (7 int), DT Mark Duda. *Noteworthy:* 1st year under Bobby Ross. Lost to Washington 21–20 in inaugural Aloha Bowl; Esiason passed for 251 yds and 2 TDs and Tice caught 6 for 85 yds, a TD, and a 2-pt conversion.
1983 (8–4) *Won:* Vanderbilt 21–14, Pittsburgh 13–7, Virginia 23–3, Syracuse 34–31, Wake Forest 36–33, Duke 38–3 (10th straight over Blue Devils), North Carolina 28–26, N.C. State 29–6. *Lost:* West Virginia 31–21, Auburn 35–23, Clemson 52–27. *Stars:* Esiason (2,322 yds and 15 TDs pass), Hill (27 pass rec for 570 yds and 7 TDs), Davis (29 pass rec for 465 yds), Badanjek (635 yds rush, 9 TDs), Joyner (908 yds rush), G Ron Solt, Atkinson (15 FGs, 73 pts), DB Clarence Baldwin (7 int), DT Pete Koch, LB Eric Wilson. *Noteworthy:* Won 6th ACC title. Lost to Tennessee 30–23 in Florida Citrus Bowl; QB Frank Reich (replacing injured Esiason in 2nd quarter) passed for 192 yds and Atkinson kicked 5 FGs.
1984 (9–3) *Won:* West Virginia 20–17, Wake Forest 38–17, N.C. State 44–21, Duke 43–7, North Carolina 34–23, Miami (Fla.) 42–40, Clemson 41–23,

Virginia 45–34. *Lost:* Syracuse 23–7 (1st to Orange in 10 games since 1972), Vanderbilt 23–14, Penn St. 25–24 (20th straight to Nittany Lions). *Stars:* C Kevin Glover, Badanjek (832 yds rush, 16 TDs, 102 pts), TB Alvin Blount (759 yds rush, 20 pass rec for 269 yds, 8 TDs), B Tommy Neal (618 yds rush, 7 TDs), Reich (1,446 yds pass), QB Stan Gelbaugh (1,123 yds pass), Hill (51 pass rec for 820 yds), frosh WR Aziz Abdur-Ra'oof (25 pass rec for 438 yds), Atkinson (17 FGs, 88 pts), soph DL Bruce Mesner, Wilson, DB Al Covington, frosh P Darryl Wright (41.4-yd avg). *Noteworthy:* Again won ACC crown. Beat Tennessee 28–27 in Sun Bowl; Reich passed for 201 yds and a TD, Neal ran for 107 yds and a TD, and Badanjek ran for 90 yds and 2 TDs.

1985 (9–3)   *Won:* Boston College 31–13, West Virginia 28–0, N.C. State 31–17, Wake Forest 26–3, Duke 40–10, North Carolina 28–10, Clemson 34–31, Virginia 33–21. *Lost:* unbeaten Penn St. 20–18, Michigan 20–0, Miami (Fla.) 29–22. *Stars:* Gelbaugh (2,475 yds and 15 TDs pass), Badanjek (676 yds and 12 TDs rush), Abdur-Ra'oof (35 pass rec for 671 yds), James Milling (26 pass rec for 415 yds), soph TE Ferrell Edmunds (21 pass rec for 314 yds), WR Eric Holder (19 pass rec for 366 yds), Blount (828 yds rush), OL J.D. Maarleveld, frosh K Dan Plocki (11 FGs), Mesner, LB Chuck Faucette, DB Keeta Covington (6 int). *Noteworthy:* Won 8th ACC crown (3rd straight). Beat Syracuse 35–18 in Cherry Bowl; Gelbaugh passed for 223 yds and 2 TDs, Abdur-Ra'oof caught 5 for 86 yds and a TD, and Blount ran for 135 yds and a score.

Bowl Summary

Aloha 0–1; Cherry 1–0; Cotton 0–1; Florida Citrus 0–1; Gator 2–0–1; Hall of Fame 1–0; Independence 0–0–1; Liberty 0–1; Orange 0–2; Peach 0–1; Sugar 1–0; Sun 1–1; Tangerine 0–1.

Bowl Record (6–9–2)

Regular Season	Bowl	Score	Opponent	Record
1947 (7–2–1)	Gator	20–20	Georgia	(7–4)
1949 (8–1)	Gator	20–7	Missouri	(7–3)
1951 (9–0)	Sugar	28–13	Tennessee	(10–0)
1953 (10–0)	Orange	0–7	Oklahoma	(10–0)
1955 (10–0)	Orange	6–20	Oklahoma	(10–0)
1973 (8–3)	Peach	16–17	Georgia	(6–4–1)
1974 (8–3)	Liberty	3–7	Tennessee	(6–3–2)
1975 (8–2–1)	Gator	13–0	Florida	(9–2)
1976 (11–0)	Cotton	21–30	Houston	(9–2)
1977 (7–4)	Hall of Fame	17–7	Minnesota	(7–4)
1978 (9–2)	Sun	0–42	Texas	(8–3)
1980 (8–3)	Tangerine	20–35	Florida	(7–4)
1982 (8–3)	Aloha	20–21	Washington	(9–2)
1983 (8–3)	Florida Citrus	23–30	Tennessee	(8–3)
1984 (8–3)	Sun	28–27	Tennessee	(7–3–1)
1985 (8–3)	Cherry	35–18	Syracuse	(7–4)
1990 (6–5)	Independence	34–34	Louisiana Tech	(8–3)

Conference Titles

Southern—1937, 1951*. **Atlantic Coast**—1953*, 1955*, 1974, 1975, 1976, 1983, 1984, 1985.

TOP 20 AP AND UPI RANKING

1949	14	1954	8–11	1975	13–11	1984	12–11
1951	3–4	1955	3–3	1976	8–11	1985	18–19
1952	13–13	1973	20–18	1978	20–U		
1953	1–1	1974	13–13	1982	20–20		

MAJOR RIVALS

Maryland has played at least 10 games with Catholic U. 8–1–2, Clemson 20–19–2, Duke 20–16, Florida 6–11, Gallaudet 9–6–1, George Washington 10–3, Georgetown 6–9, Johns Hopkins 16–11–5, Miami (Fla.) 7–7, Navy 5–14, North Carolina 25–30–1, N.C. State 23–22–4, Penn St. 1–34–1, Richmond 11–5–2, St. John's College 18–11, South Carolina 17–11, Syracuse 14–17–2, Vanderbilt 4–8, Villanova 8–2, Virginia 37–18–2, VMI 14–9–2, Virginia Tech 15–10, Wake Forest 29–11–1, Washington & Lee 13–5–2, Washington College 18–3–1, West Virginia 14–14–2, Western Maryland 18–13–1, Yale 2–8–1. Record against ACC foes met fewer than 10 times is Florida St. 0–3, Georgia Tech 1–4.

COACHES

Dean of Maryland coaches is H.C. Byrd with record of 117–82–15 for 1912–34. Other top records for at least 3 years were by D. John Markey, 18–17–4 for 1902–05; Jack Faber, 21–9 for 1935–37 with 1 SC title; Jim Tatum (1953 national Coach of Year), 73–15–4 for 1947–55 with 3 conference titles, 5 bowl teams, 3 teams unbeaten in regular season, and 1 national champion; Tom Nugent, 36–34 for 1959–65; Jerry Claiborne, 77–37–3 for 1972–81 with 3 ACC titles, 7 bowl teams, and 1 team unbeaten in regular season; and Bobby Ross, 39–19–1 for 1982–86 with 3 ACC titles and 4 bowl teams.

MISCELLANEA

First game was loss to St. John's 50–0 in 1892 . . . 1st win was over Eastern H.S. 36–0 in 1893 . . . 1st win over college foe was over Baltimore City College 18–0 in 1893 . . . highest score was over Washington College 80–0 in 1927 . . . highest since W.W. II was over Missouri 74–13 in 1954 . . . worst defeat was by Navy 76–0 in 1913 . . . worst since W.W. II was by Penn St. 48–0 in 1969 and by Florida St. 69–21 in 1992 . . . longest unbeaten string of 22 in 1950–52 ended by Mississippi 21–14 . . . 15-game win streaks in 1954–55 ended by Oklahoma 20–6 in 1956 Orange Bowl and in 1975–76 ended by Houston 30–21 in 1977 Cotton Bowl . . . longest losing string of 16 in 1966–68 broken with win over North Carolina 33–24 . . . consensus All-Americans were Bob Ward, G, 1951; Dick Modzelewski, T, and Jack Scarbath, QB, 1952; Stan Jones, T, 1953; Bob Pellegrini, C, 1955; Gary Collins, E, 1961; Randy White, DL, 1974; Joe Campbell, DT, 1976; Dale Castro, K, 1979; and J.D. Maarleveld, OL, 1985 . . . Academic All-Americans were Bernie Faloney, B, 1953; Kim Hoover, DE, 1975; and Joe Muffler, DL, 1978 . . . Outland Trophy–winners were Dick Modzelewski, T, 1952; and Randy White, DE, 1974 . . . Lombardi Award–winner was Randy White, DE, 1974.

NORTH CAROLINA (Tar Heels; Carolina Blue and White)

NOTABLE TEAMS

1892 (5–1) *Won:* Richmond 40–0 (1st meeting), Trinity (Duke) 24–0, Auburn 64–0, Vanderbilt 24–0 (1st meeting), Virginia 26–0. *Lost:* Virginia 30–18 (1st meeting).

1895 (7–1–1) *Won:* N.C. State 36–0, Richmond 34–0, Georgia 6–0, 10–6 (1st meetings), Vanderbilt 12–0, Washington & Lee 16–0, Virginia Tech 32–5 (1st meeting). *Lost:* Virginia 6–0 in finale. *Tied:* Sewanee 0–0.

1897 (7–3) *Won:* N.C. State 40–0, Guilford 16–0, Greensboro A. A. 24–0, Clemson 28–0 (1st meeting), Sewanee 12–6, Tennessee 16–0, Bingham's

School 14–0. *Lost:* Virginia Tech 4–0, unbeaten Vanderbilt 31–0, Virginia 12–0. *Noteworthy:* 1st year under W.A. Reynolds.

1898 (9–0)   *Won:* Guilford 18–0, N.C. State 34–0, Greensboro A.A. 11–0, Oak Ridge 11–0, Virginia Tech 28–6, Davidson 11–0 (1st meeting), Georgia 53–0, Auburn 29–0, Virginia 6–2. *Noteworthy:* outscored foes 201–8 in 1st undefeated season.

1901 (7–2)   *Won:* Oak Ridge 28–0, N.C. State 39–0, 30–0, Guilford 42–0, Davidson 6–0, Georgia 27–0, Auburn 10–0. *Lost:* Virginia 23–6, Clemson 22–10 in last 2 games.

1902 (5–1–3)   *Won:* Guilford 16–0, Oak Ridge 35–0, Furman 10–0, Davidson 27–0, Virginia Military Institute (VMI) 17–10. *Lost:* Georgetown 12–5. *Tied:* Virginia Tech 0–0, N.C. State 0–0, Virginia 12–12. *Noteworthy:* 1st year under H.B. Olcott.

1909 (5–2)   *Won:* Wake Forest 18–0, Tennessee 3–0, Georgetown 5–0, Richmond 22–0, Washington & Lee 6–0. *Lost:* VMI 3–0, Virginia Tech 15–0.

1911 (6–1–1)   *Won:* Wake Forest 12–3, Bingham's School 12–0, Davidson 5–0, U.S.S. Franklin 12–0, South Carolina 21–0, Washington & Lee 4–0. *Lost:* Virginia 28–0 in finale. *Tied:* Virginia Tech 0–0. *Noteworthy:* only year under Branch Bocock.

1914 (10–1)   *Won:* Richmond 41–0, Virginia Medical 65–0, Wake Forest 53–0, 12–7 (10 straight over Deacons), South Carolina 48–0, Georgia 41–6, Riverside Academy 40–0, Vanderbilt 10–9 (1st meeting since 1900), Davidson 16–3, VMI 30–7. *Lost:* Virginia 20–3 in finale. *Noteworthy:* introduced numbered jerseys to Southern football.

1922 (9–1)   *Won:* Wake Forest 62–3, Trinity (Duke) 20–0 (1st meeting since 1894), South Carolina 10–7, N.C. State 14–9, Maryland 27–3, Tulane 19–12 (1st meeting), VMI 9–7, Davidson 29–6, Virginia 10–7. *Lost:* Yale 18–0 in 2nd game. *Noteworthy:* got share of 1st SC title.

1925 (7–1–1)   *Won:* South Carolina 7–0, Duke 41–0, N.C. State 17–0, Mercer 3–0, Maryland 16–0, VMI 23–11, Davidson 13–0. *Lost:* Wake Forest 6–0 in opener. *Tied:* Virginia 3–3 in finale.

1929 (9–1)   *Won:* Wake Forest 48–0, Maryland 43–0, Georgia Tech 18–7 (1st in 5-game series dating to 1915), Virginia Tech 38–13 (1st over Gobblers in 12 games since 1904), N.C. State 32–0, South Carolina 40–0, Davidson 26–7, Virginia 41–7,

Duke 48–7. *Lost:* Georgia 19–12 (1st meeting since 1914). *Star:* G Ray Farris.

1934 (7–1–1)   *Won:* Wake Forest 21–0, Georgia 14–0, Kentucky 6–0 (1st meeting since 1910), Georgia Tech 26–0, Davidson 12–2, Duke 7–0, Virginia 25–6. *Lost:* Tennessee 19–7. *Tied:* N.C. State 7–7. *Stars:* Bs George Barclay, Don Jackson, and Charlie Shaffer (41.2-yd punting avg), soph E Dick Buck (11 pass rec for 271 yds). *Noteworthy:* won 2nd SC title in 1st year under Carl Snavely.

1935 (8–1)   *Won:* Wake Forest 14–0, Tennessee 38–13 (1st over Vols in 8 games since 1909), Maryland 33–0, Davidson 14–0, Georgia Tech 19–0, N.C. State 35–6, VMI 56–0, Virginia 61–0. *Lost:* Duke 25–0. *Stars:* Jackson (1,205 yds and 15 TDs total off, 6 int), Jim Hutchins (6 TDs), Buck.

1936 (8–2)   *Won:* Wake Forest 14–7, Tennessee 14–6, Maryland 14–0, New York U. 14–13, N.C. State 21–6, Davidson 26–6, South Carolina 14–0, Virginia 59–14. *Lost:* Tulane 21–7 (1st meeting since 1922), Duke 27–7. *Stars:* Buck (20 pass rec for 232 yds), Hutchins (7 TDs), E Andy Bershak, Tom Burnette (41.8-yd punting avg). *Noteworthy:* 1st year under Ray Wolf.

1937 (7–1–1)   *Won:* N.C. State 20–0, New York U. 19–6, Wake Forest 28–0, Tulane 13–0, Davidson 26–0, Duke 14–6, Virginia 40–0. *Lost:* Fordham 14–0. *Tied:* South Carolina 13–13. *Stars:* Bershak (Tar Heels' 1st consensus All-American), T Hank Bartos, G Elmer Wrenn, Bs Crowell Little (7 TDs) and George Watson (7 TDs, 4 int). *Noteworthy:* won 3rd SC crown.

1938 (6–2–1)   *Won:* Wake Forest 14–6, N.C. State 21–0, New York U. 7–0, Davidson 34–0, Virginia Tech 7–0, Virginia 20–0. *Lost:* Tulane 17–14, unbeaten, unscored-on Duke 14–0. *Tied:* Fordham 0–0. *Stars:* B George "Snuffy" Stirnweiss, George Radman (6 TDs), T Steve Maronic, Watson (4 int).

1939 (8–1–1)   *Won:* The Citadel 50–0, Wake Forest 36–6, Virginia Tech 13–6, New York U. 14–7, Pennsylvania 30–6 (1st meeting since 1907), N.C. State 17–0, Davidson 32–0, Virginia 19–0. *Lost:* Duke 13–3. *Tied:* unbeaten Tulane 14–14. *Stars:* Stirnweiss (779 yds all-purpose running), Jim Lalanne (944 yds and 15 TDs total off), Radman (23 pass rec for 228 yds), E Paul Severin, soph P Harry Dunkle (nation's leader with 46.6-yd avg).

1946 (8–2–1)   *Won:* Miami (Fla.) 21–0 (1st meeting), Maryland 33–0 (1st meeting since 1936), Navy

TB Charlie "Choo Choo" Justice, 1946–49

21–14 (1st meeting since 1906), Florida 40–19 (1st meeting since 1933), William & Mary 21–7, Wake Forest 26–14, Duke 22–7, Virginia 49–14. *Lost:* Tennessee 20–14. *Tied:* Virginia Tech 14–14. *Star:* frosh TB Charlie "Choo Choo" Justice (1,554 all-purpose yds, 943 yds rush, 12 TDs, 39.9-yd punting avg). *Noteworthy:* Won 4th SC title. Made 1st postseason appearance, losing to unbeaten Georgia 20–10 in Sugar Bowl as Justice was held to 37 yds rush; Walt Pupa scored TD and Bob Cox kicked 27-yd FG.

1947 (8–2) *Won:* Georgia 14–7, William & Mary 13–7, Florida 35–7, Tennessee 20–6, N.C. State 41–6, Maryland 19–0, Duke 21–0, Virginia 40–7. *Lost:* Texas 34–0 (1st meeting), Wake Forest 19–7. *Stars:* Justice (1,106 all-purpose yds, 930 yds and 14 TDs total off, 41.6-yd punting avg), Cox (22 pass rec for 297 yds), soph E Art Weiner (19 pass rec for 386 yds), T Len Szafaryn.

1948 (9–1–1) *Won:* Texas 34–7, Georgia 21–14, Wake Forest 28–6, N.C. State 14–0, Louisiana St. (LSU) 34–7 (1st meeting), Tennessee 14–7, Maryland 49–20, Duke 20–0, Virginia 34–12. *Tied:*

William & Mary 7–7. *Stars:* Justice (1,620 yds and 23 TDs total off, 2 punt returns for TDs, nation's leader with 44-yd punting avg), Weiner (31 pass rec for 481 yds and 6 TDs), Szafaryn, Hosea Rodgers (637 yds and 6 TDs rush). *Noteworthy:* 1st unbeaten season since 1898. Lost to Oklahoma 14–6 in Sugar Bowl; Justice ran for 84 yds and passed for 57 yds, and Tar Heels scored on 2-yd run by Rodgers.

1949 (7–4) *Won:* N.C. State 26–6, Georgia 21–14, South Carolina 28–13, Wake Forest 28–14, William & Mary 20–14, Duke 21–20, Virginia 14–7. *Lost:* LSU 13–7, Tennessee 35–6, unbeaten national champ Notre Dame 42–6 (1st meeting). *Stars:* Justice (1,108 yds and 14 TDs total off, 44.1-yd punting avg), Weiner (nation's leader with 52 pass rec for 762 yds and 7 TDs), Dick Bunting (6 int, 1 returned for TD), C Irv Holdash. *Noteworthy:* Won 5th and last SC title. Lost to Rice 27–13 in Cotton Bowl; Billy Hayes ran for 107 yds and Justice passed for 63 yds and a TD to Paul Rizzo, who scored other Tar Heel TD on 2-yd run.

1963 (9–2) *Won:* Virginia 11–7, Wake Forest 21–0, Maryland 14–7, N.C. State 31–10, South Carolina 7–0, Georgia 28–7 (1st over Bulldogs in 7 games since 1949), Miami (Fla.) 27–16, Duke 16–14. *Lost:* Michigan St. 31–0, Clemson 11–7. *Stars:* QB Junior Edge (1,413 yds total off), E Bob Lacey (48 pass rec for 533 yds), FB Ken Willard (648 yds and 6 TDs rush), C/LB Chris Hanburger. *Noteworthy:* Won share of 1st ACC title. Beat Air Force 35–0 in Gator Bowl; Willard ran for 94 yds and a TD and backup QB Gary Black completed all 6 of his passes for 71 yds and a TD and scored another.

1970 (8–4) *Won:* Kentucky 20–10, N.C. State 19–0, Maryland 53–20, Vanderbilt 10–7, Virginia 30–15, Virginia Military Institute (VMI) 62–13, Clemson 42–7, Duke 59–34. *Lost:* South Carolina 35–21, Tulane 24–17, Wake Forest 14–13 in consecutive mid-season games. *Stars:* RBs Don McCauley (21 TDs, 1,720 yds rush, nation's leader with 2,021 all-purpose yds) and soph Ike Oglesby (562 yds and 6 TDs rush), Lewis Jolley (20 pass rec for 358 yds and 5 TDs), OT Paul Hoolahan, DT Flip Ray, soph DB Lou Angelo (5 int). *Noteworthy:* First winning team since 1963. Lost to unbeaten Arizona St. 48–26 in Peach Bowl blizzard; McCauley ran for 143 yds and 3 TDs.

1971 (9–3) *Won:* Richmond 28–0 (1st meeting

since 1941), Illinois 27–0, Maryland 35–14, N.C. State 27–7, Wake Forest 7–3, William & Mary 36–35 (1st meeting since 1950), Clemson 26–13, Virginia 32–20, Duke 38–0. *Lost:* Tulane 37–29, Notre Dame 16–0 in successive mid-season games. *Stars:* QB Paul Miller (1,302 yds and 15 TDs total off), Jolley (1,455 yds all-purpose running, 11 TDs), Oglesby (504 yds and 5 TDs rush), OG Ron Rusnak, C Bob Thornton, OT Jerry Sain, soph P Nick Vidnovic (42.8-yd avg), DE Bill Brafford, DT Bud Grissom, LB John Bunting, DB Richard Stilley (5 int). *Noteworthy:* Won 2nd ACC title. Lost to Georgia 7–3 in Gator Bowl; Jolley ran for 77 yds and Tar Heels scored on 35-yd FG by K Ken Craven.

1972 (11–1)   *Won:* Richmond 28–18, Maryland 31–26, N.C. State 34–33, Kentucky 31–20, Wake Forest 21–0, Clemson 26–10, Virginia 23–3, Duke 14–0, East Carolina 42–19 (1st meeting), Florida 28–24. *Lost:* Ohio St. 29–14. *Stars:* Rusnak, Sain, QB Vidnovic (1,245 yds and 16 TDs total off), soph WR Jimmy Jerome (22 pass rec for 326 yds), Oglesby (707 yds rush), Craven (11 FGs), soph P Dale Lydecker (41.1-yd avg), LBs Mike Mansfield and soph Jimmy DeRatt, DE Gene Brown, DT Eric Hyman, Angelo (8 int). *Noteworthy:* Repeated as ACC champ. Beat Texas Tech 32–28 in Sun Bowl; Vidnovic passed for 215 yds, 2 TDs, and 2-pt conversion, and Ted Leverenz caught 5 for 95 yds, 2 TDs, and 2-pt conversion.

1976 (9–3)   *Won:* Miami (Ohio) 14–10, Florida 24–21, Northwestern 12–0, Army 34–32, East Carolina 12–10, Wake Forest 34–14, Clemson 27–23, Virginia 31–6, Duke 39–38. *Lost:* Missouri 24–3, N.C. State 21–13 in successive mid-season games. *Stars:* RB Mike Voight (1,407 yds and 18 TDs rush), OG Craig Funk, K Tom Biddle (13 FGs), DLs Dee Hardison and Bill Perdue, DBs Ronny Johnson and Bobby Cale (5 int). *Noteworthy:* lost to Kentucky 21–0 in Peach Bowl, gaining only 108 yds total off.

1977 (8–3–1)   *Won:* Richmond 31–0, Northwestern 41–7, Wake Forest 24–3, N.C. State 27–14, South Carolina 17–0 (1st over Gamecocks in 6 games since 1964), Maryland 16–7, Virginia 35–14, Duke 16–3. *Lost:* Kentucky 10–7, Texas Tech 10–7. *Tied:* Clemson 13–13. *Stars:* Hardison, DL Rod Broadway and Ken Sheets, soph LB Buddy Curry, DB Alan Caldwell, OG Mike Salzano, frosh HB Amos Lawrence (1,211 yds and 6 TDs rush), Biddle (15 FGs). *Noteworthy:* Bill Dooley's last

team led nation in scoring defense (7.4-pt avg) and took 4th ACC crown. Lost to Nebraska 21–17 in Liberty Bowl; soph QB Matt Kupec threw 2 TD passes.

1979 (8–3–1)   *Won:* South Carolina 28–0, Pittsburgh 17–7, Army 41–3, Cincinnati 35–14, N.C. State 35–21, Virginia 13–7, Duke 37–16. *Lost:* Wake Forest 24–19, Maryland 17–14, Clemson 19–10. *Tied:* East Carolina 24–24. *Stars:* Lawrence (1,019 yds and 9 TDs rush), Doug Paschal (835 yds and 5 TDs rush), Kupec (1,587 yds and 18 TDs pass), TE Mike Chatham (29 pass rec for 448 yds and 8 TDs), OT Steve Junkmann, P/DB Steve Streater (41.2-yd punting avg, 5 int), Curry (5 int), DB Ricky Barden. *Noteworthy:* beat Michigan 17–15 in Gator Bowl; Lawrence ran for 118 yds, Kupec passed for 161 yds and a TD, Paschal scored on 1-yd run, and Jeff Hayes kicked 32-yd FG.

1980 (11–1)   *Won:* Furman 35–13 (1st meeting since 1916), Texas Tech 9–3, Maryland 17–3, Georgia Tech 33–0 (1st over Yellow Jackets in 5 games since 1935), Wake Forest 27–9, N.C. State 28–8, East

LB Lawrence Taylor, 1977–80

Carolina 31–3, Clemson 24–19, Virginia 26–3, Duke 44–21. *Lost:* Oklahoma 41–7 (1st meeting since 1956). *Stars:* Lawrence (1,118 yds rush, 15 TDs), soph HB Kelvin Bryant (1,039 yds rush, 12 TDs), QB Rod Elkins (1,002 yds and 11 TDs pass), Chatham (20 pass rec for 239 yds), C Rick Donnalley, OG Ron Wooten, Streater (43.4-yd punting avg, 5 int), LBs Lawrence Taylor and Darrell Nicholson, DL Donnell Thompson. *Noteworthy:* Won 5th ACC title. Beat Texas 16–7 in Bluebonnet Bowl; Lawrence ran for 104 yds and a TD, and Bryant ran for 82 yds and other Tar Heel TD.

1981 (10–2) *Won:* East Carolina 56–0, Miami (Ohio) 49–7, Boston College 56–14, Georgia Tech 28–7, Wake Forest 48–10, N.C. State 21–10, Maryland 17–10, Virginia 17–14, Duke 31–10. *Lost:* South Carolina 31–13, unbeaten national champ Clemson 10–8. *Stars:* Bryant (1,015 yds rush, 18 TDs), soph RB Tyrone Anthony (699 yds and 6 TDs rush), Elkins (1,032 yds total off), Jon Richardson (28 pass rec for 373 yds), OGs David Drechsler and Ron Spruill, P Jeff Hayes (41.8-yd avg), soph DT William Fuller, LB Lee Shaffer, DBs Greg Poole and soph Walter Black (6 int). *Noteworthy:* beat Arkansas 31–27 in Gator Bowl; Bryant ran for 148 yds and a TD, and frosh RB Ethan Horton ran for 144 yds and 2 TDs.

1982 (8–4) *Won:* Vanderbilt 34–10 (1st meeting since 1970), Army 62–8, Georgia Tech 41–0, Wake Forest 24–7, N.C. State 41–9, Virginia 27–14, Bowling Green 33–14. *Lost:* Pittsburgh 7–6, Maryland 31–24, Clemson 16–13, Duke 23–17 (1st to Blue Devils since 1973). *Stars:* Bryant (1,064 yds rush), Anthony (697 yds and 6 TDs rush), Horton (576 yds and 7 TDs rush), Drechsler, Spruill, Fuller, QB Scott Stankavage (1,124 yds pass), Victor Harrison (30 pass rec for 489 yds), Mark Smith (27 pass rec for 479 yds and 5 TDs), K Brooks Barwick (20 FGs), LB Chris Ward, DE Mike Wilcher, DB Willie Harris. *Noteworthy:* beat Texas 26–10 in Sun Bowl; Horton ran for 119 yds and a TD, Rob Rogers kicked FGs

of 53 and 47 yds, and Barwick kicked 2 FGs.

1983 (8–4) *Won:* South Carolina 24–8, Memphis St. 24–10, Miami (Ohio) 48–17, William & Mary 51–20, Georgia Tech 38–21, Wake Forest 30–10, N.C. State 42–14, Duke 34–27. *Lost:* Maryland 28–26, Clemson 16–3, Virginia 17–14 (1st to Cavaliers since 1973) in consecutive late games. *Stars:* Horton (1,107 yds and 8 TDs rush), Anthony (1,063 yds and 7 TDs rush), Stankavage (1,721 yds and 16 TDs pass), Smith (40 pass rec for 580 yds and 8 TDs), soph Arnold Franklin (25 pass rec for 271 yds), Barwick (11 FGs), Fuller, Harris, OT Brian Blados. *Noteworthy:* lost to Florida St. 28–3 (1st meeting) in Peach Bowl; Stankavage passed for 150 yds but Tar Heels had only 32 yds rush and scored only on Barwick's 36-yd FG.

1992 (9–3) *Won:* Wake Forest 35–17, Furman 28–0, Army 22–9, Navy 28–14, Virginia 27–7 (1st over Cavaliers since 1986), Georgia Tech 26–14, Maryland 31–24, Duke 31–28. *Lost:* N.C. State 27–20, Florida St. 36–13 (1st meeting since 1986), Clemson 40–7. *Stars:* TB Natrone Means (1,195 yds and 13 TDs rush), soph QB Jason Stanicek (1,082 yds pass), frosh QB/P Mike Thomas (1,002 yds total off, 43.1-yd punting avg), WRs Corey Holliday (37 pass rec for 588 yds), Bucky Brooks (21 pass rec for 400 yds) and Randall Felton (22 pass rec for 279 yds), C Randall Parsons, K Tripp Pignetti (14 FGs, 70 pts), LBs Rick Steinbacher and Bernardo Harris, DBs Rondell Jones and Bracey Walker. *Noteworthy:* beat Mississippi St. 21–17 in Peach Bowl as Means ran for 128 yds and a TD, Walker blocked 2 punts (returning one 24 yds for TD), and DB Cliff Baskerville scored on 44-yd pass int return.

Bowl Summary

Aloha 0–1; Bluebonnet 1–0; Cotton 0–1; Gator 3–1; Liberty 0–1; Peach 1–3; Sugar 0–2; Sun 2–1.

Bowl Record (7–10)

Regular Season	Bowl	Score	Opponent	Record
1946 (8–1–1)	Sugar	10–20	Georgia	(10–0)
1948 (9–0–1)	Sugar	6–14	Oklahoma	(9–1)
1949 (7–3)	Cotton	13–27	Rice	(9–1)

(continued)

Regular Season	Bowl	Score	Opponent	Record
1963 (8–2)	Gator	35–0	Air Force	(7–3)
1970 (8–3)	Peach	26–48	Arizona St.	(10–0)
1971 (9–2)	Gator	3–7	Georgia	(10–1)
1972 (10–1)	Sun	32–28	Texas Tech	(8–3)
1974 (7–4)	Sun	24–26	Miss. State	(8–3)
1976 (9–2)	Peach	0–21	Kentucky	(7–4)
1977 (8–2–1)	Liberty	17–21	Nebraska	(8–3)
1979 (7–3–1)	Gator	17–15	Michigan	(8–3)
1980 (10–1)	Bluebonnet	16–7	Texas	(7–4)
1981 (9–2)	Gator	31–27	Arkansas	(8–3)
1982 (7–4)	Sun	26–10	Texas	(9–2)
1983 (8–3)	Peach	3–28	Florida State	(6–5)
1986 (7–3–1)	Aloha	21–30	Arizona	(8–3)
1992 (8–3)	Peach	21–17	Mississippi St.	(7–4)

CONFERENCE TITLES

Southern—1922*, 1934, 1937, 1946, 1949. **Atlantic Coast**—1963*, 1971, 1972, 1977, 1980.

TOP 20 AP AND UPI
(USA TODAY/CNN SINCE 1991) RANKING

1937	19	1949	16	1977	17–14	1982	18–13
1946	9	1963	U–19	1979	15–14	1992	19–20
1947	9	1971	U–18	1980	10–9		
1948	3	1972	12–14	1981	9–8		

MAJOR RIVALS

North Carolina has played at least 10 games with Clemson 13–27–1, Davidson 31–4–4, Duke 41–34–4, Florida 7–2–1, Georgetown 4–7–2, Georgia 12–16–2, Georgia Tech 12–13–3, Kentucky 5–5, Maryland 30–25–1, Navy 5–5, N.C. State 52–24–6, Notre Dame 1–15, Richmond 12–2, South Carolina 34–16–4, Tennessee 10–20–1, Tulane 3–9–2, Vanderbilt 8–5, Virginia 53–40–4, VMI 16–6–1, Virginia Tech 8–11–6, Wake Forest 58–29–2, Washington & Lee 5–3–2, William & Mary 11–0–2. Record against ACC foe Florida St. is 0–3–1.

COACHES

Dean of Tar Heel coaches is Bill Dooley with record of 69–53–2 for 1967–77, including 3 ACC titles and 6 bowl teams. Most wins were under Dick Crum, 72–41–3 for 1978–87 with 1 ACC title and 6 bowl teams. Other top records for at least 3 years were by T.C. Trenchard, 26–9–2 for 1895 and 1913–15; W.A. Reynolds, 27–7–4 for 1897–1900 with 1 unbeaten team; Bob and Bill Fetzer, 30–12–4 for 1921–25 with 1 SC title; Chuck Collins, 38–31–9 for 1926–33; Carl Snavely, 59–35–5 for 1934–35 and 1945–52 with 3 SC titles, 3 bowl teams, and 1 team unbeaten in regular season; Ray Wolf, 38–17–3 for 1936–41 with 1 SC title; Jim Tatum, 19–17–3 for 1942 and 1956–58; Jim Hickey, 36–45 for 1959–66 with 1 ACC title and 1 bowl team; and Mack Brown, 24–31–1 for 1988–92 with 1 bowl team.

MISCELLANEA

First game was loss to Wake Forest 6–4 in 1888 . . . 1st win was over Wake Forest 33–0 in 1889 . . .

highest score was over Virginia Medical 65–0 in 1914 and over Wake Forest 65–0 in 1928... highest since W.W. II was over VMI 62–13 in 1970 and over Army 62–8 in 1982...biggest margin since W.W. II was over East Carolina 56–0 in 1981 ...worst defeat was by Virginia 66–0 in 1912... worst since W.W. II was by Florida 52–2 in 1969 ...highest against Carolina since W.W. II was by Clemson 54–32 in 1974...longest unbeaten string of 17 in 1947–48 ended by Oklahoma 14–6 in 1949 Sugar Bowl...longest losing string of 12 in 1966–67 broken with win over Maryland 14–0... consensus All-Americans were Andy Bershak, E, 1937; Charlie Justice, B, 1948; Don McCauley, B, 1970; Ron Rusnak, G, 1972; Ken Huff, G, 1974; Dee Hardison, DL, 1977; Lawrence Taylor, LB, 1980; and William Fuller, DL, 1983...Academic All-Americans were Ken Willard, B, 1964; Charles Putnik, OL, 1971; and Kevin Anthony, QB, 1985.

NORTH CAROLINA STATE
(Wolfpack; Red and White)

NOTABLE TEAMS

1905 (4–1–1) *Won:* Virginia Military Institute (VMI) 5–0, South Carolina 29–0, Washington & Lee 21–0 (1st meeting), Davidson 10–0. *Lost:* Virginia 10–0. *Tied:* North Carolina 0–0.
1907 (6–0–1) *Won:* Randolph-Macon 20–0, Richmond 7–4, 11–0, Roanoke 22–0, Davidson 6–0, Virginia 10–4. *Tied:* North Carolina All Stars 5–5. *Noteworthy:* had 1st unbeaten season since 1-game schedule of 1896 in 1st year under Mickey Whitehurst.
1908 (6–1) *Won:* Wake Forest 25–0, 76–0 (1st meetings since 1895), William & Mary 24–0, Georgetown 5–0, Davidson 21–0, Virginia Tech 6–5. *Lost:* unbeaten Virginia 6–0 in mid-season.
1909 (6–1) *Won:* Maryville 39–0, Maryland A.C. 12–0, Kentucky 15–6, Maryland 31–0 (1st meeting), Washington & Lee 3–0, U.S.S. Franklin 5–0. *Lost:* Virginia Tech 18–5 in finale. *Noteworthy:* 1st year under Eddie L. Green.
1910 (4–0–2) *Won:* Eastern 33–0, Wake Forest 28–3, Virginia Tech 5–3, Richmond 53–0. *Tied:* Georgetown 0–0 (opener), Villanova 6–6 (finale). *Stars:* HB D.A. Roberson, G D.B. Floyd, C J.B. Bray.
1913 (6–1) *Won:* Davidson 26–6, Washington & Lee 6–0, Wake Forest 37–0, Virginia Medical 13–7,

Georgetown 12–0, U.S.S Franklin 54–0. *Lost:* VMI 14–7. *Noteworthy:* Green's last team.
1917 (6–2–1) *Won:* Guilford 19–0 (1st meeting since 1904), Davidson 7–3, Roanoke 28–0, Wake Forest 17–6 (10th straight over Deacons), Maryland 10–6, VMI 17–0. *Lost:* Washington & Lee 27–7, West Virginia 21–0. *Tied:* Virginia Tech 7–7. *Stars:* QB Dick Gurley, G John Ripple, T Solomon Homewood. *Noteworthy:* 1st year under Harry Hartsell.
1919 (7–2) *Won:* Guilford 80–0, Hampton Road 100–0, Roanoke 78–0, VMI 21–0, Davidson 36–6, Virginia Tech 3–0 (1st over Gobblers in 5 games since 1910), Wake Forest 21–7. *Lost:* Navy 49–0, North Carolina 13–12 (1st meeting since 1905). *Noteworthy:* 1st year under Bill Fetzer.
1920 (7–3) *Won:* Davidson 23–0, Navy 14–7, North Carolina 13–3 (1st in 14-game series dating to 1894), William & Mary 81–0 (1st meeting since 1908), Virginia Tech 14–6, Wofford 90–7, Wake Forest 49–7. *Lost:* unbeaten Penn St. 41–0 (1st meeting), unbeaten VMI 14–0, Georgetown 27–0.
1927 (9–1) *Won:* Elon 39–0, Clemson 18–6, Wake Forest 30–7, Florida 12–6 (1st meeting), North Carolina 19–6 (1st over Tar Heels since 1921), Davidson 25–6, Duke 20–18, South Carolina 34–0, Michigan St. 19–0. *Lost:* Furman 20–0 in 2nd game. *Star:* HB Jack McDowall. *Noteworthy:* won 1st SC championship.
1932 (6–1–2) *Won:* Appalachian St. 31–0, Richmond 9–0, Clemson 13–0, Florida 17–6, Davidson 7–3, Duke 6–0. *Lost:* North Carolina 13–0. *Tied:* Wake Forest 0–0, South Carolina 7–7. *Noteworthy:* 1st winning season since 1927.
1944 (7–2) *Won:* Milligan 27–7, Virginia 13–0 (1st meeting since 1908), Catawba 12–7, William & Mary 19–2, VMI 21–6 (1st meeting since 1926, 1st over Keydets in 8 games since 1919), Miami (Fla.) 28–7, Richmond 39–0. *Lost:* Clemson 13–7, Wake Forest 21–7. *Star:* soph TB Howard Turner. *Noteworthy:* 1st year under Beattie Feathers.
1946 (8–3) *Won:* Duke 13–6 (1st over Blue Devils in 13 games since 1932), Clemson 14–7, Davidson 25–0, Wake Forest 14–6 (1st over Deacons since 1938), VMI 49–7, Virginia 27–7, Florida 37–6 (1st meeting since 1934), Maryland 28–7 (1st meeting since 1924). *Lost:* Virginia Tech 14–6, Vanderbilt 7–0. *Stars:* Turner, E Al Phillips (back from military service after lettering in 1939). *Noteworthy:* made 1st postseason appearance, losing to

Oklahoma 34–13 in Gator Bowl; Turner passed 63 yds to Phillips for 1st TD and Les Palmer scored other on 8-yd run.

1957 (7–1–2) *Won:* North Carolina 7–0, Maryland 48–13, Clemson 13–7 (1st over Tigers in 6 games since 1947), Florida St. 7–0, Wake Forest 19–0 (1st over Deacons since 1949), Virginia Tech 12–0, South Carolina 29–26. *Lost:* William & Mary 7–6. *Tied:* Miami (Fla.) 0–0, Duke 14–14. *Stars:* HB Dick Christy (626 yds rush, 10 pass rec for 211 yds, 13 TDs, 83 pts), T Darrell Dess, C Jim Oddo. *Noteworthy:* won 1st ACC championship.

1963 (8–3) *Won:* Maryland 36–14, Southern Mississippi 14–0, Clemson 7–3, South Carolina 18–6, Duke 21–7 (1st over Blue Devils since 1946), Virginia 15–9, Virginia Tech 13–7, Wake Forest 42–0. *Lost:* North Carolina 31–10, Florida St. 14–0. *Stars:* QB Jim Rossi (1,296 yds total off), B Joe Scarpati (24 pass rec for 273 yds), Tony Koszarsky (5 TDs), G Bill Sullivan, T Bert Wilder. *Noteworthy:* Got share of 2nd ACC title. Lost to Mississippi St. 16–12 in Liberty Bowl after dropping behind 16–0; Rossi scored 1st TD and passed for 2nd.

1967 (9–2) *Won:* North Carolina 13–7, Buffalo 24–6, Florida St. 20–10, Houston 16–6, Maryland 31–9, Wake Forest 24–7, Duke 28–7, Virginia 30–8. *Lost:* Penn St. 13–8 (1st meeting since 1956), Clemson 14–6 in last 2 games. *Stars:* DT Dennis Byrd (1st State consensus All-American), DE Mark Capuano, DB Fred Combs, E Harry Martell (27 pass rec for 390 yds and 6 TDs), Tony Barchuck (600 yds rush), G Norman Cates, K Gerald Warren (nation's leader with 17 FGs). *Noteworthy:* beat Georgia 14–7 (1st over Bulldogs in 6 games dating to 1933) in Liberty Bowl behind two goal-line stands in final quarter; QB Jim Donnan passed for 161 yds and a TD, and Barchuk scored other Wolfpack TD.

1972 (8–3–1) *Won:* Syracuse 43–20, Duke 17–0, Wake Forest 42–13, East Carolina 38–16, South Carolina 42–24, Virginia 35–14, Clemson 42–17. *Lost:* North Carolina 34–33, Georgia 28–22, Penn St. 37–22. *Tied:* Maryland 24–24. *Stars:* QB Bruce Shaw (1,708 yds pass), Pat Kenney (38 pass rec for 832 yds and 5 TDs), RB Willie Burden, soph FB Stan Fritts (689 yds and 16 TDs rush, 106 pts), T Rick Druschel, G Bill Yoest, DB Mike Stultz. *Noteworthy:* 1st year under Lou Holtz. Beat West Virginia 49–13 (1st over Mountaineers in 5 games

since 1914) in Peach Bowl; frosh QB Dave Buckey (subbing for Shaw, who had broken leg) passed for 2 TDs (1 to twin brother Don) and scored a 3rd, Burden ran for 116 yds and a TD, and Fritts scored 3 TDs.

1973 (9–3) *Won:* East Carolina 57–8, Virginia 43–23, North Carolina 28–26, Maryland 24–22, Clemson 29–6, South Carolina 56–35, Duke 21–3, Wake Forest 52–13. *Lost:* Nebraska 31–14, Georgia 31–12, unbeaten Penn St. 35–29 (10th straight to Nittany Lions). *Stars:* Yoest, Druschel, Burden (1,014 yds rush), Fritts (13 TDs), SE Don Buckey (24 pass rec for 439 yds), Stultz, DB Bobby Pilz. *Noteworthy:* Won 6th ACC title. Beat Kansas 31–18 in Liberty Bowl; Fritts ran for 83 yds and 2 TDs, and frosh DT Jim Henderson scored on 31-yd pass int return.

1974 (9–2–1) *Won:* Wake Forest 33–15, Duke 35–21, Clemson 31–10, Syracuse 28–22, East Carolina 24–20, Virginia 22–21, South Carolina 42–27, Penn St. 12–7 (1st in 11-game series dating to 1920), Arizona St. 35–14. *Lost:* North Carolina 33–14, Maryland 20–10 in consecutive mid-season games. *Stars:* Fritts (1,169 yds and 12 TDs rush), Roland Hooks (13 TDs), Dave Buckey (1,481 yds pass), Don Buckey (26 pass rec for 452 yds), C Justus Everett, G Bob Blanchard, DB Mike Devine. *Noteworthy:* tied Houston 31–31 in Bluebonnet Bowl; Dave Buckey passed for 200 yds and a TD (to Fritts, who ran for 89 yds, another TD, and 2-pt conversion), and John Huff kicked 37-yd FG and 2 ex pts.

1977 (8–4) *Won:* Virginia 14–0, Syracuse 38–0, Wake Forest 41–14, Maryland 24–20, Auburn 17–15, South Carolina 7–3, Duke 37–32. *Lost:* East Carolina 28–23, North Carolina 27–14, Clemson 7–3 (1st to Tigers in 7 games since 1968), Penn St. 21–17. *Stars:* RB Ted Brown (14 TDs, 1,251 yds rush, 24 pass rec for 164 yds), QB Johnny Evans (1,357 yds pass), Elijah Marshall (20 pass rec for 418 yds), DBs Ralph Stringer and Richard Carter. *Noteworthy:* Beat Iowa St. 24–14 in Peach Bowl; Evans passed for 202 yds and 2 TDs and scored other TD himself, and Brown ran for 114 yds and caught 7 passes for 66 yds and a TD.

1978 (9–3) *Won:* East Carolina 29–13, Syracuse 27–19, West Virginia 29–15, Wake Forest 34–10, North Carolina 34–7, South Carolina 22–13, Duke 24–10, Virginia 24–21. *Lost:* Maryland 31–7,

Clemson 33–10, unbeaten Penn St. 19–10. *Stars:* Brown (1,350 yds and 11 TDs rush), soph K Nathan Ritter (76 pts), C Jim Ritcher, T Chris Dieterich, DT Simon Gupton, DB Woodrow Wilson. *Noteworthy:* beat Pittsburgh 30–17 in Tangerine Bowl; Brown ran for 126 yds and a TD, Ritter kicked 3 FGs (including 51-yarder), reserve QB John Isley passed 55 yds to Buster Ray for TD, and Mike Nall scored on 66-yd pass int return.

1986 (8–3–1) *Won:* East Carolina 38–10, Wake Forest 42–38, Maryland 28–16 (1st over Terps since 1979), North Carolina 35–34 (1st over Tar Heels since 1978), Clemson 27–3, South Carolina 23–22, Duke 29–15, Western Carolina 31–18 (1st meeting). *Lost:* Georgia Tech 59–21, Virginia 20–16. *Tied:* Pittsburgh 14–14. *Stars:* QB Erik Kramer (2,092 yds and 14 TDs pass), Nasrallah Worthen (41 pass rec for 686 yds), Haywood Jeffires (40 pass rec for 591 yds), Bobby Crumpler (581 yds rush), K Mike Cofer (72 pts), P Kelly Hollodick (42.3-yd avg). *Noteworthy:* 1st year under Dick Sheridan. Lost to Virginia Tech 25–24 (1st meeting since 1964) in Peach Bowl; Kramer passed for 155 yds and 2 TDs, Worthen caught 5 for 70 yds and a TD, and soph Mal Crite ran for 101 yds.

1988 (8–3–1) *Won:* Western Carolina 45–6, Wake Forest 14–6, Georgia Tech 14–6, East Tennessee St. 49–0, North Carolina 48–3, Clemson 10–3, Pittsburgh 14–3. *Lost:* Maryland 30–26, South Carolina 23–7, Virginia 19–14. *Tied:* Duke 43–43. *Stars:* QB Shane Montgomery (1,522 yds pass), Worthen (55 pass rec for 856 yds and 7 TDs), SE Danny Peebles (23 pass rec for 436 yds), frosh TB Tyrone Jackson (5 TDs rush), soph TB Chris Williams (5 TDs), DT Ray Agnew, LB Scott Auer, frosh DB Jesse Campbell (5 int), soph P Preston Poag (40.2-yd avg). *Noteworthy:* beat Iowa 28–23 in Peach Bowl; Montgomery passed for 152 yds and a TD (75 yds to Peebles), Jackson scored 2 TDs (one on 30-yd run), and Wolfpack came up with 4 int and 3 fumble recoveries.

1991 (9–3) *Won:* Virginia Tech 7–0 (1st over Gob- blers in 5 games since 1963), Kent 47–0, Wake Forest 30–3, North Carolina 24–7, Georgia Tech 28–21, Marshall 15–14, South Carolina 38–21, Duke 32–31, Maryland 20–17. *Lost:* Clemson 29–19, Virginia 42–10. *Stars:* frosh QB Geoff Bender (949 yds pass), SE Charles Davenport (33 pass rec for 558 yds), soph FB Ledel George (25 pass rec for 225 yds), TBs Anthony Barbour (769 yds rush) and soph Gary Downs (5 TDs rush), K Damon Hartman (12 FGs), DT Mark Thomas, LBs Billy Ray Haynes and soph Tyler Lawrence, DBs Sebastian Savage (5 int) and soph Mike Reid. *Noteworthy:* lost to East Carolina 37–34 in Peach Bowl after leading 34–17 early in 4th quarter; QB Terry Jordan passed for 145 yds and 2 TDs, George threw 52-yd TD pass to Davenport (6 pass rec for 118 yds), and Barbour ran for 90 yds.

1992 (9–3–1) *Won:* Iowa 24–14, Appalachian St. 35–10, Maryland 14–10, North Carolina 27–20, Texas Tech 48–13, Clemson 20–6, Virginia 31–7 (1st over Cavaliers since 1985), Duke 45–27, Wake Forest 42–14. *Lost:* Florida St. 34–13 (1st meeting since 1969), Georgia Tech 16–13. *Tied:* Virginia Tech 13–13. *Stars:* Jordan (1,963 yds pass), soph FL Eddie Goines (46 pass rec for 580 yds), SE Robert Hinton (23 pass rec for 323 yds), TE Neal Auer (27 pass rec for 275 yds), Barbour (1,204 yds and 8 TDs rush, 1,676 all-purpose yds), FB Greg Manior (634 yds and 6 TDs rush), OG Mike Gee, soph K Steve Videtich (14 FGs), MG Ricky Logo, Lawrence, LB David Merritt, Reid, DBs Ricky Turner (5 int), Savage and Dewayne Washington. *Noteworthy:* lost to Florida 27–10 in foggy Gator Bowl; Jordan passed for 213 yds and a TD (to TB Aubrey Shaw) and Videtich kicked FG.

BOWL SUMMARY

All-American 1–0; Bluebonnet 0–0–1; Copper 0–1; Gator 0–2; Liberty 2–1; Peach 3–3; Tangerine 1–0.

BOWL RECORD (7–7–1)

Regular Season	Bowl	Score	Opponent	Record
1946 (8–2)	Gator	13–34	Oklahoma	(7–3)
1963 (8–2)	Liberty	12–16	Mississippi St.	(6–2–2)

(continued)

Regular Season	Bowl	Score	Opponent	Record
1967 (8–2)	Liberty	14–7	Georgia	(7–3)
1972 (7–3–1)	Peach	49–13	West Virginia	(8–3)
1973 (8–3)	Liberty	31–18	Kansas	(7–3–1)
1974 (9–2)	Bluebonnet	31–31	Houston	(8–3)
1975 (7–3–1)	Peach	10–13	West Virginia	(8–3)
1977 (7–4)	Peach	24–14	Iowa State	(8–3)
1978 (8–3)	Tangerine	30–17	Pittsburgh	(8–3)
1986 (8–2–1)	Peach	24–25	Virginia Tech	(8–2–1)
1988 (7–3–1)	Peach	28–23	Iowa	(6–3–3)
1989 (7–4)	Copper	10–17	Arizona	(7–4)
1990 (6–5)	All-American	31–27	Southern Miss.	(8–3)
1991 (9–2)	Peach	34–37	East Carolina	(10–1)
1992 (9–2–1)	Gator	10–27	Florida	(8–4)

CONFERENCE TITLES

Southern—1927. **Atlantic Coast**—1957, 1963*, 1964, 1965*, 1968, 1973, 1979.

TOP 20 AP AND UPI
(USA TODAY/CNN SINCE 1991) RANKING

1946	18	1967	U–17	1974	11–9	1988	U–17
1947	17	1972	17–U	1977	U–19	1992	17–15
1957	15–20	1973	16–U	1978	18–19		

MAJOR RIVALS

N.C. State has played at least 10 games with Clemson 22–38–1, Davidson 30–9–6, Duke 25–38–5, East Carolina 12–7, Florida 4–9–1, Florida St. 4–9, Furman 4–8–4, Georgetown 2–6–2, Georgia Tech 5–7, Maryland 22–23–4, North Carolina 24–52–6, Penn St. 2–17, Richmond 16–1–1, South Carolina 25–25–4, Virginia 27–14–1, VMI 7–11–1, Virginia Tech 17–23–4, Wake Forest 51–29–6, Washington & Lee 5–11–1, William & Mary 10–8.

COACHES

Dean of N.C. State coaches is Earle Edwards with record of 77–88–8 for 1954–70, including 5 ACC titles and 2 bowl teams. Other top records for at least 3 years were by Eddie Green, 25–8–2 for 1909–13 with 1 unbeaten team; Gus Tebell, 21–25–2 for 1925–29 with 1 SC title; Beattie Feathers, 37–38–3 for 1944–51 with 1 bowl team; Lou Holtz, 33–12–3 for 1972–75 with 1 ACC title and 4 bowl teams; Bo Rein, 27–18–1 for 1976–79 with 1 ACC title and 2 bowl champions; and Dick Sheridan, 52–29–3 for 1986–92 with 6 bowl teams.

MISCELLANEA

First game was win over Raleigh Academy 14–6 in 1892...1st win over college foe was over Richmond 40–0 in 1895...highest score was over Hampton Road 100–0 in 1919...highest since W.W. II was over Western Carolina 67–0 in 1990...worst defeat was by Georgia Tech 128–0 in 1918...worst since W.W. II was by West Virginia 61–0 in 1953...State has won 9 straight 3 times, the most recent string in 1973–74 ended by North Carolina 33–14...longest losing string of 10 in 1953–54 broken with win over William & Mary 26–0...consensus All-Americans were Dennis Byrd, DT, 1967; Bill Yoest, OG, 1973; Ted Brown,

B, 1978; and Jim Ritcher, C, 1978–79 . . . Academic All-Americans were Roman Gabriel, QB, 1960; Joseph Scarpati, HB, 1963; Steve Warren, OT, 1967; Craig John, OG, 1971; Stan Fritts, RB, 1973; Justus Everett, C, 1973–74; and Calvin Warren, P, 1980 . . . Outland Trophy–winner was Jim Ritcher, C, 1979.

VIRGINIA (Cavaliers, Wahoos; Orange and Blue)

NOTABLE TEAMS

1890 (5–2) *Won:* Dickinson 12–0, Lafayette 20–6, Randolph-Macon 136–0 (1st meeting), Washington & Lee 46–0 (1st meeting), Trinity (Duke) 10–4 (1st meeting). *Lost:* Pennsylvania 72–0 (1st meeting), Princeton 115–0 (1st meeting).

1893 (8–3) *Won:* Richmond 34–4 (1st meeting), Washington YMCA 20–0, Johns Hopkins 28–12, Trinity (Duke) 30–0, Georgetown 58–0, Navy 12–0, Virginia Military Institute (VMI) 22–0 (1st meeting), North Carolina 16–0. *Lost:* Penn St. 6–0, Navy 28–0, Georgetown 28–14. *Noteworthy:* 1st year under John Poe.

1894 (8–2) *Won:* Richmond 48–0, 28–0, Baltimore City College 36–0, Johns Hopkins 76–0, Rutgers 20–4, Ft. Monroe 102–0, West Philadelphia A.C. 64–0, North Carolina 34–0. *Lost:* Princeton 12–0, unbeaten Penn 14–6.

1895 (9–2) *Won:* Miller School 30–0, Virginia Tech 38–0 (1st meeting), Maryland A.C. 20–0, Gallaudet 16–6, Roanoke 14–0 (1st meeting), St. Albans 14–4, Richmond 62–0, Vanderbilt 6–4 (1st meeting), North Carolina 6–0. *Lost:* Princeton 36–0, unbeaten national champ Penn 54–0. *Noteworthy:* only year under Harry Mackey.

1896 (7–2–2) *Won:* Miller School 26–2, St. John's 48–0, Virginia Tech 44–0, St. Albans 6–0, VMI 46–0, Gallaudet 6–0, North Carolina 48–0. *Lost:* Penn 20–0, unbeaten national champ Princeton 48–0. *Tied:* Hampton A.C. 10–10, 6–6. *Noteworthy:* 1st year under Martin Bergen.

1897 (6–2–1) *Won:* Franklin & Marshall 38–0, St. Albans 14–0, Georgia 17–4 (1st meeting), Gallaudet 20–4, George Washington 10–0 (1st meeting), North Carolina 12–0. *Lost:* unbeaten national champ Penn 42–0, Navy 4–0. *Tied:* unbeaten Vanderbilt 0–0.

1900 (7–2–1) *Won:* Richmond 51–0, Johns Hopkins 20–0, Washington & Lee 28–0 (1st meeting since 1890), Gallaudet 34–0, Virginia Tech 17–5, North Carolina 17–0, Sewanee 17–5. *Lost:* Carlisle Indians 17–2, Georgetown 10–0. *Tied:* VMI 0–0.

1901 (8–2) *Won:* Washington & Lee 28–0, Roanoke 68–0, St. Albans 39–0, Gallaudet 24–0, Virginia Tech 16–0, VMI 28–0, North Carolina 23–6, Sewanee 23–5. *Lost:* Penn 20–5, Georgetown 17–16. *Noteworthy:* only year under Wesley Abbott.

1902 (8–1–1) *Won:* Washington & Lee 16–0, St. Albans 15–0, Nashville 27–0, Kentucky 12–0, St. John's 22–0, Davidson 35–0, Virginia Tech 6–0, Carlisle 6–5 (only win in 7-game series between 1900 and 1910). *Lost:* Lehigh 34–6. *Tied:* North Carolina 12–12. *Noteworthy:* only year under John DeSaulles.

1903 (7–2–1) *Won:* St. Albans 16–0, Randolph-Macon 37–0 (1st meeting since 1890), Washington & Lee 16–0, Kentucky 6–0, Virginia Tech 21–0, Davidson 22–0, St. John's 48–6. *Lost:* Navy 6–5, North Carolina 16–6. *Tied:* Carlisle 6–6. *Noteworthy:* only year under Gresham Poe.

1906 (7–2–2) *Won:* St. John's 11–0, Richmond 22–0, 12–6, Randolph-Macon 38–0, Hampden-Sydney 38–5 (1st meeting), VMI 4–0, Georgetown 12–0. *Lost:* Bucknell 12–5, Carlisle 18–17. *Tied:* N.C. State 0–0, George Washington 0–0. *Noteworthy:* 1st year under Edward Hammond.

1908 (7–0–1) *Won:* William & Mary 11–0 (1st meeting), St. John's 18–9, Randolph-Macon 22–0, Davidson 12–0, N.C. State 6–0, Georgetown 6–0, North Carolina 31–0. *Tied:* Sewanee 0–0. *Noteworthy:* had 1st unbeaten season in only year under M.T. Cooke.

1909 (7–1) *Won:* William & Mary 30–0, Hampden-Sydney 37–0, Davidson 11–0, St. John's 12–0, Navy 5–0 (1st over Midshipmen in 6 games since 1893), VMI 32–0, Georgetown 21–0. *Lost:* Lehigh 11–7. *Noteworthy:* only year under John Neff.

1910 (6–2) *Won:* William & Mary 10–0, Randolph-Macon 17–0, Roanoke 21–0 (1st meeting since 1901), St. John's 29–0 (10th win in as many games in series), VMI 28–0, North Carolina 7–0. *Lost:* Carlisle 22–5, Georgetown 15–0 in successive late games. *Noteworthy:* only year under Charles Crawford.

1911 (8–2) *Won:* Hampden-Sydney 23–0, William & Mary 81–0, Randolph-Macon 31–0, St. John's 6–0, VMI 22–6, Wake Forest 29–6 (1st meeting since 1889), Johns Hopkins 34–0 (1st meeting since

1900), North Carolina 28–0. *Lost:* Swarthmore 9–8, Georgetown 9–0. *Noteworthy:* only year under Kemper Yancey.

1913 (7–1) *Won:* Randolph-Macon 40–0 (10th straight over Yellow Jackets), South Carolina 54–0, Hampden-Sydney 53–0, VMI 38–7, Georgia 13–6 (1st meeting since 1897), Vanderbilt 34–0, North Carolina 26–7. *Lost:* Georgetown 8–7. *Noteworthy:* 1st year in Lambeth Stadium.

1914 (8–1) *Won:* Randolph-Macon 39–0, Richmond 62–0, South Carolina 49–0, Georgia 28–0, Vanderbilt 20–7, St. John's 88–0, Swarthmore 47–0, North Carolina 20–3. *Lost:* Yale 21–0 (1st meeting) in 2nd game. *Stars:* QB Bobby Gooch, HB Eugene "Buck" Mayer (21 TDs, 142 pts). *Noteworthy:* only year under Joseph Wood.

1915 (8–1) *Won:* Randolph-Macon 20–0, Yale 10–0 (1st win over Ivy League school), Richmond 74–0 (10th straight over Spiders), Georgia 9–7, VMI 44–0, Vanderbilt 35–10, South Carolina 13–0, North Carolina 14–0. *Lost:* Harvard 9–0 (1st meeting). *Star:* Mayer (Virginia's—and South's—1st consensus All-American). *Noteworthy:* only year under Harry Varner.

1925 (7–1–1) *Won:* Hampden-Sydney 40–0, Georgia 7–6 (1st over Bulldogs in 8 games since 1915), Richmond 19–0, VMI 18–10, Maryland 6–0, Virginia Tech 10–0, Randolph-Macon 41–0. *Lost:* Washington & Lee 12–0. *Tied:* North Carolina 3–3. *Noteworthy:* 3rd year under "Greasy" Neale.

1926 (6–2–2) *Won:* Lynchburg 38–0, VMI 14–7, South Carolina 6–0 (1st meeting since 1916), Washington & Lee 30–7, Randolph-Macon 57–0, North Carolina 3–0. *Lost:* Georgia 27–7, Virginia Tech 6–0. *Tied:* Hampden-Sydney 0–0, Maryland 6–6.

1941 (8–1) *Won:* Hampden-Sydney 41–0, Lafayette 25–0 (1st meeting since 1891), Richmond 44–0 (1st meeting since 1925), VMI 27–7 (1st over Keydets since 1934), Virginia Tech 34–0, Washington & Lee 27–7, Lehigh 34–0, North Carolina 28–7 (1st over Tar Heels since 1932). *Lost:* Yale 21–19 in 3rd game. *Stars:* Maxwell Award–winning HB Bill Dudley (18 TDs, 856 yds and 11 TDs pass, 968 yds rush, nation's leader with 134 pts and 1,674 all-purpose yds), William Preston (20 pass rec for 303 yds), William Suhling (5 int).

1944 (6–1–2) *Won:* Hampden-Sydney 37–0, West Virginia 24–6, VMI 34–0, Maryland 18–7, Richmond 39–0, North Carolina 26–7. *Lost:* N.C. State

13–0 (1st meeting since 1908) in 2nd game. *Tied:* North Carolina Pre-Flight 13–13, unbeaten Yale 6–6. *Star:* John Duda (726 yds and 8 TDs rush). *Noteworthy:* led nation in total defense.

1945 (7–2) *Won:* Coast Guard 39–0, N.C. State 26–6, VMI 40–7, Virginia Tech 31–13, West Virginia 13–7, Richmond 45–0, Oceana Naval Air Station 40–0. *Lost:* Maryland 19–13, North Carolina 27–18 in final 2 games. *Noteworthy:* Frank Murray's last team.

1947 (7–3) *Won:* George Washington 33–13 (1st meeting since 1922), Virginia Tech 41–7, Harvard 47–0 (1st meeting since 1938, 1st win in 9-game series dating to 1915), Washington & Lee 32–7, VMI 35–6, Richmond 34–0, West Virginia 6–0. *Lost:* unbeaten Penn 19–7, N.C. State 7–2, North Carolina 40–7. *Stars:* Grover Jones (7 TDs rush), Edmund Bessell (11 pass rec for 226 yds), George Grimes (40.8-yd punting avg).

1949 (7–2) *Won:* George Washington 27–13, Miami (Ohio) 21–18, Virginia Tech 26–0, Washington & Lee 27–7, VMI 32–13, West Virginia 19–14, Penn 26–14 (1st in 15-game series dating to 1890). *Lost:* Tulane 28–14 (1st meeting), North Carolina 14–7 in last 2 games. *Stars:* FB John Papit (1,214 yds and 9 TDs rush, nation's leader with 1,611 all-purpose yds), B Ralph Shoaf, E Carlton Eliot, Stephen Osisek (11 pass rec for 205 yds), soph DL Joe Palumbo.

1950 (8–2) *Won:* George Washington 19–0, Virginia Tech 45–6, Washington & Lee 26–21, VMI 26–13, West Virginia 28–21, The Citadel 34–14, William & Mary 13–0 (1st meeting since 1940), North Carolina 44–14 (1st over Tar Heels since 1944). *Lost:* Penn 21–7, Tulane 42–18. *Stars:* Papit (949 yds and 8 TDs rush), QB Rufus Barkley (16 TDs pass), E Gene Schroeder (35 pass rec for 552 yds and 7 TDs), Palumbo, soph Harold Hoak (40.2-yd punting avg).

1951 (8–1) *Won:* George Washington 20–0, Virginia Tech 33–0, VMI 34–14, Duke 30–7 (1st meeting since 1943), The Citadel 39–0, North Carolina 34–14, South Carolina 28–27 (1st meeting since 1929), William & Mary 46–0. *Lost:* Washington & Lee 42–14 (1st to Generals in 10 games since 1937). *Stars:* Palumbo, William Chisolm (19 pass rec for 209 yds), E Tom Scott, T Bob Miller, B James Lesane.

1952 (8–2) *Won:* Vanderbilt 27–0 (1st meeting

since 1928), Virginia Tech 42–0, George Washington 50–0, VMI 33–14 (10th straight over Keydets), North Carolina 34–7, Richmond 49–0, Washington & Lee 21–14, William & Mary 20–13. *Lost:* Duke 21–7, South Carolina 21–14 in successive mid-season games. *Stars:* Scott, Billy King (6 int), B Gerald Furst (699 yds rush). *Noteworthy:* Art Guepe's last team led nation in pass defense.

1968 (7–3) *Won:* VMI 47–0, Davidson 41–14, Duke 50–20 (1st over Blue Devils in 7 games since 1958), Navy 24–0 (1st over Midshipmen in 12 games since 1909), North Carolina 41–6, Tulane 63–47, Maryland 28–23. *Lost:* Purdue 44–6, N.C. State 19–0 (10th straight to Wolfpack), South Carolina 49–28. *Stars:* B Frank Quayle (14 TDs, 1,213 yds rush, 30 pass rec for 426 yds), QB Gene Arnette (1,754 yds and 20 TDs total off), G Chuck Hammer, T Greg Shelly, LB Bob Paczkoski, Billy Schmidt (6 int). *Noteworthy:* 1st winning season since 1952.

1984 (8–2–2) *Won:* VMI 35–7, Navy 21–9, Virginia Tech 26–23 (1st over Hokies since 1979), Duke 38–10, Wake Forest 28–9, West Virginia 27–7 (1st over Mountaineers in 7 games since 1965), N.C. State 45–0. *Lost:* Clemson 55–0 (opener), Maryland 45–34 (finale). *Tied:* Georgia Tech 20–20, North Carolina 24–24. *Stars:* OT Jim Dombrowski, OG Bob Olderman, RB Howard Petty (811 yds and 8 TDs rush), soph QB Don Majkowski (1,540 yds and 13 TDs total off), Jon Muha (22 pass rec for 283 yds), Geno Zimmerlink (22 rec for 350 yds), frosh WR John Ford (19 pass rec for 545 yds and 7 TDs), MG David Bond, DT Ron Mattes, DBs Ray Daly (6 int) and Lester Lyles. *Noteworthy:* made 1st postseason appearance, beating Purdue 27–24 in Peach Bowl as Wahoos took advantage of 4 turnovers and overcame 24–14 halftime deficit; Petty ran for 114 yds and a TD, Majkowski passed for 118 yds and a TD and ran for another, and K Kenny Stadlin had 2 FGs and 3 ex pts.

1987 (8–4) *Won:* Virginia Tech 14–13, Duke 42–17, VMI 30–0, Wake Forest 35–21, Georgia Tech 23–14, North Carolina 20–17, N.C. State 34–31. *Lost:* Georgia 30–22, Maryland 21–19, Clemson 38–21, South Carolina 58–10. *Stars:* QB Scott Secules (2,311 yds and 12 TDs pass, 6 TDs rush), Ford (48 pass rec for 855 yds and 6 TDs, 7 TDs total), soph WR Tim Finkelston (31 pass rec for 430 yds), Keith Mattioli (29 pass rec for 428 yds), frosh RB Marcus Wilson (692 yds and 7 TDs rush), OT Chris

Minear, K Mark Inderlied (13 FGs, 70 pts), DE Sean Scott, LB Jeff Lageman, frosh DB Keith McMeans (nation's leader with 9 int), soph DB Kevin Cook (8 int). *Noteworthy:* beat Brigham Young 22–16 in All-American Bowl; Secules passed for 162 yds, a TD, and 2-pt conversion and ran for a TD, and RB Kevin Morgan scored on 25-yd run.

1989 (10–3) *Won:* Penn St. 14–6 (1st in 5-game series dating to 1893), Georgia Tech 17–10, Duke 49–28, William & Mary 24–12, North Carolina 50–17, Wake Forest 47–28, Louisville 16–15, N.C. State 20–9, Virginia Tech 32–25, Maryland 48–21. *Lost:* Notre Dame 36–13, Clemson 34–20. *Stars:* QB Shawn Moore (2,078 yds and 18 TDs pass, 505 yds and 9 TDs rush), WR Herman Moore (36 pass rec for 848 yds and 10 TDs), TE Bruce McGonnigal (42 pass rec for 634 yds and 6 TDs), Finkelston (20 pass rec for 442 yds), Wilson (1,098 yds rush, 20 pass rec for 161 yds, 1,543 all-purpose yds, 6 TDs), K Jake McInerney (16 FGs, 88 pts), OG Roy Brown, DEs Ray Savage and frosh Chris Slade, LB Phil Thomas, DBs Jason Wallace (5 int) and Tony Covington. *Noteworthy:* Got share of 1st ACC title. Lost to Illinois 31–21 in Florida Citrus Bowl; Shawn Moore passed for 191 yds and 2 TDs, and Herman Moore caught 5 for 56 yds and a TD.

1990 (8–4) *Won:* Kansas 59–10, Clemson 20–7 (1st in 30-game series dating to 1955), Navy 56–14, Duke 59–0, William & Mary 63–35, N.C. State 31–0, Wake Forest 49–14, North Carolina 24–10. *Lost:* unbeaten national cochamp Georgia Tech 41–38, Maryland 35–30, Virginia Tech 38–13. *Stars:* Shawn Moore (nation's passing efficiency leader with 2,262 yds and 21 TDs; 306 yds and 8 TDS rush), Herman Moore (54 pass rec for 1,190 yds and 13 TDs), WR Derek Dooley (27 pass rec for 422 yds), McGonnigal (17 pass rec for 239 yds), soph TB Terry Kirby (1,020 yds rush, 33 pass rec for 324 yds, 11 TDs), RB Nikki Fisher (848 yds and 10 TDs rush), McInerney (15 FGs, 94 pts), Slade, frosh LB P.J. Killian, P Ed Garno (42.6-yd avg). *Noteworthy:* lost to Tennessee 23–22 in Sugar Bowl after leading 16–0 at halftime when Vols scored winning TD in waning moments of game; McInerney kicked 3 FGs, and soph RB Gary Steele and Kirby each scored TDs.

1991 (8–3–1) *Won:* Navy 17–10, Duke 34–3, Kansas 31–19, North Carolina 14–9, Wake Forest 48–7,

VMI 42–0, N.C. State 42–10, Virginia Tech 38–0. *Lost:* Maryland 17–6, Georgia Tech 24–21 in early games. *Tied:* Clemson 20–20. *Stars:* Kirby (9 TDs, 887 yds and 7 TDs rush, 37 pass rec for 406 yds), Fisher (658 yds rush), QB Matt Blundin (1,902 yds and 19 TDs pass), soph TE Aaron Mundy (31 pass rec for 409 yds and 5 TDs), soph WR Larry Holmes (27 pass rec for 462 yds and 8 TDs), frosh WR Tyrone Davis (19 pass rec for 465 yds and 5 TDs), OT Ray Roberts, K Michael Husted (11 FGs, 72 pts), DT Matt Quigley, Slade, Killian, Garno

(42-yd punting avg). *Noteworthy:* lost to Oklahoma 48–14 in Gator Bowl; Blundin passed for 142 yds and both Wahoo TDs (to Davis and WR Terrence Tomlin).

BOWL SUMMARY

All-American 1–0; Florida Citrus 0–1; Gator 0–1; Peach 1–0; Sugar 0–1.

BOWL RECORD (2–3)

Regular Season	Bowl	Score	Opponent	Record
1984 (7–2–2)	Peach	27–24	Purdue	(7–4)
1987 (7–4)	All-American	22–16	Brigham Young	(9–3)
1989 (10–2)	Florida Citrus	21–31	Illinois	(9–2)
1990 (8–3)	Sugar	22–23	Tennessee	(8–2–2)
1991 (8–2–1)	Gator	14–48	Oklahoma	(8–3)

CONFERENCE TITLES

Atlantic Coast—1989*.

TOP 20 AP AND UPI RANKING

1951	13–U	1984	20–17	1989	18–15	1990	U–15

MAJOR RIVALS

Virginia has played at least 10 games with Clemson 1–30–1, Davidson 8–0–2, Duke 19–25, Georgetown 7–7–2, George Washington 12–2–1, Georgia 6–7–3, Georgia Tech 5–9–1, Hampden-Sydney 17–1–2, Maryland 18–37–2, Navy 9–27, North Carolina 41–52–4, N.C. State 14–27–1, Pennsylvania 1–15, Princeton 1–9–1, Randolph-Macon 21–0–1, Richmond 21–2–2, South Carolina 12–19–1, St. John's (Md.) 17–0, Vanderbilt 7–12–2, VMI 55–23–3, Virginia Tech 33–36–5, Wake Forest 23–11, Washington & Lee 21–13–1, West Virginia 11–10–1, William & Mary 24–5–1. Record against ACC member Florida St. is 0–1.

COACHES

Dean of Virginia coaches is George Welsh with record of 73–51–3 for 1982–92 with 1 ACC title and 5 bowl teams. Other top records for at least 3 years were by Earle "Greasy" Neale, 28–22–5 for 1923–28; Frank Murray, 41–34–5 for 1937–45; and Art Guepe, 47–17–2 for 1946–52.

MISCELLANEA

First game was win over Pantops Academy 20–0 in 1888 . . . 1st win over college foe was over Georgetown 32–0 in 1889 . . . highest score was over Randolph-Macon 136–0 in 1890 . . . highest since 1900 was over St. John's (Md.) 88–0 in 1914 . . . highest since W.W. II was over Hampden-Sydney 71–0 in 1946 . . . worst defeat was by Princeton 115–0 in 1890 . . . worst since 1900 was by Ohio St. 75–0 in 1933 . . . worst since W.W. II was by Texas 68–0 in 1977 . . . longest unbeaten string of 14 in 1944–45 ended by Maryland 19–13 . . . longest losing string of 28 in 1958–60 broken with win over William & Mary 21–6 in 1961 opener . . . consensus All-Americans were Eugene Mayer, B, 1915; Bill Dudley, B, 1941; Jim Dombrowski, OL, 1985; Herman Moore, WR, 1990; and Chris Slade, DL, 1992 . . . Academic All-Americans were Tom Kennedy, OG, 1972; Bob Meade, DT, 1975; and Tom Burns, LB, 1992 . . . Maxwell Award–winner was Bill Dudley, HB, 1941.

WAKE FOREST (Demon Deacons; Old Gold and Black)

NOTABLE TEAMS

1892 (4–0–1) *Won:* Asheville Athletics 40–0, Washington & Lee 16–0, Richmond 16–0, Tennessee 10–6. *Tied:* unbeaten Virginia Military Institute (VMI) 12–12. *Noteworthy:* coached by W.E. Sikes.

1924 (7–2) *Won:* Duke 32–0, Elon 41–0, Guilford 67–0, Lynchburg 37–7, N.C. State 12–0, North Carolina 7–6 (1st over Tar Heels in 17 games since 1891), Washington & Lee 10–8 (1st over Generals in 8 games since 1892). *Lost:* South Carolina 7–0, Florida 34–0.

1925 (6–2–1) *Won:* North Carolina 6–0, Duke 21–3, Lenoir-Rhyne 49–0, Guilford 25–0, Furman 9–0, Elon 65–0. *Lost:* Florida 24–3, N.C. State 6–0. *Tied:* Davidson 7–7. *Noteworthy:* Hank Garrity's last team.

1939 (7–3) *Won:* Elon 34–0, South Carolina 19–7, Miami (Fla.) 33–0, N.C. State 32–0, Western Maryland 66–0, Marshall 14–13, Davidson 46–7. *Lost:* North Carolina 36–6, Duke 6–0, Clemson 20–7. *Stars:* B John Polanski (nation's leader with 882 yds rush), T Rupert Pate. *Noteworthy:* led nation in rush.

1940 (7–3) *Won:* William Jewell 79–0, North Carolina 12–0 (1st over Tar Heels since 1927), Furman 19–0, Marshall 31–19, George Washington 18–0,

N.C. State 20–14, South Carolina 7–6. *Lost:* Clemson 39–0, Duke 23–0 (10th straight to Blue Devils), Texas Tech 12–7. *Star:* B Tony Gallovich.

1942 (6–2–1) *Won:* Duke 20–7 (1st over Blue Devils since 1926), Furman 14–6, Clemson 19–6 (1st over Tigers since 1936), VMI 28–0, George Washington 20–0, South Carolina 33–14. *Lost:* North Carolina 6–0, Boston College 27–0. *Tied:* N.C. State 0–0. *Stars:* B Red Cochran, T Pat Preston, G Buck Jones.

1944 (8–1) *Won:* North Carolina 7–0, Georgia 14–7, Maryland 39–0, VMI 38–7, N.C. State 21–7, Miami (Fla.) 27–0, Clemson 13–7, South Carolina 19–13. *Lost:* Duke 34–0. *Stars:* Bs Nick Sacrinty and Elmer Barbour, Ts George Owens and John Kerns, C Dick Foreman, E Dave Harris.

1950 (6–1–2) *Won:* Richmond 43–0, William & Mary 47–0, North Carolina 13–7, George Washington 13–7, Duke 13–7, South Carolina 14–7. *Lost:* unbeaten Clemson 13–12. *Tied:* Boston College 7–7, N.C. State 6–6. *Stars:* Bs Bill Miller (721 yds rush) and Guido Scarton (7 TDs), Ts Jim Staton and Ed Listopad, G Bob Auffarth, soph E Jack Lewis. *Noteworthy:* D.C. "Peahead" Walker's last team led nation in total defense.

1979 (8–4) *Won:* Appalachian St. 30–23, Georgia 22–21, East Carolina 23–20, Virginia Tech 19–14, North Carolina 24–19, Maryland 25–17 (1st over Terps since 1971), Auburn 42–38, Duke 17–14. *Lost:* N.C. State 17–14, Clemson 31–0, South Carolina 35–14. *Stars:* RB James McDougald (1,231 yds rush, 13 TDs), QB Jay Venuto (2,597 yds and 17 TDs pass), soph WR Wayne Baumgardner (61 pass rec for 1,128 yds and 9 TDs), MG James Parker. *Noteworthy:* Nation's most-improved team had 1st winning season since 1971. Made 1st postseason appearance in more than 30 years, losing to Louisiana State (LSU) 34–10 in Tangerine Bowl; scored TD on 34-yd pass from Venuto to Baumgardner.

1992 (8–4) *Won:* Appalachian St. 10–7, Vanderbilt 40–6, Maryland 30–23, Army 23–7, Clemson 18–15 (1st over Tigers since 1976), Duke 28–14, Georgia Tech 23–10. *Lost:* North Carolina 35–17, Florida St. 35–7 (1st meeting since 1973), Virginia 31–17, N.C. State 42–14. *Stars:* QB Keith West (2,039 yds and 12 TDs pass), SE Todd Dixon (51 pass rec for 750 yds and 7 TDs), TE John Henry Mills (34 pass rec for 369 yds), TBs John Leach (575 yds and 5

FB Brian Piccolo, 1962–64. Nations scoring leader (111 points) 1964.

TDs rush, 27 pass rec for 262 yds) and Ned Moultrie (717 yds and 5 TDs rush), WB Bobby Jones (18 pass rec for 305 yds), OT Ben Coleman, K Mike Green (10 FGs), DEs Maurice Miller and Mike McCrary, soph LB Kevin Giles, DBs George Coghill and Lamont Scales. *Noteworthy:* Bill Dooley's last team. Beat Oregon 39–35 in Independence Bowl after trailing 29–10 in 2nd half; West passed for 262 yds and a TD, Dixon had 5 pass rec for 166 yds and 2 TDs (including 61-yarder from Jones), Leach ran for 116 yds and 2 TDs and caught 2-pt conversion pass from West, and Moultrie scored on short run.

BOWL SUMMARY

Dixie 0–1; Gator 1–0; Independence 1–0; Tangerine 0–1.

BOWL RECORD (2–2)

Regular Season	Bowl	Score	Opponent	Record
1945 (4–3–1)	Gator	26–14	South Carolina	(2–3–3)
1948 (6–3)	Dixie	7–20	Baylor	(5–3–2)
1979 (8–3)	Tangerine	10–34	LSU	(6–5)
1992 (7–4)	Independence	39–35	Oregon	(6–5)

CONFERENCE TITLES

Atlantic Coast—None.

TOP 20 AP AND UPI RANKING

1945	19	1948	20

MAJOR RIVALS

Wake Forest has played at least 10 games with Appalachian St. 10–4–1, Boston College 3–5–2, Clemson 12–45–1, Davidson 11–15–4, Duke 23–48–2, Florida St. 2–8–1, Furman 7–11, George Washington 9–3, Georgia Tech 4–11, Guilford 11–0–1, Maryland 11–29–1, North Carolina 29–58–2, N.C. State 29–51–6, Presbyterian 5–4–1, Richmond 9–7–1, South Carolina 20–34–2, Virginia 11–23, Virginia Tech 11–20–1, William & Mary 10–9–1.

COACHES

Dean of Wake Forest coaches is D.C. "Peahead" Walker with record of 77–51–6 for 1937–50, including 2 bowl teams. Other top records for at least 3 years were by Hank Garrity, 19–7–1 for 1923–25; F.S. Miller, 18–15–4 for 1929–32; John Mackovic, 14–20 for 1978–80 with 1 bowl team; and Bill Dooley, 29–36–2 for 1987–92 with 1 bowl champion.

MISCELLANEA

First game was win over North Carolina 6–4 in 1888 . . . highest score was over Florence YMCA 80–0 in 1915 . . . highest since W.W. II was over Virginia 66–21 in 1975 . . . biggest margin since W.W. II was over Richmond 56–6 in 1951 . . . worst defeat was by N.C. State 76–0 in 1908 . . . worst since W.W. II was by Oklahoma 63–0 in 1974 . . . most pts ever against Deacons was by Clemson 82–24 in 1981 . . . longest unbeaten string of 9 in 1945–46 ended by N.C. State 14–6 . . . longest losing string of 18 in 1962–63 broken with win over South Carolina 20–19 . . . consensus All-American was Bill Armstrong, DB, 1976 . . . Wake Forest has had no Academic All-America 1st team selections.

BIG EAST CONFERENCE

One of the nation's leading basketball leagues formed a football-only conference in early 1991 to accommodate member football powers Boston College, Miami (Fla.), Pittsburgh, and Syracuse. After Miami was admitted to full league membership in 1990, a series of meetings in late 1990 and early 1991 led to football membership only for former independents Rutgers, Temple, Virginia Tech, and West Virginia. Conference competition began with the 1991 football season.

FACTS AND ODDITIES ON BIG EAST MEMBERS

Members of the nation's newest football conference have a rich football tradition. Miami gave the league a national champion in the league's first year of existence when the 1991 Hurricanes finished 11–0, then blanked Nebraska 22–0 in the Orange Bowl to earn a share of the national title. Eight other generally recognized national championships have been won by current Big East schools.

"Pop" Warner's Pittsburgh team won the national crown in 1916, outscoring foes 255–25 in an 8–0 season, and won again in a curtailed World War I schedule in 1918, outscoring four opponents 131–6. In 1937, Pittsburgh (then under John B. "Jock" Sutherland) went 9–0–1 to earn a share of the Panthers' third national title.

Syracuse won its first national championship in 1959 when Ben Schwartzwalder's powerful Orangemen finished 10–0, then beat Texas 23–14 in the Cotton Bowl. Syracuse led the nation in three offensive and two defensive team categories that season. Pittsburgh returned to the throne in 1976, finishing 11–0 behind Heisman Trophy–winner Tony Dorsett, then whipping Georgia 27–3 in the Sugar Bowl.

Miami won its first national crown in 1983, losing its opener to Florida 28–3 but then finishing 10–1 before upsetting 12–0 Nebraska 31–30 in the Orange Bowl behind freshman QB Bernie Kosar. The Hurricanes won the title again in 1987, finishing 11–0 and then beating undefeated Oklahoma 20–14 in the Orange Bowl. Miami won its third crown in 1989 with a 10–1 season (the loss was 24–10 to Florida State) followed by a 33–25 win over Alabama in the Sugar Bowl. The 1991 title was Miami's fourth in less than a decade.

Heisman Trophy winners have come from Big East schools five times. They are Syracuse HB Ernie Davis, 1961; Pittsburgh HB Tony Dorsett, 1976; Boston College QB Doug Flutie, 1984; Miami QB Vinny Testaverde, 1986; and Miami QB Gino Torretta, 1992. The Maxwell Award has gone to players from Big East members seven times. Winners were Temple QB Steve Joachim, 1974; Pittsburgh RB Tony Dorsett, 1976; Pittsburgh DE Hugh Green, 1980; Boston College QB Doug Flutie, 1984; Miami QB Vinny Testaverde, 1986; Syracuse QB Don McPherson, 1987; and Miami QB Gino Torretta, 1992.

Players from Big East schools have won the Outland Trophy four times. Winners were Pittsburgh OT Mark May, 1980; Virginia Tech DT Bruce Smith, 1984; Boston College NG Mike Ruth, 1985; and Miami DT Russell Maryland, 1990. The Lombardi Award has gone to a player from a Big East member only one time—Pittsburgh DE Hugh Green winning in 1980. Green, who played in 1978–1980, was one of only a half dozen linemen in the twentieth century to make consensus All-America three times.

Coaches of Big East schools have won national Coach of the Year awards in seven different seasons. Syracuse coaches twice took both the American Football Coaches Association (AFCA) and the Football Writers Association of America (FWAA) awards, with Floyd "Ben" Schwartzwalder winning in 1959 and Dick MacPherson in 1987. Miami also has had two winners: Howard Schnellenberger won the FWAA share in 1983, and Dennis Erickson won both awards in 1989. Pittsburgh's Johnny Majors won the FWAA award in 1973 and both awards in 1976. Don Nehlen of West Virginia earned the AFCA award in 1988.

Among coaches at current Big East schools who rank high in total victories or winning percentage are Glenn "Pop" Warner, "Jock" Sutherland, and Schwartzwalder.

Warner had a record of 313–106–32 for 1895–1938, including stints at Pitt (59–12–4 for 1915–1923 with four unbeaten teams and two national titles) and Temple (31–18–9 for 1933–1938 with one Sugar Bowl team unbeaten in regular season). Sutherland was 144–28–14 at Lafayette (1919–1923) and Pittsburgh (1924–1938), a winning percentage of .812. His record at Pitt was 111–20–12 with four Rose Bowl teams, four teams unbeaten in regular season, and one national champion. Schwartzwalder was 178–96–3 at Muhlenberg (1946–1948) and Syracuse (1949–1973). His Syracuse record was 153–91–3 with seven bowl teams and one unbeaten national champion.

Rutgers took part in the first college football game on November 6, 1869, beating visiting Princeton 6 goals to 4, but lost a rematch to the Tigers 8–0 a week later and did not beat Princeton again until 1938. The Scarlet Knights lost 33 straight games to Princeton over the 68-year span before winning 20–18. The two last met in 1980, with Rutgers winning 44–13, but Princeton leads the all-time series 53–17–1.

Pittsburgh has played Penn State 92 times in one of the nation's most-played rivalries. Through 1992 the Nittany Lions held an edge of 47–41–4 in a series that began in 1893. The two won't meet again, however, until 1997.

West Virginia ended one of the most remarkable winning streaks in college football history in 1917. Gil Dobie had not seen his team lose a game in 11 years of college coaching when he took the Navy job, having compiled a 58–0–3 record at North Dakota State and Washington between 1906 and 1916. His first Navy team outscored opponents 443–23. But on October 6, 1917, his streak came to an end when the Midshipmen were beaten 7–0 by West Virginia—their only defeat of the year.

West Virginia and Pittsburgh played in a pioneering radio broadcast by Pittsburgh station KDKA, the nation's first fully licensed commercial radio station. KDKA broadcast the 1921 contest in Pittsburgh, won by the Panthers 21–13.

Pittsburgh and Fordham, both Eastern powers at the time, played three consecutive 0–0 tie games in 1935–1937.

Schools now in the Big East have won the Lambert Trophy, symbolic of football supremacy in the Northeast, 17 times since it was inaugurated in 1936. Pittsburgh won it six times between 1936 and 1980, Syracuse six times between 1952 and 1992, Boston College four times between 1940 and 1984, and West Virginia in 1988.

Among the distinctive nicknames of the Big East members are Miami Hurricanes, Rutgers Scarlet Knights, Syracuse Orangemen (or Orange), Temple Owls, Virginia Tech Gobblers or Hokies, and West Virginia Mountaineers. More common are the Eagles of Boston College and the Panthers of Pittsburgh.

Boston College's nickname resulted from a letter to the student newspaper in 1920 from a priest dissatisfied because the school did not have an official emblem for its athletic teams; Father Edward McLaughlin suggested the name Eagles, and the student body quickly concurred. Pittsburgh student and alumni leaders met in early autumn 1909 to select a nickname for the school's athletic teams and came up with Panthers, the name of an animal indigenous to the region, and alliterative with Pittsburgh. Panthers was a unique college nickname at the time.

Temple was the first school in the nation to adopt the owl as its symbol. Dating to the 1880s, the nickname may have been adopted because Temple originally was a night school for ambitious young people of limited means. Virginia Tech introduced a gobbler mascot in 1912, and it made such an impression that sportswriters soon began applying that term to all Tech teams. However, many Tech fans prefer Hokies, derived from an 1896 cheer. That year Tech senior O. M. Stull won a contest for a new cheer to celebrate the school's name change from Virginia A&M to the Virginia Polytechnic Institute; Stull later said the term Hokie, used in the cheer, was pure imagination and did not really stand for anything.

West Virginia teams were known as Mountaineers by the World War I period; previously, game reports usually referred to WVU as the Old Gold and Blue or simply the Varsity. Miami's nickname was adopted prior to the 1927 season (the first varsity competition for the school), apparently as the result of a devastating hurricane that had struck the area on September 16, 1926. The players hoped to sweep away opponents like a hurricane.

Two members of the Big East, Rutgers and Syracuse, have only one official school color—scarlet at Rutgers, orange at Syracuse. Miami, on the other hand, has three—orange, green, and white. Miami's colors were selected in 1926 by a committee that included the daughter of three-time presidential candidate William Jennings Bryan. Ruth Bryan Owens, a member of the board of regents and a speech teacher at the university, suggested the colors of the orange tree—orange for the fruit, green for the leaves, and white for the blossom.

Syracuse adopted orange in 1890 to replace pink and blue. Boston College early in its history adopted the Papal colors of maroon and gold as the official school colors. Temple was the first school in the country to use cherry as an official color, the adoption taking place at least as early as 1888. No other Division I-A member has Temple's combination of cherry and white.

West Virginia adopted its colors, old gold and blue, at a series of meetings by student representatives in 1890—a year before the school fielded its first football team. Virginia Tech adopted its colors of Chicago maroon and burnt orange through a student committee in 1896. The colors were chosen because they were a unique combination at the time.

ALL-TIME BIG EAST CONFERENCE CHAMPIONS

Annual Champion	Big East	Regular Season and Bowl	
1991 Miami	2–0	11–0	Orange (W)
1992 Miami	4–0	11–0	Sugar (L)

BOSTON COLLEGE (Eagles; Maroon and Gold)

NOTABLE TEAMS

1896 (5–2) *Won:* Andover Academy 14–6, Exeter Academy 8–0, Holy Cross 6–2, 8–6 (1st meetings), Boston U. 10–0. *Lost:* Campello 24–0, Tufts 22–8. *Noteworthy:* 1st winning season.

1899 (8–1–1) *Won:* Exeter Academy 2–0, Massachusetts Institute of Technology (MIT) 24–0, Newton 6–0, Andover Academy 6–0, New Hampshire A.A. 6–0, Massachusetts 18–0 (1st meeting), All-College 6–0, Holy Cross 17–0. *Lost:* Brown 18–0. *Tied:* Bates 0–0.

1916 (6–2) *Won:* Neponset Wanderers 16–0, New Hampshire 19–0, Trinity 21–7, Rhode Island 39–0, Worcester Tech 49–0, Holy Cross 17–14 (1st over Crusaders in 8 games since 1899). *Lost:* Dartmouth 32–6, Tufts 13–0. *Star:* frosh Jimmy Fitzpatrick (75 pts on 8 TDs, 3 FGs, and 18 ex pts). *Noteworthy:* 1st year under Charles Brickley.

1917 (6–2) *Won:* Norwich 26–0, Naval Reserves 40–0, Tufts 20–0, Rhode Island 48–0, Holy Cross 34–6, Middlebury 31–6. *Lost:* Brown 7–2, Army 14–7 (1st meeting). *Star:* Fitzpatrick (9 TDs, 80 pts).

1918 (5–2) *Won:* Camp Devens 13–0, Norwich 6–0, Camp Bumpkin 38–7, Tufts 54–0, Minneola Aviators 25–0. *Lost:* Fordham 14–0, Harvard 14–6 (only road game) in successive mid-season games. *Stars:* playing coach and captain Frank Morrissey, soph Phil Corrigan (5 TDs).

1920 (8–0) *Won:* Fordham 20–0, Yale 21–13, Springfield 12–0, Boston U. 34–0 (1st meeting since 1896), Tufts 17–0, Marietta 13–3, Georgetown 30–0, Holy Cross 14–0. *Stars:* E Luke Urban (Eagles' 1st consensus All–American), Jim Liston (7 TDs). *Noteworthy:* 1st undefeated season.

1922 (6–2–1) *Won:* Boston U. 20–6, Fordham 27–0, Villanova 15–3 (1st meeting), Baylor 33–0, Canisius 13–7, Holy Cross 17–13. *Lost:* Detroit 10–8 (only road game), Lafayette 19–0 in consecutive early games. *Tied:* Georgetown 0–0. *Star:* soph Chuck Darling (5 TDs).

1923 (7–1–1) *Won:* Providence 28–0, Fordham 20–0, Canisius 21–0, Georgetown 21–0, Centenary 14–0, Villanova 41–0, Holy Cross 16–7. *Lost:* unbeaten Marquette 7–6 (1st meeting). *Tied:* Vermont 0–0. *Star:* Darling (9 TDs, 65 pts). *Noteworthy:* all games at home.

1925 (6–2) *Won:* Catholic U. 6–0, Haskell 7–6, Boston U. 54–7, Allegheny 14–7, Providence 51–0, Holy Cross 16–6. *Lost:* West Virginia 20–0 (1st meeting), West Virginia Wesleyan 7–6 in successive late games. *Star:* Jack Cronin (6 TDs). *Noteworthy:* all games at home.

1926 (6–0–2) *Won:* Catholic U. 28–0, Fordham 27–0, St. Louis 61–0 (only road game), West Virginia Wesleyan 27–6, Villanova 19–7, Gettysburg 39–0. *Tied:* Haskell 21–21, Holy Cross 0–0. *Star:* soph Al Weston (12 TDs). *Noteworthy:* Frank Cavanaugh's last team.

1928 (9–0) *Won:* Catholic U. 38–6, Navy 6–0 (1st meeting), Duke 19–0, Boston U. 27–7, Manhattan 60–6, Fordham 19–7, Canisius 24–0, Connecticut 51–13, Holy Cross 19–0. *Star:* Weston (8 TDs). *Noteworthy:* 1st year under Joe McKenney.

1929 (7–2–1) *Won:* Catholic U. 13–6, Maine 42–0, Dayton 23–7, Canisius 40–6, Duke 20–12, Boston U. 33–0, Holy Cross 12–0. *Lost:* Fordham 7–6 (1st to Rams in 9 games since 1918), Marquette 20–6. *Tied:* Villanova 7–7. *Star:* Ceslaus Antos (8 TDs).

1933 (8–1) *Won:* St. Anselm 22–0 (1st meeting since 1914), Loyola (Md.) 37–0, Centre 6–0, Boston U. 25–0, Georgetown 39–0, Villanova 9–0, Western Maryland 12–9, Holy Cross 13–9. *Lost:* Fordham 32–6 (only road game).

1936 (6–1–2) *Won:* Northeastern 26–6, New Hampshire 12–0, Providence 26–0, N.C. State 7–3, Western Maryland 12–7, Holy Cross 13–12. *Lost:* Temple 14–0 (1st meeting). *Tied:* Michigan St. 13–13, Boston U. 0–0. *Noteworthy:* all games at home in 1st year under Gil Dobie.

1938 (6–1–2) *Won:* Canisius 63–12, Northeastern 13–0, Detroit 9–6, Florida 33–0, Indiana 14–0, Boston U. 21–14. *Lost:* Holy Cross 29–7 in finale. *Tied:* Temple 26–26 (only road game), St. Anselm 0–0. *Star:* Vito Ananis (5 TDs). *Noteworthy:* Dobie's last team.

1939 (9–2) *Won:* Lebanon Valley 45–0, St. Joseph's 20–6, Temple 19–0, St. Anselm 28–0, Auburn 13–7, Detroit 20–13 (only road game), Boston U. 19–0, Kansas St. 38–7, Holy Cross 14–0. *Lost:* Florida 7–0. *Stars:* Ananis (11 pass rec for 222 yds and 5 TDs, 12 TDs total), Charlie O'Rourke (9 TDs pass). *Noteworthy:* 1st year under Frank Leahy. 1st postseason appearance, losing to Clem-

TB Charles "Chuckin' Charlie" O'Rourke, 1939–40

son 6–3 in Cotton Bowl after taking 3–0 lead on Alex Likachick's 24-yd FG.

1940 (11–0) *Won:* Centre 40–0, Tulane 27–7 (only road game), Temple 33–20, Idaho 60–0, St. Anselm 55–0, Manhattan 25–0, Boston U. 21–0, Georgetown 19–18, Auburn 33–7, Holy Cross 14–0. *Stars:* O'Rourke, soph FB Mike Holovak (532 yds and 11 TDs rush), Monk Maznicki (10 TDs, 80 pts), E Gene Goodreault, C Chet Gladchuck. *Noteworthy:* Led nation in scoring (32-pt avg), had 1st unbeaten season since 1928, and won 1st Lambert Trophy in last year under Leahy. Beat undefeated national cochamp Tennessee 19–13 in Sugar Bowl on TDs by Harry Connolly, Holovak, and O'Rourke (24-yd run for winning score).

1941 (7–3) *Won:* St. Anselm 78–0, Manhattan 26–13, Georgetown 14–6, Temple 31–0, Wake Forest 26–6, Boston U. 19–7, Holy Cross 14–13. *Lost:*

Tulane 21–7 (only road game), Clemson 26–13, Tennessee 14–7. *Stars:* Holovak (586 yds and 5 TDs rush), Ted Williams (606 yds and 6 TDs rush), Maznicki (7 TDs, 58 pts). *Noteworthy:* 1st year under Denny Myers.

1942 (8–2) *Won:* West Virginia 33–0 (1st meeting since 1925), Clemson 14–7, North Carolina Pre-Flight 7–6, Wake Forest 27–0, Georgetown 47–0, Temple 28–0, Fordham 56–6 (1st meeting since 1935), Boston U. 37–0. *Lost:* Holy Cross 55–12 in finale. *Stars:* Holovak (965 yds and 7 TDs yds rush), Mickey Connolly (5 TDs, 49 pts), E Dan Currivan, T Laurent Bouley, C Fred Naumetz. *Noteworthy:* Led nation in rush defense and won 2nd Lambert Trophy. All games at home. Lost to Alabama 37–21 in Orange Bowl; Holovak scored 3 TDs, including runs of 65 and 34 yds.

1943 (4–0–1) *Won:* BC Army Training 7–0, Camp Hingham 42–6, Brooklyn College 37–6, Rome Air Force 64–0. *Tied:* Harvard 6–6 in finale (only road game). *Star:* soph Jim Cahill (7 TDs). *Noteworthy:* Moody Sarno took over as wartime coach.

1954 (8–1) *Won:* Detroit 12–7, Temple 12–9 (1st meeting since 1942), Virginia Military Institute (VMI) 44–0, Fordham 21–7, Springfield 42–6, Marquette 13–7, Boston U. 7–6 (1st meeting since 1942), Holy Cross 31–13. *Lost:* Xavier (Ohio) 19–14 in mid-season. *Stars:* Ed DeSilva (635 yds rush), Tom Magnarelli (6 TDs).

1957 (7–2) *Won:* Florida St. 20–7, Quantico Marines 13–7, Dayton 41–14, Villanova 12–9, Detroit 20–16, Boston U. 27–2, Marquette 19–14. *Lost:* Navy 46–6 (1st meeting since 1928) in opener, Holy Cross 14–0 in finale. *Stars:* Jim Colclough (12 pass rec for 257 yds, 7 TDs), Alan Miller (5 TDs).

1958 (7–3) *Won:* Scranton 48–0, Marquette 21–13, Miami (Fla.) 6–2, Pacific 25–12, Detroit 40–0, Boston U. 18–13, Holy Cross 26–8. *Lost:* Syracuse 24–14 (1st meeting since 1944), Villanova 21–19, Clemson 34–12. *Stars:* Colclough (24 pass rec for 462 yds), John Flanagan (6 TDs).

1962 (8–2) *Won:* Detroit 27–0, Villanova 28–13, VMI 18–0, Houston 14–0, Vanderbilt 27–22, Texas Tech 41–13, Boston U. 41–25, Holy Cross 48–12. *Lost:* Syracuse 12–0, Navy 26–6 in successive early games. *Stars:* QB Jack Concannon (1,452 yds and 15 TDs pass), Art Graham (41 pass rec for 823 yds and 7 TDs), RB Harry Crump (641 yds rush). *Noteworthy:* 1st year under Jim Miller.

1970 (8–2) *Won:* Villanova 28–21, Navy 28–14, VMI 56–3, Army 21–13 (1st in 10-game series dating to 1917), Buffalo 65–12, Pittsburgh 21–6 (1st meeting since 1959), Massachusetts 21–10, Holy Cross 54–0. *Lost:* Penn St. 28–3, Air Force 35–10 in successive mid-season games. *Stars:* QB Frank Harris (1,595 yds and 12 TDs pass), John Bonistalli (35 pass rec for 455 yds), Fred Willis (1,007 yds and 11 TDs rush, 16 TDs total).

1971 (9–2) *Won:* Temple 17–3 (1st meeting since 1954), Navy 49–6, Richmond 24–0, Villanova 23–7, Pittsburgh 40–22, Syracuse 10–3, Northern Illinois 20–10, Massachusetts 35–0, Holy Cross 21–7. *Lost:* West Virginia 45–14 (1st meeting since 1942), Texas Tech 14–6. *Stars:* Tom Bougus (1,058 yds and 6 TDs rush), QB Ray Rippman (1,214 yds pass), Ed Rideout (7 TDs, 27 pass rec for 430 yds).

1974 (8–3) *Won:* Navy 37–0, William & Mary 31–16, Villanova 55–7, West Virginia 35–3, Tulane 27–3, Syracuse 45–0, Massachusetts 70–8, Holy Cross 38–6. *Lost:* Texas 42–19, Temple 34–7 (1st to Owls in 11 games since 1936), Pittsburgh 35–11. *Stars:* QB Mike Kruczek (1,275 yds pass), Dave Zumbach (43 pass rec for 557 yds), Keith Barnette (1,097 yds and 22 TDs rush, 134 pts), Mike Esposito (544 yds rush), OT Al Krevis.

1976 (8–3) *Won:* Texas 14–13, Tulane 27–3, Navy 17–13, West Virginia 14–3, Army 27–10, Syracuse 28–14, Massachusetts 35–0, Holy Cross 59–6. *Lost:* Florida St. 28–9, Villanova 22–3 (1st to Wildcats since 1969), Miami (Fla.) 13–6. *Stars:* Glen Capriola (1,003 yds and 7 TDs rush), Zumbach (24 pass rec for 354 yds), OG Steve Schindler, soph K Tim Moorman (12 FGs).

1982 (8–3–1) *Won:* Texas A&M 38–16, Navy 31–0, Temple 17–7, Rutgers 14–13, Army 32–17, Massachusetts 34–21, Syracuse 20–13, Holy Cross 35–10. *Lost:* West Virginia 20–13, national champ Penn St. 52–17. *Tied:* Clemson 17–17 (1st meeting since 1960). *Stars:* soph QB Doug Flutie (2,749 yds and 13 TDs pass, 265 yds rush), TE Scott Nizolek (39 pass rec for 658 yds), Jon Schoen (605 yds pass rec), frosh RB Troy Stradford (606 yds rush), frosh K Kevin Snow (11 FGs). *Noteworthy:* made 1st bowl appearance in 40 years, losing to Auburn 33–26 in Tangerine Bowl; Flutie passed for 299 yds and 2 TDs and scored another, and WR Brian Brennan caught 7 passes for 149 yds and a TD.

1983 (9–3) *Won:* Morgan St. 45–12, Clemson 31–

QB Doug Flutie, 1981–84

16, Rutgers 42–22, Temple 18–15, Yale 42–7, Penn St. 27–17 (1st in 12-game series dating to 1949), Army 34–14, Holy Cross 47–7, Alabama 20–13. *Lost:* West Virginia 27–17, Syracuse 21–10. *Stars:* Flutie (2,724 yds and 17 TDs pass, 245 yds rush), Brennan (66 pass rec for 1,149 yds and 8 TDs), TE Scott Gieselman (45 pass rec), Stradford (810 yds and 7 TDs rush). *Noteworthy:* Got 3rd Lambert Trophy, 1st since 1942. Lost to Notre Dame 19–18 in frigid Liberty Bowl; Flutie passed for 287 yds and 3 TDs.

1984 (10–2) *Won:* Western Carolina 44–24, Alabama 38–31, North Carolina 52–20, Temple 24–10, Rutgers 35–23, Army 45–31, Syracuse 24–16, Miami (Fla.) 47–45, Holy Cross 45–10. *Lost:* West Virginia 21–20, Penn St. 37–30. *Stars:* Heisman Trophy– and Maxwell Award–winner Flutie (nation's passing leader with 3,454 yds and 27 TDs), WR Gerard Phelan (64 pass rec for 971 yds), soph Kelvin Martin (12 TDs, 37 pass rec for 715 yds and 10 TDs), Stradford (666 yds rush, 37 pass rec for

422 yds, 10 TDs), Gieselman (32 pass rec for 434 yds), frosh FL Darren Flutie (9 pass rec for 214 yds), FB Steve Strachan (10 TDs), Snow (12 FGs, 82 pts), DBs Tony Thurman (nation's leader with 12 int) and Todd Russell (5 int). *Noteworthy:* Led nation in scoring (36.7-pt avg) and won 2nd straight Lambert Trophy. Beat Houston 45–28 in Cotton Bowl; Flutie passed for 180 yds and 3 TDs (to Martin, Stradford, and Phelan), Stradford ran for 196 yds and a TD, and Strachan ran for 91 yds and 2 TDs.

1986 (9–3) *Won:* California 21–15, Maryland 30–25, Louisville 41–7, West Virginia 19–10 (1st over Mountaineers in 7 games since 1977), Army 27–20, Temple 38–29, Syracuse 27–9, Holy Cross 56–26. *Lost:* Rutgers 11–9 (1st to Scarlet Knights in 7 games since 1919), unbeaten national champ Penn St. 26–14, Southern Methodist (SMU) 31–29. *Stars:* QB Shawn Halloran (2,090 yds and 17 TDs pass), Martin (41 pass rec for 545 yds and 8 TDs), Stradford (1,188 yds and 10 TDs rush), frosh K Brian Lowe (17 FGs, 81 pts). *Noteworthy:* beat Georgia 27–24 in Hall of Fame Bowl; Halloran passed for 242 yds and game-winning TD with 32 seconds left, and Stradford ran for 122 yds and a TD and had 7 pass rec for 48 yds.

1992 (8–3–1) *Won:* Rutgers 37–20, Northwestern 49–0, Navy 28–0, Michigan St. 14–0, Penn St. 35–32 (1st over Lions since 1983), Tulane 17–13 (1st meeting since 1979), Temple 45–6, Army 41–24. *Lost:* Notre Dame 54–7, Syracuse 27–10 in consecutive late games. *Tied:* West Virginia 24–24. *Stars:* QB Glenn Foley (2,231 yds and 15 TDs pass), soph TE Pete Mitchell (40 pass rec for 555 yds), soph SE Clarence Cannon (23 pass rec for 420 yds), FL Ivan Boyd (17 pass rec for 370 yds), RB Chuckie Dukes (1,387 yds and 10 TDs rush), soph FB Dwight Shirley (604 yds and 8 TDs rush), FB Darnell Campbell (5 TDs rush), OT Dan Britten, NG John Stolberg, LB Tom McManus, DB Charlie Brennan (6 int), soph P Jeff Beckley (42.2-yd avg). *Noteworthy:* 1st year under Tom Coughlin. Lost to Tennessee 38–23 in Hall of Fame Bowl; Foley passed for 268 yds, 2 TDs, and 2 conversions, Mitchell had 9 pass rec for 100 yds, 2 TDs, and 2-pt conversion, and Campbell scored on 7-yd run.

BOWL SUMMARY

Cotton 1–1; Hall of Fame 1–1; Liberty 0–1; Orange 0–1; Sugar 1–0; Tangerine 0–1.

BOWL RECORD (3–5)

Regular Season	Bowl	Score	Opponent	Record
1939 (9–1)	Cotton	3–6	Clemson	(8–1)
1940 (10–0)	Sugar	19–13	Tennessee	(10–0)
1942 (8–1)	Orange	21–37	Alabama	(7–3)
1982 (8–2–1)	Tangerine	26–33	Auburn	(8–3)
1983 (9–2)	Liberty	18–19	Notre Dame	(6–5)
1984 (9–2)	Cotton	45–28	Houston	(7–4)
1986 (8–3)	Hall of Fame	27–24	Georgia	(8–3)
1992 (8–2–1)	Hall of Fame	23–38	Tennessee	(8–3)

CONFERENCE TITLES

Big East—None. Won **Lambert Trophy** in 1940, 1942, 1983, 1984.

TOP 20 AP AND UPI RANKING

1939	11	1942	8	1984	5–4	1986	19–18
1940	5	1983	19–20				

MAJOR RIVALS

Boston College has played at least 10 games with Army 17–11, Boston U. 27–4–1, Clemson 5–7–2, Detroit 12–7, Fordham 14–11–2, Georgetown 11–5–1, Holy Cross 48–31–3, Marquette 6–6–1, Massachusetts 16–5, Miami (Fla.) 3–11, Navy 12–10, New Hampshire 6–5, Penn St. 2–19, Pittsburgh 6–11, Rutgers 8–6, St. Anselm 11–3–3, Syracuse 12–21, Temple 18–5–2, Tennessee 2–8, Tufts 3–8, Tulane 6–7, Villanova 30–14–1, Wake Forest 5–3–2, West Virginia 7–13–1. Record against Big East foe Virginia Tech is 0–0 (no games played).

COACHES

Deans of Boston College coaches are Joe Yukica and Jack Bicknell. Yukica was 68–37 for 1968–77, and Bicknell was 59–55–1 for 1981–90 with 2 Lambert Trophy winners and 4 bowl teams. Other top records for at least 3 years were by Frank Cavanaugh, 48–14–5 for 1919–26 with 2 unbeaten teams; Joe McKenney, 44–18–3 for 1928–34 with 1 perfect record; Gil Dobie, 16–6–5 for 1936–38; Dennis Myers, 35–27–4 for 1941–42 and 1946–50 with 1 Lambert Trophy winner and 1 bowl team; Amerino Sarno, 11–7–1 for 1943–45; Mike Holovak, 49–29–3 for 1951–59; and Jim Miller, 34–24 for 1962–67.

MISCELLANEA

First game was win over St. John's Institute 4–0 in 1893 . . . 1st win over college foe was over Boston U. 10–6 in 1893 . . . highest score was over St. Anselm 78–0 in 1941 . . . highest since W.W. II was over Holy Cross 76–0 in 1949 . . . worst defeat was by Colby 55–0 in 1912 . . . worst since W.W. II was by Mississippi 54–0 in 1950 . . . highest ever against Eagles was by West Virginia 59–19 in 1988 . . . longest unbeaten string of 17 in 1927–29 ended by Fordham 7–6 . . . longest winless string of 18 in 1910–12 broken with win over Connecticut 13–0 . . . consensus All-Americans were Luke Urban, E, 1920; Gene Goodreault, E, 1940; Mike Holovak, B, 1942; Doug Flutie, QB, and Tony Thurman, DB, 1984; and Mike Ruth, DL, 1985 . . . Academic All-Americans were Richard Scudellari,

LB, 1977; and Michael Degnan, DL, 1986 . . . Heisman Trophy–winner was Doug Flutie, QB, 1984 . . . Maxwell Award–winner was Doug Flutie, QB, 1984 . . . Outland Trophy–winner was Mike Ruth, DL, 1985.

MIAMI (Fla.) *(Hurricanes; Orange, Green and White)*

NOTABLE TEAMS

1926 (8–0) *Won:* Rollins 7–0, Florida Southern 12–0, Mercer 22–6, Stetson 20–0, Loyola 6–0, Havana 23–0, 23–0 (one game on Christmas Day in Havana), Howard 9–7 (New Year's Day). *Noteworthy:* played all freshman games under Howard Buck in 1st year of competition.

1933 (5–1–2) *Won:* South Georgia St. 20–0, Piedmont 71–6, Bowden 48–0, Louisville 33–7, Rollins 18–0. *Tied:* Tampa 0–0 (1st meeting), Stetson 0–0 (1st homecoming). *Noteworthy:* 1st unbeaten varsity season. Lost to Duquesne 33–7 in postseason Palm Festival game after trailing only 12–7 early in 4th quarter; scored on pass from Johnny Ott to George Reichgott.

1936 (6–2–2) *Won:* Georgia Southern 44–0, Bucknell 6–0, Rollins 26–0, Stetson 20–6 (1st in 8-game series begun in 1927), Mercer 13–0, Georgetown 10–6. *Lost:* Mississippi 14–0, South Carolina 6–3 (1st meeting). *Tied:* Tampa 0–0, Boston U. 7–7. *Star:* soph punt returner Eddie Dunn.

1938 (8–2) *Won:* Spring Hill 46–0, Tampa 32–6 (1st in 6-game series begun in 1933), Florida 19–7 (1st meeting), Rollins 19–0, Oglethorpe 44–0, Duquesne 21–7, Bucknell 19–0, Georgia 13–7. *Lost:* Drake 18–6, Catholic U. 7–0. *Stars:* Dunn (683 yds rush, 1,211 yds all-purpose running, 14 TDs), RB John Douglas.

1941 (8–2) *Won:* Elon 38–0, Tampa 20–6, Rollins 21–0, Howard 19–0, Texas Tech 6–0, West Virginia Wesleyan 34–0, South Carolina 7–6 (1st in 5-game series begun in 1936), Virginia Military Institute (VMI) 10–7. *Lost:* Florida 14–0, Alabama 21–7 (1st meeting). *Stars:* RB Walter Watt, P Howard Plasman (42.7-yd avg).

1942 (7–2) *Won:* Tampa 65–6, St. Louis 31–6, Rollins 21–0, Furman 32–13, Florida 12–0, South Carolina 13–6, West Virginia 21–13 (1st meeting). *Lost:*

Jacksonville Air Base 14–0, N.C. State 2–0. *Star:* punt returner Al Kasulin.

1943 (5–1) *Won:* Jacksonville NATTC 6–0, Camp Gordon 52–6, Charleston Coast Guard 13–6, Presbyterian 32–13, Ft. Benning 21–7. *Lost:* Jacksonville NATTC 20–0. *Star:* Arnold Tucker (6 int). *Noteworthy:* 1st year under Eddie Dunn.

1945 (9–1–1) *Won:* Chattanooga 27–7, St. Louis 21–0, Florida 7–6, Miami (Ohio) 27–13, Clemson 7–6 (1st meeting), N.C. State 21–7, Michigan St. 21–7, Auburn 33–7. *Lost:* Georgia 27–21. *Tied:* South Carolina 13–13. *Star:* frosh Harry Ghaul (13 TDs, 100 pts, 41.1-yd punting avg). *Noteworthy:* Nation's most-improved team. Beat Holy Cross 13–6 in Orange Bowl on 89-yd pass int return by Al Hudson on last play of game.

1946 (8–2) *Won:* William & Mary 13–3, Texas Christian 20–12, Florida 20–13, Chattanooga 33–13, Villanova 26–21, Miami (Ohio) 20–17, Washington & Lee 40–20, Detroit 21–7. *Lost:* North Carolina 21–0, Louisiana St. (LSU) 20–7. *Star:* Ghaul (42.1-yd punting avg).

1950 (9–1–1) *Won:* The Citadel 21–0, Villanova 18–12, Purdue 20–14, Boston U. 34–7, Pittsburgh 28–0 (1st meeting), Georgetown 42–7, Florida 20–14, Iowa 14–6, Missouri 27–9. *Tied:* Louisville 13–13. *Stars:* B Frank Smith (10 TDs), T Al Carapella. *Noteworthy:* 1st unbeaten season since 1933. Lost to unbeaten Clemson 15–14 in Orange Bowl; scored on 5-yd run by Harry Mallios and 14-yd pass from Jack Hackett to Smith.

1951 (8–3) *Won:* Florida St. 35–13 (1st meeting), Purdue 7–0, Washington & Lee 32–12, Mississippi 20–7, Chattanooga 34–7, Florida 21–6, Nebraska 19–7 (1st meeting). *Lost:* Tulane 21–7 (1st meeting), Kentucky 32–0, Pittsburgh 21–7. *Stars:* Smith (9 TDs, 764 yds rush, 1,167 yds all-purpose running), HB Jim Dooley (6 int). *Noteworthy:* beat Clemson 14–0 in Gator Bowl; Mallios scored both TDs and Dooley had 4 int.

1954 (8–1) *Won:* Furman 51–13, Baylor 19–13, Holy Cross 26–20, Mississippi St. 27–13, Maryland 9–7, Fordham 75–7, Alabama 23–7, Florida 14–0. *Lost:* Auburn 14–13. *Stars:* E Frank McDonald, Whitey Rouviere (7 int).

1956 (8–1–1) *Won:* South Carolina 14–6, Boston College 27–6, Maryland 13–6, Texas Christian (TCU) 14–0, Florida St. 20–7, Clemson 21–0, West Virginia 18–0 (1st meeting since 1942), Florida 20–7. *Lost:* Pittsburgh 14–7 in finale. *Tied:* Georgia 7–7. *Stars:* John Bookman (6 int), FB Don Bosseler (723 yds rush). *Noteworthy:* led nation in total defense and rush defense.

1961 (7–4) *Won:* Kentucky 14–7 (1st in 6-game series dating to 1948), Penn St. 25–8, North Carolina 10–0, Georgia 32–7, Tulane 6–0, Northwestern 10–6, Florida 15–6. *Lost:* Pittsburgh 10–7, Navy 17–6, Colorado 9–7. *Stars:* E Bill Miller (Hurricanes' 1st consensus All-American; 43 pass rec for 640 yds), soph QB George Mira (1,075 yds and 11 TDs total off). *Noteworthy:* lost to Syracuse 15–14 in Liberty Bowl; scored on 12-yd run by James Vollenweider and 60-yd punt return by Nick Spinelli to take 1st half 14–0 lead.

1962 (7–4) *Won:* Pitt 23–14, TCU 21–20, Florida St. 7–6, Maryland 28–24, Air Force 21–3, Kentucky 25–17, Florida 17–15. *Lost:* LSU 17–3, Alabama 36–3 (1st meeting since 1955), Northwestern 29–7. *Stars:* Mira (1,572 yds and 10 TDs pass), LB James O'Mahoney, Jim Simon (4 fumble recoveries). *Noteworthy:* lost to Nebraska 36–34 in freezing Gotham Bowl in New York despite 34–12 edge in 1st downs; Mira passed for 321 yds and 2 TDs (including 30 yds to Spinelli), and Nick Ryder scored 2 TDs.

1966 (8–2–1) *Won:* Colorado 24–3, Georgia 7–6, Indiana 14–7, Southern California 10–7, Pittsburgh 38–14, Iowa 44–0, Florida 21–16. *Lost:* Florida St. 23–20, LSU 10–8 in consecutive early games. *Tied:* Tulane 10–10. *Stars:* soph DE Ted Hendricks, DB Tom Beier. *Noteworthy:* beat Virginia Tech 14–7 in Liberty Bowl, scoring on 7-yd pass from QB Bill Miller to Joe Mira and short plunge by Doug McGee.

1967 (7–4) *Won:* Tulane 34–14, LSU 17–15 (1st in 8-game series dating to 1946), Pittsburgh 58–0, Auburn 7–0 (1st over Tigers in 5 games since 1945), Virginia Tech 14–7, Georgia Tech 49–7, Florida 20–13. *Lost:* Northwestern 12–7, Penn St. 17–8, Notre Dame 24–22. *Stars:* Hendricks (4 fumble recoveries), Jimmy Dye (6 int). *Noteworthy:* lost to Colorado 31–21 in Bluebonnet Bowl; TDs scored by Mira, Dye (77-yd pass int return), and Jerry Daanen (pass from Miller).

1980 (9–3) *Won:* Louisville 24–10, Florida A&M 49–0, Houston 14–7, Florida St. 10–9, East Carolina 23–10, Vanderbilt 24–17, North Texas St. 26–8, Florida 31–7. *Lost:* Notre Dame 32–14,

Mississippi St. 34–31, Penn St. 27–12. *Stars:* soph QB Jim Kelly (1,519 yds and 11 TDs pass), K Dan Miller (15 FGs), MG Jim Burt (4 fumble recoveries), DB Fred Marion (7 int), soph P Greg La Belle (40.6-yd avg). *Noteworthy:* beat Virginia Tech 20–10 in Peach Bowl, scoring on 15-yd pass from Kelly to Larry Brodsky and 12-yd run by Chris Hobbs.

1981 (9–2) *Won:* Florida 21–20, Houston 12–7, Vanderbilt 48–16, East Carolina 31–6, Penn St. 17–14, Florida St. 27–19, Virginia Tech 21–14, N.C. State 14–6, Notre Dame 37–15 (1st over Irish in 13 games since 1960). *Lost:* Texas 14–7, Mississippi St. 14–10 in early games. *Stars:* Kelly (2,403 yds and 13 TDs pass), Brodsky (37 pass rec for 631 yds), Mike Rodrigue (29 pass rec for 478 yds), WR Rocky Belk (15 pass rec for 451 yds), Mark Rush (26 pass rec for 356 yds), soph TE Glenn Dennison (29 pass rec for 270 yds), Miller (18 FGs, 77 pts), Marion (6 int), DT Lester Williams.

1983 (11–1) *Won:* Houston 29–7, Purdue 35–0, Notre Dame 20–0, Duke 56–17, Louisville 42–14, Mississippi St. 31–7, Cincinnati 37–7, West Virginia 20–3 (1st meeting since 1974), East Carolina 12–7, Florida St. 17–16. *Lost:* Florida 28–3 in opener. *Stars:* frosh QB Bernie Kosar (2,329 yds and 15 TDs pass), Dennison (54 pass rec for 594 yds), WR Eddie Brown (6 TDs, 30 pass rec for 640 yds and 5 TDs), Albert Bentley (722 yds rush, 1,112 all-purpose yds), K Jeff Davis (11 FGs), LBs Jay Brophy and Ken Sisk, Jack Fernandez (4 fumble recoveries). *Noteworthy:* Howard Schnellenberger's last team. Upset unbeaten Nebraska 31–30 in Orange Bowl to take 1st national championship; Kosar passed for 300 yds and 2 TDs (both to Dennison), Brown caught 6 for 115 yds, frosh TB Alonzo Highsmith and Bentley scored TDs, and Davis kicked 45-yd FG and 4 ex pts.

1985 (10–2) *Won:* Rice 48–20, Boston College 45–10, East Carolina 27–15, Cincinnati 38–0, national champ Oklahoma 27–14, Louisville 45–7, Florida St. 35–27, Maryland 29–22, Colorado St. 24–3, Notre Dame 58–7. *Lost:* Florida 35–23 in opener. *Stars:* QB Vinny Testaverde (3,238 yds and 21 TDs pass), TE Willie Smith (48 pass rec for 669 yds), soph Michael Irvin (46 pass rec for 840 yds and 9 TDs), soph Brian Blades (657 yds and 6 TDs pass rec), soph K Greg Cox (12 FGs, 82 pts), soph LB George Mira Jr. *Noteworthy:* lost to Tennessee 35–7 in Sugar Bowl; Testaverde passed for 217 yds

and a TD (18 yds to Irvin, who caught 5 for 91 yds).

1986 (11–1) *Won:* South Carolina 34–14 (1st meeting since 1960), Florida 23–15, Texas Tech 61–11, Oklahoma 28–16, Northern Illinois 34–0, West Virginia 58–14, Cincinnati 45–13, Florida St. 41–23, Pittsburgh 37–10, Tulsa 23–10, East Carolina 36–10. *Stars:* Heisman Trophy– and Maxwell Award– winner Testaverde (nation's leader with 2,557 yds and 26 TDs pass), Irvin (53 pass rec for 868 yds and 11 TDs), Mira, DT Jerome Brown, DB Bennie Blades (nation's leader with 10 int). *Noteworthy:* 1st unbeaten season since 1950. Lost national championship game to unbeaten Penn St. 14–10 in Fiesta Bowl; Testaverde passed for 285 yds, Highsmith ran for 119 yds, and Melvin Bratton scored Miami TD on short dive in 2nd quarter.

1987 (12–0) *Won:* Florida 31–4, Arkansas 51–7, Florida St. 26–25, Maryland 46–16, Cincinnati 48–10, East Carolina 41–3, Miami (Ohio) 54–3 (1st meeting since 1946), Virginia Tech 27–13, Toledo 24–14, Notre Dame 24–0, South Carolina 20–16. *Stars:* Bennie Blades, Mira, DEs Daniel Stubbs and Bill Hawkins, soph DT Greg Mark, LB Rod Carter, DB Tolbert Bain, QB Steve Walsh (2,249 yds and 19 TDs pass), Irvin (44 pass rec for 715 yds and 6 TDs), Brian Blades (5 TD pass rec), Bratton (11 TDs), Cox (17 FGs, 94 pts). *Noteworthy:* won 2nd national title by beating undefeated Oklahoma 20–14 in Orange Bowl; Walsh passed for 209 yds and 2 TDs (30 yds to Bratton, who caught 9 for 102 yds, and 23 yds to Irvin), and Cox kicked FGs of 56 and 48 yds.

1988 (11–1) *Won:* Florida St. 31–0, Michigan 31–30, Wisconsin 23–3, Missouri 55–0, Cincinnati 57–3, East Carolina 31–7, Tulsa 34–3, LSU 44–3, Arkansas 18–16, Brigham Young (BYU) 41–17. *Lost:* unbeaten national champ Notre Dame 31–30 (1st to Irish in 5 games since 1982). *Stars:* Walsh (3,115 yds and 29 TDs pass), FB Cleveland Gary (11 TDs, 480 yds rush, 57 pass rec for 655 yds), Andre Brown (47 pass rec for 746 yds and 8 TDs), WR Dale Dawkins (31 pass rec for 488 yds), soph TEs Rob Chudzinski (30 pass rec for 388 yds and 5 TDs) and Randy Bethel (16 pass rec for 245 yds and 5 TDs), soph HB Leonard Conley (26 pass rec for 303 yds), soph WR Randal Hill (21 pass rec for 338 yds), frosh K Carlos Huerta (21 FGs, 107 pts), Hawkins, Mark, soph LB Maurice Crum. *Noteworthy:* Jimmy Johnson's last team. Beat Nebraska

23–3 in Orange Bowl; Walsh passed for 277 yds and 2 TDs (22 and 42 yds to Conley), and Huerta kicked 3 FGs.

1989 (11–1)   *Won:* Wisconsin 51–3, California 31–3, Missouri 38–7, Michigan St. 26–20, Cincinnati 56–0, San Jose St. 48–16, East Carolina 40–10, Pittsburgh 24–3, San Diego St. 42–6, Notre Dame 27–10. *Lost:* Florida St. 24–10 (1st to Seminoles since 1984).   *Stars:* QBs Craig Erickson (2,007 yds and 16 TDs pass) and frosh Gino Torretta (1,325 yds and 8 TDs pass), Dawkins (54 pass rec for 833 yds and 7 TDs), WR Wesley Carroll (53 pass rec for 770 yds and 5 TDs), Hill (42 pass rec for 652 yds), frosh FB Steve McGuire (519 yds and 10 TDs rush), Conley (529 yds rush), C Bobby Garcia, OG Rod Holder, OT Mike Sullivan, Huerta (18 FGs, 101 pts), DE Mark, DTs Cortez Kennedy and Russell Maryland, Crum, LB Bernard Clark, DB Roland Smith (6 int).   *Noteworthy:* Led nation in scoring defense (9.3-pt avg) and total defense in 1st year under Dennis Erickson. Won 3rd national title by beating Alabama 33–25 in Sugar Bowl; Erickson passed for 250 yds and 3 TDs (19 yds to Carroll, 11 yds to Chudzinski, and 12 yds to Bethel), and McGuire and Alex Johnson scored on short runs.

1990 (10–2)   *Won:* California 52–24, Iowa 48–21, Florida St. 31–22, Kansas 34–0, Texas Tech 45–10, Pittsburgh 45–0, Boston College 42–12, Syracuse 33–7 (1st meeting since 1979), San Diego St. 30–28. *Lost:* BYU 28–21, Notre Dame 29–20.   *Stars:* Erickson (3,363 yds and 22 TDs pass), Carroll (61 pass rec for 952 yds and 6 TDs), soph FL Lamar Thomas (43 pass rec for 742 yds and 6 TDs), Hill (44 pass rec for 653 yds), Chudzinski (21 pass rec for 306 yds), McGuire (621 yds and 11 TDs rush), Conley (7 TDs), Sullivan, Huerta (17 FGs, 101 pts), Outland Trophy–winner Maryland, DT Shane Curry, Crum, soph LB Darrin Smith, DB Robert Bailey. *Noteworthy:* beat Texas 46–3 in Cotton Bowl as Erickson passed for 272 yds and 4 TDs, Carroll caught 8 for 135 yds and 2 TDs, Roland Smith scored on 34-yd pass int return, Hill scored on 48-yd pass, and Huerta kicked 2 FGs (including 50-yarder).

1991 (12–0)   *Won:* Arkansas 31–3, Houston 40–10 (1st meeting since 1983), Tulsa 34–10, Oklahoma St. 40–3, Penn St. 26–20, Long Beach St. 55–0, Arizona 36–9, West Virginia 27–3 (1st meeting since 1986), Florida St. 17–16, Boston College 19–14,

San Diego St. 39–12.   *Stars:* Torretta (3,095 yds and 20 TDs pass), Thomas (39 pass rec for 623 yds and 6 TDs), WR Horace Copeland (31 pass rec for 592 yds), TB Darryl Spencer (28 pass rec for 380 yds), TE Coleman Bell (27 pass rec for 376 yds), soph FB Martin Patton (7 TDs, 26 pass rec for 428 yds), soph WR Kevin Williams (6 TDs, 21 pass rec for 330 yds, 1,183 all-purpose yds), McGuire (608 yds and 9 TDs rush), OT Leon Searcy, Huerta (17 FGs, 88 pts), soph DE Rusty Medearis, Smith, LB Micheal Barrow, DBs Ryan McNeil (5 int) and Darryl Williams.   *Noteworthy:* Led nation in scoring defense (9.1-pt avg) and won inaugural Big East title in 1st unbeaten season since 1987. Beat Nebraska 22–0 in Orange Bowl to earn share of 4th national championship; Torretta passed for 257 yds and a TD (to Kevin Williams, who caught 8 for 126 yds), frosh FB Larry Jones ran for 144 yds and a TD, and Huerta kicked 3 FGs (including 54-yarder).

1992 (11–1)   *Won:* Iowa 24–7, Florida A&M 38–0, Arizona 8–7, Florida St. 19–16, Penn St. 17–14, TCU 45–10 (1st meeting since 1977), Virginia Tech 43–23 (1st meeting since 1987, 10th win in as many games in series), West Virginia 35–23, Temple 48–0 (1st meeting since 1930), Syracuse 16–10, San Diego St. 63–17.   *Stars:* Heisman Trophy– and Maxwell Award–winner Torretta (3,060 yds and 19 TDs pass), Thomas (47 pass rec for 701 yds and 10 TDs), Copeland (47 pass rec for 769 yds), Bell (43 pass rec for 634 yds), Kevin Williams (40 pass rec for 457 yds), Spencer (20 pass rec for 265 yds), soph FBs Donnell Bennett (6 TDs rush) and Larry Jones (6 TDs rush), McGuire (5 TDs rush), OT Mario Cristobal, frosh K Dane Prewitt (13 FGs), DE Kevin Patrick, DT Mark Caesar, Barrow, Smith, McNeil, P Paul Snyder (40.3-yd avg).   *Noteworthy:* Won 2nd straight Big East title. Lost national championship game to unbeaten Alabama 34–13 in Sugar Bowl (ending 5-bowl and 29-game win streaks); Toretta passed for 278 yds but had 3 int, Prewitt had FGs of 49 and 42 yds, and Kevin Williams scored on 78-yd punt return.

BOWL SUMMARY

Bluebonnet 0–1; Cotton 1–0; Fiesta 0–2; Gator 1–0; Gotham 0–1; Liberty 1–1; Orange 5–2; Peach 1–0; Sugar 1–2.

BOWL RECORD (10–9)

Regular Season	Bowl	Score	Opponent	Record
1934 (5–2–1)	Orange	0–26	Bucknell	(5–2–2)
1945 (8–1–1)	Orange	13–6	Holy Cross	(8–1)
1950 (9–0–1)	Orange	14–15	Clemson	(8–0–1)
1951 (7–3)	Gator	14–0	Clemson	(7–2)
1961 (7–3)	Liberty	14–15	Syracuse	(7–3)
1962 (7–3)	Gotham	34–36	Nebraska	(8–2)
1966 (7–2–1)	Liberty	14–7	Virginia Tech	(8–1–1)
1967 (7–3)	Bluebonnet	21–31	Colorado	(8–2)
1980 (8–3)	Peach	20–10	Virginia Tech	(8–3)
1983 (10–1)	Orange	31–30	Nebraska	(12–0)
1984 (8–4)	Fiesta	37–39	UCLA	(8–3)
1985 (10–1)	Sugar	7–35	Tennessee	(8–1–2)
1986 (11–0)	Fiesta	10–14	Penn State	(11–0)
1987 (11–0)	Orange	20–14	Oklahoma	(11–0)
1988 (10–1)	Orange	23–3	Nebraska	(11–1)
1989 (10–1)	Sugar	33–25	Alabama	(10–1)
1990 (9–2)	Cotton	46–3	Texas	(10–1)
1991 (11–0)	Orange	22–0	Nebraska	(9–1–1)
1992 (11–0)	Sugar	13–34	Alabama	(12–0)

CONFERENCE TITLES

Big East—1991, 1992.

TOP 20 AP AND UPI
(USA TODAY/CNN SINCE 1991) RANKING

1950	15–13	1962	U–18	1983	1–1	1988	2–2
1954	11–9	1966	9–10	1984	18–U	1989	1–1
1955	14–18	1967	U–16	1985	9–8	1990	3–3
1956	6–6	1980	18–U	1986	2–2	1991	1–2
1961	U–19	1981	8–U	1987	1–1	1992	3–3

MAJOR RIVALS

Miami has played at least 10 games with Alabama 3–14, Auburn 4–7, Boston College 11–3, Cincinnati 9–1, Florida 24–25, Florida St. 22–14, Georgia 4–7–1, Houston 9–7, LSU 3–8, Maryland 7–7, Notre Dame 7–15–1, Penn St. 5–6, Pittsburgh 11–8–1, Rollins 14–3–1, South Carolina 8–5–2, Stetson 4–5–2, Syracuse 6–5, Tampa 6–5–2, Tulane 6–5–1, Virginia Tech 10–0. Record against Big East foes met fewer than 10 times is Rutgers 0–0, Temple 1–1, West Virginia 7–1.

COACHES

Dean of Miami coaches is Andy Gustafson with record of 93–65–3 for 1948–63, including 4 bowl teams and 1 team unbeaten in regular season. Other top records for at least 3 years were by Tom McCann, 18–15–4 for 1931–34 with 1 Orange Bowl team; Jack Harding, 54–32–3 for 1937–42 and 1945–47 with 1 Orange Bowl champion; Charlie Tate, 34–27–3 for 1964 to early 1970 with 2 bowl teams; Howard Schnellenberger, 41–16 for 1979–83 with 2 bowl champions and 1 national title; Jimmy

Johnson, 52–9 for 1984–88 with 5 bowl teams, 2 teams unbeaten in regular season, and 1 national title; and Dennis Erickson, 44–4 for 1989–92 with 2 Big East titles, 2 unbeaten teams, 4 bowl teams (3 winners), and 2 national champions.

MISCELLANEA

First game was win over Rollins 7–0 in freshman competition in 1926 . . . 1st varsity game was win over Rollins 39–3 in 1927 . . . highest score was over Fordham 75–7 in 1954 . . . worst defeat was by Texas A&M 70–14 in 1944 . . . worst since W.W. II was by Notre Dame 44–0 in 1973 . . . highest against Hurricanes since W.W. II was by Syracuse 56–15 in 1970 . . . longest win streak of 29 in 1990–92 ended by Alabama 34–13 in 1993 Sugar Bowl . . . 16-game win streak in 1987–88 ended by Notre Dame 31–30 . . . 14-game unbeaten string in 1955–56 ended by Pittsburgh 14–7 . . . longest winless string of 9 in 1963–64 broken with win over Detroit 10–7 . . . consensus All-Americans were Bill Miller, E, 1961; Tom Beier, DB, 1966; Ted Hendricks, DE, 1967–68; Tony Cristiani, DL, 1973; Rubin Carter, MG, 1974; Fred Marion, DB, 1981; Eddie Brown, WR, 1984; Willie Smith, TE, 1985; Vinny Testaverde, QB, and Jerome Brown, DL, 1986; Bennie Blades, DB, 1986–87; Daniel Stubbs, DL, 1987; Greg Mark, DL, 1989; Russell Maryland, DL, and Maurice Crum, LB, 1990; Carlos Huerta, K, and Darryl Williams, DB, 1991; and Gino Torretta, QB, Micheal Barrow, LB, and Ryan McNeil, DB, 1992 . . . Academic All-Americans were Fran Curci, B, 1959; and Bennie Kosar, QB, 1984 . . . Heisman Trophy–winners were Vinny Testaverde, QB, 1986; and Gino Torretta, QB, 1992 . . . Maxwell Award–winners were Vinny Testaverde, QB, 1986; and Gino Torretta, QB, 1992 . . . Outland Trophy–winner was Russell Maryland, DT, 1990.

PITTSBURGH (Panthers; Blue and Gold)

NOTABLE TEAMS

1899 (3–1–1) *Won:* Grove City 16–0, Swissvale A.C. 11–0, Bethany (W.Va.) 5–0. *Lost:* J.F. Lalus A.C. 12–0 in finale. *Tied:* Westminster 11–11 in opener.

1901 (7–2–1) *Won:* West Virginia 12–0 (1st in 4-game series begun in 1895), Allegheny 11–0, Duquesne 18–0 (1st meeting), California Teachers 15–0, Geneva 12–5, Thiel 17–0, Westminster 11–0. *Lost:* Penn St. 33–0 (opener), Allegheny 15–0 (finale). *Tied:* Indiana Teachers 0–0.

1904 (10–0) *Won:* Grove City 12–0, Mt. Union 67–0, Westminster 38–0, Geneva 30–0, Susquehanna 40–0, California Normal 40–0, Waynesburg 83–0, West Virginia 53–0, Bethany (W.Va.) 21–0, Penn St. 22–5 (1st in 7-game series dating to 1893). *Noteworthy:* outscored foes 407–5 in 1st undefeated season.

1905 (10–2) *Won:* Westminster 11–0, California Normal 71–0, Dickinson 24–0, Mt. Union 57–0, Bethany (W.Va.) 48–0, Franklin & Marshall 53–0, Washington & Jefferson (W & J) 11–0 (1st meeting since 1895, 1st win in 6-game series begun in 1890), Butler YMCA 67–0, Ohio Medical 51–0, Geneva 12–0. *Lost:* Cornell 30–0, Penn St. 6–0. *Noteworthy:* Arthur Mosse's last team.

1907 (8–2) *Won:* Marietta 6–0, Carnegie Tech 6–0, Muskingum 33–0, Bucknell 12–0, Ohio Northern 16–0, West Virginia 10–0, Wooster 51–0, Penn St. 6–0. *Lost:* Cornell 18–5, W&J 9–2.

1908 (8–3) *Won:* Mt. Union 26–4, Bethany (W.Va.) 27–0, Marietta 7–0, Bucknell 22–0, St. Louis 13–0, Carnegie Tech 22–0, West Virginia 11–0, Gettysburg 6–0. *Lost:* Carlisle 6–0, Penn St. 12–6, W&J 14–0. *Noteworthy:* 1st year under Joseph Thompson.

1909 (6–2–1) *Won:* Ohio Northern 16–0, Marietta 12–0, Bucknell 18–6, Carlisle 14–3, W&J 17–3, Mt. Union 17–3. *Lost:* unbeaten Notre Dame 6–0 (1st meeting), unbeaten Penn St. 5–0. *Tied:* West Virginia 0–0.

1910 (9–0) *Won:* Ohio Northern 36–0, Westminster 18–0, Waynesburg 42–0, Georgetown 17–0, Ohio Medical 71–0, West Virginia 38–0, W&J 14–0, Carnegie Tech 35–0, Penn St. 11–0. *Noteworthy:* blanked foes 282–0 in 1st unbeaten season since 1904.

1913 (6–2–1) *Won:* Ohio Northern 67–0, West Virginia 40–0, Carlisle 12–6, Cornell 20–7, Lafayette 13–0, Penn St. 7–6. *Lost:* Bucknell 9–0, W&J 18–6. *Tied:* Navy 0–0. *Noteworthy:* 1st year under Joseph Duff.

1914 (8–1) *Won:* Cornell 9–3, Westminster 21–10, Navy 13–6, Carlisle 10–3, Georgetown 21–0,

Dickinson 96–0, Carnegie Tech 14–0, Penn St. 13–3. *Lost:* W&J 13–10. *Stars:* soph C Robert Peck, frosh FB Andy Hastings (5 TDs, 5 FGs). *Noteworthy:* Duff's last team.

1915 (8–0)   *Won:* Westminster 32–0, Navy 47–12, Carlisle 45–0, Pennsylvania 14–7 (1st meeting), Allegheny 42–7, W&J 19–0, Carnegie Tech 28–0, Penn St. 20–0. *Stars:* Peck (Panthers' 1st consensus All-American), Hastings (503 yds rush, 11 TDs, 74 pts), Guy Williamson (1,034 all-purpose yds). *Noteworthy:* 1st year under Glenn "Pop" Warner.

1916 (8–0)   *Won:* Westminster 57–0, Navy 20–19, Syracuse 30–0 (1st meeting), Penn 20–0, Carnegie Tech 14–6, Allegheny 46–0, W&J 37–0, Penn St. 31–0. *Stars:* Peck, Hastings (6 TDs, 5 FGs), James DeHart (786 yds rush), E James Herron, G Claude Thornhill. *Noteworthy:* won 1st national championship.

1917 (9–0)   *Won:* West Virginia 14–9, Bethany (W.Va.) 40–0, Lehigh 41–0, Syracuse 28–0, Penn 14–6, Westminster 25–0, W&J 13–0, Carnegie Tech 27–0, Penn St. 28–6. *Stars:* FB George McLaren (782 yds rush, 13 TDs), E H.C. Carlson, Gs Jock Sutherland and Dale Seis.

1918 (4–1)   *Won:* W&J 34–0, Penn 37–0, Georgia Tech 32–0, Penn St. 28–6. *Lost:* Cleveland Naval Reserve 10–9 in finale. *Stars:* McLaren (6 TDs), frosh B Tom Davies (5 TDs, 38 pts), T Leonard Hilty. *Noteworthy:* Won 2nd national title in schedule curtailed by W.W. I and flu epidemic.

1919 (6–2–1)   *Won:* Geneva 32–0 (1st meeting since 1905), West Virginia 26–0, Georgia Tech 16–6, Lehigh 14–0, W&J 7–6, Carnegie Tech 17–7. *Lost:* Syracuse 24–3, Penn St. 20–0 (1st to Nittany Lions since 1912). *Tied:* Penn 3–3. *Stars:* Hastings (8 TDs, 64 pts), Davies (650 yds rush).

1920 (6–0–2)   *Won:* Geneva 47–0, West Virginia 34–13, Georgia Tech 10–3, Lafayette 14–0, Penn 27–21, W&J 7–0. *Tied:* Syracuse 7–7, unbeaten Penn St. 0–0. *Stars:* Davies (1,254 all-purpose yds, 10 TDs, 77 pts), C Herb Stein.

1922 (8–2)   *Won:* Cincinnati 35–0, Syracuse 21–14, Bucknell 7–0, Penn 7–6, Geneva 62–0, W&J 19–0, Penn St. 14–0, Stanford 16–7. *Lost:* Lafayette 7–0, unbeaten West Virginia 9–6 (1st to Mountaineers in 12 games since 1903) in successive early games. *Stars:* Orville Hewitt (609 yds rush), W.H. Flanagan (7 TDs).

1925 (8–1)   *Won:* W&J 28–0, 6–0, Gettysburg 13–0, West Virginia 15–7, Carnegie Tech 12–0, Penn

14–0, Penn St. 23–7, Johns Hopkins 31–0. *Lost:* Lafayette 20–9. *Stars:* T Ralph Chase, soph HB Gibby Welch (589 yds rush), Andy Gustafson (6 TDs, 5 FGs).

1927 (8–1–1)   *Won:* Thiel 42–0, Grove City 33–0, West Virginia 40–0, Drake 32–0, Carnegie Tech 23–7, Allegheny 62–0, Nebraska 21–13, Penn St. 30–0. *Tied:* W&J 0–0. *Stars:* Welch (10 TDs, 1,641 all-purpose yds), Allan Booth (659 yds rush, 10 TDs, 81 pts), T Bill Kern. *Noteworthy:* 1st unbeaten season since 1920. Made 1st postseason appearance, losing to Stanford 7–6 in Rose Bowl; Panthers' TD came on 20-yd fumble return by Jimmy Hagan.

1928 (6–2–1)   *Won:* Thiel 20–0, Bethany (W.Va.) 53–0, Allegheny 29–0, Syracuse 18–0, W&J 25–0, Penn St. 26–0. *Lost:* West Virginia 9–6, Carnegie Tech 6–0. *Tied:* Nebraska 0–0. *Stars:* T Mike Getto, Josh Williams (777 yds and 7 TDs rush), Tony Uansa (551 yds rush).

1929 (9–1)   *Won:* Waynesburg 53–0, Duke 52–7 (1st meeting), West Virginia 27–7, Nebraska 12–7, Allegheny 40–0, Ohio St. 18–2 (1st meeting), W&J 21–0, Penn St. 20–7, Carnegie Tech 34–13. *Stars:* Uansa (964 yds rush, 10 TDs), B Thomas Parkinson, E Joe Donchess, G Ray Montgomery. *Noteworthy:* lost to Southern California 47–14 in Rose Bowl; scored on 28-yd pass from Uansa to William Wallinchus and 36-yd pass from Parkinson to Paul Collins.

1930 (6–2–1)   *Won:* Waynesburg 52–0, West Virginia 16–0, Western Reserve 52–0, Syracuse 14–0, Carnegie Tech 7–6, Penn St. 19–12. *Lost:* unbeaten national champ Notre Dame 35–19 (1st meeting since 1912), Ohio St. 16–7. *Tied:* Nebraska 0–0. *Stars:* Franklin Hood (8 TDs), Edward Baker (234 yds pass rec).

1931 (8–1)   *Won:* Miami (Ohio) 61–0, Iowa 20–0, West Virginia 34–0, Western Reserve 32–0, Penn St. 41–6, Carnegie Tech 14–6, Army 26–0 (1st meeting), Nebraska 40–0. *Lost:* Notre Dame 25–12. *Stars:* T Jesse Quatse, Warren Heller (744 yds and 11 TDs rush, 594 yds pass), Paul Reider (379 yds pass rec).

1932 (8–1–2)   *Won:* Ohio Northern 47–0, West Virginia 40–0, Duquesne 33–0 (1st meeting since 1901), Army 18–13, Notre Dame 12–0 (1st in 6-game series dating to 1909), Penn 19–12 (1st meeting since 1925), Carnegie Tech 6–0, Stanford 7–0. *Tied:* Ohio St. 0–0, Nebraska 0–0. *Stars:*

Heller (684 yds and 8 TDs rush, 450 yds pass), E Joe Skladany. *Noteworthy:* lost to unbeaten national cochamp USC 35–0 in Rose Bowl; trailed only 14–0 going into 4th quarter.

1933 (8–1) *Won:* W&J 9–0, West Virginia 21–0, Centre 37–0, Navy 34–6 (1st meeting since 1916), Notre Dame 14–0, Duquesne 7–0, Nebraska 6–0, Carnegie Tech 16–0. *Lost:* unbeaten Minnesota 7–3. *Stars:* Skladany, Howard Odell (868 all-purpose yds), Henry Weisenbaugh (5 TDs).

1934 (8–1) *Won:* W&J 26–6, West Virginia 27–6, USC 20–6, Westminster 30–0, Notre Dame 19–0, Nebraska 25–6, Navy 31–7, Carnegie Tech 20–0. *Lost:* unbeaten national cochamp Minnesota 13–7. *Stars:* Gs Chuck Hartwig and Ken Ormiston, C George Shotwell, Mike Nicksick (779 yds rush), Isadore Weinstock (9 TDs).

1935 (7–1–2) *Won:* Waynesburg 14–0, W&J 35–0, West Virginia 24–6, Penn St. 9–0, Army 29–6, Nebraska 6–0, USC 12–7. *Lost:* Notre Dame 9–6. *Tied:* Fordham 0–0 (1st meeting), Carnegie Tech 0–0. *Stars:* T Art Detzel, Herbert Randour (569 yds rush), soph Frank Patrick (9 TDs).

1936 (8–1–1) *Won:* Ohio Wesleyan 53–0, West Virginia 34–0, Ohio St. 6–0, Notre Dame 26–0, Penn St. 24–7, Nebraska 19–6, Carnegie Tech 31–14. *Lost:* Duquesne 7–0 (1st in 4-game series dating to 1901). *Tied:* Fordham 0–0. *Stars:* soph HB Marshall Goldberg (886 yds rush, 1,268 all-purpose yds, 6 TDs), T Averell Daniell, G Bill Glassford. *Noteworthy:* Won inaugural Lambert Trophy. Beat Washington 21–0 in Rose Bowl as B Bobby LaRue and Patrick led strong running attack.

1937 (9–0–1) *Won:* Ohio Wesleyan 59–0, West Virginia 20–0, Duquesne 6–0, Wisconsin 21–0, Carnegie Tech 25–14, Notre Dame 21–6, Nebraska 13–7, Penn St. 28–7, Duke 10–0 (1st meeting since 1929). *Tied:* Fordham 0–0. *Stars:* Goldberg (701 yds rush, 5 TDs), Patrick (7 TDs), T Tony Matisi, Es Art Souchak and Bill Daddio. *Noteworthy:* again won Lambert Trophy and got share of 3rd national title.

1938 (8–2) *Won:* West Virginia 19–0 (10th straight win over Mountaineers), Temple 28–6 (1st meeting), Duquesne 27–0, Wisconsin 26–6, Southern Methodist (SMU) 34–7, Fordham 24–13, Nebraska 19–0, Penn St. 26–0. *Lost:* Carnegie Tech 20–10 (1st to Tartans since 1928), unbeaten, unscored-on Duke 7–0. *Stars:* Goldberg (7 TDs), Daddio, Dick

Cassiano (739 yds and 11 TDs rush). *Noteworthy:* "Jock" Sutherland's last team.

1955 (7–4) *Won:* California 27–7, Syracuse 22–12 (1st meeting since 1930), Nebraska 21–7, Duke 26–7, Virginia 18–7, West Virginia 26–7, Penn St. 20–0. *Lost:* unbeaten national champ Oklahoma 26–14, Navy 21–0 (1st to Midshipmen in 8 games since 1912), Miami (Fla.) 21–7. *Star:* E Joe Walton (16 pass rec for 241 yds and 8 TDs). *Noteworthy:* Won 3rd Lambert Trophy. Lost to Georgia Tech 7–0 in Sugar Bowl as controversial pass interference call set up game's only TD.

1956 (7–3–1) *Won:* West Virginia 14–13, Syracuse 14–7, Duke 27–14, Oregon 14–7, Notre Dame 26–13, Army 20–7, Miami (Fla.) 14–7. *Lost:* California 14–0, Minnesota 9–6. *Tied:* Penn St. 7–7. *Stars:* Walton (21 pass rec for 360 yds and 6 TDs), QB Corny Salvaterra (6 TDs, 504 yds rush, 500 yds pass). *Noteworthy:* lost to Georgia Tech 21–14 in Gator Bowl; Salvaterra passed for 1st TD (36 yds to Dick Bowen) and scored 2nd.

1963 (9–1) *Won:* UCLA 20–0, Washington 13–6, California 35–15, West Virginia 13–10, Syracuse 35–27, Notre Dame 27–7, Army 28–0, Miami (Fla.) 31–20, Penn St. 22–21. *Lost:* Navy 24–12. *Stars:* B Paul Martha, QB Fred Mazurek (7 TDs and 646 yds rush, 949 yds pass), Joe Kuzneski (21 pass rec for 258 yds), T Ernie Borghetti.

1975 (8–4) *Won:* Georgia 19–9, William & Mary 47–0, Duke 14–0, Temple 55–6, Army 52–20, Syracuse 38–0, Notre Dame 34–20 (1st over Irish since 1963). *Lost:* national champ Oklahoma 46–10, Navy 17–0, West Virginia 17–14, Penn St. 7–6 (10th straight to Nittany Lions. *Stars:* RBs Tony Dorsett (1,544 yds and 11 TDs rush, 16 TDs total) and soph Elliott Walker (903 yds rush), Jim Corbett (24 pass rec for 322 yds). *Noteworthy:* beat Kansas 33–19 in Sun Bowl; Dorsett ran for 142 yds and 2 TDs, Walker ran for 123 yds and 2 TDs (one on 60-yd run), and QB Robert Haygood ran for 101 yds and threw a TD pass to frosh SE Gordon Jones.

1976 (12–0) *Won:* Notre Dame 31–10, Georgia Tech 42–14, Temple 21–7, Duke 44–31, Louisville 27–6, Miami (Fla.) 36–19, Navy 45–0, Syracuse 23–13, Army 37–7, West Virginia 24–16, Penn St. 24–7 (1st over Nittany Lions since 1965). *Stars:* Heisman Trophy– and Maxwell Award–winner Dorsett (nation's leader with 1,948 yds rush, 2,021 all-purpose yds and 134 pts), QB Matt Cavanaugh

(1,046 yds pass), Corbett (34 pass rec for 538 yds), K Carson Long (18 FGs), MG Al Romano, DB Bob Jury (10 int), P Larry Swider (44.2-yd avg). *Noteworthy:* Johnny Majors' last team till 1993 won 4th Lambert Trophy in 1st unbeaten season since 1937. Clinched 4th national championship by beating Georgia 27–3 in Sugar Bowl; Dorsett ran for 202 yds and a TD, Cavanaugh ran for 1 TD and passed to Jones (59 yds) for another, and Long kicked 2 FGs.

1977 (9–2–1) *Won:* William & Mary 28–6, Temple 76–0, Boston College 45–17, Navy 34–17, Syracuse 28–21, Tulane 48–0, West Virginia 44–3, Army 52–26. *Lost:* national champ Notre Dame 19–9, Penn St. 15–13. *Tied:* Florida 17–17. *Stars:* Cavanaugh (1,844 yds and 15 TDs pass), Jones (45 pass rec for 793 yds and 9 TDs), Walker (1,025 yds rush, 15 TDs), frosh QB Rick Trocano (6 TDs rush), C Tom Brzoza, DT Randy Holloway, Jury (8 int). *Noteworthy:* 1st year under Jackie Sherrill. Beat Clemson 34–3 in Gator Bowl; Cavanaugh passed for 387 yds and 4 TDs (3 to Walker), and Jones caught 10 for 163 yds and a TD.

1978 (8–4) *Won:* Tulane 24–6, Temple 20–12, North Carolina 20–16, Boston College 32–15, Florida St. 7–3, Syracuse 18–17, West Virginia 52–7, Army 35–17. *Lost:* Notre Dame 26–17, Navy 21–11, unbeaten Penn St. 17–10. *Stars:* Trocano (1,648 yds pass, 268 yds and 7 TDs rush), Gordon Jones (45 pass rec for 666 yds), RB Freddie Jacobs (634 yds and 9 TDs rush), HB Ray Jones (617 yds and 5 TDs rush), soph DE Hugh Green. *Noteworthy:* lost to N.C. State 30–17 in Tangerine Bowl as Panthers lost ball 4 times on int; Trocano passed for 182 yds, and Jacobs and Russell Carter scored TDs.

1979 (11–1) *Won:* Kansas 24–0, Temple 10–9, Boston College 28–7, Cincinnati 35–0, Washington 26–14, Navy 24–7, Syracuse 28–21, West Virginia 24–17, Army 40–0, Penn St. 29–14. *Lost:* North Carolina 17–7 in 2nd game. *Stars:* Green, DB Terry White (5 int), frosh QB Dan Marino (1,508 yds pass), Benjie Pryor (45 pass rec for 588 yds), Ralph Still (43 pass rec for 580 yds and 7 TDs), Ken Bowles (20 pass rec for 369 yds), FB Randy McMillan (802 yds rush, 10 TDs), Ray Jones (6 TDs rush), K Mark Schubert (14 FGs, 71 pts). *Noteworthy:* Won 5th Lambert Trophy. Beat Arizona 16–10 in Fiesta Bowl; Schubert kicked 3 FGs, Marino passed 12 yds to Pryor for a TD, and White had 2 int.

1980 (11–1) *Won:* Boston College 14–6, Kansas 18–3, Temple 36–2, Maryland 38–9, West Virginia 42–14, Tennessee 30–6, Syracuse 43–6, Louisville 41–23, Army 45–7, Penn St. 14–9. *Lost:* Florida St. 36–22. *Stars:* Lombardi and Maxwell award-winner Green, LB Sal Sunseri, DB Lynn Thomas (5 int), Marino (1,531 yds and 14 TDs pass), Trocano (1,401 yds pass), Pryor (47 pass rec for 574 yds), frosh FL Dwight Collins (30 pass rec for 827 yds and 10 TDs), Willie Collier (594 yds pass rec), McMillan (692 yds rush), OT Mark May (Outland Trophy winner), K David Trout (15 FGs, 84 pts). *Noteworthy:* Led nation in total defense and rush defense, and again won Lambert Trophy. Beat South Carolina 37–9 in Gator Bowl; McMillan scored 2 TDs, Trocano ran for 1 TD and passed for another, Marino passed for a TD, and Rickey Jackson made 14 solo tackles.

1981 (11–1) *Won:* Illinois 26–6, Cincinnati 38–7, South Carolina 42–28, West Virginia 17–0, Florida St. 42–14, Syracuse 23–10, Boston College 29–24, Rutgers 47–3 (1st meeting), Army 48–0, Temple 35–0. *Lost:* Penn St. 48–14 in finale. *Stars:* Marino (2,615 yds and 34 TDs pass), SE Julius Dawkins (46 pass rec for 767 yds and 16 TDs), Collins (20 pass rec for 308 yds and 5 TDs), RB Bryan Thomas (1,132 yds and 7 TDs rush, 46 pass rec for 451 yds), TE John Brown (43 pass rec for 530 yds and 8 TDs), Barry Compton (23 pass rec for 385 yds and 5 TDs), Wayne DiBartola (716 yds rush, 37 pass rec for 312 yds, 5 TDs), OT Jimbo Covert, Sunseri, DB Tom Flynn (5 int). *Noteworthy:* Sherrill's last team again led nation in total defense and rush defense. Beat Georgia 24–20 in Sugar Bowl on last-minute 33-yd pass from Marino (his 3rd TD pass) to Brown (his 2nd TD reception) for winning score; Dawkins scored on 30-yd pass and frosh K Ray Everett had 41-yd FG.

1982 (9–3) *Won:* North Carolina 7–6, Florida St. 37–17, Illinois 20–3, West Virginia 16–13, Temple 38–17, Syracuse 14–0 (10th straight over Orange), Louisville 63–14, Army 24–6, Rutgers 52–6. *Lost:* Notre Dame 31–16, national champ Penn St. 19–10. *Stars:* Marino (2,251 yds and 17 TDs pass), Thomas (955 yds rush, 54 pass rec for 404 yds), Collins (50 pass rec for 696 yds), Covert, soph OT Bill Fralic, K Eric Schubert (11 FGs, 69 pts), DT Bill Maas. *Noteworthy:* 1st year under Serafino "Foge" Fazio. Lost to unbeaten SMU 7–3 in Cotton Bowl; Marino passed for 181 yds and Schubert kicked 43-yd FG.

1983 (8–3–1) *Won:* Tennessee 13–3, Temple 35–0 (10th straight over Owls), Florida St. 17–16, Louisville 55–10, Navy 21–14, Syracuse 13–10, Notre Dame 21–16, Army 38–7. *Lost:* Maryland 13–7, West Virginia 24–21 (1st to Mountaineers since 1975) in successive early games. *Tied:* Penn St. 24–24 in finale. *Stars:* frosh QB John Congemi (1,940 yds and 16 TDs pass), Bill Wallace (45 pass rec for 727 yds and 8 TDs), Joe McCall (961 yds rush), Fralic. *Noteworthy:* lost to Ohio St. 28–23 in Fiesta Bowl; Congemi passed for 341 yds and TDs to TE Clint Wilson (who also scored on fumble recovery) and Collins, and Everett had 37-yd FG.

1987 (8–4) *Won:* Brigham Young (BYU) 27–17, N.C. State 34–0, West Virginia 6–3, Notre Dame 30–22, Navy 10–6, Rutgers 17–0, Penn St. 10–0, Kent St. 28–5. *Lost:* Temple 24–21, Boston College 13–10, unbeaten Syracuse 24–10. *Stars:* FB Craig Heyward (1,655 yds rush, 13 TDs), QB Sal Genilla (1,051 yds pass), soph FL Reggie Williams (31 pass rec for 535 yds), soph K Jeff Van Horne (10 FGs, 53 pts), LB Ezekial Gadson, frosh DT Marc Spindler. *Noteworthy:* lost to Texas 32–27 in Bluebonnet Bowl; reserve QB Larry Wanke passed for 172 yds and 3 TDs, and Heyward ran for 136 yds and a TD.

1989 (8–3–1) *Won:* Pacific 38–3, Boston College 29–10, Syracuse 30–23 (1st over Orange since 1983), Temple 27–3, Navy 31–14, East Carolina 47–42, Rutgers 46–29 (in Dublin, Ireland). *Lost:* Notre Dame 45–7, national champ Miami (Fla.) 24–3, Penn St. 16–13. *Tied:* West Virginia 31–31. *Stars:* frosh QB Alex Van Pelt (2,881 yds and 17 TDs pass), SE Henry Tuten (7 TDs, 41 pass rec for 975 yds and 6 TDs), soph RB Curvin Richards (10 TDs, 1,282 yds rush, 20 pass rec for 222 yds), soph FB Ronald Redmon (31 pass rec for 275 yds), frosh WR Olanda Truitt (19 pass rec for 383 yds), RB Adam Walker (7 TDs), C Dean Caliguire, soph K Ed Frazier (14 FGs, 77 pts), Spindler, DB Louis Riddick, P Brian Greenfield (41.7-yd avg). *Noteworthy:* Mike Gottfried's last team. Beat Texas A&M 31–28 in John Hancock Bowl under new coach Paul Hackett; Van Pelt passed for 354 yds and 2 TDs and ran for a TD, Tuten had 4 pass rec for 124 yds and a TD, and Richards ran for 156 yds and a TD.

BOWL SUMMARY

Bluebonnet 0–1; Cotton 0–1; Fiesta 1–2; Gator 2–1; John Hancock 1–0; Rose 1–3; Sugar 2–1; Sun 1–0; Tangerine 0–1.

BOWL RECORD (8–10)

Regular Season	Bowl	Score	Opponent	Record
1927 (8–0–1)	Rose	6–7	Stanford	(7–2–1)
1929 (9–0)	Rose	14–47	USC	(9–2)
1932 (8–0–2)	Rose	0–35	USC	(9–0)
1936 (7–1–1)	Rose	21–0	Washington	(7–1–1)
1955 (7–3)	Sugar	0–7	Georgia Tech	(8–1–1)
1956 (7–2–1)	Gator	14–21	Georgia Tech	(9–1)
1973 (6–4–1)	Fiesta	7–28	Arizona State	(10–1)
1975 (7–4)	Sun	33–19	Kansas	(7–4)
1976 (11–0)	Sugar	27–3	Georgia	(10–1)
1977 (8–2–1)	Gator	34–3	Clemson	(8–2–1)
1978 (8–3)	Tangerine	17–30	N.C. State	(8–3)
1979 (10–1)	Fiesta	16–10	Arizona	(6–4–1)
1980 (10–1)	Gator	37–9	South Carolina	(8–3)
1981 (10–1)	Sugar	24–20	Georgia	(10–1)
1982 (9–2)	Cotton	3–7	SMU	(10–0–1)
1983 (8–2–1)	Fiesta	23–28	Ohio State	(8–3)
1987 (8–3)	Bluebonnet	27–32	Texas	(6–5)
1989 (7–3–1)	John Hancock	31–28	Texas A&M	(8–3)

CONFERENCE TITLES

Big East—None. Won **Lambert Trophy** in 1936, 1937, 1955, 1976, 1979, 1980.

TOP 20 AP AND UPI RANKING

1936	3	1956	13–12	1977	8–7	1983	18–19
1937	1	1959	20–U	1979	7–6	1989	17–19
1938	8	1963	4–3	1980	2–2		
1952	U–15	1975	15–13	1981	4–2		
1955	11–11	1976	1–1	1982	10–9		

MAJOR RIVALS

Pittsburgh has played at least 10 games with Allegheny 8–2, Army 19–6–2, Boston College 11–6, Carnegie Tech 24–5–1, Duke 9–8, Geneva 12–6, Grove City 8–2–1, Miami (Fla.) 8–11–1, Minnesota 3–9, Navy 20–12–3, Nebraska 15–4–3, Notre Dame 16–37–1, Ohio St. 5–15–1, Oklahoma 1–9–1, Pennsylvania 10–1–1, Penn St. 41–47–4, Rutgers 9–1, Southern California 4–6, Syracuse 25–20–3, Temple 17–5–1, UCLA 5–9, Washington & Jefferson 18–13–2, Westminster 15–0–2, West Virginia 55–27–3. Record against Big East foe Virginia Tech is 0–0 (no games played).

COACHES

Dean of Pittsburgh coaches is Dr. John B. "Jock" Sutherland with record of 111–20–12 for 1924–38, including 2 Lambert Trophy winners, 4 Rose Bowl teams, 4 teams unbeaten in regular season, and 1 national champion. Other top records for at least 3 years were by Arthur St. Ledger Mosse, 20–10–1 for 1903–05 with 1 unbeaten team; Joseph H. Thompson, 30–14–2 for 1908–12 with 1 unbeaten team; Glenn S. "Pop" Warner, 59–12–4 for 1915–23 with 4 unbeaten teams and 2 national champions; John P. Michelosen, 56–49–7 for 1955–65 with 1 Lambert Trophy winner and 2 bowl teams; John Majors (1973, 1976 national Coach of Year), 33–13–1 for 1973–76 with 1 Lambert Trophy winner, 3 bowl teams, and 1 unbeaten national champion; Jackie Sherrill, 50–9–1 for 1977–81 with 2 Lambert Trophy winners and 5 bowl teams (4 winners);

Serafino "Foge" Fazio, 25–18–3 for 1982–85 with 2 bowl teams; and Mike Gottfried, 26–17–2 for 1986–89 with 2 bowl teams.

MISCELLANEA

First game was loss to Allegheny A.A. 38–0 in 1890 . . . 1st win was over Geneva 10–4 in 1890 . . . highest score was over Dickinson 96–0 in 1914 . . . highest since W.W. II was over Temple 76–0 in 1977 . . . worst defeat was by Michigan 69–0 in 1947 . . . highest score against Panthers matched in defeats by Army 69–7 in 1944 and by Notre Dame 69–13 in 1965 . . . longest win streak of 31 in 1914–18 ended by Cleveland Naval Reserve 10–9 . . . 22-game unbeaten string in 1936–38 ended by Carnegie Tech 20–10 . . . 17-game win streak in 1980–81 ended by Penn St. 48–14 . . . longest losing string of 10 in 1950–51 broken with win over West Virginia 32–12 and in 1971–72 broken with win over Boston College 35–20 . . . consensus All-Americans were Robert Peck, C, 1915–16; James Herron, E, 1916; Dale Seis, G, and John "Jock" Sutherland, G, 1917; Leonard Hilty, T, Tom Davies, B, and George McLaren, B, 1918; Herb Stein, C, 1920–21; Ralph Chase, T, 1925; Gibby Welch, B, 1927; Mike Getto, T, 1928; Joe Donchess, E, and Ray Montgomery, G, 1929; Jesse Quatse, T, 1931; Warren Heller, B, 1932; Joe Skladany, E, 1932–33; Chuck Hartwig, G, 1934; Averell Daniell, T, 1936; Tony Matisi, T, 1937; Marshall Goldberg, B, 1937–38; Joe Walton, E, 1956; John Guzik, G, 1958; Mike Ditka, E, 1960; Paul Martha, B, 1963; Tony Dorsett, RB, and Al Romano, MG, 1976; Tom

Brzoza, C, Randy Holloway, DL, and Bob Jury, DB, 1977; Hugh Green, DL, 1978–80; Mark May, OL, 1980; Sal Sunseri, LB, 1981; Jimbo Covert, OL, 1982; Bill Fralic, OL, 1983–84; Randy Dixon, OL, and Tony Woods, DL, 1986; Craig Heyward, RB, 1987; Mark Stepnoski, OL, 1988; and Brian Greenfield, P, 1990 . . . Academic All-Americans were Dick Deitrick, DT, 1952; Lou Palatella, T, 1954; Joe Walton, E, 1956; John Guzik, G, 1958; Jeff Delaney, LB, 1976; Greg Meisner, DL, 1980; Rob Fada, OG, 1981–82; J.C. Pelusi, DL, 1982; and Mark Stepnoski, OL, 1988 . . . Heisman Trophy winner was Tony Dorsett, HB, 1976 . . . Maxwell Award winners were Tony Dorsett, HB, 1976; and Hugh Green, DE, 1980 . . . Outland Trophy winner was Mark May, OT, 1980 . . . Lombardi Award winner was Hugh Green, DE, 1980.

RUTGERS (Scarlet Knights; Scarlet)

NOTABLE TEAMS

1915 (7–1) *Won:* Albright 53–0, Rensselaer Poly. Institute (RPI) 96–0, Muhlenburg 21–0, Springfield 44–13 (1st meeting), Hamilton Fish All Stars 28–7, Stevens Tech 39–3, New York U. 70–0. *Lost:* Princeton 10–0. *Stars:* FB Howard Talman (16 TDs), Elmer Bracher (1,021 yds rush), E Harry Rockafeller. *Noteworthy:* Most wins since 1891.
1917 (7–1–1) *Won:* Ursinus 25–0, Ft. Wadsworth 90–0, Lafayette 33–7 (1st meeting since 1899), Fordham 28–0, Springfield 61–0, League Island Marines 27–0, Newport Naval Reserve 14–0. *Lost:* Syracuse 14–10. *Tied:* West Virginia 7–7. *Star:* E Paul Robeson (Rutgers' 1st consensus All-American).
1918 (5–2) *Won:* Ursinus 66–0, Pelham Bay Naval Training Station 7–0, Lehigh 39–0 (1st meeting since 1908, 1st over Engineers in 14 games since 1884), Naval Transport–Hoboken 40–0, Penn St. 26–3 (1st meeting). *Lost:* Great Lakes Naval Training Station 54–14, Syracuse 21–0 in last 2 games. *Star:* Robeson.
1923 (7–1–1) *Won:* Penn Military 27–0, Villanova 44–0, Lehigh 10–0, New York U. 7–3, Richmond 56–0, Boston U. 61–0 (1st meeting), Fordham 42–0. *Lost:* West Virginia 27–7. *Tied:* Lafayette 6–6. *Stars:* HB Henry Marvin Benkert, E Homer Hazel. *Noteworthy:* Foster Sanford's last team.
1924 (7–1–1) *Won:* Villanova 14–0, Lebanon Val-

ley 56–0, St. Bonaventure 35–7, Cornell 10–0, Franklin & Marshall 30–6, Lafayette 43–7, New York U. 41–3. *Lost:* Bucknell 12–7 in finale. *Tied:* Lehigh 13–13. *Star:* FB Hazel. *Noteworthy:* 1st year under John Wallace.
1938 (7–1) *Won:* Marietta 20–0, Vermont 15–14, Springfield 6–0, Hampden-Sydney 32–0, Lehigh 13–0, Princeton 20–18 (1st over Tigers in 32 games since 1st meeting in 1869), Lafayette 6–0. *Lost:* New York U. 25–6. *Noteworthy:* 1st year under Harvey Harman.
1939 (7–1–1) *Won:* Wesleyan 13–7, Wooster 20–0, Maryland 25–12, Lehigh 20–6, New Hampshire 32–13, Lafayette 13–6, Springfield 17–7. *Lost:* Brown 13–0 in finale. *Tied:* Richmond 6–6.
1941 (7–2) *Won:* Alfred 34–0, Springfield 26–0, Lehigh 16–6, Fort Monmouth 26–0, Maryland 20–0, Connecticut 32–7, Brown 13–7. *Lost:* Syracuse 49–7 (1st meeting since 1930), Lafayette 16–0. *Noteworthy:* Harman's last team till after W.W. II.
1945 (5–2) *Won:* Muhlenburg 19–6, Rhode Island St. 39–7, Lehigh 25–0, Lafayette 32–14, New York U. 13–7 (1st meeting since 1938). *Lost:* Swarthmore 13–6 (1st meeting since 1928), Princeton 14–6 (1st meeting since 1938). *Noteworthy:* Harry Rockafeller's last team.
1946 (7–2) *Won:* Johns Hopkins 53–0, New York U. 26–0, George Washington 25–13, Harvard 13–0, Lafayette 41–2, Lehigh 55–6, Bucknell 25–0. *Lost:* Columbia 13–7 (1st meeting since 1935), Princeton 14–7 in early games. *Noteworthy:* Harman returned as coach.
1947 (8–1) *Won:* Western Reserve 20–6, Princeton 13–7, Fordham 36–6 (1st meeting since 1923), Lehigh 46–13, Harvard 31–7, Lafayette 20–0, New York U. 40–0, Brown 27–20 (1st meeting since 1941). *Lost:* Columbia 40–28 in opener. *Stars:* QB Frank Burns (11 TD passes), Bill Vigh (7 int). *Noteworthy:* won Middle 3 title.
1948 (7–2) *Won:* Colgate 34–19, Temple 34–20 (1st meeting), Princeton 22–6, Lehigh 20–6, Lafayette 34–13, New York U. 40–0, Fordham 28–19. *Lost:* Columbia 27–6, Brown 20–6. *Star:* Burns.
1958 (8–1) *Won:* Princeton 28–0 (1st over Tigers in 9 games since 1948), Colgate 21–7, Richmond 23–12, Bucknell 57–12 (1st meeting since 1946), Lehigh 44–13 (1st over Engineers in 7 games since 1949), Delaware 37–20, Lafayette 18–0, Columbia 61–0. *Lost:* Quantico Marines 13–12. *Stars:* TB Bill Austin (747 yds rush, 16 TDs, 106 pts, 6 int),

Es Bob Simms (33 pass rec for 468 yds and 9 TDs) and Charles Wermuth, G Larry Muschiatti. *Noteworthy:* Led nation in scoring (33.4-pt avg) and won 1st Middle Atlantic Conference title.
1960 (8–1) *Won:* Princeton 13–8, Connecticut 19–6, Colgate 49–12, Bucknell 23–19, Lehigh 8–0, Lafayette 36–8, Delaware 22–0, Columbia 43–2. *Lost:* Villanova 14–12. *Stars:* C Alex Kroll, RB Steve Simms (613 yds rush, 6 TDs). *Noteworthy:* Won 2nd Middle Atlantic title in 1st year under John Bateman.
1961 (9–0) *Won:* Princeton 16–13, Connecticut 35–12, Bucknell 21–6, Lehigh 32–15, Pennsylvania 20–6 (1st meeting since 1934), Lafayette 37–6, Delaware 27–19, Colgate 26–6, Columbia 32–19. *Stars:* Kroll, Simms (614 yds rush), Sam Mudie (10 TDs). *Noteworthy:* Won 3rd Middle Atlantic crown in 1st unbeaten season since 1-game schedule of 1876.
1968 (8–2) *Won:* Lafayette 37–7, Princeton 20–14 (1st over Tigers since 1961), Lehigh 29–26, Columbia 28–17, Delaware 23–14, Connecticut 27–15, Holy Cross 41–14, Colgate 55–34. *Lost:* Cornell 17–16, Army 24–0. *Stars:* Bryant Mitchell (1,204 yds and 9 TDs rush), QB Rich Policastro (15 TDs pass), Bob Stonebreaker (448 yds and 6 TDs pass rec), John Pollock (9 int), John Miller (8 int).
1974 (7–3–1) *Won:* Bucknell 16–14, Harvard 24–21, Lehigh 37–16, Air Force 20–3, Lafayette 35–0, Boston U. 6–0, Colgate 62–21. *Lost:* William & Mary 28–15 (1st meeting since 1957), Connecticut 9–7, Hawaii 28–16. *Tied:* Princeton 6–6. *Stars:* soph QB Bert Kosup (1,070 yds pass, 6 TDs rush), FB Curt Edwards (889 yds rush), C Andy Zdobylak, LB Tom Holmes, soph DE Nate Toran, DT Paul Krasnavage, DBs Ed Jones (7 int) and Tony Pawlik.
1975 (9–2) *Won:* Bucknell 47–3, Hawaii 7–3, William & Mary 24–0, Columbia 41–0, Connecticut 35–8, Lafayette 48–6, Boston U. 41–3, Colgate 56–14, Syracuse 21–10 (1st meeting since 1950, 1st win in 10-game series dating to 1914). *Lost:* Princeton 10–7, Lehigh 34–20. *Stars:* Edwards (1,157 yds and 9 TDs rush, 11 TDs total), WR Mark Twitty (544 yds and 7 TDs pass rec), Toran, DT John Alexander, DB Jim Teaton.
1976 (11–0) *Won:* Navy 13–3 (1st meeting since 1969), Bucknell 19–7, Princeton 17–0, Cornell 21–14, Connecticut 38–0, Lehigh 28–21, Columbia 47–0, Massachusetts 24–7, Louisville 34–0, Tulane

29–20, Colgate 17–9. *Stars:* Kosup (1,098 yds pass), Twitty (514 yds pass rec), soph Glen Kehler (764 yds rush), Mark Lassiter (9 TDs), OT Nick Sauter, frosh K Kennan Startzell, Henry Jenkins (nation's punt return leader with 15-yd avg), Toran, Alexander, LB Jim Hughes, Teaton. *Noteworthy:* Led nation in total defense, rush defense and scoring defense (7.4-pt avg) in 1st unbeaten season since 1961.
1977 (8–3) *Won:* Bucknell 36–14, Princeton 10–6, Cornell 30–14, Connecticut 48–18, Lehigh 20–0, William & Mary 22–21, Tulane 47–8, Boston U. 63–8. *Lost:* Penn St. 45–7 (1st meeting since 1955), Colgate 23–0, Temple 24–14 (1st meeting since 1954). *Stars:* Kosup (1,445 yds and 10 TDs pass), George Carter (391 yds pass rec), Lester Johnson (5 TDs pass rec), Kehler (866 yds rush), Mike Fisher (9 TDs), DB Bob Davis.
1978 (9–3) *Won:* Bucknell 27–13, Princeton 24–0, Yale 28–27, Connecticut 10–0, Villanova 24–9, Columbia 69–0, Massachusetts 21–11, Temple 13–10, Holy Cross 31–21. *Lost:* unbeaten Penn St. 26–10 (opener), Colgate 14–9 (finale). *Stars:* Kehler (883 yds rush), QB Bob Hering (1,193 yds pass), FL Dave Dorn (535 yds pass rec), C John Bucci, OT John Gallo, Startzell (14 FGs, 76 pts), MG Ed Steward, Hughes, LB Tim Blanchard, DBs Mark Freeman and Walt Hynoski (6 int). *Noteworthy:* made 1st postseason appearance, losing to Arizona St. 34–18 in Garden State Bowl after jumping to quick 10–0 lead on Dorn's 47-yd TD run and Startzell's 46-yd FG.
1979 (8–3) *Won:* Holy Cross 28–0, Bucknell 16–14, Princeton 38–14, Connecticut 26–14, William & Mary 24–0, Tennessee 13–7, Army 20–0 (1st meeting since 1972, 1st over Cadets in 12 games since 1891), Louisville 31–7. *Lost:* Penn St. 45–10, Temple 41–20, Villanova 32–17. *Stars:* QB Ed McMichael (1,529 yds pass), Dorn (468 yds and 5 TDs pass rec, 74 pts), soph Albert Ray (567 yds rush), Startzell (13 FGs), OT Kevin Kurdyla, DT Dino Mangiero, DB Deron Cherry (41.3-yd punting avg).
1984 (7–3) *Won:* Temple 10–9, Syracuse 19–0, Cincinnati 43–15, Army 14–7, Louisville 38–21, West Virginia 23–19 (1st over Mountaineers in 7 games since 1921), Colgate 17–7. *Lost:* Penn St. 15–12, Kentucky 27–14, Boston College 35–21. *Stars:* QB Eric Hochberg (1,905 yds pass), FL Andrew Baker (42 pass rec for 583 yds), TE Alan

Andrews (40 pass rec for 522 yds), RB Albert Smith (869 yds and 9 TDs rush), C Joe DiGilio, K Tom Angstadt (19 FGs, 77 pts), DT George Pickel, LB Roy Oake, DBs Harold Young and soph Tyronne Stowe. *Noteworthy:* 1st year under Dick Anderson.

BOWL SUMMARY

Garden State 0–1.

BOWL RECORD (0–1)

Regular Season	Bowl	Score	Opponent	Record
1978 (9–2)	Garden State	18–34	Arizona State	(8–3)

CONFERENCE TITLES

Middle 3—1947. **Middle Atlantic**—1958, 1960, 1961. **Big East**—None.

TOP 20 AP AND UPI RANKING

1958	20–U	1961	15–U	1976	17–17

MAJOR RIVALS

Rutgers has played at least 10 games with Army 10–16, Boston College 6–8, Boston U. 11–2, Brown 6–5, Bucknell 12–4, Colgate 26–15, Columbia 23–21–5, Connecticut 16–5, Cornell 5–6, Delaware 15–13–3, Fordham 8–5–1, Haverford 5–9–3, Holy Cross 8–11, Lafayette 41–30–1, Lehigh 43–30–1, Navy 3–6–1, New York U. 23–18–2, Pennsylvania 6–9, Penn St. 2–19, Pittsburgh 1–9, Princeton 17–53–1, Springfield 12–1, Stevens Tech 30–11–5, Swarthmore 5–9, Syracuse 4–18–1, Temple 11–11, Ursinus 9–8, Villanova 5–6, West Virginia 3–15–2, William & Mary 6–4, Yale 2–11. Record against Big East foes met fewer than 10 times is Miami (Fla.) 0–0 (no games played), Virginia Tech 3–0.

COACHES

Dean of Rutgers coaches is Harvey J. Harman with record of 74–44–2 for 1938–41 and 1946–55, with 1 conference title. Most wins were under Frank Burns, 78–43–1 for 1973–83 including 1 bowl team and 1 unbeaten team. Other top records for at least 3 years were by Howard Gargan, 12–10–4 for 1910–12; G. Foster Sanford, 56–32–5 for 1913–23; Harry J. Rockafeller, 33–26–1 for 1927–30 and 1942–45; J. Wilder Tasker, 31–27–5 for 1931–37; John R. Stiegman, 22–15 for 1956–59 with 1 conference title; and John F. Bateman, 73–51 for 1960–72 with 2 conference titles and 1 unbeaten team.

MISCELLANEA

First game was win over Princeton 6–4 in 1st intercollegiate football contest in 1869 . . . highest score was over RPI 96–0 in 1915 . . . highest since W.W. II was over King's Point 79–6 in 1949 . . . worst defeat was by Yale 98–0 in 1883 . . . worst since 1900 was by Lafayette 56–0 in 1927 . . . worst since W.W. II was by Boston College 48–0 in 1956 . . . highest against Scarlet Knights since 1900 was by Princeton 61–19 in 1952 . . . longest winning streak of 18 in 1975–76 ended by Penn St. 45–7 in 1977 opener . . . longest losing string of 14 in 1900–02 broken with win over Stevens Tech 10–0 . . . consensus All-Americans were Paul Robeson, E, 1917–18; and Alex Kroll, C, 1961 . . . Rutgers has had no 1st team Academic All-Americans.

SYRACUSE *(Orangemen; Orange)*

NOTABLE TEAMS

1890 (8-3) *Won:* Rochester 4-0, 8-0, Hamilton 14-10, St. John's Military Academy 18-4, 28-6, Syracuse A.A. 20-4, 14-0, 32-0. *Lost:* Hamilton 6-4, Union 26-0, 28-0.

1895 (6-2-2) *Won:* Scranton A.A. 12-0, Syracuse A.A. 24-0, 18-0, Hobart 46-0, Colgate 4-0, Rochester 30-0. *Lost:* Cornell 8-0, Syracuse A.A. 28-10. *Tied:* St. John's Military Academy 6-6, 4-4. *Noteworthy:* 1st year under George Redington.

1898 (8-2-1) *Won:* Rochester 35-0, Hobart 46-5, Case 10-0, Syracuse A.A. 28-0, 28-0, Ogdensburg 17-6, New York U. 17-0, Wyoming Seminary 11-0. *Lost:* Cornell 28-0, 30-0. *Tied:* Trinity (N.Y.) 0-0 in finale.

1900 (7-2-1) *Won:* Amherst 5-0, Cortland St. 35-0, Dickinson 6-0, New York U. 12-0, Oberlin 6-0, Rochester 68-5, St. Lawrence 70-0. *Lost:* Cornell 6-0, Princeton 43-0 in successive early games. *Tied:* Brown 6-6 (1st meeting). *Noteworthy:* 1st year under Edwin R. Sweetland.

1901 (7-1) *Won:* Clarkson 27-0 (1st meeting), Cortland St. 35-0, Rensselaer Poly. Institute (RPI) 26-0, Vermont 38-0, Amherst 28-17, Brown 20-0, Columbia 11-5 (1st meeting). *Lost:* Lafayette 5-0 (1st meeting).

1902 (6-2-1) *Won:* Cortland St. 21-0, Onondaga Indians 34-0, Clarkson 47-0, Colgate 23-0, Amherst 15-0, Williams 26-17. *Lost:* unbeaten Yale 24-0 (1st meeting), Army 46-0. *Tied:* Columbia 6-6. *Noteworthy:* Sweetland's last team.

1905 (8-3) *Won:* Alfred 52-0, Hobart 24-0, Rochester 16-0, Hamilton 27-0 (1st meeting since 1894), Colgate 11-5, Lehigh 17-0, Holy Cross 16-4 (1st meeting), Rensselaer Poly. Institute (RPI) 62-0. *Lost:* unbeaten Yale 16-0, Brown 27-0, Army 17-0.

1915 (9-1-2) *Won:* Brown 6-0 (1st meeting since 1905), Bucknell 6-0, Colgate 38-0 (1st over Red Raiders in 8 games since 1905), E. Syracuse 43-0, Michigan 14-7, Mt. Union 73-0, Occidental 35-0, Oregon St. 28-0, Rochester 82-0. *Lost:* Princeton 3-0. *Tied:* Dartmouth 0-0, Montana 6-6. *Stars:* Gs Harold White, Chris Schlachter.

1917 (8-1-1) *Won:* 47th Infantry 19-0, Rutgers 14-10, Tufts 58-0, Bucknell 42-0, Colgate 27-7, Brown 6-0, Michigan St. 21-7 (1st meeting), Ne-braska 10-9 (1st meeting). *Lost:* unbeaten Pittsburgh 28-0. *Tied:* 47th Infantry 0-0. *Star:* T Alfred Cobb.

1918 (5-1) *Won:* USN Transport 13-0, Dartmouth 34-6, Brown 53-0, Columbia 20-0 (1st meeting since 1902), Rutgers 21-0. *Lost:* unbeaten Michigan 15-0. *Stars:* G Joe Alexander, T Louis Usher.

1919 (8-3) *Won:* All-Syracuse 10-0, Vermont 27-0, Army 7-3 (1st meeting since 1912), Pittsburgh 24-3, Brown 13-0, Rutgers 14-6, Bucknell 9-0, Colgate 13-7. *Lost:* Washington & Jefferson 13-0, Indiana 12-6, Nebraska 3-0. *Star:* Alexander. *Noteworthy:* Frank O'Neill's last team.

1920 (6-2-1) *Won:* Hobart 55-7, Vermont 49-0, Johns Hopkins 45-0, Dartmouth 10-0, Washington & Jefferson 14-0, Colgate 14-0. *Lost:* Holy Cross 3-0 (1st meeting since 1905), Maryland 10-7 (1st meeting). *Tied:* unbeaten Pittsburgh 7-7. *Stars:* C Alexander, T Bertrand Gulick. *Noteworthy:* 1st year under John Meehan.

1921 (7-2) *Won:* Hobart 35-0 (15th straight over Statesmen), Ohio U. 38-0, Colgate 14-0, Dartmouth 14-7, McGill 13-0, Maryland 42-0, Brown 28-0. *Lost:* unbeaten Washington & Jefferson 17-10, Pittsburgh 30-0 in successive late games.

1922 (6-1-2) *Won:* Hobart 28-7, Muhlenberg 47-0, New York U. 34-0, Nebraska 9-6, McGill 32-0, Colgate 14-7. *Lost:* Pittsburgh 21-14. *Tied:* Brown 0-0, Penn St. 0-0 (1st meeting).

1923 (8-1) *Won:* Hobart 33-0, William & Mary 61-3, Alabama 23-0, Pittsburgh 3-0, Springfield 44-0, Penn St. 10-0, Boston U. 49-0 (1st meeting), Nebraska 7-0. *Lost:* Colgate 16-7 (1st to Red Raiders in 6 games since 1916). *Star:* E Pete MacRae.

1924 (8-2-1) *Won:* Hobart 35-0, Mercer 26-0, William & Mary 24-7, Boston College 10-0 (1st meeting), Penn St. 10-6, Niagara 23-6, Colgate 7-3, Columbia 9-6. *Lost:* West Virginia Wesleyan 7-3, Southern California 16-0. *Tied:* Pittsburgh 7-7. *Noteworthy:* Meehan's last team.

1925 (8-1-1) *Won:* Hobart 32-0, Vermont 26-0, William & Mary 33-0, Niagara 17-0, Providence 48-0, Indiana 14-0, Penn St. 7-0, Columbia 16-5. *Lost:* Colgate 19-6. *Tied:* Ohio Wesleyan 3-3. *Noteworthy:* 1st year under C.W.P. Reynolds.

1926 (7-2-1) *Won:* Hobart 18-0 (20th straight over Statesmen), Vermont 64-0, William & Mary 35-0, Penn St. 10-0, Johns Hopkins 31-0, Niagara 12-6, Columbia 19-2. *Lost:* Army 27-21 (1st meeting since 1919), Georgetown 13–7. *Tied:* Colgate 10–10. *Star:* E Vic Hanson.

1931 *(7–1–1)* *Won:* St. Lawrence 46–6, Hobart 49–0 (25th win in as many games with Statesmen), Ohio Wesleyan 48–7, Florida 33–12, Penn St. 7–0, Michigan St. 15–10 (1st meeting since 1917), Western Reserve 33–0 in 1st 7 games. *Lost:* Colgate 21–7. *Tied:* Columbia 0–0 in finale.

1934 *(6–2)* *Won:* Clarkson 28–0, Cornell 20–7, Penn St. 16–0, Brown 33–0, Michigan St. 10–0, Ohio Wesleyan 32–10 in 1st 6 games. *Lost:* Colgate 13–2, Columbia 12–0. *Star:* T James Steen.

1935 *(6–1–1)* *Won:* Clarkson 33–0, Cornell 21–14, Ohio Wesleyan 18–10, Brown 19–0, Penn St. 7–3, Columbia 14–2 in 1st 6 games. *Lost:* Colgate 27–0. *Tied:* Maryland 0–0 (1st meeting since 1921).

1952 *(7–3)* *Won:* Boston U. 34–21, Temple 27–0, Cornell 26–6, Holy Cross 20–19, Penn St. 25–7, Colgate 20–14, Fordham 26–13. *Lost:* Bolling Field 13–12, unbeaten national champ Michigan St. 48–7 (1st meeting since 1939). *Stars:* Bill Wetzel (670 yds and 5 TDs rush), QB Pat Stark (1,035 yds pass, 11 TDs rush), Joe Szombathy (21 pass rec for 178 yds), G Bob Fleck, Bruce Yancey (5 int). *Noteworthy:* Won 1st Lambert Trophy. Made 1st postseason appearance, losing to Alabama 61–6 in Orange Bowl; Stark passed for 157 yds and a TD (15 yards to Szombathy in 1st quarter).

1956 *(7–2)* *Won:* Maryland 26–12, West Virginia 27–20, Army 7–0, Boston U. 21–7, Penn St. 13–9, Holy Cross 41–20, Colgate 61–7. *Lost:* Pittsburgh 14–7. *Stars:* HB Jim Brown (986 yds rush, 14 TDs, 106 pts, 1,298 all-purpose yds), Jim Ridlon (6 int). *Noteworthy:* Won 2nd Lambert Trophy. Lost to Texas Christian (TCU) 28–27 in Cotton Bowl; Brown ran for 132 yds and 3 TDs and kicked 3 ex pts, and soph QB Chuck Zimmerman passed 27 yds to Ridlon for final Syracuse TD.

1958 *(8–2)* *Won:* Boston College 24–14 (1st meeting since 1944), Cornell 55–0, Nebraska 38–0, Penn St. 14–6, Pittsburgh 16–13, Boston U. 42–0, Colgate 47–0, West Virginia 15–12. *Lost:* Holy Cross 14–13 in 2nd game. *Stars:* Zimmerman (9 TDs), T Ron Luciano, P Ed Keiffer (40.9-yd avg). *Noteworthy:* lost to Oklahoma 21–6 in Orange Bowl, scoring in last period on 15-yd run by HB Mark Weber.

1959 *(11–0)* *Won:* Kansas 35–21, Maryland 29–0, Navy 32–6 (1st meeting), Holy Cross 42–6, West Virginia 44–0, Pittsburgh 35–0, Penn St. 20–18,

Colgate 71–0, Boston U. 46–0, UCLA 36–8. *Stars:* soph HB Ernie Davis (686 yds and 10 TDs rush), soph QB Dave Sarette (10 TDs pass), E Fred Mautino (17 pass rec for 215 yds), Gerhard Schwedes (5 TDs on pass rec, 16 TDs and 100 pts total), G Roger Davis, T Robert Yates. *Noteworthy:* Outscored foes 390–59 in 1st unbeaten season and won 1st national title and 3rd Lambert Trophy. Led nation in total off, rushing, scoring (39-pt avg), total defense, and rush defense. Beat Texas 23–14 in Cotton Bowl as Davis scored 2 TDs (one on 87-yd pass from Schwedes, who also scored on 3-yd run) and caught 2 conversion passes from Sarette.

1960 *(7–2)* *Won:* Boston U. 35–7, Kansas 14–7, Holy Cross 15–6, Penn St. 21–15, West Virginia 45–0, Colgate 46–6, Miami (Fla.) 21–14 (1st meeting). *Lost:* Pittsburgh 10–0, Army 9–6 in consecutive late games. *Stars:* Davis (877 yds and 10 TDs rush), P Tom Gilburg (41.4-yd avg).

1961 *(8–3)* *Won:* Oregon St. 19–8, West Virginia 29–14, Nebraska 28–6, Holy Cross 34–6, Pittsburgh 28–9, Colgate 51–8, Boston College 28–13. *Lost:* Maryland 22–21, Penn St. 14–0, Notre Dame 19–17. *Stars:* Heisman Trophy–winner Davis (823 yds rush, 15 TDs, 16 pass rec for 157 yds), John Snider (5 int). *Noteworthy:* beat Miami (Fla.) 15–14 in Liberty Bowl; Davis ran for 140 yds and a TD, Sarette passed for 148 yds, a 2-pt conversion, and the tying TD (both to Dick Easterly), and Ken Ericson kicked winning ex pt.

1963 *(8–2)* *Won:* Boston College 32–21, Holy Cross 48–0, UCLA 29–7, Penn St. 9–0, Oregon St. 31–8, West Virginia 15–13, Richmond 50–0, Notre Dame 14–7. *Lost:* Kansas 10–0, Pittsburgh 35–27. *Star:* Mike Koski (6 TDs).

1964 *(7–4)* *Won:* Kansas 38–6, Holy Cross 34–8, UCLA 39–0, Penn St. 21–14, Pittsburgh 21–6, Army 27–15, Virginia Tech 20–15 (1st meeting). *Lost:* Boston College 21–14 (1st to Eagles in 5 games since 1944), Oregon St. 31–13, West Virginia 28–27. *Stars:* C Pat Killorin, FB Jim Nance (951 yds rush, 13 TDs), soph HB Floyd Little (828 yds rush, 16 pass rec for 248 yds, 12 TDs). *Noteworthy:* Led nation in rush. Lost to Louisiana St. (LSU) 13–10 in Sugar Bowl, scoring on 23-yd FG by Roger Smith and 28-yd blocked punt return by Brad Clarke.

1965 *(7–3)* *Won:* Navy 14–6, Maryland 24–7, Penn St. 28–21, Holy Cross 32–6, Pittsburgh 51–13, West

Coach Ben Schwartzwalder, 1949–73, HB Jim Brown, 1954–56, and HB Ernie Davis, 1959–61

Virginia 41–19, Boston College 21–13. *Lost:* Miami (Fla.) 24–0, UCLA 24–14 (1st in 5-game series begun in 1959), Oregon St. 13–12. *Stars:* Little (19 TDs, 1,065 yds rush, 21 pass rec for 248 yds, nation's leader with 1,990 all-purpose yds), soph FB Larry Csonka (795 yds rush), Killorin, DB Charley Brown.

1966 (8–3) *Won:* Maryland 28–7, Navy 28–14, Boston College 30–0, Holy Cross 28–6, Pittsburgh 33–7, Penn St. 12–10, Florida St. 37–21, West Virginia 34–7. *Lost:* Baylor 35–12, UCLA 31–12 in 1st 2 games. *Stars:* Little (811 yds rush, 15 TDs), Csonka (1,012 yds and 7 TDs rush), T Gary Bugenhagen. *Noteworthy:* Won 4th Lambert Trophy. Lost to Tennessee 18–12 in Gator Bowl; Little ran for 216 yds and a TD, and Csonka ran for 114 yds and a score.

1967 (8–2) *Won:* Baylor 7–0, West Virginia 23–6, Maryland 7–3, California 20–14, Pittsburgh 14–7, Holy Cross 41–7, Boston College 32–20, UCLA 32–14. *Lost:* Navy 27–14 (1st in 5-game series begun in 1959), Penn St. 29–20. *Stars:* Csonka

(1,127 yds rush, 10 TDs), Tom Coughlin (26 pass rec for 257 yds), Cliff Ensley (6 int).

1987 (11–0–1) *Won:* Maryland 25–11, Rutgers 20–3, Miami (Ohio) 24–10, Virginia Tech 35–21, Missouri 24–13, Penn St. 48–21 (1st over Nittany Lions since 1970), Colgate 52–6, Pittsburgh 24–10, Navy 34–10, Boston College 45–17, West Virginia 32–31. *Stars:* Maxwell Award–winning QB Don McPherson (5 TDs rush, nation's leader with 2,341 yds and 22 TDs pass), soph RBs Robert Drummond (746 yds and 6 TDs rush) and Michael Owens (531 yds rush, 6 TDs), Tommy Kane (44 pass rec for 968 yds and 14 TDs), K Tim Vesling (15 FGs, 88 pts), NG Ted Gregory, DB Markus Paul (5 int). *Noteworthy:* Nation's most-improved team won 5th Lambert Trophy in 1st undefeated season since 1959. Tied Auburn 16–16 in Sugar Bowl; McPherson passed for 140 yds and a TD, and Vesling kicked 3 FGs.

1988 (10–2) *Won:* Temple 31–21, Virginia Tech 35–0, Maryland 20–9, Rutgers 34–20, Penn St. 24–10, East Carolina 38–14, Navy 49–21, Boston

HB Floyd Little, 1964–66

8 TDs rush), frosh K John Biskup (14 FGs), Bavaro, LB Terry Wooden, DB Rob Thomson (7 int), soph P Ken Hawkins (40.3-yd avg).   *Noteworthy:* beat Georgia 19–18 in Peach Bowl; Owens ran for 116 yds and a TD, soph QB Mark McDonald passed for 135 yds and a TD, Scharr passed for 100 yds, and Biskup kicked 32-yd FG.

1991 (10–2)   *Won:* Vanderbilt 37–10, Maryland 31–17, Florida 38–21, Tulane 24–0, Pittsburgh 31–27, Rutgers 21–7, Temple 27–6, Boston College 38–16, West Virginia 16–10.   *Lost:* Florida St. 46–14, East Carolina 23–20 in successive mid-season games. *Stars:* soph QB Marvin Graves (1,912 yds and 10 TDs pass), WR Qadry Ismail (37 pass rec for 693 yds, 7 TDs), TE Chris Gedney (25 pass rec for 322 yds), soph WR Shelby Hill (21 pass rec for 321 yds), RB David Walker (969 yds rush, 8 TDs), Biskup (17 FGs, 85 pts), DL George Rooks, soph NG Kevin Mitchell, LBs Glen Young and John Lusardi, soph P Pat O'Neill (42-yd avg).   *Noteworthy:* 1st year under Paul Pasqualoni. Beat Ohio St. 24–17 in Hall of Fame Bowl; Graves passed for 309 yds and 2 TDs (50 yds to Hill and 60 yds to WR Antonio Johnson) and ran for another, and Biskup kicked 32-yd FG.

1992 (10–2)   *Won:* East Carolina 42–21, Texas 31–21, Louisville 15–9, Rutgers 50–28, West Virginia 20–17, Temple 38–7, Pittsburgh 41–10, Virginia Tech 28–9, Boston College 27–10.   *Lost:* Ohio St. 35–12, unbeaten Miami (Fla.) 16–10.   *Stars:* Graves (2,296 yds and 14 TDs pass, 5 TDs rush), Ismail (36 pass rec for 625 yds, 1,220 all-purpose yds, 5 TDs), Gedney (34 pass rec for 587 yds and 5 TDs), Hill (29 pass rec for 480 yds), Walker (855 yds rush, 1,018 all-purpose yds), FB Al Wooten (7 TDs rush), OT Terrence Wisdom, Biskup (16 FGs, 81 pts), Mitchell, Wooden, Young, DBs Bob Grosvenor (6 int) and soph Tony Jones (5 int), O'Neill (42.3-yd punting avg).   *Noteworthy:* Won 6th Lambert Trophy. Beat Colorado 26–22 in Fiesta Bowl (5th straight bowl win) as Walker ran for 80 yds and a TD, soph Kirby Dar Dar scored on 100-yd kickoff return, Graves scored on 28-yd run, and Biskup had 2 FGs and 2 ex pts.

College 45–20, Pittsburgh 24–7.   *Lost:* Ohio St. 26–9, unbeaten West Virginia 31–9.   *Stars:* Drummond (747 yds and 6 TDs rush), FB Daryl Johnston (645 yds and 5 TDs rush, 20 pass rec for 250 yds), QB Todd Philcox (2,076 yds and 16 TDs pass), soph WR Rob Moore (44 pass rec for 797 yds and 11 TDs), Deval Glover (41 pass rec for 580 yds and 5 TDs), Pat Davis (27 pass rec for 424 yds), Owens (5 TDs), K Kevin Greene (15 FGs, 82 pts), LB David Bavaro, DB Paul, P Cooper Gardiner (42-yd avg).   *Noteworthy:* beat LSU 23–10 in Hall of Fame Bowl; Philcox passed for 130 yds and a TD, and Drummond ran for 122 yds and 2 TDs.

1989 (8–4)   *Won:* Temple 43–3, Army 10–7, Rutgers 49–28, East Carolina 18–16, Boston College 23–11, Navy 38–17, Louisville 24–13 (in Tokyo). *Lost:* Pittsburgh 30–23, Florida St. 41–10, Penn St. 34–12, West Virginia 24–17.   *Stars:* QB Bill Scharr (1,625 yds pass), Moore (53 pass rec for 1,064 yds and 9 TDs), soph WR Rob Carpenter (6 TDs, 41 pass rec for 761 yds and 5 TDs), RB Duane Kinnon (39 pass rec for 429 yds), Owens (1,018 yds and

BOWL SUMMARY

Aloha 1–0; Cherry 0–1; Cotton 1–1; Fiesta 1–0; Gator 0–1; Hall of Fame 2–0; Independence 1–0; Liberty 1–0; Orange 0–2; Peach 1–0; Sugar 0–1–1.

BOWL RECORD (8–6–1)

Regular Season	Bowl	Score	Opponent	Record
1952 (7–2)	Orange	6–61	Alabama	(9–2)
1956 (7–1)	Cotton	27–28	TCU	(7–3)
1958 (8–1)	Orange	6–21	Oklahoma	(9–1)
1959 (10–0)	Cotton	23–14	Texas	(9–1)
1961 (7–3)	Liberty	15–14	Miami (Fla.)	(7–3)
1964 (7–3)	Sugar	10–13	LSU	(7–2–1)
1966 (8–2)	Gator	12–18	Tennessee	(7–3)
1979 (6–5)	Independence	31–7	McNeese St.	(11–0)
1985 (7–4)	Cherry	18–35	Maryland	(8–3)
1987 (11–0)	Sugar	16–16	Auburn	(9–1–1)
1988 (9–2)	Hall of Fame	23–10	LSU	(8–3)
1989 (7–4)	Peach	19–18	Georgia	(6–5)
1990 (6–4–2)	Aloha	28–0	Arizona	(7–4)
1991 (9–2)	Hall of Fame	24–17	Ohio State	(8–3)
1992 (9–2)	Fiesta	26–22	Colorado	(9–1–1)

CONFERENCE TITLES

Big East—None. Won **Lambert Trophy** in 1952, 1956, 1959, 1966, 1987, 1992.

TOP 20 AP AND UPI
(USA TODAY/CNN SINCE 1991) RANKING

1952	14–U	1960	19–U	1965	U–19	1988	13–12
1956	8–8	1961	14–16	1966	U–16	1991	11–11
1958	9–10	1963	U–12	1967	U–12	1992	6–7
1959	1–1	1964	U–12	1987	4–4		

MAJOR RIVALS

Syracuse has played at least 10 games with Army 10–10, Boston College 21–12, Boston U. 12–3–1, Brown 9–3–3, Clarkson 15–0, Colgate 29–31–5, Columbia 11–9, Cornell 11–23, Dartmouth 3–6–1, Hamilton 10–3, Hobart 25–0, Holy Cross 23–5, Illinois 1–9, Lafayette 6–3–1, Maryland 17–14–2, Miami (Fla.) 5–6, Michigan 4–5–1, Michigan St. 3–9–1, Navy 19–8, Nebraska 7–5, Niagara 11–0, Penn St. 23–40–5, Pittsburgh 20–25–3, Rochester 21–3–1, Rutgers 18–4–1, St. John's 5–5–2, Syracuse A.A. 11–7–1, Temple 15–8–1, West Virginia 24–16, Yale 0–11. Record against Big East foe Virginia Tech is 4–2.

COACHES

Dean of Syracuse coaches is Floyd "Ben" Schwartzwalder (1959 national Coach of Year) with record of 153–91–3 for 1949–73, including 4 Lambert Trophy winners, 7 bowl teams, and 1 unbeaten national champion. Other top records for at least 3 years were by Frank E. Wade, 17–9–2 for 1897–99; Edwin R. Sweetland, 20–5–2 for 1900–02; Frank J. O'Neill, 52–19–6 for 1906–07, 1913–15, and 1917–19; John F. Meehan, 35–8–4 for 1920–24; Lewis P. Andreas, 15–10–3 for 1927–29; Victor A. Hanson, 33–21–5 for 1930–36; Ossie Solem, 30–27–6 for 1937–45; Frank Maloney, 32–46 for 1974–80 with 1 bowl team; and Dick MacPherson (1987 national Coach of Year), 66–46–4 for 1981–90 with 1 unbeaten Lambert Trophy winner and 5 bowl teams.

MISCELLANEA

First game was loss to Rochester 36–0 in 1889 . . . 1st win was over Rochester 4–0 in 1890 . . . highest score was over Manhattan 144–0 in 1904 . . . highest since W.W. II was over Colgate 71–0 in 1959 . . . worst defeat was by Union 71–0 in 1891 . . . worst since 1900 was by Princeton 62–0 in 1912 . . . worst since W.W. II was by Nebraska 63–7 in 1983 (also highest against Orangemen since 1900) . . . longest win streak of 15 in 1959–60 ended by Pittsburgh 10–0 . . . 14-game unbeaten string in 1986–88 ended by Ohio St. 26–9 . . . longest winless string of 13 in 1891–93 broken with win over Hamilton 16–14 . . . losing strings of 9 in 1948–49 broken with win over Lafayette 20–13 and in 1972–73 broken with win over Holy Cross 5–3 . . . consensus All-Americans were Frank Horr, T, 1908; Harold White, E, 1915; Alfred Cobb, T, 1917; Lou Usher, T, 1918; Joe Alexander, G, 1918–19; Pete McRae, E, 1923; Vic Hanson, E, 1926; Jim Brown, B, 1956; Roger Davis, G, 1959; Ernie Davis, B, 1960–61; Larry Csonka, B, 1967; Tim Green, DL, 1985; Don McPherson, QB, and Ted Gregory, DL, 1987; John Flannery, C, 1990; and Chris Gedney, TE, 1992 . . . Academic All-Americans were Fred Mautino, E, 1960; Howard Goodman, LB, 1971; Tony Romano, LB, 1983; and Tim Green, DL, 1984–85 . . . Heisman Trophy winner was Ernie Davis, HB, 1961 . . . Maxwell Award winner was Don McPherson, QB, 1987.

TEMPLE (Owls; Cherry and White)

NOTABLE TEAMS

1894 (4–1) *Won:* Philadelphia Dental College 14–6, First Regiment 26–0, Crescent A.C. 12–10, Central Pa. College 18–0. *Lost:* Ursinus 16–0. *Noteworthy:* 1st year of competition.
1903 (4–1) *Won:* Tioga A.C. 13–6, Medico 13–6, St. Joseph's 12–0, LaSalle 18–6. *Lost:* Trenton 6–0.
1907 (4–0–2) *Won:* Schuylkill Navy 21–5, Penn Military 17–6, Girard College 14–0, Loyola 13–12. *Tied:* St. Joseph's 5–5, Philadelphia Pharmacy

12–12. *Noteworthy:* resumed competition after 1–year layoff in only year under Horace Butterworth.
1911 (6–1) *Won:* Philadelphia Osteopathy 21–6, LaSalle 25–0, New York Aggies 18–12, Pratt Institute 6–0, Philadelphia Navy Yard 13–6, West Chester 7–0. *Lost:* Penn Military 30–0.
1915 (3–1–1) *Won:* Philadelphia Navy Yard 6–0, LaSalle 13–12, St. Joseph's 13–7. *Lost:* Schuylkill 21–0. *Tied:* Philadelphia Normal 0–0.
1927 (7–1) *Won:* Blue Ridge 110–0, Juniata 58–0, Gallaudet 62–0, Brown 7–0, Albright 13–0, Washington College 75–0, Bucknell 19–13 (1st meeting). *Lost:* Dartmouth 47–7.
1928 (7–1–2) *Won:* St. Thomas 12–0, Gallaudet 39–0, Western Maryland 7–0, Albright 32–0, Providence 41–0, Geneva 6–0, Washington College 73–6. *Lost:* Schuylkill 10–7. *Tied:* Villanova 0–0 (1st meeting since 1908), Bucknell 7–7.
1930 (7–3) *Won:* Thiel 13–6, St. Thomas 28–2, Bucknell 7–6, Washington & Jefferson 20–7, Wake Forest 36–0, Miami (Fla.) 34–0 (1st meeting), Lafayette 46–0. *Lost:* Villanova 8–7, Carnegie Tech 32–13, Drake 49–20.
1931 (8–1–1) *Won:* Mt. St. Mary's 33–0, Albright 19–7, Penn St. 12–0 (1st meeting), Haskell Institute 6–0, Washington & Jefferson 6–3, Villanova 13–7, Denver 18–0. *Lost:* Carnegie Tech 19–13. *Tied:* Bucknell 0–0. *Noteworthy:* beat Missouri 38–6 in postseason charity game in Kansas City.
1932 (5–1–2) *Won:* Thiel 31–0, West Virginia 14–13 (1st meeting), Bucknell 12–0, Denver 14–0, Penn St. 13–12. *Lost:* Villanova 7–0 in finale. *Tied:* Carnegie Tech 7–7, Haskell Institute 14–14. *Noteworthy:* Henry Miller's last team.
1934 (7–1–2) *Won:* Virginia Tech 34–0 (1st meeting), Texas A&M 40–6, West Virginia 28–13, Marquette 28–6, Holy Cross 14–0 (1st meeting), Carnegie Tech 34–6 (1st in 5-game series begun in 1930), Villanova 22–0. *Tied:* Indiana 6–6, Bucknell 0–0. *Noteworthy:* 1st unbeaten season since 1907. Lost to Tulane 20–14 in inaugural Sugar Bowl after taking 14–0 lead on TD pass from Glenn Frey to Danny Testa and 25-yd TD run by Dave Smukler.
1935 (7–3) *Won:* St. Joseph's 51–0, Centre 25–13, Texas A&M 14–0, Vanderbilt 6–3, Carnegie Tech 13–0, West Virginia 19–6, Marquette 26–6. *Lost:* Michigan St. 12–7, Villanova 21–14, Bucknell 7–6.
1941 (7–2) *Won:* Kansas 31–9, Virginia Military

Institute (VMI) 28–13, Georgetown 17–7, Penn St. 14–0, Bucknell 41–14, Villanova 14–13, Holy Cross 31–13. *Lost:* Boston College 31–0, Michigan St. 46–0.

1945 (7–1) *Won:* Syracuse 7–6, New York U. 59–0, Bucknell 64–0, West Virginia 28–12, Pittsburgh 6–0 (1st meeting since 1939), Lafayette 20–0, Holy Cross 14–6. *Lost:* Penn St. 27–0.

1964 (7–2) *Won:* Kings Point 34–9, Southern Connecticut 22–6, Boston U. 44–13 (1st meeting since 1955), Lafayette 38–18, Delaware 21–0 (1st over Blue Hens in 11 games since 1951), Gettysburg 32–20 (1st in 8-game series dating to 1956), Hofstra 21–6. *Lost:* Connecticut 25–7, Bucknell 31–28 in consecutive mid-season games.

1967 (7–2) *Won:* Kings Point 18–12, Boston U. 22–16, Hofstra 35–23, Delaware 26–17, Bucknell 13–8, Gettysburg 45–27, Akron 22–21. *Lost:* Buffalo 44–14, Dayton 56–6. *Noteworthy:* won Mid-Atlantic Conference title.

1970 (7–3) *Won:* Bucknell 10–3, Holy Cross 23–13 (1st meeting since 1955, 1st over Crusaders in 5 games since 1949), Boston U. 10–7, Connecticut 41–23, Xavier (Ohio) 28–15, Rhode Island 18–15, Buffalo 21–8 (1st in 10-game series dating to 1957). *Lost:* Akron 21–0, Delaware 15–13, Villanova 31–26 (1st meeting since 1943). *Star:* Bob Thornton (47 pass rec for 621 yds and 6 TDs). *Noteworthy:* 1st year under Wayne Hardin.

1971 (6–2–1) *Won:* Boston U. 34–10, Connecticut 38–0, Xavier (Ohio) 38–0, Delaware 32–27, Rhode Island 40–13, William & Mary 17–13. *Lost:* Boston College 17–3 (1st meeting since 1954), West Virginia 43–33 (1st meeting since 1948). *Tied:* Villanova 13–13. *Stars:* QB Doug Shobert (1,513 yds and 10 TDs pass), soph Randy Grossman (27 pass rec for 473 yds), Paul Loughran (5 TDs, 1,459 all-purpose yds, nation's kickoff return leader with 33.5-yd avg), K Nick Mike-Mayer (nation's leader with 12 FGs).

1973 (9–1) *Won:* Xavier (Ohio) 49–7, Akron 47–33, Holy Cross 63–34, Cincinnati 16–15 (1st meeting), Boston U. 35–15, Delaware 31–8, Rhode Island 43–0, Drake 35–10, Villanova 34–0. *Lost:* Boston College 45–0. *Stars:* Tom Sloan (1,036 yds rush), QB Steve Joachim (1,312 yds and 11 TDs pass), Grossman (39 pass rec for 683 yds), Henry Hynoski (10 TDs), Dwight Fulton (5 int).

1974 (8–2) *Won:* Rhode Island 38–7 (10th straight over Rams), Boston College 34–7 (1st over Eagles in 9 games since 1938), Marshall 31–10, Southern Illinois 59–16, Holy Cross 56–0, Delaware 21–17, West Virginia 35–21, Villanova 17–7. *Lost:* Cincinnati 22–20, Pittsburgh 35–24 (1st meeting since 1946) in consecutive late games. *Stars:* Maxwell Award–winner Joachim (nation's leader with 2,227 yds total off and in passing efficiency with 1,950 yds and 20 TDs), Pete Righi (35 pass rec for 608 yds and 8 TDs), Hynoski (1,006 yds and 7 TDs rush), K Don Bitterlich (71 pts), soph LB Joe Klecko, Bob Mizia (6 int).

1979 (10–2) *Won:* West Virginia 38–16, Drake 43–21, Delaware 31–14, Rutgers 41–20, Syracuse 49–17 (1st over Orange in 7 games since 1950), Cincinnati 35–14, Hawaii 34–31, Akron 42–6, Villanova 42–10. *Lost:* Pittsburgh 10–9, Penn St. 22–7. *Stars:* QB Brian Broomell (2,103 yds and 22 TDs pass), soph Gerald Lucear (45 pass rec for 964 yds and 13 TDs, 1,346 all-purpose yds), Mark Bright (1,036 yds and 7 TDs rush), soph LB Steve Conjar, Mark McCants (5 int), P Casey Murphy (43-yd avg). *Noteworthy:* made 1st bowl appearance in 45 years, beating California 28–17 in Garden State Bowl; Bright ran for 112 yds, Kevin Duckett ran for 92 yds and 2 TDs, and Broomell passed for other 2 TDs.

BOWL SUMMARY

Garden State 1–0; Sugar 0–1.

BOWL RECORD (1–1)

Regular Season	Bowl	Score	Opponent	Record
1934 (7–0–2)	Sugar	14–20	Tulane	(10–1)
1979 (9–2)	Garden State	28–17	California	(6–5)

CONFERENCE TITLES

Mid-Atlantic—1967. **Big East**—None.

TOP 20 AP AND UPI RANKING

1979	17–17

MAJOR RIVALS

Temple has played at least 10 games with Akron 7–4, Boston College 5–18–2, Boston U. 9–9–1, Bucknell 16–20–8, Buffalo 1–9, Carnegie Tech 4–6–1, Cincinnati 9–2–1, Delaware 13–23, Gettysburg 4–7–1, Hofstra 7–6, Holy Cross 9–12–2, Lafayette 8–1–1, LaSalle 8–1–3, Michigan St. 1–7–2, Muhlenberg 6–7, Penn Military 2–9, Penn St. 3–26–1, Pittsburgh 4–18–1, Rhode Island 11–0, Rutgers 10–12, St. Joseph's 6–4–4, Scranton 6–4, Syracuse 8–15–1, Villanova 12–13–2, West Virginia 11–13. Record against Big East foes met fewer than 10 times is Miami (Fla.) 1–1, Virginia Tech 2–4.

COACHES

Dean of Temple coaches is Wayne Hardin with record of 80–52–3 for 1970–82, including 1 Garden State Bowl champion. Other top records for at least 3 years were by H. Shindle Wingert, 13–9–3 for 1901–05 with 1 unbeaten team; Henry J. Miller, 50–15–8 for 1925–32; Glenn S. "Pop" Warner, 31–18–9 for 1933–38 with 1 Sugar Bowl team unbeaten in regular season; and George Makris, 45–44–4 for 1960–69 with 1 conference title.

MISCELLANEA

First game was win over Philadelphia Dental College 14–6 in 1894 . . . highest score was over Blue Ridge 110–0 in 1927 . . . highest since W.W. II was over Bucknell 82–28 in 1966 . . . biggest margin since W.W. II was over Holy Cross 56–0 in 1974 . . . worst defeat was by Franklin & Marshall 96–0 in 1899 . . . worst since 1900 was by

Pittsburgh 76–0 in 1977 . . . longest winning streak of 14 in 1973–74 ended by Cincinnati 22–20 . . . longest losing string of 21 in 1957–59 broken with win over Kings Point 26–13 in 1960 opener . . . consensus All-Americans were John Rienstra, OL, 1985; and Paul Palmer, RB, 1986 . . . Temple has had no 1st team Academic All-Americans . . . Maxwell Award winner was Steve Joachim, QB, 1974.

VIRGINIA TECH (Hokies, Gobblers; *Chicago Maroon and Burnt Orange*)

NOTABLE TEAMS

1894 (4–1) *Won:* Emory & Henry 16–0, Roanoke College 36–0 (1st meeting), St. Albans 42–0, 12–0. *Lost:* unbeaten Virginia Military Institute (VMI) 10–6 (1st meeting) in finale.

1896 (5–2–1) *Won:* Alleghany Institute 20–0, Roanoke 12–0, Hampden-Sydney 46–0 (1st meeting), Maryville 52–0, VMI 24–0. *Lost:* Virginia 44–0, Tennessee 6–4. *Tied:* North Carolina 0–0.

1897 (5–2) *Won:* King College 54–0, North Carolina 4–0, Roanoke 41–0, Richmond 36–0 (1st meeting), Hampden-Sydney 10–0. *Lost:* Maryland 18–4 (1st meeting), Tennessee 18–0.

1899 (4–1) *Won:* St. Albans 21–0, Tennessee 5–0, Roanoke 45–0, Washington & Lee (W&L) 35–0. *Lost:* Virginia 28–0.

1901 (6–1) *Won:* Roanoke 16–0, W&L 11–0, Georgetown 32–6, Clemson 17–11, Maryland 18–0, VMI 21–0. *Lost:* Virginia 16–0 in mid-season.

1903 (5–1) *Won:* St. Albans 29–0, N.C. State 21–0, North Carolina 21–0, Navy 11–0, VMI 17–5. *Lost:* Virginia 21–0.

1905 (9–1) *Won:* Roanoke 86–0, Cumberland 12–0, Army 16–6, Gallaudet 56–0, North Carolina 35–6, Virginia 11–0 (1st in 9-game series dating to

1895), W&L 15–0, South Carolina 34–0 (1st meeting), VMI 34–0. *Lost:* Navy 12–6.

1907 (7–2) *Won:* Roanoke 33–0, Hampden-Sydney 18–0 (1st meeting since 1897), W&L 5–0, Georgetown 20–0, VMI 22–0, George Washington 34–0 (1st meeting), North Carolina 20–6. *Lost:* Davidson 12–5, Navy 12–0.

1909 (6–1) *Won:* Clemson 6–0, Richmond 52–0, W&L 34–6, North Carolina 15–0, George Washington 17–8, N.C. State 18–5. *Lost:* Princeton 8–6 in 2nd game. *Noteworthy:* 1st year under Branch Bocock.

1910 (6–2) *Won:* Hampden-Sydney 18–0, Davidson 16–5, Western Maryland 13–0, W&L 23–0, North Carolina 20–0, George Washington 15–5. *Lost:* unbeaten Navy 3–0, unbeaten N.C. State 5–3.

1911 (6–1–2) *Won:* Hampden-Sydney 16–0, Maryland 12–0 (1st meeting since 1901), Roanoke 94–0, Tennessee 36–11, Morris Harvey 10–3, N.C. State 3–0. *Lost:* Yale 33–0. *Tied:* W&L 5–5, North Carolina 0–0. *Noteworthy:* only year under L.W. Reiss.

1913 (7–1–1) *Won:* Roanoke 26–0, Hampden-Sydney 14–0, Mississippi 34–13, VPI Stars 20–12, North Carolina 14–7, Marshall 47–0, Morris Harvey 14–0. *Lost:* W&L 21–0. *Tied:* VMI 6–6 (1st meeting since 1908).

1914 (6–2–1) *Won:* King College 35–0, Randolph-Macon 13–0 (1st meeting since 1893), Hampden-Sydney 22–0, Marshall 54–6, N.C. State 3–0, VMI 3–0. *Lost:* West Virginia Wesleyan 13–0, unbeaten W&L 7–6. *Tied:* Roanoke 7–7.

1916 (7–2) *Won:* Richmond 13–0 (1st meeting since 1909), Hampden-Sydney 10–0, N.C. State 40–0, North Carolina 14–7, Wake Forest 52–0 (1st meeting), Roanoke 41–0, VMI 23–14. *Lost:* West Virginia 20–0, Yale 19–0 in successive early games. *Noteworthy:* only year under Jack Ingersell.

1917 (6–2–1) *Won:* Hampden-Sydney 12–0, Emory & Henry 59–6, Davidson 13–7, Wake Forest 50–0, Roanoke 70–0, VMI 6–0. *Lost:* Georgetown 28–0, West Virginia 27–3. *Tied:* N.C. State 7–7. *Noteworthy:* 1st year under C.A. Bernier.

1918 (7–0) *Won:* Belmont Abbey 30–0, Camp Humphreys 33–6, W&L 13–0, Wake Forest 27–0, N.C. State 25–0, North Carolina 18–7, VMI 6–0. *Noteworthy:* outscored foes 152–13 in 1st unbeaten season.

1921 (7–3) *Won:* Hampden-Sydney 14–6 (15th straight over Tigers), William & Mary 14–0, Rich-

mond 34–0, Morris Harvey 54–7, N.C. State 7–3, Roanoke 35–0, VMI 26–7. *Lost:* unbeaten Centre 14–0, Maryland 10–7, W&L 3–0. *Noteworthy:* 1st year under B.C. Cubbage.

1922 (8–1–1) *Won:* Hampden-Sydney 38–0, King College 25–0, William & Mary 20–6, Catholic U. 73–0, Maryland 21–0, N.C. State 24–0, W&L 41–6, VMI 7–3. *Lost:* Centre 10–6. *Tied:* Davidson 7–7.

1928 (7–2) *Won:* Roanoke 34–7, Hampden-Sydney 32–7, North Carolina 16–14 (1st meeting since 1918), King College 54–0, Maryland 9–6, Virginia 20–0, W&L 13–7. *Lost:* Colgate 35–14, VMI 16–6.

1932 (8–1) *Won:* Roanoke 32–7, Georgia 7–6, Maryland 23–0, William & Mary 7–0, Kentucky 7–0, W&L 32–6, Virginia 13–0, VMI 26–0. *Lost:* Alabama 9–6 (1st meeting). *Noteworthy:* 1st year under H.B. Redd.

1942 (7–2–1) *Won:* Catawba 28–14, Furman 7–6, Davidson 16–0, W&L 19–6, Virginia 20–14, Richmond 16–7, VMI 20–6. *Lost:* William & Mary 21–7, Army 19–7. *Tied:* Kentucky 21–21. *Noteworthy:* 1st year under wartime coach H.M. McEver.

1943–1944—No team, due to W.W. II.

1954 (8–0–1) *Won:* N.C. State 30–21, Wake Forest 32–0 (1st meeting since 1919), Clemson 18–7 (1st meeting since 1946, 1st over Tigers in 5 games since 1924), Richmond 19–12, Virginia 6–0, George Washington 20–13 (1st over Colonials in 6 games since 1947), Waynesburg 20–6, VMI 46–9. *Tied:* William & Mary 7–7. *Stars:* Dickie Beard (647 yds rush), QB Billy Cranwell, E Tom Petty (9 pass rec for 236 yds and 5 TDs), T George Preas. *Noteworthy:* 1st unbeaten season since 1918.

1956 (7–2–1) *Won:* East Carolina 37–2, N.C. State 35–6, Florida St. 20–7, William & Mary 34–7, Richmond 46–14, Virginia 14–7, VMI 45–0. *Lost:* Tulane 21–14, Clemson 21–6. *Tied:* Wake Forest 13–13. *Star:* QB Jimmy Lugar (8 TDs), frosh E Carroll Dale.

1963 (8–2) *Won:* Wake Forest 27–0, Virginia 10–0, George Washington 22–8, William & Mary 28–13, Florida St. 31–23, Richmond 14–13, West Virginia 28–3, VMI 35–20. *Lost:* Kentucky 32–14 (1st meeting since 1942), N.C. State 13–7. *Stars:* QB Bob Schweickert (839 yds and 7 TDs rush, 687 yds and 6 TDs pass, 39.1-yd punting avg), Tommy Marvin (28 pass rec for 303 yds), B Sonny Utz (10 TDs). *Noteworthy:* Won only SC title.

E Carroll Dale, 1956–59

1965 (7–3) *Won:* Wake Forest 12–3, Richmond 25–7, William & Mary 9–7, George Washington 17–12, Virginia 22–14, Villanova 21–19, VMI 44–13. *Lost:* Vanderbilt 21–10 (1st meeting since 1930), Florida St. 7–6, West Virginia 31–22. *Stars:* QB Bobby Owens (1,417 yds total off, 7 TDs rush), soph Gene Fisher (30 pass rec for 387 yds).

1966 (8–2–1) *Won:* George Washington 49–0, Kentucky 7–0, Vanderbilt 21–6, Virginia 24–7, Florida St. 23–21, Wake Forest 11–0, William & Mary 20–18, VMI 70–12. *Lost:* Tulane 13–0 in opener. *Tied:* West Virginia 13–13. *Stars:* TB Tommy Francisco (753 yds rush, 14 TDs), QB Tommy Stafford (1,193 yds total off), TE Ken Barefoot (22 pass rec for 267 yds), DE George Foussekis, DB Frank Loria. *Noteworthy:* Lost to Miami (Fla.) 14–7 (1st meeting since 1953) in Liberty Bowl after taking early 7–0 lead following blocked punt.

1967 (7–3) *Won:* Tampa 13–3, William & Mary 31–7, Kansas St. 15–3, Villanova 3–0, Kentucky 24–14, Richmond 45–14, West Virginia 20–7 in 1st 7 games. *Lost:* Miami (Fla.) 14–7, Florida St. 38–15, VMI 12–10 (1st to Keydets since 1962). *Stars:* Barefoot (26 pass rec for 225 yds), K John Utin (10 FGs), Loria (1st VPI consensus All-American), DB Ron Davidson (9 int).

1968 (7–4) *Won:* William & Mary 12–0, Wake Forest 7–6, West Virginia 27–12, Florida St. 40–22, Richmond 31–18, South Carolina 17–6 (1st meeting since 1936), VMI 55–6. *Lost:* Alabama 14–7 (1st meeting since 1952), Kansas St. 34–19, Miami (Fla.) 13–8. *Stars:* Terry Smoot (820 yds and 8 TDs rush), Danny Cupp (21 pass rec for 323 yds), LB Mike Widger. *Noteworthy:* lost to Mississippi 34–17 in Liberty Bowl after taking 17–0 lead in 1st quarter; TB Ken Edwards ran for 119 yds and a TD, and Smoot ran for 91 yds and other Tech TD.

1975 (8–3) *Won:* Richmond 21–9, Auburn 23–16, Florida St. 13–10, Virginia 24–17, William & Mary 24–7, Houston 34–28, VMI 33–0, Wake Forest 40–10. *Lost:* Kentucky 27–8, Kent St. 17–11, West Virginia 10–7. *Stars:* soph RB Roscoe Coles (1,045 yds and 10 TDs rush), Phil Rogers (1,141 yds total off), Steve Galloway (18 pass rec for 378 yds).

DT Bruce Smith, 1982–84

1980 (8–4) *Won:* Wake Forest 16–7, East Tennessee St. 35–7, William & Mary 7–3, James Madison 38–6 (1st meeting), Rhode Island 34–7, Virginia 30–0, West Virginia 34–11, VMI 21–6. *Lost:* Clemson 13–10, Richmond 18–7, Florida St. 31–7. *Stars:* QB Steve Casey (1,119 yds and 13 TDs pass), Sidney Snell (43 pass rec for 568 yds and 8 TDs), RB Cyrus Lawrence (1,221 yds and 8 TDs rush), P Dave Smigelsky (39.8-yd avg). *Noteworthy:* lost to Miami (Fla.) 20–10 (1st meeting since 1974) in Peach Bowl; Lawrence scored on 1-yd run and Dennis Laury kicked 42-yd FG.

1983 (9–2) *Won:* Memphis St. 17–10, VMI 28–0, Louisville 31–0, Duke 27–14, Richmond 38–0, William & Mary 59–21, Tulane 26–10, Vanderbilt 21–10, Virginia 48–0. *Lost:* Wake Forest 13–6,

West Virginia 13–0. *Stars:* DT Bruce Smith, QB Mark Cox (1,188 yds pass), Mike Shaw (23 pass rec for 357 yds), Otis Copeland (709 yds and 7 TDs rush), soph P David Cox (41-yd avg). *Noteworthy:* Led nation in rush defense and scoring defense (8.3-pt avg).

1984 (8–4) *Won:* Wake Forest 21–20, Richmond 21–13, VMI 54–7, Duke 27–0, William & Mary 38–14, Temple 9–7 (1st meeting since 1934), Tulane 13–6, Vanderbilt 23–3. *Lost:* West Virginia 14–7, Virginia 26–23 (1st to Cavaliers since 1979), Clemson 17–10. *Stars:* Outland Trophy–winner Smith, DB Ashley Lee (7 int), Mark Cox (1,057 yds total off), Joe Jones (39 pass rec for 452 yds), soph RB Maurice Williams (574 yds and 6 TDs rush), K Don Wade (12 FGs), P David Cox (41.9-yd avg). *Noteworthy:* lost to Air Force 23–7 in Independence Bowl; Williams scored on 3-yd run.

1986 (10–1–1) *Won:* Clemson 20–14 (1st over Tigers in 10 games since 1954), Syracuse 26–17, East Tennessee St. 37–10, West Virginia 13–7 (1st over Mountaineers since 1980), Temple (by forfeit after losing 29–14 on field), Virginia 42–10, Kentucky 17–15, Richmond 17–10, Vanderbilt 29–21. *Lost:* Cincinnati 24–20 in opener. *Tied:* South Carolina 27–27 (1st meeting since 1974). *Stars:* Williams (1,029 yds and 6 TDs rush), Eddie Hunter (1,395 all-purpose yds), QB Erik Chapman (1,627 yds and 10 TDs pass), Donald Snell (34 pass rec for 661 yds and 6 TDs), soph K Chris Kinzer (22 FGs, 93 pts). *Noteworthy:* Bill Dooley's last team. Beat N.C. State 25–24 (1st meeting since 1964) in Peach Bowl (1st bowl win in 6 tries) as Kinzer kicked 40-yd FG on last play of game (to go with 46-yarder in 1st quarter); Williams ran for 129 yds and a TD, Hunter ran for 113 yds and a TD, and Chapman passed 6 yds to TE Steve Johnson for other Tech TD.

Bowl Summary

Independence 0–1; Liberty 0–2; Peach 1–1; Sun 0–1.

Bowl Record (1–5)

Regular Season	Bowl	Score	Opponent	Record
1946 (3–3–3)	Sun	6–18	Cincinnati	(8–2)
1966 (8–1–1)	Liberty	7–14	Miami (Fla.)	(7–2–1)

(continued)

Regular Season	Bowl	Score	Opponent	Record
1968 (7–3)	Liberty	17–34	Mississippi	(6–3–1)
1980 (8–3)	Peach	10–20	Miami (Fla.)	(8–3)
1984 (8–3)	Independence	7–23	Air Force	(7–4)
1986 (8–2–1)	Peach	25–24	N.C. State	(8–2–1)

CONFERENCE TITLES

Southern—1963. **Big East**—None.

TOP 20 AP AND UPI RANKING

1966	U–20	1986	20–U

MAJOR RIVALS

Virginia Tech has played at least 10 games with Alabama 0–10, Clemson 7–17–1, Davidson 10–3–1, Duke 4–7, Florida St. 10–18–1, George Washington 11–8, Hampden-Sydney 24–0, Kentucky 6–11–2, Maryland 10–15, Miami (Fla.) 0–10, North Carolina 11–8–6, N.C. State 23–17–4, Richmond 37–10–4, Roanoke 25–0–2, South Carolina 7–11–2, Virginia 36–33–5, VMI 49–25–5, Wake Forest 20–11–1, Washington & Lee 23–20–5, West Virginia 13–24–1, William & Mary 39–18–4. Record against Big East foes met fewer than 10 times is Boston College 0–0 (no games played), Pittsburgh 0–0 (no games played), Rutgers 0–3, Syracuse 2–4, Temple 4–2.

COACHES

Deans of Virginia Tech coaches are Frank Moseley and Jerry Claiborne with 10 years each. Moseley was 54–42–4 for 1951–60 with 1 unbeaten team; Claiborne was 61–39–2 for 1961–70 with 1 SC title and 2 bowl teams. Most wins were under Bill Dooley, 64–37–1 for 1978–86 with 3 bowl teams. Other top records for at least 3 years were by Branch B. Bocock, 34–14–2 for 1909–10 and 1912–15; Charles A. Bernier, 18–6–1 for 1917–19 with 1 perfect record; Ben C. Cubbage, 30–12–6 for 1921–25; Andy Gustafson, 22–13–1 for 1926–29; H.B. Redd, 43–37–8 for 1932–40; and James R. Kitts, 13–13–3 for 1941 and 1946–47 with 1 bowl team.

MISCELLANEA

First game was win over St. Albans 14–10 in 1892 . . . highest score was over Emory & Henry 99–0 in 1919 . . . highest since W.W. II was over VMI 70–12 in 1966 . . . worst defeat was by Alabama 77–6 in 1973 . . . longest unbeaten string of 12 in 1917–19 ended by Georgetown 33–7 . . . longest winless string of 18 in 1947–49 broken with win over Richmond 28–13 . . . consensus All-Americans were Frank Loria, DB, 1967; and Bruce Smith, DT, 1984 . . . Academic All-Americans were Frank Loria, DB, 1967; and Tommy Carpenito, LB, 1972 . . . Outland Trophy winner was Bruce Smith, DT, 1984.

WEST VIRGINIA (Mountaineers; Old Gold and Blue)

NOTABLE TEAMS

1895 (5–1) *Won:* Mt. Pleasant 6–0, Latrobe Independents 10–0, Pittsburgh 8–0 (1st meeting), Marietta 6–0, Washington & Lee (W&L) 28–6 (1st meeting). *Lost:* Washington & Jefferson (W&J) 4–0.

1898 (6–1) *Won:* Westminster 24–0, Marietta 6–5, 6–0, Pittsburgh 6–0, Virginia 6–0 (1st meeting), Ohio U. 16–0. *Lost:* Pittsburgh A.C. 18–0.

1903 (7–1) *Won:* Pittsburgh 24–6, Grove City 21–0, Marietta 18–0, West Virginia Wesleyan 39–0, Westminster 21–0, Bethany 11–5, W&J 6–0 (1st score and 1st win in 9-game series dating to

1891).   *Lost:* Ohio St. 34–6.   *Star:* B Paul Martin.
1905 (8–1)   *Won:* Westminster 15–0, California
(Pa.) 12–0, 17–10, Ohio U. 28–0, Bethany 46–0,
24–0, Kentucky 45–0 (1st meeting), Marietta 17–6.
Lost: Penn St. 6–0.   *Noteworthy:* 1st year under
Carl Forkum.
1919 (8–2)   *Won:* Marietta 61–0, Westminster 55–0,
Maryland 27–0 (1st meeting), Bethany 60–0, Princeton 25–0, Rutgers 30–7, Ohio Wesleyan 55–0,
W&J 7–0.   *Lost:* Pittsburgh 26–0, unbeaten Centre
14–6.   *Stars:* FB Ira Errett "Rat" Rodgers (Mountaineers' 1st consensus All-American; nation's
leader with 147 pts and 19 TDs), C Russ Bailey,
T Joe Harrick.   *Noteworthy:* Resumed competition after 1-year layoff due to flu epidemic and
W.W. I.
1922 (10–0–1) *Won:* West Virginia Wesleyan
20–3, Marietta 55–0, Pittsburgh 9–6 (1st over Panthers in 12 games since 1903), Rutgers 28–0,
Cincinnati 34–0, Indiana 33–0, Virginia 13–0, Ohio
U. 28–0, W&J 14–0.   *Tied:* W&L 12–12.   *Stars:* T
Russ Meredith, G Joe Setron, soph E Fred Graham,
soph HB Nick Nardacci, soph B Gus Ekberg.
Noteworthy: 1st unbeaten season. Made 1st post-
season appearance, beating Gonzaga 21–13 in San
Diego East-West Christmas Classic; Nardacci ran
for 120 yds and a TD and passed 16 yds to Jack
Simons for another, and Meredith scored on 80-yd
pass int return.
1923 (7–1–1)   *Won:* West Virginia Wesleyan 21–7,
Allegheny 28–0, Pittsburgh 13–7, Marshall 81–0,
Rutgers 27–7, W&L 63–0, St. Louis 49–0.   *Lost:*
W&J 7–2 in finale.   *Tied:* Penn St. 13–13 (in New
York, 1st meeting since 1909).   *Stars:* Nardacci,
Ekberg, E Charles Tallman.
1924 (8–1)   *Won:* West Virginia Wesleyan 21–6
(1st game in old Mountaineer Field), Allegheny
35–6, Centre 13–6, Geneva 55–0, Bethany 71–6,
Colgate 34–2, W&L 6–0, W&J 40–7.   *Lost:* Pittsburgh 14–7.   *Stars:* Nardacci, Graham, G Walter
"Red" Mahan, soph B Francis "Skeets" Farley.
Noteworthy: Dr. Clarence Spears' last team.
1925 (8–1)   *Won:* Allegheny 18–0, Davis & Elkins
6–0, Grove City 54–3 (1st meeting since 1906), West
Virginia Wesleyan 16–0, W&L 21–0, Boston College 20–0 (1st meeting), Penn St. 14–0 (1st in
7-game series dating to 1904), W&J 19–0.   *Lost:*
Pittsburgh 15–7.   *Stars:* Mahan, Farley, T Carl
Davis.   *Noteworthy:* 1st year under Ira Rodgers.
1928 (8–2)   *Won:* West Virginia Wesleyan 12–0,
Haskell Institute 28–7, Pittsburgh 9–6 (1st over

Panthers since 1923), W&L 22–0, Lafayette 17–0,
Fordham 18–0 (1st meeting), Oklahoma A&M
32–6, W&J 14–0.   *Lost:* Davis & Elkins 7–0 (1st in
7-game series dating to 1913), Georgetown 12–0.
Stars: HB Marshall "Little Sleepy" Glenn, T Wally
Brewster.
1937 (8–1–1)   *Won:* West Virginia Wesleyan 14–0,
W&L 6–0, Xavier (Ohio) 13–7, Waynesburg 13–0,
Western Maryland 64–0, Toledo 34–0, George
Washington 26–0.   *Lost:* unbeaten national cochamp Pittsburgh 20–0.   *Tied:* Georgetown 6–6.
Stars: QB Emmett "Kelly" Moan, soph HB Harry
"Flash" Clarke (816 yds rush), G Alex Atty, soph
T Al Baisi.   *Noteworthy:* 1st year under Marshall
Glenn. Beat Texas Tech 7–6 in Sun Bowl; Clarke
ran for 132 yds, Davey Isaac scored on 1-yd run,
and Moan kicked winning ex pt.
1948 (9–3)   *Won:* Waynesburg 29–16, Wooster
34–6, Temple 27–7, W&L 14–7, South Carolina
35–12, Ohio U. 48–6, Western Reserve 20–0, Maryland 16–14.   *Lost:* Pittsburgh 16–6, Penn St. 37–7,
Virginia 7–0.   *Stars:* QB Jimmy Walthall (1,222 yds
and 13 TDs pass), Vic Bonfili (6 TDs, 535 yds rush,
24 pass rec for 244 yds), FB Pete Zinaich (513 yds
rush), soph drop-kicking specialist Gene Simmons.
Noteworthy: 1st year under Dud DeGroot. Beat
Texas Mines (Texas–El Paso) 21–12 in Sun Bowl;
Walthall passed for 122 yds and a TD (25 yards
to Clarence Cox), and Jim Devonshire ran for 2
TDs.
1952 (7–2)   *Won:* Waynesburg 49–12, W&L 31–13,
Pittsburgh 16–0 (1st over Panthers since 1947),
George Washington 24–0, Virginia Military Institute (VMI) 39–21 (1st meeting), Virginia Tech 27–7
(1st meeting since 1917), South Carolina 13–6.
Lost: Furman 22–14, Penn St. 35–21 in early games.
Stars: frosh QB Fred Wyant (1,049 yds and 13 TDs
total off), HB/K Jack Stone (6 TDs, 60 pts), Es Paul
Bischoff (31 pass rec for 402 yds) and Bill Marker
(19 pass rec for 282 yds), OT Ben Dunkerley, DB
Bob Snider.
1953 (8–2)   *Won:* Pittsburgh 17–7, Waynesburg
47–19, W&L 40–14, George Washington 27–6, VMI
52–20, Penn St. 20–19 (1st over Nittany Lions in
7 games since 1944), Virginia Tech 12–7, N.C. State
61–0 (1st meeting since 1917).   *Lost:* South Carolina 20–14.   *Stars:* Wyant, Marker (16 pass rec for
301 yds), Stone (5 TDs, 49 pts), FB Tommy Allman
(501 yds rush), soph HB Joe Marconi (5 TDs), C
Bob Orders, G Gene Lamone, soph T Bruce Bosley.
Noteworthy: Won 1st SC title. Lost to Georgia Tech

T Sam Huff, 1952–55

42–19 in Sugar Bowl, losing ball 5 times on fumbles; scored TDs on short runs by Danny Williams, Marconi, and Allman.

1954 (8–1) *Won:* South Carolina 26–6, George Washington 13–7, Penn St. 19–14, VMI 40–6, Fordham 39–9, William & Mary 20–6 (1st meeting), N.C. State 28–3, Virginia 14–10 (1st over Cavaliers in 9 games since 1922). *Lost:* Pittsburgh 13–10 in mid-season. *Stars:* Wyant (8 TDs rush), Marconi, Lamone, Bosley, E Billy Hillen, C Chick Donaldson. *Noteworthy:* repeated as SC champ.

1955 (8–2) *Won:* Richmond 33–12, Wake Forest 46–0, VMI 47–12, William & Mary 39–13, Penn St. 21–7, Marquette 39–0, George Washington 13–7, N.C. State 27–7. *Lost:* Pittsburgh 26–7, Syracuse 20–13 (1st meeting since 1946) in consecutive late games. *Stars:* Wyant, HB Bobby Moss (807 yds and 10 TDs rush), Marconi (7 TDs), Bosley, T Sam Huff, Gs Gene Lathey and soph Chuck Howley. *Noteworthy:* won 3rd straight SC title.

1957 (7–2–1) *Won:* Virginia Tech 14–0, Boston U.

46–6, George Washington 34–14, William & Mary 19–0, Pittsburgh 7–6, Wake Forest 27–14, Syracuse 7–0. *Lost:* Wisconsin 45–13, Penn St. 27–6. *Tied:* Virginia 6–6. *Stars:* FB Larry Krutko (5 TDs), Howley, HB/P Ralph Anastasio.

1962 (8–2) *Won:* Vanderbilt 26–0, Virginia Tech 14–0, Boston U. 7–0, Pittsburgh 15–8, George Washington 27–25, William & Mary 28–13, The Citadel 49–0, Syracuse 17–6 (1st over Orangemen since 1957). *Lost:* Oregon St. 51–22, Penn St. 34–6. *Stars:* QB Jerry Yost (1,134 yds and 11 TDs pass, 1,361 yds and 16 TDs total off), Es Gene Heeter (19 pass rec for 284 yds) and Ken Herock, FB Glenn Holton (6 TDs), C Pete Goimarac.

1964 (7–4) *Won:* Richmond 20–10, The Citadel 7–3, Virginia Tech 23–10, Kentucky 26–21 (1st meeting since 1947), George Washington 20–19, William & Mary 24–14, Syracuse 28–27. *Lost:* Rice 24–0, Pittsburgh 14–0, Penn St. 37–8. *Stars:* QB Allen McCune (1,034 yds and 11 TDs pass), TE Milt Clegg (31 pass rec for 437 yds), Bob Dunlevy (18 pass rec for 279 yds), FB Dick Leftridge (534 yds and 5 TDs rush), WB Dick Madison (5 TDs, 15 pass rec for 240 yds). *Noteworthy:* Won 6th SC title. Lost to Utah 32–6 in Liberty Bowl (indoors at Atlantic City, N.J.); scored on 6-yd pass from McCune to Clegg.

1968 (7–3) *Won:* Richmond 17–0, Pittsburgh 38–15, VMI 14–7, William & Mary 20–0, The Citadel 17–0, Villanova 30–20, Syracuse 23–6. *Lost:* unbeaten Penn St. 31–20 (10th straight to Nittany Lions), Virginia Tech 27–12, Kentucky 35–16. *Stars:* soph QB Mike Sherwood (1,998 yds and 12 TDs pass), WR Oscar Patrick (50 pass rec for 770 yds and 5 TDs), soph FL Wayne Porter (37 pass rec for 493 yds), soph Jim Braxton (18 pass rec for 276 yds), RB Eddie Silverio (559 yds and 7 TDs rush), MG Carl Crennel, DE Bob Starford (5 fumble recoveries).

1969 (10–1) *Won:* Cincinnati 57–11 (1st meeting since 1940), Maryland 31–7 (1st over Terps in 7 games since 1948), Tulane 35–17 (1st meeting), VMI 32–0, Pittsburgh 49–18, Kentucky 7–6, William & Mary 31–0, Richmond 33–21, Syracuse 13–10. *Lost:* unbeaten Penn St. 20–0. *Stars:* Crennel, DBs Mike Slater (7 int) and Ron Pobolish (5 int), Sherwood, RB Bob Gresham (10 TDs, 1,155 yds rush, 15 pass rec for 147 yds), FBs Braxton (843 yds rush, 13 TDs, 113 pts) and Eddie Williams (589 yds rush). *Noteworthy:* Jim Carlen's last year. Beat South Carolina 14–3 (1st meeting since 1954) in Peach Bowl; Williams ran for 208 yds, Gresham ran for 98 yds and a TD, and Braxton scored other Mountaineer TD.

1970 (8–3) *Won:* William & Mary 43–7, Richmond 49–10, VMI 47–10, Indiana 16–10, Colorado St. 24–21, East Carolina 28–14 (1st meeting), Syracuse 28–19, Maryland 20–10. *Lost:* Duke 21–13, Pittsburgh 36–35, Penn St. 42–8. *Stars:* Sherwood (1,550 yds and 15 TDs pass, 5 TDs rush), Gresham (866 yds rush, 8 TDs), FB Pete Wood (713 yds rush, 7 TDs), Williams (524 yds and 5 TDs rush), TE Braxton (27 pass rec for 565 yds and 8 TDs, 9 TDs total, 75 pts), WB Chris Potts (31 pass rec for 346 yds), LB Dale Farley. *Noteworthy:* 1st year under Bobby Bowden.

1972 (8–4) *Won:* Villanova 25–6, Richmond 28–7, Virginia 48–10 (1st meeting since 1965), William & Mary 49–34, Tulane 31–19, Pittsburgh 38–20, VMI 50–24, Syracuse 43–12. *Lost:* Stanford 41–35, Temple 39–36, Penn St. 28–19. *Stars:* QB Bernie Galiffa (2,496 yds and 17 TDs pass), soph WRs Danny Buggs (35 pass rec for 791 yds and 8 TDs, 1,362 all-purpose yds, 14 TDs) and Marshall Mills (39 pass rec for 445 yds), FLs Nate Stephens (36 pass rec for 577 yds) and Bernie Kirchner (23 pass rec for 280 yds), RB Kerry Marbury (775 yds rush, 18 TDs), FB Brian Chiles (6 TDs), C Gerald Schultze, K Frank Nester (11 FGs, 81 pts), DB Tom Geishauser (7 int). *Noteworthy:* lost to N.C. State 49–13 (1st meeting since 1955) in Peach Bowl after taking 13–7 1st quarter lead; scored on 2 FGs by Nester and short TD pass from Galiffa to Buggs.

1975 (9–3) *Won:* Temple 50–7, California 28–10, Boston College 35–18, Southern Methodist (SMU) 28–25, Virginia Tech 10–7, Kent St. 38–13, Pittsburgh 17–14, Richmond 31–13. *Lost:* Penn St. 39–0, Tulane 16–14, Syracuse 20–19. *Stars:* RBs Artie Owens (1,055 yds rush, 6 TDs) and Dwayne Woods (6 TDs rush), FBs Ron Lee (623 yds and 10 TDs rush) and Heywood Smith (5 TDs rush), soph QB Dan Kendra (1,315 yds pass), soph WR Steve Lewis (21 pass rec for 296 yds), FL Scott MacDonald (20 pass rec for 392 yds), TE Randy Swinson (19 pass rec for 282 yds), DT Chuck Smith, LBs Ray Marshall and Steve Dunlap, soph DB Tom Pridemore (5 int). *Noteworthy:* Bowden's last team. Beat N.C. State 13–10 in Peach Bowl on 50-yd pass from Kendra (202 yds pass) to MacDonald with 7 minutes left; scored on last play of 1st half on 39-yd pass from Kendra to Owens.

1981 (9–3) *Won:* Virginia 32–18, Maryland 17–13, Colorado St. 49–3, Boston College 38–10, Virginia Tech 27–6, East Carolina 20–3 (1st meeting since 1971), Temple 24–19, Rutgers 20–3. *Lost:* Pittsburgh 17–0, Penn St. 30–7, Syracuse 27–24. *Stars:* QB Oliver Luck (2,448 yds and 16 TDs pass), TE Mark Raugh (64 pass rec for 601 yds), RBs Mickey Walczak (49 pass rec for 338 yds and 6 TDs) and Dane Conwell (5 TDs), soph WR Rich Hollins (37 pass rec for 754 yds and 6 TDs), LBs Darryl Talley and Dennis Fowlkes, DB Lind Murray (6 int). *Noteworthy:* upset Florida 26–6 in Peach Bowl; Luck passed for 107 yds and a TD (to Walczak, who also scored on 1-yd run), frosh K Paul Woodside kicked 4 FGs (including 42 and 49 yds), and Fowlkes, Talley, and DBs Steve Newberry, Tim Agee and Don Stemple sparked defense.

1982 (9–3) *Won:* Oklahoma 41–27, Maryland 19–18, Richmond 43–10, Boston College 20–13, Virginia Tech 16–6, East Carolina 30–3, Temple 20–17, Rutgers 44–17, Syracuse 26–0 (1st over Orange since 1976). *Lost:* Pittsburgh 16–13, national champ Penn St. 24–0. *Stars:* QB Jeff Hostetler (1,798 yds and 10 TDs pass), Raugh (32 pass rec for 423 yds), Darrell Miller (29 pass rec for 465 yds), Woodside (110 pts, nation's leader with 28 FGs), Talley, Fowlkes, Agee, soph WR and kick returner Willie Drewrey, frosh P Steve Superick (42.1-yd avg). *Noteworthy:* lost to Florida St. 31–12 in Gator Bowl, scoring on 2 Woodside FGs and 26-yd pass from soph QB Kevin White to Miller.

1983 (9–3) *Won:* Ohio U. 55–3 (1st meeting since 1949), Pacific 48–7, Maryland 31–21, Boston College 27–17, Pittsburgh 24–21 (1st over Panthers since 1975), Virginia Tech 13–0, Temple 27–9, Rutgers 35–7. *Lost:* Penn St. 41–23 (25th straight to Nittany Lions), national champ Miami (Fla.) 20–3 (1st meeting since 1974), Syracuse 27–16. *Stars:* Hostetler (2,345 yds and 16 TDs pass), Hollins (50 pass rec for 781 yds and 5 TDs), TE Rob Bennett (24 pass rec for 343 yds), FL Gary Mullen (20 pass rec for 363 yds), soph TB Tom Gray (6 TDs), Woodside (21 FGs, 100 pts), MG Dave Oblak, Agee, Newberry, Drewrey, Superick (40.5-yd punting avg). *Noteworthy:* beat Kentucky 20–16 in Hall of Fame Bowl; Gray ran for 149 yds, Hostetler passed for 2 TDs (to Hollins and Bennett), and Woodside kicked 2 FGs.

1984 (8–4) *Won:* Ohio U. 38–0, Louisville 30–6 (1st meeting), Virginia Tech 14–7, Pittsburgh 28–

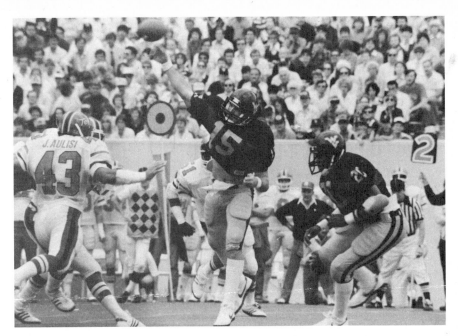

QB Jeff Hostetler, 1982–83

10, Syracuse 20–10, Boston College 21–20, Penn St. 17–14 (1st over Nittany Lions since 1955). *Lost:* Maryland 20–17, Virginia 27–7 (1st to Cavaliers in 7 games since 1965), Rutgers 23–19 (1st to Scarlet Knights in 7 games since 1921), Temple 19–17. *Stars:* White (1,727 yds pass), Drewrey (36 pass rec for 594 yds), Mullen (31 pass rec for 557 yds), Bennett, TE Todd Fisher (21 pass rec for 205 yds), FB Ron Wolfley (5 TDs), RB John Gay (5 TDs), OT Brian Jozwiak, Woodside (15 FGs, 73 pts), LBs Fred Smalls and Matt Smith, Superick (42.1-yd punting avg). *Noteworthy:* beat Texas Christian (TCU) 31–14 in Bluebonnet Bowl; White passed for 3 TDs (to Gay, Mullen, and Wolfley) and Drewrey caught 6 passes for 152 yds.

1988 (11–1) *Won:* Bowling Green 62–14, Cal St.–Fullerton 45–10, Maryland 55–24 (1st over Terps since 1983), Pittsburgh 31–10, Virginia Tech 22–10, East Carolina 30–10, Boston College 59–19, Penn St. 51–30, Cincinnati 51–13, Rutgers 35–25, Syracuse 31–9. *Stars:* soph QB Major Harris (1,915 yds and 14 TDs pass, 610 yds and 6 TDs rush), WRs Calvin Phillips (24 pass rec for 611 yds) and Reggie Rembert (23 pass rec for 516 yds and 7 TDs, 3 TDs rush), TBs Anthony B. Brown (962 yds and 7 TDs rush) and Undra Johnson (709 yds rush, 12 TDs), FB Craig Taylor (10 TDs), OTs Rick Phillips and Brian Smider, OG John Stroia, C Kevin Koken, K Charlie Baumann (20 FGs, 119 pts), DT Chris Parker, LBs Chris Haering, Theron Ellis and Renaldo Turnbull, DBs Bo Orlando, Alvoid Mays (5 int) and frosh Darrell Whitmore, P Lance Carion (41.7-yd avg). *Noteworthy:* One of nation's most-improved teams outscored foes 472–174 in 1st unbeaten season since 1922 and won 1st Lambert Trophy. Lost national championship game to unbeaten Notre Dame 34–21 in Fiesta Bowl; Harris (despite early injury) passed for 166 yds and a TD, Baumann kicked 2 FGs, and Rembert scored on 3-yd run.

1989 (8–3–1) *Won:* Ball St. 35–10, Maryland 14–10, South Carolina 45–21, Louisville 30–21, Cincinnati 69–3, Boston College 44–30, Rutgers 21–20, Syracuse 24–17. *Lost:* Virginia Tech 12–10, Penn St. 19–9. *Tied:* Pittsburgh 31–31. *Stars:* Harris (1,939 yds and 16 TDs pass, 919 yds and 6 TDs rush), Rembert (43 pass rec for 793 yds and 11 TDs), WR Greg Dykes (23 pass rec for 400 yds), TE Adrian Moss (21 pass rec for 321 yds), frosh RBs Garrett Ford Jr. (688 yds and 6 TDs rush) and

QB Major Harris, 1987–89

Carl Hayes (5 TDs), K Brad Carroll (11 FGs, 71 pts), DT Mike Fox, Haering, Turnbull, Ellis, soph LB Steve Grant, DB Preston Waters (6 int), P Greg Hertzog (43-yd avg). *Noteworthy:* lost to Clemson 27–7 in Gator Bowl; Harris passed for 119 yds and a TD (12 yds to frosh WR James Jett in 1st quarter) but had 3 int.

BOWL SUMMARY

Bluebonnet 1–0; Fiesta 0–1; Gator 0–2; Hall of Fame 1–0; John Hancock Sun 0–1; Liberty 0–1; Peach 3–1; San Diego East-West Christmas Classic 1–0; Sugar 0–1; Sun 2–0.

BOWL RECORD (8–7)

Regular Season	Bowl	Score	Opponent	Record
1922 (9–0–1)	East-West	21–13	Gonzaga	(5–2)
1937 (7–1–1)	Sun	7–6	Texas Tech	(8–3)
1948 (8–3)	Sun	21–12	Texas–El Paso	(8–1–1)
1953 (8–1)	Sugar	19–42	Georgia Tech	(8–2–1)
1964 (7–3)	Liberty	6–32	Utah	(8–2)
1969 (9–1)	Peach	14–3	South Carolina	(7–3)
1972 (8–3)	Peach	13–49	N.C. State	(7–3–1)
1975 (8–3)	Peach	13–10	N.C. State	(7–3–1)
1981 (8–3)	Peach	26–6	Florida	(7–4)

(continued)

Regular Season	Bowl	Score	Opponent	Record
1982 (9–2)	Gator	12–31	Florida State	(8–3)
1983 (8–3)	Hall of Fame	20–16	Kentucky	(6–4–1)
1984 (7–4)	Bluebonnet	31–14	TCU	(8–3)
1987 (6–5)	John Hancock Sun	33–35	Oklahoma State	(9–2)
1988 (11–0)	Fiesta	21–34	Notre Dame	(11–0)
1989 (8–2–1)	Gator	7–27	Clemson	(9–2)

CONFERENCE TITLES

Southern—1953, 1954, 1955, 1956, 1958, 1964, 1965, 1967. **Big East**—None. Won **Lambert Trophy** in 1988.

TOP 20 AP AND UPI RANKING

1953	10–13	1969	17–18	1982	19–19	1984	U–18
1954	12–U	1975	20–17	1983	16–16	1988	5–5
1955	19–17	1981	17–18				

MAJOR RIVALS

WVU has played at least 10 games with Bethany (W.Va.) 13–0–1, Boston College 13–7–1, Cincinnati 10–0–1, Davis & Elkins 9–2, Fordham 3–8, George Washington 17–7, Georgetown 4–7, Kentucky 8–11–1, Marietta 16–6–1, Maryland 14–14–2, Ohio U. 12–4, Penn St. 9–48–2, Pittsburgh 27–55–3, Richmond 21–3–1, Rutgers 15–3–2, South Carolina 7–3–1, Syracuse 16–24, Temple 13–11, Virginia 10–11–1, Virginia Military Institute 11–0, Virginia Tech 24–13–1, Washington & Jefferson 12–20–2, Washington & Lee 27–6–4, Waynesburg 16–1, Westminster 14–0, W.Va. Wesleyan 29–4–1, William & Mary 15–0–1. Record against Big East foe Miami (Fla.) is 1–7.

COACHES

Dean of West Virginia coaches is Don Nehlen (1988 national Coach of Year) with record of 92–55–4 for 1980–92 with 1 Lambert Trophy winner, 1 team unbeaten in regular season, and 7 bowl teams. Other top records for at least 3 years were by Louis Yeager, 12–9 for 1899 and 1901–02; C.A. Leuder, 17–13–3 for 1908–11; Mont McIntire, 24– 11–4 for 1916–17 and 1919–20; Dr. Clarence Spears, 30–6–3 for 1921–24 with 1 unbeaten bowl champion; Ira Errett Rodgers, 44–31–8 for 1925–30 and 1943–45; Charles Tallman, 15–12–2 for 1934–36; Marshall Glenn, 14–12–3 for 1937–39 with 1 Sun Bowl champion; Bill Kern, 24–23–1 for 1940–42 and 1946–47; Art "Pappy" Lewis, 58–38–2 for 1950–59 with 5 SC titles and 1 Sugar Bowl team; Gene Corum, 29–30–2 for 1960–65 with 2 SC titles and 1 bowl team; Jim Carlen, 25–13–3 for 1966–69 with 1 SC title and 1 Peach Bowl champion; and Bobby Bowden, 42–26 for 1970–75 with 2 bowl teams.

MISCELLANEA

First game was loss to Washington & Jefferson 72–0 in 1891 . . . 1st win was over Uniontown Independents 12–2 in 1893 . . . 1st win over college foe was over Bethany (W.Va.) 6–0 in 1894 . . . highest score was over Marshall 92–6 in 1915 . . . highest since W.W. II (biggest margin of victory ever) was over Geneva 89–0 in 1951 . . . worst defeat was by Michigan 130–0 in 1904 . . . worst since W.W. II was by Penn St. 62–14 in 1973 . . . longest unbeaten string of 19 in 1922–23 ended by Washington & Jefferson 7–2 . . . 13-game win streak in 1952–53 ended by South Carolina 20–14 . . . longest winless string of 18 in 1959–61 broken with win over Virginia Tech 28–0 . . . consensus All-Americans were Ira Rodgers, B, 1919; Bruce Bosley, T, 1955; Darryl Talley, LB, 1982; Brian Jozwiak, OL, 1985; and Mike Compton, C, 1992 . . . Academic All-Americans were Paul Bischoff, E, 1952; Fred Wyant, QB, 1954; Sam Huff, T, 1955; Kim West, K, 1970; Oliver Luck, QB, 1980–81; Jeff Hostetler, QB, 1983; and Mike Compton, C, 1992.

BIG 8 CONFERENCE

The Big 8 Conference grew out of the Missouri Valley Intercollegiate Athletic Association (MVIAA), formed on January 12, 1907, by Iowa, Kansas, Missouri, Nebraska, and Washington University of St. Louis. Iowa State University (Ames College at the time) and Drake were added in 1908. Iowa dropped out after the 1910 season to join the Big 10 Conference and was replaced in 1913 by Kansas State University (then the Kansas State College of Applied Science and Agriculture). Grinnell College joined in 1919 and the University of Oklahoma in 1920. The league expanded to 10 teams in 1925 when Oklahoma A&M College (now Oklahoma State University) withdrew from the Southwest Conference to join the Missouri Valley league.

In a meeting on May 19, 1928, at Lincoln, Nebraska, six of the seven state institutions (excluding Oklahoma A&M) formally organized as a separate conference, retaining the MVIAA title but becoming known informally as the Big 6. The remaining schools formed the Missouri Valley Conference (MVC), a polyglot league that over the years included such members as Bradley, Cincinnati, Creighton, Detroit, Houston, Illinois State, Indiana State, Louisville, Memphis State, New Mexico State, North Texas State, St. Louis, Southern Illinois, Tulsa, West Texas State, and Wichita State. The MVC expired in the late 1980s.

The Big 6 operated with Iowa State, Kansas, Kansas State, Missouri, Nebraska, and Oklahoma for nearly 20 years before the addition of the University of Colorado in December 1947 made it the Big 7. Oklahoma A&M rejoined its old MVIAA cohorts on June 1, 1957, about the time of its name change to Oklahoma State University. That brought the conference to its current eight members. The name Big 8 Conference replaced MVIAA as the league's official title in 1964.

FACTS AND ODDITIES ON BIG 8 MEMBERS

The Big 8 has a rich tradition of national champions, All-Americans, and winners of the nation's highest individual honors, especially since the 1950s. It was in 1950 that Oklahoma, coached by "Bud" Wilkinson, compiled a 10–0 record and, despite being upset 13–7 in the Sugar Bowl by "Bear" Bryant's Kentucky squad, was generally recognized as the nation's top team. It was the first time an MVIAA team had reached that pinnacle.

Wilkinson won his second national title at Oklahoma in 1955 with a 10–0 season capped by a 20–6 win over unbeaten Maryland in the Orange Bowl, then repeated in 1956 with another 10–0 team. It was 1970 before another league member, Nebraska, won a national title. That year the Cornhuskers finished 10–0–1 and beat LSU 17–12 in the Orange Bowl to earn a share of the national crown. Bob Devaney's Cornhuskers repeated as national champ in 1971 with an awesome team that won all 12 of its regular–season games, then whipped unbeaten Alabama 38–6 in the Orange Bowl to sew up the title.

Oklahoma was back with a share of its fourth title in 1974, finishing 11–0, and repeated in 1975 with a 10–1 team that beat Michigan 14–6 in the Orange Bowl. Oklahoma earned its sixth national crown in 1985, going 10–1 and then beating undefeated Penn State 25–10 in the Orange Bowl. Colorado got its first share of a national championship in 1990, finishing 10–1–1, then edging Notre Dame 10–9 in the Orange Bowl.

Six Big 8 players have won the Heisman Trophy, starting with HB Billy Vessels of Oklahoma in 1952. The others were HB Steve Owens, Oklahoma, 1969; FL Johnny Rodgers, Nebraska, 1972; HB Billy Sims, Oklahoma, 1978; HB Mike Rozier, Nebraska, 1983; and HB Barry Sanders, Oklahoma State, 1988. The Maxwell Trophy has gone to three Big 8 players: HB Tommy McDonald, Oklahoma, 1956; RB Mike Rozier, Nebraska, 1983; and RB Barry Sanders, Oklahoma State, 1988.

Nine Big 8 players—five from Nebraska and four from Oklahoma—have won the Outland Trophy, including the only player ever to win it twice. The winners were T Jim Weatherall, Oklahoma, 1951; G J. D. Roberts, Oklahoma, 1953; DT Larry Jacobson, Nebraska, 1971; MG Rich Glover, Nebraska, 1972; DT Lee Roy Selmon, Oklahoma, 1975; OG Greg Roberts, Oklahoma, 1978; C Dave Rimington, Nebraska, 1981–1982; OG Dean Steinkuhler, Nebraska, 1983; and OG Will Shields, Nebraska, 1992. The Lombardi Award has gone to Big 8 players five times. Winners were MG Rich Glover, Nebraska, 1972; DT Lee Roy Selmon, Oklahoma, 1975; C Dave Rimington, Nebraska, 1982; G Dean Steinkuhler, Nebraska, 1983; and NG Tony Casillas, Oklahoma, 1985.

National Coach of the Year awards have gone to Big 8 coaches three times. "Bud" Wilkinson of Oklahoma won the award in 1949, Bob Devaney of Nebraska won the Football Writers Association of America (FWAA) share in 1971, and Bill McCartney of Colorado won both the FWAA and the American Football Coaches Association Award in 1989.

Three Big 8 coaches rank in the top 10 in all-time winning percentage. Oklahoma's Barry Switzer (fourth at .837) was 157–29–4 for 1973–1988 with 12 conference titles, 13 bowl teams, three teams unbeaten in regular season, and three national champions. Wilkinson (eighth at .826) was 145–29–4 for 1947–1963 with 14 conference titles, eight bowl teams (6 winners), five teams unbeaten in regular season, and three national champs. Devaney (tenth at .806) was 136–30–7 at Wyoming (1957–1961) and Nebraska (1962–1972). He coached Nebraska to a record of 101–20–2 with eight conference titles, nine bowl teams, three teams unbeaten in regular season, and two national champions. Nebraska's Tom Osborne is next on the all-time list with a record of 195–46–3 for 1973–1992 (an .805 winning percentage), with nine conference titles, 20 bowl teams, and one team unbeaten in regular season.

The first consensus All-American from what is now the Big 8 was E Guy Chamberlin of Nebraska, chosen from the 1915 Cornhusker team that won all eight of its games and won the MVIAA title for the seventh time in nine years.

The NCAA began keeping official college football statistics in 1937, and the dominant player that year was Colorado's Byron "Whizzer" White. Ten years before the Buffs entered the Big 6 (making it the Big 7), White led the nation in four categories—rushing, total off, scoring, and kick scoring. He also was a basketball and baseball star and later was twice All-Pro halfback in the National Football League. But White wasn't just a winner in athletics; he was elected Phi Beta Kappa as a junior, became a Rhodes Scholar, was a decorated naval intelligence officer in World War II, was the leading graduate of the Yale Law School in 1946, and in 1962—not yet 45 years old—became the youngest man ever appointed to the U.S. Supreme Court.

Oklahoma holds the longest winning streak in college football history: 47. The Sooners started the string in early 1953 and saw it end at Norman on November 16, 1957, when Notre Dame's Dick Lynch scored on a three–yard run with less than four minutes left to give the Irish a 7–0 win. The Sooners actually had gone 48 games without defeat, having tied Pittsburgh 7–7 before winning the next 47. The loss to Notre Dame also ended an Oklahoma scoring string of 123 consecutive games. An earlier Sooner winning streak under "Bud" Wilkinson in 1948–50 had reached 31 when once–beaten Kentucky, under "Bear" Bryant, upset the Sooners 13–7 in the 1951 Sugar Bowl.

Oklahoma and Nebraska both rank in the top 10 among Division I-A teams in all-time winning percentage and total victories in college football. Nebraska holds the record for the most consecutive winning seasons: 31 from 1962 through 1992.

The series between Kansas and Missouri is the Division I-A's second longest in games played, with 101 through 1992. The series stands at 48–44–9 in favor of Missouri. The Kansas-Nebraska series is next in line at 99 games through 1992, with the Cornhuskers dominating by a margin of 75–21–3.

Two other Big 8 rivalries tie for fifteenth among the leaders in the longest series played, both of them also involving Kansas. In 90 games through 1992 the Jayhawks held an edge over Kansas State of 61–24–5 but trailed Oklahoma by a margin of 60–24–6. The Kansas-Oklahoma rivalry is the longest uninterrupted series in Division I-A college football, having been played continually since 1903. Kansas-Nebraska is second longest, with the teams meeting every year since 1906.

Oklahoma holds the record of the most consecutive wins over a major opponent in an uninterrupted series, beating Kansas State 32 straight times between 1937 and 1968. Kansas State had not actually beaten the Sooners since 1934 but had tied them 6–6 in 1936. The string started with a 19–0 Sooner victory in 1937 and ended with a 59–21 shocker by the Wildcats in 1969.

Some of the more interesting nicknames in college football have been tags on Big 8 teams at one time or another. Nebraska was known in the early days of the sport as Bugeaters, Old Gold Knights, and Antelopes. It was in 1900 that Lincoln, Nebraska, sportswriter Charles S. "Cy" Sherman started calling the team Cornhuskers, and the label caught on.

Iowa State teams were known as Cardinals until 1895. But that fall the football squad surprised Northwestern 36–0 in a game at Evanston, Illinois. An unusually large number of tornadoes (cyclones in the terminology of the day) had hit Iowa earlier that year, and the *Chicago Tribune* headline for the game story read: "Iowa Cyclone Devastates Evanstontown [*sic*]." It has been Iowa State Cyclones ever since.

Early University of Oklahoma teams were called Rough Riders or Boomers, but in 1908 the Sooners nickname was adapted from a pep club called "The Sooner Rooters." In state history, Sooners were settlers who entered Oklahoma before the run for land officially began. Another nickname unique in college football is the Jayhawks symbol at Kansas. The Jayhawk is a mythical bird of unknown origin, but the term Jayhawker was applied to Kansans in pioneer times, referring to foragers, guerillas, and, during the Civil War, Kansas soldiers. The Jayhawk appeared in a University of Kansas cheer as early as 1886.

When Missouri's first football team was organized in 1890, the athletic committee adopted the nickname Tigers in honor of a unit that had defended Columbia, Missouri, from marauders during the Civil War. Colorado adopted Buffaloes as a nickname after students rented a buffalo calf to use as a mascot for the Utah game of November 10, 1934 (Colorado won, 7–6). The new mascot was an immediate hit. Previously, Colorado teams had been referred to as the Silver and Gold.

Kansas State had been known as Aggies until Coach Chief Bender in 1915 named his team Wildcats because of their fighting spirit. The nickname was changed to Farmers in 1916, but in 1920 Coach Charles Bachman switched it back to Wildcats. Oklahoma State teams were known as Aggies in the days when the school was Oklahoma A&M, but the teams sometimes were referred to informally as Cowpokes. A change to Cowboys for the official nickname was made in the late 1950s when the school became Oklahoma State University.

Kansas originally had colors of Michigan's maize and sky blue, but in the early 1890s changed to crimson and blue. Student backers of the first Kansas football team in 1890 wanted to switch to crimson in honor of a Harvard grad who had donated money for an athletic field at the University. Some Yale alumni on the faculty insisted that Yale blue be added. A senior class committee in 1896 chose royal purple for Kansas State's color. White, though never adopted officially, has been used as a complementary color for many years.

ALL-TIME CONFERENCE CHAMPIONS
MISSOURI VALLEY INTERCOLLEGIATE
ATHLETIC ASSOCIATION

Annual Champion	League Record	Regular Season and Bowl
1907 Iowa	1–0	3–2
Nebraska	1–0	8–2
1908 Kansas	4–0	9–0
1909 Missouri	4–0–1	7–0–1
1910 Nebraska	2–0	7–1
1911 Iowa St.	2–0–1	6–1–1
Nebraska	2–0–1	5–1–2
1912 Iowa St.	2–0	6–2
Nebraska	2–0	8–1
1913 Missouri	4–0	7–1
Nebraska	3–0	8–0
1914 Nebraska	3–0	7–0–1
1915 Nebraska	4–0	8–0
1916 Nebraska	3–1	6–2
1917 Nebraska	2–0	5–2
1918 No standings, due to W.W. I		
1919 Missouri	4–0–1	5–1–2
1920 Oklahoma	4–0–1	6–0–1
1921 Nebraska	3–0	7–1
1922 Nebraska	5–0	7–1
1923 Nebraska	3–0–2	4–2–2
1924 Missouri	5–1	7–2
1925 Missouri	5–1	6–1–1
1926 Oklahoma A&M	3–0–1	3–4–1
1927 Missouri	5–1	7–2
BIG 6		
1928 Nebraska	5–0	7–1–1
1929 Nebraska	3–0–2	4–1–3
1930 Kansas	4–1	6–2
1931 Nebraska	5–0	8–2
1932 Nebraska	5–0	7–1–1
1933 Nebraska	5–0	8–1
1934 Kansas St.	5–0	7–2–1
1935 Nebraska	4–0–1	6–2–1
1936 Nebraska	5–0	7–2

(continued)

ALL-TIME CONFERENCE
CHAMPIONS BIG 8 *(continued)*

Annual Champion	League Record	Regular Season and Bowl	
1937 Nebraska	3–0–2	6–1–2	
1938 Oklahoma	5–0	10–0	Orange (L)
1939 Missouri	5–0	8–1	Orange (L)
1940 Nebraska	5–0	8–1	Rose (L)
1941 Missouri	5–0	8–1	Sugar (L)
1942 Missouri	4–0–1	8–3–1	
1943 Oklahoma	5–0	7–2	
1944 Oklahoma	4–0–1	6–3–1	
1945 Missouri	5–0	6–3	Cotton (L)
1946 Kansas	4–1	7–2–1	
Oklahoma	4–1	7–3	Gator (W)
1947 Kansas	4–0–1	8–0–2	Orange (L)
Oklahoma	4–0–1	7–2–1	
BIG 7			
1948 Oklahoma	5–0	9–1	Sugar (W)
1949 Oklahoma	5–0	10–0	Sugar (W)
1950 Oklahoma	6–0	10–0	Sugar (L)
1951 Oklahoma	6–0	8–2	
1952 Oklahoma	5–0–1	8–1–1	
1953 Oklahoma	6–0	8–1–1	Orange (W)
1954 Oklahoma	6–0	10–0	
1955 Oklahoma	6–0	10–0	Orange (W)
1956 Oklahoma	6–0	10–0	
1957 Oklahoma	6–0	9–1	Orange (W)
BIG 8			
1958 Oklahoma	6–0	9–1	Orange (W)
1959 Oklahoma	5–1	7–3	
1960 Missouri	7–0	9–1	Orange (W)
1961 Colorado	7–0	9–1	Orange (L)
1962 Oklahoma	7–0	8–2	Orange (L)
1963 Nebraska	7–0	9–1	Orange (W)
1964 Nebraska	6–1	9–1	Cotton (L)
1965 Nebraska	7–0	10–0	Orange (L)
1966 Nebraska	6–1	9–1	Sugar (L)
1967 Oklahoma	7–0	9–1	Orange (W)
1968 Kansas	6–1	9–1	Orange (L)
Oklahoma	6–1	7–3	Bluebonnet (L)
1969 Missouri	6–1	9–1	Orange (L)
Nebraska	6–1	8–2	Sun (W)
1970 Nebraska	7–0	10–0–1	Orange (W)
1971 Nebraska	7–0	12–0	Orange (W)
1972 Nebraska	5–1–1	8–2–1	Orange (W)
1973 Oklahoma	7–0	10–0–1	
1974 Oklahoma	7–0	11–0	
1975 Nebraska	6–1	10–1	Fiesta (L)
Oklahoma	6–1	10–1	Orange (W)
1976 Colorado	5–2	8–3	Orange (L)
Oklahoma	5–2	8–2–1	Fiesta (W)
Oklahoma St.	5–2	8–3	Tangerine (W)
1977 Oklahoma	7–0	10–1	Orange (L)

(continued)

ALL-TIME CONFERENCE
CHAMPIONS BIG 8 *(continued)*

Annual Champion	*League Record*	*Regular Season and Bowl*	
1978 Nebraska	6–1	9–2	Orange (L)
Oklahoma	6–1	10–1	Orange (W)
1979 Oklahoma	7–0	10–1	Orange (W)
1980 Oklahoma	7–0	9–2	Orange (W)
1981 Nebraska	7–0	9–2	Orange (L)
1982 Nebraska	7–0	11–1	Orange (W)
1983 Nebraska	7–0	12–0	Orange (L)
1984 Nebraska	6–1	9–2	Sugar (W)
Oklahoma	6–1	9–1–1	Orange (L)
1985 Oklahoma	7–0	10–1	Orange (W)
1986 Oklahoma	7–0	10–1	Orange (W)
1987 Oklahoma	7–0	11–0	Orange (L)
1988 Nebraska	7–0	11–1	Orange (L)
1989 Colorado	7–0	11–0	Orange (L)
1990 Colorado	7–0	10–1–1	Orange (W)
1991 Colorado	6–0–1	8–2–1	Blockbuster (L)
Nebraska	6–0–1	9–1–1	Orange (L)
1992 Nebraska	6–1	9–2	Orange (L)

COLORADO *(Buffaloes, Buffs; Silver, Gold and Black)*

NOTABLE TEAMS

1894 (8–1) *Won:* East Denver H.S. 46–0, Denver A.C. 12–4, Denver 44–0, 49–4, Colorado St. 67–0, West Denver H.S. 26–4, Colorado Mines 20–0, 18–0. *Lost:* Denver A.C. 20–6. *Noteworthy:* 1st head coach was Harry Heller.

1895 (5–1) *Won:* Denver Manual H.S. 36–0, Denver Wheel Club 32–0, Denver 28–0, Colorado College 38–10, Colorado Mines 14–0. *Lost:* Denver A.C. 22–10. *Noteworthy:* 1st year under Fred Folsom.

1896 (5–0) *Won:* Denver Manual H.S. 42–0, East Denver H.S. 41–0, Colorado Mines 30–0, Colorado College 50–0, Denver A.C. 8–6. *Noteworthy:* outscored foes 171–6 in 1st unbeaten season.

1897 (7–1) *Won:* East Denver H.S. 22–0, West Denver H.S. 52–0, Denver Manual H.S. 18–0, Littleton A.C. 30–0, Colorado College 8–0, Denver Wheel Club 22–0, Colorado Mines 36–2. *Lost:* Denver A.C. 8–0.

1899 (7–2) *Won:* State Prep School 6–0, Denver Manual H.S. 46–0, West Denver H.S. 21–0, East Denver H.S. 33–0, Colorado St. 63–0 (1st meeting since 1894), Denver Wheel Club 5–0, Colorado Mines 25–6. *Lost:* Colorado College 17–5, Denver A.C. 11–6 in last 2 games.

1901 (5–1–1) *Won:* State Prep School 5–0, Alumni 6–0, Denver Wheel Club 11–0, Colorado College 11–2, Colorado Mines 23–0. *Lost:* Denver A.C. 29–0. *Tied:* State Prep School 0–0. *Noteworthy:* won 1st Rocky Mountain Conference title.

1902 (5–1) *Won:* State Prep School 12–0, Denver 24–0, Colorado St. 11–6, Colorado College 12–6, Colorado Mines 28–0. *Lost:* unbeaten Nebraska 10–0. *Noteworthy:* repeated as Rocky Mountain champ.

1903 (8–2) *Won:* State Prep School 40–0, Utah 22–0 (1st meeting), Colorado St. 5–0, Colorado Mines 17–0, 23–5, Denver 10–0, Colorado College 31–6, Missouri Mines 38–0. *Lost:* Kansas 12–11 (1st meeting), unbeaten Nebraska 31–0 in successive games. *Noteworthy:* won 3rd straight Rocky Mountain crown in 1st year under Dave Cropp.

1904 (6–2–1) *Won:* Alumni 6–0, Utah 33–6, Nebraska 6–0, Colorado College 23–0, Denver 57–0,

Colorado St. 46–0. *Lost:* Colorado Mines 13–10, Stanford 33–0. *Tied:* Kansas 6–6.

1905 (8–1) *Won:* North Denver H.S. 28–0, Regis 109–0, Alumni 23–0, Wyoming 69–0, Kansas 14–0, Utah 46–5, Washburn 30–5, Haskell 39–0. *Lost:* Nebraska 18–0. *Noteworthy:* only year under Willis Keinholtz.

1908 (5–2) *Won:* Longmont H.S. 6–0, State Prep School 29–0, Colorado St. 8–0, Colorado College 14–0, Colorado Mines 15–0. *Lost:* Utah 21–14, Denver 14–10. *Noteworthy:* Folsom returned as head coach.

1909 (6–0) *Won:* State Prep School 3–0, Alumni 3–0, Colorado St. 57–0, New Mexico 53–0, Colorado College 9–0, Colorado Mines 16–0. *Noteworthy:* blanked foes 141–0 in 1st unbeaten season since 1896.

1910 (6–0) *Won:* State Prep School 20–0, Alumni 11–0, Wyoming 16–3, Utah 11–0, Colorado St. 44–0, Colorado Mines 19–0. *Noteworthy:* won 4th Rocky Mountain title.

1911 (6–0) *Won:* Alumni 11–0, Wyoming 18–3, Colorado College 8–2, Colorado St. 31–0, Utah 9–0, Colorado Mines 11–0. *Noteworthy:* again won Rocky Mountain crown.

1913 (5–1–1) *Won:* Wyoming 7–0, Alumni 6–0, Colorado St. 16–7, Utah 30–12, Colorado Mines 20–0. *Lost:* Oklahoma 14–3 in finale. *Tied:* Colorado College 0–0. *Noteworthy:* won 6th Rocky Mountain title.

1914 (5–1) *Won:* Alumni 27–3, Colorado St. 33–6, Colorado College 10–7, Utah 33–0 (1st homecoming), Denver 6–0. *Lost:* Colorado Mines 6–2.

1917 (6–2) *Won:* Alumni 6–0, Northern Colorado 54–0, Colorado St. 6–0, Colorado Mines 12–0, Colorado College 18–17, Utah 18–9. *Lost:* unbeaten Denver 7–0, unbeaten Utah St. 23–10.

1920 (4–1–2) *Won:* Denver 31–0, Wyoming 7–0, Colorado Mines 7–0, Oklahoma St. 40–7 (1st meeting). *Lost:* Utah 7–0. *Tied:* Colorado College 7–7, Colorado St. 7–7. *Noteworthy:* 1st year under Myron Witham.

1921 (4–1–1) *Won:* Denver 10–7, Colorado College 35–14, Colorado St. 10–0, Colorado Mines 10–7. *Lost:* Chicago 35–0. *Tied:* Utah 0–0.

1923 (9–0) *Won:* Brigham Young (BYU) 41–0 (1st meeting), Western St. 51–0, Northern Colorado 60–0, Denver 21–7, Colorado College 17–7, Colorado Mines 47–0, Utah 17–7, Wyoming 20–3 (10th straight over Cowboys), Colorado St. 6–3. *Note-*

worthy: won 7th Rocky Mountain title in 1st un-beaten season since 1911.

1924 (8–1–1) *Won:* Western St. 29–0, Regis 39–0 (1st game at Folsom Field), Colorado College 26–0, Wyoming 21–0, Utah 3–0, Colorado Mines 38–0, Colorado St. 36–0, Hawaii-Navy All-Stars 43–0. *Lost:* unbeaten Hawaii 13–0 on New Year's Day in Honolulu. *Tied:* Denver 0–0. *Noteworthy:* again won Rocky Mountain title.

1928 (5–1) *Won:* Northern Colorado 21–6, Colorado Mines 39–0, Colorado St. 13–7, Colorado College 24–19, Denver 7–0. *Lost:* unbeaten Utah 25–6.

1929 (5–1–1) *Won:* Regis 27–13, Northern Colorado 19–0, Colorado Mines 13–9, Colorado St. 6–0, Colorado College 13–7. *Lost:* unbeaten Utah 40–0. *Tied:* Denver 0–0.

1930 (6–1–1) *Won:* Missouri 9–0 (1st meeting), Colorado Mines 36–7, Colorado St. 7–0, Colorado College 14–13, Northern Colorado 27–7, Denver 27–7. *Lost:* unbeaten Utah 34–0. *Tied:* Utah St. 0–0.

1933 (7–2) *Won:* Chadron St. 19–0, Oklahoma St. 6–0 (1st meeting since 1920), Colorado Mines 42–0, Wyoming 40–12 (1st meeting since 1926), Colorado College 26–0, Northern Colorado 24–0, Denver 14–7. *Lost:* Colorado St. 19–6, Utah 13–6.

1934 (6–1–2) *Won:* BYU 48–6, Colorado St. 27–9, Colorado Mines 40–6, Utah 7–6 (1st over Utes since 1924), Colorado College 31–0, Denver 7–0. *Lost:* Northern Colorado 13–7. *Tied:* Kansas 0–0 (1st meeting since 1922), Missouri 0–0. *Star:* William "Kayo" Lam (906 yds and 7 TDs rush). *Noteworthy:* got share of 9th Rocky Mountain title.

1937 (8–1) *Won:* Missouri 14–6, Utah St. 33–0, BYU 14–0, Colorado St. 47–0, Colorado Mines 54–0, Utah 17–7, Colorado College 35–6, Denver 34–7. *Star:* TB Byron "Whizzer" White (Colorado's 1st consensus All-American; 42.5-yd punting avg, nation's leader with 1,596 yds total off, 1,121 yds rush, 1,970 all-purpose yds, and 122 pts on 16 TDs, 23 ex pts, and a FG). *Noteworthy:* Won 11th and last Rocky Mountain crown in 1st unbeaten season since 1923. Led nation in total off, rush, and scoring (31-pt avg). Made 1st bowl appearance, losing to Rice 28–14 in Cotton Bowl after jumping off to 14–0 1st period lead; White passed to Joe Antonio for 1st TD, returned pass int 47 yds for other, and kicked both ex pts.

1942 (7–2) *Won:* Colorado Mines 54–0, Utah St. 31–14, New Mexico 12–0, Colorado St. 34–7, Wyoming 28–7, BYU 48–0, Denver 31–6. *Lost:* Missouri 26–13, Utah 13–0. *Noteworthy:* got share of 2nd Mountain States Conference title.

1943 (5–2) *Won:* Ft. Francis Warren 38–0, Lowry AFB 19–6, Utah 35–0, 22–19, Salt Lake AFB 14–0. *Lost:* Colorado College, 16–6, 6–0. *Noteworthy:* again won Mountain States title.

1944 (6–2) *Won:* Utah 26–0, Colorado College 28–0, 40–6, New Mexico 39–0, Peru St. 40–12, Denver 16–14. *Lost:* Ft. Francis Warren 7–6, Second AFB 33–6 in 1st 2 games. *Noteworthy:* won 3rd straight (and last) Mountain States title.

1951 (7–3) *Won:* Colorado St. 28–13, Kansas 35–27, Missouri 34–13 (1st over Tigers in 11 games since 1937), Kansas St. 20–7, Iowa St. 47–20, Utah 54–0, Nebraska 36–14. *Lost:* Northwestern 35–14, Oklahoma 55–14, unbeaten Michigan St. 45–7. *Stars:* FB Merwin Hodel (597 yds and 6 TDs rush), E Chuck Mosher, Woody Shelton (14 pass rec for 254 yds), HB Tom Brookshier, T Jack Jorgenson, E Don Branby.

1952 (6–2–2) *Won:* San Jose St. 20–14, Arizona 34–19, Iowa St. 21–12, Utah 20–14, Kansas St. 34–14, Colorado St. 61–0. *Lost:* Kansas 21–12, Missouri 27–7. *Tied:* Oklahoma 21–21, Nebraska 16–16. *Stars:* P Zack Jordan (43.4-yd avg), B Ralph Curtis (664 yds and 8 TDs rush), Branby, Roger Williams (22 pass rec for 243 yds), Roy Shepherd (5 int).

1954 (7–2–1) *Won:* Drake 61–0, Colorado St. 46–0, Kansas 27–0, Arizona 40–18, Iowa St. 20–0, Utah 20–7, Kansas St. 38–14. *Lost:* Nebraska 20–6, unbeaten Oklahoma 13–6 in successive mid-season games. *Tied:* Missouri 19–19. *Stars:* soph FB John Bayuk (824 yds and 11 TDs rush), HBs Carroll Hardy (831 yds total off, 9 TDs, 41.6-yd punting avg) and Frank Bernardi.

1956 (8–2–1) *Won:* Kansas St. 34–0, Kansas 26–25, Colorado St. 47–7, Iowa St. 52–0, Nebraska 16–0, Utah 21–7, Arizona 38–7. *Lost:* Oregon 35–0, unbeaten national champ Oklahoma 27–19. *Tied:* Missouri 14–14. *Stars:* Bayuk (659 yds and 11 TDs rush), Es Jerry Leahy and Wally Merz, T Dick Stapp, soph QB Boyd Dowler (42.1-yd punting avg). *Noteworthy:* beat Clemson 27–21 in Orange Bowl; Bayuk ran for 121 yds and 2 TDs, Dowler scored on 6-yd run, soph Howard Cook scored on 26-yd run, and Bob Stransky had 2 int.

1961 (9–2) *Won:* Oklahoma St. 24–0, Kansas 20–19, Miami (Fla.) 9–7, Kansas St. 13–0, Oklahoma 22–14, Missouri 7–6, Nebraska 7–0, Iowa St. 34–0, Air Force 29–12. *Lost:* Utah 21–12 (1st to Utes in 11 games since 1948). *Stars:* QB Gale Weidner (1,101 yds pass), E Jerry Hillebrand (17 pass rec for 282 yds), Ted Woods (525 yds rush), G Joe Romig, C Walt Klinker. *Noteworthy:* Sonny Grandelius's last team. Won 1st Big 8 title. Lost to Louisiana St. (LSU) 25–7 in Orange Bowl, gaining only 143 yds total off against Tigers' "Chinese Bandits" defense; scored on 59-yd pass int return by Loren Schweninger.

1965 (6–2–2) *Won:* Fresno St. 10–7, Kansas St. 36–0, Oklahoma St. 34–11, Oklahoma 13–0, Kansas 21–14, Air Force 19–6. *Lost:* unbeaten Nebraska 38–13, Missouri 20–7. *Tied:* Wisconsin 0–0, Iowa St. 10–10. *Stars:* QB Bernie McCall (1,175 yds pass), George Lewark (18 pass rec for 278 yds), soph William Harris (680 yds rush), Frank Rogers (13 FGs), DE Sam Harris, LB Steve Sidwell, DB Hale Irwin (5 int).

1966 (7–3) *Won:* Baylor 13–7, Kansas St. 10–0, Iowa St. 41–21, Oklahoma 24–21, Missouri 26–0 (1st over Tigers since 1961), Kansas 35–18, Air Force 10–9. *Lost:* Miami (Fla.) 24–3, Oklahoma St. 11–10, Nebraska 21–19. *Stars:* G John Beard, FB Wilmer Cooks (594 yds and 10 TDs rush), Larry Plantz (22 pass rec for 354 yds), DE Bill Fairband, DB Dick Anderson (5 int), Irwin.

1967 (9–2) *Won:* Baylor 27–7, Oregon 17–13, Iowa St. 34–0, Missouri 23–9, Nebraska 21–16 (1st over Cornhuskers since 1961), Kansas 12–8, Kansas St. 40–6, Air Force 33–0. *Lost:* Oklahoma St. 10–7, Oklahoma 23–0 in successive mid-season games. *Stars:* Dick Anderson (7 int, 40.4-yd punting avg), DT Frank Bosch, DE Mike Schnitker, OT Mike Montler, OG Kirk Tracy, soph QB Bobby Anderson (625 yds and 7 TDs rush, 733 yds pass), soph Monte Huber (45 pass rec for 486 yds), Cooks (10 TDs). *Noteworthy:* beat Miami (Fla.) 31–21 in Bluebonnet Bowl; Bobby Anderson ran for 108 yds and 2 TDs, and Cooks ran for 74 yds and a TD.

1969 (8–3) *Won:* Tulsa 35–14, Indiana 30–7, Iowa St. 14–0, Missouri 31–24, Kansas 17–14, Oklahoma St. 17–14, Kansas St. 45–32. *Lost:* unbeaten Penn St. 27–3, Oklahoma 42–30, Nebraska 20–7. *Stars:* HB Bobby Anderson (954 yds rush, 19 TDs), Huber (28 pass rec for 488 yds), OG Dick Melin, DE Bill Brundige. *Noteworthy:* beat Alabama 47–33 in

QB/HB Bobby Anderson, 1967–69

Liberty Bowl; Anderson ran for 254 yds and 3 TDs, QB Jim Bratten ran for 119 yds, FB Ward Walsh scored 2 TDs, and Bob Masten and Steve Engel collaborated on 91-yd TD kickoff return.

1971 (10–2) *Won:* LSU 31–21, Wyoming 56–13 (1st meeting since 1947), Ohio St. 20–14, Kansas St. 31–21, Iowa St. 24–14, Missouri 27–7, Kansas 35–14, Oklahoma St. 40–6, Air Force 53–17. *Lost:* Oklahoma 45–17, unbeaten national champ Nebraska 31–7. *Stars:* soph RB Charlie Davis (1,386 yds and 10 TDs rush), QB Ken Johnson (1,126 yds pass), Willie Nichols (16 pass rec for 316 yds), Cliff Branch (11 TDs), OT Jake Zumbach, DE Herb Orvis, John Stearns (5 int), MG Bud Magrum. *Noteworthy:* beat Houston 29–17 in Astro-Bluebonnet Bowl; Davis ran for 202 yds and 2 TDs, and J.B. Dean Jr. kicked FG and 2 ex pts.

1972 (8–4) *Won:* California 20–10, Cincinnati 56–14, Minnesota 38–6, Kansas St. 38–17, Iowa St. 34–22, Oklahoma 20–14, Kansas 33–8, Air Force 38–7. *Lost:* Oklahoma St. 31–6, Missouri 20–17, Nebraska 33–10. *Stars:* Davis (926 yds rush, 14 TDs), Johnson (1,044 yds pass), TE J.V. Cain (30 pass rec for 407 yds), Zumbach, Magrum, Stearns,

DB Cullen Bryant (7 int). *Noteworthy:* lost to Auburn 24–3 in Gator Bowl, losing ball on 4 turnovers; Johnson passed for 169 yds and Buffs scored on Fred Lima's 33-yd FG.

1975 (9–3) *Won:* California 34–27, Wyoming 27–10, Wichita St. 52–0, Miami (Fla.) 23–10, Missouri 31–20, Iowa St. 28–27, Oklahoma St. 17–7, Kansas 24–21, Kansas St. 33–7. *Lost:* national champ Oklahoma 21–20, Nebraska 63–21. *Stars:* QB David Williams (1,282 yds pass), Dave Logan (23 pass rec for 392 yds), FB Terry Kunz (882 yds rush, 11 TDs), TE Don Hasselbeck, OT Mark Koncar, LB Gary Campbell. *Noteworthy:* lost to Texas 38–21 in Astro-Bluebonnet Bowl; Williams passed for 177 yds and 2 TDs, and Hasselbeck had 5 pass rec for 84 yds and a TD.

1976 (8–4) *Won:* Washington 21–3, Miami (Fla.) 33–3, Drake 45–24, Oklahoma St. 20–10, Iowa St. 33–14, Oklahoma 42–31, Kansas 40–17, Kansas St. 35–28. *Lost:* Texas Tech 24–7, Nebraska 24–12, Missouri 16–7. *Stars:* TB Tony Reed (1,210 yds rush, 19 pass rec for 128 yds), Jim Kelleher (15 TDs), Hasselbeck, P Stan Koleski (40-yd avg), MG Charlie Johnson, DB Mike Spivey, Odis McKinney (5 int). *Noteworthy:* Got share of 2nd Big 8 title. Lost to Ohio St. 27–10 in Orange Bowl; soph QB Jeff Knapple passed for 137 yds and a TD.

1988 (8–4) *Won:* Fresno St. 45–3, Iowa 24–21, Oregon St. 28–21, Colorado St. 27–23, Kansas 21–9, Iowa St. 24–12, Missouri 45–8, Kansas St. 56–14. *Lost:* Oklahoma St. 41–21, Oklahoma 17–14, Nebraska 7–0. *Stars:* QB Sal Aunese (1,004 yds pass, 8 TDs rush), WR Jeff Campbell (15 pass rec for 466 yds), soph RB Eric Bieniemy (1,243 yds and 10 TDs rush), TB J.J. Flannigan (522 yds and 6 TDs rush), C Erik Norgard, G Darrin Muilenburg, P Keith English (42.9-yd avg), LBs Michael Jones and Don DeLuzio, soph DE Kanavis McGhee. *Noteworthy:* lost to BYU 20–17 in Freedom Bowl; Bieniemy ran for 144 yds and 2 TDs.

1989 (11–1) *Won:* Texas 27–6, Colorado St. 45–20, Illinois 38–7, Washington 45–28, Missouri 49–3, Iowa St. 52–17, Kansas 49–17, Oklahoma 20–3 (1st over Sooners since 1976), Nebraska 27–21, Oklahoma St. 41–17, Kansas St. 59–11. *Stars:* Flannigan (1,187 yds and 18 TDs rush), soph QB Darian Hagan (1,002 yds pass, 1,004 yds and 17 TDs rush), Campbell (10 pass rec for 286 yds), soph HB Mike Pritchard (12 pass rec for 292 yds), WR M.J. Nelson (9 pass rec for 266 yds), Bieniemy (561 yds and

9 TDs rush), OGs Joe Garten and Muilenburg, OT Mark Vander Poel, K Ken Culbertson (13 FGs, 98 pts), DE Alfred Williams, soph MG Joel Steed, Jones, McGhee, soph P Tom Rouen (nation's leader with 45.8-yd avg). *Noteworthy:* Won 3rd Big 8 title in 1st unbeaten season since 1937. Lost to Notre Dame 21–6 in Orange Bowl; Hagan ran for 106 yds (including 39-yd TD run).

1990 (11–1–1) *Won:* Stanford 21–17, Texas 29–22, Washington 20–14, Missouri 33–31, Iowa St. 28–12, Kansas 41–10, Oklahoma 32–23, Nebraska 27–12, Oklahoma St. 41–22, Kansas St. 64–3. *Lost:* Illinois 23–22. *Tied:* Tennessee 31–31. *Stars:* Hagan (1,538 yds and 11 TDs pass, 442 yds and 5 TDs rush), Pritchard (28 pass rec for 733 yds and 6 TDs, 445 yds and 5 TDs rush), FB George Hemingway (14 pass rec for 217 yds), WR Rico Smith (12 pass rec for 358 yds), Bieniemy (1,628 yds and 17 TDs rush), Garten, Vander Poel, K Jim Harper (14 FGs, 83 pts), Dave McCloughan (nation's punt return leader with 16.3-yd avg), NT Garry Howe, Williams, LBs Chad Brown and soph Greg Biekert, DB Tim James (6 int), Rouen (40.8-yd punting avg). *Noteworthy:* Repeated as Big 8 champ. Edged Notre Dame 10–9 in Orange Bowl (breaking 7-game bowl losing string) to earn share of 1st national championship; Bieniemy ran for 86 yds and a TD, and Harper kicked 22-yd FG and ex pt.

1991 (8–3–1) *Won:* Wyoming 30–13 (1st meeting since 1982), Minnesota 58–0, Missouri 55–7, Oklahoma 34–17, Kansas St. 10–0, Oklahoma St. 16–12, Kansas 30–24, Iowa St. 17–14. *Lost:* Baylor 16–14, Stanford 28–21. *Tied:* Nebraska 19–19. *Stars:* Hagan (1,228 yds and 12 TDs pass, 386 yds rush), frosh WB Michael Westbrook (22 pass rec for 309 yds and 5 TDs), TE Sean Brown (24 pass rec for 300 yds), WR Mark Henry (13 pass rec for 292 yds), frosh TB Lamont Warren (830 yds and 7 TDs rush), C Jay Leeuwenburg, Steed, soph DT Leonard Renfro, Brown, Biekert, soph LB Ron Woolfork, DBs Eric Hamilton and Deon Figures, soph P Mitch Berger (40.8-yd avg). *Noteworthy:* Got share of 5th Big 8 title (3rd in a row). Lost to Alabama 30–25 in Blockbuster Bowl; Hagan passed for 210 yds and 2 TDs (including 62-yarder to Westbrook).

1992 (9–2–1) *Won:* Colorado St. 37–17, Baylor 57–38, Minnesota 21–20, Iowa 28–12, Missouri 6–0, Kansas St. 54–7, Oklahoma St. 28–0, Kansas 25–18,

Iowa St. 31–10. *Lost:* Nebraska 52–7. *Tied:* Oklahoma 24–24. *Stars:* soph QB Kordell Stewart (2,109 yds and 12 TDs pass), Westbrook (76 pass rec for 1,060 yds and 8 TDs), SE Charles Johnson (57 pass rec for 1,149 yds and 5 TDs), soph TE Christian Fauria (31 pass rec for 326 yds and 5 TDs), Warren (512 yds and 8 TDs rush), TB James Hill (6 TDs), OT Jim Hansen, Renfro, Biekert, Brown, Woolfork, Figures (6 int), DBs Ronnie Bradford and soph Chris Hudson, Berger (47-yd punting avg). *Noteworthy:* lost to Syracuse 26–22

in Fiesta Bowl; Stewart passed for 217 yds and 2 TDs (to TE Sean Embree and Johnson), and Warren scored on 6-yd run.

BOWL SUMMARY

Blockbuster 0–1; Bluebonnet 2–2; Cotton 0–1; Fiesta 0–1; Freedom 0–2; Gator 0–1; Liberty 1–1; Orange 2–3.

BOWL RECORD (5–12)

Regular Season	Bowl	Score	Opponent	Record
1937 (8–0)	Cotton	14–28	Rice	(5–3–2)
1956 (7–2–1)	Orange	27–21	Clemson	(7–1–2)
1961 (9–1)	Orange	7–25	LSU	(9–1)
1967 (8–2)	Bluebonnet	31–21	Miami (Fla.)	(7–3)
1969 (7–3)	Liberty	47–33	Alabama	(6–4)
1970 (6–4)	Liberty	3–17	Tulane	(7–4)
1971 (9–2)	Bluebonnet	29–17	Houston	(9–2)
1972 (8–3)	Gator	3–24	Auburn	(9–1)
1975 (9–2)	Bluebonnet	21–38	Texas	(9–2)
1976 (8–3)	Orange	10–27	Ohio State	(8–2–1)
1985 (7–4)	Freedom	17–20	Washington	(6–5)
1986 (6–5)	Bluebonnet	9–21	Baylor	(8–3)
1988 (8–3)	Freedom	17–20	BYU	(8–4)
1989 (11–0)	Orange	6–21	Notre Dame	(11–1)
1990 (10–1–1)	Orange	10–9	Notre Dame	(9–2)
1991 (8–2–1)	Blockbuster	25–30	Alabama	(10–1)
1992 (9–1–1)	Fiesta	22–26	Syracuse	(9–2)

CONFERENCE TITLES

Rocky Mountain—1901, 1902, 1903, 1910, 1911, 1913, 1923, 1924, 1934*, 1935*, 1937.
Mountain States—1939, 1942*, 1943, 1944. **Big 8**—1961, 1976*, 1989, 1990, 1991*.

TOP 20 AP AND UPI
(USA TODAY/CNN SINCE 1991) RANKING

1937	17	1967	U–13	1972	16–14	1990	1–2
1956	20–18	1969	16–U	1975	16–U	1991	20–20
1961	7–7	1970	U–16	1976	16–16	1992	13–13
1965	U–20	1971	3–7	1989	4–4		

MAJOR RIVALS

Colorado has played at least 10 games with Air Force 12–4, Arizona 12–1, Brigham Young 8–3–1, Colorado College 32–14–3, Colorado Mines 36–14–1, Colorado St. 49–15–2, Denver 26–14–4, Denver A.C. 3–13, Iowa St. 35–11–1, Kansas 31–18–3, Kansas St. 36–12, Missouri 21–33–3, Nebraska 14–35–2, Northern Colorado 9–2, Oklahoma 11–34–2, Oklahoma St. 19–15–1, Oregon 6–6, Utah 30–24–3, Utah St. 10–6–1, Wyoming 22–2–1.

COACHES

Dean of Colorado coaches is Fred Folsom with record of 77–23–2 for 1895–99, 1901–02, and 1908–15, including 5 Rocky Mountain Conference titles and 4 perfect records. Other top records for at least 3 years were by Myron Witham, 63–26–7 for 1920–31 with 2 Rocky Mountain titles and 1 perfect season; William Saunders, 15–7–2 for 1932–34 with 1 Rocky Mountain title; Bunnie Oakes, 25–15–1 for 1935–39 with 3 conference titles and 1 bowl team unbeaten in regular season; Frank Potts, 16–8–1 for 1940 and 1944–45 with 1 Mountain States title; Jim Yeager, 24–17–2 for 1941–43 and 1946–47 with 2 Mountain States titles; Dallas Ward, 63–41–6 for 1948–58 with 1 Orange Bowl champion; Sonny Grandelius, 20–11 for 1959–61 with 1 Big 8 title and 1 bowl team; Eddie Crowder, 67–49–2 for 1963–73 with 5 bowl teams; Bill Mallory, 35–21–1 for 1974–78 with 1 Big 8 title and 2 bowl teams; and Bill McCartney, 74–51–4 for 1982–92 with 3 Big 8 titles, 7 bowl teams, 1 team unbeaten in regular season, and 1 national champion.

MISCELLANEA

First game was loss to Denver A.C. 20–0 in 1890 . . . 1st win was over Colorado College 24–4 in 1891 . . . highest score was over Regis 109–0 in 1905 . . . highest since W.W. II was over Kansas St. 64–3 in 1990 . . . biggest margin since W.W. II equalled in wins over Colorado St. 61–0 in 1952 and Drake 61–0 in 1954 . . . worst defeat was by Colorado Mines 103–0 in 1890 . . . worst since 1900 was by Texas 76–0 in 1946 . . . highest against Buffs since 1900 was by Oklahoma 82–42 in 1980 . . . longest win streak of 21 in 1908–12 ended by Colorado St. 21–0 . . . 19-game unbeaten string in 1922–24 ended by Hawaii 13–0 on New Year's Day 1925 . . . longest losing string of 10 in 1963–64 broken with win over Iowa St. 14–7 . . . consensus All-Americans were Byron "Whizzer" White, B, 1937; Joe Romig, G, 1960–61; Dick Anderson, DB, 1967; Mike Montler, G, 1968; Bob Anderson, B, 1969; Don Popplewell, C, 1970; Cullen Bryant, DB, 1972; Barry Helton, P, 1985–86; Keith English, P, 1988; Tom Rouen, P, 1989; Joe Garten, OL, and Alfred Williams, LB, 1989–90; Eric Bieniemy, RB, 1990; Jay Leeuwenburg, C, 1991; and Deon Figures, DB, 1992 . . . Academic All-Americans were Joe Romig, G, 1960–61; Kirk Tracy, OG, 1967; Jim Cooch, DB, 1970; Rick Stearns, LB, 1973–74; Steve Young, DT, 1975; Eric McCarty, LB, 1987; and Jim Hansen, OL, 1990, 1992.

IOWA STATE (Cyclones; Cardinal and Gold)

NOTABLE TEAMS

1894 (6–1) *Won:* Fort Dodge 40–0, 46–0, Des Moines YMCA 18–4, Iowa 16–8 (1st meeting), Simpson 28–0, Panora 66–0. *Lost:* Grinnell 12–6.
1896 (8–2) *Won:* Iowa Falls 46–0, Cornell (Iowa) 50–0, Missouri 12–0, Grinnell 40–0, Des Moines YMCA 24–16, 15–0, Simpson 44–0, Eldora 62–0. *Lost:* Minnesota 18–6, Nebraska 12–4 (1st meeting).
1903 (8–1) *Won:* Highland Park 16–0, Omaha Light Guards 18–0, Coe 36–5, South Dakota 23–0, Grinnell 41–6, Simpson 11–2, Cornell (Iowa) 41–0, Drake 16–0. *Lost:* unbeaten Minnesota 46–0.
1904 (7–2) *Won:* Coe 22–0, Northern Iowa 17–0, Simpson 87–0, Grinnell 40–0, Des Moines College 16–0, Cornell (Iowa) 41–6, Drake 19–0. *Lost:* unbeaten Minnesota 32–0, Iowa City 10–6.
1906 (9–1) *Won:* Cornell (Iowa) 81–0, Coe 36–0, Des Moines College 45–0, Morningside 32–0, Nebraska 14–2, South Dakota 22–0, Grinnell 25–6, Iowa 2–0 (1st over Hawkeyes in 6 games since 1897), Drake 7–0. *Lost:* Minnesota 22–4. *Noteworthy:* A.W. Ristine's last team.
1907 (7–1) *Won:* Coe 18–0, Morningside 12–0, Cornell (Iowa) 17–0, Nebraska 13–10, Grinnell 49–0, Iowa 20–14, Drake 13–8. *Lost:* Minnesota

8–0.   *Noteworthy:* 1st year under Clyde Williams.
1911 (6–1–1)   *Won:* Coe 25–0, Missouri 6–3, Grinnell 21–6, Cornell (Iowa) 15–0, Iowa 9–0, Drake 6–0.   *Lost:* unbeaten Minnesota 5–0.   *Tied:* Nebraska 6–6.   *Star:* E A.K. Chappell.   *Noteworthy:* earned share of 1st MVC title.
1912 (6–2)   *Won:* Simpson 24–7 (1st meeting since 1905), Missouri 29–0, Grinnell 31–7 (10th straight over Pioneers), Morningside 16–3, Cornell (Iowa) 21–0, Drake 27–3.   *Lost:* Minnesota 5–0, Iowa 20–7 (1st homecoming).   *Stars:* B R.L. "Buck" Hurst, soph E Clarence Nagle.   *Noteworthy:* Williams' last team earned share of MVC title.
1915 (6–2)   *Won:* Ellsworth 31–0, Simpson 27–0, Missouri 14–6, Morningside 7–0, Iowa 16–0, Drake 28–14.   *Lost:* Minnesota 9–6, unbeaten Nebraska 21–0.   *Stars:* QB Durry Moss, G Harold McKinley.   *Noteworthy:* 1st year under Charles Mayser.
1917 (5–2)   *Won:* Simpson 47–0, Coe 7–0, Missouri 15–0, Kansas St. 10–7 (1st meeting), Drake 47–0.   *Lost:* Kansas 7–0, Iowa 6–3.   *Stars:* G Dick Barker, C Leigh Wallace.
1938 (7–1–1)   *Won:* Denver 14–7, Luther 32–7, Nebraska 8–7 (1st over Cornhuskers in 16 games since 1919), Missouri 16–13, Kansas 21–7, Marquette 7–0, Drake 14–0 in 1st 7 games.   *Lost:* unbeaten Oklahoma 10–0.   *Tied:* Kansas St. 13–13.   *Stars:* G Ed Bock (Iowa State's 1st consensus All-American), B Everett Kischer, E Charles Heileman, T Clyde Shugart.
1944 (6–1–1)   *Won:* Gustavus Adolphus 49–0, Doane 59–0, Kansas 25–0, Kansas St. 14–0, Nebraska 19–6, Drake 9–0.   *Lost:* Oklahoma 12–7.   *Tied:* Missouri 21–21.   *Stars:* E Rex Wagner, Gs Charles Wright and soph Jack Fathauer.
1959 (7–3)   *Won:* Drake 41–0, Denver 28–12, South Dakota 41–6, Colorado 27–0 (1st over Buffs since 1950), Kansas St. 26–0 (1st over Wildcats since 1952), Nebraska 18–6, San Jose St. 55–0.   *Lost:* Missouri 14–0, Kansas 7–0, Oklahoma 35–12.   *Stars:* TB Dwight Nichols (9 TDs, 746 yds rush, 1,355 yds and 17 TDs total off), FB Tom Watkins (843 yds rush, 9 TDs), E Don Webb (24 pass rec for 309 yds).
1960 (7–3)   *Won:* Drake 46–0, Detroit 44–21, Nebraska 10–7, Oklahoma St. 13–9 (1st meeting since 1926), Oklahoma 10–6 (1st over Sooners in 29 games since 1931), Kansas St. 20–7, Pacific 14–6.   *Lost:* Kansas 28–14, Colorado 21–6, Missouri 34–8 in successive mid-season games.   *Stars:* soph TB

Dave Hoppmann (844 yds and 5 TDs rush), Watkins (688 yds rush, 10 TDs), Webb (13 pass rec for 203 yds).   *Noteworthy:* led nation in pass defense.
1971 (8–4)   *Won:* Idaho 24–7, New Mexico 44–20, Kent St. 17–14, Kansas St. 24–0, Kansas 40–24, Missouri 45–17, Oklahoma St. 54–0 (1st over Cowboys since 1965), San Diego St. 48–31.   *Lost:* Colorado 24–14, Oklahoma 43–12 (10th straight to Sooners), unbeaten national champ Nebraska 37–0.   *Stars:* QB Dean Carlson (1,637 yds pass), soph TE Keith Krepfle (40 pass rec for 570 yds and 7 TDs), TB George Amundson (1,260 yds and 15 TDs rush), LB Keith Schroeder, DB John Schweizer (6 int).   *Noteworthy:* made 1st postseason appearance, losing to Louisiana St. (LSU) 33–15 in Sun Bowl; Carlson passed for 230 yds and both TDs.
1976 (8–3)   *Won:* Drake 58–14 (1st meeting since 1965), Air Force 41–6, Kent St. 47–7, Utah 44–14, Missouri 21–17, Kansas St. 45–14, Kansas 31–17,

DB Mark DouBrava, 1989–92. All Big 8 selection, 1991–92.

Nebraska 37–28 (1st over Cornhuskers since 1960). *Lost:* Oklahoma 24–10 (15th straight to Sooners), Colorado 33–14, Oklahoma St. 42–21. *Stars:* SE Luther Blue (33 pass rec for 644 yds and 5 TDs), QB Wayne Stanley (1,084 yds pass), TB Dexter Green (1,074 yds and 8 TDs rush), G Dave Greenwood, K Scott Kollman (11 FGs, 75 pts), P Rich Blabolil (42.8-yd avg), DL Maynard Stensrud, S Tony Hawkins.

1977 (8–4) *Won:* Wichita St. 35–9, Bowling Green 35–21, Dayton 17–13, Missouri 7–0, Nebraska 24–21, Kansas 41–3, Kansas St. 22–15, Oklahoma St. 21–13. *Lost:* Iowa 12–10 (1st meeting since 1934), Oklahoma 35–16, Colorado 12–7. *Stars:* Green (1,240 yds and 15 TDs rush, 25 pass rec for 203 yds), soph QB Terry Rubley (1,037 yds pass), DTs Mike Stensrud and Tom Randall, DB Kevin Hart, Blabolil (41.6-yd punting avg). *Noteworthy:* lost to N.C. State 24–14 in Peach Bowl; Green ran for

172 yds and frosh John Quinn scored 1 Cyclone TD and passed for other.

1978 (8–4) *Won:* Rice 23–19, San Diego St. 14–13, Iowa 31–0, Drake 35–7, Kansas 13–7, Kansas St. 24–0, Oklahoma St. 28–15, Colorado 20–16 (1st over Buffs since 1963). *Lost:* Nebraska 23–0, Missouri 26–13, Oklahoma 34–6 in consecutive mid-season games. *Stars:* Green (13 TDs, 1,139 yds rush), SE Stan Hixon (26 pass rec for 474 yds), Stensrud, DE Rick White, S Mike Schwartz. *Noteworthy:* Earle Bruce's last team. Lost to Texas A&M 28–12 in Hall of Fame Bowl; Green ran for 148 yds and 2 TDs.

BOWL SUMMARY

Hall of Fame 0–1; Liberty 0–1; Peach 0–1; Sun 0–1.

BOWL RECORD (0–4)

Regular Season	Bowl	Score	Opponent	Record
1971 (8–3)	Sun	15–33	LSU	(8–3)
1972 (5–5–1)	Liberty	30–31	Georgia Tech	(6–4–1)
1977 (8–3)	Peach	14–24	N.C. State	(7–4)
1978 (8–3)	Hall of Fame	12–28	Texas A&M	(7–4)

CONFERENCE TITLES

Missouri Valley—1911*, 1912*. **Big 8**—None.

TOP 20 AP AND UPI RANKING

1971	U–17

MAJOR RIVALS

Iowa State has played at least 10 games with Coe 16–2, Colorado 11–35–1, Cornell (Iowa) 14–3–1, Denver 7–3, Drake 48–17–4, Grinnell 20–10–3, Iowa 12–28, Kansas 29–37–6, Kansas St. 45–27–4, Marquette 2–8–1, Minnesota 2–21–1, Missouri 29–48–9, Nebraska 15–70–2, Northern Iowa 13–2–3, Oklahoma 5–58–2, Oklahoma St. 12–20–2, Simpson 15–1–1.

COACHES

Dean of Iowa State coaches is Clay Stapleton with record of 42–53–4 for 1958–67. Best winning percentage was by A.W. Ristine with record of 36–10–1 for 1902–06. Other top records for at least 3 years were by Glenn Warner, 18–7 for 1895–98; Clyde Williams, 33–14–2 for 1907–12 with 2 MVC titles; Charles Mayser, 21–11–2 for 1915–19; Mike Michalske, 18–18–3 for 1942–46; John Majors, 24–

30–1 for 1968–72 with 2 bowl teams; and Earle Bruce, 36–32 for 1973–78 with 2 bowl teams.

Miscellanea

First game was tie with State Center 6–6 in 1892 . . . 1st win was over Des Moines YMCA 30–0 in 1892 . . . 1st win over college foe was over Iowa 16–8 in 1894 . . . highest score was over Simpson 87–0 in 1904 . . . highest since W.W. II was over Colorado St. 69–0 in 1980 . . . worst defeat was by Oklahoma 63–0 in 1946 . . . highest against Cyclones was by Nebraska 72–29 in 1983 . . . longest unbeaten string of 10 in 1937–38 ended by Oklahoma 10–0 . . . longest losing string of 16 in 1929–30 broken with win over Simpson 6–0 in 1931 opener . . . consensus All-Americans were Ed Bock, G, 1938; and Mike Busch, TE, 1989 . . . Academic All-Americans were Max Burkett, S, 1952; and Mark Carlson, LB, 1982.

KANSAS (Jayhawks; Crimson and Blue)

Notable Teams

1891 (7–0–1) *Won:* Missouri 22–8 (1st meeting), Washburn 32–10, 38–10 (1st meetings), Kansas City YMCA 22–4, Baker 18–4, 8–0, Iowa 14–12 (1st meeting). *Tied:* Washington (Mo.) 6–6. *Noteworthy:* had 1st unbeaten season under E.M. Hopkins.

1892 (7–1) *Won:* Denver A.C. 20–6, Baker 14–0, Washburn 36–0, Illinois 26–4, Iowa 24–4, Nebraska 12–0 (1st meeting), Missouri 12–4. *Lost:* Baker 18–0. *Noteworthy:* 1st year under A.W. Shepard.

1895 (6–1) *Won:* Midland 28–0, 56–0, Emporia St. 10–0, Iowa 52–0, Doane 32–0, Nebraska 8–4. *Lost:* Missouri 10–6 in finale.

1896 (7–3) *Won:* Haskell 32–0 (1st meeting), Abilene 6–0, Emporia St. 26–0, Denver A.C. 8–6, Nebraska 18–4, Doane 16–4, Missouri 30–0. *Lost:* Iowa 6–0, Kansas City Medical 8–0, Minnesota 12–0.

1897 (8–2) *Won:* Kansas City Medical 22–8, Midland 40–0, Haskell 40–0, Warrensburg 23–0, Glasco 23–0, Iowa 56–0, St. Mary's 28–0, Missouri 16–0. *Lost:* Nebraska 6–5, Kansas City Medical 2–0. *Noteworthy:* 1st year under Wylie Woodruff.

1898 (7–1) *Won:* Haskell 15–0, Kansas City Med-ical 6–0, 6–0, Iowa St. 11–6 (1st meeting), Warrensburg 33–0, Ainsworth Medical 40–0, Missouri 12–0. *Lost:* Nebraska 18–6. *Noteworthy:* Woodruff's last year.

1899 (10–0) *Won:* Haskell 12–0, 18–0, Washburn 35–0, 23–0 (1st meetings since 1892), Ottawa 29–6, 29–0, Drake 29–5 (1st meeting), Emporia St. 35–0, Nebraska 36–20, Missouri 34–6. *Noteworthy:* had 1st unbeaten season since 1891 in only year under Fielding Yost.

1904 (8–1–1) *Won:* College of Emporia 6–0, Emporia St. 34–0, Oklahoma 16–0, Washburn 5–0, Notre Dame 24–5, Washington (Mo.) 12–0, Kansas St. 41–4, Missouri 29–0. *Lost:* Haskell 23–6. *Tied:* Colorado 6–6. *Noteworthy:* 1st year under A.R. "Bert" Kennedy.

1905 (10–1) *Won:* William Jewell 31–0, College of Emporia 45–0, Arkansas 6–0, Drury 11–0, Emporia St. 32–0, Oklahoma 34–0, Washington (Mo.) 21–0, Washburn 18–11, Kansas St. 28–0, Missouri 24–0. *Lost:* Colorado 15–0 in mid-season.

1906 (7–2–2) *Won:* William Jewell 18–0, College of Emporia 25–0, St. Mary's 18–0, Arkansas 37–5, Oklahoma 20–4, Colorado 16–0, Nebraska 8–6 (1st over Cornhuskers in 5 games since 1899). *Lost:* St. Louis 34–2, Kansas St. 6–4 (1st in 5-game series begun in 1902). *Tied:* Washburn 0–0, Missouri 0–0.

1908 (9–0) *Won:* Emporia St. 11–0, St. Mary's 24–0, Kansas St. 12–6, Oklahoma 11–0, Washington (Mo.) 10–0, Washburn 23–0, Nebraska 20–5, Iowa 10–5 (1st meeting since 1897), Missouri 10–4. *Stars:* G Howard "Tub" Reed, E Carl Pleasant, C Swede Carlson. *Noteworthy:* won 1st MVC title in 1st unbeaten season since 1899.

1909 (8–1) *Won:* Emporia St. 55–0, St. Mary's 29–0, Oklahoma 11–0, Kansas St. 5–3, Washington (Mo.) 23–0, Washburn 17–0, Nebraska 6–0, Iowa 20–7. *Lost:* unbeaten Missouri 12–6 (1st to Tigers since 1901) in finale. *Stars:* Pleasant, Carlson, soph G Ellis Davidson.

1910 (6–1–1) *Won:* Ottawa 11–0, St. Mary's 9–5, Baker 21–0 (1st meeting since 1893), Drake 6–0 (1st meeting since 1899), Washburn 21–6, Oklahoma 2–0. *Lost:* Nebraska 6–0. *Tied:* Missouri 5–5. *Stars:* Davidson, E Earl Ammons. *Noteworthy:* Kennedy's last team.

1915 (6–2) *Won:* William Jewell 20–0, Emporia St. 21–3, Drake 30–7, Kansas St. 19–7, Washburn 41–0, Missouri 8–6. *Lost:* unbeaten Oklahoma 23–14,

unbeaten Nebraska 33–0. *Star:* HB Ad Lindsey.
Noteworthy: 1st year under Herman Olcott.
1917 (6–2) *Won:* Emporia St. 33–0 (10th straight
win in series), Washburn 34–2, Iowa St. 7–0, Kansas
St. 9–0, Oklahoma 13–6, Missouri 27–3. *Lost:*
Illinois 22–0, Nebraska 13–3. *Stars:* QB Stem Foster, frosh E Dutch Lonborg, soph T George Nettels.
Noteworthy: Olcott's last team.
1923 (5–0–3) *Won:* Creighton 6–0, Oklahoma St.
9–0 (1st meeting), Oklahoma 7–3, Washington
(Mo.) 83–0, Drake 17–0. *Tied:* Nebraska 0–0, Kansas St. 0–0, Missouri 3–3. *Stars:* E Charles Black,
T Bob Mosby. *Noteworthy:* got share of 2nd MVC
title in 1st unbeaten season since 1908.
1930 (6–2) *Won:* Creighton 26–0, Haskell 33–7,
Kansas St. 14–0, Iowa St. 20–6, Oklahoma 13–0,
Missouri 32–0. *Lost:* Pennsylvania 21–6, Nebraska 16–0 in consecutive late games. *Stars:* HBs
Jim Bausch and Forrest Cox, soph FB Ormand
Beach, T Earl Foy, C Charles Smoot. *Noteworthy:*
won 1st Big 6 title.
1946 (7–2–1) *Won:* Denver 21–13, Wichita St.
14–7, Iowa St. 24–8, Oklahoma St. 14–13 (1st
meeting since 1931), Oklahoma 16–13 (1st over
Sooners since 1937), Kansas St. 34–0, Missouri
20–19. *Lost:* Nebraska 16–14, Tulsa 56–0 in consecutive mid-season games. *Tied:* Texas Christian
(TCU) 0–0 in opener. *Stars:* HB Ray Evans (7 TDs,
838 yds and 12 TDs total off), E Otto Schnellbacher
(16 pass rec for 342 yds), T Don Ettinger, soph E
Dave Schmidt, QB Lynne McNutt, G Don Fambrough. *Noteworthy:* got share of 2nd Big 6 title
in 1st year under George Sauer.
1947 (8–1–2) *Won:* Denver 9–0, Iowa St. 27–7,
South Dakota St. 86–6, Kansas St. 55–0, Nebraska
13–7, Oklahoma St. 13–7, Missouri 20–14, Arizona
54–28. *Tied:* TCU 0–0, Oklahoma 13–13. *Stars:*
Evans (7 TDs, 1,018 yds and 11 TDs total off),
Schnellbacher (17 pass rec for 361 yds), Ettinger,
Fambrough, soph FB Forrest Griffith (9 TDs).
Noteworthy: Sauer's last team shared Big 6 crown
in 1st unbeaten season since 1923. Made 1st
postseason appearance, losing to Georgia Tech
20–14 in Orange Bowl; Evans scored TDs on 12-yd
run and 12-yd pass from QB Bill Hogan but
Jayhawks fumbled at Tech's 1-yd line in final
minutes of game.
1948 (7–3) *Won:* Denver 40–0, Colorado 40–7 (1st
meeting since 1935), Iowa St. 20–7, George Washington 12–0, Nebraska 27–7, Oklahoma St. 13–7,

Kansas St. 20–14. *Lost:* TCU 14–13, Oklahoma
60–7, Missouri 21–7. *Stars:* Griffith (6 TDs), QB
Dick Gilman (14 TDs pass), E Bryan Sperry (21 pass
rec for 343 yds), G Dick Tomlinson. *Noteworthy:*
1st year under J.V. Sikes.
1951 (8–2) *Won:* TCU 27–13 (1st in 9-game series
begun in 1942), Iowa St. 53–33, Utah 26–7, Kansas
St. 33–14, Nebraska 27–7, Loyola (Calif.) 34–26,
Oklahoma St. 27–12, Missouri 41–28. *Lost:* Colorado 35–27, Oklahoma 33–21. *Stars:* DT George
Mrkonic, T Oliver Spencer, Gs George Kennard
and soph Bob Hantla, Es Bill Schaake and Orban
Tice (19 pass rec for 363 yds), Bs Bob Brandeberry
(649 yds rush), Bud Laughlin (13 TDs), Charlie
Hoag and John Konek (8 int).
1952 (7–3) *Won:* TCU 13–0, Santa Clara 21–9,
Colorado 21–12, Iowa St. 43–0, Southern Methodist
26–0, Kansas St. 26–6, Oklahoma St. 12–7. *Lost:*
Oklahoma 42–20, Nebraska 14–13, Missouri 20–19.
Stars: Spencer, Hantla, Brandeberry (9 TDs), Hoag
(16 pass rec for 380 yds), FB Galen Fiss, HB Gil
Reich, E Paul Leoni.
1968 (9–2) *Won:* Illinois 47–7, Indiana 38–20, New
Mexico 68–7, Nebraska 23–13, Oklahoma St. 49–14,

HB/QB John Hadl, 1959–61. Led Jayhawks in scoring,
punting and intercepting, 1959.

HB Gale Sayers, 1962–64

Iowa St. 46–25, Colorado 27–14, Kansas St. 38–29, Missouri 21–19. *Lost:* Oklahoma 27–23. *Stars:* QB Bobby Douglass (1,811 yds total off, 12 TDs rush), TE John Mosier, George McGowan (32 pass rec for 592 yds), soph FB John Riggins (866 yds and 6 TDs rush), Donnie Shanklin (772 yds and 8 TDs rush), T Keith Christensen, DE John Zook, LB Emery Hicks, P Bill Bell (41.9-yd avg). *Noteworthy:* Got share of 1st Big 8 title (5th conference title overall). Lost to unbeaten Penn St. 15–14 in Orange Bowl when Nittany Lions made good on 2nd try for 2-pt conversion with 15 seconds remaining; Douglass passed for 165 yds, Mosier had 5 pass rec for 77 yds, and Jayhawk TDs were scored by RB Michael Reeves and Riggins.

1981 (8–4) *Won:* Tulsa 15–11, Oregon 19–10, Kentucky 21–16, Arkansas St. 17–16, Kansas St. 17–14, Iowa St. 24–11, Colorado 27–0, Missouri 19–11. *Lost:* Oklahoma St. 20–7, Oklahoma 45–7, Nebraska 31–15. *Stars:* P Bucky Scribner (43.8-yd punting avg), LB Kyle McNorton, soph QB Frank Seurer (1,199 yds pass), WR Wayne Capers (36 pass rec for 629 yds), Garfield Taylor (728 yds rush),

QB Nolan Cromwell, 1973–76. Led Jayhawks in rushing, passing, and scoring, 1975.

soph K Bruce Kallmeyer (12 FGs), G David Lawrence. *Noteworthy:* lost to Mississippi St. 10–0 in Hall of Fame Bowl as opening kickoff fumble by Jayhawks led to only TD of game; Scribner averaged 45.2 yds on 9 punts.
1992 (8–4) *Won:* Oregon St. 49–20, Ball St. 62–10, Tulsa 40–7, Kansas St. 31–7, Iowa St. 50–47, Oklahoma 27–10 (1st over Sooners since 1984), Oklahoma St. 26–18. *Lost:* California 27–23, Nebraska 49–7, Colorado 25–18, Missouri 22–17. *Stars:* QB Chip Hilleary (1,583 yds and 12 TDs pass, 537 yds and 6 TDs rush), WR Matt Gay (30 pass rec for 425 yds), TE Dwayne Chandler (17 pass rec for 398 yds and 6 TDs), TB Maurice Douglas (899 yds and 12 TDs rush), FB Monte Cozzens (527 yds and

6 TDs rush), OT Keith Loneker, soph OG John Jones, K/P Dan Eichloff (16 FGs, 40.6-yd punting avg), DL Dana Stubblefield, DB Kwamie Lassiter. *Noteworthy:* beat Brigham Young (BYU) 23–20 in Aloha Bowl as Hilleary passed for 126 yds and ran for a TD and 2-pt conversion, Gay threw 74-yd TD pass to soph TE Rodney Harris (4 pass rec for 142 yds), and Eichloff kicked FGs of 42 and 48 yds.

BOWL SUMMARY

Aloha 1–0; Bluebonnet 1–0; Hall of Fame 0–1; Liberty 0–1; Orange 0–2; Sun 0–1.

BOWL RECORD (2–5)

Regular Season	Bowl	Score	Opponent	Record
1947 (8–0–2)	Orange	14–20	Georgia Tech	(9–1)
1961 (6–3–1)	Bluebonnet	33–7	Rice	(7–3)
1968 (9–1)	Orange	14–15	Penn State	(10–0)
1973 (7–3–1)	Liberty	18–31	N.C. State	(8–3)
1975 (7–4)	Sun	19–33	Pittsburgh	(7–4)
1981 (8–3)	Hall of Fame	0–10	Miss. State	(7–4)
1992 (7–4)	Aloha	23–20	BYU	(8–4)

CONFERENCE TITLES

Missouri Valley—1908. **Big 6**—1930, 1946*, 1947*. **Big 8**—1968*.

TOP 20 AP AND UPI RANKING

1947	12	1960	11–9	1968	7–6	1973	18–15
1951	U–20	1961	U–15				

MAJOR RIVALS

Kansas has played at least 10 games with Baker 6–3–1, Colorado 18–31–3, Drake 10–6–1, Emporia St. 16–0–1, Haskell 6–5, Iowa 7–3, Iowa St. 37–29–6, Kansas St. 61–24–5, Missouri 44–48–9, Nebraska 21–75–3, Oklahoma 24–60–6, Oklahoma St. 25–23–3, Texas Christian 5–15–4, Washburn 28–5–4, Washington (Mo.) 12–0–3.

COACHES

Dean of Kansas coaches is Jack Mitchell with record of 44–42–5 for 1958–66, including a Bluebonnet Bowl champion. Most wins were under A.R. "Bert" Kennedy, 53–9–4 for 1904–10, with 1 MVC title and 1 unbeaten team. Other top records for at least 3 years were by Hector Cowan, 15–7–1 for 1894–96; Herman Olcott, 16–7–1 for 1915–17;

Bill Hargiss, 18–16–2 for 1928–32 with 1 Big 6 title; J.V. Sikes, 35–25 for 1948–53; Pepper Rodgers, 20–22 for 1967–70 with 1 Big 8 title and 1 bowl team; Don Fambrough, 36–49–5 for 1971–74 and 1979–82 with 2 bowl teams; and Glen Mason, 22–33–1 for 1988–92 with 1 bowl team.

Miscellanea

First game was loss to Baker 22–9 in 1890 . . . 1st win was over Baker 14–12 in 1890 . . . highest score was over South Dakota St. 86–6 in 1947 . . . biggest margin was over Washington (Mo.) 83–0 in 1923 . . . worst defeat was by Nebraska 70–0 in 1986 . . . highest against Jayhawks was by Oklahoma 71–10 in 1987 . . . longest win streak of 18 in 1907–09 ended by Missouri 12–6 . . . 15-game unbeaten string in 1890–92 ended by Baker 18–0 . . . longest losing string of 17 in 1953–55 broken with win over Washington St. 13–0 . . . consensus All-Americans were Gale Sayers, B, 1963–64; John Zook, DE, 1968; and Dave Jaynes, QB, 1973 . . . Academic All-Americans were Fred Elder, T, 1964; Mike Sweatman, LB, 1967; Dave Morgan, LB, 1968; Mike McCoy, C, 1971; and Tom Fitch, S, 1976.

KANSAS STATE (Wildcats; Purple and White)

Notable Teams

1905 (6–2) **Won:** Ottawa 29–0, Kansas Wesleyan 24–0, St. Mary's 10–5, Wichita St. 11–6, Haskell 60–0, Kansas St. Teachers 10–0. **Lost:** Washburn 12–5, Kansas 28–0. **Noteworthy:** had 1st winning season in 1st year under Mike Ahearn.
1906 (5–2) **Won:** College of Emporia 35–0, Haskell 10–5, Ottawa 32–11, Kansas 6–4 (1st in 5-game series begun in 1902), Kansas St. Teachers 10–0. **Lost:** Washburn 5–4, Wichita St. 12–6 in consecutive mid-season games.
1908 (6–2) **Won:** Kansas Wesleyan 28–5, Southwestern 17–0, Creighton 31–0, Oklahoma St. 40–10 (1st meeting), Washburn 23–4, Colorado St. 33–10. **Lost:** unbeaten Kansas 12–6, Oklahoma 33–4 (1st meeting).
1909 (7–2) **Won:** Kansas Wesleyan 35–0, Southwestern 60–0, Kansas St. Teachers 44–0, Creighton 58–3, Oklahoma St. 9–0, Wichita St. 71–0, Wash-

burn 40–0. **Lost:** unbeaten Missouri 3–0 (1st meeting), Kansas 5–3 in consecutive early games.
1910 (10–1) **Won:** William Jewell 57–0, Haskell 39–0, Kansas St. Teachers 22–0, Arkansas 5–0, Drury 75–0, Missouri Mines 23–0, Creighton 6–2, Wichita St. 33–6, Baker 35–0, Washburn 33–0. **Lost:** Colorado College 15–8. **Noteworthy:** Ahearn's last team.
1912 (8–2) **Won:** Southwestern 19–7, Haskell 21–14, Kansas St. Teachers 22–7, Wichita St. 54–0, College of Emporia 28–7, Texas A&M 13–10, Washburn 21–3, Colorado 14–6 (1st meeting). **Lost:** Nebraska 30–6, Kansas 19–6 in early games. **Star:** T Jacob Holmes.
1916 (6–1–1) **Won:** Baker 20–0, Southwestern 53–0, Kansas St. Teachers 13–3, Missouri 7–6 (1st in 4-game series begun in 1909), Oklahoma 14–13 (1st in 4-game series begun in 1908), Washburn 47–0. **Lost:** Nebraska 14–0. **Tied:** Kansas 0–0. **Stars:** E Lee Randels, B Eddie Wells. **Noteworthy:** 1st year under Z.G. Clevenger.
1917 (6–2) **Won:** Baker 28–0, Oklahoma St. 23–0 (1st meeting since 1911), Missouri 7–6, Kansas St. Teachers 51–0, Washburn 38–0, Washington (Mo.) 61–0. **Lost:** Kansas 9–0, Iowa St. 10–7 (1st meeting) in consecutive mid-season games. **Star:** soph G Carl Roda.
1918 (4–1) **Won:** Baker 22–0, Fort Riley 27–7, Washburn 28–9, Iowa St. 11–0. **Lost:** Kansas 13–7 in finale.
1922 (5–1–2) **Won:** Washburn 47–0, Washington (Mo.) 22–14, Missouri 14–10, Iowa St. 12–2, Texas Christian (TCU) 45–0. **Lost:** Nebraska 21–0 (1st meeting since 1916). **Tied:** Oklahoma 7–7, Kansas 7–7 in consecutive games. **Star:** G Ray Hahn.
1931 (8–2) **Won:** Kansas St. Teachers 28–7, Missouri 20–7, Kansas 13–0, Oklahoma 14–0, West Virginia 19–0, North Dakota St. 19–6, Washburn 22–0. **Lost:** Iowa St. 7–6, Nebraska 6–3 in consecutive mid-season games. **Stars:** E Henry Cronkite, Bs Eldon Auker and soph Ralph Graham. **Noteworthy:** beat Wichita St. 20–6 (1st meeting since 1913) in postseason charity game.
1933 (6–2–1) **Won:** Kansas St. Teachers 25–0, Washington (Mo.) 20–14, Missouri 33–0, Kansas 6–0, Iowa St. 7–0, Oklahoma 14–0. **Lost:** Nebraska 9–0, Texas Tech 6–0. **Tied:** Michigan St. 0–0. **Stars:** Graham, G Homer Hanson. **Noteworthy:** A.N. "Bo" McMillan's last team.
1934 (7–2–1) **Won:** Fort Hays St. 13–0, Kansas

QB Lynn Dickey, 1968–70. Wildcats all-time leading passer with 6,208 yards and 29 TD's.

WR Michael Smith, 1988–90. Wildcats all-time leading receiver with 179 pass receptions for 2,457 yards.

13–0, Washburn 14–6, Missouri 29–0, Oklahoma 8–7, Iowa St. 20–0, Nebraska 19–7. *Lost:* Marquette 27–20, Tulsa 21–0 (1st meeting). *Tied:* Manhattan 13–13. *Stars:* soph Bs Leo Ayres and Maurice Elder, B Oren Stoner, E Ralph Churchill, T George Maddox. *Noteworthy:* won Big 6 title in only year under Lynn "Pappy" Waldorf.
1954 (7–3) *Won:* Colorado St. 29–0, Wyoming 21–13, Nebraska 7–3, Tulsa 20–13 (1st in 7-game series dating to 1934), Kansas 28–6, Drake 53–18, Iowa

St. 12–7. *Lost:* Missouri 35–7, unbeaten Oklahoma 21–0, Colorado 38–14. *Stars:* B Corky Taylor (8 TDs), T Ron Nery, G Ron Marciniak. *Noteworthy:* last year under Bill Meek.

BOWL SUMMARY

Independence 0–1.

BOWL RECORD (0–1)

Regular Season	Bowl	Score	Opponent	Record
1982 (6–4–1)	Independence	3–14	Wisconsin	(6–5)

Conference Titles

Big 6—1934. **Big 8**—None.

TOP 20 AP AND UPI RANKING

None.

Major Rivals

Kansas State has played at least 10 games with Colorado 12–36, Fort Hays St. 8–2–1, Iowa St. 27–45–4, Kansas 24–61–5, Kansas St. Teachers (Emporia St.) 13–8–3, Marquette 6–7, Missouri 18–55–5, Nebraska 10–65–2, Oklahoma 11–63–4, Oklahoma St. 15–32, Tulsa 6–11–1, Washburn 18–10–2, Wichita St. 17–4–2.

Coaches

Deans of Kansas State coaches are Charles Bachman, 33–23–9 for 1920–27, and Vince Gibson, 33–52 for 1967–74. Most wins were under Mike Ahearn, 39–12 for 1905–10. Other top records for at least 3 years were by Guy Lowman, 17–15–3 for 1911–14; Z.G. Clevenger, 19–9–2 for 1916–19; A.N. "Bo" McMillin, 29–21–1 for 1928–33; and Jim Dickey, 25–53–2 for 1978 to early 1985 with 1 bowl team.

Miscellanea

First game was loss to Fort Riley 14–0 in 1896 ... 1st win was over Dickinson County H.S. 4–0 in 1897 ... 1st win over college foe was over Kansas Wesleyan 17–5 in 1899 ... highest score was over Drury 75–5 in 1910 ... highest since W.W. II was over Oklahoma 59–21 in 1969 ... biggest margin since W.W. II was over Ft. Hays St. 55–0 in 1949 and over Baker 55–0 in 1950 ... biggest margin ever was over Wichita St. 71–0 in 1909 ... worst defeat was by Oklahoma 76–0 in 1942 ... worst since W.W. II was by Oklahoma 66–0 in 1956 ... longest winning streak of 13 in 1909–10 ended by Colorado College 15–8 ... longest winless string of 30 in 1986–89 broken with win over North Texas St. 20–17 ... longest losing string of

LB Gary Spani, 1974–77

28 in 1945–48 broken with win over Arkansas St. 37–6 ... consensus All-Americans were Gary Spani, LB, 1977; and Sean Snyder, P, 1992 ... Academic All-Americans were Don Lareau, LB, 1974; Floyd Dorsey, OG, 1977; Darren Gale, DB, 1981–82; Mark Hundley, RB, 1982; and Troy Faunce, P, 1985.

MISSOURI (Tigers; Old Gold and Black)

Notable Teams

1895 (7–1) *Won:* Sedalia A.C. 10–0, Vanderbilt 16–0, Purdue 16–6, Depauw 38–0, Northwestern 22–18, Iowa 34–0, Kansas 10–6. *Lost:* Nebraska 12–10.
1899 (9–2) *Won:* Warrensburg 21–0, Wentworth 45–0, Haskell 17–0, Nebraska 11–0, Tarkio 23–0, Amity 18–0, Christian Brothers 29–0, Missouri Valley 39–0, Washington (Mo.) 33–11. *Lost:*

Drake 11–0 (1st meeting), unbeaten Kansas 34–6.
1907 (7–2) *Won:* Central Methodist 39–0, 46–0,
Warrensburg 38–6, William Jewell 47–0, Texas 5–4,
Tarkio 70–6, Washington (Mo.) 27–0. *Lost:* Iowa
21–6, Kansas 4–0.
1908 (6–2) *Won:* Warrensburg 57–6, Rolla Miners
16–0, Iowa 10–5, Westminster 58–0, Drake 11–8,
Washington (Mo.) 40–0. *Lost:* Iowa St. 16–0 (1st
meeting since 1896), unbeaten Kansas 10–4.
Noteworthy: W.J. Monilaw's last team.
1909 (7–0–1) *Won:* Monmouth 12–6, Kansas St.
3–0 (1st meeting), Rolla Miners 13–0, Iowa 13–12,
Washington (Mo.) 5–0, Drake 22–6, Kansas 12–6
(1st over Jayhawks since 1901). *Tied:* Iowa St.
6–6. *Noteworthy:* William R. Roper's only team
won 1st MVC title in 1st unbeaten season.
1913 (7–1) *Won:* Drury 69–0, Oklahoma 20–17,
Iowa St. 21–13 (1st in 7-game series dating to 1896),
Rolla Miners 44–13, Drake 10–0, Washington (Mo.)
19–0, Kansas 3–0. *Lost:* Illinois 24–7 (1st meeting
since 1896). *Noteworthy:* got share of 2nd MVC
title in Chester L. Brewer's last year.
1916 (6–1–1) *Won:* Central Methodist 40–0,
Washington (Mo.) 13–0, Oklahoma 23–14, Texas
3–0 (1st meeting since 1907), Drake 14–0, Kansas
13–0. *Lost:* Kansas St. 7–6. *Tied:* Iowa St. 0–0.
1919 (5–1–2) *Won:* Drury 41–12, Iowa St. 10–0,
Drake 3–0, Washington (Mo.) 7–0, Kansas 13–6.
Lost: Nebraska 12–5. *Tied:* Kansas St. 6–6, Oklahoma 6–6. *Noteworthy:* Resumed competition after 1-year layoff during W.W. I. Won 3rd MVC title
in 1st year under J.F. Miller.
1920 (7–1) *Won:* Missouri Wesleyan 41–0, St.
Louis 44–0 (1st meeting since 1911), Iowa St. 14–2,
Drake 10–7 (10th straight over Bulldogs), Kansas
St. 19–7, Washington (Mo.) 14–10, Kansas 16–7.
Lost: unbeaten Oklahoma 28–7.
1921 (6–2) *Won:* Oklahoma A&M 36–0 (1st meeting since 1915), St. Louis 32–0, Iowa St. 17–14,
Drake 6–0, Washington (Mo.) 7–0, Oklahoma 24–
14. *Lost:* Kansas St. 7–5, Kansas 15–9. *Noteworthy:* James Phelan's only team.
1924 (7–2) *Won:* Chicago 3–0, Missouri Wesleyan
14–0, Iowa St. 7–0, Kansas St. 14–7, Oklahoma
10–0, Washington (Mo.) 35–0, Kansas 14–0. *Lost:*
Nebraska 14–6. *Noteworthy:* Won 4th MVC title.
Made 1st postseason appearance, losing to Southern California 20–7 in Los Angeles Christmas
Festival game.

1925 (6–1–1) *Won:* Nebraska 9–6 (1st over Cornhuskers in 11 games since 1899), Rolla Miners 32–0
(1st meeting since 1914), Kansas St. 3–0, Iowa St.
23–8, Washington (Mo.) 14–0, Oklahoma 16–14.
Lost: Kansas 10–7 in finale. *Tied:* unbeaten Tulane 6–6. *Star:* T Ed Lindenmeyer. *Noteworthy:*
repeated as MVC champ.
1926 (5–1–2) *Won:* Nebraska 14–7, Iowa St. 7–3,
West Virginia 27–0, Washington (Mo.) 45–6, Kansas 15–0. *Lost:* Oklahoma 10–7. *Tied:* Tulane
0–0, unbeaten Southern Methodist (SMU) 7–7 (1st
meeting).
1927 (7–2) *Won:* Kansas St. 13–6, Nebraska 7–6,
Washington (Mo.) 13–0, Northwestern 34–19, West
Virginia 13–0, Iowa St. 13–6, Oklahoma 20–7.
Lost: SMU 32–9, Kansas 14–7. *Noteworthy:* won
5th and last MVC title.
1936 (6–2–1) *Won:* Cape Girardeau 20–0, Iowa St.
10–0 (1st over Cyclones since 1930), St. Louis 13–7
(1st over Billikens in 7 games since 1922), Oklahoma 21–14, Washington (Mo.) 17–10 (1st over
Bears in 5 games since 1929), Kansas 19–3 (1st over
Jayhawks since 1929). *Lost:* Michigan St. 13–0,
Nebraska 20–0. *Tied:* Kansas St. 7–7. *Stars:* C
Betty Huston and G Kirk Maurice. *Noteworthy:*
1st winning team since 1929.
1939 (8–2) *Won:* Colorado 30–0, Washington
(Mo.) 14–0, Kansas St. 9–7, Iowa St. 21–6, Nebraska
27–13, New York U. 20–7, Oklahoma 7–6, Kansas
20–0. *Lost:* Ohio St. 19–0 (1st meeting). *Stars:*
TB Paul Christman (1,095 yds total off, 7 TDs rush),
T Kenneth Haas, E Roland Orf, C Charles Moser,
G Robert Waldorf. *Noteworthy:* Won 1st Big 6
title. Lost to Georgia Tech 21–7 in Orange Bowl
after Christman scored 1st TD of game in 1st
quarter.
1941 (8–2) *Won:* Colorado 21–6, Kansas St. 35–0,
Iowa St. 39–13, Nebraska 6–0, Michigan St. 19–0,
New York U. 26–0, Oklahoma 28–0, Kansas 45–6.
Lost: Ohio St. 12–7. *Stars:* HB Bob Steuber (855
yds and 9 TDs rush, 67 pts), soph FB Don Reece,
B Harry Ice, C Darold Jenkins (Missouri's 1st
consensus All-American), G Bob Jeffries, T Bud
Wallach. *Noteworthy:* Led nation in rush and
won 2nd Big 6 title. Lost to Fordham 2–0 in Sugar
Bowl on blocked punt for safety in 1st quarter.
1942 (8–3–1) *Won:* Fort Riley 31–0, St. Louis 38–7,
Colorado 26–13, Kansas St. 46–2, Iowa St. 45–6,
Nebraska 26–6, Kansas 42–13, Iowa Navy

Pre-Flight 7–0. *Lost:* Wisconsin 17–9, Great Lakes Naval Training Center 17–0, Fordham 20–12. *Tied:* Oklahoma 6–6. *Stars:* Steuber (1,098 yds rush, 356 yds pass, 18 TDs, national scoring leader with 121 pts), E Bert Ekern, G Mike Fitzgerald. *Noteworthy:* repeated as Big 6 champ.

1945 (6–4) *Won:* SMU 10–7 (1st meeting since 1927), Iowa St. 13–7, Kansas St. 41–7, Nebraska 19–0, Oklahoma 14–6, Kansas 33–12. *Lost:* Minnesota 34–0, Ohio St. 47–6, Michigan St. 14–7. *Stars:* T Jim Kekeris, C Ralph Stewart, G Robert Eigelberger, frosh E Roland Oakes, QB Leonard Brown, HB Robert Hopkins (5 TDs). *Noteworthy:* Won 4th Big 6 title (10th conference crown) in last year under Chauncey Simpson. Lost to Texas 40–27 (1st meeting since 1932) in Cotton Bowl; HB Bill Dellastatious scored 1 TD and passed 40 yds to Oakes for another, and frosh Howard Bonnett had 21-yd TD run.

1948 (8–3) *Won:* St. Louis 60–7, SMU 20–14, Navy 35–14, Iowa St. 49–7, Kansas St. 49–7 (10th straight over Wildcats), Colorado 27–13, Nebraska 33–6, Kansas 21–7. *Lost:* Ohio St. 21–7, Oklahoma 41–7. *Stars:* QB Hal Entsminger (1,084 yds total off, 9 TDs), E Mel Sheehan (23 pass rec for 346 yds), T Chester Fritz, C Robert Fuchs. *Noteworthy:* lost to unbeaten Clemson 24–23 in Gator Bowl on last quarter FG; Entsminger ran for 77 yds and 2 TDs, and HB Richard Braznell passed 20 yds to Kenneth Bounds for other Tiger TD.

1949 (7–4) *Won:* Oklahoma A&M 21–7 (1st meeting since 1921), Illinois 27–20 (1st meeting since 1913), Iowa St. 32–0, Nebraska 21–20, Colorado 20–13, Kansas 34–28, Kansas St. 34–27. *Lost:* Ohio St. 35–34, SMU 28–27, unbeaten Oklahoma 27–7. *Stars:* Braznell (766 yds rush), Gene Ackerman (40 pass rec for 576 yds), John Glorioso (8 TDs, 77 pts). *Noteworthy:* lost to Maryland 20–7 in Gator Bowl after trailing 20–0 at halftime; scored on 5-yd run by Phillip Klein.

1959 (6–5) *Won:* Michigan 20–15, Iowa St. 14–0, Nebraska 9–0, Air Force 13–0, Kansas St. 26–0, Kansas 13–9. *Lost:* Penn St. 19–8, SMU 23–2, Oklahoma 23–0, Colorado 21–20 (1st to Buffaloes since 1951). *Stars:* Melvin West (556 yds rush), E Ross Sloan, T Mike Magac. *Noteworthy:* lost to Georgia 14–0 in Orange Bowl; QB Phil Snowden passed for 152 yds and Russ Sloan had 6 pass rec for 73 yds.

1960 (11–0) *Won:* SMU 20–0, Oklahoma St. 28–7 (1st meeting since 1952), Penn St. 21–8, Air Force 34–8, Kansas St. 45–0, Iowa St. 34–8, Nebraska 28–0, Colorado 16–6, Oklahoma 41–19 (1st over Sooners since 1945), Kansas (by forfeit after losing 23–7 in finale). *Stars:* E Danny LaRose, West (650 yds rush), Donnie Smith (13 TDs), G Paul Henley, T Rockne Calhoun, Charles Snyder (5 int). *Noteworthy:* Won 1st Big 8 title (5th in league and 11th conference title overall). Beat Navy 21–14 in Orange Bowl (1st postseason win in 8 games); West ran for 108 yds, Smith ran for 93 yds and a TD, Norman Beal scored on 90-yd pass int return, and Ronald Taylor scored on 1-yd run.

1961 (7–2–1) *Won:* Washington St. 28–6, Minnesota 6–0, Oklahoma St. 10–0, Iowa St. 13–7, Nebraska 10–0, Kansas St. 27–9, Kansas 10–7. *Lost:* Colorado 7–6, Oklahoma 7–0 in successive late games. *Tied:* California 14–14. *Stars:* Ts Ed Blaine and Bill Wegener, E Conrad Hitchler, Carl Crawford (5 int).

1962 (8–1–2) *Won:* California 21–10, Arizona 17–7, Kansas St. 32–0, Oklahoma St. 23–6, Iowa St. 21–6, Nebraska 16–7, Colorado 57–0. *Lost:* Oklahoma 13–0. *Tied:* Minnesota 0–0, Kansas 3–3. *Stars:* soph HB Johnny Roland (830 yds and 13 TDs rush), T Jerry Wallach, Hitchler, G Tom Hertz, Andy Russell (6 int). *Noteworthy:* beat Georgia Tech 14–10 in Bluebonnet Bowl; Bill Tobin ran for 114 yds and a TD (on 77-yd run), and Jim Johnson scored on 21-yd run.

1963 (7–3) *Won:* Arkansas 7–6, Idaho 24–0, Kansas St. 21–11, Oklahoma St. 28–6, Iowa St. 7–0, Colorado 28–7, Kansas 9–7. *Lost:* Northwestern 23–12, Nebraska 13–12, Oklahoma 13–3. *Stars:* soph QB Gary Lane (6 TDs), E George Seals.

1965 (8–2–1) *Won:* Oklahoma St. 13–0, Minnesota 17–6, Kansas St. 28–14, Iowa St. 23–7, Colorado 20–7, Oklahoma 30–0, Kansas 44–20. *Lost:* Kentucky 7–0, unbeaten Nebraska 16–14. *Tied:* UCLA 14–14. *Stars:* Lane (9 TDs), Roland (6 int), HB Charles Brown (937 yds rush), Monroe Phelps (17 pass rec for 207 yds), soph E Russell Washington, Ts Francis Peay and Bruce Van Dyke, G Mike Eader, P Ray West (40-yd avg). *Noteworthy:* beat Florida 20–18 in Sugar Bowl; Brown ran for 120 yds and a TD, Bill Bates kicked 2 FGs and 2 ex pts, and Roland passed 11 yds to Earl Denny for TD.

1967 (7–3) *Won:* SMU 21–0 (1st meeting since 1960), Northwestern 13–6, Arizona 17–3, Iowa St. 23–7, Oklahoma St. 7–0, Kansas St. 28–6 (10th straight over Wildcats), Nebraska 10–7 (1st over Cornhuskers since 1962). *Lost:* Colorado 23–9, Oklahoma 7–0, Kansas 17–6 (1st to Jayhawks since 1960 game forfeited to Missouri). *Stars:* Barry Lischner (647 yds rush), HB Roger Wehrli, Chuck Weber (15 pass rec for 212 yds), T Washington, LB John Douglas.

1968 (8–3) *Won:* Illinois 44–0, Army 7–3, Colorado 27–14, Nebraska 16–14, Kansas St. 56–20, Oklahoma St. 42–7, Iowa St. 42–7. *Lost:* Kentucky 12–6, Oklahoma 28–14, Kansas 21–19. *Stars:* Wehrli (7 int, nation's punt return leader with 11.7-yd avg), Ts Jim Anderson and Jay Wallace, G Carl Garber, E Bill Schmitt, soph James Harrison (8 TDs), Greg Cook (693 yds rush). *Noteworthy:* beat Alabama 35–10 in Gator Bowl; Cook ran for 179 yds and a TD, and QB Terry McMillan ran for 76 yds and 3 TDs.

1969 (9–2) *Won:* Air Force 19–17, Illinois 37–6, Michigan 40–17, Nebraska 17–7, Oklahoma St. 31–21, Kansas St. 41–38, Oklahoma 44–10, Iowa St. 40–13, Kansas 69–21. *Lost:* Colorado 31–24 in mid-season. *Stars:* McMillan (1,963 yds and 18 TDs pass, 2,157 yds and 25 TDs total off), Joe Moore (1,312 yds rush), E Mel Gray (26 pass rec for 705 yds and 9 TDs), OG Mike Carroll, Ts Larron Jackson and Mark Kuhlmann, DB Dennis Poppe (6 int). *Noteworthy:* Got share of 2nd Big 8 title (12th conference crown overall). Lost to unbeaten Penn St. 10–3 in Orange Bowl as Tigers lost ball 7 times on int and twice on fumbles; scored on 33-yd FG by Henry Brown.

1973 (8–4) *Won:* Mississippi 17–0, Virginia 31–7, North Carolina 27–14, SMU 17–7, Nebraska 13–12, Oklahoma St. 13–9, Kansas St. 31–7. *Lost:* Colorado 17–13, unbeaten Oklahoma 31–3, Iowa St. 17–7, Kansas 14–13. *Stars:* Thomas Reamon (610 yds rush), E Mark Miller (17 pass rec for 256 yds), C Scott Anderson, T Jim Schnietz, K Greg Hill (13 FGs), DB John Moseley. *Noteworthy:* beat Auburn 34–17 in Sun Bowl; Ray Bybee ran for 127 yds and a TD, Reamon ran for 110 yds, Ray Smith passed for 2 TDs, and Moseley scored on 84-yd kickoff return.

1978 (8–4) *Won:* Notre Dame 3–0, Mississippi 45–14, Illinois 45–3, Iowa St. 26–13, Kansas St. 56–14, Kansas 48–0, Nebraska 35–31. *Lost:* national cochamp Alabama 38–20, Oklahoma 45–23, Colorado 28–27, Oklahoma St. 35–20. *Stars:* soph QB Phil Bradley (1,780 yds pass, 2,081 yds total off), TE Kellen Winslow (29 pass rec for 479 yds and 6 TDs), soph B James Wilder (873 yds rush, 12 TDs), Earl Gant (789 yds rush), C Pete Allard, DB Russ Calabrese. *Noteworthy:* 1st year under Warren Powers. Beat Louisiana St. 20–15 in Liberty Bowl; Wilder ran for 115 yds and a TD, Bradley passed for 117 yds and a TD, and Gant scored on 13-yd run.

1980 (8–4) *Won:* New Mexico 47–16, Illinois 53–7, San Diego St. 31–7, Oklahoma St. 30–7, Colorado 45–7, Kansas St. 13–3, Iowa St. 14–10, Kansas 31–6. *Lost:* Penn St. 29–21, Nebraska 38–16, Oklahoma 17–7. *Stars:* Bradley (1,632 yds and 12 TDs pass), Ron Fellows (33 pass rec for 586 yds), TE Andy Gibler (26 pass rec for 298 yds), Terry Hill (22 pass rec for 273 yds, 7 TDs), Ken Blair (22 pass rec for 270 yds), Wilder (839 yds rush, 9 TDs), T Howard Richards, C Brad Edelman, K Ron Verrilli (11 FGs, 67 pts), LB Lester Dickey, DBs Bill Whitaker (6 int) and Eric Wright, P Jeff Brockhaus (42.6-yd avg). *Noteworthy:* lost to Purdue 28–25 in Liberty Bowl; Bradley passed for 210 yds and Fellows scored on 92-yd kickoff return.

1981 (8–4) *Won:* Army 24–10, Rice 42–10, Louisville 34–3, Mississippi St. 14–3, Kansas St. 58–13, Colorado 30–14, Oklahoma 19–14 (1st over Sooners since 1969). *Lost:* Iowa St. 34–13, Nebraska 6–0, Oklahoma St. 16–12, Kansas 19–11. *Stars:* QB Mike Hyde (1,471 yds pass), WR James Caver (33 pass rec for 509 yds), Bob Meyer (791 yds rush), DT Jeff Gaylord, DB Kevin Potter. *Noteworthy:* beat Southern Mississippi 19–17 in Tangerine Bowl; Meyer ran for 96 yds and a TD, and Bob Lucchesi kicked 4 FGs.

BOWL SUMMARY

Bluebonnet 1–0; Cotton 0–1; Fiesta 0–1; Gator 1–2; Hall of Fame 1–0; Holiday 0–1; Liberty 1–1; Los Angeles Christmas Festival 0–1; Orange 1–3; Sugar 1–1; Sun 1–0; Tangerine 1–0.

BOWL RECORD (8–11)

Regular Season	Bowl	Score	Opponent	Record
1924 (7–1)	L.A. Festival	7–20	USC	(8–2)
1939 (9–1)	Orange	7–21	Georgia Tech	(8–2)
1941 (8–1)	Sugar	0–2	Fordham	(7–1)
1945 (6–3)	Cotton	27–40	Texas	(9–1)
1948 (8–2)	Gator	23–24	Clemson	(10–0)
1949 (7–3)	Gator	7–20	Maryland	(8–1)
1959 (6–4)	Orange	0–14	Georgia	(9–1)
1960 (9–1)	Orange	21–14	Navy	(9–1)
1962 (7–1–2)	Bluebonnet	14–10	Georgia Tech	(7–2–1)
1965 (7–2–1)	Sugar	20–18	Florida	(7–3)
1968 (7–3)	Gator	35–10	Alabama	(8–2)
1969 (9–1)	Orange	3–10	Penn State	(10–0)
1972 (6–5)	Fiesta	35–49	Arizona St.	(9–2)
1973 (7–4)	Sun	34–17	Auburn	(6–5)
1978 (7–4)	Liberty	20–15	LSU	(8–3)
1979 (6–5)	Hall of Fame	24–14	South Carolina	(8–3)
1980 (8–3)	Liberty	25–28	Purdue	(8–3)
1981 (7–4)	Tangerine	19–17	Southern Miss.	(9–1–1)
1983 (7–4)	Holiday	17–21	BYU	(10–1)

CONFERENCE TITLES

Missouri Valley—1909, 1913*, 1919, 1924, 1925, 1927. **Big 6**—1939, 1941, 1942, 1945. **Big 8**—1960, 1969*.

TOP 20 AP AND UPI RANKING

1939	6	1960	5–4	1964	U–18	1973	17–U
1941	7	1961	11–11	1965	6–6	1978	15–14
1949	20	1962	U–12	1968	9–17	1979	U–20
1959	18–19	1963	U–16	1969	6–6	1981	19–20

MAJOR RIVALS

Missouri has played at least 10 games with Colorado 33–21–3, Drake 14–4, Illinois 10–6, Indiana 5–3–2, Iowa 7–5, Iowa St. 48–28–9, Kansas 48–44–9, Kansas St. 55–18–5, Missouri–Rolla 10–1–1, Nebraska 32–51–3, Ohio St. 1–8–1, Oklahoma 22–56–5, Oklahoma St. 21–18, St. Louis 10–10–1, SMU 7–13–1, Texas 4–10, Washington (Mo.) 25–11–2.

COACHES

Dean of Missouri coaches is Don Faurot with record of 101–79–10 for 1935–42 and 1946–56, including 3 Big 6 titles and 4 bowl teams. Other top records for at least 3 years were by W.J. Monilaw, 18–6–1 for 1906–08; Chester L. Brewer, 14–8–2 for 1911–13 with 1 MVC title; Henry F. Schulte, 16–14–2 for 1914–17; Gwinn Henry, 40–28–9 for 1923–31 with 3 MVC titles and 1 bowl team; Chauncey Simpson, 12–14–2 for 1943–45 with 1 Big 6 title and 1 bowl team; Dan Devine, 93–37–7 for 1958–70 with 2 Big 8 titles and 6 bowl teams; Al Onofrio, 38–41 for 1971–77 with 2 bowl teams; and Warren Powers, 46–33–3 for 1978–84 with 5 bowl teams.

MISCELLANEA

First game was win over Picked Team 22–6 in 1890 . . . 1st win over college foe was over Washburn 36–6 in 1891 . . . highest score was over Engineers 90–0 in 1890 . . . highest since 1900 was over Tarkio 70–6 in 1907 . . . highest since W.W. II was over Kansas 69–21 in 1969 . . . biggest margin since 1900 was over Drury 69–0 in 1913 . . . biggest margin since W.W. II was over Colorado 57–0 in 1962 . . . worst defeat was by Oklahoma 77–0 in 1986 . . . longest unbeaten string of 11 in 1909–10 ended by Iowa St. 6–5 . . . longest winless string of 17 in 1933–34 broken with win over William Jewell 39–0 in 1935 opener . . . consensus All-Americans were Darold Jenkins, C, 1941; Danny LaRose, E, 1960; Johnny Roland, DB, 1965; Roger Wehrli, DB, 1968; Kellen Winslow, TE, 1978; and John Clay, OL, 1986 . . . Academic All-Americans were Tom Hertz, G, 1962; Dan Schuppan, DE, and Bill Powell, DT, 1966; Carl Garber, MG, 1968; John Weisenfels, LB, 1970; Greg Hill, K, 1972; and Van Darkow, LB, 1981.

NEBRASKA (Cornhuskers, Huskers; Scarlet and Cream)

NOTABLE TEAMS

1894 (6–2) *Won:* Lincoln H.S. 8–0 (exhibition), Grinnell 22–0, Omaha YMCA 36–6, 10–6, Kansas 12–6, Ottawa 6–0, Iowa 36–0. *Lost:* Missouri 18–14, Doane 12–0.

1897 (5–1) *Won:* Tarkio 16–0, Nebraska Wesleyan 11–0, Missouri 41–0, Kansas 10–5, Iowa 6–0. *Lost:* Iowa St. 10–0 in opener.

1898 (8–3) *Won:* Hastings 76–0, Iowa St. 23–10, Tarkio 24–0, William Jewell 38–0, Missouri 47–6, Kansas 18–6, Colorado 23–10 (1st meeting), Denver A.C. 11–10. *Lost:* Kansas City Medics 24–0, Drake 6–5 (1st meeting), Iowa 6–5. *Noteworthy:* Grinnell game cancelled. Only year under Fielding Yost.

1900 (6–1–1) *Won:* Lincoln H.S. 17–0 (exhibition), Iowa St. 30–0, Drake 8–0, Tarkio 5–0, Missouri 12–0, Grinnell 33–0, Kansas 12–0. *Lost:* unbeaten Minnesota 20–12 (1st meeting) in finale. *Tied:* Alumni 0–0 (exhibition), Kansas City Medics 0–0. *Noteworthy:* 1st year under W.C. "Bummy" Booth.

1901 (6–2) *Won:* Lincoln H.S. 22–0 (exhibition), Kirksville Osteopaths 5–0, Doane 29–0, Iowa St. 17–0, Missouri 51–0, Kansas 29–5, Haskell 18–10. *Lost:* Minnesota 19–0, unbeaten Wisconsin 18–0.

1902 (9–0) *Won:* Lincoln H.S. 27–0 (exhibition), Doane 51–0, Colorado 10–0, Grinnell 17–0, Minnesota 6–0, Missouri 12–0, Haskell 28–0, Kansas 16–0, Knox 7–0, Northwestern 12–0. *Noteworthy:* blanked opposition 159–0 in 1st unbeaten season since 2-game schedule of 1890.

1903 (10–0) *Won:* Lincoln H.S. 23–6 (exhibition), Grand Island 64–0, South Dakota 23–0, Denver 10–0, Haskell 16–0, Colorado 31–0, Iowa 17–6, Knox 33–5, Kansas 6–0, Bellevue 52–0, Illinois 16–0 (1st meeting since 1892).

1904 (7–3) *Won:* Grand Island 72–0, Lincoln H.S. 17–0 (exhibition), Grinnell 46–0, Creighton 39–0, Lincoln Medics 29–0 (exhibition), Knox 34–0, Iowa 17–6, Bellevue 51–0, Illinois 16–10. *Lost:* Colorado 6–0, unbeaten Minnesota 16–12, Haskell 14–6.

1905 (8–2) *Won:* Grand Island 30–0, Lincoln H.S. 20–0 (exhibition), South Dakota 42–6, Knox 16–0, Creighton 102–0, Iowa St. 21–0, Colorado 18–0, Doane 43–5, Illinois 24–6. *Lost:* Michigan 31–0, Minnesota 35–0. *Noteworthy:* Booth's last team.

1907 (8–2) *Won:* Peru St. 53–0, South Dakota 39–0, Grinnell 30–4, Colorado 22–8, Iowa St. 10–9, Kansas 16–6, Denver 63–0, Doane 85–0. *Lost:* Minnesota 8–5, St. Louis 34–0. *Stars:* T Bill Chaloupka, G S.T. Frum, Bs Harold Cook and John Weller. *Noteworthy:* got share of initial MVC title in 1st year under W.C. "King" Cole.

1908 (7–2–1) *Won:* Peru St. 20–0, Doane 43–0, Grinnell 20–5, Haskell 10–0, Iowa 11–8, Iowa St. 23–17, Wabash 27–6. *Lost:* unbeaten Kansas 20–5, Carlisle Indians 37–6. *Tied:* Minnesota 0–0. *Star:* B Ernest Kroger.

1910 (7–1) *Won:* Peru St. 66–0, South Dakota 12–9, Denver 27–0, Doane 6–0, Kansas 6–0, Iowa St. 24–0, Haskell 119–0. *Lost:* Minnesota 27–0. *Stars:* Bs Owen Frank and Leon Warner, E W.F. Chauner, Ts LeRoy Temple and Sylvester Shonka. *Noteworthy:* Cole's last team won 2nd MVC title.

1911 (5–1–2) *Won:* Kearney Normal 117–0, Kansas St. 59–0 (1st meeting), Missouri 34–0 (1st meeting since 1902), Doane 27–0, Kansas 29–0. *Lost:* unbeaten Minnesota 21–3. *Tied:* Iowa St. 6–6, Michigan 6–6. *Stars:* Warner, Chauner, Shonka, Gs E.B. Elliott and E.Z. Hornberger. *Noteworthy:* got share of MVC title in 1st year under "Jumbo" Stiehm.

1912 (7–1) *Won:* Bellevue 81–0, Kansas St. 30–6, Adrian 41–0, Missouri 7–0, Doane 54–6, Kansas 14–3, Oklahoma 13–9 (1st meeting). *Lost:* Minnesota 13–0. *Stars:* Bs Leonard Purdy and soph Vic Halligan, T J.D. Harmon, G J.T.M. Pearson. *Noteworthy:* got share of 3rd straight MVC crown.

1913 (8–0) *Won:* Washburn 19–0, Kansas St. 24–6, Minnesota 7–0 (1st over Gophers in 10 games since 1902), Haskell 7–6, Iowa St. 18–9, Nebraska Wesleyan 42–7, Kansas 9–0, Iowa 12–0. *Stars:* Bs Max Towle, soph Richard Rutherford and Purdy, Es Guy Mastin and Charles Beck, T Halligan. *Noteworthy:* got share of 5th MVC title in 1st unbeaten season since 1903.

1914 (7–0–1) *Won:* Washburn 14–7, Kansas St. 31–0, Michigan St. 24–0, Iowa St. 20–7, Morningside 34–7, Kansas 35–0, Iowa 16–7. *Tied:* South Dakota 0–0. *Stars:* Halligan, soph T H.H. Corey, G E.L. Abbott, C Roy Cameron, E Warren Howard, Bs Rutherford and Guy Chamberlin. *Noteworthy:* won 5th straight MVC title.

1915 (8–0) *Won:* Drake 48–13 (1st meeting since 1906), Kansas St. 31–0, Washburn 47–0, Notre Dame 20–19 (1st meeting), Iowa St. 21–0, Nebraska Wesleyan 30–0, Kansas 33–0, Iowa 52–7. *Stars:* E Chamberlin (Cornhuskers' 1st consensus All-American), Rutherford, Corey, Abbott, G Paul Shields. *Noteworthy:* won 7th MVC title in Stiehm's last year.

1916 (6–2) *Won:* Drake 53–0, Kansas St. 14–0, Oregon St. 17–7 (1st meeting), Nebraska Wesleyan 21–0, Iowa St. 3–0, Iowa 34–17. *Lost:* Kansas 7–3 (breaking 34-game unbeaten string, 1st loss to Jayhawks since 1909), Notre Dame 20–0. *Stars:* Corey, B Hugo Otopalik. *Noteworthy:* won 8th MVC title in 1st year under E.J. "Doc" Stewart.

1917 (5–2) *Won:* Nebraska Wesleyan 100–0, Iowa 47–0, Notre Dame 7–0, Missouri 52–0, Kansas 13–3. *Lost:* Michigan 20–0, Syracuse 10–9. *Stars:* Bs E.H. Schellenberg, John Cook and Paul Dobson, E Roscoe Rhodes, T Edson Shaw. *Noteworthy:* won 8th straight MVC title in Stewart's last year.

1921 (7–1) *Won:* Nebraska Wesleyan 55–0, Haskell 41–0, Oklahoma 44–0, Pittsburgh 10–0 (1st meeting), Kansas 28–0, Iowa St. 35–3, Colorado St. 70–7. *Lost:* Notre Dame 7–0. *Stars:* Bs Glen Preston and Chick Hartley, E Clarence Swanson, G John Pucelik. *Noteworthy:* won 10th MVC title in 1st year under Fred Dawson.

1922 (7–1) *Won:* South Dakota 66–0, Missouri 48–0, Oklahoma 39–7, Kansas 28–0, Kansas St. 21–0 (1st meeting since 1916), Iowa St. 54–6, Notre Dame 14–6 (1st over Irish since 1917). *Lost:* Syracuse 9–6. *Stars:* Preston, Hartley, B Dave Noble, E Leo Scherer, Ts Bub Weller and Adolph Wenke, G Joy Berquist. *Noteworthy:* again won MVC title.

1926 (6–2) *Won:* Drake 21–0, Washington (Mo.) 20–6, Kansas 20–3, Iowa St. 31–6, Kansas St. 3–0, New York U. 15–7. *Lost:* Missouri 14–7, Washington 10–6. *Stars:* B Glenn Presnell, T Lon Stiner.

1927 (6–2) *Won:* Iowa St. 6–0, Grinnell 58–0, Syracuse 21–0, Kansas 47–13, Kansas St. 33–0, New York U. 27–18. *Lost:* Missouri 7–6, unbeaten Pittsburgh 21–13 (1st meeting since 1921). *Stars:* Presnell, B Blue Howell, T Roy Randels, G Dan McMullen, C Ted James.

1928 (7–1–1) *Won:* Iowa St. 12–0, Montana St. 26–6, Syracuse 7–6, Missouri 24–0, Kansas 20–0, Oklahoma 44–6, Kansas St. 8–0. *Lost:* Army 13–3. *Tied:* Pittsburgh 0–0. *Stars:* Howell, McMullen, James, soph T Marion Broadstone, B Clair Sloan. *Noteworthy:* won initial Big 6 title (13th conference crown) in last year under E.E. Bearg.

1931 (8–2) *Won:* South Dakota 44–6, Oklahoma 13–0, Kansas 6–0, Missouri 10–7, Iowa 7–0, Kansas St. 6–3, Iowa St. 23–0. *Lost:* unbeaten Northwestern 19–7, Pittsburgh 40–0. *Stars:* soph FB George Sauer (565 yds and 6 TDs rush), B Everett Kreizinger, T Hugh Rhea, G George Koster, C Lawrence Ely. *Noteworthy:* Won 3rd Big 6 title. Beat Colorado St. 20–7 in postseason charity game in Denver.

1932 (7–1–1) *Won:* Iowa St. 12–6 (10th straight over Cyclones), Kansas 20–6, Kansas St. 6–0, Iowa 14–13, Oklahoma 5–0, Missouri 21–6, Southern Methodist (SMU) 21–14. *Lost:* Minnesota 7–6 (1st meeting since 1919). *Tied:* unbeaten Pittsburgh 0–0. *Stars:* Es Steve Hokuf and Lee Penney, Ely, T Corwin Hulbert, B Chris Mathias, Sauer (6 int). *Noteworthy:* again won Big 6 crown.

1933 (8–1) *Won:* Texas 26–0, Iowa St. 20–0, Kansas St. 9–0, Oklahoma 16–7, Missouri 26–0, Kansas 12–0 (10th straight over Jayhawks), Iowa 7–6, Oregon St. 22–0 (1st meeting since 1924). *Lost:* Pittsburgh 6–0. *Stars:* Sauer (594 yds and 6 TDs rush), Bs Bernie Masterson and Hubert Boswell,

Penney, E Bruce Kilbourne, T Gail O'Brien, G Warren DeBus, C Frank Meier. *Noteworthy:* won 3rd straight Big 6 title.

1935 (6–2–1) *Won:* Chicago 28–7, Iowa St. 20–7, Oklahoma 19–0, Missouri 19–6, Kansas 19–13, Oregon St. 26–20. *Lost:* Minnesota 12–7, Pittsburgh 6–0. *Tied:* Kansas St. 0–0. *Stars:* Bs Lloyd Cardwell and Jerry LaNoue, FB Sam Francis, E Bernard Scherer, soph T Fred Shirey. *Noteworthy:* won 6th Big 6 title.

1936 (7–2) *Won:* Iowa St. 34–0, Indiana 13–9 (1st meeting), Oklahoma 14–0, Missouri 20–0, Kansas 26–0, Kansas St. 40–0, Oregon St. 32–14. *Lost:* unbeaten national champ Minnesota 7–0, Pittsburgh 19–6. *Stars:* Francis, Cardwell, B Ron Douglas, Shirey, E Les McDonald, soph C Charles Brock. *Noteworthy:* Dana X. Bible's last team repeated as Big 6 champ.

1937 (6–1–2) *Won:* Minnesota 14–9 (1st over Gophers in 6 games since 1913), Iowa St. 20–7 (15th straight over Cyclones), Missouri 7–0, Indiana 7–0, Iowa 28–0, Kansas St. 3–0. *Lost:* unbeaten national champ Pittsburgh 13–7. *Tied:* Oklahoma 0–0, Kansas 13–13. *Stars:* Shirey, Brock, E Elmer Dohrmann, T Ted Doyle, G Bob Mehring, B Johnny Howell. *Noteworthy:* won 3rd straight Big 6 title (8th overall) in 1st year under L.McC. "Biff" Jones.

1939 (7–1–1) *Won:* Minnesota 6–0, Iowa St. 10–7, Baylor 20–0, Kansas St. 25–9, Kansas 7–0, Pittsburgh 14–13 (1st over Panthers in 13 games since 1921), Oklahoma 13–7. *Lost:* Missouri 27–13. *Tied:* Indiana 7–7. *Stars:* G Warren Alfson, Bs Herman Rohrig and Harry Hopp.

1940 (8–2) *Won:* Indiana 13–7, Kansas 53–2, Missouri 20–7, Oklahoma 13–0, Iowa 14–6, Pittsburgh 9–7, Iowa St. 21–12, Kansas St. 20–0. *Lost:* unbeaten national cochamp Minnesota 13–7 in opener. *Stars:* Alfson, E Ray Prochaska, T Forrest Behm, Hopp, Bs Walter Luther and Roy Petsch. *Noteworthy:* Won 9th Big 6 title (21st conference crown). Made 1st bowl appearance, losing to unbeaten Stanford 21–13 in Rose Bowl; took 13–7 lead in 1st half on 2-yd run by Vike Francis and 33-yd pass from Rohrig to Allen Zikmund.

1950 (6–2–1) *Won:* Minnesota 32–26 (1st over Gophers since 1939), Penn St. 19–0, Kansas 33–26, Missouri 40–34, Kansas St. 49–21, Iowa St. 20–13. *Lost:* Colorado 28–19, unbeaten national champ Oklahoma 49–35. *Tied:* Indiana 20–20. *Stars:*

soph HB Bobby Reynolds (1,631 all-purpose yds, 1,342 yds rush, nation's scoring leader with 157 pts on 22 TDs and 25 ex pts), QB Fran Nagle, T Charles Toogood, G Don Strasheim. *Noteworthy:* 1st winning team since 1940.

1954 (6–5) *Won:* Iowa St. 39–14, Oregon St. 27–7 (1st meeting since 1948), Colorado 20–6, Missouri 25–19, Kansas 41–20, Hawaii 50–0. *Lost:* Minnesota 19–7, Kansas St. 7–3, Pittsburgh 21–7, unbeaten Oklahoma 55–7. *Stars:* B Bob Smith, T Don Glantz, G Charles Bryant. *Noteworthy:* lost to Duke 34–7 in Orange Bowl as Cornhuskers were held to 110 yds total off; scored on 3-yd run by Donald Comstock.

1962 (9–2) *Won:* South Dakota 53–0, Michigan 25–13, Iowa St. 36–22, N.C. State 19–14, Kansas St. 26–6, Colorado 31–6, Kansas 40–16, Oklahoma St. 14–0. *Lost:* Missouri 16–7, Oklahoma 34–6. *Stars:* QB Dennis Claridge (10 TDs, 1,199 yds total off), T Tyrone Robertson, G Bob Brown. *Noteworthy:* 1st year under Bob Devaney. Beat Miami (Fla.) 36–34 in Gotham Bowl in New York; Willie Ross ran for 77 yds and scored 2 TDs (1 on 92-yd kickoff return), Claridge passed for 146 yds and a TD, and B Bill Thornton ran for 2 TDs.

1963 (10–1) *Won:* South Dakota St. 58–7, Minnesota 14–7, Iowa St. 21–7, Kansas St. 28–6, Colorado 41–6, Missouri 13–12 (1st over Tigers since 1956), Kansas 23–9, Oklahoma St. 20–16, Oklahoma 29–20. *Lost:* Air Force 17–13. *Stars:* Claridge (7 TDs), Dick Callahan (20 pass rec for 371 yds), Rudy Johnson (573 yds and 7 TDs rush), Brown, T Lloyd Voss. *Noteworthy:* Led nation in rush and won 1st Big 8 title (1st conference crown since 1940). Beat Auburn 13–7 in Orange Bowl; Claridge scored on 68-yd run and Dave Theisen kicked 2 FGs.

1964 (9–2) *Won:* South Dakota 56–0, Minnesota 26–21, Iowa St. 14–7, South Carolina 28–6, Kansas St. 47–0, Colorado 21–3, Missouri 9–0, Kansas 14–7, Oklahoma St. 27–14. *Lost:* Oklahoma 17–7 in finale. *Stars:* OT Larry Kramer, C Lyle Sittler, Es Tony Jeter (18 pass rec for 219 yds) and Freeman White (17 pass rec for 338 yds), HB Kent McCloughan (12 TDs), soph QB Bob Churchich (1,045 yds total off), MG Walt Barnes, DB Ted Vactor. *Noteworthy:* Repeated as Big 8 champ. Lost to unbeaten national cochamp Arkansas 10–7 in Cotton Bowl when Razorbacks scored winning TD with less than 5 minutes left; soph Harry Wilson ran for 84 yds and scored Nebraska's TD.

1965 (10–1) *Won:* Texas Christian (TCU) 34–14, Air Force 27–17, Iowa St. 44–0, Wisconsin 37–0, Kansas St. 41–0, Colorado 38–13, Missouri 16–14, Kansas 42–6, Oklahoma St. 21–17, Oklahoma 21–9. *Stars:* Wilson (672 yds and 5 TDs rush), FBs Frank Solich (580 yds rush, 1,058 all-purpose yds) and Pete Tatman (6 TDs), Charlie Winters (7 TDs), Jeter, White (28 pass rec for 458 yds and 6 TDs), T Dennis Carlson, G LaVerne Allers, Barnes, LB Mike Kennedy, DBs Larry Wachholtz and Marv Mueller (5 int). *Noteworthy:* Led nation in rush and took 3rd straight Big 8 title in 1st unbeaten season since 1915. Lost to national cochamp Alabama 39–28 in Orange Bowl; Churchich passed for 232 yds and 3 TDs (2 to Jeter) and scored once.

1966 (9–2) *Won:* TCU 14–10, Utah St. 28–7, Iowa St. 12–6, Wisconsin 31–3, Kansas St. 21–10, Colorado 21–19, Missouri 35–0, Kansas 24–13, Oklahoma St. 21–6. *Lost:* Oklahoma 10–9 in finale. *Stars:* Wilson (635 yds rush, 1,077 all-purpose yds), Churchich (1,136 yds pass), soph Tom Penney (24 pass rec for 286 yds), TE Dennis Morrison (22 pass rec), Ben Gregory (7 TDs), Allers, C Kelly Petersen, T Bob Pickens, MG Wayne Meylan, LB Lynn Senkbeil, DT Carl Stith, Wachholtz (7 int), DB Kaye Carstens. *Noteworthy:* Won 4th straight Big 8 crown (25th conference title). Lost to unbeaten Alabama 34–7 in Sugar Bowl; Churchich passed for 201 yds and a TD (to FB Dick Davis).

1969 (9–2) *Won:* Texas A&M 14–0, Minnesota 42–14, Kansas 21–17, Oklahoma St. 13–3, Colorado 20–7, Iowa St. 17–3, Kansas St. 10–7, Oklahoma 44–14. *Lost:* unbeaten USC 31–21, Missouri 17–7. *Stars:* soph QB Jerry Tagge (1,302 yds pass), TE Jim McFarland (30 pass rec for 381 yds), soph HB Jeff Kinney (546 yds and 9 TDs rush, 41 pass rec for 433 yds and 2 TDs), LB Ken Geddes, DB Dana Stephenson (7 int), DT Bob Liggett, LB Jerry Murtaugh. *Noteworthy:* Got share of 5th Big 8 title. Beat Georgia 45–6 in Sun Bowl; Van Brownson passed for 109 yds and a TD and scored another, Paul Rogers kicked 4 FGs (including 50-yarder), and Kinney ran 11 yds for TD.

1970 (11–0–1) *Won:* Wake Forest 36–12, Army 28–0, Minnesota 35–10, Missouri 21–7, Kansas 41–20, Oklahoma St. 65–31, Colorado 29–13, Iowa St. 54–29 (10th straight over Cyclones), Kansas St. 51–13, Oklahoma 28–21. *Tied:* USC 21–21.

Stars: HB Joe Orduna (834 yds, 14 TDs ru·'', Tagge (national leader in passing efficiency w 1,383 yds and 12 TDs), soph WB Johnny Rodgers (11 TDs, 1,592 all-purpose yds, 35 pass rec for 665 yds and 7 TDs), SE Guy Ingles (34 pass rec for 603 yds and 8 TDs), Rogers, OT Bob Newton, G Donnie McGhee, DT Dave Walline, MG Ed Periard, Murtaugh, DB Bill Kosch (7 int). *Noteworthy:* Again won Big 8 (15th title since Big 6 began). Beat Louisiana St. (LSU) 17–12 in Orange Bowl to earn share of 1st national championship; Tagge passed for 153 yds and scored winning TD in 4th quarter, Orduna scored a TD, and Rogers kicked a FG and 2 ex pts.

1971 (13–0) *Won:* Oregon 34–7, Minnesota 35–7, Texas A&M 34–7, Utah St. 42–6, Missouri 36–0, Kansas 55–0, Oklahoma St. 41–13 (10th straight over Cowboys), Colorado 31–7, Iowa St. 37–0, Kansas St. 44–17, Oklahoma 35–31, Hawaii 45–3. *Stars:* Tagge (314 yds and 8 TDs rush, nation's passing efficiency leader with 2,019 yds and 17 TDs), Rodgers (17 TDs, 1,983 all-purpose yds, 53 pass rec for 872 yds and 11 TDs), TE Jerry List (347 yds pass rec), Kinney (1,037 yds and 16 TDs rush), T Carl Johnson, G Dick Rupert, DE Willie Harper, DT Larry Jacobson (Outland Trophy winner), MG Rich Glover, LB Bob Terrio, DBs Kosch, Dave Mason (6 int), Jim Anderson and Joe Blahak. *Noteworthy:* Repeated as Big 8 champ and won 2nd straight national title. Beat undefeated Alabama 38–6 in Orange Bowl; Kinney ran for 99 yds and a TD, Tagge passed for 159 yds and a TD and scored another, and Rodgers scored on 77-yd punt return.

1972 (9–2–1) *Won:* Texas A&M 37–7, Army 77–7, Minnesota 49–0, Missouri 62–0, Kansas 56–0, Oklahoma St. 34–0, Colorado 33–10, Kansas St. 59–7. *Lost:* UCLA 20–17 (in opener, ending 32-game unbeaten string), Oklahoma 17–14 (in finale). *Tied:* Iowa St. 23–23. *Stars:* soph QB Dave Humm (2,074 yds and 17 TDs pass), Heisman Trophy–winner Rodgers (17 TDs, 2,011 all-purpose yds, 55 pass rec for 942 yds and 8 TDs), List (339 yds pass rec), Gary Dixon (506 yds and 8 TDs rush), K/P Rich Sanger (76 pts, 40.2-yd punting avg), OT Daryl White, Outland Trophy– and Lombardi Award– winner Glover, Harper, Blahak. *Noteworthy:* Devaney's last team won 4th straight Big 8 title (8th overall). Beat Notre Dame 40–6 (1st meeting since 1948) in Orange Bowl; Rodgers ran for 81 yds and 3 TDs, scored on 50-yd pass from Humm, and threw 52-yd TD pass to SE Frosty Anderson.

1973 (9–2–1) *Won:* UCLA 40–13, N.C. State 31–14, Wisconsin 20–16, Minnesota 48–7, Kansas 10–9, Colorado 28–16, Iowa St. 31–7, Kansas St. 50–21. *Lost:* Missouri 13–12, unbeaten Oklahoma 27–0. *Tied:* Oklahoma St. 17–17.   *Stars:* DT John Dutton, DE Steve Manstedt, Humm (1,526 yds and 12 TDs pass), Anderson (26 pass rec for 504 yds and 8 TDs), Bob Revelle (41 pass rec for 509 yds), Brent Longwell (26 pass rec for 293 yds), Rich Bahe (30 pass rec for 406 yds), Tony Davis (13 TDs, 1,008 yds rush), White. *Noteworthy:* Led nation in pass defense in 1st year under Tom Osborne. Beat Texas 19–3 in Cotton Bowl; Davis ran for 106 yds and a TD, Bahe scored on 12-yd run, and Sanger kicked 2 FGs.

1974 (9–3) *Won:* Oregon 61–7, Northwestern 49–7, Minnesota 54–0 (10th straight over Gophers), Kansas 56–0, Oklahoma St. 7–3, Colorado 31–15, Iowa St. 23–13, Kansas St. 35–7. *Lost:* Wisconsin 21–20, Missouri 21–10, unbeaten national cochamp Oklahoma 28–14. *Stars:* C Rik Bonness, OT Marvin Crenshaw, Humm (1,435 yds and 12 TDs pass), Don Westbrook (10 TDs, 1,093 all-purpose yds, 33 pass rec for 508 yds and 7 TDs), Monte Anthony (587 yds and 6 TDs rush), LB Tom Ruud, DE Bob Martin. *Noteworthy:* beat Florida 13–10 in Sugar Bowl; Davis ran for 126 yds, Anthony scored on short run, and K Mike Coyle had 2 last-quarter FGs.

1975 (10–2) *Won:* LSU 10–7, Indiana 45–0 (1st meeting since 1959), TCU 56–14, Miami (Fla.) 31–16, Kansas 16–0, Oklahoma St. 28–20, Colorado 63–21, Missouri 30–7, Kansas St. 12–0, Iowa St. 52–0. *Lost:* national champ Oklahoma 35–10 in finale. *Stars:* Bonness, Anthony (723 yds and 7 TDs rush), Davis (619 yds rush), QB Vince Ferragamo (1,153 yds and 12 TDs pass), SE Bobby Thomas (24 pass rec for 501 yds and 7 TDs), John O'Leary (8 TDs, 26 pass rec for 255 yds), TE Brad Jenkins (5 TD pass rec), Coyle (10 FGs), Martin, DT Mike Fultz, DBs Wonder Monds and Dave Butterfield. *Noteworthy:* Got share of 9th Big 8 title (30th conference crown). Lost to unbeaten Arizona St. 17–14 in Fiesta Bowl (ending 6-bowl win streak); Anthony scored both Nebraska TDs on short runs.

1976 (9–3–1) *Won:* Indiana 45–13, TCU 64–10,

Miami (Fla.) 17–9, Colorado 24–12, Kansas St. 51–0, Kansas 31–3, Oklahoma St. 14–10, Hawaii 68–3. *Lost:* Missouri 34–24, Iowa St. 37–28 (1st to Cyclones since 1960), Oklahoma 20–17. *Tied:* LSU 6–6. *Stars:* Ferragamo (2,071 yds and 20 TDs pass), SEs Chuck Malito (30 pass rec for 615 yds) and Dave Shamblin (30 pass rec for 468 yds), Thomas (30 pass rec for 561 yds and 7 TDs), soph HB Rick Berns (9 TDs, 1,180 all-purpose yds, 854 yds rush), T Bob Lingenfelter, G Dan Schmidt, K Al Eveland (11 FGs, 73 pts), Fultz, Butterfield, LB Clete Pillen, DE Ray Phillips, P Randy Lessman (40.9-yd avg). *Noteworthy:* beat Texas Tech 27–24 in Astro-Bluebonnet Bowl; Ferragamo passed for 183 yds and 2 TDs, and Berns ran for 118 yds and other 2 Cornhusker TDs.

1977 (9–3) *Won:* Alabama 31–24, Baylor 31–10, Indiana 31–13, Kansas St. 26–9, Colorado 33–15 (10th straight over Buffs), Oklahoma St. 31–14, Missouri 21–10, Kansas 52–7. *Lost:* Washington St. 19–10, Iowa St. 24–21, Oklahoma 38–7. *Stars:* C Tom Davis, G Greg Jorgensen, HB I.M. Hipp (1,301 yds and 10 TDs rush), Berns (10 TDs), soph SE/P Tim Smith (23 pass rec for 371 yds, 41.1-yd punting avg), TE Ken Spaeth (23 pass rec for 300 yds), K Billy Todd (12 FGs), DB Jim Pillen. *Noteworthy:* beat North Carolina 21–17 in Liberty Bowl; reserve QB Randy Garcia threw 2 TD passes in last quarter and Dodie Donnell ran 15 yds for other Cornhusker TD.

1978 (9–3) *Won:* California 36–26, Hawaii 56–10, Indiana 69–17, Iowa St. 23–0, Kansas St. 48–14 (10th straight over Wildcats), Colorado 52–14, Oklahoma St. 22–14, Kansas 63–21 (10th straight over Jayhawks), Oklahoma 17–14 (1st over Sooners since 1971). *Lost:* national cochamp Alabama 20–3 (opener), Missouri 35–31 (finale). *Stars:* OT Kelvin Clark, G Steve Lindquist, QB Tom Sorley (1,571 yds and 12 TDs pass, 6 TDs rush), TE Junior Miller (30 pass rec for 560 yds and 5 TDs), WR Kenny Brown (23 pass rec for 367 yds), Berns (11 TDs, 1,095 all-purpose yds), Hipp (936 yds and 7 TDs rush), Todd (10 FGs, 72 pts), Pillen, DT Rod Horn, DE George Andrews. *Noteworthy:* Led nation in total off and got share of 10th Big 8 title. Lost rematch with Oklahoma 31–24 in Orange Bowl; Sorley passed for 220 yds and 2 TDs, and Berns ran for 99 yds and a TD.

1979 (10–2) *Won:* Utah St. 35–14, Iowa 24–21 (1st meeting since 1946), Penn St. 42–17 (1st meeting since 1958), New Mexico St. 57–0, Kansas 42–0, Oklahoma St. 36–0, Colorado 38–10, Missouri 23–20, Kansas St. 21–12, Iowa St. 34–3. *Lost:* Oklahoma 17–14 in finale. *Stars:* RB Jarvis Redwine (1,042 yds rush, 9 TDs), Miller (21 pass rec for 409 yds and 7 TDs), Brown, Smith (30 pass rec for 477 yds), G John Havekost, K Dean Sukup (12 FGs, 74 pts), Horn, MG Kerry Weinmaster, DE Derrie Nelson. *Noteworthy:* lost to Houston 17–14 in Cotton Bowl as Cougars scored winning TD with 12 seconds left; Cornhuskers scored on 9-yd run by Redwine and 6-yd pass from QB Jeff Quinn to Jeff Finn.

1980 (10–2) *Won:* Utah 55–9, Iowa 57–0, Penn St. 21–7, Kansas 54–0, Oklahoma St. 48–7, Colorado 45–7, Missouri 38–16, Kansas St. 55–8, Iowa St. 35–0. *Lost:* Florida St. 18–14, Oklahoma 21–17. *Stars:* OG Randy Schleusener, soph C Dave Rimington, Quinn (1,337 yds and 14 TDs pass, 348 yds and 6 TDs rush), Redwine (1,119 yds and 9 TDs rush), soph HB Roger Craig (15 TDs), soph SE Todd Brown (28 pass rec for 416 yds), FB Andra Franklin (678 yds rush), Nelson, DT David Clark, DB Russell Gary. *Noteworthy:* Led nation in rush. Beat Mississippi St. 31–17 in Sun Bowl; Quinn passed for 157 yds and 2 TDs (including 52-yarder to Tim McCrady), and Brown scored on 23-yd run.

1981 (9–3) *Won:* Florida St. 34–14, Auburn 17–3, Colorado 59–0, Kansas St. 49–3, Missouri 6–0, Kansas 31–15, Oklahoma St. 54–7, Iowa St. 31–7, Oklahoma 37–14. *Lost:* Iowa 10–7, Penn St. 30–24. *Stars:* soph QB Turner Gill (882 yds total off), Craig (1,060 yds and 6 TDs rush), soph RB Mike Rozier (943 yds and 5 TDs rush), FB Phil Bates (8 TDs, 555 yds rush), TE Jamie Williams (22 pass rec for 282 yds), Brown (14 pass rec for 277 yds), Outland Trophy–winner Rimington, T Dan Hurley, P Grant Campbell (43.4-yd avg), DEs Tony Felici and Jimmy Williams, DBs Ric Lindquist and Jeff Krejci. *Noteworthy:* Led nation in pass defense and won 11th Big 8 title. Lost to unbeaten national champ Clemson 22–15 in Orange Bowl; Craig ran for 87 yds, a TD, and a 2-pt conversion, and Rozier passed 25 yds to Anthony Steels for TD.

1982 (12–1) *Won:* Iowa 42–7, New Mexico St. 68–0, Auburn 41–7, Colorado 40–14 (15th straight over Buffaloes), Kansas St. 42–13, Missouri 23–19, Kansas 52–0, Oklahoma St. 48–10, Iowa St. 48–10, Oklahoma 28–24, Hawaii 37–16. *Lost:* national

champ Penn St. 27–24. *Stars:* Outland Trophy– and Lombardi Award–winner Rimington, OT Randy Theiss, OG Mike Mandelko, Gill (1,182 yds and 11 TDs pass), Jamie Williams, Rozier (17 TDs, 1,689 yds and 15 TDs rush), WR Irving Fryar (5 TDs, 24 pass rec for 346 yds, 993 all-purpose yds), Brown (23 pass rec for 399 yds), Felici, LB Steve Damkroger. *Noteworthy:* Led nation in total off, rush, and scoring (41.1-pt avg) and won 12th Big 8 title (33rd conference crown). Beat LSU 21–20 in Orange Bowl; Rozier ran for 118 yds, Gill passed for 184 yds and a TD (to Rozier) and ran for another, and FB Mark Schellen scored on 5-yd run.

1983 (12–1) *Won:* Penn St. 44–6, Wyoming 56–20, Minnesota 84–13 (1st meeting since 1974), UCLA 42–10, Syracuse 63–7 (1st meeting since 1961), Oklahoma St. 14–10 (10th straight over Cowboys), Missouri 34–13, Colorado 69–19, Kansas St. 51–25 (15th straight over Wildcats), Iowa St. 72–29, Kansas 67–13 (15th straight over Jayhawks), Oklahoma 28–21. *Stars:* OG Dean Steinkuhler (Outland Trophy and Lombardi Award winner), C Mark Traynowicz, OT Scott Raridon, Heisman and Maxwell award–winner Rozier (2,486 all-purpose yds, nation's leader with 2,148 yds rush and with 174 pts on 29 TDs), Schellen (9 TDs), Gill (1,516 yds and 14 TDs pass), Fryar (10 TDs, 40 pass rec for 780 yds and 8 TDs, 1,267 all-purpose yds), LB Mike Knox, DB Bret Clark (5 int), P Scott Livingston (40.8-yd avg). *Noteworthy:* Scored 624 pts in 1st unbeaten season since 1971 and led nation in rush and scoring (52-pt avg) while repeating as Big 8 champ. Lost national championship to Miami (Fla.) 31–30 in Orange Bowl when 4th quarter rally fell short on missed 2-pt conversion try with 48 seconds left; Rozier ran for 147 yds, Jeff Smith ran for 99 yds and 2 TDs, Gill passed for 172 yds and ran for a TD, and Steinkuhler scored on a 19-yd "fumblerooskie" run.

1984 (10–2) *Won:* Wyoming 42–7, Minnesota 38–7, UCLA 42–3, Oklahoma St. 17–3, Missouri 33–23, Colorado 24–7, Kansas St. 62–14, Iowa St. 44–0, Kansas 41–7. *Lost:* Syracuse 17–9, Oklahoma 17–7. *Stars:* Clark (6 int), soph LB Marc Munford, DEs Scott Strasburger and Bill Weber, Livingston (41.2-yd punting avg), Traynowicz, OG Harry Grimminger, OT Mark Behning, OG Greg Orton, RB Doug DuBose (1,040 yds and 8 TDs rush), Smith (1,277 yds all-purpose running), Travis Turner (10 TDs). *Noteworthy:* Got share of

14th Big 8 title. Led nation in scoring defense (9.5-pt avg) and total defense. Beat LSU 28–10 in Sugar Bowl; DuBose ran for 102 yds and QB Craig Sundberg passed for 143 yds and 3 TDs (one to DuBose) and scored one himself.

1985 (9–3) *Won:* Illinois 52–25 (1st meeting since 1953), Oregon 63–0, New Mexico 38–7, Oklahoma St. 34–24, Missouri 28–20, Colorado 17–7, Kansas St. 41–3, Iowa St. 49–0, Kansas 56–6. *Lost:* Florida St. 17–13 (opener), national champ Oklahoma 27–7 (finale). *Stars:* DuBose (1,161 yds and 8 TDs rush, 1,488 all-purpose yds), FB Tom Rathman (8 TDs, 881 yds rush), Robb Schnitzler (16 pass rec for 382 yds), C Bill Lewis, OG Brian Blankenship, K Dale Klein (13 FGs, 77 pts), Munford, DT Jim Skow, P Dan Wingard (42-yd avg). *Noteworthy:* Led nation in rush. Lost to Michigan 27–23 in Fiesta Bowl; DuBose ran for 99 yds and a TD (and scored another on a pass), and frosh QB Steve Taylor ran for 76 yds and a TD.

1986 (10–2) *Won:* Florida St. 34–17, Illinois 59–14, Oregon 48–14, South Carolina 27–24, Oklahoma St. 30–10, Missouri 48–17, Kansas St. 38–0, Iowa St. 35–14, Kansas 70–0. *Lost:* Colorado 20–10 (1st to Buffs since 1967), Oklahoma 20–17. *Stars:* OT Tom Welter, Taylor (808 yds pass, 537 yds rush), RB Keith Jones (830 yds and 14 TDs rush), Dana Brinson (1,104 all-purpose yds, 14 pass rec for 208 yds), Rod Smith (nation's punt return leader with 18.9-yd avg), Munford, MG Danny Noonan, DT Chris Spachman, soph DE Broderick Thomas. *Noteworthy:* Had 25th consecutive winning season. Beat LSU 30–15 in Sugar Bowl; Taylor passed for 110 yds and a TD and ran for another, and Tyreese Knox ran for 84 yds and 2 TDs.

1987 (10–2) *Won:* Utah St. 56–12, UCLA 42–33, Arizona St. 35–28, South Carolina 30–21, Kansas 54–2, Oklahoma St. 35–0, Kansas St. 56–3, Missouri 42–7, Iowa St. 42–3 (10th straight over Cyclones), Colorado 24–7. *Lost:* unbeaten Oklahoma 17–7. *Stars:* Taylor (902 yds and 13 TDs pass, 659 yds rush), Jones (1,232 yds and 13 TDs rush), Rod Smith (21 pass rec for 329 yds), OT Kevin Lightner, OG John McCormick, Thomas, LBs LeRoy Etienne and Steve Forch, DTs Tim Rother and Neil Smith. *Noteworthy:* lost to Florida St. 31–28 in Fiesta Bowl; Taylor passed for 142 yds and scored a TD, Jones ran for 80 yds and a TD, and Brinson scored on 52-yd punt return.

1988 (11–2) *Won:* Texas A&M 23–14, Utah St.

63–12, Arizona St. 47–16, Nevada–Las Vegas 48–6, Kansas 63–10 (20th straight over Jayhawks), Oklahoma St. 63–42 (15th straight over Cowboys), Kansas St. 48–3 (20th straight over Wildcats), Missouri 26–18 (10th straight over Tigers), Iowa St. 51–16, Colorado 7–0, Oklahoma 7–3. *Lost:* UCLA 41–28. *Stars:* Taylor (1,067 yds and 11 TDs pass, 826 yds and 13 TDs rush), SE Morgan Gregory (20 pass rec for 239 yds), TE Todd Millikan (16 pass rec for 308 yds and 7 TDs), RB Ken Clark (1,497 yds and 12 TDs rush), Knox (6 TDs rush), Brinson, C Jake Young, OG Andy Keeler, OT Bob Sledge, MG Lawrence Pete, Thomas, DT Willie Griffin, Etienne, DBs Charles Fryar and Tim Jackson, P John Kroeker (40.6-yd avg). *Noteworthy:* Led nation in rush and won 15th Big 8 title (24th since Big 6 began and 36th conference crown overall). Lost to Miami (Fla.) 23–3 in Orange Bowl, gaining only 135 yds total off; scored on 50-yd FG by K Gregg Barrios.

1989 (10–2) *Won:* Northern Illinois 48–17, Utah 42–30, Minnesota 48–0, Oregon St. 35–7 (1st meeting since 1959), Kansas St. 58–7, Missouri 50–7, Oklahoma St. 48–23, Iowa St. 49–17, Kansas 51–14, Oklahoma 42–25. *Lost:* unbeaten Colorado 27–21. *Stars:* Clark (1,196 yds and 12 TDs rush), QB Gerry Gdowski (1,326 yds and 19 TDs pass, 925 yds and 13 TDs rush), Gregory (19 pass rec for 282 yds), FL Richard Bell (18 pass rec for 357 yds), soph SE Jon Bostick (12 pass rec for 289 yds and 6 TDs), soph RB Leodis Flowers (7 TDs), FB Bryan Carpenter (5 TDs), Young, OT Doug Glaser, DT Kent Wells, LB Mike Croel, DBs Bruce Pickens and Reggie Cooper. *Noteworthy:* Led nation in rush. Lost to Florida St. 41–17 in Fiesta Bowl; Gdowski passed for 154 yds and a TD, and Clark ran for 86 yds.

1990 (9–3) *Won:* Baylor 13–0, Northern Illinois 60–14, Minnesota 56–0, Oregon St. 31–7, Kansas St. 45–8, Missouri 69–21, Oklahoma St. 31–3, Iowa St. 45–13, Kansas 41–9. *Lost:* national cochamp Colorado 27–12, Oklahoma 45–10. *Stars:* Flowers (940 yds and 9 TDs rush), Bostick (19 pass rec for 375 yds), QB Mickey Joseph (11 TDs pass, 554 yds and 10 TDs rush), frosh TE Johnny Mitchell (11 pass rec for 282 yds and 7 TDs), soph FB Scott Baldwin (579 yds and 5 TDs rush), frosh RB Derek Brown (6 TDs), Barrios (14 FGs, 87 pts), DL Kenny Walker, Croel, soph DB Tyrone Byrd (5 int), soph P Mike Stigge (41.4-yd avg). *Noteworthy:* lost to unbeaten national cochamp Georgia Tech 45–21 in Florida Citrus Bowl; soph QB Tom Haase passed for 209 yds and 2 TDs, Mitchell caught 5 for 138 yds and a TD, and Brown ran 50 yds for a TD. **1991** (9–2–1) *Won:* Utah St. 59–28, Colorado St. 71–14, Arizona St. 18–9, Oklahoma St. 49–15, Kansas St. 38–31, Missouri 63–6, Kansas 59–23, Iowa St. 38–13, Oklahoma 19–14. *Lost:* unbeaten national cochamp Washington 36–21. *Tied:* Colorado 19–19. *Stars:* QB Keithen McCant (1,454 yds and 13 TDs pass, 654 yds and 7 TDs rush), Mitchell (31 pass rec for 534 yds and 5 TDs), Bostick (24 pass rec for 419 yds and 5 TDs), Brown (1,313 yds and 14 TDs rush), frosh RB Calvin Jones (900 yds and 14 TDs rush), OG Will Shields, OT Erik Wiegert, soph K Byron Bennett (11 FGs, 78 pts), soph LBs Mike Anderson and Trev Alberts, DBs Tyrone Legette, Kenny Wilhite (6 int) and Steve Carmer, Stigge (42-yd punting avg). *Noteworthy:* Led nation in rush and won 16th Big 8 title (25th in conference) in 30th consecutive winning season. Lost to unbeaten national cochamp Miami (Fla.) 22–0 in rainy Orange Bowl (1st shutout loss since 1973, 5th straight bowl loss); had only 80 yards total off. **1992** (9–3) *Won:* Utah 49–22, Middle Tennessee St. 48–7, Arizona St. 45–24, Oklahoma St. 55–0,

Missouri 34–24, Colorado 52–7, Kansas 49–7, Oklahoma 33–9, Kansas St. 38–24 (in Tokyo). *Lost:* Washington 29–14, Iowa St. 19–10 (1st to Cyclones since 1977). *Stars:* Jones (15 TDs, 1,210 yds and 14 TDs rush), Brown (1,011 yds rush), FB Lance Lewis (482 yds rush, 6 TDs), frosh QB Tommie Frazier (10 TDs pass, 7 TDs rush), QB Mike Grant (6 TDs rush, 5 TDs pass), soph SE Corey Dixon (13 pass rec for 279 yds), TEs William Washington and Gerald Armstrong (7 TDs on pass rec), Outland Trophy–winner Shields, C Jim Scott, soph OT Zach Wiegert, Bennett (71 pts), DT John Parrella, LB Travis Hill, Alberts, Wilhite, Byrd, Stigge (43.2-yd punting avg). *Noteworthy:* Repeated as Big 8 champ while leading nation in rush and turnover margin. Lost to Florida St. 27–14 in Orange Bowl; Frazier passed for 146 yds and 2 TDs, and Dixon had 5 pass rec for 123 yds and a TD.

BOWL SUMMARY

Bluebonnet 1–0; Cotton 1–2; Fiesta 0–4; Florida Citrus 0–1; Gotham 1–0; Liberty 1–0; Orange 5–8; Rose 0–1; Sugar 3–1; Sun 2–0.

BOWL RECORD (14–17)

Regular Season	Bowl	Score	Opponent	Record
1940 (8–1)	Rose	13–21	Stanford	(9–0)
1954 (6–4)	Orange	7–34	Duke	(7–2–1)
1962 (8–2)	Gotham	36–34	Miami (Fla.)	(7–3)
1963 (9–1)	Orange	13–7	Auburn	(9–1)
1964 (9–1)	Cotton	7–10	Arkansas	(10–0)
1965 (10–0)	Orange	28–39	Alabama	(8–1–1)
1966 (9–1)	Sugar	7–34	Alabama	(10–0)
1969 (8–2)	Sun	45–6	Georgia	(5–4–1)
1970 (10–0–1)	Orange	17–12	LSU	(9–2)
1971 (12–0)	Orange	38–6	Alabama	(11–0)
1972 (8–2–1)	Orange	40–6	Notre Dame	(8–2)
1973 (8–2–1)	Cotton	19–3	Texas	(8–2)
1974 (8–3)	Sugar	13–10	Florida	(8–3)
1975 (10–1)	Fiesta	14–17	Arizona St.	(11–0)
1976 (7–3–1)	Bluebonnet	27–24	Texas Tech	(10–1)
1977 (8–3)	Liberty	21–17	North Carolina	(8–2–1)
1978 (9–2)	Orange	24–31	Oklahoma	(10–1)

(continued)

Regular Season	Bowl	Score	Opponent	Record
1979 (10–1)	Cotton	14–17	Houston	(10–1)
1980 (9–2)	Sun	31–17	Mississippi St.	(9–2)
1981 (9–2)	Orange	15–22	Clemson	(11–0)
1982 (11–1)	Orange	21–20	LSU	(8–2–1)
1983 (12–0)	Orange	30–31	Miami (Fla.)	(10–1)
1984 (9–2)	Sugar	28–10	LSU	(8–2–1)
1985 (9–2)	Fiesta	23–27	Michigan	(9–1–1)
1986 (9–2)	Sugar	30–15	LSU	(9–2)
1987 (10–1)	Fiesta	28–31	Florida St.	(10–1)
1988 (11–1)	Orange	3–23	Miami (Fla.)	(10–1)
1989 (10–1)	Fiesta	17–41	Florida State	(9–2)
1990 (9–2)	Fla. Citrus	21–45	Georgia Tech	(10–0–1)
1991 (9–1–1)	Orange	0–22	Miami (Fla.)	(11–0)
1992 (9–2)	Orange	14–27	Florida St.	(10–1)

CONFERENCE TITLES

Missouri Valley—1907*, 1910, 1911*, 1912*, 1913*, 1914, 1915, 1916, 1917, 1921, 1922, 1923. **Big 6**—1928, 1929, 1931, 1932, 1933, 1935, 1936, 1937, 1940. **Big 8**—1963, 1964, 1965, 1966, 1969*, 1970, 1971, 1972, 1975*, 1978*, 1981, 1982, 1983, 1984*, 1988, 1991*, 1992.

TOP 20 AP AND UPI
(USA TODAY/CNN SINCE 1991) RANKING

1936	9	1969	11–12	1977	12–10	1985	11–10
1937	11	1970	1–3	1978	8–8	1986	5–4
1939	18	1971	1–1	1979	9–7	1987	6–6
1940	8	1972	4–9	1980	7–7	1988	10–10
1950	17–20	1973	7–11	1981	11–9	1989	11–12
1963	6–5	1974	9–8	1982	3–3	1990	U–17
1964	6–6	1975	9–9	1983	2–2	1991	15–16
1965	5–3	1976	9–7	1984	4–3	1992	14–14
1966	6–7						

MAJOR RIVALS

Nebraska has played at least 10 games with Colorado 35–14–2, Doane 16–2, Illinois 7–2–1, Indiana 7–9–3, Iowa 24–12–3, Iowa St. 71–14–2, Kansas 75–21–3, Kansas St. 65–10–2, Minnesota 20–29–2, Missouri 51–32–3, Notre Dame 6–7–1, Oklahoma 31–39–3, Oklahoma St. 30–2–1, Oregon St. 9–2, Penn St. 5–6, Pittsburgh 4–15–3, South Dakota 14–1–2, Syracuse 5–7.

COACHES

Dean of Nebraska coaches is Tom Osborne with record of 195–46–3 for 1973–92 with 9 Big 8 titles, 20 bowl teams, and 1 team unbeaten in regular season. Other top records for at least 3 years were by W.C. Booth, 46–8–1 for 1900–05 with 2 unbeaten teams; W.C. Cole, 25–8–3 for 1907–10 with 2 MVC titles; E.O. "Jumbo" Stiehm, 35–2–3 for 1911–15 with 5 MVC titles and 3 unbeaten teams;

Fred Dawson, 23–7–2 for 1921–24 with 3 MVC titles; E.E. Bearg, 23–7–3 for 1925–28 with 1 Big 6 title; Dana X. Bible, 50–15–7 for 1929–36 with 6 Big 6 titles; L.McC. "Biff" Jones, 28–14–4 for 1937–41 with 2 Big 6 titles and a Rose Bowl team; Bill Glassford, 31–35–3 for 1949–55 with 1 Orange Bowl team; and Bob Devaney (1971 national Coach of Year), 101–20–2 for 1962–72 with 8 Big 8 titles, 9 bowl teams, 3 teams unbeaten in regular season, and 2 national champions.

MISCELLANEA

First game was win over Omaha YMCA 10–0 in 1890 . . . 1st win over college foe was over Doane 18–0 in February 1891 . . . highest score was over Haskell 119–0 in 1910 . . . highest since W.W. II was over Minnesota 84–13 in 1983 . . . worst defeat was by Minnesota 61–7 in 1945 . . . worst since W.W. II was by Oklahoma 55–7 in 1954 and by Oklahoma 54–6 in 1956 . . . longest unbeaten string of 32 in 1969–71 ended by UCLA 20–17 in 1972 opener . . . 27-game win streak in 1901–04 ended by Colorado 6–0 . . . longest losing string of 7 in 1957 broken with win over Penn St. 14–7 in 1958 opener . . . consensus All-Americans were Guy Chamberlin, E, 1915; Ed Weir, T, 1924–25; George Sauer, B, 1933; Sam Francis, B, 1936; Bob Brown, G, 1963; Larry Kramer, T, 1964; Freeman White, E, and Walt Barnes, DT, 1965; LaVerne Allers, G, 1966; Wayne Meylan, MG, 1966–67; Bob Newton, T, 1970; Larry Jacobson, DT, 1971; Johnny Rodgers, FL, and Willie Harper, DE, 1971–72; Rich Glover, MG, 1972; John Dutton, DL, 1973; Marvin Crenshaw, OT, 1974; Rik Bonness, C, 1975; Dave Butterfield, DB, 1976; Kelvin Clark, OT, 1978; Junior Miller, TE, 1979; Randy Schleusener, OL, and Jarvis Redwine, RB, 1980; Dave Rimington, C, 1981–82; Mike Rozier, RB, 1982–83; Irving Fryar, WR, and Dean Steinkuhler, OL, 1983; Mark Traynowicz, C, 1984; Danny Noonan, DL, 1986; Broderick Thomas, LB, and Jake Young, C, 1988–89; and Will Shields, OG, 1992 . . . Academic All-Americans were James Huge, E, 1962; Dennis Claridge, B, 1963; Marv Mueller, DB, 1966; Randy Reeves, DB, 1969; Larry Jacobson, DT, and Jeff Kinney, HB, 1971; Frosty Anderson, E, 1973; Rik Bonness, C, and Tom Heiser, RB, 1975; Vince Ferragamo, QB, 1976; Ted

Harvey, RB, 1976–77; George Andrews, DL, and James Pillen, DB, 1978; Kelly Saalfeld, C, and Rod Horn, DL, 1979; Randy Schleusener, OG, 1979–80; Jeff Finn, TE, 1980; Randy Theiss, OT, and Eric Lindquist, DB, 1981; Dave Rimington, C, 1981–82; Rob Stuckey, DL, and Scott Strasburger, DL, 1983–84; Mark Traynowicz, C, 1984; Thomas Welter, OT, and Dale Klein, K, 1986; Jeffrey Jamrog, DL, 1987; Mark Blazek, DB, and John Kroeker, P, 1988; Gerry Gdowski, QB, and Jake Young, C, 1989; David Edeal, OL, Jim Wanek, OL, and Pat Tyrance, LB, 1990; Pat Engelbert, DL, 1991; and Mike Stigge, P, 1991–92 . . . Heisman Trophy winners were Johnny Rodgers, FL, 1972; and Mike Rozier, RB, 1983 . . . Maxwell Award winner was Mike Rozier, RB, 1983 . . . Outland Trophy winners were Larry Jacobson, DT, 1971; Rich Glover, MG, 1972; Dave Rimington, C, 1981–82; Dean Steinkuhler, OG, 1983; and Will Shields, OG, 1992 . . . Lombardi Award winners were Rich Glover, MG, 1972; Dave Rimington, C, 1982; and Dean Steinkuhler, OG, 1983.

OKLAHOMA (Sooners; Cream and Crimson)

NOTABLE TEAMS

1900 (3–1–1) *Won:* Chilocco Indians 27–0, Fort Reno 79–0, Arkansas City 10–0. *Lost:* unbeaten Texas 28–2 (1st meeting). *Tied:* Kingfisher 0–0.
1905 (7–2) *Won:* Central Normal 28–0, 58–0, Haskell Institute 18–12, Kansas City Medics 33–0, Texas 2–0 (1st in 8 games with Longhorns), Kingfisher 55–0, Bethany 29–0. *Lost:* Kansas 34–0, Washburn 9–6. *Noteworthy:* 1st year under Bennie Owen.
1908 (8–1–1) *Won:* Central Normal 51–0, Oklahoma A&M 18–0, Kingfisher 51–0, Kansas St. 33–4 (1st meeting), Arkansas 27–5, Epworth U. 24–0, Texas 50–0, Fairmont 12–4. *Lost:* unbeaten Kansas 11–0. *Tied:* Washburn 6–6.
1911 (8–0–0) *Won:* Kingfisher 104–0, Oklahoma Christian 62–0, Oklahoma A&M 22–0, Washburn 37–0, Missouri 14–6, Kansas 3–0 (1st in 9-game series begun in 1903), Alva Normal 34–6, Texas 6–3. *Noteworthy:* 1st unbeaten season since 2-game schedule of 1898.
1913 (6–2) *Won:* Kingfisher 74–0, Central Normal

83–0, Alva Normal 101–0, Kansas 21–7, Oklahoma A&M 7–0, Colorado 14–3. *Lost:* Missouri 20–17, Texas 14–6. *Star:* FB Claude Reeds.

1914 (9–1–1) *Won:* Central Normal 67–0, Kingfisher 67–0, Ada Normal 96–6, Missouri 13–0, Oklahoma A&M 23–6, Kansas St. 52–10 (1st meeting since 1908), Arkansas 35–7, Haskell 33–12, Henry Kendall 26–7. *Lost:* unbeaten Texas 32–7. *Tied:* Kansas 16–16.

1915 (10–0) *Won:* Kingfisher 67–0, Weatherford Normal 55–0, Alva Normal 102–0, Missouri 24–0, Texas 14–13, Kansas 23–14, Henry Kendall 14–13, Arkansas 24–0, Kansas St. 21–7, Oklahoma A&M 26–7. *Stars:* FB Forest Geyer, Bs Hap Johnson and Elmer Capshaw, E Homer Montgomery, T Oliver Hott, G Willis Hott. *Noteworthy:* Owen's 2nd unbeaten team won SWC title.

1918 (6–0) *Won:* Central Normal 44–0, Post Field 58–0, Kansas 33–0, Arkansas 103–0, Phillips U. 13–7, Oklahoma A&M 27–0.

1920 (6–0–1) *Won:* Central Normal 16–7, Washington (Mo.) 24–14, Missouri 28–7, Kansas 21–9, Oklahoma A&M 36–0, Drake 44–7. *Tied:* Kansas St. 7–7. *Stars:* HB Phil White, Bs Sol Swatek and Harry Hill, T Roy Smoot, soph E Howard Marsh, G Bill McKinley. *Noteworthy:* Owen's 4th unbeaten team won MVC title.

1938 (10–1) *Won:* Rice 7–6, Texas 13–0 (1st over Longhorns since 1933), Kansas 19–0, Nebraska 14–0 (1st over Cornhuskers since 1930), Tulsa 28–6, Kansas St. 26–0, Missouri 21–0, Iowa St. 10–0, Oklahoma A&M 19–0, Washington St. 28–0. *Stars:* E Waddy Young (Sooners' 1st consensus All-American), Bs Hugh McCullough (1,020 yds total off) and Earl Crowder, soph Bill Jennings (23 pass rec for 217 yds), T Gilford Duggan, Otis Rogers (6 int). *Noteworthy:* Led nation in rush defense and won 1st Big 6 title in 1st unbeaten season since 1920. Made 1st postseason appearance, losing to unbeaten Tennessee 17–0 in Orange Bowl; Sooners had only 116 yds total off.

1939 (6–2–1) *Won:* Northwestern 23–0, Texas 24–12, Kansas 27–7, Oklahoma A&M 41–0, Iowa St. 38–6, Kansas St. 13–10. *Lost:* Missouri 7–6, Nebraska 13–7 in last 2 games. *Tied:* Southern Methodist (SMU) 7–7 in opener. *Stars:* Jennings (21 pass rec for 236 yds), Duggan, E Frank Ivy, T Justin Bowers, Bs Beryl Clark and Robert Seymour.

1943 (7–2) *Won:* Norman Naval Air Station 22–6,

Oklahoma A&M 22–13, Kansas St. 37–0, Iowa St. 21–7, Kansas 26–13, Missouri 20–13, Nebraska 26–7 (1st over Cornhuskers since 1938). *Lost:* Texas 13–7, unbeaten Tulsa 20–6 in consecutive early games. *Stars:* Bs Bob Brumely and Derald Lebow, E W.G. Wooten, T Lee Kennon, G Gale Fulgham, C Bob Mayfield. *Noteworthy:* won 2nd Big 6 title.

1946 (8–3) *Won:* Texas A&M 10–7, Kansas St. 28–7 (10th straight over Wildcats), Iowa St. 63–0 (10th straight over Cyclones), Texas Christian (TCU) 14–12, Missouri 27–6, Nebraska 27–6, Oklahoma A&M 73–12. *Lost:* unbeaten Army 21–7, Texas 20–13, Kansas 16–13 (1st to Jayhawks since 1937). *Stars:* HB Joe Golding (890 yds and 13 TDs rush), frosh E Jim Owens (19 pass rec for 262 yds), C John Rapacz, Gs Plato Andros and soph Buddy Burris, E Warren Geise, soph T Homer Paine, frosh T Wade Walker. *Noteworthy:* Jim Tatum's only Oklahoma team got share of 4th Big 6 title while leading nation in rush defense. Beat N.C. State 34–13 in Gator Bowl as Eddy Davis scored 3 TDs.

1947 (7–2–1) *Won:* Detroit 24–20, Texas A&M 26–14, Iowa St. 27–9, Kansas St. 27–13, Missouri 21–12, Nebraska 14–13, Oklahoma A&M 21–13. *Lost:* Texas 34–14, TCU 20–7 in early games. *Tied:* unbeaten Kansas 13–13. *Stars:* Burris, Walker, Rapacz, soph Darrell Royal (7 int), E Jim Tyree, QB Jack Mitchell (573 yds and 8 TDs rush). *Noteworthy:* got share of 5th Big 6 title in 1st year under Bud Wilkinson.

1948 (10–1) *Won:* Texas A&M 42–14, Texas 20–14 (1st over Longhorns since 1939), Kansas St. 42–0, TCU 21–18, Iowa St. 33–6, Missouri 41–7, Nebraska 41–14, Kansas 60–7, Oklahoma A&M 19–15. *Lost:* Santa Clara 20–17 in opener. *Stars:* Burris, Walker, Paine, Mitchell (10 TDs), soph FB Leon Heath (7 TDs), HB George Thomas (835 yds and 10 TDs rush), Frankie Anderson (9 pass rec for 210 yds), Owens, soph Ed Lisak (6 int). *Noteworthy:* Won inaugural Big 7 title. Beat undefeated North Carolina 14–6 in Sugar Bowl, holding Tar Heels to 128 yds rush and intercepting 2 passes; Mitchell and Lindell Pearson scored Sooner TDs.

1949 (11–0) *Won:* Boston College 46–0, Texas A&M 33–13, Texas 20–14, Kansas 48–26, Nebraska 48–0, Iowa St. 34–7, Kansas St. 39–0, Missouri 27–7, Santa Clara 28–21, Oklahoma A&M 41–0. *Stars:* QB Royal (40.6-yd on 18 punts), Thomas (859 yds rush, nation's leader with 19 TDs and 117 pts),

Heath (684 yds and 6 TDs rush), Walker, G Stan West, Owens (15 pass rec for 207 yds), P Dick Heatly (40.7-yd avg on 41 punts). *Noteworthy:* Led nation in rush defense and won Big 7 again in 1st unbeaten season since 1938. Beat Louisiana St. (LSU) 35–0 in Sugar Bowl, holding Tigers to 38 yds rush; Heath had TD runs of 86 and 34 yds.
1950 (10–1)   *Won:* Boston College 28–0, Texas A&M 34–28, Texas 14–13, Kansas St. 58–0, Iowa St. 20–7, Colorado 27–18 (1st meeting since 1936), Kansas 33–13, Missouri 41–7, Nebraska 49–35, Oklahoma A&M 41–14.   *Stars:* QB Claude Arnold (1,339 yds and 17 TDs total off), Heath (606 yds rush, 11 pass rec for 205 yds, 6 TDs), soph HB Billy Vessels (870 yds rush, 11 pass rec for 229 yds, 15 TDs), T Jim Weatherall, G Norman McNabb, C Harry Moore, E Frankie Anderson, DB Buddy Jones.   *Noteworthy:* Again took Big 7 and won 1st national championship. Upset by Kentucky 13–7 in Sugar Bowl when Wildcats took 1st-half 13–0 lead; Vessels passed 17 yds to Merrill Green for Sooner TD.
1951 (8–2)   *Won:* William & Mary 49–7, Kansas 33–21, Colorado 55–14, Kansas St. 33–0 (15th straight over Wildcats), Missouri 34–20, Iowa St. 35–6 (15th straight over Cyclones), Nebraska 27–0, Oklahoma A&M 41–6.   *Lost:* Texas A&M 14–7, Texas 9–7.   *Stars:* Outland Trophy–winner Weatherall, C Tom Catlin, T Art James, soph G Roger Nelson, FB Buck McPhail (865 yds rush), John Reddell (13 pass rec for 362 yds), frosh Buddy Leake (13 TDs).   *Noteworthy:* won 4th straight Big 7 crown (10th conference title overall).
1952 (8–1–1)   *Won:* Pittsburgh 49–20 (1st meeting), Texas 49–20, Kansas 42–20, Kansas St. 49–6, Iowa St. 41–0, Missouri 47–7, Nebraska 34–13 (10th straight over Cornhuskers), Oklahoma A&M 54–7.   *Lost:* Notre Dame 27–21 (1st meeting).   *Tied:* Colorado 21–21.   *Stars:* Heisman Trophy–winner Vessels (18 TDs, 1,072 yds rush, nation's leader with 1,512 all-purpose yds), McPhail (1,018 yds rush), QB Eddie Crowder (704 yds pass), soph E Max Boydston (13 pass rec for 334 yds), Catlin, G J.D. Roberts, Ts Ed Rowland and Jim Davis.   *Noteworthy:* led nation in scoring (40.7-pt avg) and again won Big 7.
1953 (9–1–1)   *Won:* Texas 19–14, Kansas 45–0, Colorado 27–20, Kansas St. 34–0, Missouri 14–7, Iowa St. 47–0, Nebraska 30–7, Oklahoma A&M 42–7.   *Lost:* unbeaten national cochamp Notre Dame

28–21 in opener.   *Tied:* Pittsburgh 7–7 in 2nd game.   *Stars:* Outland Trophy–winner Roberts, B Larry Grigg (792 yds rush, 13 TDs), Boydston, T Nelson, C Kurt Burris.   *Noteworthy:* Led nation in rush and took 8th straight conference title. Upset unbeaten national cochamp Maryland 7–0 in Orange Bowl; Grigg scored on 25-yd run in 2nd quarter and Sooners twice stopped Terps inside 10-yd line in 1st half.
1954 (10–0)   *Won:* California 27–13, TCU 21–16, Texas 14–7, Kansas 65–0, Kansas St. 21–0, Colorado 13–6, Iowa St. 40–0, Missouri 34–13, Nebraska 55–7, Oklahoma A&M 14–0.   *Stars:* Burris, G Bo Bolinger, Boydston (11 pass rec for 276 yds, 40.2-yd punting avg), B Bob Herndon (588 yds and 7 TDs rush), Leake (9 TDs).   *Noteworthy:* Again won Big 7. Kept out of Orange Bowl by Big 7 rule prohibiting same team from appearing two consecutive years.
1955 (11–0)   *Won:* North Carolina 13–6, Pittsburgh 26–14, Texas 20–0, Kansas 44–6, Colorado 56–21, Kansas St. 40–7, Missouri 20–0 (10th straight over Tigers), Iowa St. 52–0, Nebraska 41–0, Oklahoma A&M 53–0 (10th straight over Aggies).   *Stars:* HBs Tommy McDonald (702 yds rush, 16 TDs) and soph Clendon Thomas (9 TDs), Bolinger, T Ed Gray, C Jerry Tubbs.   *Noteworthy:* Led nation in total off, rush, and scoring (36.5-pt avg) while winning 10th straight conference title. Beat undefeated Maryland 20–6 in Orange Bowl to earn 2nd national title; TDs scored by McDonald, Jay O'Neal, and Carl Dodd (82-yd pass int return).
1956 (10–0)   *Won:* North Carolina 36–0, Kansas St. 66–0 (20th straight over Wildcats), Texas 45–0, Kansas 34–12, Notre Dame 40–0, Colorado 27–19, Iowa St. 44–0 (20th straight over Cyclones), Missouri 67–14, Nebraska 54–6, Oklahoma A&M 53–0.   *Stars:* Thomas (817 yds rush, 12 pass rec for 241 yds, nation's scoring leader with 18 TDs for 108 pts), Maxwell Award–winner McDonald (17 TDs, 853 yds rush, 12 pass rec for 282 yds, 3 TD passes, 6 int), QB Jimmy Harris (844 yds and 12 TDs total off), Tubbs, Gray, G Bill Krisher.   *Noteworthy:* Retained both national and Big 7 titles and again led nation in total off, rush, and scoring (46.6-pt avg). Ineligible for Orange Bowl because of Big 7 no-repeat rule.
1957 (10–1)   *Won:* Pittsburgh 26–0, Iowa St. 40–14, Texas 21–7, Kansas 47–0 (10th straight over Jayhawks), Colorado 14–13, Kansas St. 13–0, Missouri

39–14, Nebraska 32–7 (15th straight over Cornhuskers), Oklahoma St. 53–6. *Lost:* Notre Dame 7–0 (ending 47-game win streak). *Stars:* Thomas (816 yds and 9 TDs rush), Krisher, C Bob Harrison, E Don Stiller. *Noteworthy:* Won 10th title in as many years of Big 7 existence. Beat Duke 48–21 in Orange Bowl, scoring 27 pts in final quarter and taking advantage of 6 Duke turnovers; David Baker (who caught a TD pass and threw another) returned pass int 94 yds for 1st score and Dick Carpenter returned intercepted lateral 73 yds for final TD.

1958 (10–1) *Won:* West Virginia 47–14, Oregon 6–0, Kansas 43–0, Kansas St. 40–6, Colorado 23–7, Iowa St. 20–0, Missouri 39–0, Nebraska 40–7, Oklahoma St. 7–0. *Lost:* Texas 15–14 (1st to Longhorns since 1951). *Stars:* Harrison, B Prentice Gautt (627 yds rush), Bobby Boyd (6 TDs), E Ross Coyle, G Dick Corbitt. *Noteworthy:* Led nation in scoring defense (4.9-pt avg) and won inaugural Big 8 title. Beat Syracuse 21–6 in Orange Bowl, scoring TDs in each of 1st 3 quarters; Brewster Hobby passed for 2nd TD and returned punt 40 yds for 3rd.

1959 (7–3) *Won:* Colorado 42–12, Missouri 23–0, Kansas 7–6, Kansas St. 36–0, Army 28–20, Iowa St. 35–12, Oklahoma St. 17–7. *Lost:* Northwestern 45–13, Texas 19–12, Nebraska 25–21 (1st to Cornhuskers since 1942). *Stars:* Gautt (674 yds rush), Boyd (10 TDs), G Jerry Thompson. *Noteworthy:* won 14th consecutive conference title.

1962 (8–3) *Won:* Syracuse 7–3, Kansas 13–7, Kansas St. 47–0, Colorado 62–0, Iowa St. 41–0, Missouri 13–0, Nebraska 34–6, Oklahoma St. 37–6. *Lost:* Notre Dame 13–7, unbeaten Texas 9–6. *Stars:* QB Monte Deere, HB Joe Don Looney (10 TDs, 852 yds rush, national punting leader with 43.4-yd avg), E John Flynn (10 pass rec for 247 yds), C Wayne Lee, G Leon Cross, T Dennis Ward. *Noteworthy:* Won 3rd Big 8 title (18th since Big 6 was formed). Lost to Alabama 17–0 in Orange Bowl.

1963 (8–2) *Won:* Clemson 31–14, USC 17–12, Kansas 21–18, Kansas St. 34–9, Colorado 35–0, Iowa St. 24–14, Missouri 13–3, Oklahoma St. 34–10. *Lost:* unbeaten national champ Texas 28–7, Nebraska 29–20. *Stars:* FB Jim Grisham (861 yds and 8 TDs rush), T Ralph Neely, Flynn, G Newt Burton, Larry Shields (6 int). *Noteworthy:* Wilkinson's last team.

1967 (10–1) *Won:* Washington St. 21–0, Maryland 35–0, Kansas St. 46–7, Missouri 7–0, Colorado 23–0, Iowa St. 52–14, Kansas 14–10, Nebraska 21–14, Oklahoma St. 38–14. *Lost:* Texas 9–7. *Stars:* MG Granville Liggins, Steve Barrett (7 int), QB Bobby Warmack (1,345 yds total off), Eddie Hinton (28 pass rec for 427 yds), soph TE Steve Zabel (22 pass rec for 333 yds), soph TB Steve Owens (808 yds and 12 TDs rush), OT Bob Kalsu. *Noteworthy:* Led nation in scoring defense (6.8-pt avg) and won 4th Big 8 title (19th title since Big 6 began) in 1st year under Chuck Fairbanks. Beat Tennessee 26–24 in Orange Bowl, building up 19–0 lead in 1st half on 3 long drives directed by Warmack, who scored 1 TD and passed for another.

1968 (7–4) *Won:* N.C. State 28–14, Iowa St. 42–7, Kansas St. 35–20, Kansas 27–23, Missouri 28–14, Nebraska 47–0, Oklahoma St. 41–7. *Lost:* Notre Dame 45–21, Texas 26–20, Colorado 41–27. *Stars:* Warmack (1,814 yds and 15 TDs total off), Hinton (60 pass rec for 967 yds and 6 TDs), Owens (1,536 yds and 21 TDs rush). *Noteworthy:* Got share of 5th Big 8 crown. Lost to SMU 28–27 in wild Astro-Bluebonnet Bowl in which 5 TDs were scored in final period; Owens ran for 113 yds and threw a TD pass.

1971 (11–1) *Won:* SMU 30–0, Pittsburgh 55–29, USC 33–20, Texas 48–27 (1st over Longhorns since 1966), Colorado 45–17, Kansas St. 75–28, Iowa St. 43–12 (10th straight over Cyclones), Missouri 20–3, Kansas 56–10, Oklahoma St. 58–14. *Lost:* unbeaten national champ Nebraska 35–31. *Stars:* QB Jack Mildren (1,140 yds and 17 TDs rush, 878 yds and 10 TDs pass), RB Greg Pruitt (1,665 yds and 17 TDs rush, 1,946 all-purpose yds), Jon Harrison (17 pass rec for 494 yds), C Tom Brahaney, LB Steve Aycock, DT Derland Moore, Joe Wylie (40.6-yd punting avg). *Noteworthy:* Led nation in total off, rush, and scoring (44.9-pt avg). Beat Auburn 40–22 in Sugar Bowl, leading 19–0 after 1st quarter and 31–0 at half; Mildren ran for 149 yds and 3 TDs, and Wylie scored on 71-yd punt return.

1972 (8–4) *Won:* Utah St. 49–0, Oregon 68–3, Clemson 52–3, Texas 27–0, Kansas St. 52–0, Iowa St. 20–6, Nebraska 17–14. *Lost:* Colorado 20–14, Missouri (forfeit after winning 17–6), Kansas (forfeit after winning 31–7), Oklahoma St. (forfeit after winning 38–15). *Stars:* Pruitt (938 yds rush, 14 TDs, 1,104 all-purpose yds), Brahaney, QB Dave

Robertson (1,332 yds and 15 TDs total off), frosh SE Tinker Owens (17 pass rec for 298 yds), John Carroll (17 pass rec for 343 yds), frosh RB Joe Washington (630 yds rush, 7 TDs), FB Leon Crosswhite, Moore, DT Lucious Selmon, soph LB Rod Shoate. *Noteworthy:* Fairbanks' last team led nation in rush. Beat Penn St. 14–0 in Sugar Bowl, holding Nittany Lions to 49 yds rush; Pruitt ran for 86 yds, Crosswhite ran for 82 yds and a TD, and Owens caught 27-yd TD pass from Robertson.

1973 (10–0–1) *Won:* Baylor 42–14, Miami (Fla.) 24–20, Texas 52–13, Colorado 34–7, Kansas St. 56–14, Iowa St. 34–17, Missouri 31–3, Kansas 48–20, Nebraska 27–0, Oklahoma St. 45–18. *Tied:* USC 7–7. *Stars:* soph QB Steve Davis (934 yds and 9 TDs pass, 887 yds and 18 TDs rush), Owens (18 pass rec for 472 yds), Washington (1,173 yds rush, 1,744 all-purpose yds, 10 TDs), Waymon Clark (1,014 yds rush), OT Eddie Foster, Shoate, MG Selmon, DB Randy Hughes. *Noteworthy:* 1st unbeaten season since 1956. Won 6th Big 8 title in 1st year under Barry Switzer. Ineligible for bowl, on NCAA probation.

1974 (11–0) *Won:* Baylor 28–11, Utah St. 72–3, Wake Forest 63–0, Texas 16–13, Colorado 49–14, Kansas St. 63–0, Iowa St. 28–10, Missouri 37–0, Kansas 45–14 (10th straight over Jayhawks), Nebraska 28–14, Oklahoma St. 44–13. *Stars:* Davis (601 yds and 11 TDs pass, 659 yds and 9 TDs rush), Owens (18 pass rec for 413 yds and 5 TDs), Washington (1,321 yds rush, 1,904 all-purpose yds, 14 TDs), C Kyle Davis, G John Roush, Shoate, Hughes, DTs Dewey and Lee Roy Selmon, DE Jimbo Elrod. *Noteworthy:* Repeated as Big 8 champ (25th conference title overall) while leading nation in total off, rush, and scoring (43-pt avg). Got share of 4th national championship but again ineligible for bowl.

1975 (11–1) *Won:* Oregon 62–7, Pittsburgh 46–10, Miami (Fla.) 20–17, Colorado 21–20, Texas 24–17, Kansas St. 25–3, Iowa St. 39–7, Oklahoma St. 27–7, Missouri 28–27, Nebraska 35–10. *Lost:* Kansas 23–3 (1st to Jayhawks since 1964). *Stars:* Davis (523 yds and 6 TDs rush), Owens (9 pass rec for 241 yds), SE Billy Brooks, Washington (871 yds rush, 1,347 all-purpose yds, 12 TDs, 50.2-yd avg on 10 punts), OT Mike Vaughan, OG Terry Webb, Outland Trophy– and Lombardi Award–winner Lee Roy Selmon, MG Dewey Selmon, Elrod, Jerry Anderson (5 int), soph DB Zac Henderson. *Noteworthy:* Got share of 3rd straight Big 8 title.

Beat Michigan 14–6 in Orange Bowl to earn 2nd straight national title; Brooks scored on 39-yd end-around play and Davis ran 10 yds for 2nd Sooner TD.

1976 (9–2–1) *Won:* Vanderbilt 24–3, California 28–17, Florida St. 24–9, Iowa St. 24–10 (15th straight over Cyclones), Kansas 28–10, Kansas St. 49–20, Missouri 27–20, Nebraska 20–17. *Lost:* Oklahoma St. 31–24 (1st field loss to Cowboys since 1966), Colorado 42–31. *Tied:* Texas 6–6. *Stars:* Kenny King (791 yds rush), Vaughan, LB Daryl Hunt, Henderson. *Noteworthy:* Won share of 9th Big 8 title. Beat Wyoming 41–7 in Fiesta Bowl; Elvis Peacock scored 2 TDs and K Uwe von Schamann kicked 2 FGs and 5 ex pts.

1977 (10–2) *Won:* Vanderbilt 25–23, Utah 62–24, Ohio St. 29–28, Kansas 24–9, Missouri 21–17, Iowa St. 35–16, Kansas St. 42–7, Oklahoma St. 61–28, Colorado 52–14, Nebraska 38–7. *Lost:* unbeaten Texas 13–6 (1st to Longhorns since 1970). *Stars:* Henderson (7 int), Hunt, soph LB George Cumby, MG Reggie Kinlaw, QB Thomas Lott (1,074 yds and 16 TDs total off), Steve Rhodes (12 pass rec for 226 yds), soph RB Billy Sims (6 TDs), G Greg Roberts, von Schamann (14 FGs, 89 pts). *Noteworthy:* Won 5th straight Big 8 title (10th overall) and led nation in rush. Upset by Arkansas 31–6 in Orange Bowl; Sooners scored in last quarter on 8-yd pass from Dean Blevins to Victor Hicks.

1978 (11–1) *Won:* Stanford 35–29, West Virginia 52–10, Rice 66–7, Missouri 45–23, Texas 31–10, Kansas 17–16, Iowa St. 34–6, Kansas St. 56–19, Colorado 28–7, Oklahoma St. 62–7. *Lost:* Nebraska 17–14 (1st to Cornhuskers since 1971). *Stars:* Outland Trophy–winner Roberts, Heisman Trophy–winner Sims (national leader with 1,762 yds rush and in scoring with 120 pts on 20 TDs), Lott (1,017 yds and 15 TDs total off), Kinlaw, Hunt, Cumby, DT Phil Tabor, DE Reggie Mathis, DB Darrol Ray (7 int). *Noteworthy:* Led nation in rush and scoring (40-pt avg) and got share of 6th straight Big 8 title. Got revenge by beating Nebraska 31–24 in Orange Bowl; Sims ran for 134 yds and 2 TDs, and Lott scored 2 TDs.

1979 (11–1) *Won:* Iowa 21–6, Tulsa 49–13 (1st meeting since 1943), Rice 63–21, Colorado 49–24, Kansas St. 38–6, Iowa St. 38–9, Oklahoma St. 38–7, Kansas 38–0, Missouri 24–22, Nebraska 17–14. *Lost:* Texas 16–7. *Stars:* Sims (1,506 yds rush, nation's leader with 132 pts on 22 TDs), QB J.C. Watts

(1,240 yds total off), Fred Nixon (13 pass rec for 257 yds), Cumby (5 int), Ray, DT John Goodman, frosh P Michael Keeling (41.9-yd avg). *Noteworthy:* Won 7th straight Big 8 title. Beat undefeated Florida St. 24–7 in Orange Bowl; Sims ran for 164 yds and a TD, Watts (127 yds rush) scored on 61-yd run, and Bud Herbert had 3 int.

1980 (10–2) *Won:* Kentucky 29–7, Colorado 82–42, Kansas St. 35–21 (10th straight over Wildcats), Iowa St. 42–7, North Carolina 41–7, Kansas 21–19, Missouri 17–7, Nebraska 21–17, Oklahoma St. 63–7. *Lost:* Stanford 31–14, Texas 20–13. *Stars:* OT Louis Oubre, G Terry Crouch, Watts (1,568 yds total off, 18 TDs rush), Bobby Grayson (14 pass rec for 389 yds), David Overstreet (678 yds and 6 TDs rush), DT Richard Turner, Keeling (41.5-yd punting avg). *Noteworthy:* Won 8th straight Big 8 crown (13th overall and 28th since Big 6 began). Beat Florida St. 18–17 in Orange Bowl as Watts passed for TD (11 yds to Rhodes) and 2-pt conversion (to TE Steve Valora) with 1:27 left; Sooners scored earlier on 53-yd FG by Keeling and 4-yd run by Overstreet.

1982 (8–4) *Won:* Kentucky 29–8, Iowa St. 13–3, Texas 28–22, Kansas 38–14, Oklahoma St. 27–9, Colorado 45–10, Kansas St. 24–10, Missouri 41–14. *Lost:* West Virginia 41–27, USC 12–0, Nebraska 28–24. *Stars:* DT Rick Bryan, DE Kevin Murphy, LB Jackie Shipp, frosh RB Marcus Dupree (905 yds and 13 TDs rush), David Carter (11 pass rec for 218 yds), G Steve Williams, Keeling (43-yd punting avg). *Noteworthy:* Lost to Arizona St. 32–21 in Fiesta Bowl; Dupree ran for 239 yds and Stanley Wilson scored 2 TDs.

1983 (8–4) *Won:* Stanford 27–14, Tulsa 28–18, Kansas St. 29–10, Oklahoma St. 21–20, Iowa St. 49–11, Kansas 45–14, Colorado 41–28, Hawaii 21–17. *Lost:* Ohio St. 24–14, unbeaten Texas 28–16, Missouri 10–0, unbeaten Nebraska 28–21. *Stars:* Bryan, Shipp, DE Kevin Murphy, DB Scott Case (8 int), frosh RB Spencer Tillman (1,047 yds rush, 10 TDs), QB Danny Bradley (1,551 yds and 12 TDs total off), George "Buster" Rhymes (32 pass rec for 747 yds).

1984 (9–2–1) *Won:* Stanford 19–7, Pittsburgh 42–10 (1st meeting since 1975), Baylor 34–15, Kansas St. 24–6, Iowa St. 12–10, Missouri 49–7, Colorado 41–17, Nebraska 17–7, Oklahoma St. 24–14. *Lost:* Kansas 28–11 (1st to Jayhawks since 1975). *Tied:* Texas 15–15. *Stars:* frosh DE Darrell Reed, MG Tony Casillas, Bradley (1,271 yds and

16 TDs total off), Steve Sewell (16 pass rec for 315 yds), frosh TE Keith Jackson (15 pass rec for 223 yds), Lydell Carr (625 yds rush). *Noteworthy:* Got share of 14th Big 8 title (32nd conference crown overall) and led nation in rush defense. Lost to Washington 28–17 in Orange Bowl; Bradley passed for 124 yds and a TD and ran for other Sooner TD.

1985 (11–1) *Won:* Minnesota 13–7, Kansas St. 41–6 (15th straight over Wildcats), Texas 14–7, Iowa St. 59–14, Kansas 48–6, Missouri 51–6, Colorado 31–0, Nebraska 27–7, Oklahoma St. 13–0, SMU 35–13. *Lost:* Miami (Fla.) 27–14. *Stars:* Lombardi Award–winner Casillas, Reed, Murphy, LB Brian Bosworth, frosh QB Jamelle Holieway (1,378 yds and 14 TDs total off), Jackson (20 pass rec for 486 yds), soph G Mark Hutson, DB Sonny Brown (5 int), K Tim Lashar (15 FGs, 88 pts). *Noteworthy:* Led nation in total defense and pass defense, and won 15th Big 8 title. Beat undefeated Penn St. 25–10 in Orange Bowl to earn 6th national title; Holieway passed 71 yds to Jackson for TD, Lashar kicked 4 FGs and an ex pt, and Carr ran 61 yds for other Sooner TD.

1986 (11–1) *Won:* UCLA 38–3, Minnesota 63–0, Kansas St. 56–10, Texas 47–12, Oklahoma St. 19–0 (10th straight over Cowboys), Iowa St. 38–0, Kansas 64–3, Missouri 77–0, Colorado 28–0 (10th straight over Buffaloes), Nebraska 20–17. *Lost:* Miami (Fla.) 28–16 in 3rd game. *Stars:* Holieway (1,352 yds and 12 TDs total off), Jackson (14 pass rec for 403 yds and 5 TDs), soph OT Anthony Phillips, Hutson, Lashar (12 FGs and 96 pts), Bosworth, Reed, DT Steve Bryan, DBs David Vickers and Rickey Dixon. *Noteworthy:* Led nation in scoring (42.4-pt avg), rush, scoring defense (6.6-pt avg), total defense, rush defense, and pass defense while winning 3rd straight Big 8 title. Beat Arkansas 42–8 in Orange Bowl; Spencer Tillman and Holieway each scored 2 TDs, including 77-yd run by Tillman.

1987 (11–1) *Won:* North Texas 69–14, North Carolina 28–0, Tulsa 65–0, Iowa St. 56–3, Texas 44–9, Kansas St. 59–10, Colorado 24–6, Kansas 71–10, Oklahoma St. 29–10, Missouri 17–13, Nebraska 17–7. *Stars:* Holieway (1,408 yds and 17 TDs total off), Jackson (13 pass rec for 358 yds), Hutson, Phillips, OT Greg Johnson, C Bob Latham, Reed, LB Dante Jones, Vickers, Dixon (8 int). *Noteworthy:* Led nation in scoring (43.5-pt avg), total off, rush, scoring defense (7.5-pt avg), total defense, rush defense, and pass defense while winning 4th straight Big 8 title (35th conference title overall). Lost national championship to unbeaten Miami (Fla.) 20–14 in Orange Bowl; Sooners scored on short run by HB Anthony Stafford and 29-yd "fumblerooskie" run by Hutson.

1988 (9–3) *Won:* North Carolina 28–0, Arizona 28–10, Iowa St. 35–7, Texas 28–10, Kansas St. 70–24, Colorado 17–14, Kansas 63–14, Oklahoma St. 31–28, Missouri 16–7. *Lost:* USC 23–7, Nebraska 7–3 (1st to Cornhuskers since 1983). *Stars:* Phillips, QB Charles Thompson (824 yds and 9 TDs rush), frosh TB Mike Gaddis (516 yds rush), FB Leon Perry (546 yds rush, 7 TDs), Stafford (6 TDs), SE Eric Bross (14 pass rec for 279 yds), soph DT Scott Evans, MG Tony Woods, DBs Scott Garl (5 int) and Kevin Thompson (6 int), P Todd Thomsen (40.9-yd avg). *Noteworthy:* Switzer's last team. Lost to Clemson 13–6 in Florida Citrus Bowl; Holieway passed for 138 yds and soph K R.D. Lashar had 2 FGs.

1990 (8–3) *Won:* UCLA 34–14, Pittsburgh 52–10, Tulsa 52–10, Kansas 31–17, Oklahoma St. 31–17, Missouri 55–10, Kansas St. 34–7 (20th straight over Wildcats), Nebraska 45–10. *Lost:* Texas 14–13, Iowa St. 33–31 (1st to Cyclones since 1961), national cochamp Colorado 32–23 in consecutive mid-season games. *Stars:* soph TB Dewell Brewer

(872 yds rush, 8 TDs), soph FB Kenyon Rasheed (661 yds rush, 10 TDs), FB Mike McKinley (534 yds rush, 6 TDs), TE Adrian Cooper (13 pass rec for 301 yds), OG Mike Sawatzky, Lashar (15 FGs, 95 pts), Evans, LB Joe Bowden, DBs Jason Belser and Greg DeQuasie (2 int returned for TDs), soph P Brad Reddell (41.6-yd punting avg). *Noteworthy:* ineligible for bowl, on NCAA probation.

1991 (9–3) *Won:* North Texas 40–2, Utah St. 55–21, Virginia Tech 27–17, Iowa St. 29–8, Kansas 41–3, Kansas St. 28–7, Missouri 56–16, Oklahoma St. 21–6 (15th straight over Cowboys). *Lost:* Texas 10–7, Colorado 34–17, Nebraska 19–14. *Stars:* Gaddis (1,240 yds rush, 14 TDs), soph QB Cale Gundy (1,228 yds pass), soph SE Corey Warren (26 pass rec for 366 yds), RB Ted Long (24 pass rec for 302 yds), OT Brian Brauninger, DE Reggie Barnes, Bowden, Belser (5 int), DB Charles Franks (5 int). *Noteworthy:* beat Virginia 48–14 in Gator Bowl; Gundy passed for 329 yds and 2 TDs (both to TE Joey Mickey), Warren caught 5 passes for 110 yds, and Gaddis ran for 104 yds and 3 TDs.

Bowl Summary

Bluebonnet 0–1–1; Fiesta 1–1; Florida Citrus 0–1; Gator 2–1; Orange 11–5; Sugar 4–1; Sun 1–0.

Bowl Record (19–10–1)

Regular Season	Bowl	Score	Opponent	Record
1938 (10–0)	Orange	0–17	Tennessee	(10–0)
1946 (7–3)	Gator	34–13	N.C. State	(8–2)
1948 (9–1)	Sugar	14–6	North Carolina	(9–0–1)
1949 (10–0)	Sugar	35–0	LSU	(8–2)
1950 (10–0)	Sugar	7–13	Kentucky	(10–1)
1953 (8–1–1)	Orange	7–0	Maryland	(10–0)
1955 (10–0)	Orange	20–6	Maryland	(10–0)
1957 (9–1)	Orange	48–21	Duke	(6–2–2)
1958 (9–1)	Orange	21–6	Syracuse	(8–1)
1962 (8–2)	Orange	0–17	Alabama	(9–1)
1964 (6–3–1)	Gator	19–36	Florida St.	(8–1–1)
1967 (9–1)	Orange	26–24	Tennessee	(9–1)
1968 (7–3)	Bluebonnet	27–28	SMU	(7–3)
1970 (7–4)	Bluebonnet	24–24	Alabama	(6–5)
1971 (10–1)	Sugar	40–22	Auburn	(9–1)

(continued)

Regular Season	Bowl	Score	Opponent	Record
1972 (10–1)	Sugar	14–0	Penn State	(10–1)
1975 (10–1)	Orange	14–6	Michigan	(8–1–2)
1976 (8–2–1)	Fiesta	41–7	Wyoming	(8–3)
1977 (10–1)	Orange	6–31	Arkansas	(10–1)
1978 (10–1)	Orange	31–24	Nebraska	(9–2)
1979 (10–1)	Orange	24–7	Florida St.	(11–0)
1980 (9–2)	Orange	18–17	Florida St.	(10–1)
1981 (6–4–1)	Sun	40–14	Houston	(7–3–1)
1982 (8–3)	Fiesta	21–32	Arizona St.	(9–2)
1984 (9–1–1)	Orange	17–28	Washington	(10–1)
1985 (10–1)	Orange	25–10	Penn State	(11–0)
1986 (10–1)	Orange	42–8	Arkansas	(9–2)
1987 (11–0)	Orange	14–20	Miami (Fla.)	(11–0)
1988 (9–2)	Fla. Citrus	6–13	Clemson	(9–2)
1991 (8–3)	Gator	48–14	Virginia	(8–2–1)

CONFERENCE TITLES

Southwest—1915. **Missouri Valley**—1920. **Big 6**—1938, 1943, 1944, 1946*, 1947*. **Big 7**—1948, 1949, 1950, 1951, 1952, 1953, 1954, 1955, 1956, 1957. **Big 8**—1958, 1959, 1962, 1967, 1968*, 1973, 1974, 1975*, 1976*, 1977, 1978*, 1979, 1980, 1984*, 1985, 1986, 1987.

TOP 20 AP AND UPI
(USA TODAY/CNN SINCE 1991) RANKING

1938	4	1954	3–3	1970	20–15	1980	3–3
1939	19	1955	1–1	1971	2–3	1981	20–14
1946	14	1956	1–1	1972	2–2	1982	16–16
1947	16	1957	4–4	1973	3–2	1984	6–6
1948	5	1958	5–5	1974	1–U	1985	1–1
1949	2	1959	15–15	1975	1–1	1986	3–3
1950	1–1	1962	8–7	1976	5–6	1987	3–3
1951	10–11	1963	10–8	1977	7–6	1988	14–14
1952	4–4	1967	3–3	1978	3–3	1990	17–U
1953	4–5	1968	11–10	1979	3–3	1991	16–14

MAJOR RIVALS

Oklahoma has played at least 10 games with Arkansas 9–4–1, Central Normal 17–1–1, Colorado 34–11–2, Iowa St. 58–5–2, Kansas 60–24–6, Kansas St. 63–11–4, Kingfisher 19–0–3, Missouri 56–22–5, Nebraska 39–31–3, Oklahoma St. 69–11–7, Pittsburgh 9–1–1, Texas 32–51–4, Texas A&M 7–5, Tulsa 10–6–1.

COACHES

Dean of Oklahoma coaches is Bennie Owen with record of 122–54–16 for 1905–26 with 2 conference titles and 4 unbeaten teams. Most wins were under Barry Switzer, 157–29–4 for 1973–88 with 12 Big 8 titles, 13 bowl teams, 3 teams unbeaten in regular season, and 3 national champions. Other top records for at least 3 years were by Tom Stidham,

27–8–3 for 1937–40 with 1 Big 6 title and an Orange Bowl team unbeaten in regular season; Dewey Luster, 27–18–3 for 1941–45 with 2 Big 6 titles; Charles "Bud" Wilkinson (1949 national Coach of Year), 145–29–4 for 1947–63 with 14 conference titles, 8 bowl teams (6 winners), 5 teams unbeaten in regular season, and 3 national champions; Chuck Fairbanks, 52–15–1 (49–18–1 by forfeit) for 1967–72 with 2 Big 8 titles and 5 bowl teams; and Gary Gibbs, 29–14–2 for 1989–92 with 1 bowl champion.

MISCELLANEA

First game was loss to Oklahoma City 34–0 in 1895 . . . 1st win was over Norman H.S. 12–0 in 1896 . . . 1st win over college foe was over Oklahoma City 16–0 in 1897 . . . highest score was over Kingfisher 179–0 in 1917 . . . highest since W.W. II was over Colorado 82–42 in 1980 . . . biggest margin since W.W. II was over Missouri 77–0 in 1986 . . . worst defeat was by Oklahoma St. 47–0 in 1945 . . . worst since W.W. II was by Notre Dame 38–0 in 1966 . . . highest ever against Sooners was by Kansas St. 59–21 in 1969 . . . longest win streak of 47 (NCAA record) and longest unbeaten string of 48 in 1953–57 ended by Notre Dame 7–0 . . . 37-game unbeaten string in 1972–75 ended by Kansas 23–3 . . . 31-game win streak in 1948–50 ended by Kentucky 13–7 in 1951 Sugar Bowl . . . longest losing string of 5 in 1961 broken with win over Kansas St. 17–6 . . . consensus All-Americans were Waddy Young, E, 1938; Buddy Burris, G, 1948; Leon Heath, B, 1950; Jim Weatherall, T, 1950–51; Billy Vessels, B, 1952; J.D. Roberts, G, 1953; Max Boydston, E, and Kurt Burris, C, 1954; Bo Bolinger, G, 1955; Jerry Tubbs, C, and Tommy McDonald, B, 1956; Bill Krisher, G, and Clendon Thomas, B, 1957; Bob Harrison, C, 1958; Jim Grisham, B, 1963; Ralph Neely, T, 1964; Carl McAdams, LB, 1965; Granville Liggins, MG, 1967; Steve Owens, B, 1969; Greg Pruitt, B, and Tom Brahaney, C, 1971–72; Lucious Selmon, DL, 1973; Rod Shoate, LB, 1973–74; John Roush, G, and Joe Washington, RB, 1974; Lee Roy Selmon, DT, Dewey Selmon, MG, and Jimbo Elrod, DE, 1975; Mike Vaughan, OT, 1976; Zac Henderson, DB, 1977; Greg Roberts, G, 1978; Billy Sims, RB, 1978–79; George Cumby, LB, 1979; Louis Oubre, OL, 1980; Terry Crouch, OL, 1981; Rick Bryan,

DL, 1982–83; Tony Casillas, DL, 1984–85; Brian Bosworth, LB, 1985–86; Keith Jackson, TE, 1986–87; Mark Hutson, OL, Dante Jones, LB, and Rickey Dixon, DB, 1987; and Anthony Phillips, OL, 1988 . . . Academic All-Americans were Tom Catlin, C, 1952; Carl Allison, E, 1954; Jerry Tubbs, C, 1956; Doyle Jennings, T, 1957; Ross Coyle, E, 1958; Wayne Lee, C, 1962; Newt Burton, G, 1963–64; Ron Shotts, HB, 1966–67; Eddie Hinton, DB, 1968; Joe Wylie, RB, 1970, 1972; Jack Mildren, QB, 1971; Randy Hughes, S, 1974; Dewey Selmon, LB, and Lee Roy Selmon, DT, 1975; Jay Jimerson, DB, 1980; and Brian Bosworth, LB, 1986 . . . Heisman Trophy winners were Billy Vessels, HB, 1952; Steve Owens, HB, 1969; and Billy Sims, HB, 1978 . . . Maxwell Award winner was Tommy McDonald, HB, 1956 . . . Outland Trophy winners were Jim Weatherall, T, 1951; J.D. Roberts, G, 1953; Lee Roy Selmon, DT, 1975; and Greg Roberts, G, 1978 . . . Lombardi Award winners were Lee Roy Selmon, DT, 1975; and Tony Casillas, NG, 1985.

OKLAHOMA STATE (Cowboys; Orange and Black)

NOTABLE TEAMS

1911 (5–2)   *Won:* Blackwell College 35–5, Central State 46–5, Kingfisher 84–0, Oklahoma City Military 30–0, Southwestern (Kansas) 61–16. *Lost:* Kansas St. 11–0, unbeaten Oklahoma 22–0.
1912 (6–2)   *Won:* Central State 18–0, Blackwell 79–0, Arkansas 13–7 (1st meeting), Baker 37–13, Oklahoma Methodist 90–0, Emporia St. 28–7. *Lost:* Oklahoma 16–0, Rolla Mines 13–7 in consecutive late games.
1914 (6–2–1)   *Won:* Phillips 134–0, Tulsa 13–6 (1st meeting), Tonkawa Preps 48–0, Baylor 60–0 (1st meeting), Arkansas 46–0, Colorado St. 7–0. *Lost:* Oklahoma 28–6, Texas A&M 24–0. *Tied:* Rice 13–13. *Noteworthy:* last year under Paul Davis.
1924 (6–1–2)   *Won:* SW Oklahoma 9–0, Kansas 3–0, Rolla Mines 23–0, Phillips 13–0, Oklahoma 6–0 (1st over Sooners since 1917), Arkansas 20–0. *Lost:* Texas Christian (TCU) 17–10. *Tied:* Creighton 20–20, unbeaten Southern Methodist (SMU) 13–13. *Noteworthy:* last year in SWC.
1930 (7–2–1)   *Won:* Wichita St. 12–0 (1st meeting), Iowa 6–0, Washington (Mo.) 28–7, Arkansas 26–0 (1st over Razorbacks in 5 games since 1924),

Oklahoma 7–0, Creighton 13–0, Tulsa 13–7. *Lost:* Oklahoma City 6–0, Haskell 13–12. *Tied:* Indiana 7–7. *Noteworthy:* won share of 1st MVC title.
1931 (8–2–1) *Won:* Bethany (Kansas) 34–9, NE Oklahoma 25–0, Arizona 31–0, Haskell 39–0, Kansas 13–7 (1st meeting since 1925), Creighton 20–0, Tulsa 7–6, Wichita St. 14–6. *Lost:* Minnesota 20–0, Oklahoma City 13–0. *Tied:* Oklahoma 0–0. *Noteworthy:* again got share of MVC crown.
1932 (9–1–2) *Won:* Phillips 13–0, SW Oklahoma 33–3, Drake 27–7, Creighton 18–7, Oklahoma City 14–6, Oklahoma 7–0, Grinnell 27–0, Arizona 13–6, Texas Mines (UTEP) 20–7. *Lost:* Jefferson 12–6. *Tied:* Central State 0–0, Tulsa 0–0. *Noteworthy:* took 3rd straight MVC title.
1933 (6–2–1) *Won:* Central State 20–12, Haskell 18–0, Tulsa 7–0, Drake 21–0, Creighton 33–13, Oklahoma 13–0. *Lost:* Colorado 6–0 (1st meeting since 1920), Oklahoma City 19–13. *Tied:* SMU 7–7 (1st meeting since 1924). *Noteworthy:* "Pappy" Waldorf's last team won 4th straight MVC crown.
1944 (8–1) *Won:* West Texas St. 41–6, Arkansas 19–0, Texas Tech 14–7, Denver 33–21, Tulsa 46–40 (1st over Hurricane since 1939), Texas 13–8, Oklahoma 28–6 (1st over Sooners since 1933). *Lost:* Navy Zoomers 15–0. *Stars:* HB Bob Fenimore (12 TDs, 897 yds rush, nation's leader in total off with 1,758 yds), Cecil Hankins (19 pass rec for 474 yds). *Noteworthy:* Won 5th MVC title. Made 1st postseason appearance, beating TCU 34–0 in Cotton Bowl; Fenimore scored twice and passed for 137 yds, and frosh FB Jim Spavital ran for 119 yds and a TD.
1945 (9–0) *Won:* Arkansas 19–14, Denver 31–7, SMU 26–12, Utah 46–6, TCU 25–12, Tulsa 12–6, Texas Tech 46–6, Oklahoma 47–0. *Stars:* Fenimore (Aggies' 1st consensus All-American; 12 TDs, 39-yd punting avg, 7 int, nation's leader with 1,641 yds total off, 1,048 yds rush, and 1,577 all-purpose yds), Neill Armstrong (312 yds pass rec). *Noteworthy:* Repeated as MVC champ in 1st unbeaten season. Beat St. Mary's 33–13 in Sugar Bowl; Fenimore ran and passed for 206 yds, scored 2 TDs, passed for a 3rd (28 yds to Hankins), and averaged 53.2 yds on 4 punts, and Jim Reynolds scored 1 TD and passed 20 yds to Joe Thomas for another.
1953 (7–3) *Won:* Hardin-Simmons 20–0, Arkansas 7–6, Wichita St. 14–7, Houston 14–7, Tulsa 28–14 (1st over Hurricane since 1948), Wyoming 20–14

(1st meeting), Kansas 41–14 (1st over Jayhawks in 8 games since 1931). *Lost:* Texas Tech 27–13 (1st meeting since 1946), Detroit 18–14, Oklahoma 42–7. *Stars:* soph FB Earl Lunsford (748 yds rush), Bill Bredde (5 int). *Noteworthy:* Got share of 8th and last MVC title.
1958 (8–3) *Won:* Denver 31–14, North Texas St. 21–14, Wichita St. 43–12, Houston 7–0, Cincinnati 19–14, Kansas St. 14–7, Kansas 6–3. *Lost:* Tulsa 24–16 (1st to Hurricane since 1952), unbeaten Air Force 33–29, Oklahoma 7–0. *Stars:* HB Duane Wood (7 TDs), E Jim Wood. *Noteworthy:* beat Florida St. 15–6 in Blue Grass Bowl; Duane Wood scored 2 TDs and Forrest Campbell ran for 130 yds on frozen field.
1976 (9–3) *Won:* Tulsa 33–21 (1st meeting since 1965), North Texas St. 16–10, Kansas 21–14, Oklahoma 31–24 (1st over Sooners since 1966), Missouri 20–19, Kansas St. 45–21, Iowa St. 42–21, Texas–El Paso 42–13. *Lost:* Arkansas 16–10, Colorado 20–10, Nebraska 14–10. *Stars:* RB Terry Miller (1,541 yds rush, 19 TDs, 114 pts), QB Charlie Weatherbie (1,197 yds total off), Sam Lisle (360 yds pass rec), C Derrel Gofourth, K Abby Daigle (9 FGs), DT Phillip Dokes, DE Daria Butler, P Cliff Parsley (43.5-yd avg). *Noteworthy:* Got share of 1st Big 8 title. Beat Brigham Young (BYU) 49–21 in Tangerine Bowl; Miller ran for 173 yds and 3 TDs, and Cowboys intercepted 4 BYU passes (Chris Dawson returned one 36 yds for TD).
1983 (8–4) *Won:* North Texas St. 20–13, Cincinnati 27–17, Texas A&M 34–15, Tulsa 9–0, Kansas 21–10, Colorado 40–14, Iowa St. 30–7. *Lost:* unbeaten Nebraska 14–10 (10th straight to Cornhuskers), Oklahoma 21–20, Kansas St. 21–20 (1st to Wildcats since 1978), Missouri 16–10. *Stars:* P John Conway (42-yd punting avg), K Larry Roach (18 FGs, 77 pts), QB Rusty Hilger (1,110 yds pass), Jamie Harris (42 pass rec for 549 yds and 6 TDs), Shawn Jones (924 yds rush), OG Kevin Igo, soph DT Leslie O'Neal, DB Chris Rockins, Adam Hinds (8 int). *Noteworthy:* Last year under Jimmy Johnson. Beat Baylor 24–14 (1st meeting since 1974) in Bluebonnet Bowl; Ernest Anderson ran for 143 yds and a TD, and Hilger passed for 137 yds and 2 TDs.
1984 (10–2) *Won:* Arizona St. 45–3, Bowling Green 31–14, San Diego St. 19–16, Tulsa 31–7, Kansas 47–10, Colorado 20–14, Kansas St. 34–6, Missouri 31–13, Iowa St. 16–10. *Lost:* Nebraska

17–3, Oklahoma 24–14. *Stars:* O'Neal, Roach (16 FGs, 77 pts), Hilger (1,843 yds pass), Harris (26 pass rec for 413 yds and 5 TDs), frosh TB Thurman Thomas (688 yds rush, 6 TDs), OG Ralph Partida, OT Paul Blair, DT Rodney Harding, LB Matt Monger, DBs Rod Brown (6 int) and soph Mark Moore. *Noteworthy:* 1st year under Pat Jones. Beat South Carolina 21–14 in Gator Bowl, scoring winning TD on 25-yd pass from Hilger to TE Barry Hanna with about a minute left; Thomas ran for 155 yds and a TD and passed for a TD (to Hilger). **1985** (8–4) *Won:* Washington 31–17, North Texas St. 10–9, Miami (Ohio) 45–10, Tulsa 25–13, Kansas 17–10, Colorado 14–11, Kansas St. 35–3, Missouri 21–19. *Lost:* Nebraska 34–24, Iowa St. 15–10 (1st to Cyclones since 1980), national champ Oklahoma 13–9. *Stars:* Thomas (1,553 yds rush, 16 TDs), QB Ronnie Williams (1,506 yds pass), Bobby Riley (33 pass rec for 610 yds) Blair, O'Neal, Moore (7 int), DB Mike Hudson. *Noteworthy:* lost to Florida St. 34–23 in Gator Bowl; Williams scored on 12-yd pass from Thomas and passed for 2 TDs (29 yds to Thomas, who had 97 yds rush, and 31 yds to

frosh WR Hart Lee Dykes, who caught 8 for 104 yds).
1987 (10–2) *Won:* Tulsa 39–28, Houston 35–0, Wyoming 35–29, SW Louisiana 36–0, Colorado 42–17, Missouri 24–20, Kansas St. 56–7, Kansas 49–17, Iowa St. 48–27. *Lost:* Nebraska 35–0, unbeaten Oklahoma 29–10. *Stars:* Thomas (1,613 yds rush, 18 TDs, 1,938 all-purpose yds), soph QB Mike Gundy (2,106 yds and 13 TDs pass), Dykes (61 pass rec for 978 yds and 8 TDs), soph RB Barry Sanders (13 TDs, 603 yds rush, 1,348 all-purpose yds, nation's leader in kickoff returns with 31.6-yd avg), P Cary Cooper (41.8-yd avg), Melvin Gilliam (5 int), soph Rod Smith (5 int). *Noteworthy:* edged West Virginia 35–33 in John Hancock Sun Bowl; Thomas ran for 157 yds and 4 TDs, and Gundy passed for 161 yds and a TD (to J.R. Dillard).
1988 (10–2) *Won:* Miami (Ohio) 52–20, Texas

RB Barry Sanders, 1986–88

QB Mike Gundy, 1986–89

A&M 52–15, Tulsa 56–35, Colorado 41–21, Missouri 49–21, Kansas St. 45–27, Kansas 63–24, Iowa St. 49–28, Texas Tech 45–42 (in Tokyo, 1st meeting since 1975). *Lost:* Nebraska 63–42 (15th straight to Cornhuskers), Oklahoma 31–28. *Stars:* Heisman Trophy– and Maxwell Award–winner Sanders (nation's leader with 2,628 yds rush, 234 pts on 39 TDs, and 3,250 all-purpose yds), Gundy (2,163 yds and 19 TDs pass), Dykes (15 TDs, 74 pass rec for 1,278 yds and 14 TDs), FL Jarod Green (20 pass rec for 309 yds), OT Byron Woodard, OG Chris Stanley, soph K Cary Blanchard (11 FGs, 100 pts), Gilliam (5 int). *Noteworthy:* Led nation in scoring (47.5-pt avg). Beat Wyoming 62–14 in Holiday Bowl; Sanders ran for 222 yds and 5 TDs, Dykes had 10 pass rec for 163 yds and a TD, and Gundy passed for 315 yds and 2 TDs.

BOWL SUMMARY

Bluebonnet 1–0; Bluegrass 1–0; Cotton 1–0; Delta 0–1; Fiesta 1–0; Gator 1–1; Holiday 1–0; Independence 0–1; John Hancock Sun 1–0; Sugar 1–0; Tangerine 1–0.

BOWL RECORD (9–3)

Regular Season	Bowl	Score	Opponent	Record
1944 (7–1)	Cotton	34–0	TCU	(7–2–1)
1945 (8–0)	Sugar	33–13	St. Mary's	(7–1)
1948 (6–3)	Delta	0–20	William & Mary	(6–2–2)
1958 (7–3)	Bluegrass	15–6	Florida State	(7–3)
1974 (6–5)	Fiesta	16–6	BYU	(7–3–1)
1976 (8–3)	Tangerine	49–21	BYU	(9–2)
1981 (7–4)	Independence	16–33	Texas A&M	(6–5)
1983 (7–4)	Bluebonnet	24–14	Baylor	(7–3–1)
1984 (9–2)	Gator	21–14	South Carolina	(10–1)
1985 (8–3)	Gator	23–34	Florida State	(8–3)
1987 (9–2)	John Hancock Sun	35–33	West Virginia	(6–5)
1988 (9–2)	Holiday	62–14	Wyoming	(11–1)

CONFERENCE TITLES

Missouri Valley Intercollegiate Athletic Association—1926. **Missouri Valley**—1930*, 1931*, 1932, 1933, 1944, 1945, 1948, 1953*. **Big 8**—1976*.

TOP 20 AP AND UPI RANKING

1945	5	1984	7–5	1987	11–12	1988	11–11
1958	19–U						

MAJOR RIVALS

Oklahoma St. has played at least 10 games with Arkansas 15–30–1, Baylor 3–10, Central St. (Okla.) 14–5–2, Colorado 15–19–1, Creighton 11–6–1, Detroit 6–7, Drake 7–2–1, Houston 8–8–1, Iowa St. 20–12–2, Kansas 23–25–3, Kansas St. 32–15, Missouri 18–21, Nebraska 2–30–1, North Texas St. 9–1, Oklahoma 11–69–7, Oklahoma City 6–9–2, Phillips U. 7–2–1, Texas 1–9, Texas A&M 4–7, TCU 10–9–2, Texas Tech 8–12–3, Tulsa 32–25–5, Washington (Mo.) 5–6–1, Wichita St. 19–5–1.

COACHES

Dean of Oklahoma St. coaches is Jim Lookabaugh with record of 58–41–6 for 1939–49, including 3 MVC titles, 3 bowl teams, and 1 unbeaten team. Other top records for at least 3 years were by Paul J. Davis, 29–16–1 for 1909–14; Lynn "Pappy" Waldorf, 34–10–7 for 1929–33 with 4 MVC titles; Jim Stanley, 35–31–2 for 1973–78 with 1 Big 8 title and 2 bowl champions; Jimmy Johnson, 30–25–2 for 1978–83 with 2 bowl teams; and Pat Jones, 56–45–2 for 1984–92 with 4 bowl teams.

MISCELLANEA

First game was loss to Kingfisher 12–0 in 1901 . . . 1st win was over N.W. Oklahoma 17–0 in 1901 . . . highest score was over Phillips 134–0 in 1914 . . . highest since W.W. II was over Southern Illinois 70–7 in 1973 . . . worst defeat was by Oklahoma 75–0 in 1904 . . . worst since W.W. II was by Oklahoma 73–12 in 1946 . . . longest unbeaten string of 14 in 1944–46 ended by Texas 54–6 . . . longest winless string of 11, in 1903–05 broken with win over Central St. 5–0, in 1919–20 broken with win over SW Oklahoma 53–0 in 1921 opener, and in 1991 broken with win over Indiana St. 35–3 in 1992 opener . . . consensus All-Americans were Bob Fenimore, B, 1945; John Ward, T, 1969; Derrel Gofourth, C, 1976; Terry Miller, RB, 1977; Rod Brown, DB, 1984; Thurman Thomas, RB, and Leslie O'Neal, DL, 1985; and Barry Sanders, RB, and Hart Lee Dykes, WR, 1988 . . . Academic All-Americans were Dale Meinert, G, 1954; Tom Wolfe, OT, 1972, 1974; Doug Tarrant, LB, 1973; and Joe Avanzini, DE, 1977 . . . Heisman Trophy winner was Barry Sanders, HB, 1988 . . . Maxwell Award winner was Barry Sanders, HB, 1988.

BIG 10 CONFERENCE

A meeting in Chicago of the presidents of seven Midwestern universities in 1895, called to discuss the regulation and control of intercollegiate athletics, led to the formation on February 8, 1896, of the "Intercollegiate Conference of Faculty Representatives," which soon became known informally as the Western Conference and later as the Big 10. The charter members of the new conference were Northwestern and Purdue Universities and the universities of Chicago, Illinois, Michigan, Minnesota, and Wisconsin.

Indiana University and the University of Iowa both were admitted on December 1, 1899. Michigan withdrew from the conference in 1907 but resumed membership in 1917. In the meantime, Ohio State University was admitted on April 6, 1912. Chicago (which had dropped football after the 1939 season) withdrew from the conference in 1946 and was replaced on May 20, 1949, by Michigan State University (first eligible for the conference title in 1953). Membership remained stable until Pennsylvania State University was admitted to membership in 1990. The Nittany Lions, however, were not eligible for the conference title until 1993.

FACTS AND ODDITIES ON BIG 10 MEMBERS

As the oldest active conference in college football, the Big 10 has a rich and varied tradition, boasting some of the top teams, players, and coaches in the sport's history.

Michigan in 1901 became the first non–Ivy League team to win a national title, outscoring opponents 501–0 in compiling a 10–0 regular-season record, then demolishing Stanford 49–0 in the first Tournament of Roses postseason game. Fielding "Hurry Up" Yost's 1902 "point-a-minute" team, which outscored opponents 644–12 in an 11–0 season, gave the Wolverines a second straight national crown. Chicago gave famed coach Amos Alonzo Stagg his only national title in 1905, wrapping up a 10–0 season by ending Michigan's 56-game unbeaten string with a 2–0 victory behind diminutive QB Walter Eckersall. It was the only national title ever won by a school not now in Division I-A or the Ivy League.

Illinois' 1923 squad, sparked by sensational sophomore TB Harold "Red" Grange, won the national title with an 8–0 mark, then was back for another national crown in 1927 with a record of 7–0–1 (the tie was with Iowa State 12–12). Michigan got a share of its third national title in 1932, when the Wolverines finished 8–0, then won outright with a 7–0–1 record in 1933 (the tie was with unbeaten Minnesota 0–0).

Minnesota took over national dominance in the middle 1930s with three consecutive championships. The Golden Gophers finished 8–0 in 1934, 8–0 in 1935, and 7–1 in 1936 (losing to Northwestern 6–0 in mid-season) and got the majority of votes for the national championship each year, earning sole possession in 1936. The Golden Gophers resumed their national dominance with consecutive titles in 1940 and 1941, finishing with 8–0 records each year under coach Bernie Bierman. They got majority support for the crown in 1940 and won outright in 1941.

Ohio State, with a 9–1 record (the loss was to Wisconsin 17–7), got a share of its first national crown in 1942. Michigan was the unanimous choice for its fifth national crown in 1948, finishing 9–0 but unavailable for postseason play because conference representatives at that time would not send the same team to the Rose Bowl two years in a row— champion or not. At that time Big 10 teams did not accept bids to other bowls.

Ohio State earned a share of its second national title in 1954, finishing 9–0 and beating the University of Southern California (USC) 20–7 in the Rose Bowl. The Buckeyes were back with another share in 1957, despite losing the season opener to Texas Christian (TCU) 18–14. Ohio State then won eight straight before beating Oregon 10–7 in the Rose Bowl. Iowa was only 7–1–1 (losing to Ohio State 38–28 and tying unbeaten Air Force 13–13) in 1958 but won the Rose Bowl over California 38–12 and got a share of its first national title. Minnesota shared the crown in 1960, despite finishing 8–1 (the loss was to Purdue 23–14) and losing to Washington 17–7 in the Rose Bowl. In 1961 Ohio State got a share of its fourth title by winning eight straight games after a season–opening 7–7 tie with TCU.

Michigan State (which had won the 1952 national title with a 9–0 record as an independent) got most of the support for the national crown in 1965 by going 10–0 behind DE Bubba Smith and DB George Webster before being upset in the Rose Bowl 14–12 by a UCLA team that the Spartans had beaten 13–3 in the season opener. Michigan State got a small piece of the title again in 1966 by finishing 9–0–1, including an epic 10–10 tie with unbeaten Notre Dame (which got the majority of votes for the national crown).

Ohio State was the overwhelming choice for the national crown in 1968, finishing 9–0 and then beating undefeated USC 27–16 in the Rose Bowl. The Buckeyes earned a share of their sixth national crown in 1970, finishing 9–0 before being stunned by Stanford 27–17 in the Rose Bowl. Ohio State seemed to have the 1975 title sewn up with an 11–0 regular-season record, but was upset by UCLA 23–10 in the Rose Bowl and had to settle for a share of the championship.

No Big 10 team has won a national title since 1975, although newest member Penn State, competing as an Eastern independent, won national crowns in 1982 (losing to Alabama 42–21 in mid-season but finishing 10–1 and then beating undefeated Georgia 27–23 in the Sugar Bowl) and in 1986 (going 11–0, then beating undefeated Miami 14–10 in the Fiesta Bowl).

The Heisman Trophy has gone to Big 10 players 11 times, including the first award (to Chicago HB Jay Berwanger) in 1935. The only player ever to win the award twice was HB Archie Griffin of Ohio State in 1974–1975. Other Big 10 winners were HB Nile Kinnick, Iowa, 1939; HB Tom Harmon, Michigan, 1940; HB Bruce Smith, Minnesota, 1941; QB Les Horvath, Ohio State, 1944; HB Vic Janowicz, Ohio State, 1950; FB Alan Ameche, Wisconsin, 1954; HB Howard Cassady, Ohio State, 1955; and WR Desmond Howard, Michigan, 1991. Penn State HB John Cappelletti won the Heisman in 1973 when the Nittany Lions were independent.

The Maxwell Award has gone to eight Big 10 players. They were HB Nile Kinnick, Iowa, 1939; HB Tom Harmon, Michigan, 1940; HB Howard Cassady, Ohio State, 1955; FB Bob Ferguson, Ohio State, 1961; DB Brad Van Pelt, Michigan State, 1972; RB Archie Griffin, Ohio State, 1975; QB Chuck Long, Iowa, 1985; and WR Desmond Howard, Michigan, 1991. Penn State players won the Maxwell Award five times before the Nittany Lions entered the Big 10, taking it with QB Rich Lucas, 1959; C Glenn Ressler, 1964; DT Mike Reid, 1969; RB John Cappelletti, 1973; and QB Chuck Fusina, 1978.

The Outland Trophy has gone to Big 10 players seven times. Winners were G Calvin Jones, Iowa, 1955; G Jim Parker, Ohio State, 1956; T Alex Karras, Iowa, 1957; G Tom Brown, Minnesota, 1960; T Bobby Bell, Minnesota, 1962; MG Jim Stillwagon, Ohio State, 1970; and OT John Hicks, Ohio State, 1973. In addition, G Ed Bagdon of Michigan State won the award in 1949, before the Spartans were eligible for the Big 10 crown, and Penn State DT Mike Reid won the Outland in 1969 when the Nittany Lions were independent.

The Lombardi Award has gone to four Big 10 players—three from Ohio State. Buckeye MG Jim Stillwagon won the first award in 1970, with OT John Hicks winning in 1973 and LB Chris Spielman in 1987. Michigan State LB Percy Snow won the award in 1989. Penn State DT Bruce Clark won the Lombardi in 1978 before State was a Big 10 member.

The first Big 10 players to make consensus All-America were Chicago B Clarence Herschberger and Michigan C William Cunningham in 1898.

One of the early Big 10 players to gain national fame was Michigan B Willie Heston, considered the best running back of college football's first 50 years by noted sportswriter Grantland Rice. As a star of Michigan's teams of 1901–1904, Heston scored 72 TDs, including 20 as a freshman and 21 as a senior. Complete statistics are not available, but he ran for more than 200 yards in a game at least four times and for more than

100 yards at least 11 times—and that was against stacked defenses that did not have to worry about the forward pass. Heston was credited with inventing the cutback, in which he started in one direction behind his blockers, then suddenly darted around to the other side. During Heston's time at Michigan the Wolverines were 43–0–1 with two national titles and a Tournament of Roses victory.

Among the all-time great players who performed for Big 10 schools was Harold "Red" Grange of Illinois, the "Galloping Ghost" of 1923–1925. The "Wheaton Iceman" (his other nickname) ran for 2,071 yds (despite missing several games with injuries during his career), completed 40 of 82 passes for 575 yds, and caught 14 passes for 253 yds. His versatility was shown in his TD total: 31, including 2 on pass receptions, 2 on punt returns, 2 on kickoff returns, and 1 on a pass interception return.

Two of Grange's performances were among the most spectacular in football history. In 1924 Illinois had won its first two games when powerful Michigan came in for the October 18 game dedicating the Illini's new Memorial Stadium. On the opening kickoff the "Wheaton Iceman" grabbed the ball and returned it 95 yds for a score. The next time he touched the ball, Grange raced 70 yds for a second TD. The third time it was 57 yds for another score, and shortly thereafter a 43-yd run gave Grange his fourth TD in less than 12 minutes of play. Taken out for a breather, Grange returned to score on a 15-yd run on his first carry of the second half, and in the 4th quarter he threw a TD pass for good measure in Illinois' 39–14 triumph. That day Grange ran for 212 yds on 15 carries, returned three kickoffs 126 yds, scored five TDs, and completed six of eight passes for 64 yds and another score.

His performance against Pennsylvania in Philadelphia the following year was also impressive. Illinois had lost three of four games that year, and Grange had been stopped short of 100 yards in each. Heavily favored Penn was unbeaten in five games. Despite a heavy rain that turned the field into a quagmire, 63,000 fans turned out for their only chance to view the two–time All-American. If they had any ideas that he was overrated, such ideas didn't last long. The first time Grange carried the ball he raced 58 yds for a TD, and before the day was over he had totaled 237 yds and two TDs on 28 carries, had caught a couple of passes for 35 yds and another score, had returned two kickoffs 79 yds, and had led the Illini to a 24–2 upset victory. Illinois did not lose again in 1925, finishing 5–3, and Grange made All-America for the third time.

Another Big 10 player considered an all-time great in the early years was Bronko Nagurski of Minnesota. One of the larger players of his day, at 230 pounds, Nagurski was quick and fast, able to play equally well on the line or in the backfield. During his 1927–1929 playing days at Minnesota, he played end, tackle, and fullback at various times and made several All-America teams, some at the tackle and some at the fullback positions. During that time the Gophers' record was 18–4–2.

Big 10 backs who made consensus All-America three times were Walter Eckersall of Chicago, 1904–1906; Charles "Chic" Harley of Ohio

State, 1916–1917, 1919; and Harold "Red" Grange of Illinois, 1923–1925. Only a half-dozen linemen have made consensus All-America three times in the 20th century, and two of them were from the Big 10—Michigan E Bennie Oosterbaan in 1925–1927 and Ohio State E Wes Fesler in 1928–1930.

National Coach of the Year awards have gone to 14 different Big 10 coaches. Lynn "Pappy" Waldorf of Northwestern won the American Football Coaches Association's first award in 1935. That award also has gone to Eddie Anderson, Iowa, 1939; Carroll Widdoes, Ohio State, 1944; Bo McMillin, Indiana, 1945; Fritz Crisler, Michigan, 1947; Bennie Oosterbaan, Michigan, 1948; Duffy Daugherty, Michigan State, 1955; Woody Hayes, Ohio State, 1957; Murray Warmath, Minnesota, 1960; John Pont, Indiana, 1967; Bo Schembechler, Michigan, 1969; and Earle Bruce, Ohio State, 1979. Clarence "Biggie" Munn of Michigan State won the award in 1952, a year before the Spartans began conference play, and Penn State's Joe Paterno won the award an unprecedented four times—in 1968, 1978, 1982, and 1986—when the Nittany Lions were independent.

The Football Writers Association of America presented its first award to Woody Hayes of Ohio State in 1957 and gave him the award again in 1968 and 1975. Other Big 10 recipients of that award were Murray Warmath, Minnesota, 1960; Duffy Daugherty, Michigan State, 1965; John Pont, Indiana, 1967; Bo Schembechler, Michigan, 1969; Alex Agase, Northwestern, 1970; and Earle Bruce, Ohio State, 1979. Paterno won the award at independent Penn State in 1978, 1982, and 1986.

Among the outstanding coaches who have directed Big 10 teams is Amos Alonzo Stagg, who holds the all-time record of 57 years as a head coach—41 of them at the University of Chicago. His Maroon teams in 1892–1932 compiled a record of 244–111–27 for a winning percentage of .674. He won seven Big 10 titles, including the league's inaugural one in 1896, and one national crown. Later, while coaching at Pacific in 1943, he won national Coach of the Year honors—at age 81!

Famed Notre Dame coach Knute Rockne was one of Stagg's admirers. Asked where he got his football system, Rockne replied, "I got my system from Jess Harper, and he got it from Amos Alonzo Stagg, and I really think that Stagg got it from God." Stagg was credited with originating the hidden ball play (later outlawed), the onside kick, the quick kick, and the end–around play, as well as such equipment as tackling dummies, blocking sleds, and padded goal posts. He had a career coaching record of 314–199–35 for 1890–1946 at Springfield, Chicago, and Pacific.

Fielding H. Yost is seventh in all-time winning percentage among major college coaches, with a record of 196–36–12 for 29 years as head coach, a winning percentage of .828. His Michigan teams for 1901–1923 and 1925–1926 were 165–29–10. The West Virginia native coached ten Big 10 champions and had eight unbeaten teams, including two national champions. Before Yost went to Michigan, the Wolverines already had developed a winning tradition, going 25–4–1 in the three years preceding his arrival. But that wasn't good enough for the cocky Yost. He threw himself into his new job with such vigor that a Detroit sportswriter said: "There is a new cry at Michigan. It's hurry, hurry, hurry! If you can't hustle, make way for someone who can!" Thus was born the nickname, "Hurry Up" Yost. In his first five years at Michigan, Yost's teams compiled a record of 55–1–1, with two national titles.

Another famous Big 10 coach in the early days was Bob Zuppke of Illinois, who compiled a record of 131–81–13 for 1913–1941, with seven conference crowns and two generally recognized national titles. Zuppke invented the screen pass and the offensive huddle, and modified and popularized the "flea flicker" with its many variations. He also was known for his psychological ploys.

In 1916 the Illini played an unbeaten Minnesota team that had rolled up such scores as 67–0 over Iowa, 81–0 over South Dakota, 49–0 over Chicago, and 53–0 over Wisconsin. Illinois had a 2–2 record and figured to lose by 50 points or more. Before the game Zuppke climbed up on a bench, looked around the room, and proclaimed: "I am Louis XIV, and you are my court. After us, the deluge." The players may not have known what he was referring to, but they cheered. Zuppke continued: "Today I want you to have some fun. Get beaten 100 to 0 if you want to, but have fun." The Illini had fun, all right. They quickly scored a TD on one of Zuppke's trick plays, then fought to an astounding 14–9 upset win. It was Minnesota's only defeat of the year.

Another effective ploy by Zuppke came when the Illini faced Michigan in 1939. A mediocre Illinois team went into the contest with a record of 0–3–1 while Michigan had hardly been tested in its first four games. But earlier in the season Michigan's Fritz Crisler, an excellent coach in his own right, had stated that his star back, Tom Harmon, was better than "Red" Grange had been. All week before the Michigan game Zuppke repeated the statement: "Crisler says Harmon is better than Grange." The team and the student body as well were fired up to stop the Michigan All-American, and Harmon had one of his poorest games as he was swarmed time and again by the aroused Illinois team. The Illini pulled off a 16–7 upset, then went on to win two of their remaining three games.

More recent Big 10 coaches who have solidified records as all-time greats were Woody Hayes of Ohio State and Glenn "Bo" Schembechler of Michigan. Hayes had an all-time coaching record of 238–72–10, with a 1951–1978 Ohio State record of 205–61–10 (a .761 winning percentage). Under Hayes, the Buckeyes won 13 Big 10 titles and five national crowns, and had six unbeaten regular seasons. Schembechler compiled a career record of 234–65–8 with a 1969–1989 record at Michigan of 194–48–5. His teams won 13 Big 10 titles.

Joe Paterno of the Big 10's newest member, Penn State, has the longest tenure among current conference coaches and leads the nation's active coaches in victories. Since 1966, all at Penn State, Paterno has compiled a record of 247–67–3.

Michigan sent a team to South Bend, Indiana, in 1887 and instructed some Notre Dame students how to play the game, then beat the home team 8–0 in an official game. The Wolverines won the first eight games in the series, but when the Fighting Irish finally beat Michigan, 11–3 in 1909, it was the Wolverines' only defeat of the year.

When Michigan played in the first Tournament of Roses game on New Year's Day, 1902, the Wolverine players rode on horse-drawn floats in the parade preceding the game. Then they hammered Stanford 49–0 in a game shortened by six minutes when Stanford players became exhausted—despite the fact that the Indians used 17 players while Michigan stuck with the starting 11.

One of the first backs to gain fame as a passer was Benny Friedman of Michigan, who threw 27 TD passes during his 1924–1926 career. The Wolverines' record for that period was 20–4.

When Francis A. Schmidt coached Ohio State during 1934–1940, he was given the nickname "Close the Gates of Mercy Schmidt" for running up scores on inferior opponents. Some of the games responsible for that nickname were wins over Western Reserve 76–0 in 1934, Drake 85–7 in 1935, New York U. 60–0 in 1936, and Chicago 61–0 in 1939.

Tom Harmon of Michigan ran for 2,110 yds during his 1938–1940 career, averaging 5.4 yds per carry. His best season rushing was 1939, when he gained 868 yds and averaged 6.7 yds per carry. When he won the Heisman and Maxwell awards as a senior in 1940, Harmon averaged "only" 4.5 yds per try (totaling 844 yds), but he also passed for 502 yds and scored 16 TDs.

Two Minnesota players of 1942 made All-America in 1943—but not for the Golden Gophers. Bill Daley and Herb Hein were assigned to different schools under World War II military training programs, and Daley was chosen All-America fullback at Michigan in 1943 while Hein made a few all-star teams at the end position at Northwestern.

As a 19-year-old sophomore in 1942, Elroy Hirsch contributed a good deal to Wisconsin's 8–1–1 season. He ran for 766 yds, had 390 more on pass receptions and runbacks, and passed for 226 yds. The following season found him at Michigan in a Marine training program. At his new school, Hirsch lettered not only in football but also in basketball, baseball, and track—the only athlete ever to letter in all of those sports at Michigan in one year. Better known as "Crazy Legs," Hirsch went on to an outstanding professional football career after World War II.

At Michigan in 1943 Hirsch had replaced Bob Chappuis, who lettered in 1942 before finding himself in active military service. As a bomber gunner Chappuis was forced to parachute over enemy-held territory in Italy when his plane was hit. He was hidden by Italian partisans until the area was liberated by the Allies. In 1946 he returned to Ann Arbor in time for the football season and picked up 1,265 yds running and passing as a single-wing tailback. In 1947 Chappuis gained 1,395 yds total offense, sparked Michigan to a 9–0 record and the Big 10 title, and had 279 yds total off in a 49–0 win over USC in the Rose Bowl. He was a unanimous All-America choice.

Three brothers named Wistert made consensus All-America at Michigan over a span of 16 years—all at the tackle position. Francis made the all-star team in 1933, Albert in 1942, and Alvin in 1948–1949.

The most-played series in Division I-A college football is that between Minnesota and Wisconsin, with 102 games through 1992. The series began in 1890 and stands at 54–40–8 in favor of Minnesota. It also is third longest in an uninterrupted series, with the teams meeting annually since 1907. The Purdue-Indiana rivalry is tied for 10th in most-played games. Between 1891 and 1992 the schools played 95 times, with Purdue holding a 58–31–6 edge.

Other long-standing rivalries involving Big 10 schools include Penn State vs. Pittsburgh (the Nittany Lions lead 47–41–4 in a series begun in 1893), Michigan vs. Ohio State (the Wolverines lead 50–33–6 in a series begun in 1897), and Michigan vs. Michigan State (the Wolverines lead 56–24–5 in a series dating to 1898). The Penn State–Pitt series, however, lapsed after the 1892 game until 1897.

The longest losing string in Division I-A football history was Northwestern's 34-game string in 1979–1982. The string ended with the Wildcats' 31–6 win over Northern Illinois on September 25, 1982. Between 1974 and 1982, Northwestern set a record of 46 consecutive road games without a win.

While competing as an independent, the Nittany Lions won the Lambert Trophy, emblematic of football supremacy in the East, nearly three times as often as any other school: Penn State won the trophy 21 times between 1947 and 1991.

The largest crowd (since the NCAA began keeping official statistics) ever to see a regular-season college football game was 106,788 on October 10, 1992, at Ann Arbor, Michigan, when Michigan beat Michigan State 35–10. The largest crowd officially to see a college game was in the 1973 Rose Bowl when 106,869 turned out to see undefeated USC beat Ohio State 42–17.

Nicknames at Big 10 schools include several unique on the college scene, including the Illinois Fighting Illini, Indiana Fightin' Hoosiers, Iowa Hawkeyes, Michigan Wolverines, Minnesota Golden Gophers, Ohio State Buckeyes, Penn State Nittany Lions, Purdue Boilermakers, and Wisconsin Badgers. Michigan State's Spartans and Northwestern's Wildcats are nicknames shared by other schools.

A number of Big 10 schools adopted their state nickname as their own, including Iowa (with Hawkeye dating to pre–Civil War days), Indiana (which later added "Fightin'" to the state nickname of Hoosiers), Michigan, Ohio State, Minnesota, and Wisconsin (the Badger nickname dating to the 1820s). Minnesota became the Golden Gophers in the early 1930s, however, when Coach Bernie Bierman's national powerhouses wore gold-colored jerseys. Illinois' Fighting Illini comes from the name of a tribe of Native Americans that inhabited the state at one time—the Illini.

Michigan State's nickname came in a roundabout way. A 1925 contest selected The Michigan Staters to officially replace Aggies as the nickname of State's athletic teams. However, in 1926 two writers on Lansing newspapers took one of the losing names from that 1925 contest, Spartans, and hung it on the baseball team during a trip south. The name fit headlines and stories better than the official nickname and soon was in use for all Michigan State teams.

Northwestern became known as Wildcats in 1924 after a write-up of the Chicago game in the *Chicago Tribune* noted that "football players had not come down from Evanston; Wildcats would be a name better suited to [Coach] Thistlethwaite's boys." An outstanding effort against Notre Dame's unbeaten national champions in the following game solidified the nickname.

Many fans are confused by Penn State's nickname, Nittany Lions, but the explanation is quite simple. The campus lies in the Nittany valley (called "Happy Valley" by Penn Staters) at the foot of Mount Nittany. Mountain lions once roamed the area, so the student body in 1906 chose the Nittany Lion as the school mascot.

Purdue's nickname was one of the insulting terms hurled by Wabash supporters during an 18–4 Purdue win in 1889; however, players preferred Boilermakers to other names that had been applied to Purdue teams, such as Cornfield Sailors, Pumpkin Shuckers, Hayseeds, Farmers, and Rail Splitters.

Purdue's first football team in 1887 adopted the orange and black colors of Princeton, a national football power at the time. However, Purdue later changed the orange to old gold. Purple (with white) was selected by a special committee in 1894 as the official school color at Northwestern.

Would you believe Penn State gridders appearing in pink uniforms? The school's original colors, chosen by a student committee in 1887, were cerise (dark pink) and black. However, several blazers made in those colors faded to black and white after a few weeks in the sun, and in 1890 Penn State students opted to change the colors to blue and white.

ALL-TIME BIG 10 CONFERENCE CHAMPIONS

Annual Champion	Big 10	Regular Season and Bowl
1896 Chicago	3–2	14–2–1
1897 Wisconsin	3–0	9–1
1898 Michigan	3–0	10–0
1899 Chicago	4–0	12–0–2
1900 Minnesta	3–0–1	8–0–1
Iowa	2–0–1	7–0–1

(continued)

ALL-TIME BIG 10 CONFERENCE CHAMPIONS (continued)

Annual Champion	Big 10	Regular Season and Bowl	
1901 Michigan	4–0	10–0	Rose (W)
Wisconsin	2–0	9–0	
1902 Michigan	5–0	11–0	
1903 Michigan	3–0–1	11–0–1	
Minnesota	3–0–1	11–0–1	
1904 Minnesota	3–0	11–0	
Michigan	2–0	10–0	
1905 Chicago	7–0	9–0	
1906 Wisconsin	3–0	5–0	
Michigan	2–0	4–1	
Minnesota	2–0	4–1	
1907 Chicago	4–0	4–1	
1908 Chicago	5–0	5–0–1	
1909 Minnesota	3–0	6–1	
1910 Illinois	4–0	7–0	
Minnesota	2–0	6–1	
1911 Minnesota	3–0–1	6–0–1	
1912 Wisconsin	5–0	7–0	
1913 Chicago	7–0	7–0	
1914 Illinois	6–0	7–0	
1915 Minnesota	3–0–1	6–0–1	
Illinois	3–0–2	5–0–2	
1916 Ohio State	4–0	7–0	
1917 Ohio State	4–0	8–0–1	
1918 Illinois	4–0	5–2	
Michigan	2–0	5–0	
Purdue	1–0	3–3	
1919 Illinois	6–1	6–1	
1920 Ohio State	5–0	7–0	Rose (L)
1921 Iowa	5–0	7–0	
1922 Iowa	5–0	7–0	
Michigan	4–0	6–0–1	
1923 Illinois	5–0	8–0	
Michigan	4–0	8–0	
1924 Chicago	3–0–3	4–1–3	
1925 Michigan	5–1	7–1	
1926 Michigan	5–0	7–1	
Northwestern	5–0	7–1	
1927 Illinois	5–0	7–0–1	
1928 Illinois	4–1	7–1	
1929 Purdue	5–0	8–0	
1930 Michigan	5–0	8–0–1	
Northwestern	5–0	7–1	
1931 Michigan	5–1	8–1–1	
Northwestern	5–1	7–1–1	
Purdue	5–1	9–1	
1932 Michigan	6–0	8–0	
1933 Michigan	5–0–1	7–0–1	
1934 Minnesota	5–0	8–0	
1935 Minnesota	5–0	8–0	
Ohio State	5–0	7–1	

(continued)

ALL-TIME BIG 10 CONFERENCE CHAMPIONS *(continued)*

Annual Champion	Big 10	Regular Season and Bowl	
1936 Northwestern	6–0	7–1	
1937 Minnesota	5–0	6–2	
1938 Minnesota	4–1	6–2	
1939 Ohio State	5–1	6–2	
1940 Minnesota	6–0	8–0	
1941 Minnesota	5–0	8–0	
1942 Ohio State	5–1	9–1	
1943 Michigan	6–0	8–1	
Purdue	6–0	9–0	
1944 Ohio State	6–0	9–0	
1945 Indiana	5–0–1	9–0–1	
1946 Illinois	6–1	7–2	Rose (W)
1947 Michigan	6–0	9–0	Rose (W)
1948 Michigan	6–0	9–0	
1949 Michigan	4–1–1	6–2–1	
Ohio State	4–1–1	6–1–2	Rose (W)
1950 Michigan	4–1–1	5–3–1	Rose (W)
1951 Illinois	5–0–1	8–0–1	Rose (W)
1952 Purdue	4–1–1	4–3–2	
Wisconsin	4–1–1	6–2–1	Rose (L)
1953 Illinois	5–1	7–1–1	
Michigan St.	5–1	8–1	Rose (W)
1954 Ohio State	7–0	9–0	Rose (W)
1955 Ohio State	6–0	7–2	
1956 Iowa	5–1	8–1	Rose (W)
1957 Ohio State	7–0	8–1	Rose (W)
1958 Iowa	5–1	7–1–1	Rose (W)
1959 Wisconsin	5–2	7–2	Rose (L)
1960 Iowa	5–1	8–1	
Minnesota	6–1	8–1	Rose (L)
1961 Ohio State	6–0	8–0–1	
1962 Wisconsin	6–1	8–1	Rose (L)
1963 Illinois	5–1–1	7–1–1	Rose (W)
1964 Michigan	6–1	8–1	Rose (W)
1965 Michigan St.	7–0	10–0	Rose (L)
1966 Michigan St.	7–0	9–0–1	
1967 Indiana	6–1	9–1	Rose (L)
Minnesota	6–1	8–2	
Purdue	6–1	8–2	
1968 Ohio State	7–0	9–0	Rose (W)
1969 Michigan	6–1	8–2	Rose (L)
Ohio State	6–1	8–1	
1970 Ohio State	7–0	9–0	Rose (L)
1971 Michigan	7–0	11–0	Rose (L)
1972 Michigan	7–1	10–1	
Ohio State	7–1	9–1	Rose (L)
1973 Michigan	8–0–1	10–0–1	
Ohio State	7–0–1	9–0–1	Rose (W)
1974 Michigan	7–1	10–1	
Ohio State	7–1	10–1	Rose (L)
1975 Ohio State	8–0	11–0	Rose (L)

(continued)

ALL-TIME BIG 10 CONFERENCE CHAMPIONS (continued)

Annual Champion	Big 10	Regular Season and Bowl	
1976 Michigan	7–1	10–1	Rose (L)
Ohio State	7–1	8–2–1	Orange (W)
1977 Michigan	7–1	10–1	Rose (L)
Ohio State	7–1	9–2	Sugar (L)
1978 Michigan	7–1	10–1	Rose (L)
Michigan St.	7–1	8–3	
1979 Ohio State	8–0	11–0	Rose (L)
1980 Michigan	8–0	9–2	Rose (W)
1981 Iowa	6–2	8–3	Rose (L)
Ohio State	6–2	8–3	Liberty (W)
1982 Michigan	8–1	8–3	Rose (L)
Ohio State	7–1	8–3	Holiday (W)
1983 Illinois	9–0	10–1	Rose (L)
1984 Ohio State	7–2	9–2	Rose (L)
1985 Iowa	7–1	10–1	Rose (L)
1986 Michigan	7–1	11–1	Rose (L)
Ohio State	7–1	9–3	Cotton (W)
1987 Michigan St.	7–0–1	8–2–1	Rose (W)
1988 Michigan	7–0–1	8–2–1	Rose (W)
1989 Michigan	8–0	10–1	Rose (L)
1990 Illinois	6–2	8–3	Hall of Fame (L)
Iowa	6–2	8–3	Rose (L)
Michigan	6–2	8–3	Gator (W)
Michigan St.	6–2	7–3–1	John Hancock (W)
1991 Michigan	8–0	10–1	Rose (L)
1992 Michigan	6–0–2	8–0–3	Rose (W)

ILLINOIS *(Fighting Illini; Orange and Blue)*

Notable Teams

1891 (6–0) *Won:* Lake Forest (by forfeit after losing 8–0), Bloomington Swifts 26–0, Eureka 40–0, Illinois Wesleyan 44–4, Knox 12–0 (1st meeting), Bloomington 20–12. *Noteworthy:* won Illinois Intercollegiate Football League title.

1892 (9–3–2) *Won:* Washington (Mo.) 22–0, Doane 20–0, Baker 26–10, Kansas City A.C. 42–0, Wisconsin (forfeit), Englewood H.S. of Chicago 38–0, Beloit (forfeit), DePauw 34–0, Chicago 28–12. *Lost:* unbeaten Purdue 12–6, Nebraska 6–0 (1st meeting), Kansas 26–4. *Tied:* Northwestern 16–16 (1st meeting), Chicago 4–4 (1st meeting).

1897 (6–2) *Won:* Eureka 26–0, 6–0, Chicago Physicians & Surgeons 6–0, Lake Forest 36–0, Purdue 34–4 (1st in 7 games with Boilermakers), Knox 64–0. *Lost:* Chicago 18–12, Carlisle Indians 23–6.

1901 (8–2) *Won:* Englewood H.S. 39–0, Marion Sims 52–0, Physicians & Surgeons 23–0, Washington (Mo.) 21–0, Chicago 24–0, Indiana 18–0, Iowa 27–0, Purdue 28–6. *Lost:* Northwestern 17–11, Minnesota 16–0. *Noteworthy:* 1st year under Edgar Holt.

1902 (10–2–1) *Won:* North Division H.S. 34–6, Englewood H.S. 45–0, Osteopaths 22–0, Monmouth 33–0, Haskell 24–10, Washington (Mo.) 44–0, Purdue 29–5, Indiana 47–0, Northwestern 17–0, Iowa 80–0. *Lost:* Chicago 6–0, Minnesota 17–5. *Tied:* Ohio St. 0–0 (1st meeting). *Noteworthy:* Holt's last year.

1903 (8–4) *Won:* Englewood H.S. 45–5, Lombard 43–0, Osteopaths 36–0, Knox 29–5, Physicians & Surgeons 40–0, Rush 64–0, Chicago Dentistry 64–0, Purdue 24–0. *Lost:* Chicago 18–6, unbeaten Minnesota 32–0, Iowa 12–0, unbeaten Nebraska 16–0 (1st meeting since 1892).

1904 (9–2–1) *Won:* Northwestern College 10–0, Wabash 23–2, Knox 11–0, Physicians & Surgeons 26–0, Washington (Mo.) 31–0, Indiana 10–0, Purdue 24–6, Ohio St. 46–0, Iowa 29–0. *Lost:* Northwestern 12–6, Nebraska 16–10. *Tied:* Chicago 6–6.

1908 (5–1–1) *Won:* Monmouth 17–6, Indiana 10–0, Iowa 22–0, Purdue 15–6, Northwestern 64–8. *Lost:* unbeaten Chicago 11–6. *Tied:* Marquette 6–6. *Star:* G F.C. VanHook.

1909 (5–2) *Won:* Millikin 23–0, Purdue 24–0, Indiana 6–5, Northwestern 35–0, Syracuse 17–8. *Lost:* Kentucky 6–2, Chicago 14–8.

1910 (7–0) *Won:* Millikin 13–0, Drake 29–0, Chicago 3–0 (1st homecoming), Purdue 11–0, Indiana 3–0, Northwestern 27–0, Syracuse 3–0. *Stars:* C J.F. Twist, G G.D. Butzer, QB Otto Seiler. *Noteworthy:* won 1st Big 10 title in 1st unbeaten season since 1891.

1914 (7–0) *Won:* Christian Brothers 37–0, Indiana 51–0, Ohio St. 37–0 (1st meeting since 1904), Northwestern 33–0, Minnesota 21–6 (1st over Gophers in 8 games since 1898), Chicago 21–7, Wisconsin 24–9 (1st meeting since 1907). *Stars:* HB Harold Pogue and Illinois' 1st 2 consensus All-Americans: G Ralph Chapman, E Perry Graves. *Noteworthy:* won 2nd Big 10 title.

1915 (5–0–2) *Won:* Haskell 36–0, Rolla Mines 75–7, Northwestern 36–6, Wisconsin 17–3, Chicago 10–0. *Tied:* Ohio St. 3–3, Minnesota 6–6. *Stars:* HB Bart Macomber, E C.K. Squier, C J.W. Watson. *Noteworthy:* got share of 2nd straight Big 10 title.

1918 (5–2) *Won:* Chanute Field 3–0, Iowa 19–0 (1st meeting since 1908), Wisconsin 22–0, Ohio St. 13–0, Chicago 29–0. *Lost:* Great Lakes 7–0, Municipal Pier 7–0 in consecutive early games. *Star:* C John Depler. *Noteworthy:* got share of 4th Big 10 title.

1919 (6–1) *Won:* Purdue 14–7, Iowa 9–7, Chicago 10–0, Minnesota 10–6, Michigan 29–7 (1st meeting since 1906, 1st win in 6-game series dating to 1898), Ohio St. 9–7. *Lost:* Wisconsin 14–10. *Stars:* G C.O. Applegran, T Burt Ingwersen. *Noteworthy:* won 5th Big 10 title.

1920 (5–2) *Won:* Drake 41–0, Iowa 20–3, Michigan 7–6, Minnesota 17–7, Chicago 3–0. *Lost:* Wisconsin 14–9, unbeaten Ohio St. 7–0 in last 2 games. *Stars:* FB Jack Crangle, E Charles Carney.

1923 (8–0) *Won:* Nebraska 24–7 (1st meeting since 1905), Butler 21–7, Iowa 9–6, Northwestern 29–0, Chicago 7–0, Wisconsin 10–0, Mississippi St. 27–0, Ohio St. 9–0. *Stars:* soph HB Harold "Red" Grange (12 TDs, 723 yds rush, 10 pass rec for 178 yds), G Jim McMillen. *Noteworthy:* won 1st national championship and got share of 6th Big 10 title.

1924 (6–1–1) *Won:* Nebraska 9–6, Butler 40–10, Michigan 39–14, DePauw 45–0, Iowa 36–0, Ohio St. 7–0. *Lost:* Minnesota 20–7. *Tied:* Chicago 21–21. *Star:* Grange (13 TDs, 743 yds rush, 433 yds pass).

1926 (6–2) *Won:* Coe 27–0, Butler 38–7, Iowa 13–6, Pennsylvania 3–0, Chicago 7–0, Wabash

27–13. *Lost:* Michigan 13–0, Ohio St. 7–6. *Star:* G Bernie Shively.

1927 (7–0–1) *Won:* Bradley 19–0, Butler 58–0, Northwestern 7–6, Michigan 14–0, Iowa 14–0, Chicago 15–6, Ohio St. 13–0. *Tied:* Iowa St. 12–12. *Stars:* G Russ Crane, C Robert Reitsch. *Noteworthy:* won 2nd national title and 7th Big 10 crown.

1928 (7–1) *Won:* Bradley 33–6, Coe 31–0, Indiana 13–7 (1st meeting since 1914), Northwestern 6–0, Butler 14–0, Chicago 40–0, Ohio St. 8–0. *Lost:* Michigan 3–0. *Stars:* HB J.A. Timm, T Albert "Butch" Nowack, G Leroy Wietz. *Noteworthy:* again won Big 10.

1929 (6–1–1) *Won:* Kansas 25–0, Bradley 45–0, Michigan 14–0, Army 17–7, Chicago 20–6, Ohio St. 27–0. *Lost:* Northwestern 7–0 (1st to Wildcats in 8 games since 1912). *Tied:* Iowa 7–7. *Star:* T Lou Gordon.

1934 (7–1) *Won:* Bradley 40–7, Washington (Mo.) 12–7, Ohio St. 14–13 (1st over Buckeyes since 1929), Michigan 7–6 (1st over Wolverines since 1929), Army 7–0, Northwestern 14–3, Chicago 6–0. *Lost:* Wisconsin 7–3.

1946 (8–2) *Won:* Pittsburgh 33–7, Purdue 43–7 (1st over Boilermakers in 5 games since 1919), Wisconsin 27–21, Michigan 13–9 (1st over Wolverines since 1939), Iowa 7–0, Ohio St. 16–7 (1st cver Buckeyes since 1934), Northwestern 20–0. *Lost:* unbeaten national champ Notre Dame 26–6, Indiana 14–7. *Stars:* G Alex Agase, HB Buddy Young, B Perry Moss. *Noteworthy:* One of nation's most-improved teams won 9th Big 10 title. Made 1st postseason appearance, beating undefeated UCLA 45–14 in Rose Bowl; Young scored 2 TDs and Illini returned 2 int for scores—68 yds by FB Russ Steger and 20 yds by Stan Green.

1950 (7–2) *Won:* Ohio U. 28–2, UCLA 14–6, Washington 20–13 (1st meeting), Indiana 20–0, Michigan 7–0, Iowa 21–7, Ohio St. 14–7. *Lost:* Wisconsin 7–6, Northwestern 14–7. *Stars:* FB Dick Raklovits (709 yds and 6 TDs rush), E Tony Klimek (13 pass rec for 200 yds), C Bill Vohaska, G Charles Brown, T Al Tate, soph DB Al Brosky (11 int).

1951 (9–0–1) *Won:* UCLA 27–13, Wisconsin 14–10, Syracuse 41–20, Washington 27–20, Indiana 21–0, Michigan 7–0, Iowa 40–13 (10th straight over Hawkeyes), Northwestern 3–0 (1st over Wildcats since 1946). *Tied:* Ohio St. 0–0. *Stars:* B John Karras (592 yds rush, 72 pts), E Rex Smith (21 pass

rec for 331 yds), Brosky (10 int), C Charles Boerio, G Chuck Studley, T Charles Ulrich. *Noteworthy:* Won 10th Big 10 title in 1st unbeaten season since 1927. Beat Stanford 40–7 (1st meeting) in Rose Bowl, scoring 27 pts in last quarter; Bill Tate scored 2 TDs and soph Stan Wallace set up 2 scores with int.

1953 (7–1–1) *Won:* Stanford 33–21, Ohio St. 41–20, Minnesota 27–7, Syracuse 20–13, Purdue 21–0, Michigan 19–3, Northwestern 39–14. *Lost:* Wisconsin 34–7. *Tied:* Nebraska 21–21 (1st meeting since 1925). *Stars:* soph HB J.C. Caroline (5 TDs, nation's leader with 1,256 yds rush and 1,470 all-purpose yds), HB Mickey Bates (11 TDs), E Rocky Ryan (16 pass rec for 308 yds), G Jan Smid. *Noteworthy:* got share of 11th Big 10 title.

1963 (8–1–1) *Won:* California 10–0, Northwestern 10–9, Minnesota 16–6, UCLA 18–12, Purdue 41–21, Wisconsin 17–7, Michigan St. 13–0. *Lost:* Michigan 14–8. *Tied:* Ohio St. 20–20. *Stars:* C/LB Dick Butkus, T Archie Sutton, soph FB Jim Grabowski (6 TDs). *Noteworthy:* Nation's most-improved team won 12th Big 10 title. Beat Washington 17–7 in Rose Bowl, overcoming 7–3 halftime deficit on TDs by James Plankenhorn (who also kicked 32-yd FG and 2 ex pts) and Grabowski (10-yd run).

1983 (10–2) *Won:* Stanford 17–7, Michigan St. 20–10, Iowa 33–0, Wisconsin 27–15, Ohio St. 17–13 (1st over Buckeyes since 1967), Purdue 35–21, Michigan 16–6 (1st over Wolverines since 1966), Minnesota 50–23, Indiana 49–21, Northwestern 56–24. *Lost:* Missouri 28–18 in opener. *Stars:* soph QB Jack Trudeau (2,446 yds pass), soph WR David Williams (59 pass rec for 870 yds and 6 TDs), Tim Brewster (59 pass rec for 628 yds), soph FB Thomas Rooks (842 yds rush), RB Dwight Beverly, OG Chris Babyar, soph OT Jim Juriga, soph K Chris White (13 FGs, 78 pts), P Chris Sigourney (40.6-yd avg), DTs Mark Butkus and Don Thorp, soph DB Craig Swoope. *Noteworthy:* Won 13th Big 10 title, 1st in 20 years. Lost to UCLA 45–9 (1st meeting since 1964) in Rose Bowl; scored on 41-yd FG by White and 5-yd pass from Trudeau to Rooks.

1989 (10–2) *Won:* USC 14–13 (1st over Trojans in 10 games since 1935), Utah St. 41–2, Ohio St. 34–14, Purdue 14–2, Michigan St. 14–10, Wisconsin 32–9, Iowa 31–7, Indiana 41–28, Northwestern 63–14. *Lost:* unbeaten Colorado 38–7, Michigan 24–10. *Stars:* QB Jeff George (2,417 yds and 19 TDs pass),

WRs Mike Bellamy (8 TDs, 51 pass rec for 761 yds and 7 TDs), Steve Williams (30 pass rec for 413 yds) and Shawn Wax (25 pass rec for 457 yds), FB Howard Griffith (39 pass rec for 297 yds, 654 yds rush, 10 TDs), DT Mel Agee, DL Mo Gardner, LB Darrick Brownlow, DBs Chris Green, Henry Jones (5 int) and soph Marion Primous, P Brian Menkhausen (41.5-yd avg). *Noteworthy:* beat Virginia 31–21 in Florida Citrus Bowl; George passed for 321 yds and 3 TDs, Bellamy had 8 pass rec for 166 yds and a TD, and Griffith ran for 93 yds and a TD.

1990 (8–4) *Won:* national cochamp Colorado 23–22, Southern Illinois 56–21, Ohio St. 31–20, Purdue 34–0, Michigan St. 15–13, Wisconsin 21–3, Indiana 24–10 (10th straight over Hoosiers), Northwestern 28–23. *Lost:* Arizona 28–16, Iowa 54–28, Michigan 22–17. *Stars:* QB Jason Verduzco (2,446 yds

and 16 TDs pass), Wax (54 pass rec for 786 yds and 6 TDs), Steven Mueller (29 pass rec for 420 yds), TE Jeff Finke (28 pass rec for 312 yds), WR Elbert Turner (23 pass rec for 310 yds), soph RB Wagner Lester (29 pass rec for 250 yds), Griffith (1,056 yds and 15 TDs rush), K Doug Higgins (14 FGs, 77 pts), Brownlow, LB Bill Henkel, Gardner, Agee. *Noteworthy:* Got share of 14th Big 10 title. Lost to Clemson 30–0 in Hall of Fame Bowl; Verduzco passed for 121 yds and Wax had 6 pass rec for 77 yds.

BOWL SUMMARY

All-American 0–1; Florida Citrus 1–0; Hall of Fame 0–1; Holiday 0–1; John Hancock 0–1; Liberty 0–1; Peach 0–1; Rose 3–1.

BOWL RECORD (4–7)

Regular Season	Bowl	Score	Opponent	Record
1946 (7–2)	Rose	45–14	UCLA	(10–0)
1951 (8–0–1)	Rose	40–7	Stanford	(9–1)
1963 (7–1–1)	Rose	17–7	Washington	(6–4)
1982 (7–4)	Liberty	15–21	Alabama	(7–4)
1983 (10–1)	Rose	9–45	UCLA	(6–4–1)
1985 (6–4–1)	Peach	29–31	Army	(8–3)
1988 (6–4–1)	All-American	10–14	Florida	(6–5)
1989 (9–2)	Florida Citrus	31–21	Virginia	(10–2)
1990 (8–3)	Hall of Fame	0–30	Clemson	(9–2)
1991 (6–5)	John Hancock	3–6	UCLA	(8–3)
1992 (6–4–1)	Holiday	17–27	Hawaii	(10–2)

CONFERENCE TITLES

Illinois Intercollegiate Football League—1891. **Big 10**—1910*, 1914, 1915*, 1918*, 1919, 1923*, 1927, 1928, 1946, 1951, 1953*, 1963, 1983, 1990*.

TOP 20 AP AND UPI RANKING

1944	15	1951	4–3	1962	U–18	1983	10–10
1946	5	1953	7–7	1963	3–4	1989	10–10
1950	13–11	1959	13–11	1964	U–16		

MAJOR RIVALS

Illinois has played at least 10 games with Chicago 23–17–4, Indiana 34–16–2, Iowa 32–21–2, Michigan 19–57–2, Michigan St. 16–14–2, Minnesota 22–25–3, Missouri 6–10, Nebraska 2–7–1, Northwestern 45–36–5, Notre Dame 0–11–1, Ohio St. 26–51–4, Purdue 38–30–6, Southern California 2–9, Stanford 4–6, Syracuse 9–1, Wisconsin 33–24–6. Record against Big 10 member Penn St. is 1–3.

COACHES

Dean of Illinois coaches is Robert C. Zuppke with record of 131–81–13 for 1913–41, including 7 Big 10 titles, 4 unbeaten teams, and 2 national champions. Other top records for at least 3 years were by George Huff, 21–16–3 for 1895–99; Arthur R. Hall, 27–10–3 for 1907–12 with 1 Big 10 title and 1 unbeaten team; Ray Eliot, 83–73–11 for 1942–59 with 3 Big 10 titles, 2 Rose Bowl champions, and 1 unbeaten team; Pete Elliott, 31–34–1 for 1960–66 with 1 Big 10 title and 1 Rose Bowl champ; Mike White, 47–41–3 for 1980–87 with 1 Big 10 title and 3 bowl teams; and John Mackovic, 30–16–1 for 1988–91 with 1 Big 10 title and 4 bowl teams.

MISCELLANEA

First game was loss to Illinois Wesleyan 16–0 in 1890 . . . 1st win was over Illinois Wesleyan 12–6 in 1890 . . . highest score was over Illinois Wesleyan 87–3 in 1912 . . . highest since W.W. II was over Northwestern 63–14 in 1989 . . . biggest margin since W.W. II was over Wisconsin 51–0 in 1965 . . . worst defeat was by Chicago 63–0 in 1906 . . . worst since W.W. II was by Iowa 59–0 in 1985 . . . highest ever against was by Michigan 70–21 in 1981 . . . longest unbeaten string of 15 in 1914–16 ended by Colgate 15–3 . . . 13-game win streak in 1909–11 ended by Chicago 24–0 . . . longest losing string of 15 in 1960–62 broken with win over Purdue 14–10 . . . consensus All-Americans were Perry Graves, E, and Ralph Chapman, G, 1914; Bart Macomber, B, 1915; John Depler, C, 1918; Charles Carney, E, 1920; James McMillen, G, 1923; Harold "Red" Grange, B, 1923–25; Bernie Shively, G, 1926; Alex Agase, G, 1946; Johnny Karras, B, 1951; J.C. Caroline, B, 1953; Bill Burrell, G, 1959; Dick Butkus, C, 1963–64; Jim Grabowski, B, 1965; David Williams, WR, 1984–85; and Moe Gardner, DL, 1989–

90 . . . Academic All-Americans were Bob Lenzini, T, 1952; Jim Grabowski, B, 1964–65; John Wright, E, 1966; Jim Rucks, DE, 1970; Bob Bucklin, DE, 1971; Dan Gregus, DL, 1980–82; Mike Hopkins, DB, 1991; and John Wright, WR, 1992.

INDIANA (Fightin' Hoosiers; Cream and Crimson)

NOTABLE TEAMS

1896 (6–2) *Won:* Knightstown 50–0, Butler 22–6, Cincinnati 16–0 (1st meeting), Wabash 38–0, Louisville A.C. 38–24, DePauw 12–0. *Lost:* DePauw 22–4, Noblesville 8–6 in 1st 2 games.

1897 (6–1–1) *Won:* Rose Poly 12–0, Bedford 40–0, Manual Training 30–0, DePauw 18–0, 14–0, Miami (Ohio) 22–6 (1st meeting). *Lost:* Purdue 20–6. *Tied:* Rose Poly 6–6 in opener.

1898 (4–1–2) *Won:* Rose Poly 16–0, Indiana Training School 20–0, Notre Dame 11–5 (1st meeting), DePauw 32–0. *Lost:* Purdue 14–0. *Tied:* Cincinnati 0–0, 11–11. *Noteworthy:* 1st year under James Horne.

1899 (6–2) *Won:* Rose Poly 16–0, Illinois 6–0 (1st meeting), Vanderbilt 20–0, Cincinnati 35–0, De Pauw 34–0, Purdue 17–5 (1st in 7-game series begun in 1891). *Lost:* Notre Dame 17–0, Northwestern 11–5 (1st meeting).

1905 (8–1–1) *Won:* Alumni 5–0, Butler 31–0, Kentucky 29–0, Washington (Mo.) 39–0, Cincinnati 47–6, Notre Dame 22–5, Wabash 40–0, Ohio St. 11–0. *Lost:* unbeaten national champ Chicago 16–5. *Tied:* Purdue 11–11. *Star:* E Benton Bloom. *Noteworthy:* 1st year under James Sheldon.

1910 (6–1) *Won:* DePauw 12–0, Chicago 6–0 (1st in 9-game series begun in 1902), Millikin 33–0, Wisconsin 12–3, Butler 33–0, Purdue 15–0. *Lost:* unbeaten, unscored-on Illinois 3–0. *Stars:* T Homer Dutter, G Allen Messick, E A.H. "Cotton" Berndt, HB Tom Gill.

1917 (5–2) *Won:* Franklin 50–0, Wabash 51–0, St. Louis 40–0, DePauw 35–0, Purdue 37–0 (1st over Boilermakers since 1910). *Lost:* Minnesota 33–9 (1st meeting since 1906), unbeaten Ohio St. 26–3 in consecutive mid-season games. *Star:* C Russ Hathaway. *Noteworthy:* 1st winning season since 1910.

1920 (5–2) *Won:* Franklin 47–0, Mississippi St. 24–0, Minnesota 21–7 (1st in 4-game series dating to 1906), Northwestern 10–7, Purdue 10–7. *Lost:* Iowa 14–7 (1st meeting since 1913), unbeaten Notre Dame 13–10. *Stars:* Gs William McCaw and Elliott Risley.

1942 (7–3) *Won:* Butler 53–0, Nebraska 12–0, Pittsburgh 19–7, Minnesota 7–0 (1st over Gophers in 10 games since 1920), Kansas St. 54–0, Purdue 20–0, Fort Knox 51–0. *Lost:* national champ Ohio St. 32–21, Iowa 14–13, Iowa Seahawks 26–6. *Stars:* HB Bill Hillenbrand (Hoosiers' 1st consensus All-American; 1,399 yds and 15 TDs total off, national punt return leader with 20.9-yd avg), frosh E Pete Pihos (21 pass rec for 294 yds), Hugh McKinnis (9 TDs), P Earl Dolaway (40.1-yd avg).

1944 (7–3) *Won:* Fort Knox 72–0, Michigan 20–0, Nebraska 54–0, Northwestern 14–7 (1st over Wildcats in 7 games since 1929), Iowa 32–0, Pittsburgh 47–0, Purdue 14–6. *Lost:* Illinois 26–18 (1st meeting since 1939), unbeaten Ohio St. 21–7, Minnesota 19–14. *Stars:* Bob Hoernschemeyer (6 TDs rush, 7 pass), Abe Addams (21 pass rec for 332 yds), C John Tavener.

1945 (9–0–1) *Won:* Michigan 13–7, Illinois 6–0, Nebraska 54–14, Iowa 52–20, Tulsa 7–2, Cornell 46–6, Minnesota 49–0, Pittsburgh 19–0, Purdue 26–0. *Tied:* Northwestern 7–7 in 2nd game. *Stars:* FB Pihos (8 TDs), Ben Raimondi (10 TDs pass), soph HB George Taliaferro (719 yds rush), Mel Grooms (12 pass rec for 223 yds), Es Bob Ravensburg and Ted Kluszewski. *Noteworthy:* won 1st Big 10 title in 1st unbeaten season.

1967 (9–2) *Won:* Kentucky 12–10 (1st meeting since 1927), Kansas 18–15, Illinois 20–7, Iowa 21–17, Michigan 27–20 (1st meeting since 1960), Arizona 42–7, Wisconsin 14–9, Michigan St. 14–13, Purdue 19–14 (1st over Boilermakers since 1962). *Lost:* Minnesota 33–7. *Stars:* soph QB Harry Gonso (931 yds pass), soph FL Jade Butcher (38 pass rec for 654 yds and 10 TDs), soph RB John Isenbarger (579 yds rush), G Gary Cassells, LBs Ken Kaczmarek and Jim Sniadecki. *Noteworthy:* Nation's most-improved team got share of 2nd Big 10 title. Made 1st postseason appearance, losing to national champ Southern California (USC) 14–3 in Rose Bowl; Gonso passed for 110 yds and David Kornowa kicked 27-yd FG.

1979 (8–4) *Won:* Iowa 30–26, Vanderbilt 44–13, Kentucky 18–10, Wisconsin 3–0, Northwestern 30–0, Minnesota 42–24, Illinois 45–14. *Lost:* Colorado 17–16, unbeaten Ohio St. 47–6, Michigan 27–21, Purdue 37–21. *Stars:* Mike Harkrader (807

yds and 6 TDs rush), QB Tim Clifford (2,078 yds and 13 TDs pass), soph TE Bob Stephenson (49 pass rec for 564 yds), Lonnie Johnson (9 TDs), soph DB Tim Wilbur (8 int). *Noteworthy:* 1st winning season since 1968. Beat undefeated Brigham Young (BYU) 38–37 in Holiday Bowl; Clifford ran for 2 TDs and passed for 171 yds and another, Stephenson had 5 pass rec for 91 yds and a TD, and Wilbur returned punt 62 yds for winning score in 4th quarter.

1987 (8–4) *Won:* Rice 35–13, Missouri 20–17, Northwestern 35–18, Ohio St. 31–10 (1st over Buckeyes in 32 games since 1951), Minnesota 18–17, Michigan 14–10 (1st over Wolverines in 16 games since 1967), Illinois 34–29, Purdue 35–14 (1st over Boilermakers since 1982). *Lost:* Kentucky 34–15, Iowa 29–21, Michigan St. 27–3. *Stars:* LBs Van Waiters and Willie Bates, Brian Dewitz (5 int), soph QB Dave Schnell (1,707 yds and 13 TDs pass), WR Ernie Jones (66 pass rec for 1,265 yds and 13 TDs), TE Tim Jorden (31 pass rec for 351 yds), soph RB Anthony Thompson (947 yds and 11 TDs rush, 20 pass rec for 214 yds), Kenny Allen (17 pass rec for 251 yds), K Pete Stoyanovich (59 pts), G Don Shrader. *Noteworthy:* lost to Tennessee 27–22 in Peach Bowl; Schnell passed for 218 yds and a TD, Jones had 7 pass rec for 150 yds and a TD, Thompson and Jorden scored on 12-yd runs, and Stoyanovich kicked 52-yd FG.

1988 (8–3–1) *Won:* Rice 41–14, Kentucky 36–15, Northwestern 48–17, Ohio St. 41–7, Minnesota 33–13, Iowa 45–34 (1st over Hawkeyes in 7 games since 1979), Purdue 52–7. *Lost:* Michigan 31–6, Illinois 21–20, Michigan St. 38–12. *Tied:* Missouri 28–28. *Stars:* Thompson (1,546 yds and 24 TDs rush, 29 pass rec for 219 yds), Schnell (1,877 yds pass, 5 TDs rush), soph WR Rob Turner (36 pass rec for 814 yds and 8 TDs), Tony Buford (30 pass rec for 564 yds), Jorden (25 pass rec for 298 yds), Stoyanovich (17 FGs, 96 pts), LB Doug Bates, P Tom Bolyard (43.1-yd avg). *Noteworthy:* beat South Carolina 34–10 in Liberty Bowl; Schnell passed for 378 yds and 2 TDs (including 88-yarder to Turner, who caught 5 for 182 yds), and Thompson ran for 140 yds and 2 TDs.

Bowl Summary

All-American 0–1; Copper 1–0; Holiday 1–0; Liberty 1–0; Peach 0–2; Rose 0–1.

BOWL RECORD (3–4)

Regular Season	Bowl	Score	Opponent	Record
1967 (9–1)	Rose	3–14	USC	(9–1)
1979 (7–4)	Holiday	38–37	BYU	(11–0)
1986 (6–5)	All-American	13–27	Florida St.	(6–4–1)
1987 (8–3)	Peach	22–27	Tennessee	(9–2–1)
1988 (7–3–1)	Liberty	34–10	South Carolina	(8–3)
1990 (6–4–1)	Peach	23–27	Auburn	(7–3–1)
1991 (6–4–1)	Copper	24–0	Baylor	(8–3)

CONFERENCE TITLES

Big 10—1945, 1967*.

TOP 20 AP AND UPI RANKING

1945	4	1967	4–6	1987	U–20	1988	20–19
1946	20	1979	19–16				

MAJOR RIVALS

Indiana has played at least 10 games with Butler 5–5, Chicago 5–20–1, Cincinnati 6–3–2, DePauw 23–7–3, Illinois 16–34–2, Iowa 20–32–4, Kentucky 14–8–1, Miami (Ohio) 8–3–1, Michigan 9–40, Michigan St. 11–30–2, Minnesota 20–31–3, Missouri 6–2–2, Nebraska 9–7–3, Northwestern 30–34–1, Notre Dame 5–23–1, Ohio St. 12–53–5, Purdue 31–58–6, Wabash 14–6, Wisconsin 16–25–2. Record against Big 10 member Penn St. is 0–0 (no games played).

COACHES

Dean of Indiana coaches is A.N. "Bo" McMillin (1945 national Coach of Year), with record of 63–48–11 for 1934–47, including 1 unbeaten Big 10 champion. Other top records for at least 3 years were by James H. Horne, 33–21–5 for 1898–1904; James M. Sheldon, 35–26–3 for 1905–13; Ewald O. "Jumbo" Stiehm, 20–18–1 for 1916–21; John Pont (1967 national Coach of Year), 31–51–1 for 1965–72 with 1 Big 10 champion and 1 Rose Bowl team; Lee Corso, 41–68–2 for 1973–82 with 1 Holiday Bowl champion; and Bill Mallory, 49–52–3 for 1984–92 with 5 bowl teams.

MISCELLANEA

First recorded game was loss to Franklin 10–8 in 1888 . . . 1st recorded win was over Louisville A.C. 30–0 in 1891 . . . 1st recorded win over college foe was over Butler 11–10 in 1892 . . . highest score was over Franklin 76–0 in 1901 . . . highest since W.W. II was over Kentucky 58–30 in 1969 and over Missouri 58–7 in 1990 . . . worst defeat was by Purdue 68–0 in 1892 . . . worst since 1900 was by Michigan 63–0 in 1925 . . . worst since W.W. II and highest ever against was by Nebraska 69–17 in 1978 . . . longest unbeaten string of 12 in 1944–45 ended by Cincinnati 15–6 in 1946 opener . . . longest losing string of 16 in 1983–84 broken with win over Louisville 41–28 in 1985 opener . . . consensus All-Americans were Bill Hillenbrand, B, 1942; John Tavener, C, 1944; Bob Ravensburg, E, 1945; Anthony Thompson, RB, 1988–89; and Vaughn Dunbar, RB, 1991 . . . Academic All-Americans were Harry Gonso, HB, 1967; Glenn Scolnik, RB, 1972; and Kevin Speer, C, 1980.

IOWA (Hawkeyes; Old Gold and Black)

NOTABLE TEAMS

1896 (7–1–1)   *Won:* Drake 32–0 (1st meeting), Kansas 6–0, Wilton 27–0, Missouri 12–0, Grinnell 15–6, Des Moines YMCA 34–0, Nebraska 6–0. *Lost:* Chicago 6–0. *Tied:* Nebraska 0–0.

1899 (8–0–1)   *Won:* Iowa Teachers 22–0, Penn College 35–0, Rush 17–0, Iowa St. 5–0, Nebraska 30–0, Grinnell 16–0, Knox 33–0, Illinois 58–0 (1st meeting). *Tied:* unbeaten Chicago 5–5. *Noteworthy:* outscored foes 221–5 in 1st undefeated season.

1900 (7–0–1)   *Won:* Upper Iowa 57–0, Iowa Teachers 68–0, Simpson 47–0, Drake 26–0, Chicago 17–0 (1st in 5-game series dating to 1894), Michigan 28–5 (1st meeting), Grinnell 63–2. *Tied:* Northwestern 5–5 in finale. *Stars:* QB Clyde Williams, T Joe Warner. *Noteworthy:* got share of title in 1st year in Big 10.

1903 (9–2)   *Won:* Cornell (Iowa) 6–0, Coe 16–0, Iowa Teachers 29–0, Drake 22–6, Grinnell 17–0, Simpson 35–2, Missouri 16–0, Illinois 12–0, Washington (Mo.) 12–2. *Lost:* unbeaten Minnesota 75–0, unbeaten Nebraska 17–6. *Noteworthy:* 1st year under John Chalmers.

1905 (8–2)   *Won:* Coe 27–0, Monmouth 40–0, Iowa Teachers 41–5, Grinnell 46–0, Des Moines 72–0, Drake 44–0, Iowa St. 8–0, St. Louis 31–0. *Lost:* unbeaten national champ Chicago 42–0, Minnesota 39–0 in consecutive early games. *Noteworthy:* Chalmers' last team.

1910 (5–2)   *Won:* Morningside 12–0, Purdue 16–0 (1st meeting), Iowa St. 2–0, Drake 21–0, Washington (Mo.) 38–0. *Lost:* Northwestern 10–5 (1st meeting since 1900), Missouri 5–0. *Noteworthy:* 1st year under Jess Hawley.

1913 (5–2)   *Won:* Iowa Teachers 45–3, Cornell (Iowa) 76–0, Northwestern 78–6, Indiana 60–0, Iowa St. 45–7. *Lost:* unbeaten Chicago 23–6, unbeaten Nebraska 12–0. *Star:* FB Ralph McGinnis.

1918 (6–2–1)   *Won:* Nebraska 12–0 (1st over Cornhuskers in 10 games since 1899), Coe 27–0, Cornell (Iowa) 34–0, Minnesota 6–0 (1st in 13-game series dating to 1891), Iowa St. 21–0, Northwestern 23–7. *Lost:* Great Lakes 10–0, Illinois 19–0 (1st meeting since 1908). *Tied:* Camp Dodge 0–0. *Stars:* G Harry Hunzelman, E Ronald Reed.

1919 (5–2)   *Won:* Nebraska 18–0, Minnesota 9–6, South Dakota 26–13, Northwestern 14–7, Iowa St. 10–0. *Lost:* Illinois 9–7, Chicago 9–6 (1st meeting

since 1914). *Stars:* soph E Les Belding (Hawkeyes' 1st consensus All-American), soph T Fred Slater, FB Fred Lohman, soph QB Aubrey Devine.

1920 (5–2)   *Won:* Indiana 14–7 (1st meeting since 1913), Cornell (Iowa) 63–0, Northwestern 20–0, Minnesota 28–7, Iowa St. 14–10. *Lost:* Illinois 20–3, Chicago 10–0 in consecutive mid-season games. *Stars:* Belding, Slater, Devine.

1921 (7–0)   *Won:* Knox 52–14, Notre Dame 10–7 (1st meeting), Illinois 14–2 (1st over Illini in 5 games since 1907), Purdue 13–6 (1st meeting since 1916), Minnesota 41–7, Indiana 41–0, Northwestern 14–0. *Stars:* Belding, Slater, Devine, FB Gordon Locke, E Max Kadesky, C John Heldt, G Chester Meade. *Noteworthy:* won 2nd Big 10 title in 1st unbeaten season since 1900.

1922 (7–0)   *Won:* Knox 61–0, Yale 6–0, Illinois 8–7, Purdue 56–0, Minnesota 28–14, Ohio St. 12–9 (1st meeting), Northwestern 37–3. *Stars:* Locke, Kadesky, G Paul Minick, T George Thompson. *Noteworthy:* got share of 3rd Big 10 title.

1924 (6–1–1)   *Won:* SE Oklahoma 43–0, Lawrence 13–5, Minnesota 13–0, Butler 7–0, Wisconsin 21–7 (1st meeting since 1917, 1st win in 7-game series dating to 1894), Michigan 9–2. *Lost:* Illinois 36–0. *Tied:* Ohio St. 0–0. *Stars:* E Lowell Otte, T John Hancock, G William Fleckenstein, QB Leland Parkin. *Noteworthy:* 1st year under Burton Ingwersen.

1928 (6–2)   *Won:* Monmouth 26–0, Chicago 13–0 (1st meeting since 1920, 1st over Maroons in 8 games since 1900), Ripon 61–6, Minnesota 7–6, South Dakota 19–0, Ohio St. 14–7. *Lost:* Wisconsin 13–0, Michigan 10–7 in last 2 games. *Stars:* T Peter Westra, C Richard Brown, G Fred Roberts, HB Willis Glassgow.

1939 (6–1–1)   *Won:* South Dakota 41–0, Indiana 32–29 (1st over Hoosiers in 8 games since 1921), Wisconsin 19–13, Purdue 4–0 (1st over Boilermakers since 1933), Notre Dame 7–6 (1st meeting since 1921), Minnesota 13–9 (1st over Gophers in 9 games since 1929). *Lost:* Michigan 27–7. *Tied:* Northwestern 7–7. *Stars:* Heisman Trophy– and Maxwell Award–winning TB Nile Kinnick (1,012 yds and 16 TDs total off, 8 int, 39.9-yd punting avg, nation's kickoff return leader with 25.1-yd avg), E Irwin Prasse, T Mike Enich. *Noteworthy:* 1st year under Dr. Eddie Anderson.

1956 (9–1)   *Won:* Indiana 27–0, Oregon St. 14–13 (1st meeting), Wisconsin 13–7, Hawaii 34–0, Purdue 21–20, Minnesota 7–0, Ohio St. 6–0, Notre Dame 48–8 (1st over Irish in 12 games since 1940). *Lost:* Michigan 17–14. *Stars:* QB Kenneth Ploen (873 yds and 11 TDs total off), Es Frank Gilliam and Jim Gibbons (17 pass rec for 255 yds), T Alex Karras, C Donald Suchy. *Noteworthy:* Nation's most-improved team won 4th Big 10 title, 1st since 1922. Made 1st bowl appearance, beating Oregon St. 35–19 in Rose Bowl rematch; Ploen ran 49 yds for 1st Iowa score and passed to Gibbons (5 pass rec for 61 yds) for final TD; Collins Hagler had TD runs of 9 and 66 yds.

1957 (7–1–1) *Won:* Utah St. 70–14, Washington St. 20–13, Indiana 47–7, Wisconsin 21–7, Northwestern 6–0 (1st meeting since 1952), Minnesota 44–20, Notre Dame 21–13. *Lost:* national cochamp Ohio St. 17–13. *Tied:* Michigan 21–21. *Stars:* Outland Trophy–winner Karras, Gibbons (36 pass rec for 587 yds), QB Randy Duncan (1,124 yds and 10 TDs pass, 5 TDs rush), G Frank Bloomquist.

1958 (8–1–1) *Won:* Texas Christian (TCU) 17–0, Indiana 34–13, Wisconsin 20–9, Northwestern 26–20, Michigan 37–14 (1st over Wolverines in 15 games since 1924), Minnesota 28–6, Notre Dame 31–21. *Lost:* Ohio St. 38–28. *Tied:* unbeaten Air Force 13–13. *Stars:* Duncan (1,406 yds and 15 TDs total off, national leader with 1,347 yds and 11 TDs pass), Don Norton (25 pass rec for 374 yds), E Curt Merz, HB Willie Fleming (11 TDs), B Ray Jauch (524 yds rush). *Noteworthy:* Led nation in total off and took 5th Big 10 title. Beat California 38–12 in Rose Bowl to earn share of 1st national title; Bob Jeter ran for 194 yds (including 81-yd TD run), Fleming ran for 85 yds and 2 TDs, and Duncan ran for 1 TD and passed for another.

1960 (8–1) *Won:* Oregon St. 22–12, Northwestern 42–0, Michigan St. 27–15, Wisconsin 28–21, Purdue 21–14, Kansas 21–7, Ohio St. 35–12, Notre Dame 28–0. *Lost:* national cochamp Minnesota 27–10 (1st to Gophers since 1954). *Stars:* QB Wilburn Hollis (11 TDs rush), HB Larry Ferguson (665 yds and 6 TDs rush), G Mark Manders. *Noteworthy:* Forest Evashevski's last team got share of 6th Big 10 crown.

1981 (8–4) *Won:* Nebraska 10–7, UCLA 20–7, Northwestern 64–0, Indiana 42–28, Michigan 9–7 (1st over Wolverines in 11 games since 1962), Purdue 33–7 (1st over Boilermakers since 1960), Wisconsin 17–7, Michigan St. 36–7. *Lost:* Iowa St. 23–13, Minnesota 12–10, Illinois 24–7. *Stars:* DE Andre Tippett, DT Mark Bortz, LB Mel Cole, MG Pat Dean, DB Lou King (8 int), P Reggie Roby (nation's leader with 49.8-yd punting avg), OT Ron Hallstrom, Phil Blatcher (708 yds and 8 TDs rush), Jeff Brown (20 pass rec for 301 yds), frosh K Tom Nichol (11 FGs). *Noteworthy:* Got share of 7th Big 10 title (1st since 1960) in 1st winning season since 1961. Lost to Washington 28–0 in Rose Bowl, turning ball over 5 times on int and fumbles.

1982 (8–4) *Won:* Arizona 17–14, Northwestern 45–7, Indiana 24–20, Minnesota 21–16 (1st over Gophers since 1977), Illinois 14–13, Wisconsin 28–14, Michigan St. 24–18. *Lost:* Nebraska 42–7, Iowa St. 19–7, Michigan 29–7, Purdue 16–7. *Stars:* frosh QB Chuck Long (1,374 yds pass), WR Dave Moritz (41 pass rec for 605 yds), Eddie Phillips (806 yds and 5 TDs rush), soph Owen Gill (683 yds and 7 TDs rush), Bortz, DB Bobby Stoops, Roby (nation's punting leader with 48.1-yd avg). *Noteworthy:* beat Tennessee 28–22 in Peach Bowl; Long passed for 304 yds and 3 TDs (2 to frosh Ronnie Harmon), Moritz caught 8 for 168 yds and a TD, and Phillips scored on short run.

1983 (9–3) *Won:* Iowa St. 51–10, Penn St. 42–34, Ohio St. 20–14 (1st over Buckeyes in 17 games since 1962), Northwestern 61–21 (10th straight over Wildcats), Purdue 31–14, Indiana 49–3, Wisconsin 34–14, Michigan St. 12–6, Minnesota 61–10. *Lost:* Illinois 33–0, Michigan 16–13. *Stars:* Long (2,434 yds and 14 TDs pass, 5 TDs rush), Moritz (50 pass rec for 912 yds and 5 TDs), Harmon (35 pass rec for 729 yds and 5 TDs), Gill (798 yds and 10 TDs rush), Phillips (778 yds and 8 TDs rush), OT John Alt, Nichol (14 FGs), DT Paul Hufford, soph LB Larry Station, DBs Mike Stoops (6 int) and soph Devon Mitchell (5 int). *Noteworthy:* lost to Florida 14–6 in frigid Gator Bowl, turning ball over 4 times on int; Long passed for 167 yds, Harmon caught 6 for 90 yds, and Nichol had 2 FGs.

1985 (10–2) *Won:* Drake 58–0, Northern Illinois 48–20, Iowa St. 57–3, Michigan St. 35–31, Wisconsin 23–13, Michigan 12–10, Northwestern 49–10, Illinois 59–0, Purdue 27–24, Minnesota 31–9. *Lost:* Ohio St. 22–13. *Stars:* Maxwell Award–winner Long (2,978 yds and 26 TDs pass), Harmon (60 pass rec for 699 yds and a TD; 1,166 yds and 9 TDs rush), Bill Happel (56 pass rec for 901 yds and 8 TDs), Scott Helverson (54 pass rec for 703 yds and 5 TDs), frosh FB David Hudson (7 TDs rush), soph K Rob Houghtlin (19 FGs, 105 pts), OT Mike Haight, Station, DT Jeff Drost, MG Hap

Peterson, DB Jay Norvell (7 int), Mitchell (5 int). *Noteworthy:* Won 8th Big 10 title. Lost to UCLA 45–28 in Rose Bowl; Long passed for 319 yds and a TD and ran for another, Harmon had 11 pass rec for 102 yds, Happel had 6 pass rec for 89 yds and a TD, and Houghtlin had 52-yd FG.

1986 (9–3) *Won:* Iowa St. 43–7, Northern Illinois 57–3, Texas–El Paso 69–7, Michigan St. 24–21, Wisconsin 17–6, Northwestern 27–20, Purdue 42–14, Minnesota 30–27. *Lost:* Michigan 20–17, Ohio St. 31–10, Illinois 20–16. *Stars:* QB Mark Vlasic (1,456 yds pass), Jim Mauro (30 pass rec for 600 yds and 5 TDs), RB Rick Bayless (1,150 yds and 10 TDs rush, 30 pass rec for 209 yds and 1 TD), Hudson (511 yds and 7 TDs rush), OT Dave Croston, soph OL Bob Kratch, Houghtlin (14 FGs), Drost, soph MG Dave Haight, DB Keaton Smiley (5 int). *Noteworthy:* beat San Diego St. 39–38 in Holiday Bowl on 41-yd FG by Houghtlin on last play of game; Vlasic passed for 222 yds and 2 TDs and ran for another, and Bayless ran for 110 yds and a TD.

1987 (10–3) *Won:* Arizona 15–14, Iowa St. 48–9, Kansas St. 38–13, Wisconsin 31–10, Purdue 38–14, Indiana 29–21, Northwestern 52–24, Ohio St. 29–27, Minnesota 34–20. *Lost:* Tennessee 23–22, Michigan St. 19–14, Michigan 37–10. *Stars:* QB Chuck Hartlieb (2,855 yds and 19 TDs pass), WR Quinn Early (63 pass rec for 1,004 yds and 10 TDs), TE Marv Cook (43 pass rec for 760 yds), Travis Watkins (33 pass rec for 534 yds), Kevin Harmon (715 yds rush, 31 pass rec for 253 yds, 7 TDs), Mike Flagg (28 pass rec for 468 yds), Hudson (8 TDs), Houghtlin (21 FGs, 104 pts), Haight, DBs Kerry Burt (7 int) and Dwight Sistrunk (5 int). *Noteworthy:* edged Wyoming 20–19 in Holiday Bowl; Hartlieb passed for 237 yds, Hudson scored on short run, and Hawkeyes also scored on 10-yd blocked punt return by Jay Hess and 33-yd pass int return by Anthony Wright.

1990 (8–4) *Won:* Cincinnati 63–10, Iowa St. 45–35, Michigan St. 12–7, Wisconsin 30–10, Michigan 24–23, Northwestern 56–14, Illinois 54–28, Purdue 38–9. *Lost:* Miami (Fla.) 48–21, Ohio St. 27–26, Minnesota 31–24. *Stars:* TB Nick Bell (1,009 yds rush, 21 pass rec for 308 yds, 14 TDs), RB Tony Stewart (844 yds rush), QB Matt Rodgers (2,228 yds and 15 TDs pass, 9 TDs rush), WRs Danan Hughes (29 pass rec for 410 yds and 5 TDs) and Jon Filloon (20 pass rec for 322 yds), TE Michael Titley (29 pass rec for 280 yds), Sean Smith (24 pass rec for 361 yds), soph FB Lew Montgomery (6 TDs rush), K Jeff Skillett (12 FGs, 82 pts), DL Matt Ruhland, LB Melvin Foster, DB Merton Hanks. *Noteworthy:* Got share of 9th Big 10 title. Lost to Washington 46–34 in Rose Bowl; Rodgers passed for 196 yds, a TD, and 2-pt conversion and ran for 2 TDs, Saunders had 5 pass rec for 99 yds and a TD, and Bell ran for 2 TDs.

1991 (10–1–1) *Won:* Hawaii 53–10, Iowa St. 29–10, Northern Illinois 58–7, Wisconsin 10–6, Illinois 24–21, Purdue 31–21, Ohio St. 16–9, Indiana 38–21, Northwestern 24–10, Minnesota 23–8. *Lost:* Michigan 43–24. *Stars:* Rodgers (2,054 yds and 14 TDs pass), Hughes (38 pass rec for 709 yds and 8 TDs), TE Alan Cross (30 pass rec for 484 yds), Filloon (29 pass rec for 343 yds), Saunders (919 yds rush, 27 pass rec for 204 yds, 11 TDs), Montgomery (34 pass rec for 267 yds, 8 TDs rush), Skillett (11 FGs), C Mike Devlin, OT Rob Baxley, DE Leroy Smith, LB John Derby. *Noteworthy:* tied Brigham Young (BYU) 13–13 in Holiday Bowl; Rodgers passed for 221 yds, Filloon had 7 pass rec for 107 yds, and Saunders ran for 103 yds and both Hawkeye TDs.

BOWL SUMMARY

Freedom 1–0; Gator 0–1; Holiday 2–0–1; Peach 1–1; Rose 2–3.

BOWL RECORD (6–5–1)

Regular Season	Bowl	Score	Opponent	Record
1956 (8–1)	Rose	35–19	Oregon St.	(7–2–1)
1958 (7–1–1)	Rose	38–12	California	(7–3)
1981 (8–3)	Rose	0–28	Washington	(9–2)
1982 (7–4)	Peach	28–22	Tennessee	(6–4–1)

(continued)

Regular Season	Bowl	Score	Opponent	Record
1983 (9–2)	Gator	6–14	Florida	(8–2–1)
1984 (7–4–1)	Freedom	55–17	Texas	(7–3–1)
1985 (10–1)	Rose	28–45	UCLA	(8–2–1)
1986 (8–3)	Holiday	39–38	San Diego St.	(8–3)
1987 (9–3)	Holiday	20–19	Wyoming	(10–2)
1988 (6–3–3)	Peach	23–28	N.C. State	(7–3–1)
1990 (8–3)	Rose	34–46	Washington	(9–2)
1991 (10–1)	Holiday	13–13	BYU	(8–3–1)

CONFERENCE TITLES

Missouri Valley—1907*. **Big 10**—1900*, 1921, 1922*, 1956, 1958, 1960*, 1981*, 1985, 1990*.

TOP 20 AP AND UPI
(USA TODAY/CNN SINCE 1991) RANKING

1939	9	1958	2–2	1984	16–15	1990	18–16
1953	9–10	1960	3–2	1985	10–9	1991	10–10
1956	3–3	1981	18–15	1986	16–15		
1957	6–5	1983	14–14	1987	16–16		

MAJOR RIVALS

Iowa has played at least 10 games with Chicago 3–9–2, Cornell (Iowa) 13–1, Drake 12–3, Grinnell 11–5–1, Illinois 21–32–2, Indiana 32–20–4, Iowa St. 28–12, Iowa Teachers 10–1, Kansas 3–7, Michigan 8–32–4, Michigan St. 13–13–2, Minnesota 29–55–2, Missouri 5–7, Nebraska 12–24–3, Northern Iowa 10–1, Northwestern 39–14–3, Notre Dame 8–13–3, Ohio St. 13–35–3, Oregon St. 7–5, Purdue 26–41–2, Wisconsin 34–34–2.

COACHES

Dean of Iowa coaches is Hayden Fry with record of 105–58–5 for 1979–92 with 3 Big 10 titles and 10 bowl teams. Other top records for at least 3 years were by Alden Knipe, 29–11–4 for 1898–1902 with 1 Big 10 title and 2 unbeaten teams; John Chalmers, 24–8 for 1903–05; Jess Hawley, 24–18 for 1910–15; Howard Jones, 42–17–1 for 1916–23 with 2 Big 10 titles and 2 unbeaten teams; Burton Ingwersen, 33–27–4 for 1924–31; Dr. Eddie Ander-son (1939 national Coach of Year), 35–33–2 for 1939–42 and 1946–49; and Forest Evashevski, 52–27–4 for 1952–60 with 3 Big 10 titles, 2 Rose Bowl champions, and a national title.

MISCELLANEA

First game was loss to Grinnell 24–0 in 1889 . . . 1st win was over Iowa Wesleyan 91–0 in 1890 . . . highest score was over Iowa Teachers 95–0 in 1914 . . . highest since W.W. II was over Utah St. 70–14 in 1957 . . . biggest margin since W.W. II was over Northwestern 64–0 in 1981 . . . worst defeat was by Michigan 107–0 in 1902 . . . worst since W.W. II was by Ohio St. 83–21 in 1950 . . . longest unbeaten string of 23 in 1898–1901 ended by Minnesota 16–0 . . . 20-game win streak in 1920–23 ended by Illinois 9–6 . . . longest losing string of 12 in 1973–74 broken with win over UCLA 21–10 . . . consensus All-Americans were Lester Belding, E, 1919; Aubrey Devine, B, 1921; Gordon Locke, B, 1922; Nile Kinnick, B, 1939; Calvin Jones, G,

1954–55; Alex Karras, T, 1957; Randy Duncan, B, 1958; Andre Tippett, DL, and Reggie Roby, P, 1981; Larry Station, LB, 1984–85; Chuck Long, QB, 1985; Marv Cook, TE, 1988; and Leroy Smith, DE, 1991 . . . Academic All-Americans were Bill Fenton, E, 1952–53; Bob Elliott, DB, 1975; and Larry Station, LB, 1985 . . . Heisman Trophy winner was Nile Kinnick, HB, 1939 . . . Maxwell Award winner was Chuck Long, QB, 1985 . . . Outland Trophy winners were Calvin Jones, G, 1955; and Alex Karras, T, 1957.

MICHIGAN *(Wolverines; Maize and Blue)*

Notable Teams

1888 (4–1) *Won:* Notre Dame 26–6, 10–4, Detroit A.C. 14–6, Albion 76–4. *Lost:* Chicago U. Club 26–4 (1st defeat since 1883).

1890 (4–1) *Won:* Albion 56–10, 16–0, Detroit A.C. 18–0, Purdue 34–6 (1st meeting). *Lost:* Cornell 20–5.

1893 (7–3) *Won:* Detroit A.C. 6–0, 26–0, Purdue 46–8, DePauw 34–0, Northwestern 72–6, Kansas 22–10, Chicago 28–10. *Lost:* Chicago 10–6, unbeaten Minnesota 34–20, Wisconsin 34–18.

1894 (9–1–1) *Won:* Albion 26–10, Olivet 48–0, Michigan Military Academy 40–6, Adrian 46–0, Case 18–8, Kansas 22–12, Oberlin 14–6, Cornell 12–4 (1st in 8-game series dating to 1889), Chicago 6–4. *Lost:* Cornell 22–0. *Tied:* Michigan Military Academy 12–12.

1895 (8–1) *Won:* Michigan Military Academy 34–0, Detroit A.C. 42–0, Adelbert 64–0, Rush Medical College 40–0, Oberlin 42–0, Purdue 12–10, Minnesota 20–0, Chicago 12–0. *Lost:* Harvard 4–0.

1896 (9–1) *Won:* Michigan Normal 18–0, Grand Rapids 44–0, Chicago Physicians & Surgeons 28–0, Rush Medical 66–0, Purdue 16–0, Lehigh 40–0, Minnesota 6–4, Oberlin 10–0, Wittenberg 28–0. *Lost:* Chicago 7–6 in finale.

1897 (6–1–1) *Won:* Michigan Normal 24–0, Ohio St. 36–0 (1st meeting), Oberlin 16–6, Purdue 34–4, Minnesota 14–0, Wittenberg 32–0. *Lost:* Chicago 21–12 in finale. *Tied:* Ohio Wesleyan 0–0. *Noteworthy:* 1st year under Gustave Ferbert.

1898 (10–0) *Won:* Michigan Normal 21–0, Kenyon 29–0, Michigan St. 39–0 (1st meeting), Western Reserve 18–0, Case 23–5, Notre Dame 23–0 (1st meeting since 1888), Northwestern 6–5, Illinois 12–5 (1st meeting), Beloit 22–0, Chicago 12–11. *Star:* C William Cunningham (Wolverines' 1st consensus All-American). *Noteworthy:* won 1st Big 10 title in 1st unbeaten season since 3-game schedule of 1887.

1899 (8–2) *Won:* Hillsdale 11–0, Albion 26–0, Western Reserve 17–0, Notre Dame 12–0, Illinois 5–0, Virginia 38–0, Case 28–6, Kalamazoo 24–9. *Lost:* Pennsylvania 11–10 (1st meeting), Wisconsin 17–5 (1st meeting since 1893). *Noteworthy:* Ferbert's last team.

1900 (7–2–1) *Won:* Hillsdale 29–0, Kalamazoo 11–0, Case 24–6, Purdue 11–6, Illinois 12–0, Indiana 12–0 (1st meeting), Notre Dame 7–0. *Lost:* unbeaten Iowa 28–5 (1st meeting), Chicago 15–6. *Tied:* Ohio St. 0–0. *Noteworthy:* only season under Langdon "Biff" Lee.

1901 (11–0) *Won:* Albion 50–0, Case 57–0, Indiana 33–0, Northwestern 29–0, Buffalo 128–0, Carlisle Indians 22–0, Ohio St. 21–0, Chicago 22–0, Beloit 89–0, Iowa 50–0. *Stars:* frosh HB Willie Heston (20 TDs), E Neil Snow. *Noteworthy:* Won 1st national championship and got share of 2nd Big 10 title while blanking foes 501–0 in 1st year under Fielding H. "Hurry Up" Yost. Beat Stanford 49–0 in 1st postseason Tournament of Roses game as Heston ran for 170 yds and Snow (at FB) ran for 107 yds and scored 5 TDs; final 8 minutes of game cancelled when Stanford pleaded exhaustion.

1902 (11–0) *Won:* Albion 88–0, Case 48–6, Michigan St. 119–0, Indiana 60–0, Notre Dame 23–0, Ohio St. 86–0, Wisconsin 6–0, Iowa 107–0, Chicago 21–0, Oberlin 63–0, Minnesota 23–6 (1st meeting since 1897). *Star:* Heston (15 TDs). *Noteworthy:* "point-a-minute" team outscored foes 644–12, repeated as national champ, and took 3rd Big 10 title.

1903 (11–0–1) *Won:* Case 31–0, Beloit 79–0, Ohio Northern 65–0, Indiana 51–0, Ferris Institute 88–0, Drake 47–0, Albion 76–0, Ohio St. 36–0, Wisconsin 16–0, Oberlin 42–0, Chicago 28–0. *Tied:* unbeaten Minnesota 6–6. *Star:* Heston (16 TDs). *Noteworthy:* scored 565 and earned share of 4th Big 10 crown.

1904 (10–0) *Won:* Case 33–0, Ohio Northern 48–0, Kalamazoo 95–0, Physicians & Surgeons 72–0, Ohio St. 31–6, American College of M&S 72–0, West Virginia 130–0, Wisconsin 28–0, Drake 36–4, Chicago 22–12. *Star:* Heston (21 TDs). *Note-*

worthy: outscored foes 567–22 and won 5th Big 10 title (4th straight).

1905 (12–1)   *Won:* Ohio Wesleyan 65–0, Kalamazoo 44–0, Case 36–0, Ohio Northern 23–0, Vanderbilt 18–0 (1st meeting), Nebraska 31–0, Albion 70–0, Drake 48–0, Illinois 33–0, Ohio St. 40–0, Wisconsin 12–0, Oberlin 75–0.   *Lost:* unbeaten national champ Chicago 2–0 (1st to Maroons since 1900) in finale, ending 56-game unbeaten string.

1906 (4–1)   *Won:* Case 28–0 (10th win in as many games in series), Ohio St. 6–0, Illinois 28–9, Vanderbilt 10–4.   *Lost:* Pennsylvania 17–0 (1st meeting since 1899) in finale.   *Noteworthy:* got share of 6th Big 10 title.

1907 (5–1)   *Won:* Case 9–0, Michigan St. 46–0 (1st meeting since 1902), Wabash 22–0, Ohio St. 22–0, Vanderbilt 8–0.   *Lost:* Penn 6–0 in finale.   *Star:* C/LB Adolph "Germany" Schulz.   *Noteworthy:* withdrew from Big 10.

1909 (6–1)   *Won:* Case 3–0, Ohio St. 33–6, Marquette 6–5, Syracuse 44–0, Penn 12–6 (1st in 5-game series dating to 1899), Minnesota 15–6 (1st meeting since 1903).   *Lost:* unbeaten Notre Dame 11–3 (1st in 9-game series dating to 1887).   *Star:* G Albert Benbrook.

1910 (3–0–3)   *Won:* Michigan St. 6–3, Syracuse 11–0, Minnesota 6–0.   *Tied:* Case 3–3, Ohio St. 3–3, Penn 0–0.   *Stars:* Benbrook, E Stanfield Wells.

1911 (5–1–2)   *Won:* Case 24–0, Michigan St. 15–3, Ohio St. 19–0, Vanderbilt 9–8, Penn 11–9.   *Lost:* Cornell 6–0 (1st meeting since 1894).   *Tied:* Syracuse 6–6, Nebraska 6–6.

1912 (5–2)   *Won:* Case 34–0, Michigan St. 55–7, Ohio St. 14–0, South Dakota 7–6, Cornell 20–7.   *Lost:* Syracuse 18–7, Penn 27–21.

1913 (6–1)   *Won:* Case 48–0, Mt. Union 14–0, Vanderbilt 33–2, Syracuse 43–7, Cornell 17–0, Penn 13–0.   *Lost:* unbeaten Michigan St. 12–7 (1st in 8-game series dating to 1898).   *Stars:* HB James Craig, T Miller Pontius.

1916 (7–2)   *Won:* Marietta 30–0, Case 19–3, Carroll 54–0, Mt. Union 26–0, Michigan St. 9–0, Syracuse 14–13, Washington (Mo.) 66–7.   *Lost:* Cornell 23–20, Penn 10–7 in last 2 games.

1917 (8–2)   *Won:* Case 41–0, Western Reserve 17–13, Mt. Union 69–0, Detroit 14–3, Michigan St. 27–0, Nebraska 20–0, Kalamazoo 62–0, Cornell 46–0.   *Lost:* Penn 16–0, Northwestern 21–12 (1st meeting since 1901) in last 2 games.   *Stars:* FB

Cedric Smith, Gs Ernest Allmendinger and Frank Culver.   *Noteworthy:* reentered Big 10.

1918 (5–0)   *Won:* Case 33–0, Chicago 13–0 (1st meeting since 1905), Syracuse 15–0, Michigan St. 21–6, Ohio St. 14–0 (1st meeting since 1912).   *Star:* FB Frank Steketee.   *Noteworthy:* got share of 7th Big 10 title in 1st unbeaten season since 1910.

1920 (5–2)   *Won:* Case 35–0 (10th straight win in series), Michigan St. 35–0, Tulane 21–0, Chicago 14–0, Minnesota 3–0.   *Lost:* Illinois 7–6, unbeaten Ohio St. 14–7.

1921 (5–1–1)   *Won:* Mt. Union 44–0, Case 65–0, Michigan St. 30–0, Illinois 3–0, Minnesota 38–0.   *Lost:* Ohio St. 14–0.   *Tied:* Wisconsin 7–7 (1st meeting since 1905).   *Star:* C Henry Vick.

1922 (6–0–1)   *Won:* Case 48–0, Ohio St. 19–0, Illinois 24–0, Michigan St. 63–0, Wisconsin 13–6, Minnesota 16–7.   *Tied:* unbeaten Vanderbilt 0–0 (1st meeting since 1914).   *Stars:* HB Harry Kipke, E Paul Goebel.   *Noteworthy:* got share of 8th Big 10 title.

1923 (8–0)   *Won:* Case 36–0, Vanderbilt 3–0, Ohio St. 23–0, Michigan St. 37–0, Iowa 9–3 (1st meeting since 1902), Quantico Marines 26–6, Wisconsin 6–3, Minnesota 10–0.   *Star:* C Jack Blott.   *Noteworthy:* Yost's 8th unbeaten team got share of 9th Big 10 crown.

1924 (6–2)   *Won:* Miami (Ohio) 55–0, Michigan St. 7–0, Wisconsin 21–0, Minnesota 13–0, Northwestern 27–0 (1st meeting since 1919), Ohio St. 16–6.   *Lost:* Illinois 39–14, Iowa 9–2.   *Star:* G Edliff Slaughter.   *Noteworthy:* only year under George Little.

1925 (7–1)   *Won:* Michigan St. 39–0 (10th straight over Spartans), Indiana 63–0 (1st meeting since 1903), Wisconsin 21–0, Illinois 3–0, Navy 54–0 (1st meeting), Ohio St. 10–0, Minnesota 35–0.   *Lost:* Northwestern 3–2.   *Stars:* QB Benny Friedman (760 yds and 13 TDs pass), soph E Bennie Oosterbaan, G Harry Hawkins, T Tom Edwards, C Robert Brown.   *Noteworthy:* won 10th Big 10 title as Yost returned as coach.

1926 (7–1)   *Won:* Oklahoma A&M 42–3, Michigan St. 55–3, Minnesota 20–0, 7–6, Illinois 13–0, Wisconsin 37–0, Ohio St. 17–16.   *Lost:* unbeaten Navy 10–0.   *Stars:* Friedman (562 yds and 9 TDs pass), Oosterbaan.   *Noteworthy:* Yost's last team got share of 11th Big 10 crown.

1927 (6–2)   *Won:* Ohio Wesleyan 33–0, Michigan St. 21–0, Wisconsin 14–0, Ohio St. 21–0, Chicago

14–0 (1st meeting since 1920), Navy 27–12. *Lost:* unbeaten national champ Illinois 14–0, unbeaten Minnesota 13–7 (1st to Gophers since 1919). *Star:* Oosterbaan. *Noteworthy:* 1st year under Tad Wieman.

1930 (8–0–1) *Won:* Denison 33–0, Michigan Normal 7–0, Purdue 14–13, Ohio St. 13–0, Illinois 15–7, Harvard 6–3, Minnesota 7–0, Chicago 16–0. *Tied:* Michigan St. 0–0. *Star:* soph QB/S Harry Newman (646 yds total off, 4 int). *Noteworthy:* got share of 12th Big 10 title.

1931 (8–1–1) *Won:* Central St. Teachers 27–0, Michigan Normal 34–0, Chicago 13–7, Illinois 35–0, Princeton 21–0, Indiana 22–0, Minnesota 6–0. *Lost:* Ohio St. 20–7. *Tied:* Michigan St. 0–0. *Star:* C Maynard Morrison. *Noteworthy:* Again got share of Big 10 title. Beat Wisconsin 16–0 in postseason charity game in Ann Arbor.

1932 (8–0) *Won:* Michigan St. 26–0, Northwestern 15–6 (1st meeting since 1925), Ohio St. 14–0, Illinois 32–0, Princeton 14–7, Indiana 7–0, Chicago 12–0, Minnesota 3–0. *Stars:* Newman (650 yds and 8 TDs total off), E Ted Petoskey, C Charles Bernard. *Noteworthy:* won 14th Big 10 title (3rd straight) and share of 3rd national crown.

1933 (7–0–1) *Won:* Michigan St. 20–6, Cornell 40–0 (1st meeting since 1917), Ohio St. 13–0, Chicago 28–0, Illinois 7–6, Iowa 10–6, Northwestern 13–0. *Tied:* unbeaten Minnesota 0–0. *Stars:* Bernard, Petoskey, T Francis Wistert. *Noteworthy:* Harry Kipke's 3rd unbeaten team won 15th Big 10 title and 2nd straight national crown.

1938 (6–1–1) *Won:* Michigan St. 14–0 (1st over Spartans since 1933), Chicago 45–7, Yale 15–13, Illinois 14–0, Penn 19–13, Ohio St. 18–0 (1st over Buckeyes since 1933). *Lost:* Minnesota 7–6. *Tied:* Northwestern 0–0. *Stars:* G Ralph Heikkinen, E Paul Kromer (6 TDs), soph TB Tom Harmon (708 yds total off). *Noteworthy:* had 1st winning season since 1933 in 1st year under Fritz Crisler.

1939 (6–2) *Won:* Michigan St. 26–13, Iowa 27–7, Chicago 85–0, Yale 27–7, Penn 19–17, Ohio St. 21–14. *Lost:* Illinois 16–7, Minnesota 20–7 in consecutive late games. *Stars:* Harmon (1,356 yds total off, 868 yds rush, nation's leader in scoring with 14 TDs and 102 pts, and with 1,108 all-purpose yds), E Forest Evashevski, Kromer (41.4-yd punting avg).

1940 (7–1) *Won:* California 41–0, Michigan St. 21–14, Harvard 26–0, Illinois 28–0, Penn 14–0, North-

western 20–13, Ohio St. 40–0. *Lost:* unbeaten national cochamp Minnesota 7–6. *Stars:* Heisman Trophy– and Maxwell Award–winner Harmon (1,346 yds total off, 844 yds rush, nation's leader in scoring with 16 TDs and 117 pts and with 1,312 all-purpose yds), E Edward Frutig.

1941 (6–1–1) *Won:* Michigan St. 19–7, Iowa 6–0, Pittsburgh 40–0, Northwestern 14–7, Illinois 20–0, Columbia 28–0. *Lost:* unbeaten national champ Minnesota 7–0. *Tied:* Ohio St. 20–20. *Stars:* FB Bob Westfall (688 yds rush), soph HB Bill Daley (685 yds rush, 9 TDs), Tom Kuzma (8 TDs).

1942 (7–3) *Won:* Great Lakes 9–0, Michigan St. 20–0, Northwestern 34–16, Illinois 28–14, Harvard 35–7, Notre Dame 32–20 (1st meeting since 1909), Iowa 28–14. *Lost:* Iowa Pre-Flight 26–14, Minnesota 16–14, national cochamp Ohio St. 21–7. *Stars:* Daley (8 TDs), Paul White (8 TDs), George Ceithaml (18 pass rec for 232 yds), T Albert Wistert, G Julius Franks.

1943 (8–1) *Won:* Camp Grant 26–0, Western Michigan 57–6, Northwestern 21–7, Minnesota 49–6 (1st over Gophers since 1932), Illinois 42–6, Indiana 23–6 (1st meeting since 1936), Wisconsin 27–0 (1st meeting since 1935), Ohio St. 45–7. *Lost:* national champ Notre Dame 35–12. *Stars:* Daley (817 yds rush, 9 TDs), B Elroy "Crazy Legs" Hirsch (11 TDs), T Mervin Pregulman. *Noteworthy:* got share of 16th Big 10 title.

1944 (8–2) *Won:* Iowa Pre-Flight 12–7, Marquette 14–0, Minnesota 28–13, Northwestern 27–0, Purdue 40–14 (1st meeting since 1930), Penn 41–19, Illinois 14–0, Wisconsin 14–0. *Lost:* Indiana 20–0, unbeaten Ohio St. 18–14. *Stars:* Bob Nussbaumer (502 yds rush), Bob Wiese (7 TDs and 41-yd punting avg), frosh E Dick Rifenberg (8 pass rec for 232 yds), Don Lund (6 int).

1945 (7–3) *Won:* Great Lakes 27–2, Michigan St. 40–0, Northwestern 20–7, Illinois 19–0, Minnesota 26–0, Purdue 27–13, Ohio St. 7–3. *Lost:* unbeaten Indiana 13–7, unbeaten national champ Army 28–7, Navy 33–7 (1st meeting since 1928).

1946 (6–2–1) *Won:* Indiana 21–0, Iowa 14–7, Minnesota 21–0, Michigan St. 55–7, Wisconsin 28–6, Ohio St. 58–6. *Lost:* unbeaten Army 20–13, Illinois 13–9 (1st to Illini since 1939). *Tied:* Northwestern 14–14. *Stars:* TB Bob Chappuis (531 yds rush, 734 yds pass), Bobby Mann (14 pass rec for 327 yds), Wiese (40-yd punting avg), E Elmer Madar, Gene Derricotte (6 int).

1947 (10–0) *Won:* Michigan St. 55–0, Stanford 49–13, Pittsburgh 69–0, Northwestern 49–21, Minnesota 13–6, Illinois 14–7, Indiana 35–0, Wisconsin 40–6, Ohio St. 21–0. *Stars:* Chappuis (976 yds and 11 TDs pass, 419 yds and 5 TDs rush), HB Chalmers "Bump" Elliott (18 pass rec, 10 TDs), Mann (357 yds on pass rec), Jack Weisenburger (773 yds and 10 TDs rush). *Noteworthy:* Crisler's last team led nation in total off, pass, and scoring (38.3-pt avg) in 1st unbeaten season since 1933; won 17th Big 10 title. Beat Southern California (USC) 49–0 in Rose Bowl; Chappuis ran for 91 yds and passed for 188 yds and 2 TDs, and Weisenburger ran for 91 yds and 3 TDs.

1948 (9–0) *Won:* Michigan St. 13–7, Oregon 14–0, Purdue 40–0, Northwestern 28–0, Minnesota 27–14, Illinois 28–20, Navy 35–0, Indiana 54–0, Ohio St. 13–3. *Stars:* soph B Chuck Ortmann (1,073 yds total off), QB Pete Elliott, Tom Peterson (9 TDs), Es Dick Rifenburg (22 pass rec for 490 yds and 8 TDs) and Leo Koceski (22 pass rec), T Alvin Wistert. *Noteworthy:* Repeated as Big 10 while leading nation in scoring defense (4.9-pt avg) in 1st year under Bennie Oosterbaan. Ineligible for Rose Bowl under Big 10 rules forbidding same team competing two consecutive years.

1949 (6–2–1) *Won:* Michigan St. 7–3, Stanford 27–7, Minnesota 14–7, Illinois 13–0, Purdue 20–12, Indiana 20–7. *Lost:* unbeaten Army 21–7, Northwestern 21–20 (1st to Wildcats in 11 games since 1937) in consecutive early games. *Tied:* Ohio St. 7–7. *Stars:* Wistert, T Allen Wahl, Ortmann (956 yds total off), FB Don Dufek (5 TDs), E Harry Allis (23 pass rec for 338 yds), Chuck Lentz (9 int). *Noteworthy:* got share of 3rd straight Big 10 title.

1950 (6–3–1) *Won:* Dartmouth 27–7, Wisconsin 26–13, Indiana 20–7, Northwestern 34–23, Ohio St. 9–3 (in snowstorm game in which Wolverines failed to get 1st down but scored as result of Buckeye errors). *Lost:* Michigan St. 14–7 (1st to Spartans in 11 games since 1937), Army 27–6, Illinois 7–0. *Tied:* Minnesota 7–7. *Stars:* Wahl, Dufek (702 yds and 9 TDs rush), soph Lowell Perry (24 pass rec for 374 yds). *Noteworthy:* Won 20th Big 10 crown (4th straight). Upset unbeaten California 14–6 in Rose Bowl; Dufek ran for 113 yds and both TDs, and Ortmann passed for 146 yds.

1955 (7–2) *Won:* Missouri 42–7, Michigan St. 14–7, Army 26–2, Northwestern 14–2, Minnesota 14–13, Iowa 33–21 (10th straight over Hawkeyes), Indiana 30–0. *Lost:* Illinois 25–6, Ohio St. 17–0. *Stars:* E Ron Kramer (12 pass rec for 224 yds), Tom Maentz (253 yds pass rec, 40.1-yd punting avg).

1956 (7–2) *Won:* UCLA 42–13, Army 48–14, Northwestern 34–20, Iowa 17–14, Illinois 17–7, Indiana 49–26, Ohio St. 19–0. *Lost:* Michigan St. 9–0, Minnesota 20–7. *Stars:* Kramer (19 pass rec for 361 yds), Terry Barr (7 TDs), John Herrnstein (7 TDs).

1964 (9–1) *Won:* Air Force 24–7, Navy 21–0, Michigan St. 17–10 (1st over Spartans since 1955), Minnesota 19–12 (1st over Gophers since 1959), Northwestern 35–0, Illinois 21–6, Iowa 34–20, Ohio St. 10–0 (1st over Buckeyes since 1959). *Lost:* Purdue 21–20. *Stars:* QB Bob Timberlake (807 yds pass, 574 yds and 8 TDs rush, 80 pts), John Henderson (31 pass rec for 427 yds and 9 TDs, 89 pts including 4 FGs and 23 ex pts), Mel Anthony (702 yds rush), T William Yearby. *Noteworthy:* Won 21st Big 10 title (1st since 1950). Beat Oregon St. 34–7 in Rose Bowl; Anthony ran for 123 yds and 3 TDs, Timberlake scored on 24-yd run, and soph Carl Ward scored on 43-yd run.

1968 (8–2) *Won:* Duke 31–10, Navy 32–9, Michigan St. 28–14, Indiana 27–22, Minnesota 33–20, Northwestern 35–0, Illinois 36–0, Wisconsin 34–9. *Lost:* California 21–7 (opener), unbeaten national champ Ohio St. 50–14 (finale). *Stars:* QB Dennis Brown (1,562 yds pass and 1,777 total off), TE Jim Mandich (43 pass rec for 576 yds), HB Ron Johnson (1,391 yds and 19 TDs rush, 116 pts), DB Tom Curtis (10 int). *Noteworthy:* "Bump" Elliott's last team.

1969 (8–3) *Won:* Vanderbilt 42–14 (1st meeting since 1923), Washington 45–7, Purdue 31–20 (1st over Boilermakers in 6 games since 1961), Minnesota 35–9, Wisconsin 35–7, Illinois 57–0, Iowa 51–6, Ohio St. 24–12. *Lost:* Missouri 40–17, Michigan St. 23–12. *Stars:* Mandich (50 pass rec for 676 yds), QB Don Moorhead (1,261 yds pass, 1,886 total off), soph RB Bill Taylor (864 yds rush), Garvie Craw (13 TDs), Curtis (8 int), DB Barry Pierson (7 int). *Noteworthy:* Got share of 22nd Big 10 title in 1st year under "Bo" Schembechler. Lost to unbeaten USC 10–3 in Rose Bowl (1st bowl loss in 5 appearances); Moorhead passed for 127 yds and Mandich had 8 pass rec for 79 yds.

1970 (9–1) *Won:* Arizona 20–9, Washington 17–3, Texas A&M 14–10, Purdue 29–0, Michigan St. 34–20, Minnesota 39–13, Wisconsin 29–15, Illinois 42–0, Iowa 55–0. *Lost:* unbeaten national co-champ Ohio St. 20–9 in finale. *Stars:* Moorhead (1,167 yds pass, 1,535 total off), Taylor (911 yds and 11 TDs rush), Paul Staroba (35 pass rec for 519 yds, 41.5-yd punting avg), OT Dan Dierdorf, MG Henry Hill, LB Marty Huff.

1971 (11–1) *Won:* Northwestern 21–6, Virginia 56–0, UCLA 38–0, Navy 46–0, Michigan St. 24–13, Illinois 35–6, Minnesota 35–7, Indiana 61–7, Iowa 63–7, Purdue 20–17, Ohio St. 10–7. *Stars:* Bill Taylor (1,297 yds rush), Glenn Doughty (16 pass rec for 203 yds), OG Reggie McKenzie, LB Mike Taylor, DB Tom Darden, soph P Barry Dotzauer (40.3-yd avg). *Noteworthy:* Led nation in rush defense and scoring defense (6.4-pt avg) in 1st unbeaten season since 1948 and won 23rd Big 10 title. Upset by Stanford 13–12 in Rose Bowl as Cardinals' Don Bunce passed for 290 yds; scored on FG by Dana Coin, 1-yd run by FB Fritz Seyferth, and safety.

1972 (10–1) *Won:* Northwestern 7–0, UCLA 26–9, Tulane 41–7, Navy 35–7, Michigan St. 10–0, Illinois 31–7, Minnesota 42–0, Indiana 21–7, Iowa 31–0, Purdue 9–6. *Lost:* Ohio St. 14–11 in finale. *Stars:* soph QB Dennis Franklin (1,329 yds total off), TE Paul Seal (18 pass rec for 243 yds), Ed Shuttlesworth (723 yds and 11 TDs rush), OT Paul Seymour, DB Randy Logan. *Noteworthy:* again led nation in scoring defense (5.2-pt avg) and got share of 24th Big 10 title.

1973 (10–0–1) *Won:* Iowa 31–7, Stanford 47–10, Navy 14–0, Oregon 24–0, Michigan St. 31–0, Wisconsin 35–6, Minnesota 34–7, Indiana 49–13, Illinois 21–6, Purdue 34–9. *Tied:* unbeaten Ohio St. 10–10 in finale. *Stars:* Franklin, Seal (14 pass rec for 254 yds), Shuttlesworth (745 yds rush), DT Dave Gallagher, DB Dave Brown. *Noteworthy:* got share of 3rd straight Big 10 title.

1974 (10–1) *Won:* Iowa 24–7, Colorado 31–0, Navy 52–0, Stanford 27–16, Michigan St. 21–7, Wisconsin 24–20, Minnesota 49–0, Indiana 21–7, Illinois 14–6, Purdue 51–0. *Lost:* Ohio St. 12–10 in finale. *Stars:* Brown, Franklin (1,223 yds total off), Gordon Bell (1,048 yds and 11 TDs rush), soph

RB Rob Lytle (802 yds rush), Gil Chapman (23 pass rec), soph Jim Smith (392 yds pass rec). *Noteworthy:* led nation in scoring defense (6.8-pt avg) and got share of 4th straight Big 10 crown.

1975 (8–2–2) *Won:* Wisconsin 23–6, Missouri 31–7, Michigan St. 16–6, Northwestern 69–0, Indiana 55–7, Minnesota 28–21, Purdue 28–0, Illinois 21–15. *Lost:* unbeaten Ohio St. 21–14 in finale. *Tied:* Stanford 19–19, Baylor 14–14 in consecutive early games. *Stars:* Bell (1,388 yds and 14 TDs rush), Smith (24 pass rec for 680 yds), Lytle (1,008 yds rush, 10 TDs), DB Don Dufek. *Noteworthy:* lost to national champ Oklahoma 14–6 in Orange Bowl as Bell (who scored Michigan's TD) was held to 53 yds rush.

1976 (10–2) *Won:* Wisconsin 40–27 (10th straight over Badgers), Stanford 51–0, Navy 70–14, Wake Forest 31–0, Michigan St. 42–10, Northwestern 38–7, Indiana 35–0, Minnesota 45–0, Illinois 38–7 (10th straight over Illini), Ohio St. 22–0 (1st over Buckeyes since 1971). *Lost:* Purdue 16–14 (1st to Boilermakers in 8 games since 1966). *Stars:* Smith (26 pass rec for 714 yds and 6 TDs), soph QB Rick Leach (1,611 yds total off), Lytle (1,402 yds rush, 13 TDs), OG Mark Donahue, LB Calvin O'Neal, DB Jerry Zuver (6 int), P John Anderson (41.5-yd avg). *Noteworthy:* Got share of 27th Big 10 title and led nation in total off, rush, scoring (38.7-pt avg), and scoring defense (7.4-pt avg). Lost to USC 14–6 in Rose Bowl as Lytle (who scored Michigan's TD) was held to 67 yds rush.

1977 (10–2) *Won:* Illinois 37–9, Duke 21–9, Navy 14–7, Texas A&M 41–3, Michigan St. 24–14, Wisconsin 56–0, Iowa 23–6, Northwestern 63–20, Purdue 40–7, Ohio St. 14–6. *Lost:* Minnesota 16–0 (1st to Gophers since 1967). *Stars:* Leach (1,723 yds total off), Donahue, C Walt Downing, Ralph Clayton (24 pass rec for 477 yds), Russell Davis (1,092 yds and 9 TDs rush), LB/P Anderson (40.5-yd punting avg). *Noteworthy:* Got share of 28th Big 10 title. Lost to Washington 27–20 in Rose Bowl; Leach passed for 239 yds and 2 TDs, and Davis ran for 79 yds and a TD.

1978 (10–2) *Won:* Illinois 31–0, Notre Dame 28–14 (1st meeting since 1943), Duke 52–0, Arizona 21–17, Wisconsin 42–0, Minnesota 42–10, Iowa 34–0, Northwestern 59–14, Purdue 24–6, Ohio St. 14–3. *Lost:* Michigan St. 24–15 (1st to Spartans since 1969). *Stars:* Leach (12 TDs rush, 1,894 yds total off), Clayton (25 pass rec for 546 yds and 8 TDs), Doug Marsh (6 TD pass rec), Harlan Huckleby (741 yds rush). *Noteworthy:* Got share of 3rd straight Big 10 title. Lost to national cochamp USC 17–10 in Rose Bowl, gaining only 99 yds rush; Leach passed for 137 yds and a TD (44 yds to TB Roosevelt Smith).

1979 (8–4) *Won:* Northwestern 49–7 (10th straight over Wildcats), Kansas 28–7, California 14–10, Michigan St. 21–7, Minnesota 31–21, Illinois 27–7, Indiana 27–21, Wisconsin 54–0. *Lost:* Notre Dame 12–10, Purdue 24–21, unbeaten Ohio St. 18–15. *Stars:* QB John Wangler (1,431 yds pass), Marsh (33 pass rec for 612 yds), frosh WR Anthony Carter (13 pass rec for 321 yds and 5 TDs, 988 all-purpose yds, 6 TDs), soph TB Butch Woolfolk (990 yds and 13 TDs rush), soph FB Stan Edwards (633 yds rush), DT Curtis Greer, LB Ron Simpkins. *Noteworthy:* lost to North Carolina 17–15 in Gator Bowl; Wangler passed for 203 yds and a TD before being injured, backup QB B.J. Dickey passed for 125 yds and a score, and Carter had 4 pass rec for 141 yds and 2 TDs.

1980 (10–2) *Won:* Northwestern 17–10, California 38–13, Michigan St. 27–23, Minnesota 37–14, Illinois 45–14, Indiana 35–0, Wisconsin 24–0, Purdue 26–0, Ohio St. 9–3. *Lost:* Notre Dame 29–27, South Carolina 17–14 in consecutive early games. *Stars:* Woolfolk (1,042 yds rush), Edwards (901 yds rush), soph TB Lawrence Ricks (850 yds rush), Wangler (1,522 yds and 16 TDs pass), Carter (46 pass rec for 750 yds and 13 TDs, 1,355 all-purpose yds), C George Lilja, soph K Ali Haji–Sheikh (11 FGs, 70 pts), LB Andy Cannavino, DBs Marion Body (5 int) and Brian Carpenter (5 int), frosh P Don Bracken (42.7-yd avg). *Noteworthy:* Won 30th Big 10 title. Beat Washington 23–6 in Rose Bowl (breaking 7-game bowl losing string); Woolfolk ran for 182 yds and a TD, Wangler passed for 145 yds and a score, and Carter caught 5 for 68 yds and a TD.

1981 (9–3) *Won:* Notre Dame 25–7, Navy 21–16, Indiana 38–17 (10th straight over Hoosiers), Michigan St. 38–20, Northwestern 38–0, Minnesota 34–13, Illinois 70–21 (15th straight over Illini), Purdue 28–10. *Lost:* Wisconsin 21–14 (1st to Badgers in 15 games since 1962), Iowa 9–7 (1st to Hawkeyes in 11 games since 1962), Ohio St. 14–9. *Stars:* Woolfolk (1,459 yds rush), Carter (44 pass rec for 825 yds and 7 TDs, 1,438 all-purpose yds, 8 TDs), soph QB Steve Smith (1,661 yds pass, 2,335 total off, 12 TDs rush), Bracken (43.3-yd punting avg), Ts Ed Muransky and William "Bubba" Paris, OG Kurt Becker, DB Tony Jackson (6 int). *Noteworthy:* beat UCLA 33–14 in Bluebonnet Bowl; Woolfolk ran for 186 yds and a TD, Smith passed for 152 yds and a score, and Carter had 6 pass rec for 127 yds and a TD.

1982 (8–4) *Won:* Wisconsin 20–9, Indiana 24–10, Michigan St. 31–17, Iowa 29–7, Northwestern 49–14, Minnesota 52–14, Illinois 16–10, Purdue 52–21. *Lost:* Notre Dame 23–17, UCLA 31–27, Ohio St. 24–14. *Stars:* Smith (2,080 yds total off, 1,735 pass), Carter (38 pass rec for 785 yds and 8 TDs, 1,416 all-purpose yds, 9 TDs), Ricks (1,388 yds rush), Craig Dunaway (35 pass rec), Haji-Sheikh (12 FGs, 77 pts). *Noteworthy:* Won 31st Big 10 crown. Lost rematch to UCLA 24–14 in Rose Bowl; Dave Hall, replacing injured QB Steve Smith in 2nd quarter, passed for 155 yds and both Michigan TDs.

1983 (9–3) *Won:* Washington St. 20–17, Wisconsin 38–21, Indiana 43–18, Michigan St. 42–0, Northwestern 35–0, Iowa 16–13, Purdue 42–10, Minnesota 58–10, Ohio St. 24–21. *Lost:* Washington 25–24, Illinois 16–6 (1st to Illini since 1966). *Stars:* Smith (1,295 yds and 13 TDs pass, 2,087 yds total off), Sim Nelson (41 pass rec for 494 yds), Rick Rogers (1,002 yds rush), C Tom Dixon, OG Stefan Humphries, K Bob Bergeron (15 FGs, 76 pts). *Noteworthy:* lost to Auburn 9–7 in Sugar Bowl; Smith passed for 125 yds and ran for the Wolverine TD.

1985 (10–1–1) *Won:* Notre Dame 20–12, South Carolina 34–3, Maryland 20–0, Wisconsin 33–6, Michigan St. 31–0, Indiana 42–15, Purdue 47–0, Minnesota 48–7, Ohio St. 27–17. *Lost:* Iowa 12–10. *Tied:* Illinois 3–3. *Stars:* QB Jim Harbaugh (nation's leader with 1,913 yds and 18 TDs pass), Eric Kattus (38 pass rec for 582 yds and 8 TDs), Paul Jokisch (37 pass rec for 681 yds), frosh FL John Kolesar (12 pass rec for 336 yds), soph RB Jamie Morris (1,030 yds rush), K Mike Gillette (16 FGs, 78 pts), soph P Monte Robbins (40.4-yd avg), DT Mike Hammerstein, DBs Brad Cochran and Ivan Hicks (6 int). *Noteworthy:* Led nation in scoring defense (6.8-pt avg). Beat Nebraska 27–23 in Fiesta Bowl; Morris ran for 156 yds, Harbaugh scored 2

TDs, and Pat Moons kicked 2 FGs and 3 ex pts.
1986 (11–2) *Won:* Notre Dame 24–23, Oregon St. 31–12, Florida St. 20–18, Wisconsin 34–17, Michigan St. 27–6, Iowa 20–17, Indiana 38–14 (15th straight over Hoosiers), Illinois 69–13, Purdue 31–7, Ohio St. 26–24, Hawaii 27–10. *Lost:* Minnesota 20–17 (1st to Gophers since 1977). *Stars:* Harbaugh (2,729 yds pass), Gerald White (38 pass rec), Ken Higgins (621 yds pass rec), frosh SE Greg McMurtry (22 pass rec for 508 yds), Kolesar (15 pass rec for 402 yds), soph TE Jeff Brown (18 pass rec for 215 yds), Morris (1,086 yds rush, 1,560 all-purpose yds), Robbins (43.6-yd punting avg), OT John Elliott, Gillette (11 FGs), DB Garland Rivers. *Noteworthy:* Got share of 32nd Big 10 title. Lost to Arizona St. 22–15 in Rose Bowl; Harbaugh passed for 172 yds and scored a TD, and Morris ran 18 yds for 1st Michigan score.
1987 (8–4) *Won:* Washington St. 44–18, Long Beach St. 49–0, Wisconsin 49–0, Iowa 37–10, Northwestern 29–6, Minnesota 30–20, Illinois 17–14. *Lost:* Notre Dame 26–7, Michigan St. 17–11, Indiana 14–10 (1st to Hoosiers in 16 games since 1967), Ohio St. 23–20. *Stars:* Morris (1,703 yds rush, 15 TDs), QB Demetrius Brown (1,251 yds and 11 TDs pass, 5 TDs rush), McMurtry (21 pass rec for 474 yds), Kolesar (16 pass rec for 331 yds), Gillette (12 FGs, 73 pts), Elliott, Robbins (43.5-yd punting avg), DT Mark Messner. *Noteworthy:* beat Alabama 28–24 in Hall of Fame Bowl; Morris ran for 234 yds and 3 TDs (one on 77-yd run), and Brown passed 20 yds to Kolesar for winning TD.
1988 (9–2–1) *Won:* Wake Forest 19–9, Wisconsin 62–14, Michigan St. 17–3, Indiana 31–6, Northwestern 52–7, Minnesota 22–7, Illinois 38–9, Ohio St. 34–31. *Lost:* unbeaten national champ Notre Dame 19–17, Miami (Fla.) 31–30 in 1st 2 games. *Tied:* Iowa 17–17. *Stars:* RB Tony Boles (1,408 yds and 9 TDs rush), soph FB Leroy Hoard (752 yds and 11 TDs rush), QBs Brown (775 yds pass) and Michael Taylor (957 yds pass), McMurtry (27 pass rec for 470 yds), Kolesar (18 pass rec for 356 yds), WR Chris Calloway (18 pass rec for 272 yds), TE Derrick Walker (15 pass rec for 260 yds), C John Vitale, OL Mike Husar, Gillette (18 FGs, 97 pts, 39.9-yd punting avg), Messner, DBs David Arnold and soph Tripp Welborne (5 int). *Noteworthy:* Took 33rd Big 10 crown. Beat USC 22–14 in Rose Bowl; Hoard ran for 142 yds and 2 TDs, and Brown passed for 144 yds and a TD.
1989 (10–2) *Won:* UCLA 24–23, Maryland 41–21, Wisconsin 24–0, Michigan St. 10–7, Iowa 26–12, Indiana 38–10, Purdue 42–27, Illinois 24–10, Minnesota 49–15, Ohio St. 28–18. *Lost:* Notre Dame 24–19 in opener. *Stars:* Boles (839 yds and 9 TDs rush, 16 pass rec for 224 yds, 1,345 all-purpose yds), Hoard (832 yds and 6 TDs rush), Taylor (1,081 yds and 11 TDs pass), soph QB Elvis Grbac (824 yds and 8 TDs pass), McMurtry (41 pass rec for 711 yds and 7 TDs), Calloway (31 pass rec for 425 yds), Walker, OG Dean Dingman, OT Tom Dohring, soph K J.D. Carlson (13 FGs, 76 pts), frosh DT Chris Hutchinson, MG Mike Teeter, LBs Bobby Abrams and soph Erick Anderson, Welborne, DBs Vada Murray and Tripp Williams, frosh P Chris Stapleton (40.3-yd avg). *Noteworthy:* Schembechler's last team won 34th Big 10 title. Lost to USC 17–10 in Rose Bowl; Hoard ran for 108 yds, Taylor passed for 115 yds, and Wolverines scored TD on 2-yd run by TB Allen Jefferson.
1990 (9–3) *Won:* UCLA 38–15, Maryland 45–17, Wisconsin 41–3, Indiana 45–19, Purdue 38–13, Illinois 22–17, Minnesota 35–18, Ohio St. 16–13. *Lost:* Notre Dame 28–24, Michigan St. 28–27, Iowa 24–23. *Stars:* Grbac (1,615 yds and 17 TDs pass), Howard (57 pass rec for 858 yds and 9 TDs), soph WR Derrick Alexander (29 pass rec for 400 yds and 5 TDs), soph TB John Vaughn (1,236 yds and 9 TDs rush), frosh TB Ricky Powers (636 yds rush), Jefferson (6 TDs rush), OL Greg Skrepenak, Dingman, Carlson (16 FGs, 90 pts), Welborne, Anderson, DB Lance Dottin (5 int). *Noteworthy:* Got share of 35th Big 10 title (3rd straight) in 1st year under Gary Moeller. Beat Mississippi 35–3 in Gator Bowl; Grbac passed for 296 yds and 4 TDs, Howard had 6 pass rec for 167 yds and 2 TDs, Vaughn ran for 128 yds, Powers ran for 112 yds, and FB Jarrod Bunch ran for 1 TD and caught a TD pass.
1991 (10–2) *Won:* Boston College 35–13, Notre Dame 24–14 (1st over Irish since 1986), Iowa 43–24, Michigan St. 45–28, Indiana 24–16, Minnesota 52–6, Purdue 42–0, Northwestern 59–14, Illinois 20–0, Ohio St. 31–3. *Lost:* Florida St. 51–31. *Stars:* Heisman Trophy– and Maxwell Award–winner Howard (23 TDs, 1,749 all-purpose yds, 61 pass rec for 950 yds and 19 TDs), Grbac (nation's leader in pass efficiency with 1,955 yds and 24

TDs), Powers (1,187 yds and 9 TDs rush), WR Yale VanDyne (35 pass rec for 478 yds), soph RB Jesse Johnson (600 yds rush, 7 TDs), frosh RB Tyrone Wheatley (8 TDs rush), Skrepenak, OG Matt Elliott, Carlson (10 FGs, 82 pts), DT Mike Evans, LBs Anderson, Brian Townsend and soph Steve Morrison. *Noteworthy:* Won 4th straight Big 10 title. Lost to unbeaten national cochamp Washington 34–14 in Rose Bowl; Grbac passed for 130 yds and a TD (9 yds to frosh FL Walter Smith), and Wheatley scored on 53-yd run.

1992 (9–0–3) *Won:* Oklahoma St. 35–3, Houston 61–7, Iowa 52–28, Michigan St. 35–10, Indiana 31–3, Minnesota 63–13, Purdue 24–17, Northwestern 40–7 (20th straight over Wildcats). *Tied:* Notre Dame 17–17 (opener), Illinois 22–22, Ohio St. 13–13 (finale). *Stars:* Grbac (nation's pass efficiency leader: 1,465 yds and 15 TDs pass), Wheatley (14 TDs, 1,523 all-purpose yds, 1,122 yds and 10 TDs rush), Johnson (792 yds rush, 5 TDs), Alexander (14 TDs, 2 on punt returns; 1,168 all-purpose yds, 47 pass rec for 722 yds and 11 TDs), TE Tony McGee (32 pass rec for 350 yds), Smith (22 pass rec for 301 yds), FB Burnie Legette, OG Joe Cocozzo, C Steve Everitt, OT Rob Doherty, DT Chris Hutchinson, Morrison, soph LB Matt Dyson, DB Corwin Brown, P Chris Stapleton (40.2-yd avg). *Noteworthy:* Won 5th straight Big 10 title in 1st undefeated season since 1973. Beat Washington 38–31 in Rose Bowl as Wheatley ran for 235 yds and 3 TDs (runs of 56, 88, and 24 yds), Grbac passed for 175 yds and 2 TDs, McGee had 6 pass rec for 117 yds and 2 TDs (including 49-yarder), and K Peter Elezovic had 41-yd FG and 5 ex pts.

Bowl Summary

Bluebonnet 1–0; Fiesta 1–0; Gator 1–1; Hall of Fame 1–0; Holiday 0–1; Orange 0–1; Rose 7–9; Sugar 0–1.

Bowl Record (11–13)

Regular Season	Bowl	Score	Opponent	Record
1901 (10–0)	Rose	49–0	Stanford	(3–1–2)
1947 (9–0)	Rose	49–0	USC	(7–1–1)
1950 (5–3–1)	Rose	14–6	California	(9–0–1)
1964 (8–1)	Rose	34–7	Oregon St.	(8–2)
1969 (8–2)	Rose	3–10	USC	(9–0–1)
1971 (11–0)	Rose	12–13	Stanford	(8–3)
1975 (8–1–2)	Orange	6–14	Oklahoma	(10–1)
1976 (10–1)	Rose	6–14	USC	(10–1)
1977 (10–1)	Rose	20–27	Washington	(9–2)
1978 (10–1)	Rose	10–17	USC	(11–1)
1979 (8–3)	Gator	15–17	North Carolina	(7–3–1)
1980 (9–2)	Rose	23–6	Washington	(9–2)
1981 (8–3)	Bluebonnet	33–14	UCLA	(7–3–1)
1982 (8–3)	Rose	14–24	UCLA	(9–1–1)
1983 (9–2)	Sugar	7–9	Auburn	(10–1)
1984 (6–5)	Holiday	17–24	BYU	(12–0)
1985 (9–1–1)	Fiesta	27–23	Nebraska	(9–2)
1986 (11–1)	Rose	15–22	Arizona St.	(9–1–1)
1987 (7–4)	Hall of Fame	28–24	Alabama	(7–4)
1988 (8–2–1)	Rose	22–14	USC	(10–1)
1989 (10–1)	Rose	10–17	USC	(8–2–1)
1990 (8–3)	Gator	35–3	Mississippi	(9–2)
1991 (10–1)	Rose	14–34	Washington	(11–0)
1992 (8–0–3)	Rose	38–31	Washington	(9–2)

Conference Titles

Big 10—1898, 1901*, 1902, 1903*, 1904*, 1906*, 1918*, 1922*, 1923*, 1925, 1926*, 1930*, 1931*, 1932, 1933, 1943*, 1947, 1948, 1949*, 1950, 1964, 1969*, 1971, 1972*, 1973*, 1974*, 1976*, 1977*, 1978*, 1980, 1982, 1986*, 1988, 1989, 1990*, 1991, 1992.

TOP 20 AP AND UPI
(USA TODAY/CNN SINCE 1991) RANKING

Year	Rank	Year	Rank	Year	Rank	Year	Rank
1938	16	1949	7	1972	6–6	1983	8–9
1939	20	1950	9–6	1973	6–6	1985	2–2
1940	3	1953	20–19	1974	3–5	1986	8–7
1941	5	1954	15–15	1975	8–8	1987	19–18
1942	9	1955	12–13	1976	3–3	1988	4–4
1943	3	1956	7–7	1977	9–8	1989	7–8
1944	8	1964	4–4	1978	5–5	1990	7–8
1945	6	1968	12–15	1979	18–19	1991	6–6
1946	6	1969	9–8	1980	4–4	1992	5–5
1947	2	1970	9–7	1981	12–10		
1948	1	1971	6–4	1982	U–15		

Major Rivals

Michigan has played at least 10 games with Albion 16–1, Case 26–0–1, Chicago 19–7, Cornell 6–12, Illinois 57–19–2, Indiana 40–9, Iowa 32–8–4, Michigan St. 56–24–5, Minnesota 57–23–3, Navy 12–5–1, Northwestern 44–11–2, Notre Dame 14–9–1, Ohio St. 50–33–6, Pennsylvania 11–8–2, Purdue 32–10, Stanford 6–3–1, Syracuse 5–4–1, Vanderbilt 9–0–1, Wisconsin 41–8–1. Record against Big 10 member Penn St. is 0–0 (no games played).

Coaches

Dean of Michigan coaches is Fielding H. "Hurry Up" Yost with record of 165–29–10 for 1901–23 and 1925–26, including 10 Big 10 titles, a Rose Bowl champion, 8 unbeaten teams, and 2 national titles. Glenn E. "Bo" Schembechler (1969 national Coach of Year) had most Wolverine victories with record of 194–48–5 for 1969–89 with 13 Big 10 titles, 17 bowl teams, and 2 teams unbeaten in regular season. Other top records for at least 3 years were by Gustave H. Ferbert, 24–3–1 for 1897–99 with 1 unbeaten Big 10 champ; Harry G. Kipke, 46–26–4 for 1929–37 with 4 Big 10 titles, 3 unbeaten teams, and 2 national champions; H.O. "Fritz" Crisler (1947 national Coach of Year), 71–16–3 for 1938–47 with 2 Big 10 titles, a Rose Bowl champ, and 1 unbeaten national champion; Bennie G. Oosterbaan (1948 national Coach of Year), 63–33–4 for 1948–58 with 3 Big 10 titles, a Rose Bowl champion, and 1 unbeaten national champ; Chalmers W. "Bump" Elliott, 51–42–2 for 1959–68 with 1 Big 10 title and 1 Rose Bowl champion; and Gary Moeller, 28–5–3 for 1990–92 with 3 Big 10 titles and 3 bowl teams.

Miscellanea

First game was win over Racine in 1879 . . . 1st win over college foe was over Stevens Institute 17–5 in 1883 . . . highest score was over West Virginia 130–0 in 1904 . . . highest since W.W. II was over Navy 70–14 in 1976 and over Illinois 70–21 in 1981 . . . biggest margin since W.W. II was 69–0, over Pittsburgh in 1947 and Northwestern in 1975 . . . worst defeat was by Cornell 56–0 in 1889 . . . worst since 1900 was by Minnesota 40–0 in 1935 . . . worst since W.W. II was by Ohio St. 50–14 in 1968 . . . highest ever against was by Cornell 58–12 in 1891 . . . highest since 1900 was by Northwestern 55–24 in 1958 . . . longest unbeaten string of 56 in 1901–05 ended by Chicago 2–0 . . . longest win streak of 29 in 1901–03 ended by Minnesota 6–6 . . . 25-game win streak in 1946–49 ended by Army 21–7 . . . 22-game unbeaten string in 1931–33 ended by Michigan St. 16–0 in 1934 opener . . . 21-game unbeaten string in 1973–74 ended by Ohio St. 12–10 . . . longest losing string of 7 in 1936–37 broken with win over Iowa 7–6 . . . consensus All-Americans were William Cunningham, C, 1898; Neil Snow, E, 1901; Willie Heston, B, 1903–04; Adolph "Germany" Schulz, C, 1907; Albert Benbrook, G, 1909–10; Stanfield Wells, E, 1910; Miller Pontius, E, and Jim Craig, B, 1913; John Maulbetsch, B, 1914; Harry Kipke, B, 1922; Jack Blott, C, 1923; Benny Friedman, B, 1925–26; Bennie Oosterbaan, E, 1925–27; Otto Pommerening, T, 1928; Harry Newman, B, 1932; Francis Wistert, T, and Charles Bernard, C, 1933; Ralph Heikkinen, G, 1938; Tom Harmon, B, 1939–40; Bob Westfall, B, 1941; Albert Wistert, T, and Julie Franks, G, 1942; Bill Daley, B, 1943; Bob Chappuis, B, 1947; Dick Rifenburg, E, 1948; Alvin Wistert, T, 1948–49; Ron Kramer, E, 1955–56; Bill Yearby, DT, 1965; Jack Clancy, E, 1966; Jim Mandich, E, and Tom Curtis, DB, 1969; Dan Dierdorf, T, 1970; Reggie McKenzie, G, and Mike Taylor, LB, 1971; Paul Seymour, T, and Randy Logan, DB, 1972; Dave Gallagher, DL, 1973; Dave Brown, DB, 1973–74; Rob Lytle, RB, 1976; Mark Donahue, G, 1976–77; Ron Simpkins, LB, 1979; Ed Muransky, OL, and Kurt Becker, OL, 1981; Anthony Carter, WR, 1981–82; Mike Hammerstein, DL, and Brad Cochran, DB, 1985; Garland Rivers, DB, 1986; John Elliott, OL, 1987; Mark Messner, DL, and John Vitale, C, 1988; Tripp Welbourne, DB, 1989–90; and Desmond Howard, WR, and Greg Skrepenak, OT, 1991 . . . Academic All-Americans were Dick Balzhiser, B, 1952; Jim Owrig, T, 1955, 1957; Bob Timberlake, QB, 1964; Dave Fisher, FB, and Dick Vidner, QB, 1966; Jim Mandich, E, 1969; Phil Seymour, DE, 1970; Bruce Elliott, DB, 1971; Bill Hart, OG, 1972; Kirk Lewis, OG, 1974; Dan Jilek, DE, 1975; Norm Betts, TE, 1981; Robert Thompson, LB, 1982; Stefan Humphries, OG, 1982–83; Clay Miller, OL, 1985; and Kenneth Higgins, WR, 1986 . . . Heisman Trophy winners were Tom Harmon, B, 1940; and Desmond Howard, WR, 1991 . . . Maxwell Award winners

were Tom Harmon, B, 1940; and Desmond Howard, WR, 1991.

MICHIGAN STATE (Spartans; Green and White)

NOTABLE TEAMS

1903 (6–1–1) *Won:* Alma 11–0, Olivet 45–0, Michigan freshmen 11–0, Kalamazoo 11–0, Hillsdale 43–0, Detroit YMCA 51–6. *Lost:* unbeaten Notre Dame 12–0. *Tied:* Albion 6–6. *Noteworthy:* 1st year under Chester Brewer.

1904 (8–1) *Won:* Michigan Deaf School 47–0, Ohio Northern 28–6, Port Huron YMCA 29–0, Hillsdale 104–0, Michigan freshmen 39–0, Olivet 35–6, Alma 40–0, Kalamazoo 58–0. *Lost:* Albion 4–0.

1905 (9–2) *Won:* Michigan Deaf School 42–0, Port Huron YMCA 43–0, Michigan freshmen 24–0, Olivet 30–0, Hillsdale 18–0, Armour Institute 18–0, Kalamazoo 30–0, Albion 46–10, Alma 18–0. *Lost:* Notre Dame 28–0, Northwestern 37–11 (1st meeting).

1906 (7–2–2) *Won:* Olivet 23–0, Albion 37–0, 5–0, Kalamazoo 38–0, DePauw 33–0, Alma 12–0, Hillsdale 35–9. *Lost:* Notre Dame 5–0, Olivet 8–6. *Tied:* Alma 0–0, Detroit A.C. 6–6.

1908 (6–0–2) *Won:* Kalamazoo 35–0, Michigan Deaf School 51–0, Wabash 6–0, Olivet 46–2, Saginaw Naval Brigade 30–6, Detroit A.C. 37–14. *Tied:* Michigan 0–0, DePaul 0–0. *Noteworthy:* 1st unbeaten season.

1909 (8–1) *Won:* Detroit 27–0, Alma 34–0, Wabash 28–0, Culver Military Academy 29–0, DePaul 51–0, Marquette 10–0 (1st meeting), Olivet 20–0, Detroit A.C. 34–0. *Lost:* unbeaten Notre Dame 17–0.

1910 (6–1) *Won:* Detroit A.C. 35–0, Alma 11–0, Lake Forest 37–0, Notre Dame 17–0 (1st in 9-game series dating to 1897), Marquette 3–2, Olivet 62–0. *Lost:* unbeaten Michigan 6–3.

1911 (5–1) *Won:* Alma 12–0, Olivet 29–3, DePauw 6–0, Mt. Union 26–6, Wabash 17–6. *Lost:* Michigan 15–3. *Noteworthy:* John Macklin's 1st year.

1912 (7–1) *Won:* Alma 14–3, Olivet 52–0, DePauw 58–0, Ohio Wesleyan 46–0, Mt. Union 61–20, Wabash 24–0, Ohio St. 35–20 (1st meeting). *Lost:* Michigan 55–7.

1913 (7–0) *Won:* Olivet 26–0, Alma 57–0, Michigan 12–7 (1st in 8-game series dating to 1898),

Wisconsin 12–7 (1st meeting), Akron 41–0, Mt. Union 13–7, South Dakota 19–7.

1914 (5–2) *Won:* Olivet 26–7, Alma 60–0, Akron 75–0, Mt. Union 21–14, Penn St. 6–3 (1st meeting). *Lost:* Michigan 3–0, unbeaten Nebraska 24–0 in consecutive early games.

1915 (5–1) *Won:* Olivet 34–0, Alma 77–12, Carroll 56–0, Michigan 24–0, Marquette 68–6. *Lost:* Oregon St. 20–0 (1st homecoming). *Stars:* HB Jerry DaPrato (Spartans' 1st consensus All-American), E Blake Miller. *Noteworthy:* Macklin's last team.

1930 (5–1–2) *Won:* Alma 28–0, Cincinnati 32–0, Colgate 14–7 (1st in 5-game series begun in 1925), Case 45–0, North Dakota St. 19–11. *Lost:* Georgetown 14–13. *Tied:* unbeaten Michigan 0–0, Detroit 0–0.

1932 (7–1) *Won:* Alma 93–0, Grinnell 27–6, Illinois Wesleyan 27–0, Fordham 19–13, Syracuse 27–13, South Dakota 20–6, Detroit 7–0 (1st over Titans in 6 games since 1923). *Lost:* unbeaten national co-champ Michigan 26–0. *Star:* HB Robert Monnett. *Noteworthy:* Jim Crowley's last team.

1934 (8–1) *Won:* Grinnell 33–20, Michigan 16–0 (1st over Wolverines since 1915), Carnegie Tech 13–0, Manhattan 39–0, Marquette 13–7, Detroit 7–6, Kansas 6–0, Texas A&M 26–13. *Lost:* Syracuse 10–0. *Star:* E Edward Klewicki.

1935 (6–2) *Won:* Grinnell 41–0, Michigan 25–6, Kansas 42–0, Washington (Mo.) 47–13, Temple 12–7 (1st meeting), Loyola (Calif.) 27–0. *Lost:* Boston College 18–6, Marquette 13–7. *Star:* G Sid Wagner.

1936 (6–1–2) *Won:* Wayne St. 27–0, Michigan 21–7, Carnegie Tech 7–0, Missouri 13–0, Kansas 41–0, Arizona 7–0. *Lost:* Marquette 13–7. *Tied:* Boston College 13–13, Temple 7–7. *Star:* C Sam Ketchman.

1937 (8–2) *Won:* Wayne St. 19–0, Michigan 19–14, Missouri 2–0, Marquette 21–7, Kansas 16–0, Temple 13–6, Carnegie Tech 13–6, San Francisco 14–0. *Lost:* Manhattan 3–0. *Stars:* HB Johnny Pingel (nation's punting leader with 42.9-yd avg), T Harry Speelman. *Noteworthy:* made 1st postseason appearance, losing to Auburn 6–0 in Orange Bowl; Spartans were outgained 312–57 in total yds.

1944 (6–1) *Won:* Scranton 40–12, Kentucky 2–0, Kansas St. 45–6, Maryland 8–0, 33–0, Wayne St. 32–0. *Lost:* Missouri 13–7. *Star:* FB Jack Breslin. *Noteworthy:* resumed competition after 1-year W.W. II layoff and led nation in pass defense.

1947 (7–2) *Won:* Mississippi St. 7–0, Washington St. 21–7, Iowa St. 20–0, Marquette 13–7, Santa Clara 28–0 (1st in 5-game series dating to 1938), Temple 14–6 (1st meeting since 1942), Hawaii 58–19. *Lost:* unbeaten national cochamp Michigan 55–0, Kentucky 7–6. *Stars:* soph HB Lynn Chandnois (6 int), E Warren Huey. *Noteworthy:* 1st year under Clarence "Biggie" Munn.

1948 (6–2–2) *Won:* Hawaii 68–21, Arizona 61–7, Oregon St. 46–21, Marquette 47–0, Iowa St. 48–7, Washington St. 40–0. *Lost:* unbeaten national champ Michigan 13–7, unbeaten Notre Dame 26–7 (1st meeting since 1921) in early games. *Tied:* Penn St. 14–14, Santa Clara 21–21. *Stars:* HB George Guerre (734 yds rush), Chandnois (678 yds and 12 TDs rush), QB Gene Glick (11 TDs pass), Ed Sobczak (20 pass rec for 465 yds and 7 TDs).

1950 (8–1) *Won:* Oregon St. 38–13, Michigan 14–7 (1st over Wolverines in 11 games since 1937), William & Mary 33–14, Marquette 34–6, Notre Dame 36–33 (1st over Irish in 6 games since 1918), Indiana 35–0 (1st meeting since 1940, 1st win in 5-game series dating to 1922), Minnesota 27–0 (1st meeting), Pittsburgh 19–0. *Lost:* Maryland 34–7 (1st in 5-game series begun in 1944). *Stars:* HB Sonny Grandelius (1,023 yds rush, 12 TDs), Robert Carey (19 pass rec for 268 yds), E Dorne Dibble, Jesse Thomas (8 int, 41.8-yd punting avg).

1951 (9–0) *Won:* Oregon St. 6–0, Michigan 25–0, Ohio St. 24–20 (1st meeting since 1912), Marquette 20–14, Penn St. 32–21, Pittsburgh 53–26, Notre Dame 35–0, Indiana 30–26, Colorado 45–7. *Stars:* QB Al Dorow, Carey (20 pass rec for 263 yds), HBs Don McAuliffe (566 yds rush, 9 TDs) and James Ellis (6 int), T Don Coleman. *Noteworthy:* 1st unbeaten season since 1913.

1952 (9–0) *Won:* Michigan 27–13, Oregon St. 17–14, Texas A&M 48–6, Syracuse 48–7 (1st meeting since 1939), Penn St. 34–7, Purdue 14–7 (1st meeting since 1942), Indiana 41–14, Notre Dame 21–3, Marquette 62–13. *Stars:* McAuliffe, Ellis, QB Tom Yewcic (10 TD passes), HB Billy Wells (585 yds rush), E Ellis Duckett (10 pass rec for 323 yds and 5 TDs), G Frank Kush, C/LB Richard Tamburo. *Noteworthy:* led nation in rush defense and won 1st national championship.

1953 (9–1) *Won:* Iowa 21–7 (1st meeting), Minnesota 21–0, Texas Christian (TCU) 26–19, Indiana 47–18, Oregon St. 34–6, Ohio St. 28–13, Michigan 14–6, Marquette 21–15. *Lost:* Purdue 6–0 (1st to

Boilermakers in 5 games since 1939). *Stars:* HB LeRoy Bolden (691 yds rush, 8 TDs), Yewcic (40.1-yd punting avg), E Don Dohoney. *Noteworthy:* Munn's last team got share of Big 10 title in 1st year of conference play. Beat UCLA 28–20 in Rose Bowl; Wells ran for 80 yds and 2 TDs, Bolden scored once, and Duckett blocked punt for TD.

1955 (9–1) *Won:* Indiana 20–13, Stanford 38–14, Notre Dame 21–7, Illinois 21–7 (1st meeting), Wisconsin 27–0 (1st over Badgers in 6 games since 1913), Purdue 27–0, Minnesota 42–14, Marquette 33–0 (10th straight over Hilltoppers). *Lost:* Michigan 14–7. *Stars:* QB Earl Morrall (1,047 yds total off, 42.9-yd punting avg), soph E Dave Kaiser (12 pass rec for 343 yds), soph HB Walt Kowalczyk (584 yds and 6 TDs rush), FB Gerald Planutis, T Norman Masters, G Carl Nystrom. *Noteworthy:* beat UCLA 17–14 in Rose Bowl on 41-yd FG by Kaiser with 7 seconds left; Clarence Peaks scored on pass from Morrall and passed to John Lewis for 2nd TD, and Kowalczyk had 88 yds rush.

1956 (7–2) *Won:* Stanford 21–7, Michigan 9–0, Indiana 53–6, Notre Dame 47–14, Wisconsin 33–0, Purdue 12–9, Kansas St. 38–17. *Lost:* Illinois 20–13, Minnesota 14–13. *Stars:* Dennis Mendyk (7 TDs), Tony Kolodziej (7 pass rec for 221 yds), C John Matsko.

1957 (8–1) *Won:* Indiana 54–0, California 19–0, Michigan 35–6, Illinois 19–14, Wisconsin 21–7, Notre Dame 34–6, Minnesota 42–13, Kansas St. 27–9. *Lost:* Purdue 20–13. *Stars:* Kowalczyk (545 yds and 9 TDs rush), Kaiser (19 pass rec for 267 yds), QB Jim Ninowski, E Sam Williams, C Dan Currie, T Pat Burke, G Ellison Kelly.

1960 (6–2–1) *Won:* Michigan 24–17, Notre Dame 21–0, Indiana 35–0, Purdue 17–13, Northwestern 21–18, Detroit 43–15 (1st meeting since 1934). *Lost:* Iowa 27–15, Ohio St. 21–10. *Tied:* Pittsburgh 7–7. *Stars:* HB Herb Adderley, QB Tom Wilson, E Fred Arbanas.

1961 (7–2) *Won:* Wisconsin 20–0, Stanford 31–3, Michigan 28–0, Notre Dame 17–7, Indiana 35–0, Northwestern 21–13, Illinois 34–7. *Lost:* Minnesota 13–0, Purdue 7–6 in consecutive late games. *Stars:* FB George Saimes (8 TDs), soph HB Sherman Lewis (6 TDs), Lonnie Sanders (15 pass rec for 247 yds), G/T David Behrman.

1963 (6–2–1) *Won:* North Carolina 31–0, Indiana 20–3, Northwestern 15–7, Wisconsin 30–13, Pur-

due 23–0, Notre Dame 12–7. *Lost:* Southern California (USC) 13–10, Illinois 13–0. *Tied:* Michigan 7–7. *Stars:* Lewis (577 yds and 3 TDs rush, 11 pass rec for 303 yds and 5 TDs), Roger Lopes (601 yds rush), E Dan Underwood, G Earl Lattimer, P Lou Bobich (40.1-yd avg).

1965 (10–1) *Won:* UCLA 13–3, Penn St. 23–0 (1st meeting since 1952), Illinois 22–12, Michigan 24–7, Ohio St. 32–7 (1st meeting since 1960), Purdue 14–10, Northwestern 49–7, Iowa 35–0 (1st meeting since 1960), Indiana 27–13, Notre Dame 12–3. *Stars:* QB Steve Juday (1,173 yds pass), HB Clint Jones (787 yds and 10 TDs rush, 26 pass rec for 308 yds and 2 TDs), E Gene Washington (40 pass rec for 638 yds), FB Robert Apisa, K Dick Kenney (11 FGs), DE Charles "Bubba" Smith, LB Ronald Goovert, MG Harold Lucas, DBs George Webster and Donald Japinga. *Noteworthy:* Won 2nd Big 10 title and got share of 2nd national crown in 1st unbeaten season since 1952 while leading nation in rush defense and scoring defense (6.2-pt avg). Upset by UCLA 14–12 in Rose Bowl rematch when 2-pt conversion tries failed after 4th quarter TDs by Apisa (38-yd run) and Juday; Jones had 113 yds rush.

1966 (9–0–1) *Won:* N.C. State 28–10, Penn St. 42–8, Illinois 26–10, Michigan 20–7, Ohio St. 11–8, Purdue 41–20, Northwestern 22–0, Iowa 56–7, Indiana 37–19. *Tied:* unbeaten national cochamp Notre Dame 10–10. *Stars:* Smith, Webster, DT Nick Jordan, LB Charles Thornhill, DB Jess Phillips, QB Jimmy Raye (1,110 yds and 10 TDs pass), Washington (27 pass rec for 677 yds and 7 TDs), Jones (784 yds rush, 6 TDs), Apisa (9 TDs), Kenney, OT Jerry West, G Anthony Conti. *Noteworthy:* repeated as Big 10 champ and got share of 3rd national crown.

1978 (8–3) *Won:* Syracuse 49–21, Michigan 24–15 (1st over Wolverines since 1969), Indiana 49–14, Wisconsin 55–2, Illinois 59–19, Minnesota 33–9, Northwestern 52–3, Iowa 42–7. *Lost:* Purdue 21–14, national cochamp USC 30–9, Notre Dame 29–25. *Stars:* QB Ed Smith (2,226 yds and 20 TDs pass), FL Kirk Gibson (42 pass rec for 806 yds and 7 TDs), SE Eugene Byrd (43 pass rec for 718 yds and 7 TDs), soph HB Steve Smith (772 yds rush), TE Mark Brammer, OT James Hinesly, DT Melvin Land, DB Thomas Graves, P Ray Stachowicz (43.1-yd avg). *Noteworthy:* got share of 4th Big 10 title.

1987 (9–2–1)   *Won:* USC 27–13, Iowa 19–14, Michigan 17–11, Northwestern 38–0, Ohio St. 13–7 (1st over Buckeyes in 9 games since 1974), Purdue 45–3, Indiana 27–3, Wisconsin 30–9.   *Lost:* Notre Dame 31–8, Florida St. 31–3 in successive early games.   *Tied:* Illinois 14–14.   *Stars:* RB Lorenzo White (1,459 yds rush, 14 TDs), QB Bobby McAllister (1,171 yds pass), WR Andre Rison (34 pass rec for 785 yds and 5 TDs), soph TB Blake Ezor (617 yds rush), OT Tony Mandarich, C Pat Shurmur, frosh K John Langeloh (17 FGs, 79 pts), soph LB Percy Snow, DBs Todd Krumm (9 int) and John Miller (8 int), P Greg Montgomery (45-yd avg).   *Noteworthy:* Led nation in rush defense and won 5th Big 10 title. Won rematch with USC 20–17 in Rose Bowl; White ran for 113 yds and both Spartan TDs, and Langeloh kicked 2 FGs and 2 ex pts.
1989 (8–4)   *Won:* Miami (Ohio) 49–0, Iowa 17–14, Purdue 28–21, Indiana 51–20, Minnesota 21–7, Northwestern 76–14, Wisconsin 31–3.   *Lost:* Notre Dame 21–13, national champ Miami (Fla.) 26–20, Michigan 10–7, Illinois 14–10.   *Stars:* Lombardi Award–winner Snow, DT Travis Davis, LBs Dixon Edwards and Carlos Jenkins, DB Harlon Barnett, QB Dan Enos (1,950 yds pass, 6 TDs rush), soph WR Courtney Hawkins (60 pass rec for 1,080 yds and 6 TDs, 1,649 all-purpose yds), WR James Bradley (22 pass rec for 437 yds), Ezor (1,120 yds and 16 TDs rush), frosh TB Tico Duckett (593 yds

rush, 5 TDs), Langeloh (10 FGs, 71 pts), OT Bob Kula, soph P Josh Butland (43.1-yd punting avg).   *Noteworthy:* beat Hawaii 33–13 in Aloha Bowl; Ezor ran for 179 yds and 3 TDs, DE Mark Vanderbeek recovered 3 fumbles, and Jenkins recovered a fumble, intercepted a pass, and blocked an ex pt.
1990 (8–3–1)   *Won:* Rutgers 34–10, Michigan 28–27, Purdue 55–33, Indiana 45–20, Minnesota 28–16, Northwestern 29–22, Wisconsin 14–9.   *Lost:* Notre Dame 20–19, Iowa 12–7, Illinois 15–13.   *Tied:* Syracuse 23–23 (1st meeting since 1978).   *Stars:* Enos (1,546 yds pass, 7 TDs rush), Bradley (31 pass rec for 506 yds), Hawkins (25 pass rec for 368 yds), Duckett (1,376 yds and 10 TDs rush), TB Hyland Hickson (1,128 yds and 13 TDs rush), OG Eric Molen, OT Roosevelt Wagner, LB Chuck Bullough, Jenkins, Edwards, Langeloh (11 FGs).   *Noteworthy:* Got share of 6th Big 10 title. Beat USC 17–16 in John Hancock Bowl; Enos passed for 131 yds and a TD (to Hawkins, who caught 6 for 106 yds), Hickson ran for a TD, and Langeloh kicked 52-yd FG and 2 ex pts.

BOWL SUMMARY

All-American 0–1; Aloha 1–0; Cherry 0–1; Gator 0–1; John Hancock 1–0; Orange 0–1; Rose 3–1.

BOWL RECORD (5–5)

Regular Season	Bowl	Score	Opponent	Record
1937 (8–2)	Orange	0–6	Auburn	(5–2–3)
1953 (8–1)	Rose	28–20	UCLA	(8–1)
1955 (8–1)	Rose	17–14	UCLA	(9–1)
1965 (10–0)	Rose	12–14	UCLA	(7–2–1)
1984 (6–5)	Cherry	6–10	Army	(7–3–1)
1985 (7–4)	All-American	14–17	Georgia Tech	(8–2–1)
1987 (8–2–1)	Rose	20–17	USC	(8–3)
1988 (6–4–1)	Gator	27–34	Georgia	(8–3)
1989 (7–4)	Aloha	33–13	Hawaii	(9–2–1)
1990 (7–3–1)	John Hancock	17–16	USC	(8–3–1)

CONFERENCE TITLES

Big 10—1953*, 1965, 1966, 1978*, 1987, 1990*.

TOP 20 AP AND UPI RANKING

1948	14	1955	2–2	1963	9–10	1987	8–8
1949	19	1956	9–10	1964	U–20	1989	16–16
1950	8–9	1957	3–3	1965	2–1	1990	16–14
1951	2–2	1959	U–16	1966	2–2		
1952	1–1	1960	15–11	1974	12–18		
1953	3–3	1961	8–9	1978	12–U		

MAJOR RIVALS

Michigan St. has played at least 10 games with Albion 11–4–3, Alma 22–4–4, Detroit 7–6–1, Illinois 14–16–2, Indiana 30–11–2, Iowa 13–13–2, Kalamazoo 9–8, Marquette 18–6–1, Michigan 24–56–5, Minnesota 20–11, Northwestern 27–10, Notre Dame 18–39–1, Ohio St. 10–17, Olivet 18–4–1, Penn St. 8–1–1, Purdue 25–20–2, Syracuse 9–3–1, Temple 7–1–2, Wisconsin 23–12.

COACHES

Dean of Michigan St. coaches is Hugh "Duffy" Daugherty (1955, 1965 national Coach of Year) with record of 109–69–5 for 1954–72, including 2 Big 10 titles, 2 bowl teams, and 2 unbeaten national champions. Other top records for at least 3 years were by Chester L. Brewer, 58–23–7 for 1903–10, 1917, and 1919 with 1 unbeaten team; John F. Macklin, 29–5 for 1911–15 with 1 perfect record; James H. Crowley, 22–8–3 for 1929–32; Charles W. Bachman, 70–34–10 for 1933–46 with 1 bowl team; Clarence "Biggie" Munn (1952 national Coach of Year), 54–9–2 for 1947–53 with 1 Big 10 title, 1 Rose Bowl champion, 2 perfect records, and 1 national champion; Denny Stolz, 19–13–1 for 1973–75; Darryl D. Rogers, 24–18–2 for 1976–79 with 1 Big 10 title; and George Perles, 62–50–4 for 1983–92 with 1 Big 10 title and 6 bowl teams.

MISCELLANEA

First game was win over Lansing H.S. 10–0 in 1896 ... 1st win over college foe was over Olivet 26–6 in 1897 ... highest score was over Olivet 109–0 in 1920 ... highest since W.W. II was over Northwestern 76–14 in 1989 ... biggest margin since W.W. II was over Arizona 75–0 in 1949 ... worst defeat was by Michigan 119–0 in 1902 ... worst defeat since W.W. II was by Michigan 55–0 in 1947 ... highest against since W.W. II was by UCLA 56–14 in 1974 ... longest win streak of 28 in 1950–53 ended by Purdue 6–0 ... 15-game win streak in 1912–14 ended by Michigan 3–0 ... longest winless string of 11 in 1916–17 broken with win over Albion 21–6 in 1918 opener ... consensus All-Americans were Jerry DaPrato, B, 1915; Sidney Wagner, G, 1935; Ed Bagdon, G, 1949; Bob Carey, E, and Don Coleman, T, 1951; Don Dohoney, E, 1953; Norman Masters, T, and Earl Morrall, B, 1955; Dan Currie, C, and Walt Kowalczyk, B, 1957; Sam Williams, E, 1958; George Saimes, B, 1962; Sherman Lewis, B, 1963; Charles "Bubba" Smith, DE, and George Webster, DB, 1965–66; Clint Jones, B, 1966; Brad VanPelt, DB, 1972; Lorenzo White, RB, 1985, 1987; Tony Mandarich, OL, 1988; and Percy Snow, LB, and Bob Kula, OL, 1989 ... Academic All-Americans were John Wilson, HB, 1952; Don Dohoney, E, 1953; Buck Nystrom, G, 1955; Blanche Martin, HB, 1957; Don Bierowicz, DT, and Don Japinga, DB, 1965; Pat Gallinagh, DT, 1966; Al Brenner, E and S, 1968; Ron Saul, OG, and Rich Saul, DE, 1969; John Shinsky, DT, 1973; Alan Davis, DB, 1979; Dean Altobelli, DB, 1985–86; Shane Bullough, LB, 1986; and Steve Wasylk, DB, 1992 ... Maxwell Award winner was Brad VanPelt, DB, 1972 ... Outland Trophy winner was Ed Bagdon, G, 1949 ... Lombardi Award winner was Percy Snow, LB, 1989.

MINNESOTA (Golden Gophers; Maroon and Gold)

NOTABLE TEAMS

1890 (5–1–1) *Won:* Wisconsin 63–0 (1st meeting), Ex-Collegiates 14–6, Shattuck 58–0, Hamline 44–0,

Grinnell 18–13. *Lost:* Ex-Collegian 14–11. *Tied:* Ex-Collegiates 0–0. *Noteworthy:* only year under Tom Eck.

1891 (3–1–1) *Won:* Wisconsin 26–12, Iowa 42–4 (1st meeting), Grinnell 22–14. *Lost:* Ex-Collegiates 4–0. *Tied:* Grinnell 12–12.

1892 (5–0) *Won:* Wisconsin 32–4, Michigan 14–6 (1st meeting), Northwestern 16–12 (1st meeting), Ex-Collegiates 18–10, Grinnell 40–24. *Star:* HB William Leary. *Noteworthy:* 1st undefeated season since 2-game schedule of 1887.

1893 (6–0) *Won:* Wisconsin 40–0, Michigan 34–20, Northwestern 16–0, Grinnell 36–6, Hamline 10–6, Kansas 12–6. *Star:* C James Madigan.

1895 (7–3) *Won:* Wisconsin 14–10, Chicago 10–6 (1st meeting), Boat Club 6–0, Ex-Collegiates 14–0, High Schools 4–0, Iowa St. 24–0 (1st meeting), Macalester 40–0. *Lost:* Michigan 20–0, Purdue 18–4, Grinnell 6–4 (1st in 7-game series begun in 1890).

1896 (8–2) *Won:* Purdue 14–0, Carleton 16–6, Ex-Collegiates 7–0, Grinnell 12–0, Minneapolis Central H.S. 50–0, Minneapolis South H.S. 34–0, Iowa St. 18–6, Kansas 12–0. *Lost:* Wisconsin 6–0, Michigan 6–4 in 1st 2 games. *Star:* E John Harrison.

1900 (10–0–2) *Won:* Wisconsin 6–5, Illinois 23–0, Northwestern 21–0, Carleton 44–0, Grinnell 26–0, St. Paul Central H.S. 26–0, Iowa St. 27–0, Macalester 66–0, Nebraska 20–12 (1st meeting), North Dakota 34–0 (1st meeting). *Tied:* Chicago 6–6, Minneapolis Central H.S. 0–0. *Star:* C Bert Page. *Noteworthy:* won share of 1st Big 10 title in 1st year under Dr. Henry Williams.

1901 (10–1) *Won:* Iowa 16–0 (1st meeting since 1891), Illinois 16–0, Northwestern 16–0, Carleton 35–0, Chicago 27–0, Haskell 28–0, St. Paul Central H.S. 16–0, Minneapolis Central H.S. 12–0, Nebraska 19–0, North Dakota St. 10–0. *Lost:* unbeaten Wisconsin 18–0 in opener. *Star:* FB Warren Knowlton.

1902 (9–2–1) *Won:* Wisconsin 11–0, Iowa 34–0, Illinois 17–5, Beloit 29–0, Carleton 33–0, Grinnell 102–0, Hamline 59–0, Minneapolis Central H.S. 28–0, Iowa St. 16–0. *Lost:* unbeaten national champ Michigan 23–6 (1st meeting since 1897), unbeaten Nebraska 6–0. *Tied:* St. Paul Central H.S. 0–0. *Star:* G John Flynn.

1903 (14–0–1) *Won:* Wisconsin 17–0, Iowa 75–0, Illinois 32–0, Beloit 46–0, Carleton 29–0, Grinnell 39–0, Hamline 65–0, Minneapolis East H.S. 37–0,

Minneapolis Central H.S. 26–6, St. Paul Central H.S. 36–0, Iowa St. 46–0, Lawrence 46–0, Macalester 112–0, North Dakota St. 11–0. *Tied:* unbeaten Michigan 6–6. *Stars:* T Fred Schacht (Gophers' 1st consensus All-American), E Ed Rogers. *Noteworthy:* scored 618, shut out 12, and got share of 2nd Big 10 title.

1904 (12–0) *Won:* Wisconsin 28–0, Iowa 11–0, Northwestern 17–0, Carleton 65–0, Grinnell 146–0, High Schools 107–0, Iowa St. 32–0, Lawrence 69–0, Nebraska 16–12, North Dakota 35–0, St. Thomas 47–0, Shattuck 75–0. *Star:* C Mose Strathern. *Noteworthy:* outscored foes 725–12 and again earned share of Big 10 crown.

1905 (10–1) *Won:* Iowa 39–0, Northwestern 72–6, High Schools 74–0, Iowa St. 42–0, Lawrence 46–0, Nebraska 35–0, North Dakota 45–0, Pillsbury/Shattuck 54–0, St. Thomas 42–0, South Dakota St. 81–0. *Lost:* Wisconsin 16–12 (breaking 27-game unbeaten string) in opener. *Star:* FB Earl Current.

1906 (4–1) *Won:* Chicago 4–2, Indiana 8–6 (1st meeting), Iowa St. 22–4, Nebraska 13–0. *Lost:* Carlisle Indians 17–0. *Star:* Current. *Noteworthy:* got share of 4th Big 10 title.

1909 (6–1) *Won:* Lawrence 25–0, Iowa 41–0, Iowa St. 18–0 (10th straight over Cyclones), Nebraska 14–0, Chicago 20–6, Wisconsin 34–6. *Lost:* Michigan 15–6 (1st meeting since 1903) in finale. *Star:* QB Johnny McGovern. *Noteworthy:* won 5th Big 10 title.

1910 (6–1) *Won:* Lawrence 34–0, South Dakota 17–0, Iowa St. 49–0, Nebraska 27–0, Chicago 24–0, Wisconsin 28–0. *Lost:* unbeaten Michigan 6–0 in finale. *Stars:* T James Walker, FB Lisle Johnston. *Noteworthy:* got share of 6th Big 10 crown.

1911 (6–0–1) *Won:* Iowa St. 5–0, South Dakota 5–0, Nebraska 21–3, Chicago 30–0, Iowa 24–6, Illinois 11–0 (1st meeting since 1903). *Tied:* Wisconsin 6–6. *Star:* FB Earl Pickering. *Noteworthy:* won 3rd straight Big 10 title.

1913 (5–2) *Won:* South Dakota 14–0, Iowa St. 25–0, North Dakota 30–0, Wisconsin 21–3, Illinois 19–9. *Lost:* unbeaten Nebraska 7–0 (1st to Cornhuskers in 10 games since 1902), unbeaten Chicago 13–7. *Star:* E Donald Aldworth.

1914 (6–1) *Won:* North Dakota 28–6, Iowa St. 26–0 (15th straight over Cyclones), South Dakota 29–7, Iowa 7–0 (10th straight over Hawkeyes), Wisconsin 14–3 (1st homecoming), Chicago 13–7.

Lost: unbeaten Illinois 21–6. *Star:* C Boles Rosenthal.

1915 (6–0–1) *Won:* North Dakota 41–0, Iowa St. 34–6, South Dakota 19–0, Iowa 51–13, Chicago 20–7, Wisconsin 20–3. *Tied:* unbeaten Illinois 6–6. *Stars:* E Bert Baston, HB Bernie Bierman. *Noteworthy:* got share of 8th Big 10 title.

1916 (6–1) *Won:* South Dakota St. 41–7, North Dakota 47–7, South Dakota 81–0, Iowa 67–0, Wisconsin 54–0, Chicago 49–0. *Lost:* Illinois 14–9. *Stars:* Baston, T George Hauser, QB Shorty Long.

1917 (4–1) *Won:* South Dakota St. 64–0, Indiana 33–9 (1st meeting since 1906), Chicago 33–0, Illinois 27–6. *Lost:* Wisconsin 10–7. *Star:* Hauser.

1923 (5–1–1) *Won:* Iowa 20–7, Northwestern 34–14, Haskell 13–12, Iowa St. 20–17 (1st meeting since 1915), North Dakota 27–0. *Lost:* unbeaten Michigan 10–0. *Tied:* Wisconsin 0–0. *Stars:* HB Earl Martineau, E Ray Ecklund.

1927 (6–0–2) *Won:* Wisconsin 13–7, Iowa 38–0, Michigan 13–7 (1st over Wolverines since 1919), Drake 27–6, North Dakota 57–10, Oklahoma A&M 40–0. *Tied:* Indiana 14–14 (1st meeting since 1922), Notre Dame 7–7. *Stars:* FB Herb Joesting, G Harold Hanson, soph T Bronko Nagurski. *Noteworthy:* 1st unbeaten season since 1915.

1928 (6–2) *Won:* Wisconsin 6–0, Chicago 33–7 (1st meeting since 1918), Indiana 21–12, Purdue 15–0 (1st meeting since 1897), Creighton 40–0, Haskell 52–0. *Lost:* Iowa 7–6, Northwestern 10–9 (1st meeting since 1923). *Stars:* E Kenneth Haycraft, G George Gibson, T/FB Nagurski.

1929 (6–2) *Won:* Wisconsin 13–12, Northwestern 26–14, Indiana 19–7, Coe 39–0, Ripon 54–0, Vanderbilt 15–6. *Lost:* Iowa 9–7, Michigan 7–6 in consecutive early games. *Stars:* Nagurski, E Robert Tanner. *Noteworthy:* last year under Dr. Clarence Spears.

1931 (7–3) *Won:* Wisconsin 14–0, Iowa 34–0, Ohio St. 19–7 (1st meeting since 1922), Cornell (Iowa) 47–7, North Dakota St. 13–7, Oklahoma A&M 20–0, Ripon 30–0. *Lost:* Michigan 6–0, unbeaten Northwestern 32–14, Stanford 13–0. *Star:* G Clarence "Biggie" Munn.

1933 (4–0–4) *Won:* South Dakota St. 19–6, Pittsburgh 7–3 (1st meeting), Iowa 19–7, Wisconsin 6–3. *Tied:* Indiana 6–6, Purdue 7–7, Northwestern 0–0, unbeaten national champ Michigan 0–0. *Stars:* HB Francis "Pug" Lund (626 yds rush), E Frank "Butch" Larson, C Roy Oen. *Noteworthy:* 1st unbeaten season since 1927.

1934 (8–0) *Won:* North Dakota St. 56–12, Nebraska 20–0, Pittsburgh 13–7, Iowa 48–12, Michigan 34–0 (1st over Wolverines since 1927), Indiana 30–0, Chicago 35–7 (1st meeting since 1928), Wisconsin 34–0. *Stars:* Lund (621 yds and 6 TDs rush), Larson, G Bill Bevan, T Ed Widseth. *Noteworthy:* won 9th Big 10 title and share of 1st national championship in 1st perfect season since 1904.

1935 (8–0) *Won:* North Dakota St. 26–6, Nebraska 12–7, Tulane 20–0, Northwestern 21–13, Purdue 29–7, Iowa 13–6, Michigan 40–0, Wisconsin 33–7. *Stars:* Widseth, T Dick Smith, QB Glenn Seidel, FB Sheldon Beise, B Vernal LeVoir. *Noteworthy:* repeated as national and Big 10 cochamps.

1936 (7–1) *Won:* Washington 14–7 (1st meeting), Nebraska 7–0, Michigan 26–0, Purdue 33–0, Iowa 52–0, Texas 47–19, Wisconsin 24–0. *Lost:* Northwestern 6–0 (ending 28-game unbeaten streak) in mid-season. *Stars:* Widseth, FB Andy Uram, HB Julius Alfonse. *Noteworthy:* took 3rd straight national championship.

1937 (6–2) *Won:* North Dakota St. 69–7, Indiana 6–0, Michigan 39–6, Iowa 35–10, Northwestern 7–0, Wisconsin 12–6. *Lost:* Nebraska 14–9 (1st to Cornhuskers in 6 games since 1913), Notre Dame 7–6. *Stars:* Uram, HB Rudy Gmitro, E Ray King. *Noteworthy:* won 11th Big 10 title.

1938 (6–2) *Won:* Washington 15–0, Nebraska 16–7, Purdue 7–0, Michigan 7–6, Iowa 28–0, Wisconsin 21–0. *Lost:* Northwestern 6–3, Notre Dame 19–0. *Stars:* G Francis Twedell, FB Larry Buhler, soph HB George Franck (42.5-yd punting avg). *Noteworthy:* repeated as Big 10 champ.

1940 (8–0) *Won:* Washington 19–14, Nebraska 13–7, Ohio St. 13–7, Iowa 34–6, Northwestern 13–12, Michigan 7–6, Purdue 33–6, Wisconsin 22–13. *Stars:* Franck (8 TDs, 39.6-yd punting avg), HB Bruce Smith (5 TDs), QB Bob Paffrath, T Urban Odson, G Helge Pukema. *Noteworthy:* got share of 4th national title and won 13th Big 10 crown.

1941 (8–0) *Won:* Washington 14–6, Illinois 34–6 (1st meeting since 1924), Pittsburgh 39–0 (1st meeting since 1934), Michigan 7–0, Northwestern 8–7, Nebraska 9–0, Iowa 34–13, Wisconsin 41–6. *Stars:* Heisman Trophy–winner Smith (766 yds total off, 5 TDs), HB Bill Daley (685 yds and 9 TDs rush), B Bob Sweiger, T Dick Wildung. *Note-*

worthy: repeated as Big 10 and national champion.
1948 (7–2) *Won:* Washington 20–0, Nebraska 39–13, Illinois 6–0, Indiana 30–7, Purdue 34–7, Iowa 28–21, Wisconsin 16–0. *Lost:* Northwestern 19–16, unbeaten national champ Michigan 27–14. *Stars:* T Leo Nomellini, E Bud Grant, B Ev Faunce (558 yds rush, 567 pass).
1949 (7–2) *Won:* Washington 48–20, Nebraska 28–6 (10th straight over Cornhuskers), Northwestern 21–7, Ohio St. 27–0 (1st over Buckeyes in 4 games since 1940), Iowa 55–7, Pittsburgh 24–7, Wisconsin 14–6. *Lost:* Michigan 14–7, Purdue 13–7 in successive mid-season games. *Stars:* Nomellini, Grant, HB Billy Bye (561 yds rush, 572 pass), C/LB Clayton Tonnemaker.
1954 (7–2) *Won:* Nebraska 19–7, Pittsburgh 46–7, Northwestern 26–7, Illinois 19–6, Michigan St. 19–13, Oregon St. 44–6, Iowa 22–20. *Lost:* Michigan 34–0, Wisconsin 27–0. *Star:* FB/HB Bob McNamara (708 yds rush). *Noteworthy:* 1st year under Murray Warmath.
1956 (6–1–2) *Won:* Washington 34–14 (1st over Huskies in 5 games since 1949), Purdue 21–14, Illinois 16–13, Michigan 20–7, Pittsburgh 9–6, Michigan St. 14–13. *Lost:* Iowa 7–0. *Tied:* Northwestern 0–0, Wisconsin 13–13. *Stars:* G Bob Hobert, B Bobby Cox (553 yds rush).
1960 (8–2) *Won:* Nebraska 26–14, Indiana 42–0, Northwestern 7–0, Illinois 21–10, Michigan 10–0, Kansas St. 48–7, Iowa 27–10, Wisconsin 26–7. *Lost:* Purdue 23–14. *Stars:* QB Sandy Stephens (9 TDs), G Tom Brown, C Greg Larson, E Tom Hall. *Noteworthy:* Nation's most-improved team got

share of 15th Big 10 title (1st since 1941) and share of 6th national crown. Made 1st postseason appearance, losing to Washington 17–7 in Rose Bowl as Stephens was intercepted 3 times; Bill Munsey ran 18 yds for Gophers' TD.
1961 (8–2) *Won:* Oregon 14–7, Northwestern 10–3, Illinois 33–0, Michigan 23–20, Michigan St. 13–0, Iowa 16–9, Purdue 10–7. *Lost:* Missouri 6–0 (opener), Wisconsin 23–21 (finale). *Stars:* Stephens (794 yds and 9 TDs pass, 487 yds and 6 TDs rush), T Bobby Bell. *Noteworthy:* beat UCLA 21–3 in Rose Bowl; Stephens scored 2 TDs and Munsey one.
1962 (6–2–1) *Won:* Navy 21–0, Illinois 17–0, Michigan 17–0, Michigan St. 28–7, Iowa 10–0, Purdue 7–6. *Lost:* Northwestern 34–22, Wisconsin 14–9. *Tied:* Missouri 0–0 in opener. *Stars:* Bell, E John Campbell, G Julian Hook. *Noteworthy:* led nation in rush defense.
1967 (8–2) *Won:* Utah 13–12, Southern Methodist (SMU) 23–3, Illinois 10–7, Michigan St. 21–0 (1st meeting since 1962), Michigan 20–15, Iowa 10–0, Indiana 33–7, Wisconsin 21–14. *Lost:* Nebraska 7–0, Purdue 41–12. *Stars:* E Bob Stein, Ts McKinley Boston and John Williams, Bs Jim Carter (519 yds rush) and Tom Sakal. *Noteworthy:* got share of 16th Big 10 title.

BOWL SUMMARY

Hall of Fame 0–1; Independence 1–0; Liberty 0–1; Rose 1–1.

BOWL RECORD (2–3)

Regular Season	Bowl	Score	Opponent	Record
1960 (8–1)	Rose	7–17	Washington	(9–1)
1961 (7–2)	Rose	21–3	UCLA	(7–3)
1977 (7–4)	Hall of Fame	7–17	Maryland	(7–4)
1985 (6–5)	Independence	20–13	Clemson	(6–5)
1986 (6–5)	Liberty	14–21	Tennessee	(6–5)

CONFERENCE TITLES

Big 10—1900*, 1903*, 1904*, 1906*, 1909, 1910*, 1911, 1915*, 1934, 1935*, 1937, 1938, 1940, 1941, 1960*, 1967*.

TOP 20 AP AND UPI RANKING

1936	1	1941	1	1954	U–20	1962	10–10
1937	5	1942	19	1956	12–9	1967	U–14
1938	10	1948	16	1960	1–1	1968	U–18
1940	1	1949	8	1961	6–6		

MAJOR RIVALS

Minnesota has played at least 10 games with Ames 11–0, Carleton 10–1, Chicago 13–5–1, Grinnell 12–2–2, Illinois 25–22–3, Indiana 31–20–3, Iowa 55–29–2, Iowa St. 21–2–1, Michigan 23–57–3, Michigan St. 11–20, Nebraska 29–20–2, North Dakota 18–0, Northwestern 44–23–5, Ohio St. 6–30, Pittsburgh 9–3, Purdue 28–20–3, Shattuck 5–5–1, Washington 10–7, Wisconsin 55–39–8. Record against Big 10 member Penn St. is 0–0 (no games played).

COACHES

Dean of Minnesota coaches is Dr. Henry L. Williams with record of 136–33–11 for 1900–21, including 8 Big 10 titles and 5 unbeaten teams. Other top records for at least 3 years were by William Spaulding, 11–7–4 for 1922–24; Dr. Clarence Spears, 28–9–3 for 1925–29 with 1 unbeaten team; Bernie Bierman, 93–35–6 for 1932–41 and 1945–50 with 6 Big 10 titles, 5 unbeaten teams, and 5 national champions; George Hauser, 15–11–1 for 1942–44; Murray Warmath (1960 national Coach of Year), 86–77–7 for 1954–71 with 2 Big 10 titles, 2 Rose Bowl teams, and 1 national champion; Cal Stoll, 39–39 for 1972–78 with 1 bowl team; and John Gutekunst, 29–37–2 for 1986–91 with 1 bowl team.

MISCELLANEA

First game was win over Hamline 4–0 in 1882 . . . highest score was over Grinnell 146–0 in 1904 . . . highest since W.W. II was over Montana 62–17 in 1985 . . . biggest margin since W.W. II was over Ohio U. 57–3 in 1982 . . . worst defeat was by Nebraska 84–13 in 1983 . . . longest unbeaten string of 28 in 1933–36 ended by Northwestern 6–0 . . . 27-game unbeaten string in 1903–04 ended by Wisconsin 16–12 in 1905 opener . . . 18-game unbeaten string in 1899–1900 ended by Wisconsin 18–0 in 1901 opener . . . 18-game win streak in 1939–42 ended by Iowa Seahawks 7–6 . . . longest losing string of 10 in 1957–58 broken with win over Michigan St. 39–12 . . . consensus All-Americans were Fred Schacht, T, 1903; John McGovern, B, 1909; James Walker, T, 1910; Bert Baston, E, 1916; George Hauser, T, 1917; Ray Ecklund, E, 1923; Herb Joesting, B, 1926–27; Bronko Nagurski, T, 1929; Biggie Munn, G, 1931; Frank Larson, E, Bill Bevan, G, and Pug Lund, B, 1934; Ed Widseth, T, 1935–36; Urban Odson, T, and George Franck, B, 1940; Bruce Smith, B, 1941; Dick Wildung, T, 1941–42; Leo Nomellini, T, 1948–49; Clayton Tonnemaker, C, 1949; Paul Giel, B, 1953; Tom Brown, G, 1960; Sandy Stephens, B, 1961; Bobby Bell, T, 1962; Carl Eller, T, 1963; and Aaron Brown, DE, 1965 . . . Academic All-Americans were Bob Hobert, T, 1956; Frank Brixius, T, 1960; Bob Stein, DE, 1968; and Barry Mayer, RB, 1970 . . . Heisman Trophy winner was Bruce Smith, HB, 1941 . . . Outland Trophy winners were Tom Brown, G, 1960; and Bobby Bell, T, 1962.

NORTHWESTERN *(Wildcats; Purple and White)*

NOTABLE TEAMS

1890 (3–1–1)   *Won:* Evanston H.S. 16–4, Wisconsin 22–10 (1st meeting), Beloit 22–6 (1st meeting). *Lost:* Alumni 24–0. *Tied:* South Division H.S. 0–0.
1896 (6–1–2)   *Won:* Englewood H.S. 25–0, Armour 40–0, Chicago A.C. 4–0, Chicago 46–6, Illinois 10–4, Chicago Physicians & Surgeons 16–6. *Lost:* Chicago 18–6. *Tied:* Wisconsin 6–6, Beloit 6–6.
1901 (8–2–1)   *Won:* Lombard 44–0, Lake Forest 12–0, Fort Sheridan 21–0, Notre Dame 2–0, Illinois 17–11, Chicago 6–5, Purdue 10–5, Naperville 30–0.

Lost: unbeaten national champ Michigan 29–0, Minnesota 16–0.   *Tied:* Beloit 11–11.

1903 (9–2–3)   *Won:* North Division H.S. 17–5, Fort Sheridan 28–0, Englewood H.S. 35–0, Naperville 22–6, Alumni 5–0, Lombard 24–0, Washington (Mo.) 23–0, Cincinnati 35–0, Illinois 12–11.   *Lost:* Chicago Dental 11–10, Carlisle Indians 28–0.   *Tied:* Chicago 0–0, unbeaten Notre Dame 0–0, Wisconsin 6–6.   *Noteworthy:* 1st year under Walter McCornack.

1904 (8–2)   *Won:* Fort Sheridan 17–0, Naperville 34–0, North Division H.S. 18–0, Lombard 55–0, Beloit 34–0, DePauw 45–0, Oshkosh Normal 97–0, Illinois 12–6.   *Lost:* Chicago 32–0, unbeaten Minnesota 17–0.

1905 (8–2–1)   *Won:* Evanston H.S. 32–0, North Division H.S. 11–0, St. Viator 41–0, Wabash 5–0, Beloit 18–2, Marquette 30–5, Ohio Northern 34–0, Michigan St. 37–11 (1st meeting).   *Lost:* unbeaten national champ Chicago 32–0, Minnesota 72–6.   *Tied:* Transylvania 0–0.   *Noteworthy:* McCornack's last team.

1906–1907—No varsity team.

1916 (6–1)   *Won:* Lake Forest 26–7, Chicago 10–0 (1st over Maroons in 12 games since 1901), Drake 40–6, Indiana 7–0, Iowa 20–13, Purdue 38–6.   *Lost:* unbeaten Ohio St. 23–3 in finale.

1917 (5–2)   *Won:* Lake Forest 48–0, Purdue 12–6, Michigan St. 39–6 (1st meeting since 1905), Iowa 25–14, Michigan 21–12 (1st meeting since 1901).   *Lost:* unbeaten Ohio St. 40–0, Chicago 7–0 in successive early games.

1926 (7–1)   *Won:* South Dakota 34–0, Carleton 31–3, Indiana 20–0, 21–0, Purdue 22–0, Chicago 38–7 (1st over Maroons in 7 games since 1918), Iowa 13–6.   *Lost:* Notre Dame 6–0 in mid-season.   *Stars:* HB Ralph "Moon" Baker (1st Northwestern consensus All-American), T Bob Johnson.   *Noteworthy:* got share of 1st Big 10 title in last year under Glenn Thistlethwaite.

1930 (7–1)   *Won:* Tulane 14–0, Ohio St. 19–2, Illinois 32–0, Centre 45–7, Minnesota 27–6, Indiana 25–0, Wisconsin 20–7.   *Lost:* unbeaten national champ Notre Dame 14–0 in finale.   *Stars:* FB Fayette "Reb" Russell, G Wade Woodworth, E Frank Baker, C Robert Clark.   *Noteworthy:* won share of 2nd Big 10 title.

1931 (7–1–1)   *Won:* Nebraska 19–7, UCLA 19–0, Ohio St. 10–0, Illinois 32–6, Minnesota 32–14,

Indiana 7–6, Iowa 19–0.   *Tied:* Notre Dame 0–0.   *Stars:* HB Ernest "Pug" Rentner, Ts Dallas Marvil and Jack Riley.   *Noteworthy:* Again got share of Big 10 title in 1st unbeaten season. Lost to Purdue 7–0 in postseason charity game.

1936 (7–1)   *Won:* Iowa 18–7, North Dakota St. 40–7, Ohio St. 14–13, Illinois 13–2, national champ Minnesota 6–0, Wisconsin 26–18, Michigan 9–0.   *Lost:* Notre Dame 26–6 in finale.   *Stars:* G Steve Reid, FB Don Geyer, E John Zitko.   *Noteworthy:* won 4th Big 10 title.

1940 (6–2)   *Won:* Syracuse 40–0, Ohio St. 6–3, Wisconsin 27–7, Indiana 20–7 (1st meeting since 1933), Illinois 32–14, Notre Dame 20–0 (1st over Irish since 1935).   *Lost:* unbeaten national co-champ Minnesota 13–12, Michigan 20–13.   *Stars:* T Alf Bauman, C Paul Hiemenz, B Ollie Hahnenstein.

1943 (6–2)   *Won:* Indiana 14–6, Great Lakes 13–0, Ohio St. 13–0, Minnesota 42–6, Wisconsin 41–0, Illinois 53–6.   *Lost:* Michigan 21–7, national champ Notre Dame 25–6.   *Stars:* TB Otto Graham (9 TDs rush, 819 yds and 13 TDs total off, 41.4-yd punting avg), E Herb Hein.

1948 (8–2)   *Won:* UCLA 19–0, Purdue 21–0, Minnesota 19–16, Syracuse 48–0, Ohio St. 21–7, Wisconsin 16–7, Illinois 20–7.   *Lost:* unbeaten national champ Michigan 28–0, unbeaten Notre Dame 12–7.   *Stars:* FB Art Murakowski (622 yds rush), C Alex Sarkisian.   *Noteworthy:* Led nation in pass defense. Made 1st postseason appearance, upsetting unbeaten California 20–14 in Rose Bowl on TDs by Frank Aschenbrenner (73-yd run), Murakowski (disputed TD on fumble at goal line), and Ed Tunnicliff (43-yd run).

1962 (7–2)   *Won:* South Carolina 37–20, Illinois 45–0, Minnesota 34–22, Ohio St. 18–14, Notre Dame 35–6, Indiana 26–21, Miami (Fla.) 29–7.   *Lost:* Wisconsin 37–6, Michigan St. 31–7 in consecutive late games.   *Stars:* QB Tom Myers (1,537 yds and 13 TDs pass), Paul Flatley (45 pass rec for 632 yds and 5 TDs), soph Steve Murphy (9 TDs), G Jack Cvercko.

Bowl Summary

Rose 1–0.

BOWL RECORD (1–0)

Regular Season	Bowl	Score	Opponent	Record
1948 (7–2)	Rose	20–14	California	(10–0)

CONFERENCE TITLES

Big 10—1926*, 1930*, 1931*, 1936.

TOP 20 AP AND UPI RANKING

1936	7	1941	11	1948	7	1959	U–16
1938	17	1943	9	1958	U–17	1962	U–16
1940	8						

MAJOR RIVALS

Northwestern has played at least 10 games with Beloit 12–3–4, Chicago 8–26–3, Illinois 36–45–5, Indiana 34–30–1, Iowa 14–39–3, Lake Forest 17–4–3, Michigan 11–44–2, Michigan St. 10–27, Minnesota 23–44–5, Notre Dame 7–35–2, Ohio St. 13–48–1, Purdue 21–40–1, Wisconsin 27–48–5. Record against Big 10 member Penn St. is 0–0 (no games played).

COACHES

Dean of Northwestern coaches is Lynn "Pappy" Waldorf (1935 national Coach of Year) with record of 49–45–7 for 1935–46, with 1 Big 10 title. Other top records for at least 3 years were by C.M. Hollister, 25–16–4 for 1899–1902; Walter McCornack, 25–6–4 for 1903–05; Glenn Thistlethwaite, 21–17–1 for 1922–26 with 1 Big 10 title; Dick Hanley, 36–26–4 for 1927–34 with 2 Big 10 titles and 1 team unbeaten in regular season; Bob Voigts, 33–39–1 for 1947–54 with 1 Rose Bowl champion; Ara Parseghian, 36–35–1 for 1956–63; and Alex Agase (1970 national Coach of Year), 32–58–1 for 1964–72.

MISCELLANEA

First game was loss to Lake Forest in 1882 . . . 1st win was over Lake Forest in 1882 . . . highest score was over Oshkosh Normal 97–0 in 1904 . . . high-est since W.W. II was over Michigan 55–24 in 1958 . . . biggest margin since W.W. II was 48–0 over Syracuse in 1948 and Illinois in 1970 . . . worst defeat was by Chicago 76–0 in 1899 . . . worst since 1900 (and highest ever against Wildcats) was by Iowa 78–6 in 1913 . . . worst since W.W. II was by Michigan 69–0 in 1975 . . . highest against since W.W. II was by Michigan St. 76–14 in 1989 . . . longest unbeaten string of 11 in 1935–36 ended by Notre Dame 26–6 . . . longest losing string of 34 in 1979–82 broken with win over Northern Illinois 31–6 . . . consensus All-Americans were Ralph Baker, B, 1926; Frank Baker, E, 1930; Jack Riley, T, Dallas Marvil, T, and Pug Rentner, B, 1931; Steve Reid, G, 1936; Alf Bauman, T, 1940; Max Morris, E, 1945; Ron Burton, B, 1959; and Jack Cvercko, G, 1962 . . . Academic All-Americans were Al Viola, G, 1956; Andy Cvercko, T, 1958; Larry Onesti, C, 1961; Paul Flatley, B, 1962; George Burman, E, 1963; Joe Zigulich, OG, 1970; Randolph Dean, E, 1976; Jim Ford, OT, 1980; Bob Dirkes, DL, and Todd Krehbiel, DB, 1986; Michael Baum, OT, 1986–88; and Ira Adler, K, 1990.

OHIO STATE (Buckeyes; Scarlet and Gray)

NOTABLE TEAMS

1892 (5–2)   *Won:* Akron 62–0, Marietta 80–0, Denison 32–0, Dayton YMCA 42–4, Kenyon 26–10. *Lost:* Oberlin 40–0 (1st meeting), Western Reserve 40–18.

1899 (9–0–1) *Won:* Otterbein 30–0, Wittenberg 28–0, Ohio U. 41–0 (1st meeting), Oberlin 6–0, Western Reserve 6–0 (1st in 6-game series begun in 1891), Marietta 17–0, Ohio Medical 12–0, Muskingum 34–0, Kenyon 5–0. *Tied:* Case 5–5 in 3rd game. *Noteworthy:* had 1st unbeaten season in 1st year under John Eckstorm.

1900 (8–1–1) *Won:* Otterbein 20–0, Ohio U. 20–0, Cincinnati 29–0, Ohio Wesleyan 47–0, Oberlin 17–0, West Virginia 27–0, Case 24–10, Kenyon 23–5. *Lost:* Ohio Medical 11–0. *Tied:* Michigan 0–0.

1902 (6–2–2) *Won:* Otterbein 5–0, Ohio U. 17–0, West Virginia 30–0, Marietta 34–0, Kenyon 51–5, Ohio Wesleyan 17–16. *Lost:* unbeaten national champ Michigan 86–0, Case 23–12. *Tied:* Illinois 0–0 (1st meeting), Indiana 6–6. *Noteworthy:* 1st year under Perry Hale.

1903 (8–3) *Won:* Otterbein 18–0, Wittenberg 28–0, Denison 24–5, Muskingum 30–0, Kenyon 59–0, West Virginia 34–6, Oberlin 27–5, Ohio Wesleyan 29–6. *Lost:* Case 12–0, unbeaten Michigan 36–0, Indiana 17–16.

1905 (8–2–2) *Won:* Heidelberg 28–0, Muskingum 40–0, Wittenberg 17–0, Denison 2–0, DePauw 32–6, Kenyon 23–0, Oberlin 36–0, Wooster 15–0. *Lost:* Michigan 40–0, Indiana 11–0. *Tied:* Otterbein 6–6, Case 0–0.

1906 (8–1) *Won:* Otterbein 41–0, Wittenberg 52–0, Muskingum 16–0, Oberlin 6–0, Kenyon 6–0, Case 9–0, Wooster 12–0, Ohio Medical 11–8. *Lost:* Michigan 6–0. *Noteworthy:* 1st year under A.E. Herrnstein.

1907 (7–2–1) *Won:* Otterbein 28–0, Muskingum 16–0, Denison 28–0, Kenyon 12–0, Oberlin 22–10, Heidelberg 23–0, Ohio Wesleyan 16–0. *Lost:* Michigan 22–0, Case 11–9. *Tied:* Wooster 6–6.

1909 (7–3) *Won:* Otterbein 14–0, Wittenberg 39–0, Wooster 74–0, Denison 29–0, Ohio Wesleyan 21–6, Vanderbilt 5–0, Kenyon 22–0. *Lost:* Michigan 33–6, Case 11–3, Oberlin 26–6. *Noteworthy:* Herrnstein's last team.

1910 (6–1–3) *Won:* Otterbein 14–5, Wittenberg 62–0, Cincinnati 23–0 (1st meeting since 1900), Western Reserve 6–0, Ohio Wesleyan 6–0, Kenyon 53–0. *Lost:* Case 14–10. *Tied:* unbeaten Michigan 3–3, Denison 5–5, Oberlin 0–0. *Noteworthy:* only year under Howard Jones.

1914 (5–2) *Won:* Ohio Wesleyan 16–2, Case 7–6, Indiana 13–3 (1st in 7-game series dating to 1901), Oberlin 39–0, Northwestern 27–0. *Lost:* unbeaten Illinois 37–0 (1st meeting since 1904), Wisconsin 7–6 in successive early games.

1915 (5–1–1) *Won:* Ohio Wesleyan 19–6, Case 14–0, Indiana 10–9, Oberlin 25–0, Northwestern 34–0. *Lost:* Wisconsin 21–0. *Tied:* unbeaten Illinois 3–3.

1916 (7–0) *Won:* Ohio Wesleyan 12–0, Oberlin 128–0, Illinois 7–6 (1st in 5-game series dating to 1902), Wisconsin 14–13 (1st in 4-game series begun in 1913), Indiana 46–7, Case 28–0, Northwestern 23–3. *Stars:* soph B Charles "Chic" Harley (1st Buckeye consensus All-American), T Robert Karch. *Noteworthy:* won 1st Big 10 title in 1st unbeaten season since 1899.

1917 (8–0–1) *Won:* Case 49–0, Ohio Wesleyan 53–0, Northwestern 40–0, Denison 67–0, Indiana 26–3, Wisconsin 16–3, Illinois 13–0, Camp Sherman 28–0. *Tied:* Auburn 0–0. *Stars:* Harley, E Charles Bolen. *Noteworthy:* repeated as Big 10 champ.

1919 (6–1) *Won:* Ohio Wesleyan 38–0, Cincinnati 46–0 (1st meeting since 1912), Kentucky 49–0, Michigan 13–3 (1st in 16-game series dating to 1897), Purdue 20–0 (1st meeting), Wisconsin 3–0. *Lost:* Illinois 9–7 in finale. *Star:* Harley.

1920 (7–1) *Won:* Ohio Wesleyan 55–0, Oberlin 37–0, Purdue 17–0, Wisconsin 13–7, Chicago 7–6 (1st meeting), Michigan 14–7, Illinois 7–0. *Stars:* G Iolas Huffman, B Gaylord Stinchcomb. *Noteworthy:* Took 3rd Big 10 title. Made 1st postseason appearance, losing to unbeaten national champ California 28–0 in Rose Bowl.

1921 (5–2) *Won:* Ohio Wesleyan 28–0, Minnesota 27–0 (1st meeting), Michigan 14–0, Chicago 7–0, Purdue 28–0. *Lost:* Oberlin 7–6 (1st to Yeomen in 9 games since 1909), Illinois 7–0. *Star:* T Huffman.

1926 (7–1) *Won:* Wittenberg 40–0 (1st meeting since 1910), Ohio Wesleyan 47–0, Columbia 32–7, Iowa 23–6 (1st in 5-game series begun in 1922), Chicago 18–0, Wilmington 13–7, Illinois 7–6. *Lost:* Michigan 17–16. *Stars:* Gs Edwin Hess and Edwin Hayes, B Martin Karow.

1933 (7–1) *Won:* Virginia 75–0, Vanderbilt 20–0, Northwestern 12–0, Indiana 21–0, Pennsylvania 20–7, Wisconsin 6–0, Illinois 7–6. *Lost:* unbeaten national champ Michigan 13–0. *Noteworthy:* Sam Willaman's last team.

1934 (7–1) *Won:* Indiana 33–0, Colgate 10–7, Northwestern 28–6, Western Reserve 76–0 (1st meeting since 1913), Chicago 33–0 (1st meeting since 1927), Michigan 34–0, Iowa 40–7 (1st meeting since 1929). *Lost:* Illinois 14–13 (1st to Illini since 1929). *Stars:* G Regis Monahan, E Merle Wendt. *Noteworthy:* 1st year under Francis A. Schmidt.

1935 (7–1) *Won:* Kentucky 19–6, Drake 85–7, Northwestern 28–7, Indiana 28–6, Chicago 20–13, Illinois 6–0, Michigan 38–0. *Lost:* Notre Dame 18–13 in mid-season. *Stars:* Wendt, G Inwood Smith, C Gomer Jones. *Noteworthy:* got share of 4th Big 10 title.

1937 (6–2) *Won:* Texas Christian (TCU) 14–0, Purdue 13–0 (1st meeting since 1924), Northwestern 7–0, Chicago 39–0, Illinois 19–0, Michigan 21–0. *Lost:* Southern California (USC) 13–12 (1st meeting), Indiana 10–0 (1st to Hoosiers in 11 games since 1924). *Star:* G Gust Zarnas.

1939 (6–2) *Won:* Missouri 19–0 (1st meeting), Northwestern 13–0, Minnesota 23–20 (1st meeting since 1931), Indiana 24–0, Chicago 61–0, Illinois 21–0. *Lost:* unbeaten Cornell 23–14, Michigan 21–14. *Stars:* B Don Scott (42.5-yd punting avg), E Esco Sarkkinen. *Noteworthy:* led nation in total off and won 5th Big 10 title.

1941 (6–1–1) *Won:* Missouri 12–7, USC 33–0, Purdue 16–14, Pittsburgh 21–14, Wisconsin 46–34 (1st meeting since 1933), Illinois 12–7. *Lost:* Northwestern 14–7. *Tied:* Michigan 20–20. *Noteworthy:* 1st year under Paul Brown.

1942 (9–1) *Won:* Fort Knox 59–0, Indiana 32–21, USC 28–12, Purdue 26–0, Northwestern 20–6, Pittsburgh 59–19, Illinois 44–20, Michigan 21–7 (1st over Wolverines since 1937), Iowa Seahawks 41–12. *Lost:* Wisconsin 17–7 (1st to Badgers in 8 games since 1918). *Stars:* Gene Fekete (10 TDs and 92 pts), B Les Horvath (6 TDs), E Robert Shaw, T Charles Csuri, G Lindell Houston. *Noteworthy:* won 6th Big 10 crown and got share of 1st national title.

1944 (9–0) *Won:* Missouri 54–0, Iowa 34–0 (1st meeting since 1934), Wisconsin 20–7, Great Lakes 26–6, Minnesota 34–14, Indiana 21–7, Pittsburgh 54–19, Illinois 26–12 (10th straight over Illini), Michigan 18–14. *Stars:* Heisman Trophy–winner Horvath (905 yds and 12 TDs rush, 345 yds pass), E Jack Dugger, G Bill Hackett, T Bill Willis. *Noteworthy:* nation's most-improved team won 7th Big 10 title in 1st unbeaten season since 1920 in 1st year under Carroll Widdoes.

1945 (7–2) *Won:* Missouri 47–6, Iowa 42–0, Wisconsin 12–0, Minnesota 20–7, Northwestern 16–14,

Pittsburgh 14–0, Illinois 27–2. *Lost:* Purdue 35–13, Michigan 7–3. *Stars:* FB Ollie Cline (936 yds and 9 TDs rush), G Warren Amling.

1949 (7–1–2) *Won:* Missouri 35–34, Indiana 46–7, Wisconsin 21–0, Northwestern 24–7, Pittsburgh 14–10, Illinois 30–17. *Lost:* Minnesota 27–0. *Tied:* USC 13–13, Michigan 7–7. *Stars:* B Gerry Krall (606 yds rush), Ray Hamilton (15 pass rec for 347 yds), Fred Morrison (9 TDs), G Jack Lininger. *Noteworthy:* Got share of 8th Big 10 title. Upset unbeaten California 17–14 in Rose Bowl on FG by Jimmy Hague with less than 2 minutes left; Morrison ran for 127 yds.

1954 (10–0) *Won:* Indiana 28–0, California 21–13, Illinois 40–7, Iowa 20–14, Wisconsin 31–14, Northwestern 14–7, Pittsburgh 26–0, Purdue 28–6, Michigan 21–7. *Stars:* HB Howard "Hopalong" Cassady (609 yds and 8 TDs rush, 12 pass rec for 137 yds), Bob Watkins (9 TDs), E Dean Dugger, Ts Dick Hilinski and Francis Machinsky. *Noteworthy:* Won 9th Big 10 title and got share of 2nd national crown in 1st undefeated season since 1944. Beat USC 20–7 in rainy, muddy Rose Bowl; Cassady ran for 92 yds and QB Bill Leggett ran for 67 yds and a TD and passed for 63 yds and another score.

1955 (7–2) *Won:* Nebraska 28–20, Illinois 27–12, Wisconsin 26–16, Northwestern 49–0, Indiana 20–13, Iowa 20–10, Michigan 17–0. *Lost:* Stanford 6–0, Duke 20–14 in early games. *Stars:* Heisman Trophy– and Maxwell Award–winner Cassady (958 yds rush, 15 TDs), G James Parker, C Ken Vargo. *Noteworthy:* won 2nd straight Big 10 title.

1957 (9–1) *Won:* Washington 35–7, Illinois 21–7, Indiana 56–0, Wisconsin 16–13, Northwestern 47–6, Purdue 20–7, Iowa 17–13, Michigan 31–14. *Lost:* TCU 18–14 in opener. *Stars:* Don Clark (737 yds rush), soph FB Bob White (552 yds rush), Frank Kremblas (8 TDs), G Aurelius Thomas, E Leo Brown. *Noteworthy:* Won 11th Big 10 title and share of 3rd national crown. Beat Oregon 10–7 in Rose Bowl on 1st quarter TD by Kremblas and 4th quarter FG by Don Sutherin; White ran for 82 yds.

1958 (6–1–2) *Won:* Southern Methodist (SMU) 23–20, Washington 12–7, Illinois 19–13, Indiana 49–8, Iowa 38–28, Michigan 20–14. *Lost:* Northwestern 21–0 (1st to Wildcats since 1948). *Tied:* Wisconsin 7–7, Purdue 14–14. *Stars:* Clark, White (859 yds and 12 TDs rush), E James Houston, T Jim Marshall.

1960 (7–2) *Won:* SMU 24–0, USC 20–0, Illinois 34–7, Wisconsin 34–7, Michigan St. 21–10, Indiana 36–7, Michigan 7–0. *Lost:* Purdue 24–21, Iowa 35–12. *Stars:* FB Bob Ferguson (853 yds and 13 TDs rush), QB Tom Matte (1,419 yds total off), Charles Bryant (17 pass rec for 336 yds), T Jim Tryer.

1961 (8–0–1) *Won:* UCLA 13–3, Illinois 44–0, Northwestern 10–0, Wisconsin 30–21, Iowa 29–13, Indiana 16–7, Oregon 22–12, Michigan 50–20. *Tied:* TCU 7–7 in opener. *Stars:* Maxwell Award–winner Ferguson (938 yds and 11 TDs rush), Bryant (15 pass rec for 270 yds), G Mike Ingram. *Noteworthy:* won 12th Big 10 title and got share of 4th national crown.

1964 (7–2) *Won:* SMU 27–8, Indiana 17–9, Illinois 26–0, USC 17–0, Wisconsin 28–3, Iowa 21–19, Northwestern 10–0. *Lost:* Penn St. 27–0, Michigan 10–0 (1st to Wolverines since 1959). *Stars:* LBs Dwight Kelley and Tom Bugel, DB Arnold Chonko (7 int), T Jim Davidson, G Dan Poretta, E Bill Spahr, soph Bo Rein (22 pass rec for 320 yds), Willard Sander (626 yds and 7 TDs rush).

1965 (7–2) *Won:* Washington 23–21, Illinois 28–14, Wisconsin 20–10, Minnesota 11–10 (1st meeting since 1950), Indiana 17–10, Iowa 38–0, Michigan 9–7. *Lost:* North Carolina 14–3, unbeaten national cochamp Michigan St. 32–7 in early games. *Stars:* QB Don Unverferth (1,061 yds pass), Rein (29 pass rec for 328 yds), Sander (8 TDs), Tom Barrington (554 yds rush), OT Doug Van Horn, C Ray Pryor, Kelley, LB John Fill.

1968 (10–0) *Won:* SMU 35–14, Oregon 21–6, Purdue 13–0, Northwestern 45–21, Illinois 31–24, Michigan St. 25–20, Wisconsin 43–8, Iowa 33–27, Michigan 50–14. *Stars:* FB Jim Otis (985 yds and 17 TDs rush), soph QB Rex Kern (1,506 yds total off), soph Bruce Jankowski (31 pass rec for 328 yds), OTs Dave Foley and Rufus Mayes, soph DB Jack Tatum. *Noteworthy:* Won 13th Big 10 title in 1st perfect season since 1954. Clinched 5th national title by beating undefeated USC 27–16 in Rose Bowl; Otis ran for 101 yds and a TD, Kern passed for 101 yds and 2 TDs (to Leo Hayden and Ray Gillian), and Jim Roman kicked 2 FGs.

1969 (8–1) *Won:* TCU 62–0, Washington 41–14, Michigan St. 54–21, Minnesota 34–7, Illinois 41–0, Northwestern 35–6, Wisconsin 62–7 (10th straight over Badgers), Purdue 42–14. *Lost:* Michigan 24–12 in finale. *Stars:* Otis (1,027 yds rush, 16 TDs), Kern (1,585 yds total off), Jankowski (23 pass rec for 404 yds), T Charles Hutchinson, C Brian Donovan, Tatum, DBs Ted Provost and Mike Sensibaugh (9 int), MG Jim Stillwagon, LB Doug Adams. *Noteworthy:* got share of 14th Big 10 title.

1970 (9–1) *Won:* Texas A&M 56–13, Duke 34–10, Michigan St. 29–0, Minnesota 28–8, Illinois 48–29, Northwestern 24–10, Wisconsin 24–7, Purdue 10–7, Michigan 20–9. *Stars:* Outland Trophy– and inaugural Lombardi Award–winner Stillwagon, Tatum, Sensibaugh (nation's leader with 8 int), DB Tim Anderson, FB John Brockington (1,142 yds and 17 TDs rush), Jankowski (12 pass rec for 235 yds), TE Jan White, T Dave Cheney, G Phil Strickland, C Tom DeLeone. *Noteworthy:* Won 3rd straight Big 10 title and got share of 6th national crown. Upset by Stanford 27–17 in Rose Bowl; Kern ran for 129 yds and Brockington ran for 101 yds and 2 TDs.

1972 (9–2) *Won:* Iowa 21–0, North Carolina 29–14, California 35–18, Illinois 26–7, Indiana 44–7, Wisconsin 28–20, Minnesota 27–19, Northwestern 27–14, Michigan 14–11. *Lost:* Michigan St. 19–12. *Stars:* FB Harold Henson (nation's scoring leader with 120 pts on 20 TDs), frosh TB Archie Griffin (772 yds rush, 1,012 all-purpose yds), QB Greg Hare (1,180 yds total off), Rick Galbos (11 pass rec for 235 yds), OT John Hicks, OG Charles Bonica, LB Randy Gradishar, DT George Hasenohri. *Noteworthy:* Got share of 16th Big 10 title. Lost to unbeaten national champ USC 42–17 in Rose Bowl; Griffin ran for 95 yds and Buckeyes TDs were scored by FB Randy Keith and John Bledsoe.

1973 (10–0–1) *Won:* Minnesota 56–7, TCU 37–3, Washington St. 27–3, Wisconsin 24–0, Indiana 37–7 (10th straight over Hoosiers), Northwestern 60–0, Illinois 30–0, Michigan St. 35–0, Iowa 55–13. *Tied:* unbeaten Michigan 10–10 in finale. *Stars:* Outland Trophy– and Lombardi Award–winner Hicks, OG Jim Kregel, OT Kurt Schumacher, Griffin (1,428 yds and 6 TDs rush), Bruce Elia (14 TDs), DE Van DeCree, Gradishar, LBs Vic Koegel and Rick Middleton, DT Pete Cusick, DB Neal Colzie. *Noteworthy:* Led nation in scoring defense (4.3-pt avg) and again got share of Big 10 title. Beat USC 42–21 in Rose Bowl; Griffin ran for 149 yds and a TD, soph FB Pete Johnson ran for 94 yds and 3 TDs, and soph QB Cornelius Greene passed for 129 yds and scored a TD and a 2-pt conversion.

1974 (10–2) *Won:* Minnesota 34–19, Oregon St. 51–10, SMU 28–9, Washington St. 42–7, Wisconsin 52–7 (15th straight over Badgers), Indiana 49–9, Northwestern 55–7, Illinois 49–7, Iowa 35–10 (10th straight over Hawkeyes), Michigan 12–10. *Lost:* Michigan St. 16–13. *Stars:* Heisman Trophy–winner Griffin (1,620 yds and 12 TDs rush), Greene (1,781 yds total off), Brian Baschnagel (19 pass rec for 244 yds), TE Doug France, Schumacher, C Steve Myers, DeCree, Cusick, Colzie (8 int), soph P Tom Skladany (45.6-yd avg). *Noteworthy:* Got share of 18th Big 10 title. Lost to national cochamp USC 18–17 in Rose Bowl as Griffin was held to 75 yds rush; Henson and Greene scored Buckeye TDs.
1975 (11–1) *Won:* Michigan St. 21–0, Penn St. 17–9 (1st meeting since 1964), North Carolina 32–7, UCLA 41–20, Iowa 49–0, Wisconsin 56–0, Purdue 35–6 (1st meeting since 1970), Indiana 24–14, Illinois 40–3, Minnesota 38–6, Michigan 21–14. *Stars:* Heisman Trophy– and Maxwell Award–winner Griffin (1,357 yds rush), Johnson (nation's leader with 150 pts on 25 TDs), Greene (1,584 yds total off), Baschnagel (24 pass rec for 362 yds), Myers, OG Ted Smith, OTs Scott Dannelley and soph Chris Ward, DBs Tim Fox and Craig Cassady (9 int), DE Bob Brudzinski, LB Ed Thompson, DT Nick Buonamici, Skladany (nation's leader with 46.7-yd punting avg). *Noteworthy:* Woody Hayes' 6th unbeaten team led nation in scoring (34-pt avg) and won 4th straight Big 10 title. Upset by UCLA 23–10 in rematch in Rose Bowl; Griffin ran for 93 yds, Johnson had 70 yds and a TD rush, and Tom Klaban kicked 42-yd FG.
1976 (9–2–1) *Won:* Michigan St. 49–21, Penn St. 12–7, Iowa 34–14, Wisconsin 30–20, Purdue 24–3, Indiana 47–7, Illinois 42–10, Minnesota 9–3. *Lost:* Missouri 22–21 (1st meeting since 1949, lst loss in 10-game series dating to 1939), Michigan 22–0. *Tied:* UCLA 10–10. *Stars:* Jeff Logan (1,248 yds rush), James Harrell (14 pass rec for 288 yds), Johnson (19 TDs), Ward, Brudzinski, Buonamici, soph LB Tom Cousineau, MG Aaron Brown, Skladany (42.4-yd punting avg). *Noteworthy:* Won share of 20th Big 10 title. Beat Colorado 27–10 in Orange Bowl; RB Ron Springs ran for 98 yds, QB Rod Gerald ran for 81 yds and a TD, and Cousineau made 13 tackles.
1977 (9–3) *Won:* Miami (Fla.) 10–0, Minnesota 38–7, SMU 35–7, Purdue 46–0, Iowa 27–6, Northwestern 35–15, Wisconsin 42–0, Illinois 35–0 (10th straight over Illini), Indiana 35–7. *Lost:* Oklahoma 29–28, Michigan 14–6. *Stars:* Ward, Springs (1,166 yds rush), Logan, Gerald (1,462 yds total off), Joel Payton (13 TDs), TE Jimmy Moore, Cousineau, Brown, DB Ray Griffin. *Noteworthy:* Got share of 6th straight Big 10 title. Lost to Alabama 35–6 in Sugar Bowl as Buckeyes were held to 263 yds total off and were intercepted 3 times; scored on 38-yd pass from Gerald to Harrell.
1979 (11–1) *Won:* Syracuse 31–8, Minnesota 21–17, Washington St. 45–29, UCLA 17–13, Northwestern 16–7, Indiana 47–6, Wisconsin 59–0 (20th straight over Badgers), Michigan St. 42–0, Illinois 44–7, Iowa 34–7 (15th straight over Hawkeyes), Michigan 18–15. *Stars:* soph QB Art Schlichter (1,816 yds and 14 TDs pass, 430 yds and 9 TDs rush), SE Doug Donley (37 pass rec for 800 yds), Calvin Murray (872 yds rush), OG Ken Fritz, K Vlade Janakievski (18 FGs, 97 pts), DBs Mike Guess and Vince Skillings, LB Jim Laughlin, DT Luther Henson. *Noteworthy:* Won 22nd Big 10 title in 1st year under Earle Bruce. Lost to unbeaten USC 17–16 in Rose Bowl; Schlichter passed for 297 yds and a TD (to frosh SE Gary Williams), and Janakievski kicked 3 FGs.
1980 (9–3) *Won:* Syracuse 31–21, Minnesota 47–0, Arizona St. 38–21, Northwestern 63–0, Indiana 27–17, Wisconsin 21–0, Michigan St. 48–16, Illinois 49–42, Iowa 41–7. *Lost:* UCLA 17–0, Michigan 9–3. *Stars:* Schlichter (1,930 yds and 15 TDs pass, 325 yds and 7 TDs rush), Donley (43 pass rec for 887 yds and 7 TDs), Williams (39 pass rec for 682 yds and 6 TDs), Murray (1,267 yds and rush, 21 pass rec for 204 yds, 8 TDs), soph FB Tim Spencer (577 yds and 8 TDs rush), QB Bob Atha (5 TDs rush), OG Joe Lukens, Janakievski (15 FGs, 90 pts), soph LB Marcus Marek, DT Jerome Foster, Skillings, DBs Todd Bell and Ray Ellis (5 int), P Tom Orosz (40.8-yd avg). *Noteworthy:* lost to Penn St. 31–19 in Fiesta Bowl; Schlichter passed for 302 yds and 3 TDs (2 to Donley, who caught 5 passes for 122 yds, and one to Williams, who caught 7 for 112 yds).
1981 (9–3) *Won:* Duke 34–13, Michigan St. 27–13, Stanford 24–19, Illinois 34–27, Indiana 29–10, Purdue 45–33, Northwestern 70–6, Michigan 14–9. *Lost:* Florida St. 36–27, Wisconsin 24–21 (1st to Badgers since 1959), Minnesota 35–31 (1st to Gophers in 13 games since 1966). *Stars:* Schlichter (2,551 yds and 17 TDs pass), Williams (50 pass rec

for 941 yds and 6 TDs), soph TE John Frank (45 pass rec for 449 yds), TB Spencer (1,217 yds and 12 TDs rush), Atha (13 FGs, 88 pts), Lukens, Marek. *Noteworthy:* Got share of 23rd Big 10 crown. Beat Navy 31–28 in Liberty Bowl; Schlichter passed for 159 yds and 2 TDs (to Williams and soph Cedric Anderson), James Gayle scored 2 TDs, and Spencer ran for 96 yds.

1982 (9–3) *Won:* Baylor 21–14, Michigan St. 31–10, Illinois 26–21 (15th straight over Illini), Indiana 49–25, Purdue 38–6, Minnesota 35–10, Northwestern 40–28, Michigan 24–14. *Lost:* Stanford 23–20, Florida St. 34–17, Wisconsin 6–0 in consecutive early games. *Stars:* Spencer (1,538 yds and 14 TDs rush), soph QB Mike Tomczak (1,602 yds pass), Williams (40 pass rec for 690 yds), Frank, Lukens, Marek, DT Jerome Foster. *Noteworthy:* beat Brigham Young (BYU) 47–17 in Holiday Bowl; Spencer ran for 167 yds and 2 TDs, Tomczak passed for 132 yds, and Gayle scored 2 TDs.

1983 (9–3) *Won:* Oregon 31–6, Oklahoma 24–14, Minnesota 69–18, Purdue 33–22, Michigan St. 21–11, Wisconsin 45–27, Indiana 56–17 (20th straight over Hoosiers), Northwestern 55–7 (10th straight over Wildcats). *Lost:* Iowa 20–14 (1st to Hawkeyes in 17 games since 1962), Illinois 17–13 (1st to Illini since 1967), Michigan 24–21. *Stars:* Tomczak (2,192 yds total off, 13 TDs pass), Frank (45 pass rec for 641 yds and 6 TDs), soph RB Keith Byars (1,126 yds rush, 21 pass rec for 338 yds, 20 TDs), LB Rowland Tatum, DB Garcia Lane. *Noteworthy:* beat Pittsburgh 28–23 (1st meeting since 1954) in Fiesta Bowl; Tomczak passed for 226 yds (including 39-yd winning TD pass to SE Thad Jemison with 39 seconds left) and scored a TD, Jemison had 8 pass rec for 131 yds, and Byars scored 2 TDs (one on 99-yd kickoff return).

1984 (9–3) *Won:* Oregon St. 22–14, Washington St. 44–0, Iowa 45–26, Minnesota 35–22, Illinois 45–38, Michigan St. 23–20, Indiana 50–7, Northwestern 52–3, Michigan 21–6. *Lost:* Purdue 28–23, Wisconsin 16–14. *Stars:* Byars (37 pass rec for 453 yds, nation's leader with 1,655 yds rush, 144 pts on 24 TDs, and 2,284 all-purpose yds), Tomczak (1,952 yds pass), soph SE Cris Carter (32 pass rec for 476 yds and 7 TDs), Mike Lanese (41 pass rec for 618 yds), OG Jim Lachey, C Kirk Lowdermilk, OT Mark Krerowicz, LB Tom Johnson, frosh P Tom Tupa (47-yd avg). *Noteworthy:* Won 24th Big 10 title. Lost to USC 20–17 in Rose Bowl; Byars ran

for 109 yds, Tomczak passed for 290 yds and a TD (to Carter, who caught 9 for 172 yds), K Rich Spangler had 3 FGs (including 52-yarder), and frosh LB Chris Spielman made 12 tackles.

1985 (9–3) *Won:* Pittsburgh 10–7, Colorado 36–13, Washington St. 48–32, Indiana 48–7, Purdue 41–27, Minnesota 23–19, Iowa 22–13, Northwestern 35–17. *Lost:* Illinois 31–28, Wisconsin 12–7, Michigan 27–17. *Stars:* QB Jim Karsatos (2,311 yds and 19 TDs pass), Carter (53 pass rec for 879 yds and 8 TDs), John Wooldridge (820 yds rush), Spangler (13 FGs, 78 pts), Spielman, Johnson, Tupa (42.5-yd punting avg). *Noteworthy:* beat BYU 10–7 in Citrus Bowl as Buckeyes intercepted 4 passes and Karsatos (196 yds pass) passed to Carter for winning TD with 7:34 left; Wooldridge ran for 92 yds.

1986 (10–3) *Won:* Colorado 13–10, Utah 64–6, Illinois 14–0, Indiana 24–22, Purdue 39–11, Minnesota 33–0, Iowa 31–10, Northwestern 30–9, Wisconsin 30–17. *Lost:* Alabama 16–10, Washington 40–7, Michigan 26–24. *Stars:* Karsatos (2,212 yds and 13 TDs pass), Carter (65 pass rec for 1,066 yds and 11 TDs), Vince Workman (1,030 yds and 8 TDs rush), frosh TB Jaymes Bryant (656 yds rush), TE Ed Taggart, C Bob Maggs, soph OG Jeff Uhlenhake, Tupa (43.6-yd punting avg), Spielman, LB Eric Kumerow, DB Sonny Gordon (7 int). *Noteworthy:* Got share of 25th Big 10 title. Beat Texas A&M 28–12 in Cotton Bowl as Buckeyes intercepted 5 passes; Karsatos passed for 195 yds, Nate Harris had 6 pass rec for 105 yds, Spielman scored on 24-yd pass int return, and Michael Kee scored on 49-yd pass int return.

1989 (8–4) *Won:* Oklahoma St. 37–13, Boston College 34–29, Indiana 35–31, Purdue 21–3, Minnesota 41–37, Northwestern 52–27, Iowa 28–0, Wisconsin 42–22. *Lost:* USC 42–3, Illinois 34–14, Michigan 28–18. *Stars:* QB Greg Frey (1,900 yds and 12 TDs pass), Jeff Graham (32 pass rec for 608 yds), FL Bobby Olive (23 pass rec for 379 yds), TE Jim Palmer (28 pass rec for 308 yds), TBs Carlos Snow (990 yds rush, 13 TDs) and frosh Dante Lee (503 yds and 6 TDs rush), soph FB Scottie Graham (977 yds rush, 11 TDs), OT Joe Staysniak, OG Jeff Davidson, LB Derek Isaman, soph P Jeff Bohlman (40.3-yd avg). *Noteworthy:* lost to Auburn 31–14 in Hall of Fame Bowl after taking early 14–3 lead; Frey passed for 232 yds and a TD.

1991 (8–4) *Won:* Arizona 38–14, Louisville 23–15, Washington St. 33–19, Wisconsin 31–16, Northwestern 34–3, Michigan St. 27–17, Minnesota 35–6 (10th straight over Gophers), Indiana 20–16. *Lost:* Illinois 10–7, Iowa 16–9, Michigan 31–3. *Stars:* Snow (772 yds and 8 TDs rush), QB Kent Graham (1,018 yds pass), FL Bernard Edwards (25 pass rec for 364 yds), SE Brian Stablein (25 pass rec for 363 yds), soph TB Butler By'not'e (631 yds and 5 TDs rush), Scottie Graham (5 TDs rush), soph OT Alan Kline, DE Alonzo Spellman, LBs Steve Tovar and soph Jason Simmons, soph DB Roger Harper. *Noteworthy:* lost to Syracuse 24–17 in Hall of Fame Bowl; QB Kirk Herbstreit passed for 174 yds and Buckeyes scored TDs on 2-yd run by Snow and blocked punt recovered in end zone by DB Foster Paulk.

1992 (8–3–1) *Won:* Louisville 20–19, Bowling Green 17–6, Syracuse 35–12, Northwestern 31–7, Michigan St. 27–17, Iowa 38–15, Minnesota 17–0, Indiana 27–10. *Lost:* Wisconsin 20–16 (1st to Badgers since 1987), Illinois 18–16 in successive mid-season games. *Tied:* unbeaten Michigan 13–13 in finale. *Stars:* Herbstreit (1,794 yds pass), Stablein (51 pass rec for 612 yds), soph SE Chris Sanders (22 pass rec for 360 yds), TE Cedric Saunders (26 pass rec for 326 yds), soph TB Robert Smith (707 yds and 8 TDs rush), TBs Raymont Harris (5 TDs rush) and frosh Eddie George (5 TDs rush), K Tim Williams (16 FGs, 77 pts), MG Greg Smith, frosh DT Dan Wilkinson, Tovar, Harper. *Noteworthy:* lost to Georgia 21–14 in Florida Citrus Bowl; TB Robert Smith ran for 112 yds and 2 TDs, and Herbstreit passed for 110 yds.

Bowl Summary

Cotton 1–0; Fiesta 1–1; Florida Citrus 1–1; Gator 0–1; Hall of Fame 0–2; Holiday 1–0; Liberty 1–1; Orange 1–0; Rose 5–7; Sugar 0–1.

Bowl Record (11–14)

Regular Season	Bowl	Score	Opponent	Record
1920 (7–0)	Rose	0–28	California	(8–0)
1949 (6–1–2)	Rose	17–14	California	(10–0)
1954 (9–0)	Rose	20–7	USC	(8–3)
1957 (8–1)	Rose	10–7	Oregon	(7–3)
1968 (9–0)	Rose	27–16	USC	(9–0–1)
1970 (9–0)	Rose	17–27	Stanford	(8–3)
1972 (9–1)	Rose	17–42	USC	(11–0)
1973 (9–0–1)	Rose	42–21	USC	(9–1–1)
1974 (10–1)	Rose	17–18	USC	(9–1–1)
1975 (11–0)	Rose	10–23	UCLA	(8–2–1)
1976 (8–2–1)	Orange	27–10	Colorado	(8–3)
1977 (9–2)	Sugar	6–35	Alabama	(10–1)
1978 (7–3–1)	Gator	15–17	Clemson	(10–1)
1979 (11–0)	Rose	16–17	USC	(10–0–1)
1980 (9–2)	Fiesta	19–31	Penn State	(9–2)
1981 (8–3)	Liberty	31–28	Navy	(7–3–1)
1982 (8–3)	Holiday	47–17	BYU	(8–3)
1983 (8–3)	Fiesta	28–23	Pittsburgh	(8–2–1)
1984 (9–2)	Rose	17–20	USC	(8–3)
1985 (8–3)	Fla. Citrus	10–7	BYU	(11–2)
1986 (9–3)	Cotton	28–12	Texas A&M	(9–2)
1989 (8–3)	Hall of Fame	14–31	Auburn	(9–2)
1990 (7–3–1)	Liberty	11–23	Air Force	(6–5)
1991 (8–3)	Hall of Fame	17–24	Syracuse	(9–2)
1992 (8–2–1)	Fla. Citrus	14–21	Georgia	(9–2)

CONFERENCE TITLES

Big 10—1916, 1917, 1920, 1935*, 1939, 1942, 1944, 1949*, 1954, 1955, 1957, 1961, 1968, 1969*, 1970, 1972*, 1973*, 1974*, 1975, 1976*, 1977*, 1979, 1981*, 1984, 1986*.

TOP 20 AP AND UPI (USA TODAY/CNN SINCE 1991) RANKING

1937	13	1954	1–2	1968	1–1	1980	15–15
1939	15	1955	6–5	1969	4–5	1981	15–12
1941	13	1956	15–U	1970	5–2	1982	12–12
1942	1	1957	2–1	1972	9–3	1983	9–8
1944	2	1958	8–7	1973	2–3	1984	13–12
1945	12	1960	8–8	1974	4–3	1985	14–11
1949	6	1961	2–2	1975	4–4	1986	7–6
1950	14–10	1962	U–13	1976	6–5	1992	18–18
1952	17–15	1964	9–9	1977	11–12		
1953	U–20	1965	U–11	1979	4–4		

MAJOR RIVALS

Ohio St. has played at least 10 games with Case 11–10–2, Chicago 10–2–2, Cincinnati 9–2, Denison 14–1–2, Illinois 51–26–4, Indiana 53–12–5, Iowa 35–13–3, Kenyon 17–6, Michigan 33–50–6, Michigan St. 17–10, Minnesota 30–6, Missouri 8–1–1, Northwestern 48–13–1, Oberlin 13–9–3, Ohio Wesleyan 26–2–1, Otterbein 13–2–3, Pittsburgh 15–5–1, Purdue 27–10–2, Southern California 9–11–1, Western Reserve 5–6–1, Wisconsin 45–13–4, Wittenberg 12–3. Record against Big 10 foe Penn St. is 2–6.

COACHES

Dean of Ohio St. coaches is Woodrow W. "Woody" Hayes (1957, 1968, 1975 national Coach of Year) with record of 205–61–10 for 1951–78, including 13 Big 10 titles, 11 bowl teams, 6 teams unbeaten in regular season, and 5 national champions. Other top records for at least 3 years were by John B.C. Eckstorm, 22–4–3 for 1899–1901 with 1 unbeaten team; A.E. Herrnstein, 28–10–1 for 1906–09; John W. Wilce, 78–33–9 for 1913–28 with 3 Big 10 titles, 1 Rose Bowl team, and 3 teams unbeaten in regular season; Sam S. Willaman, 26–10–5 for 1929–33; Francis A. Schmidt, 39–16–1 for 1934–40 with 2 Big 10 titles; Paul E. Brown, 18–8–1 for 1941–43 with 1 Big 10 and national champion; Wesley E. Fesler, 21–13–3 for 1947–50 with 1 Big 10 and Rose Bowl champion; Earle Bruce (1979 national Coach of Year), 81–26–1 for 1979–87 with 4 Big 10 titles, 8 bowl teams, and 1 team unbeaten in regular season; and John Cooper, 35–21–3 for 1988–92 with 4 bowl teams. Carroll C. Widdoes, 16–2 for 1944–45 with 1 Big 10 title, was 1944 national Coach of Year.

MISCELLANEA

First game was win over Ohio Wesleyan 20–14 in 1890 . . . highest score was over Oberlin 128–0 in 1916 . . . highest since W.W. II was over Iowa 83–21 in 1950 . . . biggest margin since W.W. II was over Northwestern 63–0 in 1980 . . . worst defeat was by Michigan 86–0 in 1902 . . . worst since W.W. II was by Michigan 58–6 in 1946 . . . longest win streak of 22 in 1967–69 ended by Michigan 24–12 . . . 19-game unbeaten string in 1973–74 ended by Michigan St. 16–13 . . . 18-game unbeaten string in 1898–1900 ended by Ohio Medical 11–6 . . . longest losing string of 5 occurred twice, in the 1890s . . . consensus All-Americans were Charles "Chic"

Harley, B, 1916–18; Charles Bolen, E, 1917; Gaylord Stinchcomb, B, 1920; Iolas Huffman, G, 1920, T, 1921; Ed Hess, G, 1925; Wes Fesler, E, 1928–30; Gomer Jones, C, 1935; Esco Sarkkinen, E, 1939; Jack Dugger, E, Bill Hackett, G, and Les Horvath, B, 1944; Warren Amling, G, 1945, T, 1946; Vic Janowicz, B, 1950; Howard "Hopalong" Cassady, B, 1954–55; Jim Parker, G, 1956; Bob White, B, 1958; Bob Ferguson, B, 1960–61; Dave Foley, OT, 1968; Jim Otis, B, 1969; Jim Stillwagon, MG, and Jack Tatum, DB, 1969–70; Randy Gradishar, LB, 1972–73; John Hicks, OT, 1973; Kurt Schumacher, OT, and Steve Myers, C, 1974; Archie Griffin, RB, 1974–75; Ted Smith, G, and Tim Fox, DB, 1975; Bob Brudzinski, DE, 1976; Chris Ward, OT, 1976–77; Tom Cousineau, LB, 1977–78; Ken Fritz, G, 1979; Marcus Marek, LB, 1982; Jim Lachey, G, and Keith Byars, RB, 1984; Cris Carter, WR, 1986; Chris Spielman, LB, 1986–87; and Tom Tupa, P, 1987 . . . Academic All-Americans were John Borton, B, 1952; Dick Hilinski, T, 1954; Bob White, B, 1958; Tom Perdue, E, 1961; Bill Ridder, MG, 1965; Dave Foley, OT, 1966, 1968; Mark Stier, LB, 1968; Bill Urbanik, DT, 1969; Rick Simon, OG, 1971; Randy Gradishar, LB, 1973; Brian Baschnagel, RB, 1974–75; Bill Lukens, OG, and Pete Johnson, RB, 1976; Jeff Logan, RB, 1977; Marcus Marek, LB, 1980; Joseph Smith, OT, 1982; John Frank, TE, 1982–83; David Crecelius, DL, 1984; Michael Lanese, WR, 1984–85; Joseph Staysniak, OL, 1989; and Leonard Hartman, OL, and Gregory Smith, DL, 1992 . . . Heisman Trophy winners were Les Horvath, QB, 1944; Vic Janowicz, HB, 1950; Howard Cassady, HB, 1955; and Archie Griffin, HB, 1974–75 . . . Maxwell Award winners were Howard Cassady, HB, 1955; Bob Ferguson, FB, 1961; and Archie Griffin, HB, 1975 . . . Outland Trophy winners were Jim Parker, G, 1956; Jim Stillwagon, MG, 1970; and John Hicks, OT, 1973 . . . Lombardi Award winners were Jim Stillwagon, MG, initial award in 1970; John Hicks, OT, 1973; and Chris Spielman, LB, 1987.

PENN STATE (Nittany Lions; Blue and White)

NOTABLE TEAMS

1891 (6–2) *Won:* Lafayette 14–4, Swarthmore 44–0, Franklin & Marshall 26–6, Gettysburg 18–0

(1st meeting), Dickinson 2–0 (forfeit), Haverford 58–0. *Lost:* Lehigh 24–4, Bucknell 12–10.
1892 (5–1) *Won:* Wyoming Seminary 40–0, Pittsburgh A.C. 16–0, Bucknell 18–0, Lafayette 18–0, Dickinson 16–0. *Lost:* Pennsylvania 20–0 in opener. *Noteworthy:* 1st year under George Hoskins.
1893 (4–1) *Won:* Virginia 6–0, Pittsburgh 32–0 (1st meeting), Bucknell 36–18, Pittsburgh A.C. 12–0. *Lost:* Penn 18–6.
1894 (6–0–1) *Won:* Gettysburg 60–0, Lafayette 72–0, Bucknell 12–6, Washington & Jefferson 6–0 (1st meeting), Oberlin 9–6, Pittsburgh A.C. 14–0. *Tied:* Navy 6–6 (1st meeting). *Noteworthy:* 1st unbeaten season since 2-game schedule of 1887.
1902 (7–3) *Won:* Dickinson Seminary 27–0, Pittsburgh 27–0, Villanova 32–0 (1st meeting), Susquehanna 55–0, Navy 6–0, Gettysburg 37–0, Dickinson 23–0. *Lost:* Pennsylvania 17–0, unbeaten Yale 11–0, Steelton YMCA 6–5. *Noteworthy:* last year under W.N. "Pop" Golden.
1905 (8–3) *Won:* Lebanon Valley 23–0 (1st meeting), California St. 29–0, Gettysburg 18–0, Villanova 29–0, Geneva 73–0, Dickinson 6–0, West Virginia 6–0, Pittsburgh 6–0. *Lost:* Carlisle Indians 11–0, unbeaten Yale 12–0, Navy 11–5.
1906 (8–1–1) *Won:* Lebanon Valley 24–0, Allegheny 26–0, Carlisle 4–0, Navy 5–0, Bellefonte Academy 12–0, Dickinson 6–0, West Virginia 10–0, Pittsburgh 6–0. *Lost:* unbeaten Yale 10–0. *Tied:* Gettysburg 0–0. *Star:* C Walter "Mother" Dunn (Lions' 1st consensus All-American).
1909 (5–0–2) *Won:* Grove City 31–0, Geneva 46–0, Bucknell 33–0, West Virginia 40–0, Pittsburgh 5–0. *Tied:* Carlisle 8–8, Penn 3–3. *Star:* frosh FB Pete Mauthe (119 pts). *Noteworthy:* had 1st unbeaten season since 1894 in 1st year under Bill Hollenback.
1911 (8–0–1) *Won:* Geneva 57–0, Gettysburg 31–0, Cornell 5–0, Villanova 18–0, Pennsylvania 22–6 (1st in 18-game series dating to 1890), St. Bonaventure 46–0, Colgate 17–9 (1st meeting), Pittsburgh 3–0. *Tied:* unbeaten Navy 0–0. *Stars:* Mauthe, E Dexter Very.
1912 (8–0) *Won:* Carnegie Tech 41–0, Washington & Jefferson 30–0 (1st meeting since 1904), Cornell 29–6, Gettysburg 25–0, Pennsylvania 14–0, Villanova 71–0, Ohio St. 37–0 (1st meeting), Pittsburgh 38–0. *Stars:* Mauthe, Very, QB E.E. "Shorty" Miller.

1915 (7–2) *Won:* Westminster 26–0, Lebanon Valley 13–0 (1st meeting since 1907), Penn 13–3, Gettysburg 27–12, West Virginia Wesleyan 28–0, Lehigh 7–0, Lafayette 33–3. *Lost:* Harvard 13–0, unbeaten Pittsburgh 20–0. *Star:* soph E Bob Higgins. *Noteworthy:* 1st year under Dick Harlow.

1916 (8–2) *Won:* Susquehanna 27–0, Westminster 55–0, Bucknell 50–7, West Virginia Wesleyan 39–0, Gettysburg 48–2, Geneva 79–0, Lehigh 10–7, Lafayette 40–0. *Lost:* Pennsylvania 15–0, unbeaten national champ Pittsburgh 31–0.

1919 (7–1) *Won:* Gettysburg 33–0, Bucknell 9–0, Ursinus 48–7, Pennsylvania 10–0, Lehigh 20–7, Cornell 20–0 (1st meeting since 1912), Pittsburgh 20–0 (1st over Panthers since 1912). *Lost:* Dartmouth 19–13. *Star:* Higgins.

1920 (7–0–2) *Won:* Muhlenberg 27–7, Gettysburg 13–0, Dartmouth 14–7 (1st homecoming), N.C. State 41–0 (1st meeting), Lebanon Valley 109–7, Pennsylvania 28–7, Nebraska 20–0 (1st meeting). *Tied:* Lehigh 7–7, unbeaten Pittsburgh 0–0 in last 2 games. *Star:* HB Charley Way. *Noteworthy:* 1st unbeaten season since 1912.

1921 (8–0–2) *Won:* Lebanon Valley 53–0, Gettysburg 24–0 (10th straight over Bullets), N.C. State 35–0, Lehigh 28–7, Georgia Tech 28–7, Carnegie Tech 28–7, Navy 13–7 (1st meeting since 1913), Washington 21–7. *Tied:* Harvard 21–21, Pittsburgh 0–0. *Star:* HB Glenn Killinger.

1922 (6–4–1) *Won:* St. Bonaventure 54–0, William & Mary 27–7, Gettysburg 20–0, Lebanon Valley 32–6, Middlebury 33–0, Carnegie Tech 10–0. *Lost:* Navy 14–0, Pennsylvania 7–6, Pittsburgh 14–0. *Tied:* Syracuse 0–0 (1st meeting). *Noteworthy:* made 1st bowl appearance, losing to Southern California (USC) 14–3 in Rose Bowl after taking early 3–0 lead on 20-yd FG by Mike Palm.

1923 (6–2–1) *Won:* Lebanon Valley 58–0, N.C. State 16–0, Gettysburg 20–0, Navy 21–3, Georgia Tech 7–0, Pennsylvania 21–0. *Lost:* Syracuse 10–0, Pittsburgh 20–3. *Tied:* West Virginia 13–13 (in New York, 1st meeting since 1909). *Stars:* HB Harry Wilson, G Joe Bedenk.

1927 (6–2–1) *Won:* Lebanon Valley 27–0, Gettysburg 34–13, Pennsylvania 20–0, Syracuse 9–6 (1st in 6-game series begun in 1922), Lafayette 40–6 (1st meeting since 1916), George Washington 13–0. *Lost:* Bucknell 13–7 (1st to Bison in 8 games since

1899), unbeaten Pittsburgh 30–0. *Tied:* New York U. 13–13.

1939 (5–1–2) *Won:* Bucknell 13–3, Lehigh 49–7, Maryland 12–0, Pennsylvania 10–0, Pittsburgh 10–0 (1st over Panthers in 17 games since 1919). *Lost:* unbeaten Cornell 47–0. *Tied:* Syracuse 6–6, Army 14–14 (1st meeting since 1900).

1940 (6–1–1) *Won:* Bucknell 9–0, West Virginia 17–13 (1st meeting since 1931), Lehigh 34–0, Temple 18–0 (1st meeting since 1932), South Carolina 12–0, New York U. 25–0. *Lost:* Pittsburgh 20–7. *Tied:* Syracuse 13–13. *Star:* C Leon Gajecki.

1941 (7–2) *Won:* Bucknell 27–13, Lehigh 40–6, New York U. 42–0, Syracuse 34–19, West Virginia 7–0, Pittsburgh 31–7, South Carolina 19–12. *Lost:* Colgate 7–0 (1st meeting since 1932), Temple 14–0.

1942 (6–1–1) *Won:* Bucknell 14–7, Lehigh 19–3, Colgate 13–10, Syracuse 18–13, Pennsylvania 13–7, Pittsburgh 14–6. *Lost:* West Virginia 24–0. *Tied:* Cornell 0–0.

1946 (6–2) *Won:* Bucknell 48–6, Syracuse 9–0, Colgate 6–2, Fordham 68–0, Temple 26–0, Navy 12–7. *Lost:* Michigan St. 19–16, Pittsburgh 14–7. *Star:* soph TB/DB Elwood Petchel (7 TDs, 4 int).

1947 (9–0–1) *Won:* Washington St. 27–6, Bucknell 54–0, Fordham 75–0, Syracuse 40–0, West Virginia 21–14, Colgate 46–0, Temple 7–0, Navy 20–7, Pittsburgh 29–0. *Stars:* Petchel, Bs Larry Joe and soph Fran Rogel (6 TDs), T Negley Norton, G Steve Suhey, soph Bill Luther (5 int), Joe Colone (40-yd punting avg). *Noteworthy:* Won 1st Lambert Trophy and led nation in total defense, rush defense (record low 17 yds per game) and scoring defense (3-pt avg) in 1st unbeaten season since 1921. Tied unbeaten Southern Methodist (SMU) 13–13 in Cotton Bowl; Rogel ran for 95 yds and Petchel threw TD passes to Larry Cooney and Wally Triplett.

1948 (7–1–1) *Won:* Bucknell 35–0 (10th straight over Bison), Syracuse 34–14, West Virginia 37–7, Colgate 32–13, Pennsylvania 13–0 (1st meeting since 1942), Temple 47–0, Washington St. 7–0. *Lost:* Pittsburgh 7–0. *Tied:* Michigan St. 14–14. *Stars:* Rogel (602 yds and 5 TDs rush), Triplett (6 TDs), Petchel (9 TDs pass, 4 int), E Sam Tamburo (17 pass rec for 301 yds). *Noteworthy:* last year under Bob Higgins.

1952 (7–2–1) *Won:* Temple 20–13, William & Mary 35–23, West Virginia 35–21, Nebraska 10–0,

Pennsylvania 14–7, Rutgers 7–6, Pittsburgh 17–0. *Lost:* unbeaten national champ Michigan St. 34–7, Syracuse 25–7. *Tied:* Purdue 20–20. *Stars:* E Jesse Arnelle (33 pass rec for 291 yds), Jack Sherry (8 int), Don Eyer (8 int).

1954 (7–2) *Won:* Illinois 14–12 (1st meeting), Syracuse 13–0, Virginia 34–7, Pennsylvania 35–13, Holy Cross 39–7, Rutgers 37–14, Pittsburgh 13–0. *Lost:* West Virginia 19–14, Texas Christian (TCU) 20–7 in consecutive mid-season games. *Star:* B Lenny Moore (13 TDs, 1,082 yds and 11 TDs rush, 1,582 all-purpose yds, 6 int).

1956 (6–2–1) *Won:* Pennsylvania 34–0, Holy Cross 43–0, Ohio St. 7–6 (1st meeting since 1912), West Virginia 16–6, Boston U. 40–7, N.C. State 14–7 (1st meeting since 1924). *Lost:* Army 14–7, Syracuse 13–9. *Tied:* Pittsburgh 7–7. *Stars:* Billy Kane (544 yds and 7 TDs rush, 16 pass rec for 232 yds), G Sam Valentine, QB/S Milt Plum (7 int).

1959 (9–2) *Won:* Missouri 19–8, Virginia Military Institute (VMI) 21–0, Colgate 58–20 (1st meeting

QB Rich Lucas, 1957–59

since 1948), Army 17–11 (1st over Cadets in 9 games since 1899), Boston U. 21–12, Illinois 20–9, West Virginia 28–10, Holy Cross 46–0. *Lost:* unbeaten national champ Syracuse 20–18, Pittsburgh 22–7 in late games. *Stars:* Maxwell Award–winning QB/DB Rich Lucas (913 yds and 5 TDs pass, 325 yds and 6 TDs rush, 5 int), Jim Kerr (6 TDs). *Noteworthy:* beat Alabama 7–0 (1st meeting) in inaugural Liberty Bowl, scoring in 2nd quarter on 18-yd pass from soph QB Galen Hall to soph HB Roger Kochman.

1960 (7–3) *Won:* Boston U. 20–0, Army 27–16, West Virginia 34–13, Maryland 28–9 (1st meeting since 1944), Holy Cross 33–8, Pittsburgh 14–3. *Lost:* Missouri 21–8, Syracuse 21–15, Illinois 10–8. *Star:* Kerr (8 TDs). *Noteworthy:* beat Oregon 41–12 in Liberty Bowl; Dick Hoak scored 2 TDs and passed for another.

1961 (8–3) *Won:* Navy 20–10, Boston U. 32–0, Syracuse 14–0, California 33–16, West Virginia 20–6, Holy Cross 34–14, Pittsburgh 47–26. *Lost:* Miami (Fla.) 25–8 (1st meeting), Army 10–6, Maryland 21–17 (1st in 8-game series dating to 1917). *Stars:* Hall (1,013 yds and 11 TDs total off), Kochman (9 TDs, 666 yds rush, 1,144 all-purpose yds), soph Junior Powell (15 pass rec for 332 yds), Jim Schwab (16 pass rec for 257 yds), E Bob Mitinger. *Noteworthy:* Won 2nd Lambert Trophy. Beat Georgia Tech 30–15 in Gator Bowl; Hall passed for 175 yds and 3 TDs, and Kochman ran for 76 yds and caught a TD pass.

1962 (9–2) *Won:* Navy 41–7, Air Force 20–6, Rice 18–7, Syracuse 20–19, California 23–21, Maryland 23–7, West Virginia 34–6, Holy Cross 48–20, Pittsburgh 16–0. *Lost:* Army 9–6. *Stars:* Kochman (8 TDs, 652 yds rush, 1,056 all-purpose yds), QB Pete Liske (1,037 yds pass, 16 TDs total off), Powell (32 pass rec for 303 yds, 5 int), E Dave Robinson, P Chuck Raisig (41.4-yd avg). *Noteworthy:* Again won Lambert Trophy. Lost to Florida 17–7 in Gator Bowl; Liske scored Lions' TD on 1-yd run.

1963 (7–3) *Won:* Oregon 17–7, UCLA 17–14, Rice 28–7, West Virginia 20–9, Maryland 17–15, Ohio St. 10–7, Holy Cross 28–14. *Lost:* Army 10–7, Syracuse 9–0, Pittsburgh 22–21. *Stars:* Liske (1,117 yds pass, 10 TDs total off), Dick Anderson (21 pass rec for 229 yds).

1967 (8–2–1) *Won:* Miami (Fla.) 17–8 (1st meeting since 1961), Boston College 50–28, West Virginia 21–14, Syracuse 29–20 (1st over Orange since 1962),

Maryland 38–3, N.C. State 13–8 (1st meeting since 1956), Ohio U. 35–14, Pittsburgh 42–6. *Lost:* Navy 23–22, UCLA 17–15 in early games. *Stars:* QB Tom Sherman (1,616 yds and 13 TDs pass), Jack Curry (41 pass rec for 681 yds), TE Ted Kwalick (33 pass rec for 563 yds), soph RB Charlie Pittman (580 yds rush, 7 TDs), Don Abbey (9 TDs, 88 pts), soph LB Dennis Onkotz (6 int, 2 returned for TDs), Tim Montgomery (6 int), B/P Bob Campbell (45.1-yd punting avg). *Noteworthy:* Won 5th Lambert Trophy. Tied Florida St. 17–17 in Gator Bowl; Sherman passed for 2 TDs (to Kwalick and Curry) and kicked FG to give Lions early 17–0 lead.

1968 (11–0) *Won:* Navy 31–6, Kansas St. 25–9, West Virginia 31–20 (10th straight over Mountaineers), UCLA 21–6, Boston College 29–0, Army 28–24, Miami (Fla.) 22–7, Maryland 57–13, Pittsburgh 65–9, Syracuse 30–12. *Stars:* Kwalick (31 pass rec for 403 yds), Pittman (950 yds and 14 TDs rush, 1,262 all-purpose yds), QB Chuck Burkhart (1,170 yds pass), Onkotz, DB Neal Smith (8 int). *Noteworthy:* Again won Lambert Trophy in 1st unbeaten season since 1947. Beat Kansas 15–14 in Orange Bowl; Campbell ran for 101 yds and

winning 2-pt conversion, Pittman scored on 13-yd run, and Burkhart passed for 154 yds and scored other Lion TD.

1969 (11–0) *Won:* Navy 45–22, Colorado 27–3, Kansas St. 17–14, West Virginia 20–0, Syracuse 15–14, Ohio U. 42–3, Boston College 38–16, Maryland 48–0, Pittsburgh 27–7, N.C. State 33–8. *Stars:* Onkotz (13.5-yd avg on punt returns, 1 returned for TD), DT Mike Reid (Outland Trophy and Maxwell Award winner), Smith (10 int), Pittman (706 yds rush, 11 TDs), Greg Edmonds (20 pass rec for 246 yds), soph HB Lydell Mitchell (616 yds and 6 TDs rush), soph FB Franco Harris (643 yds and 10 TDs rush), LB Jack Ham, soph P Bob Parsons (40.6-yd avg). *Noteworthy:* Won 3rd straight Lambert Trophy (7th overall). Beat Missouri 10–3 in Orange Bowl; Burkhart passed for 187 yds and a TD (to Mitchell, who caught 5 for 81 yds).

1970 (7–3) *Won:* Navy 55–7, Boston College 28–3, Army 38–14, West Virginia 42–8, Maryland 34–0,

DL Mike Reid, 1966, 1968–69

RB Lydell Mitchell, 1969–71

Ohio U. 32–22, Pittsburgh 35–15. *Lost:* Colorado 41–13 (ending 31-game unbeaten string), Wisconsin 29–16, Syracuse 24–7. *Stars:* Ham, soph LB John Skorupan, DB Mike Smith (5 int), Mitchell (751 yds and 6 TDs rush, 1,271 all-purpose yds), Harris (675 yds and 8 TDs rush), Edmonds (38 pass rec for 506 yds and 6 TDs).

1971 (11–1) *Won:* Navy 56–3, Iowa 44–14 (1st meeting since 1930), Air Force 16–14, Army 42–0, Syracuse 31–0, TCU 66–14, West Virginia 35–7, Maryland 63–27 (10th straight over Terps), N.C. State 35–3, Pittsburgh 55–18. *Lost:* Tennessee 31–11 in finale. *Stars:* Mitchell (29 TDs, 1,567 yds and 26 TDs rush, 1,754 all-purpose yds), Harris (684 yds and 6 TDs rush), QB John Hufnagel (1,185 yds and 10 TDs pass), Parsons (30 pass rec for 489 yds and 5 TDs), OT Dave Joyner, LB Charlie Zapiec, Gary Gray (5 int). *Noteworthy:* Won 8th Lambert Trophy. Beat Texas 30–6 in Cotton Bowl; Mitchell ran for 146 yds and a TD, Hufnagel passed for 137

RB John Cappelletti, 1971–73

yds and a TD, and Alberto Vitiello kicked 3 FGs.
1972 (10–2) *Won:* Navy 21–10, Iowa 14–10, Illinois 35–17, Army 45–0, Syracuse 17–0, West Virginia 28–19, Maryland 46–16, N.C. State 37–22, Boston College 45–26, Pittsburgh 49–27. *Lost:* Tennessee 28–21 in opener. *Stars:* Hufnagel (nation's passing efficiency leader with 2,039 yds and 15 TDs, 6 TDs rush), soph Dan Natale (30 pass rec for 460 yds and 5 TDs), RB John Cappelletti (1,117 yds rush, 13 TDs), DE Bruce Bannon, Skorupan, LB Ed O'Neil. *Noteworthy:* Again won Lambert Trophy. Lost to Oklahoma 14–0 in Sugar Bowl as Lions were held to 49 yds rush; Hufnagel passed for 147 yds.

1973 (12–0) *Won:* Stanford 20–6, Navy 39–0, Iowa 27–8, Air Force 19–9, Army 54–3, Syracuse 49–6, West Virginia 62–14 (15th straight over Mountaineers), Maryland 42–22, N.C. State 35–29 (10th straight over Wolfpack), Ohio U. 49–10, Pittsburgh 35–13. *Stars:* Heisman Trophy– and Maxwell Award–winner Cappelletti (1,522 yds and 17 TDs

LB Jack Ham, 1968–70

DL Mike Hartenstine, 1972–74

lor 41–20 in Cotton Bowl; Donchez ran for 116 yds and a TD, Shuman passed for 226 yds and a TD and scored another, frosh WR Jim Cefalo scored 1 TD and caught 49-yd pass for 2nd, and Joe Jackson scored on 50-yd kickoff return.

1975 (9–3)   *Won:* Temple 26–25 (1st meeting since 1952), Stanford 34–14, Iowa 30–10, Kentucky 10–3, West Virginia 39–0, Syracuse 19–7, Army 31–0, Maryland 15–13, Pittsburgh 7–6 (10th straight over Panthers). *Lost:* unbeaten Ohio St. 17–9, N.C. State 15–14. *Stars:* Buttle, Bahr (18 FGs, 73 pts), Woody Petchel (621 yds and 5 TDs rush), Dick Barvinchak (17 pass rec for 327 yds), OG Tom Rafferty. *Noteworthy:* Won 5th straight Lambert Trophy. Lost to Alabama 13–6 (1st meeting since 1959 Liberty Bowl) in Sugar Bowl; Bahr kicked FGs of 42 and 37 yds.

1977 (11–1)   *Won:* Rutgers 45–7 (1st meeting since 1955), Houston 31–14, Maryland 27–9 (15th straight over Terps), Utah St. 16–7, Syracuse 31–24, West Virginia 49–28, Miami (Fla.) 49–7, N.C. State 21–17,

rush), Natale (21 pass rec for 359 yds), QB Tom Shuman (1,375 yds and 13 TDs pass), Gary Hayman (30 pass rec for 525 yds, nation's punt return leader with 19.2-yd avg), DT Randy Crowder, DE Mike Hartenstine, O'Neil. *Noteworthy:* won 3rd straight Lambert Trophy. Beat Louisiana State (LSU) 16–9 in Orange Bowl; Shuman passed for 157 yds and a TD (72 yds to Chuck Herd), Cappelletti scored other Lion TD, and soph K Chris Bahr had 44-yd FG.

1974 (10–2)   *Won:* Stanford 24–20, Iowa 27–0, Army 21–14, Wake Forest 55–0, Syracuse 30–14, West Virginia 21–12, Maryland 24–17, Ohio U. 35–16, Pittsburgh 31–10. *Lost:* Navy 7–6 (1st to Midshipmen since 1967), N.C. State 12–7 (1st in 11-game series dating to 1920). *Stars:* Shuman (1,355 yds and 12 TDs pass), Tom Donchez (880 yds and 7 TDs rush, 17 pass rec for 176 yds and a TD), Jerry Jeram (17 pass rec for 259 yds), OT John Nessel, Hartenstine, LB Greg Buttle. *Noteworthy:* Won 11th Lambert Trophy. Beat Bay-

LB Greg Buttle, 1973–75

QB Chuck Fusina, 1976–78

Bahr (97 pts, nation's leader with 22 FGs), DTs Bruce Clark (Lombardi Award winner) and Matt Millen, LB Lance Mehl, DB Pete Harris (nation's leader with 10 int). *Noteworthy:* Joe Paterno's 4th unbeaten team led nation in total defense and rush defense and again won Lambert Trophy. Lost to national cochamp Alabama 14–7 in Sugar Bowl as Lions gained only 19 yds rush; Fusina passed for 163 yds and Penn St. TD (17 yds to Fitzkee).

1979 (8–4) *Won:* Rutgers 45–10, Maryland 27–7, Army 24–3, Syracuse 35–7, West Virginia 31–6, N.C. State 9–7, Temple 22–7. *Lost:* Texas A&M 27–14, Nebraska 42–17 (1st meeting since 1958), Miami (Fla.) 26–10, Pittsburgh 29–14. *Stars:* Clark, Mehl, Suhey (973 yds rush, 1,127 all-purpose yds, 7 TDs), Moore (555 yds and 9 TDs rush), frosh RB Curt Warner (1,013 all-purpose yds), QB Dayle Tate (1,179 yds pass), Brad Scovill (26 pass rec for 331 yds), K Herb Menhardt (14 FGs, 70 pts). *Noteworthy:* beat Tulane 9–6 in Liberty Bowl on 3 FGs by Menhardt; Suhey ran for 112 yds.

1980 (10–2) *Won:* Colgate 54–10 (1st meeting since 1959), Texas A&M 25–9, Missouri 29–21, Maryland 24–10, Syracuse 24–7 (10th straight over Orange), West Virginia 20–15, Miami (Fla.) 27–12, N.C. State 21–13, Temple 50–7. *Lost:* Nebraska

Temple 44–7, Pittsburgh 15–13. *Lost:* Kentucky 24–20. *Stars:* QB Chuck Fusina (2,221 yds and 15 TDs pass), Mickey Shuler (33 pass rec for 600 yds), Cefalo (28 pass rec for 507 yds and 5 TDs), Scott Fitzkee (18 pass rec for 372 yds), soph FB Matt Suhey (638 yds and 8 TDs rush), K Matt Bahr (14 FGs, 81 pts), OT Keith Dorney, MG Randy Sidler. *Noteworthy:* Won 13th Lambert Trophy. Beat Arizona St. 42–30 in Fiesta Bowl; Steve Geise ran for 111 yds, a TD, and a 2-pt conversion, Suhey scored 2 TDs, Fusina passed for 1 TD, and Bahr kicked 2 FGs and 4 ex pts.

1978 (11–1) *Won:* Temple 10–7, Rutgers 26–10, Ohio St. 19–0, SMU 26–21, TCU 58–0, Kentucky 30–0, Syracuse 45–15, West Virginia 49–21 (20th straight over Mountaineers), Maryland 27–3, N.C. State 19–10, Pittsburgh 17–10. *Stars:* Maxwell Award–winner Fusina (1,859 yds and 11 TDs pass), Fitzkee (37 pass rec for 630 yds and 6 TDs), Suhey (720 yds rush, 1,131 all-purpose yds, 9 TDs), soph Booker Moore (602 yds and 6 TDs rush), Dorney,

DL Bruce Clark, 1976–79

21–7, Pittsburgh 14–9. *Stars:* OT Bill Dugan, OG Sean Farrell, Warner (922 yds rush, 1,364 all-purpose yds, 8 TDs), Moore (707 yds rush), soph QB Todd Blackledge (1,037 yds pass), frosh FL Kenny Jackson (21 pass rec for 386 yds and 5 TDs), Scovill (18 pass rec for 277 yds), Menhardt (15 FGs, 71 pts), soph P Ralph Giacomarro (43.3-yd avg). *Noteworthy:* beat Ohio St. 31–19 in Fiesta Bowl; Warner ran for 155 yds and a TD (on 64-yd run), Blackledge passed for 117 yds and scored a TD, and Moore scored on 37-yd run.

1981 (10–2) *Won:* Cincinnati 52–0, Nebraska 30–24, Temple 30–0, Boston College 38–7 (1st meeting since 1972, 10th straight over Eagles), Syracuse 41–16, West Virginia 30–7, N.C. State 22–15, Notre Dame 24–21 (1st in 6-game series dating to 1913), Pittsburgh 48–14. *Lost:* Miami (Fla.) 17–14, Alabama 31–16. *Stars:* Warner (1,044 yds and 8 TDs rush), Blackledge (1,557 yds and 12 TDs pass, 5 TDs rush), Greg Garrity (23 pass rec for 415 yds), Kenny Jackson (19 pass rec for 440 yds and 6 TDs), soph Jon Williams (667 yds and 6 TDs rush), Farrell, K Brian Franco (15 FGs, 81 pts), Roger Jackson (5 int), Giacomarro (43.6-yd punting avg).

RB Curt Warner, 1979–82

Noteworthy: Won 15th Lambert Trophy. Beat USC 26–10 in Fiesta Bowl; Warner ran for 145 yds and 2 TDs, and Blackledge passed for 175 yds and a TD (52 yards to Garrity).

1982 (11–1) *Won:* Temple 31–14, Maryland 39–31, Rutgers 49–14 (10th straight over Scarlet Knights), Nebraska 27–24, Syracuse 28–7, West Virginia 24–0, Boston College 52–17, N.C. State 54–0, Notre Dame 24–14, Pittsburgh 19–10. *Lost:* Alabama 42–21 in mid-season. *Stars:* Warner (1,041 yds and 8 TDs rush, 1,376 all-purpose yds, 13 TDs), Williams (609 yds and 5 TDs rush), Blackledge (2,218 yds and 22 TDs pass), Kenny Jackson (41 pass rec for 697 yds and 7 TDs), Garrity (32 pass rec for 509 yds), soph K Nick Gancitano (11 FGs), Giacomarro (41.1-yd punting avg), DE Walker Lee Ashley, LB Scott Radecic, DB Mark Robinson. *Noteworthy:* Again won Lambert Trophy. Won 1st national championship by beating undefeated Georgia 27–23 in Sugar Bowl; Warner ran for 117 yds and 2 TDs, Blackledge passed for 228 yds and

DL Matt Millen, 1976–79

QB Todd Blackledge, 1980–82

Virginia 19–0, Maryland 17–15, Notre Dame 24–19, Pittsburgh 34–14. *Stars:* Shaffer (1,510 yds pass), Dozier (811 yds and 10 TDs rush, 26 pass rec for 287 yds and 2 TDs), soph RB Blair Thomas (504 yds rush, 6 TDs), OT Chris Conlin, Manca (14 FGs, 79 pts), Johnson, Conlan, Bruno (40.9-yd punting avg). *Noteworthy:* Won 18th Lambert Trophy. Beat undefeated Miami (Fla.) 14–10 in Fiesta Bowl to earn 2nd national title; Dozier ran for 99 yds and winning TD (on 6-yd run), and Shaffer scored on 4-yd run.

1987 (8–4) *Won:* Bowling Green 45–19, Cincinnati 41–0, Boston College 27–17, Temple 27–13, Rutgers 35–21 (15th straight over Scarlet Knights), West Virginia 25–21, Maryland 21–16, Notre Dame

a TD (47 yds to Garrity, who caught 4 for 116 yds), and Gancitano kicked 2 FGs and 3 ex pts.

1985 (11–1) *Won:* Maryland 20–18, Temple 27–25, East Carolina 17–10, Rutgers 17–10, Alabama 19–17, Syracuse 24–20 (15th straight over Orange), West Virginia 27–0, Boston College 16–12, Cincinnati 31–10, Notre Dame 36–6, Pittsburgh 31–0. *Stars:* LBs Shane Conlan and Rogers Alexander, DT Tim Johnson, DBs Michael Zordich and Lance Hamilton, QB John Shaffer (1,366 yds pass), Ray Roundtree (15 pass rec for 285 yds), RB D.J. Dozier (723 yds rush, 5 TDs), K Massimo Manca (21 FGs, 91 pts), P John Bruno (42.9-yd avg). *Noteworthy:* Paterno's 5th unbeaten team won 17th Lambert Trophy. Lost national championship game to Oklahoma 25–10 in Orange Bowl (breaking 5–bowl winning streak); Lions scored on 1-yd run by Tim Manoa and ex pt and 27-yd FG by Manca.

1986 (12–0) *Won:* Temple 45–15, Boston College 26–14, East Carolina 42–17, Rutgers 31–6, Cincinnati 23–17, Syracuse 42–3, Alabama 23–3, West

LB Shane Conlan, 1983–86

21–20. *Lost:* Alabama 24–13, unbeaten Syracuse 48–21 (1st to Orange since 1970), Pittsburgh 10–0. *Stars:* Thomas (1,414 yds and 11 TDs rush, 23 pass rec for 300 yds and 2 TDs), QB Matt Knizner (1,478 yds pass), OG Steve Wisniewski, soph LB Brian Chizmar, P Chris Clauss (40.5-yd avg). *Noteworthy:* lost to Clemson 35–10 in Florida Citrus Bowl; Knizner passed for 148 yds and a TD (39 yds to Mike Alexander).

1989 (8–3–1) *Won:* Temple 42–3 (15th straight over Owls), Boston College 7–3, Texas 16–12, Rutgers 17–0, Syracuse 34–12, West Virginia 19–9, Pittsburgh 16–13. *Lost:* Virginia 14–6, Alabama 17–16, Notre Dame 34–23. *Tied:* Maryland 13–13. *Stars:* Thomas (1,341 yds and 5 TDs rush), WRs David Daniels (22 pass rec for 362 yds) and soph Terry Smith (16 pass rec for 298 yds), K Ray Tarasi (19 FGs, 77 pts), C Roger Duffy, LB Andre Collins, Chizmar, DB Sherrod Rainge (6 int). *Noteworthy:*

RB Blair Thomas, 1985–87, 1989

RB D.J. Dozier, 1983–86

Won 19th Lambert Trophy. Beat BYU 50–39 in Holiday Bowl; Thomas ran for 186 yds and a TD, soph QB Tony Sacca passed for 206 yds and 2 TDs, Tarasi kicked 3 FGs, Collins returned intercepted conversion attempt 100 yds for 2 pts, and Brown returned fumble 53 yds for Lions' final TD.

1990 (9–3) *Won:* Rutgers 28–0, Temple 48–10, Syracuse 27–21, Boston College 40–21, Alabama 9–0, West Virginia 31–19, Maryland 24–10, Notre Dame 24–21, Pittsburgh 22–17. *Lost:* Texas 17–13, USC 19–14 in 1st 2 games. *Stars:* Sacca (1,866 yds and 10 TDs pass), Daniels (31 pass rec for 538 yds), Smith (29 pass rec for 530 yds), TB Leroy Thompson (573 yds and 8 TDs rush, 20 pass rec for 245 yds), FB Sam Gash (5 TDs rush), frosh K Craig Fayak (15 FGs, 74 pts), LBs Mark D'Onofrio and Keith Goganious, DBs Darren Perry (7 int) and Leonard Humphries (6 int). *Noteworthy:* Won 20th Lambert Trophy. Lost to Florida St. 24–17 in inaugural Blockbuster Bowl, losing ball 3 times on int and having FG attempt blocked; Sacca passed for 194 yds and a TD (56 yds to Daniels, who caught 7 for 154 yds), and reserve QB Tom Bill threw 37-yd TD pass to Smith (5 pass rec for 100 yds).

1991 (11–2) *Won:* Georgia Tech 34–22, Cincinnati 81–0, Brigham Young (BYU) 33–7, Boston College 28–21, Temple 24–7 (25th straight without loss to Owls), Rutgers 37–17, West Virginia 51–6, Maryland 47–7, Notre Dame 35–13, Pittsburgh 32–20. *Lost:* USC 21–10, unbeaten national cochamp Miami (Fla.) 26–20. *Stars:* Sacca (2,488 yds and 21 TDs pass), Smith (55 pass rec for 846 yds and 8 TDs), WR O.J. McDuffie (46 pass rec for 790 yds and 6 TDs, 1,367 all-purpose yds, 9 TDs total— 2 on punt returns), TB Richie Anderson (1,256

all-purpose yds, 11 TDs, 779 yds rush, 21 pass rec for 255 yds), Fayak (17 FGs, 93 pts), DT Tyoka Jackson, Goganious, D'Onofrio, LB Rich McKenzie, Perry (6 int, 2 returned for TDs), DB Lee Rubin (5 int). *Noteworthy:* Led nation in turnover margin and won 21st Lambert Trophy (3rd straight). Beat Tennessee 42–17 in Fiesta Bowl after trailing 17–7 in 3rd quarter; Sacca passed for 150 yds and 4 TDs, Anderson scored on 2-yd run, and LB Reggie Givens scored on 23-yd fumble return.

BOWL SUMMARY

Aloha 1–0; Blockbuster 0–2; Cotton 2–0–1; Fiesta 5–0; Florida Citrus 0–1; Gator 1–2–1; Holiday 1–0; Liberty 3–0; Orange 3–1; Rose 0–1; Sugar 1–3.

BOWL RECORD (17–10–2)

Regular Season	Bowl	Score	Opponent	Record
1922 (6–3–1)	Rose	3–14	USC	(9–1)
1947 (9–0)	Cotton	13–13	SMU	(9–0–1)
1959 (8–2)	Liberty	7–0	Alabama	(7–1–2)
1960 (6–3)	Liberty	41–12	Oregon	(7–2–1)
1961 (7–3)	Gator	30–15	Georgia Tech	(7–3)
1962 (9–1)	Gator	7–17	Florida	(6–4)
1967 (8–2)	Gator	17–17	Florida State	(7–2–1)
1968 (10–0)	Orange	15–14	Kansas	(9–1)
1969 (10–0)	Orange	10–3	Missouri	(9–1)
1971 (10–1)	Cotton	30–6	Texas	(8–2)
1972 (10–1)	Sugar	0–14	Oklahoma	(10–1)
1973 (11–0)	Orange	16–9	LSU	(9–2)
1974 (9–2)	Cotton	41–20	Baylor	(8–3)
1975 (9–2)	Sugar	6–13	Alabama	(10–1)
1976 (7–4)	Gator	9–20	Notre Dame	(8–3)
1977 (10–1)	Fiesta	42–30	Arizona State	(9–2)
1978 (11–0)	Sugar	7–14	Alabama	(10–1)
1979 (7–4)	Liberty	9–6	Tulane	(9–2)
1980 (9–2)	Fiesta	31–19	Ohio State	(9–2)
1981 (9–2)	Fiesta	26–10	USC	(9–2)
1982 (10–1)	Sugar	27–23	Georgia	(11–0)
1983 (7–4–1)	Aloha	13–10	Washington	(8–3)
1985 (11–0)	Orange	10–25	Oklahoma	(10–1)
1986 (11–0)	Fiesta	14–10	Miami (Fla.)	(11–0)
1987 (8–3)	Fla. Citrus	10–35	Clemson	(9–2)
1989 (7–3–1)	Holiday	50–39	BYU	(10–2)
1990 (9–2)	Blockbuster	17–24	Florida State	(9–2)
1991 (10–2)	Fiesta	42–17	Tennessee	(9–2)
1992 (7–4)	Blockbuster	3–24	Stanford	(9–3)

Conference Titles

Big 10—None. Won **Lambert Trophy** in 1947, 1961, 1962, 1964, 1967, 1968, 1969, 1971, 1972, 1973, 1974, 1975, 1977, 1978, 1981, 1982, 1985, 1986, 1989, 1990, 1991.

TOP 20 AP AND UPI (USA TODAY/CNN SINCE 1991) RANKING

1942	19	1963	U–16	1973	5–5	1982	1–1
1947	4	1964	U–14	1974	7–7	1983	U–17
1948	18	1967	10–11	1975	10–10	1985	3–3
1954	20–16	1968	2–3	1977	5–4	1986	1–1
1959	12–10	1969	2–2	1978	4–4	1989	15–14
1960	16–U	1970	18–19	1979	20–18	1990	11–10
1961	17–19	1971	5–11	1980	8–8	1991	3–3
1962	9–9	1972	10–8	1981	3–3		

Major Rivals

Penn State has played at least 10 games with Alabama 5–8, Army 13–10–2, Boston College 19–2, Bucknell 28–10, Colgate 9–4–1, Cornell 4–7–2, Dickinson 11–5–1, Gettysburg 27–0–1, Lafayette 10–5–1, Lebanon Valley 20–0, Lehigh 16–6–1, Maryland 34–1–1, Miami (Fla.) 6–5, Michigan St. 1–8–1, Navy 18–17–2, Nebraska 6–5, N.C. State 17–2, Notre Dame 8–8–1, Pennsylvania 18–25–4, Pittsburgh 47–41–4, Rutgers 19–2, Syracuse 40–23–5, Temple 26–3–1, West Virginia 48–9–2. Record against Big 10 foes met fewer than 10 times is Illinois 3–1, Indiana 0–0 (no games played), Iowa 6–3, Michigan 0–0 (no games played), Minnesota 0–0 (no games played), Northwestern 0–0 (no games played), Ohio St. 6–2, Purdue 0–1–1, Wisconsin 0–2.

Coaches

Dean of Penn St. coaches is Joe Paterno (1968, 1978, 1982, and 1986 national Coach of Year) with record of 247–67–3 for 1966–92, including 17 Lambert Trophy winners, 23 bowl teams, 6 teams unbeaten in regular season, and 2 national champions. Other top records for at least 3 years were by George Hoskins, 17–4–4 for 1892–95 with 1 unbeaten team; W.N. "Pop" Golden, 16–12–1 for 1900–02; Tom Fennell, 33–17–1 for 1904–08; Bill Hollenback, 28–9–4 for 1909 and 1911–14 with 3 unbeaten teams; Dick Harlow, 20–8 for 1915–17; Hugo Bezdek, 65–30–11 for 1918–29 with 1 Rose Bowl team and 2 unbeaten teams; Bob Higgins, 91–57–11 for 1930–48 with 1 unbeaten Lambert Trophy winner and Cotton Bowl team; and Charles A. "Rip" Engle, 104–48–4 for 1950–65 with 3 Lambert Trophy winners and 4 bowl teams (3 winners).

Miscellanea

First game was win over Bucknell 54–0 in 1887 . . . highest score was over Lebanon Valley 109–7 in 1921 . . . highest since W.W. II was over Cincinnati 81–0 in 1991 . . . worst defeat was by Lehigh 106–0 in 1889 . . . worst since 1900 was by Cornell 47–0 in 1939 . . . worst since W.W. II was by UCLA 49–11 in 1966 and by Nebraska 44–6 in 1983 . . . highest against since 1900 was by Navy 55–14 in 1944 . . . highest against since W.W. II was by West Virginia 51–30 in 1988 . . . longest unbeaten string of 31 (and win streak of 23) in 1967–70 ended by Colorado 41–13 . . . 30-game unbeaten string in 1919–22 ended by Navy 14–0 . . . 19-game unbeaten strings, in 1911–13 ended by Washington & Jefferson 17–0 and in 1977–78 ended by Alabama 14–7 in 1979 Sugar

Bowl . . . longest losing string of 7 in 1931 broken with win over Lehigh 31–0 . . . consensus All-Americans were William Dunn, C, 1906; Bob Higgins, E, 1919; Charles Way, B, 1920; Glenn Killinger, B, 1921; Harry Wilson, B, 1923; Richie Lucas, B, 1959; Glenn Ressler, G, 1964; Ted Kwalick, E, 1968; Dennis Onkotz, LB, 1968–69; Mike Reid, DT, 1969; Jack Ham, LB, 1970; Dave Joyner, T, 1971; Bruce Bannon, DE, and John Skorupan, LB, 1972; John Cappelletti, B, 1973; Mike Hartenstine, DL, 1974; Greg Buttle, LB, 1975; Keith Dorney, OT, and Chuck Fusina, QB, 1978; Bruce Clark, DL, 1978–79; Sean Farrell, OL, 1981; D.J. Dozier, RB, and Shane Conlan, LB, 1986; and O.J. McDuffie, WR, 1992 . . . Academic All-Americans were Joe Bellas, T, 1965; John Runnells, LB, 1965–66; Rich Buzin, OT, 1967; Charlie Pittman, HB, and Dennis Onkotz, LB, 1969; Dave Joyner, OT, 1971; Bruce Bannon, DE, 1972; Mark Markovich, OG, 1973; Chuck Benjamin, DT, 1976; Keith Dorney, OT, 1978; Todd Blackledge, QB, and Scott Radecic, LB, 1982; Harry Hamilton, DB, 1982, and LB, 1983; Carmen Masciantonio, LB, 1984; Lance Hamilton, DB, 1984–85; and John Shaffer, QB, 1986 . . . Heisman Trophy winner was John Cappelletti, HB, 1973 . . . Maxwell Award winners were Rich Lucas, QB, 1959; Glenn Ressler, G, 1964; Mike Reid, DT, 1969; John Cappelletti, RB, 1973; and Chuck Fusina, QB, 1978 . . . Outland Trophy winner was Mike Reid, DT, 1969 . . . Lombardi Award winner was Bruce Clark, DT, 1978.

PURDUE (Boilermakers; Old Gold and Black)

NOTABLE TEAMS

1892 (8–0) **Won:** Illinois 12–6, Wabash 72–0, Wisconsin 34–6 (1st meeting), Michigan 24–0, Butler 40–6, Indiana 68–0, Chicago 38–0 (1st meeting), DePauw 32–6. **Noteworthy:** won 2nd straight Indiana Association title.
1894 (9–1) **Won:** Light Artillery 6–4, Butler 30–0, Armour 36–0, Chicago 10–6, Illinois 22–2, Wisconsin 6–0 (forfeit), Wabash 44–0, Indiana 6–0 (forfeit), DePauw 28–0. **Lost:** Minnesota 24–0 (1st meeting). **Noteworthy:** won 4th Indiana Association crown.
1902 (7–2–1) **Won:** Franklin 56–0, DePauw 39–0, Case 5–0, Northwestern 5–0, Greer 73–0, Indiana 39–0, Butler 87–0 (1st meeting since 1894). **Lost:**

Chicago 33–0, Illinois 29–5 in successive early games. **Tied:** Notre Dame 6–6.
1904 (9–3) **Won:** North Division H.S. 5–0, Beloit 11–0, Earlham 28–11, Wabash 6–0, Missouri 11–0, Indiana Medical 34–5, Indiana 27–0, Culver Military 10–0, Notre Dame 36–0. **Lost:** Alumni 6–2, Chicago 20–0, Illinois 24–6.
1905 (6–1–1) **Won:** Wendell Phillips H.S. 33–0, Beloit 36–0, Wabash 12–0 (10th straight over Giants), Illinois 29–0 (1st over Illini since 1899), Missouri 24–0, Notre Dame 32–0. **Lost:** unbeaten national champ Chicago 19–0. **Tied:** Indiana 11–11.
1913 (4–1–2) **Won:** Wabash 26–0 (1st over Giants in 6 games since 1905), Northwestern 34–0, Rose Poly (RPI) 62–0, Indiana 42–7. **Lost:** unbeaten Chicago 6–0. **Tied:** Wisconsin 7–7, Illinois 0–0. **Noteworthy:** 1st year under Andy Smith.
1914 (5–2) **Won:** Wabash 27–3, Western Reserve 26–0, Kentucky 40–6, Northwestern 34–6, Indiana 23–13. **Lost:** Wisconsin 14–7, Chicago 21–0 in successive early games.
1924 (5–2) **Won:** Wabash 21–7, RPI 41–3, Northwestern 7–3, DePauw 36–0, Indiana 26–7 (dedication game for Ross-Ade Stadium). **Lost:** Ohio St. 7–0, Chicago 19–6. **Noteworthy:** 1st winning season since 1914.
1927 (6–2) **Won:** DePauw 15–0, Harvard 19–0, Montana St. 39–7, Northwestern 18–6, Franklin 46–0, Indiana 21–6. **Lost:** Chicago 7–6, Wisconsin 12–6 in consecutive early games.
1929 (8–0) **Won:** Kansas St. 26–14, Michigan 30–16 (1st meeting since 1900, 1st over Wolverines in 6 games since 1892), DePauw 26–7, Chicago 26–0, Wisconsin 13–0 (1st over Badgers in 11 games since 1894), Mississippi 27–7, Iowa 7–0 (1st meeting since 1923, 1st over Hawkeyes in 5 games since 1915), Indiana 32–0. **Stars:** T Elmer Sleight, HB Ralph Welch (1st Purdue consensus All-Americans). **Noteworthy:** had 1st unbeaten season since 1892 and won 2nd Big 10 title in last year under James Phelan.
1930 (6–2) **Won:** Baylor 20–7, Iowa 20–0, Wisconsin 7–6, Illinois 25–0 (1st meeting since 1919, 1st over Illini in 12 games since 1905), Chicago 26–7, Butler 33–0 (1st meeting since 1902). **Lost:** unbeaten Michigan 14–13, Indiana 7–6 (1st to Hoosiers since 1923). **Star:** T George VanBibber. **Noteworthy:** 1st year under Noble Kizer.

1931 (9–1) *Won:* Western Reserve 28–0, Coe 19–0, Illinois 7–0, Carnegie Tech 13–6, Chicago 14–6, Centenary 49–6, Iowa 22–0, Indiana 19–0. *Lost:* Wisconsin 21–14. *Stars:* E Paul Moss, C Charles Miller. *Noteworthy:* Got share of 3rd Big 10 title. Beat undefeated Northwestern 7–0 in postseason charity game in Chicago.

1932 (7–0–1) *Won:* Kansas St. 29–13, Minnesota 7–0, Wisconsin 7–6, New York U. 34–9, Chicago 37–0, Iowa 18–0, Indiana 25–7. *Tied:* Northwestern 7–7. *Stars:* Moss, FB Roy Horstmann, C Johnnie Oehler. *Noteworthy:* again shared Big 10 title.

1933 (6–1–1) *Won:* Ohio U. 13–6, Chicago 14–0, Wisconsin 14–0, Carnegie Tech 17–7, Notre Dame 19–0 (1st meeting since 1923, 1st over Irish in 9 games since 1905), Indiana 19–3. *Lost:* Iowa 14–6. *Tied:* unbeaten Minnesota 7–7. *Stars:* HBs Duane Purvis and Fred Hecker.

1938 (5–1–2) *Won:* Detroit 19–6, Butler 21–6, Wisconsin 13–7, Ohio St. 12–0 (1st in 7-game series dating to 1919), Indiana 13–6. *Lost:* Minnesota 7–0. *Tied:* Fordham 6–6, Iowa 0–0. *Stars:* HB Cecil Isbell, FB Tony Ippolito, T Joe Mihal, C Paul Humphrey.

1943 (9–0) *Won:* Great Lakes 23–13, Marquette 21–0, Illinois 40–21 (1st meeting since 1931), Camp Grant 19–0, Ohio St. 30–7, Iowa 28–7, Wisconsin 32–0, Minnesota 14–7 (1st over Gophers in 7 games since 1932), Indiana 7–0. *Stars:* FB Tony Butkovich (973 yds and 16 TDs rush), HB Babe Dimancheff, Gs Dick Barwegen and Alex Agase, soph T Tom Hughes. *Noteworthy:* nation's most-improved team got share of 4th Big 10 title in 1st undefeated season since 1932.

1945 (7–3) *Won:* Marquette 14–13, Great Lakes 20–6, Wisconsin 13–7, Iowa 40–0, Ohio St. 35–13, Pittsburgh 28–0, Miami (Ohio) 21–7 (1st meeting). *Lost:* Northwestern 26–14, Michigan 27–13, unbeaten Indiana 26–0. *Stars:* Hughes, soph E Ned Maloney.

1958 (6–1–2) *Won:* Nebraska 28–0, Rice 24–0, Michigan St. 14–6, Notre Dame 29–22, Illinois 31–8, Northwestern 23–6. *Lost:* Wisconsin 31–6. *Tied:* Ohio St. 14–14, Indiana 15–15. *Stars:* FB Bob Jarus (10 TDs), Es Tom Franckhauser (13 pass rec for 300 yds) and Richard Brooks, T Gene Selawski, G Ron Maltony.

1965 (7–2–1) *Won:* Miami (Ohio) 38–0, Notre Dame 25–21, Iowa 17–14, Michigan 17–15, Wisconsin 45–7, Minnesota 35–0, Indiana 26–21. *Lost:* unbeaten national cochamp Michigan St. 14–10, Illinois 7–0 in consecutive mid-season games. *Tied:* Southern Methodist (SMU) 14–14. *Stars:* QB Bob Griese (1,719 yds and 11 TDs pass, 5 FGs, 62 pts), E Bob Hadrick (47 pass rec for 562 yds), HB Charles King, OT Karl Singer, C Larry Kaminski, DT Jerry Shay.

1966 (9–2) *Won:* Ohio U. 42–3, SMU 35–23, Iowa 35–0, Michigan 22–21, Illinois 25–21, Wisconsin 23–0, Minnesota 16–0, Indiana 51–6. *Lost:* unbeaten national cochamp Notre Dame 26–14, unbeaten national cochamp Michigan St. 41–20. *Stars:* Griese (1,749 yds and 12 TDs pass, 215 yds and 6 TDs rush, 81 pts), Es Jim Beirne (64 pass rec for 768 yds and 8 TDs) and George Olion, soph FB Perry Williams (689 yds rush), Gs Jack Calcaterra and Chuck Erienbaugh, T Lance Olssen, soph MG Chuck Kyle, DB John Charles. *Noteworthy:* made 1st bowl appearance, beating Southern California (USC) 14–13 in Rose Bowl; Williams scored both Purdue TDs and DB George Catavolos intercepted USC 2-pt conversion pass attempt in final seconds.

QB Bob Griese, 1964–66

1967 (8–2) *Won:* Texas A&M 24–20, Notre Dame 28–21, Northwestern 25–16 (1st meeting since 1958), Ohio St. 41–6 (1st meeting since 1960), Iowa 41–22, Illinois 42–9, Minnesota 41–12, Michigan St. 21–7. *Lost:* Oregon St. 22–14, Indiana 19–14. *Stars:* HB/DB Leroy Keyes (986 yds rush, 45 pass rec for 758 yds and 6 TDs, national scoring leader with 114 pts on 19 TDs), soph QB Mike Phipps (1,800 yds and 11 TDs pass, 220 yds rush), Beirne (45 pass rec for 758 yds and 5 TDs), Williams, Olion, Olssen, Kyle, LB Dick Marvel, DB Bob Corby (6 int). *Noteworthy:* got share of 6th Big 10 title (1st since 1952).

1968 (8–2) *Won:* Virginia 44–6, Notre Dame 37–22, Northwestern 43–6, Wake Forest 28–27, Iowa 44–14, Illinois 35–17, Michigan St. 9–0, Indiana 38–35. *Lost:* unbeaten national champ Ohio St. 13–0, Minnesota 27–13. *Stars:* Keyes (1,003 yds and 14 TDs rush, 33 pass rec for 428 yds and 1 TD), Phipps (1,096 yds pass), Bob Dillingham (35 pass rec for 456 yds), Williams, Kyle, G Gary Roberts, T Bill Yanchar.

1969 (8–2) *Won:* Texas Christian (TCU) 42–35, Notre Dame 28–14, Stanford 36–35, Iowa 35–31, Northwestern 45–20, Illinois 49–22, Michigan St. 41–13, Indiana 44–21. *Lost:* Michigan 31–20, Ohio St. 42–14. *Stars:* Phipps (2,527 yds and 23 TDs pass, 218 yds and 8 TDs rush), Ashley Bell (49 pass rec for 669 yds and 11 TDs), Randy Cooper (697 yds rush), HB Stan Brown (18 TDs, nation's kickoff return leader with 26.8-yd avg), Yanchar, T Paul DeNuccio, LB Veno Paraskevas, DBs Tim Foley (5 int) and Mike Renie (5 int). *Noteworthy:* Jack Mollenkopf's last team.

1978 (9–2–1) *Won:* Michigan St. 21–14, Ohio U. 24–0, Wake Forest 14–7, Ohio St. 27–16 (1st over Buckeyes in 7 games since 1967), Illinois 13–0, Iowa 34–7, Northwestern 31–0, Indiana 20–7. *Lost:* Notre Dame 10–6, Michigan 24–6. *Tied:* Wisconsin 24–24. *Stars:* soph QB Mark Herrmann (1,738 yds and 12 TDs pass), soph TE Dave Young (26 pass rec for 372 yds), Russell Pope (35 pass rec for 292 yds), John Macon (913 yds rush), K Scott Sovereen (15 FGs, 73 pts), DE Keena Turner, MG Ken Loushin. *Noteworthy:* beat Georgia Tech 41–21 in Peach Bowl; Herrmann passed for 166 yds and 2 TDs and ran for another.

1979 (10–2) *Won:* Wisconsin 41–20, Notre Dame 28–22, Oregon 13–7, Illinois 28–14, Michigan St. 14–7, Northwestern 20–16, Iowa 20–14, Michigan 24–21, Indiana 37–21. *Lost:* UCLA 31–21, Minnesota 31–14 (1st meeting since 1974) in early games. *Stars:* Herrmann (2,074 yds and 13 TDs pass), Young (51 pass rec for 512 yds and 8 TDs), soph TB Wally Jones (754 yds rush, 27 pass rec for 267 yds, 8 TDs), OG Dave Schwann, OT Steve McKenzie, Turner, Loushin, DT Calvin Clark, DB Bill Kay (7 int). *Noteworthy:* beat Tennessee 27–22 in Bluebonnet Bowl; Herrmann passed for 303 yds and 3 TDs (2 to Young, including 17-yd winning TD pass in final moments).

1980 (9–3) *Won:* Wisconsin 12–6, Miami (Ohio) 28–3, Minnesota 21–7, Illinois 45–20, Michigan St. 36–25, Northwestern 52–31, Iowa 58–13 (20th straight over Hawkeyes), Indiana 24–23. *Lost:* Notre Dame 31–10, UCLA 23–14, Michigan 26–0. *Stars:* Herrmann (2,923 yds and 19 TDs pass), Young (nation's leader in pass rec with 67 catches for 917 yds and 8 TDs), WR Bart Burrell (66 pass rec for 1,001 yds and 8 TDs), FL Steve Bryant (50 pass rec for 892 yds), TB Jimmy Smith (657 yds rush, 9 TDs), Ben McCall (507 yds rush), K Rick Anderson (16 FGs, 86 pts), Clark, LB James Looney, DBs Kay and Robert Williams (5 int). *Noteworthy:* beat Missouri 28–25 in Liberty Bowl; Herrmann passed for 289 yds and 4 TDs (to Bryant, Young, and Burrell), and Burrell had 8 pass rec for 113 yds and 2 TDs).

BOWL SUMMARY

Bluebonnet 1–0; Liberty 1–0; Peach 1–1; Rose 1–0.

BOWL RECORD (4–1)

Regular Season	Bowl	Score	Opponent	Record
1966 (8–2)	Rose	14–13	USC	(7–3)
1978 (8–2–1)	Peach	41–21	Georgia Tech	(7–4)
1979 (9–2)	Bluebonnet	27–22	Tennessee	(7–4)
1980 (8–3)	Liberty	28–25	Missouri	(8–3)
1984 (7–4)	Peach	24–27	Virginia	(7–2–2)

Conference Titles

Indiana Association—1891, 1892, 1893, 1894. **Big 10**—1918*, 1929, 1931*, 1943*, 1952*, 1967*.

TOP 20 AP AND UPI RANKING

1943	5	1960	19–15	1967	9–9	1979	10–10
1951	U–14	1961	12–11	1968	10–11	1980	17–16
1952	18–12	1965	U–13	1969	18–18		
1958	13–11	1966	7–6	1978	13–13		

Major Rivals

Purdue has played at least 10 games with Butler 9–3, Chicago 14–27–1, DePauw 26–1, Illinois 30–38–6, Indiana 58–31–6, Iowa 41–26–2, Miami (Ohio) 8–3–1, Michigan 10–32, Michigan St. 20–25–2, Minnesota 20–28–3, Northwestern 40–21–1, Notre Dame 21–41–2, Ohio St. 10–27–2, Wabash 19–8–2, Wisconsin 25–32–7. Record against Big 10 member Penn St. is 1–0–1.

Coaches

Dean of Purdue coaches is Jack Mollenkopf with record of 84–39–9 for 1956–69, including 1 Big 10 title and 1 Rose Bowl champ. Other top records for at least 3 years were by D.M. Balliet, 22–10–2 for 1893–95 and 1901; Andrew L. Smith, 12–6–3 for 1913–15; James Phelan, 35–22–5 for 1922–29 with 1 Big 10 title and 1 unbeaten team; Noble E. Kizer, 42–13–3 for 1930–36 with 1 Big 10 title and 1 unbeaten team; Stuart Holcomb, 35–42–4 for 1947–55 with 1 Big 10 title; and Jim Young, 38–19–1 for 1977–81 with 3 bowl champions.

Miscellanea

First game was loss to Butler 48–6 in 1887 ... 1st win was over DePauw 34–10 in 1889 ... highest score was over Butler 96–0 in 1893 ... highest since 1900 was over Rose Poly 91–0 in 1912 ... highest since W.W. II was over Boston U. 62–7 in 1947 ... worst defeat was by Chicago 56–0 in 1907 and by Iowa 56–0 in 1922 ... worst since W.W. II was by Michigan 51–0 in 1974 ... highest against since W.W. II was by Michigan St. 55–33 in 1990 ...

longest unbeaten string of 20 in 1931–33 ended by Iowa 14–6 ... 16-game win streak in 1891–93 ended by Michigan 46–8 ... longest losing string of 11 in 1906–08 broken with win over Earlham 40–0 ... consensus All-Americans were Elmer Sleight, T, and Ralph Welch, B, 1929; Paul Moss, E, 1932; Duane Purvis, B, 1933; Dave Rankin, E, 1940; Alex Agase, G, 1943; Bernie Flowers, E, 1952; Bob Griese, QB, 1965; Leroy Keyes, B, 1967–68; Chuck Kyle, MG, 1968; Mike Phipps, QB, 1969; Otis Armstrong, B, and Dave Butz, DT, 1972; Dave Young, TE, and Mark Herrmann, QB, 1980; and Rod Woodson, DB, 1986 ... Academic All-Americans were Len Dawson, B, 1956; Jerry Beabout, T, 1960; Sal Ciampi, G, 1965; Jim Beirne, E, and Lance Olssen, DT, 1967; Tim Foley, DB, 1968–69; Mike Phipps, QB, and Bill Yanchar, DT, 1969; Bob Hoftiezer, DE, 1973; Ken Loushin, DL, 1979; Tim Seneff, DB, 1980–81; and Bruce Brineman, OL, 1989.

WISCONSIN (Badgers; Cardinal and White)

Notable Teams

1891 (3–1–1) **Won:** Beloit 40–4, Lake Forest 6–4, Northwestern 40–0. **Lost:** Minnesota 26–12. **Tied:** Northwestern 0–0.

1894 (6–1) **Won:** Chicago A.A. 22–4, 4–0, Chicago 30–0 (1st meeting), Iowa 44–0 (1st meeting), Beloit 46–0, Minnesota 6–0 (1st in 5 games with Gophers). **Lost:** Purdue (forfeit).

1896 (7–1–1) **Won:** Lake Forest 34–0, Madison H.S. 18–0, Rush Medical 50–0, Grinnell 54–6, Beloit 6–0, Chicago 24–0, Minnesota 6–0 in 1st 7 games. **Lost:** Carlisle Indians 18–8. **Tied:** Northwestern 6–6. **Noteworthy:** 1st year under Phil King.

1897 (9–1)   *Won:* Lake Forest 30–0, Madison H.S. 8–0, 29–0, Rush Medical 28–0, Platteville Normal 20–0, Minnesota 39–0, Beloit 11–0, Chicago 23–8, Northwestern 22–0. *Lost:* Alumni 6–0. *Noteworthy:* won 1st Big 10 title.

1898 (9–1)   *Won:* Ripon 52–0, Madison H.S. 21–0, Dixon College 76–0, Rush Medical 42–0, Beloit 17–0, Minnesota 29–0, Alumni 12–11, Whitewater Normal 22–0, Northwestern 47–0.   *Lost:* Chicago 6–0.   *Star:* Pat O'Dea (drop-kicked 10 FGs).

1899 (9–2)   *Won:* Lake Forest 45–0, Beloit 36–0, Northwestern 38–0, Rush Medical 11–0, Alumni 17–5, Illinois 23–0, Minnesota 19–0, Lawrence 58–0 (1st meeting), Michigan 17–5 (1st meeting since 1893). *Lost:* Yale 6–0, unbeaten Chicago 17–0. *Star:* O'Dea (14 FGs).

1900 (8–1)   *Won:* Ripon 50–0, Chicago Physicians & Surgeons 5–0, Beloit 11–0, Upper Iowa 64–0, Grinnell 45–0, Notre Dame 54–0 (1st meeting), Chicago 39–5, Illinois 27–0. *Lost:* unbeaten Minnesota 6–5 in mid-season.

1901 (9–0)   *Won:* Milwaukee Medical 26–0, Hyde Park H.S. 62–0, Beloit 40–0 (10th straight over Buccaneers), Knox 23–5, Kansas 50–0, Nebraska 18–0, Iowa St. 45–0, Minnesota 18–0, Chicago 35–0. *Noteworthy:* outscored foes 317–5 in 1st unbeaten season and got share of 2nd Big 10 title.

1905 (8–2)   *Won:* Company I of Marinette, Wis. 16–0, Northwestern College 49–0, Marquette 29–0, Lawrence 34–0, Notre Dame 21–0, Alumni 17–0, Minnesota 16–12, Beloit 44–0. *Lost:* unbeaten national champ Chicago 4–0, Michigan 12–0. *Noteworthy:* last year under King.

1906 (5–0)   *Won:* Lawrence 5–0, North Dakota 10–0, Iowa 18–4 (1st meeting since 1894), Illinois 16–6 (1st meeting since 1900), Purdue 29–5 (1st meeting since 1894).   *Noteworthy:* got share of 3rd Big 10 title in 1st year under Dr. C.P. Hutchins.

1907 (3–1–1)   *Won:* Iowa 6–5, Indiana 11–8 (1st meeting), Purdue 12–6. *Lost:* Illinois 15–4 in opener. *Tied:* Minnesota 17–17.

1908 (5–1)   *Won:* Lawrence 35–0, Indiana 16–0, Freshmen 24–15, Marquette 9–6, Minnesota 5–0. *Lost:* unbeaten Chicago 18–12 in finale. *Noteworthy:* 1st year under Tom Barry.

1909 (3–1–1)   *Won:* Lawrence 22–0, Indiana 6–3, Northwestern 21–11 (1st meeting since 1903). *Lost:* Minnesota 34–6. *Tied:* Chicago 6–6.

1911 (5–1–1)   *Won:* Lawrence 15–0, Ripon 24–0, Colorado College 26–0, Northwestern 28–3, Iowa 12–0 in 1st 5 games. *Lost:* Chicago 5–0. *Tied:*

unbeaten Minnesota 6–6.   *Noteworthy:* 1st year under J.R. Richards.

1912 (7–0)   *Won:* Lawrence 13–0, Northwestern 56–0, Purdue 41–0 (1st meeting since 1907), Chicago 30–12, Arkansas 64–7, Minnesota 14–0, Iowa 28–10.   *Stars:* T Robert Butler (Badgers' 1st consensus All-American), FB Al Tanberg, HB John Van Riper.   *Noteworthy:* won 4th Big 10 title in 1st year under William Juneau.

1919 (5–2)   *Won:* Ripon 37–0, Marquette 13–0, Northwestern 10–6 (1st meeting since 1912), Illinois 14–10 (1st over Illini in 7 games since 1906), Chicago 10–3. *Lost:* Minnesota 19–7, Ohio St. 3–0 in consecutive late games. *Stars:* Es Paul Meyers and Frank Weston, C Charles Carpenter, T Berthold Mann.

1920 (6–1)   *Won:* Lawrence 60–0, Michigan St. 27–0, Northwestern 27–7, Minnesota 3–0, Illinois 14–9, Chicago 3–0. *Lost:* unbeaten Ohio St. 13–7. *Stars:* Weston, Ts Ralph Scott and Howie Stark. *Noteworthy:* J.R. Richards returned as coach.

1921 (5–1–1)   *Won:* Lawrence 28–0, South Dakota St. 24–3, Northwestern 27–0, Illinois 20–0, Minnesota 35–0 in 1st 5 games. *Lost:* Chicago 3–0. *Tied:* Michigan 7–7 (1st meeting since 1905). *Stars:* FB Guy Sundt, HB Alvah Elliott, C George Bunge.

1925 (6–1–1)   *Won:* Iowa St. 30–0, Franklin 35–0, Purdue 7–0 (1st meeting since 1915), Iowa 6–0, Michigan St. 21–10, Chicago 20–7. *Lost:* Michigan 21–0. *Tied:* Minnesota 12–12. *Noteworthy:* 1st year under George Little.

1928 (7–1–1)   *Won:* Notre Dame 22–6, Cornell (Iowa) 49–0, North Dakota St. 13–7, Michigan 7–0 (1st over Wolverines in 12 games since 1899), Alabama 15–0, Chicago 25–0, Iowa 13–0. *Lost:* Minnesota 6–0 in finale. *Tied:* Purdue 19–19. *Stars:* QB Bo Cuisinier, G John Parks, T Rube Wagner.

1930 (6–2–1)   *Won:* Lawrence 53–6, Carleton 28–0, Chicago 34–0, Pennsylvania 27–0, South Dakota St. 58–7, Minnesota 14–0. *Lost:* Purdue 7–6, Northwestern 20–7. *Tied:* Ohio St. 0–0 (1st meeting since 1920). *Stars:* T Milo Lubratovich, E Milt Gantenbein, soph G Greg Kabat.

1932 (6–1–1)   *Won:* Marquette 7–2 (1st meeting since 1919), Iowa 34–0, Coe 39–0, Illinois 20–12, Minnesota 20–13, Chicago 18–7. *Lost:* unbeaten Purdue 7–6. *Tied:* Ohio St. 7–7. *Stars:* Kabat, HB Mickey McGuire (43-yd punting avg). *Noteworthy:* 1st year under Dr. Clarence Spears.

1942 (8–1–1)   *Won:* Camp Grant 7–0, Marquette

35–7, Missouri 17–9, Great Lakes 13–7, Purdue 13–0, national cochamp Ohio St. 17–7, Northwestern 20–19, Minnesota 20–6. *Lost:* Iowa 6–0. *Tied:* Notre Dame 7–7 (1st meeting since 1936). *Stars:* FB Pat Harder (5 TDs, 48 pts), E Dave Schreiner, C Fred Negus.

1951 (7–1–1) *Won:* Marquette 22–6, Purdue 31–7, Northwestern 41–0, Indiana 6–0, Penn 16–7, Iowa 34–7, Minnesota 30–6. *Lost:* unbeaten Illinois 14–10. *Tied:* Ohio St. 6–6. *Stars:* E/LB Harold Faverty, DE Pat O'Donahue, LB Deral Teteak, Bill Lane (6 int), DB Ed Withers, QB John Coatta (1,154 yds pass), Jerry Witt (17 pass rec for 371 yds and 8 TDs), frosh FB Alan "The Horse" Ameche (824 yds rush), G Bob Kennedy, T Jerry Smith. *Noteworthy:* led nation in total defense and scoring defense (5.9-pt avg).

1952 (6–3–1) *Won:* Marquette 42–19, Illinois 20–6, Iowa 42–13, Rice 21–7, Northwestern 24–20, Indiana 37–14. *Lost:* Ohio St. 23–14, UCLA 20–7. *Tied:* Minnesota 21–21. *Stars:* Ameche (946 yds and 7 TDs rush), soph QB Jim Haluska (1,410 yds and 12 TDs pass), Witt (25 pass rec for 341 yds and 7 TDs), Harland Carl (7 TDs), OT Dave Suminski, DE Don Voss, DT Kennedy, Burt Hable (5 int). *Noteworthy:* Got share of 5th Big 10 title (1st since 1912). Made 1st bowl appearance, losing to USC 7–0 in Rose Bowl; Ameche ran for 133 yds.

1953 (6–2–1) *Won:* Penn St. 20–0 (1st meeting), Marquette 13–11 (10th straight over Hilltoppers), Purdue 28–19, Iowa 10–6, Northwestern 34–13, Illinois 34–7. *Lost:* UCLA 13–0, Ohio St. 20–19. *Tied:* Minnesota 21–21. *Stars:* Ameche (801 yds and 5 TDs rush), Jim Miller (6 TDs), Norbert Esser (19 pass rec for 238 yds).

1954 (7–2) *Won:* Marquette 52–14, Michigan St. 6–0 (1st meeting since 1925), Rice 13–7, Purdue 20–6, Northwestern 34–13, Illinois 27–14, Minnesota 27–0. *Lost:* unbeaten national cochamp Ohio St. 31–14, Iowa 13–7 (1st to Hawkeyes since 1948) in successive mid-season games. *Stars:* Heisman Trophy–winner Ameche (641 yds and 9 TDs rush),

Ron Locklin (22 pass rec for 218 yds), C Gary Messner, Miller (6 int).

1958 (7–1–1) *Won:* Miami (Fla.) 20–0, Marquette 50–0 (15th straight over Hilltoppers), Purdue 31–6, Michigan St. 9–7, Northwestern 17–13, Illinois 31–12, Minnesota 27–12. *Lost:* national cochamp Iowa 20–9. *Tied:* Ohio St. 7–7. *Star:* QB/DB Dale Hackbart (9 TDs rush, 7 int).

1959 (7–3) *Won:* Stanford 16–14, Marquette 44–6, Iowa 25–16, Ohio St. 12–3 (1st over Buckeyes in 12 games since 1946), Michigan 19–10 (1st meeting since 1950, 1st over Wolverines in 7 games since 1934), Northwestern 24–19, Minnesota 11–7. *Lost:* Purdue 21–0 (1st to Boilermakers in 11 games since 1945), Illinois 9–6. *Stars:* Hackbart (955 yds total off, 6 TDs rush), T Dan Lanphear, G Jerry Stalcup, K Karl Holzwarth (nation's leader with 7 FGs). *Noteworthy:* Won 6th Big 10 title. Lost to Washington 44–8 in Rose Bowl, scoring on 4-yd run by Tom Wiesner and 2-pt conversion pass from Hackbart (who had 145 yds pass) to Al Schoonover.

1962 (8–2) *Won:* New Mexico St. 69–13, Indiana 30–6, Notre Dame 17–8 (1st meeting since 1944), Iowa 42–14, Michigan 34–12, Northwestern 37–6, Illinois 35–6, Minnesota 14–9. *Lost:* Ohio St. 14–7. *Stars:* QB Ron VanderKelen (1,181 yds and 12 TDs pass), TE Pat Richter (38 pass rec for 531 yds and 5 TDs), HB Lou Holland (11 TDs), Ralph Kurek (6 TDs). *Noteworthy:* Led nation in scoring (31.7-pt avg) and took 7th Big 10 title. Lost to unbeaten national champ USC 42–37 in Rose Bowl after trailing 42–14 in 4th period; VanderKelen passed for 401 yds and 2 TDs and ran for another, Richter caught 11 for 163 yds and a TD, and Holland caught 8 passes and ran for a TD.

BOWL SUMMARY

Garden State 0–1; Hall of Fame 0–1; Independence 1–0; Rose 0–3.

BOWL RECORD (1–5)

Regular Season	Bowl	Score	Opponent	Record
1952 (6–2–1)	Rose	0–7	USC	(9–1)
1959 (7–2)	Rose	8–44	Washington	(9–1)
1962 (8–1)	Rose	37–42	USC	(10–0)

(continued)

Regular Season	Bowl	Score	Opponent	Record
1981 (7–4)	Garden State	21–28	Tennessee	(7–4)
1982 (6–5)	Independence	14–3	Kansas St.	(6–4–1)
1984 (7–3–1)	Hall of Fame	19–20	Kentucky	(8–3)

CONFERENCE TITLES

Big 10—1897, 1901*, 1906*, 1912, 1952*, 1959, 1962.

TOP 20 AP AND UPI RANKING

1942	3	1952	11–10	1957	U–14	1961	U–18
1950	U–20	1953	15–14	1958	7–6	1962	2–2
1951	8–8	1954	9–10	1959	6–6		

MAJOR RIVALS

Wisconsin has played at least 10 games with Beloit 16–1, Chicago 19–16–5, Illinois 24–33–6, Indiana 25–16–2, Iowa 34–34–2, Lawrence 17–0–1, Marquette 32–4, Michigan 8–41–1, Michigan St. 12–23, Minnesota 39–55–8, Northwestern 48–27–5, Notre Dame 6–8–2, Ohio St. 13–45–4, Purdue 32–25–7. Record against Big 10 member Penn St. is 2–0.

COACHES

Dean of Wisconsin coaches is Harry Stuhldreher with record of 45–62–6 for 1936–48. Most wins were under Phil King, 65–11–1 for 1896–1902 and 1905, with 2 Big 10 titles and 1 perfect season. Other top records for at least 3 years were by J.R. Richards, 29–9–4 for 1911, 1917, and 1919–22; William Juneau, 18–8–2 for 1912–15 with 1 Big 10 title and 1 perfect record; Glenn Thistlethwaite, 26–16–3 for 1927–31; Ivan "Ivy" Williamson, 41–19–4 for 1949–55 with 1 Big 10 title and 1 Rose Bowl team; Milt Bruhn, 52–45–6 for 1956–66 with 2 Big 10 titles and 2 Rose Bowl teams; and Dave McClain, 46–42–3 for 1978–85 with 3 bowl teams.

MISCELLANEA

First game was loss to Calumet Club 27–0 in 1889 ...1st win (and highest score ever) was over Whitewater Normal 106–0 in 1890 ... highest score since 1900 was over Beloit 87–0 in 1903 ... highest since W.W. II was over New Mexico St. 69–13 in 1962 ... worst defeat was by Minnesota 63–0 in 1890 ... worst since 1900 was by Ohio St. 59–0 in 1969 ... highest against since 1900 was by Ohio St. 62–7 in 1969 and by Michigan 62–14 in 1988 ... longest win streak of 17 in 1900–02 ended by Michigan 6–0 ... longest winless string of 23 in 1967–69 broken with win over Iowa 23–17 ... consensus All-Americans were Robert Butler, T, 1912; Ray Keeler, G, 1913; Howard Buck, T, 1915; Charles Carpenter, C, 1919; Ralph Scott, T, 1920; Marty Below, T, 1923; Milo Lubratovich, T, 1930; Dave Schreiner, E, 1942; Alan Ameche, B, 1954; Dan Lanphear, T, 1959; Pat Richter, E, 1962; Dennis Lick, OT, 1975; and Tim Krumrie, DL, 1981 ... Academic All-Americans were Bob Kennedy, DL, 1952; Alan Ameche, B, 1953–54; Jon Hobbs, B, 1958; Dale Hackbart, B, 1959; Pat Richter, E, 1962; Ken Bowman, C, 1963; Rufus Ferguson, RB, 1972; Kyle Borland, LB, 1982; and Donald Davey, DL, 1987–90 ... Heisman Trophy winner was Alan Ameche, FB, 1954.

INDEPENDENTS

Over the past several decades a score of colleges and universities, most of them in the East and South, operated without conference affiliation on the Division I-A level in college football. A number of these were affiliated with conferences at one time or another; others have always been independent by choice or through circumstance. Among current independents that have won conference titles in the past are Cincinnati (Buckeye, MAC, MVC), East Carolina (SC), Louisville (MVC), Memphis State (MVC), Southern Mississippi (Gulf States), Tulane (SC, SEC), and Tulsa (MVC). A number of independent powers of the past no longer play intercollegiate football in the late twentieth century or else field teams on the Division II or Division III level. Some of college football's rich traditions belong to those schools and to schools that currently operate as independents.

At the beginning of the final decade of the twentieth century, a number of independents began to seek conference affiliation in large part because of television contracts tied in with conferences. In 1990, Penn State, long a major independent in the East, was admitted to membership in the Big 10 (though not eligible for the title until 1993), Florida State was admitted to the ACC (beginning league play in 1992), South Carolina entered the SEC (starting league play in 1992), and Miami (Fla.) became a member of the Big East.

The Big East, a powerful basketball conference for several years, expanded in early 1991 in accordance with the wishes of its major football-playing members—Boston College, Miami (Fla.), Pittsburgh, and Syracuse—which had competed for years as independents. Added as new members for football only were longtime independents Rutgers, Temple, Virginia Tech, and West Virginia. The league began play immediately, with Miami (Fla.) winning the inaugural championship in 1991.

In the spring of 1992 five independents—Cincinnati, East Carolina, Memphis State, Southern Mississippi, and Tulsa—formed an Independent Football Alliance to generate increased recognition for its members. In 1993 the five began playing one another on a home-and-home basis as schedules permitted. The alliance will keep statistics and establish individual awards for members.

FACTS AND ODDITIES ON INDEPENDENTS

Schools still operating as Divison I-A independents in 1993 have won 16 generally recognized national championships; most of these have been won by Notre Dame.The first independent to win a national title was Army in 1914, when the Cadets went 9–0, outscored foes 219–20, and, in the process, beat Notre Dame (20–7) for the first time. Notre Dame won its first national championship in 1924, finishing 9–0 behind the fabled Four Horsemen and then beating undefeated Stanford 27–10 in the Rose Bowl. The Irish were back to win successive national crowns in 1929–30, going 9–0 in 1929 behind QB Frank Carideo and 10–0 in 1930 (Knute Rockne's last season as coach) behind Carideo and B Marchy Schwartz.

No current independent won the national title again until Notre Dame won its fourth title in 1943; it lost its finale to a powerful Great Lakes service team 19–14 but finished 9–1 behind QB Angelo Bertelli (Notre Dame's first Heisman Trophy winner) and B Creighton Miller. The title shifted back to the East the following year when Army set a modern record, averaging 56 points per game behind the legendary backfield duo of HB Glenn Davis (Maxwell Award winner) and FB Felix "Doc" Blanchard. The Cadets finished 9–0, gave Notre Dame its worst ever defeat (59–0), and beat all foes by at least 16 points. In 1945 the Cadets repeated with a 9–0 record behind Davis and Blanchard (winner of both the Heisman Trophy and the Maxwell Award), and won all games by at least 19 points.

In 1946 Notre Dame's Fighting Irish and Earl "Red" Blaik's third straight unbeaten Army team (once more featuring Blanchard and Heisman Trophy–winner Davis) played to a 0–0 tie in an epic game at Yankee Stadium. The Cadets finished 9–0–1 to Notre Dame's 8–0–1, but most of the selectors gave the national crown to the Irish, paced by QB Johnny Lujack and T George "Moose" Connor (winner of the first Outland Trophy). In 1947 Frank Leahy's Notre Dame team finished 9–0 behind Heisman Trophy–winner Lujack, Connor, and HB Terry Brennan, and won a major share of Notre Dame's sixth national title. Two years later Notre Dame went 10–0 behind QB Bob Williams and E Leon Hart (the last lineman to win the Heisman Trophy) to win the 1949 crown. In 1953 Notre Dame was back with a 9–0–1 record (the tie was with Iowa 14–14) in Leahy's last year, and won a major share of its eighth national crown.

Notre Dame won a minor share of the national crown in 1964, Ara Parseghian's first year as Fighting Irish coach, winning 9 straight games before a season-ending loss to USC 20–17. In 1966 the Irish were back with a solid share of the title and led the nation in scoring while finishing 9–0–1 (the tie was with unbeaten defending national champ Michigan State 10–10 at East Lansing). In 1973 the Irish won a major portion of the national title, their 11th, by finishing 10–0 and then edging 11–0 Alabama 24–23 in the Sugar Bowl in one of the most exciting bowl games ever played. Notre Dame was back for its 12th national crown in 1977 despite an early season loss to Mississippi 20–13. The 10–1 Irish upset 11–0 Texas 38–10 in the Cotton Bowl to seize the title from the Longhorns. In 1988 the Fiesta Bowl matched two unbeaten independents for the national crown, with 11–0 Notre Dame beating then independent West Virginia (11–0 and winner of its first Lambert Trophy) 34–21 to give the Irish their 13th national crown.

Players from current independents have won the Heisman Trophy 12 times. Winners were Notre Dame QB Angelo Bertelli, 1943; Army FB Felix "Doc" Blanchard, 1945; Army HB Glenn Davis, 1946; Notre Dame QB John Lujack, 1947; Notre Dame E Leon Hart, 1949; Notre Dame HB John Lattner, 1953; Notre Dame QB Paul Hornung, 1956; Army HB Pete Dawkins, 1958; Navy HB Joe Bellino, 1960; Navy QB Roger Staubach, 1963; Notre Dame QB John Huarte, 1964; and Notre Dame WR Tim Brown, 1987.

The Maxwell Award has gone to players at current independent schools 12 times as well. Winners were Army HB Glenn Davis, 1944; Army FB Felix "Doc" Blanchard, 1945; Notre Dame E Leon Hart, 1949; Notre Dame HB John Lattner, 1952–1953; Navy E Ron Beagle, 1954; Navy T Bob Reifsnyder, 1957; Army HB Pete Dawkins, 1958; Navy HB Joe Bellino, 1960; Navy QB Roger Staubach, 1963; Notre Dame LB Jim Lynch, 1966; and Notre Dame DE Ross Browner, 1977.

Players from current independents have won the Outland Trophy four times. Winners were Notre Dame T George Connor, 1946; Army G Joe Steffy, 1947; Notre Dame G Bill Fischer, 1948; and Notre Dame DE Ross Browner, 1976. The Lombardi Award has gone to players at current independent schools twice, to Notre Dame DE Walt Patulski in 1971 and to Notre Dame DE Ross Browner in 1977.

Coaches at current independent schools have won national Coach of the Year honors a number of times since the American Football Coaches Association (AFCA) initiated the award in 1935.

The first independents coaches to win the AFCA award were Edward Mylin of Lafayette in 1937 and Bill Kern of Carnegie Tech in 1938. Frank Leahy in 1941 was the first Notre Dame coach to win it. Only two other Irish coaches have won national honors, Ara Parseghian taking both the AFCA award and the Football Writers Association of America (FWAA) award (initiated in 1957) in 1964, and Lou Holtz winning the FWAA award in 1988. Earl "Red" Blaik of Army was named national Coach of the Year in 1946; Army's Tom Cahill was named in 1966.

Some of the most famous coaches of all time spent all or most of their careers at independent schools. Knute Rockne of Notre Dame, more than 60 years after his death, still is considered by many to be the greatest of all college coaches. Rockne compiled a record of 105–12–5 at Notre Dame in 1918–1930, a winning percentage of .881 that has never been equaled. He directed Notre Dame to its first postseason appearance, a victory over unbeaten Stanford 27–10 in the 1925 Rose Bowl, had five unbeaten teams and three national champions, and coached 10 consensus All-America players. Yet statistics touch only the surface in discussing "the Rock." He was recognized as perhaps the most outstanding motivator football has ever seen. His halftime talks are legendary, and one of his former players at Notre Dame, Frank Leahy, stands second only to Rockne in all-time winning percentage for college coaches: .864 for 13 years, 11 of them at his alma mater. Other top Rockne disciples with outstanding winning percentages as coaches were Frank Thomas (.795 for 19 years), Jim Crowley (.761 for 13 years), Elmer Layden (.733 for 16 years), and Eddie Anderson (.606 for 39 years).

Rockne attracted good players and assistant coaches because of not only his success on the football field, but also his magnetic personality. His clinics for high school coaches, conducted at the beginning of Notre Dame's spring drills, attracted hundreds annually from across the country. He used his varsity team to demonstrate plays and formations, and many a coach hoped some day to send one of his players to Notre Dame to learn under "Rock." Rockne insisted that football should be fun. "When you're playing it," he told his team, "have a lot of fun out of it. Come out here and enjoy it. I want you to play football because you like it." He admitted, however, that winning "is the most fun of all." He stressed team play and "sacrifice, unselfish sacrifice," and his teams were noted for their speed, intelligence, and deception. Rhythm, cadence, and play execution were all important factors in Rockne's coaching system.

Rockne did not invent plays, but his Notre Dame shift revolutionized football's offense. When the NCAA rule makers began limiting movement in the shift—thereby restricting its capacity to deceive the opposing team—Rockne uttered his disgust along with some warnings about how the new limitations would change football. He said: "Without the shift, we would never have had the Four Horsemen in football. They averaged in weight 157 pounds. The shift enabled them to use their speed and their intelligence and their ability to finesse the other fellow. Now they're legislating against the shift. . . . Every year they want to slow the shift up slower and slower and slower, which in my opinion is absolutely ridiculous. Whether the referee counts 6 or whether he counts 20, the question simmers down to this: Is there any unfair advantage? In my opinion, if the shifting team stops for one second, that's long enough for anybody except the stupid defensive team, and football wasn't made for any defensive team. However, if they abolish the shift, I'll change my cut of player from the intelligent, smart, trim–ankled player that the Four Horsemen [typified] . . . and I'll go in for the cow-minded, hippopotamus type that so many schools use now, and so when you see a football picture of the Notre Dame team about four years from now, you will notice the bovine expressions and the ox-knuckle ankles predominating. . . . "

A by-product of Rockne's brand of football was fewer injuries than caused by the power style preferred by many coaches. Players who faced Notre Dame during the Rockne years claimed that the Fighting Irish were the easiest team to play—not the easiest to beat, but the easiest to play, because Notre Dame never banged the opposition into submission thereby ruining them for later games.

No one had a better reputation than Rockne for getting his teams ready for a game, or for rousing them to greater efforts through his halftime talks. Leahy said that Rockne "was a great psychologist. He knew just exactly when to criticize and when to encourage." He said that during practice "the Rock" could be "extremely complimentary, and ten seconds later he'd be saying the most sarcastic, cutting words I've ever heard."

The best-known of Rockne's halftime pep talks was the "Win one for the Gipper" story. Grantland Rice said that Rockne used the plea in the 1928 Army game in a season when the Irish were a bit undermanned for a Rockne team. Army had a 6–0 record behind All–America back Chris Cagle, and Notre Dame was 4–2, when the two teams met at Yankee Stadium. For two quarters Notre Dame fought the Cadets to a scoreless standoff; at that point Rockne decided the time was right. At halftime he related the story of the final request by his 1920 All-American, how George Gipp had looked up from his deathbed and said, "Rock, I know I'm going . . . but I'd like one last request. . . . Some day, some time, when the going isn't so easy, when the odds are against us, ask a Notre Dame team to win a game for me—for the 'Gipper.' I don't know where I'll be then, Rock, but I'll know about it and I'll be happy." Rockne let that sink in a moment, then added, "This is the day, and you are the team."

Even with emotions aroused to fever pitch, the Irish fell behind 6–0 as the result of some great running by Army's Cagle, but then drove 80 yards to tie the score. With less than three minutes left in the game, third team end Johnny O'Brien made a juggling catch of a long pass and raced to the end zone to give Notre Dame a 12–6 upset win. However, the emotional drain may have taken something out of the Irish—they lost their last two games to finish the season 5–4.

Against Navy the previous year Rockne had opened the game with his reserves (a frequent practice of his, aimed at wearing down the opposition for the starters) clad in the usual Notre Dame blue jerseys. Navy scored in the first 5 minutes, and Rockne ordered in his first team. At the last moment they whipped off their blue warmup sweaters and dashed out on the field clad in green jerseys, a morale booster that helped the Irish to a 19–6 win.

Rockne was known on occasion to stay out of the locker room at halftime after an especially poor first-half performance by his charges. Then, just before time to take the field for the second half, he would open the door, peek in, and say, "Oh, sorry. I was looking for the Notre Dame football team." Or he might say in a sarcastic tone: "So this is Notre Dame!" Either way, the comment usually got the desired results.

Another fabled coach who spent most of his career at independent schools was Glenn "Pop" Warner, one of only four men who compiled 300 or more victories primarily at the major college level. Warner had a record of 313–106–32, a winning percentage of .729, for 1895–1938 at seven schools. Included were stints of thirteen years at Carlisle Indian School, nine at Pittsburgh, and six at Temple. Warner produced five All-Americans, including the immortal Jim Thorpe, at Carlisle (where he was 109–42–8 in two stints between 1899 and 1913); had two All-Americans at Cornell in 1906; eight All-Americans and two national champions at Pittsburgh between 1915 and 1923; five All-Americans and a national champion at Stanford between 1924 and 1932; and coached a Sugar Bowl team (unbeaten in regular season) at Temple in 1934.

Warner was credited with inventing both the single-wing and double-wing systems of attack, which dominated football for nearly half a century, and also was known for his psychological ploys. When he coached at Carlisle Indian School, he often used a warrior theme to fire up his charges before a big game. A typical pregame talk would go something like this:"From the shores of Little Big Horn to the banks of Wounded Knee Creek, the spirits of your people call to you today. The men who died in Chief Joseph's retreat over the mountains, the Cherokees who marched on bleeding feet through the snow out of their ancestral lands, tell you you must win. These men playing against you today are soldiers. You are Indians. Tonight we will know whether or not you are warriors." More often than not, they proved to be warriors.

A number of independents that fielded teams in the past have given up the sport over the years, but not before adding to the richness of the game's tradition. Among such schools were Detroit, which fielded teams from 1896–1964; Marquette, with teams from 1892–1960; New York University, 1873–1952; and San Francisco, 1924–1951 and 1959–1971. But the most colorful, perhaps, was Carlisle, which fielded teams from 1893 through 1917. Carlisle played some of the best teams in the land in those years, compiling a record of 167–88–13 (a winning percentage of .647) and producing five All-Americans.

One of those, Jim Thorpe, was picked in a 1950 Associated Press poll as not only the greatest football player in the history of the sport, but also the greatest athlete of the twentieth century by its mid-point. The Sac and Fox American Indian, who also had some French and Irish ancestry, scored 53 TDs for Carlisle during his four years on the varsity at the small school in Pennsylvania, and kicked 17 FGs and 70 extra pts. Statistics can tell only part of Thorpe's football story, for complete records are not available for 15 of the games he played at Carlisle; but, during his senior year, he ran for more than 200 yds in at least five games, totaling 362 in a 34–26 loss to Pennsylvania. He was a consensus All-America pick in both his junior and senior years.

Early in his senior season, in 1912, Thorpe gained 119 yds in just seven carries against Villanova, and two games later made 184 yds and three TDs in a 33–0 win over Syracuse. In the next game he made 266 yds and two TDs in a 45–8 rout of Pittsburgh, then gained more than 220 yds in each of his last four games. Against Army he gained 238 yds on 27 carries in a 27–6 win. The Thorpe legend was built on incidents such as the one that broke that game open: Backed up deep in their own territory, the Indians went into punt formation. As Thorpe stood waiting for the ball, he muttered to referee Bill Langford, "They think I'm going to kick, both us and Army. But I ain't." Thorpe then took the snap from center, faked a punt, and raced 90 yds for a TD.

The next game, the loss to Penn, was Thorpe's biggest yardage performance. In his last two games Thorpe ran for 221 yds and four TDs in a victory over Springfield, then closed his Carlisle career with 264 yds and three TDs in a 32–0 win over Brown on Thanksgiving Day.

Notre Dame has produced more than 70 consensus All-Americans, 7 Heisman Trophy winners, 5 Maxwell Award winners, 3 Outland Trophy winners, and 2 Lombardi Award winners. Yet no Fighting Irish player is more famous than George Gipp, immortalized with his reputed deathbed plea to Coach Knute Rockne to have the boys "win one for the Gipper."

When he arrived at South Bend, however, the Michigan minister's son had visions of baseball glory, and turned to football only after Rockne persuaded him to go out for the team. Over his four-year career Gipp ran for 2,341 yds (a record that stood at Notre Dame until 1978) and completed 93 of 187 passes (an excellent percentage at the time) for another 1,769 yds. He scored 21 TDs, passed for 8, kicked 27 extra pts, and was Notre Dame's punter. During his 1917–1920 playing days Notre Dame's record was 27–2–3, 18–0 in his last two years.

Injured in the 13–10 win over Indiana in his next–to–last college game, Gipp was kept out of action in his finale at Northwestern until the final quarter when Rockne gave in to the fans' chant, "We want Gipp! We want Gipp!" The star halfback did not carry the ball in the 33–7 Notre Dame victory, but he completed five of six passes for 157 yds and two TDs in a few minutes' playing time. Within three weeks Gipp was dead of complications from strep throat, dying about the time that he was named Notre Dame's third consensus All-American.

Notre Dame also was home of the most famous backfield unit of all time—the Four Horsemen. In his *New York Times* story reporting the Irish's 13–7 win over Army on October 18, 1924, Grantland Rice wrote: "Outlined against a blue, gray October sky the Four Horsemen rode again. In dramatic lore they are known as famine, pestilence, destruction and death. These are only aliases. Their real names are: Stuhldreher, Miller, Crowley and Layden. They formed the crest of the South Bend cyclone before which another fighting Army team was swept over the precipice at the Polo Grounds this afternoon as 55,000 spectators peered down upon the bewildering panorama spread out upon the green plain below."

The week following that game Coach Rockne's student publicity aide posed the players on four plow horses from the Notre Dame farm. The photo quickly gained wide circulation, and the Four Horsemen became legendary before their senior season had reached the mid-point. Taken separately, the career or season record of each Horseman does not stand out; though it must be remembered that the canny Rockne usually started a heavier second team backfield and then inserted the fleet, smaller

Horsemen after the opposing line had been worn down a bit. Thus, they did not play full time. But as a unit, they were extremely versatile and effective.

The quarterback was Harry Stuhldreher, a 5'7", 151-pounder from Massillon, Ohio. Rockne called him a good and fearless blocker with exceptional intelligence. Stuhldreher was the best passer of the group, completing 43 of 67 passes for 744 yds and 10 TDs during his regular-season 1922–24 career. He also ran for 10 TDs, scored another on a pass reception, and had a 12th TD on a punt return. Stuhldreher was the squad's principal punt returner.

The halfbacks were Don Miller, a 5'11", 160-pounder from Defiance, Ohio, and Jimmy Crowley, a 5'11", 161-pounder from Green Bay, Wisconsin. Rockne praised Miller for his fleetness and daring, Crowley for his broken-field-running ability and his wit. Miller ran for 1,933 yds (763 as a senior) in regular season and scored 22 TDs, including four on pass rec and one on a kickoff return. He was the leading pass receiver with 31 for 590 yds. Crowley ran for 1,841 yds (739 as a senior) in regular season, passed for 544 yds and four TDs, and scored 18 TDs, three on pass rec. He also intercepted six passes and was the leading place kicker with 36 extra pts. He punted occasionally.

The fullback was Elmer Layden, a 6-foot, 162-pounder from Davenport, Iowa. Rockne said Layden had exceptional speed and kicking ability. He ran for 1,296 yds, scored 14 TDs, three on pass rec, passed for two more scores, and kicked 12 extra pts during regular season. He also averaged 36.1 yds on 113 punts and led the Horsemen with seven interceptions. Layden scored three TDs, two on long pass int returns, in Notre Dame's 27–10 Rose Bowl win over Stanford on New Year's Day 1925.

The four began playing as a unit about midway through their sophomore seasons. When they finished their careers, they had compiled a regular-season total of 5,188 yds rushing with 53 TDs, caught 73 passes for 1,254 yds and 11 TDs, completed 93 of 180 passes for 1,530 yds and 16 TDs, returned 99 punts and 31 kickoffs, kicked 50 extra pts, and intercepted 19 passes. During the three years the Four Horse-men were on the varsity, Notre Dame's regular-season record was 26–2–1. Their senior season saw a 9–0 record followed by the victory over previously unbeaten Stanford in the Rose Bowl and Notre Dame's first national championship. Three of the Horsemen made consensus All-America in 1924. The exception was Miller, who was edged out by an Illinois sophomore tailback named Harold Grange—better known as "Red."

The most famous pair of backs in the history of college football also played for an independent. They were Felix "Doc" Blanchard and Glenn Davis, who formed Army's "Mr. Inside, Mr. Outside" combination of 1944–46. The two were excellent all-round athletes, Blanchard participating in basketball, track, and wrestling and Davis in basketball, track, and baseball (captain of the latter team, he was good enough to receive a professional contract offer). Their greatest fame, however, came in football, as they sparked Army to a 27–0–1 record and two undisputed national championships.

Davis, of Claremont, California, started his varsity career a year earlier than Blanchard, gaining 634 yds rushing as a plebe. In four years he carried the ball 358 times for 2,957 yds—a remarkable career average of 8.3 yds per carry that still is unsurpassed by players with at least 300 carries. Davis averaged 11.5 yds per carry in both his sophomore and junior seasons, and won the Maxwell Award as a sophomore. When he won the Heisman Trophy as a senior, his per-carry average of 5.8 yds was the lowest of his career. However, that year he also passed for 396 yds and four TDs, caught 20 passes for 348 yds and five scores, intercepted five passes, and did the punting.

Blanchard won both the Heisman Trophy and the Maxwell Award as a junior in 1945 when he rushed for 718 yds, scored 19 TDs, returned four pass interceptions for 150 yds, and handled the punting. Both players were not only outstanding runners but good blockers and standouts on defense. Davis had 14 career interceptions, was an excellent punt returner, and scored 354 points. Blanchard was a hard-hitting linebacker as well as a fullback. He intercepted seven passes and scored 231 points.

An Army player from an earlier era, Chris "Red" Cagle (1927–29), joins Blanchard and Davis among the few players who have made consensus All-America three times in the twentieth century.

Notre Dame HB John Lattner was the only player ever to win two Maxwell Awards, taking the honor in 1952 and 1953. He ran for 732 yds and intercepted four passes as a junior in 1952, then led the Irish to a 9–0–1 record and a national championship in 1953, when he also won the Heisman Trophy.

Cincinnati's series with Miami (Ohio) is tied for sixth in the nation for most games played. Through 1992 the schools had met 97 times since 1888, with Miami holding an edge of 53–38–6.

The famed Army-Navy series stands 13th in most games played with 93 contests. The series began in 1890 and, through 1992, was dead even at 43–43–7. Independent Tulane has played 90 games with Louisiana State since 1893; through 1992 LSU led that series by 61–22–7 by its reckoning, or 60–23–7 by Tulane's reckoning. William and Mary's rivalry with Richmond is fourth in most games played among Division I-AA teams with 102; through 1992 the Tribe led 50–47–5 in the series begun in 1898.

A number of players in the early twentieth century transferred to the U.S. Military Academy after one or more years at another school. Harvard's three-time All-American, HB Charles Daly (1898–1900), made All-America again at Army in 1901, and Harry Wilson starred at Army in the mid-1920s after making All-America as a Penn State back in 1923. All-time Army great Chris Cagle (All-America 1927–1929) started his career at Southwestern Louisiana, where he set a number of records in 1925.

A Navy player is credited by some historians with introducing to the game an important piece of protection—the helmet. An elderly lady friend who saw lineman Joe Reeves take a nasty blow to the head during an 1893 game, designed a moleskin headgear for him to wear in the next contest—which he did despite the laughter and jeers of opponents. Within three years helmets were a common sight in college football games. Reeves later became an admiral and served as commander of the U.S. Fleet.

The Army–Navy game of 1893, won by Navy 6–4, was so bloody—including several free-for-all fights in the stands—that President Grover Cleveland banned the contest for five years. The series was resumed in 1899. The service academies did not meet during World War I (1917–1918), as a sign of unity. The series was interrupted again in 1928–1929 after bad feelings had again flared up. No regular-season games were scheduled in 1930 and 1931, but the teams met in charity games at New York's Yankee Stadium following the two seasons, with proceeds going to the relief of the unemployed during the early years of the Great Depression. Army won both games, 6–0 in 1930 and 17–7 in 1931. The series has continued uninterrupted since.

For more than 60 years Army has played its home games in a stadium named for the "father of West Point football," Cadet Dennis Michie. He was responsible for organizing the Army team that challenged Navy to the first interservice academy game in 1890. Dennis' father, the officer in command of West Point athletics, opposed that game. But when Army was beaten 24–0 by the more experienced Navy squad, the elder Michie ordered his son to organize a better team for a rematch in 1891. Dennis did, and Army defeated Navy 32–16 in their second meeting.

A 19-year-old Marine who had seen service in World War I got an appointment to the Naval Academy, and went out for the football team at Annapolis. He joked to teammates that Navy would never lose to Army as long as he played. Navy didn't lose many games during the three years that Swede Larson was on the varsity; its record was 18–4. Sure enough, the Midshipmen beat Army each year, 6–0 in 1919, 7–0 in 1920, and 7–0 again in 1921 when Larson was captain of the squad. Army, compiling a 19–9 record in the same period, was no slouch, either.

Larson returned to the Naval Academy as head coach in 1939 and predicted that Army would never beat a Navy team that he coached. Navy was 16–8–3 under Larson over the next three years, beating inferior Army teams 10–0 in 1939 and 14–0 in 1940, then defeating a good Cadet team 14–6 in 1941. Thus, in six games in which Larson participated as either player or coach, Navy not only won each time but shut out the Black Knights five times. Following the 1941 season and the attack on Pearl Harbor, Larson returned to active duty and never coached again.

One man is on record as having played in five Army-Navy games. He was Edward E. Farnsworth, who played for Army from 1899 through 1903. Army lost only the 1900 game during that period.

HB Glenn Davis scored 59 TDs during his 1943–1946 career at Army. Of those, 27 came on runs ranging from 37 to 87 yds. When the Cadets won the national championship in 1945, Davis and FB "Doc" Blanchard each scored at least one TD in every game of the 9–0 season. Blanchard scored 19 times and Davis 18.

An outstanding runner who never made consensus All-America was FB Ollie Matson of San Francisco, who gained 3,166 yds for the Dons in 1949–1951. He averaged 5.8 yds per carry and went on to professional football fame. In his senior year at San Francisco, Matson rushed for 1,566 yds, averaging 6.4 yds per carry, scored 21 TDs, and led the Dons to a 9–0 record.

One of the most remarkable of all football coaching records was set by Gil Dobie, who coached at Navy while Swede Larson was a player there. Dobie had not seen defeat in 11 years of college coaching when he took the Navy job in 1917, having compiled a record of 58–0–3 at North Dakota State and Washington between 1906 and 1916. His 1917 Navy team outscored opponents 443–23, but on October 6 his remarkable unbeaten string came to an end when the Midshipmen were beaten by West Virginia 7–0—the only defeat suffered by Navy that year. Dobie's record at Navy was 17–3 for 1917–1919.

Fordham, behind a line known as the "Seven Blocks of Granite," allowed its opponents only one TD all season in 1936, but that was a 1–yard run in the final game that gave New York University a 7–6 upset victory and knocked the Rams out of a likely Rose Bowl bid. Fordham and Pittsburgh, both of them Eastern and national powers at the time, played three consecutive 0–0 ties in 1935–1937.

The first time a college football game drew a crowd of at least 100,000 was in 1926 when 9–0 Navy met 7–1 Army at Chicago's Soldier Field. The two battled to a 21–21 tie before an estimated 110,000 spectators.

Several current Division I-A independents carry unusual or distinctive nicknames, including the Akron Zips, Cincinnati Bearcats, East Carolina Pirates, Notre Dame Fighting Irish, Southwestern Louisiana Ragin' Cajuns, Tulane Green Wave, and Tulsa Golden Hurricane.

Army is one of a handful of schools that have two nicknames, or three if it is kept in mind that Army itself is a nickname for the U.S. Military Academy. The official emblems of the Academy are Cadets and Black Knights. The U.S. Naval Academy, better known simply as Navy, uses the nickname Midshipmen, sometimes shortened to Middies or Mids.

The Bearcats emblem at Cincinnati may have come from a 1914 cartoon following a 14–7 win over Kentucky that showed a half-bear, half-cat-like animal harassing the Kentucky Wildcat. Two years earlier *Cincinnati Enquirer* sportswriter Jack Ryder had commented that the team played like Bearcats in another game.

Tulane was known simply as the Olive and Blue until 1919, when the school newspaper began calling the football team the Greenbacks. In

October 1920 the paper's editor, Earl Sparling (later a staff writer for the *New York World-Telegram*) published a song he had written, "The Rolling Green Wave," and various papers began using Green Wave as Tulane's nickname.

Tulsa's nickname is similar to that of Miami (Fla.) but in fact is derived from a different type of storm. Known as the Kendallites, Tigers, Orange and Black, or Presbyterians in early years, Tulsa changed its nickname as a result of a 7–0 record in 1922, when Coach Howard Archer said his team had roared through opponents like tornadoes. He suggested that they be known henceforth as the Golden Tornado. Georgia Tech, however, had that nickname at the time, so a change was made to Golden Hurricane, even though a hurricane would be hard-pressed to reach the inland Oklahoma city of Tulsa.

The nicknames of a few schools may have begun as terms of derision by opponents, but are now worn proudly. One of the most famous in this category is the Fighting Irish of Notre Dame. The name may have been first used as an insult by Northwestern fans in an 1887 game. With Notre Dame leading 5–0 at halftime in a game at Evanston, Northwestern fans began chanting, "Kill the Fighting Irish! Kill the Fighting Irish!" Because Notre Dame teams traditionally traveled the land to take on the best in all sections, such nicknames as Ramblers and Nomads were popular for a while, especially in the 1920s and 1930s, but Fighting Irish has long been carried proudly by Notre Dame athletic teams.

A number of colorful nicknames belonging to independent teams are no longer seen on the major college football scene. These include the Denver Pioneers, Georgetown Hoyas, San Francisco Dons, Santa Clara Broncos, St. Mary's Galloping Gaels, and Washington and Jefferson Presidents.

Army, Louisville, and William and Mary are among the few Division I schools with more than two official school colors. The Cadets use black, gold, and gray; Louisville red, black, and white; and William and Mary green, gold, and silver.

Over the years most of the independents in the West and the Midwest joined conferences, dropped to Division II or Division III football, or dropped the sport. Only the East and the South retained large numbers of schools operating independently of conferences before 1991, and only the East annually awards a trophy to the top team in its section. Independents have won the lion's share of the award in the past, but that can be expected to change with most former Eastern independents now in the Big East Conference.

The Lambert Trophy, since 1936 symbolic of football supremacy in the East, has been won 21 times by Penn State, though the Nittany Lions did not take their first trophy until 1947. Army is runner–up with seven Lambert Trophy winners, but has not won since 1958. Pittsburgh and Syracuse each has won the trophy six times, Navy five times, Boston College four times, and West Virginia once. Carnegie Tech and Fordham each won the award once in its early years, and Ivy League schools won it a half–dozen times between 1939 and 1970.

WINNERS OF THE LAMBERT TROPHY

Annual Champion	Regular Season	Bowl and Result
1936 Pittsburgh	7–1–1	Rose (W)
1937 Pittsburgh	9–0–1	
1938 Carnegie Tech	7–1	Sugar (L)
1939 Cornell	8–0	
1940 Boston College	10–0	Sugar (W)
1941 Fordham	7–1	Sugar (W)
1942 Boston College	8–1	Orange (L)
1943 Navy	8–1	
1944 Army	9–0	
1945 Army	9–0	
1946 Army	9–0–1	
1947 Penn State	9–0	Cotton (T)
1948 Army	8–0–1	
1949 Army	9–0	
1950 Princeton	9–0	
1951 Princeton	9–0	
1952 Syracuse	7–2	Orange (L)
1953 Army	7–1–1	
1954 Navy	7–2	Sugar (W)
1955 Pittsburgh	7–3	Sugar (L)
1956 Syracuse	7–1	Cotton (L)
1957 Navy	8–1–1	Cotton (W)
1958 Army	8–0–1	
1959 Syracuse	10–0	Cotton (W)
1960 Navy	5–4–1	
Yale	9–0	
1961 Penn State	7–3	Gator (W)
1962 Penn State	9–1	Gator (L)
1963 Navy	9–1	Cotton (L)
1964 Penn State	6–4	
1965 Dartmouth	9–0	
1966 Syracuse	8–2	Gator (L)
1967 Penn State	8–2	Gator (T)
1968 Penn State	10–0	Orange (W)
1969 Penn State	10–0	Orange (W)
1970 Dartmouth	9–0	
1971 Penn State	10–1	Cotton (W)
1972 Penn State	10–1	Sugar (L)
1973 Penn State	11–0	Orange (W)
1974 Penn State	9–2	Cotton (W)
1975 Penn State	9–2	Sugar (L)
1976 Pittsburgh	11–0	Sugar (W)
1977 Penn State	10–1	Fiesta (W)
1978 Penn State	11–0	Sugar (L)
1979 Pittsburgh	10–1	Fiesta (W)
1980 Pittsburgh	10–1	Gator (W)
1981 Penn State	9–2	Fiesta (W)
1982 Penn State	10–1	Sugar (W)
1983 Boston College	9–2	Liberty (L)
1984 Boston College	9–2	Cotton (W)
1985 Penn State	11–0	Orange (L)

(continued)

WINNERS OF THE LAMBERT TROPHY *(continued)*

Annual Champion	Regular Season	Bowl and Result
1986 Penn State	11–0	Fiesta (W)
1987 Syracuse	11–0	Sugar (T)
1988 West Virginia	11–0	Fiesta (L)
1989 Penn State	7–3–1	Holiday (W)
1990 Penn State	9–2	Blockbuster (L)
1991 Penn State	10–2	Fiesta (W)
1992 Syracuse	9–2	Fiesta (W)

ARMY (U.S. MILITARY ACADEMY) *(Cadets, Black Knights; Black, Gold and Gray)*

NOTABLE TEAMS

1891 (4–1–1) *Won:* Fordham 10–6, Stevens Tech 14–12, Schuylkill 6–0, Navy 32–16. *Lost:* Rutgers 27–6 (1st meeting). *Tied:* Princeton reserves 12–12.

1892 (3–1–1) *Won:* Stevens Tech 42–0, Trinity 24–0 (1st meeting), Princeton reserves 14–0. *Lost:* Navy 12–4 in finale. *Tied:* Wesleyan 6–6 in opener.

1895 (5–2) *Won:* Trinity 50–0, Tufts 35–0 (1st meeting), Dartmouth 6–0, Union 16–0, Brown 26–0. *Lost:* Harvard 4–0 (1st meeting), unbeaten Yale 28–8.

1897 (6–1–1) *Won:* Trinity 38–6, Wesleyan 12–9, Tufts 30–0, Lehigh 48–6, Stevens Tech 18–4, Brown 42–0. *Lost:* Harvard 10–0. *Tied:* unbeaten Yale 6–6. *Noteworthy:* 1st year under Herman Koehler.

1901 (5–1–2) *Won:* Franklin & Marshall 20–0, Trinity 17–0, Williams 15–0, Pennsylvania 24–0 (1st meeting), Navy 11–5. *Lost:* unbeaten Harvard 6–0. *Tied:* Yale 5–5, Princeton 6–6. *Stars:* T Paul Bunker, QB Charles Daly.

1902 (6–1–1) *Won:* Tufts 5–0, Dickinson 11–0, Williams 28–0, Union 56–0, Syracuse 46–0, Navy 22–8. *Lost:* Harvard 14–6. *Tied:* unbeaten Yale 6–6. *Stars:* T/HB Bunker, C Robert Boyers.

1903 (6–2–1) *Won:* Tufts 17–0, Dickinson 12–0, Vermont 32–0, Manhattan 48–0, Chicago 10–6 (1st intersectional game), Navy 40–5. *Lost:* Harvard 5–0, Yale 17–5 in successive mid-season games. *Tied:* Colgate 0–0 (1st meeting) in opener.

1904 (7–2) *Won:* Tufts 12–0, Dickinson 18–0, Yale 11–6 (1st in 12-game series dating to 1893), Williams 16–0, New York U. 41–0, Syracuse 21–5, Navy 11–0. *Lost:* Harvard 4–0, Princeton 12–6. *Stars:* B Henry Torney, C Arthur Tipton. *Noteworthy:* 1st year under Robert Boyers.

1907 (6–2–1) *Won:* Franklin & Marshall 23–0, Trinity 12–0, Rochester 30–0, Colgate 6–0, Tufts 21–0, Syracuse 23–4. *Lost:* Cornell 14–10, Navy 6–0. *Tied:* unbeaten national champ Yale 0–0. *Star:* G William Erwin.

1908 (6–1–2) *Won:* Tufts 5–0, Trinity 33–0, Colgate 6–0, Springfield 6–5 (1st meeting), Villanova 25–0 (1st meeting), Navy 6–4. *Lost:* Yale 6–0. *Tied:* Princeton 0–0, Washington & Jefferson 6–6. *Noteworthy:* 1st year under Harry Nelly.

1910 (6–2) *Won:* Tufts 24–0, Yale 9–3, Lehigh 28–0, Springfield 5–0, Villanova 13–0, Trinity 17–0. *Lost:* unbeaten national champ Harvard 6–0, unbeaten Navy 3–0. *Noteworthy:* Nelly's last team.

1911 (6–1–1) *Won:* Vermont 12–0, Rutgers 18–0 (1st meeting since 1900), Yale 6–0, Lehigh 20–0, Bucknell 20–2, Colgate 12–6. *Lost:* unbeaten Navy 3–0 in finale. *Tied:* Georgetown 0–0. *Star:* T Leland Devore.

1913 (8–1) *Won:* Stevens Tech 34–0, Rutgers 29–0, Colgate 7–6, Tufts 2–0, Albright 77–0, Villanova 55–0, Springfield 14–7, Navy 22–9 (1st Army–Navy game in New York City). *Lost:* unbeaten Notre Dame 35–13 (1st meeting). *Star:* E Louis Merillat. *Noteworthy:* 1st year under Charles Daly.

1914 (9–0) *Won:* Stevens Tech 49–0, Rutgers 13–0, Colgate 21–7, Holy Cross 14–0 (1st meeting), Villanova 41–0, Notre Dame 20–7, Maine 28–0, Springfield 13–6, Navy 20–0 (in Philadelphia). *Star:* soph C John McEwan. *Noteworthy:* won 1st national championship in 1st unbeaten season.

1916 (9–0) *Won:* Lebanon Valley 3–0, Washington & Lee 14–7, Holy Cross 17–0, Trinity 53–0, Villanova 69–7, Notre Dame 30–10, Maine 17–3, Springfield 17–2, Navy 15–7 (in New York). *Star:* HB Elmer Oliphant.

1917 (7–1) *Won:* Carnegie Tech 28–0, Virginia Military Institute (VMI) 34–0 (1st meeting), Tufts 26–3, Villanova 21–7, Carlisle Indians 28–0, Lebanon Valley 50–0, Boston College 13–7 (1st meeting). *Lost:* Notre Dame 7–2. *Star:* Oliphant (125 pts). *Noteworthy:* Navy game not played as sign of unity during W.W. I.

1920 (7–2) *Won:* Marshall 40–0, Union 35–0, Middlebury 29–0, Springfield 26–7, Tufts 28–6, Lebanon Valley 53–0, Bowdoin 90–0. *Lost:* unbeaten Notre Dame 27–17, Navy 7–0.

1922 (8–0–2) *Won:* Springfield 35–0, Lebanon Valley 12–0, Kansas 13–0, Auburn 19–6, New Hampshire 33–0, St. Bonaventure 53–0, Bates 39–0, Navy 17–14 (1st meeting in Philadelphia since 1914). *Tied:* Yale 7–7, Notre Dame 0–0. *Star:* soph C Ed Garbisch. *Noteworthy:* Daly's last team.

1923 (6–2–1) *Won:* Tennessee 41–0, Florida 20–0, Auburn 28–6, Lebanon Valley 74–0, Arkansas St. 44–0, Bethany (W.Va.) 20–6. *Lost:* Notre Dame

13–0 (in Brooklyn), unbeaten Yale 31–10. *Tied:* Navy 0–0 (in New York). *Noteworthy:* 1st year under John McEwan.

1924 (5–1–2) *Won:* St. Louis 17–0, Detroit 20–0, Boston U. 20–0 (1st meeting), Florida 14–7, Navy 12–0 (1st Army–Navy game in Baltimore). *Lost:* unbeaten national champ Notre Dame 13–7 (1st meeting in New York). *Tied:* unbeaten Yale 7–7, Columbia 14–14. *Stars:* Garbisch, G Gus Farwick.

1925 (7–2) *Won:* Detroit 31–6, Knox 26–7, Notre Dame 27–0 (1st over Irish since 1916), St. Louis 19–0, Davis & Elkins 14–6, Ursinus 44–0, Navy 10–3 (in New York). *Lost:* Yale 28–7, Columbia 21–7. *Stars:* soph HB Harry Wilson, E Charles Born. *Noteworthy:* McEwan's last year.

1926 (7–1–1) *Won:* Detroit 21–0, Davis & Elkins 21–7, Syracuse 27–21 (1st meeting since 1919), Boston U. 41–0, Yale 33–0 (1st over Bulldogs in 7 games since 1911), Franklin & Marshall 55–0, Ursinus 21–15. *Lost:* Notre Dame 7–0. *Tied:* unbeaten Navy 21–21 (in finale before estimated 110,000 in Chicago). *Stars:* Wilson, plebe HB Chris Cagle (5 TDs), soph T Bud Sprague. *Noteworthy:* 1st year under Biff Jones.

1927 (9–1) *Won:* Boston U. 13–0, Detroit 6–0, Marquette 21–12, Davis & Elkins 27–6, Bucknell 34–0, Franklin & Marshall 45–0, Notre Dame 18–0, Ursinus 13–0, Navy 14–9 (in New York). *Lost:* Yale 10–6 in mid-season. *Stars:* Sprague, Wilson, Cagle (681 yds rush, 353 yds pass, 6 TDs).

1928 (8–2) *Won:* Boston U. 35–0, Southern Methodist (SMU) 14–13, Providence 44–0, Harvard 15–0 (1st meeting since 1910, 1st over Crimson in 14-game series dating to 1895), Yale 18–6, DePauw 38–12, Carleton 32–7, Nebraska 13–3. *Lost:* Notre Dame 12–6, Stanford 26–0 (in New York, 1st meeting). *Star:* Cagle (759 yds rush, 470 yds pass, 5 TDs).

1930 (9–1–1) *Won:* Boston U. 39–0, Furman 54–0, Swarthmore 39–0, Harvard 6–0, North Dakota 33–6, Illinois 13–0 (in New York), Kentucky Wesleyan 47–2, Ursinus 18–0. *Lost:* unbeaten national champ Notre Dame 7–6 (in Chicago). *Tied:* Yale 7–7. *Star:* T Jack Price. *Noteworthy:* 1st year under Ralph Sasse. Beat Navy 6–0 in postseason charity game in New York City.

1931 (8–2–1) *Won:* Ohio Northern 60–0, Knox 67–6, Michigan St. 20–7, Colorado College 27–0, Louisiana State (LSU) 20–0, Ursinus 54–6, Notre Dame 12–0 (in New York). *Lost:* Harvard 14–13,

Pittsburgh 26–0 (1st meeting). *Tied:* Yale 6–6. *Star:* Price. *Noteworthy:* beat Navy 17–7 in postseason charity game in New York City.

1932 (8–2) *Won:* Furman 13–0, Carleton 57–0, Yale 20–0, William & Mary 33–0, Harvard 46–0, North Dakota St. 52–0, West Virginia Wesleyan 7–0, Navy 20–0 (in Philadelphia). *Lost:* unbeaten Pittsburgh 18–13, Notre Dame 21–0. *Star:* G Milt Summerfelt. *Noteworthy:* Sasse's last team.

1933 (9–1) *Won:* Mercer 19–6, VMI 32–0 (1st meeting since 1917), Delaware 52–0, Illinois 6–0 (in Cleveland), Yale 21–0, Coe 34–0, Harvard 27–0, Penn Military 12–0, Navy 12–7. *Lost:* Notre Dame 13–12 in finale. *Star:* B Jack Buckler. *Noteworthy:* 1st year under Gar Davidson.

1934 (7–3) *Won:* Washburn 19–0, Davidson 41–0, Drake 48–0, Sewanee 20–0, Yale 20–12, Harvard 27–6, The Citadel 34–0. *Lost:* Illinois 7–0, Notre Dame 12–6, Navy 3–0.

1935 (6–2–1) *Won:* William & Mary 14–0, Gettysburg 54–0, Harvard 13–0, Yale 14–8, Vermont 34–0, Navy 28–6. *Lost:* Mississippi St. 13–7, Pittsburgh 29–6 in successive mid-season games. *Tied:* Notre Dame 6–6. *Stars:* E Bill Shuler, B Charles "Monk" Meyer.

1937 (7–2) *Won:* Clemson 21–6, Columbia 21–18, Washington (Mo.) 47–7, VMI 20–7, Harvard 7–6, St. John's 47–6, Navy 6–0. *Lost:* Yale 15–7, Notre Dame 7–0. *Noteworthy:* Davidson's last team.

1938 (8–2) *Won:* Wichita St. 32–0, Virginia Tech 39–0, Harvard 20–17, Boston U. 40–0, Franklin & Marshall 20–12, Chattanooga 34–13, Princeton 19–7 (1st meeting since 1908), Navy 14–7. *Lost:* Columbia 20–18, Notre Dame 19–7. *Noteworthy:* 1st year under William Wood.

1943 (7–2–1) *Won:* Villanova 27–0, Colgate 42–0 (1st meeting since 1936), Temple 51–0, Columbia 52–0, Yale 39–7, Sampson (USN) 16–7, Brown 59–0. *Lost:* national champ Notre Dame 26–0, Navy 13–0 (1st meeting at West Point since 1892). *Tied:* Penn 13–13. *Stars:* T Frank Merritt, C Cas Myslinski, plebe HB Glenn Davis (634 yds rush, 394 yds pass, 8 TDs).

1944 (9–0) *Won:* North Carolina 46–0, Brown 59–7, Pittsburgh 69–7 (1st meeting since 1935), Coast Guard 76–0, Duke 27–7 (in New York, 1st meeting), Villanova 83–0, Notre Dame 59–0 (worst defeat in Fighting Irish history), Pennsylvania 62–7, Navy 23–7 (in Baltimore). *Stars:* Maxwell Award–winner Davis (667 yds rush, 13 pass rec for 221 yds, nation's leading scorer with 120 pts on 20 TDs), soph FB Felix "Doc" Blanchard (9 TDs, 8 pass rec for 203 yds), Gs John Green and Joe Stanowicz, QB Doug Kenna, soph E Barney Poole. *Noteworthy:* Outscored foes 504–35 (setting modern NCAA scoring record of 56 pts per game) and won 2nd national title and 1st Lambert Trophy. Led nation in rush and in scoring defense (3.9-pt avg).

1945 (9–0) *Won:* Louisville Army Air Force 32–0, Wake Forest 54–0, Michigan 28–7 (in New York), Melville, R.I. (USN) 55–13, Duke 48–13 (in New York), Villanova 54–0, Notre Dame 48–0, Pennsylvania 61–0, Navy 32–13 (in Philadelphia). *Stars:* Heisman Trophy– and Maxwell Award–winner Blanchard (718 yds rush, nation's leading scorer with 115 pts, including 19 TDs), Davis (944 yds rush, 5 pass rec for 213 yds, 18 TDs), Green, Ts Dewitt "Tex" Coulter and Albert Nemetz, E Hank Foldberg. *Noteworthy:* led nation in total off, rush, and scoring (45.8-pt avg) while winning 2nd straight Lambert Trophy and national championship.

1946 (9–0–1) *Won:* Villanova 35–0, Oklahoma 21–7, Cornell 46–21, Michigan 20–13, Columbia 48–14, Duke 19–0 (in New York), West Virginia 19–0, Pennsylvania 34–7, Navy 21–18. *Tied:* unbeaten national champ Notre Dame 0–0 (in New York). *Stars:* Heisman Trophy–winner Davis (13 TDs, 712 yds rush, 396 yds pass, 20 pass rec for 348 yds and 5 TDs, 5 int), Blanchard (10 TDs, 613 yds rush), Foldberg, QB/DB Arnold Tucker (8 int). *Noteworthy:* "Red" Blaik's 3rd straight unbeaten team won 3rd straight Lambert Trophy.

1948 (8–0–1) *Won:* Villanova 28–0, Lafayette 54–7 (1st meeting since 1942), Illinois 26–21, Harvard 20–7 (1st meeting since 1942), Cornell 27–6, Virginia Tech 49–7, Stanford 43–0 (in New York), Pennsylvania 26–20. *Tied:* Navy 21–21 in finale. *Stars:* soph B Gil Stephenson (887 yds rush), HB Bobby Stuart, QB Arnold Galiffa (802 yds total off), soph E Dan Foldberg (15 pass rec for 212 yds), G Joe Henry. *Noteworthy:* won 4th Lambert Trophy.

1949 (9–0) *Won:* Davidson 47–7, Penn St. 42–7 (1st meeting since 1939), Michigan 21–7, Harvard 54–14, Columbia 63–6, VMI 40–14 (1st meeting since 1941), Fordham 35–0, Pennsylvania 14–13, Navy 38–0. *Stars:* Galiffa (887 yds and 13 TDs pass, 201 yds and 4 TDs rush), Foldberg (20 pass

FB Felix "Doc" Blanchard, 1944–46, Coach Earl "Red" Blaik, 1941–58, and HB Glenn Davis, 1943–46

rec for 308 yds and 5 TDs). *Noteworthy:* Blaik's 5th unbeaten team led nation in scoring (39.3-pt avg) and again won Lambert Trophy.

1950 (8–1)   *Won:* Colgate 28–0 (1st meeting since 1943), Penn St. 41–7, Michigan 27–6 (in New York), Harvard 49–0, Columbia 34–0, Pennsylvania 28–13, New Mexico 51–0, Stanford 7–0. *Lost:* Navy 14–2 in finale (1st to Midshipmen since 1943). *Stars:* Foldberg (22 pass rec for 304 yds and 5 TDs), Ts Charles Shira and J.D. Kimmel, C Elmer Stout. *Noteworthy:* led nation in scoring defense (4.4-pt avg).

1953 (7–1–1)   *Won:* Furman 41–0, Dartmouth 27–0, Duke 14–13 (in New York, 1st meeting since 1946), Columbia 40–7, N.C. State 27–7, Pennsylvania 21–14, Navy 20–7. *Lost:* Northwestern 33–20. *Tied:* Tulane 0–0. *Noteworthy:* won 6th Lambert Trophy.

1954 (7–2)   *Won:* Michigan 26–7, Dartmouth 60–0, Duke 28–14, Columbia 67–12, Virginia 21–20, Yale 48–7 (1st meeting since 1943), Pennsylvania 35–0. *Lost:* South Carolina 34–20 (opener), Navy 27–20 (finale).   *Stars:* HB Tommy Bell (1,020 yds rush),

E Don Holleder, G Ralph Chesnauskas. *Noteworthy:* led nation in total off and rush.

1957 (7–2)   *Won:* Nebraska 42–0, Penn St. 27–13, Pittsburgh 29–13, Virginia 20–12, Colgate 53–7, Utah 39–33, Tulane 20–14. *Lost:* Notre Dame 23–21 (in Philadelphia, 1st meeting since 1947), Navy 14–0. *Stars:* soph HB Bob Anderson (983 yds rush, 14 TDs), HB Pete Dawkins (665 yds rush, 11 pass rec for 225 yds, 11 TDs).

1958 (8–0–1)   *Won:* South Carolina 45–8, Penn St. 26–0, Notre Dame 14–2 (1st over Irish in 4 games since 1945), Virginia 35–6, Colgate 68–6, Rice 14–7, Villanova 26–0, Navy 22–6. *Tied:* Pittsburgh 14–14 in mid-season. *Stars:* QB Joe Caldwell, "lonely end" Bill Carpenter (22 pass rec for 453 yds), Heisman Trophy– and Maxwell Award–winner Dawkins (12 TDs, 428 yds rush, 16 pass rec for 494 yds and 6 TDs), Anderson (564 yds rush, 14 pass rec for 138 yds, 6 TDs), G Bob Novogratz. *Noteworthy:* Blaik's last team (6th unbeaten one) led nation in pass and won 7th Lambert Trophy.

HB Pete Dawkins, 1957–58

HB Bob Anderson, 1957–59

1963 (7–3)   *Won:* Boston U. 30–0, Cincinnati 22–0, Penn St. 10–7, Wake Forest 47–0, Washington St. 23–0, Air Force 14–10 (in Chicago), Utah 8–7. *Lost:* Minnesota 24–8, Pittsburgh 28–0, Navy 21–15.   *Stars:* QB Rollie Stichweh, FB Don Parcells, HB John Seymour, T Bill Zadel, G Dick Nowak.

1966 (8–2)   *Won:* Kansas St. 21–6, Holy Cross 14–0 (1st meeting since 1919), Penn St. 11–0, Rutgers 14–9, Pittsburgh 28–0, George Washington 20–7, California 6–3, Navy 20–7.   *Lost:* unbeaten national cochamp Notre Dame 35–0, Tennessee 38–7. *Stars:* soph QB Steve Lindell (1,035 yds pass, 1,314 yds total off), Terry Young (37 pass rec for 539 yds), LB Townsend Clarke.   *Noteworthy:* 1st year under Tom Cahill.

1967 (8–2)   *Won:* Virginia 26–7, Boston College 21–10, SMU 24–6, Rutgers 14–3, Stanford 24–20, Air Force 10–7 (1st meeting at Air Force), Utah 22–0, Pittsburgh 21–12.   *Lost:* Duke 10–7, Navy 19–14.   *Stars:* Lindell, Young (41 pass rec for 516 yds), LB Jim Bevans (8 int).

1968 (7–3)   *Won:* The Citadel 34–14, California 10–7, Rutgers 24–0, Duke 57–25, Boston College 58–25, Pittsburgh 26–0, Navy 21–14.   *Lost:* Vanderbilt 17–13, Missouri 7–3, unbeaten Penn St. 28–24.   *Stars:* FB Charlie Jarvis (1,110 yds rush), Lindell (1,304 yds total off), LB Ken Johnson, Jim McCall (8 int).

1984 (8–3–1)   *Won:* Colgate 41–15, Duke 13–9, Harvard 33–11, Pennsylvania 48–13 (1st meeting since 1955), Air Force 24–12, Montana 45–31 (in Tokyo), Navy 28–11 (in Philadelphia, 1st over Midshipmen since 1977).   *Lost:* Rutgers 14–7, Syracuse 27–16 (1st meeting since 1972), Boston College 45–31.   *Tied:* Tennessee 24–24.   *Stars:* QB Nate Sassaman (1,002 yds rush, 1,366 yds total off), B Doug Black (1,148 yds rush), K Craig Stopa (15 FGs).   *Noteworthy:* Nation's most-improved team led nation in rush in 1st winning season since 1977. Made 1st bowl appearance, beating Michigan St. 10–6 in inaugural Cherry Bowl; Sassaman ran for 136 yds and Cadets converted Spartan mistakes into 2 scores with 4-yd TD run by HB Clarence Jones and 38-yd FG by Stopa.

1985 (9–3)   *Won:* Western Michigan 48–6, Rutgers 20–16, Pennsylvania 41–3, Yale 59–16 (1st meeting since 1955), Boston College 45–14, Colgate 45–43, Holy Cross 34–12, Memphis St. 49–7.   *Lost:* Notre

E Bill Carpenter, 1958–59

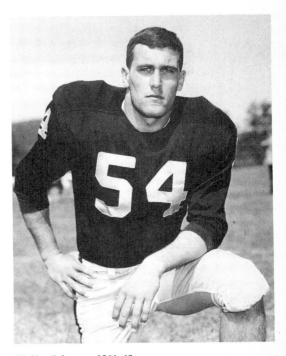

LB Ken Johnson, 1966–68

Dame 24–10, Air Force 45–7, Navy 17–7. *Stars:* Black, OG Don Smith, DB Doug Pavek (7 int). *Noteworthy:* beat Illinois 31–29 in rainy, muddy Peach Bowl; QB Rob Healy ran for 107 yds and a TD, DB Peel Chronister set up Army TDs with 2 int, and Stopa kicked 39-yd FG and 4 ex pts. **1988** (9–3) *Won:* Holy Cross 23–3, Northwestern 23–7, Bucknell 58–10, Yale 33–18, Lafayette 24–17 (10th straight over Leopards), Rutgers 34–24, Air Force 28–15, Vanderbilt 24–19, Navy 20–15. *Lost:* Washington 31–17, Boston College 38–24 (in Dublin). *Stars:* soph HB Mike Mayweather (1,022 yds and 9 TDs rush), FB Ben Barnett (679 yds and 6 TDs rush), HB Calvin Cass (582 yds rush), soph

QB Bryan McWilliams (749 yds and 8 TDs rush), SE Sean Jordan (12 pass rec for 289 yds), K Keith Walker (15 FGs, 80 pts), LBs Pat Davie and Troy Lingley, DT Will Huff, DBs O'Neal Miller and Earnest Boyd (5 int). *Noteworthy:* lost to Alabama 29–28 in John Hancock Sun Bowl; Barnett ran for 177 yds, Mayweather scored 2 TDs, and Miller scored TD on 57-yd pass int return.

BOWL SUMMARY

Cherry 1–0; John Hancock Sun 0–1; Peach 1–0.

BOWL RECORD (2–1)

Regular Season	Bowl	Score	Opponent	Record
1984 (7–3–1)	Cherry	10–6	Michigan St.	(6–5)
1985 (8–3)	Peach	31–29	Illinois	(6–4–1)
1988 (9–2)	John Hancock Sun	28–29	Alabama	(8–3)

CONFERENCE TITLES

None. Won **Lambert Trophy** in 1944, 1945, 1946, 1948, 1949, 1953, 1958.

TOP 20 AP AND UPI RANKING

1943	11	1947	11	1950	2–5	1955	20–15
1944	1	1948	6	1953	14–16	1957	18–13
1945	1	1949	4	1954	7–7	1958	3–3
1946	2						

MAJOR RIVALS

Army has played at least 10 games with Air Force 11–15–1, Boston College 11–17, Boston U. 10–0, Colgate 19–5–2, Columbia 14–4–3, Duke 8–6–1, Harvard 18–19–2, Holy Cross 16–5–1, Lafayette 14–1, Lehigh 7–2–1, Navy 43–43–7, Notre Dame 8–34–4, Pennsylvania 13–4–2, Penn St. 10–13–2, Pittsburgh 6–19–2, Princeton 4–6–3, Rutgers 16–10, Springfield 10–0, Stanford 5–5, Syracuse 10–10, Trinity 13–0, Tufts 20–0, Villanova 18–3, Virginia Military Institute 10–1, Yale 15–21–8.

COACHES

Dean of Army coaches is Earl "Red" Blaik (1946 national Coach of Year) with record of 121–33–10 for 1941–58, including 7 Lambert Trophy winners, 6 unbeaten teams, and 2 national champions. Other top records for at least 3 years were by Herman Koehler, 20–11–3 for 1897–1900; Harry Nelly, 15–5–2 for 1908–10; Charles Daly, 58–13–3 for 1913–16 and 1919–22 with 3 unbeaten teams and 1 national title; John McEwan, 18–5–3 for 1923–25; Biff Jones, 30–8–2 for 1926–29; Ralph

Sasse, 25–5–2 for 1930–32; Gar Davidson, 35–11–1 for 1933–37; Dale Hall, 16–11–2 for 1959–61; Paul Dietzel, 21–18–1 for 1962–65; Tom Cahill (1966 national Coach of Year), 40–39–2 for 1966–73; and Jim Young, 51–39–1 for 1983–90 with 3 bowl teams.

MISCELLANEA

First game was loss to Navy 24–0 in 1890 . . . 1st win was over Fordham 10–6 in 1891 . . . highest score was over Bowdoin 90–0 in 1920 . . . highest since W.W. II was over Furman 81–0 in 1955 . . . worst defeat was by Nebraska 77–7 in 1972 . . . longest unbeaten string of 32 in 1944–47 ended by Columbia 21–20 . . . 28-game unbeaten string in 1947–50 and 17-game win streak in 1949–50 ended by Navy 14–2 . . . longest win streak of 25 in 1944–46 ended by Notre Dame 0–0 . . . 16-game win streak in 1915–17 ended by Notre Dame 7–2 . . . 15-game unbeaten string in 1913–15 ended by Colgate 13–0 . . . longest winless string of 11 in 1970–71 broken with win over Georgia Tech 16–13 . . . consensus All-Americans were Charles Romeyn, B, 1898; William Smith, E, 1900; Charles Daly, B, 1901; Paul Bunker, T, B, 1901–02; Robert Boyers, C, 1902; Arthur Tipton, C, 1904; Henry Torney, B, 1904–05; William Erwin, G, 1907; Leland Devore, T, 1911; Louis Merillat, E, 1913; John McEwan, C, 1914; Elmer Oliphant, B, 1916–17; Ed Garbisch, C, 1922; Bud Sprague, T, 1926; Chris "Red" Cagle, B, 1927–29; Milt Summerfelt, G, 1932; Casimir Myslinski, C, 1943; Glenn Davis, B, and Felix "Doc" Blanchard, B, 1944–46; Tex Coulter, T, and John Green, G, 1945; Hank Foldberg, E, 1946; Joe Steffy, G, 1947; Arnold Galiffa, B, 1949; Dan Foldberg, E, 1950; Bob Anderson, B, 1957; Pete Dawkins, B, 1958; and Bill Carpenter, E, 1959 . . . Academic All-Americans were Ralph Chesnauskas, E, 1955; James Kernan, C, 1957; Pete Dawkins, HB, 1957–58; Don Usry, E, 1959; Sam Champi, DE, 1967; Bud Neswiacheny, DE, 1967; Theodore Shadid, C, 1969; Michael Thorson, DB, 1989; and Mike McElrath, DB, 1992 . . . Heisman Trophy winners were Felix "Doc" Blanchard, FB, 1945; Glenn Davis, HB, 1946; and Pete Dawkins, HB, 1958 . . . Maxwell Award winners were Glenn Davis, HB, 1944; Felix "Doc" Blanchard, FB, 1945; and Pete Dawkins, HB, 1958 . . . Outland Trophy winner was Joe Steffy, G, 1947.

CINCINNATI *(Bearcats; Red and Black)*

NOTABLE TEAMS

1897 (9–1–1) *Won:* Ohio U. 12–0, Miami (Ohio) 6–0, 10–6, Centre 4–0, 10–0, Ohio National Guard 20–0, Ohio St. 34–0, Southern A.C. 16–0, Louisiana St. (LSU) 28–0. *Lost:* Carlisle Indians 10–0. *Tied:* Nashville Guards 6–6. *Noteworthy:* only year under Tom Fennell.
1898 (5–1–3) *Won:* Miami (Ohio) 22–0, Vanderbilt 12–0, Alumni 12–0, Ohio Wesleyan 57–0, Dartmouth 17–12. *Lost:* Oberlin 5–0. *Tied:* Ohio U. 12–12, Indiana 0–0, 11–11. *Noteworthy:* only year under Frank Cavanaugh.
1899 (5–2) *Won:* Miami (Ohio) 22–0, Vanderbilt 6–0, Centre 26–0, Alumni 6–0, Ohio Wesleyan 28–5. *Lost:* Indiana 35–0, Washington & Jefferson 20–0 in consecutive mid-season games. *Noteworthy:* 1st year under Dan Reed.
1904 (7–1) *Won:* Georgetown (Ky.) 33–0 (1st meeting since 1894), Wittenberg 29–4, Miami (Ohio) 46–0, Kentucky 11–0, Ohio Medics 11–0, Tennessee 35–0, Kenyon 17–0. *Lost:* Stumps 6–0. *Noteworthy:* 1st year under Amos Foster.
1911 (6–2–1) *Won:* Transylvania 12–0, Otterbein 16–3, Kentucky 6–0 (1st meeting since 1904), Butler 23–11, Miami (Ohio) 11–0, Wittenberg 5–0. *Lost:* Earlham 9–0, Ohio St. 11–6. *Tied:* Denison 0–0. *Noteworthy:* last year under Robert Burch.
1914 (7–2) *Won:* Georgetown (Ky.) 35–0, Denison 13–0, Ohio Wesleyan 7–0, Kenyon 47–0, Kentucky 14–7, Western Reserve 20–0, Ohio U. 15–0. *Lost:* Otterbein 3–0, Miami (Ohio) 20–13.
1918 (3–0–2) *Won:* Ft. Thomas 6–0, Georgetown (Ky.) 21–7, Xavier (Ohio) 12–0 (1st meeting). *Tied:* Ohio U. 6–6, Miami (Ohio) 0–0. *Noteworthy:* 1st unbeaten season since 2-game schedule of 1888.
1932 (7–2) *Won:* Hanover 51–0, Georgetown (Ky.) 22–12, Butler 13–7, South Dakota 7–0, Denison 6–0, Wittenberg 25–6, Wabash 14–0 in 1st 7 games. *Lost:* Ohio U. 23–0, Miami (Ohio) 21–13.
1933 (7–2) *Won:* Rio Grande 20–0, South Dakota 13–0, Marshall 19–0, Butler 34–7, Ohio Wesleyan 7–0 (1st over Bishops in 5 games since 1915), Wittenberg 14–6, Ohio U. 2–0 (1st over Bobcats since 1923). *Lost:* Kentucky 3–0 (1st meeting since 1923), Miami (Ohio) 6–2. *Noteworthy:* won share of 1st Buckeye Conference title.

1934 (6–2–1) *Won:* Otterbein 45–0, Ashland 32–6, Georgetown (Ky.) 45–0, Marshall 7–0, Ohio Wesleyan 13–6, Miami (Ohio) 21–0. *Lost:* Kentucky 27–0, Vanderbilt 32–0 in consecutive early games. *Tied:* Ohio U. 0–0. *Noteworthy:* Dana King's last team won 2nd straight Buckeye Conference title.
1935 (7–2) *Won:* Dayton 25–0, South Dakota St. 38–0, Denison 35–0, Indiana 7–0 (1st meeting since 1905), Baltimore 67–0, Marshall 39–13, Miami (Ohio) 8–7. *Lost:* Ohio Wesleyan 13–12, Ohio U. 16–6. *Noteworthy:* 1st year under Russ Cohen.
1942 (8–2) *Won:* Louisville 51–0, Western Reserve 18–7, Centre 21–0, Ohio U. 26–7, Boston U. 6–0, Dayton 20–0, Xavier (Ohio) 9–0 (1st meeting since 1918), Miami (Ohio) 21–12. *Lost:* national co-champ Georgia 35–13, Tennessee 34–12. *Noteworthy:* Joe Meyer's last team.
1946 (9–2) *Won:* Indiana 15–6 (1st meeting since 1937), Marshall 39–14, Dayton 19–0, Ohio U. 19–0, Michigan St. 18–7, Xavier (Ohio) 39–0, Western Reserve 34–7, Miami (Ohio) 13–7. *Lost:* Kentucky 26–7, Tulsa 20–0 (1st meeting). *Star:* HB Roger Stephens (768 yds rush). *Noteworthy:* made 1st postseason appearance, beating Virginia Tech 18–6 in Sun Bowl.
1947 (7–3) *Won:* St. Bonaventure 20–14, Oklahoma City 20–13, Xavier (Ohio) 27–25, Ohio U. 34–0, Miami (Fla.) 20–7 (1st meeting), Western Reserve 7–6, Butler 26–19. *Lost:* Kentucky 20–0, Dayton 26–21, unbeaten Miami (Ohio) 38–7. *Stars:* Stephens (959 yds and 7 TDs rush), Alkie Richards (18 pass rec for 400 yds, 8 TDs total), T Dick Langenbeck, G John Vilkowski. *Noteworthy:* won 1st Mid-American Conference title.
1949 (7–3) *Won:* Hardin-Simmons 27–21, Western Michigan 27–6, Mississippi St. 19–0, Western Reserve 21–13, Ohio U. 34–13, Miami (Ohio) 27–6. *Lost:* Nevada–Reno 41–21, unbeaten Pacific 34–7, Kentucky 14–7. *Stars:* QB Tom O'Malley (1,617 yds and 16 TDs pass), E Jim Kelly (42 pass rec for 468 yds), Bob Stratton (6 TDs), G Lee Haslinger. *Noteworthy:* Won 2nd Mid-American Conference title in 1st year under Sid Gillman. Beat Toledo in Glass Bowl 33–13.
1950 (8–4) *Won:* Texas Western (Texas–El Paso) 32–0, Hardin-Simmons 19–7, Louisville 28–20 (1st meeting since 1942), Western Michigan 27–6, Western Reserve 48–6, Ohio U. 23–0, Pacific 14–7, Xavier (Ohio) 33–20. *Lost:* William & Mary 20–14, Kentucky 41–7, Miami (Ohio) 28–0. *Stars:* Kelly

(29 pass rec for 455 yds and 9 TDs), soph QB Gene Rossi (1,000 yds and 14 TDs pass), B Bob Stratton (539 yds and 5 TDs rush), C Frank Middendorf, soph G Bill Shalosky. *Noteworthy:* lost to West Texas St. 14–13 in Sun Bowl.
1951 (10–1) *Won:* Virginia Military Institute (VMI) 26–7, Kansas St. 34–0, Tulsa 47–35, Hawaii 34–0, Louisville 38–0, Western Reserve 41–0, Texas Western 53–18, Hardin-Simmons 13–12, Ohio U. 40–0, Miami (Ohio) 19–14. *Lost:* unbeaten Xavier (Ohio) 26–0. *Stars:* Rossi (1,444 yds and 11 TDs pass), FB Bob Dougherty (11 TDs, 528 yds and 10 TDs rush), Stratton, Shalosky, Middendorf, E Dick Jarvis, T Andy Matto, DB Glenn Sample. *Noteworthy:* won 3rd Mid-American Conference title.
1952 (8–1–1) *Won:* Dayton 25–0, Kansas St. 13–6, Xavier (Ohio) 20–13, Wabash 27–7, Western Reserve 41–2, Ohio U. 41–7, Washington & Lee 54–0, Miami (Ohio) 34–9. *Lost:* Kentucky 14–6. *Tied:* Tulsa 14–14. *Stars:* Rossi (1,559 yds and 12 TDs pass), HBs Dom Del Bene (28 pass rec for 372 yds) and soph Dick Goist, Jack Delaney (9 TDs), Joe Concilla (8 TDs), Shalosky, G Terry Boyle, T Don Grammer, DE Don Fritz, Sample, Don Polagyi (6 int). *Noteworthy:* repeated as Mid-American champ in last year in league.
1953 (9–1) *Won:* Tulsa 14–7, William & Mary 57–7, Toledo 41–7, Xavier (Ohio) 20–6, Western Reserve 66–0, Dayton 27–0, Louisville 41–0, VMI 67–0, Miami (Ohio) 14–0. *Lost:* Marquette 31–7. *Stars:* Goist (561 yds and 7 TDs rush), Concilla (9 TDs), Glen Dillhoff (13 pass rec for 265 yds), G Bob Marich. *Noteworthy:* led nation in total off.
1954 (8–2) *Won:* Detroit 21–13, Dayton 42–13, Tulsa 40–7, Marquette 30–13, Hardin-Simmons 27–13, Xavier (Ohio) 33–0, Pacific 13–7, Arizona St. 34–7 in 1st 8 games. *Lost:* Wichita St. 13–0 (1st meeting), Miami (Ohio) 21–9. *Stars:* Joe Miller (717 yds and 11 TDs rush), Goist. *Noteworthy:* Gillman's last team.
1958 (6–2–2) *Won:* Dayton 14–0, Xavier (Ohio) 14–8, Pacific 12–6, Tulsa 15–6, Marquette 15–0, Miami (Ohio) 18–7 (1st over Redskins since 1953). *Lost:* Houston 34–13, Oklahoma St. 19–14. *Tied:* Wichita St. 16–16, North Texas St. 8–8 (1st meeting). *Stars:* HBs Joe Morrison (9 TDs, 27 pass rec for 303 yds) and Ed Kovac, QB Jack Lee.
1964 (8–2) *Won:* Dayton 20–10, Detroit 19–0, Xavier (Ohio) 35–6, Tulsa 28–23, North Texas St. 27–6, Wichita St. 19–7, Miami (Ohio) 28–14 (1st

over Redskins since 1959), Houston 20–6. *Lost:* Boston College 10–0, George Washington 17–15. *Stars:* RB Brig Owens, HB Al Nelson (973 yds and 13 TDs rush, 82 pts), T Bob Taylor, G Roger Perdrix. *Noteworthy:* Won 2nd straight MVC title.
1976 (9–2) *Won:* Tulane 21–14, SW Louisiana (won by forfeit after losing 7–3), Miami (Ohio) 17–0 (1st over Redskins since 1970), Southern Mississippi 28–21, Arizona St. 14–0, Tulsa 16–7, Ohio U. 35–0, Vanderbilt 33–7, Louisville 20–6. *Lost:*

Georgia 31–17, unbeaten Maryland 21–0 in successive late games. *Stars:* Napoleon Outlaw (20 pass rec for 309 yds), soph K Steve Shultz (12 FGs), P Mike Connell (43-yd avg). *Noteworthy:* last year under Tony Mason.

BOWL SUMMARY

Sun 1–1.

BOWL RECORD (1–1)

Regular Season	Bowl	Score	Opponent	Record
1946 (8–2)	Sun	18–6	Virginia Tech	(3–3–3)
1950 (8–3)	Sun	13–14	West Texas St.	(9–1)

CONFERENCE TITLES

Buckeye—1933*, 1934. **Mid-American**—1947, 1949, 1951, 1952. **Missouri Valley**—1963, 1964.

TOP 20 AP AND UPI RANKING

None.

MAJOR RIVALS

Cincinnati has played at least 10 games with Centre 6–5–3, Dayton 15–17–1, Denison 7–14–2, Detroit 5–4–1, Georgetown (Ky.) 8–3, Hanover 10–1, Houston 2–11, Indiana 3–6–2, Kentucky 8–21–3, Kenyon 9–4, Louisville 23–11–1, Marietta 4–6–1, Memphis St. 5–13, Miami (Fla.) 1–9, Miami (Ohio) 38–53–6, North Texas St. 7–8–1, Ohio St. 2–9, Ohio U. 23–23–4, Ohio Wesleyan 9–9–1, Temple 2–9–1, Tulsa 9–16–2, West Virginia 0–10–1, Western Reserve 10–3–2, Wichita St. 14–7–2, Wittenberg 10–11–5, Xavier (Ohio) 18–12.

COACHES

Deans of Cincinnati coaches are Sid Gillman, George Blackburn, and Chuck Studley, with 6 years each. Gillman was 50–13–1 for 1949–54 with 3 MAC titles and a Sun Bowl team; Blackburn was 25–27–6 for 1955–60; and Studley was 27–33 for 1961–66 with 2 MVC titles. Other top records for at least 3 years were by Robert Burch, 16–8–2 for 1909–11; Dana King, 25–10–1 for 1931–34 with 2 Buckeye Conference titles; Joe Meyer, 27–16–3 for 1938–42; Ray Nolting, 23–15–1 for 1945–48 with 1 Sun Bowl champion; and Tony Mason, 26–18 for 1973–76.

MISCELLANEA

First game was tie with Mt. Auburn 0–0 in 1885 ... 1st win was over Mt. Auburn 26–6 in 1885 ... 1st win over college foe was over Franklin 38–0 in 1891 ... highest score was over Transylvania 124–0 in 1912 ... highest since W.W. II was over Virginia Military Institute 67–0 in 1953 ... worst defeat was by Penn St. 81–0 in 1991 ... longest win streak of 16 in 1953–54 ended by Wichita St. 13–0 ... longest winless string of 16 in 1915–17 broken with win over Ft. Thomas 6–0 in 1918 opener . . . Cincinnati has had no consensus All-America players . . . Academic All-Americans were Kari Yli-Renko, OT, 1981; Kyle Stroh, DL, 1990; and Kris Bjorson, TE, 1991.

EAST CAROLINA (Pirates; Purple and Gold)

NOTABLE TEAMS

1941 (7–0)   **Won:** Tusculum 31–0, Newport News Apprentice 39–0, Western Carolina 19–6, Newport Navy 30–0, Erskine 14–7, Bergen 13–7, Belmont Abbey 13–0. **Star:** T Jack Young. **Noteworthy:** had 1st unbeaten season in last year under John Christianbury.

1950 (7–3)   **Won:** Newport News Apprentice 21–7, Lenoir-Rhyne 27–19 (1st in 6-game series dating to 1934), Western Carolina 36–6 (1st over Catamounts in 5 games since 1941), Guilford 26–7 (1st meeting since 1940), Cherry Point Marines 20–12, High Point 26–0 (1st in 6 games since 1937), Atlantic Christian 54–7. **Lost:** Hampden-Sydney 38–26, Elon 26–16, Appalachian St. 20–0.

1953 (8–2)   **Won:** Wilson Teachers 41–0, Lenoir-Rhyne 34–0, Catawba 13–6, Elon 45–25, Western Carolina 26–7, Guilford 40–0, Appalachian St. 40–7, Stetson 40–6. **Lost:** Tampa 18–13. **Stars:** QB Dick Cherry (16 TDs pass), E Bobby Hodges (10 TDs pass rec), soph C/LB Louis Hallow. **Noteworthy:** Won North State Conference title. Lost to Morris Harvey 12–0 in Elks Bowl at Greenville; Pirates lost ball on 4 int and a fumble.

1960 (7–3)   **Won:** Newport News Apprentice 21–6, Guilford 7–0, Catawba 28–0, Elon 14–8, Western Carolina 7–6, Newberry 21–0, Richmond 22–7. **Lost:** Appalachian St. 21–17, Lenoir-Rhyne 17–0, Presbyterian 27–7 in consecutive late games. **Star:** HB Glen Bass.

1963 (9–1)   **Won:** Wake Forest 20–10 (1st meeting), Wofford 34–7, Presbyterian 24–7, Elon 6–0, Western Carolina 50–0, The Citadel 20–6 (1st meeting since 1951), Lenoir-Rhyne 21–0 (1st in series since 1954), Tampa 14–8. **Lost:** Richmond 10–7 in opener. **Stars:** FB Tom Michel (830 yds rush, 9 TDs), E Dave Bumgarner (23 pass rec for 328 yds). **Noteworthy:** Beat Northeastern 27–6 in Eastern

Bowl at Allentown, Pa.; Michel ran for 149 yds and 2 TDs, and LB Frankie Galloway starred on defense.

1964 (9–1)   **Won:** Catawba 25–0, West Chester St. 33–7, Howard 31–20, Wofford 21–0, Lenior–Rhyne 33–14, The Citadel 19–10, Furman 34–14, Presbyterian 49–8. **Lost:** Richmond 22–20 in midseason. **Stars:** TB Bill Cline (1,574 yds total off), FB Dave Alexander (869 yds rush, 16 TDs), Bumgarner (37 pass rec for 450 yds). **Noteworthy:** overcame 13–0 deficit to beat Massachusetts 14–13 in Tangerine Bowl; Cline passed for 178 yds and 2-pt conversion and scored TD.

1965 (9–1)   **Won:** West Chester St. 27–6, Richmond 34–13, Louisville 34–20, The Citadel 21–0, NE Louisiana 45–0, Lenoir-Rhyne 44–0, George Washington 21–20, Howard 35–10.   **Lost:** Furman 14–7. **Stars:** Alexander (1,029 yds rush, 1,587 yds total off, 16 TDs), E Ruffin Odom (28 pass rec for 367 yds), Bobby Ellis (5 int), soph Todd Hicks (5 int). **Noteworthy:** beat Maine 31–0 in Tangerine Bowl; Alexander ran for 170 yds and 2 TDs (1 on 55-yd run) and passed for 3rd score, and George Richardson passed for 118 yds and a TD.

1967 (8–2)   **Won:** William & Mary 27–7, Richmond 23–7, Davidson 42–17, Southern Illinois 21–8, Louisville 18–13, Parsons 27–26, Furman 34–29, Marshall 29–13. **Lost:** The Citadel 21–19, West Texas St. 37–13. **Stars:** TB Neal Hughes (1,484 yds total off), soph FB Butch Colson (1,135 yds rush, 15 TDs), E Jimmy Adkins (19 pass rec for 328 yds), G Kevin Moran, Hicks (5 int).

1972 (9–2)   **Won:** Virginia Military Institute (VMI) 30–3, Southern Illinois 16–0, Appalachian St. 35–7 (1st meeting since 1962), Richmond 21–0, The Citadel 27–21, Furman 27–21, UT-Chattanooga 33–7, William & Mary 21–15, Dayton 24–22.   **Lost:** N.C. State 38–16, North Carolina 42–19 (1st meeting). **Stars:** RB Carlester Crumpler (1,309 yds rush, 17 TDs), QB Carl Summerell (1,275 yds pass, 1,700 yds total off), SE Tim Dameron (30 pass rec for 648 yds), G Greg Troupe, E Stan Eure, soph LB Danny Kepley, DB Rusty Markland (5 int). **Noteworthy:** won 2nd SC title.

1973 (9–2)   **Won:** Southern Mississippi 13–0, Southern Illinois 42–25, Furman 14–3, Davidson 45–0, VMI 42–7, The Citadel 34–0, William & Mary 34–3, Richmond 44–14, Appalachian St. 49–14. **Lost:** N.C. State 57–8, North Carolina 28–27.

Stars: Crumpler (1,042 yds rush, 12 TDs), Summerell (1,222 yds pass, 1,507 yds total off), Eure (27 pass rec for 495 yds), Troupe, K Jim Woody, Kepley, frosh DE Cary Godette, DBs Mike Myrick and frosh Jim Bolding (7 int). *Noteworthy:* won 3rd SC title in last year under Sonny Randle.
1975 (8–3) *Won:* William & Mary 20–0, Southern Illinois 41–7, The Citadel 3–0, Western Carolina 42–14 (1st meeting since 1963), North Carolina 38–17 (1st over Tar Heels), Furman 21–10, Virginia 61–10, VMI 28–12. *Lost:* N.C. State 26–3, Appalachian St. 41–25, Richmond 17–14. *Stars:* TB Kenny Strayhorn (638 yds rush), frosh SE Terry Gallaher (7 TDs, 13 pass rec for 433 yds), soph RB Willie Hawkins (1,090 yds all-purpose running, 7 TDs), G Jimbo Walker, Godette, soph LB Harold Randolph, Bolding (nation's leader with 10 int).
1976 (9–2) *Won:* Southern Mississippi 48–0, N.C. State 23–14, William & Mary 20–19, The Citadel 22–3, Southern Illinois 49–14, VMI 17–3, Western Carolina 24–17, Richmond 20–10, Appalachian St. 35–7. *Lost:* North Carolina 12–10, Furman 17–10. *Stars:* QB Mike Weaver (1,124 yds total off), Gallaher (14 pass rec for 269 yds), Hawkins (1,036 yds all-purpose running), soph RB Eddie Hicks (897 yds rush), G Wayne Bolt, K Pete Conaty (16 FGs, 86 pts), Godette, Randolph, Bolding. *Noteworthy:* won 4th and final SC title.
1977 (8–3) *Won:* N.C. State 28–23, Duke 17–16 (1st meeting), Toledo 22–9, VMI 14–13, Southern Illinois 33–0, Richmond 35–14, The Citadel 34–16, Appalachian St. 45–14. *Lost:* South Carolina 19–16 (1st meeting), SW Louisiana 9–7 (1st meeting), William & Mary 21–17. *Stars:* QB Jimmy Southerland (1,190 yds total off, 8 TDs rush), Gallaher (27 pass rec for 512 yds), Hawkins (919 all-purpose yds), frosh FB Teddy Sutton (706 yds rush), Bolt, Randolph, DE Zack Valentine, DB Gerald Hall.
1978 (9–3) *Won:* Western Carolina 14–6, SW Louisiana 38–9, Texas-Arlington 23–17, VMI 19–6, Richmond 21–14, Appalachian St. 33–8, William & Mary 20–3, Marshall 45–0. *Lost:* N.C. State 29–13, North Carolina 14–10, Southern Mississippi 17–16. *Stars:* QB Leander Green (1,145 yds total off), SE Billy Ray Washington (17 pass rec for 515 yds and 5 TDs), Gallaher (18 pass rec for 227 yds), Sutton (621 yds rush), Valentine, Hall, DB Charlie Carter

(5 int). *Noteworthy:* beat Louisiana Tech 35–13 in Independence Bowl; Sutton ran for 143 yds and a TD, soph RB Anthony Collins scored 2 TDs, and Valentine starred on defense.
1983 (8–3) *Won:* N.C. State 22–16 (1st over Wolfpack since 1977), Murray St. 50–25, Missouri 13–6, SW Louisiana 21–18, Temple 24–11, East Tennessee St. 21–9, William & Mary 40–6, Southern Mississippi 10–6. *Lost:* Florida St. 47–46, Florida 24–17, national champ Miami (Fla.) 12–7. *Stars:* OG Terry Long (East Carolina's 1st consensus All-American), OT John Robertson, QB Kevin Ingram (1,191 yds pass), Carlton Nelson (28 pass rec for 526 yds), FL Stefon Adams (20 pass rec for 277 yds), RB Earnest Byner (862 yds rush, 1,060 all-purpose yds), Henry Williams (nation's kickoff return leader with 31.1-yd avg), P Jeff Bolch (40.3-yd avg), DE Jeff Pegues, DBs Clint Harris and soph Kevin Walker (5 int).
1991 (11–1) *Won:* Memphis St. 20–13, Central Florida 47–25, South Carolina 31–20 (1st in 9-game series dating to 1977), Akron 56–20, Syracuse 23–20, Pittsburgh 24–23, Tulane 38–28, Southern Mississippi 48–20 (1st over Eagles since 1983), Virginia Tech 24–17, Cincinnati 30–19. *Lost:* Illinois 38–31 in opener. *Stars:* QB Jeff Blake (3,073 yds and 28 TDs pass), WRs Hunter Gallimore (49 pass rec for 881 yds and 8 TDs) and Clayton Driver (28 pass rec for 464 yds and 10 TDs), TE Luke Fisher (48 pass rec for 686 yds), FL Dion Johnson (40 pass rec for 743 yds, 1,673 all-purpose yds, 6 TDs), soph K Anthony Brenner (14 FGs, 82 pts), DT Greg Gardill, soph DE Bernard Carter, LB Robert Jones, DB Greg Grandison (5 int), P John Jett (42.2-yd avg). *Noteworthy:* Last year under Bill Lewis. Overcame 34–17 deficit in last quarter to beat N.C. State 37–34 in Peach Bowl; Blake passed for 378 yds and 4 TDs (2 to Johnson) and ran for another, Fisher caught 12 passes for 144 yds (including 22-yarder for winning TD), Gallimore had 5 pass rec for 113 yds (including 55-yd TD pass), and Brenner had 27-yd FG and 4 ex pts.

BOWL SUMMARY

Independence 1–0; Peach 1–0; Tangerine 2–0.

Bowl Record (4–0)

Regular Season	Bowl	Score	Opponent	Record
1964 (8–1)	Tangerine	14–13	Massachusetts	(8–1)
1965 (8–1)	Tangerine	31–0	Maine	(8–1)
1978 (8–3)	Independence	35–13	Louisiana Tech	(6–4)
1991 (10–1)	Peach	37–34	N.C. State	(9–2)

Conference Titles

North State—1953. Southern—1966*, 1972, 1973, 1976.

TOP 20 AP AND UPI
(USA TODAY/CNN SINCE 1991) RANKING

1983	20–U	1991	9–9

Major Rivals

East Carolina has played at least 10 games with Appalachian St. 10–19, Catawba 8–3–1, The Citadel 14–4, East Tennessee St. 5–4–1, Elon 9–9, Furman 11–3, Guilford 9–5–1, Lenoir-Rhyne 6–15, Newport News Apprentice 10–1, N.C. State 7–12, Presbyterian 6–5, Richmond 13–11, South Carolina 2–8, Southern Illinois 8–2, Southern Mississippi 4–14, SW Louisiana 4–6, Western Carolina 17–13, William & Mary 11–4–1.

Coaches

Dean of East Carolina coaches is Jack Boone with record of 49–45–5 for 1952–61 with 2 minor bowl teams. Most wins were under Clarence Stasavich, 50–27–1 for 1962–69 with 1 SC title and 3 bowl champions (1 minor). Other top records for at least 3 years were by Bill Dole, 15–14–1 for 1949–51; Sonny Randle, 22–10 for 1971–73 with 2 SC titles; Pat Dye, 48–18–1 for 1974–79 with 1 SC title and a bowl champion; and Bill Lewis, 21–12–1 for 1989–91 with a Peach Bowl champion.

Miscellanea

First game was loss to Presbyterian 39–0 in 1932 ... 1st win was over Campbell 6–0 in 1933 ... highest score was over Newport News Apprentice 74–0 in 1959 ... worst defeat was by Guilford 79–0 in 1932 ... worst since W.W. II was by Southern Mississippi 65–0 in 1968 ... longest win streak of 14 in 1963–64 ended by Richmond 22–20 ... 11–game win streak in 1991 ended by Syracuse 42–21 in 1992 opener ... longest losing string of 15 in 1985–86 broken with win over Georgia Southern 35–33 ... winless string of 13 in 1938–39 broken with win over Kutztown St. 14–6 in 1940 opener ... consensus All-Americans were Terry Long, OL, 1983; and Robert Jones, LB, 1991 ... East Carolina has had no 1st team Academic All-Americans.

LOUISVILLE (Cardinals; Red, Black and White)

Notable Teams

1913 (5–1) *Won:* Bethel 48–0, Moore's Hill 77–0, Washington (Tenn.) 100–0, Cumberland 6–0, Butler 20–0. *Lost:* Kentucky 20–0 in finale.
1925 (8–0) *Won:* Evansville 20–0 (1st meeting), Western Kentucky 6–0, Hanover 24–0, Kentucky Wesleyan 6–0, Transylvania 7–0, Rose Poly (RPI) 30–0, Toledo 33–0, Marshall 7–2 (1st in 4-game series begun in 1921). *Noteworthy:* had 1st unbeaten season in 1st year under Tom King.
1926 (6–2) *Won:* Ogden 79–0, RPI 49–0, Western Kentucky 26–10, Kentucky Wesleyan 25–12, Mar-

shall 27–3, Florida Southern 13–0. *Lost:* Xavier (Ohio) 20–7 (1st meeting), Centre 6–0 in consecutive early games.

1946 (6–2) *Won:* Evansville 13–7, Wittenberg 19–0, Georgetown (Ky.) 20–0, 20–0, St. Joseph's (Ind.) 13–7, Union 25–0. *Lost:* Western Kentucky 20–19 (1st meeting since 1933), Eastern Kentucky 28–7. *Noteworthy:* Resumed varsity football after 3-year W.W. II layoff. 1st year under Frank Camp.

1947 (7–0–1) *Won:* Wittenberg 40–3, DePauw 37–0, Evansville 20–7, Western Kentucky 19–13 (1st over Hilltoppers in 9 games dating to 1926), Eastern Kentucky 14–13, SE Louisiana 23–0, Washington (Mo.) 33–20. *Tied:* St. Joseph's (Ind.) 7–7. *Noteworthy:* 1st unbeaten season since 1925.

1949 (8–3) *Won:* St. Joseph's (Ind.) 33–7, Western Kentucky 47–7, Murray St. 34–14 (1st meeting since 1933), Akron 62–6, Bradley 35–12, Catawba 41–7, Washington (Mo.) 35–12, Evansville 28–7. *Lost:* Miami (Fla.) 26–0 (1st meeting since 1933), Xavier (Ohio) 19–7, Southern Mississippi 26–21 (1st meeting). *Star:* Tom Lucia (800 yds rush).

1955 (7–2) *Won:* Wayne St. 72–0, Dayton 19–7, Evansville 29–7, Western Kentucky 20–0, Morehead St. 37–12, Eastern Kentucky 45–13, Toledo 33–13 (1st meeting since 1935). *Lost:* Murray St. 33–14, Xavier (Ohio) 49–20 in 1st 2 games. *Star:* soph Lenny Lyles (780 yds rush, 14 TDs).

1957 (9–1) *Won:* Evansville 33–7, Eastern Kentucky 40–14, Toledo 48–20, Murray St. 35–0, Dayton 33–19, Central Michigan 40–0, Ohio U. 40–7, Morehead St. 40–6. *Lost:* Kent St. 13–7. *Stars:* Lyles (1,207 yds rush, 21 TDs, 132 pts), Ed Young (10 pass rec for 263 yds). *Noteworthy:* made 1st postseason appearance, beating Drake 34–20 (1st meeting) in Sun Bowl despite losing Lyles to injury in 1st quarter; soph Ken Porco (Lyles' replacement) ran for 119 yds and a TD, and Pete Bryant ran for 80 yds and a score and threw 20-yd TD pass to Young.

1960 (7–2) *Won:* Eastern Kentucky 28–7, Bradley 40–6, Murray St. 12–6, Dayton 36–0, Western Kentucky 44–0, Marshall 7–0, Kent St. 22–8. *Lost:* Tennessee Tech 21–7, Xavier (Ohio) 29–0.

1970 (8–3–1) *Won:* North Texas St. 13–2 (1st over Eagles since 1965), Tulsa 14–8, Marshall 16–14, Kent St. 14–13, Memphis St. 40–27 (1st in 9-game series dating to 1948), Cincinnati 28–14 (1st over Bearcats in 13 games since 1922), Drake 23–14, Wichita St. 34–24. *Lost:* Florida St. 9–7 (1st meet-

ing since 1954), Southern Illinois 31–28 (1st to Salukis since 1964), Dayton 28–11. *Stars:* soph QB John Madeya (1,750 yds and 11 TDs pass), Cookie Brinkman (48 pass rec for 647 yds), Bill Gatti (981 yds rush), Larry Hart (8 TDs), soph LB Tom Jackson. *Noteworthy:* Won 1st MVC title. Tied Long Beach St. 24–24 in Pasadena Bowl; Madeya scored 2 TDs, soph Joe Welch returned pass int 65 yds for TD, soph K Scott Marcus had FG and 3 ex pts, and Paul Mattingly made 17 tackles and blocked FG attempt.

1972 (9–1) *Won:* Kent St. 34–0, Dayton 28–11, Tampa 17–14, North Texas St. 56–6, Wichita St. 46–3, Cincinnati 38–13, Southern Illinois 20–16, Memphis St. 17–0, Drake 27–0. *Lost:* Tulsa 28–26 (1st to Golden Hurricane since 1967). *Stars:* RB Howard Stevens (17 TDs, 1,294 yds rush, nation's leader with 2,132 all-purpose yds), Madeya (1,709 yds and 16 TDs pass), Gary Barnes (52 pass rec for 655 yds), Jackson. *Noteworthy:* Lee Corso's last team led nation in total defense and rush defense, and got share of 2nd MVC title.

1988 (8–3) *Won:* Memphis St. 29–18, North Carolina 38–34, Tulsa 9–3, Virginia 30–28, Tulane 38–35, Cincinnati 21–6 (1st over Bearcats since 1983), Virginia Tech 13–3, Western Kentucky 35–17. *Lost:* Maryland 27–16, Wyoming 44–9, Southern Mississippi 30–23. *Stars:* QB Jay Gruden (2,605 yds and 17 TDs pass), Deon Booker (12 TDs, 1,011 yds rush, 41 pass rec for 391 yds), soph FL Anthony Cummings (30 pass rec for 406 yds and 5 TDs), TE Chad Fortune (35 pass rec for 339 yds), HB Keith Stephens (19 pass rec for 288 yds), soph SE Eric Broomfield (17 pass rec for 303 yds), soph K Ron Bell (10 FGs), soph LB Mark Sander.

1990 (10–1–1) *Won:* Murray St. 68–0, Kansas 28–16, West Virginia 9–7 (1st in 5-game series dating to 1984), Tulsa 38–14, Memphis St. 19–17, Pittsburgh 27–20, Western Kentucky 41–7, Cincinnati 41–16, Boston College 17–10. *Lost:* Southern Mississippi 25–13. *Tied:* San Jose St. 10–10 in opener. *Stars:* QB Browning Nagle (2,150 yds and 16 TDs pass), Cummings (28 pass rec for 473 yds and 10 TDs), TE Ken McKay (33 pass rec for 471 yds), SE Fred Jones (23 pass rec for 400 yds), frosh RB Ralph Dawkins (27 pass rec for 373 yds, 542 yds rush, 6 TDs), Broomfield (13 pass rec for 251 yds), HB Curtis Lipsey (6 TDs), DE Mike Flores, Sander, LB Pat Fitzgerald, DB William Blackford (5 int), K/P Klaus Wilmsmeyer (9 FGs, 42.9-yd punting avg).

Noteworthy: beat Alabama 34–7 in Fiesta Bowl; Nagle passed for 451 yds and 3 TDs (including 70-yarder to Latrell Ware), McKay had 5 pass rec for 110 yds, and Cummings had 3 pass rec for 69 yds and 2 TDs.

BOWL SUMMARY

Fiesta 1–0; Independence 0–1; Pasadena 0–0–1; Sun 1–0.

BOWL RECORD (2–1–1)

Regular Season	Bowl	Score	Opponent	Record
1957 (8–1)	Sun	34–20	Drake	(7–1)
1970 (8–3)	Pasadena	24–24	Long Beach St.	(9–2)
1977 (7–3–1)	Independence	14–24	Louisiana Tech	(8–1–2)
1990 (9–1–1)	Fiesta	34–7	Alabama	(7–4)

CONFERENCE TITLES

Missouri Valley—1970, 1972*.

TOP 20 AP AND UPI RANKING

1972	18–16	1990	14–12

MAJOR RIVALS

Louisville has played at least 10 games with Centre 3–11–3, Cincinnati 12–23–1, Dayton 13–12, Drake 10–5–1, Eastern Kentucky 16–8–1, Evansville 13–1, Florida St. 1–11, Georgetown (Ky.) 7–10, Hanover 8–4–1, Kent St. 8–9, Marshall 16–9, Memphis St. 12–17, Murray St. 10–6, North Texas St. 6–10, Southern Illinois 7–3, Southern Mississippi 4–13–1, Transylvania 7–12, Tulsa 10–14, Western Kentucky 18–12, Wichita St. 13–4, Xavier (Ohio) 0–13.

COACHES

Dean of Louisville coaches is Frank Camp with record of 118–95–2 for 1946–68, including 1 Sun Bowl champion and 1 unbeaten team. Other top records for at least 3 years were by Tom King, 27–21 for 1925–30 with 1 unbeaten team; Lee Corso, 28–11–3 for 1969–72 with 2 MVC titles and 1 bowl team; Vince Gibson, 25–29–2 for 1975–79 with 1 bowl team; and Howard Schnellenberger, 39–48–2 for 1985–92 with 1 Fiesta Bowl champion.

MISCELLANEA

First game was win over Transylvania 32–0 in 1912 ... highest score was over Washington (Tenn.) 100–0 in 1913 ... highest since W.W. II was over Wayne St. 72–0 in 1955 ... worst defeat was by Murray St. 105–0 in 1932 ... worst defeats since W.W. II were by Florida St. 59–0 in 1953 and Southern Mississippi 65–6 in 1987 ... highest against Cardinals since W.W. II was by Memphis St. 69–19 in 1969 ... longest unbeaten string of 10 in 1925–26 ended by Xavier (Ohio) 20–7 ... longest losing string of 24 in 1931–33 broken with win over Eastern Kentucky 13–7 ... Louisville has had no consensus All-Americans and no 1st team Academic All-Americans.

MEMPHIS STATE (Tigers; Blue and Gray)

NOTABLE TEAMS

1929 (8–0–2) *Won:* Sunflower J.C. 20–0, Caruthersville J.C. 26–0, Tennessee J.C. 13–2, Cumberland

12–6, Arkansas St. 6–0, Bethel 10–0, Murray St. 27–13, Little Rock College 32–6. *Tied:* SE Missouri St. 0–0, Delta St. 0–0. *Stars:* RB Henry Evans, Ts Sam Johnson and Gene Fulghum. *Noteworthy:* won Mississippi Valley Conference title in 1st unbeaten season since 2-game schedule of 1912.
1933 (7–1–1) *Won:* SE Missouri St. 18–0, Bethel 20–13, Arkansas College 18–6, Freed-Hardeman 51–0, Middle Tennessee St. 20–6, Tennessee Tech 13–0, Union 7–0. *Lost:* Western Kentucky 19–0. *Tied:* Arkansas St. 0–0.
1938 (10–0) *Won:* Millsaps 19–0, Louisiana College 14–6, Arkansas St. 38–2, Cumberland 68–0, Middle Tennessee St. 25–7, Tennessee Tech 26–13, Arkansas A&M 50–0, Troy St. 20–6, Union 13–7, Delta St. 8–0. *Stars:* QB Elmer Vaughn, RB Thomas "Skeeter" Ellis, soph FB Paul Hicks, E Roland McMackin, G Doug Mayo, T George Zarecor. *Noteworthy:* 1st unbeaten season since 1929.
1947 (6–2–1) *Won:* Missouri Mines 13–0, Centenary 26–7, Union 21–0, Pensacola Navy 54–0, Memphis Navy 58–0, Austin Peay 40–0. *Lost:* Middle Tennessee St. 20–0, Murray St. 14–7. *Tied:* Arkansas St. 19–19 (1st meeting since 1939). *Star:* C Andy Settles. *Noteworthy:* Resumed varsity football after 4-year layoff caused by W.W. II. 1st year under Ralph Hatley.
1949 (9–1) *Won:* Tampa 70–6, Washington (Mo.) 34–0, Delta St. 47–0, Pensacola Navy 49–0, Kansas St. 21–14, Murray St. 34–6, Louisiana College 27–0, Arkansas St. 61–7, Union 35–0. *Lost:* Mississippi 40–7 (1st meeting since 1942) in opener. *Stars:* FB Alex Williams (13 TDs), Frank Berry (12 TDs), RB Keith White, E Bill Robertson.
1950 (9–2) *Won:* Union 64–0, Memphis Navy 76–7, Chattanooga 26–8, Washington (Mo.) 54–0, SW Louisiana 20–0 (1st meeting), Murray St. 23–6, Louisiana College 25–12, Arkansas St. 60–7, Louisiana Tech 6–0. *Lost:* Mississippi 39–7, Vanderbilt 29–13 (1st meeting). *Stars:* Williams (11 TDs), Robertson (12 TDs), White, soph G Percy Roberts, T Tom Nix.
1960 (8–2) *Won:* Texas-Arlington 35–0, Tennessee Tech 37–6, North Texas St. 44–0, Hardin–Simmons 42–7, Virginia Military Institute (VMI) 21–8, Abilene Christian 55–0, Chattanooga 42–0, Southern Mississippi 7–6. *Lost:* unbeaten national cochamp Mississippi 31–20, Mississippi St. 21–0. *Stars:* QB James Earl Wright (13 TD passes), soph LB John Bramlett.

1961 (8–2) *Won:* The Citadel 40–0, Tulsa 48–12 (1st meeting), Hardin-Simmons 56–0, Louisville 28–13 (1st meeting since 1952), Southern Mississippi 21–7, Abilene Christian 35–0, North Texas St. 41–0, Chattanooga 41–13. *Lost:* Mississippi St. 23–16, Furman 7–6 in consecutive late games. *Stars:* Wright (11 TD passes, 10 TDs rush), soph FB Dave Casinelli (646 yds and 9 TDs rush), Bramlett.
1962 (8–1) *Won:* Tennessee Tech 12–6, North Texas St. 14–6, Louisville 49–0, Southern Mississippi 8–6, Mississippi St. 28–7 (1st in 10-game series dating to 1951), The Citadel 60–13, Texas-Arlington 50–0, Detroit 33–8. *Lost:* unbeaten Mississippi 21–7 in 2nd game. *Stars:* Bramlett, Casinelli (826 yds and 11 TDs rush), soph QB Russ Vollmer (8 TDs, 72 pts), T Bill Hudson.
1963 (9–0–1) *Won:* Southern Mississippi 28–7, Tulsa 28–15, North Texas St. 21–0, West Texas St. 29–14, Mississippi St. 17–14, Louisville 25–0, South Carolina 9–0, Chattanooga 13–0, Houston 29–6 (1st meeting). *Tied:* unbeaten Mississippi 0–0. *Stars:* Casinelli (nation's leader with 1,016 yds rush and in scoring with 84 pts on 14 TDs), Vollmer, HB John Griffin, Ts Harry Schuh and Richard Quast, DL John Fred Robilio, soph P Olie Cordill (41.3-yd avg). *Noteworthy:* 1st unbeaten season since 1938.
1966 (7–2) *Won:* South Carolina 16–7, Southern Mississippi 6–0, Quantico Marines 20–14, Tulsa 6–0, West Texas St. 26–14, Cincinnati 26–14 (1st meeting), Houston 14–13. *Lost:* Mississippi 13–0, Wake Forest 21–7. *Stars:* Tom Wallace (6 TDs), DT Larry Duck, soph LB Bill McRight, DB Bill Brundzo (6 int).
1969 (8–2) *Won:* North Texas St. 15–13, Cincinnati 52–6, Miami (Fla.) 26–13, Utah St. 40–0, Tulsa 42–24, Southern Mississippi 37–7, Florida St. 28–26, Louisville 69–19. *Lost:* Mississippi 28–3, Tennessee 55–16. *Stars:* soph RB Paul Gowen (715 yds and 6 TDs rush), OT Mike Stark, OG Al Hotz, C John Bomer, DE Bobby Dees, DT Luis Fernandez, LBs Fred Almon and John Allen, DBs Steve Jaggard (8 int) and David Berrong (8 int). *Noteworthy:* won 2nd straight MVC title.
1973 (8–3) *Won:* Louisville 28–21, North Texas St. 24–3, Mississippi 17–13 (1st over Rebels since 1967), Tulsa 28–16, Florida St. 13–10, Virginia Tech 49–16, SW Louisiana 41–6, Cincinnati 17–13. *Lost:* Houston 35–21, Kansas St. 21–16, Southern Mississippi 13–10 (1st to Golden Eagles since 1965). *Stars:* James Thompson (46 pass rec for 517 yds), WR

Bobby Ward (43 pass rec for 774 yds and 7 TDs), frosh DB Eric Harris.

BOWL RECORD (1–0)

Regular Season	Bowl	Score	Opponent	Record
1971 (4–6)	Pasadena	28–9	San Jose St.	(5–5–1)

CONFERENCE TITLES

Mississippi Valley—1929. **Missouri Valley**—1968, 1969, 1971.

TOP 20 AP AND UPI RANKING

1963	U–14	

MAJOR RIVALS

Memphis St. has played at least 10 games with Arkansas St. 19–20–5, Bethel 7–4–2, Cincinnati 13–5, Delta St. 9–4–1, Florida St. 7–10–1, Louisiana Tech 5–5, Louisville 17–12, Middle Tennessee St. 7–12–1, Mississippi 6–38–2, Mississippi St. 9–22, Murray St. 9–9–3, North Texas St. 15–4, Southern Mississippi 15–27–1, SW Louisiana 8–2, Tennessee 0–14, Tennessee Tech 9–7–4, Tulane 7–8–1, Tulsa 12–5, Union 9–13, UT-Chattanooga 8–5, Vanderbilt 5–7, Wichita St. 10–0.

COACHES

Dean of Memphis St. coaches is Billy Murphy with record of 91–44–1 for 1958–71, including 3 MVC titles, 1 Pasadena Bowl champion, and 1 unbeaten team. Other top records for at least 3 years were by Zach Curlin, 41–60–14 for 1924–36 with 1 unbeaten MVC champ; Ralph Hatley, 59–43–5 for 1947–57 with 1 minor bowl champion; and Fred Pancoast, 20–12–1 for 1972–74.

MISCELLANEA

First game was tie with Memphis University School 0–0 in 1912...1st win was over Bolton Agricultural College 13–6 in 1912...highest score was over Somerville H.S. 115–0 in 1916...highest since W.W. II was over Memphis Navy (Naval Air Training Center) 76–7 in 1950...highest margin against college foe since W.W. II was over Tampa 70–6 in 1949 and Union 64–0 in 1950...worst defeat was by Mississippi 92–0 in 1935...worst since W.W. II was by Texas A&M 58–0 in 1978... highest against Tigers since W.W. II was by Florida St. 66–17 in 1979...longest unbeaten string of 17 in 1962–63 ended by Mississippi 30–0 in 1964 opener...longest losing string of 17 in 1981–82 broken with win over Arkansas St. 12–0...consensus All-American was Joe Allison, K, 1992... Academic All-American was Pat Jansen, DL, 1992.

NAVY (U.S. NAVAL ACADEMY)
(Midshipmen, Mids; Navy-Blue and Gold)

NOTABLE TEAMS

1889 (4–1–1) *Won:* St. John's 20–10, Johns Hopkins 36–0, Virginia 26–6 (1st meeting), Washington All-Stars 24–0. *Lost:* Lehigh 26–6 (1st meeting). *Tied:* Dickinson 0–0 (1st meeting).
1890 (5–1–1) *Won:* St. John's 45–0, Georgetown 70–4 (1st meeting), Dickinson 32–6, Gallaudet 24–0, Army 24–0 (1st meeting). *Lost:* Lehigh 24–4. *Tied:* Columbia A.C. 6–6.
1891 (5–2) *Won:* St. John's 28–6, Rutgers 21–12

(1st meeting), Gallaudet 6–0, Georgetown 16–4, Dickinson 34–4 in 1st 5 games. *Lost:* Lafayette 4–0 (1st meeting), Army 32–16.

1892 (5–2) *Won:* Lafayette 22–4, Franklin & Marshall 24–0, Rutgers 48–12, Georgetown 40–0, Army 12–4. *Lost:* Pennsylvania 16–0, Princeton 28–0 (1st meeting) in 1st 2 games.

1894 (4–1–2) *Won:* Georgetown 12–0, Carlisle Indians 8–0, Lehigh 10–0, Baltimore City College 30–6. *Lost:* unbeaten Pennsylvania 12–0. *Tied:* Elizabeth A.C. 6–6, unbeaten Penn St. 6–6 (1st meeting).

1895 (5–2) *Won:* Elizabeth A.C. 6–0, New Jersey A.C. 34–0, Franklin & Marshall 68–0, Carlisle 34–0, Virginia 1–0 (forfeit) in 1st 5 games. *Lost:* Orange A.C. 10–6, Lehigh 6–4.

1897 (8–1) *Won:* Penn reserves 22–0, Princeton reserves 6–0, Penn St. 4–0, Rutgers 1–0 (forfeit), Virginia 4–0, Maryland 38–0 (1st meeting), Lehigh 28–6, White Squadron 8–0. *Lost:* Princeton 28–0 in opener. *Noteworthy:* 1st year under Bill Armstrong.

1898 (7–1) *Won:* Bucknell 11–0 (1st meeting), Penn St. 16–11, Lafayette 18–0, Columbia A.C. 52–5, Lehigh 6–5, Virginia 6–0, Virginia Military Institute (VMI) 21–5 (1st meeting). *Lost:* Princeton 30–0.

1904 (7–2–1) *Won:* VMI 12–0, Marine Officers 68–0, Princeton 10–9 (1st in 7-game series dating to 1892), St. John's 23–0, Penn St. 20–9, Virginia 5–0, Virginia Tech 11–0. *Lost:* Swarthmore 9–0, Army 11–0. *Tied:* Dickinson 0–0. *Noteworthy:* 1st year under Paul Dashiell.

1905 (10–1–1) *Won:* VMI 34–0, St. John's 29–0, Dickinson 6–0, Western Maryland 29–0, North Carolina 38–0 (1st meeting since 1899), Maryland 17–0, Penn St. 11–5, Bucknell 34–0, Virginia 22–0, Virginia Tech 12–6. *Lost:* Swarthmore 6–5. *Tied:* Army 6–6.

1906 (8–2–2) *Won:* Maryland 12–0, St. John's 28–0, Lehigh 12–0, Western Maryland 31–0, Swarthmore 5–4, North Carolina 40–0, Virginia Tech 5–0, Army 10–0 (1st over Cadets since 1900). *Lost:* unbeaten national champ Princeton 5–0, Penn St. 5–0. *Tied:* Dickinson 0–0, Bucknell 0–0. *Star:* FB Jonas Ingram. *Noteworthy:* Dashiell's last team.

1907 (9–2–1) *Won:* St. John's 26–0, 12–0, Dickinson 15–0, Maryland 12–0, Lafayette 17–0, West Virginia 6–0, Penn St. 6–4, Virginia Tech 12–0,

Army 6–0. *Lost:* Harvard 6–0, Swarthmore 18–0. *Tied:* Vanderbilt 6–6. *Star:* E Bill Dague (Navy's 1st consensus All-American). *Noteworthy:* only year under Joe Reeves.

1908 (9–2–1) *Won:* Rutgers 18–0, St. John's 22–0, Dickinson 22–0, Maryland 57–0, Lehigh 16–0, George Washington 17–0, Villanova 30–6 (1st meeting), Penn St. 5–0, Virginia Tech 15–4. *Lost:* Carlisle 16–6, Army 6–4. *Tied:* unbeaten Harvard 6–6. *Stars:* QB Ed Lange, T Percy Northcroft.

1910 (8–0–1) *Won:* St. John's 16–0, Washington & Jefferson 15–0, Virginia Tech 3–0, Western Reserve 17–0, Lehigh 30–0, Carlisle 6–0, New York U. 9–0, Army 3–0. *Tied:* Rutgers 0–0. *Noteworthy:* had 1st unbeaten season since 1-game schedule of 1884 in last year under Frank Berrien.

1911 (6–0–3) *Won:* Johns Hopkins 27–5 (1st meeting since 1889), St. John's 21–0, Washington & Jefferson 16–0, N.C. State 17–6, West Virginia 32–0, Army 3–0. *Tied:* unbeaten national champ Princeton 0–0, Western Reserve 0–0, unbeaten Penn St. 0–0. *Star:* FB Jack Dalton. *Noteworthy:* 1st year under Doug Howard.

1913 (7–1–1) *Won:* Georgetown 23–0, Dickinson 29–0, Maryland 76–0, Lehigh 39–0, Bucknell 70–7, Penn St. 10–0, New York U. 48–0. *Lost:* Army 22–9 in finale. *Tied:* Pittsburgh 0–0. *Star:* G John "Babe" Brown.

1917 (7–1) *Won:* Davidson 27–6, Maryland 62–0, Carlisle 62–0, Haverford 89–0, Western Reserve 95–0, Georgetown 28–7, Villanova 80–3. *Lost:* West Virginia 7–0 in 2nd game. *Stars:* B Bill Ingram (21 TDs, 174 pts), E Ernest Von Heimberg. *Noteworthy:* No Army game, as sign of unity during W.W. I. 1st year under Gil Dobie.

1918 (4–1) *Won:* Newport Training Station 47–7, St. Helena Training Station 66–0, Norfolk Naval Base 37–6, Ursinus 127–0. *Lost:* Great Lakes 7–6 in finale. *Stars:* Ingram, HB Wolcott Roberts, G Lyman Perry.

1919 (7–1) *Won:* N.C. State 49–0, Johns Hopkins 66–0 (1st meeting since 1912), Bucknell 21–6, West Virginia Wesleyan 20–6 (1st meeting), Colby 121–0, Army 6–0, USS Utah 15–0. *Lost:* Georgetown 6–0. *Noteworthy:* Dobie's last team.

1920 (6–2) *Won:* Lafayette 12–7 (1st meeting since 1907), Bucknell 7–2, Western Reserve 47–0, Georgetown 21–6, South Carolina 63–0, Army 7–0. *Lost:* N.C. State 14–7, unbeaten Princeton 14–0 (1st meeting since 1911). *Noteworthy:* 1st year under Bob Folwell.

1921 (6–1) *Won:* N.C. State 40–0, Western Reserve 53–0, Princeton 13–0, Bethany (W.Va.) 21–0, Bucknell 6–0, Army 7–0. *Lost:* unbeatenPenn St. 13–7 (1st meeting since 1913).

1922 (5–2) *Won:* Western Reserve 71–0, Bucknell 14–7, Georgia Tech 13–0 (1st meeting), Penn St. 14–0, Xavier (Ohio) 52–0. *Lost:* Pennsylvania 13–7 (1st meeting since 1915), unbeaten Army 17–14. *Star:* E Wendell Taylor.

1923 (5–1–3) *Won:* William & Mary 39–10 (1st meeting), Dickinson 13–7, West Virginia Wesleyan 26–7, Colgate 9–0, Xavier (Ohio) 61–0. *Lost:* Penn St. 21–3. *Tied:* Princeton 3–3, Army 0–0. *Noteworthy:* made 1st postseason appearance, tying Washington 14–14 in Rose Bowl; Ira "Pete" McKee passed for both TDs to TB Carl Cullen (20 and 7 yds) and kicked both ex pts.

1926 (9–0–1) *Won:* Purdue 17–13, Drake 24–7, Richmond 26–0, Princeton 27–13, Colgate 13–7, Michigan 10–0, West Virginia Wesleyan 53–7, Georgetown 10–7, Loyola 35–13. *Tied:* Army 21–21 in finale (before estimated 110,000 in Chicago). *Stars:* HB Tom Hamilton (6 FGs, 42 pts), Howard Caldwell (7 TDs), T Frank Wickhorst. *Noteworthy:* 1st year under Bill Ingram.

1929 (6–2–2) *Won:* Denison 47–0, William & Mary 15–0, Duke 45–13, Wake Forest 61–0, West Virginia Wesleyan 30–6, Dartmouth 13–6. *Lost:* unbeaten national champ Notre Dame 14–7, Pennsylvania 7–2. *Tied:* Princeton 13–13, Georgetown 0–0. *Star:* Joe Clifton (5 TDs).

1934 (8–1) *Won:* William & Mary 20–7, Virginia 21–6, Maryland 16–13, Columbia 18–7, Pennsylvania 17–0, Washington & Lee 26–0, Notre Dame 10–6, Army 3–0 (1st over Cadets in 11 games since 1921). *Lost:* Pittsburgh 31–7. *Stars:* HB Fred "Buzz" Borries (10 TDs), T Slade Cutter. *Noteworthy:* 1st year under Tom Hamilton.

1940 (6–2–1) *Won:* William & Mary 19–7, Cincinnati 14–0, Princeton 12–6 (1st over Tigers in 8 games since 1931), Drake 19–0, Yale 21–0 (1st in 5-game series dating to 1901), Army 14–0. *Lost:* Pennsylvania 20–0, Notre Dame 13–7. *Tied:* Columbia 0–0. *Star:* Bill Busik (860 yds total off). *Noteworthy:* led nation in total defense.

1941 (7–1–1) *Won:* William & Mary 34–0, West Virginia 40–0 (1st meeting since 1917), Lafayette 41–2 (1st meeting since 1920), Cornell 14–0 (1st meeting), Pennsylvania 13–6, Princeton 23–0,

Army 14–6. *Lost:* unbeaten Notre Dame 20–13. *Tied:* Harvard 0–0. *Stars:* Busik (609 yds rush, 43.8-yd punting avg), Howie Clark (6 TDs). *Noteworthy:* last year under Swede Larson.

1943 (8–1) *Won:* North Carolina Pre-Flight 31–0, Cornell 46–7, Duke 14–13 (1st meeting since 1930), Penn St. 14–6 (1st meeting since 1924), Georgia Tech 28–14, Pennsylvania 24–7, Columbia 61–0, Army 13–0. *Lost:* national champ Notre Dame 33–6. *Stars:* T Don Whitmire, G George Brown, Bs Hillis Hume and Hal Hamberg. *Noteworthy:* won 1st Lambert Trophy.

1945 (7–1–1) *Won:* Villanova 49–0 (1st meeting since 1917), Duke 21–0, Penn St. 28–0, Georgia Tech 20–6, Pennsylvania 14–7, Michigan 33–7 (1st meeting since 1928), Wisconsin 36–7. *Lost:* unbeaten national champ Army 32–13 in finale. *Tied:* Notre Dame 6–6. *Stars:* Clyde Scott (7 TDs, 4 int), HB Anthony "Skip" Minisi, soph C Dick Scott, E Dick Duden (14 pass rec for 200 yds).

1952 (6–2–1) *Won:* Yale 31–7, Cornell 31–7, William & Mary 14–0 (1st meeting since 1942), Duke 16–6, Columbia 28–0, Army 7–0. *Lost:* Maryland 38–7, Notre Dame 17–6. *Tied:* Pennsylvania 7–7. *Stars:* G Steve Eisenhauer, Fred Franco (691 yds rush, 5 TDs), John Weaver (7 int). *Noteworthy:* 1st winning season since 1945.

1954 (8–2) *Won:* William & Mary 27–0, Dartmouth 42–7, Stanford 25–0, Pennsylvania 52–6, Duke 40–7, Columbia 51–6, Army 27–20. *Lost:* Pittsburgh 21–19 (1st meeting since 1934), Notre Dame 6–0. *Stars:* Maxwell Award–winner Ron Beagle (20 pass rec for 243 yds), QB George Welsh (740 yds and 10 TDs total off), Joe Gattuso (525 yds rush, 7 TDs). *Noteworthy:* Won 2nd Lambert Trophy. Beat Mississippi 21–0 in Sugar Bowl in 1st postseason appearance in 31 years; Gattuso ran for 111 yds and 2 TDs, and Welsh passed for other TD to HB Jack Weaver (106 yds rush).

1955 (6–2–1) *Won:* William & Mary 7–0, South Carolina 26–0, Pittsburgh 21–0 (1st over Panthers in 8 games since 1912), Penn St. 34–14 (1st meeting since 1947), Pennsylvania 33–0, Columbia 47–0. *Lost:* Notre Dame 21–7 (10th straight to Irish), Army 14–6. *Tied:* Duke 7–7. *Stars:* Welsh (nation's leader in pass with 1,319 yds and in total off with 1,348 yds), Beagle (30 pass rec for 451 yds), Dick Guest (6 TDs), soph FB Ned Oldham. *Noteworthy:* led nation in pass.

1956 (6–1–2) *Won:* William & Mary 39–14, Cornell 14–0, Cincinnati 13–7, Pennsylvania 54–6, Notre

Dame 33–7 (1st over Irish since 1944), Virginia 34–7 (1st meeting since 1942). *Lost:* Tulane 21–6. *Tied:* Duke 7–7, Army 7–7. *Star:* Oldham (7 TDs, 53 pts).

1957 (9–1–1) *Won:* Boston College 46–6 (1st meeting since 1928), William & Mary 33–6, California 21–6, Georgia 27–14, Pennsylvania 35–7, Notre Dame 20–6, George Washington 52–0, Army 14–0. *Lost:* North Carolina 13–7 (1st meeting since 1946). *Tied:* Duke 6–6. *Stars:* Oldham (8 TDs, 69 pts), Harry Hurst (634 yds rush), QB Tom Forrestal (1,270 yds pass), Pete Jokanovich (32 pass rec for 386 yds), T Bob Reifsnyder (Maxwell Award winner). *Noteworthy:* Won 3rd Lambert Trophy. Beat Rice 20–7 in Cotton Bowl as Midshipmen recovered 5 Owl fumbles, Oldham scored TD and kicked 2 ex pts, and Reifsnyder led defense.

1960 (9–2) *Won:* Boston College 22–7, Villanova 41–7, Washington 15–14, Southern Methodist (SMU) 26–7, Air Force 35–3 (1st meeting), Pennsylvania 27–0, Notre Dame 14–7, Virginia 41–6, Army 17–12. *Lost:* Duke 19–10. *Stars:* Heisman Trophy– and Maxwell Award–winning HB Joe Bellino (18 TDs, 110 pts, 834 yds rush, 17 pass rec for 280 yds), QB Hal Spooner, Jim Luper (22 pass rec for 307 yds). *Noteworthy:* Got share of 4th Lambert Trophy. Lost to Missouri 21–14 in Orange Bowl; E Greg Mather scored on 94-yd fumble return and Spooner passed for 176 yds and a TD (27 yds to Bellino).

1961 (7–3) *Won:* William & Mary 44–6, Miami (Fla.) 17–6, Cornell 31–7, Detroit 37–19, Notre Dame 13–10, Virginia 13–3, Army 13–7. *Lost:* Penn St. 20–10, Pittsburgh 28–14 (1st meeting since 1955), Duke 30–9. *Stars:* Mather (61 pts, nation's kicking leader with 11 FGs), QB Ron Klemick (1,035 yds pass), Jim Stewart (23 pass rec for 498 yds).

1963 (9–2) *Won:* West Virginia 51–7, William & Mary 28–0, Michigan 26–13 (1st meeting since 1958), VMI 21–12, Pittsburgh 24–12, Notre Dame 35–14, Maryland 42–7, Duke 38–25, Army 21–15.

Lost: SMU 32–28. *Stars:* Heisman Trophy– and Maxwell Award–winning QB Roger Staubach (1,474 yds and 7 TDs pass, 418 yds and 8 TDs rush), Ed "Skip" Orr (25 pass rec for 321 yds), John Sai (10 TDs), Pat Donnelly (603 yds rush). *Noteworthy:* Won 5th Lambert Trophy. Lost to unbeaten national champ Texas 28–6 in Cotton Bowl; Staubach passed for 228 yds and Orr caught 9 passes.

1978 (9–3) *Won:* Virginia 32–0, Connecticut 30–0, Boston College 19–8, Air Force 37–8, Duke 31–8, William & Mary 9–0, Pittsburgh 21–11, Army 28–0. *Lost:* Notre Dame 27–7 (15th straight to Irish), Syracuse 20–17, Florida St. 38–6. *Stars:* QB Bob Leszczynski (1,282 yds pass), Phil McConkey (22 pass rec for 532 yds and 6 TDs), Steve Callahan (766 yds rush), K Bob Tata (14 FGs), soph Fred Reitzel (5 int). *Noteworthy:* beat Brigham Young (BYU) 23–16 in inaugural Holiday Bowl as McConkey caught 65-yd TD pass from Leszczynski for clinching score; Tata kicked 3 FGs.

1980 (8–4) *Won:* Kent St. 31–3, William & Mary 45–6, Boston College 21–0, Villanova 24–15, Washington 24–10, Syracuse 6–3, Georgia Tech 19–8, Army 33–6. *Lost:* Virginia 6–3 (1st to Cavaliers in 7 games since 1968), Air Force 21–20, Notre Dame 33–0. *Stars:* TB Eddie Meyers (957 yds rush), QB Reitzel (8 TDs rush, 7 TDs pass), TEs Curt Gainer (24 pass rec for 340 yds) and Greg Pappajohn (16 pass rec for 267 yds), WR Dave Dent (20 pass rec for 274 yds), K Steve Fehr (17 FGs, 75 pts), LBs Mike Kronzer and Ted Dumbauld, Elliott Reagans (5 int), P Lex Lauletta (41.1-yd avg). *Noteworthy:* lost to Houston 35–0 in Garden State Bowl as Midshipmen were held to 200 yds total off.

Bowl Summary

Cotton 1–1; Garden State 0–1; Holiday 1–0; Liberty 0–1; Orange 0–1; Rose 0–0–1; Sugar 1–0.

Bowl Record (3–4–1)

Regular Season	Bowl	Score	Opponent	Record
1923 (5–1–2)	Rose	14–14	Washington	(10–1)
1954 (7–2)	Sugar	21–0	Mississippi	(9–1)
1957 (8–1–1)	Cotton	20–7	Rice	(7–3)
1960 (9–1)	Orange	14–21	Missouri	(9–1)
1963 (9–1)	Cotton	6–28	Texas	(10–0)

(continued)

Regular Season	Bowl	Score	Opponent	Record
1978 (8–3)	Holiday	23–16	BYU	(9–3)
1980 (8–3)	Garden State	0–35	Houston	(6–5)
1981 (7–3–1)	Liberty	28–31	Ohio State	(8–3)

CONFERENCE TITLES

None. Won **Lambert Trophy** in 1943, 1954, 1957, 1960*, 1963.

TOP 20 AP AND UPI RANKING

1936	18	1945	3	1955	18–20	1963	2–2
1941	10	1950	U–19	1956	16–19	1978	U–17
1943	4	1952	U–17	1957	5–6		
1944	4	1954	5–5	1960	4–6		

MAJOR RIVALS

Navy has played at least 10 games with Air Force 8–17, Army 43–43–7, Boston College 10–12, Bucknell 9–4–1, Columbia 13–9–1, Cornell 9–1, Dickinson 10–1–4, Duke 14–9–5, Georgetown 13–4–2, Georgia Tech 8–13, Johns Hopkins 9–3, Lafayette 7–4, Lehigh 14–6–1, Maryland 14–5, Michigan 5–12–1, North Carolina 5–5, Notre Dame 9–56–1, Pennsylvania 21–22–4, Penn St. 17–18–2, Pittsburgh 12–20–3, Princeton 12–18–6, Rutgers 6–3–1, St. John's College 18–3, Syracuse 8–19, Villanova 8–2, Virginia 27–9, William & Mary 35–6–1, Yale 4–5–1.

COACHES

Deans of Navy coaches are Eddie Erdelatz and George Welsh with 9 years each. Erdelatz was 50–26–8 for 1950–58, with 2 Lambert Trophy winners and 2 bowl champions. Welsh was 55–46–1 for 1973–81 with 3 bowl teams. Other top records for at least 3 years were by Bill Armstrong, 19–5–1 for 1897–99; Paul Dashiell, 25–5–4 for 1904–06; Frank Berrien, 21–5–3 for 1908–10 with 1 unbeaten team; Doug Howard, 25–7–4 for 1911–14 with 1 unbeaten team; Gil Dobie, 17–3 for 1917–19; Bob Folwell, 24–12–2 for 1920–24 with 1 bowl team; Bill Ingram, 32–13–4 for 1926–30 with 1 unbeaten team; Swede Larson, 16–8–3 for 1939–41; and Wayne Hardin, 38–22–2 for 1959–64 with 2 Lambert Trophy winners and 2 bowl teams.

MISCELLANEA

First game was tie with Baltimore A.C. 0–0 in 1879 ... 1st win was over Johns Hopkins 8–0 in 1882 ... highest score was over Ursinus 127–0 in 1918 ... highest since W.W. II was over Princeton 65–7 in 1953 ... worst defeat was by Michigan 70–14 in 1976 ... longest unbeaten string of 22 in 1909–12 ended by Lehigh 14–0 ... longest winless string of 15 in 1947–49 broken with win over Princeton 28–7 ... 11-game losing string in 1990–91 broken with win over Army 24–3 ... consensus All-Americans were Bill Dague, E, 1907; Percy Northcroft, T, and Ed Lange, B, 1908; Jack Dalton, B, 1911; John Brown, G, 1913; Lyman Perry, G, and Wolcott Roberts, B, 1918; Wendell Taylor, T, 1922; Frank Wickhorst, T, 1926; Edward Burke, G, 1928; Fred Borries, B, 1934; Don Whitmire, T, 1943–44; Ben Chase, G, and Bob Jenkins, B, 1944; Dick Duden, E, 1945; Ron Beagle, E, 1954–55; Joe Bellino, B, 1960; Roger Staubach, B, 1963; Chet Moeller, DB, 1975; and Napoleon McCallum, RB, 1983, 1985 ... Academic All-Americans were Steve Eisenhauer, G, 1953; Tom Forrestal, QB, 1957; Joe Tranchini, B, 1958; Dan Pike, RB, 1969; and Ted Dumbauld, LB, 1980 ... Heisman Trophy winners were Joe Bellino, HB, 1960; and Roger Staubach, QB, 1963 ... Maxwell Award winners were Ron Beagle, E, 1954; Bob Reifsnyder, T, 1957; Joe Bellino, HB, 1960; and Roger Staubach, QB, 1963.

NOTRE DAME *(Fighting Irish; Gold and Blue)*

NOTABLE TEAMS

1893 (4–1) *Won:* Kalamazoo 34–0, Albion 8–6, DeLaSalle 28–0, Hillsdale 22–10. *Lost:* Chicago 8–0 in finale.

1894 (3–1–1) *Won:* Hillsdale 14–0, Wabash 30–0 (1st meeting), Rush Medical 18–6. *Lost:* Albion 19–12 in finale. *Tied:* Albion 6–6.

1897 (4–1–1) *Won:* DePauw 4–0 (1st meeting), Chicago Dental Surgeons 62–0, St. Viator 60–0, Michigan St. 34–6 (1st meeting). *Lost:* Chicago 34–5. *Tied:* Rush Medical 0–0.

1901 (8–1–1) *Won:* Ohio Medical 6–0, Chicago Medical College 32–0, Beloit 5–0, Lake Forest 16–0, Purdue 12–6, Indiana 18–5, Chicago Physicians & Surgeons 34–0, South Bend A.C. 22–6. *Lost:* Northwestern 2–0. *Tied:* South Bend A.C. 0–0. *Star:* soph FB Louis "Red" Salmon (7 TDs).

1902 (6–2–1) *Won:* Michigan St. 33–0, Lake Forest 28–0, Indiana 11–5, Ohio Medical 6–5, American Medical 92–0, DePauw 22–0. *Lost:* unbeaten national champ Michigan 23–0, Knox 12–5. *Tied:* Purdue 6–6. *Star:* Salmon (11 TDs, 77 pts). *Noteworthy:* 1st year under James Faragher.

1903 (8–0–1) *Won:* Michigan St. 12–0, Lake Forest 28–0, DePauw 56–0, American Medical 52–0, Physicians & Surgeons 46–0, Missouri Osteopaths 28–0, Ohio Medical 35–0, Wabash 35–0 (1st meeting since 1894). *Tied:* Northwestern 0–0. *Star:* Salmon (15 TDs, 105 pts). *Noteworthy:* blanked foes 292–0 in 1st unbeaten season since 2-game schedule of 1892.

1906 (6–1) *Won:* Franklin 26–0, Hillsdale 17–0, Physicians & Surgeons 28–0, Michigan St. 5–0, Purdue 2–0, Beloit 29–0. *Lost:* Indiana 6–0. *Noteworthy:* 1st year under Thomas Barry.

1907 (6–0–1) *Won:* Physicians & Surgeons 32–0, Franklin 23–0, Olivet 22–4, Knox 22–4, Purdue 17–0, St. Vincent's (Ill.) 21–12. *Tied:* Indiana 0–0.

1908 (8–1) *Won:* Hillsdale 39–0, Franklin 64–0, Physicians & Surgeons 88–0, Ohio Northern 58–4, Indiana 11–0, Wabash 8–4, St. Viator 46–0, Marquette 6–0 (1st meeting). *Lost:* Michigan 12–6 (1st meeting since 1902). *Noteworthy:* only year under Victor Place.

1909 (7–0–1) *Won:* Olivet 58–0, Rose Poly (RPI) 60–11, Michigan St. 17–0, Pittsburgh 6–0 (1st meeting), Michigan 11–3 (1st in 9-game series dating

to 1887), Miami (Ohio) 46–0, Wabash 38–0. *Tied:* Marquette 0–0 in finale. *Noteworthy:* 1st year under Frank Longman. "Notre Dame Victory March" introduced during season.

1910 (4–1–1) *Won:* Olivet 48–0, Akron 51–0, RPI 41–3, Ohio Northern 47–0. *Lost:* Michigan St. 17–0 (1st in 9-game series dating to 1897). *Tied:* Marquette 5–5.

1911 (6–0–2) *Won:* Ohio Northern 32–6, St. Viator 43–0, Butler 27–0, Loyola (Ill.) 80–0, St. Bonaventure 34–0, Wabash 6–3. *Tied:* Pittsburgh 0–0, unbeaten Marquette 0–0. *Noteworthy:* 1st year under John Marks.

1912 (7–0) *Won:* St. Viator 116–7, Adrian 74–7, Morris Harvey 39–0, Wabash 41–6, Pittsburgh 3–0, St. Louis 47–7, Marquette 69–0. *Noteworthy:* outscored foes 389–27 in 1st perfect season since 1-game schedule of 1889.

1913 (7–0) *Won:* Ohio Northern 87–0, South Dakota 20–7, Alma 62–0, Army 35–13 (1st meeting), Penn St. 14–7 (1st meeting), Christian Brothers (St. Louis) 20–7, Texas 30–7 (1st meeting). *Stars:* QB Gus Dorais (Notre Dame's 1st consensus All-American), E Knute Rockne, FB Ray Eichenlaub. *Noteworthy:* 1st year under Jess Harper.

1914 (6–2) *Won:* Alma 56–0, Rose Poly 103–0, South Dakota 33–0, Haskell 20–7, Carlisle 48–6, Syracuse 20–0. *Lost:* Yale 28–0, unbeaten national champ Army 20–7. *Star:* HB Stan Cofall (9 TDs, 82 pts).

1915 (7–1) *Won:* Alma 32–0, Haskell 34–0, South Dakota 6–0, Army 7–0, Creighton 41–0, Texas 36–7, Rice 55–2. *Lost:* unbeaten Nebraska 20–19 (1st meeting). *Star:* Cofall (9 TDs, 71 pts).

1916 (8–1) *Won:* Case Tech 48–0, Western Reserve 48–0, Haskell 26–0, Wabash 60–0, South Dakota 21–0, Michigan St. 14–0 (1st meeting since 1910), Alma 46–0, Nebraska 20–0. *Lost:* unbeaten Army 30–10. *Stars:* Cofall (12 TDs, 84 pts), G Charlie Bachman.

1917 (6–1–1) *Won:* Kalamazoo 55–0, South Dakota 40–0, Army 7–2, Morningside 13–0, Michigan St. 23–0, Washington & Jefferson 3–0. *Lost:* Nebraska 7–0. *Tied:* Wisconsin 0–0 (1st meeting since 1905). *Star:* C Frank Rydzewski. *Noteworthy:* Harper's last team.

1919 (9–0) *Won:* Kalamazoo 14–0, Mt. Union 60–7, Nebraska 14–9, Western Michigan 53–0, Indiana 16–3 (1st meeting since 1908), Army 12–9, Michigan St. 13–0, Purdue 33–13, Morningside 14–6. *Stars:* B George Gipp (7 TDs, 729 yds rush,

TB George Gipp, 1917–20

727 yds pass), Bernie Kirk (21 pass rec for 372 yds). *Noteworthy:* Knute Rockne's 1st unbeaten team.
1920 (9–0) *Won:* Kalamazoo 39–0, Western Michigan 42–0, Nebraska 16–7, Valparaiso 28–3, Army 27–17, Purdue 28–0 (1st homecoming), Indiana 13–10, Northwestern 33–7 (1st meeting since 1903), Michigan St. 25–0. *Stars:* Gipp (8 TDs, 64 pts, 827 yds rush, 709 yds pass, 40.6-yd punting avg), Eddie Anderson (17 pass rec for 293 yds), HB Paul Castner (43.3-yd punting avg), E Roger Kiley.
1921 (10–1) *Won:* Kalamazoo 56–0, DePauw 57–10 (1st meeting since 1905), Purdue 33–0, Nebraska 7–0, Indiana 28–7, Army 28–0, Rutgers 48–0, Haskell 42–7, Marquette 21–7 (1st meeting since 1912), Michigan St. 48–0. *Lost:* unbeaten Iowa 10–7 (1st meeting). *Stars:* HB John Mohardt (12 TDs, 781 yds rush, 995 yds and 9 TDs pass), Castner (40-yd punting avg), Eddie Anderson (26 pass rec for 394 yds), Kiley, G Hunk Anderson, T Buck Shaw.
1922 (8–1–1) *Won:* Kalamazoo 46–0, St. Louis 26–0, Purdue 20–0, DePauw 34–7, Georgia Tech 13–3 (1st meeting), Indiana 27–0, Butler 31–3, Carnegie Tech 19–0 (1st meeting). *Lost:* Nebraska 14–6 in finale. *Tied:* unbeaten Army 0–0. *Stars:* FB Castner (8 TDs, 64 pts), soph HB Jim Crowley (566 yds and 5 TDs rush), soph HB Don Miller (5 TDs), soph QB Harry Stuhldreher (6 TDs), soph FB Elmer Layden (626 yds total off), G Ed DeGree.
1923 (9–1) *Won:* Kalamazoo 74–0, Lombard 14–0, Army 13–0, Princeton 25–2, Georgia Tech 35–7, Purdue 34–7, Butler 34–7, Carnegie Tech 26–0, St. Louis 13–0. *Lost:* Nebraska, 14–7 in mid-season. *Stars:* Miller (698 yds rush, 10 TDs), Crowley (536 yds rush, 39 pts), Layden (7 TDs), Red Maher (10 TDs), G Harvey Brown.
1924 (10–0) *Won:* Lombard 40–0, Wabash 34–0 (1st meeting since 1918), Army 13–7, Princeton 12–0, Georgia Tech 34–3, Wisconsin 38–3 (1st meeting since 1917, 1st win in 5-game series dating to 1900), Nebraska 34–6, Northwestern 13–6, Carnegie Tech 40–19. *Stars:* C Adam Walsh and "Four Horsemen" backfield of Miller (763 yds rush, 16 pass rec for 297 yds, 7 TDs), Crowley (739 yds rush, 12 pass rec for 265 yds, 9 TDs, 71 pts), Layden (423 yds rush, 6 TDs), Stuhldreher. *Noteworthy:* Rockne's 3rd unbeaten team won 1st national championship. Made 1st postseason appearance, beating undefeated Stanford 27–10 in Rose Bowl; Layden scored 3 TDs (2 on pass int returns of 78 and 70 yds), and Ed Hunsinger returned a fumbled Layden punt 20 yds for another TD.
1925 (7–2–1) *Won:* Baylor 41–0, Lombard 69–0, Beloit 19–3, Minnesota 19–7, Georgia Tech 13–0, Carnegie Tech 26–0, Northwestern 13–10. *Lost:* Army 27–0 (1st to Cadets since 1916), Nebraska 17–0. *Tied:* Penn St. 0–0 (1st meeting since 1913). *Star:* soph Christie Flanagan (556 yds rush, 7 TDs).
1926 (9–1) *Won:* Beloit 77–0, Minnesota 20–7, Penn St. 28–0, Northwestern 6–0, Georgia Tech 12–0, Indiana 26–0, Army 7–0, Drake 21–0, Southern California (USC) 13–12 (1st meeting). *Lost:* Carnegie Tech 19–0 (1st in 5-game series begun in 1922). *Stars:* Flanagan (535 yds rush), Bucky Dahman (6 TDs), C Art "Bud" Boeringer.
1927 (7–1–1) *Won:* Coe 28–7, Detroit 20–0, Navy 19–6 (1st meeting), Indiana 19–6, Georgia Tech 26–7, Drake 32–0, USC 7–6 (1st Notre Dame game seen by more than 100,000 fans). *Lost:* Army 18–0. *Tied:* unbeaten Minnesota 7–7. *Stars:* Flanagan (731 yds rush), G John Smith, T John Polisky.

Four Horsemen backfield of HB Don Miller, FB Elmer Layden, HB Jim Crowley, and QB Harry Stuhldreher, 1922–24

1929 (9–0) *Won:* Indiana 14–0, Navy 14–7, Wisconsin 19–0, Carnegie Tech 7–0, Georgia Tech 26–6, Drake 19–7, USC 13–12, Northwestern 26–6, Army 7–0. *Stars:* QB/S Frank Carideo (5 int), FB Joe Savoldi (597 yds rush), HB Jack Elder (7 TDs), G Jack Cannon, T Ted Twomey. *Noteworthy:* Won 2nd national title in 1st unbeaten season since 1924. Played only road games (Notre Dame Stadium under construction).

1930 (10–0) *Won:* Southern Methodist (SMU) 20–14 (1st meeting), Navy 26–2 (in Notre Dame Stadium dedication), Carnegie Tech 21–6, Pittsburgh 35–19 (1st meeting since 1912), Indiana 27–0, Pennsylvania 60–20, Drake 28–7, Northwestern 14–0, Army 7–6 (before more than 100,000 at Chicago's Soldier Field), USC 27–0. *Stars:* Carideo, Savoldi, HBs Marchy Schwartz (9 TDs, 927 yds rush, 319 yds pass) and Marty Brill, E Tom Conley, G Bert Metzger, T Al Culver. *Noteworthy:* Rockne's last team (his 5th unbeaten one) repeated as national champion.

1931 (6–2–1) *Won:* Indiana 25–0 (10th straight over Hoosiers), Drake 63–0, Pittsburgh 25–12, Car-negie Tech 19–0, Pennsylvania 49–0, Navy 20–0. *Lost:* national champ USC 16–14 (before 1st capacity crowd in Notre Dame Stadium), Army 12–0 in last 2 games. *Tied:* unbeaten Northwestern 0–0. *Stars:* Schwartz (692 yds and 5 TDs rush), T Joe Kurth, C Tommy Yarr, G Nordy Hoffmann. *Noteworthy:* 1st year under Hunk Anderson.

1932 (7–2) *Won:* Haskell 73–0, Drake 62–0, Carnegie Tech 42–0, Kansas 24–6, Northwestern 21–0, Navy 12–0, Army 21–0. *Lost:* unbeaten Pittsburgh 12–0 (1st in 6-game series dating to 1909), unbeaten national cochamp USC 13–0. *Stars:* Kurth, T Ed Krause, E Ed Kosky, soph FB George Melinkovich (503 yds and 8 TDs rush).

1935 (7–1–1) *Won:* Kansas 28–7, Carnegie Tech 14–3, Wisconsin 27–0, Pittsburgh 9–6, Navy 14–0, Ohio St. 18–13, USC 20–13. *Lost:* Northwestern 14–7 (1st to Wildcats in 12 games since 1901). *Tied:* Army 6–6. *Stars:* HBs Bill Shakespeare and Andy Pilney, E Wayne Millner.

1936 (6–2–1) *Won:* Carnegie Tech 21–7, Washington (Mo.) 14–6, Wisconsin 27–0, Ohio St. 7–2, Army 20–6, Northwestern 26–6. *Lost:* Pittsburgh

9–7, Navy 3–0.   *Tied:* USC 13–13.   *Stars:* HB Bob Wilke (6 TDs), G John Lautar.

1937 (6–2–1)   *Won:* Drake 21–0, Navy 9–7, Minnesota 7–6 (1st meeting since 1927), Army 7–0, Northwestern 7–0, USC 13–6.   *Lost:* Carnegie Tech 9–7, unbeaten national cochamp Pittsburgh 21–6.   *Tied:* Illinois 0–0 (1st meeting since 1898). *Stars:* E Chuck Sweeney, T Ed Beinor.

1938 (8–1)   *Won:* Kansas 52–0, Georgia Tech 14–6 (1st meeting since 1929), Illinois 14–6, Carnegie Tech 7–0, Army 19–7, Navy 15–0, Minnesota 19–0, Northwestern 9–7.   *Lost:* USC 13–0 in finale. *Stars:* Beinor, E Earl Brown, G Jim McGoldrick.

1939 (7–2)   *Won:* Purdue 3–0 (1st meeting since 1934), Georgia Tech 17–14, SMU 20–19 (1st meeting since 1930), Navy 14–7, Carnegie Tech 7–6, Army 14–0, Northwestern 7–0.   *Lost:* Iowa 7–6 (1st meeting since 1921), USC 20–12.   *Stars:* FB Milt Piepul (6 TDs), E Bud Kerr.

1940 (7–2)   *Won:* Pacific 25–7, Georgia Tech 26–20, Carnegie Tech 61–0, Illinois 26–0, Army 7–0, Navy 13–7, USC 10–6.   *Lost:* Iowa 7–0, Northwestern 20–0 in consecutive late games.   *Stars:* Piepul, HB Steve Juzwik (7 TDs).   *Noteworthy:* last year under Elmer Layden.

1941 (8–0–1)   *Won:* Arizona 38–7, Indiana 19–6 (1st meeting since 1933), Georgia Tech 20–0, Carnegie Tech 16–0, Illinois 49–14, Navy 20–13, Northwestern 7–6, USC 20–18.   *Tied:* Army 0–0.   *Stars:* soph QB Angelo Bertelli (1,027 yds and 8 TDs pass), Juzwik (18 pass rec for 307 yds), FB Fred Evans (11 TDs), E Bob Dove, G Bernie Crimmins. *Noteworthy:* had 1st unbeaten season since 1930 in 1st year under Frank Leahy.

1942 (7–2–2)   *Won:* Stanford 27–0 (1st meeting since 1925 Rose Bowl), Iowa Pre-Flight 28–0, Illinois 21–14, Navy 9–0, Army 13–0, Northwestern 27–20, USC 13–0.   *Lost:* Georgia Tech 13–6 (1st to Yellow Jackets in 6 games since 1928), Michigan 32–20 (1st meeting since 1909).   *Tied:* Wisconsin 7–7 (1st meeting since 1936), Great Lakes 13–13. *Stars:* Bertelli (8 int, 1,039 yds and 10 TDs pass), Bob Livingstone (17 pass rec for 272 yds), Dove, FB Corwin Clatt (698 yds and 5 TDs rush), HB Creighton Miller (5 TDs), G Harry Wright, T Bob Neff.

1943 (9–1)   *Won:* Pittsburgh 41–0 (1st meeting since 1937), Georgia Tech 55–13, Michigan 35–12, Wisconsin 50–0, Illinois 47–0, Navy 33–6, Army 26–0, Northwestern 25–6, Iowa Pre-Flight 14–13. *Lost:* Great Lakes 19–14 in finale.   *Stars:* Heisman Trophy–winner Bertelli (10 TDs pass, 45 pts), Miller

(6 int, 13 TDs, nation's leader with 911 yds rush), E John Yonakor (15 pass rec for 323 yds), soph QB John Lujack (716 yds and 8 TDs total off), T Jim White, G Pat Filley, C Herb Coleman. *Noteworthy:* won 4th national title and led nation in total off and rush.

1944 (8–2)   *Won:* Pittsburgh 58–0, Tulane 26–0, Dartmouth 64–0, Wisconsin 28–13, Illinois 13–7, Northwestern 21–0, Georgia Tech 21–0, Great Lakes 28–7.   *Lost:* Navy 32–13 (1st to Midshipmen since 1936), unbeaten national champ Army 59–0 (1st to Cadets since 1931) in successive mid-season games. *Stars:* HB Bob Kelly (681 yds and 8 TDs rush, 18 pass rec for 283 yds and 5 TDs), G Pat Killey.

1945 (7–2–1)   *Won:* Illinois 7–0, Georgia Tech 40–7, Dartmouth 34–0, Pittsburgh 39–9, Iowa 56–0 (1st meeting since 1940, 1st win in 4-game series dating to 1921), Northwestern 34–7, Tulane 32–6. *Lost:* unbeaten national champ Army 48–0, Great Lakes 39–7.   *Tied:* Navy 6–6.   *Stars:* QB Frank Dancewicz, HB Elmer Angsman (616 yds rush, 7 TDs), G John Mastrangelo.

1946 (8–0–1)   *Won:* Illinois 26–6, Pittsburgh 33–0, Purdue 49–6 (1st meeting since 1939), Iowa 41–6, Navy 28–0, Northwestern 27–0, Tulane 41–0, USC 26–6.   *Tied:* unbeaten Army 0–0 (in New York). *Stars:* Lujack (back from military service; 886 yds total off), soph HB Terry Brennan (6 TDs), FB Jim Mello (6 TDs), frosh E Leon Hart, Ts George "Moose" Connor (initial Outland Trophy winner) and Ziggy Czarobski, C George Strohmeyer, Mastrangelo, soph G Bill Fischer.   *Noteworthy:* led nation in total defense and scoring defense (2.7-pt avg) while winning 5th national title.

1947 (9–0)   *Won:* Pittsburgh 40–6, Purdue 22–7, Nebraska 31–0 (1st meeting since 1925), Iowa 21–0, Navy 27–0, Army 27–7 (1st meeting at South Bend), Northwestern 26–19, Tulane 59–6, USC 38–7. *Stars:* Lujack (930 yds and 10 TDs total off), Brennan (11 TDs), soph FB Emil "Red" Sitko (5 TDs), Hart, Connor, Czarobski, Fischer.   *Noteworthy:* got share of 6th (and 2nd straight) national title.

1948 (9–0–1)   *Won:* Purdue 28–27, Pittsburgh 40–0, Michigan St. 26–7 (1st meeting since 1921), Nebraska 44–13, Iowa 27–12, Navy 41–7, Indiana 42–6 (1st meeting since 1941), Northwestern 12–7, Washington 46–0.   *Tied:* USC 14–14 in finale. *Stars:* Outland Trophy–winner Fischer, G Marty Wendell, Hart (16 pass rec for 231 yds), QB Frank Tripucka (11 TDs pass), Sitko (742 yds and 9 TDs rush), HB Bill Gay (6 int).

1949 (10–0) *Won:* Indiana 49–6, Washington 27–7, Purdue 35–12, Tulane 46–7, Navy 40–0, Michigan St. 34–21, North Carolina 42–6 (1st meeting), Iowa 28–7, USC 32–0, SMU 27–20 (1st meeting since 1939). *Stars:* QB Bob Williams (1,437 yds and 15 TDs pass), Heisman Trophy– and Maxwell Award– winner Hart (19 pass rec for 257 yds and 5 TDs), Sitko (712 yds and 9 TDs rush), HB Billy Barrett (9 TDs), T Jim Martin. *Noteworthy:* Leahy's 5th unbeaten team (4th straight) and 4th national champion (Notre Dame's 7th) led nation in total off.

1951 (7–2–1) *Won:* Indiana 48–6, Detroit 40–6, Pittsburgh 33–0, Purdue 30–9, Navy 19–0, North Carolina 12–7, USC 19–12. *Lost:* SMU 27–20, unbeaten Michigan St. 35–0. *Tied:* Iowa 20–20. *Stars:* E Jim Mutscheller (20 pass rec for 305 yds), soph FB Neil Worden (676 yds and 8 TDs rush), soph HB/DB John Lattner (6 TDs, 5 int), T Bob Toneff.

1952 (7–2–1) *Won:* Texas 14–3 (1st meeting since 1934), Purdue 26–14, North Carolina 34–14, Navy 17–6, Oklahoma 27–21 (1st meeting), Iowa 27–0, USC 9–0. *Lost:* Pittsburgh 22–19 (1st to Panthers in 9 games since 1937), unbeaten national champ Michigan St. 21–3. *Tied:* Pennsylvania 7–7. *Stars:* Maxwell Award–winner Lattner (732 yds rush, 17 pass rec for 220 yds, 5 TDs, 4 int), Worden (504 yds and 10 TDs rush), soph HB Joe Heap (29 pass rec for 437 yds), DE Bob O'Neill.

1953 (9–0–1) *Won:* Oklahoma 28–21, Purdue 37–7, Pittsburgh 23–14, Georgia Tech 27–14 (1st meeting since 1945), Navy 38–7, Pennsylvania 28–20, North Carolina 34–14, USC 48–14, SMU 40–14. *Tied:* Iowa 14–14. *Stars:* Heisman Trophy– and Maxwell Award–winner Lattner (651 yds rush, 14 pass rec for 204 yds, 9 TDs, 4 int), QB/DB Ralph Guglielmi (792 yds and 8 TDs pass, 6 TDs rush, 5 int), Heap (22 pass rec for 335 yds and 5 TDs), Worden (859 yds and 11 TDs rush), E Don Penza, T Art Hunter. *Noteworthy:* Leahy's last team (6th unbeaten one) got share of 8th national title (Leahy's 5th).

1954 (9–1) *Won:* Texas 21–0, Pittsburgh 33–0, Michigan St. 20–19, Navy 6–0, Pennsylvania 42–7, North Carolina 42–13, Iowa 34–18, USC 23–17, SMU 26–14. *Lost:* Purdue 27–14. *Stars:* Guglielmi (1,162 yds pass, 5 TDs rush, 5 int), Heap (594 yds and 8 TDs rush, 18 pass rec for 369 yds), FB Don Schaefer (766 yds rush), E Dan Shannon, T Frank Varrichione. *Noteworthy:* 1st year under Terry Brennan.

1955 (8–2) *Won:* SMU 17–0, Indiana 19–0, Miami (Fla.) 14–0 (1st meeting), Purdue 22–7, Navy 21–7, Pennsylvania 46–14, North Carolina 27–7, Iowa 17–14. *Lost:* Michigan St. 21–7, USC 42–20. *Stars:* Schaefer (638 yds rush), HB/DB Paul Hornung (743 yds and 9 TDs pass, 472 yds and 6 TDs rush, 5 int), HB Jim Morse (17 pass rec for 424 yds), G Pat Bisceglia.

1957 (7–3) *Won:* Purdue 12–0, Indiana 26–0, Army 23–21 (1st meeting since 1947), Pittsburgh 13–7, Oklahoma 7–0 (ending Sooners' 48-game unbeaten string), USC 40–12, SMU 54–21. *Lost:* Navy 20–6, Michigan St. 34–6, Iowa 21–13. *Stars:* FB Nick Pietrosante, G Al Ecuyer. *Noteworthy:* one of nation's most-improved teams.

1964 (9–1) *Won:* Wisconsin 31–7, Purdue 34–15, Air Force 34–7 (1st meeting), UCLA 24–0, Stanford 28–6, Navy 40–0, Pittsburgh 17–15, Michigan St. 34–7 (1st over Spartans since 1954), Iowa 28–0. *Lost:* USC 20–17 in finale. *Stars:* Heisman Trophy–winning QB John Huarte (2,062 yds and 16 TDs pass), E Jack Snow (60 pass rec for 1,114 yds and 9 TDs), HBs Bill Wolski (657 yds rush, 11 TDs) and soph Nick Eddy (16 pass rec for 352 yds, 7 TDs), soph DT Kevin Hardy, LB Jim Carroll, DB Tony Carey (nation's leader with 8 int). *Noteworthy:* nation's most-improved team got share of 9th national championship in 1st year under Ara Parseghian.

1965 (7–2–1) *Won:* California 48–6, Northwestern 38–7 (1st over Wildcats in 5 games since 1948), Army 17–0 (1st meeting since 1958), USC 28–7, Navy 29–3, Pittsburgh 69–13, North Carolina 17–0. *Lost:* Purdue 25–21, unbeaten national cochamp Michigan St. 12–3. *Tied:* Miami (Fla.) 0–0 (1st meeting since 1960) in finale. *Stars:* Eddy (582 yds rush, 13 pass rec for 233 yds, 6 TDs), Wolski (8 TDs), Gs Dick Arrington and Tom Regner, LB Jim Lynch, DB Nick Rassas (6 int, nation's punt return leader with 19.1-yd avg).

1966 (9–0–1) *Won:* Purdue 26–14, Northwestern 35–7, Army 35–0, North Carolina 32–0, Oklahoma 38–0, Navy 31–7, Pittsburgh 40–0, Duke 64–0, USC 51–0. *Tied:* unbeaten national cochamp Michigan St. 10–10. *Stars:* soph QB Terry Hanratty (1,247 yds pass, 5 TDs rush), soph E Jim Seymour (48 pass rec for 862 yds and 8 TDs), Eddy (553 yds rush, 10 TDs), FB Larry Conjar, Regner, T Paul Seiler, C George Goeddeke, Maxwell Award–winner Lynch, Hardy, DT Pete Duranko, DE Alan Page, DB Tom Schoen (7 int). *Noteworthy:* got share of 10th national title and led nation in scoring (36.2-pt avg).

1967 (8–2) *Won:* California 41–8, Iowa 56–6, Illinois 47–7 (1st meeting since 1946), Michigan St. 24–12, Navy 43–14, Pittsburgh 38–0, Georgia Tech 36–3 (1st meeting since 1959), Miami (Fla.) 24–22. *Lost:* Purdue 28–21, national champ USC 24–7. *Stars:* Hanratty (1,439 yds pass, 7 TDs rush), Seymour (37 pass rec for 515 yds), FB Jeff Zimmerman (591 yds rush), G Dick Swatland, DE Hardy, LBs Mike McGill and John Pergine, Schoen, DB Jim Smithberger.

1968 (7–2–1) *Won:* Oklahoma 45–21, Iowa 51–28, Northwestern 27–7, Illinois 58–8 (10th straight over Illini), Navy 45–14, Pittsburgh 56–7, Georgia Tech 34–6. *Lost:* Purdue 37–22, Mıchigan St. 21–17. *Tied:* unbeaten USC 21–21. *Stars:* Hanratty (1,466 yds and 10 TDs pass, 279 yds and 4 TDs rush), Seymour (53 pass rec for 736 yds), HB Bob Gladieux (713 yds rush, 14 TDs), T George Kunz, LB Bob Olson, DB Chuck Zloch (5 int).

1969 (8–2–1) *Won:* Northwestern 35–10, Michigan St. 42–28, Army 45–0, Tulane 37–0, Navy 47–0, Pittsburgh 49–7, Georgia Tech 38–20, Air Force 13–6 (1st meeting since 1964). *Lost:* Purdue 28–14. *Tied:* USC 14–14. *Stars:* QB Joe Theismann (1,531 yds and 13 TDs pass, 378 yds and 6 TDs rush), soph SE Tom Gatewood (77 pass rec for 1,123 yds and 7 TDs), HB Denny Allen (612 yds rush), OT Jim Reilly, OG Larry DiNardo, C Mike Oriard, DT Mike McCoy, Olsen. *Noteworthy:* made 1st postseason appearance in 45 years, losing to unbeaten national champ Texas 21–17 (1st meeting since 1954) in Cotton Bowl; Theismann passed for 231 yds and 2 TDs (24 yds to Jim Yoder and 54 yds to Gatewood, who caught 6 for 112 yds).

1970 (10–1) *Won:* Northwestern 35–14, Purdue 48–0, Michigan St. 29–0, Army 51–10, Missouri 24–7, Navy 56–7, Pittsburgh 46–14, Georgia Tech 10–7, Louisiana St. (LSU) 3–0. *Lost:* USC 38–28 in finale. *Stars:* Theismann (2,429 yds and 16 TDs pass, 384 yds and 4 TDs rush), Gatewood (33 pass rec for 417 yds), HB Ed Gulyas (534 yds rush), DiNardo, LB Jim Wright, DBs Clarence Ellis (7 int) and Ralph Stepaniak (6 int). *Noteworthy:* upset unbeaten national cochamp Texas 24–11 in Cotton Bowl as Irish recovered 5 Longhorn fumbles; Theismann passed for 176 yds and a TD and ran for 2.

1971 (8–2) *Won:* Northwestern 50–7, Purdue 8–7, Michigan St. 14–2, Miami (Fla.) 17–0, North Carolina 16–0 (1st meeting since 1966), Navy 21–0, Pittsburgh 56–7, Tulane 21–7. *Lost:* USC 28–14, LSU 28–8. *Stars:* Gatewood (47 pass rec for 743 yds and 8 TDs), DE Walt Patulski (Lombardi Award winner), DT Mike Kadish, Ellis.

1972 (8–3) *Won:* Northwestern 37–0, Purdue 35–14, Michigan St. 16–0, Pittsburgh 42–16, Texas Christian 21–0, Navy 42–23, Air Force 21–7, Miami (Fla.) 20–17. *Lost:* Missouri 30–26, unbeaten national champ USC 45–23. *Stars:* DT Greg Marx, LB Jim O'Malley, DB Mike Townsend (nation's leader with 10 int), soph QB Tom Clements (1,163 yds pass), SE Willie Townsend (25 pass rec for 369 yds), HB Eric Penick (726 yds rush), FB Andy Huff (10 TDs), OT John Dampeer. *Noteworthy:* lost to Nebraska 40–6 (1st meeting since 1948) in Orange Bowl; Clements passed for 103 yds and the Irish TD.

1973 (11–0) *Won:* Northwestern 44–0, Purdue 20–7, Michigan St. 14–10, Rice 28–0, Army 62–3, USC 23–14 (1st over Trojans since 1966), Navy 44–7 (10th straight over Midshipmen), Pittsburgh 31–10 (10th straight over Panthers), Air Force 48–15, Miami (Fla.) 44–0. *Stars:* frosh DB Luther Bradley (6 int), Mike Townsend, LB Greg Collins, Clements (1,242 yds total off), TE Dave Casper (19 pass rec for 317 yds), SE Pete Demmerle (26 pass rec for 404 yds and 5 TDs), FB Wayne Bullock (752 yds and 10 TDs rush), K Bob Thomas (70 pts), P Brian Doherty (42.7-yd avg). *Noteworthy:* earned share of 11th national title, edging unbeaten national cochamp Alabama 24–23 in Sugar Bowl; Clements passed for 169 yds and ran for 74 yds, Bullock ran for 79 yds and a TD, soph HB Al Hunter scored on 93-yd kickoff return, and Thomas kicked 19-yd FG with 4:26 remaining.

1974 (10–2) *Won:* Georgia Tech 31–7, Northwestern 49–3, Michigan St. 19–14, Rice 10–3, Army 48–0, Miami (Fla.) 38–7, Navy 14–6, Pittsburgh 14–10, Air Force 38–0. *Lost:* Purdue 31–20, national cochamp USC 55–24. *Stars:* Clements (1,549 yds pass, 1,918 total off), Demmerle (43 pass rec for 667 yds and 6 TDs), Bullock (855 yds and 12 TDs rush), OG Gerry DiNardo, OT Steve Sylvester, DTs Mike Fanning and Steve Niehaus, Collins. *Noteworthy:* Parseghian's last team led nation in total defense and rush defense. Beat undefeated Alabama 13–11 in Orange Bowl; Bullock ran for 83 yds and a TD, and HB Mark McLane scored on 9-yd run.

1975 (8–3) *Won:* Boston College 17–3 (1st meeting), Purdue 17–0, Northwestern 31–7 (10th straight over Wildcats), North Carolina 21–14, Air Force 31–30, Navy 31–10, Georgia Tech 24–3, Miami (Fla.) 32–9. *Lost:* Michigan St. 10–3 (1st to Spartans since 1968), USC 24–17, Pittsburgh 34–20 (1st to Panthers since 1963). *Stars:* frosh FB Jerome Heavens (756 yds and 5 TDs rush), Hunter (558 yds and 8 TDs rush), soph TE Ken MacAfee (26 pass rec for 333 yds and 5 TDs), soph K Dave Reeve (11 FGs), Niehaus, Bradley, frosh P Joe Restic (43.5-yd avg). *Noteworthy:* 1st year under Dan Devine.

1976 (9–3) *Won:* Purdue 23–0, Northwestern 48–0, Michigan St. 24–6, Oregon 41–0, South Carolina 13–6, Navy 27–21, Alabama 21–18, Miami (Fla.) 40–27. *Lost:* unbeaten national champ Pittsburgh 31–10, Georgia Tech 23–14 (1st to Yellow Jackets in 7 games since 1959), USC 17–13. *Stars:* QB Rick Slager (1,281 yds and 11 TDs pass), MacAfee (34 pass rec for 482 yds), Hunter (1,058 yds rush, 13 TDs), DEs Ross Browner (Outland Trophy winner) and Willie Fry, soph LB Steve Heimkreiter, Bradley, Restic (41.7-yd punting avg). *Noteworthy:* beat Penn St. 20–9 (1st meeting since 1928) in Gator Bowl; Hunter ran for 102 yds and 2 TDs, Slager passed for 141 yds, and Reeve kicked 2 FGs.

1977 (11–1) *Won:* Pittsburgh 19–9, Purdue 31–24, Michigan St. 16–6, Army 24–0, USC 49–19, Navy 43–10, Georgia Tech 69–14, Clemson 21–17, Air Force 49–0, Miami (Fla.) 48–10. *Lost:* Mississippi 20–13 in 2nd game. *Stars:* Maxwell and Lombardi award–winner Browner, Fry, MG Bob Golic, Bradley, DB/P Restic (6 int), DB Ted Burgmeier, QB Joe Montana (1,604 yds and 11 TDs pass, 6 TDs rush), McAfee (54 pass rec for 797 yds and 6 TDs), Heavens (994 yds and 6 TDs rush), soph HB Vagas Ferguson (7 TDs), G Ernie Hughes, Reeve (13 FGs, 75 pts). *Noteworthy:* earned 12th national title, beating undefeated Texas 38–10 in Cotton Bowl; Ferguson ran for 100 yds and 2 TDs and caught a TD pass from Montana (111 yds pass), Heavens ran for 101 yds, Terry Eurick ran for 2 TDs, and Reeve had 47-yd FG.

1978 (9–3) *Won:* Purdue 10–6, Michigan St. 29–25, Pittsburgh 26–17, Air Force 38–15, Miami (Fla.) 20–0, Navy 27–7 (15th straight over Midshipmen), Tennessee 31–14, Georgia Tech 38–21. *Lost:* Missouri 3–0, Michigan 28–14 (1st meeting since 1943),

national cochamp USC 27–25. *Stars:* Ferguson (1,192 yds rush, 8 TDs), Montana (2,010 yds and 10 TDs pass, 104 yds and 6 TDs rush), SE Kris Haines (32 pass rec for 699 yds and 5 TDs), frosh TE Dean Masztak (13 pass rec for 236 yds), C Dave Huffman, LBs Golic and Heimkreiter. *Noteworthy:* beat Houston 35–34 in Cotton Bowl on 8-yd pass from Montana (163 yds and 2 TDs pass) to Haynes on last play of game and ex pt by Joe Unis; Montana ran for 2 TDs but Irish had to rally from 34–12 deficit with 23 pts in last quarter.

1980 (9–2–1) *Won:* Purdue 31–10, Michigan 29–27, Michigan St. 26–21, Miami (Fla.) 32–14, Army 30–3, Arizona 20–3, Navy 33–0, Alabama 7–0, Air Force 24–10 (10th in as many meetings with Falcons). *Lost:* USC 20–3 in finale. *Tied:* Georgia Tech 3–3. *Stars:* LB Bob Crable, DE Scott Zettek, HBs Jim Stone (908 yds and 7 TDs rush) and soph Phil Carter (822 yds and 6 TDs rush), soph WR Troy Hunter (23 pass rec for 303 yds),

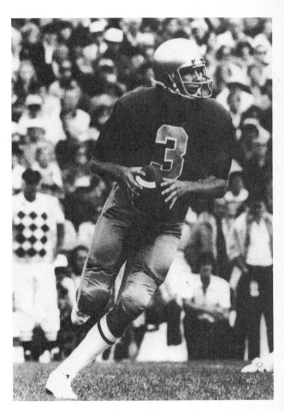

QB Joe Montana, 1975, 1977–78

Pete Holohan (21 pass rec for 296 yds), C John Scully, K Harry Oliver (18 FGs, 73 pts), soph QB/P Blair Kiel (40.1-yd punting avg). *Noteworthy:* Devine's last team. Lost to unbeaten national champ Georgia 17–10 in Sugar Bowl (breaking 5-bowl win streak); Carter ran for 109 yds and the Irish TD, and Kiel passed for 138 yds.

1987 (8–4) *Won:* Michigan 26–7, Michigan St. 31–8, Purdue 44–20, Air Force 35–14, USC 26–15, Navy 56–13, Boston College 32–25, Alabama 37–6. *Lost:* Pittsburgh 30–22, Penn St. 21–20, unbeaten national champ Miami (Fla.) 24–0. *Stars:* SE Tim Brown (Heisman Trophy winner, 7 TDs, 3 TDs on punt returns, 39 pass rec for 846 yds, 1,847 all-purpose yds), soph QB Tony Rice (7 TDs), TB Mark Green (861 yds and 6 TDs rush), soph FB Anthony Johnson (11 TDs), C Chuck Lanza, K Ted Gradel (14 FGs, 75 pts), LBs Cedric Figaro and soph Ned Bolcar, P Vince Phelan (40.9-yd avg). *Noteworthy:* lost to Texas A&M 35–10 in Cotton Bowl; QB Terry Andrysiak passed for 203 yds and a TD (to Brown, who caught 6 for 105 yds).

1988 (12–0) *Won:* Michigan 19–17, Michigan St. 20–3, Purdue 52–7, Stanford 42–14 (1st meeting since 1964), Pittsburgh 30–20, Miami (Fla.) 31–30 (1st over Hurricanes in 5 games since 1982), Air Force 41–13, Navy 22–7 (25th straight over Midshipmen), Rice 54–11, Penn St. 21–3, USC 27–10. *Stars:* Rice (1,176 yds pass, 700 yds and 9 TDs rush), soph FL Ricky Watters (15 pass rec for 286 yds, 2 TDs on punt returns), frosh SE Raghib Ismail (12 pass rec for 331 yds, nation's kickoff return leader with 36.1-yd avg and 2 TDs), soph TB Tony Brooks (667 yds rush), Green (646 yds and 7 TDs rush), Johnson (5 TDs rush), OT Andy Heck, K Reggie Ho, DE Frank Stams, DT Chris Zorich, LBs Mike Stonebreaker and Wes Pritchett. *Noteworthy:* 1st unbeaten season since 1973. Won 13th national championship, beating undefeated West Virginia 34–21 in Fiesta Bowl; Rice passed for 213 yds and 2 TDs (to Ismail and Frank Jacobs) and ran for 75 yds, and Johnson and frosh FB Rodney Culver scored on short runs.

1989 (12–1) *Won:* Virginia 36–13, Michigan 24–19, Michigan St. 21–13, Purdue 40–7, Stanford 27–17, Air Force 41–27, USC 28–24, Pittsburgh 45–7, Navy 41–0, SMU 59–6, Penn St. 34–23. *Lost:* national champ Miami (Fla.) 27–10 in finale. *Stars:* Rice (1,122 yds pass, 884 yds and 7 TDs rush), Ismail (27 pass rec for 535 yds, 1,628 all-purpose yds, 5 TDs), RB Watters (791 yds rush,

1,188 all-purpose yds, 11 TDs), Johnson (515 yds and 11 TDs rush, 13 TDs total), Culver (5 TDs rush), soph TE Derek Brown (13 pass rec for 204 yds), C Mike Heldt, OG Tim Grunhard, OT Dean Brown, frosh K/P Craig Hentrich (68 pts, 44.6-yd punting avg), Zorich, DT Jeff Alm, DE Scott Kowalkowski, Bolcar, LB Donn Grimm, DBs Todd Lyght (8 int) and Pat Terrell (5 int). *Noteworthy:* beat undefeated Colorado 21–6 in Orange Bowl; Johnson scored 2 TDs and Ismail ran for 108 yds and a TD (35-yd run).

1990 (9–3) *Won:* Michigan 28–24, Michigan St. 20–19, Purdue 37–11, Air Force 57–27, Miami (Fla.) 29–20, Pittsburgh 31–22, Navy 52–31, Tennessee 34–29, USC 10–6. *Lost:* Stanford 36–31, Penn St. 24–21. *Stars:* Ismail (32 pass rec for 699 yds, 537 yds rush, 1,723 all-purpose yds, 6 TDs), soph QB Rick Mirer (1,824 yds pass, 6 TDs rush), SE Tony Smith (15 pass rec for 229 yds), Derek Brown (15 pass rec for 220 yds), Watters (579 yds and 8 TDs rush), Culver (710 yds rush, 7 TDs), Brooks (6 TDs rush), Heldt, Lombardi Award–winner Zorich, Stonebreaker, Lyght, Hentrich (16 FGs, 89 pts, 44.9-yd punting avg). *Noteworthy:* lost to national cochamp Colorado 10–9 in Orange Bowl; Mirer passed for 141 yds and Irish scored TD on 2-yd run by Watters but had ex pt blocked.

1991 (10–3) *Won:* Indiana 49–27 (1st meeting since 1958), Michigan St. 49–10, Purdue 45–20, Stanford 42–26, Pittsburgh 42–7, Air Force 28–15, USC 24–20, Navy 38–0, Hawaii 48–42. *Lost:* Michigan 24–14 (1st to Wolverines since 1986), Tennessee 35–34, Penn St. 35–13. *Stars:* Mirer (2,117 yds and 18 TDs pass, 306 yds and 9 TDs rush), Smith (42 pass rec for 789 yds), Brown (22 pass rec for 325 yds), Brooks (894 yds rush, 6 TDs), Culver (550 yds rush), soph FL Lake Dawson (24 pass rec for 433 yds), soph FB Jerome Bettis (20 TDs, 1,162 all-purpose yds, 972 yds and 16 TDs rush), OG Mirko Jurkovic, Hentrich (63 pts, 42.9-yd punting avg), soph DT Bryant Young, LBs Demetrius DuBose and Devon McDonald, soph DB Tom Carter. *Noteworthy:* beat Florida 39–28 in Sugar Bowl; Bettis ran for 150 yds and 3 TDs (including runs of 49 and 39 yds), Mirer passed for 154 yds, 2 TDs (including 40 yds to Dawson), and 2-pt conversion, and Smith caught 7 passes for 75 yds.

1992 (10–1–1) *Won:* Northwestern 42–7 (1st meeting since 1976), Michigan St. 52–31, Purdue 48–0, Pittsburgh 52–21, Brigham Young (BYU) 42–16,

Navy 38–7, Boston College 54–7, Penn St. 17–16, USC 31–23 (10th straight over Trojans). *Lost:* Stanford 33–16. *Tied:* unbeaten Michigan 17–17. *Stars:* Mirer (1,876 yds and 15 TDs pass), Dawson (25 pass rec for 462 yds), FL Ray Griggs (17 pass rec for 312 yds), TE Irv Smith (20 pass rec for 262 yds), Brooks (14 TDs, 1,343 yds and 13 TDs rush), Bettis (12 TDs, 825 yds and 10 TDs rush), Lee Becton (5 TDs), OG Aaron Taylor, Hentrich (10 FGs, 74 pts, 43.8-yd punting avg), DuBose, Carter (5 int), DB Jeff Burris (5 int). *Noteworthy:* beat undefeated Texas A&M 28–3 in Cotton Bowl as Mirer passed for 119 yds and 2 TDs (40 yds to Dawson and 26 yds to Bettis, who also ran for 75 yds and 2 TDs), and Brooks ran for 115 yds.

Bowl Summary

Aloha 0–1; Cotton 4–2; Fiesta 1–0; Gator 1–0; Liberty 1–0; Orange 2–2; Rose 1–0; Sugar 2–1.

Bowl Record (12–6)

Regular Season	Bowl	Score	Opponent	Record
1924 (9–0)	Rose	27–10	Stanford	(7–0–1)
1969 (8–1–1)	Cotton	17–21	Texas	(10–0)
1970 (9–1)	Cotton	24–11	Texas	(10–0)
1972 (8–2)	Orange	6–40	Nebraska	(8–2–1)
1973 (10–0)	Sugar	24–23	Alabama	(11–0)
1974 (9–2)	Orange	13–11	Alabama	(11–0)
1976 (8–3)	Gator	20–9	Penn St.	(7–4)
1977 (10–1)	Cotton	38–10	Texas	(11–0)
1978 (8–3)	Cotton	35–34	Houston	(9–2)
1980 (9–1–1)	Sugar	10–17	Georgia	(11–0)
1983 (6–5)	Liberty	19–18	Boston College	(9–2)
1984 (7–4)	Aloha	20–27	SMU	(9–2)
1987 (8–3)	Cotton	10–35	Texas A&M	(9–2)
1988 (11–0)	Fiesta	34–21	West Virginia	(11–0)
1989 (11–1)	Orange	21–6	Colorado	(11–0)
1990 (9–2)	Orange	9–10	Colorado	(10–1–1)
1991 (9–3)	Sugar	39–28	Florida	(10–1)
1992 (9–1–1)	Cotton	28–3	Texas A&M	(12–0)

Conference Titles

None.

TOP 20 AP AND UPI
(USA TODAY/CNN SINCE 1991) RANKING

1936	8	1948	2	1965	9–8	1976	12–12
1937	9	1949	1	1966	1–1	1977	1–1
1938	5	1951	U–13	1967	5–4	1978	7–6
1939	13	1952	3–3	1968	5–8	1980	9–10
1941	3	1953	2–2	1969	5–9	1987	17–U
1942	6	1954	4–4	1970	2–5	1988	1–1
1943	1	1955	8–9	1971	13–15	1989	2–3
1944	9	1957	10–9	1972	14–12	1990	6–6
1945	9	1958	17–14	1973	1–4	1991	13–12
1946	1	1959	17–U	1974	6–4	1992	4–4
1947	1	1964	3–3	1975	U–17		

MAJOR RIVALS

Notre Dame has played at least 10 games with Air Force 17–4, Army 34–8–4, Carnegie Tech 15–4, Georgia Tech 25–4–1, Illinois 11–0–1, Indiana 23–5–1, Iowa 13–8–3, Miami (Fla.) 15–7–1, Michigan 9–14–1, Michigan St. 39–18–1, Navy 56–9–1, Nebraska 7–6–1, North Carolina 15–1, Northwestern 35–7–2, Penn St. 8–8–1, Pittsburgh 37–16–1, Purdue 41–21–2, Southern California 37–23–4, Southern Methodist 10–3, Wabash 10–1, Wisconsin 8–6–2.

COACHES

Dean of Notre Dame coaches is the legendary Knute Rockne with record of 105–12–5 for 1918–30, including 5 unbeaten teams, a Rose Bowl champion, and 3 national titles. Other top records for at least 3 years were by Frank E. Hering, 12–6–1 for 1896–98; Jesse C. Harper, 34–5–1 for 1913–17 with 1 unbeaten team; Hunk Anderson, 16–9–2 for 1931–33; Elmer Layden, 47–13–3 for 1934–40; Frank Leahy (1941 national Coach of Year), 87–11–9 for 1941–43 and 1946–53 with 6 unbeaten teams and 5 national champions; Terry Brennan, 32–18 for 1954–58; Ara Parseghian (1964 national Coach of Year), 95–17–4 for 1964–74 with 5 bowl teams, 2 unbeaten teams, and 3 national champions; Dan Devine, 53–16–1 for 1975–80 with 4 bowl teams and 1 national champion; Gerry Faust, 30–26–1 for 1981–85 with 2 bowl teams; and Lou Holtz, 66–18–1 for 1986–92 with 6 bowl teams and 1 unbeaten national champion.

MISCELLANEA

First game was loss to Michigan 8–0 in 1887 . . . 1st win was over Harvard School of Chicago 20–0 in 1888 . . . 1st win over college foe was over Northwestern 9–0 in 1889 . . . highest score was over American Medical 142–0 in 33-minute game in 1905 . . . highest scores since W.W. II were over Pittsburgh 69–13 in 1965 and Georgia Tech 69–14 in 1977 . . . biggest margin since W.W. II was over Duke 64–0 in 1966 . . . worst defeat was by Army 59–0 in 1944 . . . worst since W.W. II was by Miami (Fla.) 58–7 in 1985 . . . longest unbeaten string of 39 in 1946–50 ended by Purdue 28–14 . . . 27-game

unbeaten string in 1910–14 ended by Yale 28–0 . . . 26-game unbeaten string in 1929–31 ended by USC 16–14 . . . longest win streak of 23 in 1988–89 ended by Miami (Fla.) 27–10 . . . 20-game win streak in 1919–21 ended by Iowa 10–7 . . . longest losing string of 8 in 1960 broken with win over USC 17–0 . . . consensus All-Americans were Gus Dorais, B, 1913; Frank Rydzewski, C, 1917; George Gipp, B, 1920; Eddie Anderson, E, 1921; Harry Stuhldreher, B, Jimmy Crowley, B, and Elmer Layden, B, 1924; Bud Boeringer, C, 1926; John Smith, G, 1927; Jack Cannon, G, 1929; Frank Carideo, B, 1929–30; Marchy Schwartz, B, 1930–31; Tommy Yarr, C, 1931; Joe Kurth, T, 1932; Jack Robinson, C, 1934; Wayne Millner, E, 1935; Chuck Sweeney, E, 1937; Ed Beinor, T, 1938; Bob Dove, E, 1941–42; John Yonakor, E, Jim White, T, Pat Filley, G, Angelo Bertelli, B, and Creighton Miller, B, 1943; George Connor, T, and John Lujack, B, 1946–47; Bill Fischer, G, 1947–48; Leon Hart, E, and Emil Sitko, B, 1948–49; Bob Williams, B, 1949; Jerry Groom, C, 1950; Johnny Lattner, B, 1952–53; Art Hunter, T, 1953; Ralph Guglielmi, B, 1954; Paul Hornung, B, 1955; Al Ecuyer, G, 1957; Monty Stickles, E, 1959; Jack Snow, E, and John Huarte, B, 1964; Dick Arrington, G, and Nick Rassas, B, 1965; Tom Regner, G, Nick Eddy, B, Alan Page, DE, and Jim Lynch, LB, 1966; Tom Schoen, DB, 1967; George Kunz, T, and Terry Hanratty, QB, 1968; Mike McCoy, DT, 1969; Tom Gatewood, E, and Larry DiNardo, G, 1970; Walt Patulski, DE, and Clarence Ellis, DB, 1971; Greg Marx, DT, 1972; Dave Casper, TE, and Mike Townsend, DB, 1973; Pete Demmerle, WR, and Gerry DiNardo, G, 1974; Steve Niehaus, DT, 1975; Ken MacAfee, TE, and Ross Browner, DE, 1976–77; Luther Bradley, DB, 1977; Dave Huffman, C, and Bob Golic, LB, 1978; Vagas Ferguson, RB, 1979; John Scully, C, 1980; Bob Crable, LB, 1980–81; Tim Brown, WR, 1987; Frank Stams, DL, 1988; Mike Stonebreaker, LB, 1988, 1990; Todd Lyght, DB, and Chris Zorich, DL, 1989–90; Raghib Ismail, WR, 1990; Mirko Jurkovic, OG, 1991; and Aaron Taylor, OG, 1992 . . . Academic All-Americans were Joe Heap, B, 1952–54; Don Schaefer, B, 1955; Bob Wetoska, E, 1958; Bob Lehmann, G, 1963; Tom Regner, OG, and Jim Lynch, LB, 1966; Jim Smithberger, DB, 1967; George Kunz, OT, 1968; Jim Reilly, OT, 1969; Larry DiNardo, OG, and Joe Theismann, QB, 1970; Tom Gatewood, E, 1970–71; Greg Marx, DT, 1971–72;

Mike Creaney, E, 1972; David Casper, E, Robert Thomas, K, and Gary Potempa, LB, 1973; Pete Demmerle, E, and Reggie Barnett, DB, 1974; Ken MacAfee, E, and Dave Vinson, OG, 1977; Joe Restic, DB, 1977–78; Tom Gibbons, DB, and Bob Burger, OG, 1980; John Krimm, DB, 1981; Greg Dingens, DL, 1985; and Ted Gradel, K, and Vince Phelan, P, 1987 . . . Heisman Trophy winners were Angelo Bertelli, QB, 1943; John Lujack, QB, 1947; Leon Hart, E, 1949; John Lattner, HB, 1953; Paul Hornung, QB, 1956; John Huarte, QB, 1964; and Tim Brown, WR, 1987 . . . Maxwell Award winners were Leon Hart, E, 1949; John Lattner, HB, 1952–53; Jim Lynch, LB, 1966; and Ross Browner, DE, 1977 . . . Outland Trophy winners were George Connor, T, 1946 (initial award); Bill Fischer, G, 1948; and Ross Browner, DE, 1976 . . . Lombardi Award winners were Walt Patulski, DE, 1971; Ross Browner, DE, 1977; and Chris Zorich, NT, 1990.

SOUTHERN MISSISSIPPI (Golden Eagles; Black and Gold)

NOTABLE TEAMS

(Many scores are not available before 1937.)
1919 (4–1–2)—Resumed football after 2-year layoff during W.W. I. Lost only to Meridian College.
1936 (7–2–1) *Won:* Memphis St. 25–0, among others. *Tied:* SW Louisiana 14–14. *Noteworthy:* Pooley Hubert's last team.
1937 (7–3) *Won:* Louisiana College 19–0, Spring Hill 33–0, SW Louisiana 13–0, Jacksonville St. 58–0, Troy St. 53–0, Union 34–0, Appalachian St. 7–0. *Lost:* Louisiana Tech 7–0, NW Louisiana 3–0, East Texas St. 14–6. *Noteworthy:* 1st year under Reed Green.
1938 (7–2) *Won:* Arkansas A&M 39–0, Troy St. 19–0, Delta St. 44–0, Millsaps 47–0, Louisiana College 7–0, SW Louisiana 15–6, Union 32–0. *Lost:* Mississippi 14–0 (1st meeting since 1933), NW Louisiana 6–0.
1941 (9–0–1) *Won:* Georgia Teachers 70–0, Louisiana Tech 19–7, SE Louisiana 43–6, Millsaps 20–0, Spring Hill 26–7, Louisiana College 13–6, NW Louisiana 21–7, Delta St. 27–7, St. Mary's (Texas) 7–0. *Tied:* SW Louisiana 0–0. *Noteworthy:* 1st unbeaten season since 2-game schedule of 1912.
1946 (7–3) *Won:* Louisiana Tech 7–6, Jacksonville

St. 65–0, SW Louisiana 6–0, Oklahoma City 20–6, Stephen F. Austin 7–0, Louisiana College 65–0, Univ. of Havana 55–0. *Lost:* Auburn 13–12 (1st meeting), NW Louisiana 7–6, SE Louisiana 20–0. *Noteworthy:* returned to competition after 3-year layoff during W.W. II.
1947 (7–3) *Won:* Auburn 19–13, Louisiana Tech 7–6, SW Louisiana 15–7, Stephen F. Austin 20–7, NW Louisiana 20–0, Union 18–0, SE Louisiana 35–0. *Lost:* Alabama 34–7 (1st meeting), Oklahoma City 21–6, Mississippi St. 14–7 (1st meeting since 1935). *Stars:* frosh Bubba Phillips (659 yds rush, 5 TDs), Hindu Reynolds (12 pass rec for 230 yds), E Jay Smith.
1948 (7–3) *Won:* Austin College 41–0, SW Louisiana 26–6, Oklahoma City 55–20, NW Louisiana 38–14, Louisiana Tech 20–6, SE Louisiana 27–0, Union 47–8. *Lost:* Auburn 20–14, Trinity (Texas) 26–9, Alabama 27–0. *Stars:* Phillips (831 yds and 6 TDs rush), Cliff Coggin (19 pass rec for 455 yds and 6 TDs). *Noteworthy:* Green's last year.
1949 (7–3) *Won:* Delta St. 20–13, McMurry 55–32, SW Louisiana 25–0, Chattanooga 33–20 (1st meeting), NW Louisiana 67–28, Oklahoma City 27–21, Louisville 26–21 (1st meeting). *Lost:* Kentucky 71–7, Louisiana Tech 34–13, Alabama 34–26. *Stars:* Coggin (53 pass rec for 1,087 yds and 9 TDs), Phillips (9 TDs, 8 int), Bobby Holmes (1,096 yds and 10 TDs total off). *Noteworthy:* 1st year under Thad "Pie" Vann.
1952 (10–2) *Won:* Memphis St. 27–20 (1st meeting since 1936), Tampa 52–25, SW Louisiana 32–12, SE Louisiana 20–12, Chattanooga 27–14, NW Louisiana 39–13, Florida St. 50–21 (1st meeting), Louisiana Tech 52–0, Louisville 55–26, Stetson 42–0. *Lost:* Alabama 20–6 in opener. *Stars:* FB Bucky McElroy (1,069 yds rush), Bob McKellar (22 pass rec for 379 yds and 5 TDs), Hugh Laurin Pepper (1,227 yds rush, 14 TDs), Billy Jarrell (14 TDs pass). *Noteworthy:* made 1st postseason appearance, losing to Pacific 26–7 in Sun Bowl; Pepper scored on 2-yd run and DT J.T. Shepard starred on defense.
1953 (9–2) *Won:* Alabama 25–19 (1st in 7-game series begun in 1947), Parris Island Marines 40–0, Tampa 42–6, SW Louisiana 41–14, SE Louisiana 7–0, Florida St. 21–0, Louisiana Tech 30–0, Georgia 14–0, Chattanooga 33–19. *Lost:* Memphis St. 27–13. *Stars:* Pepper (677 yds rush, 12 TDs), Hub Waters (21 pass rec for 350 yds). *Noteworthy:* lost to Texas–El Paso 37–14 in Sun Bowl; scored on

13-yd pass from Jarrell to Tommie Wood and 13-yd run by Fred Smallwood.

1955 (9–1)   *Won:* Elon 39–0, Louisiana Tech 7–6, North Texas St. 26–0, SE Louisiana 33–0, Memphis St. 34–14, Abilene Christian 40–0, North Dakota St. 58–0, Dayton 19–13, Florida St. 21–6.   *Lost:* Chattanooga 10–0.   *Stars:* Lawrence Meeks (7 TDs), C Les Clark.

1956 (7–2–1)   *Won:* Louisiana Tech 14–0, Dayton 23–6, SE Louisiana 21–14, Memphis St. 27–0, Chattanooga 33–0, Abilene Christian 36–6, Trinity (Texas) 20–13 in 1st 7 games.   *Lost:* Florida St. 20–19.   *Tied:* Alabama 13–13.   *Stars:* Bo Dickinson (670 yds rush, 6 TDs, 40.4-yd punting avg), Jerry Taylor (17 pass rec for 284 yds and 5 TDs), T Don Owens.   *Noteworthy:* lost to West Texas St. 20–13 (1st meeting) in Tangerine Bowl after taking 13–0 lead in 2nd quarter on 51-yd run by J.C. Arban on statue-of-liberty play and 53-yd pass from Bobby Hughes to Taylor.

1957 (8–3)   *Won:* Louisiana Tech 7–0, Trinity (Texas) 13–0, West Texas St. 34–0, SE Louisiana 14–0, Memphis St. 14–6, Chattanooga 20–0, Abilene Christian 7–0, Florida St. 20–0.   *Lost:* Houston 27–12, Alabama 29–2.   *Noteworthy:* lost to East Texas St. 10–9 in Tangerine Bowl after leading 9–7 at halftime; QB George Sekul scored on 1-yd plunge.

1958 (9–0)   *Won:* Louisiana Tech 14–0, Trinity (Texas) 15–0, Memphis St. 24–22, SE Louisiana 33–6, West Texas St. 15–0, Abilene Christian 22–0, N.C. State 26–14, Virginia Tech 41–0, Chattanooga 20–13.   *Stars:* Es Bob Yencho (11 pass rec for 230 yds) and Hugh McInnis, Buddy Supple (551 yds rush), Bobby Lance (5 TDs).   *Noteworthy:* 1st unbeaten season since 1942.

1961 (8–2)   *Won:* Texas-Arlington 30–7 (1st meeting), SW Louisiana 22–6 (1st meeting since 1953), Chattanooga 24–7, Arkansas St. 20–0, Abilene Christian 33–6, Louisiana Tech 7–0, Florida St. 12–0, Trinity (Texas) 22–14.   *Lost:* Memphis St. 21–7, N.C. State 7–6.   *Stars:* QB Don Fuell (1,095 yds total off, 9 TDs rush, 12 extra pts), Charley Dedwyler (20 pass rec for 276 yds).

1962 (9–1)   *Won:* Texas-Arlington 28–7, Richmond 29–8 (1st meeting), SW Louisiana 29–0 (10th straight over Cajuns), Chattanooga 31–13, N.C. State 30–0, Abilene Christian 30–0, Arkansas St. 20–7, Trinity (Texas) 33–6, Louisiana Tech 29–18.   *Lost:* Memphis St. 8–6 in mid-season.   *Stars:* QB Billy Coleman (1,211 yds and 14 TDs total off),

Johnny Sklopan (511 yds rush, 7 TDs), Billy Lyons (16 pass rec for 272 yds).

1965 (7–2)   *Won:* SE Louisiana 15–0 (1st meeting since 1959), Memphis St. 21–16, Richmond 28–7, Virginia Military Institute (VMI) 3–0, Auburn 3–0, Chattanooga 17–0 (10th straight over Moccasins), Louisiana Tech 31–7.   *Lost:* Mississippi St. 27–9, William & Mary 3–0.   *Stars:* QB Vic Purvis (1,128 yds total off, 6 TDs rush), Robert Brown (17 pass rec for 262 yds), Billy Devrow (8 int), soph P Dickie Dunaway (41.1-yd avg).   *Noteworthy:* led nation in total defense.

1975 (8–3)   *Won:* Weber St. 14–10, Mississippi St. (by forfeit after losing 7–3 on field), Memphis St. 21–7, Texas-Arlington 34–7, Louisiana Tech 24–14, Lamar 43–3, Cal St.–Fullerton 70–0, Brigham Young (BYU) 42–14.   *Lost:* Bowling Green 16–14, Mississippi 24–8, Alabama 27–6.   *Stars:* QB Jeff Bower (1,086 yds total off), Greg Pieper (29 pass rec for 446 yds), soph TB Ben Garry (846 yds rush, 10 TDs), OT Jerry Fremin, NG Randy Latta, DL Norris Thomas.   *Noteworthy:* 1st year under Bobby Collins.

1980 (9–3)   *Won:* Tulane 17–14, Louisiana Tech 38–11, East Carolina 35–7, Mississippi 28–22, Mississippi St. 42–14, Arkansas St. 35–0, Lamar 36–10, Richmond 33–12.   *Lost:* Alabama 42–7, Auburn 31–0, Louisville 6–3.   *Stars:* TB Sammy Winder (996 yds rush, nation's scoring leader with 120 pts on 20 TDs), soph QB Reggie Collier (1,268 yds pass, 464 yds rush), TE Marvin Harvey (28 pass rec for 359 yds), Mike Livings (23 pass rec for 294 yds), soph Don Horn (20 pass rec for 342 yds), C James Watson, soph DE George Tillman, LB Ron Brown, DB Hanford Dixon, soph P Bruce Thompson (40.8-yd avg).   *Noteworthy:* beat McNeese St. 16–14 in Independence Bowl (1st bowl win in 5 tries) as Mike Woodard scored on 1-yd plunge with 1:17 remaining; Eagles scored in 1st quarter on 36-yd FG by Winston Walker and 14-yd TD run by Clemson Terrell.

1981 (9–2–1)   *Won:* SW Louisiana 33–0 (1st meeting since 1974, 15th straight over Cajuns), Tulane 21–3, Richmond 17–10, Texas–Arlington 52–9, Memphis St. 10–0, North Texas St. 22–0, Mississippi St. 7–6, Florida St. 58–14 (1st over Seminoles in 8 games since 1961), Lamar 45–14.   *Lost:* Louisville 13–10.   *Tied:* Alabama 13–13.   *Stars:* Collier (1,005 yds and 12 TDs rush, 1,004 yds pass), Winder (1,029 yds and 12 TDs rush), Raymond Powell (20 pass rec for 254 yds), Horn (15 pass rec for 237 yds), soph K Steve Clark, LB Greg Kelly, Danny Jackson (5 int), Thompson (39.3-yd punting avg).   *Noteworthy:* Collins' last team led nation in scoring defense (8.1-pt avg). Lost to Missouri 19–17 in Tangerine Bowl; scored on FG by Clark, 4-yd run by Winder, and 74-yd pass from David Sellers to soph WR Louis Lipps.

1988 (10–2)   *Won:* Stephen F. Austin 21–7, Virginia Tech 35–13, East Carolina 45–42, Louisville 30–23, Tulane 38–13, Mississippi St. 38–21, SW Louisiana 27–14, Memphis St. 34–27, Louisiana Tech 26–19. *Lost:* Florida St. 49–13, Auburn 38–8.   *Stars:* soph QB Brett Favre (2,271 yds and 16 TDs pass), WRs Alfred Williams (39 pass rec for 601 yds), Darryl Tillman (25 pass rec for 409 yds) and Eugene Rowell (20 pass rec for 308 yds), soph TB Eddie Ray Jackson (30 pass rec for 289 yds), Rickey Bradley (665 yds rush, 8 TDs), K Chris Seroka (14 FGs, 75 pts), LB George Hill, DB James Henry, frosh P Scott Bryant (40-yd avg). *Noteworthy:* 1st year under Curley Hallman. Beat Texas–El Paso 38–18 in Independence Bowl; Henry returned punts 65 yds and 45 yds for

TDs, and Shelton Gandy also scored 2 TDs for Eagles.

1990 (8–4)   *Won:* Delta St. 12–0 (1st meeting since 1950), Alabama 27–24 (1st over Tide in 6 games since 1982), Louisville 25–13, East Carolina 16–7, Tulane 20–14, Memphis St. 23–7, SW Louisiana 14–13, Auburn 13–12 (1st over Tigers in 9 games since 1977).   *Lost:* Georgia 18–17, Mississippi St. 13–10, Virginia Tech 20–16.   *Stars:* Favre (1,572 yds pass), Jackson (25 pass rec for 358 yds), soph WR Greg Reed (23 pass rec for 257 yds), Smith (657 yds rush, 6 TDs), K Jim Taylor (15 FGs), LBs Arnie Williams and soph Rod Lynch, DBs Kerry Valrie (6 int) and Simmie Carter.   *Noteworthy:* Hallman's last team. Lost to N.C. State 31–27 in All-American Bowl in 1st game under Jeff Bower; Favre passed for 341 yds and 2 TDs.

Bowl Summary

All-American 0–1; Independence 2–0; Sun 0–2; Tangerine 0–3.

Bowl Record (2–6)

Regular Season	Bowl	Score	Opponent	Record
1952 (10–1)	Sun	7–26	Pacific	(6–3–1)
1953 (9–1)	Sun	14–37	Texas–El Paso	(7–2)
1956 (7–1–1)	Tangerine	13–20	West Texas St.	(7–2)
1957 (8–2)	Tangerine	9–10	East Texas St.	(8–1)
1980 (8–3)	Independence	16–14	McNeese State	(10–1)
1981 (9–1–1)	Tangerine	17–19	Missouri	(7–4)
1988 (9–2)	Independence	38–18	Texas–El Paso	(10–2)
1990 (8–3)	All-American	27–31	N.C. State	(6–5)

Conference Titles

Gulf States—1950, 1951.

TOP 20 AP AND UPI RANKING

1981	U–19

Major Rivals

Southern Mississippi has played at least 10 games with Alabama 4–23–2, Auburn 5–15, Delta St. 10–3–1, East Carolina 14–4, Florida St. 8–12–1, Louisiana College 12–3, Louisiana Tech 29–13, Louisville 13–4–1, Memphis St. 27–15–1, Millsaps

2–7–5, Mississippi 6–18, Mississippi College 0–10, Mississippi St. 14–12–1, NW Louisiana 10–11, Richmond 14–2, SE Louisiana 17–3, SW Louisiana 30–10–1, Spring Hill 7–9–1, UT–Chattanooga 16–3, Texas–Arlington 10–0, Tulane 10–4, West Texas St. 8–3.

COACHES

Dean of Southern Mississippi coaches is Thad "Pie" Vann with record of 139–59–2 for 1949–68, including 2 conference titles, 4 bowl teams, and 1 unbeaten team. Other top records for at least 3 years were by Pooley Hubert, 24–19–5 for 1932–36; Reed Green, 59–20–4 for 1937–42 and 1946–48 with 2 unbeaten teams; Bobby Collins, 48–30–2 for 1975–81 with 2 bowl teams; Jim Carmody, 37–29 for 1982–87; and Curley Hallman, 23–11 for 1988–90 with 2 bowl teams.

MISCELLANEA

Beat Hattiesburg Boy Scouts and Mobile Military Academy in 1st 2 games in 1912 . . . highest score since 1937 was over NW Louisiana 76–0 in 1951 . . . worst defeat was by SW Louisiana 66–0 in 1923 . . . worst defeat and highest margin against since W.W. II was by Kentucky 71–7 in 1949 . . . longest unbeaten string of 19 in 1940–46 (no games in 1943–45) ended by Auburn 13–12 . . . longest losing string of 9 in 1976 broken with win over Memphis St. 14–12 . . . Southern Mississippi has had no consensus All-Americans and no 1st team Academic All-Americans.

TULANE (Green Wave; Olive Green and Sky Blue)

NOTABLE TEAMS

1900 (5–0) *Won:* Southern A.C. 23–0, Alabama 6–0, Louisiana St. (LSU) 29–0 (1st over Tigers in 5 games since 1893), Millsaps 35–0, Mississippi 12–0. *Noteworthy:* blanked foes 105–0 in 1st undefeated season.
1901 (5–1) *Won:* Meridian 1–0 (forfeit), Mississippi St. 24–6 (1st meeting), LSU 23–0, YMCA 35–0, Mississippi 25–11. *Lost:* Mobile 2–0.
1904 (5–2) *Won:* Louisiana Tech 11–0, Mississippi

St. 10–0, Marion Military 10–0, LSU 5–0, Mississippi 2–0. *Lost:* Sewanee 18–0, Alabama 5–0.
1908 (7–1) *Won:* Centre 10–0, YMCA 11–0, Mississippi 10–0, Mississippi St. 33–0, Baylor 10–2, Texas 28–16, Washington (Mo.) 11–0. *Lost:* Baylor 6–0.
1918 (4–1–1) *Won:* Camp Shelby 7–0, Camp Beauregard 13–6, Spring Hill 32–0, SW Louisiana 74–0. *Lost:* Camp Pike 10–7. *Tied:* Pensacola Naval Air Base 0–0. *Noteworthy:* abbreviated W.W. I schedule.
1919 (6–2–1) *Won:* Jefferson 27–0, SW Louisiana 73–0, Spring Hill 21–0, Mississippi 27–12 (1st meeting since 1914), Mississippi College 49–0, Florida 14–2 in 1st 6 games. *Lost:* LSU 27–6, Washington & Lee 7–0. *Tied:* Georgia 7–7 (1st meeting).
1920 (6–2–1) *Won:* SW Louisiana 79–0, Mississippi College 29–0, Mississippi 32–0, Florida 14–0, Mississippi St. 6–0 (1st meeting since 1914), LSU 21–0. *Lost:* Michigan 21–0, Detroit 7–0. *Tied:* Rice 0–0.
1924 (8–1) *Won:* SW Louisiana 14–0, Mississippi College 32–7, Louisiana Tech 42–14, Vanderbilt 21–13, Spring Hill 33–0, Auburn 14–6, Tennessee 26–7, LSU 13–0. *Lost:* Mississippi St. 14–0. *Stars:* G Milton Levy, B Charles Flournoy.
1925 (9–0–1) *Won:* Louisiana College 77–0, Mississippi 26–7, Mississippi St. 25–3, Northwestern 18–7, Auburn 13–0, Louisiana Tech 37–9, Sewanee 14–0, LSU 16–0, Centenary 14–0. *Tied:* Missouri 6–6. *Stars:* Flournoy (19 TDs, 128 pts), Levy. *Noteworthy:* 1st unbeaten season since 1900.
1929 (9–0) *Won:* Louisiana Normal 40–6, Texas A&M 13–10, SW Louisiana 60–0 (1st meeting since 1924), Georgia Tech 20–14 (1st in 6-game series dating to 1916), Mississippi St. 34–0, Georgia 21–15, Auburn 52–0, Sewanee 18–0, LSU 21–0. *Stars:* B Willis Banker (13 TDs, 21 extra pts), C Lloyd Roberts. *Noteworthy:* won 1st SC title.
1930 (8–1) *Won:* SW Louisiana 84–0 (10th straight over Cajuns), Texas A&M 19–9, Birmingham Southern 21–0, Georgia Tech 28–0, Mississippi St. 53–0, Auburn 21–0, Georgia 25–0, LSU 12–7. *Lost:* Northwestern 14–0 in 2nd game. *Stars:* Roberts, E Jerry Dalrymple. *Noteworthy:* got share of 2nd straight SC title.
1931 (11–1) *Won:* Mississippi 31–0, Texas A&M 7–0, Spring Hill 40–0, Vanderbilt 19–0, Georgia Tech 33–0, Mississippi St. 59–7, Auburn 27–0, Georgia 20–7, Sewanee 40–0, LSU 34–7, Washington St. 28–14. *Stars:* Dalrymple (1st Tulane consensus All-American), Don Zimmerman (899 yds rush, 560

yds pass, 1,885 all-purpose yds), G John Scafide. *Noteworthy:* Bernie Bierman's last team won 3rd straight SC crown. Made 1st postseason appearance, losing to national champ Southern California (USC) 21-12 in Rose Bowl; Harry Glover ran for 139 yds and a TD, and Zimmerman passed to Vern Hayes for other Tulane score.

1932 (6-2-1) *Won:* Texas A&M 26-14, Georgia 34-25, South Carolina 6-0, Georgia Tech 20-14, Kentucky 6-3, Sewanee 26-0. *Lost:* unbeaten Auburn 19-7 (1st to Tigers since 1926), LSU 14-0 (1st to Tigers since 1926). *Tied:* Vanderbilt 6-6. *Stars:* Zimmerman, Scafide. *Noteworthy:* 1st year under Ted Cox.

1934 (10-1) *Won:* Chattanooga 41-0, Auburn 13-0, Florida 28-12 (1st meeting since 1922), Georgia 7-6, Georgia Tech 20-12, Mississippi 15-0, Kentucky 20-7, Sewanee 32-0, LSU 13-12. *Lost:* Colgate 20-6 in mid-season. *Stars:* B Claude "Monk" Simons Jr., C Homer Robinson. *Noteworthy:* Got share of 1st SEC title. Beat undefeated Temple 20-14 in inaugural Sugar Bowl, overcoming 14-0 deficit on TD by Simons on 85-yd kickoff return and 2 TD pass rec by Dick Hardy (from soph B Howard "Bucky" Bryan and Barney Mintz).

1938 (7-2-1) *Won:* North Carolina 17-14, Rice 26-17 (1st meeting since 1921), Mercer 51-0, Mississippi St. 27-0 (1st meeting since 1933), Georgia 28-6, Sewanee 38-0, LSU 14-0. *Lost:* Clemson 13-10, Alabama 3-0. *Tied:* Auburn 0-0. *Star:* B Warren Brunner.

1939 (8-1-1) *Won:* Clemson 7-6, Auburn 12-0, Fordham 7-0, Mississippi 18-6, Alabama 13-0, Columbia 25-0, Sewanee 52-0, LSU 33-20. *Tied:* North Carolina 14-14. *Stars:* E Ralph Wenzel, B Bob Kellogg, T Harley McCollum, P Stan Nyhan (44.5-yd avg). *Noteworthy:* Got share of 2nd SEC title in 1st unbeaten season since 1931. Lost to unbeaten national champ Texas A&M 14-13 in Sugar Bowl; scored on 75-yd punt return by Kellogg and short run by Monette Butler but had 2nd ex pt try blocked.

1948 (9-1) *Won:* Alabama 21-14, South Carolina 14-0, Mississippi 20-7, Auburn 21-6, Mississippi St. 9-0, Virginia Military Institute (VMI) 28-7, Baylor 35-13, Cincinnati 6-0, LSU 46-0. *Lost:* Georgia Tech 13-7 in 2nd game. *Stars:* FB Eddie Price (1,178 yds rush, 10 TDs), soph T Paul Lea.

1949 (7-2-1) *Won:* Alabama 28-14, Georgia Tech 18-0 (1st over Yellow Jackets in 7 games since 1934), SE Louisiana 40-0, Auburn 14-6, Mississippi St. 54-6, Vanderbilt 41-14 (1st meeting since 1942), Virginia 28-14. *Lost:* unbeaten national champ Notre Dame 46-7, LSU 21-0. *Tied:* Navy 21-21. *Stars:* Price (1,137 yds rush, 11 TDs), Lea, Jimmy Glisson (9 int). *Noteworthy:* won 3rd and last SEC title.

1950 (6-2-1) *Won:* Louisiana College 64-0, Mississippi 27-20, Auburn 28-0, Navy 27-0, Virginia 42-18, Vanderbilt 35-6. *Lost:* Alabama 26-14, Notre Dame 13-9. *Tied:* LSU 14-14. *Stars:* Lea, T Jerome Helluin, B Harold Waggoner (663 yds rush).

1970 (8-4) *Won:* Georgia 17-14, Illinois 23-9, Cincinnati 6-3, North Carolina 24-17, Vanderbilt 10-7, Miami (Fla.) 31-6, N.C. State 31-0. *Lost:* Texas Tech 21-14, Air Force 24-3, Georgia Tech 20-6, LSU 26-14 (15th straight to Tigers). *Stars:* TB David Abercrombie (993 yds rush), soph QB Mike W. Walker (1,038 yds pass), FL Steve Barrios (20 pass rec for 505 yds), DT Mike Walker, LB Rick Kingrea, DBs Joe Bullard and Paul Ellis (9 int). *Noteworthy:* Last year under Jim Pittman. Made 1st postseason appearance in 30 years, beating Colorado 17-3 in Liberty Bowl; Kingrea set up FG with 44-yd pass int return and Abercrombie returned 2nd half kickoff 66 yds to set up own short TD plunge.

1973 (9-3) *Won:* Boston College 21-16, VMI 42-0, Pittsburgh 24-6, Duke 24-17, North Carolina 16-0, Georgia Tech 23-14, Navy 17-15, Vanderbilt 24-3, LSU 14-0 (1st over Tigers since 1948). *Lost:* Kentucky 34-7, Maryland 42-9. *Stars:* QB Steve Foley (601 yds rush, 824 yds pass), C Steve Wade, NG Mark Olivari, DT Charles Hall, DE Mike Truax, DB David Lee. *Noteworthy:* lost to Houston 47-7 in Astro-Bluebonnet Bowl; scored on 32-yd pass from Buddy Gilbert to Tom Fortner.

1979 (9-3) *Won:* Stanford 33-10, TCU 33-19, SMU 24-17, Vanderbilt 42-14, Southern Mississippi 20-19 (1st meeting), Georgia Tech 12-7 (1st over Yellow Jackets since 1973), Boston College 43-8, Mississippi 49-15, LSU 24-13 (1st over Tigers since 1973). *Lost:* Rice 21-17 (1st meeting since 1971), West Virginia 27-17. *Stars:* QB Roch Hontas (2,345 yds and 21 TDs pass, 6 TDs rush), Alton Alexis (47 pass rec for 557 yds and 5 TDs), soph TE Rodney Holman (47 pass rec for 477 yds and 5 TDs), Darrell Griffin (5 TDs on pass rec), K Ed Murray (11 FGs, 68 pts), C Chris Doyle, DE Bob Becnel.

Noteworthy: Had 1st winning season since 1973 in last year under Larry Smith. Lost to Penn St. 9-6 in Liberty Bowl in driving rainstorm when Nittany Lions kicked winning FG with 18 seconds left; Tulane scored on 2 FGs by Murray.

BOWL SUMMARY

Bluebonnet 0-1; Hall of Fame 0-1; Independence 0-1; Liberty 1-1; Rose 0-1; Sugar 1-1.

BOWL RECORD (2-6)

Regular Season	Bowl	Score	Opponent	Record
1931 (11-0)	Rose	12-21	USC	(9-1)
1934 (10-1)	Sugar	20-14	Temple	(7-0-2)
1939 (8-0-1)	Sugar	13-14	Texas A&M	(10-0)
1970 (7-4)	Liberty	17-3	Colorado	(6-4)
1973 (9-2)	Bluebonnet	7-47	Houston	(10-1)
1979 (9-2)	Liberty	6-9	Penn St.	(7-4)
1980 (7-4)	Hall of Fame	15-34	Arkansas	(6-5)
1987 (6-5)	Independence	12-24	Washington	(6-4-1)

CONFERENCE TITLES

Southern—1929, 1930*, 1931. **Southeastern**—1934*, 1939*, 1949.

TOP 20 AP AND UPI RANKING

1938	19	1948	13	1970	17-U	1973	20-15
1939	5	1950	20-U				

MAJOR RIVALS

Tulane has played at least 10 games with Alabama 10-25-3, Auburn 17-13-6, Boston College 7-6, Clemson 6-4, Florida 6-13-2, Florida St. 0-10, Georgia 10-14-1, Georgia Tech 13-35, Kentucky 6-9, LSU 23-60-7, Memphis St. 8-7-1, Miami (Fla.) 5-6-1, Mississippi 28-36, Mississippi College 9-3, Mississippi St. 24-25-2, North Carolina 9-3-2, Rice 10-11-1, Sewanee 13-6, Southern Methodist 6-4, Southern Mississippi 4-10, SW Louisiana 17-2, Texas 1-15-1, Texas A&M 5-10, Vanderbilt 28-17-3.

COACHES

Dean of Tulane coaches is Clark Shaughnessy with record of 59-28-7 for 1915-20 and 1922-26, including 1 unbeaten team. Other top records for at least 3 years were by Bernie Bierman, 36-10-2 for 1927-31 with 3 SC titles, 1 Rose Bowl team, and 2 teams unbeaten in regular season; Ted Cox, 28-10-2 for 1932-35 with 1 SEC title and 1 Sugar Bowl champion; Lowell Dawson, 36-19-4 for 1936-41 with 1 SEC title, 1 Sugar Bowl team, and 1 team unbeaten in regular season; Henry E. Frnka, 31-23-4 for 1946-51 with 1 SEC title; Jim Pittman, 21-30-1 for 1966-70 with 1 Liberty Bowl champion; Bennie Ellender, 27-29 for 1971-75 with 1 bowl team; and Vince Gibson, 17-17 for 1980-82 with 1 bowl team.

MISCELLANEA

First game was loss to Southern A.C. 12-0 in 1893 . . . 1st win was over LSU 34-0 in 1893 . . . highest score was over SW Louisiana 95-0 in 1912 . . . highest since W.W. II was over Louisiana College 64-0 in 1950 . . . worst defeat was by Florida St. 70-7 in 1992 . . . highest against was by Florida St. 73-14 in 1987 ... longest win streak of 18 in 1930-31 ended by USC 21-12 in 1932 Rose Bowl ... longest losing string of 17 in 1961-63 broken with win over South Carolina 20-7 ... consensus All-Americans were Jerry Dalrymple, E, 1931; Don Zimmerman, B, 1932; Harley McCollum, T, 1939; and Ernie Blandin, T, 1941 ... Academic All-American was Dave Hebert, DB, 1971.

TULSA *(Golden Hurricane; Old Gold, Royal Blue and Crimson)*

NOTABLE TEAMS

1913 (5-1) *Won:* NE Oklahoma 34-0, University Prep School 43-0, Euchee Indians 92-0, Haskell Indian School 58-0 (1st meeting), Oklahoma City 18-0. *Lost:* Pittsburg (Kansas) 32-25. *Noteworthy:* only year under George Evans.
1914 (6-2) *Won:* NW Oklahoma 33-0 (1st meeting), University Prep School 58-0, Pittsburg (Kansas) 63-0, East Central Okla. 12-0, Oklahoma Military 54-0, Oklahoma City 39-0. *Lost:* Oklahoma A&M 13-6 (1st meeting), Oklahoma 26-7 (1st meeting). *Noteworthy:* 1st year under Sam McBirney.
1915 (6-1-1) *Won:* Oklahoma Mines 61-0, NE Oklahoma 55-0, NW Oklahoma 26-6, East Central Okla. 49-3, SE Oklahoma 45-7, Haskell 7-3. *Lost:* unbeaten Oklahoma 14-13. *Tied:* Oklahoma A&M 0-0. *Star:* T Madison Blevins.
1916 (10-0) *Won:* Phillips U. 51-7 (1st meeting), Cumberland (Tenn.) 81-0, Oklahoma 16-0, NW Oklahoma 59-7, Pittsburg (Kansas) 49-3, Oklahoma A&M 17-13, K.C. Veterinary College 48-10, Haskell 46-10, Shawnee Catholic U. 82-0, Missouri Mines 117-0. *Stars:* Blevins, QB Ivan Grove, HB John Young. *Noteworthy:* McBirney's last team outscored foes 566-50 in 1st unbeaten season since 1-game schedule of 1895.
1919 (8-0-1) *Won:* Oklahoma Baptist 152-0 (1st meeting), SW Oklahoma 60-0, Oklahoma 27-0, NW Oklahoma 75-0, Arkansas 63-7 (1st in 7-game series dating to 1899), Trinity (Texas) 70-0, Camp Burleson 71-7, Central Oklahoma 67-6 (1st meeting). *Tied:* Oklahoma A&M 7-7. *Stars:* Grove (196 pts), E Young. *Noteworthy:* Outscored foes 592-27 in 1st year under Francis Schmidt.
1920 (10-0-1) *Won:* Shawnee Catholic U. 121-0, Oklahoma Mines 151-0, Chilocco Indians 88-0, Oklahoma A&M 20-14, East Central Okla. 10-0,

Central Oklahoma 3-0, Oklahoma Baptist 81-7, NW Oklahoma 14-7, Kingfisher 89-0, Missouri Mines 45-0. *Tied:* Phillips U. 0-0. *Noteworthy:* outscored opponents 622-28.
1922 (7-0) *Won:* Texas Christian (TCU) 21-0, Arkansas A&M 14-12, SE Oklahoma 26-9, Texas A&M 13-10, Oklahoma Baptist 34-9, Arkansas 13-6, Central Oklahoma 14-0. *Noteworthy:* 1st year under Howard Acher.
1925 (6-2) *Won:* Eastern Oklahoma J.C. 7-3, Tennessee Medics 27-7, NW Oklahoma 42-13, Phillips U. 6-0, General Normal 20-8, SE Oklahoma 19-7. *Lost:* Haskell 33-3, Arkansas 20-7. *Star:* QB Murl "Tuffy" Cline. *Noteworthy:* 1st year under Elmer Henderson.
1926 (7-2) *Won:* Arkansas 14-7 (1st homecoming), SE Oklahoma 33-10, NW Oklahoma 35-0, Oklahoma A&M 28-0, Phillips U. 19-0, Oklahoma City 13-0 (1st meeting since 1914), NE Oklahoma 17-0. *Lost:* Oklahoma Baptist 12-3 (1st in 5-game series dating to 1919), Haskell 27-7. *Star:* Cline.
1927 (8-1) *Won:* Parsons 19-6, South Dakota 33-12, DePaul 30-6, Oklahoma A&M 28-26, Oklahoma City 7-0, Oklahoma Baptist 21-7, SE Oklahoma 32-0, Haskell 24-14 (1st over Indians in 7 games since 1916). *Lost:* Phillips U. 13-7. *Star:* T Elno Jones.
1928 (7-2-1) *Won:* NW Oklahoma 19-0, DePaul 27-0, Wichita St. 46-0 (1st meeting), Oklahoma City 13-8, SE Oklahoma 51-0, Oklahoma A&M 31-0, Haskell 33-6. *Lost:* unbeaten Detroit 19-14 (1st meeting), Phillips U. 27-26 in consecutive games. *Tied:* Oklahoma Baptist 13-13. *Stars:* Jones, QB/E Roy Selby.
1930 (7-2) *Won:* Arkansas 26-6 (1st game in new Skelly Stadium), Hendrix 27-0, Phillips U. 25-0, George Washington 14-7, Oklahoma Baptist 14-6, Missouri Mines 18-0, Oklahoma City 33-7. *Lost:* Haskell 34-7, Oklahoma A&M 13-7 in last 2 games. *Stars:* B Chet Benefiel, FB Ishmael Pilkington.
1931 (8-3) *Won:* Hendrix 26-0, TCU 13-0 (1st meeting since 1922), Oklahoma Baptist 25-0, Creighton 28-0, Mexico U. 89-0, George Washington 24-7, Phillips U. 31-7, Haskell 6-0. *Lost:* Oklahoma A&M 7-6, Oklahoma City 14-0 (1st to Chiefs in 9 games since 1912), Oklahoma 20-7 (1st meeting since 1919). *Stars:* Pilkington, HB Billy Boehm, soph G Bill Volok.
1932 (7-1-1) *Won:* Washburn 20-0, Phillips U. 21-2, George Washington 29-14, Oklahoma Baptist

39-13, Missouri Mines 26-0, Mississippi 26-0, Oklahoma City 14-0. *Lost:* Oklahoma 7-0. *Tied:* Oklahoma A&M 0-0. *Stars:* Boehm, Volok.

1933 (6-1)   *Won:* Washburn 7-0, Oklahoma 20-6, Kansas 7-0, Oklahoma City 39-0, Arkansas 7-0, George Washington 13-6. *Lost:* Oklahoma A&M 7-0. *Star:* Volok.

1937 (6-2-2)   *Won:* Oklahoma 19-7, Central Oklahoma 42-6, Oklahoma A&M 27-0, George Washington 14-13, Drake 41-9, Washington (Mo.) 32-7. *Lost:* TCU 20-13, Arkansas 28-7. *Tied:* Rice 0-0, Manhattan 0-0. *Stars:* QB Morris White, Es Buster Baze and Curly Hayes, C George Adams, G Lester Graham. *Noteworthy:* won 3rd straight MVC title.

1940 (7-3)   *Won:* Washburn 37-6, Creighton 32-0, St. Louis 19-6, TCU 7-0 (1st over Horned Frogs in 7 games since 1931), Detroit 7-0, Catholic U. 12-6, Oklahoma A&M 19-6. *Lost:* Texas A&M 41-6, Baylor 20-6, Arkansas 27-21. *Stars:* soph QB Glenn Dobbs (698 yds total off), FB Lester Moore, E Bill Grimmett, T Charles Greene, C/LB Rich Morgan (nation's leader with 7 int). *Noteworthy:* won 5th MVC title.

1941 (8-2)   *Won:* Creighton 19-7, St. Louis 33-7, Oklahoma A&M 16-0, Wichita St. 13-7, North Dakota St. 61-6, Baylor 20-13, Drake 20-6. *Lost:* TCU 6-0 (opener), Arkansas 13-6 (finale). *Stars:* FB Dobbs (739 yds total off), Bs Cal Purdin (13 pass rec for 217 yds, 5 TDs) and N.A. Keithly, Es Elston Campbell and Saxon Judd, Morgan, Greene. *Noteworthy:* Won 6th MVC title in 1st year under Henry Frnka. Made 1st postseason appearance, beating Texas Tech 6-0 (1st meeting) in Sun Bowl; Dobbs passed for 239 yds and the TD (6 yds to Judd).

1942 (10-1)   *Won:* Waco AFB 84-0, Oklahoma 23-0, Randolph AFB 68-0, Washington (Mo.) 40-0, St. Louis 41-0, Drake 40-0, Oklahoma A&M 34-6, Baylor 24-0, Creighton 33-19, Arkansas 40-7 (1st over Razorbacks since 1933). *Stars:* TB Dobbs (1,066 yds pass, 361 yds rush, 48.3-yd punting avg), Judd (35 pass rec for 509 yds and 9 TDs), Purdin, E Johnny Green. *Noteworthy:* Led nation in pass, scoring (42.7-pt avg), and scoring defense (3.2-pt avg) in 1st unbeaten season since 1922. Took 3rd straight MVC title. Lost to Tennessee 14-7 in Sugar Bowl; scored on 9-yd pass from Dobbs to Purdin.

1943 (6-1-1)   *Won:* Southern Methodist (SMU) 20-7, Texas Tech 34-7, Oklahoma 20-6, Utah 55-0, Oklahoma A&M 55-6, Arkansas 61-0. *Tied:*

Southwestern (Texas) 6-6. *Stars:* G Ellis Jones, T C.G. Stanley, Barney White (16 pass rec for 188 yds and 5 TDs), Bs Clyde LeForce (5 TDs, 59 pts) and Charley Mitchell. *Noteworthy:* Won 8th MVC crown. Lost to Georgia Tech 20-18 in Sugar Bowl after leading 18-7 at halftime; scored on pass from LeForce to Ed Shedlosky, 79-yd run by Jimmy Ford, and 6-yd run by LeForce.

1944 (8-2)   *Won:* North Texas St. 47-6 (1st meeting), Kansas 27-0, Texas Tech 34-7, Mississippi 47-0, Southwestern (Texas) 51-6, Arkansas 33-2, Miami (Fla.) 48-2. *Lost:* Oklahoma A&M 46-40 (1st to Aggies since 1939), Iowa Pre-Flight 47-27 in consecutive mid-season games. *Stars:* Mitchell, White (29 pass rec for 531 yds), B Camp Wilson (662 yds rush), Perry Moss (7 TDs, 65 pts), Jones, C Felto Prewitt, G Carl Buda, Bill Farrett (5 int). *Noteworthy:* Led nation in total off and pass. Beat Georgia Tech 26-12 in Orange Bowl, grabbing quick 14-0 lead on 2 TDs by Shedlosky; Wilson scored final TD on 90-yd kickoff return.

1945 (8-3)   *Won:* Wichita St. 61-0, West Texas St. 32-0 (1st meeting), Drake 19-0, Texas Tech 18-7, Nevada-Reno 40-0, Baylor 26-7, Arkansas 45-13, Hondo AFB 20-18. *Lost:* unbeaten Indiana 7-2, unbeaten Oklahoma A&M 12-6 in successive mid-season games. *Stars:* Prewitt, T Forrest Griggs, E Dick Moseley, Wilson (662 yds rush, 10 TDs), B Hardy Brown. *Noteworthy:* Frnka's last team. Lost to Georgia 20-6 in Oil Bowl as Bulldogs' Charles Trippi passed 65 yds for 1 TD and returned a punt 68 yds for another in 4th quarter; Tulsa scored on 1-yd run by Wilson.

1946 (9-1)   *Won:* Wichita St. 33-13, New Mexico A&M 52-0 (1st meeting), Drake 48-13, Texas Tech 21-6, Kansas 56-0, Cincinnati 20-0 (1st meeting), Oklahoma A&M 20-18, Baylor 17-0, Arkansas 14-13. *Lost:* Detroit 20-14 (1st meeting since 1940). *Stars:* LeForce (5 TDs, 67 pts), Brown, frosh B Paul Barry (548 yds rush), E Bill Kemplin, T Nelson Greene, C Bob Hellinghausen, G Vic Jordan. *Noteworthy:* Won 9th MVC title in 1st year under J.O. Brothers.

1950 (9-1-1)   *Won:* McMurry 20-13, Georgetown 21-7, Villanova 27-7, Bradley 74-7, Oklahoma A&M 27-13, Texas Tech 39-7, Wichita St. 48-0, Arkansas 28-13, Houston 28-21 (1st meeting). *Lost:* San Francisco 23-14 in 2nd game. *Tied:* Detroit 13-13. *Stars:* Jake Roberts (954 yds rush), Jack Crocker (10 TDs), soph QB Ronnie Morris (1,014 yds pass), Fred

Smith (34 pass rec for 425 yds), T Dave Rakestraw, C Jim Beasley, Gene Helwig (5 int). *Noteworthy:* won 11th MVC title.

1951 (9-2) *Won:* Hawaii 58-0, Houston 46-27, Marquette 27-21, Wichita St. 33-0, Oklahoma A&M 35-7, Kansas St. 42-26, Texas Tech 21-14, Detroit 34-20, Hardin-Simmons 33-14 (1st meeting). *Lost:* Cincinnati 47-35, Arkansas 24-7. *Stars:* Howie Waugh (1,118 yds and 7 TDs rush), Morris (1,572 yds total off), soph Tom Miner (31 pass rec for 459 yds), Bill Parsons (14 TDs), Beasley, OLs Marv Matuszak and Jim Prewitt. *Noteworthy:* led nation in total offense and again took MVC title.

1952 (8-2-1) *Won:* Hardin-Simmons 56-27, Kansas St. 26-7, Wichita St. 28-0, Oklahoma A&M 23-21, Villanova 42-6, Detroit 62-21, Arkansas 44-34, Texas Tech 26-20. *Lost:* Houston 33-7. *Tied:* Cincinnati 14-14. *Stars:* Waugh (10 TDs, nation's leader with 1,372 yds rush), Morris (1,571 yds and 23 TDs total off), B Dick Kercher, E Willie Roberts, Matuszak. *Noteworthy:* Brothers' last team led nation in total off and rush. Lost to Florida 14-13 in Gator Bowl; Morris passed for 132 yds and Roberts and Waugh each scored TDs.

1956 (7-2-1) *Won:* New Mexico A&M 27-6 (1st meeting since 1946), Marquette 54-0, Detroit 3-0, Hardin-Simmons 27-0, Pacific 14-13, Texas Tech 10-7, Wichita St. 14-6. *Lost:* Cincinnati 7-6, Houston 14-0. *Tied:* Oklahoma A&M 14-14. *Stars:* B Dick Hughes (618 yds rush 6 TDs), C Max Black, T Dean Slayton, soph Ronnie Morris (5 int).

1958 (7-3) *Won:* Arkansas 27-14 (1st over Razorbacks in 5 games since 1952), Arizona 34-0, Oklahoma St. 24-16 (1st over Cowboys since 1952), Drake 59-0, Houston 25-20, Texas Tech 9-7, Wichita St. 25-6. *Lost:* Hardin-Simmons 14-0, North Texas St. 8-7, Cincinnati 15-6. *Stars:* Morris (624 yds rush), FB Bob Brumble (8 TDs), Billy Neal (14 pass rec for 200 yds), E Dick Brown, T Opie Brandy.

1964 (9-2) *Won:* Southern Illinois 63-7, Houston 31-23, Louisville 58-0, Oklahoma St. 61-14, Memphis St. 19-7, North Texas St. 47-0, Toledo 39-16, Wichita St. 21-7. *Lost:* unbeaten national co-champ Arkansas 31-22, Cincinnati 28-23. *Stars:* QB Jerry Rhome (258 yds and 8 TDs rush, nation's leader with 2,870 yds and 32 TDs pass and with 3,128 yds total off), E Howard Twilley (110 pts, nation's leader with 95 pass rec for 1,178 yds and 13 TDs), HB Bob Daugherty (9 TDs), E Mark Maddox, C John Osmond, soph DT Willie Townes,

MG Eddie Dukes, LB Dwight Claxton, DE Garry Porterfield, Jeff Jordan (7 int). *Noteworthy:* Led nation in total off, pass, and scoring (38.4-pt avg). Beat Mississippi 14-7 in Bluebonnet Bowl; Rhome scored 1 TD and passed for 252 yds and other TD (35 yards to Eddie Fletcher).

1965 (8-3) *Won:* Houston 14-0, Memphis St. 32-28, North Texas St. 27-20, Cincinnati 49-6, Southern Illinois 55-12, Louisville 51-18, Wichita St. 13-3, Colorado St. 48-20. *Lost:* Arkansas 20-12, Oklahoma St. 17-14 in successive early games. *Stars:* QB Bill Anderson (nation's leader with 3,343 yds total off and 3,464 yds and 30 TDs pass), Twilley (Tulsa's 1st consensus All-American; nation's leader with 134 pass rec for 1,779 yds and 16 TDs and in scoring with 127 pts), FL Neal Sweeney (78 pass rec for 883 yds and 8 TDs), Osmond, OG Richard Tyson, OT Joe Brooks, Townes, DT Tom McGuire, Claxton, LB Darrell Wolff, DB Charles Hardt. *Noteworthy:* Led nation in total off and pass and won 14th MVC crown. Lost to Tennessee 27-6 in Bluebonnet Bowl, losing ball 3 times on fumbles and 4 times on int; scored on 1-yd run by Gary McDermott.

1967 (7-3) *Won:* Arkansas 14-12 (1st over Razorbacks since 1958), Idaho St. 58-0, Tampa 77-0, Cincinnati 35-6, Wichita St. 14-0, Houston 22-13, Louisville 35-23. *Lost:* Southern Illinois 16-13, Wake Forest 31-24, North Texas St. 54-12. *Stars:* LB Bob Junko, DT Willie Crittendon, soph DB Doug Wyatt, Ken Wiginton (7 int), Cee Ellison (661 yds rush), QB Mike Stripling (1,271 yds and 11 TDs pass), Rich Eber (78 pass rec for 1,168 yds and 10 TDs, 13 TDs total), OT Carl Martin.

1974 (8-3) *Won:* North Texas St. 31-6, Wichita St. 35-13, West Texas St. 17-14, Tampa 31-21, Louisville 37-7, New Mexico St. 28-7, Drake 52-14, Houston 30-14 (1st over Cougars in 6 games since 1967). *Lost:* Kansas St. 31-14, Arkansas 60-0, Tennessee 17-10. *Stars:* QB Jeb Blount (1,831 yds and 15 TDs pass), Steve Largent (52 pass rec for 884 yds and 14 TDs), Thomas Bailey (6 TDs), OG Wes Hamilton, OT Greg Fairchild, K Arthur Bennett, DT Mack Lancaster, DL Ken Thomas, LBs Al Humphrey and Byron Franklin, DB Buddy Tate, P Rick Engles (40.5-yd avg). *Noteworthy:* won 17th MVC title.

1978 (9-2) *Won:* Arkansas St. 21-20, Virginia Tech 35-33, SW Louisiana 10-3, Kansas St. 24-14 (1st over Wildcats in 7 games since 1952), Louisville 24-7, Cincinnati 27-26, Drake 44-20, West Texas St. 44-23,

Wichita St. 27-13. *Lost:* Arkansas 21-13, New Mexico St. 23-20 (1st to Aggies in 6 games since 1960). *Stars:* QB Dave Rader (1,683 yds and 14 TDs pass), Rickey Watts (34 pass rec for 730 yds and 5 TDs), Sherman Johnson (826 yds and 6 TDs rush), OT Doug Panfil, C Steve Nicholson, soph DE Don Blackmon, DB Lovie Smith, P Eddie Hare (43.1-yd punting avg). *Noteworthy:* nation's most-improved team.

1980 (8-3) *Won:* Cincinnati 31-13, Kansas St. 3-0, North Texas St. 28-27, TCU 23-17, West Texas St. 44-24, Indiana St. 30-7, Southern Illinois 41-7, New Mexico St. 21-20. *Lost:* Wichita St. 23-10, Arkansas 13-10, Florida St. 45-2. *Stars:* Blackmon, LBs Robert Tennon and Reggie Epps, DB Charles Caulfield (6 int), QB Kenny Jackson (1,208 yds pass), Paul Johns (29 pass rec for 420 yds), Ken Session (662 yds and 5 TDs rush), RB Kenneth Lacy, OT Denver Johnson, OG Chris Kelly, K Stu Crum (11 FGs). *Noteworthy:* won 20th MVC title.

1982 (10-1) *Won:* Air Force 35-17, Oklahoma St. 25-15 (1st over Cowboys in 5 games since 1964), Kansas 20-15, New Mexico St. 31-14, Southern Illinois 22-3, Drake 34-18, Wichita St. 30-21, West Texas St. 59-21, Indiana St. 48-14, North Texas St. 38-20. *Lost:* Arkansas 38-0. *Stars:* RB Michael Gunter (1,164 yds and 11 TDs rush), FB Ken Lacy (1,097 yds rush), SE Kirk Phillips (18 pass rec for 374 yds), OG Steve Cox, C David Imes, OT Sid Abramowitz, Crum (21 FGs, 100 pts), frosh DT Kevin Lilly, LB Cliff Abbott, Timmy Gibbs (5 int), DB Brent Dennis, P Steve Cook (41.1-yd avg). *Noteworthy:* won 22nd MVC title.

1983 (8-3) *Won:* San Diego St. 34-9, NW Louisiana 26-19, New Mexico St. 24-10, Illinois St. 39-25,

Texas Tech 59-20 (1st meeting since 1972), Wichita St. 30-19, Drake 22-13, West Texas St. 31-16. *Lost:* Arkansas 17-14, Oklahoma 28-18, Oklahoma St. 9-0. *Stars:* Gunter (1,198 yds and 14 TDs rush), John Green (22 pass rec for 365 yds), OG John Kasperski, OT Rod Patten, C David Pearson, DT Tom Baldwin, DE Byron Jones, Abbott, Dennis, Nate Harris (5 int). *Noteworthy:* again won MVC crown.

1991 (10-2) *Won:* SW Missouri St. 34-13, Oklahoma St. 13-7, Texas A&M 35-34, SW Louisiana 34-20, Memphis St. 33-28, Southern Mississippi 13-10, Louisville 40-0, Ohio U. 45-13, SMU 31-26. *Lost:* Kansas 23-17 (1st meeting since 1982, 1st loss in 7-game series dating to 1933), unbeaten national cochamp Miami (Fla.) 34-10. *Stars:* QB T.J. Rubley (2,054 yds and 18 TDs pass), FL Chris Penn (37 pass rec for 792 yds and 5 TDs, 1,098 all-purpose yds), SE Brian Thompson (30 pass rec for 398 yds), TE Fallon Wacasey (26 pass rec for 346 yds), TBs Chris Hughley (1,326 yds rush, 9 TDs) and Ron Jackson (674 yds rush), OG Jerry Ostroski, K Eric Lange (16 FGs, 75 pts), DE Tracy Scroggins, LBs Mike White and Barry Minter. *Noteworthy:* Nation's most-improved team. Beat San Diego St. 28-17 in Freedom Bowl; Jackson ran for 211 yds and 4 TDs.

Bowl Summary

Bluebonnet 1-1; Freedom 1-0; Gator 0-1; Independence 0-2; Oil 0-1; Orange 1-0; Sugar 0-2; Sun 1-0.

Bowl Record (4-7)

Regular Season	Bowl	Score	Opponent	Record
1941 (7-2)	Sun	6-0	Texas Tech	(9-1)
1942 (10-0)	Sugar	7-14	Tennessee	(8-1-1)
1943 (6-0-1)	Sugar	18-20	Georgia Tech	(7-3)
1944 (7-2)	Orange	26-12	Georgia Tech	(8-2)
1945 (8-2)	Oil	6-20	Georgia	(8-2)
1952 (8-1-1)	Gator	13-14	Florida	(7-3)
1964 (8-2)	Bluebonnet	14-7	Mississippi	(5-4-1)
1965 (8-2)	Bluebonnet	6-27	Tennessee	(7-1-2)
1976 (7-3-1)	Independence	16-20	McNeese State	(9-2)
1989 (6-5)	Independence	24-27	Oregon	(7-4)
1991 (9-2)	Freedom	28-17	San Diego St.	(8-3-1)

CONFERENCE TITLES

Missouri Valley—1935*, 1936*, 1937, 1938, 1940, 1941, 1942, 1943, 1946, 1947, 1950, 1951, 1962, 1965, 1966*, 1973*, 1974, 1975, 1976*, 1980, 1981*, 1982, 1983, 1984, 1985.

TOP 20 AP AND UPI RANKING

1942	4	1946	17	1964	U-18
1943	15	1950	19-U	1965	U-16
1945	17	1952	12-U	1974	U-19

MAJOR RIVALS

Tulsa has played at least 10 games with Arkansas 17-49-3, Central (Okla.) St. 8-3, Cincinnati 16-9-2, Detroit 6-10-1, Drake 20-1, Hardin-Simmons 9-3, Haskell 5-8, Houston 14-15, Kansas St. 11-6-1, Louisville 14-10, Memphis St. 5-12, New Mexico St. 15-2, North Texas St. 14-6, NE Oklahoma 5-6, NW Oklahoma 9-0-1, Oklahoma City 10-2, Oklahoma 6-10-1, Oklahoma Baptist 9-1-1, Oklahoma St. 26-31-5, Phillips U. 8-3-2, Texas Christian 4-10, Texas Tech 12-11, West Texas St. 13-1-1, Wichita St. 32-13-1.

COACHES

Dean of Tulsa coaches is Elmer Henderson with record of 70-25-5 for 1925-35, including 1 MVC title. Other top records for at least 3 years were by Sam McBirney, 25-6-1 for 1908 and 1914-16 with 1 unbeaten team; Francis Schmidt, 24-3-2 for 1919-21 with 2 unbeaten teams; Howard Archer, 12-11-2 for 1922-24; Vic Hurt, 15-9-5 for 1936-38 with 3 MVC titles; Henry Frnka, 40-9-1 for 1941-45 with 3 MVC titles, 5 bowl teams, and 2 teams unbeaten in regular season; J.O. Brothers, 45-25-4 for 1946-52 with 4 MVC titles and 1 bowl team; Bobby Dobbs, 30-28-2 for 1955-60; Glenn Dobbs, 45-37 for 1961-68 with 3 MVC titles and 2 bowl teams; F.A. Dry, 31-18-1 for mid-1972 through 1976 with 4 MVC titles and 1 bowl team; John Cooper, 57-31 for 1977-84 with 5 MVC titles; and Dave Rader, 23-23 for 1988-91 with 2 bowl teams.

MISCELLANEA

First game was win over Bacone Indians in 1895 (no score recorded) . . . 1st win over college foe was defeat of Arkansas in 1898 (no score recorded) . . . highest score was over Oklahoma Baptist 152-0 in 1919 . . . highest since W.W. II was over Tampa 77-0 in 1967 . . . worst defeat was by Houston 100-6 in 1968 . . . longest unbeaten string of 23 in 1919-21 ended by TCU 16-0 . . . longest losing string of 15 in 1953-55 broken with win over Hardin-Simmons 41-19 . . . consensus All-Americans were Howard Twilley, E, 1965; Jerry Ostroski, OL, 1991 . . . Academic All-Americans were Howard Twilley, E, 1964-65; and Mack Lancaster, DT, 1974.

WILLIAM & MARY *(Indians, Tribe; Green, Gold and Silver)*

NOTABLE TEAMS

1923 (7–3) *Won:* Norfolk Fire Dept. 21–0, Guilford 74–0 (1st meeting), Trinity (Duke) 21–0, Randolph-Macon 27–0, Hampden-Sydney 20–0, Delaware 14–0 (1st meeting since 1915), Richmond 27–6. *Lost:* Navy 39–10 (1st meeting), Syracuse 63–6, Roanoke 9–7. *Noteworthy:* 1st year under J.W. Tasker.

1924 (6–2–1) *Won:* Lenoir-Rhyne 27–0, Randolph-Macon 27–7, Trinity (Duke) 21–3, King 27–0, Albright 27–0, Richmond 20–6. *Lost:* Navy 14–7, Syracuse 24–7 in successive early games. *Tied:* Roanoke 7–7.

1926 (7–3) *Won:* Randolph-Macon 35–0, Loyola (Md.) 19–0, George Washington 14–0 (1st meeting since 1921), Lynchburg 48–0, Wake Forest 13–6, Richmond 14–0. *Lost:* Syracuse 35–0, Harvard 27–7, Columbia 13–10. *Noteworthy:* beat Chattanooga 9–6 in postseason game.

1929 (8–2) *Won:* St. Johns 19–0, Emory & Henry 7–6, Bridgewater 59–0, George Washington 51–6, Roanoke 19–6, Catholic U. 36–13, Richmond 25–0,

Hampden-Sydney 20–6. *Lost:* Navy 15–0, Virginia Tech 25–14 (1st meeting since 1922).

1930 (7–2–1) *Won:* Guilford 24–0, Wofford 19–0, Bridgewater 81–0, Emory & Henry 27–0, Roanoke 39–0, Richmond 19–0, Hampden-Sydney 13–0. *Lost:* Navy 19–6, Virginia Tech 7–6. *Tied:* Harvard 13–13. *Star:* Red Maxey (99 pts)

1932 (8–4) *Won:* Roanoke 6–0, Randolph-Macon 27–13, Navy 6–0 (1st in 7-game series begun in 1923), Guilford 47–0, Washington & Lee 7–0, Bridgewater 77–0, Virginia Military Institute (VMI) 20–7 (1st meeting since 1919, 1st win in 12-game series dating to 1905), Emory & Henry 18–6. *Lost:* Virginia Tech 7–0, Army 33–0, George Washington 12–6 (1st to Colonials in 5 games since 1897), Richmond 18–7.

1939 (6–2–1) *Won:* Guilford 31–6, Newport News Apprentice 39–6, Hampden-Sydney 26–0, Randolph-Macon 19–6, Washington & Lee 18–14, Richmond 7–0. *Lost:* Navy 31–6, Virginia 26–6 (1st score against Cavaliers in 11-game series dating to 1908). *Tied:* Virginia Tech 6–6. *Noteworthy:* 1st year under Carl Voyles.

1940 (6–2–1) *Won:* Newport News Apprentice 42–0, Virginia Tech 20–13, Hampden-Sydney 41–0, Virginia 13–6 (1st in 12-game series dating to 1908), Randolph-Macon 46–6, Richmond 16–0. *Lost:* N.C. State 16–0 (1st meeting since 1920), Navy 19–7 in 1st 2 games. *Tied:* VMI 0–0.

1941 (8–2) *Won:* Newport News Apprentice 53–0, Randolph-Macon 57–7, Virginia Tech 16–7, Hampden-Sydney 28–0, George Washington 48–0 (1st meeting since 1932), Dartmouth 3–0, VMI 21–0, Richmond 33–3. *Lost:* Navy 7–0, N.C. State 13–0. *Stars:* G Buster Ramsey, B Harvey Johnson.

1942 (9–1–1) *Won:* Hampden-Sydney 27–0, Navy 3–0 (1st over Midshipmen since 1932), Virginia Tech 21–7, George Washington 61–0, Dartmouth 35–14, Randolph-Macon 40–0, VMI 27–6, Richmond 10–0, Oklahoma 14–7. *Lost:* North Carolina Pre-Flight 14–0. *Tied:* Harvard 7–7. *Stars:* Johnson, Ramsey, E Glenn Know, T Marvin Bass. *Noteworthy:* Voyles' last team won 1st SC title.

1943 No team, due to W.W. II.

1946 (8–2) *Won:* Ft. McClelland 61–0, The Citadel 51–12 (1st meeting), Virginia Tech 49–0, Washington & Lee 34–18 (1st meeting since 1939), VMI 41–0, Maryland 41–7, George Washington 20–0, Richmond 40–0. *Lost:* Miami (Fla.) 13–3, North Carolina 21–7. *Stars:* G Knox Ramsey, E Bob

FB Jack Cloud, 1946–49

Steckroth, frosh FB Jack Cloud (66 pts), soph TB Tommy Korczowski.

1947 (9–2) *Won:* Davidson 21–0 (1st meeting since 1933), The Citadel 56–7, Virginia Tech 21–7, Boston U. 47–13 (1st meeting), Wake Forest 21–0 (1st meeting since 1928), VMI 28–20, Washington & Lee 45–6, Bowling Green 20–0, Richmond 35–0. *Lost:* North Carolina 13–7. *Stars:* Cloud (17 TDs), Steckroth, Ramsey, C Tommy Thompson, Jack Bruce (nation's leader with 9 int). *Noteworthy:* Won 2nd SC title. Made 1st bowl appearance, losing to Arkansas 21–19 in Dixie Bowl at Birmingham, Ala.; Cloud scored 2 TDs and Stan Magdziak passed 6 yds to Henry Bland for other Tribe TD.

1948 (7–2–2) *Won:* Davidson 14–6, VMI 31–0, Virginia Tech 30–0, Richmond 14–6, N.C. State 26–6 (1st in 8-game series dating to 1906), Arkansas 9–0. *Lost:* Wake Forest 21–12, St. Bonaventure 7–6. *Tied:* unbeaten North Carolina 7–7, Boston College 14–14. *Stars:* Cloud, Thompson. *Noteworthy:* beat Oklahoma A&M 20–0 in Delta Bowl at Memphis, Tenn.; Korczowski passed for 2 TDs (12 yds to Lou Hoitsma and 22 yds to Bruce), and T Lou Creekmur scored on 70-yd pass int return.

1951 (7–3) *Won:* Boston U. 34–25, Wake Forest 7–6, N.C. State 35–28, Richmond 20–14, Pennsylvania 20–12, Virginia Tech 28–7 (10th straight over Gobblers), Duke 14–13. *Lost:* Oklahoma 49–7, VMI 20–7, Virginia 46–0. *Stars:* B Ed Mioduszewski, G Sam Lupo, soph T George Parazzo. *Noteworthy:* only year under Marvin Bass.

1986 (9–3) *Won:* Colgate 42–21, VMI 37–22, Bucknell 30–13, Harvard 24–0, Lehigh 44–34, Delaware 24–18, Virginia 41–37 (1st meeting since 1976), Princeton 32–14, Richmond 21–14. *Lost:* James Madison 42–33, Holy Cross 31–7. *Stars:* QB Ken Lambiotte (2,475 yds and 22 TDs pass), TB Michael Clemons (1,065 yds and 10 TDs rush, 72 pass rec for 516 yds and 6 TDs, 2,334 all-purpose yds), FLs Harry Mehre (871 yds pass rec) and Dave Szydlik (56 pass rec for 769 yds), OT Archie Harris, frosh K/P Steve Christie (12 FGs, 72 pts, 40.6-yd punting avg), LB Dave Pocta. *Noteworthy:* lost rematch to Delaware 51–17 in NCAA Division I-AA playoffs.

1989 (8–3–1) *Won:* Colgate 17–13, VMI 24–17, Delaware 27–24, Boston U. 13–10 (1st meeting since 1984), Lehigh 55–39, East Tennessee St. 34–28, James Madison 24–21, Richmond 22–10. *Lost:* Virginia 24–12, Villanova 20–17. *Tied:* Princeton 31–31. *Stars:* QB Craig Argo (1,858 yds and 11 TDs pass), TB Alan Williams (43 pass rec for 359 yds), WRs Ray Kingsfield (41 pass rec for 614 yds), Mark Compher (21 pass rec for 401 yds) and Chris Hogarth (18 pass rec for 312 yds), soph RB Robert Green (36 pass rec for 277 yds, 618 yds and 5 TDs rush), TE Matt Shiffler (22 pass rec for 277 yds), FB Tyrone Shelton (944 yds and 7 TDs rush), Christie (21 FGs, 90 pts, 40-yd punting avg), soph LB Mark Hughes. *Noteworthy:* lost to Furman 24–10 in Division I-AA playoffs.

1990 (10–3) *Won:* Villanova 37–14 (1st over Wildcats in 6 games since 1972), Connecticut 24–7, Delaware 22–12, VMI 59–47, Bucknell 45–17, Lehigh 38–17, Furman 38–28, James Madison 31–21,

TB Michael Clemons, 1983–86

Richmond 31–10. *Lost:* The Citadel 34–31 (1st meeting since 1978), Virginia 63–35. *Stars:* Green (1,408 yds and 19 TDs rush, 42 pass rec for 324 yds), Shelton (1,082 yds rush, 23 pass rec for 268 yds), Compher (64 pass rec for 1,180 yds and 8 TDs), Kingsfield (44 pass rec for 609 yds and 5 TDs), QB Chris Hakel (3,414 yds and 22 TDs pass, 11 TDs rush), Michael Locke (27 pass rec for 359 yds and 7 TDs), Williams (6 TDs), OG Reggie White, K Dan Mueller (14 FGs, 89 pts), DE Mark Willson, LB Brad Uhl, Hughes, DB Palmer Scarritt. *Noteworthy:* beat Massachusetts 38–0 and lost to Central Florida 52–38 in Division I-AA playoffs.

1992 (9–2) *Won:* VMI 21–16, Boston U. 31–21, Harvard 36–16, Brown 51–6, Pennsylvania 21–19, Towson St. 43–15, Colgate 44–26, Lehigh 26–13, Richmond 34–19. *Lost:* Virginia 33–7, James Madison 21–14 in successive late games. *Stars:* QB Shawn Knight (1,892 yds and 11 TDs pass, 244 yds and 6 TDs rush), WRs Corey Ludwig (33 pass rec for 506 yds) and Michael Tomlin (22 pass rec for 560 yds), TE Joe Person (18 pass rec for 333 yds), frosh RBs Derek Fitzgerald (835 yds and 11 TDs rush, 23 pass rec for 244 yds) and Troy Keen (6 TDs rush), K Chris Dawson (10 FGs, 66 pts), DE Alex Utecht, LBs Adrian Rich, Keith Booker and soph Jason Miller, Scarritt, DB Marc Richards.

BOWL RECORD (1–2)

Regular Season	Bowl	Score	Opponent	Record
1947 (9–1)	Dixie	19–21	Arkansas	(5–4–1)
1948 (6–2–2)	Delta	20–0	Oklahoma State	(6–3)
1970 (5–6)	Tangerine	12–40	Toledo	(11–0)

CONFERENCE TITLES

Southern—1942, 1947, 1970.

TOP 20 AP AND UPI RANKING

1942	14	1947	14	1948	17

MAJOR RIVALS

William & Mary has played at least 10 games with Boston U. 6–4–1, The Citadel 18–7, Davidson 9–4–1, Delaware 6–10, East Carolina 4–11–1, Furman 6–6, George Washington 12–9–2, Guilford 10–0, Hampden-Sydney 17–22, James Madison 9–5, Navy 6–35–1, N.C. State 8–10, North Carolina 0–11–2, Randolph-Macon 22–19–1, Richmond 50–47–5, Roanoke 11–3–1, Rutgers 4–6, Villanova 6–4–1, VMI 35–33–2, Virginia 5–24–1, Virginia Tech 18–39–4, Wake Forest 9–10–1, Washington & Lee 4–6–1, West Virginia 0–15–1. Yankee Conference foes met fewer than 10 times: Connecticut 3–0, Maine 0–0, Massachusetts 1–0, New Hampshire 1–0, Rhode Island 0–0.

COACHES

Dean of William & Mary coaches is Jimmye Laycock with record of 82–64–2 for 1980–92 with 3 Division I-AA playoff teams. Other top records for at least 3 years were by J.W. Tasker, 31–17–2 for 1923–27; Branch Bocock, 26–20–3 for 1928–30 and 1936–37; John Kellison, 24–24–2 for 1931–34 and 1938; Carl M. Voyles, 29–7–3 for 1939–42 with 1 SC title; Rube McCray, 44–21–3 for 1944–50 with 1 SC title and 2 bowl teams; and Lou Holtz, 13–20 for 1969–71 with 1 SC title and 1 bowl team.

BOWL SUMMARY

Delta 1–0; Dixie 0–1; Tangerine 0–1.

MISCELLANEA

First game was loss to Norfolk YMCA 16–0 in 1893 . . . 1st win was over Capital City A.C. 6–4 in 1893 . . . 1st win over college foe was over Randolph-Macon 5–0 in 1898 . . . highest score was over Bridgewater 95–0 in 1931 . . . highest since W.W. II was over Ft. McClelland 61–0 in 1946 (though beat Japan All-Stars 73–3 in Epson Ivy Bowl in 1988) . . . highest score against college foe since W.W. II was over VMI 59–47 in 1990 . . . biggest margin over college foe since W.W. II was over Virginia Tech 54–0 in 1950 . . . worst defeat was by Delaware 93–0 in 1915 . . . worst defeats since W.W. II were by Cincinnati 57–7 in 1953 and West Virginia 56–6 in 1958 . . . highest against since W.W. II was by Virginia 63–35 in 1990 . . . longest unbeaten strings of 9, in 1942 ended by North Carolina Pre-Flight 14–0 and in 1985–86 by James Madison 42–33 . . . longest winless string of 15 in 1955–57 broken with win over Virginia Tech 13–7 . . . William & Mary has had no consensus All-Americans in Division I-A; Division I-AA All-Americans were Mario Shaffer, OL, 1983; Michael Clemons, RB, 1986; and Steve Christie, P, 1989 . . . Academic All-Americans were John Gerdelman, RB, 1974; Ken Smith, DB, 1975, 1977; Robert Musculus, TE, 1978; Mark Kelso, DB, 1984; Chris Gessner, DB, 1988; and Jeff Nielsen, LB, 1990.

PACIFIC-10 CONFERENCE

The Pacific-10 Conference has its roots in the formation of the original Pacific Coast Conference (PCC) on December 2, 1915, when the universities of California, Oregon, Oregon State, and Washington banded together to form a league in a meeting at the Oregon Hotel in Portland. Football competition began in the autumn of 1916, with Washington State University added in 1917, Stanford University in 1918, the universities of Idaho and Southern California (USC) in 1922, the University of Montana in 1924, and the University of California at Los Angeles (UCLA) in 1928. Montana dropped out of the conference in 1950, and Idaho did not rejoin a similar league formed after the dissolution of the PCC in 1959. In that year the Athletic Association of Western Universities (AAWU) was formed, involving California, Southern California, Stanford, UCLA, and Washington. The new league largely resumed the shape of the old PCC with the additions of Washington State in 1962 and Oregon and Oregon State in 1964. In 1968 the name Pacific-8 was adopted for the new league.

Membership was stable for a decade until the universities of Arizona and Arizona State were admitted on July 1, 1978. The conference name was changed to Pacific-10 at that time.

FACTS AND ODDITIES ON PACIFIC-10 MEMBERS

Pacific Coast teams have won or shared 13 national titles, with USC winning 8 times. California was the first PCC team to win a national championship, taking the 1920 crown by outscoring regular-season opponents 482–14 while compiling an 8–0 record, then beating undefeated Ohio State 28–0 in the Rose Bowl. The next PCC team to win the title was Stanford, which got a share of the national crown in 1926 with a 10–0 record followed by a 7–7 tie with unbeaten national cochamp Alabama in the Rose Bowl. USC got a share of its first national crown in 1928, tying California 0–0 but beating nine other foes. The Trojans won the title again in 1931 with a 9–1 regular-season record (the loss was to St. Mary's 13–7 in the opener), topped by a 21–12 win over 11–0 Tulane in the Rose Bowl.

The 1932 Trojans finished 9–0 to repeat as national champion, then beat undefeated Pittsburgh 35–0 in the Rose Bowl.

California got a share of its second national title in 1937, finishing 9–0–1 (the tie was with Washington 0–0) and then beating undefeated Alabama 13–0 for the Tide's first Rose Bowl loss in five games. PCC teams were shut out of the national title picture for the next 16 years, but UCLA brought a share of the crown back west in 1954 with a 9–0 record. Nearly a decade later, in 1962, USC won its fourth national title with a 10–0 record followed by a wild 42–37 win over Wisconsin in the Rose Bowl. The Trojans were back with another title in 1967, finishing 9–1 (the loss was to Oregon State 3–0) and then beating Indiana 14–3 in the Rose Bowl.

In 1972 USC put together one of the stronger teams in college football history, outscoring regular-season foes 425–117 in an 11–0 season and then beating Ohio State 42–17 in the Rose Bowl. That gave the Trojans their sixth national crown. They were back in 1974 with a share of the title, losing to Arkansas 22–7 in the season opener and tying California 15–15, but beating nine other foes before edging Ohio State 18–17 in the Rose Bowl. USC got a share of its eighth national title in 1978 with an 11–1 record (losing a mid-season game to Arizona State 20–7) before beating Michigan 17–10 in the Rose Bowl.

In 1991 Washington became the first Pacific Coast team to win a national crown in more than a dozen years. The Huskies finished 11–0, then beat Michigan 34–14 in the Rose Bowl to clinch a share of their first national title.

Seven Pacific Coast players, four of them from USC, have won the Heisman Trophy. Oregon State QB Terry Baker was the league's first Heisman winner in 1962. He was followed by USC HB Mike Garrett, 1965; UCLA QB Gary Beban, 1967; USC HB O. J. Simpson, 1968; Stanford QB Jim Plunkett, 1970; USC HB Charles White, 1979; and USC HB Marcus Allen, 1981. The Maxwell Award has gone to Pacific Coast players six times, with USC players taking half. That award went to Baker in 1962, Beban in 1967, Simpson in 1968, Plunkett in 1970, White in 1979, and Allen in 1981.

Only two Pacific Coast players have won the Outland Trophy—OT Ron Yary of USC in 1967 and DT Steve Emtman of Washington in 1991. And only two have won the Lombardi Award—OG Brad Budde of USC in 1979 and Emtman in 1991.

National Coach of the Year awards have gone to Pacific Coast coaches eight times. Clark Shaughnessy of Stanford was the first PCC coach to win the award, taking it in 1940. The next also was a Stanford coach, Chuck Taylor, in 1951. Henry "Red" Sanders of UCLA won in 1954; John McKay of USC won in 1962 and 1972; Tommy Prothro of UCLA won the American Football Coaches Association (AFCA) version of the award in 1965; and Don James of Washington won the AFCA share in 1977 and both the AFCA and the Football Writers Association of America

(FWAA) awards in 1991. In addition, Frank Kush of Arizona State won the AFCA share in 1975 before the Sun Devils joined the Pacific Conference.

One of only four coaches to win 300 or more games in major college football was Glenn "Pop" Warner (313–106–32 at 6 schools between 1895 and 1938), who coached Stanford to a record of 71–17–8 for 1924–1932 with three Rose Bowl teams and a national champion. Credited with inventing both the single-wing and double-wing systems of offense that dominated football for nearly half a century, Warner became famous as coach of tiny Carlisle Indian School and Pittsburgh before moving to Stanford.

Coaches who won at least 100 games at Pacific Coast schools were Howard Jones, Kush, James, and Terry Donahue.

Jones, who had an overall record of 194–64–21 at 6 schools between 1908 and 1940, was 121–36–13 at USC in 1925–1940 with 7 PCC titles, 5 Rose Bowl teams, 3 unbeaten teams, and 3 national champions. Kush was 176–54–1 at Arizona State in 1958–1979 with 9 conference titles, 7 bowl teams (6 winners), and 2 unbeaten teams. James, through 1992, was 153–57–2 at Washington since 1975 with 6 conference titles, 14 bowl teams (10 winners), and one unbeaten national champion. Donahue, through 1992, was 131–59–8 at UCLA since 1976 with 4 Pacific-10 titles and 11 bowl teams (8 winners).

Only a handful of players have made consensus All-America three times in their college careers, but the list includes a pair of UCLA teammates, LB Jerry Robinson in 1976–1978 and DB Kenny Easley in 1978–1980. No West Coast player made consensus All-America until 1921, when California E Brick Muller and T Dan McMillan both were selected.

Orenthal James Simpson had to wear leg braces as a child as the result of a calcium deficiency and was called "Pencil Legs" before becoming better known to football fans as "O. J." He led the nation in rushing in both 1967 and 1968 and, with a career game average of 164.4 yds, still ranks among college football's all-time leaders. In two years at USC, he ran for 3,124 yds, averaging 5 yds a carry, and added 299 yds in two Rose Bowl games.

Washington won 9 of its 10 games in 1959 and then trounced Wisconsin 44–8 in the Rose Bowl—the first time in seven years the Pacific Coast team had defeated the Big 10 representative in the annual bowl matchup. The quarterback who directed the effective Washington attack that season (and who intercepted six passes on defense as well) was Bob Schloredt—who had only one eye.

Washington recorded the longest unbeaten string in college football history, of 63 games (including 4 ties), but most of the string was accomplished before the PCC was formed. It started in the 1907 finale with a tie with Idaho 0–0 and finally was broken by California 27–0 in the second game of 1917. Gil Dobie was coach of the Huskies for most of that stretch, compiling a record of 58–0–3 for 1908–1916.

UCLA set a record by scoring in 245 consecutive games in 1971–1992. The Bruins' streak began during a loss to Oregon State 34–17 in the fourth game of the 1971 season and ended with a loss to Arizona State 20–0 in the seventh game of 1992. During the scoring string, the Bruins' record was 162–71–12.

Among the most-played games in the nation are the Oregon–Oregon St. and California–Stanford series. Through 1992 Oregon led the former 47–39–10 and Stanford led the latter 47–37–11.

USC won its first nine postseason games—eight in the Rose Bowl—before losing to unbeaten Alabama 34–14 in the 1946 Rose Bowl game. During that streak USC beat undefeated teams seven straight times.

In the early 1970s, Stanford pulled off successive Rose Bowl upsets under two excellent passing quarterbacks. In the 1971 contest, Heisman Trophy– and Maxwell Award–winner Jim Plunkett passed for 265 yds, completing 20 of 30, to lead the Indians to a 27–17 shocker over unbeaten Ohio State. The following year Don Bunce completed 24 of 44 passes for 290 yds as Stanford stunned unbeaten Michigan 13–12.

Pacific-10 schools have some of the more unusual nicknames on the college football scene, such as the Arizona State Sun Devils, Oregon Ducks, Oregon State Beavers, USC Trojans, UCLA Bruins, and Washington Huskies. And what of the Stanford Cardinal, adopted when Indians was dropped as the nickname in 1972 as a result of complaints that the Indian symbol used as an athletic mascot was offensive to Native Americans? Former Stanford QB Jim Plunkett (who himself has an American Indian heritage) said he would always be proud to be a Stanford Indian. "What is a Cardinal?" he said. "Is it a bird, color, or religious figure?" Among more familiar nicknames are the Arizona Wildcats, California Golden Bears, and Washington State Cougars.

California's Golden Bear was adopted as a nickname in 1895, when a blue silk banner emblazoned with a golden grizzly bear was made to accompany the school's track and field team on an eight-meet tour of the Midwest and East. The flag inspired "The Golden Bear" song, written that year by Professor Charles Mills Gayley. USC teams were called Methodists or Wesleyans in the early years, but in 1912 athletic director Warren Bovard asked *Los Angeles Times* sports editor Owen Bird to select a more appropriate nickname. Bird chose Trojans because USC at the time showed a splendid fighting spirit while regularly facing bigger and better-equipped squads.

Arizona's nickname resulted from a gallant effort in a 14–0 loss at Occidental in 1914. Student correspondent Bill Henry (a senior at Occidental) wrote in a story for the *Los Angeles Times* that the Arizona men had "showed the fight of Wildcats." The Arizona student body liked the compliment so much that a resolution was adopted that henceforth Arizona teams would be called Wildcats. Henry later became a columnist for the *Los Angeles Times* and in 1964 was honored by the University of Arizona as "Father of the Arizona Wildcats."

Arizona State teams were known as Bulldogs until the student newspaper in the fall of 1946 ran frequent appeals to change the nickname to Sun Devils (similar to the region's dust devils). On November 8 of that year, the student body voted 819–196 to make the change. Oregon at one time carried the unique nickname Webfoots but gradually switched to the more conventional, though still unusual, nickname of Ducks.

California's official colors were adopted when the university was established in 1868, 14 years before the beginning of intercollegiate competition at Berkeley. Most of the university's founders were Yale graduates, and they selected Yale blue along with gold to represent the "Golden State." Washington's colors were adopted in 1892 by a student assembly vote. Purple and gold won over red, white, and blue when one faction argued that the national colors should not be degraded by everyday use.

Arizona's school colors were sage green and silver until football was established in 1899. The student manager, Quintus J. Anderson, requested that the school colors be changed that year when he made a good deal with a local merchant for game sweaters of solid blue with red trim. It has been cardinal red and navy blue ever since.

ALL-TIME PACIFIC-10 CONFERENCE CHAMPIONS
PACIFIC COAST CONFERENCE

Annual Champion	Record	Regular Season and Bowl	
1916 Washington	3–0–1	6–0–1	
1917 Washington St.	3–0	6–0	
1918 California	2–0	7–2	
1919 Oregon	2–1	5–1–3	
Washington	2–1	5–1	
1920 California	3–0	8–0	Rose (W)
1921 California	4–0	8–0–1	Rose (T)
1922 California	4–0	9–0	
1923 California	5–0	9–0–1	
1924 Stanford	3–0–1	7–0–1	Rose (L)
1925 Washington	5–0	10–0–1	Rose (L)
1926 Stanford	4–0	10–0	Rose (T)
1927 USC	4–0–1	8–1–1	
Stanford	4–0–1	7–2–1	Rose (W)
1928 USC	4–0–1	9–0–1	
1929 USC	6–1	9–2	Rose (W)
1930 Washington St.	6–0	9–0	Rose (L)
1931 USC	7–0	9–1	Rose (W)
1932 USC	6–0	9–0	Rose (W)
1933 Oregon	4–1	9–1	
Stanford	4–1	8–1–1	Rose (L)
1934 Stanford	5–0	9–0–1	Rose (L)
1935 California	4–1	9–1	
Stanford	4–1	7–1	Rose (W)
UCLA	4–1	8–2	

(continued)

PACIFIC COAST CONFERENCE (continued)

Annual Champion	Record	Regular Season and Bowl	
1936 Washington	7–0–1	7–1–1	Rose (L)
1937 California	6–0–1	9–0–1	Rose (W)
1938 California	6–1	10–1	
USC	6–1	8–2	Rose (W)
1939 USC	5–0–2	7–0–2	Rose (W)
UCLA	5–0–3	6–0–4	
1940 Stanford	7–0	9–0	Rose (W)
1941 Oregon St.	7–2	7–2	Rose (W)
1942 UCLA	6–1	7–3	Rose (L)
1943 USC	5–0	7–2	Rose (W)
1944 USC	3–0–2	7–0–2	Rose (W)
1945 USC	5–1	7–3	Rose (L)
1946 UCLA	7–0	10–0	Rose (L)
1947 USC	6–0	7–1–1	Rose (L)
1948 California	6–0	10–0	Rose (L)
Oregon	7–0	9–1	Cotton (L)
1949 California	7–0	10–0	Rose (L)
1950 California	5–0–1	9–0–1	Rose (L)
1951 Stanford	6–1	9–1	Rose (L)
1952 USC	6–0	9–1	Rose (W)
1953 UCLA	6–1	8–1	Rose (L)
1954 UCLA	6–0	9–0	
1955 UCLA	6–0	9–1	Rose (L)
1956 Oregon St.	6–1–1	7–2–1	Rose (L)
1957 Oregon	6–2	7–3	Rose (L)
Oregon St.	6–2	8–2	
1958 California	6–1	7–3	Rose (L)

ASSOCIATION OF WESTERN UNIVERSITIES

1959 USC	3–1	8–2	
UCLA	3–1	5–4–1	
Washington	3–1	9–1	Rose (W)
1960 Washington	4–0	9–1	Rose (W)
1961 UCLA	3–1	7–3	Rose (L)
1962 USC	4–0	10–0	Rose (W)
1963 Washington	4–1	6–4	Rose (L)
1964 Oregon St.	3–1	8–2	Rose (L)
USC	3–1	7–3	
1965 UCLA	4–0	7–2–1	Rose (W)
1966 USC	4–1	7–3	Rose (L)
1967 USC	6–1	9–1	Rose (W)

PACIFIC-8

1968 USC	6–0	9–0–1	Rose (L)
1969 USC	6–0	9–0–1	Rose (W)
1970 Stanford	6–1	8–3	Rose (W)
1971 Stanford	6–1	8–3	Rose (W)

(continued)

PACIFIC COAST CONFERENCE *(continued)*

Annual Champion	Record	Regular Season and Bowl	
1972 USC	7–0	11–0	Rose (W)
1973 USC	7–0	9–1–1	Rose (L)
1974 USC	6–0–1	9–1–1	Rose (W)
1975 California	6–1	8–3	
UCLA	6–1	8–2–1	Rose (W)
1976 USC	7–0	10–1	Rose (W)
1977 Washington	6–1	7–4	Rose (W)

PACIFIC-10

1978 USC	6–1	11–1	Rose (W)
1979 USC	6–0–1	10–0–1	Rose (W)
1980 Washington	6–1	9–2	Rose (L)
1981 Washington	6–2	9–2	Rose (W)
1982 UCLA	5–1–1	9–1–1	Rose (W)
1983 UCLA	6–1–1	6–4–1	Rose (W)
1984 USC	7–1	8–3	Rose (W)
1985 UCLA	6–2	8–2–1	Rose (W)
1986 Arizona St.	5–1–1	9–1–1	Rose (W)
1987 USC	7–1	8–3	Rose (L)
UCLA	7–1	9–2	Aloha (W)
1988 USC	8–0	9–2	Rose (L)
1989 USC	6–0–1	8–2–1	Rose (W)
1990 Washington	7–1	9–2	Rose (W)
1991 Washington	8–0	11–0	Rose (W)
1992 Stanford	6–2	9–3	Blockbuster (W)
Washington	6–2	9–2	Rose (L)

ARIZONA *(Wildcats; Cardinal and Navy)*

Notable Teams

1901 (4–1)   *Won:* Tucson Indian School 22–0, 47–6, 40–0, Phoenix Indian School 6–0.   *Lost:* Phoenix Indian School 13–0.

1902 (5–0)   *Won:* Tucson Indian School 17–0, 43–0, Fort Grant 28–0, Arizona St. 12–0, Ft. Huachuca 34–0.   *Noteworthy:* blanked foes 134–0 in 1st unbeaten season.

1903   No varsity football.

1908 (5–0)   *Won:* Tucson Indians 27–0, 43–0, 36–0, 20–0, New Mexico 10–5 (1st meeting).   *Noteworthy:* 1st varsity team since 1905.

1910 (5–0)   *Won:* Tucson H.S. 21–0, 18–6, El Paso Military 29–0, New Mexico St. 18–2, New Mexico 1–0 (forfeit).

1911 (3–1–1)   *Won:* New Mexico 6–0, El Paso Military 5–0, Tucson H.S. 5–0.   *Lost:* New Mexico St. 3–0.   *Tied:* Tucson H.S. 0–0.

1914 (4–1)   *Won:* Douglas YMCA 21–0, Arizona St. 34–0 (1st meeting since 1902), New Mexico St. 10–0, Pomona 7–6 (1st homecoming).   *Lost:* Occidental 14–0.   *Noteworthy:* 1st year under J.F. "Pop" McKale.

1919 (7–1)   *Won:* Arizona St. 59–0, Phoenix Indians 60–0, Soldiers 20–0, New Mexico St. 33–0, Whittier 1–0 (forfeit), Texas–El Paso 46–0, Occidental 27–0.   *Lost:* Pomona 19–7.   *Noteworthy:* resumed play after 1-year layoff during W.W. I.

1920 (6–1)   *Won:* Phoenix Indians 51–20, Camp Harry Jones 167–0, Texas–El Paso 60–7, New Mexico St. 41–0, New Mexico 28–7, Redlands 34–0.   *Lost:* Pomona 31–0.

1921 (7–2)   *Won:* Bisbee Legion 84–13, Phoenix Indians 75–0, Texas–El Paso 74–0, New Mexico St. 31–0, New Mexico 24–0, New Mexico Military J.C. 110–0, Whittier 7–0.   *Lost:* Texas A&M 17–13.   *Noteworthy:* made 1st postseason appearance, losing to Centre 38–0 in San Diego East-West Christmas Classic.

1926 (5–1–1)   *Won:* Phoenix J.C. 54–0, Arizona St. 35–0, New Mexico St. 7–0, Whittier 16–6, New Mexico 21–0 in 1st 5 games.   *Lost:* Occidental 9–7 (1st meeting since 1919).   *Tied:* Colorado St. 3–3 (1st meeting).

1928 (5–1–2)   *Won:* Pomona 13–6 (1st meeting since 1920), Arizona St. 39–0, Texas–El Paso 12–6, New Mexico St. 40–0, Whittier 28–7.   *Lost:* un-beaten national cochamp USC 78–7.   *Tied:* UCLA 7–7, New Mexico 6–6.

1929 (7–1)   *Won:* Occidental 16–7, Cal Tech 35–0 (1st game in Arizona Stadium), Texas–El Paso 19–0, New Mexico St. 28–0, Arizona St. 26–0, New Mexico 6–0, Whittier 40–0.   *Lost:* Pomona 15–12.

1930 (6–1–1)   *Won:* Cal Tech 26–12, Arizona St. 6–0, Occidental 21–0, Pomona 20–0, New Mexico 33–0, Colorado St. 16–0.   *Lost:* Rice 21–0.   *Tied:* Texas–El Paso 0–0.   *Noteworthy:* McKale's last team.

1934 (7–2–1)   *Won:* San Diego St. 7–0, Colorado St. 7–3, Whittier 14–7, New Mexico 14–6, Oklahoma City U. 26–6, Arizona St. 32–6, Pacific 31–7.   *Lost:* Loyola (Calif.) 6–0, Texas Tech 13–7.   *Tied:* New Mexico St. 0–0.   *Stars:* QB Ted Bland, E Bud Robinson, soph T Earle Nolan.

1935 (7–2)   *Won:* Arizona St. 26–0, Whittier 45–0, New Mexico St. 9–6, Oklahoma City U. 27–0, Texas Tech 7–6, New Mexico 38–6, Drake 53–0.   *Lost:* Centenary 14–7, Loyola (Calif.) 13–6 in early games.   *Stars:* Bland, B Ken Knox, E Roy Wallace, T Harry Clayton, G Joe Mullen, C Charles Cochran.   *Noteworthy:* won 1st Border Conference title.

1937 (8–2)   *Won:* Arizona St. 20–6, Oklahoma St. 22–13, New Mexico St. 27–12, Loyola (Calif.) 13–6, New Mexico 23–0, Kansas 9–7, Colorado St. 47–0, Oregon 20–6 (1st meeting).   *Lost:* Texas Tech 20–0, Centenary 18–13 in successive early games.   *Stars:* FB Walter Nielsen, B Bronko Smilanich, E Harry Parker, T George Rogers, C Tom Greenfield.   *Noteworthy:* last year under "Tex" Oliver.

1940 (7–2)   *Won:* Northern Arizona 41–0, New Mexico St. 41–0, Centenary 29–6, Oklahoma St. 24–0, Texas–El Paso 20–13, Loyola (Calif.) 20–13, Marquette 17–14.   *Lost:* Utah 24–0, New Mexico 13–12.   *Stars:* B John Black, E Henry Stanton, soph T Jack Irish, G Bill Flake, Dick Taylor (6 int).

1941 (7–3)   *Won:* New Mexico St. 47–0, Nevada-Reno 26–7, New Mexico 31–6, Arizona St. 20–7, Texas–El Paso 33–14, Northern Arizona 41–0, Kansas St. 28–21 (1st meeting).   *Lost:* unbeaten Notre Dame 38–7, Oklahoma St. 41–14, unbeaten Utah 12–6.   *Stars:* Stanton (nation's leader with 50 pass rec for 820 yds), Irish, G Stan Petropolis, P Emil Banjaucic (40.5-yd avg).   *Noteworthy:* led nation in pass and got share of 3rd and last Border Conference crown.

1945 (5–0)   *Won:* Northern Arizona 52–6, San Diego St. 46–0, 28–0 (1st meetings since 1934),

Williams Field 30–0, Cal Poly-SLO 37–6. *Noteworthy:* resumed competition after 2-year layoff during W.W. II with 1st unbeaten season since 1910.

1954 (7–3) *Won:* New Mexico St. 58–0, Utah 54–20, Idaho 35–13, New Mexico 41–7, West Texas St. 48–12, Arizona St. 54–14, Wyoming 42–40 (1st meeting since 1947). *Lost:* Colorado 40–18, Texas Tech 28–14, Texas–El Paso 41–21. *Stars:* soph TB Art Luppino (nation's leader with 2,193 all-purpose yds, 1,359 yds rush, 166 pts and in kickoff returns with 31.6-yd avg), T Buddy Lewis, frosh G Ed Brown, C Paul Hatcher.

1960 (7–3) *Won:* Wyoming 21–19, New Mexico 26–14, West Texas St. 21–14, Idaho 32–3, Texas–El Paso 28–14, Kansas St. 35–16, Arizona St. 35–7 (1st over Sun Devils since 1955). *Lost:* Utah 13–3, Colorado 35–19, Tulsa 17–16. *Stars:* Bs Bobby Lee Thompson (732 yds rush), Joe Hernandez (12 TDs).

1961 (8–1–1) *Won:* Colorado St. 28–6, Hardin-Simmons 53–7, Oregon 15–6 (1st meeting since 1955), New Mexico 22–21, Wyoming 20–15, Idaho 43–7, Texas–El Paso 48–15, Arizona St. 22–13. *Lost:* West Texas St. 27–23. *Tied:* Nebraska 14–14. *Stars:* Thompson (752 yds rush, 1,575 all-purpose yds, 13 TDs), QB Eddie Wilson (1,294 yds and 10 TDs pass).

1968 (8–3) *Won:* Iowa St. 21–12, New Mexico 19–8, Texas–El Paso 25–0, Brigham Young (BYU) 19–3, Washington St. 28–14, Air Force 14–10, Utah 16–15, Wyoming 14–7. *Lost:* Indiana 16–13, Arizona St. 30–7. *Stars:* DT Tom Nelson, DE Frank Jenkins, DB Rich Moriarty (8 int), Ron Gardin (48 pass rec for 892 yds), OT John Matischak. *Noteworthy:* Darrell Mudra's last team. Lost to Auburn 34–10 in Sun Bowl; scored on 37-yd FG by Steve Hurley and 12-yd pass from Bruce Lee to soph Hal Arnason.

1973 (8–3) *Won:* Colorado St. 31–0, Wyoming 21–7, Indiana 26–10, Iowa 23–20, New Mexico 22–14, Utah 42–21, Texas–El Paso 35–18, BYU 24–10. *Lost:* Texas Tech 31–17, Air Force 27–26, Arizona St. 55–19. *Stars:* soph QB Bruce Hill (1,529 yds pass, 1,915 yds total off), soph FL "T" Bell (47 pass rec for 790 yds), FB Jim Upchurch (1,184 yds rush), HB Willie Hamilton, OT Jim O'Connor, LB Ransom Terrell, DB Roussell Williams, P Mitch Hoopes (43.9-yd avg). *Noteworthy:* got share of 2nd WAC title in 1st year under Jim Young.

1974 (9–2) *Won:* San Diego St. 17–10, Indiana 35–20, New Mexico 15–10, Texas–El Paso 42–13, Utah 41–8, Colorado St. 34–21, Air Force 27–24, Wyoming 21–14, Arizona St. 10–0 (1st over Sun Devils since 1964). *Lost:* Texas Tech 17–8, BYU 37–13 (1st to Cougars since 1969). *Stars:* Hill (1,814 yds and 18 TDs pass, 2,118 yds total off), Bell (53 pass rec for 700 yds, 1,574 all-purpose yds, 11 TDs), SE Scott Piper (46 pass rec for 671 yds), Upchurch (1,004 yds rush), OT Brian Murray, DT Mike Dawson, LB Mark Jacobs, DB Dennis Anderson (7 int), Williams (6 int), Hoopes (41.8-yd punting avg).

1975 (9–2) *Won:* Pacific 16–0, Wyoming 14–0, Northwestern 41–6, Texas–El Paso 36–0, Texas Tech 32–28 (1st over Red Raiders in 5 games since 1959), BYU 36–20, San Diego St. 31–24, Colorado St. 31–9, Utah 38–14. *Lost:* New Mexico 44–34, unbeaten Arizona St. 24–21. *Stars:* Hill (1,747 yds pass, 2,021 yds total off), Bell (1,296 all-purpose yds), Piper (45 pass rec for 718 yds), Murray, K Lee Pistor (15 FGs, 80 pts), Dawson, LB Obra Erby, Anderson (43.4-yd punting avg).

1985 (8–3–1) *Won:* Toledo 23–10, Washington St. 12–7, California 23–17, Southern Methodist (SMU) 28–6, San Jose St. 41–0, Oregon St. 27–6, Oregon 20–8, Arizona St. 16–13. *Lost:* Colorado 14–13 (1st meeting since 1960), Stanford 28–17, UCLA 24–19. *Stars:* DBs Allan Durden (6 int) and soph Chuck Cecil (6 int), LB Byron Evans, QB Alfred Jenkins (1,767 yds pass), K Max Zendejas (22 FGs, 89 pts). *Noteworthy:* tied Georgia 13–13 in Sun Bowl; Jenkins passed for 133 yds, Zendejas kicked 2 FGs (including 52-yarder) and an ex pt, and Martin Rudolph returned pass int 35 yds for TD.

1986 (9–3) *Won:* Houston 37–3, Colorado St. 37–10, Oregon 41–17, Colorado 24–21, Oregon St. 23–12 (10th straight over Beavers), California 33–16, Washington St. 31–6, Arizona St. 34–17. *Lost:* UCLA 32–25, USC 20–13, Stanford 29–24 (in Tokyo). *Stars:* Jenkins (1,573 yds and 10 TDs pass), RB David Adams (1,226 yds rush), soph C Joe Tofflemire, frosh K Gary Coston (21 FGs, 97 pts), Evans, Cecil (6 int). *Noteworthy:* Last year under Larry Smith. Beat North Carolina 30–21 in Aloha Bowl (1st bowl win in 6 tries); Jenkins passed for 187 yds and a TD (to Jon Horton), Adams ran for 81 yds and a TD, Coston had 2 FGs, and Jeff Valder had 52-yd FG.

1989 (8–4) *Won:* Stanford 19–3, Oklahoma 6–3,

Washington 20–17, UCLA 42–7 (1st over Bruins in 5 games since 1983), Washington St. 23–21, Pacific 38–14, Arizona St. 28–10. *Lost:* Texas Tech 24–14, Oregon 16–10 (1st to Ducks in 5 games since 1983), California 29–28, USC 24–3. *Stars:* LBs Chris Singleton and Donnie Salum, DT Anthony Smith, DBs Darryl Lewis (5 int) and Jeff Hammerschmidt, RBs David Eldridge (788 yds and 8 TDs rush) and Reggie McGill (507 yds rush), QB Ron Veal (5 TDs rush), OT Glenn Parker, K Doug Pfaff (14 FGs), P John Nies (41.5-yd avg). *Noteworthy:* beat N.C.

State 17–10 in inaugural Copper Bowl; scored on 37-yd pass from Veal to WR Olatide Ogunfiditimi, 85-yd pass int return by DB Scott Geyer, and FG and 2 ex pts by Coston.

BOWL SUMMARY

Aloha 1–1; Copper 1–0; Fiesta 0–1; John Hancock 0–1; Salad 0–1; East-West Christmas Classic 0–1; Sun 0–1–1.

BOWL RECORD (2–6–1)

Regular Season	Bowl	Score	Opponent	Record
1921 (7–1)	East–West Classic	0–38	Centre	(9–0)
1948 (6–4)	Salad	13–14	Drake	(6–3)
1968 (8–2)	Sun	10–34	Auburn	(6–4)
1979 (6–4–1)	Fiesta	10–16	Pittsburgh	(10–1)
1985 (8–3)	Sun	13–13	Georgia	(7–3–1)
1986 (8–3)	Aloha	30–21	North Carolina	(7–3–1)
1989 (7–4)	Copper	17–10	N.C. State	(7–4)
1990 (7–4)	Aloha	0–28	Syracuse	(6–4–2)
1992 (6–4–1)	John Hancock	15–20	Baylor	(6–5)

CONFERENCE TITLES

Border—1935, 1936, 1941*. **Western Athletic**—1964*, 1973*. **Pacific-10**—None.

TOP 20 AP AND UPI

1975	18–13	1986	11–10

MAJOR RIVALS

Arizona has played at least 10 games with Arizona St. 37–28–1, Brigham Young 10–8–1, California 5–7–2, Colorado 1–12, Colorado St. 13–2–1, Hardin-Simmons 4–6, Idaho 8–2, Marquette 4–6, New Mexico 42–18–3, New Mexico St. 30–5–1, Oregon 10–8, Oregon St. 13–2–1, Pomona 6–4, San Diego St. 6–5, Southern California 3–16, Stanford 7–5, Texas–El Paso 34–11–2, Texas Tech 4–26–2, UCLA 6–10–2, Utah 13–16–2, Washington 3–7–1, Washington St. 13–8, Whittier 9–3, Wyoming 12–10.

COACHES

Dean of Arizona coaches is J.F. "Pop" McKale with record of 80–32–6 for 1914–30 with 1 bowl team. Other top records for at least 3 years were by G.A. "Tex" Oliver, 32–11–4 for 1933–37 with 2 Border Conference titles; Miles W. Casteel, 45–26–3 for 1939–48 with 1 Border Conference title, 1 bowl team, and 1 unbeaten team; Warren Woodson, 26–22–2 for 1952–56; Jim LaRue, 41–37–2 for 1959–66 with 1 WAC title; James C. Young, 31–13 for 1973–76 with 1 WAC title; Larry Smith, 48–28–3 for 1980–86 with 2 bowl teams; and Dick Tomey, 36–29–4 for 1987–92 with 3 bowl teams.

MISCELLANEA

First game was tie with Tucson Town Team 0–0 in 1899 . . . 1st win was over Tucson Indians 22–5 in 1899 . . . 1st win over college foe was over Arizona St. 12–0 in 1902 . . . highest score was over Camp Harry Jones 167–0 in 1920 . . . highest against college foe was over New Mexico Military J.C. 110–0 in 1921 . . . highest since W.W. II was over Arizona St. 67–0 in 1946 and over New Mexico St. 67–13 in 1951 . . . worst defeat was by Michigan St. 75–0 in 1949 . . . highest against was by USC 78–7 in 1928 . . . longest unbeaten string of 11 in 1960–61 ended by West Texas St. 27–23 . . . longest winless string of 10 in 1956–57 broken with win over Marquette 17–14 . . . consensus All-Americans were Ricky Hunley, LB, 1982–83; Chuck Cecil, DB, 1987; Darryl Lewis, DB, 1990; and Rob Waldrop, DL, 1992 . . . Academic All-Americans were Mike Moody, OG, 1968; Jon Abbott, DT/LB, 1975–77; Jeff Whitton, DL, 1979; and Chuck Cecil, DB, 1987.

ARIZONA STATE *(Sun Devils; Maroon and Gold)*

NOTABLE TEAMS

1924 (6–1–1) *Won:* Phoenix H.S. 24–0, Phoenix Indians 13–10, Phoenix College 32–0, 30–6, Northern Arizona 20–16, Arizona freshmen 23–13. *Lost:* Phoenix College Alumni 27–3. *Tied:* Sherman Indians 13–13.
1925 (6–2) *Won:* Sacaton Indians 55–0, Phoenix College 32–0, Northern Arizona 3–0, Arizona freshmen 20–6, Phoenix Indians 11–7, Phoenix H.S. 18–6. *Lost:* Arizona 13–3, Texas–El Paso 27–12 (1st meeting).
1926 (4–1–1) *Won:* Sacaton Indians 35–0, Phoenix College 28–7, Gila J.C. 20–0, Northern Arizona 14–0. *Lost:* Arizona 35–0. *Tied:* Phoenix Indians 0–0 (1st homecoming).
1931 (6–2) *Won:* Sacaton Indians 66–0, New Mexico St. 25–7, Northern Arizona 20–6 (1st over Lumberjacks in 7 games since 1926), Arizona 19–6 (1st over Wildcats in 10 games since 1899), Fresno St. 7–0, Arizona All-Stars 13–7. *Lost:* Texas–El Paso 27–13, Northern Arizona 13–7. *Stars:* HB Norris Steverson, E Dick Wilburg, G Paul Griffin. *Noteworthy:* won 1st Border Conference title.

1939 (8–2–1) *Won:* San Diego St. 20–0, West Texas St. 19–0 (1st meeting), Cal Poly 35–0, Whittier 28–0, New Mexico St. 7–0 (1st over Aggies since 1933), Texas–El Paso 27–7, Northern Arizona 41–6 (1st over Lumberjacks in 6 games since 1935), New Mexico 28–6. *Lost:* Hardin-Simmons 19–7, San Diego Marines 18–0. *Stars:* HB Joe Hernandez, FB Wayne Pitts, Gs Al Sanserino, Noble Riggs. *Noteworthy:* Won 2nd Border Conference title. Made 1st postseason appearance, tying Catholic U. 0–0 in Sun Bowl as fumbles and int negated big statistical edge by Arizona St.
1940 (7–2–2) *Won:* Cal Poly 21–13, West Texas St. 19–13, New Mexico 13–6, New Mexico St. 42–6, Northern Arizona 12–0, Northern Colorado 41–0, North Dakota 30–12. *Lost:* Hardin-Simmons 17–0. *Tied:* Texas–El Paso 0–0, Gonzaga 7–7. *Stars:* Sanserino, C Ray Green, E Sam Andrews, HB Hascall Henshaw. *Noteworthy:* Repeated as Border Conference champ. Lost to Western Reserve 26–13 in Sun Bowl; scored on 10-yd pass from Hernandez to Pitts and 94-yd run by Henshaw.
1949 (7–3) *Won:* Pepperdine 33–13, Northern Arizona 62–6, Brigham Young (BYU) 49–21, New Mexico 28–19, New Mexico St. 68–32, Arizona 34–7 (1st over Wildcats in 12 games since 1931), Utah St. 27–12. *Lost:* Hardin-Simmons 34–13, Loyola Marymount 27–7. *Star:* HB Wilford "Whizzer" White (935 yds rush, 17 pass rec for 334 yds, 11 TDs). *Noteworthy:* lost to Xavier (Ohio) 33–21 in Salad Bowl; Cecil Coleman passed for 1 TD (to White) and ran for another, and White also scored on 5-yd run.
1950 (9–2) *Won:* BYU 41–13, New Mexico 41–6, Northern Arizona 63–0, Utah St. 28–0, New Mexico St. 49–0, San Diego St. 31–13 (1st meeting since 1939), Arizona 47–13, Colorado St. 21–13 (1st meeting), Idaho 48–21. *Lost:* Hardin-Simmons 41–14 (10th straight to Cowboys). *Stars:* White (22 TDs, 136 pts, nation's leader with 1,502 yds rush and with 2,065 all-purpose yds), Bob Rippel (27 pass rec for 380 yds), T Sam Duca, Hank Rich (nation's leader with 12 int). *Noteworthy:* Ed Doherty's last team led nation in total off and rush. Lost to Miami (Ohio) 34–21 in Salad Bowl; White scored 2 TDs (on 27-yd pass from Manuel Aja and 15-yd run), and soph HB Marvin Wahlin scored on 4-yd run.
1955 (8–2–1) *Won:* Midwestern St. 28–7, San Diego Navy 42–0, San Diego St. 46–0, Hardin-

Simmons 69–14, West Texas St. 27–7, Texas–El Paso 20–13, New Mexico St. 26–6, Hawaii 39–6. *Lost:* San Jose St. 27–20, Arizona 7–6. *Tied:* Wichita St. 20–20 (1st meeting since 1946). *Stars:* QB Dave Graybill (1,079 yds pass), E Charlie Mackey (35 pass rec for 470 yds and 5 TDs), HB Gene Mitcham (27 pass rec for 552 yds), frosh RB Leon Burton (694 yds rush, 10 TDs), T John Jankans. *Noteworthy:* 1st year under Dan Devine.

1956 (9–1) *Won:* Wichita St. 37–9, North Texas St. 27–7, New Mexico St. 28–7, Idaho 41–0, Hardin-Simmons 26–13, San Jose St. 47–13, San Diego St. 61–0, Arizona 20–0, Pacific 19–6. *Lost:* Texas–El Paso 28–0. *Stars:* Mitcham (14 pass rec for 256 yds), Mackey, Bobby Mulgado (721 yds rush, 8 TDs), Burton (532 yds and 5 TDs rush).

1957 (10–0) *Won:* Wichita St. 28–0, Idaho 19–7, San Jose St. 44–6, Hardin-Simmons 35–26, San Diego St. 66–0, New Mexico St. 21–0, Texas–El Paso 43–7, Montana St. 53–13, Pacific 41–0, Arizona 47–7. *Stars:* Burton (nation's leader with 1,126 yds rush and in scoring with 96 pts), Mulgado (681 yds and 8 TDs rush, 6 int, nation's leader in punt returns with 19.1-yd avg), QB John Hangartner (1,203 yds and 14 TDs pass), Clancy Osborne (20 pass rec for 351 yds), soph E Bill Spanko, C Dave Fonner, G Ken Kerr. *Noteworthy:* Devine's last team led nation in total off and scoring (39.7-pt avg), and took 5th Border Conference title in 1st unbeaten season since 4-game schedule of 1904.

1958 (7–3) *Won:* Hawaii 47–6, West Texas St. 16–13, Detroit 27–6, New Mexico St. 23–19, Texas–El Paso 27–0, Arizona 47–0, Marquette 42–18. *Lost:* Pacific 34–16, Hardin-Simmons 14–6 (1st to Cowboys since 1953), San Jose St. 21–20. *Stars:* Burton (642 yds and 9 TDs rush), Hangartner (1,208 yds pass), Karl Kiefer (22 pass rec for 324 yds), Spanko (21 pass rec for 463 yds), Mulgado, Osborne, T Bart Jankans. *Noteworthy:* 1st year under Frank Kush.

1959 (10–1) *Won:* West Texas St. 43–22, Utah St. 34–12 (1st meeting since 1951), Montana St. 31–14, Colorado St. 24–9 (1st meeting since 1952), New Mexico St. 35–31 (15th straight over Aggies), Texas–El Paso 20–7, BYU 27–8, Hardin-Simmons 14–8, Arizona 15–9, Hawaii 14–6. *Lost:* San Jose St. 24–15. *Stars:* Spanko (15 pass rec for 231 yds, 4 int), soph HB Nolan Jones (689 yds rush, 11 TDs, 100 pts), Bob Rembert (15 pass rec for 232 yds), T Jess Bradford, soph P Joe Zuger (44.8-yd avg). *Noteworthy:* won 6th Border Conference title.

1960 (7–3) *Won:* Colorado St. 39–0, West Texas St. 14–3, Washington St. 24–21 (1st meeting), Hardin-Simmons 28–0, BYU 31–0, Texas–El Paso 24–0, N.C. State 25–22. *Lost:* San Jose St. 12–7, unbeaten New Mexico St. 27–24 (1st to Aggies in 16 games since 1938), Arizona 35–7 (1st to Wildcats since 1955). *Stars:* Jones (582 yds rush, 8 TDs, 93 pts), FB Clay Freney, T George Flint, Bradford, G Dick Locke, C Fred Rhodes, Zuger (40.3-yd punting avg).

1961 (7–3) *Won:* Wichita St. 21–7, Colorado St. 14–6, West Texas St. 28–11, Oregon St. 24–23 (1st meeting), Hardin-Simmons 47–0, Texas–El Paso 48–28, Detroit 40–6. *Lost:* Utah 28–26 (1st meeting), San Jose St. 32–26, Arizona 22–13. *Stars:* Jones (8 TDs, 77 pts), E Roger Locke (14 pass rec for 222 yds), soph Charley Taylor (13 pass rec for 235 yds), Freney, Flint, Dick Locke, Rhodes, T Larry Reeves, Zuger (nation's leader with 10 int and with 42.1-yd punting avg). *Noteworthy:* won 7th and last Border Conference title.

1962 (7–2–1) *Won:* Wichita St. 21–10, Colorado St. 35–0, San Jose St. 44–8, Texas–El Paso 35–7, Utah St. 34–15, Utah 35–7, New Mexico St. 45–20. *Lost:* West Texas St. 15–14 (1st to Buffaloes in 10 games since 1947), Arizona 20–17. *Tied:* Washington St. 24–24. *Stars:* QB John Jacobs (1,263 yds and 14 TDs pass), Dale Keller (20 pass rec for 358 yds and 5 TDs), HB Tony Lorick (704 yds rush), WB/DB Taylor (8 TDs, 4 int), Roger Locke. *Noteworthy:* led nation in total off.

1963 (8–1) *Won:* New Mexico St. 14–13, Colorado St. 50–7, West Texas St. 24–16, Texas–El Paso 27–0, Utah 30–22, San Jose St. 21–19, Wyoming 35–6 (1st meeting since 1951), Arizona 35–6. *Lost:* Wichita St. 33–13 (1st to Shockers in 6 games since 1946) in opener. *Stars:* Lorick (805 yds rush, 9 TDs, 4 int), Taylor, Herman Harrison (23 pass rec for 371 yds). *Noteworthy:* Idaho game cancelled because of Kennedy assassination.

1964 (8–2) *Won:* Utah St. 24–8, West Texas St. 34–8, Wichita St. 24–18, Texas–El Paso 42–13, Colorado St. 34–6, Kansas St. 21–6, San Jose St. 28–16, Idaho 14–0. *Lost:* Utah 16–3, Arizona 30–6. *Stars:* QB John Torok (2,356 yds and 20 TDs pass), Ben Hawkins (42 pass rec for 718 yds and 5 TDs), Jerry Smith (42 pass rec for 618 yds and 5 TDs), HB Larry Todd.

1967 (8–2) *Won:* San Jose St. 27–16, Wisconsin 42–16, Texas–El Paso 33–32, New Mexico 56–23, Washington St. 31–20, Utah 49–32, BYU 31–22,

Arizona 47–7. *Lost:* Oregon St. 27–21, unbeaten Wyoming 15–13. *Stars:* FB Max Anderson (1,183 yds rush, 12 TDs), Ken Dyer (39 pass rec for 654 yds), QB Ed Roseborough (1,494 yds and 12 TDs pass), C George Hummer, MG Curley Culp, LB Ron Pritchard, DB Wes Plummer (8 int).
1968 (8–2) *Won:* Wisconsin 55–7, Texas–El Paso 31–19, Washington St. 41–14, New Mexico 63–28, Utah 59–21, BYU 47–12, San Jose St. 66–0, Arizona 30–7. *Lost:* Wyoming 14–13, Oregon St. 28–9. *Stars:* FB Art Malone (1,431 yds rush, 16 TDs), Fair Hooker (42 pass rec for 665 yds and 6 TDs), Hummer, G Jim Kane, DT John Helton, Pritchard, DB Paul Ray Powell (7 int). *Noteworthy:* led nation in rush defense.
1969 (8–2) *Won:* Minnesota 48–26, BYU 23–7, San Jose St. 45–11, Wyoming 30–14, New Mexico 48–17, Texas–El Paso 42–19, Colorado St. 79–7, Arizona 38–24. *Lost:* Oregon St. 30–7, Utah 24–23. *Stars:* QB Joe Spagnola (1,488 yds and 10 TDs pass), soph E Calvin Demery (45 pass rec for 816 yds), HB Dave Buchanan (908 yds rush, 15 TDs), Malone (770 yds and 8 TDs rush), soph T Tom Tomco, G Gary Venturo, soph DE Junior Ah You, LB Mike Kennedy, DBs Seth Miller (nation's leader with 11 int) and Tom Julian (6 int), P Jim McCann (41.8-yd avg). *Noteworthy:* won 1st WAC title.
1970 (11–0) *Won:* Colorado St. 38–9 (10th straight over Rams), Kansas St. 35–13, Wyoming 52–3, Washington St. 37–30, BYU 27–3, Texas–El Paso 42–13, San Jose St. 46–10, Utah 37–14, New Mexico 33–21 (10th straight over Lobos), Arizona 10–6. *Stars:* Spagnola (1,991 yds and 18 TDs pass), SE J.D. Hill (58 pass rec for 908 yds and 10 TDs, 14 TDs total), soph WB Steve Holden (nation's punt return leader with 19.2-yd avg), Bob Thomas (900 yds rush), C Tomco, Venturo, Ah You, DT Bob Davenport, DB Windlan Hall (6 int), McCann (42.2-yd punting avg). *Noteworthy:* Led nation in total off and repeated as WAC champ in 1st unbeaten season since 1957. Beat North Carolina 48–26 in Peach Bowl blizzard (1st bowl win in 5 tries); Thomas scored 3 TDs, Spagnola passed 67 yds to Hill for another, Monroe Eley scored 2 TDs, and Holden scored once.
1971 (11–1) *Won:* Houston 18–17, Utah 42–21, Texas–El Paso 24–7 (15th straight over Miners), Colorado St. 42–0, New Mexico 60–28, Air Force 44–28, BYU 38–13, Wyoming 52–19, San Jose St. 49–6, Arizona 31–0. *Lost:* Oregon St. 24–18. *Stars:* Ah You, Hall (6 int), soph QB Danny White

(1,393 yds and 15 TDs pass, 40.2-yd punting avg), Demery (39 pass rec for 586 yds), TE Joe Petty, Holden, soph HB Woody Green (1,209 yds rush, 11 TDs), Tomco, K Don Ekstrand (75 pts). *Noteworthy:* Won 3rd straight WAC title. Beat Florida St. 45–38 in inaugural Fiesta Bowl on 1-yd TD run by Green (101 yds and 3 TDs rush) with 34 seconds left; White passed for 250 yds and 2 TDs (including 55-yarder to Holden, who also scored on 68-yd punt return), and Ekstrand kicked FG and 5 ex pts.
1972 (10–2) *Won:* Houston 33–28, Kansas St. 56–14, Oregon St. 38–7 (1st over Beavers in 6 games since 1961), Utah 59–48, BYU 49–17, Texas–El Paso 55–14, New Mexico 60–7, San Jose St. 51–21, Arizona 38–21. *Lost:* Wyoming 45–43, Air Force 39–31. *Stars:* Green (Sun Devils' 1st consensus All-American; 1,363 yds rush, 15 TDs), White (1,930 yds and 21 TDs pass, 222 yds and 7 TDs rush, 43-yd punting avg), Holden (38 pass rec for 858 yds and 12 TDs), Petty, FB Brent McClanahan, Ben Malone (6 TDs), C Ron Lou, soph LB Bob Breunig. *Noteworthy:* Led nation in total off and scoring (46.6-pt avg) and won 4th straight WAC title. Beat Missouri 49–35 in Fiesta Bowl; Green ran for 202 yds and 4 TDs, McClanahan ran for 171 yds and a TD, and White passed for 266 yds and 2 TDs.
1973 (11–1) *Won:* Oregon 26–20, Washington St. 20–9, Colorado St. 67–14, New Mexico 67–24, San Jose St. 28–3, BYU 52–12, Oregon St. 44–14, Wyoming 47–0, Texas–El Paso 54–13, Arizona 55–19. *Lost:* Utah 36–31. *Stars:* Green (1,182 yds and 9 TDs rush, 22 pass rec for 328 yds and 5 TDs), White (253 yds and 5 TDs rush, 43.4-yd punting avg, nation's leader in passing efficiency with 2,609 yds and 23 TDs), Morris Owens (50 pass rec for 1,076 yds and 9 TDs), Greg Hudson (54 pass rec for 788 yds and 7 TDs), Malone (1,186 yds rush, 15 TDs), OT Steve Gunther, OG John Houser, DEs Sam Johnson and Larry Shorty, Breunig, Kory Schuknecht (5 int), soph DB Mike Haynes. *Noteworthy:* Again led nation in total off and scoring (44.6-pt avg) and got share of WAC title. Beat Pittsburgh 28–7 in Fiesta Bowl; Green ran for 131 yds and 3 TDs, and White passed for 269 yds, including 38-yd TD pass to Hudson.
1975 (12–0) *Won:* Washington 35–12 (1st meeting), Texas Christian (TCU) 33–10, BYU 20–0, Idaho 29–3, New Mexico 16–10 (15th straight over Lobos), Colorado St. 33–3, Texas–El Paso 24–6, Utah 40–14, Wyoming 21–20, Pacific 55–14, Ari-

zona 24–21. *Stars:* HB Fred Williams (1,316 yds rush, 9 TDs), soph QB Dennis Sproul (1,058 yds pass), WR John Jefferson (44 pass rec for 805 yds and 5 TDs), DT Willie Scroggins, LB Larry Gordon, Haynes, DB Mike Martinez (7 int). *Noteworthy:* Nation's most-improved team won 6th WAC title. Beat Nebraska 17–14 in Fiesta Bowl after trailing 14–6 going into 4th period; Danny Kush kicked 3 FGs, including game winner late in 4th quarter, and Fred Mortensen passed 10 yds to Jefferson (8 pass rec for 113 yds) for TD, then passed to Larry Mucker for 2-pt conversion.

1977 (9–3) *Won:* Northwestern 35–3, Oregon St. 33–31, New Mexico 45–24, Air Force 37–14, Texas–El Paso 66–3, Utah 47–19, Wyoming 45–0, BYU 24–13, Arizona 23–7. *Lost:* Missouri 15–0, Colorado St. 25–14 (1st in 16-game series dating to 1950). *Stars:* Sproul (1,667 yds and 13 TDs pass), Jefferson (9 TDs, 53 pass rec for 912 yds and 8 TDs), Mike Harris (738 yds rush), John Harris (5 int). *Noteworthy:* Got share of 7th and last WAC title. Lost to Penn St. 42–30 in Fiesta Bowl (breaking 5–bowl win streak); Sproul passed for 3 TDs (2 to Ron Washington).

1978 (9–3) *Won:* Pacific 42–7, BYU 24–17, Texas–El Paso 27–0, Northwestern 56–14, Southern California (USC) 20–7 (1st meeting), California 35–21, Oregon St. 44–22, Arizona 18–17. *Lost:* Washington St. 51–26 (1st to Cougars in 5 games since 1966), Washington 41–7, Stanford 21–14 (1st meeting). *Stars:* QB Mark Malone (1,305 yds and 11 TDs pass, 705 yds rush), Chris DeFrance (31 pass rec for 617 yds and 5 TDs), frosh RB Newton Williams (526 yds rush), DE Al Harris, DB Kim Anderson (7 int). *Noteworthy:* beat Rutgers 34–18 in inaugural Garden State Bowl; Malone passed for 268 yds and 3 TDs and scored other 2 Sun Devil TDs, and soph John Mistler had 7 pass rec for 148 yds and a TD.

1981 (9–2) *Won:* Utah 52–10, Wichita St. 33–21 (1st meeting since 1965), Washington 26–7, Oregon 24–0, California 45–17, Stanford 62–36, San Jose St. 31–24 (1st meeting since 1973), Colorado St. 52–7, Arizona 24–13. *Lost:* Washington St. 24–21, UCLA 34–24. *Stars:* QB Mike Pagel (2,484 yds and 29 TDs pass), WR Bernard Henry (39 pass rec for 647 yds and 8 TDs), RB Gerald Riggs (891 yds rush), Robert Weathers (711 yds rush), frosh K Luis Zendejas (16 FGs, 93 pts), LB Vernon Maxwell, DB Mike Richardson (6 int), P Mike Black (42.5-yd avg). *Noteworthy:* Led na-

tion in total off. Ineligible for bowl, on NCAA probation.

1982 (10–2) *Won:* Oregon 34–3, Utah 23–10, Houston 24–10, California 15–0, Kansas St. 30–7, Stanford 21–17, Texas–El Paso 37–6, USC 17–10, Oregon St. 30–16. *Lost:* Washington 17–13, Arizona 28–18 in last 2 games. *Stars:* Maxwell, Richardson, DE Jim Jeffcoat, QB Todd Hons (2,009 yds pass), soph Doug Allen (29 pass rec for 408 yds), frosh Darryl Clack (577 yds and 7 TDs rush), Zendejas (21 FGs, 90 pts), Black (44.2-yd punting avg). *Noteworthy:* Led nation in total defense. Beat Oklahoma 32–21 in Fiesta Bowl; Hons passed for 329 yds and a TD (52 yards to Ron Brown), Clack scored on 15-yd run, and Zendejas kicked 3 FGs (including 54-yarder).

1985 (8–4) *Won:* Pacific 27–0, USC 24–0, Utah 34–27, Utah St. 42–10, Washington St. 21–16, California 30–8, Washington 36–7, Stanford 21–14. *Lost:* Michigan St. 12–3, UCLA 40–17, Arizona 16–13. *Stars:* DB David Fulcher (6 int), QB Jeff Van Raaphorst (2,200 yds and 10 TDs pass), soph SE Aaron Cox (40 pass rec for 788 yds and 5 TDs), Mike Crawford (684 yds rush), soph Darryl Harris (5 TDs), K Kent Bostrom (15 FGs, 74 pts), frosh P Mike Schuh (41.7-yd avg). *Noteworthy:* 1st year under John Cooper. Lost to Arkansas 18–17 in Holiday Bowl; Bostrom kicked 3 FGs, Van Raaphorst passed for 167 yds and a TD (16 yards to Cox), and Crawford ran for 103 yds.

1986 (10–1–1) *Won:* Michigan St. 20–17, SMU 30–0, UCLA 16–9 (1st in 8-game series dating to 1976), Oregon 37–17, USC 29–20, Utah 52–7, Washington 34–21, California 49–0, Wichita St. 52–6. *Lost:* Arizona 34–17 in finale. *Tied:* Washington St. 21–21. *Stars:* Van Raaphorst (2,181 yds and 17 TDs pass), Cox (35 pass rec for 695 yds), Harris (1,042 yds and 9 TDs rush), OG Randall McDaniel, OT Danny Villa, Bostrom (18 FGs, 97 pts), DE Skip McClendon, DB Scott Stephen. *Noteworthy:* Won 1st Pacific-10 title. Beat Michigan 22–15 in Rose Bowl; Van Raaphorst passed for 193 yds and 2 TDs (both to FL Bruce Hill), Harris ran for 109 yds, and Bostrom kicked 3 FGs.

BOWL SUMMARY

Fiesta 5–1; Freedom 1–0; Garden State 1–0; Holiday 0–1; Peach 1–0; Rose 1–0; Salad 0–2; Sun 0–1–1.

BOWL RECORD (9–5–1)

Regular Season	Bowl	Score	Opponent	Record
1939 (8–2)	Sun	0–0	Catholic Univ.	(8–1)
1940 (7–1–2)	Sun	13–26	Western Reserve	(7–1)
1949 (7–2)	Salad	21–33	Xavier (Ohio)	(9–1)
1950 (9–1)	Salad	21–34	Miami (Ohio)	(8–1)
1970 (10–0)	Peach	48–26	North Carolina	(8–3)
1971 (10–1)	Fiesta	45–38	Florida State	(8–3)
1972 (9–2)	Fiesta	49–35	Missouri	(6–5)
1973 (10–1)	Fiesta	28–7	Pittsburgh	(6–4–1)
1975 (11–0)	Fiesta	17–14	Nebraska	(10–1)
1977 (9–2)	Fiesta	30–42	Penn State	(10–1)
1978 (8–3)	Garden State	34–18	Rutgers	(9–2)
1982 (9–2)	Fiesta	32–21	Oklahoma	(8–3)
1985 (8–3)	Holiday	17–18	Arkansas	(9–2)
1986 (9–1–1)	Rose	22–15	Michigan	(11–1)
1987 (6–4–1)	Freedom	33–28	Air Force	(9–3)

CONFERENCE TITLES

Border—1931, 1939, 1940, 1952, 1957, 1959, 1961. **Western Athletic**—1969, 1970, 1971, 1972, 1973*, 1975, 1977*. **Pacific-10**—1986.

TOP 20 AP AND UPI RANKING

1957	12–12	1970	6–8	1975	2–2	1982	6–6
1962	U–18	1971	8–6	1977	18–18	1986	4–5
1963	U–13	1972	13–13	1978	U–19	1987	20–U
1967	U–20	1973	9–10	1981	16–U		

MAJOR RIVALS

Arizona State has played at least 10 games with Arizona 28–37–1, Brigham Young 18–5, California 7–7, Colorado St. 19–1, Hardin-Simmons 8–13, New Mexico 22–5–1, New Mexico St. 20–6–1, Northern Arizona 16–14–4, Oregon 10–3, Oregon St. 14–6–1, Phoenix Indians 11–6–1, Phoenix Union High 9–5–1, San Jose St. 17–11, Southern California 6–5, Texas–El Paso 31–13–3, UCLA 2–9–1, Utah 15–6, Utah St. 8–3, Washington 5–9, Washington St. 12–7–2, West Texas St. 13–7, Wichita St. 9–2–1, Wyoming 9–6. Pacific-10 foe met fewer than 10 times: Stanford 6–3.

COACHES

Dean of Sun Devil coaches is Frank Kush (1975 national Coach of Year) with record of 176–54–1 for 1958 to mid-1979, including 9 conference titles, 7 bowl teams (6 winners), and 2 unbeaten teams. Other top records for at least 3 years were by Fred Irish, 12–8 for 1897–1906; Aaron McCreary, 25–17–4 for 1923–29 with 1 unbeaten team; Ted Shipkey, 12–10–2 for 1930–32 with 1 conference title; Dixie Howell, 23–15–4 for 1938–41 with 2 conference titles and 2 bowl teams; Ed Doherty, 25–17 for 1947–50 with 2 bowl teams; Clyde Smith, 15–13–1 for 1952–54 with 1 conference title; Dan Devine, 27–3–1 for 1955–57 with 1 conference title and 1 unbeaten team; Darryl Rogers, 37–18–1 for 1980–84 with 1 bowl champion; John Cooper, 25–9–2 for

1985–87 with 1 Pac–10 title and 3 bowl teams; and Larry Marmie, 22–21–1 for 1988–91.

MISCELLANEA

First game was loss to Phoenix Indians 38–20 in 1897 . . . 1st win was over Phoenix Indians 6–0 in 1899 . . . 1st win over college foe was over Arizona 11–2 in 1899 . . . highest score was over Colorado St. 79–7 in 1969 . . . biggest margin tied by win over Glendale H.S. 72–0 in 1914 . . . worst defeat was by Nevada (Reno) 74–2 in 1946 . . . longest win streak of 21 in 1969–71 ended by Oregon St. 24–18 . . . longest winless string of 11 in 1937–38 broken with win over Cal-Davis 13–0 . . . consensus All-Americans were Woody Green, B, 1972–73; John Jefferson, WR, 1977; Al Harris, DL, 1978; Mike Richardson, DB, 1981–82; Vernon Maxwell, DE, 1982; Luis Zendejas, K, 1983; David Fulcher, DB, 1984–85; Danny Villa, OL, 1986; and Randall McDaniel, OL, 1987 . . . Academic All-Americans were Ken Dyer, E, 1966; and Mark Tingstad, LB, 1988.

CALIFORNIA (Golden Bears; Blue and Gold)

NOTABLE TEAMS

1885 (4–0–1)   *Won:* Merions 13–0, 4–0, 4–0, Wasps 2–0. *Tied:* Wasps 0–0.
1886 (6–2–1)   *Won:* Wasps 20–2, 1–0 (forfeit), Orions 29–2, Hastings Law College (2 forfeits), Reliance 10–0. *Lost:* Orions 12–10, Reliance 7–4. *Tied:* Reliance 12–12.
1888 (6–1)   *Won:* San Francisco Club 26–0, 20–0, 36–0, Posens 14–0, Wasps (2 forfeits). *Lost:* Volunteers 10–6.
1889 All scheduled games cancelled because of heavy rains.
1893 (5–1–1)   *Won:* Reliance Club 30–0, 22–10, San Francisco All-Stars 14–12, Olympic Club 22–10, 12–6. *Lost:* Reliance Club 16–4. *Tied:* unbeaten Stanford 6–6.
1895 (3–1–1)   *Won:* Reliance Club 12–0, 8–0, Olympic Club 20–0. *Lost:* Reliance Club 4–0 in opener. *Tied:* unbeaten Stanford 6–6.
1896 (6–2–2)   *Won:* Olympic Club 24–8, Reliance Club 16–10, Los Angeles A.C. 14–0, Redlands H.S. 32–0, San Diego H.S. 52–0, Whittier School 10–6.

Lost: Reliance Club 12–2, Stanford 20–0.   *Tied:* Olympic Club 0–0, Reliance Club 0–0.
1898 (8–0–2)   *Won:* Olympic Club 17–0, 18–0, Washington Volunteers 4–0, 44–0, Kansas Volunteers 33–0, St. Mary's 51–0 (1st meeting), Stanford 22–0 (1st in 8-game series begun in 1892), Multnomah A.C. 27–0. *Tied:* Iowa Volunteers 0–0, Olympic Club 5–5. *Noteworthy:* 1st unbeaten season since 4-game schedule of 1890.
1899 (7–1–1)   *Won:* Olympic Club 6–0, 15–0, League of the Cross 11–0, Nevada-Reno 24–0 (1st meeting), Oregon 12–0 (1st meeting), San Jose St. 44–0 (1st meeting), Stanford 30–0. *Lost:* Carlisle Indians 2–0 in finale. *Tied:* Olympic Club 0–0.
1901 (9–0–1)   *Won:* Olympic Club 5–0, 6–0, 6–5, Reliance 6–0, Nevada-Reno 12–0, Mare Island Marines 16–0, Stanford 2–0, Southern California All-Stars 38–0, Perris Indians 15–10. *Tied:* Reliance 0–0 in opener.
1902 (8–0)   *Won:* Alumni Club 12–0, 44–0, Reliance 16–0, 17–0, '98–'99 Alumni 5–0, Nevada-Reno 29–0, Stanford 16–0, Perris Indians 29–12.
1903 (6–1–2)   *Won:* Naval Academy (not Annapolis) 51–0, Reliance 7–0, 5–0, Chemawa Indians 40–0, Alumni 6–0, Multnomah A.C. 11–0. *Lost:* Nevada-Reno 6–0 (1st in 5-game series begun in 1899). *Tied:* Reliance 0–0, unbeaten Stanford 6–6.
1904 (6–1–1)   *Won:* Sherman Indians 6–0, Olympic Club 10–0, Multnomah A.C. 20–0, Oregon 12–0, Pomona 5–0, Nevada-Reno 16–0 in 1st 6 games. *Lost:* Stanford 18–0. *Tied:* Washington 6–6 (1st meeting).
1905 (4–1–2)   *Won:* St. Vincent's 23–0, Sherman Indians 21–0, Oregon St. 10–0 (1st meeting), Nevada-Reno 16–0. *Lost:* unbeaten Stanford 12–5 in finale. *Tied:* Willamette 0–0, Oregon 0–0.
1909 (12–3–1)   *Won:* Reliance 39–0, 30–0, Barbarians 6–3, 6–0, Olympic Club 16–0, 19–0, Southern California All-Stars 19–3, Vancouver 24–3, 39–0, 14–3, Nevada-Reno 24–8, Stanford 19–13 (1st over Indians since 1902). *Lost:* Barbarians 6–3, Vancouver 3–0, 5–0. *Tied:* Castaways 10–10. *Noteworthy:* 1st year under James Schaeffer.
1910 (12–0–2)   *Won:* Barbarians 9–0, 32–5, 26–0, 22–0, Olympic Club 17–3, 16–0, 40–10, 18–0, St. Mary's 6–0, Nevada-Reno 62–0, Stanford 25–6, Victoria All-Stars 3–0. *Tied:* Victoria All-Stars 0–0, 3–3.
1911 (11–2–1)   *Won:* Barbarians 11–0, 31–3, 14–3, Olympic Club 8–0, 16–8, 18–3, 60–0, Nevada-Reno

29–0, British Columbia All-Stars 21–0, 24–0, Stanford 21–3. *Lost:* Victoria All-Stars 6–3, 8–0. *Tied:* Victoria All-Stars 0–0.

1912 (10–2–1) *Won:* Barbarians 8–3, 16–0, 16–3, Olympic Club 5–3, 9–0, 5–0, Nevada-Reno 34–0, St. Mary's 21–0, Australian Waratahs 6–5, USC 18–0 (1st meeting). *Lost:* Australian Waratahs 18–0, 23–3. *Tied:* Stanford 3–3.

1914 (14–1) *Won:* Olympic Club 8–3, 13–3, Titans 8–3, 17–3, 18–0, Barbarians 12–5, 11–0, UC Alumni 17–5, 22–3, 27–3, St. Mary's 28–0, 24–3, Santa Clara 25–0, Nevada-Reno 38–3. *Lost:* Stanford 26–8.

1918 (7–2) *Won:* San Francisco Presidio 13–7, Fort Scott 1–0 (forfeit), St. Mary's 40–14, Oregon 6–0, Stanford 67–0, San Pedro Navy 20–0, Southern California (USC) 33–7. *Lost:* Fort MacDowell 21–7, Mather Field 13–0. *Star:* soph Albert "Pesky" Sprott (13 TDs). *Noteworthy:* won 1st PCC title.

1919 (6–2–1) *Won:* Olympic Club 12–0, St. Mary's 19–0, Occidental 61–0, Oregon St. 21–14, USC 14–13, Stanford 14–10. *Lost:* Washington St. 14–0 (1st meeting), Washington 7–0. *Tied:* Olympic Club 6–6.

1920 (9–0) *Won:* Olympic Club 21–0, Mare Island Marines 88–0, St. Mary's 27–0, Nevada-Reno 79–7 (1st meeting since 1915), Utah 63–0, Oregon St. 17–7, Washington St. 49–0, Stanford 38–0. *Stars:* Sprott (15 TDs), soph Jesse "Duke" Morrison (17 TDs, 104 pts), Irving "Crip" Toomey (7 TDs, 39 extra pts), soph E Harold "Brick" Muller. *Noteworthy:* Outscored foes 482–14 in 1st unbeaten season since 1910, won 2nd PCC title, and became 1st West Coast team to win national championship. Made 1st postseason appearance, beating undefeated Ohio St. 28–0 in Rose Bowl; jumped to 21–0 1st–half lead highlighted by TD run by Sprott and 50-yd TD trick play pass from Muller to Brodie Stephens.

1921 (9–0–1) *Won:* St. Mary's 21–0, Olympic Club 14–0, Nevada-Reno 51–6 (10th straight over Wolf Pack), Pacific Fleet 21–10, Oregon 39–0, Washington St. 14–0, USC 38–7, Washington 72–3, Stanford 42–7. *Stars:* Muller and T Dan McMillan (Bears' 1st consensus All-Americans). *Noteworthy:* Repeated as PCC champ. Tied unbeaten Washington & Jefferson 0–0 in muddy Rose Bowl; W&J had game's only TD nullified by holding penalty.

1922 (9–0) *Won:* Santa Clara 45–14 (1st meeting since 1914), Mare Island Marines 80–0, St. Mary's

41–0, Olympic Club 25–0, USC 12–0, Washington St. 61–0, Washington 45–7, Nevada-Reno 61–13, Stanford 28–0. *Stars:* Muller, Morrison (18 TDs, 131 pts). *Noteworthy:* won 3rd straight PCC title.

1923 (9–0–1) *Won:* Alumni All-Stars 3–0, St. Mary's 49–0, Santa Clara 48–0, Olympic Club 16–0, Oregon St. 26–0, Washington St. 9–0, USC 13–7, Washington 9–0, Stanford 9–0. *Tied:* Nevada-Reno 0–0. *Noteworthy:* won 5th PCC title (4th straight).

1924 (8–0–2) *Won:* Santa Clara 13–7, St. Mary's 17–7, Pomona 28–0, Olympic Club 9–3, Washington St. 20–7, USC 7–0, Nevada-Reno 27–0, Pennsylvania 14–0. *Tied:* Washington 7–7, unbeaten Stanford 20–20. *Star:* C Edwin "Babe" Horrell. *Noteworthy:* Andy Smith's 5th straight unbeaten team.

1927 (7–3) *Won:* Santa Clara 14–6, Nevada-Reno 54–0, St. Mary's 13–0, Oregon 16–0, Olympic Club 6–5, Montana 33–13 (1st meeting), Pennsylvania 27–13. *Lost:* USC 13–0, Washington 6–0, Stanford 13–6. *Stars:* E Irv Phillips, T Fred Coltrin.

1928 (6–2–2) *Won:* Santa Clara 22–0, St. Mary's 7–0, Washington St. 13–3, Oregon 13–0, Washington 6–0, Nevada-Reno 60–0. *Lost:* Olympic Club 12–0. *Tied:* unbeaten national cochamp USC 0–0, Stanford 13–13. *Stars:* Phillips, HB Ben Lom, T Stephen Bancroft. *Noteworthy:* lost to unbeaten national cochamp Georgia Tech 8–7 in Rose Bowl when C Roy Riegels returned pass int wrong way to set up winning Georgia Tech safety.

1929 (7–1–1) *Won:* Santa Clara 27–6 (10th straight over Broncos), Washington St. 14–0, Pennsylvania 12–7, Olympic Club 21–19, USC 15–7, Montana 53–18, Washington 7–0. *Lost:* Stanford 21–6 in finale. *Tied:* unbeaten St. Mary's 0–0. *Stars:* Lom, Riegels, G Bert Schwarz, E Robert Norton.

1931 (8–2) *Won:* Santa Clara 6–2, Olympic Club 6–0, Washington St. 13–7, Nevada-Reno 25–6, Washington 13–0, Idaho 18–0 (1st meeting), Stanford 6–0 (1st over Indians since 1923), Georgia Tech 19–6. *Lost:* St. Mary's 14–0 (1st to Gaels since 1926), national champ USC 6–0. *Stars:* HB Rusty Gill, E Ralph Stone. *Noteworthy:* 1st year under William Ingram.

1935 (9–1) *Won:* UC-Davis 47–0, Whittier 6–0, St. Mary's 10–0, Oregon 6–0 (1st meeting since 1928), Santa Clara 6–0, USC 21–7, UCLA 14–2, Washington 14–0, Pacific 39–0. *Lost:* Stanford 13–0 in finale. *Stars:* T Larry Lutz, soph C Bob Herwig,

E Jack Brittingham, HB Floyd Blower. *Noteworthy:* got share of 6th PCC title in 1st year under "Stub" Allison.

1937 (10–0–1) *Won:* St. Mary's 30–7, Oregon St. 24–6, Washington St. 27–0, UC-Davis 14–0, Pacific 20–0, USC 20–6, UCLA 27–14, Oregon 26–0, Stanford 13–0. *Tied:* Washington 0–0. *Stars:* Herwig, G Vard Stockton, E Perry Schwartz, HBs Sam Chapman and Vic Bottari (585 yds rush, 12 TDs, 4 int), QB John Meek. *Noteworthy:* One of nation's most-improved teams got 7th PCC crown and share of 2nd national title in 1st unbeaten season since 1924. Beat undefeated Alabama 13–0 in Rose Bowl (1st Tide loss in 5 Rose Bowl games) as Bottari scored 2 TDs.

1938 (10–1) *Won:* St. Mary's 12–7, Washington St. 27–3, UC-Davis 48–0, Pacific 39–0, UCLA 20–7, Washington 14–7, Oregon St. 13–7, Oregon 20–0, Stanford 6–0, Georgia Tech 13–0. *Lost:* USC 13–7 (1st to Trojans since 1933). *Stars:* Bottari (578 yds and 8 TDs rush, 466 yds and 7 TDs pass, 61 pts), FB Dave Anderson, T Dave De Varona, E Willard Dolman. *Noteworthy:* got share of 8th PCC title.

1947 (9–1) *Won:* Santa Clara 33–7 (1st meeting since 1942), Navy 14–7, St. Mary's 45–6, Wisconsin 48–7, Washington St. 21–6, UCLA 6–0, Washington 13–7, Montana 60–14, Stanford 21–18. *Lost:* USC 39–14 in mid-season. *Stars:* FBs Jackie Jensen (705 yds total off, 7 int) and John Graves (466 yds rush), Jack Swaner (5 TDs), Bill Montagne (5 TDs), Ted Kenfield (5 TDs), Frank Van Deren (15 pass rec for 302 yds), soph G Rod Franz. *Noteworthy:* had nation's most-improved team in 1st year under Lynn "Pappy" Waldorf.

1948 (10–1) *Won:* Santa Clara 41–19, Navy 21–7, St. Mary's 20–0, Wisconsin 40–14, Oregon St. 42–0, Washington 21–0, USC 13–7, UCLA 28–13, Washington St. 44–14, Stanford 7–6. *Stars:* Franz, T Jim Turner, Van Deren, Jensen (1,010 yds and 6 TDs rush), Swaner (784 yds and 12 TDs rush), John Cunningham (14 pass rec for 222 yds), LB Jon Baker, Paul Keckley (7 int). *Noteworthy:* Got share of 9th PCC title in 1st unbeaten season since 1937. Lost to Northwestern 20–14 in Rose Bowl, scoring on TDs by Jensen (67-yd run) and Swaner; Wildcats took 13–7 halftime lead when awarded TD though California claimed Art Murakowski fumbled on 1-yd line before reaching end zone.

1949 (10–1) *Won:* Santa Clara 21–7, St. Mary's

29–7, Oregon St. 41–0, Wisconsin 35–20, USC 16–10, Washington 21–7, UCLA 35–21, Washington St. 33–14, Oregon 41–14, Stanford 33–14. *Stars:* Franz, Turner, T Jim Cullom, G Forrest Klein, QB Bob Celeri (1,081 yds pass), Dan Begovich (14 pass rec for 275 yds), RB Jim Monachino (781 yds rush, 15 TDs), DB Carl Van Heuit (5 int). *Noteworthy:* Won 10th PCC title. Lost to Ohio St. 17–14 in Rose Bowl on FG with less than 2 minutes left; Monachino scored Bear TDs on runs of 7 and 44 yds.

1950 (9–1–1) *Won:* Santa Clara 27–9, Oregon 28–7, Pennsylvania 14–7 (1st meeting since 1929), USC 13–7, Oregon St. 27–0, St. Mary's 40–25, Washington 14–7, UCLA 35–0, San Francisco 13–7. *Tied:* Stanford 7–7 in finale. *Stars:* Monachino, soph Johnny Olszewski (950 yds rush), FB Pete Schabarum (11 TDs), E Jim Minahen, G Les Richter, T Bob Karpe, DE Ed Bartlett, Van Heuit. *Noteworthy:* Won 3rd straight PCC crown (11th overall). Lost to Michigan 14–6 in Rose Bowl as 73-yd TD run by Schabarum was nullified by penalty; scored on 39-yd pass from Jim Marinos to Bob Cummings.

1951 (8–2) *Won:* Santa Clara 34–0, Pennsylvania 35–0, Minnesota 55–14, Washington St. 42–35, Oregon St. 35–14, Washington 37–28, Oregon 28–26, Stanford 20–7. *Lost:* USC 21–14, UCLA 21–7 (1st to Bruins since 1946). *Stars:* Richter, Karpe, C Charles Harris, Olszewski (651 yds rush), Don Robison (9 TDs), Dave Hood (18 pass rec for 215 yds), Dick Lee (6 int), DB Dick LemMon.

1952 (7–3) *Won:* Pacific 34–13 (1st meeting since 1944), Missouri 28–14, Minnesota 49–13, Oregon 41–7, Santa Clara 27–7, Washington St. 28–13, Stanford 26–0. *Lost:* USC 10–0, UCLA 28–7, Washington 22–7 (1st to Huskies since 1946) in consecutive late games. *Stars:* Olszewski (845 yds and 7 TDs rush), Don Johnson (7 TDs), Bill Powell (7 TDs), soph HB Paul Larson (5 TDs).

1958 (7–4) *Won:* Washington St. 34–14, Utah 36–21, USC 14–12, Oregon 23–6 (1st over Ducks since 1952), UCLA 20–17 (1st over Bruins since 1950), Washington 12–7, Stanford 16–15. *Lost:* Pacific 24–20 (1st meeting since 1952), Michigan St. 32–12, Oregon St. 14–8. *Stars:* QB Joe Kapp (1,391 yds total off, 616 yds and 5 TDs rush), HB Jack Hart (6 TDs, 32 pass rec for 395 yds). *Noteworthy:* Won 12th PCC title in league's last year. Lost to national cochamp Iowa 38–12 in Rose Bowl; Hart scored both Golden Bear TDs.

1975 (8–3) *Won:* Washington St. 33–21, San Jose St. 27–24, Oregon 34–7, Oregon St. 51–24, USC 28–14 (1st over Trojans since 1970), Washington 27–24, Air Force 31–14, Stanford 48–15. *Lost:* Colorado 34–27, West Virginia 28–10, UCLA 28–14. *Stars:* RB Chuck Muncie (1,460 yds rush, 39 pass rec for 392 yds, 15 TDs), QB Joe Roth (1,880 yds and 14 TDs pass), WR Steve Rivera (57 pass rec for 790 yds), OT Ted Albrecht. *Noteworthy:* led nation in total off and got share of only Pacific-8 title (13th conference crown).

1977 (8–3) *Won:* Tennessee 27–17, Air Force 24–14, Missouri 28–21, San Jose St. 52–3, Oregon St. 41–17, UCLA (by forfeit after losing 21–19), USC 17–14, Oregon 48–16. *Lost:* Washington St. 17–10, Washington 50–31 (1st to Huskies since 1972), Stanford 21–3. *Stars:* QB Charlie Young (1,875 yds and 12 TDs pass), Jesse Thompson (51 pass rec for 797 yds and 5 TDs), TE George Freitas (50 pass rec for 673 yds), soph Paul Jones (805 yds and 6 TDs rush), K Jim Breech (16 FGs, 82 pts), DL Ralph DeLoach, P Dan Melville (42.3-yd avg). *Noteworthy:* Mike White's last team.

1991 (10–2) *Won:* Pacific 86–24, Purdue 42–18, Arizona 23–21, UCLA 27–24, Oregon 45–7, San Jose St. 41–20, USC 52–30 (1st over Trojans since 1985), Oregon St. 27–14 (1st over Beavers in 6 games since 1983), Arizona St. 25–6. *Lost:* unbeaten national cochamp Washington 24–17, Stanford 38–21. *Stars:* QB Mike Pawlawski (2,517 yds and 21 TDs), soph WR Sean Dawkins (40 pass rec for 723 yds and 11 TDs), WRs Brian Treggs (43 pass rec for 643 yds) and Mike Caldwell (27 pass rec for 342 yds), TBs Russell White (1,177 yds and 14 TDs rush, 1,724 all-purpose yds) and soph Lindsey Chapman (675 yds and 6 TDs rush), C Steve Gordon, OT Troy Auzenne, soph K Doug Brien (98 pts, nation's leader with 19 FGs), NG Mack Travis, LBs Cornell Collier and frosh Jerrott Willard, DBs David Wilson (5 int), Chris Cannon (5 int) and Wolf Barber, P Chris Noonan (40-yd avg). *Noteworthy:* Last year under Bruce Snyder. Beat Clemson 37–13 in Florida Citrus Bowl; Pawlawski passed for 230 yds and a TD, White ran for 103 yds and a TD, Treggs scored on 72-yd punt return, and Brien kicked 3 FGs.

BOWL SUMMARY

Copper 1–0; Florida Citrus 1–0; Garden State 0–1; Rose 2–5–1.

BOWL RECORD (4–6–1)

Regular Season	Bowl	Score	Opponent	Record
1920 (8–0)	Rose	28–0	Ohio State	(7–0)
1921 (9–0)	Rose	0–0	Wash. & Jeff.	(10–0)
1928 (6–1–2)	Rose	7–8	Georgia Tech	(9–0)
1937 (9–0–1)	Rose	13–0	Alabama	(9–0)
1948 (10–0)	Rose	14–20	Northwestern	(7–2)
1949 (10–0)	Rose	14–17	Ohio State	(6–1–2)
1950 (9–0–1)	Rose	6–14	Michigan	(5–3–1)
1958 (7–3)	Rose	12–38	Iowa	(7–1–1)
1979 (7–5)	Garden State	17–28	Temple	(9–2)
1990 (6–4–1)	Copper	17–15	Wyoming	(9–3)
1991 (9–2)	Fla. Citrus	37–13	Clemson	(9–1–1)

CONFERENCE TITLES

Pacific Coast—1918, 1920, 1921, 1922, 1923, 1935*, 1937, 1938*, 1948*, 1949, 1950, 1958. **Pacific-8**—1975*. **Pacific-10**—None.

TOP 20 AP AND UPI
(USA TODAY/CNN SINCE 1991) RANKING

1937	2	1948	4	1951	12–12	1975	14–15
1938	14	1949	3	1958	16–16	1991	8–7
1947	15	1950	5–4				

MAJOR RIVALS

California has played at least 10 games with Arizona 7–5–2, Arizona St. 7–7, Nevada-Reno 21–1–1, Oregon 35–21–2, Oregon St. 27–20, Pacific 12–3, St. Mary's 28–8–2, San Jose St. 25–6, Santa Clara 17–5, Southern California 25–50–5, Stanford 37–47–11, UCLA 22–40–1, Washington 32–38–4, Washington St. 34–17–5.

COACHES

Deans of California coaches are Andy Smith and Lynn "Pappy" Waldorf with 10 years each. Smith was 74–16–7 for 1916–25 with 5 PCC titles, 2 Rose Bowl teams, 5 unbeaten teams, and 1 national title. Waldorf was 67–32–4 for 1947–56 with 3 PCC titles, 3 Rose Bowl teams, and 3 teams unbeaten in regular season. Other top records for at least 3 years were by Oscar Taylor, 13–10–1 for 1906–08; James Schaeffer, 73–16–8 for 1909–15 with 1 unbeaten team; Nibs Price, 27–17–3 for 1926–30 with 1 Rose Bowl team; Bill Ingram, 27–14–4 for 1931–34; Leonard "Stub" Allison, 58–42–2 for 1935–44 with 3 PCC titles, and 1 unbeaten Rose Bowl and national champion; Mike White, 35–30–1 for 1972–77 with 1 Pacific-8 title; and Bruce Snyder, 29–24–4 for 1987–91 with 2 bowl champions.

MISCELLANEA

First game was loss to Phoenix Club 7–4 in 1882 . . . 1st win was over Phoenix Club 7–6 in 1882 . . . 1st game with college foe was loss to Stanford 14–10 in 1892 spring game . . . 1st win over college foe was over St. Mary's 51–0 in 1898 . . . highest score was over St. Mary's 127–0 in 1920 . . . highest since W.W. II was over Pacific 86–24 in 1991 . . . worst defeat was by USC 74–0 in 1930 . . . worst since W.W. II was by Alabama 66–0 in 1973 . . . longest unbeaten string of 50 in 1920–25 ended by Olympic Club 15–0 . . . 18-game unbeaten string

in 1937–38 ended by USC 13–7 . . . 14-game win streak in 1947–48 ended by Northwestern 20–14 in 1949 Rose Bowl . . . longest losing string of 8, in 1959 broken with win over Stanford 20–17, in 1962 with win over Iowa St. 15–8 in 1963 opener, and in 1986 with win over Stanford 17–11 . . . consensus All-Americans were Dan McMillan, T, 1921; Brick Muller, E, 1921–22; Edwin Horrell, C, 1924; Irv Phillips, E, 1928; Ted Beckett, G, 1930; Larry Lutz, T, 1935; Sam Chapman, B, 1937; Vic Bottari, B, 1938; Jackie Jensen, B, 1948; Rod Franz, G, 1949; Les Richter, G, 1950–51; Ed White, MG, 1968; Sherman White, DT, 1971; Steve Bartkowski, QB, 1974; Chuck Muncie, RB, and Steve Rivera, E, 1975; Ron Rivera, LB, 1983; Russell White, RB, 1991; and Sean Dawkins, WR, 1992 . . . Academic All-Americans were Bob Crittenden, MG, 1967; Robert Richards, OT, 1970; and Harvey Salem, OT, 1982.

OREGON *(Ducks; Lemon Yellow and Emerald Green)*

NOTABLE TEAMS

1906 (5–0–1) *Won:* Idaho 12–0, Willamette 4–0, Washington 16–6, Multnomah A.C. 8–4, Whitworth 10–0. *Tied:* Oregon St. 0–0. *Noteworthy:* 1st unbeaten season since 4-game schedule of 1895.
1907 (5–1) *Won:* Pacific (Ore.) 52–0, Idaho 21–5, Willamette 11–0, Washington 6–0, Multnomah A.C. 10–5. *Lost:* Oregon St. 4–0 (1st to Beavers in 8 games since 1897).
1908 (5–2) *Won:* Alumni 4–0, Willamette 15–0, Idaho 27–21, Oregon St. 8–0, Multnomah A.C. 10–0. *Lost:* Whitman 16–10, unbeaten Washington 15–0 (1st to Huskies since 1903) in consecutive mid-season games.
1910 (4–1) *Won:* Alumni 16–6, Puget Sound 115–0, Idaho 29–0, Oregon St. 12–0. *Lost:* Multnomah A.C. 5–0 in finale.
1915 (7–2) *Won:* Idaho 19–7, Whitman 21–0, Willamette 49–0, Pacific (Ore.) 47–0 (1st meeting since

1907), USC 34–0 (1st meeting), Oregon St. 9–0, Multnomah A.C. 15–2. *Lost:* Multnomah A.C. 16–7, unbeaten Washington St. 28–3 in 1st 2 games.

1916 (7–0–1) *Won:* Willamette 97–0, Multnomah A.C. 28–0, 27–0, California 39–14 (1st meeting since 1905), Washington St. 12–0, Oregon St. 27–0. *Tied:* unbeaten Washington 0–0. *Stars:* QB Shy Huntington, E Brick Mitchell, T John Beckett, G W.C. Snyder, C Jake Risley. *Noteworthy:* 1st undefeated season since 1906. Made 1st postseason appearance, beating Pennsylvania 14–0 in Rose Bowl as Huntington passed for 1st TD (15 yds to R.L. Tergurt) and ran 1 yd for 2nd.

1919 (5–2) *Won:* Multnomah A.C. 23–0, 15–7, Idaho 26–6, Washington 24–13, Oregon St. 9–0. *Lost:* Washington St. 7–0. *Stars:* QB Bill Steers, G Ken Bartlett. *Noteworthy:* Got share of 1st PCC title. Lost to unbeaten national champ Harvard 7–6 in Rose Bowl; Hollis Huntington ran for 122 yds and a TD.

1921 (5–1–3) *Won:* Willamette 7–3, Pacific (Ore.) 21–7 (1st meeting since 1915), Multnomah A.C. 21–7, Hawaii 47–0, Pearl Harbor 35–5. *Lost:* unbeaten California 39–0. *Tied:* Idaho 7–7, Washington St. 7–7, Oregon St. 0–0.

1922 (6–1–1) *Won:* Willamette 37–0, Whitman 6–3, Idaho 6–3, Pacific (Ore.) 27–0, Washington St. 13–0, Oregon St. 10–0. *Lost:* Multnomah A.C. 20–0. *Tied:* Washington 3–3. *Stars:* T Carl Vonder Ahe, G Tiny Shields.

1928 (9–2) *Won:* Pacific (Ore.) 45–0, Willamette 38–6, Washington 27–0, Western Oregon 24–0, Oregon St. 12–0, Montana 31–6 (1st meeting), UCLA 26–6 (1st meeting), Honolulu 13–2, Hawaii 6–0. *Lost:* Stanford 26–12 (10th straight to Indians), California 13–0. *Stars:* soph HB John Kitzmiller, G George Stadelman.

1929 (7–3) *Won:* Pacific (Ore.) 58–0, Willamette 34–0, Idaho 34–7, Washington 14–0, UCLA 27–0, Oregon St. 16–0, Hawaii 7–0. *Lost:* Stanford 33–7, unbeaten St. Mary's 31–6 (1st meeting), Florida 20–6. *Star:* T Austin Colbert. *Noteworthy:* last year under John McEwan.

1930 (7–2) *Won:* Pacific (Ore.) 20–0, Willamette 51–0, Linfield 6–0, Drake 14–7, Washington 7–0, Idaho 20–6, UCLA 7–0 in 1st 7 games. *Lost:* Oregon St. 15–0, St. Mary's 7–6. *Star:* Kitzmiller. *Noteworthy:* 1st year under Dr. Clarence W. Spears.

1931 (6–2–2) *Won:* Western Oregon 21–6, Wil- lamette 20–0, Idaho 9–0, Washington 13–0, New York U. 14–6, UCLA 13–6. *Lost:* national champ USC 53–0 (1st meeting since 1920), St. Mary's 16–0. *Tied:* North Dakota 0–0, Oregon St. 0–0. *Star:* T George Christenson. *Noteworthy:* last year under Spears.

1933 (9–1) *Won:* Linfield 53–0, Gonzaga 14–0, Columbia 14–7, Washington 6–0, Idaho 19–0, UCLA 7–0, Utah 23–7 (1st meeting), Oregon St. 13–3, St. Mary's 13–7 (1st over Gaels in 5-game series begun in 1929). *Lost:* USC 26–0. *Star:* FB Mike Mikulak. *Noteworthy:* got share of 2nd PCC title.

1947 (7–3) *Won:* Montana St. 27–14, Washington 6–0, San Francisco 34–7, Idaho 34–7, Washington St. 12–6, Stanford 21–6 (1st meeting since 1941), Oregon St. 14–6 (1st over Beavers in 6 games since 1940). *Lost:* Texas 38–13, Nevada-Reno 13–6, UCLA 24–7 in consecutive early games. *Stars:* HB Jake Leicht (930 yds rush, 7 TDs, 56 pts), QB Norm Van Brocklin (939 yds pass, 40.1-yd punting avg), Dan Garza (21 pass rec for 365 yds), C Brad Ecklund. *Noteworthy:* Had 1st winning season since 1935 in 1st year under Jim Aiken.

1948 (9–2) *Won:* Santa Barbara 55–7, Stanford 20–12, Idaho 15–8 (15th straight over Vandals), USC 8–7, Washington St. 33–7, St. Mary's 14–13 (1st meeting since 1935), Washington 13–7, UCLA 26–7, Oregon St. 10–0. *Lost:* unbeaten national champ Michigan 14–0. *Stars:* Van Brocklin (1,010 yds pass), Dick Wilkins (27 pass rec for 520 yds and 5 TDs), Garza, George Bell (648 yds rush), Johnny McKay (8 TDs), Ecklund. *Noteworthy:* Got share of 3rd PCC title. Lost to Southern Methodist (SMU) 21–13 in Cotton Bowl; Van Brocklin passed for 145 yds and a TD (24 yds to Wilkins), and Bob Sanders scored on 1-yd run.

1957 (7–4) *Won:* Idaho 9–6, UCLA 21–0 (1st over Bruins in 8 games since 1948), San Jose St. 26–0, Washington St. 14–13, California 24–6, Stanford 27–26 (1st over Indians since 1952), USC 16–7. *Lost:* Pittsburgh 6–3, Washington 13–6, Oregon St. 10–7. *Stars:* HB Jim Shanley (664 yds rush, 9 TDs), Ron Stover (24 pass rec for 247 yds), G Harry Mondale. *Noteworthy:* Got share of 4th PCC title. Lost to national cochamp Ohio St. 10–7 in Rose Bowl; Stover caught 10 passes for 144 yds and Shanley scored on 5-yd run.

1959 (8–2) *Won:* Stanford 28–27, Utah 21–6, Washington St. 14–6, San Jose St. 35–12, Air Force 21–3 (1st meeting), Idaho 45–7, California 20–18,

Washington St. 7–6. *Lost:* Washington 13–12, Oregon St. 15–7. *Stars:* HB Willie West (8 TDs), Dave Powell (5 TDs), Cleveland Jones (17 pass rec for 205 yds), C Bob Peterson.

1960 (7–3–1) *Won:* Idaho 33–6 (10th straight over Vandals), Utah 20–17, San Jose St. 33–0, Washington St. 21–12, California 20–0, Stanford 27–6, West Virginia 20–6. *Lost:* Michigan 21–0, Washington 7–6. *Tied:* Oregon St. 14–14. *Stars:* QB Dave Grosz, Jones (25 pass rec for 402 yds, 5 TDs), Dave Grayson (631 yds rush), G Dave Urell, soph T Steve Barnett. *Noteworthy:* lost to Penn St. 41–12 in Liberty Bowl; Grosz passed for 178 yds and scored 1st Oregon TD, and Grayson ran for 93 yds and scored on 10-yd run.

1963 (8–3) *Won:* Stanford 36–7, West Virginia 35–0, Idaho 41–21, Arizona 28–12, Washington St. 21–7, Indiana 28–22, Oregon St. 31–14 (1st over Beavers since 1958). *Lost:* Penn St. 17–7, Washington 26–19, San Jose St. 13–7 (1st in 8-game series dating to 1953). *Stars:* QB Bob Berry (1,675 yds and 16 TDs pass), Dick Imwalle (23 pass rec for 401 yds), HB Mel Renfro (444 yds rush, 18 pass rec for 260 yds, 6 TDs). *Noteworthy:* beat SMU 21–14 in Sun Bowl; Berry passed for 146 yds and

RB Mel Renfro, 1961–63

2 TDs (to Imwalle and Paul Burleson) and Dennis Keller scored on 9-yd run to give Ducks 21–0 halftime lead.

1964 (7–2–1) *Won:* Brigham Young (BYU) 20–13, Pittsburgh 22–13, Penn St. 22–14, Idaho 14–8, Arizona 21–0, Washington 7–0, Indiana 29–21. *Lost:* Stanford 10–8 (1st to Indians since 1956), Oregon St. 7–6. *Tied:* Washington St. 21–21. *Stars:* Berry (1,478 yds and 15 TDs pass), Ray Palm (42 pass rec for 570 yds), C Dave Tobey, G Mark Richards.

1989 (8–4) *Won:* California 35–19, Iowa 44–6, Arizona 16–10 (1st over Wildcats in 5 games since 1983), Arizona St. 27–7 (1st in 10-game series dating to 1966), Long Beach St. 52–10, UCLA 38–20, Oregon St. 30–21. *Lost:* Stanford 18–17, Washington St. 51–38 (1st to Cougars since 1984), Washington 20–14, BYU 45–41. *Stars:* TB Derek Loville (959 yds and 13 TDs rush, 1,236 all-purpose yds, 14 TDs), QB Bill Musgrave (3,081 yds and 22 TDs pass), SEs Terry Obee (46 pass rec for 741 yds and 5 TDs, 1,151 all-purpose yds) and Joe Reitzug (34 pass rec for 511 yds), FL Tony Hargain (40 pass rec for 686 yds and 5 TDs), FBs Latin Berry (542 yds rush, 27 pass rec for 292 yds) and Dondre Bausley (26 pass rec for 273 yds), TE Kolya Tefft (5 TDs), soph K Gregg McCallum (24 FGs, 109 pts), LB Mark Kearns, DBs Chris Oldham (8 int) and Derek Horton (5 int). *Noteworthy:* made 1st postseason appearance in 26 years, beating Tulsa 27–24 in Independence Bowl; Musgrave passed for 320 yds and 2 TDs and scored another, Reitzug had 6 pass rec for 121 yds and a TD, Hargain had 5 pass rec for 100 yds and a TD, and McCallum kicked 2 FGs and 3 ex pts.

1990 (8–4) *Won:* San Diego St. 42–21, Idaho 55–23 (1st meeting since 1970), BYU 32–16, Utah St. 52–7, Arizona St. 27–7, Stanford 31–0, UCLA 28–24, Oregon St. 6–3. *Lost:* Arizona 22–17, Washington 38–17, California 28–3. *Stars:* Musgrave (2,219 yds and 14 TDs pass), Reitzug (35 pass rec for 542 yds), TE Jeff Thomason (30 pass rec for 396 yds and 6 TDs), SE Michael McClellan (27 pass rec for 377 yds), frosh TB Sean Burwell (996 yds and 8 TDs rush, 28 pass rec for 286 yds and 1 TD), soph TB Ngalu Kelemeni (26 pass rec for 242 yds and 1 TD, 5 TDs rush), McCallum (14 FGs, 74 pts), NT Marcus Woods, DE Matt LaBounty, soph LB Joe Farwell, DBs Daryle Smith (6 int) and soph Eric Castle, frosh P Tommy Thompson (40.7-yd avg).

Noteworthy: lost to Colorado St. 32–31 in Freedom Bowl when 2-pt conversion pass failed with 1:01 left in game; Musgrave passed for 392 yds, 3 TDs, and 2-pt conversion, and McClellan had 9 pass rec for 148 yds and a TD.

BOWL SUMMARY

Cotton 0–1; Freedom 0–1; Independence 1–1; Liberty 0–1; Rose 1–2; Sun 1–0.

BOWL RECORD (3–6)

Regular Season	Bowl	Score	Opponent	Record
1916 (6–0–1)	Rose	14–0	Pennsylvania	(7–2–1)
1919 (5–1)	Rose	6–7	Harvard	(8–0–1)
1948 (9–1)	Cotton	13–21	SMU	(8–1–1)
1957 (7–3)	Rose	7–10	Ohio State	(8–1)
1960 (7–2–1)	Liberty	12–41	Penn State	(6–3)
1963 (7–3)	Sun	21–14	SMU	(4–6)
1989 (7–4)	Independence	27–24	Tulsa	(6–5)
1990 (8–3)	Freedom	31–32	Colorado St.	(8–4)
1992 (6–5)	Independence	35–39	Wake Forest	(7–4)

CONFERENCE TITLES

Pacific Coast—1919*, 1933*, 1948*, 1957*. **Pacific-10**—None.

TOP 20 AP AND UPI

1948	9	1957	U–17

MAJOR RIVALS

Oregon has played at least 10 games with Air Force 7–3–1, Arizona 8–10, Arizona St. 3–10, California 22–34–2, Colorado 6–6, Idaho 49–3–4, Multnomah A.C. 11–20–3, Oregon St. 47–39–10, Pacific (Ore.) 14–0–2, St. Mary's 3–7, San Jose St. 11–6, Southern California 10–31–2, Stanford 19–38–1, UCLA 16–33, Utah 14–6, Washington 28–53–5, Washington St. 33–30–7, Whitman 7–3, Willamette 22–1–1.

COACHES

Deans of Oregon coaches are Len Casanova, 82–73–8 for 1951–66, with 1 PCC title and 3 bowl teams; and Rich Brooks, 77–99–4 for 1977–92 with 3 bowl teams. Other top records for at least 3 years were by Hugo Bezdek, 25–10–3 for 1913–17 with 1 unbeaten Rose Bowl champion; Shy Huntington, 26–12–6 for 1918–23 with 1 PCC title and 1 Rose Bowl team; John McEwan, 20–13–2 for 1926–29; Prink Callison, 33–23–2 for 1932–37 with 1 PCC title; and Jim Aiken, 21–20 for 1947–50 with 1 PCC title and 1 Cotton Bowl team.

MISCELLANEA

First game was win over Albany College 44–2 in 1894 . . . highest score was over Puget Sound 115–0 in 1910 . . . highest since W.W. II was over Nevada–Las Vegas 59–6 in 1992 . . . biggest margin since W.W. II was over Washington 58–0 in 1973 . . . worst defeat was by Washington 66–0 in 1974 . . . highest against was by Oklahoma 68–3 in 1972 . . . longest unbeaten string of 16 in 1915–17 ended by Washington St. 26–3 . . . longest losing string of 14 in 1974–75 broken with win over Utah 18–7 . . . consensus All-American was Mel Renfro, B, 1962 . . . Academic All-Americans were Steve Barnett, OT, 1962; Tim Casey, LB, 1965; Mike Preacher, P, 1986; and Bill Musgrave, QB, 1990.

OREGON STATE (Beavers; Orange and Black)

NOTABLE TEAMS

1893 (4–1) *Won:* Albany College 62–0, Monmouth College 36–22, 28–0, Multnomah A.C. 6–0. *Lost:* Portland 26–12. *Noteworthy:* 1st year of competition.
1902 (4–1–1) *Won:* Willamette 67–0, 21–0, McMinnville 33–0, Pacific (Ore.) 31–0 (1st meeting). *Lost:* Washington 16–5. *Tied:* Oregon 0–0. *Noteworthy:* 1st games since regents prohibited athletics in 1900.
1906 (4–1–2) *Won:* Albany A.C. 24–0, Alumni 16–0, Pacific (Ore.) 28–0, Columbia A.C. 9–0. *Lost:* Willamette 4–0 in finale. *Tied:* Washington 0–0, unbeaten Oregon 0–0. *Noteworthy:* 1st year under F.S. Norcross.
1907 (6–0) *Won:* Astoria 26–0, Whitman 6–0, Pacific (Ore.) 49–0, Oregon 4–0 (1st over Ducks in 8 games since 1897), Willamette 42–0, St. Vincent College 10–0. *Noteworthy:* blanked foes 137–0 in 1st unbeaten season since 2-game schedule of 1897.
1911 (5–2) *Won:* Pacific (Ore.) 26–0, Chemawa Indians 75–6, Washington St. 6–0, Willamette 5–3, Whitman 5–3. *Lost:* Alumni 3–2, unbeaten Washington 34–0.
1914 (7–0–2) *Won:* Alumni 12–0, Rooks 12–0, Multnomah A.C. 10–6, Willamette 64–0, Washington St. 7–0, Idaho 26–0, USC 38–6 (1st meeting). *Tied:* unbeaten Washington 0–0, Oregon 3–3. *Noteworthy:* 1st unbeaten season since 1907.
1925 (7–2) *Won:* Willamette 51–0, Gonzaga 22–0, Whitman 62–0, Montana 27–7 (1st meeting), Pacific (Ore.) 56–0, Oregon 24–13, Idaho 16–7. *Lost:* Stanford 26–10, USC 28–0.
1926 (7–1) *Won:* Multnomah A.C. 67–0, Montana 49–0, Gonzaga 23–6, California 27–7 (1st in 6-game series dating to 1905), Idaho 3–0, Oregon 16–0, Marquette 29–0. *Lost:* USC 17–7. *Stars:* Ts Percy Locey and Jim Dixon.
1930 (7–3) *Won:* Willamette 48–0, Gonzaga 16–0, Cal Aggies 20–0, Pacific (Ore.) 57–0, Oregon 15–0, UCLA 19–0 (1st meeting), West Virginia 12–0. *Lost:* USC 27–7, Stanford 13–7, unbeaten Washington St. 14–7. *Star:* E Bill McKalip.
1933 (6–2–2) *Won:* Ashland Normal 21–0, Willamette 21–0, Montana 20–0, San Francisco 12–7, Washington St. 2–0 (1st over Cougars since 1927), Fordham 9–6. *Lost:* Oregon 13–3, Nebraska 22–0

(1st meeting since 1924). *Tied:* Gonzaga 0–0, USC 0–0. *Stars:* HB Norman "Red" Franklin, T Ade Schwammel. *Noteworthy:* 1st year under Lon Stiner.
1939 (9–1–1) *Won:* Stanford 12–0, Idaho 7–6, Portland 14–12, Washington 13–7, Washington St. 13–0, Oregon 19–14, California 21–0, Hawaiian All Stars 28–0, Hawaii 39–6. *Lost:* unbeaten USC 19–7. *Tied:* unbeaten UCLA 13–13. *Stars:* FB Jim Kisselburgh (8 TDs rush), G Eberle Schultz.
1941 (8–2) *Won:* Washington 9–6, Stanford 10–0, Idaho 33–0, UCLA 19–0, California 6–0, Montana 27–0, Oregon 12–7. *Lost:* USC 13–7, Washington St. 7–0. *Stars:* QB George Peters, HB Don Durdan (5 TDs), C Quentin Greenough. *Noteworthy:* Won 1st PCC title. Made 1st postseason appearance, upsetting unbeaten Duke 20–16 in Rose Bowl transplanted to Durham, N.C., because of fears of Japanese attack on West Coast following Pearl Harbor; Beavers scored on 15-yd run by Durdan, 31-yd pass from Bob Dethman to George Zellick, and 68-yd pass from Dethman to Gene Gray.
1946 (7–1–1) *Won:* Portland 35–0, USC 6–0 (1st over Trojans in 8 games since 1935), Washington St. 13–12 (1st over Cougars in 5 games since 1940), Idaho 34–0, California 28–7, Oregon 13–0, Washington 21–12. *Lost:* unbeaten UCLA 50–7 in opener. *Tied:* Stanford 0–0. *Stars:* frosh HB Ken Carpenter (589 yds rush, 5 TDs), C Bill Gray.
1949 (7–3) *Won:* Utah 27–7, Washington 7–3, Montana 63–14, Washington St. 35–6, Idaho 35–25, Michigan St. 25–20, Oregon 20–10. *Lost:* UCLA 35–13, unbeaten California 41–0, Stanford 27–7. *Stars:* Carpenter (1,297 all-purpose yds, 689 yds rush, 9 TDs), Stan McGuire (17 pass rec for 308 yds), Bill Sheffield (9 int). *Noteworthy:* 1st year under Kip Taylor.
1956 (7–3–1) *Won:* Missouri 19–13, California 21–13, Washington St. 21–0, UCLA 21–7 (1st over Bruins since 1948), Washington 28–20, Stanford 20–9, Idaho 14–10. *Lost:* USC 21–13, Iowa 14–13 (1st meeting) in consecutive early games. *Tied:* Oregon 14–14. *Stars:* HB Earnel Durden (508 yds rush), T John Witte (1st Oregon St. consensus All-American). *Noteworthy:* Won 2nd PCC title. Lost rematch with Iowa 35–19 in Rose Bowl; TB Joe Francis passed for 130 yds and a TD (35 yards to Sterling Hammack) and ran for 73 yds, and other Beaver TDs came on short runs by Tom Berry and soph Nub Beamer.
1957 (8–2) *Won:* USC 20–0 (1st over Trojans in 8

games since 1946), Kansas 34–6, Northwestern 22–13, Idaho 20–0, Washington St. 39–25, California 21–19, Stanford 24–14, Oregon 10–7. *Lost:* UCLA 26–7, Washington 19–6 in successive midseason games. *Stars:* Francis (9 TDs), Beamer (760 yds and 8 TDs rush), Bob DeGrant (19 pass rec for 239 yds), C Buzz Randall. *Noteworthy:* got share of 3rd PCC title.

1962 (9–2) *Won:* Iowa St. 39–35, Stanford 27–0, Pacific 40–6, West Virginia 51–22, Idaho 32–0 (10th straight over Vandals), Washington St. 18–12, Colorado St. 24–14, Oregon 20–17. *Lost:* Iowa 28–8, Washington 14–13 in early games. *Stars:* QB Terry Baker (Heisman Trophy and Maxwell Award winner; 1,738 yds and 15 TDs pass, 538 yds and 9 TDs rush, nation's leader with 2,276 yds total off), FL Vern Burke (nation's leader with 69 pass rec for 1,007 yds and 10 TDs), soph T Rich Koeper, soph DB Dan Espalin (9 int). *Noteworthy:* beat Villanova 6–0 in cold, snowy Liberty Bowl; scored on 99-yd 1st-quarter run by Baker (137 yds rush, 123 yds pass).

1964 (8–3) *Won:* Colorado 14–7, Baylor 13–6, Washington 9–7, Idaho 10–7, Syracuse 31–13, Washington St. 24–7, Indiana 24–14, Oregon 7–6. *Lost:* Northwestern 7–3, Stanford 16–7. *Stars:* Koeper, Espalin, QB Paul Brothers (1,036 yds pass), Olvin Moreland (35 pass rec for 428 yds), LB Jack O'Billovich. *Noteworthy:* Tommy Prothro's last team earned share of Pacific-8 title in 1st year in league (4th conference title overall). Lost to Michigan 34–7 in Rose Bowl, though scoring 1st on 5-yd

TD pass from Brothers to Doug McDougal.

1966 (7–3) *Won:* Iowa 17–3 (1st in 6-game series dating to 1956), Idaho 14–7, Arizona St. 18–17 (1st meeting since 1961), Washington St. 41–13, Arizona 31–12 (1st meeting), Washington 24–13, Oregon 20–15. *Lost:* Michigan 41–0, USC 21–0, Northwestern 14–6 in early games. *Stars:* FB Pete Pifer (1,088 yds and 12 TDs rush), Bob Grim (25 pass rec for 289 yds), OT Jim Wilkin, DT Skip Diaz, P Gary Houser (42.6-yd avg).

1967 (7–2–1) *Won:* Stanford 13–7, Arizona St. 27–21, Iowa 38–18, Purdue 22–14, Washington St. 35–7, national champ USC 3–0, Oregon 14–10. *Lost:* Washington 13–6, Brigham Young (BYU) 31–13 in early games. *Tied:* UCLA 16–16 (1st meeting since 1958). *Stars:* QB Steve Preece (1,113 yds pass), Roger Cantlon (14 pass rec for 214 yds), FB Bill Enyart (851 yds and 8 TDs rush), OL Jon Sandstrom and Dave Marlette, soph DT Jess Lewis, Houser (43.4-yd punting avg).

1968 (7–3) *Won:* Utah 24–21, Washington 35–21, Arizona St. 28–9, Washington St. 16–8, Stanford 29–7, UCLA 45–21, Oregon 41–19. *Lost:* Iowa 21–20, Kentucky 35–34, unbeaten USC 17–13. *Stars:* Enyart (1,304 yds and 17 TDs rush), Billy Main (14 TDs), Cantlon (23 pass rec for 409 yds), OG Clyde Smith, C John Didion, DT Sandstrom.

BOWL SUMMARY

Liberty 1–0; Rose 1–2.

BOWL RECORD (2–2)

Regular Season	Bowl	Score	Opponent	Record
1941 (7–2)	Rose	20–16	Duke	(9–0)
1956 (7–2–1)	Rose	19–35	Iowa	(8–1)
1962 (8–2)	Liberty	6–0	Villanova	(7–2)
1964 (8–2)	Rose	7–34	Michigan	(8–1)

CONFERENCE TITLES

Pacific Coast—1941, 1956, 1957*. **Pacific-8**—1964*. **Pacific-10**—None.

TOP 20 AP AND UPI RANKING

1941	12	1962	U–16	1966	U–19	1968	15–13
1956	10–13	1964	8–8	1967	7–8		

MAJOR RIVALS

Oregon St. has played at least 10 games with Arizona 2–13–1, Arizona St. 6–14–1, California 20–27, Idaho 34–7, Iowa 5–7, Montana 12–1–2, Multnomah A.C. 7–11–4, Nebraska 2–9, Oregon 39–47–10, Pacific (Ore.) 12–0–2, Southern California 7–46–4, Stanford 16–41–3, UCLA 10–31–4, Utah 8–4–1, Washington 26–46–4, Washington St. 36–41–3, Whitman 12–0, Willamette 21–2.

COACHES

Dean of Oregon St. coaches is Lon Stiner with record of 74–49–17 for 1933–42 and 1945–48 with 1 PCC and Rose Bowl champion. Other top records for at least 3 years were by F.S. Norcross, 14–4–3 for 1906–1908; E.J. Stewart, 15–5–5 for 1913–15 with 1 unbeaten team; Paul J. Schissler, 48–30–2 for 1924–32; Tommy Prothro, 63–37–2 for 1955–64 with 3 conference titles and 3 bowl teams; and Dee Andros, 51–64–1 for 1965–75.

MISCELLANEA

First game was win over Albany College 62–0 in 1893 . . . highest score was over Willamette 76–0 in 1931 . . . highest since W.W. II was over Idaho 66–18 in 1959 . . . biggest margin since W.W. II was over Hawaii 59–0 in 1976 . . . worst defeat was by USC 63–0 in 1985 (matching high against Beavers by Stanford 63–9 in 1981) . . . longest unbeaten string of 15 in 1913–15 ended by Washington St. 29–0 . . . longest winless string of 19 in 1981–82 broken with win over Montana 30–10 . . . longest losing string of 15 in 1990–91 broken with win over Oregon 14–3 . . . 14-game losing string, in 1979–80 broken with win over Fresno St. 31–28 in 1981 opener and in 1981–82 with tie with Washington St. 14–14 . . . consensus All-Americans were John Witte, T, 1956; Ted Bates, T, 1958; Terry Baker, B, 1962; Vern Burke, E, 1963; and John Didion, C, 1968 . . . Academic All-Americans were Terry Baker, B, 1962; and Bill Enyart, FB, 1967–68 . . . Heisman Trophy winner was Terry Baker, QB, 1962 . . . Maxwell Award winner was Terry Baker, QB, 1962.

SOUTHERN CALIFORNIA
(Trojans; Cardinal and Gold)

NOTABLE TEAMS

1897 (5–1) *Won:* Loyola (Calif.) 34–0 (1st meeting since 1890), Los Angeles H.S. 10–0, Chaffey College 38–0, Pomona 6–0 (1st meeting), Ventura 12–0. *Lost:* San Diego YMCA 18–0.

1898 (5–1–1) *Won:* Pasadena A.C. 17–0, Pomona 14–11, 7th Regiment 34–0, Phoenix Indians 27–11, Santa Barbara A.C. 5–0. *Lost:* Los Angeles H.S. 6–0. *Tied:* Los Angeles H.S. 0–0 in opener.

1904 (6–1) *Won:* Los Angeles H.S. 42–0, Cal Tech 35–0, Occidental 36–4, Whittier Reform 60–6, Loyola (Calif.) (forfeit), Southern California Prep 26–0. *Lost:* Sherman Institute 17–0. *Noteworthy:* 1st year under Harvey Holmes.

1907 (5–1) *Won:* Los Angeles H.S. 6–0, Whittier Reform 57–0, Santa Ana H.S. 51–0, Whittier 46–0 (1st meeting), USS Colorado 16–4. *Lost:* Los Angeles H.S. 16–6 in finale. *Noteworthy:* last year under Holmes.

1908 (3–1–1) *Won:* Whittier 15–0, Arrowhead A.C. 28–0, Occidental 14–0. *Lost:* Los Angeles H.S. 12–0 in opener. *Tied:* Pomona 6–6.

1910 (7–0–1) *Won:* Long Beach H.S. 22–6, Chaffey H.S. 65–6, Cal Tech 9–0, San Diego H.S. 32–0, Redlands 35–0, Occidental 6–0, Whittier 11–3. *Tied:* Pomona 9–9 in finale.

1911–1913 Played rugby instead of American football.

1919 (4–1) *Won:* Pomona 6–0, Occidental 27–0, Utah 28–7, Stanford 13–0. *Lost:* California 14–13. *Noteworthy:* 1st year under Elmer "Gloomy Gus" Henderson.

1920 (6–0) *Won:* Cal Tech 46–7 (1st meeting since 1910), Stanford 10–0, Occidental 48–7, Pomona 7–0, Nevada-Reno 38–7, Oregon 21–0 (1st meeting since 1915). *Noteworthy:* 1st unbeaten season since 1910.

1921 (10–1) *Won:* USS Arizona 62–0, USS New York 35–0, Cal Tech 70–0, Submarine Base 34–0, 28–0, Occidental 42–0, Pomona 35–7, Whittier 14–0, Oregon St. 7–0 (1st meeting since 1916), Washington St. 28–7 (1st meeting). *Lost:* unbeaten California 38–7.

1922 (10–1) *Won:* Alumni 20–0, USS Mississippi 20–0, Pomona 54–13, Arizona 15–0 (1st meeting since 1917), Nevada-Reno 6–0, Occidental 46–0, Stanford 6–0, Idaho 14–0 (1st meeting), Washington St. 41–3. *Lost:* unbeaten California 12–0. *Noteworthy:* made 1st postseason appearance, beating Penn St. 14–3 in Rose Bowl on TDs by Gordon Campbell and Roy Baker.

1923 (6–2) *Won:* Cal Tech 18–7, Pomona 23–7, Nevada-Reno 33–0, Stanford 14–7, Arizona 69–6, Idaho 9–0. *Lost:* Washington 22–0 (1st meeting), unbeaten California 13–7.

1924 (9–2) *Won:* Cal Tech 78–6, Pomona 14–0, Arizona 29–0, Oregon St. 17–3, Nevada-Reno 21–7, Whittier 51–0, Idaho 13–0, Syracuse 16–0. *Lost:* California 7–0, St. Mary's 14–10 (1st meeting since 1917) in consecutive mid-season games. *Noteworthy:* Henderson's last team. Beat Missouri 20–7 in Los Angeles Christmas Festival game on TDs by Hayden Pythian, Wallace Newman, and Henry Lefebvre.

1925 (11–2) *Won:* Whittier 74–0, Cal Tech 32–0, Pomona 80–0, Utah 28–2, Arizona 56–0, Idaho 51–7, Santa Clara 29–9 (1st meeting), Montana 27–7 (1st meeting), Iowa 18–0 (1st meeting), Oregon St. 28–0, St. Mary's 12–0. *Lost:* Stanford 13–9 (1st to Indians in 6 games since 1905), Washington St. 17–12. *Stars:* G Brice Taylor, B Mort Kaer (576 yds rush, 19 TDs). *Noteworthy:* 1st year under Howard Jones.

1926 (8–2) *Won:* Whittier 74–0, Santa Clara 42–0, Washington St. 16–7, Occidental 28–6, California 27–0 (1st over Bears in 10 games since 1915), Oregon St. 17–7, Idaho 28–6, Montana 61–0. *Lost:* unbeaten national cochamp Stanford 13–12, Notre Dame 13–12 (1st meeting). *Star:* Kaer (Trojans' 1st consensus All-American; 852 yds rush, 12 TDs).

1927 (8–1–1) *Won:* Occidental 33–0, Santa Clara 52–12, Oregon St. 13–12, Cal Tech 51–0, California 13–0, Colorado 46–7, Washington St. 27–0, Washington 33–13. *Lost:* Notre Dame 7–6. *Tied:* Stanford 13–13. *Stars:* B Morley Drury (1,163 yds rush, 11 TDs, 76 pts), T Jesse Hibbs. *Noteworthy:* got share of 1st PCC title.

1928 (9–0–1) *Won:* Utah St. 40–12, Oregon St. 19–0, St. Mary's 19–6, Occidental 19–0, Stanford 10–0, Arizona 78–7, Washington St. 27–13, Idaho 28–7, Notre Dame 27–14. *Tied:* California 0–0. *Stars:* Hibbs, C Nate Barragar, Bs Don Williams (681 yds rush, 7 TDs) and Lloyd Thomas. *Noteworthy:* won 2nd straight PCC title and share

of 1st national championship in 1st undefeated season since 1920.

1929 (10–2) *Won:* UCLA 76–0 (1st meeting), Oregon St. 21–7, Washington 48–0, Occidental 64–0, Stanford 7–0, Nevada-Reno 66–0, Idaho 72–0, Washington St. 27–7, Carnegie Tech 45–13. *Lost:* California 15–7, unbeaten national champ Notre Dame 13–12. *Stars:* Barragar, E Francis Tappaan, Bs Russ Saunders (972 yds rush, 14 TDs) and Marsh Duffield. *Noteworthy:* Won 3rd straight PCC crown. Beat undefeated Pittsburgh 47–14 in Rose Bowl; Saunders threw 3 TD passes (2 to E Harry Edelson) and Duffield scored 2 TDs and passed for another.

1930 (8–2) *Won:* UCLA 52–0, Oregon St. 27–7, Utah St. 65–0, Stanford 41–12, Denver 33–13, California 74–0, Hawaii 52–0, Washington 32–0. *Lost:* unbeaten Washington St. 7–6 (1st to Cougars since 1925), unbeaten national champ Notre Dame 27–0. *Stars:* Duffield, soph B Orv Mohler (983 yds rush, 17 TDs), B Erny Pinckert, E Garrett Arbelbide, G Johnny Baker.

1931 (10–1) *Won:* Oregon St. 30–0, Washington St. 38–6, Oregon 53–0 (1st meeting since 1920), California 6–0, Stanford 19–0, Montana 69–0, Notre Dame 16–14, Washington 44–7, Georgia 60–0. *Lost:* St. Mary's 13–7 in opener. *Stars:* Pinckert, HB Gus Shaver (936 yds rush, 16 TDs, 100 pts), Baker, C Stan Williamson, T Ernie Smith, E Ray Sparling. *Noteworthy:* Won 4th PCC title and 2nd national crown. Beat undefeated Tulane 21–12 in Rose Bowl; Pinckert ran for 2 TDs (25 and 30 yds) and Sparling scored other Trojan TD.

1932 (10–0) *Won:* Utah 35–0, Washington St. 20–0, Oregon St. 10–0 (10th straight over Beavers), Loyola (Calif.) 6–0 (1st meeting since 1909), Stanford 13–0, California 27–7, Oregon 33–0, Washington 9–6, Notre Dame 13–0. *Stars:* Smith, T Tay Brown, G Aaron Rosenberg, Mohler, soph B Irvine "Cotton" Warburton, B Homer Griffith (8 TDs). *Noteworthy:* Repeated as national and PCC champs. Beat undefeated Pittsburgh 35–0 in Rose Bowl, breaking open close game with 21 pts in last quarter; Warburton scored 2 TDs.

1933 (10–1–1) *Won:* Occidental 39–0, Whittier 51–0 (1st meeting since 1926), Loyola (Calif.) 18–0, Washington St. 33–0, St. Mary's 14–7, California 6–3, Oregon 26–0, Notre Dame 19–0, Georgia 31–0, Washington 13–7. *Lost:* Stanford 13–7 (1st to

Indians since 1926). *Tied:* Oregon St. 0–0. *Stars:* Warburton (885 yds rush, 12 TDs), Rosenberg, G Larry Stevens.

1938 (9–2) *Won:* Oregon St. 7–0, Ohio St. 14–7, Washington St. 19–6, Stanford 13–2, Oregon 31–7, California 13–7 (1st over Bears since 1933), UCLA 42–7, Notre Dame 13–0. *Lost:* Alabama 19–7, Washington 7–6. *Stars:* G Harry Smith, B Grenny Lansdell (920 yds total off, 5 TDs). *Noteworthy:* Got share of 6th PCC title. Upset unbeaten, unscored-on Duke 7–3 in Rose Bowl when 4th string TB Doyle Nave threw 19-yd TD pass to soph 2nd string E Al Krueger in game's waning moments.

1939 (8–0–2) *Won:* Washington St. 27–0, Illinois 26–0, California 26–0, Oregon St. 19–7, Stanford 33–0, Notre Dame 20–12, Washington 9–7. *Tied:* Oregon 7–7 (opener), unbeaten UCLA 0–0 (finale). *Stars:* Lansdell (742 yds rush, 1,221 yds total off, 9 TDs), B Bob Hoffman, Smith, Ts Phil Gaspar and Howard Stoecker. *Noteworthy:* Got share of 7th PCC title. Beat undefeated, unscored-on Tennessee 14–0 in Rose Bowl; Amby Schindler scored 1st TD and passed to Krueger for 2nd.

1943 (8–2) *Won:* UCLA 20–0, 26–13, California 7–0, 13–0, St. Mary's Pre-Flight 13–0, San Francisco 34–0, Pacific 6–0. *Lost:* San Diego Navy 10–7, March Field 35–0 in consecutive late games. *Stars:* B Mickey McCardle, George Callanan (6 TDs), E Ralph Heywood, C Bill Gray. *Noteworthy:* Won 8th PCC title. Beat undefeated Washington 29–0 in Rose Bowl; Jim Hardy threw 3 TD passes and Callanan and frosh Gordon Gray each scored twice.

1944 (8–0–2) *Won:* Pacific 18–6, St. Mary's Pre-Flight 6–0, Washington 38–7, St. Mary's 34–7 (1st meeting since 1933), San Diego Navy 28–21, California 32–0, UCLA 40–13. *Tied:* UCLA 13–13, California 6–6 in early games. *Stars:* Hardy (856 yds total off, 10 TDs pass), Gordon Gray (7 TDs), Callanan, T John Ferraro. *Noteworthy:* Repeated as PCC champ. Beat undefeated Tennessee 25–0 in Rose Bowl; Hardy passed for 2 TDs and ran for a 3rd.

1945 (7–4) *Won:* UCLA 13–6, 26–15, California 13–2, 14–0, St. Mary's Pre-Flight 26–14, Pacific 52–0, Oregon St. 34–7. *Lost:* San Diego Navy 33–6, Washington 13–7, St. Mary's 26–0. *Star:* Ted Tannehill (574 yds rush, 7 TDs). *Noteworthy:* Won 3rd straight PCC title (10th overall). Lost to

unbeaten Alabama 34–14 in Rose Bowl for 1st postseason loss in 10 appearances (9 in Rose Bowl); Trojan TDs were by Harry Adelman and Don Clark.

1947 (7–2–1) *Won:* Washington St. 21–0, Ohio St. 32–0, Oregon St. 48–6, California 39–14, Washington 19–0, Stanford 14–0, UCLA 6–0. *Lost:* unbeaten national cochamp Notre Dame 38–7 in finale. *Tied:* Rice 7–7. *Stars:* Ferraro, T Bob Hendren, E Paul Cleary, B Don Doll, Jack Kirby (5 TDs). *Noteworthy:* Won 11th PCC title. Lost to unbeaten Michigan 49–0 in Rose Bowl.

1951 (7–3) *Won:* Washington St. 31–21, San Diego Navy 41–7, Washington 20–13, Oregon St. 16–14, California 21–14, Texas Christian (TCU) 28–26, Army 28–6 in 1st 7 games. *Lost:* Stanford 27–20, UCLA 21–7, Notre Dame 19–12. *Stars:* Bs Frank Gifford (841 yds rush, 303 yds pass, 7 TDs, 74 pts) and Johnny Williams, LB Pat Cannamela, Dick Nunis (6 int), soph P Des Koch (43.3-yd avg). *Noteworthy:* 1st year under Jess Hill.

1952 (10–1) *Won:* Washington St. 35–7, Northwestern 31–0, Army 22–0, San Diego Navy 20–6, Oregon St. 28–6, California 10–0, Stanford 54–7, Washington 33–0, UCLA 14–12. *Lost:* Notre Dame 9–0 in finale. *Stars:* HB/DB Jim Sears (1,030 yds total off, 6 TDs), HB Jim Psaltis (9 int), Tom Nickoloff (25 pass rec for 372 yds), E Bob Hooks, G Elmer Wilhoite, C Lou Welsh, T Bob Van Doren, LB George Timberlake, Koch (nation's leader with 43.5-yd punting avg). *Noteworthy:* Led nation in scoring defense (4.7-pt avg) and won 12th and last PCC title. Beat Wisconsin 7–0 in Rose Bowl on 22-yd TD pass from reserve QB Rudy Bukich to Al Carmichael in 3rd quarter.

1954 (8–4) *Won:* Washington St. 39–0, Pittsburgh 27–7 (1st meeting since 1935), Northwestern 12–7, Oregon 24–14, California 29–27, Oregon St. 34–0, Stanford 21–7, Washington 41–34. *Lost:* TCU 20–7, unbeaten national cochamp UCLA 34–0, Notre Dame 23–17. *Stars:* soph HB Jon Arnett (835 all-purpose yds, 6 TDs), E Leon Clarke (13 pass rec for 232 yds), T Ed Fouch. *Noteworthy:* lost to unbeaten national cochamp Ohio St. 20–7 in rainy, muddy Rose Bowl; Arnett ran for 123 yds in 9 carries and Trojans scored on 86-yd punt return by B Aramis Dandoy.

1956 (8–2) *Won:* Texas 44–20, Oregon St. 21–13, Wisconsin 13–6, Washington 35–7, Washington St. 28–12, California 20–7, UCLA 10–7, Notre Dame

28–20. *Lost:* Stanford 27–19, Oregon 7–0. *Stars:* Arnett (625 yds rush, 8 TDs), B C.R. Roberts (775 yds rush), Tony Ortega (7 pass rec for 223 yds), Ernie Zampese (6 int, 41.2-yd punting avg). *Noteworthy:* Hill's last team.

1959 (8–2) *Won:* Oregon St. 27–6, Pittsburgh 23–0, Ohio St. 17–0, Washington 22–15, Stanford 30–28, California 14–7, West Virginia 36–0, Baylor 17–8 in 1st 8 games. *Lost:* UCLA 10–3, Notre Dame 16–6. *Stars:* E Marlin McKeever, G Mike McKeever (Marlin's twin), T Ron Mix, B Jerry Traynham (583 yds rush), Clark Holden (5 TDs), Willie Wood (5 int). *Noteworthy:* last year under Don Clark.

1962 (11–0) *Won:* Duke 14–7, Southern Methodist (SMU) 33–3, Iowa 7–0, California 32–6, Illinois 28–16, Washington 14–0, Stanford 39–14, Navy 13–6, UCLA 14–3, Notre Dame 25–0 (1st over Irish since 1956). *Stars:* QB Pete Beathard (10 TDs pass, 1,238 yds total off), E Hal Bedsole (33 pass rec for 827 yds and 11 TDs), HB/DB Willie Brown (574 yds rush, 5 int), T Gary Kirner, LB Damon Bame. *Noteworthy:* Nation's most-improved team won 2nd AAWU title and 4th national crown in 1st unbeaten season since 1944. Beat Wisconsin 42–37 in Rose Bowl; Beathard passed for 4 TDs, 2 to Bedsole, to build up 42–14 lead by early 4th quarter.

1963 (7–3) *Won:* Colorado 14–0, Michigan St. 13–10, Ohio St. 32–3, California 36–6, Stanford 25–11, Oregon St. 28–22, UCLA 26–6. *Lost:* Oklahoma 17–12 (1st meeting), Notre Dame 17–14, Washington 22–7. *Stars:* Bame, Kirner, Brown (34 pass rec for 448 yds, 7 TDs), Beathard (1,036 yds total off), soph TB Mike Garrett (833 yds rush).

1964 (7–3) *Won:* Colorado 21–0, Oklahoma 40–14, Texas A&M 31–7, California 26–21, Stanford 15–10, UCLA 34–13, national cochamp Notre Dame 20–17. *Lost:* Michigan St. 17–7, Ohio St. 17–0, Washington 14–13. *Stars:* QB Craig Fertig (1,671 yds and 11 TDs pass), Fred Hill (33 pass rec for 436 yds), Garrett (948 yds rush, 10 TDs, 17 pass rec for 225 yds), OG Bill Fisk, OT Bob Svihus, DE Jeff Smith, DB Gary Hill. *Noteworthy:* got share of 3rd AAWU title.

1965 (7–2–1) *Won:* Wisconsin 26–6, Oregon St. 26–12, Washington 34–0, Stanford 14–0, California 35–0, Pittsburgh 28–0, Wyoming 56–6. *Lost:* Notre Dame 28–7, UCLA 20–16. *Tied:* Minnesota 20–20. *Stars:* Heisman Trophy–winner Garrett (16 TDs, nation's leader with 1,440 yds rush), QB Troy Winslow (1,019 yds and 11 TDs pass), Dave Moton (29 pass rec for 493 yds and 5 TDs), C Paul Johnson, OG Frank Lopez, OT Chuck Arrobio, DE Jim Walker, soph DT Ron Yary, LB Smith, DB Nate Shaw.

1966 (7–4) *Won:* Texas 10–6, Wisconsin 38–3, Oregon St. 21–0, Washington 17–14, Stanford 21–7, Clemson 30–0, California 35–9. *Lost:* Miami (Fla.) 10–7, UCLA 14–7, unbeaten national cochamp Notre Dame 51–0. *Stars:* Winslow (1,023 yds pass), E Ron Drake (52 pass rec for 607 yds), Don McCall (560 yds rush), HB Rod Sherman (6 TDs, 42 pass rec for 445 yds), OT Yary, OG Jim Homan, DE Ray May, NG Larry Petrill, Shaw (5 int). *Noteworthy:* Won 4th AAWU title. Lost to Purdue

TB Mike Garrett, 1963–65

14–13 in Rose Bowl when 2-pt conversion attempt failed with less than 3 minutes remaining; McCall scored 1st Trojan TD and Winslow passed 19 yds to Sherman for 2nd.

1967 (10–1)   *Won:* Washington St. 49–0 (1st meeting since 1958), Texas 17–13, Michigan St. 21–17, Stanford 30–0 (10th straight over Indians), Notre Dame 24–7, Washington 23–6, Oregon 28–6 (1st meeting since 1958), California 31–12, UCLA 21–20. *Lost:* Oregon St. 3–0.   *Stars:* TB O.J. Simpson (11 TDs, nation's leader with 1,415 yds rush and 1,700 all-purpose yds), Outland Trophy–winner Yary, QB Steve Sogge (1,032 yds pass), E Earl Mc-Cullouch (30 pass rec for 540 yds and 5 TDs), DE Tim Rossovich, LB Adrian Young, DB Mike Battle (5 int, nation's punt return leader with 12.1-yd avg).   *Noteworthy:* Won 5th title in last year of AAWU. Beat Indiana 14–3 in Rose Bowl to clinch 5th national title; Simpson ran for 128 yds and both Trojan TDs.

1968 (9–1–1)   *Won:* Minnesota 29–20, Northwestern 24–7, Miami (Fla.) 28–3, Stanford 27–24, Washington 14–7, Oregon 20–13, California 35–17 (10th straight over Bears), Oregon St. 17–13, UCLA 28–16.   *Tied:* Notre Dame 21–21 in finale.   *Stars:* Heisman Trophy– and Maxwell Award–winner Simpson (22 TDs, nation's leader with 1,709 yds rush and 1,966 all-purpose yds), Sogge (1,454 yds pass), Jim Lawrence (26 pass rec for 386 yds), E Bob Klein, OT Sid Smith, OG Fred Khasigian, DE Jim Gunn, Battle, Gerry Shaw (6 int).   *Noteworthy:* Won inaugural Pacific-8 title. Lost to unbeaten national champ Ohio St. 27–16 in Rose Bowl; Simpson ran for 171 yds (including 80-yd TD run) but Trojans lost ball 5 times on turnovers.

1969 (10–0–1)   *Won:* Nebraska 31–21, Northwestern 48–6, Oregon St. 31–7, Stanford 26–24, Georgia Tech 29–18, California 14–9, Washington St. 28–7, Washington 16–7, UCLA 14–12.   *Tied:* Notre Dame 14–14 in mid-season.   *Stars:* TB Clarence Davis (1,351 yds rush, 9 TDs), soph QB Jim Jones (1,220 yds and 13 TDs pass), Sam Dickerson (24 pass rec for 473 yds and 6 TDs), Smith, Khasigian, Gunn, DT Al Cowlings, DB Tyrone Hudson (6 int).   *Noteworthy:* Repeated as Pacific-8 champ. Beat Michigan 10–3 in Rose Bowl; scored on FG by Ron Ayala and 33-yd pass from Jones to Bobby Chandler.

1972 (12–0)   *Won:* Arkansas 31–10, Oregon St. 51–6, Illinois 55–20, Michigan St. 51–6, Stanford

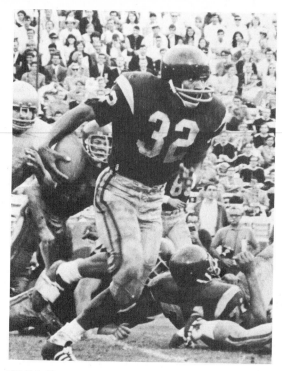

TB O.J. Simpson, 1967–68

30–21, California 42–14, Washington 34–7, Oregon 18–0, Washington St. 44–3, UCLA 24–7, Notre Dame 45–23.   *Stars:* soph TB Anthony Davis (1,034 yds rush, 1,661 all-purpose yds, 17 TDs), QB Mike Rae (1,754 yds pass, 2,001 yds total off), FL Lynn Swann (21 pass rec for 435 yds), TE Charles Young (23 pass rec for 378 yds), FB Sam Cunningham, OT Pete Adams, C Dave Brown, DT John Grant, DL James Sims, LB Richard Wood, DB Artimus Parker (6 int).   *Noteworthy:* One of nation's most-improved teams won 3rd Pacific-8 title (20th conference crown overall). Beat Ohio St. 42–17 in Rose Bowl to clinch 6th national title; Cunningham scored 4 TDs, Davis ran for 157 yds and a TD, Rae passed for 229 yds and kicked 6 ex pts, Swann caught 6 passes for 108 yds and a TD, and Young caught 6 passes for 82 yds.

1973 (9–2–1)   *Won:* Arkansas 17–0, Georgia Tech 23–6, Oregon St. 21–7, Washington St. 46–35, Oregon 31–10, California 50–14, Stanford 27–26, Washington 42–19, UCLA 23–13.   *Lost:* unbeaten national cochamp Notre Dame 23–14 (1st to Irish since 1966). *Tied:* unbeaten Oklahoma 7–7. *Stars:* Wood, Sims, Parker (8 int), DL Monte Doris, soph DB Danny Reece (8 int), Davis (1,038 yds rush, 1,441 all-purpose yds, 13 TDs), Swann (7 TDs, 37 pass rec for 667 yds and 6 TDs), QB Pat Haden (1,832 yds and 13 TDs pass), E Jim Obradovich, OTs Booker Brown and Steve Riley. *Noteworthy:* Repeated as Pacific-8 champ. Lost to unbeaten Ohio St. 42–21 in Rose Bowl; Haden passed for 229 yds and Johnny McKay caught 6 for 83 yds.

1974 (10–1–1) *Won:* Pittsburgh 16–7 (1st meeting since 1965), Iowa 41–3, Washington St. 54–7, Oregon 16–7, Oregon St. 31–10, Stanford 34–10, Washington 42–11 (10th straight over Huskies), UCLA 34–9, Notre Dame 55–24 (after trailing 24–6 at half). *Lost:* Arkansas 22–7 in opener. *Tied:* California 15–15. *Stars:* Davis (1,354 yds rush, 18 TDs, 110 pts, nation's kickoff return leader with 42.5-yd avg), Haden (13 TDs pass), McKay (34 pass rec for 550 yds and 8 TDs), Obradovich, OG Bill Bain, soph OT Marvin Powell, Wood, DB Charles Phillips (7 int). *Noteworthy:* Won 3rd straight Pacific-8 title. Beat Ohio St. 18–17 in Rose Bowl to earn share of 7th national title; Haden passed for 181 yds and both Trojan TDs (including 38-yarder to McKay and 2-pt conversion toss to soph Shelton Diggs to win game in final quarter), Obradovich caught 1st Trojan TD pass in 4th quarter, and Chris Limahelu kicked 1st quarter FG.

1975 (8–4) *Won:* Duke 35–7, Oregon St. 24–7, Purdue 19–6, Iowa 27–16, Washington St. 28–10, Oregon 17–3, Notre Dame 24–17 in 1st 7 games. *Lost:* California 28–14 (1st to Bears since 1970), Stanford 13–10, Washington 8–7 (1st to Huskies since 1964), UCLA 25–22 (1st to Bruins since 1970). *Stars:* TB Ricky Bell (14 TDs, nation's leader with 1,875 yds rush), soph Randy Simmrin (26 pass rec for 478 yds), Powell, DL Gary Jeter, LB Kevin Bruce, Reece, Clint Strozier (5 int). *Noteworthy:* Last year under John McKay. Beat Texas A&M 20–0 in Liberty Bowl; soph FB Mosi Tatupu and Bell (on 76-yd screen pass) scored TDs.

1976 (11–1) *Won:* Oregon 53–0, Purdue 31–13, Iowa 55–0, Washington St. 23–14 (10th straight over Cougars), Oregon St. 56–0, California 20–6, Stanford 48–24, Washington 20–3, UCLA 24–14, Notre Dame 17–13. *Lost:* Missouri 46–25 in opener. *Stars:* Bell (1,417 yds and 14 TDs rush), QB Vince Evans (1,440 yds and 10 TDs pass), Diggs (37 pass rec for 655 yds and 8 TDs), frosh RB

Charles White (744 yds rush, 1,104 all-purpose yds, 10 TDs), Powell, OG Donnie Hickman, Jeter, LBs Rod Martin and Clay Matthews, DB Dennis Thurman (8 int). *Noteworthy:* Won 6th Pacific-8 title in 1st year under John Robinson. Beat Michigan 14–6 in Rose Bowl; White (filling in for injured Bell) ran for 114 yds and a TD, and Evans scored other Trojan TD.

1977 (8–4) *Won:* Missouri 27–10, Oregon St. 17–10, TCU 51–0, Washington St. 41–7, Oregon 33–15, Stanford 49–0, UCLA 29–27. *Lost:* Alabama 21–20, national champ Notre Dame 49–19, California 17–14, Washington 28–10. *Stars:* White (1,291 yds rush, 8 TDs), QB Rob Hertel (2,145 yds and 19 TDs pass), Simmrin (41 pass rec for 840 yds and 5 TDs), Calvin Sweeney (33 pass rec for 564 yds and 6 TDs), OGs Pat Howell and soph Brad Budde, K Frank Jordan (14 FGs), DL Walt Underwood, Matthews, Thurman, Ricky Odom (5 int). *Noteworthy:* beat Texas A&M 47–28 in Bluebonnet Bowl; Hertel passed for 4 TDs (2 to Sweeney), White ran for 187 yds and caught a TD pass, and Dwight Ford ran 94 yds for another score.

1978 (12–1) *Won:* Texas Tech 17–9, Oregon 37–10, Alabama 24–14, Michigan St. 30–9, Oregon St. 38–7 (10th straight over Beavers), California 42–17, Stanford 13–7, Washington 28–10, UCLA 17–10, Notre Dame 27–25, Hawaii 21–5. *Lost:* Arizona St. 20–7 (1st meeting). *Stars:* White (14 TDs, 1,760 yds rush, nation's leader with 2,096 all-purpose yds), Lynn Cain (977 yds rush), QB Paul McDonald (1,690 yds and 19 TDs pass), Sweeney (32 pass rec for 644 yds), WR Kevin Williams, Howell, Budde, OT Anthony Munoz, DL Rich Dimler, LB Dennis Johnson, DB Dennis Smith (7 int), P Marty King (41.7-yd avg). *Noteworthy:* Took initial Pacific-10 title. Beat Michigan 17–10 in Rose Bowl to earn share of 8th national title; White ran for 99 yds and disputed 3-yd TD plunge, soph TE Hoby Brenner scored other Trojan TD, and Jordan kicked FG.

1979 (11–0–1) *Won:* Texas Tech 21–7, Oregon St. 42–5, Minnesota 48–14, Louisiana St. (LSU) 17–12, Washington St. 50–21, Notre Dame 42–23, California 24–14, Arizona 34–7 (1st meeting since 1928), Washington 24–17, UCLA 49–14. *Tied:* Stanford 21–21. *Stars:* Heisman Trophy– and Maxwell Award–winner White (19 TDs, nation's leader with 1,803 yds rush and 1,941 all-purpose yds), McDonald (2,223 yds and 18 TDs pass),

Danny Garcia (29 pass rec for 492 yds), soph RB Marcus Allen (606 yds rush, 20 pass rec for 273 yds, 8 TDs), Brenner, Lombardi Award–winner Budde, OL Roy Foster and Keith Van Horne, Johnson, LB Riki Gray, Smith, DB Ronnie Lott. *Noteworthy:* Won 2nd Pacific-10 title (25th conference crown overall) in 1st unbeaten season since 1972. Beat undefeated Ohio St. 17–16 in Rose Bowl; White ran for 247 yds and winning TD (with 1:32 remaining), Williams scored 1st Trojan TD, and K Eric Hipp had FG and 2 ex pts.

1980 (8–2–1) *Won:* Tennessee 20–17, South Carolina 23–13, Minnesota 24–7, Arizona St. 23–21, Arizona 27–10, California 60–7, Stanford 34–9, Notre Dame 20–3. *Lost:* Washington 20–10 (ending 28–game unbeaten string), UCLA 20–17 (1st to Bruins since 1975) in consecutive late games. *Tied:* Oregon 7–7. *Stars:* Allen (14 TDs, 1,563 yds rush, 30 pass rec for 231 yds, nation's leader with 1,794 all-purpose yds), QB Gordon Adams (1,237 yds pass), soph Jeff Simmons (21 pass rec for 309 yds), Van Horne, Foster, DL Dennis Edwards, soph NG George Achica, LB Chip Banks, Smith, Lott (nation's leader with 8 int). *Noteworthy:* banned from bowl play by Pacific-10 penalty.

1981 (9–3) *Won:* Tennessee 43–7, Indiana 21–0, Oklahoma 28–24, Oregon St. 56–22, Stanford 25–17, Notre Dame 14–7, Washington St. 41–17, California 21–3, UCLA 22–21. *Lost:* Arizona 13–10 (1st to Wildcats in 10-game series dating to 1916), Washington 13–3. *Stars:* Heisman Trophy– and Maxwell Award–winner Allen (29 pass rec for 217 yds, nation's leader with 2,342 yds rush, with 2,559 all-purpose yds, and in scoring with 138 pts on 23 TDs), Simmons (28 pass rec for 543 yds), QB John Mazur (1,128 yds pass), Foster, soph C Tony Slaton, OG Bruce Matthews, frosh K Steve Jordan (11 FGs, 65 pts), Achica, Edwards, Banks, P Dave Pryor (41.1-yd avg). *Noteworthy:* lost to Penn St. 26–10 in Fiesta Bowl (breaking 6-bowl win streak); scored on 20-yd pass int return by Banks and FG by Jordan.

1982 (8–3) *Won:* Indiana 28–7, Oklahoma 12–0, Oregon 38–7, Stanford 41–21, Oregon St. 38–0, California 42–0, Arizona 48–41, Notre Dame 17–13. *Lost:* Florida 17–9, Arizona St. 17–10, UCLA 20–19. *Stars:* Matthews, Slaton, OT Don Mosebar, soph QB Sean Salisbury (1,062 yds pass), Simmons (56 pass rec for 973 yds and 5 TDs), Todd Spencer (596 yds rush), Jordan (11 FGs, 68 pts), Achica, soph

TB Marcus Allen, 1978–81

LB Jack Del Rio, DB Joey Browner, Troy West (5 int), Pryor (42.8-yd punting avg). *Noteworthy:* Robinson's last team until 1993. Banned from bowl play by NCAA penalty.

1984 (9–3) *Won:* Utah St. 42–7, Arizona St. 6–3, Washington St. 29–27 (15th straight over Cougars), Oregon 19–9, Arizona 17–14, California 31–7, Stanford 20–11, Washington 16–7. *Lost:* LSU 23–3, UCLA 29–10, Notre Dame 19–7. *Stars:* RB Fred Crutcher (1,083 yds and 10 TDs rush), QB Tim Green (1,448 yds pass), Hank Norman (39 pass rec for 643 yds), OL Ken Ruettgers, Jordan (17 FGs, 73 pts), Del Rio, LB Duane Bickett, DL Tony Colorito, DB Tommy Haynes (5 int). *Noteworthy:* Won 3rd Pacific-10 title (26th conference crown). Beat Ohio St. 20–17 in Rose Bowl; Green threw TD passes to Joe Cormier and Timmie Ware, and Jordan kicked two 51-yd FGs.

1987 (8–4) *Won:* Boston College 23–17, California 31–14, Oregon St. 48–14, Washington 37–23, Washington St. 42–7, Stanford 39–24, Arizona 12–10,

UCLA 17–13. *Lost:* Michigan St. 27–13, Oregon 34–27 (1st to Ducks in 13 games since 1971), Notre Dame 26–15. *Stars:* QB Rodney Peete (2,460 yds and 19 TDs pass), SEs Erik Affholter (44 pass rec for 649 yds) and soph John Jackson (37 pass rec for 578 yds and 7 TDs), RB Steven Webster (1,109 yds rush), frosh TB Scott Lockwood (5 TDs rush), OT Dave Cadigan, TE Paul Green, frosh K Quinn Rodriguez (13 FGs, 74 pts), Cleveland Colter (6 int). *Noteworthy:* Got share of 4th Pacific-10 title in 1st year under Larry Smith. Lost rematch with Michigan St. 20–17 in Rose Bowl as Trojans had 5 turnovers; Peete passed for 249 yds and 2 TDs (both to Ken Henry).

1988 (10–2) *Won:* Boston College 34–7, Stanford 24–20, Oklahoma 23–7, Arizona 38–15, Oregon 42–14, Washington 28–27, Oregon St. 41–20, California 35–3, Arizona St. 50–0, UCLA 31–22. *Lost:* unbeaten national champ Notre Dame 27–10 in finale. *Stars:* Peete (2,654 yds and 18 TDs pass), Affholter (68 pass rec for 952 yds and 8 TDs), Jackson (48 pass rec for 609 yds and 5 TDs), soph FL Gary Wellman (21 pass rec for 377 yds), TE Scott Galbraith (21 pass rec for 311 yds), TB Aaron Emanuel (545 yds rush, 9 TDs), Lockwood (527 yds and 5 TDs rush), FB Leroy Holt (540 yds rush, 6 TDs), OG Mark Tucker, Rodriguez (14 FGs, 76 pts), DT Tim Ryan, DL Dan Owens, soph LB Scott Ross, Colter, soph DB Mark Carrier. *Noteworthy:* Repeated as Pacific-10 champ. Lost to Michigan 22–14 in Rose Bowl after taking 14–3 halftime lead on 2 short TD runs by Peete; Trojans lost ball 5 times on turnovers.

1989 (9–2–1) *Won:* Utah St. 66–10, Ohio St. 42–3, Washington St. 18–17, Washington 24–16, California 31–15, Stanford 19–0 (10th straight over Cardinal), Oregon St. 48–6, Arizona 24–3. *Lost:* Illinois 14–13 (1st to Illini in 10 games since 1935), Notre Dame 28–24. *Tied:* UCLA 10–10. *Stars:*

frosh QB Todd Marinovich (2,578 yds and 16 TDs pass), Jackson (62 pass rec for 964 yds and 5 TDs), TB Ricky Ervins (39 pass rec for 221 yds, 1,395 yds rush, 11 TDs), Holt (28 pass rec for 269 yds, 619 yds rush), Galbraith (27 pass rec for 241 yds), Wellman (23 pass rec for 427 yds and 6 TDs), C Brad Leggett, Tucker, OG Brent Parkinson, Rodriguez (11 FGs, 73 pts), Owens, Ryan, LBs Delmar Chesley and Junior Seau, Carrier (7 int). *Noteworthy:* Won 6th Pacific-10 crown (29th title overall) and led nation in rush defense. Beat Michigan 17–10 in Rose Bowl; Ervins ran for 126 yds and a TD, Marinovich passed for 178 yds and scored a TD, and Rodriguez kicked 34-yd FG.

1990 (8–4–1) *Won:* Syracuse 34–16, Penn St. 19–14, Ohio St. 35–26, Washington St. 30–17, Stanford 37–22, Arizona St. 13–6, Oregon St. 56–7, UCLA 45–42. *Lost:* Washington 31–0 (1st to Huskies since 1985), Arizona 35–26 (1st to Wildcats in 7 games since 1981), Notre Dame 10–6. *Tied:* California 31–31. *Stars:* Marinovich (2,249 yds and 12 TDs pass), Wellman (63 pass rec for 996 yds), SE Larry Wallace (20 pass rec for 274 yds), soph TB Mazio Royster (1,043 yds and 8 TDs rush), Lockwood (516 yds rush), Tucker, OT Pat Harlow, Rodriguez (16 FGs), LB Kurt Barber, Ross, soph DB Stephon Pace, P Ron Dale (40.7-yd avg). *Noteworthy:* lost to Michigan St. 17–16 in John Hancock Bowl; Marinovich passed for 174 yds and a TD, Royster ran for 125 yds, and Rodriguez kicked FGs of 52, 54, and 43 yds.

BOWL SUMMARY

Aloha 0–1; Bluebonnet 1–0; Fiesta 0–1; Florida Citrus 0–1; Freedom 0–1; John Hancock 0–1; Liberty 1–0; Los Angeles Christmas Festival 1–0; Rose 19–8.

BOWL RECORD (22–13)

Regular Season	Bowl	Score	Opponent	Record
1922 (9–1)	Rose	14–3	Penn State	(6–3–1)
1924 (8–2)	Christmas Fest.	20–7	Missouri	(7–1)
1929 (9–2)	Rose	47–14	Pittsburgh	(9–0)
1931 (9–1)	Rose	21–12	Tulane	(11–0)
1932 (9–0)	Rose	35–0	Pittsburgh	(8–0–2)

(continued)

Regular Season	Bowl	Score	Opponent	Record
1938 (8–2)	Rose	7–3	Duke	(9–0)
1939 (7–0–2)	Rose	14–0	Tennessee	(10–0)
1943 (7–2)	Rose	29–0	Washington	(4–0)
1944 (7–0–2)	Rose	25–0	Tennessee	(7–0–1)
1945 (7–3)	Rose	14–34	Alabama	(9–0)
1947 (7–1–1)	Rose	0–49	Michigan	(9–0)
1952 (9–1)	Rose	7–0	Wisconsin	(6–2–1)
1954 (8–3)	Rose	7–20	Ohio State	(9–0)
1962 (10–0)	Rose	42–37	Wisconsin	(8–1)
1966 (7–3)	Rose	13–14	Purdue	(8–2)
1967 (9–1)	Rose	14–3	Indiana	(9–1)
1968 (9–0–1)	Rose	16–27	Ohio State	(9–0)
1969 (9–0–1)	Rose	10–3	Michigan	(8–2)
1972 (11–0)	Rose	42–17	Ohio State	(9–1)
1973 (9–1–1)	Rose	21–42	Ohio State	(9–0–1)
1974 (9–1–1)	Rose	18–17	Ohio State	(10–1)
1975 (7–4)	Liberty	20–0	Texas A&M	(10–1)
1976 (10–1)	Rose	14–6	Michigan	(10–1)
1977 (7–4)	Bluebonnet	47–21	Texas A&M	(8–3)
1978 (11–1)	Rose	17–10	Michigan	(10–1)
1979 (10–0–1)	Rose	17–16	Ohio State	(11–0)
1981 (9–2)	Fiesta	10–26	Penn State	(9–2)
1984 (8–3)	Rose	20–17	Ohio State	(9–2)
1985 (6–5)	Aloha	3–24	Alabama	(8–2–1)
1986 (7–4)	Florida Citrus	7–16	Auburn	(9–2)
1987 (8–3)	Rose	17–20	Michigan St.	(8–2–1)
1988 (10–1)	Rose	14–22	Michigan	(8–2–1)
1989 (8–2–1)	Rose	17–10	Michigan	(10–1)
1990 (8–3–1)	John Hancock	16–17	Michigan St.	(7–3–1)
1992 (6–4–1)	Freedom	7–24	Fresno St.	(8–4)

CONFERENCE TITLES

Pacific Coast—1927*, 1928, 1929, 1931, 1932, 1938*, 1939*, 1943, 1944, 1945, 1947, 1952. **Athletic Association of Western Universities**—1959*, 1962, 1964*, 1966, 1967. **Pacific-8**—1968, 1969, 1972, 1973, 1974, 1976. **Pacific-10**—1978, 1979, 1984, 1987*, 1988, 1989.

TOP 20 AP AND UPI RANKING

1938	7	1959	14–12	1970	15–19	1979	2–2
1939	3	1961	10–10	1971	20–U	1980	11–12
1944	7	1962	1–1	1972	1–1	1981	14–13
1945	11	1963	U–16	1973	8–7	1982	15–U
1947	8	1965	10–9	1974	2–1	1984	10–9
1952	5–4	1966	U–18	1975	17–19	1987	18–17
1954	17–11	1967	1–1	1976	2–2	1988	7–9
1955	13–12	1968	4–2	1977	13–12	1989	8–9
1956	18–15	1969	3–4	1978	2–1	1990	20–U

MAJOR RIVALS

Southern California has played at least 10 games with Arizona 16–3, Arizona St. 5–6, California 50–25–5, Cal Tech 11–1–1, Illinois 9–2, Loyola (Calif.) 6–3–1, Notre Dame 23–37–4, Occidental 16–5–2, Ohio St. 11–9–1, Oregon 31–10–2, Oregon St. 46–7–4, Pittsburgh 6–4, Pomona 13–4–4, Stanford 47–20–3, UCLA 34–21–7, Washington 39–23–3, Washington St. 44–5–4, Whittier 11–1.

COACHES

Deans of USC coaches are John McKay and Howard H. Jones with 16 years each. McKay (1962, 1972 national Coach of Year) was 127–40–8 for 1960–75 with 9 conference titles, 9 bowl teams, 4 teams unbeaten in regular season, and 4 national champions. Jones was 121–36–13 for 1925–40 with 7 PCC titles, 5 Rose Bowl champions, 3 unbeaten teams, and 3 national champions. Other top records for at least 3 years were by Harvey R. Holmes, 19–5–3 for 1904–07 with 1 unbeaten team; Dean B. Cromwell, 21–8–6 for 1909–10 and 1916–18 with 1 unbeaten team; Elmer C. "Gloomy Gus" Henderson, 45–7 for 1919–24 with 2 bowl champions and 1 unbeaten team; Newell J. "Jeff" Cravath, 54–28–8 for 1942–50 with 4 PCC titles, 4 Rose Bowl teams, and 1 unbeaten team; Jesse T. Hill, 45–17–1 for 1951–56 with 1 PCC title and 2 Rose Bowl teams; John Robinson, 67–14–2 for 1976–82 with 3 conference titles, 5 bowl teams, 1 unbeaten team, and 1 national champion; Ted Tollner, 26–20–1 for 1983–86 with 1 Pacific-10 title and 3 bowl teams; and Larry Smith, 44–25–3 for 1987–92 with 3 Pacific-10 titles and 5 Bowl teams.

MISCELLANEA

First game was win over Alliance A.C. 16–0 in 1888 . . . 1st win over college foe was over Loyola (Calif.) 40–0 in 1889 . . . highest score was over Pomona 80–0 in 1925 . . . highest since W.W. II was over Washington St. 70–33 in 1970 . . . biggest margin since W.W. II was over Oregon St. 63–0 in 1985 . . . worst defeat was by Notre Dame 51–0 in 1966 . . . highest against Trojans was by California 52–30 in 1991 . . . longest unbeaten string of 28 in 1978–80

ended by Washington 20–10 . . . 27-game unbeaten string in 1931–33 ended by Stanford 13–7 . . . longest win streak of 25 in 1931–33 ended by Oregon St. 0–0 . . . 23-game unbeaten string in 1971–73 ended by Notre Dame 23–14 . . . 18-game unbeaten string in 1974–75 ended by California 28–14 . . . 17-game unbeaten string in 1938–40 ended by Stanford 21–7 . . . 15-game win streaks, in 1920–21 ended by California 38–7 and in 1976–77 by Alabama 21–20 . . . longest winless string of 8 in 1941–42 broken with win over Washington St. 26–12 . . . consensus All-Americans were Mort Kaer, B, 1926; Jesse Hibbs, T, and Morley Drury, B, 1927; Erny Pinckert, B, 1930; John Baker, G, and Gus Shaver, B, 1931; Ernie Smith, T, 1932; Aaron Rosenberg, G, and Cotton Warburton, B, 1933; Harry Smith, G, 1939; Ralph Heywood, E, 1943; John Ferraro, T, 1944; Paul Cleary, E, 1947; Elmer Wilhoite, G, and Jim Sears, B, 1952; Hal Bedsole, E, 1962; Mike Garrett, B, 1965; Nate Shaw, DB, 1966; Ron Yary, T, 1966–67; Tim Rossovich, DE, and Adrian Young, TE, 1967; O.J. Simpson, B, 1967–68; Jim Gunn, DE, 1969; Charlie Weaver, DE, 1970; Charles Young, TE, 1972; Lynn Swann, WR, Booker Brown, OT, and Artimus Parker, DB, 1973; Richard Wood, LB, 1973–74; Anthony Davis, RB, 1974; Ricky Bell, RB, 1975–76; Gary Jeter, DT, 1976; Dennis Thurman, DB, 1976–77; Pat Howell, G, 1978; Charles White, RB, 1978–79; Brad Budde, G, 1979; Keith Van Horne, OL, and Ronnie Lott, DB, 1980; Roy Foster, OL, and Marcus Allen, RB, 1981; Don Mosebar, OL, Bruce Matthews, OL, and George Achica, MG, 1982; Tony Slaton, C, 1983; Jack Del Rio, LB, 1984; Jeff Bregel, OL, 1985–86; Tim McDonald, DB, 1986; Dave Cadigan, OL, 1987; and Mark Carrier, DB, and Tim Ryan, DL, 1989 . . . Academic All-Americans were Dick Nunis, DB, 1952; Mike McKeever, G, 1959–60; Marlin McKeever, E, 1960; Charles Arrobio, T, 1965; Steve Sogge, QB, 1967–68; Harry Khasigian, OG, 1969; Pat Haden, QB, 1973–74; Rich Dimler, DL, 1978; Paul McDonald, QB, Keith Van Horne, OT, and Brad Budde, OG, 1979; Duane Bickett, LB, 1984; Matt Koart, DL, 1985; Jeff Bregel, OG, 1986; and John Jackson, WR, 1988–89 . . . Heisman Trophy winners were Mike Garrett, HB, 1965; O.J. Simpson, HB, 1968; Charles White, HB, 1979; and Marcus Allen, HB, 1981 . . . Maxwell Award winners were O.J. Simpson, RB, 1968; Charles White, RB, 1979; and Marcus Allen, RB, 1981 . . . Outland

Trophy winner was Ron Yary, T, 1967 . . . Lombardi Award winner was Brad Budde, G, 1979.

STANFORD (Cardinal; Cardinal and White)

NOTABLE TEAMS

1893 (8–0–1) *Won:* Olympic Club 46–0, 24–11, Reliance Club 34–0, 18–0, Tacoma 48–0, Port Townsend 50–0, Washington 40–0 (1st meeting), Multnomah A.C. 18–0. *Tied:* California 6–6. *Noteworthy:* only year under "Pop" Bliss.

1895 (4–0–1) *Won:* Olympic Club 4–0, 10–2, 6–0, Reliance Club 8–0. *Tied:* California 6–6 in finale. *Noteworthy:* Walter Camp's last team.

1897 (4–1) *Won:* Reliance Club 6–4, 8–6, 12–6, California 28–0. *Lost:* Reliance Club 10–0.

1900 (7–2–1) *Won:* Reliance Club 6–0, 6–0, 44–0, San Jose St. 35–0, 24–0 (1st meetings), Oregon 34–0 (1st meeting), California 5–0. *Lost:* Alumni 14–0, Nevada-Reno 6–0. *Tied:* Multnomah A.C. 0–0. *Noteworthy:* only year under Fielding Yost.

1901 (3–2–2) *Won:* Olympic Club 6–0, Reliance Club 10–0, Nevada-Reno 12–0. *Lost:* unbeaten California 2–0 in finale. *Tied:* Reliance Club 0–0, Olympic Club 6–6. *Noteworthy:* only year under C.M. Fickert. Lost to unbeaten, unscored-on national champ Michigan 49–0 in 1st Tournament of Roses postseason game.

1902 (6–1) *Won:* Reliance Club 12–0, 12–0, 23–5, Alumni 18–0, Nevada-Reno 11–5, Utah 35–11. *Lost:* unbeaten California 16–0.

1903 (8–0–3) *Won:* Pensacola 17–0, 34–0, Reliance Club 34–0, 17–0, Fort Baker 57–0, Chemawa Indians 33–0, Multnomah A.C. 11–0, Sherman Indians 18–0. *Tied:* Reliance Club 0–0, Nevada-Reno 0–0, California 6–6. *Noteworthy:* had 1st unbeaten season since 1895 in 1st year under J.F. Lanagan.

1904 (7–2–1) *Won:* Pensacola 34–0, Olympic Club 12–0, Nevada-Reno 17–0, Oregon 35–0, Utah St. 57–0, California 18–0, Colorado 33–0. *Lost:* Olympic Club 5–0, Sherman Indians 5–0. *Tied:* Multnomah A.C. 0–0.

1905 (8–0) *Won:* St. Vincent 10–0, Willamette 12–0, 15th Infantry 51–0, Oregon 10–4, Nevada-Reno 21–0, Sherman Indians 6–4, Southern California (USC) 16–0 (1st meeting), California 12–5.

1906–1917 Played rugby instead of American football.

1923 (7–2) *Won:* Mare Island 82–0, Nevada-Reno 27–0, Santa Clara 55–6, Occidental 42–0, Olympic Club 40–7, Oregon 14–3, Idaho 17–7 (1st meeting). *Lost:* USC 14–7, unbeaten California 9–0.

1924 (7–1–1) *Won:* Occidental 20–6, Olympic Club 7–0, Oregon 28–13, Idaho 3–0, Santa Clara 20–0, Utah 30–0, Montana 41–3 (1st meeting). *Tied:* unbeaten California 20–20. *Stars:* E Jim Lawson (Indians' 1st consensus All-American), FB Ernie Nevers. *Noteworthy:* Won 1st PCC title in 1st year under Glenn "Pop" Warner. Lost to unbeaten national champ Notre Dame 27–10 in Rose Bowl; Nevers ran for 114 yds on heavily taped injured ankles and Indians scored on 27-yd FG by Murray Cuddeback and 7-yd pass from soph Ed Walker to soph Ted Shipkey.

1925 (7–2) *Won:* Santa Clara 20–3, Occidental 28–0, USC 13–9 (1st football win over Trojans in 5 games since 1905), Oregon St. 26–10, Oregon 35–13, UCLA 82–0 (1st meeting), California 27–14 (1st over Bears since resuming American football in 1919). *Lost:* Olympic Club 9–0, unbeaten Washington 13–0. *Star:* Nevers (710 yds and 9 TDs rush).

1926 (10–0–1) *Won:* Fresno St. 44–0, Cal Tech 13–0, Occidental 19–0, Olympic Club 7–3, Nevada-Reno 33–9, Oregon 19–12, USC 13–12, Santa Clara 33–14, Washington 29–10, California 41–6. *Star:* Shipkey. *Noteworthy:* Won 2nd PCC title and got share of 1st national championship. Tied unbeaten national cochamp Alabama 7–7 in Rose Bowl when Crimson Tide scored in last minute; Indians scored in 1st period on 20-yd pass from George Bogue to Ed Walker.

1927 (8–2–1) *Won:* Fresno St. 44–7, Olympic Club 7–6, Nevada-Reno 20–2, Oregon St. 20–6, Oregon 19–0, Washington 13–7, California 13–6. *Lost:* St. Mary's 16–0, Santa Clara 13–6 (1st to Broncos since resuming American football in 1919). *Tied:* USC 13–13. *Noteworthy:* Earned share of 3rd PCC title. Beat undefeated Pittsburgh 7–6 in Rose Bowl as Walt Heinecke blocked Panthers' ex pt attempt in 3rd quarter; Indians' Frank Wilton scored later on fumble return and Biff Hoffman kicked winning point.

1928 (8–3–1) *Won:* West Coast Army 21–8, Oregon 26–12 (10th in as many games with Ducks), UCLA 45–7, Idaho 47–0, Fresno St. 47–0, Santa Clara 31–0, Washington 12–0, Army 26–0 (1st meeting). *Lost:* YMI 7–0, Olympic Club 12–6, unbeaten national cochamp USC 10–0. *Tied:* California 13–13. *Stars:* Gs Seraphim Post and Don Robesky.

1929 (9–2) *Won:* West Coast Army 45–0, Olympic Club 6–0, Oregon 33–7, UCLA 57–0, Oregon St. 40–7, Cal Tech 39–0, Washington 6–0, California 21–6, Army 34–13. *Lost:* USC 7–0, Santa Clara 13–7. *Star:* HB/DB Phil Moffatt (9 TDs, 8 int).

1930 (9–1–1) *Won:* West Coast Army 32–0, Olympic Club 18–0, Santa Clara 20–0, Oregon St. 13–7, UCLA 20–0, Washington 25–7, Cal Tech 57–7, California 41–0, Dartmouth 14–7. *Lost:* USC 41–12. *Tied:* Minnesota 0–0. *Star:* Moffatt (10 TDs, 9 int).

1931 (7–2–2) *Won:* West Coast Army 46–0, Santa Clara 6–0, Minnesota 13–0, Oregon St. 25–7, UCLA 12–6, Nevada-Reno 26–0 (17th straight without defeat against Wolf Pack), Dartmouth 32–6. *Lost:* national champ USC 19–0, California 6–0 (1st to Bears since 1923). *Tied:* Olympic Club 0–0, Washington 0–0.

1933 (8–2–1) *Won:* San Jose St. 27–0 (1st meeting since 1900), UCLA 3–0, Santa Clara 7–0, San Francisco 20–13, Olympic Club 21–0, USC 13–7 (1st over Trojans since 1926), Montana 33–7 (1st meeting since 1924), California 7–3. *Lost:* Washington 6–0. *Tied:* Northwestern 0–0. *Star:* G Bill Corbus. *Noteworthy:* Got share of 4th PCC title in 1st year under C. E. Thornhill. Upset by Columbia 7–0 in muddy Rose Bowl; soph FB Bobby Grayson ran for 152 yds.

1934 (9–1–1) *Won:* San Jose St. 48–0, Oregon St. 17–0 (10th in as many games with Beavers), Northwestern 20–0, San Francisco 3–0, USC 16–0, UCLA 27–0, Washington 24–0, Olympic Club 40–0, California 9–7. *Tied:* Santa Clara 7–7. *Stars:* Grayson (646 yds and 10 TDs rush, 5 int), E Monk Moscrip, Ts Bob Reynolds and Bones Hamilton. *Noteworthy:* Repeated as PCC champ in 1st undefeated season since 1926. Lost to unbeaten national cochamp Alabama 29–13 in Rose Bowl; scored on TDs by Grayson and Elzo Van Dellen.

1935 (8–1) *Won:* San Jose St. 35–0, San Francisco 10–0, Washington 6–0, Santa Clara 9–6, USC 3–0, Montana 32–0, California 13–0. *Lost:* UCLA 7–6. *Stars:* Grayson (551 yds rush, 280 yds pass), Moscrip. *Noteworthy:* Got share of 3rd straight PCC title (6th overall). Upset undefeated national cochamp Southern Methodist (SMU) 7–0 in Rose

Bowl; soph QB Bill Paulman ran 1 yd for only TD in 1st quarter.

1940 (10–0) *Won:* San Francisco 27–0, Oregon 13–0, Santa Clara 7–6 (1st over Broncos since 1935), Washington St. 26–14, USC 21–7, UCLA 20–14, Washington 20–10, Oregon St. 28–14, California 13–7 (1st over Bears since 1935). *Stars:* QB Frankie Albert (648 yds pass, 36 pts), HB Hugh Gallarneau, FB Norm Standlee. *Noteworthy:* Nation's most-improved team won 7th PCC title in 1st year under Clark Shaughnessy. Beat Nebraska 21–13 in Rose Bowl, scoring on 9-yd run by Gallarneau, 41-yd pass from Albert to Gallarneau, and 39-yd punt return by HB Pete Kmetovic.

1951 (9–2) *Won:* Oregon 27–20, San Jose St. 26–13, Michigan 23–13, UCLA 21–7, Santa Clara 21–14, Washington 14–7, Washington St. 21–13, USC 27–20, Oregon St. 35–14. *Lost:* California 20–7 in finale. *Stars:* E Bill McColl (42 pass rec for 607 yds and 7 TDs), QB Gary Kerkorian. *Noteworthy:* Won 8th PCC title in 1st year under Chuck Taylor. Lost to unbeaten Illinois 40–7 in Rose Bowl after scoring on 84-yd 1st quarter drive sparked by 5 consecutive pass completions by Kerkorian.

1969 (7–2–1) *Won:* San Jose St. 63–21, Oregon 28–0, Washington St. 49–0, Oregon St. 33–0, Washington 21–7, Air Force 47–34, California 29–28. *Lost:* Purdue 36–35, unbeaten USC 26–24 in successive early games. *Tied:* UCLA 20–20. *Stars:* QB Jim Plunkett (2,673 yds and 20 TDs pass, 113 yds rush), FL Randy Vataha (35 pass rec for 691 yds), Howie Williams (10 TDs), E Bob Moore, C John Sande, K Steve Horowitz (10 FGs, 71 pts), LB Don Parish, DB Rick Keller.

1970 (9–3) *Won:* Arkansas 34–28, San Jose St. 34–3 (10th straight over Spartans), Oregon 33–10, USC 24–14 (1st over Trojans since 1957), Washington St. 63–16, UCLA 9–7 (1st over Bruins since 1962), Oregon St. 48–10, Washington 29–22. *Lost:* Purdue 26–14, Air Force 31–14 (1st to Falcons in 5 games since 1960), California 22–14. *Stars:* Heisman Trophy– and Maxwell Award–winner Plunkett (2,715 yds and 18 TDs pass, 183 yds and 3 TDs rush), Moore, Vataha, OT Steve Jibb, DL Dave Tipton, LB Jeff Siemon. *Noteworthy:* Won 1st Pacific-8 title (9th conference crown). Upset unbeaten national cochamp Ohio St. 27–17 in Rose Bowl; Plunkett passed for 265 yds and a TD (10 yds to Vataha), Washington had 6 pass rec for 80 yds, and Siemon and Tipton starred on defense.

1971 (9–3) *Won:* Missouri 19–0, Army 38–3, Oregon 38–17, Washington 17–6, USC 33–18, Oregon St. 31–24, UCLA 20–9, California 14–0. *Lost:* Duke 9–3, Washington St. 24–23 (1st to Cougars in 5 games since 1964), San Jose St. 13–12 (1st to Spartans since 1960). *Stars:* QB Don Bunce (2,265 yds and 13 TDs pass, 248 yds rush), Miles Moore (38 pass rec for 816 yds), soph K Rod Garcia (14 FGs, 66 pts), DL Pete Lazetich and Larry Butler, Siemon, DB Benny Barnes (7 int). *Noteworthy:* John Ralston's last team repeated as Pacific-8 champ. Upset unbeaten Michigan 13–12 in Rose Bowl; Bunce passed for 290 yds, RB Jackie Brown scored on 24-yd run, and Garcia kicked FGs of 42 and 31 yds (2nd with 12 seconds left).

1977 (9–3) *Won:* Tulane 21–17, Illinois 37–24, Oregon 20–10, UCLA 32–28 (1st over Bruins since 1971), Washington St. 31–29, Oregon St. 26–7, San Jose St. 31–26, California 21–3. *Lost:* Colorado 27–21, Washington 45–21 (1st to Huskies since 1966), USC 49–0. *Stars:* QB Guy Benjamin (nation's leader with 2,521 yds and 19 TDs pass), WR James Lofton (53 pass rec for 931 yds and 12 TDs), frosh RB Darrin Nelson (1,069 yds rush, 50 pass rec for 524 yds, 6 TDs), frosh K Ken Naber (12 FGs), OT Gordon King, LB Gordon Ceresino. *Noteworthy:* 1st year under Bill Walsh. Beat Louisiana St. (LSU) 24–14 in Sun Bowl; Benjamin passed for 269 yds and 3 TDs, and Ceresino starred on defense.

1978 (8–4) *Won:* San Jose St. 38–9, Illinois 35–10, Tulane 17–14, Washington St. 43–27, Oregon St. 24–6 (10th straight over Beavers), Arizona St. 21–14 (1st meeting), California 30–10. *Lost:* Oklahoma 35–29 (1st meeting), UCLA 27–26, Washington 34–31, national cochamp USC 13–7. *Stars:* Ceresino, Naber (12 FGs, 65 pts), Nelson (1,061 yds rush, 50 pass rec for 446 yds, 10 TDs), QB Steve Dils (nation's leader with 2,943 yds and 22 TDs pass), soph WR Ken Margerum (53 pass rec for 942 yds and 9 TDs). *Noteworthy:* Walsh's last team till 1992. Overcame 22–0 deficit to beat Georgia 25–22 in Bluebonnet Bowl; Dils passed for 3 TDs (2 to Margerum and 1 to Nelson), Ceresino starred on defense, and Naber kicked winning 24-yd FG.

1986 (8–4) *Won:* Texas 31–20, San Jose St. 28–10, Oregon St. 17–7, San Diego St. 17–10, Oregon 41–7, Washington St. 42–12, UCLA 28–23, Arizona 29–24 (in Tokyo). *Lost:* Washington 24–14, USC 10–0,

California 17–11. *Stars:* RB Brad Muster (13 TDs, 1,053 yds rush, 61 pass rec for 565 yds), QB John Paye (2,261 yds and 14 TDs pass), Jeff James (52 pass rec for 779 yds and 8 TDs), DL Tony Leiker, LB Dave Wyman, Toi Cook (7 int). *Noteworthy:* lost to Clemson 27–21 in Gator Bowl; Muster ran for 70 yds, caught 4 passes for 53 yds, and scored 3 TDs, and QB Greg Ennis (subbing for injured Paye) passed for 168 yds.

1991 (8–4) *Won:* Colorado 28–21, Cornell 56–6, USC 24–21 (1st over Trojans since 1975), Oregon St. 40–10, Oregon 33–13, UCLA 27–10, Washington St. 49–14, California 38–21. *Lost:* unbeaten national cochamp Washington 42–7, Arizona 28–23, Notre Dame 42–26. *Stars:* FB Tommy Vardell (1,084 yds and 20 TDs rush, 23 pass rec for 217 yds), RB Glyn Milburn (598 yds rush, 40 pass rec for 454 yds, 1,301 all-purpose yds, 6 TDs), soph QB Steve Stenstrom (1,683 yds and 15 TDs pass), WRs Chris Walsh (66 pass rec for 934 yds and 6 TDs) and Jon Pinckney (27 pass rec for 448 yds and 5 TDs), OT Bob Whitfield, LBs Ron George and Dave Garnett, DB Seyon Albert. *Noteworthy:* Had 1st winning season since 1986 in last year under Dennis Green. Lost to Georgia Tech 18–17 in Aloha Bowl when Tech scored TD and 2-pt conversion with 14 seconds left; Stenstrom passed for 170 yds, Vardell ran for 104 yds and both Cardinal TDs, and soph K Aaron Mills had 38-yd FG.

1992 (10–3) *Won:* Oregon 21–7, Northwestern 35–24, San Jose St. 37–13, Notre Dame 33–16, UCLA 19–7, Oregon St. 27–21, USC 23–9, Washington St. 40–3, California 41–21. *Lost:* unbeaten Texas A&M 10–7, Arizona 21–6, Washington 41–7. *Stars:* Stenstrom (2,399 yds and 14 TDs pass), SE Mike Cook (51 pass rec for 649 yds), Milburn (13 TDs, 3 on punt returns; 2,121 all-purpose yds, 851 yds and 8 TDs rush, 37 pass rec for 405 yds and 2 TDs), soph FL Justin Armour (36 pass rec for 626 yds and 7 TDs), FB J.J. Lasley (5 TDs, 38 pass rec for 380 yds), TE Ryan Wetnight (26 pass rec for 313 yds), RB Ellery Roberts (627 yds and 6 TDs rush), OG Chris Dalman, C Glen Cavanaugh, frosh K Eric Abrams (16 FGs, 79 pts), DE Estevan Avila, George, Garnett, DBs John Lynch, Vaughn Bryant (5 int) and Darrien Gordon, P Paul Stonehouse (41.8-yd avg). *Noteworthy:* Got share of 1st Pacific-10 title (11th conference crown) as Bill Walsh returned as coach. Beat Penn St. 24–3 in

Blockbuster Bowl as Stenstrom passed for 210 yds and 2 TDs (to Wetnight and 40 yds to Milburn), Roberts ran for 98 yds, Lasley scored on 5-yd run, Abrams had FG and 3 ex pts, and Gordon starred on defense.

BOWL SUMMARY

Aloha 0–1; Blockbuster 1–0; Bluebonnet 1–0; Gator 0–1; Rose 5–5–1; Sun 1–0.

BOWL RECORD (8–7–1)

Regular Season	Bowl	Score	Opponent	Record
1901 (3–1–2)	Rose	0–49	Michigan	(10–0)
1924 (7–0–1)	Rose	10–27	Notre Dame	(9–0)
1926 (10–0)	Rose	7–7	Alabama	(9–0)
1927 (7–2–1)	Rose	7–6	Pittsburgh	(8–0–1)
1933 (8–1–1)	Rose	0–7	Columbia	(7–1)
1934 (9–0–1)	Rose	13–29	Alabama	(9–0)
1935 (7–1)	Rose	7–0	SMU	(12–0)
1940 (9–0)	Rose	21–13	Nebraska	(8–1)
1951 (9–1)	Rose	7–40	Illinois	(8–0–1)
1970 (8–3)	Rose	27–17	Ohio State	(9–0)
1971 (8–3)	Rose	13–12	Michigan	(11–0)
1977 (8–3)	Sun	24–14	LSU	(8–3)
1978 (7–4)	Bluebonnet	25–22	Georgia	(9–1–1)
1986 (8–3)	Gator	21–27	Clemson	(7–2–2)
1991 (8–3)	Aloha	17–18	Georgia Tech	(7–5)
1992 (9–3)	Blockbuster	24–3	Penn State	(7–4)

CONFERENCE TITLES

Pacific Coast—1924, 1926, 1927*, 1933*, 1934, 1935*, 1940, 1951. **Pacific-8**—1970, 1971. **Pacific-10**—1992*.

TOP 20 AP AND UPI
(USA TODAY/CNN SINCE 1991) RANKING

1940	2	1953	19–17	1969	19–14	1977	15–15
1942	12	1955	16–20	1970	8–10	1978	17–16
1951	7–7	1968	U–20	1971	10–16	1992	9–9

MAJOR RIVALS

Stanford has played at least 10 games with Arizona 5–7, Army 5–5, California 47–37–11, Illinois 6–4, Michigan 3–6–1, Nevada-Reno 16–1–2, Oregon 38–19–1, Oregon St. 41–16–3, San Jose St. 37–10–1, Santa Clara 22–11–2, Southern California 20–47–3, UCLA 27–33–3, Washington 31–32–4, Washington St. 25–19–1. Record against Pacific-10 foe met fewer than 10 times: Arizona St. 3–6.

COACHES

Deans of Stanford coaches are Glenn "Pop" Warner and John Ralston with 9 years each.

Warner was 71–17–8 for 1924–32 with 3 PCC titles, 3 Rose Bowl teams, 2 teams unbeaten in regular season, and 1 national champion. Ralston was 55–36–3 for 1963–71 with 2 Pacific-8 titles and 2 Rose Bowl champions. Other top records for at least 3 years were by Walter Camp, 12–3–3 for 1892 and 1894–95 with 2 unbeaten teams; James F. Lanagan, 23–2–4 for 1903–05 with 2 unbeaten teams (had 26–8–1 rugby record in 1906–08); C.E. Thornhill, 35–25–7 for 1933–39 with 3 PCC titles, 3 Rose Bowl teams, and 1 team unbeaten in regular season; Charles A. Taylor (1951 national Coach of Year), 40–29–2 for 1951–57 with 1 PCC title and 1 Rose Bowl team; Jack Christiansen, 30–22–3 for 1972–76; Jack Elway, 25–29–2 for 1984–88 with 1 bowl team; Dennis Green, 16–18 for 1989–91 with 1 bowl team; and Bill Walsh, 27–10 for 1977–78 and 1992 with 1 Pacific-10 title and 3 bowl champions. Clark Shaughnessy (1940 national Coach of Year) was 16–3 for 1940–41 with 1 PCC title and 1 unbeaten Rose Bowl champion.

MISCELLANEA

First game was win over Hopkins Academy 10–6 in 1891 . . . 1st win over college foe was over California 14–10 in 1891 . . . highest scores of 82–0 were over Mare Island Marines in 1923 and UCLA in 1925 . . . highest since W.W. II was over Hawaii 74–20 in 1949 . . . biggest margin since W.W. II was over Idaho 63–0 in 1949 . . . worst defeat was by Mare Island Marines 80–0 in unofficial game in 1918 . . . worst by college foe was by UCLA 72–0 in 1954 . . . longest unbeaten string of 15 in 1925–27 ended by St. Mary's 16–0 . . . 13-game win streak in 1939–41 ended by Oregon St. 10–0 . . . longest losing string of 19 in 1959–60 broken with win over Tulane 9–7 in 1961 opener . . . consensus All-Americans were Jim Lawson, E, 1924; Ernie Nevers, B, 1925; Seraphim Post, G, and Don Robesky, G, 1928; Bill Corbus, G, 1932–33; Bob Reynolds, T, 1934; Bobby Grayson, B, 1934–35; James Moscrip, E, 1935; Frank Albert, B, 1940–41; Chuck Taylor, G, 1942; Bill McColl, E, 1950–51; John Brodie, QB, 1956; Jim Plunkett, QB, 1970; Jeff Siemon, LB, 1971; Pat Donovan, DL, 1974; Guy Benjamin, QB, 1977; Ken Margerum, WR, 1979–80; John Elway, QB, 1982; Brad Muster, RB, 1986; and Bob Whitfield, OT, 1991 . . . Academic All-Americans were John Sande, C, and Terry Ewing, DB, 1970; Don Stevenson, RB, 1975–76; Guy Benjamin, QB, 1977; Vince Mulroy, WR, and Jim Stephens, OG, 1978; Pat Bowe, TE, Milt McColl, LB, and Joe St. Geme, DB, 1979; Darrin Nelson, RB, 1981; John Bergren, DL, 1981–83; Matt Soderlund, LB, 1985; Brad Muster, RB, 1987; Ed McCaffrey, WR, 1990; and Tom Vardell, RB, 1991 . . . Heisman Trophy winner was Jim Plunkett, QB, 1970 . . . Maxwell Award winner was Jim Plunkett, QB, 1970.

UCLA (Bruins; Blue and Gold)

NOTABLE TEAMS

1927 (6–2–1) *Won:* Santa Barbara St. 33–0, Fresno St. 7–0, Whittier 25–6 (1st in 8-game series dating to 1920), Occidental 8–0, Redlands 32–0, Cal Tech 13–0 (1st in 8-game series dating to 1920). *Lost:* Arizona 16–13 (1st meeting), Drake 25–6 in last 2 games. *Tied:* Pomona 7–7.

1934 (7–3) *Won:* Pomona 14–0, San Diego St. 20–0, Montana 16–0, Cal Aggies 49–0, St. Mary's 6–0, Oregon St. 25–7, Loyola (Calif.) 13–6. *Lost:* Oregon 26–3, California 3–0, unbeaten Stanford 27–0. *Star:* G Verdi Boyer.

1935 (8–2) *Won:* Utah St. 39–0, Oregon St. 20–7, Stanford 7–6, Oregon 33–6, Hawaii 19–6, Loyola (Calif.) 14–6, Idaho 13–6, St. Mary's 13–7. *Lost:* California 14–2, unbeaten national cochamp Southern Methodist (SMU) 21–0 in successive mid-season games. *Stars:* HB Chuck Cheshire, C Sherman Chavoor. *Noteworthy:* got share of 1st PCC title.

1939 (6–0–4) *Won:* Texas Christian (TCU) 6–2, Washington 14–7, Montana 20–6, Oregon 16–6, California 20–7, Washington St. 24–7. *Tied:* Stanford 14–14, Santa Clara 0–0 (1st meeting), Oregon St. 13–13, undefeated Southern California (USC) 0–0. *Stars:* TB Kenny Washington (811 yds and 5 TDs rush, 559 yds and 7 TDs pass, nation's leader with 1,370 yds total off), E Woody Strode (15 pass rec for 218 yds). *Noteworthy:* had 1st unbeaten season in 1st year under Edwin C. Horrell and got share of 2nd PCC title.

1942 (7–4) *Won:* Oregon St. 30–7 (1st over Beavers since 1936), California 21–0, Santa Clara 14–6, Stanford 20–7, Washington 14–10, Idaho 40–13, USC 14–7 (1st in 9-game series dating to 1929).

Lost: TCU 7–6, St. Mary's Pre-Flight 18–7, Oregon 14–7. *Stars:* B Bob Waterfield (1,033 yds and 12 TDs pass, 7 int), Milt Smith (19 pass rec for 310 yds), Al Solari (526 yds rush), G Jack Lescoulie. *Noteworthy:* Won 3rd PCC title. Made 1st post-season appearance, losing to Georgia 9–0 in Rose Bowl after battling to 0–0 tie through 3 quarters.
1946 (10–1) *Won:* Oregon St. 50–7, Washington 39–13, Stanford 26–6, California 13–6, Santa Clara 33–7, St. Mary's 46–20, Oregon 14–0, Montana 61–7, USC 13–6 (1st over Trojans in 7 games since 1942), Nebraska 18–0 (1st meeting). *Stars:* B Ernie Case (1,033 yds and 11 TDs pass), E Burr Baldwin (UCLA's 1st consensus All-American; 18 pass rec for 374 yds), Gene Rowland (540 yds rush), Ts Don Malmberg and Bill Chambers, C Don Paul, frosh Ernie Johnson (6 int), Ben Reiges (6 int). *Noteworthy:* Won 4th PCC title in 1st unbeaten season since 1939. Lost to Illinois 45–14 in Rose Bowl, scoring on short run by Case and 103-yd kickoff return by Al Hoisch.
1952 (8–1) *Won:* Oregon 13–6, TCU 14–0, Washington 32–7, Rice 20–0, Stanford 24–14, Wisconsin 20–7, California 28–7, Oregon St. 57–0. *Lost:* USC 14–12 in finale. *Stars:* TB Paul Cameron, Es Ike Jones (25 pass rec for 270 yds and 5 TDs), Ernie Stockert and Myron Berliner, Ts Chuck Doud and soph Jack Ellena, Gs Ed Flynn and soph Jim Salsbury, LB Donn Moomaw, Bill Stits (8 int), soph P Bob Heydenfeldt (40-yd avg).
1953 (8–2) *Won:* Oregon St. 41–0, Kansas 19–7, Oregon 12–0, Wisconsin 13–0, Washington St. 44–7, California 20–7, Washington 22–6, USC 13–0. *Lost:* Stanford 21–20. *Stars:* Cameron (672 yds and 12 TDs rush, 326 yds and 5 TDs pass, 41.3-yd punting avg), Stits (9 pass rec for 208 yds and 6 TDs), Doud, Ellena. *Noteworthy:* Won 5th PCC title. Lost to Michigan St. 28–20 in Rose Bowl after leading 14–7 at half; Cameron passed for 2 TDs (to Stits and soph Rommie Loudd) and scored other Bruin TD.
1954 (9–0) *Won:* San Diego Naval Training Center 67–0, Kansas 32–7, Maryland 12–7, Washington 21–20, Stanford 72–0, Oregon St. 61–0, California 27–6, Oregon 41–0, USC 34–0. *Stars:* Ellena, Salsbury, G Sam Boghosian, FB Bob Davenport (11 TDs), HB Primo Villanueva (886 yds total off), Jim Decker (508 yds rush), E Bob Long, Heydenfeldt (39.9-yd punting avg). *Noteworthy:* Won share of 1st national title and repeated as PCC champ while

leading nation in scoring (40.8-pt avg), rush defense, and scoring defense (4.4-pt avg). Ineligible for Rose Bowl under PCC's no-repeat rule of the time.
1955 (9–2) *Won:* Texas A&M 21–0, Washington St. 55–0, Oregon St. 38–0, Stanford 21–13, Iowa 33–13, California 47–0, Pacific 34–0, Washington 19–17, USC 17–7. *Lost:* unbeaten Maryland 7–0. *Stars:* Loudd, Gs Hardiman Cureton and Jim Brown, C Steve Palmer, HB Sam Brown (892 yds rush, 69 pts), Davenport, P Ronnie Knox (41-yd avg). *Noteworthy:* Won 3rd straight PCC crown (7th overall). Lost to Michigan St. 17–14 in Rose Bowl on last quarter FG; Davenport and Doug Peters scored Bruin TDs on short runs.
1956 (7–3) *Won:* Utah 13–7, Oregon 6–0, Washington St. 28–0 (10th straight over Cougars), California 34–20, Stanford 14–13, Washington 13–9, Kansas 13–0. *Lost:* Michigan 42–13 (1st meeting), Oregon St. 21–7 (1st to Beavers since 1948), USC 10–7. *Stars:* soph Dick Wallen (23 pass rec for 308 yds), G Esker Harris, C Jim Matheny, soph P Kirk Wilson (nation's leader with 49.3-yd avg).
1957 (8–2) *Won:* Air Force 47–0 (1st meeting), Illinois 16–6, Washington 19–0, Oregon St. 26–7, California 16–14, Washington St. 19–13, Pacific 21–0, USC 20–9. *Lost:* Oregon 21–0 (1st to Ducks in 8 games since 1948), Stanford 20–6. *Stars:* Wallen (20 pass rec for 303 yds, 4 int), T Bill Leeka, Wilson (42-yd punting avg, 4 int). *Noteworthy:* last year under "Red" Sanders.
1960 (7–2–1) *Won:* Pittsburgh 8–7, Stanford 26–8, N.C. State 7–0, California 28–0, Air Force 22–0, Utah 16–9, Duke 27–6. *Lost:* Washington 10–8, USC 17–6. *Tied:* Purdue 27–27. *Stars:* HB Bill Kilmer (42.3-yd punting avg, 1,086 yds and 8 TDs pass, 803 yds and 8 TDs rush, nation's leader with 1,889 yds total off), Marv Luster (17 pass rec for 250 yds), G Jack Metcalf, Ts Steve Bauwens and Marshall Shirk.
1961 (7–4) *Won:* Air Force 19–6, Vanderbilt 28–21, Pittsburgh 20–6, Stanford 20–0, California 35–15, TCU 28–7, USC 10–7. *Lost:* Michigan 29–6, unbeaten national cochamp Ohio St. 13–3 (1st meeting), Washington 17–13. *Stars:* Mike Haffner (703 yds rush), HB Bobby Smith (88 pts, 966 yds total off), Kermit Alexander (14 pass rec for 297 yds), C Ron Hull. *Noteworthy:* Won 2nd AAWU title. Lost to Minnesota 21–3 in Rose Bowl after scoring first on 28-yd FG by Smith.

1965 (8–2–1) *Won:* Penn St. 24–22, Syracuse 24–14, California 56–3, Air Force 10–0, Washington 28–24, Stanford 30–13, USC 20–16. *Lost:* unbeaten national cochamp Michigan St. 13–3 in opener, Tennessee 37–34 (1st meeting) in finale. *Tied:* Missouri 14–14. *Stars:* soph QB Gary Beban (1,336 yds and 9 TDs pass, 576 yds and 12 TDs rush), Es Kurt Altenberg (32 pass rec for 599 yds) and Jim Colletto, HB Mel Farr (785 yds rush, 8 TDs), Gs Russ Banducci and John Richardson, DB Bob Stiles (9 int). *Noteworthy:* Won 3rd AAWU title (10th conference crown overall) in 1st year under Tommy Prothro. Upset Michigan St. 14–12 in Rose Bowl rematch (1st bowl win in 6 tries); Beban scored both TDs on short runs in 2nd quarter and Kurt Zimmerman kicked ex pts.
1966 (9–1) *Won:* Pittsburgh 57–14, Syracuse 31–12, Missouri 24–15, Rice 27–24, Penn St. 49–11, California 28–15, Air Force 38–13, Stanford 10–0, USC 14–7. *Lost:* Washington 16–3. *Stars:* Beban (1,245 yds pass, 454 yds and 10 TDs rush), Harold Busby (29 pass rec for 474 yds), Farr (809 yds rush, 10 TDs), Richardson, G Rich Deakers, LB Don Manning (5 int), Andy Herrera (5 int).
1967 (7–2–1) *Won:* Tennessee 20–16, Pittsburgh 40–8, Washington St. 51–23, (1st meeting since 1958), Penn St. 17–15, California 37–14, Stanford 21–16, Washington 48–0. *Lost:* unbeaten USC 21–20, Syracuse 32–14 in last 2 games. *Tied:* Oregon St. 16–16 (1st meeting since 1958). *Stars:* Heisman Trophy– and Maxwell Award–winner Beban (1,359 yds and 8 TDs pass, 227 yds and 11 TDs rush), Dave Nuttall (37 pass rec for 612 yds and 5 TDs), soph Greg Jones (662 yds rush), C John Erquiaga, G Dennis Murphy, DT Larry Slagle, soph P/K Zenon Andrusyshyn (nation's leader with 44.2-yd punting avg), Manning, Sandy Green (6 int), DB Mark Gustafson.
1969 (8–1–1) *Won:* Oregon St. 37–0, Pittsburgh 42–8, Wisconsin 34–23, Northwestern 36–0, Washington St. 46–14, California 32–0, Washington 57–14, Oregon 13–10 (1st meeting since 1958). *Lost:* unbeaten USC 14–12 in finale. *Tied:* Stanford 20–20. *Stars:* QB Dennis Dummit (1,963 yds and 15 TDs pass), E Gwen Cooper (38 pass rec for 734 yds and 9 TDs), Jones (761 yds rush, 10 TDs), OG Dennis Alumbaugh, DE Wes Grant, DT Floyd Reese, LB Mike Ballou, DB Ron Carver (6 int), Andrusyshyn (42.1-yd punting avg). *Noteworthy:* nation's most-improved team.

1972 (8–3) *Won:* Nebraska 20–17, Pittsburgh 38–28, Oregon 65–20, Arizona 42–31, Oregon St. 37–7, California 49–13, Washington St. 35–20, Stanford 28–23. *Lost:* Michigan 26–9, Washington 30–21, unbeaten national champ USC 24–7. *Stars:* QB Mark Harmon (1,018 yds total off), RBs Kermit Johnson (952 yds and 7 TDs rush) and James McAlister, Brad Lyman (13 pass rec for 211 yds), OG Steve Klosterman, OT Bruce Walton, K Efren Herrera (63 pts), DE Fred McNeill, Jimmy Allen (6 int), DB Allan Ellis, P Bruce Barnes (43.3-yd avg).
1973 (9–2) *Won:* Iowa 55–18, Michigan St. 34–21, Utah 66–16, Stanford 59–13, Washington St. 24–13, California 61–21, Washington 62–13, Oregon 27–7, Oregon St. 56–14. *Lost:* Nebraska 40–13 (opener), USC 23–13 (finale). *Stars:* Johnson (1,129 yds rush, 16 TDs, 1,446 all-purpose yds), soph QB John Sciarra (999 yds total off), Norm Andersen (19 pass rec for 315 yds), OTs Ed Kezirian and Al Oliver, Klosterman, McNeill, DE Cal Peterson, LB Fulton Kuykendall, Allen, DBs James Bright and John Nanoski (6 int), P Mike Fryer (40.5-yd avg). *Noteworthy:* Pepper Rodgers's last team led nation in rush.
1975 (9–2–1) *Won:* Iowa St. 37–21, Tennessee 34–28, Stanford 31–21, Washington St. 37–23, California 28–14, Oregon 50–17, Oregon St. 31–9, USC 25–22 (1st over Trojans since 1970). *Lost:* unbeaten Ohio St. 41–20, Washington 17–13. *Tied:* Air Force 20–20. *Stars:* Sciarra (1,101 yds and 6 TDs pass, 806 yds and 14 TDs rush), Wendell Tyler (1,388 yds rush), Wally Henry (17 pass rec for 287 yds), OGs Randy Cross and Phil McKinnely, NG Chris Frazier, Barney Person (5 int). *Noteworthy:* Dick Vermeil's last team got share of only Pacific-8 title (11th conference crown overall). Upset Ohio St. 23–10 in Rose Bowl rematch as Sciarra passed for 212 yds and 2 TDs (both to Henry, including 67-yarder), and Tyler ran 54 yds for another score.
1976 (9–2–1) *Won:* Arizona St. 28–10 (1st meeting), Arizona 37–9, Air Force 40–7, Stanford 38–20, Washington St. 62–3 (10th straight over Cougars), California 35–19, Washington 30–21, Oregon 46–0, Oregon St. 45–14. *Lost:* USC 24–14 in finale. *Tied:* Ohio St. 10–10. *Stars:* Tyler (1,003 yds rush), RB Theotis Brown (1,092 yds rush, 78 pts), QB Jeff Dankworth (1,681 yds total off), Henry (22 pass rec for 370 yds), TE Rick Walker, C Mitch Kahn, K/P Frank Corral (44.1-yd punting avg), soph DT Manu Tuiasosopo, soph LB Jerry Robinson, DBs

Levi Armstrong and Oscar Edwards. *Noteworthy:* 1st year under Terry Donahue. Lost to Alabama 36–6 in Liberty Bowl; scored on 61-yd run by Brown.

1978 (8–3–1)   *Won:* Washington 10–7, Tennessee 13–0, Minnesota 17–3, Stanford 27–26, Washington St. 45–31, California 45–0, Arizona 24–14, Oregon 23–21.   *Lost:* Kansas 28–24, Oregon St. 15–13 (1st to Beavers since 1971), national cochamp USC 17–10.   *Stars:* Robinson, NG Tuiasosopo, soph DB Kenny Easley (7 int), Brown (1,283 yds rush), QB Rick Bashore, Severn Reece (15 pass rec for 340 yds), K Peter Boermeester (15 FGs, 75 pts). *Noteworthy:* tied Arkansas 10–10 in Fiesta Bowl on 41-yd FG and ex pt by Boermeester and 15-yd TD run by Steve Bukich; RB James Owens had 121 yds rush.

1980 (9–2)   *Won:* Colorado 56–14, Purdue 23–14, Wisconsin 35–0, Ohio St. 17–0, Stanford 35–21, California 32–9, Arizona St. 23–14, USC 20–17 (1st over Trojans since 1975), Oregon St. 34–3 (in Tokyo).   *Lost:* Arizona 23–17 (1st to Wildcats in 6 games since 1927), Oregon 20–14 (1st to Ducks in 9 games since 1970) in consecutive mid-season games.   *Stars:* TB Freeman McNeil (1,105 yds rush, 11 TDs), soph QB Tom Ramsey (1,116 yds pass), soph WR Cormac Carney (33 pass rec for 581 yds), TE Tim Wrightman (17 pass rec for 236 yds), OG Larry Lee, DT Irv Eatman, LB Avon Riley, Jimmy Turner (5 int), Easley, P Matt McFarland (40.1-yd avg).

1982 (10–1–1)   *Won:* Long Beach St. 41–10, Wisconsin 51–26, Michigan 31–27 (1st in 6-game series dating to 1956), Colorado 34–6, Washington St. 42–17, California 47–31, Oregon 40–12, Stanford 38–35, USC 20–19.   *Lost:* Washington 10–7.   *Tied:* Arizona 24–24.   *Stars:* Ramsey (3,124 yds total off, nation's leader with 2,824 yds and 21 TDs pass), Carney (46 pass rec for 779 yds), FL JoJo Townsell (41 pass rec for 718 yds and 10 TDs), TE Paul Bergmann (41 pass rec for 577 yds), frosh K John Lee (14 FGs, 81 pts), NG Karl Morgan, Lupe Sanchez (5 int), soph P Kevin Buenafe (40.7-yd avg).   *Noteworthy:* Won 1st Pacific-10 title (12th conference crown overall). Beat Michigan 24–14 in Rose Bowl rematch; scored on TDs by Ramsey (162 yds pass), Danny Andrews, and Blanchard Montgomery (11-yd pass int return), and 39-yd FG by Lee.

1983 (7–4–1)   *Won:* Stanford 39–21, Washington St. 24–14, California 20–16, Washington 27–24,

DB Kenny Easley, 1977–80

Oregon 24–13, USC 27–17.   *Lost:* Georgia 19–8, unbeaten Nebraska 42–10, Brigham Young (BYU) 37–35, Arizona 27–24.   *Tied:* Arizona St. 26–26. *Stars:* QB Rick Neuheisel (2,245 yds and 13 TDs pass), SE Mike Sherrard (48 pass rec for 709 yds), Bergmann (44 pass rec for 499 yds), TB Kevin Nelson (898 yds rush), OT Duval Love, Lee (15 FGs, 72 pts), LB Neal Dellocono, DB Don Rogers (7 int), Sanchez, Buenafe (42.1-yd punting avg). *Noteworthy:* Repeated as Pacific-10 champ. Beat Illinois 45–9 in Rose Bowl; Neuheisel passed for 298 yds and 4 TDs (including 2 to soph Karl Dorrell and 53-yarder to Mike Young), Nelson ran 28 yds for TD, and Lee kicked FG and 6 ex pts.

1984 (9–3)   *Won:* San Diego St. 18–15 (1st meeting since 1934), Long Beach St. 23–17, Colorado 33–16, Washington St. 27–24, California 17–14, Arizona St. 21–13, Oregon St. 26–17, USC 29–10.   *Lost:* Nebraska 42–3, Stanford 23–21, Oregon 20–18. *Stars:* Buenafe (43.2-yd punting avg), Lee (104 pts, nation's leader with 29 FGs), QB Steve Bono (1,576 yds pass), Sherrard (43 pass rec for 729 yds), Danny Andrews (605 yds rush), Love, LB Tommy Taylor, frosh James Washington (5 int), soph Craig

Rutledge (5 int). *Noteworthy:* beat Miami (Fla.) 39–37 in Fiesta Bowl on 22-yd FG by Lee (3 FGs, including 51-yarder, and 4 ex pts) with 51 seconds left; frosh TB Gaston Green ran for 144 yds and 2 TDs (one on 72-yd run), Bono passed for 243 yds and 2 TDs, and Sherrard had 5 pass rec for 94 yds and a TD.

1985 (9–2–1) *Won:* BYU 27–24, San Diego St. 34–16, Arizona St. 40–17, Stanford 34–9, Washington St. 31–30, California 34–7, Arizona 24–9, Oregon St. 41–0. *Lost:* Washington 21–14, USC 17–13. *Tied:* Tennessee 26–26 (1st meeting since 1978). *Stars:* QB David Norrie (1,819 yds and 10 TDs pass), Dorrell (39 pass rec for 565 yds), Green (712 yds rush), Lee (21 FGs, 96 pts), OG Mike Hartmeier, soph NG Terry Turney, DT Mark Walen, Taylor, Washington (5 int). *Noteworthy:* Led nation in rush defense and won 3rd Pacific-10 title. Beat Iowa 45–28 in Rose Bowl; frosh Eric Ball ran for 227 yds and 4 TDs (3 on runs of 30 or more yds), and Matt Stevens passed for 189 yds and a TD.

1986 (8–3–1) *Won:* San Diego St. 45–14, Long Beach St. 41–23, Arizona 32–25, California 36–10 (15th straight over Bears), Washington St. 54–16, Oregon St. 49–0, USC 45–25. *Lost:* Oklahoma 38–3, Arizona St. 16–9 (1st in 8-game series dating to 1976), Stanford 28–23. *Tied:* Washington 17–17. *Stars:* Green (1,405 yds rush, 102 pts), Stevens (1,869 yds and 11 TDs pass), Willie Anderson (36 pass rec for 675 yds), K David Franey (16 FGs), Turney, Rutledge (6 int), soph P Harold Barkate (42.4-yd avg). *Noteworthy:* beat BYU 31–10 in Freedom Bowl; Green ran for 266 yds and 3 TDs (including 79-yd run) and passed for 4th (to Dorrell), and Franey kicked 49-yd FG.

1987 (10–2) *Won:* San Diego St. 47–14, Fresno St. 17–0, Arizona 34–24, Stanford 49–0, Oregon 41–10, California 42–18, Arizona St. 31–23, Oregon St. 52–17, Washington 47–14. *Lost:* Nebraska 42–33, USC 17–13. *Stars:* Green (1,098 yds and 11 TDs rush), QB Troy Aikman (2,354 yds and 16 TDs pass), Anderson (48 pass rec for 903 yds and 6 TDs), soph FL Mike Farr (24 pass rec for 294 yds), soph TE Charles Arbuckle (22 pass rec for 246 yds), OT David Richards, soph K Alfredo Velasco (18 FGs, 100 pts), Turney, LBs Carnell Lake and Ken Norton, Barkate (41.7-yd punting avg). *Noteworthy:* Got share of 4th Pacific-10 title (15th conference crown overall). Beat Florida 20–16 in

Aloha Bowl; Velasco kicked 2 FGs and 2 ex pts, Brian Brown scored on short run, and Aikman passed for 173 yds and other UCLA TD (to Danny Thompson).

1988 (10–2) *Won:* San Diego St. 59–6, Nebraska 41–28, Long Beach St. 56–3, Washington 24–17, Oregon St. 38–21, California 38–21, Arizona 24–3, Oregon 16–6, Stanford 27–17. *Lost:* Washington St. 34–30 (1st to Cougars in 7 games since 1979), USC 31–22. *Stars:* Aikman (2,599 yds and 23 TDs pass), Farr (62 pass rec for 652 yds), soph SE Reggie Moore (38 pass rec for 627 yds and 6 TDs), Dave Keating (23 pass rec for 341 yds and 5 TDs), soph TE Corwin Anthony (5 TDs on pass rec), Ball (784 yds and 6 TDs rush), soph TB Shawn Wills (622

RB Gaston Green, 1984–87

yds and 5 TDs rush), C Frank Cornish, Velasco (17 FGs, 94 pts), Lake, Marcus Turner (5 int), DB Darryl Henley, Barkate (42.2-yd punting avg). *Noteworthy:* beat Arkansas 17–3 in Cotton Bowl; scored on TDs by Mark Estwick and Anthony (pass from Aikman, who had 172 yds pass), and FG and 2 ex pts by Velasco.

1991 (9–3) *Won:* BYU 27–23, San Diego St. 37–12 (15th straight without loss to Aztecs), Arizona 54–14, Oregon St. 44–7, Arizona St. 21–16, Washington St. 44–3, Oregon 16–7, USC 24–21 (1st over Trojans since 1986). *Lost:* Tennessee 30–16, California 27–24, Stanford 27–10. *Stars:* soph QB Tommy Maddox (2,505 yds and 16 TDs pass), SEs Sean LaChapelle (68 pass rec for 987 yds and 11 TDs) and soph Michael Moore (16 pass rec for 283 yds), FL Paul Richardson (28 pass rec for 390 yds), TB Kevin Williams (1,089 yds rush, 9 TDs), soph OT Vaughn Parker, K Louis Perez (13 FGs, 74 pts), DE Mike Chalenski, LB Arnold Ale, DBs Carlton Gray (10 int) and Matt Darby. *Noteworthy:* beat Illinois 6–3 in John Hancock Bowl (8th straight bowl win) on 2 FGs by Perez; Maddox passed for 176 yds.

BOWL SUMMARY

Aloha 1–0; Bluebonnet 0–1; Cotton 1–0; Fiesta 1–0–1; Freedom 1–0; John Hancock 1–0; Liberty 0–1; Rose 5–5.

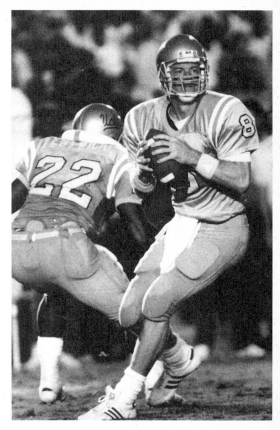

QB Troy Aikman, 1987–88

BOWL RECORD (10–7–1)

Regular Season	Bowl	Score	Opponent	Record
1942 (7–3)	Rose	0–9	Georgia	(10–1)
1946 (10–0)	Rose	14–45	Illinois	(7–2)
1953 (8–1)	Rose	20–28	Michigan St.	(8–1)
1955 (9–1)	Rose	14–17	Michigan St.	(8–1)
1961 (7–3)	Rose	3–21	Minnesota	(7–2)
1965 (7–2–1)	Rose	14–12	Michigan St.	(10–0)
1975 (8–2–1)	Rose	23–10	Ohio State	(11–0)
1976 (9–1–1)	Liberty	6–36	Alabama	(8–3)
1978 (8–3)	Fiesta	10–10	Arkansas	(9–2)
1981 (7–3–1)	Bluebonnet	14–33	Michigan	(8–3)
1982 (9–1–1)	Rose	24–14	Michigan	(8–3)
1983 (6–4–1)	Rose	45–9	Illinois	(10–1)
1984 (8–3)	Fiesta	39–37	Miami (Fla.)	(8–4)
1985 (8–2–1)	Rose	45–28	Iowa	(10–1)
1986 (7–3–1)	Freedom	31–10	BYU	(8–4)

(continued)

Regular Season	Bowl	Score	Opponent	Record
1987 (9–2)	Aloha	20–16	Florida	(6–5)
1988 (9–2)	Cotton	17–3	Arkansas	(10–1)
1991 (8–3)	John Hancock	6–3	Illinois	(6–5)

CONFERENCE TITLES

Pacific Coast—1935*, 1939*, 1942, 1946, 1953, 1954, 1955. **Athletic Association of Western Universities**—1959*, 1961, 1965. **Pacific-8**—1975*. **Pacific-10**—1982, 1983, 1985, 1987*.

TOP 20 AP AND UPI
(USA TODAY/CNN SINCE 1991) RANKING

1939	7	1955	4–4	1972	15–17	1983	17–13
1942	13	1957	U–18	1973	12–9	1984	9–10
1946	4	1961	16–U	1975	5–5	1985	7–6
1951	17–17	1965	4–5	1976	15–15	1986	14–14
1952	6–6	1966	5–5	1978	14–12	1987	9–11
1953	5–4	1967	U–10	1980	13–14	1988	6–6
1954	2–1	1969	13–10	1982	5–5	1991	19–18

MAJOR RIVALS

UCLA has played at least 10 games with Air Force 6–4–1, Arizona 10–6–2, Arizona St. 9–2–1, California 41–21–1, Cal Tech 5–6–1, Occidental 4–6, Oregon 33–16, Oregon St. 31–10–4, Pittsburgh 9–5, Pomona 8–5–1, St. Mary's 7–5, San Diego St. 15–0–1, Southern California 21–34–7, Stanford 33–27–3, Tennessee 3–5–2, Washington 26–24–2, Washington St. 31–9–1.

COACHES

Dean of UCLA coaches is Terry Donahue with record of 131–59–8 for 1976–92, including 4 Pacific-10 titles and 11 bowl teams (8–2–1 record in bowls). Other top records for at least 3 years were by William H. Spaulding, 72–51–8 for 1925–38 with 1 PCC title; Edwin C. Horrell, 24–31–6 for 1939–44 with 2 PCC titles, 1 Rose Bowl team, and 1 unbeaten team; Bert LaBrucherie, 23–16 for 1945–48 with 1 PCC title and 1 Rose Bowl team unbeaten in regular season; Henry "Red" Sanders (1954 national Coach of Year), 66–19–1 for 1949–57 with 3 PCC titles, 2 Rose Bowl teams, and 1 unbeaten national champion; William F. Barnes, 31–34–3 for mid-1958–1964 with 2 AAWU titles and 1 Rose Bowl team; Tommy Prothro (1965 national Coach of Year), 41–18–3 for 1965–70 with 1 AAWU title and 1 Rose Bowl champion; and Pepper Rodgers, 19–12–1 for 1971–73.

MISCELLANEA

First game was loss to Manual Arts H.S. 74–0 in 1919 . . . 1st win was over Occidental frosh 7–2 in 1919 . . . 1st win over college varsity foe was over San Diego St. 24–6 in 1922 . . . highest score was over Stanford 72–0 in 1954 . . . worst defeat was by Whittier 103–0 in 1920 . . . worst since W.W. II was by Washington 61–20 in 1970 . . . longest unbeaten string of 14 in 1975–76 ended by USC 24–14 . . . longest losing string of 16 in 1919–21 broken with win over San Diego St. 24–6 in 1922 opener . . . consensus All-Americans were Burr Baldwin, E, 1946; Donn Moomaw, C, 1952; Paul Cameron, B, 1953; Jack Ellena, T, 1954; Hardiman Cureton, B, 1955; Dick Wallen, B, 1957; Mel Farr, B, 1966; Gary

Beban, B, and Don Manning, LB, 1967; Mike Ballou, LB, 1969; Kermit Johnson, B, 1973; John Sciarra, QB, 1975; Jerry Robinson, LB, 1976–78; Kenny Easley, DB, 1978–80; Tim Wrightman, TE, 1981; Don Rogers, DB, 1983; John Lee, K, 1985; Troy Aikman, QB, and Darryl Henley, DB, 1988; and Carlton Gray, DB, 1992 . . . Academic All-Americans were Ed Flynn, G, and Donn Moomaw, LB, 1952; Ira Pauly, C, 1953; Sam Boghosian, G, 1954; Ray Armstrong, E, 1966; John Sciarra, QB, 1975; John Fowler, LB, 1977; Tim Wrightman, TE, 1981; Cormac Carney, WR, 1981–82; Mike Hartmeier, OG, 1985; and Carlton Gray, DB, 1992 . . . Heisman Trophy winner was Gary Beban, QB, 1967 . . . Maxwell Award winner was Gary Beban, QB, 1967.

WASHINGTON *(Huskies; Purple and Gold)*

NOTABLE TEAMS

1895 (4–0–1) *Won:* Seattle A.C. 12–0, Vashon College 44–4, 34–0, Tacoma A.C. 8–4. *Tied:* Seattle A.C. 0–0.

1899 (4–1–1) *Won:* Pt. Townsend H.S. 16–0, Everett A.C. 33–0, Wilson Business College 11–0, Whitman 6–5. *Lost:* Pt. Townsend A.C. 11–0. *Tied:* All-Seattle 5–5.

1902 (5–1) *Won:* All-Seattle 24–0, Oregon St. 16–5, Idaho 10–0, Whitman 11–5, Washington St. 16–0. *Lost:* Multnomah A.C. 7–0. *Noteworthy:* 1st year under Jim Knight.

1903 (6–1) *Won:* Oregon St. 5–0, Whitman 35–0, Washington St. 10–0, Oregon 6–5, Nevada-Reno 2–0, Idaho 5–0. *Lost:* Multnomah A.C. 6–0 in finale.

1906 (4–1–4) *Won:* USS Philadelphia 5–0, Whitworth 8–0, Seattle H.S. 4–0, Idaho 16–9. *Lost:* unbeaten Oregon 16–6. *Tied:* Seattle A.C. 10–10, Oregon St. 0–0, Whitman 0–0, Willamette 0–0 (1st meeting).

1908 (6–0–1) *Won:* Lincoln H.S. 22–0, Washington H.S. 23–5, Whitworth 24–4, Whitman 6–0, Oregon 15–0, Oregon St. 32–0. *Tied:* unbeaten Washington St. 6–6. *Noteworthy:* had 1st undefeated season since 1895 in 1st year under Gil Dobie.

1909 (7–0) *Won:* USS Milwaukee 52–0, Queen Anne H.S. 34–0, Lincoln H.S. 20–0, Idaho 50–0,

Whitman 17–0, Oregon St. 21–0, Oregon 20–6.

1910 (6–0) *Won:* Lincoln H.S. 20–0, College of Puget Sound 51–0 (1st meeting), Idaho 29–0, Washington St. 16–0, Whitman 12–8, Oregon St. 22–0.

1911 (7–0) *Won:* Lincoln H.S. 42–0, Fort Worden 90–0, College of Puget Sound 35–0, Idaho 17–0, Oregon St. 34–0, Oregon 29–3, Washington St. 30–6.

1912 (6–0) *Won:* College of Puget Sound 53–0, Bremerton Sailors 55–0, Idaho 24–0, Oregon St. 9–3, Oregon 30–14, Washington St. 19–0.

1913 (7–0) *Won:* Everett H.S. 26–0, All-Navy 23–7, Whitworth 100–0, Oregon St. 47–0, Whitman 40–6, Oregon 10–7, Washington St. 20–0.

1914 (6–0–1) *Won:* Aberdeen H.S. 33–6, Rainier Valley A.C. 81–0, Washington Park A.C. 45–0, Whitman 28–7, Oregon 10–0, Washington St. 45–0. *Tied:* unbeaten Oregon St. 0–0 (ending 39-game win streak).

1915 (7–0) *Won:* Ballard Meteors 31–0, Washington Park A.C. 64–0, Gonzaga 21–7, Whitman 27–0, California 72–0, 13–7 (1st meetings since 1904), Colorado 46–0.

1916 (6–0–1) *Won:* Ballard Meteors 28–0, Bremerton Submarine Base 62–0, Whitman 37–6, Oregon St. 35–0, California 13–3, 14–7. *Tied:* unbeaten Oregon 0–0 (1st PCC game). *Star:* G Louis Seagraves. *Noteworthy:* Dobie's last team won inaugural PCC title.

1919 (5–1) *Won:* USS New York 35–0, Whitman 120–0, Washington St. 13–7, Pacific Fleet 14–0, California 7–0. *Lost:* Oregon 24–13. *Noteworthy:* Claude Hunt's last team got share of 2nd PCC title.

1922 (6–1–1) *Won:* USS Idaho 49–0, Montana 26–0, Idaho 2–0 (1st meeting since 1912), Oregon St. 14–3, Washington St. 16–13, Stanford 12–8. *Lost:* unbeaten California 45–7. *Tied:* Oregon 3–3.

1923 (10–1–1) *Won:* USS Mississippi 35–0, USS New York 42–7, Willamette 54–0, Whitman 19–0, Southen California (USC) 22–0 (1st meeting), College of Puget Sound 24–0, Oregon St. 14–0, Montana 26–14, Washington St. 24–7, Oregon 26–7. *Lost:* unbeaten California 9–0. *Stars:* soph HB George Wilson, G James Bryan. *Noteworthy:* made 1st postseason appearance, tying Navy 14–14 in Rose Bowl; scored on 14-yd run by Wilson, 12-yd pass from Fred Abel to Bryan, and 2 ex pts by Lester Sherman.

1924 (8–1–1)   *Won:* West Seattle A.C. 32–0, USS Maryland 33–0, Willamette 57–0, Whitman 55–0, Montana 52–7, Oregon St. 6–3, College of Puget Sound 96–0, Washington St. 14–0.   *Lost:* Oregon 7–3.   *Tied:* unbeaten California 7–7.   *Star:* Wilson (13 TDs).

1925 (10–1–1)   *Won:* Willamette 108–0, USS Oklahoma 59–0, West Seattle A.C. 56–0, Montana 30–10, Whitman 64–2, Washington St. 23–0, Stanford 13–0, California 7–0 (1st over Bears in 5 games since 1919), College of Puget Sound 80–7, Oregon 15–14.   *Tied:* Nebraska 6–6.   *Star:* Wilson (Huskies' 1st consensus All-American; 14 TDs).   *Noteworthy:* Won 3rd PCC title in 1st unbeaten season since 1916. Lost to unbeaten national cochamp Alabama 20–19 in Rose Bowl; Wilson ran for 139 yds and passed for 2 TDs (to E John Cole and QB George Guttormsen) but sat out 22 minutes with injuries, during which Tide scored its 20 points.

1926 (8–2)   *Won:* Bremerton Navy 20–0, Willamette 28–0, College of Puget Sound 33–0, Oregon 23–9, Idaho 26–0, Whitman 44–0, California 13–7, Nebraska 10–6.   *Lost:* Washington St. 9–6 (1st to Cougars since 1921), unbeaten national cochamp Stanford 29–10.

1927 (9–2)   *Won:* Willamette 32–6, USS Idaho 27–0, 48–0, College of Puget Sound 40–0, Montana 32–0, Washington St. 14–0, Whitman 61–7, California 6–0, Oregon 7–0.   *Lost:* Stanford 13–7, USC 33–13.   *Star:* HB Chuck Carroll (15 TDs).

1932 (6–2–2)   *Won:* Gonzaga 19–7, Montana 26–13, Whitman 33–7, Stanford 18–13, UCLA 19–0 (1st meeting), West Seattle A.C. 66–0.   *Lost:* California 7–6, unbeaten national cochamp USC 9–6.   *Tied:* Oregon 0–0, Washington St. 0–0.   *Star:* E Dave Nisbet.

1934 (6–1–1)   *Won:* Idaho 13–0 (10th straight over Vandals), Oregon 16–6 (1st over Ducks since 1927), California 13–7, Oregon St. 14–7, College of Puget Sound 34–0, USC 14–7 (1st over Trojans in 7 games since 1923).   *Lost:* unbeaten Stanford 24–0.   *Tied:* Washington St. 0–0.

1936 (7–2–1)   *Won:* Idaho 22–0, UCLA 14–0, Oregon St. 19–7, California 13–0, Oregon 7–0, USC 12–0, Washington St. 40–0.   *Lost:* national champ Minnesota 14–7 (1st meeting) in opener.   *Tied:* Stanford 14–14.   *Stars:* G Max Starcevich, T Vic Markov, HB Jim Cain.   *Noteworthy:* Won 4th PCC title. Lost to Pittsburgh 21–0 in Rose Bowl, gaining only 153 yds total off.

1937 (7–2–2)   *Won:* Iowa 14–0, USC 7–0, Idaho 21–7, UCLA 26–0, Oregon 14–0, Hawaii 53–13 (in Pineapple Bowl), Honolulu Townies 35–6.   *Lost:* Oregon St. 6–3, Stanford 13–7.   *Tied:* Washington St. 7–7, unbeaten national cochamp California 0–0.   *Star:* Markov.

1940 (7–2)   *Won:* Idaho 21–0, Oregon 10–0, Oregon St. 19–0, California 7–6, USC 14–0, UCLA 41–0, Washington St. 33–0.   *Lost:* unbeaten national cochamp Minnesota 19–14, unbeaten Stanford 20–10.   *Stars:* E Jay MacDowell, C Rudy Mucha, G Ray Frankowski.

1943 (4–1)   *Won:* Whitman 35–6 (1st meeting since 1932), Spokane Air Command 47–12, 41–7, March Field 27–7.   *Star:* Jay Stoves (nation's leader with 7 int).   *Noteworthy:* Had 1st unbeaten season since 1925 in schedule abbreviated by W.W. II. Lost to USC 29–0 in Rose Bowl after trailing only 7–0 at halftime.

1950 (8–2)   *Won:* Kansas St. 33–7, Minnesota 28–13 (1st in 8-game series dating to 1936), UCLA 21–20, Oregon St. 35–6, Stanford 21–7, Oregon 27–12, USC 28–13 (1st over Trojans since 1945), Washington St. 52–21.   *Lost:* Illinois 20–13 (1st meeting), unbeaten California 14–7.   *Stars:* QB Don Heinrich (nation's leader with 1,846 yds and 14 TDs pass), Bill Earley (28 pass rec for 473 yds), FB Hugh McElhenny (1,107 yds rush, 16 pass rec for 236 yds, 1,644 all-purpose yds, 14 TDs), HB Rollie Kirkby, G Ted Holzknecht, C Mike Michael, E Joe Cloidt, DB Dick Sprague (7 int).

1952 (7–3)   *Won:* Idaho 39–14, Minnesota 19–13, Oregon 49–0, Stanford 27–14, Oregon St. 38–13, California 22–7 (1st over Bears since 1946), Washington St. 33–27.   *Lost:* UCLA 32–7, Illinois 48–14, USC 33–0.   *Stars:* Heinrich (back from year's layoff from injury; nation's leader with 1,647 yds and 13 TDs pass), E George Black (42 pass rec for 637 yds and 7 TDs), Jack Nugent (5 TDs rush), T Lou Yourkowski.   *Noteworthy:* last year under Howard Odell.

1959 (10–1)   *Won:* Colorado 21–12, Idaho 23–0, Utah 51–6, Stanford 10–0, Oregon 13–12, UCLA 23–7 (1st over Bruins since 1951), Oregon St. 13–6, California 20–0, Washington St. 20–0.   *Lost:* USC 22–15.   *Stars:* QB/S/P Bob Schloredt (8 TDs rush, 5 TDs pass, 6 int, 40-yd punting avg), Lee Folkins (12 pass rec for 214 yds), HB Don McKeta, G Chuck Allen, T Kurt Gegner, HB/DB George Fleming (6 int). *Noteworthy:* Nation's most-improved team won share of inaugural AAWU title. Beat Wisconsin 44–8 in Rose Bowl; Schloredt passed for 102 yds and a TD and ran for 81 yds and a score, and Fleming scored on 53-yd punt return and kicked 36-yd FG and 5 ex pts.

1960 (10–1)   *Won:* Pacific 55–6, Idaho 41–12, Stanford 29–10, UCLA 10–8, Oregon St. 30–29, Oregon 7–6, USC 34–0 (1st over Trojans since 1955), California 27–7, Washington St. 8–7.   *Lost:* Navy 15–14.   *Stars:* Fleming (5 TDs), McKeta, FB Ray Jackson, soph HB Charlie Mitchell (5 TDs rush), Pat Claridge (13 pass rec for 252 yds), Allen, Gegner, C Roy McKasson.   *Noteworthy:* Repeated as AAWU champ. Upset national cochamp Minnesota 17–7 in Rose Bowl; Schloredt (who sat out most of regular season with injuries) scored one TD and passed for another, and Fleming kicked 44-yd FG and 2 ex pts.

1962 (7–1–2)   *Won:* Illinois 28–7, Kansas St. 41–0, Oregon St. 14–13, Stanford 14–0, California 27–0, UCLA 30–0, Washington St. 26–21.   *Lost:* unbeaten national champ USC 14–0.   *Tied:* Purdue 7–7, Oregon 21–21.   *Stars:* Mitchell, soph FB Junior Coffey (581 yds and 8 TDs rush), C Ray Mansfield, soph G/LB Rick Redman, T Rod Scheyer.

1963 (6–5)   *Won:* Oregon St. 34–7, Stanford 19–11, Oregon 26–19, USC 22–7, California 39–26, Washington St. 16–0.   *Lost:* Air Force 10–7, Pittsburgh 13–6, Iowa 17–7, UCLA 14–0.   *Stars:* Coffey (6 TDs), QB Bill Douglas (1,242 yds total off), Redman, T Mike Briggs.   *Noteworthy:* Won 3rd AAWU title (7th conference crown overall). Lost to Illinois 17–7 in Rose Bowl; took early 7–3 lead on 7-yd TD run by Dave Kopay.

1971 (8–3)   *Won:* UC–Santa Barbara 65–7, Purdue 38–35, Texas Christian (TCU) 44–26, Illinois 52–14, Oregon St. 38–14, UCLA 23–12, California 30–7, Washington St. 28–20.   *Lost:* Stanford 17–6, Oregon 23–21, USC 13–12.   *Stars:* QB Sonny Sixkiller (2,068 yds and 13 TDs pass), WR Tom Scott (35 pass rec for 820 yds and 6 TDs, 1,366 all-purpose yds), soph Pete Taggares (5 TDs rush), DL Gordy Guinn, DB Cal Jones, P Gene Willis (40.6-yd avg).

1972 (8–3)   *Won:* Pacific 13–6, Duke 14–6, Purdue 22–21, Illinois 31–11, Oregon 23–17, California 35–21, Oregon St. 23–16, UCLA 30–21.   *Lost:* Stanford 24–0, unbeaten national champ USC 34–7,

Washington St. 27–10.   *Stars:* Sixkiller (1,125 yds pass), John Brady (30 pass rec for 450 yds), Taggares (11 TDs), Guinn, Jones, Tony Bonwell (7 int), Roberto Jourdan (6 int).

1977 (10–2)   *Won:* Mississippi St. (by forfeit, after losing 27–18), San Jose St. 24–3, Oregon 54–0, Stanford 45–21 (1st over Cardinal since 1966), Oregon St. 14–6, UCLA (by forfeit, after losing 20–12), California 50–31, USC 28–10, Washington St. 35–15.   *Lost:* Syracuse 22–20, Minnesota 19–17.   *Stars:* QB Warren Moon (1,584 yds and 11 TDs pass, 1,850 yds total off), Spider Gaines (30 pass rec for 660 yds and 6 TDs), soph TB Joe Steele (865 yds and 10 TDs rush, 1,263 all-purpose yds), G Jeff Toews, C Blair Bush, K Steve Robbins (14 FGs, 79 pts), DT Dave Browning, LB Michael Jackson, DB Nesby Glasgow.   *Noteworthy:* Won only Pacific-8 title (8th conference crown overall). Beat Michigan 27–20 in Rose Bowl; Moon passed for 188 yds and a TD and scored 2 TDs, Gaines caught 4 passes for 122 yds and a TD, and Robbins kicked 2 FGs.

1979 (10–2)   *Won:* Wyoming 38–2, Utah 41–7, Oregon 21–17, Fresno St. 49–14, Oregon St. 41–0, Arizona St. (by forfeit, after losing 12–7), UCLA 34–14, California 28–24, Washington St. 17–7.   *Lost:* Pittsburgh 26–14, unbeaten USC 24–17.   *Stars:* Steele (694 yds rush, 12 TDs), frosh Paul Skansi (31 pass rec for 378 yds), frosh SE Aaron Williams (14 pass rec for 234 yds), C Tom Turnure, DT Doug Martin, LBs Bruce Harrell and Antowaine Richardson, DB Mark Lee, P Rich Camarillo (40.7-yd avg).   *Noteworthy:* beat Texas 14–7 in Sun Bowl, scoring both TDs in 2nd quarter on 18-yd pass from QB Tom Flick to Skansi and 4-yd run by frosh TB Willis Ray Mackey.

1980 (9–3)   *Won:* Air Force 50–7, Northwestern 45–7, Oklahoma St. 24–18, Oregon St. 41–6, Stanford 27–24, Arizona St. 25–0, Arizona 45–22, USC 20–10, Washington St. 30–23.   *Lost:* Oregon 34–10 (1st to Ducks since 1973), Navy 24–10.   *Stars:* Flick (2,178 yds and 15 TDs pass), Skansi (33 pass rec for 419 yds), Williams (28 pass rec for 595 yds and 5 TDs), FL Anthony Allen (28 pass rec for 425 yds), TE David Bayle (36 pass rec for 315 yds), SE Ron Blacken (13 pass rec for 250 yds), TB Kyle Stevens (706 yds and 7 TDs rush), FB Toussaint Tyler (670 yds and 10 TDs rush), soph K Chuck Nelson (18 FGs, 85 pts), LB Ken Driscoll.   *Noteworthy:* Won 1st Pacific-10 title (9th conference crown overall). Lost to Michigan 23–6 in Rose Bowl; Flick passed for 282 yds and Huskies scored on 2 FGs by Nelson.

1981 (10–2) *Won:* Pacific 34–14, Kansas St. 20–3, Oregon 17–3, California 27–26, Oregon St. 56–17, Texas Tech 14–7, Stanford 42–31, USC 13–3, Washington St. 23–10. *Lost:* Arizona St. 26–7, UCLA 31–0. *Stars:* soph QB Steve Pelluer (1,138 yds pass), Allen (29 pass rec for 389 yds), Ron Jackson (623 yds rush), Nelson (16 FGs, 77 pts), DT Fletcher Jenkins, LB Mark Jerue, DB Ray Horton, P Jeff Partridge (40-yd avg). *Noteworthy:* Repeated as Pacific-10 champ. Beat Iowa 28–0 in Rose Bowl; frosh TB Jacque Robinson ran for 142 yds and 2 TDs, Pelluer passed for 142 yds and 2-pt conversion, and Jerue and Driscoll starred on defense.

1982 (10–2) *Won:* Texas–El Paso 55–0, Arizona 23–13, Oregon 37–21, San Diego St. 46–25, California 50–7, Oregon St. 34–17, Texas Tech 10–3, UCLA 10–7, Arizona St. 17–13. *Lost:* Stanford 43–31 (1st to Cardinal in 5 games since 1976), Washington St. 24–20 (1st to Cougars since 1973). *Stars:* Pelluer (1,229 yds and 10 TDs pass), Skansi (50 pass rec for 631 yds), Allen (42 pass rec for 558 yds and 6 TDs), Robinson (926 yds and 7 TDs rush), Nelson (25 FGs, 109 pts), LBs Mark Stewart and Tony Caldwell, Partridge (42.1-yd punting avg). *Noteworthy:* beat Maryland 21–20 in inaugural Aloha Bowl; QB Tim Cowan passed for 350 yds and 3 TDs (all to Allen, including 71-yarder), and Nelson kicked 3 ex pts.

1983 (8–4) *Won:* Northwestern 34–0, Michigan 25–24, Navy 27–10, Oregon St. 34–7, Stanford 32–15, Oregon 32–3, Arizona 23–22, USC 24–0. *Lost:* Louisiana St. (LSU) 40–14, UCLA 27–24, Washington St. 17–6. *Stars:* Pelluer (2,212 yds and 11 TDs pass), Mark Pattison (38 pass rec for 400 yds), Sterling Hinds (826 yds and 5 TDs rush), OG Rick Mallory, frosh K Jeff Jaeger (20 FGs, 87 pts), DT Ron Holmes. *Noteworthy:* lost to Penn St. 13–10 in Aloha Bowl; Pelluer passed for 153 yds and Danny Greene scored on 57-yd punt return.

1984 (11–1) *Won:* Northwestern 26–0, Michigan 20–11, Houston 35–7, Miami (Ohio) 53–7, Oregon St. 19–7 (10th straight over Beavers), Stanford 37–15, Oregon 17–10, Arizona 28–12, California 44–14, Washington St. 38–29. *Lost:* USC 16–7. *Stars:* Robinson (901 yds rush, 14 TDs), QB Hugh Millen (1,051 yds pass), Greene (29 pass rec for 395

yds), Jaeger (22 FGs, 96 pts), Holmes, LBs Tim Meamber and Fred Small, DB Jim Rodgers, Joe Kelly (5 int). *Noteworthy:* Led nation in turnover margin. Beat Oklahoma 28–17 in Orange Bowl; Robinson ran for 135 yds and a TD, Millen and QB Paul Sicuro each threw a TD pass, and FB Rick Fenney ran 6 yds for final TD.

1986 (8–3–1) *Won:* Ohio St. 40–7, Brigham Young (BYU) 52–21, California 50–18, Stanford 24–14, Bowling Green 48–0, Oregon 38–3, Oregon St. 28–12, Washington St. 44–23. *Lost:* USC 20–10, Arizona St. 34–21. *Tied:* UCLA 17–17. *Stars:* QB Chris Chandler (1,994 yds and 20 TDs pass), SE Lonzell Hill (43 pass rec for 721 yds and 8 TDs), Vince Weathersby (880 yds rush, 1,065 all-purpose yds), Fenney, TE Rod Jones, OG Mike Zandofsky, Jaeger (17 FGs, 93 pts), DT Reggie Rogers, DB Tim Peoples, P Thane Cleland (41.2-yd avg). *Noteworthy:* lost to Alabama 28–6 in Sun Bowl after trailing only 7–6 at halftime; Chandler passed for 199 yds and Jaeger kicked 2 FGs.

1989 (8–4) *Won:* Texas A&M 19–6, Purdue 38–9, Oregon 20–14, California 29–16, UCLA 28–27, Oregon St. 51–14, Washington St. 20–9. *Lost:* Arizona 20–17, unbeaten Colorado 45–28, USC 24–16, Arizona St. 34–32. *Stars:* QB Cary Conklin (2,569 yds and 16 TDs pass), SE Andre Riley (53 pass rec for 1,039 yds), TB Greg Lewis (45 pass rec for 350 yds, 1,100 yds rush, 11 TDs), TE Bill Ames (34 pass rec for 276 yds), soph FL Orlando McKay (30 pass rec for 443 yds), soph SE Mario Bailey (25 pass rec for 357 yds), C Bern Brostek, K John McCallum (14 FGs, 70 pts), soph LB James Clifford, DB Eugene Burkhalter (5 int). *Noteworthy:* beat Florida 34–7 in Freedom Bowl; Conklin passed for 217 yds and 2 TDs (to Bailey and Riley), frosh Jaime Fields recovered blocked punt in end zone for TD, and McCallum kicked 2 FGs and 3 ex pts.

1990 (10–2) *Won:* San Jose St. 20–17, Purdue 20–14, USC 31–0 (1st over Trojans since 1985), Arizona St. 42–14, Oregon 38–17, Stanford 52–16, California 46–7 (10th straight over Bears), Arizona 54–10, Washington St. 55–10. *Lost:* national cochamp Colorado 20–14, UCLA 25–22. *Stars:* soph QB Mark Brunell (1,732 yds and 14 TDs pass, 444 yds and 10 TDs rush, 70 pts), Bailey (40 pass rec for 667 yds and 6 TDs), Lewis (1,279 yds and 8 TDs rush, 20 pass rec for 345 yds and 1 TD), McKay (19 pass rec for 337 yds), soph TB Beno Bryant (8

TDs), OL Jeff Pahukoa and Dean Kirkland, DE Travis Richardson, soph DT Steve Emtman, LBs Donald Jones and Chico Fraley, DBs Eric Briscoe (6 int) and Charles Mincy, P Channing Wyles (41-yd avg). *Noteworthy:* Led nation in turnover margin and rush defense; won 3rd Pacific-10 title (11th conference crown). Beat Iowa 46–34 in Rose Bowl; Brunell passed for 163 yds and 2 TDs (both to Bailey) and scored 2 TDs, Lewis ran for 128 yds, and Mincy scored on 37-yd pass int return.

1991 (12–0) *Won:* Stanford 42–7, Nebraska 36–21, Kansas St. 56–3, Arizona 54–0, Toledo 48–0, California 24–17, Oregon 29–7, Arizona St. 44–16, USC 14–3, Oregon St. 58–6, Washington St. 56–21. *Stars:* soph QB Billy Joe Hobert (2,271 yds and 22 TDs pass, 5 TDs rush), Mario Bailey (62 pass rec for 1,037 yds and 17 TDs), McKay (47 pass rec for 627 yds and 6 TDs), TE Aaron Pierce (23 pass rec for 280 yds), Bryant (943 yds rush, 9 TDs, 1,330 all-purpose yds), TB Jay Barry (718 yds rush, 11 TDs), C Ed Cunningham, OT Lincoln Kennedy, Outland Trophy– and Lombardi Award–winner Emtman, Fraley, Jones, LB Dave Hoffmann, DBs Walter Bailey (7 int, 2 returned for TDs) and Dana Hall, P John Werdel (40.8-yd avg). *Noteworthy:* Won 4th Pacific-10 title in 1st unbeaten season since war-abbreviated 1943 schedule. Beat Michigan 34–14 in Rose Bowl to earn share of 1st national title; Hobert ran for a TD and passed for 192 yds, 2 TDs (to frosh TE Mark Bruener and Pierce), and 2-pt conversion (to Pierce), and Brunell threw 38-yd TD pass to Mario Bailey (6 pass rec for 126 yds).

1992 (9–3) *Won:* Arizona St. 31–7, Wisconsin 27–10, Nebraska 29–14, USC 17–10, California 35–16, Oregon 24–3, Pacific 31–7, Stanford 41–7, Oregon St. 45–16. *Lost:* Arizona 16–3 (breaking 22-game win streak), Washington St. 42–23. *Stars:* Brunell (1,301 yds pass, 8 TDs rush), FL Joe Kralik (33 pass rec for 487 yds), Jason Shelley (20 pass rec for 382 yds), soph TB Napoleon Kaufman (1,045 yds and 6 TDs rush, 1,450 all-purpose yds), Kennedy, K Travis Hanson (10 FGs, 66 pts), DE Andy Mason, Hoffmann, LB James Clifford, Walter Bailey, DBs Shane Pahukoa and Tommie Smith. *Noteworthy:* Got share of 3rd straight Pacific-10 title. Lost to unbeaten Michigan 38–31 in Rose Bowl; Brunell passed for 308 yds and 2 TDs (64 yds to Shelley, who had 3 pass rec for 100 yds, and 18 yds to Bruener), and Hanson had 44-yd FG and 4 ex pts.

BOWL SUMMARY

Aloha 1–1; Freedom 2–0; Independence 1–0; Orange 1–0; Rose 6–6–1; Sun 1–1.

BOWL RECORD (12–8–1)

Regular Season	Bowl	Score	Opponent	Record
1923 (10–1)	Rose	14–14	Navy	(5–1–2)
1925 (10–0–1)	Rose	19–20	Alabama	(9–0)
1936 (7–1–1)	Rose	0–21	Pittsburgh	(7–1–1)
1943 (4–0)	Rose	0–29	USC	(7–2)
1959 (9–1)	Rose	44–8	Wisconsin	(7–2)
1960 (9–1)	Rose	17–7	Minnesota	(8–1)
1963 (6–4)	Rose	7–17	Illinois	(7–1–1)
1977 (7–4)	Rose	27–20	Michigan	(10–1)
1979 (9–2)	Sun	14–7	Texas	(9–2)
1980 (9–2)	Rose	6–23	Michigan	(9–2)
1981 (9–2)	Rose	28–0	Iowa	(8–3)
1982 (9–2)	Aloha	21–20	Maryland	(8–3)
1983 (8–3)	Aloha	10–13	Penn State	(7–4–1)
1984 (10–1)	Orange	28–17	Oklahoma	(9–1–1)
1985 (6–5)	Freedom	20–17	Colorado	(7–4)
1986 (8–2–1)	Sun	6–28	Alabama	(9–3)

(continued)

Regular Season	Bowl	Score	Opponent	Record
1987 (6–4–1)	Independence	24–12	Tulane	(6–5)
1989 (7–4)	Freedom	34–7	Florida	(7–4)
1990 (9–2)	Rose	46–34	Iowa	(8–3)
1991 (11–0)	Rose	34–14	Michigan	(10–1)
1992 (9–2)	Rose	31–38	Michigan	(8–0–3)

CONFERENCE TITLES

Pacific Coast—1916, 1919*, 1925, 1936. **Athletic Association of Western Universities**—1959*, 1960, 1963. **Pacific-8**—1977. **Pacific-10**—1980, 1981, 1990, 1991, 1992*.

TOP 20 AP AND UPI
(USA TODAY/CNN SINCE 1991) RANKING

1936	5	1960	6–5	1979	11–11	1986	18–17
1940	10	1962	U–14	1980	16–17	1989	U–20
1943	12	1963	U–15	1981	10–7	1990	5–5
1950	11–15	1971	19–U	1982	7–7	1991	2–1
1959	8–7	1977	10–9	1984	2–2	1992	11–10

MAJOR RIVALS

Washington has played at least 10 games with Arizona 7–3–1, Arizona St. 9–5, California 38–32–4, Idaho 30–2–2, Minnesota 7–10, Montana 16–1–1, Oregon 53–28–5, Oregon St. 46–26–4, Puget Sound 13–0, Southern California 23–39–3, Stanford 32–31–4, UCLA 24–26–2, Washington St. 54–25–6, Whitman 29–2–3, Willamette 9–0–1.

COACHES

Deans of Washington coaches are Don James (1977, 1991 national Coach of Year) and Jim Owens. James was 153–57–2 for 1975–92, with 6 conference titles, 14 bowl teams (10 winners), and 1 unbeaten national champion. Owens was 99–82–6 for 1957–74, with 3 AAWU titles and 3 Rose Bowl teams. Other top records for at least 3 years were by Jim Knight, 15–4–1 for 1902–04; Gilmour Dobie, 58–0–3 for 1908–16 with 1 PCC title and 9 unbeaten teams (6 perfect records); Claude J. Hunt, 7–4–1 for 1917–19 with 1 PCC title; Enoch Bagshaw, 63–22–6 for 1921–29 with 1 PCC title and 2 Rose Bowl teams; James M. Phelan, 65–37–8 for 1930–41 with 1 PCC title and 1 Rose Bowl team; and Ralph Welch, 27–20–3 for 1942–47 with 1 Rose Bowl team unbeaten in regular season.

MISCELLANEA

First game was loss to Alumni 7–0 in 1889 . . . 1st win was over Seattle A.C. 14–0 in 1892 . . . 1st win over college foe was over Whitman 46–0 in 1894 . . . highest score was over Whitman 120–0 in 1919 . . . highest since W.W. II was over Oregon 66–0 in 1974 . . . worst defeat was by California 72–3 in 1921 . . . worst since W.W. II was by Oregon 58–0 in 1973 . . . highest against since W.W. II was by UCLA 62–13 in 1973 . . . longest unbeaten string of 63 (college football record) in 1907–17 ended by California 27–0 . . . longest win string of 39 in 1908–14 ended by Oregon St. 0–0 . . . 22-game win streak in 1990–92 broken by Arizona 16–3 . . . 14-game unbeaten string in 1924–25 ended by Alabama 20–19 in 1926 Rose Bowl . . . longest losing string of 10 in 1968–69 broken with win over Washington St. 30–21 . . . consensus All-Americans were George Wilson, B, 1925; Charles Carroll, B, 1928; Max Starcevich, G, 1936; Rudy Mucha, C, 1940; Ray Frankowski, G, 1941; Rick Redman, G, 1963–64; Tom Greenlee, DT, 1966; Al Worley, DB, 1968; Chuck Nelson, K, 1982; Ron Holmes, DL, 1984; Jeff Jaeger, K, and Reggie Rogers, DL, 1986; Mario Bailey, WR, and Steve Emtman, DL, 1991; and Lincoln Kennedy, OT, 1992 . . . Academic All-Americans were Jim Houston, E, 1955; Mike Briggs, T, 1963; Rick Redman, G, 1964; Steve Bramwell, DB, 1965; Bruce Harrell, LB, 1979; Mark Jerue, LB, 1981; Chuck Nelson, K, 1981–82; David Rill, LB, 1986–87; and Ed Cunningham, OL, 1991.

WASHINGTON STATE (Cougars;
Crimson and Gray)

NOTABLE TEAMS

1900 (4–0–1) *Won:* Lewiston A.A. 2–0, Spokane A.C. 6–0, 21–0, Walla Walla A.C. 5–0. *Tied:* Washington 5–5 (1st meeting) in finale.

1901 (4–1) *Won:* Lewiston Normal 16–0, Washington 10–0, Oregon 16–0 (1st meeting), Whitman 5–2. *Lost:* Idaho 5–0.

1906 (6–0) *Won:* Blair Business College 11–0, Montana 5–0, Spokane A.C. 8–0, 8–0, Idaho 10–0, Whitman 6–0. *Noteworthy:* had 1st unbeaten season since 1900 in 1st year under John Bender.

1907 (7–1) *Won:* Eastern Washington 46–0, Blair Business College 86–0, Montana 38–0, Spokane A.C. 70–0, Washington 11–5, Whitman 16–8, St. Louis 11–0. *Lost:* Idaho 5–4.

1908 (4–0–2) *Won:* Eastern Washington 78–0, Spokane YMCA 33–0, Bremerton Navy 44–0, Whitman 4–0. *Tied:* unbeaten Washington 6–6, Idaho 4–4. *Noteworthy:* only year under Walter Rheinschild.

1909 (4–1) *Won:* Puget Sound 74–0, Idaho 18–0, Whitworth 38–0, Whitman 23–6. *Lost:* Denver 11–6 in finale.

1915 (7–0) *Won:* Oregon 28–3, Oregon St. 29–0, Idaho 41–0, Montana 27–7, Whitman 17–0, Gonzaga 48–0. *Noteworthy:* Had 1st undefeated season since 1908 in 1st year under William Dietz. Made 1st postseason appearance, beating Brown 14–0 in muddy Rose Bowl; Ralph Boone and Carl Dietz scored on short runs in 2nd half.

1917 (6–0–1) *Won:* Oregon 26–3, Whitman 19–0, Idaho 19–0, Oregon St. 6–0, Montana 28–0, Washington 14–0 (1st over Huskies in 7 games since 1907). *Tied:* 362nd Infantry 0–0 in opener. *Stars:* HB Benton Bangs, E Clarence Zimmerman, T Walter Herried, G Silas Stites. *Noteworthy:* Won 1st PCC title in Dietz's last year.

1919 (5–2) *Won:* Multnomah A.C. 49–0, California 14–0 (1st meeting), Idaho 37–0, Oregon 7–0, Montana 42–14. *Lost:* Washington 13–7, Oregon St. 6–0 in consecutive late games. *Stars:* Herried, soph C Earl Dunlap, E Roy Hanley, FB Lloyd Gillis. *Noteworthy:* 1st year under Gus Welch.

1920 (5–1) *Won:* Gonzaga 35–0, Idaho 14–7, Montana 31–0, Oregon St. 28–0, Nebraska 21–20. *Lost:* unbeaten national champ California 49–0. *Stars:* Gillis, Dunlap, G Fred Hamilton.

1926 (6–1) *Won:* College of Idaho 35–0, Montana 14–6, Washington 9–6 (1st over Huskies since 1921), Idaho 6–0, Oregon 7–0, Gonzaga 7–0 (1st over Bulldogs in 5 games since 1922). *Lost:* Southen California (USC) 16–7. *Noteworthy:* 1st year under O.E. Hollingbery.

1928 (7–3) *Won:* Whitman 33–6 (1st meeting since 1917), Gonzaga 3–0, Montana 26–6, Oregon St. 9–7, College of Idaho 51–0, Idaho 26–0, UCLA 38–0 (1st meeting). *Lost:* California 13–3, unbeaten national cochamp USC 27–13, Washington 6–0. *Star:* T Mel Dressel.

1929 (10–2) *Won:* College of Idaho 48–0, Mt. St. Charles 38–0, Washington 20–13, Whitman 58–6, Oregon St. 9–0, Idaho 41–7, Montana 13–0 (10th straight over Grizzlies), Gonzaga 27–0, Honolulu Townies 12–0, Hawaii 28–7. *Lost:* California 14–0, USC 27–7. *Stars:* FB Elmer Schwartz, C Mel Hein.

1930 (9–1) *Won:* College of Idaho 47–12, California 16–0 (1st over Bears in 9 games since 1919), USC 7–6 (1st over Trojans since 1925), Gonzaga 24–0, Montana 61–0, Oregon St. 14–7, Idaho 33–7, Washington 3–0, Villanova 13–0. *Stars:* Schwartz, Hein, T Glenn "Turk" Edwards, G Harold Ahlskog. *Noteworthy:* Won 2nd PCC title in 1st undefeated season since 1917. Lost to unbeaten Alabama 24–0 in Rose Bowl, dropping behind 21–0 in 2nd quarter.

1932 (7–1–1) *Won:* College of Idaho 40–0, Willamette 30–0, California 7–2, Oregon St. 7–6, Montana 31–0, Idaho 12–0, UCLA 3–0. *Lost:* unbeaten national cochamp USC 20–0. *Tied:* Washington 0–0. *Star:* HB George Sander.

1942 (6–2–2) *Won:* Stanford 6–0, Oregon 7–0, Montana 68–16, Oregon St. 26–13, Michigan St. 25–13, Idaho 7–0 (15th straight over Vandals). *Lost:* USC 26–12, Texas A&M 21–0. *Tied:* 2nd Air Force 6–6, Washington 0–0 in successive late games. *Star:* FB Bob Kennedy (813 yds rush, 11 TDs). *Noteworthy:* Hollingbery's last team.

1945 (6–2–1) *Won:* Idaho 43–12, 21–0, Oregon St. 33–0, 13–6, Oregon 20–13, Washington 7–0 (1st over Huskies in 5 games since 1939). *Lost:* Washington 6–0, Oregon 26–13 in successive early games. *Tied:* California 7–7. *Stars:* G Rod Giske, Bill Lippincott (7 int). *Noteworthy:* resumed football under Phil Sarboe after 2-year W.W. II layoff.

1951 (7–3) *Won:* Santa Clara 34–20, Oklahoma St. 27–13, Oregon St. 26–13, Oregon 41–6, Idaho 9–6, Montana 47–10, Washington 27–25. *Lost:* USC 31–21, California 42–35, Stanford 21–13. *Stars:* Bud Roffler (9 TDs, 80 pts), Es Ed Barker (46 pass rec for 864 yds and 9 TDs) and Don Steinbrunner.

1958 (7–3) *Won:* Stanford 40–6, Idaho 8–0, Oregon 6–0, UCLA 38–20 (1st over Bruins in 11 games since 1937), Oregon St. 7–0, Pacific 34–0, Washington 18–14. *Lost:* Northwestern 29–28, California 34–14, USC 14–6. *Stars:* FB Chuck Morrell, G Marv Nelson.

1965 (7–3) *Won:* Iowa 7–0, Minnesota 14–13, Villanova 24–14, Arizona 21–3, Indiana 8–7, Oregon St. 10–8 (1st over Beavers since 1959), Oregon 27–7. *Lost:* Idaho 17–13, Arizona St. 7–6, Washington 27–9. *Stars:* DT Wayne Foster, DB Bill Gaskins (5 int), FB Larry Eilmes, C Ron Vrilcak.

1981 (8–3–1) *Won:* Montana St. 33–21, Colorado 14–10, Arizona St. 24–21, Pacific 31–0, Oregon St. 23–0, Arizona 34–19, Oregon 39–7, California 19–0. *Lost:* USC 41–17, Washington 23–10. *Tied:* UCLA 17–17. *Stars:* RBs Tim Harris (931 yds and 5 TDs rush), Mike Martin (9 TDs rush) and Robert Williams (5 TDs rush), QBs Clete Casper (1,008 yds pass, 5 TDs rush) and soph Ricky Turner (456 yds and 8 TDs rush), Jeff Keller (39 pass rec for 535 yds), Paul Escalera (20 pass rec for 259 yds), TE Pat Beach (17 pass rec for 230 yds), SE Terrence Jones (11 pass rec for 247 yds), NG Matt Elisara, Nate Bradley (5 int), DB Paul Sorensen, P Tim Davey (40.5-yd avg). *Noteworthy:* made 1st postseason appearance in 51 years, losing to BYU 38–36 in Holiday Bowl after trailing 24–7 at halftime;

Turner ran for 92 yds and 2 TDs, and Don LaBomme, Williams, and Martin each scored once.

1988 (9–3) *Won:* Illinois 44–7, Minnesota 41–9, Tennessee 52–24, California 44–13, UCLA 34–30 (1st over Bruins in 7 games since 1979), Stanford 24–21, Oregon St. 36–27, Washington 32–31. *Lost:* Oregon 43–28, Arizona 45–28, Arizona St. 31–28. *Stars:* QB Timm Rosenbach (308 yds and 9 TDs rush, nation's leader with 2,791 yds and 23 TDs pass), WR Tim Stallworth (63 pass rec for 1,151 yds and 8 TDs), Victor Wood (35 pass rec for 470 yds), TE Doug Wellsandt (26 pass rec for 375 yds), William Pellum (18 pass rec for 276 yds), RBs Steve Broussard (1,280 yds rush, 22 pass rec for 152 yds, 12 TDs) and soph Rich Swinton (1,018 yds rush, 7 TDs), K Jason Hanson (15 FGs, 91 pts), OL Mark Utley, DB Artie Holmes. *Noteworthy:* Had one of nation's most-improved teams in last year under Dennis Erickson. Beat Houston 24–22 in Aloha Bowl, scoring all pts in 2nd quarter; Rosenbach (306 yds pass) passed to Wood (who also scored on 5-yd fumble return) for 1 TD and scored another, Stallworth had 8 pass rec for 120 yds,

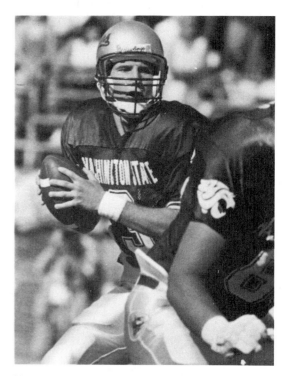

QB Timm Rosenbach, 1987–88

OG Mike Utley, 1985–88

Broussard had 139 yds rush, and Hanson kicked FG and 3 ex pts.

1992 (9–3) *Won:* Montana 25–13 (1st meeting since 1979), Arizona 23–20, Fresno St. 39–37, Temple 51–10, Oregon St. 35–10, UCLA 30–17, Arizona St. 20–18, Washington 42–23. *Lost:* USC 31–21, Oregon 34–17, Stanford 40–3. *Stars:* QB Drew Bledsoe (2,770 yds and 18 TDs pass), FLs C.J. Davis (55 pass rec for 890 yds and 5 TDs) and Calvin Schexnayder (20 pass rec for 286 yds and 5 TDs), SE Deron Pointer (6 TDs, 32 pass rec for 550 yds and 5 TDs), WR Phillip Bobo (36 pass rec for 453 yds), TEs Brett Carolan (32 pass rec for 368 yds) and Clarence Williams, RB Shaumbe Wright-Fair (1,207 yds and 11 TDs rush), OG Bob Garman, K Aaron Price (12 FGs), LBs Anthony McClanahan and soph Ron Childs, soph DE DeWayne Patterson, soph DBs Greg Burns (5 int) and Torey Hunter. *Noteworthy:* beat Utah 31–28 in Copper Bowl as Bledsoe passed for 476 yds and 2 TDs (87 and 48 yds to Bobo, who had 7 pass rec for 212 yds), Davis had 8 pass rec for 134 yds, Wright-Fair ran for 123 yds and 2 TDs, and Price had 4th-quarter FG and 4 ex pts.

BOWL SUMMARY

Aloha 1–0; Copper 1–0; Holiday 0–1; Rose 1–1.

BOWL RECORD (3–2)

Regular Season	Bowl	Score	Opponent	Record
1915 (6–0)	Rose	14–0	Brown	(5–3–1)
1930 (9–0)	Rose	0–24	Alabama	(9–0)
1981 (8–2–1)	Holiday	36–38	BYU	(10–2)
1988 (8–3)	Aloha	24–22	Houston	(9–2)
1992 (8–3)	Copper	31–28	Utah	(6–5)

CONFERENCE TITLES

Pacific Coast—1917, 1930. **Pacific-10**—None.

TOP 20 AP AND UPI
(USA TODAY/CNN SINCE 1991) RANKING

1941	19	1951	18–14	1988	16–16	1992	15–17
1942	17	1972	19–17				

Major Rivals

Washington St. has played at least 10 games with Arizona 8–13, Arizona St. 7–12–2, California 17–34–5, Gonzaga 18–5–3, Idaho 62–14–3, Montana 31–2, Oregon 32–31–7, Oregon St. 41–36–3, Pacific 7–5, San Jose St. 6–4–1, Southern California 5–44–4, Stanford 19–25–1, UCLA 9–31–1, Washington 25–54–6, Whitman 18–3–1.

Coaches

Dean of Washington St. coaches is O.E. Hollingbery with record of 93–53–14 for 1926–42, including 1 PCC title and 1 Rose Bowl team unbeaten in regular season. Other top records for at least 3 years were by John R. Bender, 21–12 for 1906–07 and 1912–14 with 2 unbeaten teams; William H. Dietz, 17–2–1 for 1915–17 with 1 PCC title, 1 Rose Bowl champion, and 2 unbeaten teams; Gus Welch, 16–10–1 for 1919–22; Jim Walden, 44–52–4 for 1978–86 with 1 bowl team; and Mike Price, 22–23 for 1989–92 with 1 bowl champion.

Miscellanea

First game was win over Idaho 10–0 in 1894 . . . highest score was over Blair Business College 86–0 in 1907 . . . highest against 4-year college was over Idaho 84–27 in 1975 . . . biggest margin against 4-year college was over Puget Sound 74–0 in 1909 . . . worst defeat was by California 61–0 in 1922 . . . worst since W.W. II was by UCLA 62–3 in 1976 . . . highest against was by USC 70–33 in 1970 . . . longest unbeaten string of 14 in 1907–09 ended by Denver 11–6 . . . 13-game unbeaten string in 1916–19 ended by Washington 13–7 . . . longest win streak of 11 in 1929–30 ended by Alabama 24–0 in 1931 Rose Bowl . . . longest losing string of 11 in 1970–71 broken with win over Minnesota 31–20 . . . consensus All-Americans were Rueben Mayes, RB, 1984; Mark Utley, OL, 1988; and Jason Hanson, K, 1989 . . . Academic All-Americans were Jason Hanson, K, 1989, P, 1990, and K, 1991; and Lee Tilleman, DL, 1990.

SOUTHEASTERN CONFERENCE

The Southeastern Conference (SEC) has roots as far back as 1894, when representatives of seven schools formed the Southeastern Intercollegiate Athletic Association (SIAA) on December 22 at a meeting in Atlanta, Georgia. Twelve more members were added during the first year of operations, and by 1920 the SIAA included 30 schools. A meeting at Gainesville, Florida, on December 12–13 of that year saw the larger schools form a new league under the name Southern Conference (SC). That conference, in turn, grew to 23 members by 1928. Between 1894 and 1928 the sprawling SIAA and SC included members from Virginia to Texas.

At a meeting in Knoxville, Tennessee, on December 8–9, 1932, the 13 most western and southern members of the SC broke off to form the SEC. Charter members were the universities of Alabama, Auburn, Florida, Georgia, Georgia Tech, Kentucky, Louisiana State, Mississippi, Mississippi State, Sewanee, Tennessee, Tulane, and Vanderbilt. League play began with the 1933 football season. Sewanee, never having won an SEC game, withdrew from the conference on December 13, 1940, and the league eventually was pared to 10 members with the withdrawals of Georgia Tech on June 1, 1964, and Tulane on June 1, 1966.

The SEC underwent a major new expansion in 1990 with the admission of the universities of Arkansas and South Carolina, both of which began league play in 1992. The expanded league was divided into East and West divisions that year, with the winners meeting in a playoff for the SEC title. Undefeated Alabama beat Florida 28–21 in the first playoff title game.

FACTS AND ODDITIES ON SOUTHEASTERN CONFERENCE MEMBERS

Nearly a score of national championships have been won by teams that were at one time members of the SEC, starting with Georgia Tech in 1917. That Tech team, coached by John Heisman, outscored opponents 494–17 in a 9–0 season but turned down a Rose Bowl bid so that many of its members could join the armed forces during that World War I year.

Alabama got a share of its first national title in 1925 by outscoring foes 277–7 in a 9–0 season, then edged unbeaten Washington 20–19 in the Rose Bowl behind future cowboy-movie star Johnny Mack Brown. The Crimson Tide repeated in 1926, earning a share of the national crown with a 9–0 record, then tied unbeaten national cochamp Stanford 7–7 in the Rose Bowl. Georgia Tech was back in 1928, finishing 9–0 to earn a share of the title before edging California 8–7 in the Rose Bowl with the help of the "wrong-way" run by the Bears' Roy Riegels.

The first conference team to win the national title after formation of the SEC was Alabama in 1934. The Tide got a share of its third national crown by compiling a 9–0 record behind B Dixie Howell and E Don Hutson, then beat undefeated Stanford 29–13 in the Rose Bowl. Tennessee got a share of its first title in 1938, finishing 10–0 and then beating undefeated Oklahoma 17–0 in the Orange Bowl. In 1942 Georgia got a share of its first crown despite a loss to Auburn 27–13. The Bulldogs finished 10–1 behind B Frank Sinkwich, then beat UCLA 9–0 in the Rose Bowl.

Nearly a decade later, in 1951, Tennessee returned the national crown to the SEC by finishing 10–0, but was upset by unbeaten Maryland 28–13 in the Sugar Bowl. Auburn got a share of its first national title in 1957, relying on an outstanding defense to finish 10–0 under Coach Ralph "Shug" Jordan. The following season Louisiana State, with its famed "Chinese Bandits" defense, got a major share of the crown with a 10–0 record followed by a win over Clemson 7–0 in the Sugar Bowl. Mississippi earned a share of the national title in 1960 with a 9–0–1 record (the tie was with LSU 6–6) followed by a win over Rice 14–6 in the Sugar Bowl.

In 1961 Alabama got a share of its fourth national title (its first under "Bear" Bryant), with a 10–0 season topped by a win over Arkansas 10–3 in the Sugar Bowl. The Tide was back for a share of the crown in 1964, despite a loss to Texas 21–17 in the Orange Bowl, as QB Joe Namath directed 'Bama to a 10–0 regular-season record. The SEC's newest member, Arkansas, shared the national crown that year while still a member of the Southwest Conference. The Razorbacks went 10–0 in regular season, then beat Nebraska 10–7 in the Cotton Bowl.

Alabama got a share of its third title in five years in 1965. The Tide finished 8–1–1 after losing the opener to Georgia 18–17, then beat undefeated Nebraska 39–28 in the Orange Bowl. The Crimson Tide got a share of their seventh national title in 1973 with an 11–0 regular-season record, though 'Bama lost to unbeaten national cochamp Notre Dame 24–23 in the Sugar Bowl in one of the most exciting bowl games ever played. In 1978 Alabama earned a share of its eighth national crown, losing to USC 24–14 early in the season but finishing 10–1 and then upsetting unbeaten Penn State 14–7 in the Sugar Bowl with a memorable 4th quarter goal-line stand. The Tide repeated as national champion in 1979 (Bryant's sixth national title) by compiling an 11–0 regular-season record and beating Arkansas 24–9 in the Sugar Bowl. Georgia gave the SEC its third straight national title in 1980 with an 11–0 record behind freshman RB Herschel Walker, and beat Notre Dame 17–10 in the Sugar Bowl.

After the longest spell without a national crown in the conference's history, Alabama returned the title to the SEC in 1992. The Crimson Tide finished 11–0 in the regular season, beat Georgia 28–21 in the 1st SEC championship playoff game, and then upset undefeated defending national champ Miami (Florida) 34–13 in the Sugar Bowl to earn their 10th national title.

A half-dozen SEC players have won the Heisman Trophy, starting with HB Frank Sinkwich of Georgia in 1942. The others were HB Billy Cannon, LSU, 1959; QB Steve Spurrier, Florida, 1966; QB Pat Sullivan, Auburn, 1971; HB Herschel Walker, Georgia, 1982; and HB Bo Jackson, Auburn, 1985. The award also was won by George Rogers of South Carolina in 1980 when the Gamecocks were independent. The Maxwell Award has gone to SEC players twice, both times to Georgia players. HB Charley Trippi won in 1946 and HB Herschel Walker in 1982.

Five SEC players have won the Outland Trophy, starting with T Bob Gain of Kentucky in 1950. The other recipients were G Zeke Smith, Auburn, 1958; T Steve DeLong, Tennessee, 1964; T Bill Stanfill, Georgia, 1968; and DT Tracy Rocker, Auburn, 1988. Two Arkansas players, G Bill Brooks in 1954 and T Loyd Phillips in 1966, won the award while the Razorbacks were in the Southwest Conference. The Lombardi Award has gone to SEC players twice, to LB Cornelius Bennett of Alabama in 1986 and to DT Tracy Rocker of Auburn in 1988.

National Coach of the Year awards have gone to SEC coaches nine times, with Alabama's Paul "Bear" Bryant winning three. Bryant won the American Football Coaches Association (AFCA) share of the award in 1961, 1971, and 1973. Other winners were Bill Alexander of Georgia Tech, 1942; Bowden Wyatt, Tennessee, 1956; Paul Dietzel, LSU, 1958; Charles McClendon, LSU, the AFCA share in 1970; Vince Dooley, Georgia, 1980; and Gene Stallings, Alabama, 1992. In addition, Frank Broyles of Arkansas won a share of the AFCA award in 1964 while in the Southwest Conference.

The SEC has had a number of coaches known for winning records at the same school over a long period of time, the most famous of whom, Bryant, compiled one of the outstanding coaching records in college football history. The "Bear's" overall record was 323–85–17, a winning percentage of .780, for 1945–1982. Most of those games were as an SEC head coach, eight years at Kentucky and 25 at his alma mater, Alabama. Bryant won 15 conference titles (14 in the SEC), had 29 bowl teams, coached eight teams unbeaten in regular season, and won six national titles (all at Alabama).

Another outstanding record was compiled by Robert R. Neyland at Tennessee. Neyland coached the Volunteers to a 173–31–12 record for 1926–1934, 1936–1940, and 1946–1952, with six conference titles (five in the SEC), eight bowl teams, nine teams unbeaten in regular season, and two national champions. He stands sixth on the all-time list of successful college football coaches with a winning percentage of .829.

Other SEC coaches with top winning percentages over a long period were Dan McGugin, Bobby Dodd, John Vaught, and Vince Dooley.

McGugin's career at Vanderbilt, covering 1904–1917 and 1919–1934, was spent almost entirely before the SEC was formed. He compiled a record of 197–55–19, a winning percentage of .762. A brother-in-law of Michigan coach Fielding H. "Hurry Up" Yost, McGugin saw Yost's Wolverines give his teams their only defeats in 1905, 1906, 1907, and 1911; in nine tries against his more famous brother-in-law, McGugin's best result was a 0–0 tie in 1922, when both Vanderbilt and Michigan were unbeaten.

Dodd spent his entire head-coaching career at Georgia Tech, where he was 165–64–8 for 1945–1966, a winning percentage of .713. He won two SEC titles and had thirteen bowl teams and two unbeaten seasons. Vaught spent his entire coaching career at Mississippi, compiling a record of 190–61–12 for 1947–1970 and part of 1973, a winning percentage of .745. Included were six SEC titles, eighteen bowl teams, four teams unbeaten in regular season, and one national title. Dooley's entire head-coaching career was at Georgia, where he compiled a record of 201–77–10 for 1964–1988, a winning percentage of .715. He had six SEC champions, twenty bowl teams, three teams unbeaten in regular season, and one national champion.

The man for whom the Heisman Trophy is named, John Heisman, was a head coach for 36 years, including two stints at schools that would be charter members of the SEC. His longest stint was at Georgia Tech, which went 102–29–7 under Heisman in 1904–1919, including a national champion. Earlier, he had coached Auburn to a record of 12–4–2 in 1895–1899.

While Arkansas was still in the Southwest Conference, Frank Broyles directed the Razorbacks to a record of 149–62–6, a winning percentage of .700, for 1958–1976. He won seven SWC titles and had 10 bowl teams.

Auburn shares in two of the most-played rivalries in college football. The Tigers' series with Georgia is tied for eighth in most games played, at 96. Through 1992 Auburn held an edge of 45–44–7. Auburn's series with former SEC member Georgia Tech has lapsed since 1987 but still ranks 12th on the most-played list, with Auburn holding a 47–39–4 lead. Tied for 15th on the most-played list is Louisiana State's series with former SEC member Tulane; through 1992 the series stood at 61–22–7 in favor of LSU (though Tulane claims it was 60–23–7).

An unusual display of sportsmanship took place in the 1939 contest between those fierce rivals. The Green Wave went into the game unbeaten and looking for a Sugar Bowl bid, while the Tigers were playing mainly for pride. The contest was scoreless when Tulane E Ralph Wenzel caught a long pass along the sideline near the LSU 5-yard line and trotted into the end zone for an apparent TD. The play had caught the small officiating crew of the time by surprise, and none of them was near Wenzel when he made the catch. The nearest official signaled a touchdown, but as he approached Wenzel, the Tulane player tossed him the ball and said, "I think I stepped over the line while running for the touchdown. I think the fair thing to do is to tell you." As it turned out Tulane scored anyway and went on to a 33–20 victory, but Wenzel wanted no part of a tainted TD—however great the pressure to win.

The last major college football team to go through a season unbeaten, untied, and unscored-on was SEC member Tennessee in that same season of 1939. However, the Volunteers were beaten in the Rose Bowl by Southern California 14–0.

Alabama holds the NCAA record for consecutive home victories, with 57 straight. The string started with a win over Houston 21–13 in the second home game of 1963, and was broken by Southern Mississippi 38–29 in the last home game of 1982.

SEC members have some nicknames common to the college football scene—Tigers at both Auburn and LSU, Bulldogs at Georgia and Mississippi State, and Wildcats at Kentucky. However, there are nicknames of more unusual kinds at Alabama, Arkansas, Florida, Mississippi, South Carolina, Tennessee, and Vanderbilt.

Alabama was known as the Thin Red Line late in the first decade of the twentieth century, but about the time of World War I the sports editor of the *Birmingham Age-Herald*, Hugh Roberts, began calling the team the Crimson Tide. Zipp Newman of the *Birmingham News* joined in popularizing the name, which caught on quickly. 'Bama fans also sometimes refer to their team as the Red Elephants, an informal nickname dating to 1930 when *Atlanta Journal* sportswriter Everett Strupper compared Alabama linemen to elephants in a 64–0 demolishing of Mississippi. Soon Strupper and other writers were calling the team Red Elephants because of the color of their jerseys. An elephant mascot still appears at Alabama games.

Arkansas was called the Cardinals till the close of the 1909 season. At a postseason rally celebrating a 7–0 record that year, Coach Hugo Bezdek referred to his team as "a wild band of razorbacks." The name quickly caught on with fans and writers.

Auburn adopted its Tigers nickname from a verse in Oliver Goldsmith's 1770 poem, "The Deserted Village," "where crouching tigers wait their hapless prey"; the poem also notes that "Sweet Auburn" is the loveliest village of the plain. LSU adopted Tigers in 1896 during a 6–0 season, the name being derived from a battalion of Confederate soldiers known as the Louisiana Tigers during the Civil War. The 1955 "4th quarter ball club" inspired the Fighting Tigers nickname now used.

Florida's nickname developed in a roundabout way. In 1907 a merchant from Gainesville, Florida, Phillip Miller, was visiting his son at the University of Virginia when he got the idea of ordering, from a

Charlottesville firm, some banners and pennants to sell at home in his drugstore. The Virginia company was happy to fill the order, but inquired what mascot or emblem should be used. Florida had just begun football the year before and had no nickname. Miller's son Austin, the U. Va. student, suggested the alligator because it was native to Florida and not used as a mascot by any other team. Thus, banners and pennants displaying alligators in various poses were made up and sent to Miller's store in Gainesville. The symbol caught on, though the name later was shortened to Gators.

Southern sportswriters in 1936 were asked to supply a nickname for the athletic teams at Mississippi, already called "Ole Miss." The student newspaper sent several suggested names to sportswriters throughout the region, and their overwhelming choice was Rebels, suggested by Judge Ben Guider of Vicksburg. Mississippi State's Bulldog nickname dates back at least to 1905 but has been the official emblem only since 1961, when university officials, with alumni support, confirmed Bulldogs as the official nickname. Between 1935 and 1960 State's teams usually were called Maroons, and before that Bulldogs had been shared with Aggies.

South Carolina football teams at the turn of the century were known as Game Cocks, but the Columbia, S.C., morning newspaper, *The State,* shortened the name to one word in 1903, and in recent years the name has evolved into Fighting Gamecocks. The state had been closely connected with the breeding and training of fighting gamecocks since colonial days.

Tennessee adopted Volunteers from the state nickname, the Volunteer state, which dated to the early 19th century when General Andrew Jackson mustered many volunteers from the state to fight Indians, and later the British in the Battle of New Orleans. Vanderbilt's nickname, Commodores, was first used in 1897 by William E. Beard, a member of the *Nashville Banner* editorial staff who had been a quarterback on Vandy's 1892 team. It was a natural because the school had been founded in 1873 by a $1 million grant from Commodore Cornelius Vanderbilt.

LSU's 1893 baseball team wore royal purple and old gold uniforms for a victory over Tulane. That autumn Coach Charles Coates and some of his players purchased purple and gold ribbons to adorn their gray jerseys for LSU's first football game. The school later followed Coates' suggestion to adopt purple and gold as official colors.

Mississippi's first team in 1893 thought the combination of Harvard's crimson and Yale's blue would enable the school to have "the spirit of both these good colleges," though the Ole Miss colors since have been modified to red and blue. South Carolina adopted garnet and black, colors of the gamecock mascot, near the turn of the century. A member of Tennessee's first football team in 1891, Charles Moore, selected orange and white for the school colors because of the profusion of daisies that grew on the Knoxville campus.

ALL-TIME SOUTHEASTERN CONFERENCE CHAMPIONS

Annual Champion	SEC Record	Regular Season and Bowl	
1933 Alabama	5–0–1	7–1–1	
1934 Alabama	7–0	9–0	Rose (W)
Tulane	8–0	9–1	Sugar (W)
1935 Louisiana St.	5–0	9–1	Sugar (L)
1936 Louisiana St.	6–0	9–0–1	Sugar (L)
1937 Alabama	6–0	9–0	Rose (L)
1938 Tennessee	7–0	10–0	Orange (W)
1939 Georgia Tech	6–0	7–2	Orange (W)
Tennessee	6–0	10–0	Rose (L)
Tulane	5–0	8–0–1	Sugar (L)
1940 Tennessee	5–0	10–0	Sugar (L)
1941 Mississippi St.	4–0–1	8–1–1	
1942 Georgia	6–1	10–1	Rose (W)
1943 Georgia Tech	3–0	7–3	Sugar (W)
1944 Georgia Tech	4–0	8–2	Orange (L)
1945 Alabama	6–0	9–0	Rose (W)
1946 Georgia	5–0	10–0	Sugar (W)
Tennessee	5–0	9–1	Orange (L)
1947 Mississippi	6–1	8–2	Delta (W)
1948 Georgia	6–0	9–1	Orange (L)
1949 Tulane	5–1	7–2–1	
1950 Kentucky	5–1	10–1	Sugar (W)
1951 Georgia Tech	7–0	10–0–1	Orange (W)
Tennessee	5–0	10–0	Sugar (L)
1952 Georgia Tech	6–0	11–0	Sugar (W)
1953 Alabama	4–0–3	6–2–3	Cotton (L)
1954 Mississippi	5–1	9–1	Sugar (L)
1955 Mississippi	5–1	9–1	Cotton (W)
1956 Tennessee	6–0	10–0	Sugar (L)
1957 Auburn	7–0	10–0	
1958 Louisiana St.	6–0	10–0	Sugar (W)
1959 Georgia	7–0	9–1	Orange (W)
1960 Mississippi	5–0–1	9–0–1	Sugar (W)
1961 Alabama	7–0	10–0	Sugar (W)
Louisiana St.	6–0	9–1	Orange (W)
1962 Mississippi	6–0	9–0	Sugar (W)
1963 Mississippi	5–0–1	7–0–2	Sugar (L)
1964 Alabama	8–0	10–0	Orange (L)
1965 Alabama	6–1–1	8–1–1	Orange (W)
1966 Alabama	6–0	10–0	Sugar (W)
Georgia	6–0	9–1	Cotton (W)
1967 Tennessee	6–0	9–1	Orange (L)
1968 Georgia	5–0–1	8–0–2	Sugar (L)
1969 Tennessee	5–1	9–1	Gator (L)
1970 Louisiana St.	5–0	9–2	Orange (L)
1971 Alabama	7–0	11–0	Orange (L)
1972 Alabama	7–1	10–1	Cotton (L)
1973 Alabama	8–0	11–0	Sugar (L)

(continued)

ALL-TIME SOUTHEASTERN
CONFERENCE CHAMPIONS (continued)

Annual Champion	SEC Record	Regular Season and Bowl	
1974 Alabama	6–0	11–0	Orange (L)
1975 Alabama	6–0	10–1	Sugar (W)
1976 Georgia	5–1	10–1	Sugar (L)
Kentucky	5–1	7–4	Peach (W)
1977 Alabama	7–0	10–1	Sugar (W)
1978 Alabama	6–0	10–1	Sugar (W)
1979 Alabama	6–0	11–0	Sugar (W)
1980 Georgia	6–0	11–0	Sugar (W)
1981 Alabama	6–0	9–1–1	Cotton (L)
Georgia	6–0	10–1	Sugar (L)
1982 Georgia	6–0	11–0	Sugar (L)
1983 Auburn	6–0	10–1	Sugar (W)
1984 Florida[a]	5–0–1	9–1–1	
1985 Tennessee	5–1	8–1–2	Sugar (W)
1986 Louisiana St.	5–1	9–2	Sugar (L)
1987 Auburn	5–0–1	9–1–1	Sugar (T)
1988 Auburn	6–1	10–1	Sugar (L)
Louisiana St.	6–1	8–3	Hall of Fame (L)
1989 Alabama	6–1	10–1	Sugar (L)
Auburn	6–1	9–2	Hall of Fame (W)
Tennessee	6–1	10–1	Cotton (W)
1990 Tennessee	5–1–1	8–2–2	Sugar (W)
1991 Florida	7–0	10–1	Sugar (L)
1992[b] Florida	6–2	8–4	Gator (W)
Alabama[c]	8–0	12–0	Sugar (W)

[a]Title later vacated as result of conference action.
[b]SEC started division play (East Division champ listed 1st, West Division champ 2nd).
[c]SEC playoff winners.

ALABAMA *(Crimson Tide; Crimson and White)*

NOTABLE TEAMS

1904 (7–3) *Won:* Florida 29–0 (1st meeting), Mississippi St. 6–0, Nashville U. 17–0, Georgia 16–5, Louisiana St. (LSU) 11–0, Tulane 6–0, Pensacola A.C. 10–5. *Lost:* Clemson 18–0, unbeaten Auburn 29–5, Tennessee 5–0.

1906 (5–1) *Won:* Maryville 6–0, Howard 14–0 (1st meeting), Mississippi St. 16–4, Auburn 10–0, Tennessee 51–0. *Lost:* Vanderbilt 78–0. *Noteworthy:* 1st year under J.W.H. Pollard.

1907 (5–1–2) *Won:* Maryville 17–0, Mississippi 20–0 (1st meeting since 1901), Centre 12–0, LSU 6–4, Tennessee 5–0. *Lost:* Sewanee 54–4. *Tied:* Georgia 0–0, Auburn 6–6.

1908 (6–1–1) *Won:* Wetumpka 27–0, Howard 17–0, Cincinnati 16–0, Chattanooga 23–6, Haskell Institute 9–8, Tennessee 4–0. *Lost:* Georgia Tech 11–6. *Tied:* Georgia 6–6.

1909 (5–1–2) *Won:* Union 16–0, Howard 14–0, Clemson 3–0, Georgia 14–0, Tennessee 10–0. *Lost:* LSU 12–6 in finale. *Tied:* Mississippi 0–0, Tulane 5–5. *Noteworthy:* Pollard's last team.

1915 (6–2) *Won:* Howard 44–0, Birmingham Southern 67–0, Mississippi College 40–0, Tulane 16–0, Sewanee 23–10 (1st over Tigers in 10 games since 1894), Mississippi 53–0. *Lost:* unbeaten Georgia Tech 21–7, Texas 20–0 (1st meeting since 1902) in consecutive late games. *Star:* FB W.T. VandeGraaf. *Noteworthy:* 1st year under Thomas Kelly.

1919 (8–1) *Won:* Birmingham Southern 27–0, Mississippi 49–0, Howard 48–0, Marion Institute 61–0, Sewanee 40–0, LSU 23–0 (1st meeting since 1909), Georgia 6–0, Mississippi St. 14–6 (1st over State in 5 games since 1906). *Lost:* Vanderbilt 16–12. *Noteworthy:* resumed competition under Xen Scott after 1-year layoff during W.W. I.

1920 (10–1) *Won:* Southern Military Academy 59–0, Marion Institute 49–0, Birmingham Southern 45–0, Mississippi College 57–0, Howard 33–0, Sewanee 21–0, Vanderbilt 14–7 (1st in 6-game series dating to 1903), LSU 21–0 (1st homecoming), Mississippi St. 24–7, Case College 40–0. *Lost:* unbeaten Georgia 21–14. *Star:* FB Riggs Stephenson.

1923 (7–2–1) *Won:* Union 12–0, Mississippi 56–0,

Sewanee 7–0, Spring Hill 59–0, Kentucky 16–8, LSU 30–3, Georgia 36–0. *Lost:* Syracuse 23–0, Florida 16–6. *Tied:* Georgia Tech 0–0. *Noteworthy:* 1st year under Wallace Wade.

1924 (8–1) *Won:* Union 55–0, Furman 20–0, Mississippi College 51–0, Sewanee 14–0, Georgia Tech 14–0 (1st over Tech in 5 games since 1914), Mississippi 61–0, Kentucky 42–7, Georgia 33–0. *Lost:* Centre 17–0. *Noteworthy:* won 1st SC title.

1925 (10–0) *Won:* Union 53–0, Birmingham Southern 50–7, LSU 42–0, Sewanee 27–0, Georgia Tech 7–0, Mississippi St. 6–0, Kentucky 31–0, Florida 34–0, Georgia 27–0. *Stars:* B Johnny Mack Brown, QB Pooley Hubert. *Noteworthy:* Outscored foes 277–7 in 1st unbeaten season since 1-game schedule of 1897; repeated as SC champ and earned share of 1st national title. Made 1st postseason appearance, beating undefeated Washington 20–19 in Rose Bowl with 20 pts in 3rd quarter after trailing 12–0 at halftime; Hubert scored 1 TD and passed 30 yds for another to Brown, who also scored on 59-yd pass from Grant Gillis.

1926 (9–0–1) *Won:* Millsaps 54–0, Vanderbilt 19–7 (1st meeting since 1921), Mississippi St. 26–7, Georgia Tech 21–0, Sewanee 2–0, LSU 24–0, Kentucky 14–0, Florida 49–0, Georgia 33–6. *Stars:* G Bill Buckler, E Hoyt Winslett. *Noteworthy:* Won 3rd straight SC title and again got share of national crown. Tied unbeaten national cochamp Stanford 7–7 in Rose Bowl; scored in last minutes of game on short run by HB Jimmy Johnson and conversion by Herschel Caldwell following blocked punt by Clarke "Babe" Pearce.

1930 (10–0) *Won:* Howard 43–0, Mississippi 64–0 (10th straight over Ole Miss), Sewanee 25–0, Tennessee 18–6, Vanderbilt 12–7, Kentucky 19–0, Florida 20–0, LSU 33–0, Georgia 13–0. *Stars:* T Fred Sington (Crimson Tide's 1st consensus All-American), HB John "Flash" Suther. *Noteworthy:* Wade's last team got share of 4th SC title. Beat undefeated Washington St. 24–0 in Rose Bowl; Suther scored on 61-yd trick pass from E Jimmy Moore, Monk Campbell scored 2 TDs (one on 43-yd run), and J.B. Whitworth kicked 30-yd FG.

1931 (9–1) *Won:* Howard 42–0, Mississippi 55–6, Mississippi St. 53–0, Sewanee 33–0, Kentucky 9–7, Florida 41–0, Clemson 74–7 (1st meeting since 1913), Vanderbilt 14–6. *Lost:* unbeaten Tennessee 25–0. *Star:* FB Johnny Cain. *Noteworthy:* 1st year under Frank Thomas. Beat Chattanooga 49–0 in postseason charity game in Chattanooga.

1932 (8–2) *Won:* Southwestern (Tenn.) 45–6, Mississippi St. 53–0, George Washington 28–6, Mississippi 24–13, Kentucky 12–7 (10th straight over Wildcats), Virginia Tech 9–6 (1st meeting), Vanderbilt 20–0, St. Mary's 6–0. *Lost:* unbeaten Tennessee 7–3, Georgia Tech 6–0. *Star:* Cain.

1933 (7–1–1) *Won:* Oglethorpe 34–0, Mississippi St. 18–0, Tennessee 12–6, Kentucky 20–0, Virginia Tech 27–0, Georgia Tech 12–9, Vanderbilt 7–0. *Lost:* Fordham 2–0. *Tied:* Mississippi 0–0. *Stars:* G Tom Hupke, HB Dixie Howell (630 yds and 9 TDs rush). *Noteworthy:* won inaugural SEC title.

1934 (10–0) *Won:* Howard 24–0, Sewanee 35–6 (10th straight over Tigers), Mississippi St. 41–0, Tennessee 13–6, Georgia 26–6, Kentucky 34–14, Clemson 40–0, Georgia Tech 40–0, Vanderbilt 34–0. *Stars:* Howell (840 yds and 10 TDs rush, 597 yds and 3 TDs pass, 42.1-yd punting avg), E Don Hutson (19 pass rec for 326 yds), T Bill Lee, G Charlie Marr. *Noteworthy:* Got shares of 2nd SEC title and 3rd national crown. Beat undefeated Stanford 29–13 in Rose Bowl; Howell passed for 160 yds, including 59-yd TD pass to Hutson (6 pass rec for 165 yds and 2 TDs, including 54-yarder from Joe Riley), ran 67 yds for another TD, and had 43.8-yd punting avg.

1935 (6–2–1) *Won:* George Washington 39–0, Tennessee 25–0, Georgia 17–7, Kentucky 13–0, Clemson 33–0, Georgia Tech 38–7. *Lost:* Mississippi St. 20–7 (1st to State in 13 games since 1914), Vanderbilt 14–6 (1st to Commodores since 1929). *Tied:* Howard 7–7. *Stars:* QB Riley Smith, T James Whatley.

1936 (8–0–1) *Won:* Howard 34–0, Clemson 32–0, Mississippi St. 7–0, Loyola (La.) 13–6, Kentucky 14–0, Tulane 34–7 (1st meeting since 1921), Georgia Tech 20–16, Vanderbilt 14–6. *Tied:* Tennessee 0–0. *Stars:* Smith, G Arthur White.

1937 (9–1) *Won:* Howard 41–0, Sewanee 65–0, South Carolina 20–0 (1st meeting), Tennessee 14–7, George Washington 19–0, Kentucky 41–0 (15th straight over Wildcats), Tulane 9–6, Georgia Tech 7–0, Vanderbilt 9–7. *Stars:* HB Joe Kilgrow (5 TDs), Charley Holm (607 yds rush), E Erwin Warren, G Leroy Monsky, T James Ryba. *Noteworthy:* Won 3rd SEC title. Lost to unbeaten national cochamp California 13–0 in Rose Bowl (1st loss in 5 postseason games); lost 4 fumbles and had 4 int.

1938 (7–1–1) *Won:* Southern California (USC) 19–7, Howard 34–0, N.C. State 14–0, Sewanee 32–0, Kentucky 26–6, Tulane 3–0, Vanderbilt 7–0. *Lost:* unbeaten national cochamp Tennessee 13–0 (1st to Vols since 1932). *Tied:* Georgia Tech 14–14. *Star:* Holm. *Noteworthy:* led nation in total defense.

1940 (7–2) *Won:* Spring Hill 26–0, Mercer 20–0, Howard 31–0, Kentucky 25–0, Tulane 13–6, Georgia Tech 14–13, Vanderbilt 25–21. *Lost:* unbeaten Tennessee 27–12, unbeaten Mississippi St. 13–0. *Stars:* Paul Spencer (503 yds rush, 8 TDs), B Jimmy Nelson, E Holt Rast, T Fred Davis.

1941 (9–2) *Won:* SW Louisiana 47–6, Howard 61–0, Tennessee 9–2, Georgia 27–14 (1st meeting since 1935), Kentucky 30–0, Tulane 19–14, Georgia Tech 20–0, Miami (Fla.) 21–7 (1st meeting). *Lost:* Mississippi St. 14–0, Vanderbilt 7–0. *Stars:* Rast (13 pass rec for 207 yds), Nelson (755 yds total off, 8 TDs), G John Wyhonic. *Noteworthy:* beat Texas A&M 29–21 in Cotton Bowl though outgained 309–75 in total yds and made only one 1st down; Tide intercepted 7 passes and recovered 5 fumbles while Nelson scored TDs on 72-yd punt return and 21-yd run, Rast returned pass int 10 yds for TD, and Russ Craft scored on short run.

1942 (8–3) *Won:* SW Louisiana 54–0, Mississippi St. 21–6, Pensacola Naval Air Station 27–0, Tennessee 8–0, Kentucky 14–0, South Carolina 29–0, Vanderbilt 27–7. *Lost:* national cochamp Georgia 21–10, Georgia Tech 7–0, Georgia Navy Pre-Flight 35–19. *Stars:* Craft (7 TDs), Sam Sharp (13 pass rec for 240 yds), C Joe Domnanovich, T Don Whitmire. *Noteworthy:* beat Boston College 37–21 in Orange Bowl after dropping behind 14–0 in 1st quarter; Bobby Tom Jenkins scored 2 TDs (one on 40-yd run), and Johnny August passed for 1 TD and ran for another.

1944 (5–2–2) *Won:* Howard 63–7, Millsaps 55–0, Kentucky 41–0, Mississippi 34–6 (1st meeting since 1933), Mississippi St. 19–0. *Lost:* Georgia 14–7. *Tied:* LSU 27–27 (1st meeting since 1930), unbeaten Tennessee 0–0. *Stars:* frosh TB Harry Gilmer (768 yds total off, 5 TDs), frosh FB Lowell Tew (6 TDs). *Noteworthy:* Returned to competition after 1-year W.W. II layoff. Lost to Duke 29–26 in Sugar Bowl; FB Norwood Hodges scored 2 TDs, Gilmer passed for one, and frosh QB Hugh Morrow scored on 75-yd pass int return.

1945 (10–0) *Won:* Keesler Army Air Force 21–0, LSU 26–7, South Carolina 55–0, Tennessee 25–7,

Georgia 28–14, Kentucky 60–19, Vanderbilt 71–0, Pensacola Naval Air Station 55–6, Mississippi St. 55–13. *Stars:* Gilmer (905 yds and 13 TDs pass, 552 yds and 9 TDs rush, 1,457 yds total off), Tew (715 yds rush), frosh E Rebel Steiner (18 pass rec for 315 yds), soph FB Fred Grant (11 TDs), C Vaughn Mancha, T Tom Whitley. *Noteworthy:* Led nation in total defense and rush defense and won 4th SEC title in 1st unbeaten season since 1937. Beat USC 34–14 in Rose Bowl (Trojans' 1st loss in 10 bowl games); Gilmer ran for 116 yds and a TD and passed for another, QB Hal Self scored 2 TDs, and Tew and Hodges each scored once.
1947 (8–3) *Won:* Mississippi Southern 34–7 (1st meeting), Duquesne 26–0, Tennessee 10–0, Georgia 17–7, Kentucky 13–0, Georgia Tech 14–7 (1st meeting since 1942), LSU 41–12, Miami (Fla.) 21–6. *Lost:* Tulane 21–20, Vanderbilt 14–7 in consecutive early games. *Stars:* Gilmer (7 TDs, 915 yds total off), Tew (571 yds rush), Steiner (23 pass rec for 295 yds), C John Wozniak. *Noteworthy:* 1st year under "Red" Drew. Lost to Texas 27–7 (1st meeting since 1922) in Sugar Bowl, scoring on 8-yd pass from Gilmer to soph E Ed White and conversion by Morrow.
1950 (9–2) *Won:* Chattanooga 27–0 (1st meeting since 1931), Tulane 26–14, Furman 34–6, Mississippi St. 14–7, Georgia 14–7, Mississippi Southern 53–0, Georgia Tech 54–19, Florida 41–13, Auburn 34–0. *Lost:* Vanderbilt 27–22, Tennessee 14–9 in early games. *Stars:* TB Ed Salem (1,252 yds total off, 10 TDs pass), E Al Lary (35 pass rec for 756 yds and 10 TDs), soph HB Bobby Marlow (882 yds rush), G Mike Mizerany, C Pat O'Sullivan.
1952 (10–2) *Won:* Mississippi Southern 20–6, LSU 21–20, Miami (Fla.) 21–7 (1st meeting since 1947), Virginia Tech 33–0 (1st meeting since 1933), Mississippi St. 42–19, Georgia 34–19, Chattanooga 42–28, Maryland 27–7, Auburn 21–0. *Lost:* Tennessee 20–0, unbeaten Georgia Tech 7–3. *Stars:* Marlow (950 yds rush), soph HB Bobby Luna (6 TDs, 72 pts), G Jerry Watford, soph DB Cecil Ingram (nation's leader with 10 int). *Noteworthy:* Nation's most-improved team. Trounced Syracuse 61–6 in Orange Bowl as FB Tommy Lewis and Luna (7 ex pts) each scored 2 TDs, QB Clell Hobson passed for 2 TDs, Ingram scored on 80-yd punt return, and Marvin Hill scored on 60-yd pass int return.
1953 (6–3–3) *Won:* Vanderbilt 21–12 (1st over Commodores in 6 games since 1946), Tulsa 41–13,

Georgia 33–12, Chattanooga 21–14, Georgia Tech 13–6, Auburn 10–7. *Lost:* Mississippi Southern 25–19 (1st in 7-game series begun in 1947), unbeaten national cochamp Maryland 21–0. *Tied:* LSU 7–7, Tennessee 0–0, Mississippi St. 7–7. *Stars:* soph QB Bart Starr, HB Corky Tharp (607 yds rush). *Noteworthy:* Won 5th SEC title. Lost to Rice 28–6 in Cotton Bowl, scoring on short plunge by Lewis in 1st quarter.
1959 (7–2–2) *Won:* Houston 3–0, Chattanooga 13–0, Mississippi St. 10–0, Tulane 19–7, Georgia Tech 9–7, Memphis St. 14–7, Auburn 10–0 (1st over Tigers since 1953). *Lost:* Georgia 17–3 in opener. *Tied:* Vanderbilt 7–7, Tennessee 7–7. *Star:* soph QB Pat Trammell (818 yds total off). *Noteworthy:* Led nation in pass defense. Lost to Penn St. 7–0 (1st meeting) in inaugural Liberty Bowl; Nittany Lions scored on fake FG play in 2nd quarter.
1960 (8–1–2) *Won:* Georgia 21–6, Vanderbilt 21–0 (1st over Commodores since 1954), Houston 14–0, Mississippi St. 7–0, Furman 51–0, Georgia Tech 16–15, Tampa 34–6, Auburn 3–0. *Lost:* Tennessee 20–7. *Tied:* Tulane 6–6. *Stars:* Trammell, soph HB Butch Wilson (13 pass rec for 204 yds). *Noteworthy:* tied Texas 3–3 in Bluebonnet Bowl, scoring on Tommy Brooker's 30-yd FG in 3rd quarter.
1961 (11–0) *Won:* Georgia 32–6, Tulane 9–0, Vanderbilt 35–6, N.C. State 26–7, Tennessee 34–3 (1st over Vols since 1954), Houston 17–0, Mississippi St. 24–0, Richmond 66–0, Georgia Tech 10–0, Auburn 34–0. *Stars:* Trammell (1,314 yds total off, 9 TDs), FB Mike Fracchia (652 yds rush), SE Richard Williamson (11 pass rec for 206 yds), DT Billy Neighbors, C/LB Leroy Jordan. *Noteworthy:* Led nation in total defense and scoring defense (2.2-pt avg) and got shares of 6th SEC title (10th conference crown overall) and 4th national title (1st under "Bear" Bryant). Beat Arkansas 10–3 (1st meeting) in Sugar Bowl, scoring on 12-yd run by Trammell and ex pt and 32-yd FG by soph Tim Davis.
1962 (10–1) *Won:* Georgia 35–0, Tulane 44–6, Vanderbilt 17–7, Houston 14–3, Tennessee 27–7, Tulsa 35–6, Mississippi St. 20–0, Miami (Fla.) 36–3 (1st meeting since 1955), Auburn 38–0. *Lost:* Georgia Tech 7–6. *Stars:* soph QB Joe Namath (1,192 yds and 13 TDs pass, 228 yds and 4 TDs rush), Williamson (24 pass rec for 492 yds), HB Cotton Clark (15 TDs), Jordan. *Noteworthy:* beat Oklahoma 17–0 in Orange Bowl; Namath passed

25 yds to Williamson for 1st TD, Clark ran 15 yds for 2nd, and Davis kicked FG and 2 ex pts.

1963 (9–2) *Won:* Georgia 32–7, Tulane 28–0, Vanderbilt 21–6, Tennessee 35–0, Houston 21–13, Mississippi St. 20–19, Georgia Tech 27–11, Miami (Fla.) 17–12. *Lost:* Florida 10–6 (1st meeting since 1951), Auburn 10–8 (1st to Tigers since 1958). *Stars:* Namath (966 yds total off, 5 TDs rush), HB Benny Nelson (612 yds rush, 10 TDs), E Jimmy Dill (19 pass rec for 319 yds). *Noteworthy:* beat undefeated Mississippi 12–7 (1st meeting since 1944) in Sugar Bowl as Davis kicked 4 FGs (including 46 and 48 yds) and Tide recovered 6 fumbles and intercepted 3 passes.

1964 (10–1) *Won:* Georgia 31–3, Tulane 36–6, Vanderbilt 24–0, N.C. State 21–0, Tennessee 19–8, Florida 17–14, Mississippi St. 23–6, LSU 17–9 (1st meeting since 1958), Georgia Tech 24–7, Auburn 21–14. *Stars:* Namath (890 yds total off, 6 TDs rush), HB David Ray (19 pass rec for 271 yds, 12 FGs, 71 pts), FB Steve Bowman (536 yds rush), OG Wayne Freeman, DT Dan Kearley. *Noteworthy:* Won 7th SEC title and got share of 5th national crown. Lost to Texas 21–17 in Cotton Bowl; gimpy-legged Namath passed for 255 yds and 2 TDs (to soph Wayne Trimble and soph E Ray Perkins) and Ray kicked 26-yd FG and 2 ex pts.

1965 (9–1–1) *Won:* Tulane 27–0, Mississippi 17–16, Vanderbilt 22–7, Florida St. 21–0, Mississippi St. 10–7, LSU 31–7, South Carolina 35–14, Auburn 30–3. *Lost:* Georgia 18–17 (1st to Bulldogs since 1959) in opener. *Tied:* Tennessee 7–7. *Stars:* QB Steve Sloan (nation's passing efficiency leader with 1,453 yds and 10 TDs), SE Tommy Tolleson (32 pass rec for 374 yds), Bowman (770 yds rush), Ray (48 pts), C Paul Crane, DE Creed Gilmer, soph DB Bobby Johns. *Noteworthy:* Again won SEC title and got share of national crown. Beat undefeated Nebraska 39–28 in Orange Bowl; Sloan passed for 2 TDs and 2-pt conversion (all to Perkins), Bowman scored 2 TDs on short runs, and Ray kicked FG and 4 ex pts.

1966 (11–0) *Won:* Louisiana Tech 34–0, Mississippi 17–7, Clemson 26–0 (1st meeting since 1936), Tennessee 11–10, Vanderbilt 42–6, Mississippi St. 27–14, LSU 21–0, South Carolina 24–0, Southern Mississippi 34–0 (1st meeting since 1957), Auburn 31–0. *Stars:* Perkins (33 pass rec for 490 yds and 7 TDs), QB Kenny Stabler (1,353 yds total off), OT Cecil Dowdy, OG John Calvert, K Steve Davis (10

FGs, 55 pts), DT Richard Cole, DB Dickey Thompson, Johns. *Noteworthy:* Got share of 3rd straight SEC title (9th overall) and led nation in scoring defense (3.7-pt avg). Beat Nebraska 34–7 in Sugar Bowl; Stabler passed for 218 yds and a TD (45 yards to Perkins) and scored on 14-yd run, Les Kelley and Trimble scored on short runs, and Davis kicked 2 FGs and 4 ex pts.

1967 (8–2–1) *Won:* Southern Mississippi 25–3, Mississippi 21–7, Vanderbilt 35–21, Clemson 13–10, Mississippi St. 13–0 (10th straight over Bulldogs), LSU 7–6, South Carolina 17–0, Auburn 7–3. *Lost:* Tennessee 24–13 (1st to Vols since 1960). *Tied:* Florida St. 37–37. *Stars:* Stabler (1,214 yds pass), SE Dennis Homan (54 pass rec for 820 yds and 9 TDs), OG Bruce Stephens, DE Mike Ford, LB Mike Hall, Johns. *Noteworthy:* lost to Texas A&M 20–16 in cold, drizzly Cotton Bowl, giving up ball 5 times on turnovers; Stabler scored both TDs on short runs and Davis had 36-yd FG.

1968 (8–3) *Won:* Virginia Tech 14–7 (1st meeting since 1952), Southern Mississippi 17–14, Vanderbilt 31–7, Clemson 21–14, Mississippi St. 20–13, LSU 16–7, Miami (Fla.) 14–6, Auburn 24–16. *Lost:* Mississippi 10–8 (1st to Rebels in 19 games since 1910), Tennessee 10–9. *Stars:* soph QB Scott Hunter (1,471 yds and 10 TDs pass), soph SE George Ranager (31 pass rec for 499 yds), OG Alvin Samples, MG Sam Gellerstedt, Ford, Hall. *Noteworthy:* lost to Missouri 35–10 in Gator Bowl after trailing only 14–7 entering final quarter; scored on 38-yd pass int return by Donnie Sutton and 28-yd FG by Mike Dean.

1971 (11–1) *Won:* USC 17–10, Southern Mississippi 42–6, Florida 38–0, Mississippi 40–6, Vanderbilt 42–0, Tennessee 32–15 (1st over Vols since 1966), Houston 34–20, Mississippi St. 41–10, LSU 14–7, Miami (Fla.) 31–3, Auburn 31–7. *Stars:* HB Johnny Musso (1,088 yds and 16 TDs rush, 100 pts), SE David Bailey (21 pass rec for 286 yds and 5 TDs), OG John Hannah, C Jimmy Grammer, OT Jim Krapf, DE Robin Parkhouse, LB Tom Surlas, DB Steve Higginbotham. *Noteworthy:* Won 10th SEC title in 1st unbeaten season since 1966. Lost to unbeaten national champ Nebraska 38–6 in Orange Bowl; scored in 3rd quarter on short run by QB Terry Davis.

1972 (10–2) *Won:* Duke 35–12, Kentucky 35–0 (1st meeting since 1947), Vanderbilt 48–21, Georgia 25–7 (1st meeting since 1965), Florida 24–7, Tennessee 17–10, Southern Mississippi 48–11, Mississippi St. 58–14 (15th straight over Bulldogs), LSU 35–21, Virginia Tech 52–13. *Lost:* Auburn 17–16 in finale. *Stars:* Hannah, C Krapf, OT Buddy Brown, Terry Davis, FB Steve Bisceglia (603 yds rush), SE Wayne Wheeler (30 pass rec for 573 yds and 5 TDs), DE John Mitchell, LB Chuck Strickland, DB Bobby McKinney, P Greg Gantt. *Noteworthy:* Repeated as SEC champ (15th conference title overall). Lost to Texas 17–13 in Cotton Bowl, scoring on 31-yd run by HB Wilbur Jackson and FGs of 50 and 30 yds by Bill Davis.

1973 (11–1) *Won:* California 66–0, Kentucky 28–14, Vanderbilt 44–0, Georgia 28–14, Florida 35–14, Tennessee 42–21, Virginia Tech 77–6, Mississippi St. 35–0, Miami (Fla.) 43–13, LSU 21–7, Auburn 35–0. *Stars:* QB Gary Rutledge (1,150 yds total off), Wheeler (19 pass rec for 530 yds), Jackson (752 yds rush), Bill Davis (75 pts), Brown, OT Steve Sprayberry, DT Mike Raines, soph LB Woody Lowe, DBs David McMakin and Mike Washington, Gantt. *Noteworthy:* Won 3rd straight SEC title and got share of 7th national crown. Lost to unbeaten national cochamp Notre Dame 24–23 in Sugar Bowl; scored on 6-yd run by HB Randy Billingsley, 5-yd run by Jackson, 25-yd pass from soph HB Mike Stock to soph QB Richard Todd, and 2 ex pts and 39-yd FG by Davis.

1974 (11–1) *Won:* Maryland 21–16, Southern Mississippi 52–0, Vanderbilt 23–10, Mississippi 35–21, Florida St. 8–7, Tennessee 28–6, Texas Christian (TCU) 41–3, Mississippi St. 35–0, LSU 30–0, Miami (Fla.) 28–7, Auburn 17–13. *Stars:* Todd, soph FB Calvin Culliver (708 yds rush, 8 TDs), HB Willie Shelby, frosh SE Ozzie Newsome (20 pass rec for 374 yds), C Sylvester Croom, OG John Rogers, DE Leroy Cook, Lowe, Washington, DB Ricky Davis. *Noteworthy:* Won 4th straight SEC title. Lost to Notre Dame 13–11 in Orange Bowl after dropping behind 13–0; scored on 48-yd pass from Todd to soph SE Russ Schamun, 2-pt conversion pass from Todd to TE George Pugh, and 21-yd FG by Danny Ridgeway.

1975 (11–1) *Won:* Clemson 56–0 (1st meeting since 1969), Vanderbilt 40–7, Mississippi 32–6, Washington 52–0, Tennessee 30–7, TCU 45–0, Mississippi St. 21–10, LSU 23–10, Southern Mississippi 27–6, Auburn 28–0. *Lost:* Missouri 20–7 in opener. *Stars:* Todd (1,090 yds total off, 9 TDs), Newsome (21 pass rec for 363 yds and 5 TDs), soph

FB Johnny Davis (820 yds rush), OG David Gerasimchuk, Cook, DT Bob Baumhower, Lowe, LB Conley Duncan, DBs Tyrone King, Alan Pizzitola and Wayne Rhodes. *Noteworthy:* Won 5th straight SEC title (14th overall) and led nation in scoring defense (6-pt avg). Beat Penn St. 13–6 (1st meeting since 1959 Liberty Bowl) in Sugar Bowl (ending 8-game winless bowl string); Todd passed for 205 yds, Stock scored on 11-yd run, and Ridgeway kicked 2 FGs.

1976 (9–3) *Won:* Southern Methodist (SMU) 56–3, Vanderbilt 42–14, Southern Mississippi 24–8 (10th straight over Eagles), Tennessee 20–13, Louisville 24–3, Mississippi St. 34–17, LSU 28–17, Auburn 38–7. *Lost:* Mississippi 10–7, Georgia 21–0, Notre Dame 21–18. *Stars:* soph QB Jeff Rutledge (1,018 yds total off), Newsome (25 pass rec for 529 yds and 6 TDs), Davis (668 yds rush), Gerasimchuk, DT Charley Hannah, Baumhower. *Noteworthy:* beat UCLA 36–6 in Liberty Bowl on TDs by soph LB Barry Krauss (44-yd pass int return), Davis, soph HB Tony Nathan (pass from QB Jack O'Rear), and FB Rick Watson, and 3 FGs by Bucky Berrey.

1977 (11–1) *Won:* Mississippi 34–13, Vanderbilt 24–12, Georgia 18–10, USC 21–20, Tennessee 24–10, Louisville 55–6, Mississippi St. 37–7 (20th straight over Bulldogs), LSU 24–3, Miami (Fla.) 36–0, Auburn 48–21. *Lost:* Nebraska 31–24. *Stars:* Rutledge (1,207 yds pass, 1,518 yds total off), Newsome (36 pass rec for 804 yds), Davis (931 yds rush), Nathan (15 TDs), soph OT Jim Bunch, soph C Dwight Stephenson, DB Mike Kramer. *Noteworthy:* Won 15th SEC title. Beat Ohio St. 35–6 in Sugar Bowl; Rutledge passed for 109 yds, 2 TDs, and 2-pt conversion (to Nathan, who ran for 1 TD), and Davis ran for 95 yds and 2 TDs.

1978 (11–1) *Won:* Nebraska 20–3, Missouri 38–20, Vanderbilt 51–28, Washington 20–17, Florida 23–12, Tennessee 30–17, Virginia Tech 35–0, Mississippi St. 35–14, LSU 31–10, Auburn 34–16. *Lost:* national cochamp USC 24–14. *Stars:* Rutledge (1,078 yds and 13 TDs pass), SE Keith Pugh (20 pass rec for 446 yds), Nathan (770 yds rush), Stephenson, Bunch, OT Mike Brock, DEs Wayne Hamilton and soph E.J. Junior, DT Marty Lyons, Krauss, DB Murray Legg. *Noteworthy:* Won 16th SEC title (20th conference crown). Upset unbeaten Penn St. 14–7 in Sugar Bowl to earn share of 8th national title; scored on 30-yd pass from Rutledge to SE Bruce Bolton with 8 seconds left in 1st half and 8-yd run by soph RB Major Ogilvie in 3rd period, then made goal-line stand in 4th quarter to preserve win.

1979 (12–0)   *Won:* Georgia Tech 30–6 (1st meeting since 1964), Baylor 45–0, Vanderbilt 66–3 (10th straight over Commodores), Wichita St. 38–0, Florida 40–0, Tennessee 27–17, Virginia Tech 31–7, Mississippi St. 24–7, LSU 3–0, Miami (Fla.) 30–0 (10th straight over Hurricanes), Auburn 25–18. *Stars:* Bunch, Stephenson, Brock, Pugh (25 pass rec for 433 yds), QB Steadman Shealy (1,508 yds total off), Ogilvie, K Alan McElroy (15 FGs, 77 pts), Junior, DTs Byron Braggs and David Hannah, soph LB Thomas Boyd, DBs Don McNeal and soph Jim Bob Harris. *Noteworthy:* Bryant's 7th unbeaten team led nation in scoring defense (5.3-pt avg) and won 3rd straight SEC title. Beat Arkansas 24–9 in Cotton Bowl to earn 9th national championship; Ogilvie scored 2 TDs, FB Steve Whitman scored one, and McElroy kicked FG and 3 ex pts.

1980 (10–2)   *Won:* Georgia Tech 26–3, Mississippi 59–35, Vanderbilt 41–0, Kentucky 45–0 (1st meeting since 1973, 10th straight over Wildcats), Rutgers 17–13, Tennessee 27–0 (10th straight over Vols), Southern Mississippi 42–7, LSU 28–7 (10th straight over Tigers), Auburn 34–18. *Lost:* Mississippi St. 6–3 (1st to Bulldogs since 1957), Notre Dame 7–0. *Stars:* Junior, Boyd, Braggs, Harris, soph DB Tommy Wilcox, RB Billy Jackson (606 yds and 5 TDs rush), Ogilvie (8 TDs rush), soph K Peter Kim (12 FGs, 71 pts). *Noteworthy:* beat Baylor 30–2 in Cotton Bowl on TDs by Ogilvie, QB Donald Jacobs, and RB Mark Nix, and 3 FGs by Kim.

1981 (9–2–1)   *Won:* LSU 24–7, Kentucky 19–10, Vanderbilt 28–7, Mississippi 38–7, Tennessee 38–19, Rutgers 31–7, Mississippi St. 13–10, Penn St. 31–16, Auburn 28–17. *Lost:* Georgia Tech 24–21 (1st to Yellow Jackets in 5 games since 1962). *Tied:* Southern Mississippi 13–13. *Stars:* Boyd, Wilcox, Harris, NG Warren Lyles, DE Mike Pitts, DB Jeremiah Castille, TE Bart Krout, Kim (15 FGs, 70 pts), soph SE Joey Jones (12 pass rec for 373 yds), OT Bob Cayavec. *Noteworthy:* Got share of 18th SEC title (22nd conference crown). Lost to Texas 14–12 in Cotton Bowl (breaking 6-bowl win string); scored on 6-yd pass from soph QB Walter Lewis to soph SE Jesse Bendross, FG and ex pt by Kim, and safety.

1982 (8–4)   *Won:* Georgia Tech 45–7, Mississippi 42–14, Vanderbilt 24–21, Arkansas St. 34–7, na-

tional champ Penn St. 42–21, Cincinnati 21–3, Mississippi St. 20–12. *Lost:* Tennessee 35–28 (1st to Vols since 1970), LSU 20–10 (1st to Tigers since 1970), Southern Mississippi 38–29 (1st to Eagles in 14 games since 1954), Auburn 23–22 (1st to Tigers since 1972). *Stars:* Lewis (1,515 yds pass), Jones (25 pass rec for 502 yds and 6 TDs), Bendross (499 yds pass rec), soph FBs Ricky Moore (600 yds rush) and Craig Turner (12 TDs), OT Joe Beazley, C Steve Mott, Pitts, Castille, Wilcox. *Noteworthy:* Bryant's last team. Beat Illinois 21–15 in Liberty Bowl in Bryant's last game; scored on TDs by Moore, Bendross, and Turner, and 3 ex pts by Kim.

1983 (8–4)   *Won:* Georgia Tech 20–7, Mississippi 40–0, Vanderbilt 44–24, Memphis St. 44–13, Mississippi St. 35–18, LSU 32–26, Southern Mississippi 28–16. *Lost:* Penn St. 34–28 (1st to Nittany Lions in 5 games since 1959 Liberty Bowl), Tennessee 41–34, Boston College 20–13, Auburn 23–20. *Stars:* Lewis (1,991 yds and 14 TDs pass), Jones (31 pass rec for 468 yds and 5 TDs), Moore (947 yds rush), frosh K Van Tiffin (14 FGs, 82 pts), OG Mike Adcock. *Noteworthy:* 1st year under Ray Perkins. Beat SMU 28–7 in Sun Bowl; Moore scored 2 TDs and Lewis passed for one (19 yds to Jones) and scored another.

1985 (9–2–1)   *Won:* Georgia 20–16, Texas A&M 23–10, Cincinnati 45–10, Vanderbilt 40–20, Memphis St. 28–9, Mississippi St. 44–28, Southern Mississippi 24–13, Auburn 25–23. *Lost:* unbeaten Penn St. 19–17, Tennessee 16–14 in consecutive mid-season games. *Tied:* LSU 14–14. *Stars:* QB Mike Shula (2,009 yds and 16 TDs pass), SE Albert Bell (37 pass rec for 648 yds and 8 TDs), frosh HB Gene Jelks (588 yds and 5 TDs rush), Tiffin (17 FGs, 84 pts), NG Curt Jarvis, DT Jon Hand, LB Cornelius Bennett, DB Freddie Robinson, frosh P Chris Mohr (45.1-yd avg). *Noteworthy:* beat USC 24–3 in Aloha Bowl on TDs by Turner, soph SE Clay Whitehurst (on 24-yd pass from Shula) and Bell (14-yd run), and 48-yd FG and 3 ex pts by Tiffin.

1986 (10–3)   *Won:* Ohio St. 16–10, Vanderbilt 42–10, Southern Mississippi 31–17, Florida 21–7 (1st meeting since 1979), Notre Dame 28–10, Memphis St. 37–0, Tennessee 56–28, Mississippi St. 38–3, Temple 24–14. *Lost:* unbeaten national champ Penn St. 23–3, LSU 14–10, Auburn 21–17. *Stars:* Shula (1,486 yds and 13 TDs pass), Bell (26 pass rec for 315 yds), Jelks (509 yds rush), soph HB Bobby Humphrey (1,471 yds rush, 17 TDs, 104 pts),

OG Bill Condon, C Wes Neighbors, Tiffin, Jarvis, Lombardi Award–winner Bennett, Robinson. *Noteworthy:* Perkins' last team. Beat Washington 28–6 in Sun Bowl; Humphrey had 159 yds rush and 3 TDs (including 64-yd run), and Shula passed for 176 yds and 2 TDs (32 yds to Richardson and 18 yds to Humphrey).

1988 (9–3) *Won:* Temple 37–0, Vanderbilt 44–10, Kentucky 31–27 (1st meeting since 1981), Tennessee 28–20, Penn St. 8–3, Mississippi St. 53–34, SW Louisiana 17–0, Texas A&M 30–10. *Lost:* Mississippi 22–12 (1st to Rebels in 6 games since 1976), LSU 19–18, Auburn 15–10. *Stars:* QB David Smith (1,592 yds pass), SE Greg Payne (33 pass rec for 442 yds), TEs Lamonde Russell (29 pass rec for 404 yds) and Howard Cross (19 pass rec for 226 yds), FL Marco Battle (28 pass rec for 367 yds), TB Murry Hill (778 yds and 5 TDs rush, 1,061 all-purpose yds), HB David Casteal (6 TDs rush), OG Larry Rose, soph K Philip Doyle (19 FGs, 91 pts), LB Derrick Thomas, DBs Kermit Kendrick (6 int), Lee Ozmint (6 int) and John Mangum (5 int), Mohr (42.6-yd punting avg). *Noteworthy:* beat Army 29–28 in John Hancock Sun Bowl; Smith passed for 412 yds and 2 TDs (to Battle and Payne), Casteal ran for a TD, and Doyle kicked 3 FGs and 2 ex pts.

1989 (10–2) *Won:* Memphis St. 35–7, Kentucky 15–3, Vanderbilt 20–14, Mississippi 62–27, SW Louisiana 24–17, Tennessee 47–30, Penn St. 17–16, Mississippi St. 23–10, LSU 32–16, Southern Mississippi 37–14. *Lost:* Auburn 30–20 in finale. *Stars:* QB Gary Hollingsworth (2,379 yds and 14 TDs pass), Russell (51 pass rec for 622 yds, 5 TDs), soph FB Kevin Turner (48 pass rec for 465 yds), TB Siran Stacy (36 pass rec for 371 yds, 1,079 yds rush, 18 TDs), Battle (33 pass rec for 388 yds), soph SE Craig Sanderson (20 pass rec for 319 yds), soph FL Prince Wimbley (19 pass rec for 253 yds), C Roger Shultz, OT Terrill Chatman, Doyle (100 pts, nation's leader with 22 FGs), LB Keith McCants, Mangum (5 int), DB Efrum Thomas (5 int). *Noteworthy:* Bill Curry's last team got share of 19th SEC title. Lost to national champ Miami (Fla.) 33–25 in Sugar Bowl (1st meeting since 1979, 1st loss to Hurricanes in 11 games since 1955; Hollingsworth threw 3 TD passes (to Battle, Russell, and Wimbley) and 2-pt conversion (to Russell), and Doyle kicked 45-yd FG.

1991 (11–1) *Won:* Temple 41–3, Georgia 10–0,

Vanderbilt 48–17, UT-Chattanooga 53–7 (1st meeting since 1959), Tulane 62–0 (1st meeting since 1965), Tennessee 24–19, Mississippi St. 13–7, LSU 20–17, Memphis St. 10–7, Auburn 13–6. *Lost:* Florida 35–0 in 2nd game. *Stars:* Stacy (967 yds and 10 TDs rush, 1,144 all-purpose yds), QB Danny Woodson (982 yds total off), frosh FL David Palmer (17 pass rec for 314 yds, 1,113 all-purpose yds, 7 TDs including 3 on punt returns), soph SE Kevin Lee (11 pass rec for 276 yds), DL Robert Stewart, DE John Copeland, LB John Sullins, DBs George Teague (6 int) and soph Antonio Langham (5 int), P Tank Williamson (40.1-yd avg). *Noteworthy:* beat Colorado 30–25 in Blockbuster Bowl; frosh QB Jay Barker passed for 154 yds and 3 TDs (to Stacy, Lee, and Palmer, who also scored on 52-yd punt return), and Stacy ran for 111 yds.

1992 (13–0) *Won:* Vanderbilt 25–8, Southern Mississippi 17–10, Arkansas 38–11 (1st meeting since 1980 Sugar Bowl), Louisiana Tech 13–0, South Carolina 48–7 (1st meeting since 1967), Tulane 37–0, Tennessee 17–10, Mississippi 31–10, LSU 31–11, Mississippi St. 30–21, Auburn 17–0. *Stars:* Barker (1,614 yds pass), Palmer (24 pass rec for 297 yds), Lee (21 pass rec for 286 yds), soph SE Curtis Brown (20 pass rec for 327 yds), Wimbley (21 pass rec for 248 yds), RBs Derrick Lassic (11 TDs, 905 yds and 10 TDs rush), Chris Anderson (8 TDs, 573 yds rush) and soph Sherman Williams (8 TDs rush), C Tobie Sheils, frosh K Michael Proctor (19 FGs, 94 pts), Copeland, DE Eric Curry, LBs Antonio London, Lemanski Hall, Derrick Oden and soph Michael Rogers, Langham (6 int), Teague (6 int), DB Chris Donnelly. *Noteworthy:* Won West Division of SEC in 1st undefeated season since 1979, then beat Florida 28–21 in 1st SEC playoff game to take 20th SEC title; led nation in rush defense and total defense. Beat undefeated Miami (Fla.) 34–13 in Sugar Bowl to earn 10th national title as Lassic ran for 135 yds and 2 TDs, Teague scored on 31-yd pass int return, Williams scored on 2-yd run, and Proctor had 2 FGs and 4 ex pts.

BOWL SUMMARY

Aloha 1–0; Blockbuster 1–0; Bluebonnet 0–0–2; Cotton 2–4; Fiesta 0–1; Gator 0–1; Hall of Fame 0–1; John Hancock Sun 1–0; Liberty 2–2; Orange 4–3; Rose 4–1–1; Sugar 8–4; Sun 2–0.

BOWL RECORD (25–17–3)

Regular Season	Bowl	Score	Opponent	Record
1925 (9–0)	Rose	20–19	Washington	(10–0–1)
1926 (9–0)	Rose	7–7	Stanford	(10–0)
1930 (9–0)	Rose	24–0	Washington St.	(9–0)
1934 (9–0)	Rose	29–13	Stanford	(9–0–1)
1937 (9–0)	Rose	0–13	California	(9–0–1)
1941 (8–2)	Cotton	29–21	Texas A&M	(9–2)
1942 (7–3)	Orange	37–21	Boston College	(8–1)
1944 (5–1–2)	Sugar	26–29	Duke	(5–4)
1945 (9–0)	Rose	34–14	USC	(7–3)
1947 (8–2)	Sugar	7–27	Texas	(9–1)
1952 (9–2)	Orange	61–6	Syracuse	(7–2)
1953 (6–2–3)	Cotton	6–28	Rice	(8–2)
1959 (7–1–2)	Liberty	0–7	Penn State	(8–2)
1960 (8–1–1)	Bluebonnet	3–3	Texas	(7–3)
1961 (10–0)	Sugar	10–3	Arkansas	(8–2)
1962 (9–1)	Orange	17–0	Oklahoma	(8–2)
1963 (8–2)	Sugar	12–7	Mississippi	(7–0–2)
1964 (10–0)	Orange	17–21	Texas	(9–1)
1965 (8–1–1)	Orange	39–28	Nebraska	(10–0)
1966 (10–0)	Sugar	34–7	Nebraska	(9–1)
1967 (8–1–1)	Cotton	16–20	Texas A&M	(6–4)
1968 (8–2)	Gator	10–35	Missouri	(7–3)
1969 (6–4)	Liberty	33–47	Colorado	(7–3)
1970 (6–5)	Bluebonnet	24–24	Oklahoma	(7–4)
1971 (11–0)	Orange	6–38	Nebraska	(12–0)
1972 (10–1)	Cotton	13–17	Texas	(9–1)
1973 (11–0)	Sugar	23–24	Notre Dame	(10–0)
1974 (11–0)	Orange	11–13	Notre Dame	(9–2)
1975 (10–1)	Sugar	13–6	Penn State	(9–2)
1976 (8–3)	Liberty	36–6	UCLA	(9–1–1)
1977 (10–1)	Sugar	35–6	Ohio State	(9–2)
1978 (10–1)	Sugar	14–7	Penn State	(11–0)
1979 (11–0)	Sugar	24–9	Arkansas	(10–1)
1980 (9–2)	Cotton	30–2	Baylor	(10–1)
1981 (9–1–1)	Cotton	12–14	Texas	(9–1–1)
1982 (7–4)	Liberty	21–15	Illinois	(7–4)
1983 (7–4)	Sun	28–7	SMU	(10–1)
1985 (8–2–1)	Aloha	24–3	USC	(6–5)
1986 (8–2–1)	Sun	28–6	Washington	(8–2–1)
1987 (7–4)	Hall of Fame	24–28	Michigan	(7–4)
1988 (8–3)	John Hancock Sun	29–28	Army	(9–2)
1989 (10–1)	Sugar	25–33	Miami (Fla.)	(10–1)
1990 (7–4)	Fiesta	7–34	Louisville	(9–1–1)
1991 (10–1)	Blockbuster	30–25	Colorado	(8–2–1)
1992 (12–0)	Sugar	34–13	Miami (Fla.)	(11–0)

CONFERENCE TITLES

Southern—1924, 1925, 1926, 1930*. **Southeastern**—1933, 1934*, 1937, 1945, 1953, 1961*, 1964, 1965, 1966*, 1971, 1972, 1973, 1974, 1975, 1977, 1978, 1979, 1981*, 1989*, 1992.

TOP 20 AP AND UPI
(USA TODAY/CNN SINCE 1991) RANKING

1936	4	1959	10–13	1971	4–2	1981	7–6
1937	4	1960	9–10	1972	7–4	1982	U–17
1938	13	1961	1–1	1973	4–1	1983	15–12
1941	20	1962	5–5	1974	5–2	1985	13–14
1942	10	1963	8–9	1975	3–3	1986	9–9
1945	2	1964	1–1	1976	11–9	1988	17–17
1947	6	1965	1–4	1977	2–2	1989	9–7
1950	16–17	1966	3–3	1978	1–2	1991	5–5
1952	9–9	1967	8–7	1979	1–1	1992	1–1
1953	13–11	1968	17–12	1980	6–6		

MAJOR RIVALS

Alabama has played at least 10 games with Auburn 33–23–1, Birmingham Southern 11–0, Clemson 11–3, Florida 17–8, Georgia 33–22–4, Georgia Tech 28–21–3, Howard 20–0–1, Kentucky 30–1–1, Louisiana St. 37–14–5, Miami (Fla.) 14–3, Mississippi 32–6–2, Mississippi St. 63–11–3, Penn St. 8–5, Sewanee 17–10–3, Southern Mississippi 23–4–2, Tennessee 41–27–7, Tulane 25–10–3, Vanderbilt 48–18–4, Virginia Tech 10–0. Record against SEC members played fewer than 10 times is: Arkansas 3–0, South Carolina 8–0.

COACHES

Dean of Alabama coaches is Paul "Bear" Bryant (1961, 1971, 1973 national Coach of Year) with record of 232–46–9 in 1958–82, including 13 SEC titles, 24 bowl teams, 7 teams unbeaten in regular season, and 6 national titles. Other top records for at least 3 years were by J.W.H. Pollard, 20–4–5 for 1906–09; D.V. Graves, 21–12–3 for 1911–14; Thomas Kelly, 17–7–1 for 1915–17; Xen C. Scott, 29–9–3 for 1919–22; Wallace Wade, 61–13–3 for 1923–30 with 4 SC titles, 3 unbeaten Rose Bowl teams, and 2 national champions; Frank Thomas, 115–24–7 for 1931–46 with 4 SEC titles, 6 bowl teams, 4 teams unbeaten in regular season, and 1 national champion; Harold D. "Red" Drew, 55–29–7 for 1947–54 with 1 SEC title and 3 bowl teams; Ray Perkins, 32–15–1 for 1983–86 with 3 bowl champions; Bill Curry, 26–10 for 1987–89 with 1 SEC title and 3 bowl teams; and Gene Stallings (1992 national Coach of Year), 31–6 for 1990–92

with 1 SEC title, 3 bowl teams, and 1 unbeaten national champion.

MISCELLANEA

First game was win over Birmingham H.S. 56–0 in 1892 . . . 1st win over college foe was over Tulane 18–6 in 1894 . . . highest score was over Marion Institute 110–0 in 1922 . . . highest since W.W. II was over Delta St. 89–0 in 1951 . . . worst defeat was by Vanderbilt 78–0 in 1906 . . . worst since W.W. II was by Auburn 40–0 in 1957 . . . highest against since W.W. II was by Auburn 49–26 in 1969 . . . longest win streak of 28 in 1978–80 ended by Mississippi St. 6–3 . . . 26-game unbeaten string in 1960–62 ended by Georgia Tech 7–6 . . . 24-game unbeaten string in 1924–27 ended by Georgia Tech 13–0 . . . 23-game win streak in 1991–92 current entering 1993 season . . . longest winless string of 20 in 1954–56 broken with win over Mississippi St. 13–12 . . . consensus All-Americans were Fred Sington, T, 1930; Don Hutson, E, Bill Lee, T, and Dixie Howell, B, 1934; Riley Smith, B, 1935; Leroy Monsky, G, 1937; Holt Rast, E, 1941; Joe Domnanovich, C, 1942; Vaughn Mancha, C, 1945; Billy Neighbors, T, 1961; Lee Roy Jordan, C, 1962; Paul Crane, C, 1965; Ray Perkins, E, and Cecil Dowdy, T, 1966; Dennis Homan, E, and Bobby Johns, DB, 1967; Johnny Musso, B, 1971; John Hannah, G, 1972; Buddy Brown, G, 1973; Woodrow Lowe, LB, 1974; Leroy Cook, DL, 1974–75; Ozzie Newsome, WR, 1977; Marty Lyons, DL, 1978; Jim Bunch, T, 1979; E.J. Junior, DL, 1980; Tommy Wilcox, DB, 1981; Mike Pitts, DL, 1982; Cornelius Bennett, LB, 1986; Derrick Thomas, LB, 1988; Keith McCants,

LB, 1989; Philip Doyle, K, 1990; and John Copeland, DL, and Eric Curry, DL, 1992 . . . Academic All-Americans were Tommy Brooker, E, and Pat Trammell, B, 1961; Gaylon McCollough, C, 1964; Steve Sloan, QB, and Dennis Homan, HB, 1965; Steve Davis, K, and Bob Childs, LB, 1967; Johnny Musso, RB, 1970–71; Randy Hall, DT, 1973–74; Danny Ridgeway, K, 1975; Major Ogilvie, RB, 1979; and Mike Pitts, DL, 1982 . . . Lombardi Award winner was Cornelius Bennett, LB, 1986.

ARKANSAS *(Razorbacks; Cardinal and White)*

NOTABLE TEAMS

1899 (3–1–1) *Won:* Drury 10–0, Tulsa 11–0 (1st meeting), Joplin H.S. 11–10. *Lost:* Oklahoma 11–5 (1st meeting). *Tied:* Tulsa 0–0. *Noteworthy:* 1st year under Colbert Searles.

1909 (7–0) *Won:* Henderson St. 24–0, Drury 12–6, Fairmount College 23–6, Oklahoma 21–6, Louisiana St. (LSU) 16–0 (1st in 5-game series dating to 1901), Ouachita 56–0, Washington (Mo.) 34–0. *Star:* FB Clinton Milford. *Noteworthy:* 1st unbeaten season since 3-game schedule of 1897.

1910 (7–1) *Won:* Drury 33–0, Henderson St. 63–0, Southwestern (Texas) 13–12, Texas A&M 5–0 (1st meeting since 1903), Washington (Mo.) 50–0, Missouri-Rolla 6–2, LSU 51–0. *Lost:* Kansas St. 5–0.

1911 (6–2–1) *Won:* SW Missouri St. 100–0, Drury 65–5, Hendrix 45–0 (1st meeting), Missouri-Rolla 44–3, Washington (Mo.) 3–0, LSU 11–0. *Lost:* Texas 12–0, Kansas St. 3–0. *Tied:* Southwestern (Texas) 0–0.

1913 (7–2) *Won:* Henderson St. 3–0, Hendrix 26–0, Oklahoma St. 3–0, Baylor 34–0, Austin College 26–7, Ouachita 14–3, Tulane 14–0. *Lost:* LSU 12–7, Mississippi 21–10 (1st meeting since 1908) in successive late games. *Noteworthy:* 1st year under E.T. Pickering.

1917 (5–1–1) *Won:* Central Missouri St. 34–0, Hendrix 19–0, Missouri-Rolla 32–0, Tulsa 19–7 (1st meeting since 1902), LSU 14–0 in 1st 5 games. *Lost:* Texas 20–0 (10th straight to Longhorns). *Tied:* Oklahoma 0–0. *Star:* B Gene Davidson.

1923 (6–2–1) *Won:* Arkansas St. Teachers 32–0, Drury 26–0, Rice 23–0, LSU 26–13, Phillips 32–0, Oklahoma St. 13–0. *Lost:* Baylor 14–0, unbeaten

Southern Methodist (SMU) 13–6. *Tied:* Ouachita 0–0. *Star:* E Charles Corgan.

1924 (7–2–1) *Won:* NE Oklahoma 54–6, SW Missouri St. 47–0, Hendrix 34–3, Mississippi 20–0, LSU 10–7, Phillips 28–6, Texas Christian (TCU) 20–0. *Lost:* Baylor 13–0, Oklahoma St. 20–0. *Tied:* unbeaten SMU 14–14. *Star:* HB Herman Bagby.

1927 (8–1) *Won:* College of Ozarks 32–0, Baylor 13–6, Missouri-Rolla 34–0 (1st meeting since 1920), LSU 28–0, TCU 10–3, Oklahoma St. 33–20, Austin College 42–0, Hendrix 20–7. *Lost:* unbeaten Texas A&M 40–6 (1st meeting since 1912). *Stars:* B George Cole (11 TDs, 85 pts), E Glen Rose.

1928 (7–2) *Won:* College of Ozarks 21–0, Baylor 14–0, Texas A&M 27–12, LSU 7–0, Missouri-Rolla 45–6, Oklahoma Baptist 57–0, Southwestern (Texas) 73–0. *Lost:* Mississippi 25–0, Texas 20–7 (1st meeting since 1919). *Stars:* B Bevo Beavers (14 TDs), G Clyde Van Sickle. *Noteworthy:* last year under Francis Schmidt.

1929 (7–2) *Won:* College of Ozarks 37–0, Henderson St. 30–7, Texas A&M 14–13, LSU 32–0, East Central Oklahoma 52–7, Centenary 13–2, Oklahoma St. 32–6. *Lost:* Texas 27–0, Baylor 31–20 in successive early games. *Star:* E Wear Schoonover (33 pass rec for 342 yds and 7 TDs). *Noteworthy:* 1st year under Fred Thomsen.

1933 (7–3–1) *Won:* College of Ozarks 40–0, Oklahoma Baptist 42–7, TCU 13–0, Baylor 19–7, SMU 3–0, Hendrix 63–0, Texas 20–6 (1st in 15-game series dating to 1894). *Lost:* unbeaten LSU 20–0, Rice 7–6, Tulsa 7–0. *Stars:* B Tom Murphy, E Paul Rucker, T John Measel. *Noteworthy:* Won 1st SWC title but later forfeited for using ineligible player. Made 1st postseason appearance, tying unbeaten Centenary 7–7 in Dixie Classic at Dallas; scored on 24-yd pass from Murphy to Elvin Geiser and Geiser's ex pt.

1936 (7–3) *Won:* Pittsburg St. 53–0, Baylor 14–10, Texas A&M 18–0, Rice 20–14 (1st over Owls since 1930), SMU 17–0, Tulsa 23–13, Texas 6–0. *Lost:* TCU 18–14, George Washington 13–6, unbeaten LSU 19–7. *Stars:* B Jack Robbins, E James Benton (35 pass rec for 489 yds and 6 TDs). *Noteworthy:* won 1st official SWC title.

1937 (6–2–2) *Won:* Central St. (Okla.) 25–0, Texas 21–10, SMU 13–0, Texas A&M 26–13, Mississippi 32–6 (1st meeting since 1924), Tulsa 28–7. *Lost:* Baylor 20–14, Rice 26–20. *Tied:* TCU 7–7, George Washington 0–0. *Stars:* Robbins (975 yds and 12

TDs total off), Benton (nation's leader with 48 pass rec for 814 yds and 7 TDs), Dwight Sloan (1,074 yds pass), soph Kay Eakin (40-yd punting avg). *Noteworthy:* led nation in pass.

1946 (6–3–2) *Won:* NW Louisiana 21–14, TCU 34–14, Baylor 13–0, Texas A&M 7–0, Rice 7–0, SMU 13–0. *Lost:* Texas 20–0, Mississippi 9–7, Tulsa 14–13. *Tied:* Oklahoma St. 21–21. *Stars:* soph B Clyde "Smackover" Scott, E Alton Baldwin. *Noteworthy:* Got share of 2nd SWC title in 1st year under John Barnhill; 1st winning season since 1937. Tied LSU 0–0 (1st meeting since 1936) in snowy, cold Cotton Bowl though outgained 271–54 in total yds and 15–1 in 1st downs; Baldwin starred on defense.

1954 (8–3) *Won:* Tulsa 41–0, TCU 20–13, Baylor 21–20, Texas 20–7, Mississippi 6–0, Texas A&M 14–7, Rice 28–15 (1st over Owls since 1946), Houston 19–0. *Lost:* SMU 21–14, LSU 7–6 in consecutive late games. *Stars:* QB/S/P George Walker (6 int, 40.8-yd punting avg), B Henry Moore, G Bud Brooks (Outland Trophy winner). *Noteworthy:* Bowden Wyatt's last team won 3rd SWC title. Lost to Georgia Tech 14–6 in Cotton Bowl after taking 6–0 1st half lead on 1-yd run by Walker.

1959 (9–2) *Won:* Tulsa 28–0, Oklahoma St. 13–7, TCU 3–0, Baylor 23–7, Texas A&M 12–7, Rice 14–10, SMU 17–14, Texas Tech 27–8. *Lost:* Texas 13–12, Mississippi 28–0 in successive mid-season games. *Stars:* B Jim Mooty, C/LB Wayne Harris. *Noteworthy:* Got share of 4th SWC title. Beat Georgia Tech 14–7 in Gator Bowl; Mooty ran for 99 yds (including 19-yd run for winning TD) and Joe Paul Alberty scored on 1-yd run.

1960 (8–3) *Won:* Oklahoma St. 9–0, Tulsa 48–7, TCU 7–0, Texas 24–23, Texas A&M 7–3, Rice 3–0, SMU 26–3, Texas Tech 34–6. *Lost:* Baylor 28–14, unbeaten national cochamp Mississippi 10–7. *Stars:* Harris, HB Lance Alworth (13 pass rec for 264 yds, nation's punt return leader with 17.1-yd avg). *Noteworthy:* Again won SWC title. Lost to Duke 7–6 in Cotton Bowl, scoring on 49-yd punt return by Alworth.

1961 (8–3) *Won:* Tulsa 6–0, TCU 28–3, Baylor 23–13, NW Louisiana 42–7, Texas A&M 15–8, Rice 10–0, SMU 21–7, Texas Tech 28–0. *Lost:* Mississippi 16–0, Texas 33–7. *Stars:* Alworth (516 yds rush, 18 pass rec for 320 yds, 5 TDs, nation's punt return leader with 12-yd avg), T John Childress, G Dean Garrett. *Noteworthy:* Got share of 3rd

straight SWC title (6th overall). Lost to unbeaten national cochamp Alabama 10–3 (1st meeting) in Sugar Bowl; scored on 23-yd FG by Mickey Cissell in 3rd quarter.

1962 (9–2) *Won:* Oklahoma St. 34–7, Tulsa 42–14, TCU 42–14, Baylor 28–21, Hardin-Simmons 49–7, Texas A&M 17–7, Rice 28–14, SMU 9–7, Texas Tech 34–0. *Lost:* unbeaten Texas 7–3. *Stars:* Bs Billy Moore (585 yds rush, 14 TDs), Jesse Branch and Danny Brabham, T Jerry Mazzanti, G Ray Trail. *Noteworthy:* lost to unbeaten Mississippi 17–13 in Sugar Bowl; scored on 2 FGs and ex pt by soph K Tom McKnelly and 5-yd pass from Moore to Branch.

1964 (11–0) *Won:* Oklahoma St. 14–10, Tulsa 31–22, TCU 29–6, Baylor 17–6, Texas 14–13, Wichita St. 17–0, Texas A&M 17–0, Rice 21–0, SMU 44–0, Texas Tech 17–0. *Stars:* E Jerry Lamb, B Ken Hatfield (nation's punt return leader with 16.7-yd avg), QB Fred Marshall, Ts Glen Ray Hines and Jim Williams, G Jim Johnson, soph DT Loyd Phillips, C/LB Ronnie Caveness. *Noteworthy:* Won 7th SWC title and led nation in scoring defense (5.7-pt avg) in 1st unbeaten season since 1909. Beat Nebraska 10–7 in Cotton Bowl to earn share of 1st national title; Marshall passed for 131 yds, Bobby Burnett scored on 3-yd run, McKnelly kicked ex pt and 31-yd FG, and Caveness sparked defense.

1965 (10–1) *Won:* Oklahoma St. 28–14, Tulsa 20–12, TCU 28–0, Baylor 38–7, Texas 27–24, North Texas St. 55–20, Texas A&M 31–0, Rice 31–0, SMU 24–3, Texas Tech 42–24. *Stars:* Burnett (947 yds rush, 16 TDs), B Harry Jones (622 yds rush, 7 TDs), Es Bobby Crockett and Bobby Roper, Hines, Williams, K Ronny South (60 pts), Phillips, DBs Jack Brasuell and soph Tommy Trantham, P Bobby Nix (40.7-yd avg). *Noteworthy:* Led nation in scoring (32.4-pt avg) and won 2nd straight SWC title. Lost to LSU 14–7 (1st meeting since 1956) in Cotton Bowl after taking early 7–0 lead on 19-yd pass from QB Jon Brittenum to Crockett and ex pt by South.

1966 (8–2) *Won:* Oklahoma St. 14–10 (10th straight over Cowboys), Tulsa 27–8, TCU 21–0, Texas 12–7, Wichita St. 41–0, Texas A&M 34–0, Rice 32–20, SMU 22–0. *Lost:* Baylor 7–0, Texas Tech 21–16 (1st in 10-game series begun in 1957). *Stars:* Outland Trophy–winner Phillips, Brittenum (1,103 yds pass), E Hartford Hamilton, T Dick

Cunningham, C Melvin Gibbs, DBs Martine Bercher and soph Gary Adams (7 int).

1968 (10–1)   **Won:** Oklahoma St. 32–15, Tulsa 56–13, TCU 17–7 (10th straight over Horned Frogs), Baylor 35–19, North Texas St. 17–15, Texas A&M 25–22, Rice 46–21, SMU 35–29, Texas Tech 42–7. **Lost:** Texas 39–29.   **Stars:** Adams (5 int), Jerry Moore (6 int), LB Cliff Powell, soph QB Bill Montgomery (1,595 yds and 10 TDs pass, 239 yds and 4 TDs rush), soph E Chuck Dicus (38 pass rec for 589 yds and 8 TDs), Max Peacock (39 pass rec for 497 yds and 7 TDs), Bill Burnett (859 yds rush, 16 TDs), C Rodney Brand, OG Jim Barnes. **Noteworthy:** Nation's most-improved team got share of 9th SWC title. Beat undefeated Georgia 16–2 (1st meeting) in Sugar Bowl, recovering 5 fumbles and intercepting 4 passes; Dicus caught 12 passes for 169 yds and a TD (27 yds from Montgomery), and K Bob White had 3 FGs.

1969 (9–2)   **Won:** Oklahoma St. 39–0, Tulsa 55–0, TCU 24–6, Baylor 21–7, Wichita St. 52–14, Texas A&M 35–13, Rice 30–6, SMU 28–15, Texas Tech 33–0.   **Lost:** unbeaten national champ Texas 15–14 in finale.   **Stars:** Powell, Burnett (900 yds rush, 20 TDs), Montgomery (1,333 yds pass), Dicus (42 pass rec for 688 yds), B Terry Stewart, Brand, G Jerry Dossey, T Rick Kersey, soph K Bill McClard. **Noteworthy:** Led nation in scoring defense (7.6-pt avg). Lost to Mississippi 27–22 in Sugar Bowl; Montgomery passed for 338 yds and 2 TDs (including 47-yarder to Dicus), FB Bruce Maxwell ran for 103 yds and caught a TD pass, Burnett scored on 12-yd run, and McClard had 35-yd FG.

1970 (9–2)   **Won:** Oklahoma St. 23–7, Tulsa 49–7, TCU 49–14, Baylor 41–7, Wichita St. 62–0, Texas A&M 45–6, Rice 38–14, SMU 36–3, Texas Tech 24–10.   **Lost:** Stanford 34–28 in opener, unbeaten national cochamp Texas 42–7 in finale.   **Stars:** Montgomery (1,662 yds and 10 TDs pass), Dicus (38 pass rec for 577 yds), McClard (10 FGs, 80 pts), DTs Dick Bumpas and Bruce James, DB David Hogue (6 int).

1971 (8–3–1)   **Won:** California 51–20, Oklahoma St. 31–10, TCU 49–15, Baylor 35–7, Texas 31–7 (1st over Longhorns since 1966), North Texas St. 60–21, SMU 18–13, Texas Tech 15–0.   **Lost:** Tulsa 21–20, Texas A&M 17–9.   **Tied:** Rice 24–24.   **Stars:** QB Joe Ferguson (2,203 yds and 11 TDs pass), E Mike Reppond (56 pass rec for 986 yds), soph Dickey

Morton (831 yds and 5 TDs rush), T Mike Kelson, C Ron Revard, E Ronnie Jones, McClard (12 FGs, 71 pts), soph LB Danny Rhodes, Louis Campbell (7 int).   **Noteworthy:** lost to Tennessee 14–13 (1st meeting since 1907) in Liberty Bowl; Ferguson passed for 200 yds and a TD (36 yards to Jim Hodge), McClard kicked 2 FGs and ex pt, and Campbell had 3 int.

1975 (10–2)   **Won:** Air Force 35–0, Tulsa 31–15, TCU 19–8, Baylor 41–3, Utah St. 31–0, Rice 20–16, SMU 35–7, Texas Tech 31–14, Texas A&M 31–6. **Lost:** Oklahoma St. 20–13, Texas 24–18.   **Stars:** Ike Forte (983 yds and 10 TDs rush), soph K Steve Little (11 FGs), G R.C. Thielemann, C Richard LaFarque, DE Ivan Jordan, P Tommy Cheyne (43-yd avg).   **Noteworthy:** Got share of 10th SWC title. Beat Georgia 31–10 in Cotton Bowl after dropping behind 10–0; Forte ran for 119 yds and 2 TDs, Little kicked FG and 4 ex pts, and LB Hal McAfee had 12 tackles, a pass int, and 2 fumble recoveries.

1977 (11–1)   **Won:** New Mexico St. 53–10, Oklahoma St. 28–6, Tulsa 37–3, TCU 42–6, Houston 34–0, Rice 30–7, Baylor 35–9, Texas A&M 26–20, SMU 47–7, Texas Tech 17–14.   **Lost:** unbeaten Texas 13–9.   **Stars:** RB Ben Cowins (1,192 yds rush, 14 TDs), QB Ron Calcagni (1,147 yds pass, 546 yds rush), G Leotis Harris, Little (19 FGs, 94 pts, 44.3-yd punting avg), DT Jimmy Walker, LB Larry Jackson, DB Howard Sampson.   **Noteworthy:** 1st year under Lou Holtz. Beat Oklahoma 31–6 (1st meeting since 1926) in Orange Bowl; RB Roland Sales ran for 205 yds and 2 TDs, Barnabas White scored on 20-yd run, and Little kicked FG and 4 ex pts.

1978 (9–2–1)   **Won:** Vanderbilt 48–17 (1st meeting since 1950), Oklahoma St. 19–7, Tulsa 21–13, TCU 42–3 (20th straight over Horned Frogs), Rice 37–7, Baylor 27–14, Texas A&M 26–7, SMU 27–14, Texas Tech 49–7.   **Lost:** Texas 28–21, Houston 20–9 in successive mid-season games.   **Stars:** Cowins (1,006 yds and 6 TDs rush), Calcagni (807 yds pass, 448 yds rush), OT Greg Kolenda, soph K Ish Ordonez (13 FGs, 78 pts), Walker, DT Dan Hampton, DB Vaughn Lusby, soph P Bruce Lahay (40.5-yd avg).   **Noteworthy:** tied UCLA 10–10 in Fiesta Bowl after leading 10–0 at halftime on 4-yd TD run by Sales and FG and ex pt by Ordonez; Walker had 10 tackles.

1979 (10–2) *Won:* Colorado St. 36–3, Oklahoma St. 27–7, Tulsa 33–8, TCU 16–13, Texas Tech 20–6, Texas 17–14 (1st over Longhorns since 1971), Rice 34–7, Baylor 29–20, Texas A&M 22–10, SMU 31–7. *Lost:* Houston 13–10. *Stars:* QB Kevin Scanlon (1,212 yds pass), WR Robert Farrell, Kolenda, Ordonez (80 pts, nation's leader with 18 FGs), DB Kevin Evans, P Steve Cox (43.8-yd avg). *Noteworthy:* Got share of 11th SWC title. Lost to unbeaten national champ Alabama 24–9 (1st meeting since 1962 Sugar Bowl) in Sugar Bowl; Scanlon passed for 245 yds and a TD, and Ordonez had 34-yd FG.

1981 (8–4) *Won:* Tulsa 14–10, Northwestern 38–7, Mississippi 27–13 (1st meeting since 1970 Sugar Bowl), Texas Tech 26–14, Texas 42–11, Rice 41–7, Baylor 41–39, Texas A&M 10–7. *Lost:* TCU 28–24 (1st to Horned Frogs since 1958), Houston 20–17, SMU 32–18. *Stars:* DT Billy Ray Smith, OG Steve Korte, K Bruce Lahay (88 pts, nation's coleader with 19 FGs). *Noteworthy:* lost to North Carolina 31–27 in foggy Gator Bowl; frosh QB Brad Taylor passed for 307 yds, 2 TDs (66 yds to Derek Holloway and 7 yds to Darryl Mason), and 2-pt conversion.

1982 (9–2–1) *Won:* Tulsa 38–0, Navy 29–17, Mississippi 14–12, TCU 35–0, Texas Tech 21–3, Houston 38–3, Rice 24–6, Texas A&M 35–0. *Lost:* Baylor 24–17, Texas 33–7. *Tied:* unbeaten SMU 17–17. *Stars:* Korte, OT Alfred Mohammed, C Jay Bequette, Taylor (1,073 yds pass), Holloway (21 pass rec for 529 yds), Smith, NG Richard Richardson, DB Danny Walters. *Noteworthy:* Led nation in scoring defense (10.5-pt avg). Beat Florida 28–24 (1st meeting) in Bluebonnet Bowl after trailing 17–7 at halftime; RB Gary Anderson ran for 161 yds and 2 TDs, and Jones ran for 1 TD and passed for another.

1985 (10–2) *Won:* Mississippi 24–19, Tulsa 24–0, New Mexico St. 45–13, TCU 41–0, Texas Tech 30–7, Houston 57–27, Rice 30–15, Baylor 20–14, SMU 15–9. *Lost:* Texas 15–13, Texas A&M 10–6. *Stars:* SE James Shibest, frosh HB James Rouse (550 yds rush, 9 TDs), OG Limbo Parks, soph NG Tony Cherico, DB Greg Lasker, P Greg Horne (42.6-yd punting avg). *Noteworthy:* beat Arizona St. 18–17 in Holiday Bowl on 37-yd FG by frosh K Kendall Trainor with 21 seconds left; QB Mark Calcagni passed for 117 yds and ran for 45

yds, and Razorbacks scored TDs on 9-yd run by Derrick Thomas and 17-yd run by Bobby Joe Edmonds.

1986 (9–3) *Won:* Mississippi 21–0, Tulsa 34–17 (10th straight over Golden Hurricane), New Mexico St. 42–11, TCU 34–17, Texas 21–14 (1st over Longhorns since 1981), Houston 30–13, Rice 45–14, Texas A&M 14–10, SMU 41–0. *Lost:* Texas Tech 17–7 (1st to Red Raiders since 1976), Baylor 29–14. *Stars:* Shibest, Trainor (10 FGs), soph OG Freddie Childress, Cherico, Charles Washington (5 int), Horne (nation's leader with 47.2-yd punting avg). *Noteworthy:* lost to Oklahoma 42–8 in Orange Bowl; scored on 2-yd run by Thomas and 2-pt conversion pass from John Bland to Shibest in last quarter.

1987 (9–4) *Won:* Mississippi 31–10, Tulsa 30–15, TCU 20–10, Texas Tech 31–0, Houston 21–17, Rice 38–14, Baylor 10–7, New Mexico 43–25, Hawaii 38–20. *Lost:* unbeaten national champ Miami (Fla.) 51–7, Texas 16–14, Texas A&M 14–0. *Stars:* Cherico, Trainor (13 FGs, 71 pts), Rouse (1,004 yds rush, 17 TDs), frosh FL Derek Russell (16 pass rec for 297 yds). *Noteworthy:* lost to Georgia 20–17 in Liberty Bowl on FG on last play of game; QB Greg Thomas scored both Arkansas TDs, and Trainor had 43-yd FG and and 2 ex pts.

1988 (10–2) *Won:* Pacific 63–14, Tulsa 30–26, Mississippi 21–13, TCU 53–10, Texas Tech 31–10, Texas 27–24, Houston 26–21, Rice 21–14, Baylor 33–3, Texas A&M 25–20. *Lost:* Miami (Fla.) 18–16 in finale. *Stars:* Trainor (102 pts, nation's leader with 24 FGs), soph QB Quinn Grovey (515 yds and 7 TDs rush, 966 yds pass), TE Billy Winston, SE Tim Horton (16 pass rec for 319 yds), Russell (15 pass rec for 396 yds), soph FB Barry Foster (660 yds rush, 11 TDs), OT Jim Mabry, NT Wayne Martin, LBs Kerry Owens and LaSalle Harper, DBs Steve Atwater and Patrick Williams (6 int), P Allen Meacham (41.6-yd avg). *Noteworthy:* Won 12th SWC title. Lost to UCLA 17–3 in Cotton Bowl, scoring on Trainor's 49-yd FG in 3rd quarter; Harper had pass int, fumble recovery, and 20 tackles.

1989 (10–2) *Won:* Tulsa 26–7, Mississippi 24–17, Texas–El Paso 39–7, TCU 41–19, Texas Tech 45–13, Houston 45–39, Rice 38–17, Baylor 19–10, Texas A&M 23–22, SMU 38–24. *Lost:* Texas 24–20.

Stars: Grovey (1,149 yds pass, 565 yds and 8 TDs rush), Horton (23 pass rec for 453 yds), Russell (17 pass rec for 284 yds, 6 TDs), Winston (16 pass rec for 252 yds), Rouse (869 yds and 7 TDs rush), Foster (833 yds and 7 TDs rush), Mabry, C Elbert Crawford, frosh K Todd Wright (20 FGs, 98 pts), soph LB Mick Thomas, Williams. *Noteworthy:* Ken Hatfield's last team won 13th and last SWC title. Lost to Tennessee 31–27 (1st meeting since 1971 Liberty Bowl) in Cotton Bowl; Grovey passed for 207 yds and a TD (67 yds to Winston), Russell had 7 pass rec for 105 yds, Rouse ran for 134 yds and a TD, and Foster ran for 103 yds and 2 TDs.

BOWL SUMMARY

Bluebonnet 1–0; Cotton 2–5–1; Dixie Bowl 1–0; Dixie Classic 0–0–1; Fiesta 0–0–1; Gator 1–1; Hall of Fame 1–0; Holiday 1–0; Independence 0–1; Liberty 0–3; Orange 1–1; Sugar 1–4.

BOWL RECORD (9–15–3)

Regular Season	Bowl	Score	Opponent	Record
1933 (7–3)	Dixie Classic	7–7	Centenary	(8–0–3)
1946 (6–3–1)	Cotton	0–0	LSU	(9–1)
1947 (5–4–1)	Dixie	21–19	William & Mary	(9–1)
1954 (8–2)	Cotton	6–14	Georgia Tech	(7–3)
1959 (8–2)	Gator	14–7	Georgia Tech	(6–4)
1960 (8–2)	Cotton	6–7	Duke	(7–3)
1961 (8–2)	Sugar	3–10	Alabama	(10–0)
1962 (9–1)	Sugar	13–17	Mississippi	(9–0)
1964 (10–0)	Cotton	10–7	Nebraska	(9–1)
1965 (10–0)	Cotton	7–14	LSU	(7–3)
1968 (9–1)	Sugar	16–2	Georgia	(8–0–2)
1969 (9–1)	Sugar	22–27	Mississippi	(7–3)
1971 (8–2–1)	Liberty	13–14	Tennessee	(9–2)
1975 (9–2)	Cotton	31–10	Georgia	(9–2)
1977 (10–1)	Orange	31–6	Oklahoma	(10–1)
1978 (9–2)	Fiesta	10–10	UCLA	(8–3)
1979 (10–1)	Sugar	9–24	Alabama	(11–0)
1980 (6–5)	Hall of Fame	34–15	Tulane	(7–4)
1981 (8–3)	Gator	27–31	North Carolina	(9–2)
1982 (8–2–1)	Bluebonnet	28–24	Florida	(8–3)
1984 (7–3–1)	Liberty	15–21	Auburn	(8–4)
1985 (9–2)	Holiday	18–17	Arizona State	(8–3)
1986 (9–2)	Orange	8–42	Oklahoma	(10–1)
1987 (9–3)	Liberty	17–20	Georgia	(8–3)
1988 (10–1)	Cotton	3–17	UCLA	(9–2)
1989 (10–1)	Cotton	27–31	Tennessee	(10–1)
1991 (6–5)	Independence	15–24	Georgia	(8–3)

CONFERENCE TITLES

Southwest—1933 (forfeited for use of ineligible player), 1936, 1946*, 1954, 1959*, 1960, 1961*, 1964, 1965, 1968*, 1975*, 1979*, 1988, 1989. **Southeastern**—None.

TOP 20 AP AND UPI RANKING

1936	18	1962	6–6	1971	16–20	1985	12–12
1937	14	1964	2–2	1975	7–6	1986	15–16
1946	16	1965	3–2	1977	3–3	1988	12–13
1954	10–8	1966	U-13	1978	11–10	1989	13–13
1959	9–9	1968	6–9	1979	8–9		
1960	7–7	1969	7–3	1981	U-16		
1961	9–8	1970	11–12	1982	9–8		

MAJOR RIVALS

Arkansas has played at least 10 games with Baylor 35–33–2, Drury 13–5–2, Hendrix 15–0–2, Houston 12–6, Louisiana St. 13–23–2, Mississippi 19–19–1, Missouri-Rolla 15–4, Oklahoma 4–9–1, Oklahoma St. 30–15–1, Rice 35–29–3, Southern Methodist 33–28–5, Texas 19–54, Texas A&M 38–24–3, Texas Christian 43–23–2, Texas Tech 28–7, Tulsa 50–15–3. Record against SEC foes played fewer than 10 times: Alabama 0–3, Auburn 0–1–1, Florida 1–0, Georgia 2–3, Kentucky 0–1, Mississippi St. 0–3, South Carolina 1–0, Tennessee 1–2, Vanderbilt 2–1.

COACHES

Dean of Arkansas coaches is Frank Broyles (1964 national Coach of Year) with record of 144–58–5 for 1958–76, including 7 SWC titles, 10 bowl teams, 2 teams unbeaten in regular season, and 1 national champion. Other top records for at least 3 years were by Hugo Bezdek, 29–13–1 for 1908–12 with 1 perfect record; Francis Schmidt, 42–20–3 for 1922–28; Fred Thomsen, 55–61–1 for 1929–41 with 1 SWC title and 1 bowl team; John Barnhill, 22–17–3 for 1946–49 with 1 SWC title and 2 bowl teams; Jack Mitchell, 17–12–1 for 1955–57; Lou Holtz (1977 national Coach of Year), 60–21–2 for 1977–83 with 1 SWC title and 6 bowl teams; and Ken Hatfield, 55–17–1 for 1984–89 with 2 SWC titles and 6 bowl teams.

MISCELLANEA

First game was win over Fort Smith H.S. 42–0 in 1894 . . . 1st win over college foe was over Ouachita 24–0 in 1897 . . . highest score was over SW Missouri St. 100–0 in 1911 . . . highest since W.W. II was over NW Louisiana St. 64–0 in 1947 . . . worst defeat was by Oklahoma 103–0 in 1918 . . . worst since W.W. II was by Rice 47–0 in 1953 . . . highest against since W.W. II was by Houston 62–28 in 1990 . . . longest win streak of 22 in 1963–65 ended by LSU 14–7 in 1966 Cotton Bowl . . . longest losing string of 7 in 1952–53 broken with win over TCU 13–6 . . . consensus All-Americans were Clyde Scott, B, 1948; Bud Brooks, G, 1954; Glen Ray Hines, T, 1965; Loyd Phillips, DT, 1965–66; Jim Barnes, G, 1968; Rodney Brand, C, 1969; Dick Bumpas, DT, 1970; Leotis Harris, G, and Steve Little, K, 1977; Greg Kolenda, T, 1979; Billy Ray Smith, DL, DE, 1981–82; Steve Korte, OG, 1982; Kendall Trainor, K, and Wayne Martin, DL, 1988; and Jim Mabry, OL, 1989 . . . Academic All-Americans were Gerald Nesbitt, FB, 1957; Lance Alworth, B, 1961; Ken Hatfield, B, 1964; Randy Stewart, C, Jim Lindsey, HB, and Jack Brasuell, DB, 1965; Bob White, K, 1968; Bill Burnett, HB, and Terry Stewart, DB, 1969; and Brad Shoup, DB, 1978 . . . Outland Trophy winners were Bud Brooks, G, 1954; and Loyd Phillips, T, 1966.

AUBURN (Tigers; Burnt Orange and Navy Blue)

NOTABLE TEAMS

1893 (3–0–2) *Won:* Alabama 32–22, 40–16 (1st meetings), Vanderbilt 30–10 (1st meeting). *Tied:* Sewanee 14–14 (1st meeting), Georgia Tech 0–0. **1899** (3–1–1) *Won:* Georgia Tech 63–0, Montgomery 41–0, Clemson 34–0 (1st meeting). *Lost:* unbeaten Sewanee 11–10. *Tied:* Georgia 0–0. *Noteworthy:* last year under John Heisman.

1904 (5–0) *Won:* Clemson 5–0, Nashville 10–0, Georgia Tech 12–0, Alabama 29–5, Georgia 17–6. *Star:* soph FB Humphrey Foy. *Noteworthy:* had 1st unbeaten season since 4-game schedule of 1900 in 1st year under Mike Donahue.

1907 (6–2–1) *Won:* Howard 23–0, Maryville 29–0, Gordon 34–0, Georgia Tech 12–6, Clemson 12–0, Mercer 63–0. *Lost:* Sewanee 12–6, Georgia 6–0. *Tied:* Alabama 6–6. *Noteworthy:* only year under W.S. Keinholz.

1908 (6–1) *Won:* Howard 18–0, Gordon 42–0, Mercer 23–0, Sewanee 6–0 (1st over Tigers in 7 games since 1896), Georgia Tech 44–0, Georgia 23–0. *Lost:* unbeaten Louisiana St. (LSU) 10–2 (1st meeting since 1903). *Stars:* frosh T John Davis, E Walker Reynolds, HB L. Hardage.

1909 (5–2) *Won:* Howard 11–0, Gordon 46–0, Mercer 23–5, Georgia Tech 17–5, Georgia 9–0. *Lost:* Vanderbilt 17–0, Sewanee 12–11. *Star:* T Harry Esslinger.

1910 (6–1) *Won:* Mississippi St. 6–0 (1st meeting since 1905), Howard 78–0, Clemson 17–0, Georgia Tech 16–0, Tulane 33–0, Georgia 26–0. *Lost:* Texas 9–0 (1st meeting) in mid-season. *Stars:* FB Brad Streit, C E.L. Caton.

1912 (6–1–1) *Won:* Mercer 56–0, Florida 27–13 (1st meeting), Clemson 27–6, Mississippi St. 7–0, Georgia Tech 27–7, LSU 7–0 in 1st 6 games. *Lost:* Georgia 12–6 (1st to Bulldogs since 1907) in finale. *Tied:* Vanderbilt 7–7. *Stars:* T M.E. Meadows, frosh G J.H. Thigpen.

1913 (8–0) *Won:* Mercer 53–0, Florida 55–0, Mississippi St. 34–0, Clemson 20–0, LSU 7–0, Georgia Tech 20–0, Vanderbilt 13–6 (1st over Commodores in 7 games since 1893), Georgia 21–7. *Stars:* QB Kirk Newell, FB F.U. "Red" Harris, E Henry Robinson, G F.W. Lockwood. *Noteworthy:* won 1st Southern Intercollegiate Athletic Association title in 1st undefeated season since 1904.

1914 (8–0–1) *Won:* Marion 39–0, Florida 20–0, Clemson 28–0, North Alabama A.C. 60–0, Mississippi St. 19–0, Georgia Tech 14–0, Vanderbilt 6–0, Carlisle Indians 7–0. *Tied:* Georgia 0–0. *Stars:* Thigpen, T G.E. Taylor, C John Pitts, E Richard Kearley. *Noteworthy:* blanked foes 193–0 and repeated as SIAA champ.

1915 (6–2) *Won:* Marion 78–0, Florida 7–0, Clemson 14–0, Mississippi St. 26–0, Georgia 12–0, Mercer 45–0 in 1st 6 games. *Lost:* Vanderbilt 17–0,

unbeaten Georgia Tech 7–0 (1st to Tech since 1906). *Stars:* Taylor, G George Steed.

1916 (6–2) *Won:* Howard 35–0, Mercer 92–0, Clemson 28–0, Mississippi St. 7–3, Georgia 3–0, Florida 20–0 in 1st 6 games. *Lost:* Vanderbilt 20–9, unbeaten Georgia Tech 33–7. *Star:* E R.J. "Moon" Ducote.

1917 (6–2–1) *Won:* Howard 53–0, Camp Sherman 13–0, Clemson 7–0, Mississippi St. 13–6, Florida 68–0, Vanderbilt 31–7. *Lost:* Davidson 21–7, unbeaten national champ Georgia Tech 68–7. *Tied:* unbeaten Ohio St. 0–0. *Stars:* FB Ducote, G Pete Bonner.

1919 (8–1) *Won:* Marion 37–0, Howard 19–6, Camp Gordon 25–13, Clemson 7–0 (10th straight over Tigers), Georgia 7–0, Spring Hill 10–0, Mississippi St. 7–0 (10th straight over Maroons), Georgia Tech 14–7 (1st over Tech since 1914). *Lost:* Vanderbilt 7–6. *Star:* Bonner. *Noteworthy:* won 3rd SIAA title.

1920 (7–2) *Won:* Marion 27–0, Howard 88–0, Ft. Benning 14–2, Clemson 21–0, Vanderbilt 56–6, Birmingham Southern 49–0 (1st meeting), Washington & Lee 77–0. *Lost:* unbeaten Georgia 7–0 (1st to Bulldogs in 6 games since 1912), Georgia Tech 34–0. *Stars:* C Noah Caton, G C.C. Warren.

1922 (8–2) *Won:* Marion 61–0, Howard 72–0, Spring Hill 19–6, Mercer 50–6, Ft. Benning 30–0, Georgia 7–3, Tulane 19–0, Centre 6–0. *Lost:* unbeaten Army 19–6, Georgia Tech 14–6. *Star:* HB John Shirey. *Noteworthy:* last year under Mike Donahue.

1932 (9–0–1) *Won:* Birmingham Southern 61–0, Erskine 77–0, Duke 18–7, Georgia Tech 6–0, Tulane 19–7 (1st over Green Wave since 1926), Mississippi 14–7, Howard 25–0, Florida 21–6 (1st over Gators in 6 games since 1917), Georgia 14–7 (1st over Bulldogs since 1922). *Tied:* South Carolina 20–20 in finale. *Stars:* HB Jimmy Hitchcock (Tigers' 1st consensus All-American), E David Arial. *Noteworthy:* won 1st SC title in last year in league; 1st unbeaten season since 1914.

1935 (8–2) *Won:* Birmingham Southern 25–7, Tulane 10–0, Kentucky 23–0, Duke 7–0, Georgia Tech 33–7, Oglethorpe 51–0, Georgia 19–7, Florida 27–6. *Lost:* Tennessee 13–6 (1st meeting since 1929), LSU 6–0. *Stars:* C Walter Gilbert, T Haygood Paterson.

1936 (7–2–2) *Won:* Birmingham Southern 45–0, Tennessee 6–0, Detroit 6–0, Georgia 20–13, Georgia Tech 13–12, Loyola 44–0, Florida 13–0. *Lost:*

Santa Clara 12–0, unbeaten LSU 19–6. *Tied:* Tulane 0–0. *Stars:* Gilbert, E Joel Eaves. *Noteworthy:* made 1st postseason appearance, tying Villanova 7–7 in Bacardi Bowl in Havana; HB Billy Hitchcock ran 40 yds for Tigers' TD.

1937 (6–2–3) *Won:* Birmingham Southern 19–0, Mississippi St. 33–7 (1st meeting since 1930), Georgia Tech 21–0, Tennessee 20–7, Florida 14–0. *Lost:* Rice 13–7, LSU 9–7. *Tied:* Tulane 0–0, Villanova 0–0, Georgia 0–0. *Star:* G Ralph Sivell. *Noteworthy:* beat Michigan St. 6–0 in Orange Bowl on short TD run by Ralph O'Gwynne set up by 60-yd punt return by George Kenmore and 32-yd pass from Kenmore to O'Gwynne.

1953 (7–3–1) *Won:* Stetson 47–0, Mississippi 13–0, Tulane 34–7, Florida 16–7, Miami (Fla.) 29–20 (1st meeting since 1945), Georgia 39–18 (1st over Bulldogs since 1942), Clemson 45–19. *Lost:* Georgia Tech 36–6, Alabama 10–7. *Tied:* Mississippi St. 21–21. *Stars:* T Frank D'Agostino, Bobby Freeman (5 int), E Jim Pyburn (25 pass rec for 379 yds). *Noteworthy:* lost to Texas Tech 35–13 in Gator Bowl; scored on TDs by Bobby Duke and Vince Dooley.

1954 (8–3) *Won:* Chattanooga 45–0, Florida St. 33–0 (1st meeting), Tulane 27–0, Miami (Fla.) 14–13, Georgia 35–0, Clemson 27–6, Alabama 28–0 (1st over Tide since 1949). *Lost:* Florida 19–13, Kentucky 21–14 (1st meeting since 1935), Georgia Tech 14–7 in consecutive early games. *Stars:* Pyburn (28 pass rec for 460 yds), QB Freeman (1,132 yds total off), FB Joe Childress (836 yds rush, 65 pts). *Noteworthy:* beat Baylor 33–13 in Gator Bowl; Childress ran for 134 yds and 2 TDs, HB Fob James ran 43 yds for a TD, and Freeman passed for 1 TD and scored another.

1955 (8–2–1) *Won:* Chattanooga 15–6, Florida 13–0, Georgia Tech 14–12 (1st over Yellow Jackets since 1940), Furman 52–0, Mississippi St. 27–26, Georgia 16–13, Clemson 21–0, Alabama 26–0. *Lost:* Tulane 27–13. *Tied:* Kentucky 14–14. *Stars:* Childress, James (879 yds rush), soph E Jimmy Phillips (14 pass rec for 272 yds), D'Agostino. *Noteworthy:* lost to Vanderbilt 25–13 in Gator Bowl as Tigers lost 5 fumbles; scored TDs on 38-yd pass from QB Howell Tubbs to James and 4-yd pass to Phillips from Jimmy Cook.

1956 (7–3) *Won:* Furman 41–0, Kentucky 13–0, Houston 12–0, Mississippi St. 27–20, Georgia 20–0, Florida St. 13–7, Alabama 34–7. *Lost:* unbeaten

Tennessee 35–7 (1st meeting since 1939), Georgia Tech 28–7, Florida 20–0. *Stars:* soph RB Tommy Lorino (692 yds rush), Phillips (23 pass rec for 383 yds), Tubbs.

1957 (10–0) *Won:* Tennessee 7–0, Chattanooga 40–7, Kentucky 6–0, Georgia Tech 3–0, Houston 48–7, Florida 13–0, Mississippi St. 15–7, Georgia 6–0, Florida St. 29–7, Alabama 40–0. *Stars:* Phillips (15 pass rec for 357 yds), Billy Atkins (11 TDs, 82 pts), E Jerry Wilson. *Noteworthy:* Won 1st SEC title and got share of 1st national championship in 1st undefeated season since 1932; led nation in total defense, rush defense, and scoring defense (2.8-pt avg). Ineligible for bowl, on NCAA probation.

1958 (9–0–1) *Won:* Tennessee 13–0, Chattanooga 30–8, Kentucky 8–0, Maryland 20–7, Florida 6–5, Mississippi St. 33–14, Georgia 21–6, Wake Forest 21–7, Alabama 14–8. *Tied:* Georgia Tech 7–7. *Stars:* G Zeke Smith (Outland Trophy winner), C/LB Jackie Burkett, T Cleve Wester, Wilson (16 pass rec for 207 yds). *Noteworthy:* Again led nation in total defense and rush defense. Ineligible for bowl, on NCAA probation.

1959 (7–3) *Won:* Hardin-Simmons 35–12, Kentucky 33–0, Georgia Tech 7–6, Miami (Fla.) 21–6, Florida 6–0, Mississippi St. 31–0, Southern Mississippi 28–7 (1st meeting since 1948). *Lost:* Tennessee 3–0, Georgia 14–13, Alabama 10–0 (1st to Tide since 1953). *Stars:* Smith, Burkett, T Ken Rice, soph QB Bobby Hunt (552 yds rush).

1960 (8–2) *Won:* Kentucky 10–7, Chattanooga 10–0, Georgia Tech 9–7, Miami (Fla.) 20–7, Florida 10–7, Mississippi St. 27–12, Georgia 9–6, Florida St. 57–21. *Lost:* Tennessee 10–3 in opener, Alabama 3–0 in finale. *Stars:* Rice, FB Ed Dyas (63 pts, nation's leader with 13 FGs), Bryant Harvard (6 int).

1963 (9–2) *Won:* Houston 21–14, Tennessee 23–19, Kentucky 14–13, Chattanooga 28–0, Georgia Tech 29–21, Florida 19–0, Georgia 14–0, Florida St. 21–15, Alabama 10–8 (1st over Tide since 1958). *Lost:* Mississippi St. 13–10. *Stars:* QB Jimmy Sidle (1,006 yds pass, 706 yds rush, 10 TDs), FB Tucker Frederickson, George Rose (15 pass rec for 202 yds). *Noteworthy:* lost to Nebraska 13–7 in Orange Bowl; scored on 13-yd run by Sidle (96 yds rush) and ex pt by Woody Woodall.

1969 (8–3) *Won:* Wake Forest 57–0, Kentucky 44–3, Clemson 51–0, Georgia Tech 17–14, Florida

38–12, Mississippi St. 52–13, Georgia 16–3, Alabama 49–26 (1st over Tide since 1963). *Lost:* Tennessee 45–19, LSU 21–20 (1st meeting since 1942). *Stars:* soph QB Pat Sullivan (1,686 yds and 16 TDs pass, 206 yds and 7 TDs rush), soph SE Terry Beasley (34 pass rec for 610 yds and 6 TDs), Connie Frederick (32 pass rec for 515 yds and 5 TDs), HB Mickey Zofko (565 yds rush), C Tom Banks, K John Riley (10 FGs, 69 pts), LB Mike Kolen, DBs Buddy McClinton (9 int) and Larry Willingham (7 int). *Noteworthy:* lost to Houston 36–7 in Astro-Bluebonnet Bowl, scoring on 36-yd pass from Zofko to Frederick; Sullivan passed for 132 yds.

1970 (9–2) *Won:* Southern Mississippi 33–14 (1st meeting since 1965), Tennessee 36–23, Kentucky 33–15, Clemson 44–0, Georgia Tech 31–7, Florida 63–14, Mississippi St. 56–0, Alabama 33–28. *Lost:* LSU 17–9, Georgia 31–17. *Stars:* Sullivan (2,586 yds and 17 TDs pass, 270 yds and 9 TDs rush, nation's leader with 2,856 yds total off), Beasley (12 TDs, 52 pass rec for 1,051 yds and 11 TDs), Zofko (34 pass rec for 443 yds), WB Dick Schmalz (44 pass rec for 647 yds and 7 TDs), Alvin Bresler (23 pass rec for 530 yds), soph K Gardner Jett (10 FGs, 71 pts), LB Bobby Strickland, Willingham (4 int), soph DB Dave Beck (6 int). *Noteworthy:* Led nation in pass. Beat Mississippi 35–28 in Gator Bowl; Sullivan passed for 351 yds and 2 TDs and ran 37 yds for a TD, Beasley had 8 pass rec for 143 yds and a TD, Wallace Clark ran for 108 yds, Zofko scored on 6-yd run, and Willingham scored on 55-yd punt return.

1971 (9–2) *Won:* UT-Chattanooga 60–7, Tennessee 10–9, Kentucky 38–6, Southern Mississippi 27–14, Georgia Tech 31–14, Clemson 35–13, Florida 40–7, Mississippi St. 30–21, Georgia 35–20. *Lost:* unbeaten Alabama 31–7 in finale. *Stars:* Heisman Trophy–winner Sullivan (2,012 yds and 20 TDs pass), Beasley (55 pass rec for 846 yds and 12 TDs), Schmalz (44 pass rec for 647 yds and 7 TDs), Robby Robinett (21 pass rec for 170 yds), DT Tommy Yearout, DE Bob Brown, P David Beverly. *Noteworthy:* lost to Oklahoma 40–22 in Sugar Bowl, dropping behind 31–0 by halftime as Sooners took advantage of 2 int and a fumble; Sullivan passed for 250 yds and a TD (to Sandy Cannon), Beasley had 6 pass rec for 117 yds, and Harry Unger scored 2 TDs on short runs.

1972 (10–1) *Won:* Mississippi St. 14–3, UT-

Chattanooga 14–7, Tennessee 10–6, Mississippi 19–13, Georgia Tech 24–14, Florida St. 27–14 (1st meeting since 1963), Florida 26–20, Georgia 27–10, Alabama 17–16. *Lost:* LSU 35–7. *Stars:* TB Terry Henley (843 yds rush, 11 TDs), OT Mac Lorendo, DE Danny Sanspree, DT Benny Sivley, Beck (6 int), David Langner (8 int). *Noteworthy:* beat Colorado 24–3 in Gator Bowl; scored on TDs by QB Wade Whatley, TE Rob Spivey (22-yd pass from soph WB Mike Fuller), and Dan Nugent (16-yd pass from Beck).

1974 (10–2) *Won:* Louisville 16–3, UT–Chattanooga 52–0, Tennessee 21–0, Miami (Fla.) 3–0 (1st meeting since 1968), Kentucky 31–13, Georgia Tech 31–22, Florida St. 38–6, Mississippi St. 24–20, Georgia 17–13. *Lost:* Florida 25–14, unbeaten Alabama 17–13. *Stars:* soph QB Phil Gargis (687 yds rush, 518 yds pass), Tom Gossom (20 pass rec for 294 yds), soph Secdrick McIntyre (839 yds rush), C Lee Gross, DE Rusty Deen, LB Ken Bernich, DB Fuller. *Noteworthy:* beat Texas 27–3 in Gator Bowl; Gargis passed for 2 TDs and 2-pt conversion.

1979 (8–3) *Won:* Kansas St. 26–18, Southern Mississippi 31–9, N.C. State 44–31, Vanderbilt 52–35, Georgia Tech 38–14, Florida 19–13, Mississippi St. 14–3, Georgia 33–13. *Lost:* Tennessee 35–17, Wake Forest 42–38, unbeaten national champ Alabama 25–18. *Stars:* RBs Joe Cribbs (1,120 yds rush, 94 pts) and James Brooks (1,208 yds rush, 72 pts), QB Charlie Trotman (1,115 yds total off), Byron Franklin (19 pass rec for 373 yds), OT George Stephenson, K Jorge Portela (13 FGs, 70 pts), DT Frank Warren.

1982 (9–3) *Won:* Wake Forest 28–10, Southern Mississippi 21–19, Tennessee 24–14, Kentucky 18–3 (1st meeting since 1975), Georgia Tech 24–0, Mississippi St. 35–17, Rutgers 30–7, Alabama 23–22 (1st over Tide since 1972). *Lost:* Nebraska 41–7, Florida 19–17, unbeaten Georgia 19–14. *Stars:* QB Randy Campbell (1,061 yds pass, 284 yds rush), frosh RB Bo Jackson (829 yds and 9 TDs rush), RB Lionel James (779 yds and 7 TDs rush, nation's punt return leader with 15.8-yd avg), OG David Jordan, K Al Del Greco (13 FGs), NG Dowe Aughtman, DT Doug Smith, soph LB Gregg Carr, DBs David King (6 int) and Bob Harris (5 int), frosh P Lewis Colbert (40.6-yd avg). *Noteworthy:* beat Boston College 33–26 in Tangerine Bowl, taking 33–10 lead after 3 quarters; James ran for 101 yds and Jackson scored 2 TDs.

1983 (11–1) *Won:* Southern Mississippi 24–3, Tennessee 37–14, Florida St. 27–24 (1st meeting since 1977), Kentucky 49–21, Georgia Tech 31–13, Mississippi St. 28–13, Florida 28–21, Maryland 35–23, Georgia 13–7, Alabama 23–20. *Lost:* unbeaten Texas 20–7. *Stars:* Jackson (1,213 yds rush, 14 TDs), Campbell (1,103 yds total off), James (728 yds rush), frosh FB Tommie Agee (606 yds rush), Jordan, OT Pat Arrington, Del Greco (12 FGs, 72 pts), Aughtman, Smith, DT Donnie Humphrey, Carr, King, Colbert (40.9-yd punting avg). *Noteworthy:* Won 2nd SEC title. Beat Michigan 9–7 in Sugar Bowl; Jackson ran for 130 yds and Del Greco kicked 3 FGs.

1984 (9–4) *Won:* Southern Mississippi 35–12, Tennessee 28–10, Mississippi 17–13 (1st meeting since 1977), Florida St. 42–41, Georgia Tech 48–34, Mississippi St. 24–21, Cincinnati 60–0, Georgia 21–12. *Lost:* Miami (Fla.) 20–18 (1st meeting since 1978), Texas 35–27, Florida 24–3, Alabama 17–15. *Stars:* Jackson (5 TDs), soph TB Brent Fullwood (628 yds and 7 TDs rush, 1,167 all-purpose yds), frosh Freddie Weygand (32 pass rec for 796 yds), OG Jeff Lott, K Robert McGinty (12 FGs), NG Harold Hallman, DT Ben Thomas, Carr, Colbert (40-yd punting avg). *Noteworthy:* beat Arkansas 21–15 (1st meeting) in Liberty Bowl; Jackson scored 2 TDs (including 39-yd run) and frosh DB Kevin Porter scored on 35-yd pass int return.

1985 (8–4) *Won:* SW Louisiana 49–7, Southern Mississippi 29–18, Mississippi 41–0, Florida St. 59–27, Georgia Tech 17–14, Mississippi St. 21–9, East Carolina 35–10, Georgia 24–10. *Lost:* Tennessee 38–20, Florida 14–10, Alabama 25–23. *Stars:* Heisman Trophy–winner Jackson (1,786 yds and 17 TDs rush), Fullwood (684 yds and 6 TDs rush), Weygand (19 pass rec for 367 yds), WR Trey Gainous (16 pass rec for 251 yds), C Ben Tamburello, OT Steve Wallace, Hallman, DT Gerald Williams, DB Tom Powell (6 int), Colbert (45.8-yd punting avg). *Noteworthy:* lost to Texas A&M 36–16 in Cotton Bowl; Jackson ran for 129 yds and a TD and scored 2nd TD on 73-yd pass from QB Pat Washington.

1986 (10–2) *Won:* UT-Chattanooga 42–14, East Carolina 45–0, Tennessee 34–8, Western Carolina 55–6, Vanderbilt 31–9 (1st meeting since 1979), Georgia Tech 31–10, Mississippi St. 35–6, Cincinnati 52–7, Alabama 21–17. *Lost:* Florida 18–17, Georgia 20–16. *Stars:* Fullwood (1,391 yds and 10

TDs rush), Gainous (19 pass rec for 207 yds), QB Jeff Burger (1,671 yds pass), soph WR Lawyer Tillman (35 pass rec for 730 yds and 6 TDs), Tamburello, OT Stacy Searels, K Chris Knapp (10 FGs, 79 pts), soph DT Tracy Rocker, LBs Aundray Bruce and Kurt Crain. *Noteworthy:* beat Southern California (USC) 16–7 in Florida Citrus Bowl; Fullwood ran for 152 yds and a TD, and Burger passed for TD to soph TE Walter Reeves.

1987 (9–1–2) *Won:* Texas 31–3, Kansas 49–0, North Carolina 20–10, Vanderbilt 48–15, Georgia Tech 20–10, Mississippi St. 38–7, Florida 29–6, Georgia 27–11, Alabama 10–0. *Lost:* Florida St. 34–6. *Tied:* Tennessee 20–20. *Stars:* Burger (2,066 yds and 13 TDs pass), Tillman (32 pass rec for 600 yds and 6 TDs), Duke Donaldson (43 pass rec for 398 yds), Reeves, Searels, soph K Win Lyle (15 FGs, 77 pts), Rocker, Bruce, Crain, DB Kevin Porter, P Brian Shulman. *Noteworthy:* Won 3rd SEC title. Tied unbeaten Syracuse 16–16 in Sugar Bowl on 30-yd FG by Lyle with :01 left; Lyle had earlier FGs of 40 and 41 yds, and Tigers scored TD on 17-yd pass from Burger (171 yds pass) to Tillman (6 pass rec for 125 yds).

1988 (10–2) *Won:* Kentucky 20–10 (10th straight over Wildcats, 1st meeting since 1983), Kansas 56–7, Tennessee 38–6, North Carolina 47–21, Akron 42–0, Mississippi St. 33–0, Florida 16–0, Southern Mississippi 38–8, Georgia 20–10, Alabama 15–10. *Lost:* LSU 7–6 (1st meeting since 1981). *Stars:* Outland Trophy– and Lombardi Award–winner Rocker, NG Benji Roland, DT Ron Stallworth, LB Quentin Riggins, DBs Carlo Cheattom and Greg Staples (5 int), QB Reggie Slack (2,230 yds pass), Weygand (38 pass rec for 577 yds), soph WR Greg Taylor (28 pass rec for 282 yds), Tillman (19 pass rec for 400 yds), soph TB Stacy Danley (877 yds and 7 TDs rush), soph TB/FB James Joseph (668 yds rush, 6 TDs), FB Vincent Harris (5 TDs rush), Reeves, OG Rodney Garner, OT Jim Thompson, Lyle (14 FGs, 78 pts), Shulman (41.2-yd punting avg). *Noteworthy:* Got share of 2nd straight SEC title while leading nation in total defense, rush defense, and scoring defense (7.2-pt avg). Lost to Florida St. 13–7 in Sugar Bowl; scored on 20-yd pass from Slack to Reeves.

1989 (10–2) *Won:* Pacific 55–0, Southern Mississippi 24–3, Kentucky 24–12, LSU 10–6, Mississippi St. 14–0, Florida 10–7, Louisiana Tech 38–23, Georgia 20–3, Alabama 30–20. *Lost:* Tennessee 21–14,

Florida St. 22–14. *Stars:* Slack (1,996 yds and 11 TDs pass), WR Alexander Wright (30 pass rec for 714 yds and 6 TDs, 7 TDs total), Taylor (25 pass rec for 353 yds), Joseph (26 pass rec for 227 yds, 817 yds rush), Danley (652 yds rush), frosh TB Darrell Williams (5 TDs rush), C John Hudson, soph OG Ed King, Lyle (16 FGs, 75 pts), DT David Rocker, Riggins, soph LBs Darrel Crawford and Craig Ogletree, DB John Wiley. *Noteworthy:* Got share of 3rd straight SEC title (5th overall). Beat Ohio St. 31–14 in Hall of Fame Bowl; Slack passed for 141 yds and 3 TDs (2 to Taylor) and scored other Tiger TD.
1990 (8–3–1) *Won:* Cal State–Fullerton 38–17, Mississippi 24–10 (1st meeting since 1985), Louisiana Tech 16–14, Vanderbilt 56–6, Florida St. 20–17, Mississippi St. 17–16, Georgia 33–10. *Lost:* Florida 48–7, Southern Mississippi 13–12 (1st to Eagles in 8 games since 1977), Alabama 16–7 (1st

to Tide since 1985). *Tied:* Tennessee 26–26. *Stars:* frosh QB Stan White (2,242 yds and 14 TDs pass), Taylor (46 pass rec for 650 yds and 7 TDs, 8 TDs total), WR Herbert Casey (25 pass rec for 439 yds), King, OL Rob Selby, K Jim Von Wyl (17 FGs, 78 pts), Rocker, Crawford, frosh LB James Willis, Wiley, DB Corey Barlow. *Noteworthy:* beat Indiana 27–23 in Peach Bowl; White passed for 351 yds and a TD and ran for 2 TDs, Casey had 7 pass rec for 159 yds, and Von Wyl had 2 FGs.

BOWL SUMMARY

Bacardi 0–0–1; Bluebonnet 0–1; Cotton 0–1; Florida Citrus 1–0; Gator 4–2; Hall of Fame 1–0; Liberty 1–1; Orange 1–1; Peach 1–0; Sugar 1–2–1; Sun 1–1; Tangerine 1–0.

BOWL RECORD (12–9–2)

Regular Season	Bowl	Score	Opponent	Record
1936 (7–2–1)	Bacardi	7–7	Villanova	(7–2)
1937 (5–2–3)	Orange	6–0	Michigan State	(8–2)
1953 (7–2–1)	Gator	13–35	Texas Tech	(10–1)
1954 (7–3)	Gator	33–13	Baylor	(7–3)
1955 (8–1–1)	Gator	13–25	Vanderbilt	(7–3)
1963 (9–1)	Orange	7–13	Nebraska	(9–1)
1965 (5–4–1)	Liberty	7–13	Mississippi	(6–4)
1968 (6–4)	Sun	34–10	Arizona	(8–2)
1969 (8–2)	Bluebonnet	7–36	Houston	(8–2)
1970 (8–2)	Gator	35–28	Mississippi	(7–3)
1971 (9–1)	Sugar	22–40	Oklahoma	(10–1)
1972 (9–1)	Gator	24–3	Colorado	(8–3)
1973 (6–5)	Sun	17–34	Missouri	(7–4)
1974 (9–2)	Gator	27–3	Texas	(8–3)
1982 (8–3)	Tangerine	33–26	Boston College	(8–2–1)
1983 (10–1)	Sugar	9–7	Michigan	(9–2)
1984 (8–4)	Liberty	21–15	Arkansas	(7–3–1)
1985 (8–3)	Cotton	16–36	Texas A&M	(9–2)
1986 (9–2)	Florida Citrus	16–7	USC	(7–4)
1987 (9–1–1)	Sugar	16–16	Syracuse	(11–0)
1988 (10–1)	Sugar	7–13	Florida State	(10–1)
1989 (9–2)	Hall of Fame	31–14	Ohio State	(8–3)
1990 (7–3–1)	Peach	27–23	Indiana	(6–4–1)

CONFERENCE TITLES

Southern Intercollegiate Athletic Association — 1913, 1914, 1919. **Southern** — 1932. **Southeastern** — 1957, 1983, 1987, 1988*, 1989*.

TOP 20 AP AND UPI RANKING

1942	16	1959	U-19	1971	12–5	1984	14–14
1953	17-U	1960	13–14	1972	5–7	1986	6–8
1954	13-U	1963	5–6	1974	8–6	1987	7–7
1955	10–8	1968	16-U	1979	16-U	1988	8–7
1957	1–2	1969	20–15	1982	14–14	1989	6–6
1958	4–4	1970	10–9	1983	3–3	1990	19–19

MAJOR RIVALS

Auburn has played at least 10 games with Alabama 23–33–1, Birmingham Southern 13–3, Clemson 31–11–2, Florida 37–30–2, Florida St. 13–4–1, Georgia 45–44–7, Georgia Tech 47–39–4, Howard 23–0–1, Kentucky 20–5–1, Louisiana St. 11–15–1, Mercer 11–0, Miami (Fla.) 7–4, Mississippi 11–6, Mississippi St. 46–18–2, Sewanee 4–6–2, Southern Mississippi 15–5, Tennessee 22–18–3, Tulane 13–17–6, UT-Chattanooga 19–0, Vanderbilt 14–19–1. Record against SEC members met fewer than 10 times: Arkansas 1–0–1, South Carolina 2–1–1.

COACHES

Dean of Auburn coaches is Ralph "Shug" Jordan with record of 176–83–6 for 1951–75, including 1 SEC title, 12 bowl teams, 2 unbeaten teams, and 1 national champion. Other top records for at least 3 years were by John Heisman, 12–4–2 for 1895–99 with 1 unbeaten team; Mike Donahue, 99–35–5 for 1904–06 and 1908–22 with 3 SIAA titles and 3 unbeaten teams; Chet Wynne, 22–15–2 for 1930–33 with 1 unbeaten SC champion; Jack Meagher, 48–37–10 for 1934–42 with 2 bowl teams; Doug Barfield, 29–25–1 for 1976–80; and Pat Dye, 99–38–4 for 1981–92 with 4 SEC titles and 9 bowl teams.

MISCELLANEA

First game was win over Georgia 10–0 in 1892 . . . highest score was over Georgia Tech 94–0 in 1894 . . . highest since 1900 was over Mercer 92–0 in 1916 . . . highest since W.W. II was over Florida 63–14 in 1970 . . . biggest margin since W.W. II was over Cincinnati 60–0 in 1984 . . . worst defeat was by North Carolina 64–0 in 1892 . . . worst since 1900 (and highest ever against) was by Georgia Tech 68–7 in 1917 . . . worst since W.W. II was by Alabama 55–0 in 1948 . . . longest unbeaten string of 24 in 1956–58 ended by Tennessee 3–0 in 1959 opener . . . 23-game unbeaten string in 1913–15 ended by Vanderbilt 17–0 . . . longest winless string of 16 in 1926–28 broken with win over Howard 25–6 . . . consensus All-Americans were Jimmy Hitchcock, B, 1932; Jimmy Phillips, E, 1957; Zeke Smith, G, 1958; Ken Rice, T, 1960; Tucker Frederickson, B, 1964; Buddy McClinton, DB, 1969; Larry Willingham, DB, 1970; Pat Sullivan, QB, and Terry Beasley, E, 1971; Ken Bernich, LB, 1974; Bo Jackson, RB, 1983, 1985; Gregg Carr, LB, 1984; Ben Tamburello, C, and Brent Fullwood, RB, 1986; Aundray Bruce, LB, 1987; Tracy Rocker, DL, 1987–88; and Ed King, OL, and David Rocker, DL, 1990 . . . Academic All-Americans were Jimmy Phillips, E, 1957; Jackie Burkett, C, 1959; Ed Dyas, B, 1960; Bill Cody, LB, 1965; Buddy McClinton, DB, 1969; Bobby Davis, LB, 1974; Chuck Fletcher, DT, 1975; Chris Vacarella, RB, 1976; and Gregg Carr, LB, 1984 . . . Heisman Trophy winners were Pat Sullivan, QB, 1971; and Bo Jackson, RB, 1985 . . . Outland Trophy winners were Zeke Smith, G, 1958; and Tracy Rocker, DT, 1988 . . . Lombardi Award winner was Tracy Rocker, DT, 1988.

FLORIDA (Gators; Orange and Blue)

NOTABLE TEAMS

1907 (4–1–1) *Won:* Columbia A.C. 6–0, Jacksonville A.C. 21–0, 17–0, Rollins 9–4. *Lost:* Mercer 6–0. *Tied:* Rollins 0–0.
1909 (6–1–1) *Won:* Gainesville A.C. 5–0, Rollins 14–0, 28–3, Olympics 11–0, 28–0, Tallahassee A.C. 26–0. *Lost:* Stetson 26–0. *Tied:* Stetson 5–5. *Noteworthy:* 1st year under G.E. Pyle.
1910 (6–1) *Won:* Gainesville Guards 23–0, Georgia A&M 52–0, The Citadel 6–2 (1st meeting),

Rollins 38–0, Charleston 34–0, Columbia College 33–0. *Lost:* Mercer 13–0.

1911 (5–0–1) *Won:* The Citadel 15–3, Clemson 9–5 (1st meeting), Columbia College 9–0, Stetson 27–0, College of Charleston 21–0. *Tied:* South Carolina 6–6 (1st meeting). *Noteworthy:* 1st undefeated season.

1914 (5–2) *Won:* Kings College 36–0, Southern 59–0, Wofford 36–0, The Citadel 7–0, Mercer 14–0. *Lost:* unbeaten Auburn 20–0, Sewanee 26–0. *Noteworthy:* 1st year under Charles McCoy.

1922 (7–2) *Won:* Rollins 19–0, American Legion 14–0, Howard 57–0, Oglethorpe 12–0, Clemson 47–14, Tulane 27–6, Mississippi College 58–0. *Lost:* Furman 7–6, Harvard 24–0. *Noteworthy:* last year under William Kline.

1923 (6–1–2) *Won:* Rollins 28–0, Wake Forest 16–7, Mercer 19–7, Stetson 27–0, Southern 53–0, Alabama 16–6. *Lost:* Army 20–0 in opener. *Tied:* Georgia Tech 7–7 (1st meeting since 1913), Mississippi St. 13–13 (1st meeting). *Stars:* HB Ark Newton, T Robbie Robinson, soph G Goldy Goldstein. *Noteworthy:* 1st year under J.A. VanFleet.

1924 (6–2–2) *Won:* Rollins 77–0, Wake Forest 34–0, Southern 27–0, Mississippi St. 27–0, Drake 10–0, Washington & Lee 16–6. *Lost:* Army 14–7, Mercer 10–0 in successive games. *Tied:* Georgia Tech 7–7, Texas 7–7. *Stars:* Goldstein, QB Edgar Jones. *Noteworthy:* VanFleet's last team.

1925 (8–2) *Won:* Mercer 24–0, Southern 9–0, Hampden-Sydney 22–6, Wake Forest 24–3, Rollins 65–0, Clemson 42–0, Mississippi St. 12–0, Washington & Lee 17–14. *Lost:* Georgia Tech 23–7, unbeaten national cochamp Alabama 34–0. *Stars:* Goldstein, Jones (108 pts). *Noteworthy:* 1st year under H.L. Sebring.

1927 (7–3) *Won:* Southern 26–7, Auburn 33–6 (1st meeting since 1917, 1st win in 7-game series dating to 1912), Kentucky 27–6, Mercer 32–6, Alabama 13–6, Washington & Lee 20–7, Maryland 7–3 (1st meeting). *Lost:* Davidson 12–0, N.C. State 12–6 (1st meeting), Georgia 28–0.

1928 (8–1) *Won:* Southern 26–0, Auburn 27–0, Mercer 73–0, N.C. State 14–7, Sewanee 71–6, Georgia 26–6 (1st in 7-game series dating to 1915), Clemson 27–6, Washington & Lee 60–6. *Lost:* unbeaten Tennessee 13–12 in finale. *Stars:* QB Clyde Crabtree, E Dale Van Sickle. *Noteworthy:* 1st year under Charles Bachman.

1929 (8–2) *Won:* Southern 54–0, Virginia Military

Institute 18–7, Auburn 19–0, Georgia 18–6, Clemson 13–7, South Carolina 20–7 (1st meeting since 1921), Washington & Lee 25–7, Oregon 20–6. *Lost:* Georgia Tech 19–6, Harvard 14–0.

1952 (8–3) *Won:* Stetson 33–6 (1st meeting since 1939), The Citadel 33–0, Clemson 54–13 (1st meeting since 1937), Georgia 30–0, Auburn 31–21, Miami (Fla.) 43–6, Kentucky 27–0 (1st over Wildcats in 5 games since 1937). *Lost:* unbeaten Georgia Tech 17–14, Vanderbilt 20–13, Tennessee 26–12 (1st meeting since 1944). *Stars:* DT Charlie LaPradd, G Joe D'Agostino, Buford Long (14 TDs), FB Rick Casares. *Noteworthy:* made 1st postseason appearance, beating Tulsa 14–13 in Gator Bowl; Casares scored TD and kicked 2 ex pts, and John Hall scored on 37-yd pass from Leffie Robinson.

1957 (6–2–1) *Won:* Wake Forest 27–0, Kentucky 14–7, Louisiana St. (LSU) 22–14, Georgia 22–0, Vanderbilt 14–7, Miami (Fla.) 14–0. *Lost:* Mississippi St. 29–20, unbeaten national cochamp Auburn 13–0. *Tied:* Georgia Tech 0–0. *Stars:* HB Jim Roundtree, Jimmy Dunn (6 int).

1960 (9–2) *Won:* George Washington 30–7, Florida St. 3–0, Georgia Tech 18–17, Vanderbilt 12–0, LSU 13–10, Georgia 22–14, Tulane 21–6, Miami (Fla.) 18–0. *Lost:* Rice 10–0, Auburn 10–7. *Stars:* E Pat Patchen, G Vic Miranda, Don Goodman (5 TDs rush). *Noteworthy:* 1st year under Ray Graves. Beat Baylor 13–12 in Gator Bowl; scored on TDs by Goodman and soph Larry Travis (recovered fumble in end zone), and ex pt by soph William Cash.

1964 (7–3) *Won:* Southern Methodist (SMU) 24–8, Mississippi St. 16–13, Mississippi 30–14 (1st meeting since 1958, 1st over Rebels in 5 games since 1945), South Carolina 37–0, Auburn 14–0, Miami (Fla.) 12–10, LSU 20–6. *Lost:* unbeaten national cochamp Alabama 17–14, Georgia 14–7 (1st to Bulldogs since 1959), Florida St. 16–7 (1st in 7-game series begun in 1958). *Stars:* HB Larry DuPree, soph QB Steve Spurrier (1,089 yds total off), SE Charley Casey (47 pass rec for 673 yds), G Larry Gagner, LB Bill Richbourg, DB Bruce Bennett.

1965 (7–4) *Won:* Northwestern 24–14, LSU 14–7, Mississippi 17–0, N.C. State 28–6, Georgia 14–10, Tulane 51–13, Florida St. 30–17. *Lost:* Mississippi St. 18–13 (1st to Bulldogs in 5 games since 1958), Auburn 28–17, Miami (Fla.) 16–13. *Stars:* Spurrier (1,893 yds and 14 TDs pass, 230 yds rush, 41-yd punting avg), Casey (58 pass rec for 809 yds and 8 TDs), Jack Harper (1,127 all-purpose yds), Gagner, E Lynn Matthews, G Larry Beckman, Bennett. *Noteworthy:* lost to Missouri 20–18 in Sugar Bowl; Spurrier passed for 352 yds and 2 TDs (to Harper and Casey, who caught 5 for 108 yds).

1966 (9–2) *Won:* Northwestern 43–7, Mississippi St. 28–7, Vanderbilt 13–0, Florida St. 22–19, N.C. State 17–10, LSU 28–7, Auburn 30–27, Tulane 31–10. *Lost:* Georgia 27–10, Miami (Fla.) 21–16. *Stars:* Heisman Trophy–winner Spurrier (Florida's 1st consensus All-American; 2,012 yds and 16 TDs pass, 40.8-yd punting avg), FL Richard Trapp (63 pass rec for 872 yds and 7 TDs), soph RB Larry Smith (742 yds and 9 TDs rush, 1,010 all-purpose yds), G Jim Benson, C Bill Cart. *Noteworthy:* beat Georgia Tech 27–12 in Orange Bowl; Smith ran for 187 yds and a TD (on 94-yd run), Spurrier passed

QB Steve Spurrier, 1964–66

for 160 yds, and Fred McKeel scored 2 TDs on short runs.

1969 (9–1–1) *Won:* Houston 59–34, Mississippi St. 47–35, Florida St. 21–6, Tulane 18–17, North Carolina 52–2, Vanderbilt 41–20, Kentucky 31–6, Miami (Fla.) 35–16. *Lost:* Auburn 38–12. *Tied:* Georgia 13–13. *Stars:* soph QB John Reaves (nation's leader with 2,896 yds and 24 TDs pass), soph FL Carlos Alvarez (88 pass rec for 1,329 yds and 12 TDs), RB Tommy Durrance (731 yds and 12 TDs rush, 18 TDs total), G Mac Steen, DB Steve Tannen, DE David Ghesquiere. *Noteworthy:* Graves' last team. Beat Tennessee 14–13 (1st meeting since 1955) in Gator Bowl; Reaves passed for 161 yds and a TD (to Alvarez), James Kelley returned fumble 8 yds for score, and soph Richard Franco kicked 2 ex pts.

1974 (8–4) *Won:* California 21–17, Maryland 17–10, Mississippi St. 29–13, LSU 24–14 (1st over Tigers in 5 games since 1966), Florida St. 24–14, Duke 30–13, Auburn 25–14, Miami (Fla.) 31–7. *Lost:* Vanderbilt 24–10 (1st to Commodores in 9 games since 1959), Georgia 17–16, Kentucky 41–24 (1st to Wildcats in 9 games since 1956). *Stars:* SE Lee McGriff (36 pass rec for 698 yds and 7 TDs), frosh B Tony Green (856 yds and 6 TDs rush, 1,115 all-purpose yds), DE Preston Kendrick, LBs Ralph Ortega and Glen Cameron, DB Randy Talbot (7 int). *Noteworthy:* lost to Nebraska 13–10 in Sugar Bowl after leading 10–0 at halftime on 21-yd TD run by Green and ex pt and 40-yd FG by soph K David Posey.

1975 (9–3) *Won:* SMU 40–14, Mississippi St. 27–10, LSU 34–6, Vanderbilt 35–0, Florida St. 34–8, Duke 24–16, Auburn 31–14, Kentucky 48–7, Miami (Fla.) 15–11. *Lost:* N.C. State 8–7, Georgia 10–7. *Stars:* FB Jimmy DuBose (1,307 yds and 6 TDs rush), soph WR Wes Chandler (20 pass rec for 457 yds and 5 TDs), QB Don Gaffney, OT Mike Williams, Posey, LB Sammy Green. *Noteworthy:* lost to Maryland 13–0 in Gator Bowl; DuBose ran for 95 yds.

1976 (8–4) *Won:* Houston 49–14, Mississippi St. 34–30, LSU 28–23, Florida St. 33–26, Tennessee 20–18, Auburn 24–19, Rice 50–22, Miami (Fla.) 19–10. *Lost:* North Carolina 24–21, Georgia 41–27, Kentucky 28–9. *Stars:* Chandler (44 pass rec for 967 yds and 10 TDs), QB Jimmy Fisher (1,511 yds and 10 TDs pass, 288 yds rush), Willie Wilder (654 yds and 9 TDs rush), frosh LB Scot Brantley, DB Alvin Cowans. *Noteworthy:* lost to Texas

A&M 37–14 in Sun Bowl; scored TDs on 29-yd run by Chandler and 1-yd run by QB Terry LeCount. **1980** (8–4)   *Won:* California 41–13, Georgia Tech 45–12, Mississippi St. 21–15, Mississippi 15–3 (1st meeting since 1973), Louisville 13–0, Auburn 21–10, Kentucky 17–15. *Lost:* LSU 24–7, unbeaten national champ Georgia 26–21, Miami (Fla.) 31–7, Florida St. 17–13. *Stars:* WRs Cris Collinsworth (40 pass rec for 599 yds) and soph Tyrone Young (24 pass rec for 468 yds), frosh QB Wayne Peace (1,271 yds pass), TE Chris Faulkner (24 pass rec for 259 yds), soph FB James Jones (657 yds rush), K Brian Clark (15 FGs), LB David Little, P Mark Dickert (41.7-yd avg). *Noteworthy:* Nation's most-improved team. Beat Maryland 35–20 in Tangerine Bowl; Peace passed for 271 yds and 2 TDs (both to Collinsworth, who caught 8 for 166 yds) and scored another TD, and Jones and soph Johnell Brown each scored on short runs.
1982 (8–4)   *Won:* Miami (Fla.) 17–14, Southern California (USC) 17–9, Mississippi St. 27–17, West Texas St. 77–14, Auburn 19–17, Kentucky 39–13, Tulane 21–14 (1st meeting since 1969), Florida St. 13–10. *Lost:* LSU 24–13, Vanderbilt 31–29 (1st meeting since 1975), unbeaten Georgia 44–0. *Stars:* Peace (2,053 yds pass), WR Dwayne Dixon (45 pass rec for 589 yds), Lorenzo Hampton (1,027 all-purpose yds), Jones (752 yds rush), LB Wilber Marshall, Randy Clark (6 int), frosh P Ray Criswell (42.8-yd avg). *Noteworthy:* lost to Arkansas 28–24 (1st meeting) in Bluebonnet Bowl; QB Robert Hewko passed for 234 yds and 3 TDs, and Dixon caught 8 for 106 yds.
1983 (9–2–1)   *Won:* national champ Miami (Fla.) 28–3, Indiana St. 17–13, Mississippi St. 35–12, LSU 31–17, Vanderbilt 29–10, East Carolina 24–17, Kentucky 24–7, Florida St. 53–14. *Lost:* Auburn 28–21, Georgia 10–9 in successive late games. *Tied:* USC 19–19. *Stars:* Peace (2,079 yds and 10 TDs pass), Dixon (47 pass rec for 596 yds), soph RB Neal Anderson (835 yds and 9 TDs rush), C Phil Bromley, K Bobby Raymond (20 FGs, 89 pts), Marshall, LB Fred McCallister, DB Tony Lilly, Criswell (47.4-yd punting avg). *Noteworthy:* beat Iowa 14–6 in Gator Bowl; Anderson ran for 84 yds and a TD, and Douglas Drew recovered fumble in end zone for other Gator TD.
1984 (9–1–1)   *Won:* Tulane 63–21, Mississippi St. 27–12, Syracuse 16–0, Tennessee 43–30 (1st meeting since 1977), Cincinnati 48–17, Auburn 24–3,

Georgia 27–0 (1st over Bulldogs since 1977), Kentucky 25–17, Florida St. 27–17. *Lost:* Miami (Fla.) 32–20. *Tied:* LSU 21–21. *Stars:* frosh QB Kerwin Bell (1,644 yds and 16 TDs pass), Anderson (916 yds and 7 TDs rush), John Williams (793 yds rush, 21 pass rec for 276 yds), OT Lomas Brown, Bromley, Raymond (23 FGs, 103 pts), soph WR Ricky Nattiel (nation's punt return leader with 15.7-yd avg), MG Tim Newton, LB Alonzo Johnson, Criswell (43.6-yd punting avg). *Noteworthy:* Galen Hall replaced Charley Pell as coach after 1st 3 games (1–1–1 record). Won 1st SEC title but had to vacate later because of recruiting violations. Ineligible for bowl, NCAA probation.
1985 (9–1–1)   *Won:* Miami (Fla.) 35–23, Mississippi St. 36–22, LSU 20–0, Tennessee 17–10, SW Louisiana 45–0, Virginia Tech 35–18, Auburn 14–10, Kentucky 15–13, Florida St. 38–14. *Lost:* Georgia 24–3. *Tied:* Rutgers 28–28. *Stars:* Anderson (1,034 yds and 8 TDs rush, 1,400 all-purpose yds), Bell (2,687 yds and 21 TDs pass), Williams (44 pass rec for 369 yds), OG Jeff Zimmerman, K Jeff Dawson (17 FGs, 78 pts), Johnson, Criswell (44.7-yd punting avg). *Noteworthy:* ineligible for bowl, NCAA probation.
1990 (9–2)   *Won:* Oklahoma St. 50–7, Alabama 17–13, Furman 27–3, Mississippi St. 34–21, LSU 34–8, Akron 59–0, Auburn 48–7, Georgia 38–7, Kentucky 47–15. *Lost:* Tennessee 45–3 (1st meeting since 1985, 1st loss to Vols in 5 games since 1971), Florida St. 45–30. *Stars:* soph QB Shane Matthews (2,952 yds and 23 TDs pass), TE Kirk Kirkpatrick (55 pass rec for 770 yds and 7 TDs), WRs Ernie Mills (41 pass rec for 770 yds and 10 TDs), Terence Barber (35 pass rec for 431 yds) and soph Tre Everett (20 pass rec for 291 yds), RBs Willie McClendon (27 pass rec for 266 yds, 631 yds rush, 8 TDs) and frosh Errict Rhett (845 yds rush, 5 TDs), K Arden Czyzewski (15 FGs, 87 pts), LBs Jerry Odom, Tim Paulk and Huey Richardson, soph DB Will White (7 int). *Noteworthy:* 1st year under Steve Spurrier. Ineligible for bowl, NCAA probation.
1991 (10–2)   *Won:* San Jose St. 59–21, Alabama 35–0, Mississippi St. 29–7, LSU 16–0, Tennessee 35–18, Northern Illinois 41–10, Auburn 31–10, Georgia 45–13, Kentucky 35–26, Florida St. 14–9 (1st over Seminoles since 1986). *Lost:* Syracuse 38–21. *Stars:* Matthews (3,130 yds and 28 TDs pass), soph WR Willie Jackson (51 pass rec for 725

yds and 10 TDs), WR Harrison Houston (33 pass rec for 618 yds and 8 TDs), Alonzo Sullivan (28 pass rec for 414 yds), Everett (19 pass rec for 407 yds and 6 TDs), Rhett (1,109 yds and 10 TDs rush), Czyzewski (11 FGs), C Cal Dixon, OG Hesham Ismail, DT Brad Culpepper, Paulk, LB Ephesians Bartley, White, frosh P Shayne Edge (43.3-yd avg). *Noteworthy:* Won 1st official SEC title. Lost to Notre Dame 39–28 in Sugar Bowl after leading 16–7 at half; Matthews passed for 370 yds and 2 TDs (to Jackson and Houston), and Czyzewski kicked 5 FGs.

1992 (9–4) *Won:* Kentucky 35–19, LSU 28–21, Auburn 24–9, Louisville 31–17, Georgia 26–24, Southern Mississippi 24–20, South Carolina 14–9 (1st meeting since 1964), Vanderbilt 41–21. *Lost:* Tennessee 31–14, Mississippi St. 30–6 (1st to Bulldogs since 1986), Florida St. 45–24. *Stars:* Matthews (3,205 yds and 23 TDs pass), Willie Jackson (62 pass rec for 772 yds and 8 TDs), Rhett (903 yds and 9 TDs rush, 55 pass rec for 400 yds and 1 TD),

Houston (29 pass rec for 472 yds, 958 all-purpose yds), frosh WR Jack Jackson (35 pass rec for 462 yds), soph WR Aubrey Hill (20 pass rec for 348 yds), soph DT Henry McMillian, LBs Carlton Miles and Ed Robinson, LB/DB Monty Grow, White, soph DB Larry Kennedy, Edge (40.8-yd punting avg). *Noteworthy:* Won East Division of SEC, then lost to unbeaten national champ Alabama 28–21 in 1st SEC playoff title game. Beat N.C. State 27–10 in foggy Gator Bowl as Matthews passed for 247 yds and 2 TDs (to Willie Jackson and Houston) and scored another, Rhett ran for 182 yds, and soph K Judd Davis had 2 FGs.

BOWL SUMMARY

All-American 1–0; Aloha 0–1; Bluebonnet 0–1; Freedom 0–1; Gator 6–2; Orange 1–0; Peach 0–1; Sugar 0–3; Sun 0–1; Tangerine 1–1.

BOWL RECORD (9–11)

Regular Season	Bowl	Score	Opponent	Record
1952 (7–3)	Gator	14–13	Tulsa	(8–1–1)
1958 (6–3–1)	Gator	3–7	Mississippi	(8–2)
1960 (8–2)	Gator	13–12	Baylor	(8–2)
1962 (6–4)	Gator	17–7	Penn State	(9–1)
1965 (7–3)	Sugar	18–20	Missouri	(7–2–1)
1966 (8–2)	Orange	27–12	Georgia Tech	(9–1)
1969 (8–1–1)	Gator	14–13	Tennessee	(9–1)
1973 (7–4)	Tangerine	7–16	Miami (Ohio)	(10–0)
1974 (8–3)	Sugar	10–13	Nebraska	(8–3)
1975 (9–2)	Gator	0–13	Maryland	(8–2–1)
1976 (8–3)	Sun	14–37	Texas A&M	(9–2)
1980 (7–4)	Tangerine	35–20	Maryland	(8–3)
1981 (7–4)	Peach	6–26	West Virginia	(8–3)
1982 (8–3)	Bluebonnet	24–28	Arkansas	(8–2–1)
1983 (8–2–1)	Gator	14–6	Iowa	(9–2)
1987 (6–5)	Aloha	16–20	UCLA	(9–2)
1988 (6–5)	All-American	14–10	Illinois	(6–4–1)
1989 (7–4)	Freedom	7–34	Washington	(7–4)
1991 (10–1)	Sugar	28–39	Notre Dame	(9–3)
1992 (8–4)	Gator	27–10	N.C. State	(9–2–1)

CONFERENCE TITLES

Southeastern—1991. (Vacated 1984 crown.)

TOP 20 AP AND UPI
(USA TODAY/CNN SINCE 1991) RANKING

1952	15-U	1965	U-12	1974	15–12	1985	5-U
1957	17-U	1966	U-11	1980	U-19	1990	13-U
1958	14–15	1969	14–17	1983	6–6	1991	7–8
1959	19-U	1973	U-19	1984	3–7	1992	10–11
1960	18–16						

MAJOR RIVALS

Florida has played at least 10 games with Alabama 8–17, Auburn 30–37–2, The Citadel 12–0, Clemson 9–3–1, Florida St. 23–11–1, Georgia 25–43–2, Georgia Tech 9–23–6, Kentucky 26–17, Louisiana St. 18–18–3, Maryland 11–6, Mercer 10–6–1, Miami (Fla.) 25–24, Mississippi 7–9–1, Mississippi St. 29–16–2, North Carolina 2–7–1, N.C. State 9–4–1, Rollins 13–2–1, South Carolina 7–3–3, Southern 13–1, Stetson 15–2–2, Tennessee 7–15, Tulane 13–6–2, Vanderbilt 15–9–2. Record against SEC member met fewer than 10 times: Arkansas 0–1.

COACHES

Deans of Florida coaches are Bob Woodruff and Ray Graves with 10 years each. Most wins were under Graves, with record of 70–31–4 for 1960–69 with 5 bowl teams (4 winners). Woodruff was 53–42–6 for 1950–59 with 2 bowl teams. Other top records for at least 3 years were by Jack Forsythe, 14–6–2 for 1906–08; G.E. Pyle, 26–7–3 for 1909–13 with 1 unbeaten team; William Kline, 19–8–2 for 1920–22; H.L. Sebring, 17–11–2 for 1925–27; Charles Bachman, 27–18–3 for 1928–32; D.K. Stanley, 14–13–2 for 1933–35; Doug Dickey, 58–43–2 for 1970–78 with 4 bowl teams; Charley Pell, 33–26–3 for 1979 to part of 1984 with 4 bowl teams; Galen Hall, 43–22–1 for most of 1984 through 1989 with 3 bowl teams; and Steve Spurrier, 28–8 for 1990–92 with 1 SEC title and 2 bowl teams.

MISCELLANEA

First game was win over Gainesville A.C. 16–6 in 1906 . . . 1st win over college foe was over Rollins 6–0 in 1906 . . . highest score was over Florida Southern 144–0 in 1913 . . . highest since W.W. II was over West Texas St. 77–14 in 1982 . . . biggest margin since W.W. II was over Montana St. 69–0 in 1988 . . . worst defeat was by Georgia 75–0 in 1942 . . . worst since W.W. II was by Georgia 51–0 in 1968 . . . highest against Gators since W.W. II was by Auburn 63–14 in 1970 . . . longest win streak of 18 in 1984–85 ended by Georgia 24–3 . . . 13-game unbeaten string in 1923–24 ended by Army 14–7 . . . longest losing string of 13 in 1945–47 broken with win over N.C. State 7–6 . . . winless string of 13 in 1978–79 broken with win over California 41–13 in 1980 opener . . . consensus All-Americans were Steve Spurrier, QB, 1966; Carlos Alvarez, E, 1969; Sammy Green, LB, 1975; David Little, LB, 1980; Wilber Marshall, LB, 1982–83; Lomas Brown, OT, 1984; Louis Oliver, DB, 1988; Emmitt Smith, RB, 1989; and Brad Culpepper, DL, 1991 . . . Academic All-Americans were Charles Casey, E, 1965; Carlos Alvarez, WR, 1969, 1971; David Posey, K, 1976; Wes Chandler, B, 1977; Cris Collinsworth, WR, 1980; and Brad Culpepper, DL, 1991 . . . Heisman Trophy winner was Steve Spurrier, QB, 1966.

GEORGIA (Bulldogs; Red and Black)

NOTABLE TEAMS

1894 (5–1) *Won:* South Carolina 40–0 (1st meeting), Wofford 10–0, Augusta A.C. 66–0, Auburn 10–8, Savannah A.C. 22–0. *Lost:* Sewanee 12–8 (1st meeting) in opener.
1910 (6–2–1) *Won:* Locust Grove 101–0, Gordon 79–0, Alabama 22–0, Tennessee 35–5, Mercer 21–0, Georgia Tech 11–6 (1st over Tech in 6 games since 1903). *Lost:* Sewanee 15–12, Auburn 26–0. *Tied:* Clemson 0–0. *Star:* frosh HB Bob McWhorter. *Noteworthy:* 1st year under W.A. Cunningham.
1911 (7–1–1) *Won:* Alabama Presbyterian 51–0,

South Carolina 38–0, Alabama 11–3, Sewanee 12–3 (1st over Tigers in 7 games since 1896), Mercer 8–5, Clemson 22–0, Georgia Tech 5–0. *Lost:* Vanderbilt 17–0 (1st meeting since 1903). *Tied:* Auburn 0–0. *Stars:* McWhorter, G D.R. Peacock.

1912 (6–1–1) *Won:* Chattanooga 33–0 (1st meeting), The Citadel 33–0, Alabama 13–9, Clemson 27–6, Georgia Tech 20–0, Auburn 12–6. *Lost:* Vanderbilt 46–0. *Tied:* Sewanee 13–13. *Star:* McWhorter.

1913 (6–2) *Won:* Alabama Presbyterian 108–0, Dahlonega 51–0, Alabama 20–0, North Carolina 19–6 (1st meeting since 1901), Clemson 18–15, Georgia Tech 14–0. *Lost:* Virginia 13–6 (1st meeting since 1897), unbeaten Auburn 21–7. *Star:* McWhorter.

1920 (8–0–1) *Won:* The Citadel 40–0, South Carolina 37–0, Furman 7–0, Oglethorpe 27–3, Auburn 7–0 (1st over Tigers in 6 games since 1912), Florida 56–0, Alabama 21–14, Clemson 55–0. *Tied:* Virginia 0–0. *Stars:* E Owen Reynolds, C Bum Day, T Artie Pew. *Noteworthy:* had 1st undefeated season since 4-game schedule of 1896 in 1st year under H.J. Stegeman.

1921 (7–2–1) *Won:* Mercer 28–0 (1st meeting since 1911), Furman 27–7, Oglethorpe 14–0, Auburn 7–0, Virginia 21–0, Alabama 22–0, Clemson 28–0. *Lost:* Harvard 10–7, Dartmouth 7–0. *Tied:* unbeaten Vanderbilt 7–7 (1st meeting since 1912). *Stars:* Reynolds, Day, Pew, G Hugh Whelchel.

1924 (7–3) *Won:* Mercer 26–7 (10th win in as many games in series), South Carolina 18–0, Furman 22–0, Vanderbilt 3–0 (1st over Commodores in 8 games since 1898), Tennessee 33–0, Virginia 7–0, Auburn 6–0. *Lost:* unbeaten Yale 7–6, Alabama 33–0, Centre 14–7. *Stars:* T Jim Taylor, E Ralph Thompson.

1927 (9–1) *Won:* Virginia 32–0, Yale 14–10 (1st in 5-game series begun in 1923), Furman 32–0, Auburn 33–0, Tulane 31–0 (1st meeting since 1919), Florida 28–0, Clemson 32–0, Mercer 26–7, Alabama 20–6 (1st over Tide since 1921). *Lost:* Georgia Tech 12–0 in finale. *Stars:* Es Tom Nash (Georgia's 1st consensus All-American) and Ivey "Chick" Shiver, FB Hertis McCrary. *Noteworthy:* 1st year under George Woodruff.

1930 (7–2–1) *Won:* Oglethorpe 31–6, Mercer 51–0 (15th straight over Bears), Yale 18–14, North Carolina 26–0, Auburn 39–7, New York U. 7–6, Georgia Tech 13–0. *Lost:* Tulane 25–0, unbeaten Alabama 13–0 in successive late games. *Tied:* Florida 0–0. *Stars:* Es Vernon "Catfish" Smith and Herb Maffett, Gs Ralph Maddox and Milton Leathers, FB Jack Roberts.

1931 (8–2) *Won:* Virginia Tech 40–0, Yale 26–7, North Carolina 32–6, Vanderbilt 9–0 (1st meeting since 1926), Florida 33–6, New York U. 7–6, Auburn 12–6, Georgia Tech 35–6. *Lost:* unbeaten Tulane 20–7, national champ Southern California (USC) 60–0. *Stars:* Smith, QB Austin Downes.

1933 (8–2) *Won:* N.C. State 20–10 (1st meeting), Tulane 26–13 (1st over Green Wave since 1928), North Carolina 30–0, Mercer 13–12, New York U. 25–0, Florida 14–0, Yale 7–0, Georgia Tech 7–6. *Lost:* Auburn 14–6, USC 31–0. *Stars:* E Graham Batchelor, G LeRoy Moorehead.

1934 (7–3) *Won:* Stetson 42–0, Furman 7–2, Florida 14–0, Yale 14–7, N.C. State 27–0, Auburn 18–0, Georgia Tech 7–0. *Lost:* North Carolina 14–0, Tulane 7–6, unbeaten national cochamp Alabama 26–6 in successive early games. *Stars:* FB George Chapman, G John Brown, C John McKnight.

1941 (9–1–1) *Won:* Mercer 81–0, South Carolina 34–6 (10th straight over Gamecocks), Columbia 7–3, Auburn 7–0, Florida 19–3, Centre 47–6, Dartmouth 35–0, Georgia Tech 21–0. *Lost:* Alabama 27–14. *Tied:* Mississippi 14–14. *Stars:* TB Frank Sinkwich (713 yds and 11 TDs pass, nation's leader with 1,103 yds and 7 TDs rush), HB Lamar Davis (12 TDs), QB Cliff Kimsey, E George Poschner, G Walter Ruark. *Noteworthy:* made 1st postseason appearance, beating Texas Christian (TCU) 40–26 in Orange Bowl; Sinkwich passed for 243 yds and 3 TDs (including 61 yds to Melvin Conger and 60 yds to Kimsey) and ran for 139 yds and a TD (43-yd run), and Kenneth Keuper scored 2 TDs.

1942 (11–1) *Won:* Kentucky 7–6, Jacksonville Naval Air Base 14–0, Furman 40–7, Mississippi 48–13, Tulane 40–0, Cincinnati 35–13, Alabama 21–10 (1st meeting since 1935), Florida 75–0, Chattanooga 40–0, Georgia Tech 34–0. *Lost:* Auburn 27–13. *Stars:* Heisman Trophy–winner Sinkwich (795 yds and 16 TDs rush, 1,392 yds and 10 TDs pass, nation's leader with 2,187 yds total off), soph TB Charley Trippi (672 yds and 8 TDs rush, 567 yds pass), Davis (8 TDs pass rec), Poschner, T Gene Ellenson. *Noteworthy:* Led nation in total off and won 1st SEC title and share of 1st national championship. Beat UCLA 9–0 in Rose Bowl; Trippi ran for 115 yds and Sinkwich scored Georgia's TD before being injured.

1944 (7–3)   *Won:* Presbyterian 67–0, Kentucky 13–12, Daniel Field 57–6, Alabama 14–7, Florida 38–12, Auburn 49–13, Clemson 21–7 (1st meeting since 1937).   *Lost:* Wake Forest 14–7, LSU 15–7, Georgia Tech 44–0.   *Stars:* frosh G Herb St. John, soph Reid Moseley (nation's leader with 32 pass rec for 506 yds).

1945 (9–2)   *Won:* Murray St. 49–0, Clemson 20–0, Miami (Fla.) 27–21, Kentucky 48–6, Chattanooga 34–7, Florida 34–0, Auburn 35–0, Georgia Tech 33–0.   *Lost:* LSU 32–0, unbeaten Alabama 28–14 in consecutive mid-season games.   *Stars:* Moseley (nation's leader with 31 pass rec for 662 yds), Trippi (9 TDs rush, 41.4-yd avg on 14 punts), St. John, T Mike Castronis.   *Noteworthy:* beat Tulsa 20–6 in Oil Bowl; Trippi passed 64 yds to John Donaldson for a TD and returned punt 68 yds for another.

1946 (11–0)   *Won:* Clemson 35–12, Temple 35–7, Kentucky 28–13, Oklahoma A&M 33–13, Furman 70–7, Alabama 14–0, Florida 33–14, Auburn 41–0, Chattanooga 48–27, Georgia Tech 35–7.   *Stars:* Maxwell Award–winner Trippi (744 yds and 14 TDs rush, 622 yds and 5 TDs pass, 6 int), St. John, soph QB/S John Rauch (779 yds and 14 TDs pass, 7 TDs rush, 6 int), E Joe Tereshinski.   *Noteworthy:* Led nation in scoring (37.2-pt avg) and got share of 2nd SEC title. Beat North Carolina 20–10 in Sugar Bowl; Rauch scored 2 TDs and Trippi passed 67 yds to soph E Dan Edwards for another.

1948 (9–2)   *Won:* Chattanooga 14–7, Kentucky 35–12, LSU 22–0, Miami (Fla.) 42–21, Alabama 35–0, Florida 20–12, Auburn 42–14, Furman 33–0, Georgia Tech 21–13.   *Lost:* unbeaten North Carolina 21–14.   *Stars:* Rauch (1,307 yds pass), Edwards, HB Joe Geri, T Porter Payne, G Homer Hobbs, Eli Maricich (8 int).   *Noteworthy:* Won 3rd SEC title. Lost to Texas 41–28 in Orange Bowl (1st bowl loss in 6 games); Rauch passed for 161 yds and a TD, Geri scored twice and kicked 4 ex pts, and Alvin Bodine scored on 71-yd pass int return.

1959 (10–1)   *Won:* Alabama 17–3, Vanderbilt 21–6, Hardin-Simmons 35–6, Mississippi St. 15–0, Kentucky 14–7, Florida St. 42–0, Florida 21–10 (1st over Gators since 1954), Auburn 14–13 (1st over Tigers since 1952), Georgia Tech 21–14.   *Lost:* South Carolina 30–14.   *Stars:* QB Fran Tarkenton, E Jimmy Vickers, G Pat Dye, HB/P Bobby Walden

(40.3-yd punting avg).   *Noteworthy:* Won 4th SEC title. Beat Missouri 14–0 in Orange Bowl; Tarkenton threw 2 TD passes (20 yds to soph HB Bill McKenny and 33 yds to Aaron Box).

1966 (10–1)   *Won:* Mississippi St. 20–17 (1st meeting since 1961), Virginia Military Institute (VMI) 43–7, South Carolina 7–0, Mississippi 9–3 (1st meeting since 1955), Kentucky 27–15, North Carolina 28–3, Florida 27–10, Auburn 21–13, Georgia Tech 23–14.   *Lost:* Miami (Fla.) 7–6.   *Stars:* DTs George Patton and soph Bill Stanfill, DE Larry Kohn, DB Lynn Hughes, FB Ronnie Jenkins, G Don Hayes, OT Edgar Chandler, K Bobby Etter.   *Noteworthy:* Got share of 5th SEC title. Beat Southern Methodist (SMU) 24–9 in Cotton Bowl; Kent Lawrence ran for 149 yds and a TD (74-yd run), Billy Payne scored on 20-yd pass from Kirby Moore, and Jenkins scored on 1-yd run.

1967 (7–4)   *Won:* Mississippi St. 30–0, Clemson 24–17, South Carolina 21–0, VMI 56–6, Kentucky 31–7, Auburn 17–0, Georgia Tech 21–14.   *Lost:* Mississippi 29–20, Houston 15–14, Florida 17–16.   *Stars:* Jenkins, Chandler, Stanfill, Kohn, DB Jake Scott (6 int).   *Noteworthy:* lost to N.C. State 14–7 in Liberty Bowl; scored on 1-yd run by Jenkins in 2nd quarter.

1968 (8–1–2)   *Won:* Clemson 31–13, South Carolina 21–20, Mississippi 21–7, Vanderbilt 32–6, Kentucky 35–14, Florida 51–0, Auburn 17–3, Georgia Tech 47–8.   *Tied:* Tennessee 17–17 (1st meeting since 1937), Houston 10–10.   *Stars:* Outland Trophy–winner Stanfill, Scott (10 int), DE Billy Payne, soph QB Mike Cavan (1,619 yds pass), SE Lawrence, soph Charles Whittemore (40 pass rec for 608 yds), E Dennis Hughes, T David Rholetter, P Spike Jones (41.2-yd avg).   *Noteworthy:* Led nation in scoring defense (9.8-pt avg) and won 6th SEC title in 1st undefeated season since 1946. Upset by Arkansas 16–2 (1st meeting) in Cotton Bowl; offense stymied by 3 fumbles and pass int.

1971 (11–1)   *Won:* Oregon St. 56–25, Tulane 17–7, Clemson 28–0, Mississippi St. 35–7, Mississippi 38–7, Vanderbilt 24–0, Kentucky 34–0, South Carolina 24–0, Florida 49–7, Georgia Tech 28–24.   *Lost:* Auburn 35–20.   *Stars:* soph QB Andy Johnson (870 yds and 13 TDs rush), G Royce Smith, T Tom Nash, C Kendell Keith, DE Mixon Robinson, LB Chip Wisdom, DB Buz Rosenberg (2 punts returned for TDs).   *Noteworthy:* One of nation's most-improved teams. Beat North Carolina 7–3 in

Gator Bowl; Jimmy Poulos ran for 161 yds and Georgia's TD (25-yd run in 3rd quarter).

1975 (9–3)   *Won:* Mississippi St. 28–6, South Carolina 28–20, Clemson 35–7, Vanderbilt 47–3, Kentucky 21–13, Richmond 28–24, Florida 10–7, Auburn 28–13, Georgia Tech 42–26.   *Lost:* Pittsburgh 19–9, Mississippi 28–13 (1st to Rebels since 1970). *Stars:* RBs Glynn Harrison (894 yds and 5 TDs rush) and soph Kevin McLee (806 yds and 10 TDs rush), QB Ray Goff (5 TDs rush), G Randy Johnson, soph LB Ben Zambiasi, DB Bill Krug.   *Noteworthy:* lost to Arkansas 31–10 in Cotton Bowl after entering 4th period tied 10–10; scored on 35-yd FG by K Allan Leavitt and 21-yd pass from QB Matt Robinson to FL Gene Washington.

1976 (10–2)   *Won:* California 36–24, Clemson 41–0, South Carolina 20–12, Alabama 21–0, Vanderbilt 45–0, Kentucky 31–7, Cincinnati 31–17, Florida 41–27, Auburn 28–0, Georgia Tech 13–10.   *Lost:* Mississippi 21–17.   *Stars:* McLee (1,058 yds and 6 TDs rush), Goff (724 yds and 10 TDs rush), Robinson (609 yds and 7 TDs pass), Washington, soph TB Willie McClendon (5 TDs rush), OG Joel Parrish, OT Mike Wilson, Leavitt (11 FGs, 70 pts), DE Dicky Clark, Zambiasi, Krug.   *Noteworthy:* Got share of 7th SEC title. Lost to unbeaten national champ Pittsburgh 27–3 in Sugar Bowl, dropping behind 21–0 by halftime; scored on 25-yd FG by Leavitt in 3rd quarter.

1978 (9–2–1)   *Won:* Baylor 16–14, Clemson 12–0, Mississippi 42–3, LSU 24–17 (1st meeting since 1953), Vanderbilt 31–10, Kentucky 17–16, VMI 41–3, Florida 24–22, Georgia Tech 29–28.   *Lost:* South Carolina 27–10 (1st to Gamecocks in 16 games since 1959).   *Tied:* Auburn 22–22.   *Stars:* McClendon (1,312 yds and 13 TDs rush), frosh WR Lindsay Scott (36 pass rec for 484 yds), OG Matt Braswell, OT Mack Guest, soph K Rex Robinson (15 FGs, 74 pts), LB Ricky McBride, soph DB Scott Woerner.   *Noteworthy:* lost to Stanford 25–22 in Bluebonnet Bowl after leading 22–0 early in 3rd period following 2 TD pass rec by FL Carmon Prince and 31-yd FG by Robinson.

1980 (12–0)   *Won:* Tennessee 16–15 (1st meeting since 1973), Texas A&M 42–0, Clemson 20–16, TCU 34–3, Mississippi 28–21, Vanderbilt 41–0, Kentucky 27–0, South Carolina 13–10, Florida 26–21, Auburn 31–21, Georgia Tech 38–20.   *Stars:* frosh TB Herschel Walker (1,616 yds and 15 TDs rush), QB Buck Belue (1,314 yds and 11 TDs pass, 5 TDs rush), Scott (19 pass rec for 374 yds), soph TE Norris Brown (12 pass rec for 253 yds), OG Tim Morrison, OT Nat Hudson, Robinson (16 FGs, 84 pts), DT Jimmy Payne, DL Eddie Weaver, Woerner (5 int, nation's leader in punt returns with 15.7-yd avg), DB Jeff Hipp (nation's coleader with 8 int).   *Noteworthy:* Won 8th SEC title in 1st undefeated season since 1968. Beat Notre Dame 17–10 in Sugar

1980 National Champions

Bowl to nail down 2nd national championship; Walker ran for 150 yds and both Georgia TDs, and Robinson kicked 46-yd FG.

1981 (10–2) *Won:* Tennessee 44–0, California 27–13, South Carolina 24–0, Mississippi 37–7, Vanderbilt 53–21, Kentucky 21–0, Temple 49–3, Florida 26–21, Auburn 24–13, Georgia Tech 44–7. *Lost:* unbeaten national champ Clemson 13–3. *Stars:* Walker (1,891 yds rush, 20 TDs), Belue (1,603 yds and 12 TDs pass), Scott (42 pass rec for 728 yds and 6 TDs), Brown (18 pass rec for 380 yds), soph TE Clarence Kay (18 pass rec for 253 yds), frosh K Kevin Butler (94 pts, nation's coleader with 19 FGs), Weaver, Payne, LB Tommy Thurson, P Jim Broadway (41.1-yd avg). *Noteworthy:* Got share of 9th SEC title. Lost to Pittsburgh 24–20 in Sugar Bowl on 4th down 33-yd TD pass with 35 seconds left; Walker scored twice and Belue passed 6 yds to Kay for final Bulldog TD.

1982 (11–1) *Won:* Clemson 13–7, Brigham Young (BYU) 17–14, South Carolina 34–18, Mississippi St. 29–22 (1st meeting since 1975), Mississippi 33–10, Vanderbilt 27–13, Kentucky 27–14, Memphis St. 34–3, Florida 44–0, Auburn 19–14, Georgia Tech 38–18. *Stars:* Heisman Trophy– and Maxwell Award–winner Walker (1,752 yds rush, 17 TDs), C Wayne Radloff, OT Jimmy Harper, Butler (17 FGs, 85 pts), DE Freddie Gilbert, Payne, Thurson, DBs Terry Hoage (nation's leader with 12 int) and soph Jeff Sanchez (9 int). *Noteworthy:* Won 3rd straight SEC title (10th overall). Lost to national champ Penn St. 27–23 in Sugar Bowl; Walker ran for 103 yds and a TD, QB John Lastinger passed for 2 TDs (to Herman Archie and Kay), and Butler kicked FG and 2 ex pts.

1983 (10–1–1) *Won:* UCLA 19–8, South Carolina 31–13, Mississippi St. 20–7, Mississippi 36–11, Vanderbilt 20–13 (10th straight over Commodores), Kentucky 47–21, Temple 31–14, Florida 10–9, Georgia Tech 27–24. *Lost:* Auburn 13–7. *Tied:* Clemson 16–16. *Stars:* Thurson, Hoage, Gilbert, LB Knox Culpepper, Kay, OT Guy McIntyre, Butler (18 FGs, 82 pts), P Chip Andrews (40.2-yd avg). *Noteworthy:* Upset unbeaten Texas 10–9 in Cotton Bowl; Lastinger ran 17 yds for TD in last quarter and Butler kicked ex pt to go along with 43-yd 1st quarter FG.

1986 (8–4) *Won:* Duke 31–7, South Carolina 31–26, Mississippi 14–10 (10th straight over Rebels), Vanderbilt 38–16, Kentucky 31–9, Richmond 28–

TB Herschel Walker, 1980–82

13, Auburn 20–16, Georgia Tech 31–24. *Lost:* Clemson 31–28, LSU 23–14 (1st meeting since 1979), Florida 31–19. *Stars:* QB James Jackson (1,475 yds pass, 410 yds rush), Lars Tate (17 TDs, 954 yds rush, 22 pass rec for 214 yds), OT Wilbur Strozier, soph K Steve Crumley (14 FGs, 75 pts), DL Henry Harris, LB John Brantley, DB John Little, P Cris Carpenter (44.1-yd avg). *Noteworthy:* lost to Boston College 27–24 in Hall of Fame Bowl on 5-yd pass with 32 seconds left in game; Jackson passed for 178 yds and ran for 2 TDs, and Gary Moss returned pass int 81 yds for other Bulldog TD.

1987 (9–3) *Won:* Virginia 30–22 (1st meeting since 1979), Oregon St. 41–7, South Carolina 13–6, Mississippi 31–14, Vanderbilt 52–24, Kentucky 17–14

(10th straight over Wildcats), Florida 23–10, Georgia Tech 30–16. *Lost:* Clemson 21–20, LSU 26–23, Auburn 27–11. *Stars:* Tate (1,016 yds rush), Jackson (1,026 yds pass, 519 yds rush), frosh TB Rodney Hampton (890 yds rush, 6 TDs), OG Kim Stephens, Crumley (14 FGs), Brantley. *Noteworthy:* beat Arkansas 20–17 in Liberty Bowl on 39-yd FG by frosh K John Kasay on last play of game; Jackson passed for 148 yds and ran for 72 yds and a TD, Kasay had 2 FGs and 2 ex pts, and Tate scored on 1-yd run.

1988 (9–3) *Won:* Tennessee 28–17 (1st meeting since 1981), TCU 38–10, Mississippi St. 42–35 (1st meeting since 1983), Mississippi 36–12, Vanderbilt 41–22, William & Mary 59–24, Florida 26–3, Georgia Tech 24–3. *Lost:* South Carolina 23–10, Kentucky 16–10 (1st to Wildcats since 1977), Auburn 20–10. *Stars:* Worley (1,216 yds rush, 18 TDs), Hampton (719 yds rush, 7 TDs), QB Wayne Johnson (1,095 yds total off), SE John Thomas (23 pass rec for 354 yds), FB Keith Henderson (5 TDs, 20 pass rec for 297 yds), frosh FL Arthur Marshall (10 pass rec for 317 yds), TE Troy Sadowski, C Todd Wheeler, NG Bill Goldberg, LBs Richard Tardits and Terrie Lee Webster, DB Ben Smith. *Noteworthy:* Last year under Vince Dooley. Beat Michigan St. 34–27 in Gator Bowl; Johnson passed for 227 yds and 3 TDs (2 to Hampton, who also ran for 109 yds and scored on 32-yd run, and to TE Kirk Warner), and Crumley kicked 39-yd FG.

1991 (9–3) *Won:* Western Carolina 48–0, LSU 31–10 (1st over Tigers in 4 games since 1979), Cal St.–Fullerton 27–14, Clemson 27–12, Mississippi 37–17, Kentucky 49–27, Auburn 37–27 (1st over Tigers since 1986), Georgia Tech 18–15. *Lost:* Alabama 10–0, Vanderbilt 27–25 (1st to Commodores since 1973), Florida 45–13. *Stars:* frosh QB Eric Zeier (1,984 yds pass), soph SE Andre Hastings (48 pass rec for 683 yds and 5 TDs, 1,050 all-purpose yds), Marshall (39 pass rec for 524 yds), soph TB Garrison Hearst (968 yds and 9 TDs rush), TB Larry Ware (680 yds rush, 6 TDs), FB Mack Strong (7 TDs, 16 pass rec for 208 yds), frosh K Kanon Parkman (12 FGs), LB Dwayne Simmons, DB Chuck Carswell, soph P Scot Armstrong (41.9-yd avg). *Noteworthy:* beat Arkansas 24–15 in Independence Bowl; Zeier passed for 228 yds and 2 TDs (to Marshall and Hastings, who caught 4 for 94 yds and also scored on 53-yd run), and Parkman kicked 39-yd FG.

1992 (10–2) *Won:* South Carolina 28–6, Cal St.–Fullerton 56–0, Mississippi 37–11, Arkansas 27–3 (1st meeting since 1987), Georgia Southern 34–7, Vanderbilt 30–20, Kentucky 40–7, Auburn 14–10, Georgia Tech 31–17. *Lost:* Tennessee 34–31, Florida 26–24. *Stars:* Zeier (2,248 yds and 12 TDs pass), Hearst (nation's leader with 21 TDs and 126 pts; 1,547 yds and 19 TDs rush, 22 pass rec for 324 yds and 2 TDs), Hastings (1,474 all-purpose yds, 52 pass rec for 860 yds and 5 TDs), TE Shannon Mitchell (20 pass rec for 308 yds), K Todd Peterson (13 FGs, 80 pts), DT Greg Jackson, NG Casey Barnum, LBs Mitch Davis and frosh Randall Godfrey, DBs Greg Tremble and Al Jackson. *Noteworthy:* beat Ohio St. 21–14 in Florida Citrus Bowl as Zeier passed for 242 yds, Hastings had 8 pass rec for 113 yds, Hearst ran for 163 yds and 2 TDs, and RB Frank Harvey scored on short run.

BOWL SUMMARY

Bluebonnet 0–1; Cotton 2–1; Florida Citrus 1–0–1; Gator 2–0–1; Hall of Fame 0–1; Independence 1–0; Liberty 1–1; Oil 1–0; Orange 2–1; Peach 1–1; Presidential Cup 0–1; Rose 1–0; Sugar 2–4; Sun 1–1–1; Tangerine 0–1.

BOWL RECORD (15–13–3)

Regular Season	Bowl	Score	Opponent	Record
1941 (8–1–1)	Orange	40–26	TCU	(7–3)
1942 (10–1)	Rose	9–0	UCLA	(7–3)
1945 (8–2)	Oil	20–6	Tulsa	(8–2)
1946 (10–0)	Sugar	20–10	North Carolina	(8–1–1)
1947 (7–4)	Gator	20–20	Maryland	(7–2–1)

(continued)

Regular Season	Bowl	Score	Opponent	Record
1948 (9–1)	Orange	28–41	Texas	(6–3–1)
1950 (6–2–3)	Presidential Cup	20–40	Texas A&M	(6–4)
1959 (9–1)	Orange	14–0	Missouri	(6–4)
1964 (6–3–1)	Sun	7–0	Texas Tech	(6–3–1)
1966 (9–1)	Cotton	24–9	SMU	(8–2)
1967 (7–3)	Liberty	7–14	N.C. State	(8–2)
1968 (8–0–2)	Sugar	2–16	Arkansas	(9–1)
1969 (5–4–1)	Sun	6–45	Nebraska	(8–2)
1971 (10–1)	Gator	7–3	North Carolina	(9–2)
1973 (6–4–1)	Peach	17–16	Maryland	(8–3)
1974 (6–5)	Tangerine	10–21	Miami (Ohio)	(9–0–1)
1975 (9–2)	Cotton	10–31	Arkansas	(9–2)
1976 (10–1)	Sugar	3–27	Pittsburgh	(11–0)
1978 (9–1–1)	Bluebonnet	22–25	Stanford	(7–4)
1980 (11–0)	Sugar	17–10	Notre Dame	(9–1–1)
1981 (10–1)	Sugar	20–24	Pittsburgh	(10–1)
1982 (11–0)	Sugar	23–27	Penn State	(10–1)
1983 (9–1–1)	Cotton	10–9	Texas	(11–0)
1984 (7–4)	Fla. Citrus	17–17	Florida State	(7–3–1)
1985 (7–3–1)	Sun	13–13	Arizona	(8–3)
1986 (8–3)	Hall of Fame	24–27	Boston College	(8–3)
1987 (8–3)	Liberty	20–17	Arkansas	(9–3)
1988 (8–3)	Gator	34–27	Michigan State	(6–4–1)
1989 (6–5)	Peach	18–19	Syracuse	(7–4)
1991 (8–3)	Independence	24–15	Arkansas	(6–5)
1992 (9–2)	Fla. Citrus	21–14	Ohio State	(8–2–1)

CONFERENCE TITLES

Southeastern—1942, 1946*, 1948, 1959, 1966*, 1968, 1976*, 1980, 1981*, 1982.

TOP 20 AP AND UPI
(USA TODAY/CNN SINCE 1991) RANKING

1941	14	1965	U–15	1976	10–10	1987	13–14
1942	2	1966	4–4	1978	16–15	1988	15–15
1945	18	1967	U–18	1980	1–1	1991	17–19
1946	3	1968	8–4	1981	6–5	1992	8–8
1948	8	1971	7–8	1982	4–4		
1959	5–5	1975	19–19	1983	4–4		

MAJOR RIVALS

Georgia has played at least 10 games with Alabama 22–33–4, Auburn 44–45–7, The Citadel 9–0–1, Clemson 37–17–4, Florida 43–25–2, Florida St. 5–4–1, Furman 21–2, Georgia Tech 47–35–5, Kentucky 35–9–2, Louisiana St. 7–12–1, Mercer 22–0, Miami (Fla.) 7–4–1, Mississippi 21–9–1, Mississippi St. 12–5, North Carolina 16–12–2, Sewanee 5–7–1, South Carolina 34–9–2, Tennessee 10–10–2, Tulane 14–10–1, Vanderbilt 35–16–2, Virginia 7–6–3, Yale 6–5. Record against SEC member met fewer than 10 times: Arkansas 3–2.

COACHES

Dean of Georgia coaches is Vince Dooley (1980 national Coach of Year) with record of 201–77–10 for 1964–88, including 6 SEC titles, 20 bowl teams, 3 teams unbeaten in regular season, and 1 national champion. Other top records for at least 3 years were by W.A. Cunningham, 43–18–9 for 1910–19; H.J. Stegeman, 20–6–3 for 1920–22 with 1 unbeaten team; George Woodruff, 30–16–1 for 1923–27; Harry Mehre, 59–34–6 for 1928–37; Wallace "Wally" Butts, 140–86–9 for 1939–60 with 4 SEC titles, 8 bowl teams, 1 unbeaten team, and 1 national champion; and Ray Goff, 29–18 for 1989–92 with 3 bowl teams.

MISCELLANEA

First game was win over Mercer 50–0 in 1892 . . . highest score was over Alabama Presbyterian 108–0 in 1913 . . . highest since W.W. II was over The Citadel 76–0 in 1958 . . . worst defeat was by Southern California 60–0 in 1931 . . . worst since W.W. II was by Georgia Tech 48–6 in 1951 . . . longest win streak of 19 in 1981–82 ended by Penn State 27–23 in 1983 Sugar Bowl . . . 15-game win streaks, in 1945–47 ended by North Carolina 14–7 and in 1979–81 by Clemson 13–3 . . . longest losing string of 8 in 1904–05 broken with win over Dahlonega 16–12 . . . consensus All-Americans were Tom Nash, E, 1927; Vernon Smith, E, 1931; Frank Sinkwich, B, 1941–42; Charley Trippi, B, 1946; Ed Chandler, T, 1967; Bill Stanfill, DT, and Jake Scott, DB, 1968; Royce Smith, G, 1971; Randy Johnson, G, 1975; Joel Parrish, G, 1976; Herschel Walker, RB, 1980–82; Terry Hoage, DB, 1982–83; Kevin Butler, K, and Jeff Sanchez, DB, 1984; Pete Anderson, C, 1985; Tim Worley, RB, 1988; and Garrison Hearst, RB, 1992 . . . Academic All-Americans were Fran Tarkenton, B, 1960; Bob Etter, K, 1965–66; Lynn Hughes, DB, 1966; Bill Stanfill, DT, 1968; Tom Nash, OT, and Mixon Robinson, DE, 1971; Jeff Lewis, LB, 1977; Terry Hoage, DB, 1982–83; and Tim Ruddy, OL, and Todd Peterson, K, 1992 . . . Heisman Trophy winners were Frank Sinkwich, HB, 1942; and Herschel Walker, RB, 1982 . . . Maxwell Award winners were Charley Trippi, HB, 1946; and Herschel Walker, RB, 1982 . . . Outland Trophy winner was Bill Stanfill, DT, 1968.

KENTUCKY (Wildcats; Blue and White)

NOTABLE TEAMS

1894 (5–2) **Won:** Georgetown (Ky.) 40–6, Miami (Ohio) 28–6 (1st meeting), Jeffersonville A.C. 64–0, Transylvania 44–0, Central U. 38–10. **Lost:** Cincinnati 32–4 (1st meeting), Centre 67–0. **Noteworthy:** won Kentucky Intercollegiate League title.
1898 (7–0) **Won:** Transylvania 18–0, Georgetown (Ky.) 28–0, Company H, 8th Mass. 59–0, Louisville A.C. 16–0, Centre 6–0, 160th Indiana 17–0, Newcastle A.C. 36–0. **Noteworthy:** Blanked foes 180–0 in 1st undefeated season. Coach was W.R. Bass.
1903 (7–1) **Won:** Cynthiana 39–0, Xavier (Ohio) 21–0 (1st meeting), Berea College 17–0, Kentucky Military 18–0, Miami (Ohio) 47–0, Georgetown (Ky.) 51–0, Marietta 11–5. **Lost:** Transylvania 17–0 in finale.
1904 (9–1) **Won:** Paris A.C. 28–0, Indiana 12–0 (1st meeting since 1893), Central U. 40–0, 81–0, Berea 42–0, Bethany (W.Va.) 6–0, Kentucky Military 11–0, Georgetown (Ky.) 35–0, Transylvania 21–4. **Lost:** Cincinnati 11–0. **Noteworthy:** 1st year under F.E. Schacht.
1907 (9–1–1) **Won:** Kentucky Wesleyan 17–0, Winchester A.C. 6–0, Louisville Manual Training School 30–0, Morris Harvey 29–0, Hanover 40–0, Maryville 5–2 (1st meeting), Georgetown (Ky.) 38–0, Centre 11–0, Transylvania 5–0. **Lost:** Vanderbilt 40–0. **Tied:** Tennessee 0–0.
1909 (9–1) **Won:** Kentucky Wesleyan 18–0, Berea 28–0, Illinois 6–2, Tennessee 17–0, Rose Poly (RPI) 43–0, Georgetown (Ky.) 22–6, St. Mary's College 29–0, Transylvania 77–0, Centre 15–6. **Lost:** N.C. State 15–6. **Noteworthy:** 1st year under E.R. Sweetland.
1910 (7–2) **Won:** Ohio U. 12–0, Maryville 12–5, North Carolina 11–0 (1st meeting), Kentucky Wesleyan 42–0, Georgetown (Ky.) 37–0, Tulane 10–3 (1st meeting), Tennessee 10–0 in 1st 7 games. **Lost:** St. Louis 9–0, unbeaten Centre 12–6.
1911 (7–3) **Won:** Maryville 13–0, Morris Harvey 12–0, Miami (Ohio) 12–0 (1st meeting since 1903), Lexington H.S. 17–0, Georgetown (Ky.) 18–0, Centre 8–5, Tennessee 12–0. **Lost:** Cincinnati 6–0 (1st

meeting since 1904), Vanderbilt 18–0, Transylvania 12–5. *Noteworthy:* only year under P.P. Douglas.
1912 (7–2) *Won:* Maryville 34–0, Marshall 13–6, Cincinnati 19–13, Louisville 41–0 (1st meeting), Hanover 64–0, Tennessee 13–6, YMI of Cincinnati 56–0. *Lost:* Miami (Ohio) 13–8 (1st in 6-game series dating to 1894), Virginia Military Institute (VMI) 3–2 (1st meeting since 1892). *Noteworthy:* Sweetland returned for final year as coach.
1913 (6–2) *Won:* Butler 21–7, Ohio Northern 21–0, Cincinnati 27–7, Earlham 28–10, Wilmington 33–0, Louisville 20–0. *Lost:* Illinois 21–0, Tennessee 13–7 (1st to Vols since 1908). *Noteworthy:* 1st year under Alpha Brumage.
1915 (6–1–1) *Won:* Butler 33–0, Earlham 54–13, Cincinnati 27–6, Louisville 15–0, Purdue 7–0, Tennessee 6–0 (1st homecoming). *Lost:* Mississippi St. 12–0. *Tied:* Sewanee 7–7 (1st meeting since 1908). *Stars:* B William Rodes, T C.C. Schrader. *Noteworthy:* 1st year under J.J. Tigert.
1916 (4–1–2) *Won:* Butler 39–3, Centre 68–0 (1st meeting since 1911), Cincinnati 32–0, Mississippi St. 13–3. *Lost:* Vanderbilt 45–0 (1st meeting since 1911). *Tied:* Sewanee 0–0, unbeaten Tennessee 0–0. *Star:* Rodes. *Noteworthy:* Tigert's last team.
1929 (6–1–1) *Won:* Maryville 40–0, Washington & Lee 20–6, Carson-Newman 58–0, Centre 33–0, Clemson 44–6, VMI 23–12. *Lost:* Alabama 24–13. *Tied:* unbeaten Tennessee 6–6.
1939 (6–2–1) *Won:* VMI 21–0, Vanderbilt 21–13 (1st in 17-game series dating to 1896), Oglethorpe 59–0, Georgia 13–6 (1st meeting), Xavier (Ohio) 21–0, West Virginia 13–6 (1st meeting since 1905). *Lost:* Georgia Tech 13–6, unbeaten, unscored-on Tennessee 19–0. *Tied:* Alabama 7–7. *Stars:* E Bill McCubbin, T John Eibner.
1946 (7–3) *Won:* Mississippi 20–7, Cincinnati 26–7, Xavier (Ohio) 70–0, Vanderbilt 10–7 (1st over Commodores in 5 games since 1939), Michigan St. 39–14, Marquette 35–0, West Virginia 13–0. *Lost:* unbeaten Georgia 28–13, Alabama 21–7, Tennessee 7–0. *Stars:* frosh HB Don "Dopey" Phelps (7 TDs), soph E Wallace "Wah Wah" Jones, C Jay Rhodemyre. *Noteworthy:* had one of nation's most-improved teams in 1st year under Paul "Bear" Bryant.
1947 (8–3) *Won:* Cincinnati 20–0, Xavier (Ohio) 20–7, Georgia 26–0 (1st over Bulldogs in 6 games since 1939), Vanderbilt 14–0, Michigan St. 7–6, West Virginia 15–6, Evansville 36–0. *Lost:* Mis-

sissippi 14–7, Alabama 13–0, Tennessee 13–6. *Stars:* Rhodemyre, T Wash Serini, G Leo Yarutis, Phelps (5 TDs, 20 pass rec for 224 yds). *Noteworthy:* made 1st postseason appearance, beating Villanova 24–14 in Great Lakes Bowl in Cleveland; Bill Boler scored 2 TDs (15-yd run and 49-yd pass int return), Jim Howe scored on 29-yd run, and QB George Blanda kicked 27-yd FG and 3 ex pts.
1949 (9–3) *Won:* Mississippi Southern 71–7, Louisiana St. (LSU) 19–0 (1st meeting), Mississippi 47–0, Georgia 25–0, The Citadel 44–0, Cincinnati 14–7, Xavier (Ohio) 21–7, Florida 35–0, Miami (Fla.) 21–6. *Lost:* Southern Methodist (SMU) 20–7, Tennessee 6–0. *Stars:* T Bob Gain, C Harry Ulinski, soph QB Babe Parilli (1,081 yds pass), E Al Bruno (12 pass rec for 224 yds), Bill Leskovar (722 yds and 5 TDs rush), Phelps (7 TDs), Jerry Claiborne (9 int). *Noteworthy:* Led nation in total defense and scoring defense (4.8-pt avg). Lost to Santa Clara 21–13 in Orange Bowl; scored TDs on 2-yd run by Wilbur Jamerson and 52-yd pass from Parilli (128 yds pass) to soph Emery Clark.
1950 (11–1) *Won:* North Texas St. 25–0, LSU 14–0, Mississippi 27–0, Dayton 40–0, Cincinnati 41–7, Villanova 34–7, Georgia Tech 28–14 (1st meeting since 1942), Florida 40–6, Mississippi St. 48–21 (1st meeting since 1944), North Dakota 83–0. *Lost:* Tennessee 7–0 in finale. *Stars:* Kentucky's 1st consensus All Americans—Outland Trophy-winner Gain and Parilli (1,627 yds and 23 TDs pass, 5 TDs rush)—along with Bruno (38 pass rec for 589 yds and 10 TDs), Leskovar (673 yds rush), Jamerson (12 TDs), E Ben Zaranka, C/LB Doug Moseley, Gs Bill Wannamaker and Pat James, P Dom Fucci (40.9-yd avg). *Noteworthy:* Won 1st SEC title. Upset unbeaten national champ Oklahoma 13–7 in Sugar Bowl; Gain and DE Walt Yowarski starred on defense, and Jamerson scored 2 TDs (22-yd pass from Parilli and 1-yd run).
1951 (8–4) *Won:* Tennessee Tech 72–13, Mississippi St. 27–0, Villanova 35–13, Florida 14–6, Miami (Fla.) 32–0, Tulane 37–0 (1st meeting since 1935, 1st over Green Wave in 5 games since 1910), George Washington 47–13. *Lost:* Texas 7–6, Mississippi 21–17, unbeaten Georgia Tech 13–7, unbeaten national champ Tennessee 28–0. *Stars:* Parilli (1,643 yds and 19 TDs pass), soph E Steve Meilinger (41 pass rec for 576 yds and 8 TDs), Tom Fillion (671 yds rush), Harry Jones (5 TDs, 62 pts),

Moseley (5 int), G Gene Donaldson, T Jim MacKenzie. *Noteworthy:* beat Texas Christian (TCU) 20–7 in Cotton Bowl; Parilli passed for 2 TDs (both to Clark) and Ed Hamilton scored on 3-yd run.
1953 (7–2–1) *Won:* Florida 26–13, Mississippi St. 32–13, Villanova 19–0, Rice 19–13, Vanderbilt 40–14 (1st meeting since 1948), Memphis St. 20–7, Tennessee 27–21 (1st over Vols in 18 games since 1935). *Lost:* Texas A&M 7–6, Mississippi 22–6 in 1st 2 games. *Tied:* LSU 6–6. *Stars:* Meilinger (18 pass rec for 308 yds, 838 all-purpose yds, 4 int), B Ralph Paolone (620 yds rush), soph QB Bob Hardy (5 TDs), G Ray Correll. *Noteworthy:* Bryant's last team.
1954 (7–3) *Won:* LSU 7–6, Auburn 21–14 (1st meeting since 1935), Georgia Tech 13–6, Villanova 28–3, Vanderbilt 19–7, Memphis St. 33–7, Tennessee 14–13. *Lost:* Maryland 20–0 (1st meeting since 1931), Mississippi 28–9, Florida 21–7. *Stars:* Hardy (1,009 yds total off), Es Bradley Mills and Howard Schnellenberger (19 pass rec for 254 yds). *Noteworthy:* 1st year under Blanton Collier.
1976 (9–3) *Won:* Oregon St. 38–13, West Virginia 14–10, Penn St. 22–6, Mississippi St. (by forfeit after losing 14–7), LSU 21–7, Vanderbilt 14–0, Florida 28–9, Tennessee 7–0 (1st over Vols since 1964). *Lost:* Kansas 37–16, Georgia 31–7, unbeaten Maryland 24–14. *Stars:* QB Derrick Ramsey (771 yds and 10 TDs rush, 1,430 yds total off), Chris Hill (606 yds rush), OT Warren Bryant, DE Art Still, soph LB Jim Kovach, Dave Hayden (5 int), DB Mike Siganos. *Noteworthy:* Got share of 2nd SEC title. Made 1st bowl appearance in 25 years, beating North Carolina 21–0 in Peach Bowl; TB

Rod Stewart ran for 104 yds and all 3 Kentucky TDs, and LB Mike Martin led defense.
1977 (10–1) *Won:* North Carolina 10–7, West Virginia 28–13, Penn St. 24–20, Mississippi St. 24–7, LSU 33–13, Georgia 33–0, Virginia Tech 32–0, Vanderbilt 28–6, Florida 14–7, Tennessee 21–17. *Lost:* Baylor 21–6. *Stars:* Ramsey (618 yds and 13 TDs rush, 1,510 yds total off), WR Dave Trosper (25 pass rec for 340 yds), OG Tom Dornbrook, Still, soph NG Richard Jaffe, DT Jerry Blanton, Martin, Siganos, DB Dallas Owens. *Noteworthy:* ineligible for SEC title and postseason play, on NCAA probation.
1984 (9–3) *Won:* Kent St. 42–0, Indiana 48–14, Tulane 30–26, Rutgers 27–14, Mississippi St. 17–13 (1st meeting since 1977), North Texas St. 31–7, Vanderbilt 27–18, Tennessee 17–2. *Lost:* LSU 36–10, Georgia 37–7, Florida 25–17. *Stars:* RB George Adams (1,085 yds and 13 TDs rush, 33 pass rec for 330 yds and 1 TD), soph QB Billy Ransdell (1,748 yds and 11 TDs pass), LB Cam Jacobs, DB/P Paul Calhoun (7 int, 44.6-yd punting avg). *Noteworthy:* beat Wisconsin 20–19 in Hall of Fame Bowl after trailing 16–7 at halftime; soph Marc Logan scored TDs on 9-yd run and 27-yd pass from Ransdell, and frosh K Joey Worley kicked 2 ex pts and FGs of 22 and 52 yds.

BOWL SUMMARY

Cotton 1–0; Great Lakes 1–0; Hall of Fame 1–1; Orange 0–1; Peach 1–0; Sugar 1–0.

BOWL RECORD (5–2)

Regular Season	Bowl	Score	Opponent	Record
1947 (7–3)	Great Lakes	24–14	Villanova	(6–2–1)
1949 (9–2)	Orange	13–21	Santa Clara	(7–2–1)
1950 (10–1)	Sugar	13–7	Oklahoma	(10–0)
1951 (7–4)	Cotton	20–7	TCU	(6–4)
1976 (7–4)	Peach	21–0	North Carolina	(9–2)
1983 (6–4–1)	Hall of Fame	16–20	West Virginia	(8–3)
1984 (8–3)	Hall of Fame	20–19	Wisconsin	(7–3–1)

CONFERENCE TITLES

Kentucky Intercollegiate League—1894. **Southeastern**—1950, 1976*.

TOP 20 AP AND UPI RANKING

1949	11	1951	15–17	1953	16–15	1977	6–U
1950	7–7	1952	20–19	1976	18–19	1984	19–19

MAJOR RIVALS

Kentucky has played at least 10 games with Alabama 1–30–1, Auburn 5–20–1, Central U. 4–10–1, Centre 11–18–1, Cincinnati 21–8–3, Clemson 7–3, Florida 17–26, Georgetown (Ky.) 23–1, Georgia 9–35–2, Georgia Tech 7–11–1, Indiana 8–14–1, Louisiana St. 11–31–1, Maryville 19–0–1, Mississippi 11–23–1, Mississippi St. 13–7, Miami (Ohio) 6–4–1, North Carolina 5–5, Sewanee 7–3–3, Tennessee 23–56–9, Transylvania 14–6–1, Tulane 9–6, Vanderbilt 29–32–4, Virginia Military Institute 12–4, Virginia Tech 11–6–2, Washington & Lee 9–7–2, West Virginia 11–8–1, Xavier (Ohio) 18–2. Record against SEC members met fewer than 10 times: Arkansas 1–0, South Carolina 2–1–1.

COACHES

Dean of Kentucky coaches is Fran Curci with record of 47–51–2 for 1973–81, including 1 SEC title and 1 bowl team. Winningest coach was Paul "Bear" Bryant with record of 60–23–5 for 1946–53, including 1 SEC title and 4 bowl teams (3 winners). Other top records for at least 3 years were by J. White Guyn, 17–7–1 for 1906–08; E.R. Sweetland, 23–5 for 1909–10 and 1912; W.J. Juneau, 13–10–2 for 1920–22; Harry Gamage, 32–25–5 for 1927–33; C.A. Wynne, 20–19 for 1934–37; Blanton Collier, 41–36–3 for 1954–61; and Jerry Claiborne, 41–46–3 for 1982–89 with 2 bowl teams.

MISCELLANEA

First game was victory over Transylvania in 1881 . . . highest score was over Wilmington 87–0 in 1914 . . . highest since W.W. II was over North Dakota 83–0 in 1950 . . . worst defeat was by St. Louis 82–0 in 1905 . . . worst defeats since W.W. II of 45–0 were by Tennessee in 1970 and Alabama in 1980 . . . highest against since W.W. II was by Indiana 58–30 in 1969 . . . longest win string of 12 in 1909–10 ended by St. Louis 9–0 . . . longest winless string of 11 and losing string of 8 in 1982 broken with win over Central Michigan 31–14 in 1983 opener . . . also had 8-game losing string in 1966–67 broken with win over West Virginia 22–7 . . . consensus All-Americans were Bob Gain, T, 1950; Babe Parilli, B, 1950–51; Lou Michaels, T, 1956–57; Sam Ball, T, 1965; and Art Still, DL, 1977 . . . Academic All-Americans were Tom Ranieri, LB, 1974; Mark Keene, C, and Jim Kovach, LB, 1978; and Ken Pietrowiak, C, 1985 . . . Outland Trophy winner was Bob Gain, T, 1950.

LOUISIANA STATE (Fighting Tigers; Purple and Gold)

NOTABLE TEAMS

1896 (6–0) **Won:** Centenary 46–0, Tulane 6–0, Mississippi 12–4, Texas 14–0 (1st meeting), Mississippi St. 52–0 (1st meeting), Southern A.C. 6–0. **Noteworthy:** outscored foes 136–4 under Allen Jeardeau in 2nd straight unbeaten season (following 3-game schedule in 1895).

1901 (5–1) **Won:** Louisiana Tech 57–0 (1st meeting), Mississippi 46–0, Tulane 11–0, New Orleans YMCA 38–0, Arkansas 15–0 (1st meeting). **Lost:** Auburn 28–0 (1st meeting). **Noteworthy:** 1st year under W.S. Borland.

1902 (6–1) **Won:** SW Louisiana 42–0 (1st meeting), Texas 5–0, Auburn 5–0, Mississippi 6–0, Mississippi St. 6–0 (1st meeting since 1896), Alabama 11–0 (1st meeting since 1895). **Lost:** Vanderbilt 27–5 (1st meeting).

1907 (7–3) **Won:** Louisiana Tech 28–0, Howard 57–0, Arkansas 17–12, Mississippi St. 23–11, Mississippi 23–0, Baylor 48–0 (1st meeting), Havana U. 56–0 (in Cuba). **Lost:** Texas 12–5, Texas A&M 11–5, Alabama 6–4. **Noteworthy:** 1st year under Edgar Wingard.

1908 (10–0) **Won:** New Orleans YMGC 41–0, New Orleans Jackson Branch 81–5, Texas A&M 26–0, Southwestern (Tenn.) 55–0, Auburn 10–2 (1st meeting since 1903), Mississippi St. 50–0, Baylor 89–0, Haskell 32–0, Louisiana Tech 22–0, Arkansas

36–4. *Star:* Doc Fenton (125 pts). *Noteworthy:* last year under Wingard.

1909 (6–2) *Won:* New Orleans Jackson Branch 70–0, Mississippi 10–0, Mississippi St. 15–0, Louisiana Tech 23–0, Transylvania 52–0, Alabama 12–6. *Lost:* Sewanee 15–6, unbeaten Arkansas 16–0 (1st in 5-game series dating to 1901).

1913 (6–1–2) *Won:* Louisiana Tech 20–2, SW Louisiana 26–0, Jefferson 45–6, Baylor 50–0, Arkansas 12–7 (1st over Razorbacks since 1908), Tulane 40–0. *Lost:* unbeaten Auburn 7–0. *Tied:* Mississippi St. 0–0, Texas A&M 7–7 (1st meeting since 1908). *Star:* L.H. "Dutch" Dupont (15 TDs). *Noteworthy:* last year under Pat Dwyer.

1915 (6–2) *Won:* Jefferson 42–0, Mississippi College 14–0, Mississippi 28–0, Mississippi St. 10–0 (1st over Bulldogs in 5 games since 1909), Arkansas 13–7, Tulane 12–0. *Lost:* unbeaten Georgia Tech 36–7 (1st meeting), Rice 6–0 (1st meeting).

1916 (7–1–2) *Won:* SW Louisiana 24–0, Jefferson 59–0, Texas A&M 13–0, Mississippi College 50–7, Arkansas 17–7, Mississippi St. 13–3, Mississippi 41–0. *Lost:* Sewanee 7–0. *Tied:* Rice 7–7, Tulane 14–14 in last 2 games. *Noteworthy:* last year under E.T. McDonald (co-coached by I.R. Pray and Dana X. Bible).

1919 (6–2) *Won:* SW Louisiana 39–0, Jefferson 38–0, Mississippi 13–0, Arkansas 20–0, Mississippi College 24–0, Tulane 27–6. *Lost:* Mississippi St. 6–0, Alabama 23–0 (1st meeting since 1909). *Noteworthy:* returned to competition after 1-year layoff during W.W.I.

1921 (6–1–1) *Won:* NW Louisiana 78–0, Texas A&M 6–0, Spring Hill 41–7, Arkansas 10–7, Mississippi 21–0, Mississippi St. 17–14. *Lost:* Tulane 21–0. *Tied:* Alabama 7–7. *Noteworthy:* last year under Branch Bocock.

1928 (6–2–1) *Won:* SW Louisiana 46–0, Louisiana College 41–0, Mississippi St. 31–0, Spring Hill 30–7, Mississippi 19–6, Georgia 13–12 (1st meeting). *Lost:* Arkansas 7–0, Alabama 13–0. *Tied:* Tulane 0–0. *Star:* QB Hank Stovall. *Noteworthy:* 1st year under Russ Cohen.

1933 (7–0–3) *Won:* Rice 13–0, Millsaps 40–0, Arkansas 20–0, South Carolina 30–7, Mississippi 31–0 (1st SEC win), Mississippi St. 21–6, Tennessee 7–0 (1st meeting since 1926). *Tied:* unbeaten Centenary 0–0, Vanderbilt 7–7 (1st meeting since 1910), Tulane 7–7. *Stars:* T Jack Torrance, C John Kent. *Noteworthy:* 1st undefeated season since 1908.

1934 (7–2–2) *Won:* Auburn 20–6 (1st meeting since 1927), Arkansas 16–0, Vanderbilt 29–0, Mississippi St. 25–3, George Washington 6–0, Mississippi 14–0, Oregon 14–13. *Lost:* Tulane 13–12, Tennessee 19–13 in successive late games. *Tied:* Rice 9–9, Southern Methodist (SMU) 14–14 in 1st 2 games. *Stars:* Bs Abe Mickal and Walter Sullivan (6 TDs), T Justin Rukas. *Noteworthy:* last year under "Biff" Jones.

1935 (9–2) *Won:* Texas 18–6 (1st meeting since 1910), Manhattan 32–0, Arkansas 13–7, Vanderbilt 7–2, Auburn 6–0, Mississippi St. 28–13, Georgia 13–0 (1st meeting since 1928), SW Louisiana 56–0, Tulane 41–0. *Lost:* Rice 10–7 in opener. *Stars:* E Gaynell Tinsley (Tigers' 1st consensus All-American), C Marvin Stewart, Rukas, Mickal, Bs Jesse Fatherree and Bill Crass (6 TDs). *Noteworthy:* Won 1st SEC title in 1st year under Bernie Moore. Made 1st postseason appearance, losing to Texas Christian (TCU) 3–2 in muddy Sugar Bowl.

1936 (9–1–1) *Won:* Rice 20–7, Georgia 47–7, Mississippi 13–0, Arkansas 19–7, Vanderbilt 19–0, Mississippi St. 12–0, Auburn 19–6, SW Louisiana 93–0, Tulane 33–0. *Tied:* Texas 6–6 in 2nd game. *Stars:* Tinsley (48 pts), Stewart, G Wardell Leisk, B Pat Coffee. *Noteworthy:* Repeated as SEC champ. Lost to Santa Clara 21–14 in Sugar Bowl, dropping behind 14–0 in 1st quarter.

1937 (9–2) *Won:* Florida 19–0 (1st meeting), Texas 9–0, Rice 13–0, Mississippi 13–0, Loyola (La.) 52–6, Mississippi St. 41–0, Auburn 9–7, NW Louisiana 52–0 (1st meeting since 1926), Tulane 20–0. *Lost:* Vanderbilt 7–6. *Stars:* T Eddie Gatto, soph E Ken Kavanaugh (11 pass rec for 310 yds, 5 TDs), Bs Pinky Rohm (9 TDs), Jabbo Stell (9 TDs) and Young Bussey (1,083 yds total off). *Noteworthy:* lost to unbeaten Santa Clara 6–0 in Sugar Bowl.

1942 (7–3) *Won:* NW Louisiana 40–0, Texas A&M 16–7 (1st meeting since 1923), Mississippi St. 16–6, Mississippi 21–7 (1st over Rebels since 1937), Georgia Navy 34–0, Fordham 26–13, Tulane 18–6. *Lost:* Rice 27–14, Tennessee 26–0, Auburn 25–7. *Stars:* Alvin Dark (989 yds total off), Jim McLeod (15 pass rec for 278 yds), B Walter Gorinski (6 TDs).

1943 (6–3) *Won:* Georgia 34–27, 27–6 (1st meetings since 1936), Rice 20–7, Louisiana Army 28–7, TCU 14–0. *Lost:* Texas A&M 28–13, Georgia Tech 42–7 (1st meeting since 1927), Tulane 27–0. *Stars:* B Steve Van Buren (847 yds rush, nation's leader with 98 pts on 14 TDs), T Joe Hartley, G Carl Janneck, E Charles Webb. *Noteworthy:* beat Texas A&M 19–14 in rematch in Orange Bowl as

Van Buren ran and passed for 2 TDs in 1st quarter and ran 63 yds for winning TD in 3rd period. **1945** (7–2) *Won:* Rice 42–0, Texas A&M 31–12, Georgia 32–0, Vanderbilt 39–7, Mississippi 32–13, Georgia Tech 9–7 (1st in 6-game series dating to 1915), Tulane 33–0. *Lost:* unbeaten Alabama 26–7, Mississippi St. 27–20. *Stars:* FB Gene Knight (667 yds rush, 51 pts), G Felix Trapani, E Clyde Lindsey.

1946 (9–1–1) *Won:* Rice 7–6, Mississippi St. 13–6, Texas A&M 33–9, Vanderbilt 14–0, Mississippi 34–21, Alabama 31–21 (1st over Tide in 13 games since 1909), Miami (Fla.) 20–7 (1st meeting), Fordham 40–0, Tulane 41–27. *Lost:* Georgia Tech 26–7. *Stars:* QB Y.A. Tittle (780 yds and 13 TDs pass), Lindsey, HB Al Heroman (5 TDs), Gs Fred Hall and soph Wren Worley, T Ed Champagne. *Noteworthy:* tied Arkansas 0–0 in Cotton Bowl in rain, sleet, and snow; Tigers had edge of 15–1 in 1st downs and 271–54 in total yds.

1949 (8–3) *Won:* Rice 14–7, Texas A&M 34–0, North Carolina 13–7, Mississippi 34–7, Vanderbilt 33–13, Mississippi St. 34–7, SE Louisiana 48–7, Tulane 21–0. *Lost:* Kentucky 19–0 (1st meeting), Georgia 7–0 in early games. *Stars:* QB Carroll Griffith, E Sam Lyle (20 pass rec for 268 yds), FB Zollie Toth, G Allen Hover, T Ray Collins. *Noteworthy:* lost to unbeaten Oklahoma 35–0 in Sugar Bowl, gaining only 38 yds rush.

1958 (11–0) *Won:* Rice 26–6, Alabama 13–3, Hardin-Simmons 20–6, Miami (Fla.) 41–0 (1st meeting since 1946), Kentucky 32–7, Florida 10–7, Mississippi 14–0 (1st over Rebels since 1950), Duke 50–18, Mississippi St. 7–6, Tulane 62–0. *Stars:* HBs Billy Cannon (686 yds rush, 11 TDs, 74 pts) and Johnny Robinson (16 pass rec for 235 yds), QB Warren Rabb, FB J.W. Brodnax, E Billy Hendrix, C Max Fugler, soph T/C Charles Strange. *Noteworthy:* Won 3rd SEC title in 1st unbeaten season since 1936. Beat Clemson 7–0 in Sugar Bowl to earn share of 1st national championship; scored on 9-yd pass from Cannon to soph E Mickey Mangham in 3rd quarter.

1959 (9–2) *Won:* Rice 26–3, TCU 10–0, Baylor 22–0, Miami (Fla.) 27–3, Kentucky 9–0, Florida 9–0, Mississippi 7–3, Mississippi St. 27–0, Tulane 14–6. *Lost:* Tennessee 14–13 (1st meeting since 1953, 10th straight loss to Vols). *Stars:* Heisman Trophy–winner Cannon (598 yds rush, 11 pass rec for 161 yds, 7 TDs, 39.9-yd punting avg, 4 int),

Rabb, Robinson, Mangham, Strange. *Noteworthy:* lost to Mississippi 21–0 in Sugar Bowl rematch, failing to get past Rebel 38-yd line.

1961 (10–1) *Won:* Texas A&M 16–7, Georgia Tech 10–0, South Carolina 42–0, Kentucky 24–14, Florida 23–0, Mississippi 10–7, North Carolina 30–0, Mississippi St. 14–6, Tulane 62–0. *Lost:* Rice 16–3 in opener. *Stars:* HBs Wendell Harris (94 pts) and Jerry Stovall (405 yds rush, 9 pass rec for 135 yds), FB Earl Gross, Gs Roy Winston and Monk Gillot, T Billy Joe Booth. *Noteworthy:* Earned share of 4th SEC title in last year under Paul Dietzel. Beat Colorado 25–7 in Orange Bowl on TDs by Charley White Cranford, Jimmy Field, and Gene Sykes, and 30-yd FG by Harris.

1962 (9–1–1) *Won:* Texas A&M 21–0, Georgia Tech 10–7, Miami (Fla.) 17–3, Kentucky 7–0, Florida 23–0, TCU 5–0, Mississippi St. 28–0, Tulane 38–3. *Lost:* unbeaten Mississippi 15–7. *Tied:* Rice 6–6. *Stars:* Stovall (368 yds rush, 9 pass rec for 203 yds, 11 TDs), T Fred Miller, G Robbie Hucklebridge, C Dennis Gaubatz. *Noteworthy:* Led nation in scoring defense (3.4-pt avg) in 1st year under Charles McClendon. Beat Texas 13–0 in Cotton Bowl; scored on 22-yd run by Field and 2 FGs by QB Lynn Amedee.

1963 (7–4) *Won:* Texas A&M 14–6, Georgia Tech 7–6, Miami (Fla.) 3–0, Kentucky 28–7, Florida 14–0, TCU 28–14, Tulane 20–0. *Lost:* Rice 21–12, unbeaten Mississippi 37–3, Mississippi St. 7–6 (1st to Bulldogs since 1957). *Stars:* FB Don Schwab (553 yds rush, 6 TDs), E Billy Truax, Hucklebridge. *Noteworthy:* lost to Baylor 14–7 in Bluebonnet Bowl, giving up both Bear TDs in last quarter; HB Buddy Soefker scored for Tigers on 8-yd run in 1st quarter.

1964 (8–2–1) *Won:* Texas A&M 9–6, Rice 3–0, North Carolina 20–3, Kentucky 27–7, Mississippi 11–10, Mississippi St. 14–10, Tulane 13–3. *Lost:* unbeaten national cochamp Alabama 17–9 (1st meeting since 1958), Florida 20–6. *Tied:* Tennessee 3–3 (1st meeting since 1959). *Stars:* Schwab (583 yds rush), FL Doug Moreau (33 pass rec for 391 yds, 73 pts, nation's leader with 13 FGs), T Remi Prudhomme, C Richard Granier, DT George Rice, LB Mike Vincent. *Noteworthy:* beat Syracuse 13–10 in Sugar Bowl; Moreau scored on 57-yd pass from Billy Ezell and kicked 28-yd FG, and Rice tackled Syracuse runner for safety.

1965 (8–3) *Won:* Texas A&M 10–0, Rice 42–14,

Miami (Fla.) 34–27, Kentucky 31–21, South Carolina 21–7, Mississippi St. 37–20, Tulane 62–0 (10th straight over Green Wave). *Lost:* Florida 14–7, Mississippi 23–0, national cochamp Alabama 31–7. *Stars:* Moreau (29 pass rec for 468 yds, 59 pts), HB Joe Labruzzo (509 yds rush), Rice, T Dave McCormick. *Noteworthy:* upset unbeaten Arkansas 14–7 in Cotton Bowl; Labruzzo scored twice on short runs.

1967 (7–3–1) *Won:* Rice 20–14, Texas A&M 17–6, Florida 37–6, Kentucky 30–7, Mississippi St. 55–0, Tulane 41–27. *Lost:* Miami (Fla.) 17–15 (1st in 8-game series dating to 1946), Tennessee 17–14, Alabama 7–6. *Tied:* Mississippi 13–13. *Stars:* QB Nelson Stokley, TB Tommy Allen (535 yds rush), Tommy Morel (28 pass rec for 404 yds), soph FB/P Eddie Ray (42.8-yd punting avg), C Barry Wilson, DE John Garlington, LB Benny Griffin, DB Sammy Grezaffi. *Noteworthy:* beat undefeated Wyoming 20–13 in chilly, rainy Sugar Bowl; Stokley threw 2 TD passes (both to Morel) and soph Glenn Smith scored on 1-yd run.

1968 (8–3) *Won:* Texas A&M 13–12, Rice 21–7, Baylor 48–16, Kentucky 13–3, TCU 10–7, Mississippi St. 20–16, Tulane 34–10. *Lost:* Miami (Fla.) 30–0, Mississippi 27–24, Alabama 16–7. *Stars:* Morel (42 pass rec for 564 yds), T Bill Fortier, C Godfrey Zaunbrecher, soph LB Mike Anderson, DB Garry Kent. *Noteworthy:* beat Florida St. 31–27 (1st meeting) in rainy inaugural Peach Bowl, scoring winning TD on 2-yd run by Maurice LeBlanc with 2:39 left; QB Mike Hillman directed Tigers to winning rally in 2nd half.

1969 (9–1) *Won:* Texas A&M 35–6, Rice 42–0, Baylor 63–8, Miami (Fla.) 20–0, Kentucky 37–10, Auburn 21–20 (1st meeting since 1942), Alabama 20–15 (1st over Tide in 6 games since 1958), Mississippi St. 61–6, Tulane 27–0. *Lost:* Mississippi 26–23. *Stars:* LB George Bevan, soph DB Tommy Casanova, Hillman (1,180 yds pass), Lonny Myles (43 pass rec for 559 yds), Ray (591 yds rush), Zaunbrecher, K Mark Lumpkin. *Noteworthy:* led nation in rush defense.

1970 (9–3) *Won:* Rice 24–0, Baylor 31–10, Pacific 34–0, Kentucky 14–7 (10th straight over Wildcats), Auburn 17–9, Alabama 14–9, Mississippi St. 38–7, Tulane 26–14 (15th straight over Green Wave), Mississippi 61–17 (1st over Rebels since 1964). *Lost:* Texas A&M 20–18 (1st to Aggies in 11 games since 1956), Notre Dame 3–0 (1st meeting). *Stars:*

QB Buddy Lee (1,162 yds pass), FL Andy Hamilton (39 pass rec for 870 yds and 6 TDs), TB Art Cantrelle (892 yds rush), G Mike Demarie, DTs John Sage and Ronnie Estay, Anderson, Casanova, DB Craig Burns (8 int). *Noteworthy:* Led nation in rush defense and won 5th SEC title. Lost to unbeaten national cochamp Nebraska 17–12 in Orange Bowl; soph QB Bert Jones passed for 182 yds and Tigers scored on 31-yd pass from Lee to Al Coffee and 2 FGs by Lumpkin.

1971 (9–3) *Won:* Texas A&M 37–0, Wisconsin 38–28, Rice 38–3, Florida 48–7, Kentucky 17–13, Mississippi St. 28–3, Notre Dame 28–8, Tulane 36–7. *Lost:* Colorado 31–21, Mississippi 24–22, unbeaten Alabama 14–7. *Stars:* Jones (945 yds and 9 TDs pass), Hamilton (45 pass rec for 854 yds and 9 TDs), TE Jay Michaelson (72 pts), Cantrelle (649 yds rush), Demarie, Estay, Casanova. *Noteworthy:* beat Iowa St. 33–15 in Sun Bowl; Jones passed for 227 yds and 3 TDs and scored another, Hamilton had 6 pass rec (one for TD), and Michaelson caught TD pass and kicked 2 FGs.

1972 (9–2–1) *Won:* Pacific 31–13, Texas A&M 42–17, Wisconsin 27–7, Rice 12–6, Auburn 35–7, Kentucky 10–0, Mississippi 17–16, Mississippi St. 28–14, Tulane 9–3. *Lost:* Alabama 35–21. *Tied:* Florida 3–3. *Stars:* Jones (1,446 yds and 14 TDs pass), SE Gerald Keigley (27 pass rec for 433 yds and 7 TDs), soph TE Brad Boyd, Chris Dantin (707 yds rush), G Tyler Lafauci, DT John Wood, LB Warren Capone, soph DB Mike Williams. *Noteworthy:* lost to Tennessee 24–17 (1st meeting since 1967) in Astro-Bluebonnet Bowl after trailing 24–3 at halftime; Tiger TDs came on runs by Jones and soph TB Brad Davis.

1973 (9–3) *Won:* Colorado 17–6, Texas A&M 28–23, Rice 24–9, Florida 24–3, Auburn 20–6, Kentucky 28–21, South Carolina 33–29 (1st meeting since 1966), Mississippi 51–14, Mississippi St. 26–7 (10th straight over Bulldogs). *Lost:* unbeaten national cochamp Alabama 21–7, Tulane 14–0 (1st to Green Wave since 1948) in last 2 games. *Stars:* QB Mike Miley, Davis (904 yds rush), Boyd (16 pass rec for 259 yds), Lafauci, T Richard Brooks, DE Binks Miciotto, LB Bo Harris, Capone, Williams. *Noteworthy:* lost to unbeaten Penn St. 16–9 in Orange Bowl; scored TD on 3-yd run by Steve Rogers.

1977 (8–4) *Won:* Rice 77–0, Florida 36–14, Vanderbilt 28–15, Oregon 56–17, Mississippi 28–21, Mississippi St. 27–24, Tulane 20–17, Wyoming

66–17. *Lost:* Indiana 24–21, Kentucky 33–13, Alabama 24–3. *Stars:* TB Charles Alexander (1,686 yds and 17 TDs rush, 104 pts), soph QB Steve Ensminger, soph SE Carlos Carson (23 pass rec for 552 yds and 10 TDs), B Kelly Simmons, OT Robert Dugas, G Craig Duhe, soph DE John Adams, LB Steve Ripple. *Noteworthy:* lost to Stanford 24–14 in Sun Bowl; Alexander ran for 197 yds and a TD.

1978 (8–4) *Won:* Indiana 24–17, Wake Forest 13–11, Rice 37–7, Florida 34–21, Kentucky 21–0, Mississippi 30–8, Tulane 40–21, Wyoming 24–17. *Lost:* Georgia 24–17 (1st meeting since 1953), national cochamp Alabama 31–10, Mississippi St. 16–14. *Stars:* Alexander (1,172 yds and 14 TDs rush, 28 pass rec for 263 yds and 2 TDs, 98 pts), QB David Woodley, Mike Quintela (30 pass rec for 352 yds), Dugas, C Jay Whitley, soph DE Lyman White, Adams, DTs Kent Broha and soph George Atiyeh, DBs Willie Teal and soph Chris Williams (8 int). *Noteworthy:* lost to Missouri 20–15 in Liberty Bowl after trailing 20–3 at halftime; Alexander ran for 133 yds and a TD, and Woodley passed for 123 yds and ran for a TD.

1982 (8–3–1) *Won:* Oregon St. 45–7, Rice 52–13, Florida 24–13, Kentucky 34–10, South Carolina 14–6, Mississippi 45–8, Alabama 20–10 (1st over Tide since 1970), Florida St. 55–21. *Lost:* Mississippi St. 27–24, Tulane 31–28 in late games. *Tied:* Tennessee 24–24 (1st meeting since 1975). *Stars:* QB Alan Risher (1,834 yds and 17 TDs pass), soph SE Eric Martin (45 pass rec for 817 yds and 7 TDs), TE Malcolm Scott, frosh TB Dalton Hilliard (901 yds rush, 16 TDs), soph OT Lance Smith, NG Ramsey Dardar, DT Leonard Marshall, LBs Al Richardson and Lawrence Williams, DB James Britt. *Noteworthy:* lost to Nebraska 21–20 in Orange Bowl after leading 17–7 in 3rd period; Hilliard ran for 2 TDs and K Juan Carlos Betanzos had FGs of 28 and 49 yds.

1984 (8–3–1) *Won:* Wichita St. 47–7, Arizona 27–26, Southern California (USC) 23–3, Vanderbilt 34–27 (1st meeting since 1977), Kentucky 36–10, Mississippi 32–29, Alabama 16–14, Tulane 33–15. *Lost:* Notre Dame 30–22, Mississippi St. 16–14. *Tied:* Florida 21–21. *Stars:* Hilliard (1,268 yds rush, 14 TDs, 1,615 all-purpose yds), QB Jeff Wickersham (2,165 yds and 12 TDs pass), Martin (47 pass rec for 668 yds), Smith, LBs Shawn Burks and soph Michael Brooks, DBs Jeffery Dale and

Liffort Hobley (6 int). *Noteworthy:* 1st year under Bill Arnsparger. Lost to Nebraska 28–10 in Sugar Bowl after jumping to 10–0 lead on FG by Ronnie Lewis and TD by Hilliard (who ran for 86 yds despite flu).

1985 (9–2–1) *Won:* North Carolina 23–13, Colorado St. 17–3, Vanderbilt 49–7, Kentucky 10–0, Mississippi 14–0, Mississippi St. 17–15, Notre Dame 10–7, Tulane 31–19, East Carolina 35–15. *Lost:* Florida 20–0. *Tied:* Alabama 14–14. *Stars:* Hilliard (1,134 yds rush, 14 TDs, 1,447 all-purpose yds), Wickersham (2,145 yds pass), TB Garry James (50 pass rec for 414 yds), soph WR Wendell Davis (31 pass rec for 471 yds), OT Curt Gore, Burks, Brooks, DEs Roland Barbay and Karl Wilson, DB Norman Jefferson. *Noteworthy:* lost to Baylor 21–7 in Liberty Bowl; scored first on 79-yd punt return by Jefferson.

1986 (9–3) *Won:* Texas A&M 35–17 (1st meeting since 1975), Florida 28–17, Georgia 23–14 (1st meeting since 1979), Kentucky 25–16, North Carolina 30–3, Alabama 14–10, Mississippi St. 47–0, Notre Dame 21–19, Tulane 37–17. *Lost:* Miami (Ohio) 21–12, Mississippi 21–19. *Stars:* frosh QB Tommy Hodson (2,261 yds and 19 TDs pass), Davis (80 pass rec for 1,244 yds and 11 TDs), frosh TB Harvey Williams (700 yds and 6 TDs rush), TE Brian Kinchen, OG Eric Andolsek, OT John Hazard, frosh K David Browndyke (14 FGs), NG Henry Thomas, Barbay, Wilson, LB Toby Caston. *Noteworthy:* Won 6th SEC title in last year under Arnsparger. Lost to Nebraska 30–15 in Sugar Bowl; scored on TDs by Williams and FL Tony Moss (24-yd pass from Hodson), and 2-pt conversion pass from Hodson to frosh TB Alvin Lee.

1987 (10–1–1) *Won:* Texas A&M 17–3, Cal St.-Fullerton 56–12, Rice 49–16, Florida 13–10, Georgia 26–23, Kentucky 34–9, Mississippi 42–13, Mississippi St. 34–14, Tulane 41–36. *Lost:* Alabama 22–10. *Tied:* Ohio St. 13–13. *Stars:* Hodson (2,125 yds and 15 TDs pass), Davis (72 pass rec for 993 yds and 7 TDs), Williams (1,001 yds and 11 TDs rush, 20 pass rec for 188 yds and 1 TD), soph FB Victor Jones (7 TDs rush), soph TB Eddie Fuller (5 TDs), C Nacho Albergamo, Andolsek, Kinchen, Browndyke (14 FGs, 83 pts), NG Darrell Phillips, LBs Nicky Hazard and Ron Sancho, DB Greg Jackson, P Matt DeFrank (41.6-yd avg). *Noteworthy:* 1st year under Mike Archer. Beat South Carolina 30–13 in Gator Bowl; Hodson passed for 224 yds and 3 TDs, and Davis caught 9 for 132 yds and 3 TDs.

1988 (8–4) *Won:* Texas A&M 27–0, Tennessee 34–9 (1st meeting since 1983), Auburn 7–6 (1st meeting since 1981), Kentucky 15–12, Mississippi 31–20, Alabama 19–18 (1st meeting since 1981), Mississippi St. 20–3, Tulane 44–14. *Lost:* Ohio St. 36–33, Florida 19–6, Miami (Fla.) 44–3 (1st meeting since 1969). *Stars:* Hodson (2,074 yds and 13 TDs pass), WR Tony Moss (55 pass rec for 957 yds and 6 TDs), SE Lee (40 pass rec for 537 yds), Fuller (32 pass rec for 375 yds and 5 TDs, 647 yds and 2 TDs rush), Browndyke (19 FGs, 77 pts), OT Ralph Norwood, Phillips, Sancho, LBs Verge Ausberry and Eric Hill, Jackson (7 int, 2 returned for TDs), P Rene Bourgeois (41.9-yd avg). *Noteworthy:* Got share of 7th SEC title. Lost to Syracuse 23–10 in Hall of Fame Bowl; Hodson passed for 192 yds and Tigers scored on 19-yd run by soph TB Calvin Windom and ex pt and 35-yd FG by Browndyke.

BOWL SUMMARY

Bluebonnet 0–2; Cotton 2–0–1; Gator 1–0; Hall of Fame 0–1; Liberty 0–2; Orange 2–3; Peach 1–0; Sugar 3–7; Sun 1–1; Tangerine 1–0.

BOWL RECORD (11–16–1)

Regular Season	Bowl	Score	Opponent	Record
1935 (9–1)	Sugar	2–3	TCU	(11–1)
1936 (9–0–1)	Sugar	14–21	Santa Clara	(8–1)
1937 (9–1)	Sugar	0–6	Santa Clara	(8–0)
1943 (5–3)	Orange	19–14	Texas A&M	(7–1–1)
1946 (9–1)	Cotton	0–0	Arkansas	(6–3–1)
1949 (8–2)	Sugar	0–35	Oklahoma	(10–0)
1958 (10–0)	Sugar	7–0	Clemson	(8–2)
1959 (9–1)	Sugar	0–21	Mississippi	(9–1)
1961 (9–1)	Orange	25–7	Colorado	(9–1)
1962 (8–1–1)	Cotton	13–0	Texas	(9–0–1)
1963 (7–3)	Bluebonnet	7–14	Baylor	(7–3)
1964 (7–2–1)	Sugar	13–10	Syracuse	(7–3)
1965 (7–3)	Cotton	14–7	Arkansas	(10–0)
1967 (6–3–1)	Sugar	20–13	Wyoming	(10–0)
1968 (7–3)	Peach	31–27	Florida State	(8–2)
1970 (9–2)	Orange	12–17	Nebraska	(10–0–1)
1971 (8–3)	Sun	33–25	Iowa State	(8–3)
1972 (9–1–1)	Bluebonnet	17–24	Tennessee	(9–2)
1973 (9–2)	Orange	9–16	Penn State	(11–0)
1977 (8–3)	Sun	14–24	Stanford	(8–3)
1978 (8–3)	Liberty	15–20	Missouri	(7–4)
1979 (6–5)	Tangerine	34–10	Wake Forest	(8–3)
1982 (8–2–1)	Orange	20–21	Nebraska	(11–1)
1984 (8–2–1)	Sugar	10–28	Nebraska	(9–2)
1985 (9–1–1)	Liberty	7–21	Baylor	(8–3)
1986 (9–2)	Sugar	15–30	Nebraska	(9–2)
1987 (9–1–1)	Gator	30–13	South Carolina	(8–3)
1988 (8–3)	Hall of Fame	10–23	Syracuse	(9–2)

CONFERENCE TITLES

Southern — 1932. **Southeastern** — 1935, 1936, 1958, 1961*, 1970, 1986, 1988*.

TOP 20 AP AND UPI RANKING

1936	2	1959	3–3	1970	7–6	1984	15–16
1937	8	1961	4–3	1971	11–10	1985	20–20
1945	15	1962	7–8	1972	11–10	1986	10–11
1946	8	1964	7–7	1973	13–14	1987	5–5
1949	9	1965	8–14	1982	11–11	1988	19–U
1958	1–1	1969	10–7				

MAJOR RIVALS

LSU has played at least 10 games with Alabama 14–37–5, Arkansas 23–13–2, Auburn 15–11–1, Baylor 8–3, Florida 18–18–3, Georgia 12–7–1, Georgia Tech 5–12, Kentucky 31–11–1, Louisiana Tech 15–1, Miami (Fla.) 8–3, Mississippi 45–32–4, Mississippi College 9–0–1, Mississippi St. 51–32–3, NW Louisiana 10–0, Rice 36–13–5, South Carolina 12–1, SW Louisiana 19–0, Tennessee 3–17–3, Texas 7–8–1, Texas A&M 26–17–3, Tulane 61–22–7, Vanderbilt 16–7–1.

COACHES

Dean of LSU coaches is Charles McClendon (1970 national Coach of Year) with record of 137–59–7 for 1962–79, including 1 SEC title and 13 bowl teams. Other top records for at least 3 years were by W.S. Borland, 15–7 for 1901–03; James K. "Pat" Dwyer, 16–7–2 for 1911–13; E.T. McDonald, 14–7–1 for 1914–16; Irving R. Pray, 11–9 for 1916, 1919, and 1922; Mike Donahue, 23–19–3 for 1923–27; Russ Cohen, 23–13–1 for 1928–31; Lawrence M. "Biff" Jones, 20–5–6 for 1932–34 with 1 SC title and 1 unbeaten team; Bernie H. Moore, 83–39–6 for 1935–47 with 2 SEC titles, 5 bowl teams, and 1 team unbeaten in regular season; Gaynell "Gus" Tinsley, 35–34–6 for 1948–54 with 1 Sugar Bowl team; Paul Dietzel (1958 national Coach of Year), 46–24–3 for 1955–61 with 2 SEC titles, 3 bowl teams, and 1 unbeaten national champion; Jerry Stovall, 22–21–2 for 1980–83 with 1 Orange Bowl team; Bill Arnsparger, 26–8–2 for 1984–86 with 1 SEC title and 3 bowl teams; and Mike Archer, 27–18–1 for 1987–90 with 1 SEC title and 2 bowl teams.

MISCELLANEA

First game was loss to Tulane 34–0 in 1893 . . . 1st win was over Natchez A.C. 36–0 in 1894 . . . 1st win over college foe was over Centenary 30–0 in 1894 . . . highest score was over SW Louisiana 93–0 in 1936 . . . highest since W.W. II was over Rice 77–0 in 1977 . . . worst defeat was by Texas A&M 63–9 in 1914 . . . worst since W.W. II was by Tulane 46–0 in 1948 . . . highest against since W.W. II was by Mississippi 55–31 in 1980 . . . longest win streak of 19 in 1957–59 ended by Tennessee 13–12 . . . 16-game unbeaten string in 1961–62 ended by Mississippi 15–7 . . . 15-game win streak in 1907–09 ended by Sewanee 15–6 . . . longest losing string of 7 in 1992 broken with win over Tulane 24–12 . . . longest winless string of 7 in 1955–56 broken with win over Oklahoma St. 13–0 . . . consensus All-Americans were Gaynell Tinsley, E, 1935–36; Ken Kavanaugh, E, 1939; Sid Fournet, T, 1954; Billy Cannon, B, 1958–59; Roy Winston, G, 1961; Jerry Stovall, B, 1962; Mike Anderson, LB, 1970; Tommy Casanova, DB, 1970–71; Bert Jones, QB, 1972; Charles Alexander, RB, 1977–78; and Wendell Davis, WR, and Nacho Albergamo, C, 1987 . . . Academic All-Americans were Mickey Mangham, E, 1959; Charles "Bo" Strange, C, 1960; Billy Booth, T, 1961; Jay Michaelson, K, 1971; Tyler Lafauci, OG, and Joe Winkler, DB, 1973; Brad Davis, RB, 1974; Rogert Dugas, OT, 1977; and Juan Carlos Betanzos, K, 1984 . . . Heisman Trophy winner was Billy Cannon, HB, 1959.

MISSISSIPPI (Rebels; Cardinal Red and Navy Blue)

NOTABLE TEAMS

1893 (4–1) *Won:* Southwest Baptist University (Union) 56–0, 36–0, Memphis A.C. 16–0, Tulane

12–4. *Lost:* Southern A.C. 24–0. *Noteworthy:* 1st varsity season.

1894 (6–1) *Won:* St. Thomas Hall 62–0, Alabama 6–0 (1st meeting), Memphis A.C. 12–0, Tulane 8–2, Southern A.C. 6–0 (forfeit), Louisiana State (LSU) 26–6 (1st meeting). *Lost:* Vanderbilt 40–0 (1st meeting). *Star:* FB William Henry Cook.

1910 (7–1) *Won:* Memphis H.S. 10–0, Memphis Medical 2–0, 44–0, Tulane 16–0, Mississippi College 24–0, Alabama 16–0 (1st over Tide in 6 games since 1894), Mississippi St. 30–0. *Lost:* unbeaten Vanderbilt 9–2. *Star:* HB John McCall.

1935 (9–3) *Won:* Millsaps 20–0, Memphis St. 92–0, Southwestern (Tenn.) 33–0, Sewanee 33–0, Florida 27–6, St. Louis 21–7, Centre 26–0, Centenary 6–0, Mississippi St. 14–6. *Lost:* Marquette 33–7, Tennessee 14–13. *Stars:* HB Rab Rodgers (10 TDs), FB Ray Hapes (12 TDs), T Bill Richardson. *Noteworthy:* made 1st postseason appearance, losing to Catholic U. 20–19 in Orange Bowl though leading in total yds 300–153; scored on 67-yd run by Ned Peters, 1-yd run by Dave Bernard, and 24-yd pass from Herb Baumsten to James "Buster" Poole.

1938 (9–2) *Won:* LSU 20–7 (1st over Tigers in 9 games since 1927), Louisiana Tech 27–7, Southern Mississippi 14–0, Centenary 47–14, George Washington 25–0, St. Louis 14–12, Sewanee 39–0, Arkansas 20–14, Mississippi St. 19–6. *Lost:* Vanderbilt 13–7 (1st meeting since 1930), unbeaten national cochamp Tennessee 47–0. *Stars:* HB/DB/P Parker Hall (7 int, 40.1-yd punting avg, 807 yds rush, nation's leader with 1,420 all-purpose yds and in scoring with 73 pts on 11 TDs and 7 ex pts), QB Kimble Bradley. *Noteworthy:* 1st year under Harry Mehre.

1939 (7–2) *Won:* LSU 14–7, Southwestern (Tenn.) 41–0, Centenary 34–0, St. Louis 42–0, Vanderbilt 14–7 (1st in 20-game series dating to 1894), Southern Mississippi 27–7, Memphis St. 46–7. *Lost:* unbeaten Tulane 18–6, Mississippi St. 18–6. *Stars:* soph TB Junie Hovious, QB Bill Schneller, soph FB Merle Hapes (5 int), C Winkey Autrey.

1940 (9–2) *Won:* Union 37–0, LSU 19–6, Southwestern (Tenn.) 27–6, Georgia 28–14 (1st meeting), Duquesne 14–6, Vanderbilt 13–7, Holy Cross 34–7, Memphis St. 38–7, Miami (Fla.) 21–7. *Lost:* Arkansas 21–20, unbeaten Mississippi St. 19–0. *Stars:* Hapes (718 yds and 10 TDs rush, 1,081 yds and 14 TDs total off, 48.7-yd punting

avg), Hovious (7 int, 65 pts, 1,031 yds and 11 TDs total off, nation's leader in punt returns with 15.1-yd avg).

1941 (6–2–1) *Won:* Southwestern (Tenn.) 27–0, Holy Cross 21–0, Tulane 20–13 (1st over Green Wave in 13 games since 1914), Marquette 12–6, LSU 13–12, Arkansas 18–0. *Lost:* Georgetown 16–6 (opener), Mississippi St. 6–0 (finale). *Tied:* Georgia 14–14. *Stars:* Hovious (943 yds total off, 5 int), Hapes (6 TDs, 44.7-yd punting avg), E Bill Eubanks, Gs Homer Hazel and Oscar Britt, T Chet Kozel.

1947 (9–2) *Won:* Kentucky 14–7, Florida 14–6, South Carolina 33–0 (1st meeting), Tulane 27–14 (1st meeting since 1941), LSU 20–18, Tennessee 43–13 (1st in 20-game series dating to 1902), Chattanooga 52–0, Mississippi St. 33–14. *Lost:* Vanderbilt 10–6, Arkansas 19–14. *Stars:* TB Charles Conerly (Rebels' 1st consensus All-American; 40.1-yd punting avg, 417 yds and 9 TDs rush, nation's leader with 1,367 yds and 18 TDs pass), E Barney Poole (nation's leader with 52 pass rec for 513 yds and 8 TDs), T Bill Erickson, soph Bobby Wilson (5 int). *Noteworthy:* Won 1st SEC title in 1st year under John Vaught. Beat Texas Christian (TCU) 13–9 in Delta Bowl; Conerly passed for 187 yds and 2 last-quarter TDs (to Joe Johnson and HB Dixie Howell) to overcome 9–0 halftime deficit.

1948 (8–1) *Won:* Florida 14–0, Kentucky 20–7, Vanderbilt 20–7, Boston College 32–13, LSU 49–19, Chattanooga 34–7, Tennessee 16–13, Mississippi St. 34–7. *Lost:* Tulane 20–7. *Stars:* Poole (18 pass rec for 253 yds), Howell (5 TDs), QB Farley Salmon, G Johnny Crawford, Wilson (5 int).

1952 (8–1–2) *Won:* Memphis St. 54–6 (10th straight over Tigers), Auburn 20–7, Tulane 20–14, Arkansas 34–7 (1st meeting since 1947), LSU 28–0, Houston 6–0 (1st meeting), Maryland 21–14, Mississippi St. 20–14. *Tied:* Kentucky 13–13, Vanderbilt 21–21. *Stars:* QB Jimmy Lear (975 yds pass, 231 yds rush), FB Harol Lofton (698 yds and 8 TDs rush), HB Wilson Dillard (621 yds and 8 TDs rush), T Kline Gilbert, Gs Crawford Mims and Jerry May, E James Mask, Jack Reed (5 int). *Noteworthy:* 1st undefeated season. Lost to unbeaten Georgia Tech 24–7 in Sugar Bowl after jumping off to 7–0 lead on 4-yd TD run by Dillard; Lear passed for 122 yds.

1953 (7–2–1) *Won:* Chattanooga 39–6, Kentucky 22–6, Vanderbilt 28–6, Tulane 45–14, Arkansas

28–0, LSU 27–16, North Texas St. 40–7. *Lost:* Auburn 13–0, unbeaten national cochamp Maryland 38–0. *Tied:* Mississippi St. 7–7. *Stars:* Mims, Lofton, FB Robert McCool (564 yds and 7 TDs rush), soph HB Earl Blair (7 TDs).

1954 (9–2) *Won:* North Texas St. 35–12, Kentucky 28–9, Villanova 52–0, Vanderbilt 22–7, Tulane 34–7, LSU 21–6, Memphis St. 51–0, Houston 26–0, Mississippi St. 14–0. *Lost:* Arkansas 6–0. *Stars:* QB Eagle Day (1,051 yds total off), McCool, HB Allen Muirhead (10 TDs), T Rex Reed Boggan, E Dave Dickerson. *Noteworthy:* Led nation in total defense and won 2nd SEC title. Lost to Navy 21–0 in Sugar Bowl; outgained 442–121 in total yds.

1955 (10–1) *Won:* Georgia 26–13 (1st meeting since 1942), North Texas St. 33–0, Vanderbilt 13–0, Tulane 27–13, Arkansas 17–7, LSU 29–26, Memphis St. 39–6, Houston 27–11, Mississippi St. 26–0. *Lost:* Kentucky 21–14. *Stars:* Day (952 yds and 10 TDs total off), FB/K Paige Cothren (6 TDs, 74 pts), HB Billy Kinard, G Buddy Alliston, C Gene Dubuisson, John Blalack (5 int). *Noteworthy:* Repeated as SEC champ. Beat TCU 14–13 in Cotton Bowl; Day passed for 137 yds, Cothren ran for 79 yds and a TD and kicked 2 ex pts, and soph HB Billy Lott scored on 5-yd run with 4:22 remaining.

1956 (7–3) *Won:* North Texas St. 45–0, Kentucky 37–7, Houston 14–0, Vanderbilt 16–0, LSU 46–17, Memphis St. 26–0, Mississippi St. 13–7. *Lost:* Tulane 10–3 (1st to Green Wave since 1950), Arkansas 14–0, unbeaten Tennessee 27–7 (1st meeting since 1951). *Stars:* Cothren (560 yds rush), QB Raymond Brown (8 TDs), T Billy Yelverton, C Jerry Stone, G Charles Duck.

1957 (9–1–1) *Won:* Trinity (Texas) 44–0, Kentucky 15–0, Hardin-Simmons 34–7, Vanderbilt 28–0, Tulane 50–0, Houston 20–7, LSU 14–12, Tennessee 14–7 (1st over Vols in 5 games since 1948). *Lost:* Arkansas 12–6 in mid-season. *Tied:* Mississippi St. 7–7 in finale. *Stars:* Brown (7 TDs), Lott, G Jackie Simpson, T Gene Hickerson, E Don Williams. *Noteworthy:* beat Texas 39–7 in Sugar Bowl; Brown ran for 157 yds and 2 TDs (including 92-yd run) and passed for a 3rd (to Williams), and soph QB Billy Brewer passed for a TD.

1958 (9–2) *Won:* Memphis St. 17–0, Kentucky 27–6, Trinity (Texas) 21–0, Tulane 19–8, Hardin-Simmons 24–0, Arkansas 14–12, Houston 56–7, Mississippi St. 21–0. *Lost:* unbeaten national cochamp LSU 14–0 (1st to Tigers since 1950), Ten-

nessee 18–16. *Stars:* QB Bobby Franklin (10 TDs pass, 6 TDs rush), FB Charlie Flowers (546 yds rush, 44.7-yd avg on 10 punts), E Larry Grantham. *Noteworthy:* beat Florida 7–3 (1st meeting since 1948) in Gator Bowl; scored on opening drive on 1-yd run by soph FB Jim Anderson (subbing for injured Flowers).

1959 (10–1) *Won:* Houston 16–0, Kentucky 16–0, Memphis St. 43–0 (15th straight over Tigers), Vanderbilt 33–0, Tulane 53–7, Arkansas 28–0, Chattanooga 58–0, Tennessee 37–7, Mississippi St. 42–0. *Lost:* LSU 7–3 in mid-season. *Stars:* Flowers (733 yds and 11 TDs rush), QB Jake Gibbs (755 yds and 6 TDs pass, 228 yds and 7 TDs rush), G Marvin Terrell, E Johnny Brewer, Grantham. *Noteworthy:* Led nation in scoring defense (2.1-pt avg). Beat LSU 21–0 in Sugar Bowl rematch; Franklin passed for 148 yds and two 2nd half TDs (to Grantham and HB George Blair), and Rebels scored in 1st half on 43-yd TD pass from Gibbs to HB James Lee "Cowboy" Woodruff.

1960 (10–0–1) *Won:* Houston 42–0, Kentucky 21–6, Memphis St. 31–20, Vanderbilt 26–0, Tulane 26–13, Arkansas 10–7, Chattanooga 45–0, Tennessee 24–3, Mississippi St. 35–9. *Tied:* LSU 6–6 in mid-season. *Stars:* Gibbs (970 yds and 12 TDs pass, 246 yds and 5 TDs rush), WB Bobby Crespino (30 pass rec for 408 yds), TB Anderson (7 TDs), Brewer, G Richard Price, T Bob Benton. *Noteworthy:* Won 4th SEC title. Beat Rice 14–6 in Sugar Bowl to earn share of 1st national title; Gibbs ran for Rebel TDs in 1st and 4th quarters.

1961 (9–2) *Won:* Arkansas 16–0, Kentucky 20–6, Florida St. 33–0, Houston 47–7, Tulane 41–0, Vanderbilt 47–0, Chattanooga 54–0, Tennessee 24–10, Mississippi St. 37–7. *Lost:* LSU 10–7. *Stars:* FB Billy Ray Adams (575 yds rush, 10 TDs), QB Doug Elmore (1,086 yds and 10 TDs total off), T Jim Dunaway, Gs Treva "Bookie" Bolin and Billy Ray Jones, E Ralph Smith. *Noteworthy:* Led nation in total off. Lost to Texas 12–7 in Cotton Bowl (breaking 5-bowl win streak); QB Glynn Griffing passed for 163 yds and a TD (20 yards to soph E Reed Davis).

1962 (10–0) *Won:* Memphis St. 21–7, Kentucky 14–0, Houston 40–7 (10th straight over Cougars), Tulane 21–0, Vanderbilt 35–0, LSU 15–7, Chattanooga 52–7, Tennessee 19–6, Mississippi St. 13–6. *Stars:* Griffing (11 TDs pass, 1,160 yds total off), WB Louis Guy (8 TDs), TB Chuck Morris, Dunaway,

G Don Dickson. *Noteworthy:* Led nation in total defense and won 5th SEC title. Beat Arkansas 17–13 in Sugar Bowl; Griffing passed for 242 yds and a TD (33 yards to Guy, who caught 5 for 107 yds) and ran for another, and soph Billy Irwin kicked 30-yd FG and 2 ex pts.

1963 (7–1–2) *Won:* Kentucky 31–7, Houston 20–6, Tulane 21–0, Vanderbilt 27–7 (10th straight over Commodores), LSU 37–3, Tampa 41–0, Tennessee 20–0. *Tied:* unbeaten Memphis St. 0–0 (opener), Mississippi St. 10–10 (finale). *Stars:* QB Perry Lee Dunn (946 yds and 11 TDs total off), C Kenny Dill, T Whaley Hall, soph G Stan Hindman, E Allen Brown, Jimmy Heidel (5 int), P Frank Lambert (41.2-yd avg). *Noteworthy:* Won 6th SEC title and led nation in rush defense and scoring defense (3.7-pt avg). Lost to Alabama 12–7 (1st meeting since 1944) in Sugar Bowl; Dunn passed for 125 yds and Rebel TD (5 yds to Larry Smith).

1966 (8–3) *Won:* Memphis St. 13–0, Kentucky 17–0, Southern Mississippi 14–7 (1st meeting since 1939), Houston 27–6, LSU 17–0, Tennessee 14–7, Vanderbilt 34–0, Mississippi St. 24–0. *Lost:* unbeaten Alabama 17–7, Georgia 9–3 (1st meeting since 1955) in consecutive early games. *Stars:* TB Doug Cunningham (653 yds and 5 TDs rush), FB Bobby Wade (599 yds rush), C Chuck Hinton, MG/K Jimmy Keyes (10 FGs), DE Jerry Richardson, DT Jim Urbanek, LB Lee Garner, Gerald Warfield (8 int). *Noteworthy:* lost to Texas 19–0 in Bluebonnet Bowl, losing ball 4 times on int.

1969 (8–3) *Won:* Memphis St. 28–3, Georgia 25–17, Southern Mississippi 69–7 (10th straight over Eagles), LSU 26–23, Chattanooga 21–0, Tennessee 38–0, Mississippi St. 48–22. *Lost:* Kentucky 10–9, Alabama 33–32, Houston 25–11. *Stars:* QB Archie Manning (1,762 yds and 9 TDs pass, 502 yds and 14 TDs rush), SEs Floyd Franks (54 pass rec for 720 yds) and Riley Myers (26 pass rec for 262 yds), soph TE Jim Poole Jr. (43 pass rec for 456 yds), OG Skip Jernigan, DE Hap Farber, DT Buz Morrow, MG Larry Thomas, DB Glenn Cannon (7 int), P Julian Fagan (41.5-yd avg). *Noteworthy:* beat Arkansas 27–22 (1st meeting since 1963 Sugar Bowl) in Sugar Bowl; Manning passed for 273 yds and a TD (30 yds to WB Vernon Studdard) and scored on 18-yd run, FB John Bowen scored on 69-yd run, and soph K Cloyce Hinton had FGs of 52 and 36 yds.

1970 (7–4) *Won:* Memphis St. 47–13, Kentucky 20–17, Alabama 48–23, Georgia 31–21, Vanderbilt 26–16, Houston 24–13, UT-Chattanooga 44–7. *Lost:* Southern Mississippi 30–14 (1st in 11-game series dating to 1913), Mississippi St. 19–14 (1st to Bulldogs since 1964), LSU 61–17 (1st to Tigers since 1964). *Stars:* Manning (1,481 yds and 14 TDs pass, 113 yds and 6 TDs rush), Franks (46 pass rec for 668 yds and 7 TDs), Poole (32 pass rec for 333 yds), FB/TB Randy Reed (31 pass rec for 325 yds, 668 yds rush), Studdard (29 pass rec for 397 yds), TB Bob Knight (8 TDs), Jernigan, OT Worthy McClure, DE Dennis Coleman, LB Fred Brister, DB Ray Heidel (7 int). *Noteworthy:* Vaught's last full year. Lost to Auburn 35–28 in Gator Bowl; Manning (with broken left arm) passed for 180 yds and a TD (34 yds to Franks) and ran for 95 yds and a score, and Poole had 9 pass rec for 111 yds and a TD (23 yds from QB Brent Chumbler, who ran for other Rebel TD).

1971 (10–2) *Won:* Long Beach St. 29–13, Memphis St. 49–21, Kentucky 34–20, Southern Mississippi 20–6, Vanderbilt 28–7, LSU 24–22, Tampa 28–27, UT-Chattanooga 49–10, Mississippi St. 48–0. *Lost:* unbeaten Alabama 40–6, Georgia 38–7 in consecutive early games. *Stars:* Poole (19 pass rec for 324 yds), soph QB Norris Weese (1,138 yds and 10 TDs total off), Myers (27 pass rec for 390 yds and 5 TDs), TB Steve Ainsworth (629 yds and 11 TDs rush), DT Elmer Allen, LB Paul Dongieux. *Noteworthy:* 1st year under Billy Kinard. Beat Georgia Tech 41–18 in Peach Bowl; Weese passed for 116 yds and a TD (to Myers) and scored another, Ainsworth ran for 119 yds, FB Jim Porter scored 2 TDs, and Hinton kicked 2 FGs and 5 ex pts.

1986 (8–3–1) *Won:* Memphis St. 28–6, Tulane 35–10, Kentucky 33–13 (1st meeting since 1978), SW Louisiana 21–20, Vanderbilt 28–12, LSU 21–19, Mississippi St. 24–3. *Lost:* Arkansas 21–0, Georgia 14–10 (10th straight to Bulldogs), Tennessee 22–10. *Tied:* Arkansas St. 10–10. *Stars:* soph QB Mark Young (1,154 yds pass), WR J.R. Ambrose (32 pass rec for 578 yds), SE Ricky Myers (30 pass rec for 468 yds and 5 TDs), DT Mike Fitzsimmons, LB Jeff Herrod, Don Price (5 int), DBs Jeff Noblin and frosh Stevon Moore, P Bill Smith (44.2-yd punting avg). *Noteworthy:* beat Texas Tech 20–17 in Independence Bowl; Young passed for 343 yds, Ambrose had 8 pass rec for 102 yds, soph K Bryan Owen had 2 FGs, and Willie Goodloe and FB Joe Mickles scored on short runs.

1989 (8–4) *Won:* Memphis St. 20–13, Florida 24–19, Arkansas St. 34–31, Georgia 17–14 (1st over Bulldogs since 1976), Tulane 32–28, Vanderbilt 24–16, Mississippi St. 21–11. *Lost:* Arkansas 24–17, Alabama 62–27, LSU 35–30, Tennessee 33–21. *Stars:* QB John Darnell (2,326 yds and 11 TDs pass), WR Willie Green (41 pass rec for 816 yds), FL Pat Coleman (32 pass rec for 595 yds and 5 TDs, 1,218 all-purpose yds), TE Rich Gebbia (18 pass rec for 268 yds), soph TB Randy Baldwin (642 yds rush, 22 pass rec for 170 yds, 10 TDs), FB Ed Thigpen (5 TDs rush), frosh K Brian Lee (10 FGs), LBs Tony Bennett and Shawn Cobb, soph DB Chauncey Godwin (6 int). *Noteworthy:* beat Air Force 42–29 in Liberty Bowl; Baldwin ran for 177 yds and 2 TDs, and Darnell passed for 261 yds and a TD.
1990 (9–3) *Won:* Memphis St. 23–21, Arkansas 21–17 (1st over Razorbacks since 1983), Tulane 31–21, Kentucky 35–29, Georgia 28–12, Arkansas St. 42–13, Vanderbilt 14–13, LSU 19–10, Mississippi St. 21–9. *Lost:* Auburn 24–10 (1st meeting since 1985), Tennessee 22–13. *Stars:* Baldwin (970 yds rush, 13 TDs), soph QB Tom Luke (853 yds pass, 519 yds rush), SE Darrick Owens (18 pass rec for 305 yds), Tyrone Montgomery (15 pass rec for 386 yds), DT Kelvin Pritchett. *Noteworthy:* lost to Michigan 35–3 in Gator Bowl; scored on

51-yd FG by Lee and soph QB Russ Shows passed for 165 yds.
1992 (9–3) *Won:* Auburn 45–21 (1st over Tigers in 10 games since 1965 Liberty Bowl), Tulane 35–9, Kentucky 24–14, Arkansas 17–3, LSU 32–0, Memphis St. 17–12, Louisiana Tech 13–6, Mississippi St. 17–10. *Lost:* Vanderbilt 31–9, Georgia 37–11, unbeaten national champ Alabama 31–10. *Stars:* Shows (1,400 yds and 9 TDs pass, 5 TDs rush), SE Eddie Small (39 pass rec for 558 yds), soph FL Germaine Kohn (29 pass rec for 377 yds), TB Cory Philpot (994 yds rush), FB Marvin Courtney (5 TDs), OG Everett Lindsay, Lee (15 FGs, 70 pts), soph DE Abdul Jackson, DT Chad Brown, LBs Dewayne Dotson and Cassius Ware, DBs Johnny Dixon and Danny Boyd (5 int). *Noteworthy:* beat Air Force 13–0 in Liberty Bowl as Shows passed for 163 yds, soph TB Dou Innocent scored on 5-yd run, Lee had 2 FGs, and Ware starred on defense.

Bowl Summary

Bluebonnet 0–2; Cotton 1–1; Delta 1–0; Gator 1–2; Independence 1–1; Liberty 4–0; Orange 0–1; Peach 1–0; Sugar 5–3; Sun 0–1.

Bowl Record (14–11)

Regular Season	Bowl	Score	Opponent	Record
1935 (9–2)	Orange	19–20	Catholic U.	(7–1)
1947 (8–2)	Delta	13–9	TCU	(4–4–2)
1952 (8–0–2)	Sugar	7–24	Georgia Tech	(11–0)
1954 (9–1)	Sugar	0–21	Navy	(7–2)
1955 (9–1)	Cotton	14–13	TCU	(9–1)
1957 (8–1–1)	Sugar	39–7	Texas	(6–3–1)
1958 (8–2)	Gator	7–3	Florida	(6–3–1)
1959 (9–1)	Sugar	21–0	LSU	(9–1)
1960 (9–0–1)	Sugar	14–6	Rice	(7–3)
1961 (9–1)	Cotton	7–12	Texas	(9–1)
1962 (9–0)	Sugar	17–13	Arkansas	(9–1)
1963 (7–0–2)	Sugar	7–12	Alabama	(8–2)
1964 (5–4–1)	Bluebonnet	7–14	Tulsa	(8–2)
1965 (6–4)	Liberty	13–7	Auburn	(5–4–1)
1966 (8–2)	Bluebonnet	0–19	Texas	(6–4)
1967 (6–3–1)	Sun	7–14	Texas–El Paso	(6–2–1)
1968 (6–3–1)	Liberty	34–17	Virginia Tech	(7–3)
1969 (7–3)	Sugar	27–22	Arkansas	(9–1)

(continued)

Regular Season	Bowl	Score	Opponent	Record
1970 (7–3)	Gator	28–35	Auburn	(8–2)
1971 (9–2)	Peach	41–18	Georgia Tech	(6–5)
1983 (6–5)	Independence	3–9	Air Force	(9–2)
1986 (7–3–1)	Independence	20–17	Texas Tech	(7–4)
1989 (8–3)	Liberty	42–29	Air Force	(8–3–1)
1990 (9–2)	Gator	3–35	Michigan	(8–3)
1992 (8–3)	Liberty	13–0	Air Force	(7–4)

CONFERENCE TITLES

Southeastern—1947, 1954, 1955, 1960, 1962, 1963.

TOP 20 AP AND UPI
(USA TODAY/CNN SINCE 1991) RANKING

1941	17	1955	9–10	1961	5–5	1966	U-12
1947	13	1957	7–8	1962	3–3	1969	8–13
1948	15	1958	11–12	1963	7–7	1970	20-U
1952	7–7	1959	2–2	1964	U-20	1971	15–20
1954	6–6	1960	2–3	1965	U-17	1992	16–16

MAJOR RIVALS

Mississippi has played at least 10 games with Alabama 6–32–2, Arkansas 19–19–1, Arkansas St. 12–1–2, Auburn 6–11, Florida 9–7–1, Georgia 9–21–1, Houston 15–3, Kentucky 23–11–1, Louisiana St. 32–45–4, Memphis St. 38–6–2, Mississippi College 8–4–1, Mississippi St. 52–31–6, Sewanee 6–8–1, Southern Mississippi 18–6, Southwestern (Tenn.) 20–1–2, Tennessee 18–39–1, Tulane 36–28, Union 14–0–1, UT-Chattanooga 13–1, Vanderbilt 34–31–2. Record against SEC member played fewer than 10 times: South Carolina 4–5.

COACHES

Dean of Mississippi coaches is John H. Vaught with record of 190–61–12 for 1947–70 and part of 1973, including 6 SEC titles, 18 bowl teams, 4 teams unbeaten in regular season, and 1 national championship. Other top records for at least 3 years were by Dr. N.P. Stauffer, 17–7–2 for 1909–11; Edward L. Walker, 38–38–8 for 1930–37 with 1 Orange Bowl team; Harry J. Mehre, 39–26–1 for 1938–45; and Billy Brewer, 62–50–3 for 1983–92 with 5 bowl teams.

MISCELLANEA

First game was win over Southwest Baptist University (Union) 56–0 in 1893 . . . highest score was over Southwest Baptist (Union) 114–0 in 1904 . . . highest since W.W. II was over Southern Mississippi 69–7 in 1969 . . . worst defeat was by Vanderbilt 91–0 in 1915 . . . worst since W.W. II was by Georgia 49–0 in 1974 . . . highest against since W.W. II was by LSU 61–17 in 1970 . . . longest unbeaten string of 21 in 1959–61 ended by LSU 10–7 . . . 19-game unbeaten string in 1962–63 ended by Alabama 12–7 in 1964 Sugar Bowl . . . longest winless string of 11 in 1916–17 broken with win over Mississippi College 21–0 . . . consensus All-Americans were Charley Conerly, B, 1947; Crawford Mims, G, 1953; Charlie Flowers, B, 1959; Jake Gibbs, B, 1960; Jim Dunaway, T, 1962; Jim Miller, P, 1979; and Everett Lindsay, OL, 1992 . . . Academic All-Americans were Harold Easterwood, C, 1954; Robert Khayat, T, and Charlie Flowers, B, 1959; Doug Elmore, B, 1961; Stan

Hindman, G, 1965; Steve Hindman, HB, 1968; Julius Fagan, K, 1969; Greg Markow, DE, 1974; Robert Fabris, E, and George Plasketes, DE, 1977; Ken Toler, WR, 1980; Danny Hoskins, OG, 1986–87; Wesley Walls, TE, 1988; Todd Sandroni, DB, 1989; and James Singleton, DL, 1992.

MISSISSIPPI STATE (Bulldogs; Maroon and White)

NOTABLE TEAMS

1903 (3–0–2) *Won:* Alabama 11–0, Meridian A.C. 43–0, Louisiana St. (LSU) 11–0. *Tied:* Mississippi 6–6, Tulane 0–0. *Noteworthy:* had 1st undefeated season in 1st year under Dan Martin.

1910 (7–2) *Won:* Mississippi College 24–0 (1st meeting), Memphis U. 6–0, LSU 3–0 (1st over Tigers in 6 games since 1903), Tennessee 48–0, Tulane 10–0 (1st in 7-game series dating to 1901), Birmingham Southern 46–0, Howard 82–0. *Lost:* Auburn 6–0 (1st meeting since 1905), Mississippi 30–0.

1911 (7–2–1) *Won:* Mississippi College 27–6, Southwestern (Tenn.) 30–0, Howard 48–0, Birmingham Southern 62–0, LSU 6–0, Mississippi 6–0, Havana A.C. 12–0. *Lost:* Auburn 11–5, Tulane 5–4. *Tied:* Alabama 6–6 (1st meeting since 1906).

1913 (6–1–1) *Won:* Howard 66–0, Mississippi College 1–0 (forfeit), Transylvania 31–0, Texas A&M 6–0, Tulane 32–0, Alabama 7–0. *Lost:* unbeaten Auburn 34–0. *Tied:* LSU 0–0. *Noteworthy:* last year under W.D. Chadwick.

1914 (6–2) *Won:* Marion Military 54–0, Cumberland 77–0, Georgia 9–0 (1st meeting), Mercer 66–0, Tulane 61–0, Alabama 9–0. *Lost:* Kentucky 17–13 (1st meeting), Auburn 19–0 in consecutive early games. *Star:* Harry McArthur (15 TDs). *Noteworthy:* 1st year under E.C. Hayes.

1917 (6–1) *Won:* Marion Military 18–6, Mississippi College 68–0, Mississippi 41–14, Kentucky 14–0, LSU 9–0, Haskell 7–6. *Lost:* Auburn 13–6. *Noteworthy:* 1st year under S.L. Robinson.

1919 (6–2) *Won:* Spring Hill 12–6, Mississippi College 56–7, Tennessee 6–0, Howard 39–0, LSU 6–0, Mississippi 33–0. *Lost:* Auburn 7–0 (10th straight to Tigers), Alabama 14–6 (1st meeting since 1914) in last 2 games. *Noteworthy:* Robinson's last team.

1935 (8–3) *Won:* Howard 19–6, Millsaps 45–0, Alabama 20–7 (1st over Tide in 13 games since 1914), Loyola (La.) 6–0, Xavier (Ohio) 7–0, Army 13–7, Mississippi Southern 20–0 (1st meeting), Sewanee 25–0. *Lost:* Vanderbilt 14–9, LSU 28–13, Mississippi 14–6. *Stars:* FB Ike Pickle, Fred Walters (5 TDs), Fred Hight (5 TDs), E Chuck Gelatka, G Willie Stone. *Noteworthy:* had 1st winning season since 1927 in 1st year under Ralph Sasse.

1936 (7–3–1) *Won:* Millsaps 20–0, Howard 35–0, Loyola (La.) 32–0, Sewanee 68–0, Mississippi 26–6 (1st over Rebels since 1925), Mercer 32–0, Florida 7–0 (1st meeting since 1925). *Lost:* unbeaten Alabama 7–0, unbeaten LSU 12–0. *Tied:* Texas Christian (TCU) 0–0. *Stars:* Pickle (5 TDs, 40 pts), Gelatka, T Alex Lott. *Noteworthy:* made 1st bowl appearance, losing to Duquesne 13–12 in Orange Bowl on 72-yd TD pass in last quarter; State scored on 10-yd run by Pickle and 40-yd pass from TB Charles "Pee Wee" Armstrong to Walters.

1939 (8–2) *Won:* Howard 45–0, Arkansas 19–0 (1st meeting since 1916), Florida 14–0, Southwestern (Tenn.) 37–0, Birmingham Southern 28–0, LSU 15–12 (1st over Tigers since 1930), Millsaps 40–0, Mississippi 18–6. *Lost:* Auburn 7–0, Alabama 7–0. *Stars:* HB Harvey Johnson (592 yds rush, 10 TDs), E Buddy Elrod, C Shag Goolsby. *Noteworthy:* 1st year under Allyn McKeen.

1940 (10–0–1) *Won:* Florida 27–7, SW Louisiana 20–0, Howard 40–7, N.C. State 26–10, Southwestern (Tenn.) 13–0, LSU 22–7, Millsaps 46–13, Mississippi 19–0, Alabama 13–0. *Tied:* Auburn 7–7 in 3rd game. *Stars:* Johnson (721 yds rush), FB Jack Nix, TB Billy Jefferson (5 TDs), Walter Craig (5 TDs), Granville Harrison (5 TDs), Elrod, G Hunter Corhern, T John Tripson. *Noteworthy:* 1st unbeaten season since 1903. Beat Georgetown 14–7 in Orange Bowl; scored on blocked punt recovery in end zone by Tripson and 2-yd run by Jefferson.

1941 (8–1–1) *Won:* Florida 6–0, Alabama 14–0, Union 56–7, Southwestern (Tenn.) 20–6, Auburn 14–7 (1st over Tigers in 5 games since 1930), Millsaps 49–6, Mississippi 6–0, San Francisco 26–13. *Lost:* unbeaten Duquesne 16–0. *Tied:* LSU 0–0. *Stars:* FB Blondy Black (651 yds rush, 6 TDs), T Bill Arnold. *Noteworthy:* won 1st SEC title.

1942 (8–2) *Won:* Union 35–2, Vanderbilt 33–0 (1st meeting since 1935, 1st win in 7-game series dating to 1904), Florida 26–12, Auburn 6–0, Tulane 7–0 (1st over Green Wave in 7 games since 1927), Duquesne 28–6, Mississippi 34–13, San Francisco 19–7. *Lost:* Alabama 21–6, LSU 16–6 in consecutive early games. *Stars:* Black (646 yds rush, 7 TDs), E Bob Patterson, Gs Raymond Ray and Curtis Patterson.

1944 (6–2) *Won:* Jackson Air Force Base 41–0, Millsaps 56–0, Arkansas A&M 49–20, LSU 13–6, Kentucky 26–0 (1st meeting since 1917), Auburn 26–21. *Lost:* Alabama 19–0, Mississippi 13–8 (1st to Rebels in 5 games since 1938) in last 2 games. *Stars:* frosh TB Tom "Shorty" McWilliams (14 TDs, 43.8-yd avg on 13 punts), Ts Hillery Horne and frosh Dub Garrett, E Bill Hildebrand. *Noteworthy:* resumed competition after 1-year layoff during W.W. II.

1946 (8–2) *Won:* Chattanooga 41–7, Michigan St. 6–0, San Francisco 48–20, Tulane 14–7, Murray St. 69–0, Auburn 33–0, NW Louisiana 27–0, Mississippi 20–0. *Lost:* LSU 13–6, Alabama 24–7. *Stars:* McWilliams, soph TB Harper Davis, Walter Matulich (7 TDs), Garrett, G Mike Harris, Billy Murphy (5 int, 41.6-yd punting avg).

1947 (7–3) *Won:* Chattanooga 19–0, San Francisco 21–14, Duquesne 34–0, Hardin-Simmons 27–7, Tulane 20–0, Auburn 14–0, Southern Mississippi 14–7 (1st meeting since 1935). *Lost:* Michigan St. 7–0, LSU 21–6, Mississippi 33–14. *Stars:* McWilliams (6 TDs, 625 yds rush, 360 yds pass), Davis (6 TDs, 15 pass rec for 229 yds), Garrett.

1957 (6–2–1) *Won:* Memphis St. 10–6, Arkansas St. 47–13, Florida 29–20, Alabama 25–13, Tulane 27–6, LSU 14–6. *Lost:* Tennessee 14–9, unbeaten national cochamp Auburn 15–7. *Tied:* Mississippi 7–7. *Stars:* QB Billy Stacy, Molly Halbert (7 TDs), E John Benge, OL Jack Benson, T Sam Latham, C Jimmy Dodd.

1963 (7–2–2) *Won:* Howard 43–0, Tennessee 7–0, Tulane 31–10, Houston 20–0, Auburn 13–10, LSU 7–6 (1st over Tigers since 1957). *Lost:* unbeaten Memphis St. 17–10, Alabama 20–19 in consecutive mid-season games. *Tied:* Florida 9–9, unbeaten Mississippi 10–10. *Stars:* QB/S Sonny Fisher (5 int), soph FB Hoyle Granger, Ode Burrell (840 all-purpose yds, 7 TDs), G Pat Watson, T Tommy Neville, E Tommy Inman. *Noteworthy:* beat N.C. State 16–12 in frigid Liberty Bowl; scored on TDs by Inman (11-yd run with blocked punt) and

Fisher (3-yd run), and 43-yd FG and ex pt by G Justin Canale.

1974 (9–3) *Won:* William & Mary 49–7, Georgia 38–14, Kansas St. 21–16, Lamar 37–21, Memphis St. 29–28 (1st meeting since 1965), Louisville 56–7, LSU 7–6 (1st over Tigers since 1963), Mississippi 31–13. *Lost:* Florida 29–13, unbeaten Alabama 35–0, Auburn 24–20. *Stars:* DT Jimmy Webb (Bulldogs' 1st consensus All-American), QB Rocky Felker (1,147 yds pass, 446 yds and 7 TDs rush), Howard Lewis (21 pass rec for 330 yds), soph TB Walter Packer (994 yds and 6 TDs rush), frosh FB Dennis Johnson (524 yds and 7 TDs rush), soph OG Sam Nichols. *Noteworthy:* beat North Carolina 26–24 in foggy Sun Bowl; Packer ran for 183 yds and 2 TDs, Terry Vitrano ran for 164 yds and a TD, Vic Nickels kicked 2 FGs, and Webb made 12 tackles.

1976 (9–2, 0–11 by forfeit) *Won:* North Texas St. 7–0, Louisville 30–21, Cal Poly–Pomona 38–0, Kentucky 14–7, Memphis St. 42–33, Southern Mississippi 14–6, Auburn 28–19 (1st over Tigers since 1963), LSU 21–13, Mississippi 28–11. *Lost:* Florida 34–30, Alabama 34–17. *Stars:* QB Bruce Threadgill (1,361 yds total off), Robert Chatman (15 pass rec for 277 yds), Johnson (859 yds rush, 7 TDs), Packer (633 yds and 6 TDs rush), Nichols, C Richard Keys, K Kinney Jordan (10 FGs), MG Harvey Hull, LB Ray Costict, DB Stan Black, Harry Davison (5 int). *Noteworthy:* all wins forfeited by NCAA ruling.

1980 (9–3) *Won:* Memphis St. 34–7, Louisiana Tech 31–11, Vanderbilt 24–14 (1st meeting since 1973), Illinois 28–21, Miami (Fla.) 34–31, Auburn 24–21, Alabama 6–3 (1st over Tide since 1957), LSU 55–31, Mississippi 19–14. *Lost:* Florida 21–15, Southern Mississippi 42–14. *Stars:* SEs Mardye McDole (19 pass rec for 289 yds, 978 all-purpose yds, 7 TDs) and soph Glen Young (11 pass rec for 218 yds), frosh QB John Bond (720 yds and 5 TDs rush, 849 yds pass), soph HB Michael Haddix (724 yds rush, 6 TDs), FB Donald Ray King (642 yds and 6 TDs rush), OT Alan Massey, soph OG Wayne Harris, DE Tyrone Keys, DT Glen Collins, LB Johnie Cooks, Larry Friday (5 int), soph P/K Dana Moore (40.5-yd punting avg, 11 FGs). *Noteworthy:* lost to Nebraska 31–17 in Sun Bowl, dropping behind 17–0 at halftime; Bond ran for 1 TD and passed to Haddix for other.

1981 (8–4) *Won:* Memphis St. 20–3, Vanderbilt 29–9, Florida 28–7, Colorado St. 37–27, Miami (Fla.) 14–10, Auburn 21–17, LSU 17–9. *Lost:* Missouri 14–3, Alabama 13–10, Southern Mississippi 7–6, Mississippi 21–17. *Stars:* Collins, Cooks, soph DE Billy Jackson, DB Rob Fesmire, Bond (1,214 yds total off), Young (19 pass rec for 263 yds, 979 all-purpose yds, nation's punt return leader with 16.2-yd avg), Haddix (622 yds rush), Harris, Moore (10 FGs, 41.7-yd punting avg). *Noteworthy:* beat Kansas 10–0 in Hall of Fame Bowl; scored on 17-yd run by Bond and 22-yd FG by Moore, and Cooks and Collins starred on defense.

BOWL SUMMARY

Hall of Fame 1–0; Liberty 1–1; Orange 1–1; Peach 0–1; Sun 1–1.

BOWL RECORD (4–4)

Regular Season	Bowl	Score	Opponent	Record
1936 (7–2–1)	Orange	12–13	Duquesne	(7–2)
1940 (9–0–1)	Orange	14–7	Georgetown	(8–1)
1963 (6–2–2)	Liberty	16–12	N.C. State	(8–2)
1974 (8–3)	Sun	26–24	North Carolina	(7–4)
1980 (9–2)	Sun	17–31	Nebraska	(9–2)
1981 (7–4)	Hall of Fame	10–0	Kansas	(8–3)
1991 (7–4)	Liberty	15–38	Air Force	(9–3)
1992 (7–4)	Peach	17–21	North Carolina	(8–3)

CONFERENCE TITLES

Southeastern—1941.

TOP 20 AP AND UPI RANKING

1940	9	1957	14-U	1974	17–17	1980	19-U
1941	16	1963	U-11	1976	20-U	1981	U-17
1942	18						

MAJOR RIVALS

Mississippi St. has played at least 10 games with Alabama 11–63–3, Arkansas St. 15–0, Auburn 18–46–2, Florida 16–29–2, Georgia 5–12, Houston 6–6, Howard 16–1–1, Kentucky 7–13, Louisiana St. 32–51–3, Memphis St. 22–9, Millsaps 14–2–1, Mississippi 31–52–6, Mississippi College 16–3, Southern Mississippi 12–14–1, Southwestern (Tenn.) 9–3, Tennessee 14–22–1, Tulane 25–24–2, Vanderbilt 7–6–2. Record against SEC members played fewer than 10 times: Arkansas 3–0, South Carolina 0–1.

COACHES

Dean of Mississippi St. coaches is Allyn McKeen with record of 65–19–3 for 1939–48, including 1 SEC title and an unbeaten Orange Bowl champion. Other top records for at least 3 years were by W.D. Chadwick, 29–12–2 for 1909–13; E.C. Hayes, 15–8–2 for 1914–16; Sid Robinson, 15–5 for 1917–19; Ralph Sasse, 20–10–2 for 1935–37 with 1 Orange Bowl team; Paul Davis, 20–28–2 for 1962–66 with 1 bowl champion; Bob Tyler, 21–44–2 for 1973–78 with 1 bowl champion; and Emory Bellard, 37–42 for 1979–85 with 2 bowl teams.

MISCELLANEA

First game was loss to Southern Baptist U. 21–0 in 1895 . . . 1st win was over Mississippi 17–0 in 1901 . . . highest score was over Howard 82–0 in 1910 . . . highest since W.W. II was over Murray St. 69–0 in 1946 . . . worst defeat was by Houston 74–0 in 1969 . . . longest unbeaten string of 21 in 1939–41 ended by Duquesne 16–0 . . . longest losing string of 27 (17 by NCAA-decreed forfeits) in 1975–77 broken with win over West Texas St. 28–0 in 1978 opener . . . longest on-field winless string of 17 in 1967–68 broken with win over Richmond 17–14 in 1969 opener . . . consensus All-American was Jimmy Webb, DL, 1974 . . . Academic All-Americans were Jackie Parker, B, 1953; Ron Bennett, E, 1956; Frank Dowsing, DB, 1972; Jimmy Webb, DE, 1973; Will Coltharp, DE, 1976; and Stacy Russell, DB, 1989.

SOUTH CAROLINA *(Fighting Gamecocks; Garnet and Black)*

NOTABLE TEAMS

1902 (6–1) *Won:* Guilford 10–0, North Carolina Military 60–0, Bingham 28–0, Clemson 12–6 (1st over Tigers in 5 games since 1896), St. Albans 5–0, Charleston Military 80–0. *Lost:* Furman 10–0. *Noteworthy:* 1st year under C.R. Williams.
1903 (8–2) *Won:* Columbia YMCA 24–0, Welsh Neck 89–0, Georgia 17–0, Guilford 29–0, Tennessee 24–0 (1st meeting), Davidson 29–12 (1st in 5-game series begun in 1898), Charleston 16–0, Georgia Tech 16–0. *Lost:* North Carolina 17–0 (1st meeting), N.C. State 6–5.
1921 (5–1–2) *Won:* Erskine 13–7, Newberry 7–0, Presbyterian 48–0, Clemson 21–0, The Citadel 13–0. *Lost:* Furman 7–0. *Tied:* North Carolina 7–7, Florida 7–7.
1924 (7–3) *Won:* Erskine 47–0, N.C. State 10–0, Presbyterian 29–0, Clemson 3–0, The Citadel 14–3, North Carolina 10–7 (1st in 13-game series dating to 1903), Wake Forest 7–0. *Lost:* Georgia 18–0, Furman 10–0, Sewanee 10–0. *Noteworthy:* last year under Sol Metzger.
1925 (7–3) *Won:* Erskine 33–0, N.C. State 7–6, Wofford 6–0, Clemson 33–0, The Citadel 30–6, Presbyterian 21–0, Centre 20–0. *Lost:* North Carolina 7–0, Virginia Tech 6–0 (1st meeting since

1905), Furman 2–0. *Noteworthy:* 1st year under Branch Bocock.
1928 (6–2–2) *Won:* Erskine 19–0, Chicago 6–0, Virginia 24–13, Maryland 21–7, Presbyterian 13–0, Furman 6–0 (1st over Purple Hurricane since 1922). *Lost:* Clemson 32–0, N.C. State 18–7. *Tied:* The Citadel 0–0, North Carolina 0–0. *Noteworthy:* 1st year under Billy Laval.
1943 (5–2) *Won:* Newberry 19–7 (1st meeting since 1923), Presbyterian 20–7 (1st meeting since 1937), Clemson 33–6, Charleston Coast Guard 20–0, Wake Forest 13–2. *Lost:* 176th Infantry 13–7, North Carolina 21–6. *Stars:* G Ernie Bauer, T Dom Fusci. *Noteworthy:* only year under J.P. Moran.
1947 (6–2–1) *Won:* Newberry 27–6, Furman 26–8, Clemson 21–19, Miami (Fla.) 8–0, The Citadel 12–0, Wake Forest 6–0. *Lost:* Maryland 19–13, Mississippi 33–0 (1st meeting) in consecutive early games. *Tied:* Duke 0–0.
1953 (7–3) *Won:* The Citadel 25–0, Virginia 19–0, Furman 27–13, Clemson 14–7 (1st ACC win), North Carolina 18–0 (1st over Tar Heels in 5 games since 1944), West Virginia 20–14, Wofford 49–0. *Lost:* Duke 20–7 (1st ACC game), unbeaten national cochamp Maryland 24–6, Wake Forest 19–13. *Stars:* QB Johnny Gramling (1,045 yds pass), B Gene Wilson (502 yds rush), G Frank Mincevich, E Clyde Bennett, C/LB Leon Cunningham.
1956 (7–3) *Won:* Wofford 26–13, Duke 7–0 (1st over Blue Devils in 13 games since 1931), North Carolina 14–0, Virginia 27–13, Furman 13–6, Maryland 13–0 (1st over Terps in 7 games since 1946), Wake Forest 13–0. *Lost:* Miami (Fla.) 14–6 (1st meeting since 1949), Clemson 7–0, N.C. State 14–7 (1st meeting since 1935). *Stars:* QB King Dixon, soph B Alex Hawkins, T Sam DeLuca, E Buddy Frick. *Noteworthy:* 1st year under Warren Giese.
1958 (7–3) *Won:* Duke 8–0, Georgia 24–14 (1st meeting since 1941, 1st over Bulldogs in 11 games since 1904), Clemson 26–6, Furman 32–7, Virginia 28–14, N.C. State 12–7 (1st over Wolfpack in 5 games since 1933), Wake Forest 24–7. *Lost:* unbeaten Army 45–8, North Carolina 6–0, Maryland 10–6. *Stars:* Hawkins, FB John Saunders, T Ed Pitts.
1969 (7–4) *Won:* Duke 27–20, North Carolina 14–6, N.C. State 21–16, Virginia Tech 17–16, Maryland 17–0, Wake Forest 24–6, Clemson 27–13. *Lost:* Georgia 41–16, Florida St. 34–9, Tennessee

29–14. *Stars:* QB Tommy Suggs (1,342 yds pass), FL Fred Zeigler (52 pass rec for 658 yds), FB Warren Muir (917 yds rush), OT Dave DeCamilla, K Billy DuPre, DT Jimmy Poston, DB Pat Watson. *Noteworthy:* Won only ACC title. Lost to West Virginia 14–3 (1st meeting since 1954) in Peach Bowl; scored on 37-yd FG by DuPre.

1979 (8–4) *Won:* Western Michigan 24–7, Duke 35–0, Georgia 27–20, Oklahoma St. 23–16, Mississippi 21–14, N.C. State 30–28, Wake Forest 35–14, Clemson 13–9. *Lost:* North Carolina 28–0, Notre Dame 18–17, unbeaten Florida St. 27–7 (1st meeting since 1973). *Stars:* RB George Rogers (1,548 yds rush, 9 TDs), FL Zion McKinney, MG Fred Sinclair. *Noteworthy:* lost to Missouri 24–14 in Hall of Fame Bowl; Rogers ran for 133 yds and QB Garry Harper passed to McKinney for 1 TD and scored other Gamecock TD on 11-yd run.

1980 (8–4) *Won:* Pacific 37–0, Wichita St. 73–0, Michigan 17–14, N.C. State 30–10, Duke 20–7, Cincinnati 49–7, The Citadel 45–24 (1st meeting since 1965), Wake Forest 39–38. *Lost:* Southern California 23–13, unbeaten national champ Georgia 13–10, Clemson 27–6. *Stars:* Heisman Trophy–winner Rogers (Gamecocks' 1st consensus All-American; 14 TDs, national leader with 1,781 yds rush), Harper (1,266 yds pass), Willie Scott (34 pass rec for 469 yds), Horace Smith (26 pass rec for 455 yds), Tim Gillespie (17 pass rec for 249 yds), K Eddie Leopard (12 FGs, 78 pts), LB Walt Kater. *Noteworthy:* lost to Pittsburgh 37–9 in Gator Bowl; Rogers ran for 113 yds and Gamecocks scored on 39-yd FG by Leopard and 14-yd pass from QB Gordon Beckham to Gillespie.

1984 (10–2) *Won:* The Citadel 31–24, Duke 21–0, Georgia 17–10 (1st over Bulldogs since 1979), Kansas St. 49–17, Pittsburgh 45–21, Notre Dame 36–32, East Carolina 42–20 (1st meeting since 1977), N.C. State 35–28, Florida St. 38–26, Clemson 22–21 (1st over Tigers since 1979). *Lost:* Navy 38–21. *Stars:* QB Mike Hold (1,385 yds pass), Thomas Dendy (634 yds rush), OG Del Wilkes, LBs James Seawright and Carl Hill, DBs Bryant Gilliard (8 int) and Joe Brooks. *Noteworthy:* lost to Oklahoma St. 21–14 in Gator Bowl after taking 14–13 lead in 3rd period; scored on 24-yd pass from Quinton Lewis to Chris Wade and 57-yd pass from Hold to Ira Hillary.

WR Sterling Sharpe, 1983, 1985–87

1987 (8–4) *Won:* Appalachian St. 24–3, Western Carolina 31–6, Virginia Tech 40–10, Virginia 58–10, East Carolina 34–12, N.C. State 48–0, Wake Forest 30–0, Clemson 20–7. *Lost:* Georgia 13–6, Nebraska 30–21, unbeaten national champ Miami (Fla.) 20–16. *Stars:* soph QB Todd Ellis (3,206 yds and 10 TDs pass), WR Sterling Sharpe (56 pass rec for 852 yds), soph RB Harold Green (1,022 yds and 15 TDs rush, 29 pass rec for 262 yds and 1 TD), C Waddy Myers, frosh K Collin Mackie (106 pts, national leader with 23 FGs), NG Roy Hart, DT Brendan McCormack, DBs Greg Philpot and Brad Edwards (8 int, 2 returned for TDs), soph P Rodney Price (42.1-yd avg). *Noteworthy:* lost to

DB Brad Edwards, 1984–87

Louisiana St. (LSU) 30–13 in Gator Bowl; Ellis passed for more than 300 yds but was intercepted 4 times, Green ran for 72 yds and a TD, and Mackie had FGs of 44 and 39 yds.

1988 (8–4)   *Won:* North Carolina 31–10 (1st meeting since 1983), Western Carolina 38–0, East Carolina 17–0, Georgia 23–10, Appalachian St. 35–9, Virginia Tech 26–24, N.C. State 23–7, Navy 19–7. *Lost:* Georgia Tech 34–0 (1st meeting since 1978), Florida St. 59–0, Clemson 29–10.   *Stars:* Ellis (2,353 yds pass), Green (36 pass rec for 315 yds, 606 yds rush), WRs Carl Platt (34 pass rec for 460 yds) and frosh Robert Brooks (34 pass rec for 508 yds, 5 TDs), soph RB Mike Dingle (19 pass rec for 228 yds, 5 TDs), C Randy Harwell, OT Mark Fryer, Mackie (19 FGs, 82 pts), DE Kevin Hendrix, soph LB Patrick Hinton (5 int), DBs Ron Rabune and Robert Robinson. *Noteworthy:* Last year under Joe Morrison. Lost to Indiana 34–10 in Liberty Bowl; scored on 34-yd return of blocked punt by Mike Tolbert and 43-yd FG by Mackie.

BOWL SUMMARY

Gator 0–4; Hall of Fame 0–1; Liberty 0–1; Peach 0–1; Tangerine 0–1.

BOWL RECORD (0–8)

Regular Season	Bowl	Score	Opponent	Record
1945 (2–3–3)	Gator	14–26	Wake Forest	(4–3–1)
1969 (7–3)	Peach	3–14	West Virginia	(9–1)
1975 (7–4)	Tangerine	7–20	Miami (Ohio)	(10–1)
1979 (8–3)	Hall of Fame	14–24	Missouri	(6–5)
1980 (8–3)	Gator	9–37	Pittsburgh	(10–1)
1984 (10–1)	Gator	14–21	Oklahoma State	(9–2)
1987 (8–3)	Gator	13–30	LSU	(9–1–1)
1988 (8–3)	Liberty	10–34	Indiana	(7–3–1)

CONFERENCE TITLES

Atlantic Coast—1969. **Southeastern**—None.

TOP 20 AP AND UPI
(USA TODAY/CNN SINCE 1991) RANKING

1958	15-U	1987	15–15	1984	11–13

MAJOR RIVALS

South Carolina has played at least 10 games with The Citadel 39–7–3, Clemson 33–53–4, Davidson 6–13, Duke 17–24–3, East Carolina 8–2, Erskine 15–1, Florida 3–7–3, Florida St. 3–15, Furman 26–20–1, Georgia 9–34–2, Georgia Tech 9–12, Louisiana St. 1–12, Maryland 11–17, Miami (Fla.) 5–8–2, Newberry 11–1–1, North Carolina 16–34–4, N.C. State 25–25–4, Presbyterian 12–3, Tennessee 2–7–2, Virginia 20–11–1, Virginia Tech 11–7–2, Wake Forest 34–20–2, West Virginia 3–7–1, Wofford 15–4. Record with SEC members played fewer than 10 times: Alabama 0–8, Arkansas 0–1, Auburn 1–2–1, Kentucky 1–2–1, Mississippi 5–4, Mississippi St. 1–0, Vanderbilt 2–0.

COACHES

Dean of South Carolina coaches is Rex Enright with record of 64–69–7 for 1938–42 and 1946–55. Other top records for at least 3 years were by N.B. Edgerton, 19–13–3 for 1912–15; Sol Metzger, 26–18–2 for 1920–24; Billy Laval, 39–26–6 for 1928–34; Warren Giese, 28–21–1 for 1956–60; Paul Dietzel, 42–53–1 for 1966–74 with 1 ACC title and 1 bowl team; Jim Carlen, 45–36–1 for 1975–81 with 3 bowl teams; Joe Morrison, 39–28–2 for 1983–88 with 3 bowl teams; and Sparky Woods, 20–21–3 for 1989–92.

MISCELLANEA

First game was loss to Furman 44–0 in 1892 . . . 1st win was over Furman 14–10 in 1895 . . . highest score was over Welsh Neck 89–0 in 1903 . . . highest since W.W. II was over Wichita St. 73–0 in 1980 . . . worst defeat was by Navy 63–0 in 1920 . . . worst since W.W. II was by Florida St. 59–0 in 1988 . . . longest unbeaten string of 10 in 1914–15 ended by Virginia 13–0 . . . longest winless string of 15 in 1963–64 broken with win over The Citadel 17–14 . . . consensus All-Americans were

George Rogers, RB, 1980; and Del Wilkes, OG, 1984 . . . Academic All-Americans were Mark Fryer, OT, 1987–88; and Joe Reaves, LB, 1991 . . . Heisman Trophy winner was George Rogers, HB, 1980.

TENNESSEE (Volunteers, Vols; Orange and White)

NOTABLE TEAMS

1897 (4–1) *Won:* King 28–0, Williamsburg 6–0, Virginia Tech 18–0, Bristol A.C. 12–0. *Lost:* North Carolina 16–0.
1898 No team, due to Spanish-American War.
1899 (5–2) *Won:* King 11–5, Kentucky 12–0, Georgia 5–0 (1st meeting), Washington & Lee 11–0, Transylvania 41–0. *Lost:* Virginia Tech 5–0, unbeaten Sewanee 51–0 (1st meeting since 1892) in consecutive early games.
1902 (6–2) *Won:* King 12–0, Maryville 34–0, Sewanee 6–0 (1st in 5-game series begun in 1891), Nashville 10–0, Mississippi 11–10 (1st meeting), Georgia Tech 10–6 (1st meeting). *Lost:* Vanderbilt 12–5, Clemson 11–0. *Stars:* B Nash Buckingham, E Joey Beane. *Noteworthy:* 1st year under H.F. Fisher.
1907 (7–2–1) *Won:* Tennessee Military 30–0, Georgia 15–0, Clemson 4–0 (1st in 6-game series dating to 1901), Maryville 34–0, Chattanooga 57–0, Mississippi St. 11–4 (1st meeting), Arkansas 14–2 (1st meeting). *Lost:* Georgia Tech 6–4, Alabama 5–0. *Tied:* Kentucky 0–0. *Stars:* B Walker Leach, G N.W. Dougherty, T Roscoe Word. *Noteworthy:* 1st year under George Levene.
1908 (7–2) *Won:* North Carolina 12–0 (1st meeting since 1900), Maryville 39–5, Kentucky 7–0, Georgia 10–0, Georgia Tech 6–5, Clemson 6–5, Chattanooga 35–6. *Lost:* Vanderbilt 16–9, Alabama 4–0. *Stars:* Leach, Dougherty.
1914 (9–0) *Won:* Carson-Newman 89–0, King 55–3, Clemson 27–0 (1st meeting since 1908), Louisville 66–0, Alabama 17–7 (1st over Tide in 8 games

since 1904), Chattanooga 67–0, Vanderbilt 16–14 (1st in 13-game series dating to 1892), Sewanee 14–7 (1st over Tigers in 7 games since 1902), Kentucky 23–6. *Stars:* G Mush Kerr, B Russ Lindsay, E Alonzo Carroll, T Farmer Kelly. *Noteworthy:* 1st undefeated season since 4-game schedule of 1896; won Southern Intercollegiate Athletic Association title.

1916 (8–0–1) *Won:* Tusculum 33–0, Maryville 32–6, Clemson 14–0, South Carolina 26–0 (1st meeting since 1903), Florida 24–0 (1st meeting), Chattanooga 12–7, Vanderbilt 10–6 (1st homecoming), Sewanee 17–0. *Tied:* Kentucky 0–0 in finale. *Stars:* Es Graham Vowell and Lloyd Wolfe, B Buck Hatcher. *Noteworthy:* 1st year under John Bender.

1917–1918 No team, due to W.W. I.

1920 (7–2) *Won:* Emory & Henry 45–0, Maryville 47–0, Chattanooga 35–0, Clemson 26–0, Transylvania 49–0, Sewanee 20–0, Kentucky 14–7. *Lost:* Vanderbilt 20–0, Mississippi St. 13–7. *Star:* T Hatcher. *Noteworthy:* Bender's last team.

1921 (6–2–1) *Won:* Emory & Henry 27–0 (1st game on Shields Watkins Stadium field), Maryville 7–0 (10th straight over Scots), Chattanooga 21–0, Florida 9–0, Mississippi St. 14–7 (1st over Bulldogs in 5 games since 1907), Sewanee 21–0. *Lost:* Dartmouth 14–3, unbeaten Vanderbilt 14–0. *Tied:* Kentucky 0–0. *Star:* soph B Roe Campbell. *Noteworthy:* 1st year under M.B. Banks.

1922 (8–2) *Won:* Emory & Henry 50–0 (1st game in orange jerseys), Carson-Newman 32–7 (1st meeting since 1915), Maryville 21–0, Camp Benning 15–0, Mississippi 49–0 (1st meeting since 1902), Mississippi St. 31–3, Sewanee 18–7, Kentucky 14–7. *Lost:* Georgia 7–3 (1st meeting since 1910), unbeaten Vanderbilt 14–6. *Stars:* Campbell (10 TDs), B Rufe Clayton, E Tarzan Holt, G Roy Striegel.

1926 (8–1) *Won:* Carson-Newman 13–0, North Carolina 34–0 (1st meeting since 1919), Louisiana St. (LSU) 14–7, Maryville 6–0 (15th straight over Scots), Centre 30–7, Mississippi St. 33–0, Sewanee 12–0, Kentucky 6–0. *Lost:* Vanderbilt 20–3. *Star:* G John Barnhill. *Noteworthy:* 1st year under Robert R. "Bob" Neyland.

1927 (8–0–1) *Won:* Carson-Newman 33–0, North Carolina 26–0, Maryville 7–0, Mississippi 21–7, Transylvania 57–0, Virginia 42–0, Sewanee 32–12, Kentucky 20–0. *Tied:* Vanderbilt 7–7. *Stars:* B

Dick Dodson, Barnhill, T Dave McArthur. *Noteworthy:* won 1st SC title.

1928 (9–0–1) *Won:* Maryville 41–0, Centre 41–7, Mississippi 13–12, Alabama 15–13 (1st meeting since 1914), Washington & Lee 26–7, Carson-Newman 57–0, Sewanee 37–0, Vanderbilt 6–0 (1st over Commodores in 9 games since 1916), Florida 13–12 (1st meeting since 1921). *Tied:* Kentucky 0–0. *Star:* soph B Gene McEver (13 TDs).

1929 (9–0–1) *Won:* Centre 40–6, Chattanooga 20–0 (1st meeting since 1921), Mississippi 52–7, Alabama 6–0, Washington & Lee 30–0, Auburn 27–0 (1st meeting since 1900), Carson-Newman 73–0 (10th straight in series), Vanderbilt 13–0, South Carolina 54–0 (1st meeting since 1919). *Tied:* Kentucky 6–6. *Stars:* McEver (Volunteers' 1st consensus All-American; 21 TDs), QB Bobby Dodd, Es Paul Hug and Fritz Brandt.

1930 (9–1) *Won:* Maryville 54–0, Centre 18–0, Mississippi 27–0, North Carolina 9–7, Clemson 27–0 (1st meeting since 1920), Carson-Newman 34–0, Vanderbilt 13–0, Kentucky 8–0, Florida 13–6. *Lost:* unbeaten Alabama 18–6 (ending 33-game undefeated string). *Stars:* Dodd, B Buddy Hackman, G Harry Thayer.

1931 (9–0–1) *Won:* Maryville 33–0, Clemson 44–0, Mississippi 38–0, Alabama 25–0, North Carolina 7–0, Duke 25–2 (1st meeting since 1893), Carson-Newman 31–0, Vanderbilt 21–7. *Tied:* Kentucky 6–6 in finale. *Stars:* McEver (10 TDs), soph HB Beattie Feathers (609 yds rush, 8 TDs, 5 int), G Herman Hickman, T Ray Saunders. *Noteworthy:* beat New York U. 13–0 in postseason charity game in New York City.

1932 (9–0–1) *Won:* Chattanooga 13–0, Mississippi 33–0, North Carolina 20–7, Alabama 7–3, Maryville 60–0 (20th straight over Scots), Duke 16–13, Mississippi St. 31–0 (1st meeting since 1926), Kentucky 26–0, Florida 32–13. *Tied:* Vanderbilt 0–0. *Stars:* Feathers (616 yds rush, 12 TDs, 39.4-yd punting avg), E Van Rayburn. *Noteworthy:* got share of 2nd SC title in last year in league.

1933 (7–3) *Won:* Virginia Tech 27–0, Mississippi St. 20–0 (1st SEC game), Florida 13–6, George Washington 13–0, Mississippi 35–6 (10th straight over Rebels), Vanderbilt 33–6, Kentucky 27–0. *Lost:* Duke 10–2, Alabama 12–6, unbeaten LSU 7–0 (1st meeting since 1926). *Stars:* Feathers (663 yds rush, 13 TDs, 40.4-yd punting avg), C Sheriff Maples.

1934 (8–2) *Won:* Centre 32–0, North Carolina 19–7, Mississippi 27–0, Duke 14–6, Mississippi St. 14–0, Vanderbilt 13–6, Kentucky 19–0, LSU 19–13. *Lost:* unbeaten national cochamp Alabama 13–6, Fordham 13–12. *Star:* G Murray Warmath.

1936 (6–2–2) *Won:* Chattanooga 13–0, Duke 15–13, Georgia 46–0 (1st meeting since 1925), Maryville 34–0, Vanderbilt 26–13, Kentucky 7–6. *Lost:* North Carolina 14–6, Auburn 6–0 in consecutive early games. *Tied:* unbeaten Alabama 0–0, Mississippi 0–0. *Star:* B Phil Dickens.

1938 (11–0) *Won:* Sewanee 26–3 (10th straight over Tigers), Clemson 20–7 (1st meeting since 1931), Auburn 7–0, Alabama 13–0, The Citadel 44–0, LSU 14–6, Chattanooga 45–0, Vanderbilt 14–0, Kentucky 46–0, Mississippi 47–0. *Stars:* TB George Cafego (645 yds rush), E Bowden Wyatt, soph G Bob Suffridge. *Noteworthy:* Won 1st SEC title and share of 1st national championship. Made 1st bowl appearance, beating undefeated Oklahoma 17–0 in Orange Bowl; scored on TDs by soph Bob Foxx (8-yd run) and Babe Wood (15-yd run), and 22-yd FG by Wyatt.

1939 (10–1) *Won:* N.C. State 13–0, Sewanee 40–0, Chattanooga 28–0 (10th straight over Moccasins), Alabama 21–0, Mercer 17–0, LSU 20–0, The Citadel 34–0, Vanderbilt 13–0, Kentucky 19–0, Auburn 7–0. *Stars:* Cafego (443 yds rush), Foxx, Suffridge, G Ed Molinski, T Abe Shires, C James Rike. *Noteworthy:* Blanked opponents 212–0 to lead nation in scoring defense and got share of 2nd SEC title (5th conference crown). Lost to unbeaten Southern California (USC) 14–0 in Rose Bowl as Cafego sat out game with injury; gave up TDs in 2nd and 4th quarters.

1940 (10–1) *Won:* Mercer 49–0, Duke 13–0, Chattanooga 53–0, Alabama 27–12, Florida 14–0 (1st meeting since 1933), LSU 28–0, Southwestern (Tenn.) 41–0, Virginia 41–14, Kentucky 33–0, Vanderbilt 20–0. *Stars:* Suffridge, Molinski, Shires, Foxx. *Noteworthy:* Neyland's 8th unbeaten team again led nation in scoring defense (2.6-pt avg) and won 3rd straight SEC title. Lost to unbeaten Boston College 19–13 in Sugar Bowl; scored TDs on short runs by Van Thompson and Buist Warren.

1941 (8–2) *Won:* Furman 32–6, Dayton 26–0, Cincinnati 21–6, LSU 13–6, Howard 28–6, Boston College 14–7, Kentucky 20–7, Vanderbilt 26–7. *Lost:* unbeaten Duke 19–0, Alabama 9–2. *Star:* T Don Edmiston. *Noteworthy:* John Barnhill took

over as coach with Neyland called to active military service.

1942 (9–1–1) *Won:* Fordham 40–14, Dayton 34–6, Furman 52–7, LSU 26–0, Cincinnati 34–12, Mississippi 14–0, Kentucky 26–0, Vanderbilt 19–7. *Lost:* Alabama 8–0. *Tied:* South Carolina 0–0 (1st meeting since 1929) in opener. *Stars:* E Al Hust, P Bobby Cifers (nation's leader with 42.9-yd avg). *Noteworthy:* beat undefeated Tulsa 14–7 in Sugar Bowl; Bill Gold and Clyde Fuson scored TDs on short runs and Denver Crawford blocked punt out of end zone for safety.

1943 No team, due to W.W. II.

1944 (7–1–1) *Won:* Kentucky 26–13, 21–7, Mississippi 20–7, Florida 40–0, Clemson 26–7 (1st meeting since 1938), LSU 13–0, Temple 27–14. *Tied:* Alabama 0–0. *Stars:* G Bob Dobelstein, B Buster Stephens. *Noteworthy:* lost to unbeaten USC 25–0 in Rose Bowl; trailed only 12–0 going into 4th quarter.

1945 (8–1) *Won:* Wake Forest 7–6, William & Mary 48–13, Chattanooga 30–0, Villanova 33–2, North Carolina 20–6 (1st meeting since 1936), Mississippi 34–0, Kentucky 14–0 (10th straight over Wildcats), Vanderbilt 45–0. *Lost:* unbeaten Alabama 25–7. *Star:* Dobelstein. *Noteworthy:* Barnhill's last team.

1946 (9–2) *Won:* Georgia Tech 13–9 (1st meeting since 1911), Duke 12–7 (1st meeting since 1941), Chattanooga 47–7, Alabama 12–0, North Carolina 20–14, Mississippi 18–14, Boston College 33–13, Kentucky 7–0, Vanderbilt 7–6. *Lost:* Wake Forest 19–6. *Star:* T Dick Huffman. *Noteworthy:* Got share of 4th SEC title as Neyland returned as coach. Lost to Rice 8–0 in Orange Bowl, giving up all points in 1st quarter on blocked punt out of end zone and 50-yd run.

1949 (7–2–1) *Won:* Mississippi St. 10–0, Chattanooga 39–7, Tennessee Tech 36–6, North Carolina 35–6, Mississippi 35–7, Kentucky 6–0, Vanderbilt 26–20. *Lost:* Duke 21–7, Georgia Tech 30–13. *Tied:* Alabama 7–7. *Stars:* E Bud Sherrod, soph TB Hank Lauricella (569 yds total off), J.W. Sherrill (12 int).

1950 (11–1) *Won:* Southern Mississippi 56–0, Duke 28–7, Chattanooga 41–0, Alabama 14–9, Washington & Lee 27–20, North Carolina 16–0, Tennessee Tech 48–14, Mississippi 35–0, Kentucky 7–0, Vanderbilt 43–0. *Lost:* Mississippi St. 7–0. *Stars:* Sherrod, Lauricella (766 yds total off), soph Andy Kozar (648 yds rush, 11 TDs), G Ted Daffer,

Bert Rechichar (9 pass rec for 205 yds, 7 int), Gordon Polofsky (6 int). *Noteworthy:* Led nation in pass defense. Beat Texas 20–14 in Cotton Bowl after trailing 14–7 at half; scored on 5-yd pass from Harold "Herky" Payne to John Gruble (set up by 75-yd run by Lauricella, who had 131 yds rush) in 1st quarter and 2 short runs by Kozar in 4th period.

1951 (10–1) *Won:* Mississippi St. 14–0, Duke 26–0, Chattanooga 42–13, Alabama 27–13, Tennessee Tech 68–0, North Carolina 27–0, Washington & Lee 60–14, Mississippi 46–21, Kentucky 28–0, Vanderbilt 35–27. *Stars:* Lauricella (881 yds and 8 TDs rush, 352 yds and 5 TDs pass), Payne (14 TDs), Kozar (11 TDs), Rechichar, Daffer, G John Michels, Ts Bill Pearman and Doug Atkins. *Noteworthy:* Got share of 5th SEC title and won 2nd national crown. Upset by unbeaten Maryland 28–13 in Sugar Bowl, dropping behind 21–6 by halftime; Payne passed to Rechichar for 1st Vol TD and scored other on 2-yd run.

1952 (8–2–1) *Won:* Mississippi St. 14–7, Chattanooga 26–6, Alabama 20–0, Wofford 50–0, North Carolina 41–14, LSU 22–3 (1st meeting since 1944), Florida 26–12 (1st meeting since 1944), Vanderbilt 46–0. *Lost:* Duke 7–0. *Tied:* Kentucky 14–14. *Stars:* Kozar (660 yds rush, 7 TDs), John Davis (14 pass rec for 297 yds), Atkins, Michels, G Francis Holohan, E Mack Franklin. *Noteworthy:* Neyland's last team led nation in total defense. Lost to Texas 16–0 in Cotton Bowl, dropping behind 9–0 by halftime and finishing with minus 14 yds rush.

1956 (10–1) *Won:* Auburn 35–7 (1st meeting since 1939), Duke 33–20, Chattanooga 42–20, Alabama 24–0, Maryland 34–7, North Carolina 20–0, Georgia Tech 6–0, Mississippi 27–7, Kentucky 20–7, Vanderbilt 27–7. *Stars:* TB Johnny Majors (549 yds and 7 TDs rush, 552 yds and 5 TDs pass, 43-yd punting avg), E Kyle "Buddy" Cruze (20 pass rec for 357 yds), FB Tommy Bronson (562 yds rush, 8 TDs), T John Gordy. *Noteworthy:* Won 6th SEC title. Upset by Baylor 13–7 in Sugar Bowl, losing ball 4 times on int; scored on 1-yd run by Majors in 3rd quarter.

1957 (8–3) *Won:* Mississippi St. 14–9, Chattanooga 28–13, Alabama 14–0, Maryland 16–0, North Carolina 35–0, Georgia Tech 21–6, Vanderbilt 20–6. *Lost:* unbeaten national cochamp Auburn 7–0, Mississippi 14–7 (1st to Rebels in 5 games since 1948), Kentucky 20–6. *Stars:* B Bobby Gordon (526 yds

rush, 9 TDs, 42.7-yd punting avg), G Bill Johnson. *Noteworthy:* beat Texas A&M 3–0 in Gator Bowl on 17-yd 4th quarter FG by Sammy Burklow.

1960 (6–2–2) *Won:* Auburn 10–3, Tampa 62–7, Alabama 20–7, Chattanooga 35–0, North Carolina 27–14, Vanderbilt 35–0. *Lost:* Georgia Tech 14–7, unbeaten national cochamp Mississippi 24–3 in successive late games. *Tied:* Mississippi St. 0–0, Kentucky 10–10. *Star:* Glen Glass (8 TDs).

1965 (8–1–2) *Won:* Army 21–0, South Carolina 24–3 (1st meeting since 1942), Houston 17–8, Georgia Tech 21–7, Kentucky 19–3, Vanderbilt 21–3, UCLA 37–34 (1st meeting). *Lost:* Mississippi 14–13. *Tied:* Auburn 13–13, Alabama 7–7. *Stars:* LB Frank Emanuel, E Bobby Frazier, Johnny Mills (23 pass rec for 328 yds). *Noteworthy:* beat Tulsa 27–6 in steady downpour in Bluebonnet Bowl, gaining possession on 4 int and 3 fumbles; soph QB Dewey Warren scored 2 TDs on short runs and passed 4 yds to Hal Wantland for another, and FB Stan Mitchell scored on 11-yd run.

1966 (8–3) *Won:* Auburn 28–0, Rice 23–3, South Carolina 29–17, Army 38–7, Chattanooga 28–10, Kentucky 28–19, Vanderbilt 28–0. *Lost:* Georgia Tech 6–3, unbeaten Alabama 11–10, Mississippi 14–7. *Stars:* LB Paul Naumoff, Warren (nation's passing efficiency leader with 1,716 yds and 18 TDs), Mills (48 pass rec for 725 yds), E Austin Denney (7 TDs), C Bob Johnson, P Ron Widby (nation's leader with 43.8-yd avg). *Noteworthy:* beat Syracuse 18–12 in Gator Bowl, building 18–0 halftime lead on 2 FGs by Gary Wright and 2 TD passes by Warren (to Denney and soph WB Richmond Flowers).

1967 (9–2) *Won:* Auburn 27–13, Georgia Tech 24–13, Alabama 24–13 (1st over Tide since 1960), LSU 17–14, Tampa 38–0, Tulane 35–14, Mississippi 20–7 (1st over Rebels since 1958), Kentucky 17–7, Vanderbilt 41–14. *Lost:* UCLA 20–16 in opener. *Stars:* Warren (1,053 yds pass), Flowers (41 pass rec for 585 yds), Walter Chadwick (645 yds rush, 11 TDs), B Albert Dorsey, Johnson, G Charles Rosenfelder, T John Boynton, Mike Jones (7 int). *Noteworthy:* Won 7th SEC title. Lost to Oklahoma 26–24 in Orange Bowl after trailing 19–0 at halftime; scored on 36-yd pass int return by Jimmy Glover, 5-yd run by Charley Fulton, 1-yd run by Warren, and FG and 3 ex pts by Karl Kremser.

1968 (8–2–1) *Won:* Memphis St. 24–17 (1st meeting), Rice 52–0, Georgia Tech 24–7, Alabama 10–9, UCLA 42–18, Mississippi 31–0, Kentucky 24–7,

Vanderbilt 10–7. *Lost:* Auburn 28–14. *Tied:* unbeaten Georgia 17–17 (1st meeting since 1937). *Stars:* Rosenfelder, soph C Chip Kell, QB Bubba Wyche (1,539 yds and 14 TDs pass), E Ken DeLong (34 pass rec for 393 yds), B Jim Weatherford, FB Richard Pickens (736 yds rush), LB Steve Kiner, Bill Young (9 int), P Herman Weaver (40.4-yd avg). *Noteworthy:* lost to Texas 36–13 in Cotton Bowl, dropping behind 28–0 by halftime; sub soph QB Bobby Scott passed for both TDs (to Gary Kreis and Mike Price).

1969 (9–2) *Won:* UT-Chattanooga 31–0, Auburn 45–19, Memphis St. 55–16, Georgia Tech 26–8, Alabama 41–14, Georgia 17–3, South Carolina 29–14, Kentucky 31–26, Vanderbilt 40–27. *Lost:* Mississippi 38–0. *Stars:* Scott (1,352 yds pass), Kreis (38 pass rec for 609 yds and 5 TDs), soph FB Curt Watson (807 yds rush), G Kell, DeLong, T Frank Yanossy, soph K George Hunt (10 FGs), Kiner, LB Jack Reynolds, Tim Priest (7 int), Weaver (41.2-yd punting avg). *Noteworthy:* Doug Dickey's last team won 8th SEC title. Lost to Florida 14–13 (1st meeting since 1955) in Gator Bowl; Watson ran for 121 yds, Scott passed to Lester McClain for TD, and Hunt kicked 2 FGs.

1970 (11–1) *Won:* Southern Methodist (SMU) 28–3, Army 48–3, Georgia Tech 17–6, Alabama 24–0, Florida 38–7, Wake Forest 41–7, South Carolina 20–18, Kentucky 45–0, Vanderbilt 24–6, UCLA 28–17. *Lost:* Auburn 36–23 in 2nd game. *Stars:* Scott (1,697 yds and 14 TDs pass), Joe Thompson (37 pass rec for 502 yds), Watson (791 yds rush), Kell, C Mike Bevans, Hunt (10 FGs, 72 pts), LB Jackie Walker, DB Bobby Majors (10 int), Priest. *Noteworthy:* 1st year under Bill Battle. Beat Air Force 34–13 in Sugar Bowl, jumping off to 24–7 lead in 1st quarter; Don McCleary scored 2 TDs, Scott passed for one, Majors scored on 57-yd punt return, and Hunt kicked 2 FGs and 4 ex pts while defense made 4 int and 4 fumble recoveries.

1971 (10–2) *Won:* UC–Santa Barbara 48–6, Florida 20–13, Georgia Tech 10–6, Mississippi St. 10–7 (1st meeting since 1964), Tulsa 38–3, South Carolina 35–6, Kentucky 21–7, Vanderbilt 19–7, Penn St. 31–11. *Lost:* Auburn 10–9, unbeaten Alabama 32–15 in early games. *Stars:* Walker, Majors, LB Ray Nettles, Conrad Graham (5 int), Watson (766 yds rush), Thompson (15 pass rec for 247 yds), Hunt (12 FGs). *Noteworthy:* beat Arkansas 14–13 (1st meeting since 1907) in Liberty Bowl on 17-yd TD run by Watson late in 4th quarter; soph Bill

Rudder scored on 2-yd run in 1st quarter, and Hunt kicked 2 ex pts.

1972 (10–2) *Won:* Georgia Tech 34–3, Penn St. 28–21 (1st night game in Neyland Stadium), Wake Forest 45–6, Memphis St. 38–7, Hawaii 34–2, Georgia 14–0, Mississippi 17–0, Kentucky 17–7, Vanderbilt 30–10. *Lost:* Auburn 10–6, Alabama 17–10 in early games. *Stars:* soph QB Condredge Holloway (1,073 yds total off), Haskel Stanback (890 yds rush, 12 TDs), Emmon Love (20 pass rec for 280 yds), G Bill Emendorfer, T John Wagster, K Ricky Townsend (12 FGs), LB Jamie Rotella, Graham (7 int). *Noteworthy:* beat LSU 24–17 (1st meeting since 1967) in Astro-Bluebonnet Bowl, opening up 24–3 halftime lead; Holloway ran for 74 yds and 2 TDs and passed for 94 yds and another, and Townsend kicked FG and 3 ex pts.

1973 (8–4) *Won:* Duke 21–17 (1st meeting since 1956), Army 37–18, Auburn 21–0, Kansas 28–27, Georgia Tech 20–14, Texas Christian (TCU) 39–7, Kentucky 16–14, Vanderbilt 20–17. *Lost:* unbeaten national cochamp Alabama 42–21, Georgia 35–31 (1st to Bulldogs in 7 games since 1924), Mississippi 28–18. *Stars:* Holloway (1,149 yds pass, 433 yds rush), frosh Stanley Morgan (22 pass rec for 511 yds), Stanback (682 yds rush), Townsend (11 FGs), LB Art Reynolds, DB Eddie Brown (5 int), P Neil Clabo (43.6-yd avg). *Noteworthy:* lost to Texas Tech 28–19 in Gator Bowl; Stanback ran for 95 yds and a TD and caught TD pass from Holloway, and Townsend kicked 2 FGs.

1981 (8–4) *Won:* Colorado St. 42–0, Auburn 10–7, Georgia Tech 10–7, Memphis St. 28–9, Wichita St. 24–21, Mississippi 28–20, Vanderbilt 38–34. *Lost:* Georgia 44–0, USC 43–7, Alabama 38–19, Kentucky 21–10. *Stars:* QB Steve Alatorre (1,171 yds pass), Anthony Hancock (32 pass rec for 437 yds and 5 TDs), WR Willie Gault (22 pass rec for 479 yds, 5 TDs), James Berry (500 yds and 6 TDs rush), C Lee North, LB Lemont Holt Jeffers, frosh P Jimmy Colquitt (43.8-yd avg). *Noteworthy:* beat Wisconsin 28–21 in Garden State Bowl; Alatorre passed for 315 yds and a TD (43 yds to Hancock, who caught 11 passes) and 2-pt conversion and scored a TD, Gault scored on 97-yd kickoff return, and frosh K Fuad Reveiz had 2 FGs.

1983 (9–3) *Won:* New Mexico 31–6, The Citadel 45–6, LSU 20–6, Alabama 41–34, Georgia Tech 37–3, Rutgers 7–0, Kentucky 10–0, Vanderbilt 34–24. *Lost:* Pittsburgh 13–3, Auburn 37–14, Mississippi 13–10. *Stars:* QB Alan Cockrell (1,683 yds and 13 TDs pass), Clyde Duncan (33 pass rec for 640 yds), soph WR Tim McGee (19 pass rec for 286 yds), Johnnie Jones (1,116 yds rush), G Bill Mayo, C Glenn Streno, Reveiz (17 FGs, 78 pts), DT Reggie White, LB Alvin Toles, Colquitt (42-yd punting avg). *Noteworthy:* beat Maryland 30–23 in Florida Citrus Bowl; Jones ran for 154 yds and 2 TDs, Cockrell passed for 185 yds and a TD, and soph Sam Henderson scored on 19-yd run.

1985 (9–1–2) *Won:* Auburn 38–20, Wake Forest 31–29, Alabama 16–14, Rutgers 40–0, Memphis St. 17–7 (10th win in as many games with Tigers), Mississippi 34–14, Kentucky 42–0, Vanderbilt 30–0. *Lost:* Florida 17–10. *Tied:* UCLA 26–26 (1st meeting since 1978), Georgia Tech 6–6. *Stars:* QB Tony Robinson (1,246 yds pass), McGee (50 pass rec for 947 yds and 7 TDs), Keith Davis (684 yds rush), T Bruce Wilkerson, K Carlos Reveiz (24 FGs, 102 pts), LB Dale Jones, DB Chris White (nation's coleader with 9 int). *Noteworthy:* Won 9th SEC title and led nation in turnover margin. Beat Miami (Fla.) 35–7 in Sugar Bowl; QB Daryl Dickey passed for 131 yds and a TD, Jeff Powell scored on 60-yd run, and other Tennessee TDs came on recovered fumble in end zone by McGee, 1-yd run by Henderson, and 6-yd run by soph Charles Wilson.

1987 (10–2–1) *Won:* Iowa 23–22, Colorado St. 49–3, Mississippi St. 38–10, California 38–12, Georgia Tech 29–15, Louisville 41–10, Mississippi 55–13, Kentucky 24–22, Vanderbilt 38–36. *Lost:* Alabama 41–22, Boston College 20–18 (1st to Eagles in 7 games since 1941 Sugar Bowl). *Tied:* Auburn 20–20. *Stars:* frosh RB Reggie Cobb (1,197 yds rush, 1,721 all-purpose yds, 20 TDs), QB Jeff Francis (1,512 yds pass), soph WRs Thomas Woods (26 pass rec for 335 yds) and Terence Cleveland (23 pass rec for 417 yds and 5 TDs), frosh WR Alvin Harper (15 pass rec for 247 yds), OG Harry Galbreath, DT Mark Hovanic, LB Keith DeLong, DB Terry McDaniel, P Bob Garmon (41.1-yd avg). *Noteworthy:* beat Indiana 27–22 in Peach Bowl; Francis passed for 2 TDs (45 yds to Anthony Miller and 15 yds to Cleveland), and Cobb ran for 2 TDs.

1989 (11–1) *Won:* Colorado St. 17–14, UCLA 24–6 (1st over Bruins in 5 games since 1970), Duke 28–6, Auburn 21–14, Georgia 17–14 (1st over Bulldogs in 5 games since 1972), LSU 45–39, Akron 52–9, Mississippi 33–21, Kentucky 31–10, Vanderbilt 17–10. *Lost:* Alabama 47–30. *Stars:* soph QB Andy Kelly (1,299 yds pass), Woods (34 pass rec for 511

yds), FB Greg Amsler (23 pass rec for 244 yds, 7 TDs), frosh RB Chuck Webb (1,236 yds and 12 TDs rush), Cobb (616 yds and 6 TDs rush), G Eric Still, OTs Antone Davis and Charles McRae, K Greg Burke (13 FGs, 75 pts), DE Marion Hobby, soph LB Darryl Hardy, DB Preston Warren, P Kent Elmore (40.2-yd avg). *Noteworthy:* Got share of 10th SEC title. Beat Arkansas 31–27 (1st meeting since 1971) in Cotton Bowl; Webb ran for 250 yds and 2 TDs (including 78-yd run), Kelly passed for 150 yds and 2 TDs (including 84-yarder to WR Anthony Morgan), and Burke kicked FG and 4 ex pts.

1990 (9–2–2) *Won:* Pacific 55–7, Mississippi St. 40–7, Texas–El Paso 56–0, Florida 45–3 (1st meeting since 1985, 1st over Gators in 5 games since 1971), Temple 41–20, Mississippi 22–13, Kentucky 42–28, Vanderbilt 49–20. *Lost:* Alabama 9–6, Notre Dame 34–29. *Tied:* national cochamp Colorado 31–31, Auburn 26–26. *Stars:* Kelly (2,241 yds and 14 TDs pass), Harper (37 pass rec for 567 yds and 8 TDs), soph WR Carl Pickens (53 pass rec for 917 yds and 6 TDs), TB Tony Thompson (1,261 yds and 16 TDs rush), Davis, Burke (19 FGs, 107 pts), DT Carey Bailey, LB Earnest Fields, Hardy, DBs Dale Carter (5 int, nation's kickoff return leader with 29.8-yd avg) and Jeremy Lincoln, frosh P Joey Chapman (41.9-yd avg). *Noteworthy:* edged Virginia 23–22 in Sugar Bowl after trailing 16–0 at halftime as Thompson (151 yds and 2 TDs rush) scored winning TD on short plunge with 31 seconds left; Kelly passed to Pickens for other Vol TD, and Burke kicked FG and 2 ex pts.

1991 (9–3) *Won:* Louisville 28–11, UCLA 30–16, Mississippi St. 26–24, Auburn 30–21, Memphis St. 52–24, Notre Dame 35–34, Mississippi 36–25, Kentucky 16–7, Vanderbilt 45–0. *Lost:* Florida 35–18, Alabama 24–19 in successive mid-season games. *Stars:* Kelly (2,759 yds and 15 TDs pass), Pickens (6 TDs, 49 pass rec for 877 yds and 5 TDs), WRs J.J. McCleskey (35 pass rec for 391 yds) and soph Corey Fleming (5 TDs on pass rec), soph WB Craig Faulkner (35 pass rec for 509 yds), frosh RBs James Stewart (939 yds and 8 TDs rush) and Aaron Hayden (704 yds rush, 8 TDs), TE Mark Adams, OG Tom Myslinski, frosh K John Becksvoort (15 FGs, 73 pts), DEs Chuck Smith and Chris Mims, Hardy, Fields, LB Shon Walker, Carter, Lincoln, frosh P Tom Hutton (41.9-yd avg). *Noteworthy:* lost to Penn St. 42–17 in Fiesta Bowl (breaking 5-bowl win string) after leading 17–7 in 3rd period; Kelly passed for 273 yds and a TD (44 yds to

Fleming), Pickens had 8 pass rec for 100 yds, and Stewart ran for 84 yds and a TD.

1992 (9–3) *Won:* SW Louisiana 38–3, Georgia 34–31, Florida 31–14, Cincinnati 40–0, LSU 20–0, Memphis St. 26–21, Kentucky 34–13, Vanderbilt 29–25 (10th straight over Commodores). *Lost:* Arkansas 25–24, unbeaten national champ Alabama 17–10, South Carolina 24–23 (1st meeting since 1971, 1st loss to Gamecocks in 10 games since initial contest in 1903) in successive mid-season games. *Stars:* soph QB Heath Shuler (1,712 yds and 10 TDs pass, 286 yds and 11 TDs rush), Fleming (40 pass rec for 490 yds), Faulkner (31 pass rec for 462 yds), TB Charlie Garner (928 yds rush), Stewart (8 TDs), OT Mike Stowell, Becksvoort (16 FGs, 83 pts), DEs Todd Kelly and James Wilson, LBs Reggie Ingram and soph Ben Talley, frosh DB Jason Parker, Hutton (41.1-yd punting avg).

Noteworthy: Majors' last team (Phillip Fulmer coached Vols to wins in 1st 3 games while Majors was recuperating from operation). Under Fulmer, beat Boston College 38–23 in Hall of Fame Bowl as Shuler passed for 245 yds and 2 TDs (including 69-yarder to soph RB Mose Phillips) and ran for 2 TDs, Fleming had 5 pass rec for 102 yds and 2 TDs (27 yds from Shuler and 28 yds from soph QB Jerry Colquitt), and Becksvoort had FG and 5 ex pts.

BOWL SUMMARY

Bluebonnet 2–1; Cotton 2–2; Fiesta 0–1; Florida Citrus 1–0; Garden State 1–0; Gator 2–2; Hall of Fame 1–0; Liberty 3–0; Orange 1–2; Peach 1–1; Rose 0–2; Sugar 4–3; Sun 0–1.

BOWL RECORD (18–15)

Regular Season	Bowl	Score	Opponent	Record
1938 (10–0)	Orange	17–0	Oklahoma	(10–0)
1939 (10–0)	Rose	0–14	USC	(7–0–2)
1940 (10–0)	Sugar	13–19	Boston College	(10–0)
1942 (8–1–1)	Sugar	14–7	Tulsa	(10–0)
1944 (7–0–1)	Rose	0–25	USC	(7–0–2)
1946 (9–1)	Orange	0–8	Rice	(8–2)
1950 (10–1)	Cotton	20–14	Texas	(9–1)
1951 (10–0)	Sugar	13–28	Maryland	(9–0)
1952 (8–1–1)	Cotton	0–16	Texas	(8–2)
1956 (10–0)	Sugar	7–13	Baylor	(8–2)
1957 (7–3)	Gator	3–0	Texas A&M	(8–2)
1965 (7–1–2)	Bluebonnet	27–6	Tulsa	(8–2)
1966 (7–3)	Gator	18–12	Syracuse	(8–2)
1967 (9–1)	Orange	24–26	Oklahoma	(9–1)
1968 (8–1–1)	Cotton	13–36	Texas	(8–1–1)
1969 (9–1)	Gator	13–14	Florida	(8–1–1)
1970 (10–1)	Sugar	34–13	Air Force	(9–2)
1971 (9–2)	Liberty	14–13	Arkansas	(8–2–1)
1972 (9–2)	Bluebonnet	24–17	LSU	(9–1–1)
1973 (8–3)	Gator	19–28	Texas Tech	(10–1)
1974 (6–3–2)	Liberty	7–3	Maryland	(8–3)
1979 (7–4)	Bluebonnet	22–27	Purdue	(9–2)
1981 (7–4)	Garden State	28–21	Wisconsin	(7–4)
1982 (6–4–1)	Peach	22–28	Iowa	(7–4)
1983 (8–3)	Florida Citrus	30–23	Maryland	(8–3)
1984 (7–3–1)	Sun	27–28	Maryland	(8–3)
1985 (8–1–2)	Sugar	35–7	Miami (Fla.)	(10–1)
1986 (6–5)	Liberty	21–14	Minnesota	(6–5)
1987 (9–2–1)	Peach	27–22	Indiana	(8–3)

(continued)

Regular Season	Bowl	Score	Opponent	Record
1989 (10–1)	Cotton	31–27	Arkansas	(10–1)
1990 (8–2–2)	Sugar	23–22	Virginia	(8–3)
1991 (9–2)	Fiesta	17–42	Penn State	(10–2)
1992 (8–3)	Hall of Fame	38–23	Boston College	(8–2–1)

CONFERENCE TITLES

Southern Intercollegiate Athletic Association—1914. **Southern**—1927, 1932*.
Southeastern—1938, 1939*, 1940, 1946*, 1951*, 1956, 1967, 1969, 1985, 1989*, 1990.

TOP 20 AP AND UPI
(USA TODAY/CNN SINCE 1991) RANKING

1936	17	1946	7	1965	7–7	1973	19–U
1938	2	1949	17	1966	U–14	1974	20–15
1939	2	1950	4–3	1967	2–2	1985	4–4
1940	4	1951	1–1	1968	13–7	1987	14–13
1941	18	1952	8–8	1969	15–11	1989	5–5
1942	7	1956	2–2	1970	4–4	1990	8–7
1944	12	1957	13–16	1971	9–9	1991	14–15
1945	14	1960	U–19	1972	8–11	1992	12–12

MAJOR RIVALS

Tennessee has played at least 10 games with Alabama 27–41–7, Auburn 18–22–3, Boston College 8–2, Carson-Newman 12–0, Centre 10–3–2, Clemson 11–5–2, Duke 12–13–2, Florida 15–7, Georgia 10–10–2, Georgia Tech 24–17–2, Kentucky 56–23–9, Louisiana St. 17–3–3, Maryville 25–1–1, Memphis St. 14–0, Mississippi 39–18–1, Mississippi St. 22–14–1, North Carolina 20–10–1, Sewanee 12–10, South Carolina 7–2–2, UT-Chattanooga 36–2–2, UCLA 5–3–2, Vanderbilt 55–26–5. Record with SEC member played fewer than 10 times: Arkansas 2–1.

COACHES

Dean of Tennessee coaches is Robert E. Neyland with record of 173–31–12 for 1926–34, 1936–40, and 1946–52, including 7 conference titles, 7 bowl teams, 9 teams unbeaten in regular season, and 3 national champions. Other top records for at least 3 years were by George Levene, 15–10–3 for 1907–09; Z.G. Clevenger, 26–15–2 for 1911–15 with 1 unbeaten SIAA champion; John R. Bender, 18–5–4 for 1916–20 with 1 unbeaten team; M.B. Banks, 27–15–3 for 1921–25; John Barnhill, 32–5–2 for 1941–45 with 2 bowl teams and 1 team unbeaten in regular season; Bowden Wyatt (1956 national Coach of Year), 49–29–4 for 1955–62 with 1 SEC title, 2 bowl teams, 1 team unbeaten in regular season; Doug Dickey, 46–15–4 for 1964–69 with 2 SEC titles and 5 bowl teams; Bill Battle, 59–22–2 for 1970–76 with 5 bowl teams (4 winners); and Johnny Majors, 116–62–8 for 1977–92 with 3 SEC titles and 12 bowl teams.

MISCELLANEA

First game was loss to Sewanee 24–0 in 1891 . . . 1st win was over Maryville 25–0 in 1892 . . . highest score was over American U. 104–0 in 1905 . . . highest since W.W. II was over Tennessee Tech 68–0 in 1951 . . . worst defeat was by Duke 70–0 in 1893 . . . worst since 1900 was by Alabama 51–0 in 1906 and by Vanderbilt 51–0 in 1909 . . . worst since W.W. II was by Georgia 44–0 in 1981 . . . highest against since 1900 was by Alabama 56–28 in

1986 . . . longest unbeaten string of 33 in 1926–30 ended by Alabama 18–6 . . . 28-game unbeaten string in 1930–33 ended by Duke 10–2 . . . longest win streak of 23 in 1937–39 ended by USC 14–0 in 1940 Rose Bowl . . . 20-game win streak in 1950–51 ended by Maryland 28–13 in 1952 Sugar Bowl . . . longest losing string of 7 in 1892–93 broken with win over Maryville 32–0 . . . consensus All-Americans were Gene McEver, B, 1929; Beattie Feathers, B, 1933; Bowden Wyatt, E, 1938; Ed Molinski, G, and George Cafego, B, 1939; Bob Suffridge, G, 1940; Dick Huffman, T, 1946; Hank Lauricella, B, 1951; John Michels, G, 1952; John Majors, B, 1956; Frank Emanuel, LB, 1965; Paul Naumoff, LB, 1966; Bob Johnson, C, 1967; Charles Rosenfelder, G, 1968; Steve Kiner, LB, 1968–69; Chip Kell, G, 1969–70; Bobby Majors, DB, 1971; Larry Seivers, E, 1975–76; Roland James, DB, 1979; Reggie White, DL, 1983; Bill Mayo, G, 1984; Tim McGee, WR, 1985; Eric Still, OL, 1989; Antone Davis, OL, 1990; and Dale Carter, DB, 1991 . . . Academic All-Americans were Charles Rader, T, 1956; Bill Johnson, G, 1957; Mack Gentry, DT, 1965; Bob Johnson, C, 1967; Tim Priest, DB, 1970; Timothy Irwin, OT, 1980; and Mike Terry, DL, 1982 . . . Outland Trophy winner was Steve De-Long, T, 1964.

VANDERBILT (Commodores; Black and Gold)

NOTABLE TEAMS

1893 (6–1) *Won:* Memphis A.C. 68–0, Sewanee 10–8, 10–0, Georgia 35–0 (1st meeting), Louisville A.C. 36–12, Central U. (Ky.) 12–0 (1st meeting). *Lost:* unbeaten Auburn 30–10 (1st meeting).
1894 (7–1) *Won:* Memphis A.C. 64–0, Centre 6–0 (1st meeting), Auburn 20–4, Mississippi 40–0 (1st meeting), Central U. (Ky.) 34–6, Cumberland 62–0, Sewanee 12–0. *Lost:* Louisville A.C. 10–8.
1897 (6–0–1) *Won:* Kentucky St. 24–0, 50–0, Central U. (Ky.) 14–0, Virginia Military Institute (VMI) 12–0, North Carolina 31–0, Sewanee 10–0. *Tied:* Virginia 0–0 in finale. *Noteworthy:* blanked foes 141–0 in 1st undefeated season since 1-game schedule of 1890.
1899 (7–2) *Won:* Cumberland 32–0, Miami (Ohio) 12–0, Mississippi 11–0, Bethel 22–0, Texas 6–0 (1st meeting), Central U. (Ky.) 21–16, Nashville 5–0.

Lost: Cincinnati 6–0, Indiana 20–0 in consecutive early games.
1901 (6–1–1) *Won:* Kentucky 22–0, Central U. (Ky.) 25–0, Georgia 47–0, Auburn 44–0 (1st meeting since 1895), Tennessee 22–0, Nashville 10–0. *Lost:* Washington (Mo.) 12–11. *Tied:* Sewanee 0–0. *Noteworthy:* 1st year under W.H. Watkins.
1902 (8–1) *Won:* Cumberland 45–0, Mississippi 29–0, Central U. (Ky.) 24–17, Tennessee 12–5, Washington (Mo.) 33–12, Kentucky 16–5, Tulane 23–5 (1st meeting), Louisiana St. (LSU) 27–5 (1st meeting). *Lost:* Sewanee 11–5 in finale. *Noteworthy:* Watkins' last team.
1903 (6–1–1) *Won:* Alabama 30–0 (1st meeting), Tennessee 40–0, Mississippi 33–0, Georgia 33–0, Washington (Mo.) 41–0, Sewanee 10–5. *Lost:* Cumberland 6–0 in opener. *Tied:* Texas 5–5. *Star:* FB John Tigert. *Noteworthy:* only year under J.H. Henry.
1904 (9–0) *Won:* Mississippi St. 61–0 (1st meeting), Georgetown (Ky.) 66–0, Mississippi 69–0, Missouri Mines 29–4, Central U. (Ky.) 97–0, Centre 22–0, Tennessee 22–0, Nashville 81–0, Sewanee 27–0. *Stars:* frosh HB John "Honus" Craig, FB/E Ed Hamilton, G J.H. "Bull" Brown, frosh C J.N. "Stein" Stone. *Noteworthy:* had 1st undefeated season since 1897 in 1st year under Dan McGugin, outscoring foes 474–4.
1905 (7–1) *Won:* Maryville 97–0, Alabama 34–0, Tennessee 45–0, Texas 33–0, Auburn 54–0, Clemson 41–0, Sewanee 68–4. *Lost:* Michigan 18–0 (1st meeting). *Stars:* Craig, FB Owsley Manier, QB Frank Kyle, soph E Bob Blake, Hamilton, Stone, G Hillsman Taylor, Ts Robert Patterson and Dan Blake.
1906 (8–1) *Won:* Kentucky 28–0, Mississippi 29–0, Alabama 78–0, Texas 45–0, Rose Poly (RPI) 33–0, Georgia Tech 37–6 (1st meeting since 1892), Carlisle Indians 4–0, Sewanee 20–0. *Lost:* Michigan, 10–4. *Stars:* Craig, Manier, QB Sam Costen, Es Dan Blake and Bob Blake, Stone, T Joe Prichard, G Walter Chorn.
1907 (5–1–1) *Won:* Kentucky 40–0, RPI 65–10, Mississippi 60–0, Georgia Tech 54–0, Sewanee 17–12. *Lost:* Michigan 8–0. *Tied:* Navy 6–6. *Stars:* Craig, Costen, Bob Blake, E Vaughan Blake, Stone, G Horace Sherrell.
1908 (7–2–1) *Won:* Southwestern (Tenn.) 11–5, Maryville 32–0, RPI 32–0, Clemson 41–0, Missis-

sippi 29–0, Tennessee 16–9, Washington (Mo.) 28–0. *Lost:* Michigan 24–6, Ohio St. 17–6. *Tied:* Sewanee 6–6. *Stars:* frosh QB Ray Morrison, Vaughn Blake, T Louis Hasslock.

1909 (7–3) *Won:* Southwestern (Tenn.) 52–0, Mercer 28–5, RPI 28–3, Auburn 17–0, Mississippi 17–0 (10th straight over Rebels), Tennessee 51–0, Washington (Mo.) 12–0. *Lost:* Alumni 3–0, Ohio St. 5–0, Sewanee 16–5 (1st to Tigers since 1902). *Stars:* Morrison, Ts Malvern Griffin and soph Ewing Freeland, soph G W.E. "Frog" Metzger.

1910 (8–0–1) *Won:* Mooney School 34–0, RPI 23–0, Castle Heights 14–0, Tennessee 18–0, Mississippi 9–2, LSU 22–0 (1st meeting since 1902), Georgia Tech 23–0, Sewanee 23–6. *Tied:* Yale 0–0. *Stars:* Morrison, HB Bill Neely, Freeland, Metzger. *Noteworthy:* 1st undefeated season since 1904.

1911 (8–1) *Won:* Birmingham Southern 40–0, Maryville 46–0, RPI 33–0, Central U. (Ky.) 45–0, Georgia 17–0 (1st meeting since 1903), Kentucky 18–0, Mississippi 21–0, Sewanee 31–0. *Lost:* Michigan 9–8. *Stars:* Morrison, HB Lewie Hardage, Freeland, Metzger, C Hugh "Buddy" Morgan.

1912 (8–1–1) *Won:* Bethel 105–0, Maryville 100–3, RPI 54–0, Georgia 46–0, Mississippi 24–0, Virginia 13–0 (1st meeting since 1898), Central U. (Ky.) 23–0, Sewanee 16–0. *Lost:* unbeaten national champ Harvard 9–3. *Tied:* Auburn 7–7. *Stars:* Hardage, soph FB Ammie Sikes, Morgan, E Enoch Brown, T Tom Brown.

1915 (9–1) *Won:* Middle Tennessee 51–0 (1st meeting), Southwestern (Tenn.) 47–0, Georgetown (Ky.) 75–0, Cumberland 60–0, Henderson-Brown 100–0, Mississippi 91–0, Tennessee 35–0, Auburn 17–0, Sewanee 27–3. *Lost:* Virginia 35–10. *Stars:* QB Irby "Rabbit" Curry, soph T Josh Cody, G Pryor "Pigiron" Williams. *Noteworthy:* Outscored foes 514–38.

1916 (7–1–1) *Won:* Southwestern (Tenn.) 86–0, Transylvania 42–0, Kentucky 45–0, Mississippi 35–0 (15th straight over Rebels), Virginia 27–6, RPI 67–0, Auburn 20–9. *Lost:* Tennessee 10–6. *Tied:* Sewanee 0–0. *Stars:* Curry, Cody, Williams.

1919 (5–1–2) *Won:* Union (Tenn.) 41–0, Auburn 7–6, Alabama 16–12, Virginia 10–6, Sewanee 33–21. *Lost:* Georgia Tech 20–0. *Tied:* Tennessee 3–3, Kentucky 0–0. *Stars:* Cody, T Tom Lipscomb, E Tom Zerfoss.

1921 (7–0–1) *Won:* Middle Tennessee 34–0, Mer-

cer 42–0, Kentucky 21–14, Texas 20–0 (1st meeting since 1906), Tennessee 14–0, Alabama 14–0, Sewanee 9–0. *Tied:* Georgia 7–7.

1922 (8–0–1) *Won:* Middle Tennessee 38–0, Henderson-Brown 33–0, Texas 20–10, Mercer 25–0, Tennessee 14–6, Kentucky 9–0, Georgia 12–0, Sewanee 26–0. *Tied:* unbeaten Michigan 0–0 (1st meeting since 1914). *Star:* E Lynn Bomar. *Noteworthy:* McGugin's 4th unbeaten team.

1926 (8–1) *Won:* Middle Tennessee 69–0, Bryson 48–0, Texas 7–0, Georgia 14–13, Southwestern (Tenn.) 50–0, Georgia Tech 13–7, Tennessee 20–3, Sewanee 13–0. *Lost:* unbeaten national cochamp Alabama 19–7 in 2nd game. *Stars:* QB Bill Spears, FB Bill Hendrix, T Fred McKibbon.

1927 (8–1–2) *Won:* Chattanooga 45–18 (1st meeting), Ouachita 39–10, Centre 53–6, Tulane 32–0, Kentucky 34–6, Maryland 39–20 (1st meeting), Sewanee 26–6, Alabama 14–7. *Lost:* Texas 13–6. *Tied:* Georgia Tech 0–0, unbeaten Tennessee 7–7 in successive late games. *Stars:* Spears, E Larry Creson, C Vernon Sharp.

1928 (8–2) *Won:* Chattanooga 20–0, Colgate 12–7, Texas 13–12, Tulane 13–6, Virginia 34–0 (1st meeting since 1920), Kentucky 14–7, Centre 26–0, Sewanee 13–0. *Lost:* unbeaten national cochamp Georgia Tech 19–7, unbeaten Tennessee 6–0 (1st to Vols in 12 games since 1914) in consecutive late games. *Stars:* E Dick Abernathy, G John "Bull" Brown.

1929 (7–2) *Won:* Mississippi 19–7, Ouachita 26–6, Auburn 41–2, Maryville 33–0, Alabama 13–0, Georgia Tech 23–7, Sewanee 26–6. *Lost:* Minnesota 15–6, unbeaten Tennessee 13–0. *Stars:* Brown, E Bill Schwartz.

1930 (8–2) *Won:* Chattanooga 39–0, Minnesota 33–7, Virginia Tech 40–0 (1st meeting), Spring Hill 27–6, Mississippi 24–0, Georgia Tech 6–0, Auburn 27–0, Maryland 22–7. *Lost:* unbeaten Alabama 12–7, Tennessee 13–0.

1932 (6–1–2) *Won:* Mercer 20–7, North Carolina 39–7, Western Kentucky 26–0, Georgia 12–6, Georgia Tech 12–0, Maryland 13–0. *Lost:* Alabama 20–0 in finale. *Tied:* Tulane 6–6, unbeaten Tennessee 0–0. *Stars:* C Pete Gracey, T Charles "Tex" Leyendecker.

1935 (7–3) *Won:* Union (Tenn.) 34–0, Mississippi St. 14–9, Cumberland 32–7, Georgia Tech 14–13, Sewanee 46–0, Tennessee 13–7 (1st over Vols since

1926), Alabama 14–6 (1st over Tide since 1929). *Lost:* Temple 6–3, Fordham 13–7, LSU 7–2 in successive mid-season games. *Stars:* QB Rand Dixon, E Willie Geny, G Sam Brown, T Rannie Throgmorton. *Noteworthy:* 1st year under Ray Morrison.

1937 (7–2) *Won:* Kentucky 12–0 (1st meeting since 1928), Chicago 18–0, Southwestern (Tenn.) 17–6, Southern Methodist (SMU) 6–0, LSU 7–6, Sewanee 41–0 (10th straight over Tigers), Tennessee 13–7. *Lost:* Georgia Tech 14–0 (1st to Yellow Jackets since 1928), unbeaten Alabama 9–7. *Stars:* HB Lunsford Hollins, C Carl Hinkle, G Ed Merlin, T Buford Ray.

1941 (8–2) *Won:* Purdue 3–0, Tennessee Tech 42–0, Kentucky 39–15, Georgia Tech 14–7, Princeton 46–7, Sewanee 20–0, Louisville 68–0, Alabama 7–0 (1st over Tide since 1935). *Lost:* Tulane 34–14 (1st meeting since 1932), Tennessee 26–7. *Stars:* C Bob Gude, B Jack Jenkins. *Noteworthy:* nation's most-improved team.

1943 (5–0) *Won:* Tennessee Tech 30–0, 47–7, Camp Campbell 40–14, Milligan 26–6, Carson-Newman 12–6. *Star:* B Harry Robinson. *Noteworthy:* Schedule restricted by W.W. II. E.H. Alley coached Commodores to 1st undefeated season since 1922 with "Red" Sanders on active duty with U.S. Navy.

1948 (8–2–1) *Won:* Kentucky 26–7, Yale 35–0, Auburn 47–0, LSU 48–7, Marshall 56–0, Maryland 34–0, Tennessee 28–6 (1st over Vols in 9 games since 1937), Miami (Fla.) 33–6 in last 8 games. *Lost:* Georgia Tech 13–0 (1st meeting since 1941), Mississippi 20–7. *Tied:* Alabama 14–14. *Stars:* C John Clark, G Ken Cooper, T Dutch Cantrell, Bs Herb Rich, Dean Davidson (9 TDs) and Lee Nalley

(nation's punt return leader with 18.4-yd avg). *Noteworthy:* Sanders' last team.

1955 (8–3) *Won:* Alabama 21–6, Chattanooga 12–0, Middle Tennessee 46–0, Virginia 34–7, Kentucky 34–0, Tulane 20–7, Florida 21–6. *Lost:* Georgia 14–13, Mississippi 13–0, Tennessee 20–14. *Stars:* HB Charley Horton (12 TDs), soph B Phil King (628 yds rush), E Joe Stephenson, G Larry Frank. *Noteworthy:* made 1st bowl appearance, beating Auburn 25–13 in Gator Bowl as Commodores recovered 5 Tiger fumbles; Don Orr passed for 1 TD (to Stephenson) and scored another, and King and Horton each scored TDs on short runs.

1982 (8–4) *Won:* Memphis St. 24–14, Tulane 24–21 (1st over Green Wave since 1975), Florida 31–29 (1st meeting since 1975), Mississippi 19–10, Kentucky 23–10 (1st over Wildcats since 1975), Virginia Tech 45–0, UT-Chattanooga 27–16, Tennessee 28–21 (1st over Vols since 1975). *Lost:* North Carolina 34–10 (1st meeting since 1970), Alabama 24–21, unbeaten Georgia 27–13. *Stars:* QB Whit Taylor (2,481 yds and 22 TDs pass), TE Allama Matthews (61 pass rec for 797 yds and 14 TDs), TB Norman Jordan (56 pass rec for 470 yds), soph K Ricky Anderson (14 FGs, 73 pts), DE Steve Bearden, soph DB Manuel Young, Leonard Coleman (8 int), P Jim Arnold (45.8-yd avg). *Noteworthy:* lost to Air Force 36–28 in Hall of Fame Bowl after leading 28–17 going into 4th quarter; Taylor passed for 452 yds and 4 TDs (3 to Jordan, who caught 20 passes for 173 yds).

BOWL SUMMARY

Gator 1–0; Hall of Fame 0–1; Peach 0–0–1.

BOWL RECORD (1–1–1)

Regular Season	Bowl	Score	Opponent	Record
1955 (7–3)	Gator	25–13	Auburn	(8–1–1)
1974 (7–3–1)	Peach	6–6	Texas Tech	(6–4–1)
1982 (8–3)	Hall of Fame	28–36	Air Force	(7–5)

CONFERENCE TITLES

Southern—1923. **Southeastern**—None.

TOP 20 AP AND UPI
(USA TODAY/CNN SINCE 1991) RANKING

1948	12

MAJOR RIVALS

Vanderbilt has played at least 10 games with Alabama 18–48–4, Auburn 19–14–1, Central U. (Ky.) 13–1–1, Florida 9–15–2, Georgia 16–35–2, Georgia Tech 15–16–3, Kentucky 32–29–4, Louisiana St. 7–16–1, Maryland 8–4, Memphis St. 7–5, Michigan 0–9–1, Middle Tennessee 12–0, Mississippi 31–34–2, Mississippi St. 6–7–2, North Carolina 5–8, Sewanee 40–8–4, Tennessee 26–55–5, Tennessee Tech 10–0–1, Texas 8–3–1, Tulane 17–28–3, Virginia 12–7–2. Record against SEC members met fewer than 10 times: Arkansas 1–2, South Carolina 0–2.

COACHES

Dean of Vanderbilt coaches is Dan McGugin with record of 197–55–19 for 1904–17 and 1919–34, including 1 SC title and 4 unbeaten teams. Other top records for at least 3 years were by R.G. Acton, 10–7–3 for 1896–98 with 1 unbeaten team; Ray Morrison, 29–22–2 for 1918 and 1935–39; Henry R. "Red" Sanders, 36–22–2 for 1940–42 and 1946–48; Bill Edwards, 21–19–2 for 1949–52; Art Guepe, 39–54–7 for 1953–62 with 1 Gator Bowl champion; and George MacIntyre, 25–52–1 for 1979–85 with 1 bowl team.

MISCELLANEA

First game was win over Nashville U. 40–0 in 1890 . . . highest score was over Bethel 105–0 in 1912 . . . highest since W.W. II was over Tennessee Tech 68–0 in 1947 . . . worst defeat was by Georgia Tech 83–0 in 1917 . . . worst since W.W. II was by Alabama 66–3 in 1979 . . . longest unbeaten string of 21 in 1920–23 ended by Michigan 3–0 . . . 18-game unbeaten string and longest winning streak of 13 in 1903–05 ended by Michigan 18–0 . . . longest losing string of 16 in 1961–62 broken with win over Tulane 20–0 . . . consensus All-Americans were Lynn Bomar, E, 1923; Henry Wakefield, E, 1924; Pete Gracey, C, 1932; George Deiderich, G, 1958; Jim Arnold, P, 1982; and Ricky Anderson, P, 1984 . . . Academic All-Americans were Ben Donnell, C, 1958; Jim Burns, DB, 1968; Doug Martin, E, 1974; Damon Regen, LB, 1975; Greg Martin, K, 1977; and Phil Roach, WR, 1983.

SOUTHWEST CONFERENCE

Representatives of the universities of Arkansas, Baylor, Louisiana State, Oklahoma A&M, Southwestern (Texas), Texas, and Texas A&M met in Dallas, Texas, on May 6, 1914, to draw up a constitution and by-laws for an organization to "enlarge and more closely relate the athletic activities of the larger institutions of the states represented." The action had arisen from a need for higher academic and ethical standards for student athletes. LSU withdrew from membership at the organizational meeting, but Oklahoma and Rice were added as charter members at a second meeting later that year, on December 8, in Houston. Thus was formed the Southwest Intercollegiate Athletic Conference, which in 1916 became simply the Southwest Athletic Conference.

Rice was only a provisional member the first year of play, 1915, and did not become a permanent member until 1918, the year Southern Methodist University joined the conference. Southwestern withdrew after the 1916 season, Oklahoma after 1919, and Oklahoma A&M after 1925. Phillips University of Oklahoma was a member for one year only, in 1920. Texas Christian University was added in 1923, and from 1926 through 1955 the conference operated with seven members. Texas Tech University was admitted in 1956, becoming eligible for the football title in 1958, and the University of Houston became a member in 1971, with eligibility for the football title in 1976.

Conference membership remained at nine until charter member Arkansas withdrew to join the Southeastern Conference effective with completion of the 1991 season. The Razorbacks began SEC play in 1992.

FACTS AND ODDITIES ON SWC MEMBERS

Southwest Conference members have won the national title seven times, beginning with SMU in 1935. That year the Mustangs finished 12–0 and earned a share of the national crown before being upset by Stanford 7–0 in the Rose Bowl. TCU got a share of the title in 1938, finishing 10–0 behind the passing of little Davey O'Brien (Heisman Trophy and Maxwell Award winner), then beating Carnegie Tech 15–7 in the Sugar Bowl. Texas A&M

kept the national crown in the SWC in 1939, finishing 10–0, then edging unbeaten Tulane 14–13 in the Sugar Bowl.

It was nearly 25 years before the national title went to a SWC team again, Texas winning its first title in 1963 by going 10–0, then beating Navy (led by Heisman Trophy– and Maxwell Award–winner Roger Staubach) 28–6 in the Cotton Bowl. Arkansas kept a portion of the title in the conference in 1964, finishing 10–0 before edging Nebraska 10–7 in the Cotton Bowl. Texas won its second national crown in 1969, finishing the season 10–0 by edging previously unbeaten Arkansas 15–14 in the regular-season finale, then winning the Cotton Bowl 21–17 over a Notre Dame team making that school's first bowl appearance since the days of the Four Horsemen. The Longhorns became the first SWC team to repeat as national champion with a share of the 1970 title despite losing to Notre Dame 24–11 in the Cotton Bowl. Texas had finished the regular season 10–0.

No SWC team has won the national title since.

The Heisman Trophy has gone to SWC players five times, starting with TCU TB Davey O'Brien in 1938. Other winners were SMU HB Doak Walker, 1948; Texas A&M HB John David Crow, 1957; Texas HB Earl Campbell, 1977; and Houston QB Andre Ware, 1989. Three SWC players have won the Maxwell Award—O'Brien in 1938, Walker in 1947, and Texas LB Tommy Nobis in 1965.

The Outland Trophy has gone to SWC players five times, with Texas players winning three and Arkansas players the other two. Texas winners were T Scott Appleton in 1963, G Tommy Nobis in 1965, and DT Brad Shearer in 1977. Arkansas winners were G Bill Brooks in 1954 and T Loyd Phillips in 1966. Three SWC players have won the Lombardi Award: Houston DT Wilson Whitley in 1976, Texas DT Kenneth Sims in 1981, and Texas DT Tony Degrate in 1984.

National Coach of the Year awards have gone to SWC coaches in six different years, with Darrell Royal of Texas taking half of them. Royal won the Football Writers Association of America (FWAA) award in 1961, both the FWAA and the American Football Coaches Association (AFCA) awards in 1963, and a share of the AFCA award in 1970. Frank Broyles of Arkansas won a share of the AFCA award in 1964, Grant Teaff of Baylor won both awards in 1974, and Lou Holtz of Arkansas won the FWAA award in 1977.

Royal had one of the notable all-time winning percentages among major college coaches with a record of 184–60–5 for a career that spanned 1954–1976, most of it at Texas. His Longhorn teams from 1957–1976 were 167–47–5 with 11 SWC titles, 16 bowl appearances, and two national championships. A contemporary of Royal's, Broyles, compiled a record of 149–62–6 for 1958–1976, all at Arkansas. He won seven SWC titles and one national crown, and had 10 bowl teams.

The fabled Paul "Bear" Bryant coached for a while in the SWC, compiling a record at Texas A&M between 1954 and 1957 of 25–14–2 with one unbeaten conference champion. Another famous coach who spent part of his career in the SWC was Francis A. "Close the Gates of Mercy" Schmidt, who had an overall record of 158–57–11 for 24 years of coaching. In the middle of his career Schmidt coached Arkansas to a 42–20–3 record from 1922 to 1928 and TCU to a 46–6–5 record from 1929 to 1933. At the latter he had two unbeaten conference champions.

Dana X. Bible spent much of his long career in the Southwest, including stints at Texas A&M (1917, 1919–1928) and Texas (1937–1946). At A&M he had a record of 72–19–8 with five conference titles and three unbeaten teams. At Texas he was 63–31–3 with three conference titles. Jess Neely, who had 207 career victories as a coach, earned most of those at Rice from 1940 to 1966. He was 144–124–10 at Rice with four conference titles and six bowl teams.

No SWC player was a consensus All-American until Baylor G Barton Koch was selected in 1930. However, some of the SWC stars of 40 and 50 years ago are still considered among college football's all-time greats.

"Slingin' Sammy" Baugh, TCU tailback in 1934–1936, had remarkable passing statistics for his era. "The Tall Texan" passed for 3,384 yds and 39 TDs in his three-year career, leading the Horned Frogs to successive victories in the Sugar and Cotton bowls during his last two seasons. Baugh also was a superb punter, averaging 40.9 yds per punt, and an excellent safetyman (intercepting 12 passes in three years), skills he carried over into a long professional career with the Redskins.

Baugh's successor, 5'–7", 150-pound Davey O'Brien, threw only 33 passes as the backup in 1936, though he intercepted five passes on defense. But he made up for lost time in the next two years, finishing with career totals of 2,628 yds and 24 TDs passing in regular season as well as intercepting 16 passes. In his senior season, 1938, he led the Horned Frogs to a 10–0 record, a Sugar Bowl win (in which he passed for 225 yds and a TD), and a national title, and was given two awards Baugh had not received—the Heisman Trophy and the Maxwell Award.

Not as well known now but considered among the best at the time was Bobby Wilson, who led SMU to a 12–0 regular-season record and a share of the national title in 1935. He topped the season with a spectacular 36-yd TD pass reception in the final minutes to beat previously undefeated TCU 20–14. Wilson was one of SMU's first consensus All-Americans.

A decade later, the SWC had two backs who got headlines around the country. QB Bobby Layne of Texas led the Longhorns to a 31–8 record in 1944–1947, including a conference title and two major bowl victories. He passed for 3,145 yds and 22 TDs in his career, ran for 845 yds, and intercepted 11 passes. In the 1946 Cotton Bowl he passed for two TDs, scored four (one on a 50-yd pass reception), and kicked four extra pts in a 40–27 win over Missouri. In the 1948 Sugar Bowl he passed for 183 yds and a TD and scored another in a 27–7 win over Alabama.

In his senior season Layne had to share the spotlight with SMU's versatile sophomore TB, Doak Walker. In 1947–1949 the Mustangs had a record of 22–5–3 and won two conference titles behind Walker. In the 1948 Cotton Bowl he threw a 53-yd TD pass, scored the other SMU touchdown, and kicked an extra point in a 13–13 tie with undefeated Penn State. In the 1949 Cotton Bowl he scored a TD, kicked two extra points, and had a 79-yd punt in a 21–13 win over Oregon. During his career (he also played as a freshman in 1945), Walker passed for 1,654 yds and 14 TDs, ran for 1,928 yds, scored 38 TDs, caught 27 passes for 454 yds and 4 TDs, kicked 57 extra pts and a field goal, intercepted 8 passes, averaged 39.3 yards per punt, and was one of SMU's primary punt and kickoff returners. He won the Maxwell Award in his sophomore year and the Heisman Trophy in his junior season, and was one of a handful of backs who have been consensus All-American three times.

TCU star Jim Swink was noted for his long runs when he led the nation in scoring in 1955 with 125 points. His 20 TDs came on plays averaging 24 yards.

The SWC was long known as a balanced league in which any team could beat another on a given day. The longest winning streak any member has had was 30 games by Texas in 1968–1970.

Southwest Conference members are involved in some of the nation's most-played rivalries. Tied for fourth on the all-time list are the Baylor–TCU and Texas–Texas A&M series. Through 1992 each series had been played 99 times, with Baylor and TCU tied at 46–46–7, while Texas led Texas A&M by a margin of 64–30–5.

Among the unique nicknames carried by SWC schools are Texas Longhorns, TCU Horned Frogs, and Texas Tech Red Raiders. The Owls of Rice and Mustangs of SMU are nicknames not all that common on the college football scene, while Baylor (Bears) and Houston (Cougars) have more conventional nicknames. Texas A&M still clings to the nickname Aggies, once popular for all "A&M" schools but now used by only a few.

Texas' nickname apparently was chosen by Alex Weisburg, editor-in-chief of *The Daily Texan*, in 1903 when he ordered the paper's writers to call the team the Longhorns in every sports article "and we'll soon have it named." The name became official within a few years. Texas Christian adopted Horned Frog for its school annual in 1897, and the plural form gradually became the nickname for TCU's athletic teams. A committee from two student literary societies picked the horned frog (a small lizard with hornlike spines) as a typically Texan namesake.

Baylor held a student-body poll for a nickname in 1914, and Bears edged Buffaloes for the honor. Students also voted for the nickname at SMU, selecting Mustangs in an election on October 25, 1917. Rice's nickname, Owls, is derived from the university's heraldic shield, which includes the Owls of Athena as they appear on an ancient Greek coin.

Houston's first athletic coach, John R. Bender, went to Houston when it was still a junior college in 1927 and gave his teams the Cougars nickname from his old Washington State connection. When Houston began intercollegiate athletics as a 4-year institution in 1946, it adopted Cougars as its official nickname. Texas Tech teams began with Matadors in 1925 because the head coach's wife, Mrs. E.Y. Freeland, liked the name. But in the 1930s the sports editor of the *Lubbock Morning Avalanche* began calling the team the Red Raiders because of the players' all-red uniforms and a schedule that had Tech playing road games from Los Angeles to Pittsburgh. Coach Pete Cawthon and the players liked the new tag and adopted it. Texas Tech's colors of scarlet and black, however, still date to Mrs. Freeland's idea of a matador's red cape and black costume.

Texas' colors of burnt orange and white, officially adopted on May 10, 1900, had been used by the school's baseball team as early as 1884. TCU's colors were adopted in 1896 by a student committee that selected purple for "royalty" and white for "a clean game." Rice's uniforms do not always reflect the official colors: Confederate gray enlivened by a tinge of lavender, and a blue deeper than Oxford blue. Those colors were selected by the designer of the Institute seal, who wanted the shield to harmonize with state and national colors.

ALL-TIME SOUTHWEST CONFERENCE CHAMPIONS

Annual Champion	SWC Record	Regular Season and Bowl	
1915 Oklahoma[a]	3–0	10–0	
1916 Texas[b]	5–1	7–2	
1917 Texas A&M	2–0	8–0	
1918 Texas[b]	4–0	9–0	
1919 Texas A&M	4–0	10–0	
1920 Texas	5–0	9–0	
1921 Texas A&M	3–0–2	6–1–2	
1922 Baylor	5–0	8–3	
1923 SMU	5–0	9–0	
1924 Baylor	4–0–1	7–2–1	
1925 Texas A&M	4–1	7–1–1	
1926 SMU	5–0	8–0–1	
1927 Texas A&M	4–0–1	8–0–1	
1928 Texas	5–1	7–2	
1929 TCU	4–0–1	9–0–1	
1930 Texas	4–1	8–1–1	
1931 SMU	5–0–1	9–1–1	
1932 TCU	6–0	10–0–1	
1933 Arkansas[c]	4–1	7–3–1	
1934 Rice	5–1	9–1–1	
1935 SMU	6–0	12–0	Rose (L)
1936 Arkansas	5–1	7–3	
1937 Rice	4–1–1	5–3–2	Cotton (W)
1938 TCU	6–0	10–0	Sugar (W)
1939 Texas A&M	6–0	10–0	Sugar (W)
1940 SMU	5–1	8–1–1	
Texas A&M	5–1	8–1	Cotton (W)
1941 Texas A&M	5–1	9–1	Cotton (L)
1942 Texas	5–1	8–2	Cotton (W)

(continued)

ALL-TIME SOUTHWEST CONFERENCE
CHAMPIONS *(continued)*

Annual Champion	SWC Record	Regular Season and Bowl	
1943 Texas	5–0	7–1	Cotton (T)
1944 TCU	3–1–1	7–2–1	Cotton (L)
1945 Texas	5–1	9–1	Cotton (W)
1946 Arkansas	5–1	6–3	Cotton (T)
Rice	5–1	8–2	Orange (W)
1947 SMU	5–0–1	9–0–1	Cotton (T)
1948 SMU	5–0–1	8–1–1	Cotton (W)
1949 Rice	6–0	9–1	Cotton (W)
1950 Texas	6–0	9–1	Cotton (L)
1951 TCU	5–1	6–4	Cotton (L)
1952 Texas	6–0	8–2	Cotton (W)
1953 Rice	5–1	8–2	Cotton (W)
Texas	5–1	7–3	
1954 Arkansas	5–1	8–2	Cotton (L)
1955 TCU	5–1	9–1	Cotton (L)
1956 Texas A&M	6–0	9–0–1	
1957 Rice	5–1	7–3	Cotton (L)
1958 TCU	5–1	8–2	Cotton (T)
1959 Arkansas	5–1	8–2	Gator (W)
Texas	5–1	9–1	Cotton (L)
TCU	5–1	8–2	Bluebonnet (L)
1960 Arkansas	6–1	8–2	Cotton (L)
1961 Arkansas	6–1	8–2	Sugar (L)
Texas	6–1	9–1	Cotton (W)
1962 Texas	6–0–1	9–0–1	Cotton (L)
1963 Texas	7–0	10–0	Cotton (W)
1964 Arkansas	7–0	10–0	Cotton (W)
1965 Arkansas	7–0	10–0	Cotton (L)
1966 SMU	6–1	8–2	Cotton (L)
1967 Texas A&M	6–1	6–4	Cotton (W)
1968 Arkansas	6–1	9–1	Sugar (W)
Texas	6–1	8–1–1	Cotton (W)
1969 Texas	7–0	10–0	Cotton (W)
1970 Texas	7–0	10–0	Cotton (L)
1971 Texas	6–1	8–2	Cotton (L)
1972 Texas	7–0	9–1	Cotton (W)
1973 Texas	7–0	8–2	Cotton (L)
1974 Baylor	6–1	8–3	Cotton (L)
1975 Arkansas	6–1	9–2	Cotton (W)
Texas	6–1	9–2	Bluebonnet (W)
Texas A&M	6–1	10–1	Liberty (L)
1976 Houston	7–1	9–2	Cotton (W)
Texas Tech	7–1	10–1	Bluebonnet (L)
1977 Texas	8–0	11–0	Cotton (L)
1978 Houston	7–1	9–2	Cotton (L)
1979 Arkansas	7–1	10–1	Sugar (L)
Houston	7–1	10–1	Cotton (W)
1980 Baylor	8–0	10–1	Cotton (L)
1981 SMU	7–1	10–1	
1982 SMU	7–0–1	10–0–1	Cotton (W)

(continued)

ALL-TIME SOUTHWEST CONFERENCE CHAMPIONS *(continued)*

Annual Champion	SWC Record	Regular Season and Bowl	
1983 Texas	8–0	11–0	Cotton (L)
1984 Houston	6–2	7–4	Cotton (L)
SMU	6–2	9–2	Aloha (W)
1985 Texas A&M	7–1	9–2	Cotton (W)
1986 Texas A&M	7–1	9–2	Cotton (L)
1987 Texas A&M	6–1	9–2	Cotton (W)
1988 Arkansas	7–0	10–1	Cotton (L)
1989 Arkansas	7–1	10–1	Cotton (L)
1990 Texas	8–0	10–1	Cotton (L)
1991 Texas A&M	8–0	10–1	Cotton (L)
1992 Texas A&M	7–0	12–0	Cotton (L)

[a]Baylor forfeited claim to cochampionship for using ineligible player.
[b]No official champion recognized.
[c]Arkansas forfeited championship for using ineligible player; no champion named.

BAYLOR *(Bears; Green and Gold)*

NOTABLE TEAMS

1910 (6–1–1) *Won:* Austin 31–0, Haskell 52–3, Texas Christian (TCU) 52–0, 10–3, Polytechnic 39–0, Southwestern (Texas) 27–5 (1st meeting). *Lost:* Texas 1–0 (forfeit). *Tied:* Daniel Baker 0–0 in opener. *Noteworthy:* 1st year under Ralph Glaze.

1915 (7–1) *Won:* Howard Payne 3–0, Rice 26–0 (1st SWC game), Trinity (Texas) 49–0, Southwestern (Texas) 10–0, Oklahoma A&M 12–6, Daniel Baker 34–0, TCU 51–0. *Lost:* Sewanee 16–3. *Noteworthy:* Got share of inaugural SWC title (later forfeited for using ineligible player).

1916 (9–1) *Won:* San Marcos 76–0, Southern Methodist (SMU) 61–0 (1st meeting), Trinity (Texas) 37–0, Howard Payne 47–0, Texas 7–3 (1st in 12-game series dating to 1901), Southwestern (Texas) 20–0, Oklahoma A&M 10–7, Austin 26–0, TCU 32–14. *Lost:* Texas A&M 3–0. *Stars:* HB Lucian Roach, FB Theron Fouts (60 pts), E John Reid.

1917 (6–2–1) *Won:* Howard Payne 17–0, Trinity (Texas) 55–0, Oklahoma A&M 17–0, Hardin-Simmons 103–0 (1st meeting since 1909), Texas 3–0, Southwestern (Texas) 26–0. *Lost:* unbeaten Texas A&M 7–0, TCU 34–0. *Tied:* SMU 0–0. *Stars:* T Jack Roach, C J. Johnson.

1921 (8–3) *Won:* Austin 17–13, John Tarleton 35–0, Rice 17–14, Phillips 34–6, Southwestern (Texas) 16–0, Hardin-Simmons 21–0, SMU 28–0 (1st over Mustangs since 1916), Mississippi College 24–0. *Lost:* Boston College 23–7, Texas A&M 14–3, Arkansas 13–12 (1st meeting since 1913). *Stars:* TB Wesley Bradshaw (119 pts, including 14 TDs and 6 FGs), FB John Tanner, T Russell Blailock.

1922 (8–3) *Won:* North Texas St. 55–0 (1st meeting), Hardin-Simmons 42–0, Rice 31–0, Arkansas 60–13, Mississippi College 40–7, Texas A&M 13–7 (1st over Aggies in 11 games since 1908), Oklahoma A&M 10–0, SMU 24–0. *Lost:* Boston College 33–0, Haskell 21–20, Phillips 47–0 (last 2 played as doubleheader). *Stars:* Bradshaw (63 pts, including 5 FGs), Tanner, Blailock, G "Cop" Weathers. *Noteworthy:* won 1st official SWC title.

1923 (5–1–2) *Won:* Hardin-Simmons 14–0, North Texas St. 23–7, Howard Payne 20–6, Arkansas 14–0, Ouachita 16–3 in 1st 5 games. *Lost:* unbeaten SMU 16–0 in finale. *Tied:* Texas A&M 0–0, unbeaten Texas 7–7. *Star:* T Roy Williamson.

1924 (7–2–1) *Won:* Hardin-Simmons 10–6, North Texas St. 30–0, Arkansas 13–0, Texas A&M 15–7, Texas 28–10, St. Edwards 20–7, Rice 17–9. *Lost:* Austin 7–3 (1st to Kangaroos in 6 games since 1912), Central Oklahoma 13–6. *Tied:* unbeaten SMU 7–7. *Stars:* HB Ralph Pittman, QB Bill Coffey, Gs Jack Sisco and "Bear" Walker, soph T Sam Coates. *Noteworthy:* won 2nd SWC title.

1928 (8–2) *Won:* S.F. Austin 31–0, North Texas St. 45–0, Trinity (Texas) 33–0, Centenary 28–6, St. Edwards 48–7, TCU 7–6 (1st over Horned Frogs in 5 games since 1919), SMU 2–0 (1st over Mustangs since 1922), Rice 25–14. *Lost:* Arkansas 14–0, Texas 6–0. *Star:* HB Virgil Gilliland.

1935 (8–3) *Won:* Southwestern (Texas) 39–0 (1st meeting since 1927), Hardin-Simmons 14–0, Texas A&I 6–0, Arkansas 13–6, Oklahoma City U. 2–0, Texas A&M 14–6 (1st over Aggies in 5 games since 1926), Centenary 20–0 (1st over Gentlemen in 6 games since 1928), Rice 8–0. *Lost:* TCU 28–0, Texas 25–6, unbeaten national cochamp SMU 10–0.

1937 (7–3) *Won:* Southwestern (Texas) 39–2, Oklahoma City U. 33–0, Arkansas 20–14, Centenary 20–0, Texas A&M 13–0, TCU 6–0, Loyola (Calif.) 27–13. *Lost:* Texas 9–6, SMU 13–7, Rice 13–7. *Stars:* QB Billy Patterson, E Sam Boyd.

1938 (7–2–1) *Won:* Southwestern (Texas) 33–0, Arkansas 9–6, Texas 14–3, Loyola (Calif.) 35–2, Rice 21–6, Centenary 14–0, Oklahoma A&M 20–6. *Lost:* unbeaten national cochamp TCU 39–7, SMU 21–6. *Tied:* Texas A&M 6–6. *Stars:* Patterson (1,334 yds and 13 TDs pass), Boyd (nation's leader with 32 pass rec for 537 yds and 5 TDs).

1939 (7–3) *Won:* Southwestern (Texas) 34–0, Oklahoma A&M 13–0, Arkansas 19–7, TCU 27–0, Texas 20–0, Centenary 13–6, Rice 10–7. *Lost:* Nebraska 20–0, unbeaten national champ Texas A&M 20–0 (1st to Aggies since 1934), SMU 21–0. *Stars:* C Robert Nelson, G Leonard Akin.

1949 (8–2) *Won:* South Carolina 20–6, Mississippi St. 14–6, Arkansas 35–13, Texas Tech 28–7, Texas A&M 21–0, TCU 40–14, SMU 35–26, Wyoming 32–13. *Lost:* Texas 20–0, Rice 21–7. *Stars:* QB Adrian Burk (nation's leader with 1,428 yds and 14 TDs pass), E J.D. Ison (42 pass rec for 457 yds and 6 TDs), G Donald Mouser, DL Chuck Stone, DB Bobby Griffin (6 int). *Noteworthy:* Last year under Bob Woodruff.

1950 (7–3) *Won:* Mississippi St. 14–7, Houston

34–7 (1st meeting), Texas Tech 26–12, Texas A&M 27–20, TCU 20–14, SMU 3–0, Rice 33–7 (1st over Owls since 1945). *Lost:* unbeaten Wyoming 7–0, Arkansas 27–6, Texas 27–20. *Stars:* QB Larry Isbell (1,220 yds pass, 41.1-yd punting avg), E Harold Riley (35 pass rec for 539 yds), James Jeffrey (569 yds rush), Buddy Parker (9 TDs), soph DL Bill Athey, DB Johnny Curtis. *Noteworthy:* 1st year under George Sauer.

1951 (8–2–1) *Won:* Houston 19–0, Tulane 27–14, Arkansas 9–7, Texas Tech 40–20, Texas 18–6 (1st over Longhorns in 10 games since 1939), Wake Forest 42–0, SMU 14–13, Rice 34–13. *Lost:* TCU 20–7. *Tied:* Texas A&M 21–21. *Stars:* Isbell (1,430 yds and 10 TDs pass), E Stan Williams (37 pass rec for 598 yds and 6 TDs), soph HB Jerry Coody (570 yds rush), Don Carpenter (42 pts), DT Ken Casner, Athey, Robert Reid (11 int), Red Donaldson (7 int). *Noteworthy:* lost to unbeaten Georgia Tech 17–14 in Orange Bowl after leading 14–7 at halftime on TDs by FB Dick Parma (107 yds rush) and Coody.

1953 (7–3) *Won:* California 25–0, Miami (Fla.) 21–13, Arkansas 14–7, Vanderbilt 47–6, Texas A&M 14–13, TCU 25–7, SMU 27–21. *Lost:* Texas 21–20, Houston 37–7, Rice 41–19. *Stars:* Coody, L.G. "Long Gone" Dupre (593 yds rush, 8 TDs), QB Cotton Davidson (1,092 yds pass), Wayne Hopkins (351 yds pass rec), T James Ray Smith.

1954 (7–4) *Won:* Houston 53–13, Vanderbilt 25–19, Washington 34–7, Texas A&M 20–7, TCU 12–7, Texas 13–7, SMU 33–21. *Lost:* Miami (Fla.) 19–13, Arkansas 21–20, Rice 20–14. *Stars:* QB Billy Hooper, E Henry Gremminger (323 yds pass rec), soph Del Shofner (545 yds rush), Smith. *Noteworthy:* lost to Auburn 33–13 in Gator Bowl; scored on 1-yd plunge by FB Reuben Saage and 38-yd run by Dupre.

1956 (9–2) *Won:* California 7–6, Texas Tech 27–0, Maryland 14–0, Arkansas 14–7, Texas 10–7, Nebraska 26–7, SMU 26–0, Rice 46–13. *Lost:* unbeaten Texas A&M 19–13, TCU 7–6 in successive mid-season games. *Stars:* Shofner (10 TDs, 40.7-yd punting avg), E Jerry Marcontell, G Bill Glass. *Noteworthy:* 1st year under Sam Boyd. Upset unbeaten Tennessee 13–7 in Sugar Bowl; Shofner ran for 88 yds and intercepted a pass, and Bears scored on 12-yd pass from QB Bobby Jones to Marcontell and 1-yd run by soph QB Buddy Humphrey.

1960 (8–3) *Won:* Colorado 26–0, LSU 7–3, Arkan-

sas 28–14, Texas Tech 14–7 (10th straight over Red Raiders), Texas A&M 14–0, Southern California (USC) 35–14, SMU 20–7, Rice 12–7. *Lost:* TCU 14–6, Texas 12–7 in consecutive mid-season games. *Stars:* HB Ronnie Bull (9 TDs), QB Ronnie Stanley (1,151 yds pass), soph Ronnie Goodwin (25 pass rec for 407 yds), E Bobby Lane. *Noteworthy:* lost to Florida 13–12 in Gator Bowl; QB Bobby Ply passed for 162 yds and a TD (11 yds to Goodwin, who caught 7 passes) and Bull scored on 3-yd run.

1963 (8–3) *Won:* Houston 27–0, Arkansas 14–10, Texas Tech 21–17, Texas A&M 34–7, TCU 32–13, Rice 21–12, SMU 20–6. *Lost:* Oregon St. 22–15, unbeaten national champ Texas 7–0, Kentucky 19–7. *Stars:* QB Don Trull (119 yds and 10 TDs rush, nation's leader with 2,157 yds and 12 TDs pass), FL Larry Elkins (nation's leader with 70 pass rec for 873 yds and 8 TDs), T Bobby Crenshaw. *Noteworthy:* beat LSU 14–7 in Bluebonnet Bowl; Trull passed for 255 yds and 2 TDs (both to E James Ingram, who had 11 pass rec for 163 yds).

1974 (8–4) *Won:* Oklahoma St. 31–14, Florida St. 21–17, Arkansas 21–17 (1st over Razorbacks since 1966), TCU 21–7, Texas 34–24 (1st over Longhorns since 1956), Texas Tech 17–10 (1st over Red Raiders since 1968), SMU 31–14 (1st over Mustangs since 1965), Rice 24–3. *Lost:* unbeaten national co-champ Oklahoma 28–11, Missouri 28–21, Texas A&M 20–0. *Stars:* RB Steve Beaird (1,104 yds rush, 16 TDs), QB Neal Jeffrey (1,314 yds pass), Alcy Jackson (436 yds pass rec), E Philip Kent, C Aubrey Schulz, LB Derrell Luce, DBs Ken Quesenberry, frosh Ronald Burns and Tommy Turnipseede. *Noteworthy:* Nation's most-improved team won 3rd SWC title (1st in 50 years) in 1st winning season since 1963. Lost to Penn St. 41–20 in Cotton Bowl after trailing only 17–14 going into last quarter; Jeffrey passed for 134 yds and a TD (35 yds to E Ricky Thompson, who also caught 11-yd TD pass from soph reserve QB Mark Jackson), Beaird ran for 84 yds and a TD, and Quesenberry had 12 tackles and a pass int.

1979 (8–4) *Won:* Lamar 20–7, Texas A&M 17–7, Texas Tech 27–17 (1st over Red Raiders since 1974), SMU 24–21, Army 55–0, TCU 16–3, Rice 45–14. *Lost:* unbeaten national champ Alabama 45–0, Houston 13–10, Arkansas 29–20, Texas 13–0. *Stars:* soph RB Walter Abercrombie (886 yds and 6 TDs rush), FB Dennis Gentry (511 yds rush), OG Billy Glass, K Robert Bledsoe (13 FGs), LB Mike

Singletary, DE Andrew Melontree, frosh P Ron Stowe (41.1-yd avg). *Noteworthy:* beat Clemson 24–18 in cold, wet Peach Bowl; frosh QB Mike Brannan passed for 2 TDs (to Bo Taylor and Robert Holt), QB Mickey Elam threw TD pass to Raymond Cockrell, and Bledsoe kicked FG and 3 ex pts.
1980 (10–2) *Won:* Lamar 42–7, West Texas St. 43–15, Texas Tech 11–3, Houston 24–12 (1st over Cougars in 5 games since 1963), SMU 32–28, Texas A&M 46–7, TCU 21–6, Arkansas 42–15 (1st over Razorbacks since 1974), Rice 16–6, Texas 16–0. *Lost:* San Jose St. 30–22. *Stars:* Singletary, LB Doak Field, DEs Max McGeary and soph Charles Benson, DTs Joe Campbell and Tommy Tabor, DB Vann McElroy (nation's coleader with 8 int), QB Jay Jeffrey (1,096 yds pass, 453 yds and 5 TDs rush), Holt (29 pass rec for 464 yds), SE Mike Fisher (22 pass rec for 494 yds and 6 TDs), Abercrombie (1,187 yds rush, 10 TDs), Gentry (883 yds rush, 6 TDs), frosh Alfred Anderson (9 TDs rush), OG Frank Ditta. *Noteworthy:* Won 4th SWC title. Lost to Alabama 30–2 in Cotton Bowl; lost ball 4 times on fumbles and 3 times on int.
1985 (9–3) *Won:* Wyoming 39–18, USC 20–13, Texas Tech 31–0, Houston 24–21, SMU 21–14 (1st over Mustangs since 1980), Texas A&M 20–15, TCU 45–0, Rice 34–10. *Lost:* Georgia 17–14, Arkansas 20–14, Texas 17–10. *Stars:* QB Tom Muecke (1,448 yds and 11 TDs pass), soph SE Matt Clark (540 yds pass rec), OT Mark Cochran, C John Adickes, OG Mark Bates, frosh K Terry Syler (11 FGs), DE Derek Turner, DT Steve Grumbine, LB Ray Berry, DBs Thomas Everett and Ron Francis (6 int), P Buzzy Sawyer (44.8-yd avg). *Noteworthy:* beat LSU 21–7 in Liberty Bowl; QB Cody Carlson passed for 161 yds, 2 TDs (to Clark and John Simpson, who caught 3 for 117 yds), and 2-pt conversion (to Clark), Syler kicked 2 FGs, and Francis had a pass int, fumble recovery, and 6 tackles.
1986 (9–3) *Won:* Wyoming 31–28, Louisiana Tech 38–7, Texas Tech 45–14, Houston 27–13, TCU 28–17, Arkansas 29–14, Rice 23–17, Texas 18–13. *Lost:* USC 17–14, SMU 27–21, Texas A&M 31–30. *Stars:* Everett (6 int), Francis (8 int), Berry, Grumbine, DE Kevin Marsh, Bates, Adickes, OT Joel Porter, Carlson (2,284 yds and 10 TDs pass, 356 yds rush), Clark (418 yds pass rec), Syler (12 FGs). *Noteworthy:* beat Colorado 21–9 in Bluebonnet Bowl; Carlson passed for 136 yds and a TD (to FL Darnell Chase), Derrick McAdoo scored 2 TDs on short runs, and Berry made 12 tackles.
1991 (8–4) *Won:* Texas–El Paso 27–7, Colorado 16–14, Missouri 47–21, SMU 45–7, Houston 38–21, TCU 26–9, Arkansas 9–5, Texas 21–11. *Lost:* Rice 20–17, Texas A&M 34–12, Texas Tech 31–24. *Stars:* soph QB J.J. Joe (1,853 yds pass, 6 TDs rush), SEs Melvin Bonner (34 pass rec for 836 yds) and Lee Miles (31 pass rec for 471 yds), TB David Mims (852 yds rush, 5 TDs), soph FBs Robert Strait (551 yds and 6 TDs rush) and John Henry (521 yds and 6 TDs rush), OGs Monte Jones and John Turnpaugh, K Jeff Ireland (11 FGs), DL Santana Dotson, LBs Le'Shai Maston and Curtis Hafford, Mike McFarland (6 int). *Noteworthy:* lost to Indiana 25–0 in Copper Bowl; Joe passed for 131 yds.

BOWL SUMMARY

Bluebonnet 2–1; Copper 0–1; Cotton 0–2; Dixie 1–0; Gator 0–2; Gotham 1–0; John Hancock 1–0; Liberty 1–0; Orange 0–1; Peach 1–0; Sugar 1–0.

BOWL RECORD (8–7)

Regular Season	Bowl	Score	Opponent	Record
1948 (5–3–2)	Dixie	20–7	Wake Forest	(6–3)
1951 (8–1–1)	Orange	14–17	Georgia Tech	(10–0–1)
1954 (7–3)	Gator	13–33	Auburn	(7–3)
1956 (8–2)	Sugar	13–7	Tennessee	(10–0)
1960 (8–2)	Gator	12–13	Florida	(8–2)
1961 (5–5)	Gotham	24–9	Utah State	(9–0–1)
1963 (7–3)	Bluebonnet	14–7	LSU	(7–3)

(continued)

Regular Season	Bowl	Score	Opponent	Record
1974 (8–3)	Cotton	20–41	Penn State	(9–2)
1979 (7–4)	Peach	24–18	Clemson	(8–3)
1980 (10–1)	Cotton	2–30	Alabama	(9–2)
1983 (7–3–1)	Bluebonnet	14–24	Oklahoma State	(7–4)
1985 (8–3)	Liberty	21–7	LSU	(9–1–1)
1986 (8–3)	Bluebonnet	21–9	Colorado	(6–5)
1991 (8–3)	Copper	0–25	Indiana	(6–4–1)
1992 (6–5)	John Hancock	20–15	Arizona	(6–4–1)

CONFERENCE TITLES

Southwest—1915* (forfeited for use of ineligible player), 1922, 1924, 1974, 1980.

TOP 20 AP AND UPI RANKING

1949	20	1956	11–11	1974	14–14	1980	14–13
1950	U–15	1960	12–11	1976	U–19	1985	17–15
1951	9–9	1963	U–20	1979	14–15	1986	12–13
1954	18–U						

MAJOR RIVALS

Baylor has played at least 10 games with Arkansas 33–35–2, Austin College 6–3–1, Centenary 5–7, Hardin-Simmons 13–1, Houston 12–12–1, Louisiana St. 3–8, Oklahoma St. 10–3, Rice 41–30–2, St. Edwards 11–1, Southern Methodist 30–36–7, Southwestern (Texas) 13–6–1, Texas 21–57–4, Texas A&M 29–51–9, Texas Christian 46–46–7, Texas Tech 31–19–1, Trinity (Texas) 15–6–1.

COACHES

Dean of Baylor coaches is Grant Teaff (1974 national Coach of Year) with record of 128–105–6 for 1972–92 with 2 SWC titles and 8 bowl teams. Other top records for at least 3 years were by Ralph Glaze, 12–10–3 for 1910–12; G.P. Mosley, 30–16–4 for 1914–19; Frank Bridges, 35–18–6 for 1920–25 with 2 SWC titles; Morley Jennings, 83–60–6 for 1926–40; Bob Woodruff, 19–10–2 for 1947–49 with 1 bowl champion; George Sauer, 38–21–3 for 1950–55 with 2 bowl teams; Sam Boyd, 15–15–1 for 1956–58 with 1 Sugar Bowl champion; and John Bridgers, 49–53–1 for 1959–68 with 3 bowl teams.

MISCELLANEA

First game was win over Toby's Business College 20–0 in 1899 . . . 1st win over college foe was over Austin College 11–6 in 1900 . . . highest score was over Hardin-Simmons 103–0 in 1917 . . . highest since W.W. II was over TCU 56–21 in 1983 . . . biggest margin since W.W. II was over Army 55–0 in 1979 . . . worst defeat was by LSU 89–0 in 1908 . . . worst since W.W. II was by Houston 66–10 in 1989 . . . longest win streak of 10 in 1936–37 ended by Texas 9–6 . . . longest losing string of 11 in 1969–70 broken with win over Army 10–7 . . . consensus All-Americans were Barton Koch, G, 1930; Bill Glass, G, 1956; Lawrence Elkins, E, 1963–64; Gary Green, DB, 1976; Mike Singletary, LB, 1979–80; Thomas Everett, DB, 1986; and Santana Dotson, DL, 1991 . . . Academic All-Americans were Ronnie Bull, RB, 1961; Don Trull, B, 1962–63; Cris Quinn, DE, 1976; and Mike Welch, DB, 1989–90.

HOUSTON (Cougars; Scarlet and White)

NOTABLE TEAMS

1952 (8–2) *Won:* Arkansas 17–7 (1st meeting), Oklahoma St. 10–7, Tulsa 33–7, Arizona St. 6–0, Texas Tech 20–7, Baylor 28–6, Detroit 33–19, Wyoming 20–0. *Lost:* Texas A&M 21–13 (1st meeting), unbeaten Mississippi 6–0 (1st meeting). *Stars:* E Vic Hampel (19 pass rec for 396 yds), HBs Ken Pridgeon (5 TDs) and S.M. Meeks (5 TDs), OG Bob Chuoke, DTs J.D. Kimmel and Buddy Gillioz, LB Paul Carr, Jackie Howton (6 int). *Noteworthy:* won 1st MVC title.

1956 (7–2–1) *Won:* Mississippi St. 18–7 (1st meeting), Oklahoma St. 13–0, Wichita St. 41–16, Tulsa 14–0, Villanova 26–13, Texas Tech 20–7, Detroit 39–7. *Lost:* Mississippi 14–0, Auburn 12–0. *Tied:* unbeaten Texas A&M 14–14. *Stars:* QB/K Don Flynn, FB Donnie Carraway, G Rudy Spitzenberger, T Dalva Allen, P Owen Mulholland (40.3-yd avg). *Noteworthy:* won 2nd MVC title.

1966 (8–2) *Won:* Florida St. 21–7, Washington St. 21–7, Oklahoma St. 35–9 (1st meeting since 1961), Mississippi St. 28–0 (1st over Bulldogs since 1960), Tampa 48–9, Tulsa 73–14, Kentucky 56–18, Utah 34–14. *Lost:* Mississippi 27–6, Memphis St. 14–13. *Stars:* RB Dick Post (1,061 yds and 5 TDs rush), QB Bo Burris (1,666 yds and 22 TDs pass), SE/P/K Ken Hebert (38 pass rec for 800 yds and 11 TDs, 41.3-yd punting avg, nation's leader with 113 pts), RB Warren McVea (648 yds rush), Gus Hollomon (6 int), Tom Paciorek (6 int). *Noteworthy:* led nation in total off.

1967 (7–3) *Won:* Florida St. 33–13, Michigan St. 37–7, Wake Forest 50–6, Mississippi St. 43–6, Georgia 15–14, Memphis St. 35–18, Idaho 77–6. *Lost:* N.C. State 16–6, Mississippi 14–13, Tulsa 22–13. *Stars:* Hebert (28 pass rec for 626 yds and 7 TDs, 86 pts, 43.5-yd punting avg), McVea (699 yds rush), FB Paul Gipson (1,100 yds and 11 TDs rush), QB Dick Woodall (1,224 yds and 12 TDs pass), OG Rich Stotter (Cougars' 1st consensus All-American), LB Greg Brezina. *Noteworthy:* led nation in total off and rush.

1968 (6–2–2) *Won:* Tulane 54–7, Cincinnati 71–33, Mississippi 29–7, Memphis St. 27–7, Idaho 77–3, Tulsa 100–6 (NCAA scoring record). *Lost:* Oklahoma St. 21–17, Florida St. 40–20. *Tied:* Texas 20–20 (1st meeting since 1953), unbeaten Georgia

10–10. *Stars:* Gipson (1,550 yds rush, 14 TDs), Carlos Bell (691 yds rush), soph WR Elmo Wright (12 TDs, 43 pass rec for 1,198 yds and 11 TDs), DE Jerry Drones, DB Johnny Peacock, Paul Shires (10 int). *Noteworthy:* led nation in total off, rush, and scoring (42.5-pt avg).

1969 (9–2) *Won:* Mississippi St. 74–0, Arizona 34–17, Mississippi 25–11, Miami (Fla.) 38–36, Tulsa 47–14, N.C. State 34–13, Wyoming 41–14, Florida St. 41–13. *Lost:* Florida 59–34, Oklahoma St. 24–18 in 1st 2 games. *Stars:* Wright (90 pts, 63 pass rec for 1,275 yds and 14 TDs), soph QB Gary Mullins (1,433 yds and 13 TDs pass, 398 yds rush), RB Jim Strong (1,293 yds and 11 TDs rush), OG Bill Bridges, Drones, LB Glenn Graef, L.D. Rowden (8 int), P Mike Parrott (40.7-yd avg). *Noteworthy:* beat Auburn 36–7 in Bluebonnet Bowl; Strong ran for 184 yds and 2 TDs, and Mullins passed for 120 yds and ran for 54 yds and a TD.

1970 (8–3) *Won:* Syracuse 42–15, Mississippi St. 31–14, Oregon St. 19–16, Tulsa 21–9, Wyoming 28–0, Wake Forest 26–2, Florida St. 53–21, Miami (Fla.) 36–3. *Lost:* Oklahoma St. 26–17, Alabama 31–21, Mississippi 24–13. *Stars:* Wright (47 pass rec for 874 yds and 9 TDs), Mullins (1,046 yds and 10 TDs pass), Tommy Mozisek (935 yds and 11 TDs rush), Robert Newhouse (788 yds rush), LB Charlie Hall, Ronny Peacock (5 int), DB Richard Harrington, Parrott (41.5-yd punting avg).

1971 (9–3) *Won:* Rice 23–21 (1st meeting), Cincinnati 12–3, San Jose St. 34–20, Villanova 42–9, Florida St. 14–7, Memphis St. 35–7, Virginia Tech 56–29, Miami (Fla.) 27–6, Utah 42–16. *Lost:* Arizona St. 18–17 (1st meeting since 1953), unbeaten Alabama 34–20. *Stars:* Mullins (1,616 yds and 14 TDs pass), TE Riley Odoms (45 pass rec for 730 yds and 8 TDs), Newhouse (1,757 yds and 12 TDs rush), Nick Holm (6 int), soph P Hal Roberts (40.3-yd avg). *Noteworthy:* lost to Colorado 29–17 in Bluebonnet Bowl; Newhouse ran for 168 yds and 2 TDs, and Mullins passed for 173 yds.

1973 (11–1) *Won:* Rice 24–6, South Carolina 27–19, Memphis St. 35–21, San Diego St. 14–9, Virginia Tech 54–27, Miami (Fla.) 30–7, Florida St. 34–3, Colorado St. 28–20, Wyoming 35–0, Tulsa 35–16. *Lost:* Auburn 7–0. *Stars:* QB D.C. Nobles (1,148 yds pass, 591 yds and 5 TDs rush), Bryan Willingham (16 pass rec for 328 yds), FB Leonard Parker (1,123 yds and 12 TDs rush), LB Deryl Ray McGallion, Jeff Bouche (5 int), DB Robert Giblin

(5 int). *Noteworthy:* beat Tulane 47–7 in Blue-bonnet Bowl; Nobles passed for 201 yds and scored a TD, RB Marshall Johnson ran for 114 yds (including 75-yd TD run), soph Donnie McGraw ran for 108 yds and 2 TDs, and Parker ran for 2 TDs.

1974 (8–3–1) *Won:* Rice 21–0, Virginia Tech 49–12, South Carolina 24–14, Villanova 35–0, Cincinnati 27–6, Georgia 31–24, Memphis St. 13–10, Florida St. 23–8. *Lost:* Arizona St. 30–9, Miami (Fla.) 20–3, Tulsa 30–14 (1st to Golden Hurricane in 6 games since 1967). *Stars:* RB John Housman (988 yds and 8 TDs rush), DE Mack Mitchell, Giblin. *Noteworthy:* tied N.C. State 31–31 in Bluebonnet Bowl; Housman ran for 134 yds and 2 TDs, soph QB Bubba McGallion passed for 178 yds and a TD (73 yds to soph Eddie Foster), and soph K Lennard Coplin had FG and 4 ex pts.

1976 (10–2) *Won:* Baylor 23–5 (1st meeting since 1963), Texas A&M 21–10 (1st meeting since 1965), West Texas St. 50–7, Southern Methodist (SMU) 29–6, Texas Christian (TCU) 49–21 (1st meeting), Texas 30–0 (1st meeting since 1968), Texas Tech 27–19 (1st meeting since 1959), Rice 42–20, Miami (Fla.) 21–16. *Lost:* Florida 49–14, Arkansas 14–7 (1st meeting since 1954). *Stars:* DT Wilson Whitley (Lombardi Award winner), DB Anthony Francis (nation's leader with 10 int), Mark Mohr (6 int), LB Paul Humphreys, soph NG Robert Oglesby, DE Vincent Greenwood, soph QB Danny Davis (1,348 yds and 11 TDs pass, 420 yds and 5 TDs rush), Foster (26 pass rec for 524 yds), RB Alois Blackwell (934 yds and 8 TDs rush), TE Don Bass, OT Val Belcher, Coplin. *Noteworthy:* Nation's most-improved team won share of SWC title in 1st year of league competition. Beat undefeated Maryland 30–21 in Cotton Bowl, jumping off to 21–0 1st quarter lead; Blackwell ran for 149 yds and 2 TDs (including 33-yd run), Dyral Thomas ran for 104 yds and a TD, Davis passed for 108 yds and a TD (33 yds to Bass), and Coplin kicked FG and 3 ex pts.

1978 (9–3) *Won:* Utah 42–25, Florida St. 27–21, Baylor 20–18, Texas A&M 33–0, SMU 42–28, Arkansas 20–9, TCU 63–6, Texas 10–7, Rice 49–25. *Lost:* Memphis St. 17–3, Texas Tech 22–21. *Stars:* Davis (1,053 yds pass, 349 yds and 5 TDs rush), WR Willis Adams (29 pass rec for 534 yds), RB Emmett King (1,095 yds and 5 TDs rush), FB Randy Love (1,019 yds and 9 TDs rush), C Chuck Brown, OG Dennis Greenawalt, OT Melvin Jones, soph DT Hosea Taylor, LB David Hodge, DB Elvis Bradley. *Noteworthy:* Won 2nd SWC title. Lost to Notre Dame 35–34 in Cotton Bowl as Irish scored on Joe Montana pass on last play of game and kicked winning ex pt; Davis ran for 76 yds and 2 TDs and passed for a 3rd (15 yds to Adams), and K Kenny Hatfield had FG and 4 ex pts.

1979 (11–1) *Won:* UCLA 24–16, Florida 14–10, West Texas St. 49–10, Baylor 13–10, Texas A&M 17–14, SMU 37–10, Arkansas 13–10, TCU 21–10, Texas Tech 14–10, Rice 63–0. *Lost:* Texas 21–13. *Stars:* QB Delrick Brown (1,114 yds total off), RB Terald Clark (1,063 yds and 7 TDs rush), TE Garrett Jurgajtis (23 pass rec for 275 yds), soph SE Lonell Phea (12 pass rec for 261 yds), soph FB David Barrett (6 TDs rush), Greenawalt, Jones, Hatfield (11 FGs), Oglesby, Taylor, DT Leonard Mitchell, Hodge, Bradley, DB Donnie Love (5 int), soph P Mark Ford (40.3-yd avg). *Noteworthy:* Got share of 3rd SWC title. Beat Nebraska 17–14 in Cotton Bowl; backup QB Terry Elston passed for 119 yds and a TD (6 yds to Eric Herring) and scored on 8-yd run, and Hatfield kicked 41-yd FG and 2 ex pts.

1984 (7–5) *Won:* Miami (Ohio) 30–17, Baylor 27–17, Texas A&M 9–7, SMU 29–20, Texas 29–15, Texas Tech 24–17, Rice 38–26. *Lost:* Washington 35–7, Louisville 30–28, Arkansas 17–3, TCU 21–14 (1st in 9-game series begun in 1976). *Stars:* soph QB Gerald Landry (1,503 yds and 12 TDs pass, 384 yds rush), TE Carl Hilton (38 pass rec for 517 yds and 5 TDs), SE Larry Shepherd (38 pass rec for 503 yds), RB Raymond Tate (864 yds and 6 TDs rush), OG Ray Rogers, K Mike Clendenen (18 FGs, 72 pts), DT T.J. Turner, LB Bryant Winn, DBs Audrey McMillian and DeWayne Bowden (6 int). *Noteworthy:* Got share of 4th SWC title. Lost to Boston College 45–28 in Cotton Bowl; Landry passed for 154 yds and a TD (15 yds to Shepherd), and Cougars also scored on 98-yd kickoff return by Earl Allen, 2-yd run by Tate, and 25-yd pass int return by McMillian.

1988 (9–3) *Won:* Louisiana Tech 60–0, Missouri 31–7, Baylor 27–24, Tulsa 82–28, TCU 40–12, Texas 66–15, Wyoming 34–10, Texas Tech 30–29, Rice 45–14. *Lost:* Texas A&M 30–16, Arkansas 26–21. *Stars:* soph QB Andre Ware (2,507 yds and 25 TDs pass), QB David Dacus (1,597 yds and 13 TDs pass), WRs Jason Phillips (nation's leader with 108 pass rec for 1,444 yds and 15 TDs), James Dixon (102 pass rec for 1,103 yds and 11 TDs) and soph Brian Williams (34 pass rec for 538 yds and 5 TDs), RBs Kimble Anders (6 TDs, 33 pass rec for 377 yds) and soph Chuck Weatherspoon (1,004 yds rush, 11 TDs), OT Joey Banes, OG Byron Forsythe, frosh K Roman Anderson (19 FGs, 108 pts), DTs Glenn Montgomery and Alfred Oglesby, LB Lamar Lathon, DBs Johnny Jackson and Alton Montgomery, P Simon Rodriguez (41.4-yd avg). *Noteworthy:* lost to Washington St. 24–22 in Aloha Bowl; Dacus passed for 153 yds and 2 TDs (53 yds to WR Kevin Mason and 2 yds to Weatherspoon, who also scored on 1-yd run), and Anderson kicked 27-yd FG and ex pt.

1989 (9–2) *Won:* Nevada–Las Vegas 69–0, Arizona St. 36–7, Temple 65–7, Baylor 66–10, SMU 95–21, TCU 55–10, Texas 47–9, Texas Tech 40–24, Rice 64–0. *Lost:* Texas A&M 17–13, Arkansas 45–

39. *Stars:* Heisman Trophy–winner Ware (4,699 yds and 46 TDs pass, nation's leader with 4,661 yds total off), WRs Emmanuel Hazard (nation's leader with 142 pass rec for 1,689 yds and 22 TDs), Paul Smith (26 pass rec for 694 yds and 9 TDs), Williams (26 pass rec for 631 yds) and Patrick Cooper (8 TDs, 35 pass rec for 468 yds and 7 TDs), Weatherspoon (58 pass rec for 735 yds, 1,146 yds rush, 13 TDs), Anders (60 pass rec for 621 yds, 5 TDs), Forsythe, Banes, Anderson (22 FGs, 131 pts), DE Craig Veasey, Oglesby, DBs Cornelius Price (nation's coleader with 12 int, 2 returned for TDs), and Chris Ellison (6 int). *Noteworthy:* Jack Pardee's last team outscored foes 589–150 and led nation in total off, pass, scoring (53.5-pt avg), and turnover margin. Ineligible for bowl, on NCAA probation.

1990 (10–1) *Won:* Nevada–Las Vegas 37–9, Texas Tech 51–35, Rice 24–22, Baylor 31–15, Texas A&M

QB Andre Ware, 1987–89

QB David Klingler, 1989–91

36–31 (1st over Aggies since 1984), SMU 44–17, Arkansas 62–28 (1st over Razorbacks since 1981), TCU 56–35, Eastern Washington 84–21, Arizona St. 62–45 (in Tokyo). *Lost:* Texas 45–24. *Stars:* QB David Klingler (5,140 yds and 54 TDs pass, nation's leader with 5,221 yds total off), Hazard (nation's leader in pass rec with 78 for 946 yds and 9 TDs), Weatherspoon (49 pass rec for 560 yds and 6 TDs, 1,097 yds and 7 TDs rush, 2,038 all-purpose yds), soph WRs Tracy Good (67 pass rec for 616 yds and 5 TDs) and Marcus Grant (37 pass rec for 662 yds and 6 TDs), Cooper (39 pass rec for 755 yds and 10 TDs), WRs Craig Alexander (35 pass rec for 429 yds), Verlond Brown (27 pass rec for 436 yds and

5 TDs) and John Brown III (17 pass rec for 431 yds and 7 TDs), Anderson (19 FGs, 115 pts), LBs Reggie Burnette, soph Eric Blount and frosh Ryan McCoy, DB Jerry Parks (nation's leader with 8 int). *Noteworthy:* Led nation in total off, pass, and scoring (46.5-pt avg) in 1st year under John Jenkins. Again ineligible for bowl.

Bowl Summary

Aloha 0–1; Bluebonnet 2–1–1; Cotton 2–2; Garden State 1–0; Salad 1–0; Sun 0–1; Tangerine 1–0.

Bowl Record (7–5–1)

Regular Season	Bowl	Score	Opponent	Record
1951 (5–5)	Salad	26-21	Dayton	(7–2)
1962 (6–4)	Tangerine	49–21	Miami (Ohio)	(8–1–1)
1969 (8–2)	Bluebonnet	36–7	Auburn	(8–2)
1971 (9–2)	Bluebonnet	17–29	Colorado	(9–2)
1973 (10–1)	Bluebonnet	47–7	Tulane	(9–2)
1974 (8–3)	Bluebonnet	31–31	N.C. State	(9–2)
1976 (9–2)	Cotton	30–21	Maryland	(11–0)
1978 (9–2)	Cotton	34–35	Notre Dame	(8–3)
1979 (10–1)	Cotton	17–14	Nebraska	(10–1)
1980 (6–5)	Garden State	35–0	Navy	(8–3)
1981 (7–3–1)	Sun	14–40	Oklahoma	(6–4–1)
1984 (7–4)	Cotton	28–45	Boston College	(9–2)
1988 (8–3)	Aloha	22–24	Washington St.	(8–3)

Conference Titles

Missouri Valley—1952, 1956, 1957, 1959*. **Southwest**—1976*, 1978, 1979*, 1984*.

TOP 20 AP AND UPI RANKING

1952	U–19	1969	12–16	1974	19–11	1988	18–U
1966	U–17	1970	19–13	1976	4–4	1989	14–U
1967	U–19	1971	17–14	1978	10–11	1990	10–U
1968	18–20	1973	9–13	1979	5–5		

Major Rivals

Houston has played at least 10 games with Arkansas 6–12, Baylor 12–12–1, Cincinnati 11–2, Florida St. 12–2–2, Miami (Fla.) 7–9, Mississippi 3–15, Mississippi St. 6–6, North Texas St. 4–7, Oklahoma St. 8–8–1, Rice 18–4, Southern Methodist 8–8,

Texas 7–10–2, Texas A&M 12–16–3, Texas Christian 13–4, Texas Tech 17–7–1, Tulsa 15–14.

COACHES

Dean of Houston coaches is Bill Yeoman with record of 160–108–8 for 1962–86, including 4 SWC titles and 11 bowl teams. Other top records for at least 3 years were by Clyde Lee, 37–32–2 for 1948–54 with 1 MVC title and 1 bowl champion; Harold Lahar, 24–23–2 for 1957–61 with 2 MVC titles; Jack Pardee, 22–11–1 for 1987–89 with 1 bowl team; and John Jenkins, 18–15 for 1990–92.

MISCELLANEA

First game was loss to SW Louisiana 13–7 in 1946 . . . first win was over West Texas St. 14–12 in 1946 . . . highest score was over Tulsa 100–6 (modern NCAA record) in 1968 . . . worst defeat was by Michigan 61–7 in 1992 . . . highest against tied in loss to Texas Tech 61–14 in 1954 . . . longest win streak of 10, in 1969–70 ended by Oklahoma St. 26–17 and in 1972–73 by Auburn 7–0 . . . longest losing string of 8, in 1947 broken with win over Texas A&I 14–0 and in 1975 with win over Tulsa 42–30 . . . consensus All-Americans were Rich Stotter, G, 1967; Bill Bridges, G, 1969; Elmo Wright, E, 1970; Wilson Whitley, DT, 1976; Leonard Mitchell, DL, 1980; Jason Phillips, WR, 1988; and Andre Ware, QB, 1989 . . . Academic All-Americans were Horst Paul, E, 1964; Mark Mohr, DB, 1976; and Kevin Rollwage, OT, 1976–77 . . . Heisman Trophy winner was Andre Ware, QB, 1989 . . . Lombardi Award winner was Wilson Whitley, DT, 1976.

RICE (Owls; Blue and Gray)

NOTABLE TEAMS

1916 (6–1–2) *Won:* Austin 40–0, Southwestern (Texas) 54–0, Texas A&M 20–0, Tulane 23–13 (1st meeting), Southern Methodist (SMU) 146–3 (1st meeting), Arizona 47–7. *Lost:* Texas 16–2 in opener. *Tied:* Texas Christian (TCU) 7–7, Louisiana St. (LSU) 7–7.
1917 (7–1) *Won:* Illinois Medics 31–0, TCU 26–0, Austin 53–13, Texas 13–0 (1st in 4-game series begun in 1914), Haskell Institute 55–13, South-

western (Texas) 34–13, Tulane 16–0. *Lost:* unbeaten Texas A&M 10–0 in finale.
1919 (8–1) *Won:* Trinity (Texas) 12–0, Baylor 8–0 (1st meeting since 1914), Southwestern (Texas) 22–0, Austin 54–0, SMU 21–14, Sewanee 19–7, Howard Payne 7–0, Arkansas 40–7 (1st meeting). *Lost:* Texas 32–7. *Star:* E Shirley Brick.
1930 (8–4) *Won:* Southwestern (Texas) 32–6, Sam Houston St. 13–12 (10th straight over Bearkats), St. Edwards 20–0, Arizona 21–0, Texas 6–0 (1st over Longhorns since 1924), Sewanee 12–0, Texas A&M 7–0 (1st over Aggies since 1923), Iowa St. 13–7. *Lost:* Arkansas 7–6 (1st meeting since 1925), TCU 20–0, SMU 32–0, Baylor 35–14. *Star:* G Bill Morgan. *Noteworthy:* 1st winning season since 1920.
1932 (7–3) *Won:* Texas A&I 20–0, LSU 10–8 (1st meeting since 1925), SMU 13–0 (1st over Mustangs in 7 games since 1921), Loyola (La.) 14–7, Creighton 41–7, Arkansas 12–7, Baylor 12–0. *Lost:* Texas 18–6, Texas A&M 14–7, unbeaten TCU 16–6.
1934 (9–1–1) *Won:* Loyola (La.) 12–0, Purdue 14–0, SMU 9–0, Creighton 47–13, Texas 20–9, Texas A&I 27–0, Arkansas 7–0, Texas A&M 25–6, Baylor 32–0. *Lost:* TCU 7–2. *Tied:* LSU 9–9. *Stars:* HB Bill Wallace, FB John McCauley, E Leche Sylvester, T Ralph Miller. *Noteworthy:* Won 1st SWC title in 1st year under Jimmy Kitts.
1935 (8–3) *Won:* St. Mary's (Texas) 38–0, LSU 10–7, Duquesne 27–7, Creighton 14–0, Texas 28–19, George Washington 41–6, Arkansas 20–7, Texas A&M 17–10. *Lost:* unbeaten national cochamp SMU 10–0, TCU 27–6, Baylor 6–0. *Stars:* McCauley, Wallace, Sylvester.
1937 (6–3–2) *Won:* Texas 14–7, Auburn 13–7, Arkansas 26–7, Baylor 13–7, SMU 15–7. *Lost:* Oklahoma 6–0, LSU 13–0, TCU 7–2 (10th straight to Horned Frogs). *Tied:* Tulsa 0–0, Texas A&M 6–6. *Noteworthy:* Won 2nd SWC title. Made 1st postseason appearance, upsetting unbeaten Colorado 28–14 in Cotton Bowl after trailing 14–0 at end of 1st quarter; soph Ernie Lain passed for 3 TDs (to Jake Scheuhle, soph B Olie Cordill, and Frank Steen) and ran for another, and Jack "Red" Vestal kicked 4 ex pts.
1940 (7–3) *Won:* Centenary 25–0, LSU 23–0 (1st over Tigers since 1935), Texas 13–0, Texas A&I 9–6, Arkansas 14–7, TCU 14–6 (1st over Horned Frogs in 13 games since 1924), Baylor 21–12. *Lost:* Tulane 15–6, Texas A&M 25–0, SMU 7–6. *Stars:* T Moose Hartman, C Ken Whitlow. *Noteworthy:* 1st year under Jess Neely.

1942 (7–2–1) *Won:* Corpus Christi Navy 18–7, LSU 27–14, Texas Tech 19–7 (1st meeting), Arkansas 40–9, TCU 21–0, Baylor 20–0, SMU 13–7. *Lost:* Tulane 18–7, Texas 12–7 in consecutive early games. *Tied:* Texas A&M 0–0. *Stars:* B Dick Dwelle, G Weldon Humble.

1946 (9–2) *Won:* Southwestern (Texas) 48–0, Tulane 25–6, SMU 21–7, Texas 18–13, Texas Tech 41–6, Texas A&M 27–10, TCU 13–0, Baylor 38–6. *Lost:* LSU 7–6, Arkansas 7–0. *Stars:* Humble (back from military service; Owls' 1st consensus All-American), Bs Carl "Buddy" Russ, Huey Keeney. *Noteworthy:* Got share of 3rd SWC title. Beat Tennessee 8–0 in Orange Bowl, scoring all points in 1st quarter on 50-yd run/lateral play by Russ and Keeney, and punt blocked through end zone by frosh T Ralph Murphy.

1949 (10–1) *Won:* Clemson 33–7, New Mexico 55–0, SMU 41–27, Texas 17–15, Texas Tech 28–0, Arkansas 14–0, Texas A&M 13–0, TCU 20–14, Baylor 21–7. *Lost:* LSU 14–7. *Stars:* C Joe Watson, Murphy, E James "Froggie" Williams (20 pass rec for 368 yds and 6 TDs). *Noteworthy:* Won 4th SWC title. Beat North Carolina 27–13 in Cotton Bowl; Tobin Rote passed for 140 yds and 2 TDs, Williams caught 4 for 55 yds and a TD and kicked 3 ex pts, and soph Bill Burkhalter ran for 74 yds and a TD and caught 44-yd TD pass.

1953 (9–2) *Won:* Florida 20–16, Cornell 28–3, Hardin-Simmons 40–0, Texas 18–13, Arkansas 47–0, Texas A&M 34–7, TCU 19–6, Baylor 41–19. *Lost:* SMU 12–7, Kentucky 19–13. *Stars:* Kosse Johnson (944 yds rush, 10 TDs), HB Dicky Maegle (833 yds rush, 10 TDs), Dan Hart (15 pass rec for 239 yds), T John Hudson, G Kenny Paul, C Leo Rucka, DL Richard Chapman. *Noteworthy:* Got share of 5th SWC title. Beat Alabama 28–6 in Cotton Bowl as Maegle ran for 265 yds and scored 3 TDs on runs of 79, 95, and 34 yds, and Buddy Grantham scored on 7-yd run; Maegle's 95-yarder was "interrupted" by off-the-bench tackle by Tide's Tommy Lewis at Alabama 42-yd line, but referee Cliff Shaw ruled a TD.

1954 (7–3) *Won:* Florida 34–14, Cornell 41–20, Texas 13–7, Vanderbilt 34–13, Texas A&M 29–19 (10th straight over Aggies), TCU 6–0, Baylor 20–14. *Lost:* Wisconsin 13–7, SMU 20–6, Arkansas 28–15 (1st to Razorbacks since 1946). *Stars:* Maegle (905 yds rush, 18 pass rec for 198 yds, 12 TDs, nation's punt return leader with 19.5-yd avg), Paul.

1957 (7–4) *Won:* LSU 20–14, Stanford 34–7, SMU 27–21 (1st over Mustangs since 1951), Arkansas 13–7, Texas A&M 7–6, TCU 20–0, Baylor 20–0. *Lost:* Duke 7–6, Texas 19–14, Clemson 20–7. *Stars:* Buddy Dial (21 pass rec for 508 yds), QB/S King Hill (798 yds and 4 TDs pass, 446 yds and 5 TDs rush, 4 int), G Matt Gorges, T Larry Whitmire. *Noteworthy:* Won 6th SWC title. Lost to Navy 20–7 in Cotton Bowl (1st loss in 5 bowl games), losing 5 fumbles; scored on 8-yd pass from QB Frank Ryan to Ken Williams.

1960 (7–4) *Won:* Tulane 10–7 (1st meeting since 1947), Florida 10–0, SMU 47–10, Texas 7–0, Texas Tech 30–6 (1st meeting since 1952), Texas A&M 21–14, TCU 23–0. *Lost:* Georgia Tech 16–13, Arkansas 3–0, Baylor 12–7. *Stars:* G Rufus King, E Johnny Burrell (20 pass rec for 266 yds), QB Billy Cox (6 TDs). *Noteworthy:* lost to unbeaten national cochamp Mississippi 14–6 in Sugar Bowl though outgaining Rebels 281–186 in total yds; scored on 2-yd run by Butch Blume.

1961 (7–4) *Won:* LSU 16–3, Florida 19–10, SMU 10–0, Texas Tech 42–7, Texas A&M 21–7, TCU 35–16, Baylor 26–14. *Lost:* Georgia Tech 24–0, Texas 34–7, Arkansas 10–0. *Stars:* Burrell, Blume (6 TDs, 4 int), B Roland Jackson (5 TDs rush), T Robert Johnston. *Noteworthy:* lost to Kansas 33–7 in Bluebonnet Bowl after trailing only 12–7 at half; scored on 5-yd pass from QB Randy Kerbow to Burrell.

Bowl Summary

Bluebonnet 0–1; Cotton 3–1; Orange 1–0; Sugar 0–1.

Bowl Record (4–3)

Regular Season	Bowl	Score	Opponent	Record
1937 (5–3–2)	Cotton	28–14	Colorado	(8–0)
1946 (8–2)	Orange	8–0	Tennessee	(9–1)

(continued)

Regular Season	Bowl	Score	Opponent	Record
1949 (9–1)	Cotton	27–13	North Carolina	(7–3)
1953 (8–2)	Cotton	28–6	Alabama	(6–2–3)
1957 (7–3)	Cotton	7–20	Navy	(8–1–1)
1960 (7–3)	Sugar	6–14	Mississippi	(9–0–1)
1961 (7–3)	Bluebonnet	7–33	Kansas	(6–3–1)

CONFERENCE TITLES

Southwest—1934, 1937, 1946*, 1949, 1953*, 1957.

TOP 20 AP AND UPI RANKING

1937	18	1947	18	1953	6–6	1957	8–7
1946	10	1949	5	1954	19–19	1961	17–U

MAJOR RIVALS

Rice has played at least 10 games with Arkansas 29–35–3, Baylor 30–41–2, Houston 4–18, Louisiana St. 13–36–5, Sam Houston St. 15–1, Southern Methodist 28–41–1, Southwestern (Texas) 16–5, Texas 20–58–1, Texas A&M 27–47–3, Texas Christian 30–38–3, Texas Tech 19–23–1, Tulane 11–10–1.

COACHES

Dean of Rice coaches is Jess Neely with record of 144–124–10 for 1940–66, including 4 SWC titles and 6 bowl teams. Other top records for at least 3 years were by Phil Arbuckle, 52–30–8 for 1912–17 and 1919–23 with 1 unbeaten team; Jack Meagher, 26–26 for 1929–33; and Jimmy Kitts, 33–29–4 for 1934–39 with 2 SWC titles and 1 Cotton Bowl champion.

MISCELLANEA

First game was win over Houston H.S. 7–0 in 1912 . . . 1st win over college foe was over Sam Houston St. 20–6 in 1912 . . . highest score was over SMU 146–3 in 1916 . . . highest since W.W. II was 55–0 over New Mexico in 1949 and Virginia Military Institute in 1969 . . . worst defeat was by Austin College 81–0 in 1912 . . . worst since W.W. II was by LSU 77–0 in 1977 . . . longest unbeaten string of 15 in 1916–17 ended by Texas A&M 10–0 . . . longest losing string of 18 in 1987–88 broken with win over SMU 35–6 in 1989 opener . . . consensus All-Americans were Weldon Humble, G, 1946; James Williams, E, 1949; Dicky Maegle, B, 1954; Buddy Dial, E, 1958; Tommy Kramer, QB, 1976; and Trevor Cobb, RB, 1991 . . . Academic All-Americans were Richard Chapman, DL, 1952–53; Dicky Maegle, B, 1954; Steve Bradshaw, DL, 1969; LaMont Jefferson, LB, 1979; and Brian Patterson, DB, 1983.

SOUTHERN METHODIST
(Mustangs; Red and Blue)

NOTABLE TEAMS

1923 (9–0) **Won:** North Texas St. 41–0, Henderson-Brown 33–0, Austin 10–3, Missouri Mines 35–0, Texas A&M 10–0, Texas Christian (TCU) 40–0 (1st on-field win in 7-game series dating to 1915), Arkansas 13–6, Oklahoma A&M 9–0, Baylor 16–0. **Stars:** Bs Logan Stollenwerck and Lawrence "Smack" Reisor, E Jimmie Stewart, G Johnny Mac Brooks, C Buddy King. **Noteworthy:** 1st undefeated team outscored foes 207–9 and won 1st SWC title.
1924 (5–1–4) **Won:** North Texas St. 7–0, Trinity (Texas) 14–3, Austin 7–0, Texas 10–6 (1st in 4-game series dating to 1916), TCU 6–0. **Tied:** Texas

A&M 7–7, Arkansas 14–14, Baylor 7–7, Oklahoma A&M 13–13.   *Stars:* Reisor, E Gene Bedford, King. *Noteworthy:* made 1st postseason appearance, losing to West Virginia Wesleyan 9–7 in Dixie Classic (Cotton Bowl forerunner) in Dallas; ended 19-game unbeaten string.
1926 (8–0–1)   *Won:* North Texas St. 42–0, Trinity (Texas) 48–0, Centenary 37–0, Texas A&M 9–7, Texas 21–17, Rice 20–0 (1st meeting since 1921), Baylor 31–3, TCU 14–13 (1st homecoming).   *Tied:* Missouri 7–7 (1st meeting).   *Star:* B Gerald Mann. *Noteworthy:* won 2nd SWC title.
1927 (7–2)   *Won:* North Texas St. 68–0, Howard Payne 32–0, Rice 34–6, Missouri 32–9, Texas 14–0, Baylor 34–0, TCU 28–6.   *Lost:* Centenary 21–12, unbeaten Texas A&M 39–13.   *Stars:* Mann, Redman Hume (17 TDs, 109 pts).
1929 (6–0–4)   *Won:* North Texas St. 13–3, Austin 16–0 (1st meeting since 1924), Mississippi 52–0, Texas A&M 12–7, Baylor 25–6, Rice 34–0.   *Tied:* Howard Payne 13–13, Nebraska 0–0, Texas 0–0, unbeaten TCU 7–7.   *Stars:* G Choc Sanders, soph T Marion Hammon, soph B Weldon Mason. *Noteworthy:* Ray Morrison's 4th undefeated team.
1931 (9–1–1)   *Won:* North Texas St. 13–0, Hardin-Simmons 27–10, Centenary 19–0, Arkansas 42–6 (1st meeting since 1925), Rice 21–12, Texas 9–7, Texas A&M 8–0, Baylor 6–0, Navy 13–7.   *Lost:* St. Mary's 7–2 in finale.   *Tied:* TCU 0–0.   *Stars:* Mason, Hammon, T Willis Tate, G Al Neeley, C Al Delcambre.   *Noteworthy:* Won 3rd SWC title.
1934 (8–2–2)   *Won:* North Texas St. 33–0, Austin 33–0, Oklahoma A&M 41–0, Fordham 26–14, Texas A&M 28–0, Arkansas 10–6, TCU 19–0 (1st over Horned Frogs since 1927).   *Lost:* Rice 9–0, Baylor 13–6.   *Tied:* LSU 14–14, Texas 7–7.   *Stars:* Bs Bobby Wilson and Harry Shuford, T Clyde Carter, G J.C. Wetsel.   *Noteworthy:* Morrison's last team. Beat Washington (Mo.) 7–0 in postseason charity game in St. Louis.
1935 (12–1)   *Won:* North Texas St. 39–0, Austin 60–0, Tulsa 14–0, Washington (Mo.) 35–6, Rice 10–0, Hardin-Simmons 18–6, Texas 20–0, UCLA 21–0, Arkansas 17–6, Baylor 10–0, TCU 20–14, Texas A&M 24–0.   *Stars:* Wilson (13 TDs) and Wetsel (Mustangs' 1st consensus All-Americans), Shuford, Ts Truman Spain and Maurice Orr. *Noteworthy:* Won 4th SWC title and share of 1st national championship in 1st year under Matty Bell. Upset by Stanford 7–0 in Rose Bowl on 1st

quarter TD; outgained Indians but fumbled away best scoring chance.
1940 (8–1–1)   *Won:* UCLA 9–6, North Texas St. 20–7, Auburn 20–13, Texas 21–13, Arkansas 28–0, Baylor 7–4, TCU 16–0, Rice 7–6.   *Lost:* Texas A&M 19–7.   *Tied:* Pittsburgh 7–7.   *Star:* B Preston Johnston.   *Noteworthy:* got share of 5th SWC title.
1947 (9–0–2)   *Won:* Santa Clara 22–6, Missouri 35–19, Oklahoma A&M 21–14, Rice 14–0, UCLA 7–0, Texas 14–13 (1st over Longhorns since 1940), Texas A&M 13–0 (1st over Aggies since 1938), Arkansas 14–6, Baylor 10–0.   *Tied:* TCU 19–19 in finale.   *Stars:* soph TB Doak Walker (Maxwell Award winner; 653 yds rush, 344 yds pass, 11 TDs, 87 pts, nation's leader in kickoff returns with 38.7-yd avg), E Sid Halliday, G Earl Cook, T John Hamberger, soph Paul Page (7 int). *Noteworthy:* Won 6th SWC title in 1st unbeaten season since 1935. Tied unbeaten Penn St. 13–13 in Cotton Bowl; Walker passed 53 yds to

TB Doak Walker, 1945, 1947–49

Page for a TD, scored on 2-yd run, and kicked ex pt.

1948 (9–1–1)   *Won:* Pittsburgh 33–14, Texas Tech 41–6, Rice 33–7, Santa Clara 33–0, Texas 21–6, Texas A&M 20–14, Arkansas 14–12, Baylor 13–6. *Lost:* Missouri 20–14.   *Tied:* TCU 7–7 in finale. *Stars:* Heisman Trophy–winner Walker (537 yds rush, 318 yds and 6 TDs pass, 14 pass rec for 264 yds, 11 TDs, 88 pts, 42.1-yd punting avg), Gil Johnson (1,026 yds pass), soph HB Kyle Rote (504 yds rush, 19 pass rec for 214 yds, 7 TDs).   *Noteworthy:* Repeated as SWC champ. Beat Oregon 21–13 in Cotton Bowl, scoring on 1-yd run by Walker (who kicked 2 ex pts), 36-yd run by Rote (93 yds rush), and 8-yd run by Gene "Chicken" Roberts; Mustangs had quick kicks of 79 yds by Walker and 84 yds by Rote.

1966 (8–3)   *Won:* Illinois 26–7, Navy 21–3, Rice 28–24, Texas Tech 24–7, Texas 13–12, Texas A&M 21–14, Baylor 24–22 (1st over Bears since 1959), TCU 21–0 (1st over Horned Frogs since 1958). *Lost:* Purdue 35–23, Arkansas 22–0.   *Stars:* QB Mac White (606 yds and 6 TDs rush), soph FL Jerry Levias (9 TDs, 18 pass rec for 420 yds and 7 TDs), G Lynn Thornhill, T Ronnye Medlen, MG John LaGrone, LBs Billy Bob Stewart and Jerry Griffin. *Noteworthy:* Won 8th SWC title in 1st winning season since 1959.Lost to Georgia 24–9 in Cotton Bowl; Levias ran for 149 yds and Mustangs scored on 22-yd FG by Dennis Partee and 1-yd run by soph B Mike Richardson.

1968 (8–3)   *Won:* Auburn 37–28, N.C. State 35–14, TCU 21–14, Rice 32–24, Texas Tech 39–18, Texas A&M 36–23, Baylor 33–17.   *Lost:* unbeaten national champ Ohio St. 35–14, Texas 38–7, Arkansas 35–29.   *Stars:* soph QB Chuck Hixson (nation's leader with 3,103 yds and 21 TDs pass), Levias (9 TDs, 80 pass rec for 1,131 yds and 8 TDs), Mike Fleming (53 pass rec for 588 yds and 7 TDs), Richardson (1,034 yds and 8 TDs rush, 49 pass rec for 581 yds and 3 TDs), T Terry May, Jim Livingston (8 int).   *Noteworthy:* beat Oklahoma 28–27 (1st meeting since 1939) in Astro-Bluebonnet Bowl, scoring 22 pts in final quarter; Hixson passed for 2 TDs (to Levias and Fleming) and 2-pt conversion (to Pinky Clements), Richardson scored 2 TDs, and Reid Lesser kicked 2 ex pts.

1980 (8–4)   *Won:* North Texas St. 28–9, TCU 17–14, Texas-Arlington 52–16 (1st meeting since 1964), Tulane 31–21, Texas 20–6 (1st over Longhorns since 1966), Texas A&M 27–0 (1st over Aggies since 1974), Rice 34–14, Arkansas 31–7.   *Lost:* Baylor 32–28, Houston 13–11, Texas Tech 14–0.   *Stars:* soph TBs Eric Dickerson (928 yds rush, 6 TDs) and Craig James (896 yds and 6 TDs rush), Anthony Smith (25 pass rec for 329 yds), C Lance Pederson, OT Lee Spivey, K Eddie Garcia (11 FGs), DT Harvey Armstrong, DB John Simmons (7 int, 2 returned for TDs), P Eric Kaifes (44.6-yd avg). *Noteworthy:* 1st winning season since 1974. Lost to Brigham Young (BYU) 46–45 in Holiday Bowl on 41-yd pass on last play of game after leading 45–25 with 4 minutes left; James had TD runs of 42 and 45 yds and caught TD pass, Dickerson ran for 110 yds and 2 TDs, and Garcia kicked FGs of 42 and 44 yds and 4 ex pts.

1981 (10–1)   *Won:* Texas-Arlington 48–0, North Texas St. 34–7, Grambling 59–27, TCU 20–9 (10th straight over Horned Frogs), Baylor 37–20,

HB Kyle Rote, 1948–50

Houston 38–22, Texas A&M 27–7, Rice 33–12, Texas Tech 30–6, Arkansas 32–18. *Lost:* Texas 9–7. *Stars:* Dickerson (1,428 yds and 19 TDs rush), James (1,147 yds and 9 TDs rush), soph QB Lance McIlhenny (1,066 yds pass, 241 yds rush), Jackie Wilson (20 pass rec for 397 yds), OG Perry Hartnett, C Gordon McAdams, Garcia (18 FGs, 91 pts), Armstrong, LBs Eric Ferguson and Gary Moten, DBs Wes Hopkins, soph Russell Carter (7 int) and James Mobley, Kaifes (42-yd punting avg). *Noteworthy:* Won 9th SWC title in last year under Ron Meyer. Ineligible for bowl, on NCAA probation.

1982 (11–0–1) *Won:* Tulane 51–7, Texas–El Paso 31–10, TCU 16–13, North Texas St. 38–10, Baylor 22–19, Houston 20–14, Texas 30–17, Texas A&M 47–9, Rice 41–14, Texas Tech 34–27. *Tied:* Arkansas 17–17 in finale. *Stars:* Dickerson (1,617 yds and 17 TDs rush), James (938 yds rush, 11 pass rec for 208 yds, 7 TDs, 44.9-yd punting avg), McIlhenny (1,077 yds total off, 10 TDs pass), OG Joe Beard, K Jeff Harrell (13 FGs, 79 pts), Moten, Carter, Hopkins (6 int), DB Blane Smith.

Noteworthy: Won 10th SWC title and had 1st unbeaten season since 1947 in 1st year under Bobby Collins. Beat Pittsburgh 7–3 in wet, cold Cotton Bowl; scored on 9-yd run by McIlhenny in last quarter.

1983 (10–2) *Won:* Louisville 24–6, Grambling 20–13, TCU 21–17, Texas-Arlington 34–0, Baylor 42–26, Texas A&M 10–7, Rice 20–6, Texas Tech 33–7, Arkansas 17–0, Houston 34–12 (in Tokyo). *Lost:* unbeaten Texas 15–12. *Stars:* McIlhenny (1,233 yds and 11 TDs pass), frosh WR Ron Morris (41 pass rec for 688 yds), TE Ricky Bolden, soph TB Reggie Dupard (1,249 yds and 9 TDs rush), OTs Andrew Campbell and Brian O'Meara, C Chris Jackson, Harrell (13 FGs), DT Michael Carter, LB Anthony Beverley, Russell Carter (7 int), DB Fred Nichols. *Noteworthy:* lost to Alabama 28–7 in Sun Bowl; scored on 15-yd pass from McIlhenny to Marquis Pleasant.

1984 (10–2) *Won:* Louisville 41–7, North Texas St. 24–6, TCU 56–17, Baylor 24–20, Texas A&M 28–20, Rice 31–17, Texas Tech 31–0, Arkansas 31–28, Nevada–Las Vegas 38–21. *Lost:* Houston 29–20,

TB Craig James, 1979–82

TB Eric Dickerson, 1979–82

Texas 13–7 in consecutive mid-season games. *Stars:* Dupard (1,157 yds rush, 16 TDs), QB Don King (1,598 yds pass), Morris (27 pass rec for 554 yds), Campbell, Jackson, OT Dale Hellestrae, soph NT Jerry Ball, Beverley, soph P Dodge Carter (43-yd avg). *Noteworthy:* Got share of 11th SWC title. Beat Notre Dame 27–20 (1st meeting since 1958) in Aloha Bowl, scoring 10 pts in last quarter; scored on 7-yd run by soph Jeff Atkins, 12-yd pass from King to Cobby Morrison, 2-yd run by Dupard (103 yds rush), and FGs of 47 and 30 yds and 3 ex pts by soph K Brandy Brownlee.

BOWL SUMMARY

Aloha 1–0; Bluebonnet 1–0; Cotton 2–1–1; Dixie Classic 0–1; Holiday 0–1; Rose 0–1; Sun 0–2.

BOWL RECORD (4–6–1)

Regular Season	Bowl	Score	Opponent	Record
1924 (5–0–4)	Dixie Classic	7–9	W.Va. Wesleyan	(8–2)
1935 (12–0)	Rose	0–7	Stanford	(7–1)
1947 (9–0–1)	Cotton	13–13	Penn State	(9–0)
1948 (8–1–1)	Cotton	21–13	Oregon	(9–1)
1963 (4–6)	Sun	14–21	Oregon	(7–3)
1966 (8–2)	Cotton	9–24	Georgia	(9–1)
1968 (7–3)	Bluebonnet	28–27	Oklahoma	(7–3)
1980 (8–3)	Holiday	45–46	BYU	(11–1)
1982 (10–0–1)	Cotton	7–3	Pittsburgh	(9–2)
1983 (10–1)	Sun	7–28	Alabama	(7–4)
1984 (9–2)	Aloha	27–20	Notre Dame	(7–4)

CONFERENCE TITLES

Texas Intercollegiate Athletic Association—1918. **Southwest**—1923, 1926, 1931, 1935, 1940*, 1947, 1948, 1966, 1981, 1982, 1984*.

TOP 20 AP AND UPI RANKING

1940	16	1954	U–17	1968	14–16	1982	2–2
1947	3	1958	18–18	1980	20–20	1983	12–11
1948	10	1966	10–9	1981	5–U	1984	8–8

MAJOR RIVALS

Southern Methodist has played at least 10 games with Arkansas 28–33–5, Austin 9–4–1, Baylor 36–30–7, Georgia Tech 2–8–1, Houston 8–8, Missouri 13–7–1, North Texas St. 27–3–1, Notre Dame 3–10, Rice 41–28–1, Texas 22–44–4, Texas A&M 29–38–6, Texas Christian 35–31–7, Texas Tech 16–22, Tulane 4–6.

COACHES

Dean of SMU coaches is Ray Morrison with record of 84–44–22 for 1915–16 and 1922–34, including 3 SWC titles, 1 bowl team, and 4 teams unbeaten in regular season. Other top records for at least 3 years were by Madison "Matty" Bell, 79–40–8 for 1935–41 and 1945–49 with 4 SWC titles, 3 bowl teams, 2 teams unbeaten in regular season, and

1 national champion; Hayden Fry, 49–66–1 for 1962–72 with 1 SWC title and 3 bowl teams; Dave Smith, 16–15–2 for 1973–75; Ron Meyer, 34–32–1 for 1976–81 with 1 SWC title and 1 bowl team; and Bobby Collins, 43–14–1 for 1982–86 with 2 SWC titles, 3 bowl teams, and 1 unbeaten team.

Miscellanea

First game was loss to TCU 43–0 in 1915 . . . 1st win was over Hendrix 13–2 in 1915 . . . highest score was over Daniel Baker 70–0 in 1920 . . . highest since W.W. II was over Grambling 59–27 in 1981 . . . biggest margin since W.W. II was over Rice 58–0 in 1978 . . . worst defeat was by Rice 146–3 in 1916 . . . worst since W.W. II was by Houston 95–21 in 1989 . . . longest unbeaten string of 21 in 1981–83 ended by Texas 15–12 . . . 19-game unbeaten string in 1922–24 ended by West Virginia Wesleyan 9–7 in Dixie Classic on New Year's Day 1925 . . . 15-game unbeaten string in 1946–48 ended by Missouri 20–14 . . . longest win streak of 14, in 1934–35 ended by Stanford 7–0 in 1936 Rose Bowl and in 1981–82 by Arkansas 17–17 . . . longest winless string of 13, in 1915–16 broken with win over Meridian 20–7 in 1917 opener and in 1959–61 with win over Air Force 9–7 . . . consensus All-Americans were J.C. Wetsel, G, and Bobby Wilson, B, 1935; Doak Walker, B, 1947–49; Kyle Rote, B, 1950; Dick Hightower, C, 1951; John LaGrone, MG, 1966; Jerry Levias, E, 1968; Robert Popelka, DB, 1972; Louie Kelcher, G, 1974; Emanuel Tolbert, WR, 1978; John Simmons, DB, 1980; Eric Dickerson, RB, 1982; Russell Carter, DB, 1983; and Reggie Dupard, RB, 1985 . . . Academic All-Americans were Dave Powell, E, 1952; Darrell Lafitte, G, 1953; Raymond Berry, E, 1954; David Hawk, G, 1955; Tom Koenig, G, 1957–58; Raymond Schoenke, T, 1962; John LaGrone, MG, and Lynn Thornhill, OG, 1966; Jerry Levias, E, 1968; Cleve Whitener, LB, 1972; and Brian O'Meara, OT, 1983 . . . Heisman Trophy winner was Doak Walker, HB, 1948 . . . Maxwell Award winner was Doak Walker, HB, 1947.

TEXAS (Longhorns; Burnt Orange and White)
Notable Teams

1894 (6–1) **Won:** Texas A&M 38–0 (1st meeting), Tulane 12–0 (1st meeting), Austin YMCA 6–0, 24–0,

Arkansas 54–0 (1st meeting), San Antonio 57–0. **Lost:** Missouri 28–0 (1st meeting).

1895 (5–0) **Won:** Dallas 10–0, Austin YMCA 24–0, Tulane 16–0, San Antonio 38–0, Galveston 8–0. **Noteworthy:** blanked foes 96–0 in 1st undefeated season since 4-game schedule of 1893.

1897 (6–2) **Won:** San Antonio 10–0, 12–0, Texas Christian (TCU) 18–10 (1st meeting), Houston (not University) 42–6, Ft. Worth 38–0, Dallas 20–16. **Lost:** Dallas 22–4, Ft. Worth 6–0.

1898 (5–1) **Won:** TCU 16–0, 29–0, Texas A&M 48–0, Galveston 17–0, Dallas 26–0. **Lost:** Sewanee 4–0 in mid-season.

1899 (6–2) **Won:** Dallas 11–6, San Antonio 28–0, Texas A&M 6–0, Tulane 11–0, 32–0, Louisiana St. (LSU) 29–0. **Lost:** unbeaten Sewanee 12–0, Vanderbilt 6–0 (1st meeting) in successive midseason games.

1900 (6–0) **Won:** Oklahoma 28–2 (1st meeting), Vanderbilt 22–0, Texas A&M 5–0, 11–0, Missouri 17–11, Kansas City Medics 30–0. **Noteworthy:** 1st year under S.H. Thompson.

1901 (8–2–1) **Won:** Houston (not University) 32–0, Oklahoma 12–6, 11–0, Texas A&M 17–0, 32–0, Baylor 23–0 (1st meeting), Dallas A.C. 12–0, Missouri 11–0. **Lost:** Kirksville 48–0, Kansas 12–0 in successive late games. **Tied:** Nashville U. 5–5. **Noteworthy:** Thompson's last year.

1903 (5–1–2) **Won:** School for Deaf 17–0, Baylor 48–0, Arkansas 15–0 (1st meeting since 1894), Oklahoma 11–5, Texas A&M 29–6. **Lost:** Haskell 6–0. **Tied:** Oklahoma 6–6, Vanderbilt 5–5. **Noteworthy:** 1st year under Ralph Hutchinson.

1904 (6–2) **Won:** TCU 40–0 (1st meeting since 1898), Trinity (Texas) 24–0, Washington (Mo.) 23–0, Oklahoma 40–10, Baylor 58–0, Texas A&M 34–6. **Lost:** Haskell 4–0, Chicago 68–0.

1906 (9–1) **Won:** 26th Infantry 21–0, TCU 22–0, West Texas Military Academy 28–0, Arkansas 11–0, Oklahoma 10–9, Haskell 28–0 (1st in 5-game series begun in 1902), Daniel Baker 40–0, Washington (Mo.) 17–6, Texas A&M 24–0. **Lost:** Vanderbilt 45–0. **Noteworthy:** only year under H.R. Schenker.

1907 (6–1–1) **Won:** LSU 12–5 (1st meeting since 1902), Haskell 45–10, Arkansas 26–6, Baylor 27–11, Oklahoma 29–10, Texas A&M 11–6. **Lost:** Missouri 5–4 (1st meeting since 1901). **Tied:** Texas A&M 0–0 in opener.

1910 (6–2) **Won:** Southwestern (Texas) 11–6,

Haskell 68–3, Transylvania 48–0, Auburn 9–0, Baylor 1–0 (forfeit), LSU 12–0. *Lost:* Texas A&M 14–8, Oklahoma 3–0.

1911 (5–2) *Won:* Southwestern (Texas) 11–2, Baylor 11–0, Arkansas 12–0, Texas A&M 6–0, Auburn 18–5. *Lost:* Sewanee 6–5 (1st meeting since 1905), unbeaten Oklahoma 6–3. *Noteworthy:* 1st year under Dave Allerdice.

1912 (7–1) *Won:* TCU 30–10, Austin College 3–0, Haskell 14–7, Baylor 19–7, Mississippi 53–14, Southwestern (Texas) 28–3, Arkansas 48–0. *Lost:* Oklahoma 21–6.

1913 (7–1) *Won:* Polytechnic 14–7, Austin College 27–6, Baylor 77–0 (10th straight over Bears), Sewanee 13–7, Southwestern (Texas) 52–0, Oklahoma 14–6, Kansas St. 46–0. *Lost:* unbeaten Notre Dame 30–7 (1st meeting) in finale.

1914 (8–0) *Won:* Trinity (Texas) 30–0, Baylor 57–0, Rice 41–0 (1st meeting), Oklahoma 32–7, Southwestern (Texas) 70–0, Haskell 23–7, Mississippi 66–7, Wabash 39–0. *Star:* B Len Barrell (121 pts on 14 TDs, 34 ex pts, and a FG). *Noteworthy:* 1st unbeaten season since 1900.

1916 (7–2) *Won:* Southern Methodist (SMU) 74–0 (1st meeting), Rice 16–2, Oklahoma A&M 14–6 (1st meeting), Oklahoma 21–7, Arkansas 52–0, Southwestern (Texas) 17–3, Texas A&M 21–7. *Lost:* Baylor 7–3 (1st in 12-game series dating to 1901), Missouri 3–0 (1st meeting since 1907) in consecutive mid-season games. *Stars:* C Gustave "Pig" Dittmar, G Alva Carlton, E Maxey Hart, Bs Rip Lang and Billy Trabue (8 TDs). *Noteworthy:* won 1st SWC title in only year under Eugene Van Gent.

1918 (9–0) *Won:* TCU 19–0, Radio School 25–0, 22–7, Ream Flying Field 26–2, Oklahoma A&M 27–5, Auto Mechanics School 22–0, Rice 14–0, SMU 32–0, Texas A&M 7–0. *Noteworthy:* won 2nd SWC title.

1920 (9–0) *Won:* Hardin-Simmons 63–0, Southwestern (Texas) 27–0, Howard Payne 41–7, Oklahoma A&M 21–0, Austin College 54–0, Rice 21–0, Phillips 27–0, SMU 21–3, Texas A&M 7–3. *Stars:* Bs Grady Watson and Kyle "Icky" Elam (9 TDs), E Hook McCullough, T Tom Dennis, soph C Swede Swenson. *Noteworthy:* won 3rd SWC title in 1st year under Berry Whitaker.

1921 (6–1–1) *Won:* St. Edwards 33–0, Austin College 60–0, Howard Payne 21–0, Rice 56–0, Southwestern (Texas) 44–0, Mississippi St. 54–7. *Lost:* unbeaten Vanderbilt 20–0 (1st meeting since 1906).

Tied: Texas A&M 0–0. *Stars:* Swenson, Dennis, McCullough, Bs Bud McCallum and H.C. "Bully" Gilstrap (8 TDs).

1922 (7–2) *Won:* Austin College 19–0, Phillips 41–10, Oklahoma A&M 19–7, Alabama 19–10, Rice 29–0, Southwestern (Texas) 26–0, Oklahoma 32–7. *Lost:* unbeaten Vanderbilt 20–10, Texas A&M 14–7. *Stars:* Swenson, T Joe Ward, B Ivan Robertson (55 pts on 3 TDs, 9 FGs and 10 ex pts). *Noteworthy:* last year under Whitaker.

1923 (8–0–1) *Won:* Austin College 31–0, Phillips 51–0, Tulane 33–0 (1st meeting since 1909), Vanderbilt 16–0 (1st over Commodores in 6 games since 1900), Southwestern (Texas) 44–0, Rice 27–0, Oklahoma 26–14, Texas A&M 6–0. *Tied:* Baylor 7–7. *Stars:* T Ed Bluestein, C F.M. Bralley, Bs Jim Marley (10 TDs) and Oscar Eckhardt. *Noteworthy:* won 4th SWC title in 1st year under E.J. Stewart.

1925 (6–2–1) *Won:* Southwestern (Texas) 33–0, Mississippi 25–0, Auburn 33–0, Rice 27–6, Baylor 13–3, Arizona 20–0. *Lost:* Vanderbilt 14–6, Texas A&M 28–0. *Tied:* SMU 0–0. *Stars:* Bs Mack Saxon and soph Rufus King (8 TDs), E Matt Newell, C H.C. Pfannkuche.

1927 (6–2–1) *Won:* SW Oklahoma 43–0, Trinity (Texas) 20–6, Vanderbilt 13–6, Rice 27–0, Baylor 13–12, Kansas St. 41–7. *Lost:* SMU 14–0, unbeaten Texas A&M 28–7. *Tied:* TCU 0–0. *Stars:* C John "Pottie" McCullough, G Ike Sewell. *Noteworthy:* 1st year under Clyde Littlefield.

1928 (7–2) *Won:* St. Edwards 32–0, Texas Tech 12–0 (1st meeting), Arkansas 20–7 (1st meeting since 1919), Rice 13–6, Baylor 6–0, TCU 6–0, Texas A&M 19–0. *Lost:* Vanderbilt 13–12, SMU 6–2. *Stars:* King (6 TDs), soph B Dexter Shelley, E Bill Ford, T Gordy Brown. *Noteworthy:* won 4th SWC title.

1930 (8–1–1) *Won:* SW Texas St. 36–0, Texas Mines (Texas–El Paso) 28–0, Howard Payne 26–0, Oklahoma 17–7, SMU 25–7 (1st over Mustangs in 7 games since 1920), Baylor 14–0, TCU 7–0, Texas A&M 26–0. *Lost:* Rice 6–0 (1st to Owls since 1924). *Tied:* Centenary 0–0. *Stars:* Shelley (5 TDs), soph Bs Harrison Stafford and Ernie Koy, E Lester Peterson, soph T Claude "Ox" Blanton, G Grover "Ox" Emerson. *Noteworthy:* won 5th SWC title.

1932 (8–2) *Won:* Daniel Baker 26–0, Missouri 65–0, Oklahoma 17–10, Rice 18–6, SMU 14–6,

Baylor 19–0, Arkansas 34–0, Texas A&M 21–0. *Lost:* Centenary 13–6, unbeaten TCU 14–0. *Stars:* Koy, Stafford, soph B Bohn Hilliard (12 TDs, 76 pts).

1934 (7–2–1) *Won:* Texas Tech 12–6 (1st meeting since 1928), Notre Dame 7–6 (1st meeting since 1915), Oklahoma 19–0, Baylor 25–6, TCU 20–19, Arkansas 19–12, Texas A&M 13–0. *Lost:* Centenary 9–6, Rice 20–9. *Tied:* SMU 7–7. *Stars:* Hilliard (5 TDs, 41 pts), T Charley Coates, E Phil Sanger. *Noteworthy:* 1st year under Jack Chevigny.

1940 (8–2) *Won:* Colorado 39–7, Indiana 13–6, Oklahoma 19–16, Arkansas 21–0, Baylor 13–0, TCU 21–14, Texas A&M 7–0, Florida 26–0. *Lost:* Rice 13–0, SMU 21–13 in successive mid-season games. *Stars:* Bs Pete Layden (496 yds and 7 TDs rush, 581 yds pass), Jack Crain (7 int) and Noble Doss (7 int), E Mal Kutner (16 pass rec for 237 yds).

1941 (8–1–1) *Won:* Colorado 34–6, LSU 34–0 (1st over Tigers in 5 games since 1910), Oklahoma 40–7, Arkansas 48–14, Rice 40–0, SMU 34–0 (1st over Mustangs since 1933), Texas A&M 23–0, Oregon 71–7. *Lost:* TCU 14–7. *Tied:* Baylor 7–7. *Stars:* Crain (11 TDs, 92 pts), Layden (536 yds rush), Kutner, Spec Sanders (17 pass rec for 241 yds), soph E Joe Parker, G Chal Daniel. *Noteworthy:* led nation in scoring (33.8-pt avg).

1942 (9–2) *Won:* Corpus Christi Naval Air Station 40–0, Kansas St. 64–0, Oklahoma 7–0, Arkansas 47–6, Rice 12–7, SMU 21–7, Baylor 20–0, Texas A&M 12–6. *Lost:* Northwestern 3–0, TCU 13–7. *Stars:* Bs Roy Dale McKay (701 yds rush, 492 yds pass, 39-yd punting avg) and Jackie Field (8 TDs, 58 pts), T Stan Mauldin. *Noteworthy:* Led nation in total defense and won 6th SWC title. Made 1st postseason appearance, beating Georgia Tech 14–7 in Cotton Bowl; Longhorns stopped Tech drive at 3-yd line in closing moments of game.

1943 (7–1–1) *Won:* Blackland Army Air Force 65–6, Oklahoma 13–7, Arkansas 34–0, Rice 58–0, SMU 20–0, TCU 46–7, Texas A&M 27–13. *Lost:* Southwestern (Texas) 14–7 (1st meeting since 1933, 1st loss in series in 19 games since 1908). *Stars:* Bs Ralph Park (8 TDs, 59 pts), J.R. Calahan, soph Ralph Ellsworth (507 yds rush) and Joe Magliolo, Parker, G Franklin Butler. *Noteworthy:* Repeated as SWC champ. Tied Randolph Field 7–7 in Cotton Bowl.

1945 (10–1) *Won:* Bergstrom Field 13–7, South-western (Texas) 46–0, Texas Tech 33–0 (1st meeting since 1937), Oklahoma 12–7, Arkansas 34–7, SMU 12–7, Baylor 21–14, TCU 20–0, Texas A&M 20–10. *Lost:* Rice 7–6 in mid-season. *Stars:* soph TB Bobby Layne (543 yds total off in 4 games played), E Hub Bechtol (Longhorns' 1st consensus All-American; 25 pass rec for 289 yds and 7 TDs), frosh C Dick Harris. *Noteworthy:* Won 8th SWC title. Beat Missouri 40–27 (1st meeting since 1932) in Cotton Bowl; Layne ran for 3 TDs, caught 50-yd pass from Ellsworth for another, passed for 2 TDs (48 yds and 15 yds to Joe William Baumgardner), and kicked 4 ex pts.

1946 (8–2) *Won:* Missouri 42–0, Colorado 76–0, Oklahoma A&M 54–6, Oklahoma 20–13, Arkansas 20–0, SMU 19–3, Baylor 22–7, Texas A&M 24–7. *Lost:* Rice 18–13, TCU 14–0. *Stars:* Layne (1,122 yds and 6 TDs pass, 338 yds and 8 TDs rush, 42.1-yd avg on 12 punts, 6 int), Jim Canady (17 pass rec for 420 yds), Bechtol, Harris. *Noteworthy:* last year under Dana Bible.

1947 (10–1) *Won:* Texas Tech 33–0, Oregon 38–13, North Carolina 34–0, Oklahoma 34–14, Arkansas 21–6, Rice 12–0, Baylor 28–7, TCU 20–0, Texas A&M 32–13. *Lost:* unbeaten SMU 14–13. *Stars:* Layne (965 yds and 9 TDs pass), E Max Baumgardner (15 pass rec for 234 yds), Byron Gillory (8 TDs), Harris, P Frank Guess (39.5-yd avg). *Noteworthy:* 1st year under Blair Cherry. Beat Alabama 27–7 in Sugar Bowl after 1st half 7–7 standoff; Layne passed for 183 yds and a TD and scored another, and Longhorns also scored on blocked punt recovered in end zone by G Vic Vasicek and 18-yd pass int return by E Lewis Holder.

1948 (7–3–1) *Won:* LSU 33–0 (1st meeting since 1941), New Mexico 47–0, Arkansas 14–6 (10th straight over Razorbacks), Rice 20–7, Baylor 13–10, TCU 14–7. *Lost:* unbeaten North Carolina 34–7, Oklahoma 20–14 (1st to Sooners since 1939), SMU 21–6. *Tied:* Texas A&M 14–14. *Stars:* Harris, T George Petrovich, B Ray Borneman (700 yds rush), soph E Ben Proctor (15 pass rec for 205 yds), Randy Clay (5 TDs, 50 pts). *Noteworthy:* beat Georgia 41–28 in Orange Bowl; took 13–7 1st quarter lead and outscored Bulldogs 14–7 in last period to clinch win.

1950 (9–2) *Won:* Texas Tech 28–14, Purdue 34–26, Arkansas 19–14, Rice 35–7, SMU 23–20, Baylor 27–20, TCU 21–7, Texas A&M 17–0, LSU 21–6.

Lost: unbeaten national champ Oklahoma 14–13. *Stars:* Byron Townsend (841 yds rush, 14 TDs), Proctor (24 pass rec for 453 yds), G Bud McFadin, T Ken Jackson, LB Don Menasco, DB Bobby Dillon. *Noteworthy:* Won 9th SWC title in Cherry's last year. Lost to Tennessee 20–14 in Cotton Bowl (1st loss in 6 bowl games) after leading 14–7 entering 4th period; scored on 5-yd run by Townsend and 35-yd pass from Ben Tompkins (who also kicked 2 ex pts) to soph B Gib Dawson.

1951 (7–3) *Won:* Kentucky 7–6, Purdue 14–0, North Carolina 45–20, Oklahoma 9–7, Rice 14–6, SMU 20–13, TCU 32–21. *Lost:* Arkansas 16–14 (1st to Razorbacks since 1938), Baylor 18–6 (1st to Bears in 10 games since 1939), Texas A&M 22–21 (1st to Aggies since 1939). *Stars:* Dawson (671 yds rush, 9 TDs, 62 pts), E Tom Stolhandske, G Harley Sewell, LB June Davis, Dillon. *Noteworthy:* 1st year under Ed Price.

1952 (9–2) *Won:* LSU 35–14, North Carolina 28–7, Arkansas 44–7, Rice 20–7, SMU 31–14, Baylor 35–33, TCU 14–7, Texas A&M 32–12. *Lost:* Notre Dame 14–3 (1st meeting since 1934), Oklahoma 49–20 in consecutive early games. *Stars:* DE Bill Georges, Sewell, G Phil Branch, Dawson, Stolhandske (30 pass rec for 519 yds), Bs Billy Quinn (13 TDs), James "T." Jones (1,018 yds pass) and Dick Ochoa (819 yds rush). *Noteworthy:* Won 10th SWC title. Beat Tennessee 16–0 in Cotton Bowl, holding Vols to minus 14 yds rush; scored on safety and short runs by Dawson and Quinn.

1953 (7–3) *Won:* Villanova 41–12, Houston 28–7 (1st meeting), Arkansas 16–7, SMU 16–7, Baylor 21–20, TCU 13–3, Texas A&M 21–12. *Lost:* LSU 20–7 (1st to Tigers in 5 games since 1938), Oklahoma 19–14, Rice 18–13. *Stars:* Branch, Delano Womack (7 TDs), Dougal Cameron (518 yds rush), Es Carlton Massey and Gilmer Spring. *Noteworthy:* got share of 11th SWC title.

1957 (6–4–1) *Won:* Georgia 26–7, Tulane 20–6, Arkansas 17–0, Rice 19–14, TCU 14–2, Texas A&M 9–7. *Lost:* South Carolina 27–21, Oklahoma 21–7, SMU 19–12. *Tied:* Baylor 7–7. *Stars:* B Walt Fondren (40.8-yd punting avg), soph HB Rene Ramirez (5 TDs). *Noteworthy:* Had one of nation's most-improved teams in 1st year under Darrell Royal. Lost to Mississippi 39–7 in Sugar Bowl; scored on 1-yd run by soph George Blanch in last quarter.

1958 (7–3) *Won:* Georgia 13–8, Tulane 21–20, Texas Tech 12–7, Oklahoma 15–14 (1st over Soon-ers since 1951), Arkansas 24–6, Baylor 20–15, Texas A&M 27–0. *Lost:* Rice 34–7, SMU 26–10, TCU 22–8. *Stars:* QB Bobby Lackey (5 TDs, 41 pts, 40-yd punting avg), Bob Bryant (14 pass rec for 233 yds).

1959 (9–2) *Won:* Nebraska 20–0, Maryland 26–0, California 33–0, Oklahoma 19–12, Arkansas 13–12, Rice 28–6, SMU 21–0, Baylor 13–12, Texas A&M 20–17. *Lost:* TCU 14–9. *Stars:* Lackey (5 TDs, 45 pts), Ramirez, soph HB Jack Collins (41.3-yd punting avg), E Monte Lee, G Maurice Doke. *Noteworthy:* Got share of 12th SWC title. Lost to unbeaten national champ Syracuse 23–14 in Cotton Bowl; Lackey passed for TD (69 yds to Collins) and 2-pt conversion (to Richard Schulte) and ran for other Texas TD.

1960 (7–3–1) *Won:* Maryland 34–0, Texas Tech 17–0, Oklahoma 24–0, SMU 17–7, Baylor 12–7, TCU 3–2, Texas A&M 21–14. *Lost:* Nebraska 14–13, Arkansas 24–23, Rice 7–0. *Stars:* G Lee, HB James Saxton (407 yds rush, 9 pass rec for 185 yds), QB Mike Cotten (5 TDs), P Bobby Nunis (40.3-yd avg). *Noteworthy:* tied Alabama 3–3 in Bluebonnet Bowl on 20-yd FG by Dan Petty in last quarter.

1961 (10–1) *Won:* California 28–3, Texas Tech 42–14, Washington St. 41–8, Oklahoma 28–7, Arkansas 33–7, Rice 34–7, SMU 27–0, Baylor 33–7, Texas A&M 25–0. *Lost:* TCU 6–0. *Stars:* Saxton (846 yds rush, 9 TDs), Cotten, Jerry Cook (9 TDs), E Bob Moses, T Don Talbert, C David Kristynik. *Noteworthy:* Got share of 13th SWC title. Beat Mississippi 12–7 in Cotton Bowl on 1st half TDs by Saxton (1-yd run) and Collins (16-yd pass from Cotten).

1962 (9–1–1) *Won:* Oregon 25–13, Texas Tech 34–0, Tulane 35–8, Oklahoma 9–6, Arkansas 7–3, SMU 6–0, Baylor 27–12, TCU 14–0, Texas A&M 13–3. *Tied:* Rice 14–14. *Stars:* Cook (7 TDs), B Tommy Ford, G Johnny Treadwell, T Scott Appleton. *Noteworthy:* Again won SWC crown in 1st unbeaten season since 1923. Lost to LSU 13–0 (1st meeting since 1954) in Cotton Bowl; Longhorns never got inside LSU 25-yd line.

1963 (11–0) *Won:* Tulane 21–0, Texas Tech 49–7, Oklahoma St. 34–7 (1st meeting since 1946), Oklahoma 28–7, Arkansas 17–13, Rice 10–6, SMU 17–12, Baylor 7–0, TCU 17–0, Texas A&M 15–13. *Stars:* Ford (738 yds rush, 9 TDs), Outland Trophy-winner Appleton, soph G/LB Tommy Nobis. *Noteworthy:* Won 3rd straight SWC title (15th overall). Beat Navy 28–6 in Cotton Bowl to earn 1st national championship; QB Duke Carlisle passed for 213 yds and 2 TDs (58 yds and 63 yds to soph Phil Harris) and ran for 54 yds, and Appleton led defense that held Navy QB Roger Staubach to minus 47 yds rush.

1964 (10–1)   *Won:* Tulane 31–0, Texas Tech 23–0, Army 17–6, Oklahoma 28–7, Rice 6–3, SMU 7–0, Baylor 20–14, TCU 28–13, Texas A&M 26–7.   *Lost:* unbeaten national cochamp Arkansas 14–13. *Stars:* Nobis, Bs Harold Philipp and Ernie Koy (574 yds rush, 8 TDs), Es Pete Lammons (13 pass rec for 204 yds) and Dan Mauldin, C Olen Underwood, T Clayton Lacy, DE Knox Nunnally, DB Joe Dixon.   *Noteworthy:* beat undefeated national cochamp Alabama 21–17 in Orange Bowl, taking 21–7 halftime lead; Koy scored on runs of 79 yds and 1 yd, and George Sauer scored on 69-yd pass from James Hudson.

1968 (9–1–1)   *Won:* Oklahoma St. 31–3, Oklahoma 26–20, Arkansas 39–29, Rice 38–14, SMU 38–7, Baylor 47–26, TCU 47–21, Texas A&M 35–14. *Lost:* Texas Tech 31–22 in 2nd game.   *Tied:* Houston 20–20 (1st meeting since 1953).   *Stars:* TB Chris Gilbert (1,132 yds rush, 13 TDs, 82 pts), soph FB Steve Worster (806 yds and 13 TDs rush), QB James Street (1,099 yds pass), Charles "Cotton" Speyrer (26 pass rec for 449 yds), E Deryl Comer, OG Danny Abbott, DTs Loyd Wainscott and Leo Brooks, LB Glen Halsell, P Bill Bradley (40.3-yd avg).   *Noteworthy:* Got share of 16th SWC title. Beat Tennessee 36–13 in Cotton Bowl after taking 28–0 halftime lead; Street passed for 2 TDs (both 79-yarders to Speyrer) and 2-pt conversion (to Speyrer), and Worster ran for 85 yds and a TD.

1969 (11–0)   *Won:* California 17–0, Texas Tech 49–7, Navy 56–17, Oklahoma 27–17, Rice 31–0, SMU 45–14, Baylor 56–14, TCU 69–7, Texas A&M 49–12, Arkansas 15–14.   *Stars:* Street, Speyrer (30 pass rec for 492 yds), Worster (649 yds and 9 TDs rush), soph B Jim Bertelsen (740 yds rush, 13 TDs), HB Tom Campbell, OTs Bob McKay and Bobby Wuensch, DE Bill Atessis, DT Leo Brooks, Halsell. *Noteworthy:* Led nation in rush and won 2nd national title while repeating as SWC champ. Beat Notre Dame 21–17 (1st meeting since 1954) in Cotton Bowl after falling behind 10–0 in 2nd quarter; Worster ran for 155 yds, Bertelsen ran for 81 yds and a TD, Street passed for 107 yds, Ted

Koy and Billy Dale scored on short runs, and James "Happy" Feller kicked 3 ex pts.

1970 (10–1)   *Won:* California 56–15, Texas Tech 35–13, UCLA 20–17, Oklahoma 41–9, Rice 45–21, SMU 42–15, Baylor 21–14, TCU 58–0, Texas A&M 52–14, Arkansas 42–7.   *Stars:* Worster (898 yds rush, 14 TDs), Bertelsen, Danny Lester (17 pass rec for 365 yds), Wuensch, soph OT Jerry Sisemore, OG Bobby Mitchell, Atessis, DT Ray Dowdy, LBs Scott Henderson and Bill Zapalac.   *Noteworthy:* Led nation in scoring (41.2-pt avg) and rush, won 3rd straight SWC title, and got share of 3rd national crown. Lost to Notre Dame 24–11 in Cotton Bowl (breaking 5-bowl win streak) when neither team scored in 2nd half; QB Eddie Phillips ran for 164 yds and passed for 199 yds, and Longhorns scored on 23-yd FG by Feller, 2-yd run by Bertelsen, and 2-pt conversion pass from Phillips to Lester.

1971 (8–3)   *Won:* UCLA 28–10, Texas Tech 28–0, Oregon 35–7, Rice 39–10, SMU 22–18, Baylor 24–0, TCU 31–0, Texas A&M 34–14.   *Lost:* Oklahoma 48–27 (1st to Sooners since 1966), Arkansas 31–7 (1st to Razorbacks since 1966) in consecutive early games.   *Stars:* Bertelsen (879 yds rush), QB Donnie Wigginton (14 TDs), soph Pat Kelly (17 pass rec for 226 yds), Sisemore, soph OG Don Crosslin, Dowdy, DT Greg Ploetz, LBs Randy Braband and Tommy Woodard, DB Alan Lowry.   *Noteworthy:* Took 4th straight SWC title. Lost to Penn St. 30–6 in Cotton Bowl; led 6–3 at halftime on 2 FGs by Steve Valek.

1972 (10–1)   *Won:* Miami (Fla.) 23–10, Texas Tech 25–20, Utah St. 27–12, Arkansas 35–15, Rice 45–9, SMU 17–9, Baylor 17–3 (15th straight over Bears), TCU 27–0, Texas A&M 38–3.   *Lost:* Oklahoma 27–0.   *Stars:* QB Lowry (11 TDs), soph RB Roosevelt Leaks (1,099 yds and 8 TDs rush), B Mike Rowan, Jim Moore (23 pass rec for 413 yds), Sisemore, OG Travis Roach, C Bill Wyman, DE Malcolm Minnick, Braband, LB Glen Gaspard. *Noteworthy:* Won 5th straight SWC title (20th overall). Beat Alabama 17–13 in Cotton Bowl after trailing 13–3 at halftime; Lowry scored TDs on runs of 3 and 34 yds, Leaks ran for 120 yds, and soph Billy "Sure" Schott kicked FG and 2 ex pts.

1973 (8–3)   *Won:* Texas Tech 28–12, Wake Forest 41–0, Arkansas 34–6, Rice 55–13, SMU 42–14, Baylor 42–6, TCU 52–7, Texas A&M 42–13.   *Lost:* Miami (Fla.) 20–15, unbeaten Oklahoma 52–13.

Stars: Leaks (1,415 yds rush, 14 TDs), Kelly (19 pass rec for 268 yds), Wyman, Crosslin, soph OT Bob Simmons, Minnick, DE Bill Rutherford, DT Doug English, Gaspard, LB Wade Johnston, DB Jay Arnold. *Noteworthy:* Won 6th straight SWC crown. Lost to Nebraska 19–3 in Cotton Bowl after taking 3–0 lead on 22-yd FG by Schott.

1974 (8–4) *Won:* Boston College 42–19, Wyoming 34–7, Washington 35–21, Arkansas 38–7, Rice 27–6, SMU 35–15, TCU 81–16, Texas A&M 32–3. *Lost:* Texas Tech 26–3 (1st to Red Raiders since 1968), unbeaten national cochamp Oklahoma 16–13, Baylor 34–24 (1st to Bears since 1956). *Stars:* frosh FB Earl Campbell (928 yds rush, 6 TDs), Simmons, OG Bruce Hebert, Schott (65 pts), English. *Noteworthy:* lost to Auburn 27–3 in Gator Bowl; Campbell ran for 91 yds and Longhorns scored on 35-yd FG by Schott in 1st quarter.

1975 (10–2) *Won:* Colorado St. 46–0, Washington 28–10, Texas Tech 42–18, Utah St. 61–7, Arkansas 24–18, Rice 41–9 (10th straight over Owls), SMU 30–22, Baylor 37–21, TCU 27–11. *Lost:* national champ Oklahoma 24–17, Texas A&M 20–10 (1st to Aggies since 1967). *Stars:* Campbell (1,118 yds rush, 13 TDs), QB Marty Akins, soph E Alfred Jackson (32 pass rec for 596 yds), Simmons, OG Will Wilcox, DT Brad Shearer, LB Bill Hamilton, DB Raymond Clayborn, frosh P/K Russell Erxleben (41.4-yd punting avg). *Noteworthy:* Got share of 22nd SWC title. Scored 24 pts in 3rd quarter and beat Colorado 38–21 in Bluebonnet Bowl after trailing 21–7 at halftime; Campbell ran for 95 yds and caught 2-pt conversion pass from Akins (who passed for TD to Jackson), and Erxleben had 55-yd FG and 3 ex pts.

1977 (11–1) *Won:* Boston College 44–0, Virginia 68–0, Rice 72–15, Oklahoma 13–6, Arkansas 13–9, SMU 30–14, Texas Tech 26–0, Houston 35–21, TCU 44–14 (10th straight over Horned Frogs), Baylor 29–7, Texas A&M 57–28. *Stars:* Heisman Trophy–winner Campbell (nation's leader with 1,744 yds rush, 114 pts on 19 TDs, and 1,855 all-purpose yds), soph FL Johnny "Lam" Jones (21 pass rec for 543 yds), Jackson, Erxleben (45.9-yd punting avg), OG Rick Ingraham, OT David Studdard, Outland Trophy–winner Shearer, LB Lance Taylor, soph DB Johnnie Johnson. *Noteworthy:* Won 23rd SWC title in 1st year under Fred Akers. Lost national championship to Notre Dame 38–10 in Cotton Bowl; Campbell ran for 116 yds and Longhorns

scored on 42-yd FG by Erxleben and 13-yd pass from Randy McEachern to Mike Lockett.

1978 (9–3) *Won:* Rice 34–0, Wyoming 17–3, Texas Tech 24–7, North Texas St. 26–16, Arkansas 28–21, SMU 22–3, TCU 41–0, Texas A&M 22–7. *Lost:* Oklahoma 31–10, Houston 10–7, Baylor 38–14. *Stars:* Erxleben (13 FGs, 63 pts, 43.4-yd punting avg), "Lam" Jones (25 pass rec for 446 yds), OG Jim Yarbrough, DE Dwight Jefferson, DT Steve McMichael, Taylor, Johnson. *Noteworthy:* beat Maryland 42–0 in Sun Bowl; frosh RB A.J. "Jam" Jones ran for 100 yds and 2 TDs, Johnny "Ham" Jones ran for 104 yds and a TD, "Lam" Jones scored on 7-yd run and 29-yd pass from Mark McBath (who also scored on 2-yd run), and Erxleben kicked 6 ex pts.

1979 (9–3) *Won:* Iowa St. 17–9, Missouri 21–0 (1st meeting since 1946), Rice 26–9, Oklahoma 16–7, SMU 30–6, Texas Tech 14–6, Houston 21–13, TCU 35–10, Baylor 13–10. *Lost:* Arkansas 17–14 (1st to Razorbacks since 1971), Texas A&M 13–7. *Stars:* "Jam" Jones (918 yds rush), "Lam" Jones (36 pass rec for 535 yds), TE Lawrence Sampleton, C Wes Hubert, soph K John Goodson (17 FGs, 72 pts), McMichael, soph LB Doug Shankle, Johnson, DBs Ricky Churchman and Derrick Hatchett. *Noteworthy:* lost to Washington 14–7 in Sun Bowl; Brad Beck ran for 98 yds and scored on 5-yd pass from QB Donnie Little.

1981 (10–1–1) *Won:* Rice 31–3, North Texas St. 23–10, Miami (Fla.) 14–7, Oklahoma 34–14, SMU 9–7, Texas Tech 26–9, TCU 31–15, Baylor 34–12, Texas A&M 21–13. *Lost:* Arkansas 42–11. *Tied:* Houston 14–14. *Stars:* "Jam" Jones (834 yds rush, 6 TDs), QB Rich McIvor (918 yds pass), Little (18 pass rec for 338 yds), soph TB John Walker (714 yds rush, 6 TDs), OT Terry Tausch, OG Joe Shearin, C Mike Baab, K Raul Allegre (15 FGs, 70 pts), DT Kenneth Sims (Lombardi Award winner), Shankle, LB Bruce Scholtz, William Graham (7 int), Goodson (41.7-yd punting avg). *Noteworthy:* beat Alabama 14–12 in Cotton Bowl on 2 ex pts by Allegre; scored last quarter TDs on 30-yd run by QB Robert Brewer and 8-yd run by frosh Terry Orr.

1982 (9–3) *Won:* Utah 21–12, Missouri 21–0, Rice 34–7, Texas Tech 27–0, Houston 50–0, TCU 38–21 (15th straight over Horned Frogs), Baylor 31–23, Texas A&M 53–16, Arkansas 33–7. *Lost:* Oklahoma 28–22, unbeaten SMU 30–17 in consecutive early games. *Stars:* Brewer (1,415 yds pass), B

Darryl Clark (1,049 yds rush), FL Herkie Walls (25 pass rec for 702 yds), OT Bryan Millard, OG Doug Dawson, Allegre (12 FGs, 77 pts), DE Kiki DeAyala, DB Mossy Cade, P Mike Poujol (41.8-yd avg). *Noteworthy:* lost to North Carolina 26–10 in Sun Bowl after leading 10–3 entering 4th quarter; scored on blocked punt recovered in end zone by Ronnie Mullins and 24-yd FG and ex pt by Allegre. **1983** (11–1)   *Won:* Auburn 20–7, North Texas St. 26–6, Rice 42–6, Oklahoma 28–16, Arkansas 31–3, SMU 15–12, Texas Tech 20–3, Houston 9–3, TCU 20–14, Baylor 24–21, Texas A&M 45–13. *Stars:* Dawson, Brent Duhon (13 pass rec for 344 yds), C Mike Reuther, frosh K Jeff Ward (15 FGs, 76 pts), DE Eric Holle, DT Tony Degrate, LB Jeff Leiding, Cade, DBs Jerry Gray and Fred Acorn, soph P John Teltschik (40.9-yd avg). *Noteworthy:* Led nation in total defense and won 24th SWC title in 1st unbeaten season since 1977. Lost to Georgia 10–9 in Cotton Bowl when Bulldogs scored TD with 3:22 remaining; Texas scored on FGs of 23, 40, and 27 yds by Ward.
1985 (8–4)   *Won:* Missouri 21–17, Stanford 38–34, Rice 44–16 (20th straight over Owls), Arkansas 15–13, Texas Tech 34–21, Houston 34–24, TCU 20–0, Baylor 17–10. *Lost:* national champ Oklahoma 14–7, SMU 44–14, Texas A&M 42–10. *Stars:* Ward (19 FGs, 84 pts), Teltschik (45.2-yd punting avg), Charles Hunter (717 yds rush), Everett Gay (22 pass rec for 431 yds), C Gene Chilton, LB Ty

Allert. *Noteworthy:* lost to Air Force 24–16 in Bluebonnet Bowl; soph QB Bret Stafford passed for 88 yds and a TD (34 yds to William Harris) and ran for 63 yds, and Ward kicked 3 FGs and ex pt.
1990 (10–2)   *Won:* Penn St. 17–13, Rice 26–10 (25th straight over Owls), Oklahoma 14–13, Arkansas 49–17, SMU 52–3, Texas Tech 41–22, Houston 45–24, TCU 38–10, Baylor 23–13, Texas A&M 28–27 (1st over Aggies since 1983). *Lost:* national co-champ Colorado 29–22. *Stars:* soph QB Peter Gardere (2,131 yds and 11 TDs pass), WRs Johnny Walker (40 pass rec for 565 yds) and Keith Cash (33 pass rec for 605 yds and 6 TDs), TE Kerry Cash (22 pass rec for 285 yds), soph TB Adrian Walker (6 TDs rush), RBs Chris Samuels (26 pass rec for 253 yds), frosh Butch Hadnot (541 yds and 8 TDs rush) and frosh Phil Brown (508 yds rush), K Michael Pollak (20 FGs, 99 pts), soph DL Shane Dronett, DBs Stan Richard and soph Lance Gunn, P Alex Waits (42.6-yd avg). *Noteworthy:* Won 25th SWC title. Lost to Miami (Fla.) 46–3 in Cotton Bowl; scored on 29-yd FG by Pollak in 2nd quarter.

BOWL SUMMARY

Bluebonnet 3–2–1; Cotton 9–9–1; Freedom 0–1; Gator 0–1; Orange 2–0; Sugar 1–1; Sun 1–2.

BOWL RECORD (16–16–2)

Regular Season	Bowl	Score	Opponent	Record
1942 (8–2)	Cotton	14–7	Georgia Tech	(9–1)
1943 (7–1)	Cotton	7–7	Randolph Field	(9–1)
1945 (9–1)	Cotton	40–27	Missouri	(6–3)
1947 (9–1)	Sugar	27–7	Alabama	(8–2)
1948 (6–3–1)	Orange	41–28	Georgia	(9–1)
1950 (9–1)	Cotton	14–20	Tennessee	(10–1)
1952 (8–2)	Cotton	16–0	Tennessee	(8–1–1)
1957 (6–3–1)	Sugar	7–39	Mississippi	(8–1–1)
1959 (9–1)	Cotton	14–23	Syracuse	(10–0)
1960 (7–3)	Bluebonnet	3–3	Alabama	(8–1–1)
1961 (9–1)	Cotton	12–7	Mississippi	(9–1)
1962 (9–0–1)	Cotton	0–13	LSU	(8–1–1)
1963 (10–0)	Cotton	28–6	Navy	(9–1)
1964 (9–1)	Orange	21–17	Alabama	(10–0)
1966 (6–4)	Bluebonnet	19–0	Mississippi	(8–2)

(continued)

Regular Season	Bowl	Score	Opponent	Record
1968 (8–1–1)	Cotton	36–13	Tennessee	(8–1–1)
1969 (10–0)	Cotton	21–17	Notre Dame	(8–1–1)
1970 (10–0)	Cotton	11–24	Notre Dame	(9–1)
1971 (8–2)	Cotton	6–30	Penn State	(10–1)
1972 (9–1)	Cotton	17–13	Alabama	(10–1)
1973 (8–2)	Cotton	3–19	Nebraska	(8–2–1)
1974 (8–3)	Gator	3–27	Auburn	(9–2)
1975 (9–2)	Bluebonnet	38–21	Colorado	(9–2)
1977 (11–0)	Cotton	10–38	Notre Dame	(10–1)
1978 (8–3)	Sun	42–0	Maryland	(9–2)
1979 (9–2)	Sun	7–14	Washington	(9–2)
1980 (7–4)	Bluebonnet	7–16	North Carolina	(10–1)
1981 (9–1–1)	Cotton	14–12	Alabama	(9–1–1)
1982 (9–2)	Sun	10–26	North Carolina	(7–4)
1983 (11–0)	Cotton	9–10	Georgia	(9–1–1)
1984 (7–3–1)	Freedom	17–55	Iowa	(7–4–1)
1985 (8–3)	Bluebonnet	16–24	Air Force	(11–1)
1987 (6–5)	Bluebonnet	32–27	Pittsburgh	(8–3)
1990 (10–1)	Cotton	3–46	Miami (Fla.)	(9–2)

CONFERENCE TITLES

Southwest—1916, 1918 (unofficial), 1920, 1928, 1930, 1942, 1943, 1945, 1950, 1952, 1953*, 1959*, 1961*, 1962, 1963, 1968*, 1969, 1970, 1971, 1972, 1973, 1975*, 1977, 1983, 1990.

TOP 20 AP AND UPI RANKING

1941	4	1957	11–11	1969	1–1	1978	9–9
1942	11	1959	4–4	1970	3–1	1981	2–4
1943	14	1960	U–17	1971	18–12	1982	17–18
1945	10	1961	3–4	1972	3–5	1983	5–5
1947	5	1962	4–4	1973	14–8	1987	U–19
1950	3–2	1963	1–1	1974	17–U	1990	12–11
1952	10–11	1964	5–5	1975	6–7		
1953	11–8	1968	3–5	1977	4–5		

MAJOR RIVALS

Texas has played at least 10 games with Arkansas 54–19, Baylor 57–21–4, Haskell 6–5, Houston 10–7–2, Louisiana St. 8–7–1, Missouri 10–4, Oklahoma 51–32–4, Oklahoma St. 9–1, Rice 58–20–1, Southern Methodist 44–22–4, Southwestern (Texas) 20–2, Texas A&M 64–30–5, Texas Christian 57–20–1, Texas Tech 33–9, Tulane 15–1–1, Vanderbilt 3–8–1.

COACHES

Dean of Texas coaches is Darrell Royal (1961, 1963, 1970 national Coach of Year) with record of 167–47–5 for 1957–76, including 11 SWC titles, 16 bowl teams, 4 teams unbeaten in regular season, and 3 national champions. Other top records for at least 3 years were by Ralph Hutchinson, 16–7–2 for 1903–05; Dave Allerdice, 33–7 for 1911–15 with 1 unbeaten team; Bill Juneau, 19–7 for 1917–19 with 1 SWC title and 1 unbeaten team; Berry Whitaker, 22–3–1 for 1920–22 with 1 SWC title and 1 unbeaten team; E.J. Stewart, 24–9–3 for 1923–26 with 1 unbeaten team; Clyde Littlefield, 44–18–6 for 1927–33 with 2 SWC titles; Dana X. Bible, 63–31–3 for 1937–46 with 3 SWC titles and 3 Cotton Bowl teams; Blair Cherry, 32–10–1 for 1947–50 with 1 SWC title and 3 bowl teams; Ed Price, 33–27–1 for 1951–56 with 2 SWC titles and 1 Cotton Bowl champion; Fred Akers, 86–31–2 for 1977–86 with 2 SWC titles, 9 bowl teams, and 2 teams unbeaten in regular season; and David McWilliams, 31–26 for 1987–91 with 1 SWC title and 2 bowl teams.

Miscellanea

First game was win over Dallas U. 18–16 in 1893 . . . highest score was over Daniel Baker 92–0 in 1915 . . . highest since W.W. II was over TCU 81–16 in 1974 . . . biggest margin since W.W. II was over Colorado 76–0 in 1946 . . . worst defeat was by Chicago 68–0 in 1904 . . . worst since W.W. II was by Houston 66–15 in 1988 . . . longest win streak of 30 in 1968–70 ended by Notre Dame 24–11 in 1971 Cotton Bowl . . . 15-game win streak in 1963–64 ended by Arkansas 14–13 . . . longest losing string of 10 in 1937–38 broken with win over Texas A&M 7–6 . . . consensus All-Americans were Hubert Bechtol, E, 1945–46; Bobby Layne, B, 1947; Bud McFadin, G, 1950; Carlton Massey, E, 1953; Jimmy Saxton, B, 1961; Johnny Treadwell, G, 1962; Scott Appleton, T, 1963; Tommy Nobis, LB, 1965; Chris Gilbert, B, 1968; Bob McKay, T, 1969; Bobby Wuensch, T, Steve Worster, B, and Bill Atessis, DE, 1970; Jerry Sisemore, T, 1971–72; Bill Wyman, C, and Roosevelt Leaks, B, 1973; Bob Simmons, T, 1975; Earl Campbell, RB, and Brad Shearer, DL, 1977; Johnnie Johnson, DB, 1978–79; Steve Mc-Michael, DL, 1979; Kenneth Sims, DL, 1980–81; Terry Tausch, OL, 1981; Doug Dawson, OL, and Jeff Leiding, LB, 1983; Jerry Gray, DB, 1983–84; and Tony Degrate, DL, 1984 . . . Academic All-Americans were Maurice Doke, G, 1959; Johnny Treadwell, G, 1961–62; Pat Culpepper, B, 1962; Duke Carlisle, B, 1963; Gene Bledsoe, OT, 1966; Mike Perrin, DE, 1967; Corby Robertson, LB, 1967–68; Scott Henderson, LB, 1968–70; Bill Zapalac, DE, 1969–70; Steve Oxley, OT, and Mike Bayer, DB, 1972; Tommy Keel, S, 1972–73; Doug

Dawson, OG, 1983; and Lee Brockman, DL, 1988 . . . Heisman Trophy winner was Earl Campbell, HB, 1977 . . . Maxwell Award winner was Tommy Nobis, LB, 1965 . . . Outland Trophy winners were Scott Appleton, T, 1963; Tommy Nobis, G, 1965; and Brad Shearer, DT, 1977 . . . Lombardi Award winners were Kenneth Sims, DT, 1981; and Tony Degrate, DT, 1984.

TEXAS A&M (Aggies; Maroon and White)

Notable Teams

1902 (7–0–2) *Won:* St. Edwards 11–0, Baylor 11–6, 22–0, Tulane 17–5, Texas Christian (TCU) 22–0, Trinity (Texas) 34–0, Texas 11–0 (1st in 9-game series dating to 1894). *Tied:* Trinity (Texas) 0–0, Texas 0–0. *Noteworthy:* Had 1st unbeaten season since 3-game schedule of 1896. 1st year under J.E. Platt.

1905 (7–2) *Won:* Houston (not University) 29–0, TCU 20–0, 24–11, Baylor 42–0, 17–5, Trinity (Texas) 24–0, Austin College 18–11 (1st meeting since 1898). *Lost:* Transylvania 29–6, Texas 27–0. *Noteworthy:* 1st year under W.E. Bachman.

1906 (6–1) *Won:* TCU 42–0, 22–0 (10th straight over Horned Frogs), Daniel Baker 34–0, Tulane 18–0, Haskell Institute 32–6, Louisiana St. (LSU) 22–12 (1st meeting since 1899). *Lost:* Texas 24–0 in finale. *Noteworthy:* Bachman's last team.

1907 (6–1–1) *Won:* Fort Worth U. 34–0, LSU 11–5, Haskell 5–0, TCU 32–5, Tulane 18–6, Oklahoma 19–0. *Lost:* Texas 11–6 in finale. *Tied:* Texas 0–0 in 2nd game.

1909 (7–0–1) *Won:* Austin College 17–0, Haskell 15–0, Baylor 9–6, Texas 23–0, 5–0 (1st over Longhorns in 9 games since 1902), Trinity (Texas) 47–0, Oklahoma 14–8. *Tied:* TCU 0–0 in 2nd game. *Noteworthy:* 1st year under Charles Moran.

1910 (8–1) *Won:* Marshall School 17–0, Austin College 27–5, TCU 35–0, 23–6, Transylvania 33–0, Texas 14–8, Southwestern (Texas) 6–0, Tulane 17–0. *Lost:* Arkansas 5–0 (1st meeting since 1903).

1911 (6–1) *Won:* Southwestern (Texas) 22–0, Austin College 33–0, Auburn 16–0, Mississippi 17–0, Baylor 22–11, Dallas U. 24–0. *Lost:* Texas 6–0.

1912 (8–1) *Won:* Daniel Baker 50–0, Trinity (Texas) 59–0, Arkansas 27–0, Austin College 57–0, Oklahoma 28–6, Mississippi St. 41–7, Tulane 41–0, Baylor 53–0. *Lost:* Kansas St. 13–10.

1914 (6–1–1) *Won:* Austin College 32–0, TCU 40–0, LSU 63–9, Rice 32–7 (1st meeting), Oklahoma A&M 24–0, Mississippi 14–7. *Lost:* Haskell 10–0. *Tied:* Trinity (Texas) 0–0. *Noteworthy:* Moran's last team.

1915 (6–2) *Won:* Austin College 40–0, Trinity (Texas) 62–0, TCU 13–10, Missouri Mines 33–3, Haskell 21–7, Texas 13–0 (1st SWC win). *Lost:* Rice 7–0 (1st SWC game), Mississippi St. 7–0. *Stars:* E John Garrity, G N.M. Braumiller.

1917 (8–0) *Won:* Austin College 66–0, Dallas U. 98–0, Southwestern (Texas) 20–0, LSU 27–0, Tulane 35–0 (1st meeting since 1912), Baylor 7–0, Texas 7–0, Rice 10–0. *Stars:* HB Rip Collins, soph FB Jack Mahan, E Tim Griesenbeck, T Ox Ford, soph G E.S. Wilson. *Noteworthy:* Blanked foes 270–0 in 1st unbeaten season since 1909 and won 1st SWC title in 1st year under Dana X. Bible.

1918 (6–1–1) *Won:* Ream Field 6–0, Camp Travis 12–6, 60–0, Baylor 19–0, Southwestern (Texas) 7–0, Camp Mabry 19–6. *Lost:* unbeaten Texas 7–0. *Tied:* Remount Station 0–0. *Noteworthy:* only year under D.V. Graves (Bible on active military service).

1919 (10–0) *Won:* Sam Houston St. 77–0, San Marcos St. 28–0, Southern Methodist (SMU) 16–0, Howard Payne 12–0, Trinity (Texas) 42–0, Oklahoma A&M 28–0 (1st meeting since 1914), Baylor 10–0, TCU 48–0, Southwestern (Texas) 7–0, Texas 7–0. *Stars:* Mahan, HB R.G. Higginbotham, E Scott Alexander, Wilson, soph G W.E. Murrah, T C.R. Drake. *Noteworthy:* blanked foes 275–0 and won 2nd SWC title as Bible returned as coach.

1920 (6–1–1) *Won:* Daniel Baker 110–0, SMU 3–0, Phillips U. 47–0, Oklahoma A&M 35–0, Baylor 24–0, Rice 7–0. *Lost:* unbeaten Texas 7–3 in finale. *Tied:* LSU 0–0. *Stars:* Mahan, Higginbotham, Murrah, Drake, frosh E T.F. Wilson.

1921 (6–1–2) *Won:* Howard Payne 14–7, SMU 13–0, Arizona 17–13, Oklahoma A&M 23–7, Baylor 14–3. *Lost:* LSU 6–0. *Tied:* Rice 7–7, Texas 0–0. *Stars:* Murrah, Wilson, B Sam Sanders. *Noteworthy:* Won 3rd SWC title. Made 1st postseason appearance, beating undefeated Centre 22–14 in Dixie Classic at Dallas; Wilson scored on 15-yd pass from T.L. Miller and on 5-yd run, and W.E. Winn scored on 45-yd pass int return.

1924 (7–2–1) *Won:* John Tarleton St. 40–0, Trinity (Texas) 33–0 (1st meeting since 1919), Southwest-ern (Texas) 54–0 (10th win in as many games in series), Sewanee 7–0, Arkansas A&M 40–0, TCU 28–0 (1st meeting since 1919), Rice 13–6. *Lost:* Baylor 15–7, Texas 7–0. *Tied:* unbeaten SMU 7–7. *Stars:* B W.W. Wilson, E Neeley Allison.

1925 (7–1–1) *Won:* Trinity (Texas) 20–10, South-western (Texas) 23–6, SMU 7–0, Sam Houston St. 77–0, Baylor 13–0, Rice 17–0, Texas 28–0. *Lost:* TCU 3–0 (1st to Horned Frogs in 20 games since 1897). *Tied:* Sewanee 6–6. *Stars:* Wilson, soph HB Joel Hunt, Ts L.G. Dietrich and Barlow Irvin, G W.M. Dansby. *Noteworthy:* Won 4th SWC title.

1927 (8–0–1) *Won:* Trinity (Texas) 45–0, South-western (Texas) 31–0, Sewanee 18–0, Arkansas 40–6 (1st meeting since 1912), Texas Tech 47–6 (1st meeting), SMU 39–13, Rice 14–0, Texas 28–7. *Tied:* TCU 0–0. *Stars:* Hunt (19 TDs, 128 pts), E J.B. Sikes, Ts A.C. Sprott and W.S. Lister, Gs J.G. Holmes and E.E. Fegari. *Noteworthy:* won 5th SWC title in 1st undefeated season since 1919.

1931 (7–3) *Won:* Southwestern (Texas) 33–0, John Tarleton St. 21–0, Iowa 29–0, Baylor 33–7, Cen-tenary 7–0, Rice 7–0, Texas 7–6. *Lost:* unbeaten Tulane 7–0, TCU 6–0, SMU 8–0. *Stars:* QB Cliff Domingue, E Charlie Malone, G Carl Moulden.

1936 (8–3–1) *Won:* Sam Houston St. 39–6, Hardin-Simmons 3–0, Rice 3–0, TCU 18–7 (1st over Horned Frogs since 1924), SMU 22–6 (1st over Mustangs since 1927), San Francisco 38–14, Utah 20–7, Manhattan 13–6. *Lost:* Arkansas 18–0, Cen-tenary 3–0, Texas 7–0. *Tied:* Baylor 0–0. *Stars:* G Joe Routt, T Roy Young, C Charles DeWare.

1939 (11–0) *Won:* Oklahoma A&M 32–0 (1st meet-ing since 1921), Centenary 14–0 (1st over Gen-tlemen in 6 games since 1931), Santa Clara 7–3, Villanova 33–7, TCU 20–6, Baylor 20–0 (1st over Bears since 1934), Arkansas 27–0, SMU 6–2, Rice 19–0, Texas 20–0. *Stars:* FB John Kimbrough (10 TDs, 5 int), HB Jim Thomason, E Herb Smith, G Marshall Robnett, T Joe Boyd. *Noteworthy:* Na-tion's most-improved team led country in total defense and rush defense; won 6th SWC title and 1st national championship in 1st unbeaten season since 1927. Edged unbeaten Tulane 14–13 (1st meeting since 1933) in Sugar Bowl; Kimbrough ran for 152 yds and scored 2 TDs, Walemon Price kicked game-winning ex pts, and Smith blocked Tulane's 2nd ex pt try.

1940 (9–1) *Won:* Texas A&I 26–0, Tulsa 41–6, UCLA 7–0, TCU 21–7, Baylor 14–7, Arkansas 17–0,

SMU 19–7, Rice 25–0. *Lost:* Texas 7–0 in finale. *Stars:* Kimbrough (611 yds rush, 7 TDs, 5 int), Thomason, E James Sterling, Robnett, T Ernie Pannell. *Noteworthy:* Again led nation in rush defense and got share of 7th SWC title. Edged Fordham 13–12 in Cotton Bowl; Marion Pugh passed for 97 yds and a TD, and Kimbrough ran for 56 yds and a TD.

1941 (9–2) *Won:* Sam Houston St. 54–0, Texas A&I 41–0, New York U. 49–7, TCU 14–0, Baylor 48–0, Arkansas 7–0, SMU 21–10, Rice 19–6, Washington St. 7–0. *Lost:* Texas 23–0. *Stars:* Sterling, C/LB Bill Sibley (10 int), Ts Derace Moser and Martin Ruby. *Noteworthy:* Won 3rd straight SWC title. Lost to Alabama 29–21 in Cotton Bowl though outgaining Tide 309–75 in total yds and 13–1 in 1st downs; Aggies lost ball 7 times on int and 5 times on fumbles but scored on 23-yd pass from soph Leo Daniels to Bob Crowley, 43-yd pass from Moser to Sterling, and 1-yd run and 3 ex pts by J.D. Webster.

1943 (7–2–1) *Won:* Bryan Air Force Base 48–6, Texas Tech 13–0, LSU 28–13, TCU 13–0, Arkansas 13–0, SMU 22–0, Rice 20–0. *Lost:* Texas 27–13 in finale. *Tied:* North Texas A.C. 0–0. *Stars:* Bs Marian Flanagan (nation's punt return leader with 9.7-yd avg) and Jim Hallmark, E M.E. Settegast, T Goble Bryant. *Noteworthy:* lost rematch with LSU 19–14 in Orange Bowl as Tigers' Steve Van Buren ran and passed for all 3 LSU TDs; Hallmark passed for both Aggie TDs.

1955 (7–2–1) *Won:* LSU 28–0 (1st meeting since 1949), Houston 21–3, Nebraska 27–0, TCU 19–16, Baylor 19–7 (1st over Bears since 1947), SMU 13–2 (1st over Mustangs since 1950), Rice 20–12 (1st over Owls since 1944). *Lost:* UCLA 21–0 (opener), Texas 21–6 (finale). *Tied:* Arkansas 7–7. *Stars:* E Gene Stallings, FB Jack Pardee, B Loyd Taylor (31 pts), G Dennis Goehring, P Ed Dudley (40.1-yd avg). *Noteworthy:* Nation's most-improved team.

1956 (9–0–1) *Won:* Villanova 19–0, LSU 9–6, Texas Tech 40–7, TCU 7–6, Baylor 19–13, Arkansas 27–0, SMU 33–7, Rice 21–7, Texas 34–21 (1st over Longhorns since 1951). *Tied:* Houston 14–14. *Stars:* Pardee, HB John David Crow (561 yds rush, 10 TDs), QB Roddy Osborne (568 yds rush), soph E John Tracey, Goehring, T Charles Krueger, C Loyd Hale. *Noteworthy:* Won 9th SWC title in 1st

undefeated season since 1939. Ineligible for bowl, on NCAA probation.

1957 (8–3) *Won:* Maryland 21–13, Texas Tech 21–0, Missouri 28–0, Houston 28–6, TCU 7–0, Baylor 14–0, Arkansas 7–6, SMU 19–6. *Lost:* Rice 7–6, Texas 9–7 in last 2 games. *Stars:* Heisman Trophy–winner Crow (562 yds rush, 6 TDs, 5 int), SE Osborne (48 pts), E Bobby Marks, Krueger. *Noteworthy:* 'Bear" Bryant's last team. Lost to Tennessee 3–0 in wet, muddy Gator Bowl on 17-yd FG with 5:30 left.

1967 (7–4) *Won:* Texas Tech 28–24, TCU 20–0, Baylor 21–3, Arkansas 33–21 (1st over Razorbacks since 1957), Rice 18–3, Texas 10–7 (1st over Longhorns since 1956) in last 6 games. *Lost:* SMU 20–17, Purdue 24–20, LSU 17–6, Florida St. 19–18. *Stars:* QB Ed Hargett (1,526 yds and 14 TDs pass), TE Bob Long (24 pass rec for 541 yds and 8 TDs), soph HB Larry Stegent (568 yds rush), OT Dan Schneider, SE/DB Tommy Maxwell, DT Rolf Krueger, DE Grady Allen, LB Bill Hobbs (7 int), P Steve O'Neal (42-yd avg). *Noteworthy:* Won 10th SWC title in 1st winning season since 1957. Upset Alabama 20–16 in cold, wet Cotton Bowl with help of 5 turnovers; Hargett passed for 2 TDs (to Stegent and Maxwell), and HB Wendell Housley scored on 3-yd run.

1974 (8–3) *Won:* Clemson 24–0, LSU 21–14, Washington 28–15, Texas Tech 28–7 (1st over Red Raiders since 1967), TCU 17–0, Baylor 20–0, Arkansas 20–10, Rice 37–7. *Lost:* Kansas 28–10, SMU 18–14, Texas 32–3. *Stars:* RB Bubba Bean (938 yds rush), HB Skip Walker (9 TDs), OT Glenn Bujnoch, K Randy Haddox, DT Warren Trahan, LBs Ed Simonini and Garth TenNapel, DBs Pat Thomas (6 int) and Tim Gray, P Mark Stanley (42-yd avg).

1975 (10–2) *Won:* Mississippi 7–0, LSU 39–8, Illinois 43–13, Kansas St. 10–0, Texas Tech 38–9, TCU 14–6, Baylor 19–10, SMU 36–3, Rice 33–14, Texas 20–10 (1st over Longhorns since 1967). *Lost:* Arkansas 31–6 in finale. *Stars:* Simonini, TenNapel, Thomas, DTs Edgar Fields and Jimmy Dean, DEs Blake Schwarz and Tank Marshall, LB Robert Jackson, DBs Jackie Williams and Lester Hayes (6 int), frosh K Tony Franklin (12 FGs), Bean (944 yds rush), frosh FB George Woodard (604 yds rush), TE Richard Osborne, Bujnoch, OG Bruce Welch. *Noteworthy:* Got share of 11th SWC title while leading nation in total defense and rush defense. Lost to Southern California (USC) 20–0 in Liberty Bowl, giving up all pts in 1st half.

1976 (10–2)   *Won:* Virginia Tech 19–0, Kansas St. 34–14, Illinois 14–7, Baylor 24–0, Rice 57–34, SMU 36–0, Arkansas 31–10, TCU 59–10, Texas 27–3. *Lost:* Houston 21–10 (1st meeting since 1965), Texas Tech 27–16.   *Stars:* Dean, Fields, Marshall, Jackson, Hayes (8 int), Woodard (1,153 yds rush, 17 TDs), frosh TB Curtis Dickey (726 yds rush), TE Gary Haack (21 pass rec for 265 yds), OT Frank Myers, OG Dennis Swilley, Franklin (81 pts, nation's leader with 17 FGs).   *Noteworthy:* beat Florida 37–14 in Sun Bowl; Woodard ran for 124 yds, 2 TDs, and 2-pt conversion and caught 15-yd TD pass from QB David Walker (who also scored on 9-yd run), and Franklin kicked 3 FGs (including 62-yarder) and 2 ex pts.

1977 (8–4)   *Won:* Kansas 28–14, Virginia Tech 27–6, Texas Tech 33–17, Baylor 38–31, Rice 28–14, SMU 38–21, TCU 52–23, Houston 27–7.   *Lost:* Michigan 41–3, Arkansas 26–20, unbeaten Texas 57–28.   *Stars:* Woodard (1,107 yds rush, 13 TDs), Dickey (978 yds rush, 17 pass rec for 231 yds, 1,510 all-purpose yds), Walker (1,144 yds total off), Myers, C Mark Dennard, OT Cody Risien, Franklin (16 FGs, 86 pts), DB Carl Grulich, soph P David Appleby (43.3-yd avg).   *Noteworthy:* lost to USC 47–28 in Bluebonnet Bowl after taking early 14–0 lead; Woodard scored 2 TDs and other Aggie scores came on TDs by frosh QB Mike Mosley and Adger Armstrong.

1978 (8–4)   *Won:* Kansas 37–10, Boston College 37–2, Memphis St. 58–0, Texas Tech 38–9, Rice 38–21, SMU 20–17, TCU 15–7.   *Lost:* Houston 33–0, Baylor 24–6 (1st to Bears since 1972), Arkansas 26–7, Texas 22–7.   *Stars:* Dickey (1,146 yds rush), Mosley (1,157 yds pass), TE Russell Mikeska (29 pass rec for 429 yds), Risien, Franklin (11 FGs), DE Jacob Green.   *Noteworthy:* Tom Wilson became coach in mid-season after Emory Bellard had compiled 4–2 record. Beat Iowa St. 28–12 in Hall of Fame Bowl; Dickey ran for 276 yds and a TD, and other Aggie scores came on 1-yd run by David Brothers, 4-yd pass from Mosley to SE Gerald Carter, 5-yd run by Armstrong, and 4 ex pts by Franklin.

1985 (10–2)   *Won:* NE Louisiana 31–17, Tulsa 45–10, Texas Tech 28–27, Houston 43–16, Rice 43–28, SMU 19–17 (1st over Mustangs since 1979), Ar-

kansas 10–6, TCU 53–6, Texas 42–10.   *Lost:* Alabama 23–10, Baylor 20–15.   *Stars:* QB Kevin Murray (1,965 yds and 13 TDs pass), FL Jeff Nelson (51 pass rec for 651 yds), FB Anthony Toney (845 yds rush, 74 pts), OT Doug Williams, OG Randy Dausin, K Eric Franklin (15 FGs, 74 pts), DE Rod Saddler, LB Johnny Holland, DB Domingo Bryant, P Todd Tschantz (42.6-yd avg).   *Noteworthy:* Won 12th SWC title. Beat Auburn 36–16 in Cotton Bowl; Toney had TD runs of 21 yds and 1 yd, soph HB Keith Woodside scored on 22-yd run and 9-yd pass from Murray, Harry Johnson ran 11 yds for TD and kicked 26-yd FG, and frosh K Scott Slater had 26-yd FG.

1986 (9–3)   *Won:* North Texas St. 48–28, Southern Mississippi 16–7, Texas Tech 45–8, Houston 19–7, Baylor 31–30, Rice 45–10, SMU 39–35, TCU 74–10, Texas 16–3.   *Lost:* LSU 35–17 (1st meeting since 1975), Arkansas 14–10.   *Stars:* Murray (2,463 yds and 17 TDs pass), TE Rod Bernstine (65 pass rec for 710 yds and 5 TDs), Woodside (52 pass rec for 603 yds and 5 TDs), Shea Walker (40 pass rec), FB Roger Vick (960 yds rush, 10 TDs), OT Louis Cheek, Slater (21 FGs, 100 pts), DE Jay Muller, Holland, DBs Kip Corrington and Terrance Brooks.   *Noteworthy:* Repeated as SWC champ. Lost to Ohio St. 28–12 in Cotton Bowl as Buckeyes intercepted 5 passes, returning 2 for TDs; Murray passed for 143 yds and Vick ran for 113 yds and a TD.

1987 (10–2)   *Won:* Washington 29–12, Southern Mississippi 27–14, Houston 22–17, Baylor 34–10, Rice 34–21, Louisiana Tech 32–3, Arkansas 14–0, TCU 42–24 (15th straight over Horned Frogs), Texas 20–13.   *Lost:* LSU 17–3, Texas Tech 27–21.   *Stars:* Slater (15 FGs, 70 pts), Woodside (25 pass rec for 237 yds), SE Rod Harris, frosh RB Darren Lewis (668 yds rush), C Matt Wilson, Cheek, DL Sammy O'Brient, LB John Roper, Corrington, frosh P Sean Wilson (40.5-yd avg).   *Noteworthy:* Won 3rd straight SWC title (14th overall). Beat Notre Dame 35–10 in Cotton Bowl; frosh QB Bucky Richardson ran for 96 yds and 2 TDs, Slater kicked 2 FGs and 3 ex pts, Lewis passed 24 yds to Tony Thompson for TD, and frosh Larry Horton scored on 2-yd run.

1989 (8–4)   *Won:* LSU 28–16, TCU 44–7, Southern Mississippi 31–14, Houston 17–13, Baylor 14–11, Rice 45–7, SMU 63–14, Texas 21–10.   *Lost:*

Washington 19–6, Texas Tech 28–24, Arkansas 23–22. *Stars:* Lewis (961 yds and 11 TDs rush), soph FB Robert Wilson (590 yds rush, 7 TDs), QB Lance Pavlas (1,681 yds and 10 TDs pass), WR Percy Waddle (36 pass rec for 600 yds and 5 TDs), TE Mike Jones (36 pass rec for 501 yds), OT Richmond Webb, K Layne Talbot (11 FGs, 71 pts), LBs Aaron Wallace and William Thomas, DBs Mickey Washington and soph Kevin Smith (9 int). *Noteworthy:* 1st year under R.C. Slocum. Lost to Pittsburgh 28–23 in John Hancock Bowl; Wilson ran for 145 yds and Keith McAfee scored 2 TDs. **1990** (9–3–1) *Won:* Hawaii 28–13, SW Louisiana 63–14, North Texas 40–8, Texas Tech 28–24, Rice 41–15 (10th straight over Owls), SMU 38–17, Arkansas 20–16, TCU 56–10. *Lost:* LSU 17–8, Houston 36–31 (1st to Cougars since 1984), Texas 28–27 (1st to Longhorns since 1983). *Tied:* Baylor 20–20. *Stars:* Lewis (1,691 yds rush, 19 TDs), Robert Wilson (724 yds rush, 6 TDs), RB Randy Simmons (5 TDs rush), Richardson (847 yds and 4 TDs pass, 670 yds and 8 TDs rush), Pavlas (871 yds and 8 TDs pass), SE Gary Oliver (28 pass rec for 455 yds), FL Shane Garrett (24 pass rec for 469 yds), Talbot (10 FGs, 80 pts), LB Anthony Williams, Thomas, Smith (7 int, 2 returned for TDs), DB Larry Horton, Sean Wilson (42.4-yd punting avg). *Noteworthy:* Trounced Brigham Young (BYU) 65–14 in Holiday Bowl; Richardson ran for 2 TDs, passed for another and caught a TD pass, Lewis scored 2 TDs and threw a TD pass, and Pavlas threw 2 TD passes. **1991** (10–2) *Won:* LSU 45–7, SW Louisiana 34–7, Texas Tech 37–14, Baylor 34–12, Houston 27–18, Rice 38–21, TCU 44–7, Arkansas 13–3, SMU 65–6, Texas 31–14. *Lost:* Tulsa 35–34. *Stars:* Richardson (1,492 yds and 8 TDs pass, 448 yds and 10 TDs rush), frosh RB Greg Hill (1,216 yds and 12 TDs rush), soph WR Tony Harrison (31 pass rec

for 577 yds and 6 TDs), frosh WR Brian Mitchell (19 pass rec for 519 yds), OT Keith Alex, soph K Terry Venetoulias (13 FGs, 88 pts), LBs Quentin Coryatt, soph Jason Atkinson and Marcus Buckley, frosh DE Sam Adams, DBs Smith (2 punts returned for TDs) and Derrick Frazier. *Noteworthy:* Won 15th SWC title and led nation in total defense. Lost to Florida St. 10–2 in rainy, cold Cotton Bowl; Aggies lost 6 fumbles but Hill ran for 71 yds and A&M scored when Coryatt tackled Seminole QB Casey Weldon in end zone for safety in 1st quarter. **1992** (12–1) *Won:* Stanford 10–7, LSU 31–22, Tulsa 19–9, Missouri 26–13, Texas Tech 19–17, Rice 35–9, Baylor 19–13, SMU 41–7, Louisville 40–18, Houston 38–30, TCU 37–10 (20th straight over Horned Frogs), Texas 34–13. *Stars:* Hill (17 TDs, 1,339 yds and 15 TDs rush), soph TB Rodney Thomas (856 yds and 13 TDs rush), frosh QB Corey Pullig (953 yds pass), Harrison (22 pass rec for 454 yds), soph FL Ryan Mathews (21 pass rec for 359 yds), TE Greg Schorp (24 pass rec for 280 yds), C Chris Dausin, OG John Ellisor, Venetoulias (16 FGs, 87 pts), Adams, DE Eric England, Buckley, Atkinson, DBs Patrick Bates and Aaron Glenn (6 int), soph P David Davis (43.8-yd avg). *Noteworthy:* Repeated as SWC champ in 1st undefeated season since 1956. Lost to Notre Dame 28–3 in Cotton Bowl; Aggies scored on 41-yd FG by Venetoulias.

Bowl Summary

Bluebonnet 0–1; Cotton 4–4; Dixie Classic 1–0; Gator 0–1; Hall of Fame 1–0; Holiday 1–0; Independence 1–0; John Hancock 0–1; Liberty 0–1; Orange 0–1; Presidential Cup 1–0; Sugar 1–0; Sun 1–0.

Bowl Record (11–9)

Regular Season	Bowl	Score	Opponent	Record
1921 (5–1–2)	Dixie Classic	22–14	Centre	(9–0)
1939 (10–0)	Sugar	14–13	Tulane	(8–1–1)
1940 (8–1)	Cotton	13–12	Fordham	(7–1)
1941 (9–1)	Cotton	21–29	Alabama	(8–2)
1943 (7–1–1)	Orange	14–19	LSU	(5–3)
1950 (6–4)	Presidential Cup	40–20	Georgia	(6–2–3)

(continued)

Regular Season	Bowl	Score	Opponent	Record
1957 (8–2)	Gator	0–3	Tennessee	(7–3)
1967 (6–4)	Cotton	20–16	Alabama	(8–1–1)
1975 (10–1)	Liberty	0–20	USC	(7–4)
1976 (9–2)	Sun	37–14	Florida	(8–3)
1977 (8–3)	Bluebonnet	21–47	USC	(7–4)
1978 (7–4)	Hall of Fame	28–12	Iowa State	(8–3)
1981 (6–5)	Independence	33–16	Oklahoma St.	(7–4)
1985 (9–2)	Cotton	36–16	Auburn	(8–3)
1986 (9–2)	Cotton	12–28	Ohio State	(9–3)
1987 (9–2)	Cotton	35–10	Notre Dame	(8–3)
1989 (8–3)	John Hancock	28–31	Pittsburgh	(7–3–1)
1990 (8–3–1)	Holiday	65–14	BYU	(10–2)
1991 (10–1)	Cotton	2–10	Florida State	(10–2)
1992 (12–0)	Cotton	3–28	Notre Dame	(9–1–1)

CONFERENCE TITLES

Southwest—1917, 1919, 1921, 1925, 1927, 1939, 1940*, 1941, 1956, 1967, 1975*, 1985, 1986, 1987, 1991, 1992.

TOP 20 AP AND UPI
(USA TODAY/CNN SINCE 1991) RANKING

1939	1	1957	9–10	1978	19–18	1989	20–U
1940	6	1974	16–15	1985	6–7	1990	15–13
1941	9	1975	11–12	1986	13–12	1991	12–13
1955	17–14	1976	7–8	1987	10–9	1992	7–6
1956	5–5						

MAJOR RIVALS

Texas A&M has played at least 10 games with Arkansas 24–38–3, Austin College 12–0, Baylor 51–29–9, Houston 16–12–3, Louisiana St. 17–26–3, Oklahoma 5–7, Oklahoma St. 7–4, Rice 47–27–3, Southern Methodist 38–29–6, Southwestern (Texas) 18–0, Texas 30–64–5, Texas Christian 52–29–7, Texas Tech 29–21–1, Trinity (Texas) 18–1–2, Tulane 10–5.

COACHES

Dean of Texas A&M coaches is Homer H. Norton with record of 82–53–9 for 1934–47, including 3 SWC titles, 4 bowl teams, and 1 undefeated national champion. Other top records for at least 3 years were by J.E. Platt, 18–5–1 for 1902–04 with 1 unbeaten team; Charles B. Moran, 38–8–4 for 1909–14 with 1 unbeaten team; Dana X. Bible, 72–19–9 for 1917 and 1919–28 with 5 SWC titles, 1 bowl champion, and 3 unbeaten teams; Madison Bell, 24–21–3 for 1929–33; Paul "Bear" Bryant, 25–14–2 for 1954–57 with 1 SWC title, 1 bowl team, and 1 unbeaten team; Gene Stallings, 27–45–1 for 1965–71 with 1 SWC title and 1 Cotton Bowl champion; Emory Bellard, 48–27 for 1972 to mid-1978 with 1 SWC title and 3 bowl teams; Tom Wilson, 21–19 for mid-1978–1981 with 2 bowl teams; Jackie Sherrill, 52–28–1 for 1982–88 with 3 SWC titles and 3 Cotton Bowl teams; and R.C. Slocum, 39–10–1 for 1989–92 with 2 SWC titles and 4 bowl teams.

MISCELLANEA

First game was win over Galveston H.S. 14–6 in 1894 . . . 1st win over college foe was over Austin College 22–4 in 1896 . . . highest score was over Daniel Baker 110–0 in 1920 . . . highest since W.W. II was over TCU 74–10 in 1986 . . . worst defeat was by Texas 48–0 in 1898 . . . worst since 1900 was by Baylor 46–0 in 1901 . . . worst since W.W. II was by Ohio St. 56–13 in 1970 . . . highest ever against was by Texas 57–28 in 1977 . . . longest unbeaten string of 18, in 1918–20 ended by Texas 7–3 and in 1956–57 by Rice 7–6 . . . longest winless string of 15 in 1947–49 broken with win over Texas Tech 26–7 . . . consensus All-Americans were Joe Routt, G, 1937; John Kimbrough, B, 1939–40; Marshall Robnett, G, 1940; John David Crow, B, 1957; Dave Elmendorf, DB, 1970; Pat Thomas, DB, 1974–75; Ed Simonini, LB, 1975; Tony Franklin, K, and Robert Jackson, LB, 1976; Johnny Holland, LB, 1985; John Roper, DL, 1987; Darren Lewis, RB, 1990; Kevin Smith, DB, 1991; and Marcus Buckley, LB, 1992 . . . Academic All-Americans were Jack Pardee, B, 1956; Bill Luebbehusen, LB, 1971; Kevin Monk, LB, 1976–77; and Kip Corrington, DB, 1985–87 . . . Heisman Trophy winner was John David Crow, HB, 1957.

TEXAS CHRISTIAN UNIVERSITY (Horned Frogs; Purple and White)

NOTABLE TEAMS

1912 (8–1) *Won:* Britten Training School 16–0, Southwestern (Texas) 20–0, Baylor 22–0 (1st over Bears in 5 games since 1909), Austin College 7–0, Polytechnic 33–3, 21–7, Howard Payne 53–0, Trinity (Texas) 48–13. *Lost:* Texas 30–10. *Noteworthy:* only year under W.T. Stewart.
1916 (6–2–1) *Won:* Meridian 7–0, Austin College 28–2, Southern Methodist (SMU) 48–3, Trinity (Texas) 35–0, Daniel Baker 23–0, Howard Payne 42–0. *Lost:* Southwestern (Texas) 41–13, Baylor 32–14. *Tied:* Rice 7–7. *Noteworthy:* 1st year under Milton Daniel.
1917 (8–2) *Won:* Meridian 20–0, First Texas Artillery 14–7, SMU 21–0, Trinity (Texas) 20–6, Southwestern (Texas) 20–6, Austin College 59–0, 111th Ambulance 6–0, Baylor 34–0. *Lost:* Rice 26–0, 2nd

Texas 132nd Infantry 14–7. *Noteworthy:* last year under Daniel.
1920 (9–1) *Won:* SE Oklahoma 20–0, Austin College 9–7, Arkansas 19–2 (1st meeting), Trinity (Texas) 20–7, Phillips U. 3–0, Missouri Osteopaths 19–3, Baylor 21–9, Hardin-Simmons 31–2 (1st meeting), Southwestern (Texas) 21–16. *Noteworthy:* Had 1st undefeated season since 1-game schedule of 1899 in 1st year under W.L. Driver. Made 1st postseason appearance, losing to Centre 63–7 in Fort Worth Classic.
1925 (7–1–1) *Won:* East Texas St. 31–0, Daniel Baker 12–0, Hardin-Simmons 28–16, Abilene Christian 21–9, Texas A&M 3–0 (1st over Aggies in 20 games since 1897), Arkansas 3–0, Austin College 21–0. *Lost:* Oklahoma A&M 22–7. *Tied:* Baylor 7–7 (1st meeting since 1920). *Stars:* QB Herman Clark, C Johnny Washmon, T Harold Brewster.
1926 (6–1–2) *Won:* Daniel Baker 5–3, Centenary 24–14, Austin College 7–0, Oklahoma A&M 3–0, Texas Tech 28–16 (1st meeting), Arkansas 10–7. *Lost:* unbeaten SMU 14–13 in finale. *Tied:* Baylor 7–7, Texas A&M 13–13. *Stars:* Clark, FB Bernard Williams, E Raymond "Rags" Matthews, Washmon, Brewster, T Luther Scarborough, G Raymond Wolf.
1928 (8–2) *Won:* East Texas St. 21–0, Daniel Baker 19–0, Hardin-Simmons 19–3, Austin College 21–0, Texas A&M 6–0, Texas Tech 28–6, Rice 7–0, SMU 15–6 (1st over Mustangs in 6 games since 1921). *Lost:* Baylor 7–6, Texas 6–0. *Stars:* QB Howard Grubbs, Austin Griffith (6 TDs), G Mike Brumbelow, T Jake Williams. *Noteworthy:* last year under Madison Bell.
1929 (9–0–1) *Won:* Daniel Baker 61–0, Hardin-Simmons 20–0, Centenary 28–0, Texas A&M 13–7, Texas Tech 22–0, North Texas St. 25–0 (1st meeting since 1919), Rice 24–0, Texas 15–12 (1st in 15-game series dating to 1897), Baylor 34–7. *Tied:* unbeaten SMU 7–7 in finale. *Stars:* Grubbs (836 yds pass), Clyde Roberson (12 pass rec for 288 yds), HB Cy Leland (680 yds and 13 TDs rush), FB Harlos Green, Brumbelow, C Noble Atkins. *Noteworthy:* Won 1st SWC title and had 1st unbeaten season since 1920 in 1st year under Francis A. Schmidt.
1930 (9–2–1) *Won:* North Texas St. 47–0, East Texas St. 40–0, Austin College 33–7, Arkansas 40–0, Texas A&M 3–0, Texas Tech 26–0, Abilene Christian 62–0, Rice 20–0, SMU 13–0. *Lost:* Texas 7–0, Baylor 35–14 in consecutive late games. *Tied:*

Hardin-Simmons 0–0. *Stars:* Leland (583 yds rush, 10 TDs), Atkins, soph T Ben Boswell, Hubert Dennis (6 int).

1931 (9–2–1) *Won:* Texas Military 40–0, North Texas St. 33–6, Louisiana St. (LSU) 3–0, Austin College 38–0, Texas A&M 6–0, Hardin-Simmons 6–0, Arkansas 7–0, Rice 7–6, Baylor 19–6. *Lost:* Tulsa 13–0, Texas 10–0. *Tied:* SMU 0–0. *Stars:* G Johnny Vaught, E Madison Pruitt, HB Blanard Spearman.

1932 (10–0–1) *Won:* North Texas St. 14–2, Daniel Baker 55–0, Arkansas 34–12, Texas A&M 17–0, Austin College 68–0, Baylor 27–0, Hardin-Simmons 27–0, Texas 14–0, Rice 16–6, SMU 8–0. *Tied:* LSU 3–3 in 2nd game. *Stars:* Vaught, Boswell, C J.W. Townsend, G Lon Evans, T Foster Howell, Pruitt, Spearman, Richard Oliver (12 TDs rush). *Noteworthy:* Won 2nd SWC title.

1933 (9–2–1) *Won:* Austin College 33–0, Daniel Baker 28–6, North Texas St. 13–0, Hardin-Simmons 20–0, Texas A&M 13–7, North Dakota 19–7, Texas 30–0, Rice 26–3, SMU 26–6. *Lost:* Arkansas 13–0, Baylor 7–0. *Tied:* unbeaten Centenary 0–0. *Stars:* Bs Charley Casper (10 TDs, 17 pass rec for 293 yds), Johnny Kitchen and soph Jimmy Lawrence, soph C Darrell Lester, T Cy Perkins. *Noteworthy:* Schmidt's last team.

1934 (8–4) *Won:* Daniel Baker 33–7, North Texas St. 27–0, Tulsa 14–12, Texas A&M 13–0, Baylor 34–12, Loyola (La.) 7–0, Rice 7–2, Santa Clara 9–7. *Lost:* Arkansas 24–10, Centenary 13–0, Texas 20–19, SMU 19–0 (1st to Mustangs since 1927). *Stars:* Lester, Lawrence (7 TDs), soph TB Sammy Baugh (883 yds and 11 TDs pass, 114 yds and 2 TDs rush, 42.3-yd punting avg), soph E Walter Roach (23 pass rec for 297 yds). *Noteworthy:* 1st year under Dutch Meyer.

1935 (12–1) *Won:* Howard Payne 41–0, North Texas St. 28–11, Arkansas 13–7, Tulsa 13–0, Texas A&M 19–14, Centenary 27–7, Baylor 28–0, Loyola (La.) 14–0, Texas 28–0, Rice 27–6, Santa Clara 10–6. *Lost:* unbeaten national cochamp SMU 20–14. *Stars:* Lester (TCU's 1st consensus All-American), Baugh (1,240 yds and 18 TDs pass, 195 yds and 3 TDs rush, 43-yd punting avg), Lawrence (23 pass rec for 218 yds, 8 TDs, 7 int), L.D. "Dutch" Meyer (23 pass rec for 246 yds), Roach, G Tracy Kellow. *Noteworthy:* Beat LSU 3–2 in rainy Sugar Bowl on 26-yd FG by Taldon Manton in 2nd period; Baugh punted 14 times for 44.6-yd avg.

1936 (9–2–2) *Won:* Howard Payne 6–0, Arkansas 18–14, Tulsa 14–7, Baylor 28–0, Texas 27–6, Centenary 26–0, Rice 13–0, Santa Clara 9–0. *Lost:* Texas Tech 7–0 (1st meeting since 1930, 1st loss in 6-game series dating to 1926), Texas A&M 18–7 (1st to Aggies since 1924). *Tied:* Mississippi St. 0–0, SMU 0–0. *Stars:* Baugh (1,261 yds and 10 TDs pass, 5 int on defense), Roach (26 pass rec for 289 yds), Harold McClure (6 TDs), soph TB/S Davey O'Brien (5 int), soph C Ki Aldrich. *Noteworthy:* Beat Marquette 16–6 in Cotton Bowl; Baugh passed for 100 yds and a TD (50 yds to Meyer, who also caught 18-yd TD pass from Vic Montgomery), and kicked 33-yd FG and ex pt.

1938 (11–0) *Won:* Centenary 13–0, Arkansas 21–14, Temple 28–6, Texas A&M 34–6, Marquette 21–0, Baylor 39–7, Tulsa 21–0, Texas 28–6, Rice 29–7, SMU 20–7. *Stars:* Heisman Trophy– and Maxwell Award–winner O'Brien (6 int, 390 yds and 3 TDs rush, 28 extra pts, nation's leader with 1,457 yds and 19 TDs pass and in total off with 1,847 yds), Earl Clark (20 pass rec for 395 yds and 6 TDs), soph FB Connie Sparks (10 TDs), E Don Looney, Aldrich, T I.B. Hale, G Forrest Kline. *Noteworthy:* Nation's most-improved team led nation in pass, won 3rd SWC title, and got share of 1st national championship. Beat Carnegie Tech 15–7 in Sugar Bowl; O'Brien passed for 225 yds and a TD (44 yds to E Durward Horner) and kicked FG, and Sparks scored on 1-yd run.

1941 (7–3–1) *Won:* Tulsa 6–0, Arkansas 9–0, Indiana 20–14, Baylor 23–12, Centenary 35–7, Texas 14–7, SMU 15–13. *Lost:* Texas A&M 14–0, Fordham 28–14 in successive early games. *Tied:* Rice 0–0. *Stars:* Frank Kring (6 TDs), E Bruce Alford, T Derrell Palmer, G Bill Crawford. *Noteworthy:* lost to Georgia 40–26 in Orange Bowl after trailing 40–7 in 3rd quarter; Kyle Gillespie passed for 2 TDs (including 52 yds to Kring) and ran for another, and Alford caught 2 TD passes and blocked a punt.

1942 (7–3) *Won:* UCLA 7–6, Arkansas 13–6, Kansas 41–6 (1st meeting), Texas A&M 7–2, Pensacola Naval Air Station 21–0, Texas 13–7, SMU 14–6. *Lost:* Baylor 10–7, Texas Tech 13–6 (1st meeting since 1936), Rice 26–0. *Stars:* Palmer, Alford, Van Hall (27 pass rec for 235 yds).

1944 (7–3–1) *Won:* Kansas 7–0, South Plains Army Air Force 34–0, Texas A&M 13–7, Chatham Army Air Force 19–7, Texas Tech 14–0, Texas 7–6, Rice 9–6. *Lost:* Oklahoma 34–19, SMU 9–6. *Tied:* Arkansas 6–6. *Stars:* Ts Clyde Flowers and Jim

Cooper, HB Norman Cox, Merle Gibson (19 pass rec for 378 yds and 6 TDs). *Noteworthy:* Won 4th SWC title. Lost to Oklahoma A&M 34–0 in Cotton Bowl, dropping behind 14–0 in 1st quarter.
1951 (6–5)   *Won:* Nebraska 28–7, Arkansas 17–7, Texas A&M 20–14, Baylor 20–7 (1st over Bears since 1946), Rice 22–6, SMU 13–2.   *Lost:* Kansas 27–13, Texas Tech 33–19, Southern California (USC) 28–26, Texas 32–21.   *Stars:* Bobby Jack Floyd (8 TDs rush), soph TB Ray McKown, Bob Blair (14 pass rec for 320 yds), Gs Herbert Zimmerman and Alton Taylor, T Doug Conaway, C/LB Keith Flowers, Ronald Fraley (6 pass int). *Noteworthy:* Won 5th SWC title. Lost to Kentucky 20–7 in Cotton Bowl; Floyd ran for 115 yds (including 43-yd TD run).
1955 (9–2)   *Won:* Kansas 47–14, Texas Tech 32–0, Arkansas 26–0, Alabama 21–0, Miami (Fla.) 21–19, Baylor 28–6, Texas 47–20, Rice 35–0, SMU 20–13. *Lost:* Texas A&M 19–16.   *Stars:* HB Jim Swink (1,283 yds rush, nation's leader in scoring with 20 TDs and 125 pts and coleader with 1,702 all-purpose yds), QB Charles Curtis, E Bryan Engram, C Hugh Pitts, T Norman Hamilton.   *Noteworthy:* Won 6th SWC title. Lost to Mississippi 14–13 in Cotton Bowl after leading 13–7 at halftime; Swink ran for 107 yds and both TCU TDs (including 39-yd run).
1956 (8–3)   *Won:* Kansas 32–0, Arkansas 41–6, Alabama 23–6, Baylor 7–6, Texas 46–0, Rice 20–17, SMU 21–17.   *Lost:* unbeaten Texas A&M 7–6, Miami (Fla.) 14–0, Texas Tech 21–7.   *Stars:* Swink (665 yds rush, 19 pass rec for 390 yds, 6 TDs), Ken Wineburg (7 TDs), E O'Day Williams, Hamilton. *Noteworthy:* beat Syracuse 28–27 in Cotton Bowl (breaking 5-bowl losing string); Curtis passed for 176 yds and 2 TDs and scored on 7-yd run, Swink caught 4 passes for 60 yds and ran for a TD, Harold Pollard kicked 4 ex pts, and Chico Mendoza blocked ex pt try.
1958 (8–2–1)   *Won:* Kansas 42–0, Arkansas 12–7, Texas Tech 26–0, Texas A&M 24–8, Baylor 22–0,

Marquette 36–8, Texas 22–8, Rice 21–10.   *Lost:* national cochamp Iowa 17–0, SMU 20–13.   *Stars:* HB Marvin Lasater, FB Jack Spikes (580 yds rush), Marshall Harris (19 pass rec for 265 yds), T Don Floyd, G Sherrill Headrick, C Dale Walker. *Noteworthy:* Won 7th SWC title. Tied unbeaten Air Force 0–0 in Cotton Bowl; Spikes ran for 108 yds but Frogs fumbled 8 times and lost 3.
1959 (8–3)   *Won:* Kansas 14–7, Texas Tech 14–8, Texas A&M 39–6, Pittsburgh 13–3, Baylor 14–0, Texas 14–9, Rice 35–6, SMU 19–0.   *Lost:* LSU 10–0, Arkansas 3–0 in consecutive early games.   *Stars:* Spikes (660 yds rush), Lasater (6 TDs), Harry Moreland (6 TDs), Floyd, T Bob Lilly. *Noteworthy:* Got share of 8th SWC title. Lost to Clemson 23–7 in inaugural Bluebonnet Bowl after leading 7–3 going into last quarter; scored on 19-yd pass from Jack Reding to Moreland.
1984 (8–4)   *Won:* Utah St. 62–18, Kansas St. 42–10, Arkansas 32–31, Rice 45–24, North Texas St. 34–3 (1st meeting since 1935), Baylor 38–28, Houston 21–14 (1st in 9-game series begun in 1976), Texas Tech 27–16.   *Lost:* SMU 26–17, Texas 44–23, Texas A&M 35–21.   *Stars:* RB Kenneth Davis (1,611 yds and 15 TDs rush, 13 pass rec for 200 yds and 2 TDs), WR James Maness (40 pass rec for 871 yds), QB Anthony Gulley (1,022 yds pass), TE Dan Sharp (42 pass rec for 596 yds and 7 TDs), frosh HB Tony Jeffery (840 yds rush), P James Gargus (40.6-yd avg), DBs Sean Thomas (8 int) and Byron Linwood. *Noteworthy:* 1st winning season since 1971. Lost to West Virginia 31–14 in Bluebonnet Bowl, dropping behind 31–7 by halftime; Gulley passed for 150 yds and both TCU scores (5 yds to Sharp and 20 yds to WR Keith Burnett).

BOWL SUMMARY

Bluebonnet 0–2; Cotton 2–3–1; Delta 0–1; Ft. Worth Classic 0–1; Orange 0–1; Sugar 2–0; Sun 0–1.

BOWL RECORD (4–9–1)

Regular Season	Bowl	Score	Opponent	Record
1920 (9–0)	Ft. Worth Classic	7–63	Centre	(7–2)
1935 (11–1)	Sugar	3–2	LSU	(9–1)

(continued)

Regular Season	Bowl	Score	Opponent	Record
1936 (8–2–2)	Cotton	16–6	Marquette	(7–1)
1938 (10–0)	Sugar	15–7	Carnegie Tech	(7–1)
1941 (7–3)	Orange	26–40	Georgia	(8–1–1)
1944 (7–2–1)	Cotton	0–34	Oklahoma St.	(7–1)
1947 (4–4–2)	Delta	9–13	Mississippi	(8–2)
1951 (6–4)	Cotton	7–20	Kentucky	(7–4)
1955 (9–1)	Cotton	13–14	Mississippi	(9–1)
1956 (7–3)	Cotton	28–27	Syracuse	(7–1)
1958 (8–2)	Cotton	0–0	Air Force	(9–0–1)
1959 (8–2)	Bluebonnet	7–23	Clemson	(8–2)
1965 (6–4)	Sun	12–13	Texas–El Paso	(7–3)
1984 (8–3)	Bluebonnet	14–31	West Virginia	(7–4)

CONFERENCE TITLES

Southwest—1929, 1932, 1938, 1944, 1951, 1955, 1958, 1959*.

TOP 20 AP AND UPI RANKING

1936	16	1938	1	1955	6–6	1958	10–9
1937	16	1951	11–10	1956	14–14	1959	7–8

MAJOR RIVALS

TCU has played at least 10 games with Arkansas 23–43–2, Austin College 18–5, Baylor 46–46–7, Centenary 8–4–1, Daniel Baker 11–4, Hardin-Simmons 9–1–2, Houston 4–13, Kansas 15–5–4, North Texas St. 13–2, Oklahoma St. 9–10–2, Rice 38–30–3, Southern Methodist 31–35–7, Southwestern (Texas) 7–5, Texas 20–57–1, Texas A&M 29–52–7, Texas Tech 21–25–3, Trinity (Texas) 15–4–2, Tulsa 10–4.

COACHES

Dean of TCU coaches is Dutch Meyer with record of 109–79–13 for 1934–52, including 3 SWC titles, 7 bowl teams, and 1 unbeaten national champion. Other top records for at least 3 years were by Madison A. Bell, 33–17–5 for 1923–28; Francis A. Schmidt, 46–6–5 for 1929–33 with 2 SWC titles and 2 unbeaten teams; Abe Martin, 74–64–7 for 1953–66 with 3 SWC titles and 5 bowl teams; and Jim Wacker, 40–58–2 for 1983–91 with 1 bowl team.

MISCELLANEA

First game was win over Toby's Business College 8–6 in 1896 . . . 1st win over college foe was over Dallas U. 6–0 in 1897 . . . highest score was over Austin College 68–0 in 1932 . . . highest since W.W. II was over Utah St. 62–18 in 1984 . . . biggest margin since W.W. II was over New Mexico 60–7 in 1991 . . . worst defeat was by Texas 72–0 in 1915 . . . worst since W.W. II and highest ever against was by Texas 81–16 in 1974 . . . longest unbeaten string of 20 in 1928–30 ended by Texas 7–0 . . . 16-game unbeaten string in 1931–33 ended by Arkansas 13–0 . . . longest win streak of 14 in 1937–38 ended by UCLA 6–3 in 1939 opener . . . longest losing string of 20 in 1974–75 broken with win over Rice 28–21 . . . 15-game losing string in 1976–77 broken with win over Rice 35–15 . . . consensus All-Americans were Darrell

Lester, C, 1935; Sammy Baugh, B, 1936; Ki Aldrich, C, and Davey O'Brien, B, 1938; Jim Swink, B, 1955; Don Floyd, T, 1959; Bob Lilly, T, 1960; Kenneth Davis, RB, 1984; and Kelly Blackwell, TE, 1991 . . . Academic All-Americans were Marshall Harris, T, 1952; Hugh Pitts, C, 1955; Jim Swink, B, 1955–56; John Nikkel, E, 1957; Jim Ray, OG, 1968; Scott Walker, C, 1972; Terry Drennan, DB, 1974; and John McClean, DL, 1980 . . . Heisman Trophy winner was Davey O'Brien, TB, 1938 . . . Maxwell Award winner was Davey O'Brien, TB, 1938.

TEXAS TECH (Red Raiders; Scarlet and Black)

NOTABLE TEAMS

1925 (6–1–2) **Won:** Montezuma 30–0, Clarendon 13–7, Sul Ross 21–7, Wayland 120–0, Abilene Christian 10–7, West Texas St. 13–12. **Lost:** Howard Payne 29–0. **Tied:** McMurry 0–0, Austin 3–3. **Noteworthy:** coached by E.Y. Freeland in 1st year of competition.
1926 (6–1–3) **Won:** McMurry 7–0, St. Edwards 7–6, Clarendon 14–0, Abilene Christian 28–7, Howard Payne 27–6, West Texas St. 7–2. **Lost:** Texas Christian (TCU) 28–16 (1st meeting). **Tied:** Schreiner 0–0, Hardin-Simmons 0–0 (1st meeting), Daniel Baker 0–0.
1932 (10–2) **Won:** Panhandle A&M 44–0, Southern Methodist (SMU) 6–0 (1st meeting), Austin College 64–0, Arizona 21–0 (1st meeting), New Mexico Normal 43–7, Colorado Mines 21–0, Notre Dame "B" team 39–0, Trinity (Texas) 79–0, Baylor 14–2, New Mexico 39–6. **Lost:** Texas A&M 7–0 (1st meeting since 1927), Hardin-Simmons 13–12. **Noteworthy:** won unofficial Border Conference title.
1933 (8–1) **Won:** Dixie U. 33–0, Arizona 7–0, Louisiana Tech 40–10, Haskell 26–6, Texas Mines (Texas–El Paso) 12–0, Hardin-Simmons 7–0, Baylor 13–0, Kansas St. 6–0. **Lost:** SMU 14–0 in opener. **Stars:** Es Elva Baker and Matt Hitchcock. **Noteworthy:** again won unofficial Border Conference title.
1934 (7–2–1) **Won:** McMurry 24–7, Baylor 14–7, Oklahoma City 20–0, Texas Mines (Texas–El Paso) 27–0, Hardin-Simmons 13–0, DePaul 48–19, Arizona 14–7. **Lost:** Texas 12–6 (1st meeting since 1928), Loyola (La.) 12–7. **Tied:** North Dakota St.

20–20. **Stars:** HB G.C. Dowell, C Lawrence Priddy, G Pete Owens. **Noteworthy:** won 3rd straight unofficial Border Conference crown.
1937 (8–4) **Won:** Northern Arizona 6–0, Arizona 20–0, New Mexico 27–0 (1st meeting since 1932), Oklahoma A&M 14–6, Duquesne 13–0, Loyola (La.) 25–6, Centenary 7–2, Creighton 27–0. **Lost:** Texas 25–12, Montana 13–6, Detroit 34–0 in consecutive early games. **Stars:** E Herschel Ramsey, HB Elmer Tarbox (6 int), Gs Floyd Owens and Lewis Jones. **Noteworthy:** Won 1st official Border Conference title. Made 1st postseason appearance, losing to West Virginia 7–6 in Sun Bowl; scored on 4-yd run by Charlie Calhoun in 2nd quarter.
1938 (10–1) **Won:** Montana St. 35–0, Wyoming 39–0, Duquesne 7–6, Oklahoma City 60–0, Montana 19–13, Texas Mines (Texas–El Paso) 14–7, Loyola (La.) 55–0, Gonzaga 7–0, New Mexico 17–7, Marquette 21–2. **Stars:** Tarbox (nation's leader with 11 int), Jones. **Noteworthy:** 1st unbeaten season. Lost to St. Mary's (Calif.) 20–13 in Cotton Bowl.
1940 (9–1–1) **Won:** Loyola (Calif.) 19–0, Montana 32–19, Brigham Young (BYU) 21–20, Marquette 20–13, Miami (Fla.) 61–14, Centenary 26–6, Wake Forest 12–7, St. Louis 7–6, San Francisco 23–21. **Lost:** New Mexico 19–14 (1st in 6-game series dating to 1931). **Tied:** Oklahoma A&M 6–6. **Noteworthy:** last year under Pete Cawthon.
1941 (9–2) **Won:** Abilene Christian 34–0, Oklahoma A&M 16–6, Loyola (Calif.) 14–0, Centenary 25–0, New Mexico 36–0, Creighton 13–6, St. Louis 46–6, Hardin-Simmons 7–0 (1st meeting since 1934), Wake Forest 35–6. **Lost:** Miami (Fla.) 6–0. **Stars:** QB Tyrus Bain, FB Charles Dvoracek. **Noteworthy:** 1st year under Dell Morgan. Lost to Tulsa 6–0 (1st meeting) in Sun Bowl, giving up TD in 4th quarter; had only 104 yds total off and 4 1st downs.
1946 (8–3) **Won:** West Texas St. 26–14, Texas A&M 6–0 (1st in 7-game series dating to 1927), SMU 7–0, Baylor 13–6, Denver 21–6, New Mexico 27–0, Oklahoma A&M 14–7, Arizona 16–0. **Lost:** Tulsa 21–6, Rice 41–6, unbeaten Hardin-Simmons 21–6. **Stars:** HB Roger Smith, FB Ed Robnett, Ts Bernie Winkler and Clyde Hall, G Floyd Lawhorn, C Roland Nabors. **Noteworthy:** 1st winning season since 1941.
1948 (7–3) **Won:** West Texas St. 19–0, Texas A&M 20–14, Tulsa 41–20, Arizona 31–0, Texas Western

(Texas–El Paso) 46–6, New Mexico 14–7, Hardin-Simmons 28–20. *Lost:* SMU 41–6, Baylor 13–0, Rice 14–7. *Stars:* QB Ernest Hawkins, E Bill Kelley, Ts Marshall Gettys and John Andrews, Gs Dan Pursel and Dorrell McCurry. *Noteworthy:* won 5th official Border Conference title.

1953 (11–1) *Won:* West Texas St. 40–14, Texas Western (Texas–El Paso) 27–6, Oklahoma A&M 27–13 (1st meeting since 1946), Pacific 34–7, New Mexico St. 71–0, Mississippi St. 27–20, Arizona 52–27 (10th straight over Wildcats), Tulsa 49–7, Houston 41–21, Hardin-Simmons 46–12. *Lost:* Texas A&M 27–14. *Stars:* Bobby Cavazos (747 yds rush, 80 pts), Don Lewis (11 TDs), QB Jack Kirkpatrick, soph FB James Sides, E Vic Spooner, Ts Jimmy Williams and soph Jerry Walker, G Don Gray. *Noteworthy:* Nation's most-improved team led country in scoring (38.9-pt avg) and won 8th Border Conference title. Beat Auburn 35–13 in Gator Bowl; Cavazos scored TDs on runs of 2 yds and 59 yds and caught 30-yd TD pass from Kirkpatrick, who also passed 53 yds to Paul Erwin for TD.

1954 (7–2–1) *Won:* Texas A&M 41–9 (1st over Aggies in 5 games since 1948), West Texas St. 33–7, Texas Western (Texas–El Paso) 55–28, Arizona 28–14, Tulsa 55–13, Houston 61–14, Hardin-Simmons 61–19. *Lost:* Louisiana St. (LSU) 20–13, Pacific 20–7 in successive mid-season games. *Tied:* Oklahoma A&M 13–13. *Stars:* Sides, HBs Ronnie Herr (8 TDs), Rick Spinks and Walter Bryan, QB Jerry Johnson, Es Claude Harland and Dean White (10 pass rec for 252 yds), Walker, Ts Bill Herchmann and Bob Kilcullen, Gs Hal Broadfoot and Arlen Wesley, C Dwayne West. *Noteworthy:* repeated as Border Conference champ.

1955 (7–3–1) *Won:* Texas 20–14 (1st meeting since 1950, 1st win in 8-game series dating to 1928), Oklahoma A&M 24–6, West Texas St. 27–24, Arizona 27–7, Tulsa 34–7, Pacific 13–7, Hardin-Simmons 16–14. *Lost:* TCU 32–0, Houston 7–0. *Tied:* Texas Western (Texas–El Paso) 27–27. *Stars:* Sides, HB Don Schmidt (508 yds rush, 7 TDs), Walker, Herchmann, Broadfoot. *Noteworthy:* Won 3rd straight (10th and last) Border Conference title. Lost to Wyoming 21–14 in Sun Bowl; Herr and Hugh Fewin scored Red Raider TDs.

1965 (8–3) *Won:* Kansas 26–7, Texas A&M 20–16, TCU 28–24, Oklahoma St. 17–14 (1st meeting since 1957), SMU 26–24, Rice 27–0 (1st over Owls in 13 games since 1944), New Mexico St. 28–9, Baylor 34–22. *Lost:* Texas 33–7, unbeaten Arkansas 42–24. *Stars:* HB Donny Anderson (705 yds and 10 TDs rush, 60 pass rec for 797 yds and 7 TDs), QB Tom Wilson (2,119 yds and 18 TDs pass), Jerry Shipley (47 pass rec for 563 yds). *Noteworthy:* lost to Georgia Tech 31–21 in Gator Bowl after leading 21–16 entering 4th quarter; Wilson passed for 283 yds and Anderson ran for 85 yds and a TD and caught 9 passes for 138 yds.

1970 (8–4) *Won:* Tulane 21–14, Kansas 23–0, UC–Santa Barbara 63–21, Texas A&M 21–7, SMU 14–10, Rice 3–0, TCU 22–14, Baylor 7–3. *Lost:* unbeaten national cochamp Texas 35–13, Mississippi St. 20–16, Arkansas 24–10. *Stars:* HB Doug McCutchen (1,068 yds rush), QB Charles Napper (979 yds pass), E Johnny Odom (26 pass rec for 331 yds), DE Bruce Dowdy, DT Wayne McDermand, DB Ken Perkins. *Noteworthy:* 1st year under Jim Carlen. Lost to Georgia Tech 17–9 in Sun Bowl after dropping behind 10–0 by halftime.

1972 (8–4) *Won:* Utah 29–2, New Mexico 41–16, Tulsa 35–18, Texas A&M 17–14, Arizona 35–10, SMU 17–3, Rice 10–6, Baylor 13–7. *Lost:* Texas 25–20, TCU 31–7, Arkansas 24–14. *Stars:* QB Joe Barnes (1,142 yds pass), E Andre Tillman (21 pass rec for 285 yds), George Smith (740 yds rush), K Don Grimes (12 FGs, 70 pts), C Russell Ingram, NG Don Rives, soph Larry Williams (nation's kickoff return leader with 30.8-yd avg). *Noteworthy:* lost to North Carolina 32–28 in Sun Bowl after leading 21–16 going into 4th quarter; Smith ran for 172 yds and 3 TDs (including runs of 65 and 46 yds) and Barnes passed 15 yds to Tillman for other Red Raider TD.

1973 (11–1) *Won:* Utah 29–22, New Mexico 41–7, Oklahoma St. 20–7, Texas A&M 28–16, Arizona 31–17, SMU 31–14, Rice 19–6, TCU 24–10, Baylor 55–24, Arkansas 24–17 (1st over Razorbacks since 1967). *Lost:* Texas 28–12. *Stars:* Barnes (568 yds rush, 978 yds pass), Tillman (26 pass rec for 428 yds and 5 TDs), frosh TB Larry Isaac (10 TDs), OT Tom Furgerson, G Dennis Allen, Grimes, MG David Knaus, soph DT Ecomet Burley, DBs Kenneth Wallace and Danny Willis. *Noteworthy:* beat Tennessee 28–19 in Gator Bowl (breaking 5-bowl losing string); Barnes passed for 2 TDs (79 yds to Williams and 7 yds to Tillman) and ran for another, and Isaac scored on 3-yd run.

1976 (10–2) *Won:* Colorado 24–7, New Mexico 20–16, Texas A&M 27–16, Rice 37–13, Arizona 52–27, Texas 31–28, TCU 14–10, SMU 34–7, Arkansas 30–7, Baylor 24–21. *Lost:* Houston 27–19 (1st meeting since 1959). *Stars:* QB Rodney Allison (1,458 yds pass), E Sammy Williams (32 pass rec for 601 yds), Isaac (685 yds rush), OG Mike Sears, OT Dan Irons, K Brian Hall (15 FGs, 78 pts), DE Harold Buell, LB Thomas Howard, DB Greg Frazier (5 int). *Noteworthy:* Got share of 1st SWC title. Lost to Nebraska 27–24 in Bluebonnet Bowl; Billy Taylor caught 2 TD passes from Allison and ran 8 yds for other Red Raider TD, and Hall kicked 28-yd FG and 3 ex pts.

1989 (9–3) *Won:* Arizona 24–14, New Mexico 27–20, Oklahoma St. 31–15, Texas A&M 27–24, Rice 41–25, Texas 24–17, TCU 37–7, SMU 48–24 (1st over Mustangs in 7 games since 1980). *Lost:* Baylor 29–15, Arkansas 45–13, Houston 40–24. *Stars:* RBs James Gray (1,509 yds rush, 20 TDs) and soph Anthony Lynn (568 yds and 6 TDs rush), soph QB Jamie Gill (1,464 yds and 12 TDs pass), SE Travis Price (23 pass rec for 389 yds and 5 TDs), TE Kevin Sprinkles (15 pass rec for 249 yds), OT Charles Odiorne, OG Nathan Richburg, C Len Wright, soph K Lin Elliott, DE Tom Mathiasmeier, DT Charles Perry, LB Charles Rowe, frosh DB Tracy Saul (8 int), P Jamie Simmons (41.4-yd avg). *Noteworthy:* beat Duke 49–21 in All-American Bowl; Gray ran for 280 yds and 4 TDs (including 54-yd run).

Bowl Summary

All-American 1–0; Bluebonnet 0–1; Cotton 0–1; Gator 2–1; Independence 0–1; Peach 0–0–1; Raisin 0–1; Sun 1–7; Tangerine 0–1.

Bowl Record (4–13–1)

Regular Season	Bowl	Score	Opponent	Record
1937 (8–3)	Sun	6–7	West Virginia	(7–1–1)
1938 (10–0)	Cotton	13–20	St. Mary's	(6–2)
1941 (9–1)	Sun	0–6	Tulsa	(7–2)
1947 (6–4)	Sun	12–13	Miami (Ohio)	(8–0–1)
1949 (7–4)	Raisin	13–20	San Jose St.	(8–4)
1951 (6–4)	Sun	25–14	Pacific	(6–4)
1953 (10–1)	Gator	35–13	Auburn	(7–2–1)
1955 (7–2–1)	Sun	14–21	Wyoming	(7–3)
1964 (6–3–1)	Sun	0–7	Georgia	(6–3–1)
1965 (8–2)	Gator	21–31	Georgia Tech	(6–3–1)
1970 (8–3)	Sun	9–17	Georgia Tech	(8–3)
1972 (8–3)	Sun	28–32	North Carolina	(10–1)
1973 (10–1)	Gator	28–19	Tennessee	(8–3)
1974 (6–4–1)	Peach	6–6	Vanderbilt	(7–3–1)
1976 (10–1)	Bluebonnet	24–27	Nebraska	(7–3–1)
1977 (7–4)	Tangerine	17–40	Florida State	(9–2)
1986 (7–4)	Independence	17–20	Mississippi	(7–3–1)
1989 (8–3)	All-American	49–21	Duke	(8–3)

Conference Titles

Border—1937, 1942*, 1944, 1947, 1948, 1949, 1951, 1953, 1954, 1955. **Southwest**—1976*.

TOP 20 AP AND UPI RANKING

1938	11	1965	U–10	1976	13–13
1953	12–12	1973	11–11	1989	19–16

MAJOR RIVALS

Texas Tech has played at least 10 games with Arizona 26–4–2, Arkansas 7–28, Baylor 19–31–1, Hardin-Simmons 14–7–3, Houston 7–17–1, New Mexico 27–5–2, Oklahoma St. 12–8–3, Rice 23–19–1, Southern Methodist 22–16, Texas 9–33, Texas A&M 21–29–1, Texas Christian 25–21–3, Texas–El Paso 11–6–1, Tulsa 11–12, West Texas St. 20–7.

COACHES

Dean of Texas Tech coaches is Pete Cawthon with record of 76–32–6 for 1930–40, including 1 official Border Conference title, 2 bowl teams, and 1 team unbeaten in regular season. Other top records for at least 3 years were by E.Y. Freeland, 21–10–6 for 1925–28; Dell Morgan, 55–49–3 for 1941–50 with 5 Border Conference titles and 3 bowl teams; DeWitt Weaver, 49–51–5 for 1951–60 with 4 Border Conference titles and 3 bowl teams; J.T. King, 44–45–3 for 1961–69 with 2 bowl teams; Jim Carlen, 37–20–2 for 1970–74 with 4 bowl teams; Steve Sloan, 23–12 for 1975–77 with 1 SWC title and 2 bowl teams; and Spike Dykes, 35–32–1 for 1986–92 with 2 bowl teams.

MISCELLANEA

First game was tie with McMurry 0–0 in 1925 . . . 1st win was over Montezuma 30–0 in 1925 . . . highest score was over Wayland 120–0 in 1925 . . . highest since W.W. II was over New Mexico St. 71–0 in 1953 . . . worst defeat was by Miami (Fla.) 61–11 in 1986 . . . longest unbeaten string of 13 in 1973–74 ended by Texas A&M 28–7 . . . longest winless string of 10 in 1981–82 broken with win over Air Force 31–30 . . . longest losing string of 8, in 1956–57 broken with win over Arizona 28–6 and in 1962 with win over Colorado 21–12 . . . consensus All-Americans were E.J. Holub, C, 1960; Donny Anderson, B, 1965; Dan Irons, T, 1977; Gabriel Rivera, DL, 1982; and Mark Bounds, P, 1991 . . . Academic All-Americans were Jeff Jobe, E, 1972; Maury Buford, P, 1979; and Chuck Alexander, DB, 1983.

WESTERN ATHLETIC CONFERENCE

The Western Athletic Conference (WAC) was founded on July 1, 1962, by several of the schools that had made up the defunct Skyline 8 and Border conferences. It is the most geographically diverse league in the country, with members ranging from Wyoming southward to New Mexico and from Colorado westward to Hawaii. The charter members were the universities of Arizona, Arizona State, Brigham Young, New Mexico, Utah, and Wyoming. Colorado State and Texas–El Paso were admitted in 1967 and began football competition in 1968. The conference was stable for 10 years after that until Arizona and Arizona State withdrew in 1978 to join the Pacific-10. In that same year, San Diego State was admitted to membership in the WAC. The University of Hawaii was added in 1979 and Air Force Academy in 1980. Membership was stable for another decade until Fresno State University was admitted in June 1991 as the 10th member, effective July 1, 1992.

FACTS AND ODDITIES ON WAC MEMBERS

The first national champion to come out of the WAC was Brigham Young in 1984. The Cougars were 12–0 behind QB Robbie Bosco, then beat Michigan 24–17 in the Holiday Bowl to finish as the nation's only undefeated team.

The first WAC player to win the Heisman Trophy was Brigham Young QB Ty Detmer in 1990. In the same year, Detmer became the first WAC player to win the Maxwell Award.

No WAC player has won the Lombardi Award, but the Outland Trophy has gone to conference players three times. DT Jason Buck of Brigham Young won in 1986, DT Chad Hennings of Air Force in 1987, and G Mohammed Elewonibi of Brigham Young in 1989.

National Coach of the Year honors went to WAC coaches for three consecutive years in the mid-1980s. Ken Hatfield of Air Force won the American Football Coaches Association (AFCA) part of the award in 1983. Both the AFCA and the Football Writers Association of America shares went to LaVell Edwards of Brigham Young in 1984 and to Fisher DeBerry of Air Force in 1985.

Edwards ranks among the nation's leaders in both coaching victories and winning percentage for a career. He had a record of 191–67–3 for 1972–1992, all at BYU. Included were 14 WAC titles and 17 bowl teams.

The first consensus All-American from a WAC member after the formation of the conference was DL Mike Bell of Colorado State in 1978, although Air Force T Brock Strom made the consensus team in 1958 before the conference was formed, and Falcon E Ernie Jennings was named in 1970, before Air Force became a WAC member.

Utah is part of one of the longest-played series in college football. The Utes' series with Utah State is tied for 15th longest at 90 games, with Utah leading 59–27–4 through 1992.

WAC members have some of the more intriguing nicknames carried by major college football teams, including the Hawaii Rainbow Warriors, the New Mexico Lobos, the San Diego State Aztecs, the Texas–El Paso Miners, and the Utah Utes. More common nicknames are found at Air Force (Falcons), Brigham Young (Cougars), Colorado State (Rams), Fresno State (Bulldogs), and Wyoming (Cowboys).

Cowboys was applied to Wyoming athletic teams as early as 1891, two years before the university's first official football game. In a pickup game with the Cheyenne Soldiers, one of the Wyoming players trotted onto the field in a checkered shirt and a stetson. Someone yelled, "Hey, look at the cowboy!" and the name stuck. New Mexico's athletic teams had been referred to simply as the University boys until 1921, when government trapper Jim Young presented a wolf cub to the university as a mascot. The Spanish name for wolves, *lobos,* was adopted as the official nickname.

Texas–El Paso's nickname dates from the founding of the institution in 1914 as the Texas State School of Mines and Metallurgy. Although the school became part of the University of Texas system in 1919, its name remained Texas Mines until 1949, then became Texas Western, and finally Texas–El Paso in 1967. The first class of cadets at Air Force in September 1955 chose the falcon as the school symbol because its characteristics of speed, courage, keen eyesight, alertness, and noble carriage were considered to be attributes that typify the U.S. Air Force.

Before 1923 Hawaii teams were nicknamed Deans, but in the final game of that season Hawaii upset Oregon State 7–0 when a rainbow (long a sign of magical powers in the islands) appeared over the field. Reporters then started calling Hawaii teams the Rainbows. The nickname evolved into Rainbow Warriors, officially adopted in 1974.

Hawaii's colors also have an unusual derivation. Back in the days when it took weeks to ship materials to the islands, a group of faculty wives were deciding on decorations and color schemes for the school's social calendar. They decided that basic white always would be available and that Hawaii's lush growth of tropical fruits could always provide green. Hence, the choice of green and white.

ALL-TIME WESTERN ATHLETIC
CONFERENCE CHAMPIONS

Annual Champion	WAC Record	Regular Season and Bowl	
1962 New Mexico	2–1–1	7–2–1	
1963 New Mexico	3–1	6–4	
1964 Arizona	3–1	6–3–1	
New Mexico	3–1	9–2	
Utah	3–1	8–2	Liberty (W)
1965 Brigham Young	4–1	6–4	
1966 Wyoming	5–0	9–1	Sun (W)
1967 Wyoming	5–0	10–0	Sugar (L)
1968 Wyoming	6–1	7–3	
1969 Arizona St.	6–1	8–2	
1970 Arizona St.	7–0	10–0	Peach (W)
1971 Arizona St.	7–0	9–1	Fiesta (W)
1972 Arizona St.	5–1	8–2	Fiesta (W)
1973 Arizona	6–1	8–3	
Arizona St.	6–1	10–1	Fiesta (W)
1974 Brigham Young	6–0–1	7–3–1	Fiesta (L)
1975 Arizona St.	7–0	11–0	Fiesta (W)
1976 Brigham Young	6–1	8–3	Tangerine (L)
Wyoming	6–1	8–3	Fiesta (L)
1977 Arizona St.	6–1	9–2	Fiesta (L)
Brigham Young	6–1	9–2	
1978 Brigham Young	5–1	9–2	Holiday (L)
1979 Brigham Young	7–0	11–0	Holiday (L)
1980 Brigham Young	6–1	11–1	Holiday (W)
1981 Brigham Young	7–1	10–2	Holiday (W)
1982 Brigham Young	7–1	8–3	Holiday (L)
1983 Brigham Young	7–0	10–1	Holiday (W)
1984 Brigham Young	8–0	12–0	Holiday (W)
1985 Air Force	7–1	11–1	Bluebonnet (W)
Brigham Young	7–1	11–2	Florida Citrus (L)
1986 San Diego St.	7–1	8–3	Holiday (L)
1987 Wyoming	8–0	10–2	Holiday (L)
1988 Wyoming	8–0	10–2	Holiday (L)
1989 Brigham Young	7–1	10–2	Holiday (L)
1990 Brigham Young	7–1	10–2	Holiday (L)
1991 Brigham Young	7–0–1	8–3–1	Holiday (T)
1992 Hawaii	7–2	10–2	Holiday (W)

AIR FORCE (U.S. AIR FORCE ACADEMY) *(Falcons; Blue and Silver)*

NOTABLE TEAMS

1956 (6–2–1) *Won:* San Diego U. 46–0, Colorado College 53–14, Western St. 48–13, Colorado Mines 49–6, Eastern New Mexico 34–7, Northern Colorado 21–0 in 1st 6 varsity games. *Lost:* Idaho St. 13–7, Brigham Young (BYU) 34–21. *Tied:* Whittier 14–14. *Stars:* FB Larry Thomson (788 yds rush, 12 TDs, 87 pts), E Tom Jozwiak (13 pass rec for 260 yds). *Noteworthy:* coached by Buck Shaw.
1958 (9–0–2) *Won:* Detroit 37–6, Colorado St. 36–6, Stanford 16–0, Utah 16–14, Oklahoma St. 33–29, Denver 10–7, Wyoming 21–6, New Mexico 45–7, Colorado 20–14 (1st meeting). *Tied:* national cochamp Iowa 13–13. *Stars:* T Brock Strom (Falcons' 1st consensus All-American), soph QB Rich Mayo (1,019 yds and 11 TDs pass), E Bob Brickley (25 pass rec for 281 yds), HBs Steve Galios (527 yds rush) and soph Mike Quinlan (8 TDs). *Noteworthy:* Nation's most-improved team had 1st unbeaten season in 1st year under Ben Martin. Made 1st postseason appearance, tying Texas Christian (TCU) 0–0 in rainy Cotton Bowl.
1963 (7–4) *Won:* Washington 10–7, Colorado St. 69–0, Nebraska 17–13, Boston College 34–7, UCLA 48–21, New Mexico 30–8, Colorado 17–14. *Lost:* Southern Methodist (SMU) 10–0, Maryland 21–14, Army 14–10. *Stars:* QB Terry Isaacson (946 yds pass, 801 yds rush, 13 TDs), E Fritz Greenlee (15 pass rec for 323 yds), C Joe Rodwell. *Noteworthy:* lost to North Carolina 35–0 in Gator Bowl; Isaacson passed for 85 yds and ran for 44 yds.
1968 (7–3) *Won:* Wyoming 10–3, Navy 26–20, Colorado St. 31–0, Pittsburgh 27–14, North Carolina 28–15, Tulsa 28–8, Colorado 58–35 (1st over Buffaloes since 1963). *Lost:* Florida 23–20, Stanford 23–13, Arizona 14–10. *Stars:* QB Gary Baxter (1,036 yds pass), E Charlie Longnecker (45 pass rec for 622 yds and 5 TDs), soph FL Ernie Jennings (23 pass rec for 375 yds, 1,026 all-purpose yds), TB Curtis Martin (8 TDs).
1970 (9–3) *Won:* Idaho 45–7, Wyoming 41–17, Missouri 37–14, Colorado St. 37–22, Tulane 24–3, Navy 26–3, Boston College 35–10, Arizona 23–20, Stanford 31–14. *Lost:* Oregon 46–35, Colorado 49–19. *Stars:* Jennings (19 TDs, 74 pass rec for 1,289 yds and 17 TDs, 1,545 all-purpose yds), QB

Bob Parker (2,789 yds and 21 TDs pass), TB Brian Bream (1,276 yds rush, nation's leader with 120 pts on 20 TDs), Jimmy Smith (7 int), P Scott Hamm (41.2-yd avg). *Noteworthy:* lost to Tennessee 34–13 in Sugar Bowl, dropping behind 24–7 in 1st period; Parker passed for 239 yds and a TD (27 yds to E Paul Bassa, who caught 10 for 114 yds).
1983 (10–2) *Won:* Colorado St. 34–13, Texas Tech 28–13, Navy 44–17, Texas–El Paso 37–25, Utah 33–31 (1st meeting since 1958), Army 41–20, Hawaii 45–10, Notre Dame 23–22, San Diego St. 38–7. *Lost:* Wyoming 14–7, BYU 46–28 in successive early games. *Stars:* QB Marty Louthan (16 TDs), FB John Kershner (934 yds and 8 TDs rush), RB Mike Brown, WR Mike Kirby, OL Scott Wachenheim and Mark Melcher, C Don Oberdieck, K Sean Pavlich, DT Chris Funk, DB Greg Zolinger, P Jeff Kubiak. *Noteworthy:* Last year under Ken Hatfield. Beat Mississippi 9–3 in rainy Independence Bowl on FGs of 44, 39, and 27 yds by Pavlich.
1984 (8–4) *Won:* San Diego St. 34–16, Northern Colorado 75–7, Colorado St. 52–10, Navy 29–22, Notre Dame 21–7, New Mexico 23–9, Texas–El Paso 38–12. *Lost:* Wyoming 26–20, Utah 28–17, unbeaten national champ BYU 30–25, Army 24–12. *Stars:* Oberdieck, Melcher, OG Fred Buttrell, HB Jody Smith, Funk, NG Larry Nicklas, soph LB Terry Maki, DB Scott Thomas, soph P Mark Simon. *Noteworthy:* 1st year under Fisher DeBerry. Beat Virginia Tech 23–7 in Independence Bowl; QB Bart Weiss ran for 93 yds and a TD, Brown and Cedric Simmons each scored TDs on short runs, and Carlos Mateos kicked FG and 2 ex pts.
1985 (12–1) *Won:* Texas–El Paso 48–6, Wyoming 49–7, Rice 59–17, New Mexico 49–12, Notre Dame 21–15, Navy 24–7, Colorado St. 35–19, Utah 37–15, San Diego St. 31–10, Army 45–7, Hawaii 27–20. *Lost:* BYU 28–21. *Stars:* Weiss (1,449 yds pass, 1,032 yds rush), Kelly Pittman (14 TDs), WR Ken Carpenter, TE Hugh Brennan, OT Kraig Evenson, C Rusty Wilson, DTs John Ziegler and Chad Hennings, Maki, LB Mike Chandler, Thomas, DB Tom Rotello (8 int, 2 returned for TDs), Simon (nation's leader with 47.3-yd punting avg). *Noteworthy:* Got share of 1st WAC title. Beat Texas 24–16 in Bluebonnet Bowl; Pat Evans ran for 129 yds and a TD, Greg Pshsniak and Weiss scored TDs on short runs, and Tom Ruby kicked 40-yd FG.
1987 (9–4) *Won:* TCU 21–10, San Diego St. 49–7,

Colorado St. 27–19, Utah 48–27, Navy 23–13, Texas–El Paso 35–7, Army 27–10, New Mexico 73–26, Hawaii 34–31. *Lost:* Wyoming 27–13, Notre Dame 35–14, BYU 24–13. *Stars:* Outland Trophy–winner Hennings, DL John Steed, LB Rip Burgwald, soph QB Dee Dowis (1,315 yds and 10 TDs rush), RB Anthony Roberson, OL Roy Garcia and Blake Gettys. *Noteworthy:* lost to Arizona St. 33–28 in Freedom Bowl after falling behind 24–14 at halftime; reserve soph QB Lance McDowell passed for 2 TDs to soph WR Steve Senn in last quarter.

1989 (8–4–1) *Won:* San Diego St. 52–36, Wyoming 45–7, Northwestern 48–31, Texas–El Paso 43–26, Colorado St. 46–21, Navy 35–7, Army 29–3, Utah 42–38. *Lost:* Notre Dame 41–27, TCU 27–9, BYU 44–35. *Tied:* Hawaii 35–35. *Stars:* Dowis (1,286 yds and 18 TDs rush, 1,285 yds and 7 TDs pass), Senn (30 pass rec for 586 yds), TE Trent Van Hulzen (26 pass rec for 529 yds), FB Rodney Lewis (1,063 yds and 7 TDs rush), HB Greg Johnson (703 yds rush, 17 TDs), soph K Joe Wood (10 FGs, 78 pts), LBs Brian Hill and Terry Walker. *Noteworthy:* lost to Mississippi 42–29 in Liberty Bowl; Dowis ran for 92 yds and a TD but had to leave game in 3rd quarter, and backup QB McDowell passed for 2 TDs to Senn in 4th quarter.

1991 (10–3) *Won:* Weber St. 48–31, Colorado St. 31–26, Utah 24–21, San Diego St. 21–20, Wyoming 51–28, Navy 46–6 (10th straight over Midshipmen), Texas–El Paso 20–13, Army 25–0, Hawaii 24–20. *Lost:* BYU 21–7, Notre Dame 28–15, New Mexico 34–32 (1st to Lobos in 5 games since 1982). *Stars:* QB Rob Perez (1,157 yds and 10 TDs rush, 732 yds and 6 TDs pass), WR Scott Hufford (8 pass rec for 334 yds), FB Jason Jones (771 yds and 7 TDs rush), soph HB Obasi Onuoha (6 TDs), OT Steed Lobotzke, Wood (17 FGs, 88 pts), LBs Hill, Vergil Simpson and Kette Dornbusch, DB Carlton McDonald (6 int), P Jason Christ (45.7-yd avg). *Noteworthy:* beat Mississippi St. 38–15 in Liberty Bowl; Perez ran for 114 yds and a TD, Jones ran for 73 yds and a score, and other TDs came on 35-yd fumble return by DB Shanon Yates, 31-yd run by Hufford, and fumble recovery in end zone by Simpson.

Bowl Summary

Bluebonnet 1–0; Cotton 0–0–1; Freedom 0–1; Gator 0–1; Hall of Fame 1–0; Independence 2–0; Liberty 2–2; Sugar 0–1.

Bowl Record (6–5–1)

Regular Season	Bowl	Score	Opponent	Record
1958 (9–0–1)	Cotton	0–0	TCU	(8–2)
1963 (7–3)	Gator	0–35	North Carolina	(8–2)
1970 (9–2)	Sugar	13–34	Tennessee	(10–1)
1982 (7–5)	Hall of Fame	36–28	Vanderbilt	(8–3)
1983 (9–2)	Independence	9–3	Mississippi	(6–5)
1984 (7–4)	Independence	23–7	Virginia Tech	(8–3)
1985 (11–1)	Bluebonnet	24–16	Texas	(8–3)
1987 (9–3)	Freedom	28–33	Arizona State	(6–4–1)
1989 (8–3–1)	Liberty	29–42	Mississippi	(8–3)
1990 (6–5)	Liberty	23–11	Ohio State	(7–3–1)
1991 (9–3)	Liberty	38–15	Mississippi St.	(7–4)
1992 (7–4)	Liberty	0–13	Mississippi	(8–3)

Conference Titles

Western Athletic—1985*.

TOP 20 AP AND UPI RANKING

1958	6–8	1983	13–15	1985	8–5

MAJOR RIVALS

Air Force has played at least 10 games with Army 15–11–1, Brigham Young 1–14, Colorado 4–12, Colorado St. 20–10–1, Hawaii 7–4–1, Navy 17–8, New Mexico 9–5, Notre Dame 4–17, Oregon 3–7–1, San Diego St. 10–3, Texas–El Paso 11–1, UCLA 4–6–1, Utah 9–3, Wyoming 14–14–3. Record against new WAC member Fresno St.: 0–0 (no games played).

COACHES

Dean of Air Force coaches is Ben Martin with record of 96–103–9 for 1958–77, including 3 bowl teams and 1 unbeaten team. Other top records for at least 3 years were by Ken Hatfield (1983 national Coach of Year), 27–31–1 for 1979–82 with 1 bowl champion; and Fisher DeBerry (1985 national Coach of Year), 72–38–1 for 1983–92 with 1 WAC title and 8 bowl teams.

MISCELLANEA

First varsity game was win over San Diego U. 46–0 in 1956 . . . highest score was over Northern Colorado 75–7 in 1984 . . . biggest margin was over Colorado St. 69–0 in 1963 . . . worst defeat was by Notre Dame 49–0 in 1977 . . . highest against was by Notre Dame 57–27 in 1990 . . . longest unbeaten string of 14 in 1958–59 ended by Oregon 20–3 . . . longest win string of 13 in 1984–85 ended by Brigham Young 28–20 . . . longest winless string of 12 in 1974–75 broken with win over Army 33–3 . . . longest losing string of 11 in 1978–79 broken with win over Army 28–7 . . . consensus All-Americans were Brock Strom, T, 1958; Ernie Jennings, E, 1970; Scott Thomas, DB, 1985; Chad Hennings, DL, 1987; and Carlton McDonald, DB, 1992 . . . Academic All-Americans were Brock Strom, T, 1958; Rich Mayo, B, 1959–60; Ernie Jennings, E, 1970; Darryl Haas, LB, K, 1971; Bob Homburg, DE, and Mark

Prill, LB, 1972; Joe Debes, OT, 1973–74; Steve Hoog, WR, 1978; Mike France, LB, 1981; Jeff Kubiak, P, 1983; Chad Hennings, DL, 1986–87; David Hlatky, OL, 1989; Chris Howard, RB, 1990; and Grant Johnson, LB, 1992 . . . Outland Trophy winner was Chad Hennings, DL, 1987.

BRIGHAM YOUNG (Cougars; Royal Blue and White)

NOTABLE TEAMS

1932 (8–1) *Won:* Montana St. 6–0, Western St. 28–6 (10 wins in as many games in series), Occidental 46–0, Colorado St. Teachers 20–2, Wyoming 25–0, Idaho St. 32–0, Utah St. 18–6, South Dakota 13–7. *Lost:* Utah 29–0.

1966 (8–2) *Won:* San Jose St. 19–9, Colorado St. 27–24, Utah St. 27–7, New Mexico 33–6, Arizona 16–14, Texas Western (Texas–El Paso) 53–33, Utah 35–13, Pacific 38–0. *Lost:* Arizona St. 10–7, Wyoming 47–14. *Stars:* QB Virgil Carter (2,182 yds and 21 TDs pass, 363 yds and 9 TDs rush, nation's leader with 2,545 yds total off), WR Phil Odle (58 pass rec for 920 yds and 5 TDs), FB John Ogden (906 yds rush), G Grant Wilson, LB Curt Belcher, DB Bobby Roberts (7 int).

1976 (9–3) *Won:* Colorado St. 42–18, Arizona 23–16, San Diego St. 8–0 (1st meeting since 1970), Southern Mississippi 63–19, Utah St. 45–14, Arizona St. 43–21, Texas–El Paso 40–27, New Mexico 21–8, Utah 34–12. *Lost:* Kansas St. 13–3, Wyoming 34–29. *Stars:* QB Gifford Nielsen (3,192 yds and 29 TDs pass), Todd Christensen (51 pass rec for 510 yds), RB Jeff Blanc (625 yds rush), TE Brian Billick, OL Dave Hubbard, K Dave Taylor (15 FGs, 79 pts), DL Mekeli Ieremia and Bill Rice, LBs Rod Wood and Blake Murdock, DB Dana Wilgar. *Noteworthy:* Led nation in pass and got share of 3rd WAC title. Lost to Oklahoma St. 49–21 in Tangerine Bowl, losing ball on 4 int and a fumble; Nielsen passed for 209 yds and a

TD, and Dave Lowry scored on 100-yd kickoff return.

1977 (9–2)   *Won:* Kansas St. 39–0, Utah St. 65–6, New Mexico 54–19, Colorado St. 63–17, Wyoming 10–7, Arizona 34–14, Utah 38–8, Long Beach St. 30–27, Texas–El Paso 68–19.   *Lost:* Oregon St. 24–19, Arizona St. 24–13.   *Stars:* Christensen (50 pass rec for 603 yds and 5 TDs), Nielsen (1,167 yds and 16 TDs pass), soph QB Marc Wilson (2,418 yds and 24 TDs pass), WRs Mike Chronister and John VanDerWouden (43 pass rec), OTs Keith Uperesa and Lance Reynolds, K Dev Duke (73 pts), LBs Ieremia and Mark Bernsten, DB Jason Coloma. *Noteworthy:* again led nation in pass and got share of 4th WAC crown.

1978 (9–4)   *Won:* Oregon St. 10–6, Colorado St. 32–6, New Mexico 27–23, Oregon 17–16, Texas–El Paso 44–0, Wyoming 48–14, San Diego St. 21–3, Hawaii 31–13, Nevada–Las Vegas 28–24 (in Yokohama, Japan).   *Lost:* Arizona St. 24–16, Utah St. 24–7, Utah 23–22 (1st to Utes since 1971).   *Stars:* Wilson (1,499 yds pass), soph QB Jim McMahon (1,307 yds pass, 248 yds rush), Chronister (52 pass rec for 850 yds), Bill Ring (520 yds rush, 11 TDs), OL Tom Bell and Al Gaspard, DL Mat Mendenhall and Ross Varner, LB Larry Miller, Coloma. *Noteworthy:* Won 3rd straight WAC title. Lost to Navy 23–16 in inaugural Holiday Bowl after leading 16–10 going into final quarter; McMahon passed for 133 yds and a TD (10 yds to Chronister) and scored another.

1979 (11–1)   *Won:* Texas A&M 18–17, Weber St. 48–3, Texas–El Paso 31–7, Hawaii 38–15, Utah St. 48–24, Wyoming 54–14, New Mexico 59–7, Colorado St. 30–7, Long Beach St. 31–17, Utah 27–0, San Diego St. 63–14.   *Stars:* Wilson (Cougars' 1st consensus All-American; 3,720 yds and 29 TDs pass, nation's leader with 3,580 yds total off), WR Lloyd Jones, RB Homer Jones (46 pass rec for 404 yds), FB Eric Lane (595 yds rush), TE/P Clay Brown (nation's leader with 45.3-yd punting avg), Bell, OL Nick Eyre and Danny Hansen, OG Scott Nielsen, K Brent Johnson (10 FGs, 82 pts), DE Glen Titensor, LBs Glen Redd and Gary Kama, DBs John Neal and Bill Schoepflin.   *Noteworthy:* Again won WAC title while leading nation in total off, pass, and scoring (40.6-pt avg) in 1st unbeaten season. Lost to Indiana 38–37 in Holiday Bowl; Wilson passed for 380 yds and 2 TDs.

1980 (12–1)   *Won:* San Diego St. 35–11, Wisconsin

28–3, Long Beach St. 41–25, Wyoming 52–17, Utah St. 70–46, Hawaii 34–7, Texas–El Paso 83–7 (10th straight over Miners), North Texas St. 41–23, Colorado St. 45–14, Utah 56–6, Nevada–Las Vegas 54–14.   *Lost:* New Mexico 25–21 (1st to Lobos since 1971).   *Stars:* McMahon (6 TDs rush, nation's leader with 4,571 yds and 47 TDs pass and with 4,627 yds total off), Scott Phillips (60 pass rec for 689 yds), Lloyd Jones, Lane (43 pass rec), Brown (48 pass rec, 39.9-yd punting avg), Eyre, OG Calvin Close, Titensor, DE Brad Anae, Redd, Schoepflin, soph Tom Holmoe (7 int), DB Mark Brady. *Noteworthy:* Again led nation in total off, pass, and scoring (46.7-pt avg) and won 5th straight WAC title. Beat Southern Methodist (SMU) 46–45 in Holiday Bowl (1st bowl win in 5 tries) after trailing 45–25 with 4:07 left; McMahon passed for 446 yds and 4 TDs (including 46-yarder to Brown to tie game with 3 seconds left), and soph K Kurt Gunther kicked winning ex pt.

1981 (11–2)   *Won:* Long Beach St. 31–8, Air Force 45–21 (1st meeting since 1975), Texas–El Paso 65–8, Colorado 41–20 (1st meeting since 1947), Utah St. 32–26, San Diego St. 27–7, New Mexico 31–7, Colorado St. 63–14, Hawaii 13–3, Utah 56–28. *Lost:* Nevada–Las Vegas 45–41, Wyoming 33–20 (1st to Cowboys since 1976).   *Stars:* McMahon (nation's leader with 3,555 yds and 30 TDs pass and with 3,458 yds total off), soph TE Gordon Hudson (67 pass rec for 960 yds and 10 TDs), WRs Dan Plater (62 pass rec for 891 yds and 5 TDs), Neil Balholm (31 pass rec for 465 yds), Glen Kozlowski (29 pass rec for 376 yds and 5 TDs) and Scott Collie (26 pass rec for 404 yds), TB Scott Pettis (48 pass rec for 490 yds and 4 TDs, 499 yds and 5 TDs rush), FB Waymon Hamilton (32 pass rec for 387 yds, 16 TDs), Close, Gunther (10 FGs, 87 pts), Anae, LB Kyle Whittingham, P Mike Mees (40.9-yd avg).   *Noteworthy:* Led nation in pass and scoring (38.7-pt avg) and won 6th straight WAC title. Beat Washington St. 38–36 in Holiday Bowl after jumping to 24–7 halftime lead; McMahon passed for 342 yds and 3 TDs, and Hudson caught 7 for 126 yds and a TD.

1982 (8–4)   *Won:* Nevada–Las Vegas 27–0, Texas–El Paso 51–3, New Mexico 40–12, Hawaii 39–25, Colorado St. 34–18, Wyoming 23–13, San Diego St. 58–8, Utah 17–12.   *Lost:* unbeaten Georgia 17–14, Air Force 39–38 (1st in 5-game series dating to 1956), Utah St. 20–17.   *Stars:* Hudson (67 pass rec for 928 yds and 6 TDs), QB Steve Young (3,100 yds and 18 TDs pass, 407 yds and 10 TDs rush), Casey Tiumalu (681 yds rush), C Bart Oates, OG Lloyd Eldredge, OT Vince Stroth, Gunther (11 FGs, 74 pts), NG Chuck Ehin, DT Mike Morgan, LB Todd Shell, Holmoe, Mees (45.6-yd punting avg). *Noteworthy:* Won 7th straight WAC title. Lost to Ohio St. 47–17 in Holiday Bowl after trailing only 17–10 at halftime; Young passed for 341 yds and 2 TDs, and Hudson caught 7 for 81 yds and a TD.

1983 (11–1)   *Won:* Bowling Green 63–28, Air Force 46–28, UCLA 37–35, Wyoming 41–10, New Mexico 66–21, San Diego St. 47–12, Utah St. 38–34, Texas–El Paso 31–9, Colorado St. 24–6, Utah 55–7.   *Lost:* Baylor 40–36 in opener.   *Stars:* Young (444 yds and 8 TDs rush, nation's leader with 3,902 yds and 33 TDs pass and with 4,346 yds total off), Hudson (44 pass rec for 596 yds and 6 TDs), Tiumalu (60 pass rec for 583 yds, 851 yds rush), Kirk Pendleton (50 pass rec), Eddie Stinnett (50 pass rec), OT Rex Burningham, K/P Lee Johnson (11 FGs, 85 pts, 50.6-yd avg on 24 punts), DE Brandon Flint, Shell, DB Jon Young.   *Noteworthy:* Led nation in total off and pass while winning 10th WAC title (8th in a row). Beat Missouri 21–17 in Holiday Bowl; Young passed for 314 yds and a TD (33 yds to Stinnett), ran 10 yds for a TD, and scored other Cougar TD on 15-yd pass from Stinnett.

1984 (13–0)   *Won:* Pittsburgh 20–14, Baylor 47–13, Tulsa 38–15, Hawaii 18–13, Colorado St. 52–9, Wyoming 41–38, Air Force 30–25, New Mexico 48–0, Texas–El Paso 42–9, San Diego St. 34–3, Utah 24–14, Utah St. 38–13.   *Stars:* QB Robbie Bosco (3,875 yds and 33 TDs pass, nation's leader with 3,932 yds total off), Kozlowski (55 pass rec for 879 yds and 11 TDs), TE David Mills (60 pass rec for 1,023 yds and 7 TDs), Kelly Smith (46 pass rec), soph FB Lakei Heimuli (796 yds rush), C Trevor Matich, OG Craig Garrick, Johnson (13 FGs, 82 pts, 45.5-yd punting avg), DE Jim Herrmann, LB Marv Allen, DB Kyle Morrell.   *Noteworthy:* Led nation in total off and pass while winning 9th straight WAC crown. Beat Michigan 24–17 in Holiday Bowl to win 1st national championship; Bosco (despite severe 1st quarter ankle injury) passed for 343 yds and 2 TDs (7 yds to Kozlowski and 13 yards to Smith for winning score with 1:23 left), Smith scored on 5-yd run, and Johnson kicked 31-yd FG and 3 ex pts.

1985 (11–3)   *Won:* Boston College 28–14, Wash-ington 31–3, Temple 26–24, Colorado St. 42–7 (10th straight over Rams), San Diego St. 28–0, New Mexico 45–23, Wyoming 59–0, Utah St. 44–0, Air Force 28–21, Utah 38–28, Hawaii 26–6.   *Lost:* UCLA 27–24, Texas–El Paso 23–16 (1st to Miners since 1970).   *Stars:* Bosco (4,273 yds and 30 TDs pass), WR Mark Bellini (63 pass rec for 1,008 yds and 14 TDs), Heimuli (66 pass rec for 459 yds, 857 yds rush, 14 TDs), TE Trevor Molini (63 pass rec), Smith (49 pass rec), OT Dave Wright, DT Jason Buck, LBs Kurt Gouveia and Leon White, P Kevin Towle (41.2-yd avg).   *Noteworthy:* Led nation in pass and total off while taking share of 10th straight WAC title (12th overall). Lost to Ohio St. 10–7 in Florida Citrus Bowl, losing ball 6 times on turnovers; Bosco passed for 261 yds, including 38-yd TD pass to David Miles.

1987 (9–4)   *Won:* Texas 22–17, New Mexico 45–25, Utah St. 45–24, Hawaii 16–14, Air Force 24–13, San Diego St. 38–21, Texas–El Paso 37–24, Utah 21–18, Colorado St. 30–26 (in Melbourne, Australia).   *Lost:* Pittsburgh 27–17, Texas Christian (TCU) 33–12, Wyoming 29–27 (1st to Cowboys since 1981).   *Stars:* QBs Bob Jensen (1,833 yds and 10 TDs pass) and Sean Covey (1,668 yds pass), TE Darren Handley (52 pass rec for 636 yds), frosh HB Matt Bellini (51 pass rec for 548 yds), OG John Borgia, K Leonard Chitty (18 FGs, 86 pts), NG David Futrell, LB Thor Salanoa, DBs Rodney Rice (6 int) and Troy Long, P Pat Thompson (43.3-yd avg).   *Noteworthy:* lost to Virginia 22–16 in All-American Bowl; Kyle Whittingham scored on 8-yd run and 1-yd pass rec, Chitty had 20-yd FG, and Miles had 188 yds on pass rec.

1988 (9–4)   *Won:* Texas 47–6, Texas–El Paso 31–27, Utah St. 38–3, Colorado St. 42–7, TCU 31–18, Hawaii 24–23 (10th straight over Rainbow Warriors), New Mexico 65–0, Air Force 49–31.   *Lost:* Wyoming 24–14, San Diego St. 27–15, Utah 57–28 (1st to Utes since 1978), Miami (Fla.) 41–17.   *Stars:* Covey (2,607 yds and 13 TDs pass), frosh QB Ty Detmer (1,252 yds and 13 TDs pass), WRs Chuck Cutler (64 pass rec for 1,039 yds and 10 TDs) and Jeff Frandsen (20 pass rec for 417 yds), Bellini (51 pass rec for 786 yds, 11 TDs), Handley (34 pass rec for 430 yds), FB Fred Whittingham (27 pass rec for 220 yds, 513 yds rush), OT Brian White, LB Bob Davis, Rice (6 int), Thompson (44.8-yd punting avg).   *Noteworthy:* beat Colorado 20–17 in Free-dom Bowl; Detmer passed for 129 yds and a TD

QB Ty Detmer, 1988–91

(to Cutler) in 2nd half, Jason Chaffetz kicked 2 FGs in 4th quarter, and Bellini ran for 78 yds and caught 4 passes for 41 yds.

1989 (10–3) *Won:* New Mexico 24–3, Navy 31–10, Utah St. 37–10, Wyoming 36–20, Colorado St. 45–16, Texas–El Paso 49–24, Oregon 45–41, Air Force 44–35, Utah 70–31, San Diego St. 48–27. *Lost:* Washington St. 46–41, Hawaii 56–14 (1st to Rainbow Warriors in 11 games since 1974). *Stars:* Detmer (6 TDs rush, nation's leader with 4,560 yds and 32 TDs pass), TE Chris Smith (60 pass rec for 1,090 yds and 5 TDs), Bellini (43 pass rec for 700 yds, 12 TDs), WR Andy Boyce (39 pass rec for 712 yds), Whittingham (34 pass rec for 465 yds, 582 yds rush, 11 TDs), Frandsen (32 pass rec for 596 yds and 9 TDs), HB Stacey Corley (9 TDs), OG Mohammed Elewonibi (Outland Trophy winner), Chaffetz (10 FGs, 83 pts), Davis, DBs Brian Mitchell (5 int) and Eric Bergeson, soph P Earl Kauffman (42-yd avg). *Noteworthy:* Won 13th WAC title. Lost to Penn St. 50–39 in Holiday Bowl; Detmer passed for 576 yds and 2 TDs and scored 2 TDs, Bellini had 10 pass rec for 124 yds, Boyce had 8 pass rec for 127 yds and a TD, WR Brent Nyberg had 8 pass rec for 117 yds and a TD, Whittingham scored on 10-yd run, and Chaffetz kicked 2 FGs.

1990 (10–3) *Won:* Texas–El Paso 30–10, Miami (Fla.) 28–21, Washington St. 50–36, San Diego St. 62–34, Colorado St. 52–9, New Mexico 55–31 (10th straight over Lobos), Air Force 54–7, Wyoming 45–14, Utah 45–22, Utah St. 45–10. *Lost:* Oregon 32–16, Hawaii 59–28. *Stars:* Heisman Trophy- and Maxwell Award–winner Detmer (5,188 yds and 41 TDs pass), Boyce (79 pass rec for 1,241 yds and 13 TDs), Smith (68 pass rec for 1,156 yds), Bellini (59 pass rec for 601 yds), Nyberg (47 pass rec for 816 yds), RB Peter Tuipulotu (637 yds and 9 TDs rush, 28 pass rec for 253 yds and 2 TDs), soph WR Micah Matsuzaki (26 pass rec for 493 yds and 6 TDs), Corley (8 TDs), OL Neal Fort, C Bob Stephens, Kauffman (11 FGs, 91 pts, 43.3-yd punting avg), DT Rich Kaufusi, LBs Rocky Biegel and Alema Fitisemanu, Mitchell, soph DB Derwin Gray (6 int). *Noteworthy:* Won 14th WAC title. Lost to Texas A&M 65–14 in Holiday Bowl; Detmer passed for 120 yds and a TD before leaving game with injury early in 3rd quarter.

1991 (8–3–2) *Won:* Air Force 21–7, Utah St. 38–10, Texas–El Paso 31–29, Hawaii 35–18, New Mexico 41–23, Colorado St. 40–17, Wyoming 56–3, Utah 48–17. *Lost:* Florida St. 44–28, UCLA 27–23, Penn St. 33–7 in 1st 3 games. *Tied:* San Diego St. 52–52. *Stars:* Detmer (4,031 yds and 35 TDs pass; nation's leader with 4,001 yds total off), soph WR Eric Drage (46 pass rec for 1,018 yds and 10 TDs), Tuipulotu (619 yds rush, 8 TDs, 41 pass rec for 587 yds), TE Byron Rex (38 pass rec for 547 yds), Matsuzaki (26 pass rec for 437 yds), WRs Nati Valdez (24 pass rec for 338 yds) and soph Tyler Anderson (14 pass rec for 293 yds), frosh RB Jamal Willis (520 yds rush, 8 TDs, 942 all-purpose yds), OG Bryan May, frosh DT Randy Brock, LB Shad Hansen, Biegel, Gray. *Noteworthy:* Won 15th

WAC title (3rd straight). Tied Iowa 13–13 in Holiday Bowl; Detmer passed for 350 yds and both TDs (9 yds to Tuipulotu, who caught 8 for 85 yds, and 29 yds to Anderson).

BOWL SUMMARY

All-American 0–1; Aloha 0–1; Fiesta 0–1; Florida Citrus 0–1; Freedom 1–1; Holiday 4–5–1; Tangerine 0–1.

BOWL RECORD (5–11–1)

Regular Season	Bowl	Score	Opponent	Record
1974 (7–3–1)	Fiesta	6–6	Oklahoma State	(6–5)
1976 (9–2)	Tangerine	21–49	Oklahoma State	(8–3)
1978 (9–3)	Holiday	16–23	Navy	(8–3)
1979 (11–0)	Holiday	37–38	Indiana	(7–4)
1980 (11–1)	Holiday	46–45	SMU	(8–3)
1981 (10–2)	Holiday	38–36	Washington State	(8–2–1)
1982 (8–3)	Holiday	17–47	Ohio State	(8–3)
1983 (10–1)	Holiday	21–17	Missouri	(7–4)
1984 (12–0)	Holiday	24–17	Michigan	(6–5)
1985 (11–2)	Florida Citrus	7–10	Ohio State	(8–3)
1986 (8–4)	Freedom	10–31	UCLA	(7–3–1)
1987 (9–3)	All-American	16–22	Virginia	(7–4)
1988 (8–4)	Freedom	20–17	Colorado	(8–3)
1989 (10–2)	Holiday	39–50	Penn State	(7–3–1)
1990 (10–2)	Holiday	14–65	Texas A&M	(8–3–1)
1991 (8–3–1)	Holiday	13–13	Iowa	(10–1)
1992 (8–4)	Aloha	20–23	Kansas	(7–4)

CONFERENCE TITLES

Western Athletic—1965, 1974, 1976*, 1977*, 1978, 1979, 1980, 1981, 1982, 1983, 1984, 1985*, 1989, 1990, 1991.

TOP 20 AP AND UPI RANKING

1977	20–16	1981	13–11	1984	1–1	1989	U–18
1979	13–12	1983	7–7	1985	16–17	1990	U–17
1980	12–11						

MAJOR RIVALS

BYU has played at least 10 games with Air Force 14–1, Arizona 8–10–1, Arizona St. 5–18, Colorado 3–8–1, Colorado St. 28–23–3, Denver 7–15, Hawaii 12–7, Montana 10–4, Montana St. 10–7, New Mexico 30–11–1, Northern Colorado 7–4–1, San Diego St. 13–5–1, San Jose St. 4–9, Texas–El Paso 24–6–1, Utah 24–40–4, Utah St. 33–32–3, Western St. 20–0, Wyoming 32–28–3. Record against new WAC member Fresno St.: 2–3.

COACHES

Dean of BYU coaches is LaVell Edwards (1984 national Coach of Year) with record of 191–67–3 for 1972–92, including 14 WAC titles, 17 bowl teams, 2 teams unbeaten in regular season, and 1 national champion. Other top records for at least 3 years were by G. Ott Romney, 42–31–5 for 1928–36; Eddie Kimball, 34–32–8 for 1937–48; and Tom Hudspeth, 39–42–1 for 1964–71 with 1 WAC title.

MISCELLANEA

First game was loss to Utah St. 42–3 in 1922 . . . 1st win was over Wyoming 7–0 in 1922 . . . highest score was over Texas–El Paso 83–7 in 1980 . . . worst defeat was by Texas A&M 65–14 in 1990 Holiday Bowl . . . longest win streak of 25 in 1983–85 ended by UCLA 27–24 . . . 17-game win streak in 1980–81 ended by Nevada–Las Vegas 45–41 . . . longest winless string of 14 in 1955–56 broken with win over New Mexico 33–12 . . . longest losing string of 11 in 1949 broken with win over Idaho St. 14–13 in 1950 opener . . . consensus All-Americans were Marc Wilson, QB, 1979; Nick Eyre, OL, 1980; Jim McMahon, QB, 1981; Gordon Hudson, TE, 1982–83; Steve Young, QB, 1983; Jason Buck, DL, 1986; Mohammed Elewonibi, OL, 1989; and Chris Smith, TE, and Ty Detmer, QB, 1990 . . . Academic All-Americans were Steve Stratton, RB, 1973; Scott Phillips, RB, 1980; Dan Platter, WR, 1981; Chuck Cutler, WR, 1987–88; Tim Clark, DL, 1988; Fred Whittingham, RB, 1989; Andy Boyce, WR, 1990; and Ty Detmer, QB, 1991 . . . Heisman Trophy winner was Ty Detmer, QB, 1990 . . . Maxwell Award winner was Ty Detmer, QB, 1990 . . . Outland Trophy winners were Jason Buck, DT, 1986; and Mohammed Elewonibi, OG, 1989.

COLORADO STATE (Rams; Green and Gold)

NOTABLE TEAMS

1903 (5–1) *Won:* Colorado Mines 10–2 (1st in 6-game series dating to 1893), Colorado College 8–5 (1st in 4-game series dating to 1900), Wyoming 17–0, Denver 16–6, Utah 16–6. *Lost:* Colorado 5–0 in opener. *Noteworthy:* had 1st winning season in last year under C.J. Griffith.
1915 (7–0) *Won:* Colorado 23–6, Utah 21–9, Utah

St. 59–0, Colorado Mines 35–0 (1st over Orediggers in 10 games since 1903), Wyoming 48–0, Colorado College 24–13 (1st over Tigers in 5 games since 1906), Denver 33–3. *Stars:* E Ralph Robinson, soph C Charles Shepardson, G Frank Wilson. *Noteworthy:* won 1st Rocky Mountain Conference title in 1st unbeaten season.
1916 (6–0–1) *Won:* Wyoming 40–0, Utah St. 53–0, Colorado College 14–12, Denver 21–13, Utah 12–6, Colorado 32–14. *Tied:* Colorado Mines 0–0. *Stars:* Robinson, Shepardson, T Horace Doke, G Ray West. *Noteworthy:* repeated as Rocky Mountain champ.
1919 (7–1) *Won:* Wyoming 28–0, 14–0, Utah 34–21, Colorado 49–7, Denver 33–3, Utah St. 27–7, Colorado Mines 33–6. *Lost:* Colorado College 13–0 in finale. *Stars:* soph HB Duane Hartshorn, FB Harry Scott, T H.L. "Hap" Dotson. *Noteworthy:* won 3rd Rocky Mountain title.
1920 (6–1–1) *Won:* Wyoming 13–0, 42–0, Colorado Mines 27–0, Utah St. 21–0, Colorado College 28–0, Denver 14–0. *Lost:* Nebraska 7–0. *Tied:* Colorado 7–7. *Stars:* Hartshorn, Scott, Dotson, E Charles Bresnahan, G Roy Ratekin. *Noteworthy:* repeated as Rocky Mountain champ.
1925 (9–1) *Won:* Regis 34–0, Brigham Young (BYU) 21–7, Denver 17–0, Colorado College 7–3, Utah St. 13–0, Northern Colorado 43–18, Colorado 12–0, Colorado Mines 41–10, Wyoming 40–0. *Lost:* unbeaten Hawaii 41–0 (1st meeting) on New Year's Day. *Stars:* QB Kenny Hyde, FB Otto Kayser, soph HB Fay Rankin, Gs Julius Wagner and Glen Clark. *Noteworthy:* won 5th Rocky Mountain title.
1926 (6–2–1) *Won:* Regis 39–0, Colorado Mines 53–0, Denver 7–6, Colorado College 19–6, Colorado 3–0, BYU 19–6. *Lost:* unbeaten Utah 10–6 (1st meeting since 1919), Utah St. 13–0 in successive mid-season games. *Tied:* Arizona 3–3 (1st meeting). *Stars:* Rankin, FB Rollie Caldwell.
1927 (7–1) *Won:* Northern Colorado 33–0, BYU 29–0, Utah 12–0, Utah St. 6–0, Colorado Mines 37–6, Colorado 39–7, Colorado College 20–7. *Lost:* Denver 6–0 (1st to Pioneers since 1921). *Stars:* Rankin, Caldwell, E Glen Davis, Gs Lynn Pitcher and soph Ed Graves, C Carlisle Vickers. *Noteworthy:* won 6th Rocky Mountain title.
1928 (6–2) *Won:* Northern Colorado 26–6, BYU 15–6, Utah St. 7–6, Denver 15–0, Colorado Mines

46–20 (10th straight over Orediggers), Colorado College 35–13. *Lost:* unbeaten Utah 6–0, Colorado 13–7. *Stars:* Graves, Vickers, Es Dan Beattie and Frank Prince.

1933 (5–1–1) *Won:* Wyoming 7–0, Colorado 19–6, Colorado Mines 19–0, Utah St. 3–0, Colorado College 30–7. *Lost:* Utah 13–0 in finale. *Tied:* Denver 0–0. *Stars:* HBs Wilbur "Red" White and Ralph Maag, QB Bud Dammann, E Glenn Morris. *Noteworthy:* got share of 7th Rocky Mountain title.

1934 (6–2–1) *Won:* Northern Colorado 12–0, Denver 2–0, Colorado Mines 56–0, Wyoming 16–0, Utah 14–6 (1st over Utes since 1927), Colorado College 40–6. *Lost:* Arizona 7–3, Colorado 27–9. *Tied:* Utah St. 21–21. *Stars:* White, E Chet Cruikshank, C Floyd Mencimer. *Noteworthy:* again got share of Rocky Mountain crown.

1948 (8–3) *Won:* Colorado College 25–6, New Mexico St. 41–6, Utah St. 9–7, Denver 14–10 (1st over Pioneers in 12 games since 1934), Wyoming 21–20, Colorado Mines 33–0, BYU 20–0, Colorado 29–25 (1st over Buffs in 13 games since 1933). *Lost:* Drake 31–29, Utah 12–3. *Stars:* QB Bob Hainlen, HBs Eddie Hanna and Ollie Woods, E George Jones, Ts Thurman McGraw, Don Hoch and Don "Tuffy" Mullison, soph G Dale Dodrill. *Noteworthy:* made 1st postseason appearance, losing to unbeaten Occidental 21–20 in Raisin Bowl; Hanna scored on runs of 71 and 79 yds, and Hainlen passed to Keith Thompson for other TD.

1949 (9–1) *Won:* Colorado College 14–7, Denver 14–13, Montana 27–12, Colorado Mines 27–7, Utah St. 28–6, Utah 21–12 (1st over Utes in 13 games since 1934), BYU 16–14, New Mexico St. 45–0, Colorado 14–7. *Lost:* Wyoming 8–0 (1st to Cowboys in 9 games since 1937). *Stars:* McGraw, Dodrill, Jones.

1955 (8–2) *Won:* New Mexico 25–0, Denver 20–19, Wyoming 14–13, Utah St. 26–9, Montana 12–7, Oklahoma St. 20–13, BYU 35–0, Colorado 10–0. *Lost:* Arizona 70–7 (1st meeting since 1937), Utah 27–6. *Stars:* HB Gary Glick (579 yds and 8 TDs rush, 248 yds pass, 66 pts, 5 int), Gary Sanders (24 pass rec for 351 yds), G Dan Mirich, C Bob Weber. *Noteworthy:* won only Skyline 8 title.

1966 (7–3) *Won:* South Dakota 45–14, Utah St. 10–7 (1st over Aggies since 1959), Air Force 41–21

(1st over Falcons in 7 games since 1957), Wyoming 12–10 (1st over Cowboys since 1955), New Mexico 45–6, West Texas St. 35–26, Iowa St. 34–10. *Lost:* BYU 27–24, Tulsa 20–6, Wichita St. 37–23. *Stars:* Oscar Reed (946 yds and 10 TDs rush), Bob Wolfe (890 yds pass), Tom Pack (21 pass rec for 313 yds), Jim Richardson (5 int), soph DB Bill Kishman (5 int). *Noteworthy:* 1st winning season since 1959.

1977 (9–2–1) *Won:* Pacific 20–3, Hawaii 20–16 (1st meeting since 1965), Northern Colorado 48–10, Utah 44–3 (1st over Utes in 9 games since 1959), Texas–El Paso 41–31, New Mexico 14–9, Arizona 35–14 (1st in 12-game series dating to 1926), Arizona St. 25–14 (1st in 16-game series dating to 1950), Utah St. 13–10. *Lost:* BYU 63–17, Wyoming 29–13. *Tied:* West Texas St. 21–21. *Stars:* QB Dan Graham (1,692 yds and 17 TDs pass), Mark Bell (40 pass rec for 797 yds and 9 TDs), Larry Jones (790 yds and 7 TDs rush), K Tom Drake (11 FGs), DT Mike Bell, DE Al Baker, DB Cliff Featherstone (7 int), P Mike Deutsch (43.6-yd avg).

1990 (9–4) *Won:* Air Force 35–33 (1st over Falcons since 1982), Montana St. 41–5, Texas–El Paso 38–20, Utah 22–13, New Mexico 47–7, Wyoming 17–8, Tulsa 31–13, Hawaii 30–27. *Lost:* Arizona St. 31–20, Arkansas 31–20, BYU 52–9, Louisiana Tech 31–30. *Stars:* QBs Kevin Verdugo (1,153 yds pass) and Mike Gimenez (1,103 yds pass), soph SE Greg Primus (54 pass rec for 945 yds), FL Mark Holmes (22 pass rec for 361 yds), TBs Brian Copeland (945 yds and 5 TDs rush, 20 pass rec for 190 yds and 2 TDs) and Tony Alford (679 yds and 8 TDs rush), FB Todd Yert (592 yds and 16 TDs rush), OG John Laurita, K Mike Brown (10 FGs), DT Eric Schaller, LBs Eric Tippeconnic and soph Otis Hamilton, Selwyn Jones (6 int), DBs Andy Byrne and soph Sylvester Mabry (5 int), P Tim Luke (40.5-yd avg). *Noteworthy:* made 1st bowl appearance in 42 years, edging Oregon 32–31 in Freedom Bowl by stopping Ducks' 2-pt conversion try with 1:01 left; scored 4th quarter TDs on 49-yd pass from Gimenez (who ran for 1st TD of game) to Primus and 52-yd run by Yert.

BOWL SUMMARY

Freedom 1–0; Raisin 0–1.

BOWL RECORD (1–1)

Regular Season	Bowl	Score	Opponent	Record
1948 (8–2)	Raisin	20–21	Occidental	(8–0)
1990 (8–4)	Freedom	32–31	Oregon	(8–3)

CONFERENCE TITLES

Rocky Mountain—1915, 1916, 1919, 1920, 1925, 1927, 1933*, 1934*. **Skyline 8**—1955. **Western Athletic**—None.

TOP 20 AP AND UPI RANKING

None.

MAJOR RIVALS

Colorado St. has played at least 10 games with Air Force 10–20–1, Arizona 2–13–1, Arizona St. 1–19, Brigham Young 23–28–3, Colorado 15–49–2, Colorado College 20–6–5, Colorado Mines 27–16–2, Denver 28–26–5, Hawaii 8–9, Montana 10–6, New Mexico 23–19, Northern Colorado 16–0–1, Pacific 7–3, San Diego St. 4–9, Texas–El Paso 20–9, Utah 16–45–2, Utah St. 32–30–2, Wyoming 43–36–5. Record against new WAC member Fresno St.: 0–1.

COACHES

Dean of Colorado St. coaches is Harry Hughes with record of 125–92–18 for 1911–41, including 8 Rocky Mountain Conference titles and 2 unbeaten teams. Other top records for at least 3 years were by Bob Davis, 54–33–2 for 1947–55 with 1 Skyline 8 title and 1 bowl team; Sark Arslanian, 46–52–4 for 1973–81; and Earle Bruce, 22–24–1 for 1989–92 with 1 bowl champion.

MISCELLANEA

First game was loss to Longmont Academy 12–8 in 1893 . . . 1st win was over Longmont Academy 24–16 in 1893 . . . 1st win over college foe was over Denver 60–10 in 1893 . . . highest score was over Kansas St. Teachers 77–0 in 1967 . . . worst defeat was by Arizona St. 79–7 in 1969 . . . longest un-

beaten string of 14 in 1915–16 ended by Wyoming 6–0 in 1917 opener . . . longest win streak of 11 in 1915–16 ended by Colorado Mines 0–0 . . . longest losing string of 26 in 1960–62 broken with win over Pacific 20–0 in 1963 opener . . . 14-game losing string in 1980–82 broken with win over Wyoming 9–3 . . . consensus All-American was Mike Bell, DL, 1978 . . . Academic All-Americans were Gary Glick, B, 1955; Tom French, OT, 1969; and Steve Bartalo, RB, 1986.

FRESNO STATE (Bulldogs; Cardinal and Blue)

NOTABLE TEAMS

1922 (7–1–2) **Won:** Tulare H.S. 12–0, Lemoore H.S. 25–9, Loyola 1–0 (forfeit), Reedley H.S. 21–0, Cal Poly–San Luis Obispo (SLO) 20–0 (1st meeting), Bakersfield J.C. 31–6, Pacific 12–7. **Lost:** Stanford frosh 7–3. **Tied:** Modesto J.C. 0–0, UC-Davis 0–0 (1st meeting). **Noteworthy:** won 1st California Coast Conference title.
1923 (7–2) **Won:** Reedley H.S. 39–0, Caruthers Legion 39–0, Sacramento J.C. 53–18, UC-Davis 26–14, Modesto J.C. 7–6, Redlands 10–6, Bakersfield J.C. 32–6. **Lost:** Nevada–Reno 46–3 (1st meeting), San Diego St. 12–2 (1st meeting). **Noteworthy:** repeated as California Coast champ.
1924 (7–2) **Won:** California Christian 31–0, Bakersfield J.C. 9–0, Modesto J.C. 41–6, Mare Island

Navy 10–0, Cal Poly–SLO 22–6, Pacific 12–0, San Diego St. 7–0. *Lost:* Nevada–Reno 16–0, Chico St. 16–0.

1930 (8–0) *Won:* California Christian 19–7, Redlands 31–26, Loyola 12–7, Chico St. 13–7, Pacific 19–0, UC-Davis 27–7, San Jose St. 27–12, Nevada-Reno 6–0. *Star:* E Myron Anderson. *Noteworthy:* won 1st Far Western Conference title in 1st unbeaten season.

1934 (7–2–1) *Won:* San Francisco St. 33–6, USC JVs 7–0, Northern Arizona 26–14, Pacific 7–6, UC-Davis 40–13, Cal Tech 66–0, Nevada-Reno 33–0. *Lost:* California JVs 12–6, Santa Clara 19–0 (1st meeting since 1928). *Tied:* San Jose St. 7–7. *Noteworthy:* got share of 2nd Far Western title.

1937 (8–1–1) *Won:* Willamette 7–0, California JVs 20–7, Whittier 24–0, UC-Davis 19–0, Chico St. 40–7, Nevada-Reno 46–8, Pacific 20–0. *Lost:* Hardin-Simmons 14–7. *Tied:* USC JVs 13–13 in opener. *Noteworthy:* Won 4th Far Western title. Made 1st postseason appearance, edging Arkansas St. 27–26 in Little All-American Bowl in Los Angeles; Ken Gleason passed for TDs to Toby Heeb (who also scored on 15-yd run) and Granny Holbrook (who also scored on 7-yd run), Ray Sturgill kicked 3 ex pts, and Frank McClurg blocked Arkansas St.'s final ex pt try.

1938 (7–3) *Won:* San Diego Marines 34–14, California JVs 27–7, Arkansas St. 34–0, Nevada-Reno 27–0, UC-Davis 37–7, Hawaii 15–13 (1st meeting), UC–Santa Barbara 28–0 (1st meeting since 1928). *Lost:* Pacific 18–13, San Francisco 14–6, Texas Mines (Texas–El Paso) 26–6 (1st meeting).

1939 (9–1) *Won:* Texas Mines (Texas–El Paso) 10–7, UC–Santa Barbara 13–6, Nevada-Reno 45–0, California JVs 28–7, San Francisco 21–2, Pacific 7–0, Portland 27–13, Hawaii 38–2, Healani A.C. 21–6. *Lost:* unbeaten San Jose St. 42–7 (1st meeting since 1934). *Stars:* soph C Bob Burgess, E Jack Mulkey.

1940 (9–2–1) *Won:* Whittier 13–7, UC–Santa Barbara 20–6, West Texas St. 15–6, Pacific 3–0, Nevada-Reno 7–6, Texas Mines (Texas–El Paso) 16–6, Colorado St. 28–0, Healani A.C. 20–0. *Lost:* San Jose St. 14–7, Arkansas St. 13–0. *Tied:* San Diego St. 0–0 (1st meeting since 1931). *Stars:* Burgess, Mulkey. *Noteworthy:* beat Hawaii 3–0 in Pineapple Bowl on New Year's Day in Honolulu on 18-yd 4th period FG by Dale Mickelwait.

1942 (9–1) *Won:* Whittier 51–0, Occidental 53–6, San Diego St. 66–0, March Field 20–0, Fort Ord 80–0, Pacific 13–0, Nevada-Reno 33–0, San Jose St. 6–0 (1st over Spartans in 7 games since 1931), Loyola 27–6. *Lost:* San Francisco 33–13. *Star:* Jackie Fellows (21 TDs pass). *Noteworthy:* won 2nd straight California Collegiate Athletic Association title.

1943 No team, due to W.W. II.

1946 (8–4) *Won:* Santa Clara 20–7 (1st meeting since 1935, 1st win in 6-game series dating to 1925), Hawaiian All-Stars 13–6, UC–Santa Barbara 20–13 (1st meeting since 1941), Loyola 28–0, Pacific 13–12, Idaho 13–12, Molii Bears 41–0, Leilehau Alumni 18–6. *Lost:* Oklahoma City 46–7, San Diego St. 7–0, Hawaii 7–2 (1st meeting since 1940), San Jose St. 13–2. *Stars:* T Bob Hoffman, G Jean Lamour. *Noteworthy:* final year under Jimmy Bradshaw.

1952 (8–2) *Won:* UC-Davis 41–7, Pepperdine 60–7, Utah St. 27–21 (1st meeting), Occidental 20–9, San Diego St. 49–33, Nevada-Reno 59–32, San Francisco St. 48–20, Whittier 21–14. *Lost:* San Jose St. 40–6, Pacific 50–0. *Stars:* FB Larry Willoughby (1,092 yds and 11 TDs rush), E Bill Raine (16 pass rec for 372 yds and 6 TDs), T Ledeo Fanucchi, soph G Willard Whitaker. *Noteworthy:* 1st year under Clark Van Galder.

1954 (7–3) *Won:* Cal St.–L.A. 49–19, Utah St. 23–13, Nevada-Reno 52–6, UC-Santa Barbara 26–20, San Diego St. 20–0, Cal Poly–SLO 16–13, San Francisco St. 39–20. *Lost:* Hawaii 25–20, San Diego Marines 20–0, San Jose St. 28–0. *Stars:* Whitaker, T Lyman Ehrlich, frosh FB Dean Philpott (527 yds rush), HBs Duke Snider and Don Driscoll (10 TDs rush). *Noteworthy:* Won 3rd California Collegiate title (1st since 1942).

1955 (9–1) *Won:* San Francisco St. 20–12, Willamette 33–7, San Diego Navy 52–0, Nevada-Reno 42–9, San Diego Marines 20–0, San Diego St. 20–6, Cal Poly–SLO 34–6, San Jose St. 19–13 (1st over Spartans since 1947), Hawaii 20–18. *Lost:* Utah St. 39–13. *Stars:* Philpott, E Darryl Rogers, T Alan Kirchof, P John Steinborn (40-yd avg). *Noteworthy:* repeated as California Collegiate champ.

1956 (8–2) *Won:* Brigham Young (BYU) 26–13 (1st meeting), Willamette 27–12, San Diego Marines 2–0, San Francisco St. 28–0, Hawaii 39–20, Cal Poly–SLO 21–13, San Diego St. 50–7, San Jose St. 30–14. *Lost:* Pacific 21–14, Idaho 24–12. *Stars:* Philpott (807 yds and 10 TDs rush), Rogers (19 pass rec for 254 yds), HB L.C. Taylor, Kirchof, C Don Kloppenburg, OL Nick Brown, T Bill Harvey,

Steinborn (40.6-yd punting avg). *Noteworthy:* Won 3rd straight California Collegiate title (5th overall).

1959 (7–3) *Won:* BYU 27–16, UC–Santa Barbara 28–12, Cal Poly–SLO 28–13, San Diego St. 38–13, Long Beach St. 29–8, Cal St.–L.A. 21–0, Hawaii 22–13. *Lost:* San Diego Marines 13–6, San Jose St. 40–14, Pacific 18–13. *Stars:* HB Dale Messer (56 pts, 17 pass rec for 297 yds), soph C/G Doug Brown, T Jack Mattox. *Noteworthy:* Won 7th California Collegiate title in 1st year under Cecil Coleman.

1960 (9–1) *Won:* Hawaii 17–7, UC–Santa Barbara 33–15, Abilene Christian 20–19, Cal Poly–SLO 33–0, Cal St.–L.A. 35–13, San Diego St. 60–0, Long Beach St. 21–3, San Jose St. 21–3, Pacific 32–7 (1st over Tigers in 11 games since 1946). *Lost:* Montana St. 22–20. *Stars:* Messer (811 yds rush, 30 pass rec for 655 yds, 1,815 all-purpose yds, 18 TDs), QB Bob Van Galder, HB Larry Iwasaki, Brown, T Sonny Bishop, C J.R. Williams, E John Webster, Jim Sanderson (6 int). *Noteworthy:* Won 3rd straight California Collegiate title.

1961 (10–0) *Won:* Montana St. 16–13, UC–Santa Barbara 22–14, Pacific 20–19, Cal Poly–SLO 42–13, Cal St.–L.A. 35–6, San Diego St. 27–6, Long Beach St. 37–14, Abilene Christian 21–7, San Jose St. 36–27. *Stars:* Brown, Williams, Bishop, T Monte Day, E Jay Buckert, QB Jon Anabo, Gerald Houser (26 pass rec for 316 yds), HB Bill Kendrick. *Noteworthy:* Won 9th California Collegiate title (4th straight) in 1st undefeated season since 1930. Beat Bowling Green 36–6 in Mercy Bowl at Los Angeles; QB Beau Carter ran for 2 TDs and passed for 246 yds and 2 TDs, and Jan Barrett had 6 pass rec for 161 yds and 2 TDs.

1962 (7–3) *Won:* Whitworth 48–7, UC–Santa Barbara 37–0, Cal Poly–SLO 51–6, Cal St.–L.A. 34–0, Long Beach St. 50–0, San Jose St. 20–14, Pacific 18–13. *Lost:* Abilene Christian 26–14, San Diego St. 29–26 (1st to Aztecs since 1951), Montana St. 21–20. *Stars:* Anabo (1,184 yds and 11 TDs pass), Carter, Barrett (20 pass rec for 482 yds), soph James Long (70 pts), Es Larry Fogelson and Jan Farris (7 TDs pass rec), Day, Williams.

1966 (7–3) *Won:* Hawaii 28–27, Northern Arizona 14–12, Cal St.–Northridge 18–17, Cal Poly–SLO 14–7, Cal St.–L.A. 14–7, Pacific 16–14, San Jose St. 15–13. *Lost:* Montana St. 55–6, unbeaten San Di-

ego St. 34–14, Long Beach St. 28–20. *Stars:* QB Danny Robinson, Ernie Nolte (35 pass rec for 551 yds), G Terry Pitts, G/DE Sylvester Greenwood, DT Gary Cohagan, DL Dick Lowe, DBs Dave Plump (9 int) and soph Mike Freeman. *Noteworthy:* 1st year under Darryl Rogers.

1968 (7–4) *Won:* Portland St. 30–13, Cal St.–Northridge 35–12, Cal Poly–SLO 17–0, Cal St.–L.A. 42–20, Long Beach St. 34–28 (1st over 49ers since 1962), Montana St. 31–16, Pacific 10–3. *Lost:* Idaho St. 38–23, San Jose St. 25–21, San Diego St. 42–12. *Stars:* QB Ron Hudson (1,047 yds pass), Mike White (33 pass rec for 461 yds, 1,214 all-purpose yds), FB Mike Flores (724 yds rush, 6 TDs), OT John Stahl, G Hank Corda, T Tony Welch, DT Ron Remington, LB Tom McCall, Freeman (6 int), Ervin Hunt (6 int). *Noteworthy:* Won 10th and last California Collegiate title. Lost to Humboldt St. 29–14 in muddy Camellia Bowl at Sacramento, scoring on 2 short TD runs by Walt Jensen; lost ball 7 times on int.

1970 (8–4) *Won:* Cal St.–Hayward 28–12, UC–Santa Barbara 25–10 (1st meeting since 1962), Pacific 34–14, Cal St.–Northridge 21–7, Cal Poly–SLO 23–17, Cal St.–L.A. 51–6, Northern Arizona 40–7, San Jose St. 27–19. *Lost:* Montana St. 26–12, San Diego St. 56–14, Long Beach St. 50–14, Hawaii 49–0. *Stars:* QB Karl Francis (1,783 yds and 17 TDs pass), WR Gary Boreham (43 pass rec for 941 yds and 11 TDs, 1,859 all-purpose yds, 74 pts), John Sexton (53 pass rec for 753 yds and 9 TDs), Henry Woodson (822 yds and 10 TDs rush), T Cleo McCutcheon, G Steve Verry, LB Tom Flanagan, DBs Carl Ray Harris (14 int) and Jack Erdman (9 int).

1977 (9–2) *Won:* Boise St. 42–7, Cal Poly–SLO 52–3 (1st over Mustangs since 1972), San Diego St. 34–14 (1st over Aztecs since 1971), Pacific 24–10, San Jose St. 45–24 (1st over Spartans since 1972), Idaho St. 28–7, Long Beach St. 23–14, Cal St.–Fullerton 44–19, Santa Clara 35–7 (1st over Broncos in 6 games since 1946). *Lost:* SW Louisiana 34–13, Montana St. 24–14. *Stars:* QB Dean Jones (746 yds and 10 TDs rush, 941 yds pass), WR Tony Jackson (25 pass rec for 507 yds), RB Steve Franklin (789 yds rush), K Vince Petrucci (10 FGs, 76 pts), OGs Chuck Shearn and Dave Applegate, OT Rick Stannard, C Steve Shearn, DTs Larry Fister and Simon Peterson, DBs Bob Glazebrook, Willy Robinson and Curtis Minor. *Noteworthy:* won 1st PCAA title in 1st winning season since 1972.

1982 (11–1) *Won:* Cal Poly–SLO 26–6, Oregon 10–4, Weber St. 25–9, Utah St. 31–6 (1st over Aggies in 6 games since 1954), Pacific 49–30, San Jose St. 39–27 (1st over Spartans since 1977), Long Beach St. 40–22, Cal St.–Fullerton 31–14, Montana St. 45–14, Nevada–Las Vegas 30–28. *Lost:* Nevada-Reno 40–26 (1st meeting since 1954). *Stars:* QB Jeff Tedford (2,993 yds and 24 TDs pass), SE Henry Ellard (16 TDs, 62 pass rec for 1,510 yds and 15 TDs), WR Stephone Paige (48 pass rec for 943 yds and 8 TDs), OT Ed Carter, OG Mike Forrest, C John Blacksill, K Scott Darrow (8 FGs), DE Kevin Jones, DBs Matt McKnight (6 int) and Eric Fox (6 int), P Rusty Karraker (41-yd avg). *Noteworthy:* Won 2nd PCAA title in 1st winning season since 1977. Beat Bowling Green 29–28 in California Bowl on 2-yd pass from Tedford to Vince Wesson and conversion by Darrow with 11 seconds left; Tedford passed for 373 yds and 3 TDs, Paige caught 15 for 246 yds and a TD and scored on 4-yd run, and Darrow passed for 2-pt conversion and kicked 3 ex pts.

1985 (11–0–1) *Won:* Nevada–Las Vegas 26–6, Oregon St. 33–24, Cal Poly–SLO 59–10, San Jose St. 37–17, New Mexico St. 48–21, Utah St. 38–19, Cal St.–Fullerton 42–7, Pacific 43–37, Long Beach St. 33–31, Wichita St. 47–6. *Tied:* Hawaii 24–24. *Stars:* QB Kevin Sweeney (2,789 yds and 17 TDs pass), SE Stephen Baker (893 yds pass rec, 1,287 all-purpose yds), TBs James Williams (1,111 yds and 14 TDs rush, 1,309 all-purpose yds) and frosh Kelly Skipper (11 TDs rush), FL Gene Taylor (7 TDs pass rec), OT David Lerma, OG Barry Grove, soph K Barry Belli (18 FGs, 107 pts), NG Chris Pacheco, DBs Michael Stewart, Anthony Dollarhide and soph Rod Webster (8 int), P Mike Mancini (43.9-yd avg). *Noteworthy:* One of nation's most-improved teams won 3rd PCAA title in 1st unbeaten season since 1961. Trounced unbeaten Bowling Green 51–7 in California Bowl; Sweeney passed for 3 TDs (2 to Taylor and 1 to Baker), Skipper ran for 2 TDs, and Mancini averaged 47.4 yds on 7 punts.

1986 (9–2) *Won:* Montana St. 55–2, Oregon St. 27–0, Louisiana Tech 34–10, New Mexico St. 17–14, Pacific 10–9, Long Beach St. 25–12, Cal St.–Fullerton 30–20, Nevada–Las Vegas 36–7, Utah St.

14–7. *Lost:* San Jose St. 45–41, Hawaii 24–13. *Stars:* Sweeney (2,363 yds and 15 TDs pass), Baker (33 pass rec for 785 yds and 7 TDs, 1,263 all-purpose yds), Williams (885 yds and 8 TDs rush), Taylor, OG Mike Chuhlantseff, OT Mike Withycombe, Belli (21 FGs, 96 pts), DE Jethro Franklin, LBs Cliff Hannemann and David Grayson, Stewart.

1988 (10–2) *Won:* New Mexico 68–21, New Mexico St. 41–0, McNeese St. 49–0, Cal St.–Fullerton 23–10, Utah St. 51–10, San Jose St. 17–15, Pacific 34–0, Nevada–Las Vegas 31–14, Long Beach St. 31–3. *Lost:* Colorado 45–3, Oregon St. 21–10. *Stars:* frosh QB Mark Barsotti (1,795 yds pass), Andre Alexander (33 pass rec for 703 yds), FB Myron Jones (746 yds rush), Skipper, TE Craig Jones, OT Jeff Truschel, OG Jeff Skidmore, K Steve Loop (18 FGs, 101 pts), NG Chuck McCutchen, LBs Tracy Rogers and soph Ron Cox, DBs Tony Harris and James D. Williams. *Noteworthy:* Won 1st Big West title. Beat Western Michigan 35–30 in California Bowl; Barsotti passed for 2 TDs to Alexander (55 yds and 38 yds), RB Darrell Rosette ran for 149 yds and 2 TDs (including 65-yd run), Jones scored on 26-yd run, and Loop kicked 5 ex pts.

1989 (11–1) *Won:* Utah 52–22 (1st meeting since 1980), Montana 52–37, Pacific 27–14, Long Beach St. 52–0, Oregon St. 35–18, Utah St. 34–7, Cal St.–Fullerton 33–19, Nevada–Las Vegas 31–17, San Jose St. 31–30, New Mexico St. 45–5. *Lost:* New Mexico 45–22 in finale. *Stars:* Barsotti (1,987 yds and 15 TDs pass, 244 yds rush), TB Aaron Craver (1,313 yds and 9 TDs rush), Myron Jones (15 TDs, 875 yds rush), FL Dwight Pickens, Loop (13 FGs, 93 pts), Cox, Williams. *Noteworthy:* Won 2nd straight Big West title. Beat Ball St. 27–6 in California Bowl; Barsotti threw 91-yd TD pass to Stephen Shelley, Cox scored on 58-yd pass int return, and Loop kicked 2 FGs and 3 ex pts.

1990 (8–2–1) *Won:* Eastern Michigan 41–10, New Mexico 24–17, Utah 31–7, New Mexico St. 42–3 (10th straight over Aggies), Cal St.–Fullerton 38–3, Long Beach St. 28–16 (10th straight over 49ers), Nevada–Las Vegas 45–18, Pacific 48–17. *Lost:* Northern Illinois 73–18, San Jose St. 42–7. *Tied:* Utah St. 24–24. *Stars:* Barsotti (2,534 yds pass, 248 yds and 5 TDs rush), Craver (18 TDs, 1,003 yds and 17 TDs rush, 34 pass rec for 259 yds), FL Kelvin Means (40 pass rec for 492 yds, 1,173 all-purpose yds), SE Chris Gawley (32 pass rec for 645 yds), soph FB Lorenzo Neal (580 yds and 9 TDs rush, 15 pass rec for 214 yds), OT Jesse Hardwick, OG Melvin Johnson, frosh K Derek Mahoney (10 FGs, 74 pts), DE Nick Ruggeroli, DBs Marquez Pope, Taylor Cooper, Tony Brown, and Mark Adams. **1991** (10–2) **Won:** Northern Illinois 55–7, Washington St. 34–30, Oregon St. 24–20, New Mexico 94–17, Long Beach St. 42–14, New Mexico St. 42–28, Nevada–Las Vegas 48–22, Pacific 59–14, Cal St.–Fullerton 38–7, San Jose St. 31–28. *Lost:* Utah St. 20–19. **Stars:** Barsotti (1,491 yds and 16 TDs pass, 6 TDs rush), Means (32 pass rec for 435 yds, 1,015 all-purpose yds, 6 TDs), Neal (759 yds rush, 9 TDs), soph TBs Ron Rivers (984 yds and 5 TDs rush, 22 pass rec for 207 yds) and Anthony Daigle (509 yds rush, 11 TDs), TE Marty Thompson (29 pass rec for 450 yds and 7 TDs), soph FLs Michael Ross (20 pass rec for 375 yds) and Malcolm Seabron (19 pass rec for 365 yds), Hardwick, Johnson, Mahoney (11 FGs, 96 pts), NG Zack Rix, DE Judd Foell, LBs Darren Boyer and Jeff Thiesen, Pope, Brown. *Noteworthy:* Led nation in total off and scoring (44.2-pt avg); got share of 3rd Big West title in last year in league. Lost to Bowling Green 28–21 in California Bowl (snapping 5-bowl win streak); Barsotti ran for 1 TD and passed to Thompson for another, and Daigle scored on 57-yd run.

1992 (9–4) **Won:** Pacific 42–21, Colorado St. 52–21 (1st WAC game, 1st meeting since 1940), Louisiana Tech 48–14, New Mexico 31–28, Wyoming 42–31 (1st meeting), Utah 41–15, San Diego St. 45–41 (1st meeting since 1979), Texas–El Paso (1st meeting since 1940). *Lost:* Oregon St. 46–36, Washington St. 39–37, BYU 36–24 (1st meeting since 1959), Hawaii 47–45 (1st meeting since 1986). **Stars:** soph QB Trent Dilfer (2,828 yds and 20 TDs pass), Seabron (41 pass rec for 974 yds and 9 TDs), SE Tydus Winans (33 pass rec for 438 yds), Ross (23 pass rec for 459 yds), Thompson (17 pass rec for 276 yds), Charlie Jones (15 pass rec for 305 yds), Neal (913 yds and 9 TDs rush), Rivers (903 yds and 8 TDs rush), Daigle (680 yds and 16 TDs rush), Hardwick, Mahoney (10 FGs, 41-yd punting avg), Rix, Tommy Jones (5 int). *Noteworthy:* Led nation in scoring (40.5-pt avg). Beat Southern California (USC) in Freedom Bowl 24–7 as Dilfer passed for 164 yds, Rivers ran for 104 yds and a TD, Neal and Daigle scored on short runs, and Mahoney had 43-yd FG and 3 ex pts.

BOWL SUMMARY

California 4–1; Freedom 1–0; Mercy 1–0; Raisin 0–1.

BOWL RECORD (6–2)

Regular Season	Bowl	Score	Opponent	Record
1945 (4–5–2)	Raisin	12–13	Drake	(4–4–1)
1961 (9–0)	Mercy	36–6	Bowling Green	(8–1)
1982 (10–1)	California	29–28	Bowling Green	(7–4)
1985 (10–0–1)	California	51–7	Bowling Green	(11–0)
1988 (9–2)	California	35–30	Western Michigan	(9–2)
1989 (10–1)	California	27–6	Ball State	(7–2–2)
1991 (10–1)	California	21–28	Bowling Green	(10–1)
1992 (8–4)	Freedom	24–7	USC	(6–4–1)

CONFERENCE TITLES

California Coast—1922, 1923. **Far Western**—1930, 1934*, 1935, 1937. **California Collegiate Athletic Association**—1941, 1942, 1954, 1955, 1956, 1958, 1959, 1960, 1961, 1968. **Pacific Coast Athletic Association**—1977, 1982, 1985. **Big West**—1988, 1989, 1991*. **Western Athletic**—None.

TOP 20 AP AND UPI RANKING

1985	U–16

MAJOR RIVALS

Fresno State has played at least 10 games with Cal Poly–San Luis Obispo 30–10–2, Cal St.–Fullerton 13–6, Cal St.–Los Angeles 15–3, Hawaii 13–11–1, Long Beach St. 21–13, Montana St. 11–16, Nevada–Las Vegas 9–4, Nevada-Reno 16–10–1, New Mexico St. 11–0, Pacific 40–26–2, San Diego St. 17–22–4, San Francisco St. 9–1, San Jose St. 24–32–3, UC–Davis 11–5–1, UC-Santa Barbara 15–4–1, Santa Clara 2–9–1, Utah St. 8–9–1. Record against WAC foes met fewer than 10 times: Air Force 0–0, Brigham Young 3–2, Colorado St. 1–0, New Mexico 5–3, Texas–El Paso 3–1, Utah 3–1, Wyoming 1–0.

COACHES

Dean of Fresno State coaches is Jim Sweeney with record of 124–47–2 for 1976–77 and 1980–92, including 6 conference titles, 6 bowl teams (5 winners), and 1 unbeaten team. Other top records for at least 3 years were by Arthur Jones, 36–26–7 for 1921–28 with 2 conference titles; Stan Borleske, 16–17–2 for 1929–32 with 1 conference title and 1 perfect record; Leo Harris, 18–9–1 for 1933–35 with 2 conference titles; Jimmy Bradshaw, 59–18–5 for 1936–42 and 1946 with 3 conference titles and 2 minor bowl teams; Clark Van Galder, 46–22–2 for 1952–58 with 4 conference titles; Cecil Coleman, 37–13 for 1959–63 with 3 conference titles and 1 unbeaten bowl champion; and Darryl Rogers, 43–32–1 for 1966–72 with 1 conference title and 2 minor bowl teams.

MISCELLANEA

First game was win over Cal Tech 12–0 in 1921 . . . highest score was over New Mexico 94–17 in 1991 . . . biggest margin was over Fort Ord 80–0 in 1942 . . . worst defeat was by Santa Clara 83–0 in 1928 . . . worst since W.W. II was by North Texas St. 62–0 in 1951 . . . highest against Bulldogs since W.W. II was by Northern Illinois 73–18 in 1990 . . .

longest win streak of 17 in 1988–89 broken by New Mexico 45–22 . . . 15-game unbeaten string in 1985–86 broken by San Jose St. 45–41 . . . 13-game win streak in 1960–62 broken by Abilene Christian 26–14 . . . longest winless string of 13 in 1928–29 broken with win over Pacific 20–6 . . . Fresno State has had no consensus All-Americans and no 1st team Academic All-Americans.

HAWAII (Rainbows, Rainbow Warriors; Green and White)

NOTABLE TEAMS

1915 (5–1–1) *Won:* McKinley H.S. 17–0, 19–0, Punahou Academy 15–13, Mills 50–0, Kamehameha H.S. 20–16. *Lost:* Kamehameha H.S. 7–0 in opener. *Tied:* Punahou Academy 0–0. *Noteworthy:* played 1st varsity games since 1911 in only year under John Peden.

1917 (4–0–1) *Won:* Kamehameha H.S. 7–6, 12–0, McKinley H.S. 48–0, Punahou Academy 21–0. *Tied:* Punahou Academy 0–0 in opener. *Noteworthy:* had 1st unbeaten season in 1st year under Dave Crawford.

1919 (4–0–1) *Won:* Outrigger Canoe Club 27–7, Schofield 10–6, Luke Field 68–0, Town Team 27–2. *Tied:* Outrigger Canoe Club 6–6 in opener. *Noteworthy:* Crawford's last team.

1920 (6–2) *Won:* Pearl Harbor Navy 19–0, Luke Field 47–0, Punahou Academy 21–0, Schofield 41–0, Palama 7–0, Waikiki 23–14. *Lost:* Outrigger Canoe Club 3–0, Nevada-Reno 14–0 (1st game with continental U.S. team). *Noteworthy:* only year under Raymond Elliot.

1922 (5–1–1) *Won:* Field Artillery 20–0, Fort Ruger 88–0, National Guard 40–0, Palama 27–0, Pomona 25–6 (1st win over continental U.S. team). *Lost:* Navy (service team) 13–10. *Tied:* Town Team 6–6.

1923 (5–1–2) *Won:* Coast Defense 83–6, Town Team 13–0, Hawaii Army 27–7, National Guard 10–0, Oregon St. 7–0 (on New Year's Day). *Lost:*

Pomona 14–7 (1st game in continental U.S.).   *Tied:* Pearl Harbor Navy 19–19, Town Team 6–6.

1924 (8–0)   *Won:* 13th Field Artillery 41–0, Town Team 21–6, 19–0, Army (service team) 37–0, Navy (service team) 16–3, Occidental 18–3, Healani 20–0, Colorado 13–0.   *Noteworthy:* outscored foes 188–12 in 1st perfect season.

1925 (10–0)   *Won:* 11th Field Artillery 68–0, 27th Infantry 20–0, National Guard 86–0, Healani 74–0, Palama 42–0, Pearl Harbor Navy 43–0, Town Team 14–6, Occidental 13–0, Colorado St. 41–0 (1st meeting), Washington St. 20–11.   *Star:* P John Morse (43.5-yd avg).

1927 (5–2)   *Won:* Oahu Blues 20–13, Pearl Harbor Navy 24–7, Town Team 10–0, Occidental 20–0, Utah St. 21–20.   *Lost:* Alumni 3–2 in opener, Santa Clara 18–12 (1st meeting) in finale.

1930 (5–2)   *Won:* Alumni 12–6, Honolulu A.C. 28–0, St. Louis Alumni 19–7, Brigham Young (BYU) 49–13 (1st meeting), Idaho 37–0.   *Lost:* Town Team 7–0, Southern California (USC) 52–0 in consecutive mid-season games.

1934 (6–0)   *Won:* McKinley Alumni 13–0, Town Team 26–7, Kamehameha Alumni 33–0, St. Louis Alumni 20–0, Denver 36–14, California 14–0. *Noteworthy:* 1st unbeaten season since 1925.

1941 (8–1)   *Won:* Portland 33–6, Pacific 14–0, Hawaii Bears 20–6, 27–13, Na Alii 19–6, 33–14, Healani 21–6, Willamette 20–6.   *Lost:* Healani 26–6.   *Star:* B Nolle Smith.

1942–1945 No team, due to W.W. II.

1946 (8–2)   *Won:* Hawaiian Pine 14–6, Kaala 44–0, Olympic 27–0, Lanakila 73–6, Pacific 19–13, Fresno St. 7–2, Healani 58–6, Utah 19–16 (Pineapple Bowl, 1st meeting since 1939).   *Lost:* Nevada-Reno 26–7, Stanford 18–7 in consecutive late games.   *Noteworthy:* 1st year under Tom Kaulukukui.

1956 (7–3)   *Won:* Prep All-Stars 21–7, Pearl Harbor Navy 59–7, Humboldt St. 33–6 (1st meeting), Hawaii Rams 32–7, Southern Oregon 59–0, Lewis & Clark 45–6, San Jose St. 20–0.   *Lost:* Iowa 34–0, Fresno St. 39–20, Hawaii Marines 7–2.

1962 (6–2)   *Won:* Old Timers 19–14, Cal Western 14–8, Kaimuki Spartans 27–0, Tantalus Rangers 13–0, Waikiki Surfers 19–0, Willamette 14–12. *Lost:* Cal St.–L.A. 10–6, San Jose St. 19–0.   *Noteworthy:* resumed competition after 1-year layoff in 1st year under Jim Asato.

1968 (7–3)   *Won:* Humboldt St. 34–20, Puget Sound 38–28, British Columbia 48–0, Santa Clara

23–12, Whitworth 54–14, Linfield 35–13, Nevada-Reno 21–0.   *Lost:* UC–Santa Barbara 49–14, Cal St.–L.A. 46–33, California 17–12.   *Stars:* QB Larry Arnold (1,821 yds and 19 TDs pass), TE McKinley Reynolds (48 pass rec for 675 yds and 6 TDs), FL Rich Leon (56 pass rec for 626 yds and 5 TDs), Emory Holmes (648 yds rush), Ralph Kaspari (7 TDs rush), LB Tim Buchanan.   *Noteworthy:* 1st year under Dave Holmes.

1970 (9–2)   *Won:* U.S. International 14–13, Long Beach St. 23–14, Santa Clara 39–24, Cal Poly–Pomona 29–10, Cal St.–L.A. 31–7, Nevada–Las Vegas 28–21, Linfield 19–17, Pacific 14–0 (1st over Tigers in 9 games since 1946), Fresno St. 49–0. *Lost:* UC–Santa Barbara 22–20, New Mexico Highlands 21–10.   *Stars:* TB Larry Sherrer (722 yds and 9 TDs rush), FB Bill Massey (708 yds and 9 TDs rush), Dave Patterson (16 pass rec for 221 yds), TE Henry Sovio (29 pass rec for 339 yds), C Ed Foote, OG Jim Kalili, LB Randy Ingraham.

1972 (8–3)   *Won:* Portland St. 38–13, Cal Lutheran 38–10, Puget Sound 27–10, Cal St.–Fullerton 49–15 (1st meeting), Montana 30–3, Northern Arizona 20–13, Linfield 36–17, San Jose St. 28–14 (1st meeting since 1962).   *Lost:* Tennessee 34–2, Grambling 46–7, Stanford 39–7.   *Stars:* RB Albert Holmes (1,146 yds and 12 TDs rush), QB Mike Biscotti, WR Golden Richards (23 pass rec for 414 yds and 5 TDs), Don Weir (17 pass rec for 262 yds), John Conley (18 pass rec for 254 yds), OG Tom Johnson, DT Levi Stanley, DE Jim Stone, LB Bill Letz, DB Jeris White.

1973 (9–2)   *Won:* Washington 10–7, Fresno St. 13–10, Texas Southern 24–21, Cal St.–L.A. 16–9, Puget Sound 30–7, Nevada–Las Vegas 31–29, Cal St.–Northridge 28–3, Santa Clara 40–9, Utah 7–6 (1st meeting since 1967, 1st over Utes in 7 games since 1946).   *Lost:* Pacific 28–3, San Jose St. 23–3 in consecutive late games.   *Stars:* Stanley, White, DB Harold Stringert, QB Casey Ortez (1,385 yds and 10 TDs pass), WR Allen Brown (46 pass rec for 735 yds), Elton Shintaku (23 pass rec for 319 yds), Albert Holmes (715 yds and 6 TDs rush), Regis Grice (583 yds rush), OT Scott Haneberg, K Reinhold Stuprich (15 FGs).   *Noteworthy:* Holmes' last team.

1980 (8–3)   *Won:* Abilene Christian 41–0, Pacific 25–14, West Virginia 16–13, New Mexico 31–14, Cal St.–Fullerton 31–21, San Diego St. 31–6 (1st meeting since 1953), Nevada–Las Vegas 24–19, Air Force

20–12 (1st meeting since 1966). *Lost:* Wyoming 45–20, Texas–El Paso 34–14 (1st to Miners in 5 games since 1952), BYU 34–7. *Stars:* TB Gary Allen (884 yds rush, 26 pass rec for 257 yds), David Toloumu (5 TDs rush), Ron Pennick (23 pass rec for 282 yds), Merv Lopes (19 pass rec for 257 yds), C Ed Riewerts, OG Jesse Sapolu, frosh NG Falaniko Noga, DB Blane Gaison.

1981 (9–2) *Won:* Cal St.–Fullerton 38–12, Idaho 21–6, Wyoming 14–9, New Mexico 23–13, San Diego St. 28–10, Nevada–Las Vegas 57–21, Texas–El Paso 35–7, Colorado St. 59–6, South Carolina 33–10. *Lost:* BYU 13–3, Pacific 23–17 in consecutive late games. *Stars:* Allen (11 TDs, 1,006 yds rush, 21 pass rec for 367 yds), Toloumu (821 all-purpose yds, 8 TDs), RB Anthony Edgar (645 yds and 9 TDs rush), QB Tim Lyons (1,002 yds total off), Lopes (23 pass rec for 313 yds), Pennick (22 pass rec for 311 yds), WR Duane Coleman (13 pass rec for 226 yds), Reiwerts, Sapolu, K Lee Larsen (12 FGs, 72 pts), Noga, DL Itai Sataua, LB Andy Moody, DB Dana McLemore.

1988 (9–3) *Won:* Iowa 27–24, Colorado St. 31–23, San Jose St. 36–27 (1st meeting since 1978), Utah 48–20, San Diego St. 32–30, Long Beach St. 34–31, New Mexico 45–3, Air Force 19–14 (1st over Falcons in 5 games since 1982), Oregon 41–17. *Lost:* Texas–El Paso 42–25, BYU 24–23 (10th straight to Cougars), Wyoming 28–22. *Stars:* QB Warren Jones (2,268 yds and 19 TDs pass, 669 yds and 8 TDs rush), WRs Chris Roscoe (44 pass rec for 859 yds and 9 TDs) and soph Larry Khan-Smith (1,010 all-purpose yds), Junior Lopati (28 pass rec for 400 yds), soph FL Dane McArthur (19 pass rec for 289 yds), FL Clayton Mahuka (16 pass rec for 317 yds), RB Heikoti Fakava (860 yds rush, 14 TDs), OL Amosa Amosa, Larry Jones and Mark Nua, frosh K Jason Elam (19 FGs, 95 pts), DL Dana Directo and Joe Seumalo, soph LB David Maeva, DB Mike Tresler, P Kyle Ah Loo (40.7-yd avg).

1989 (9–3–1) *Won:* Tulane 31–26, Long Beach St. 63–10, Utah 67–20, New Mexico 60–14, San Diego St. 31–24, BYU 56–14 (1st over Cougars in 11 games since 1974), Texas–El Paso 26–7, Pacific 34–26, Oregon St. 23–21. *Lost:* Wyoming 20–15, Colorado St. 31–16. *Tied:* Air Force 35–35. *Stars:* QB Garrett Gabriel (2,145 yds and 17 TDs pass, 246 yds and 5 TDs rush), Roscoe (47 pass rec for 1,043 yds and 9 TDs), McArthur (35 pass rec for 408 yds), FL Dan Ahuna (25 pass rec for 263 yds), frosh RB Jamal Farmer (1,007 yds rush, 19 TDs), Elam (20 FGs, 106 pts), LB Joaquin Barnett, DB Walter Briggs (9 int), Ah Loo (42.7-yd punting avg). *Noteworthy:* made 1st postseason appearance but lost to Michigan St. 33–13 in Aloha Bowl, turning ball over 8 times; Gabriel passed for 197 yds and 2 TDs, and Roscoe had 7 pass rec for 71 yds and a TD.

1992 (11–2) *Won:* Oregon 24–21, Air Force 6–3, BYU 36–32, Fresno St. 47–45 (1st meeting since 1986), Nevada–Las Vegas 55–25 (1st meeting since 1984), Texas–El Paso 41–21, Colorado St. 24–13, Wyoming 42–18, Tulsa 38–9, Pittsburgh 36–23. *Lost:* Utah 38–17 (1st to Utes since 1985), San Diego St. 52–28. *Stars:* QBs Michael Carter (540 yds and 11 TDs rush, 787 yds and 6 TDs pass) and Ivin Jasper (5 TDs rush), RB Travis Sims (1,498 yds and 9 TDs rush), WR Darrick Branch (25 pass rec for 491 yds and 5 TDs), C Lene Amosa, OG Doug Vaioleti, Elam (16 FGs, 92 pts, 44.5-yd punting avg), DT Maa Tanuvasa, DB Bryan Addison. *Noteworthy:* Nation's most-improved team won 1st WAC title. Beat Illinois 27–17 in Holiday Bowl as Carter ran for 105 yds and passed for 115 yds and a TD (53 yds to Branch), Sims ran for 113 yds and 2 TDs, and Elam had FGs of 45 and 37 yds.

BOWL SUMMARY

Aloha 0–1; Holiday 1–0.

BOWL RECORD (1–1)

Regular Season	Bowl	Score	Opponent	Record
1989 (9–2–1)	Aloha	13–33	Michigan State	(7–4)
1992 (10–2)	Holiday	27–17	Illinois	(6–4–1)

CONFERENCE TITLES

Western Athletic—1992.

TOP 20 AP AND UPI
(USA TODAY/CNN SINCE 1991) RANKING

1992	20–19

MAJOR RIVALS

Hawaii has played at least 10 games with Air Force 4–7–1, Brigham Young 7–12, Cal St.–Fullerton 10–1, Cal St.–L.A. 6–6, Colorado St. 9–8, Denver 5–5, Fresno St. 11–13–1, Humboldt St. 5–6, Nevada–Las Vegas 8–3, New Mexico 14–3, Pacific 10–16, San Diego St. 7–9–2, San Jose St. 7–11–1, Santa Clara 7–4, Texas–El Paso 12–9, Utah 11–13, Wyoming 8–7.

COACHES

Dean of Hawaii coaches is Otto "Proc" Klum with record of 84–51–7 for 1921–39, including 3 unbeaten teams. Other top records for at least 3 years were by David Crawford, 11–1–2 for 1917–19 with 2 unbeaten teams; Tommy Kaulukukui, 34–18–3 for 1946–50 (and 8–1 as cocoach with Luke Gill in 1941); Jimmy Asato, 15–12 for 1962–64; Dave Holmes, 46–17–1 for 1968–73; Dick Tomey, 63–46–3 for 1977–86; and Bob Wagner, 45–27–2 for 1987–92 with 2 bowl teams.

MISCELLANEA

First game was win over McKinley H.S. 6–5 in 1909 . . . 1st win over college foe was over Oahu College (Punahou Academy) 3–2 in 1910 . . . 1st win over continental U.S. foe was over Pomona 25–6 in 1922 . . . highest score was 101–0, over Field Artillery and over Healani, both in 1926 . . . highest since W.W. II was over Islanders 98–7 in 1949 . . . highest score against college foe was over Utah 67–20 in 1989 . . . biggest margin over college foe was over Prairie View 65–0 in 1979 . . . worst defeat was by Pacific 75–0 in 1949 . . . longest unbeaten string of 21 and longest win streak of 20 in 1923–26 ended by Alumni 2–0 . . . longest winless string of 8 in 1964–65 broken with win over Cal Western 10–8 . . . Hawaii has had no Division I consensus All-Americans and no 1st team Academic All-Americans.

NEW MEXICO (Lobos; Cherry and Silver)

NOTABLE TEAMS

1905 (5–1–1) *Won:* Albuquerque H.S. 16–0, 15–0, Menaul H.S. 15–0, Albuquerque Indian School 27–0, Santa Fe Indian School 12–0. *Lost:* unbeaten New Mexico St. 40–0 (1st meeting since 1894) in finale. *Tied:* Menaul H.S. 5–5. *Noteworthy:* 1st year under Martin Angel.
1908 (5–1) *Won:* Albuquerque Indian School 33–0, 12–6, New Mexico Mines 30–6, New Mexico Military 16–12 (1st meeting), New Mexico St. 10–6. *Lost:* unbeaten Arizona 10–5 (1st meeting) in finale. *Noteworthy:* only year under H.H. Conwell.
1914 (3–1–1) *Won:* Albuquerque Indian School 46–0, 18–7, New Mexico Military 9–7. *Lost:* New Mexico Military 12–3 in opener. *Tied:* New Mexico St. 7–7.
1919 (3–0–2) *Won:* New Mexico Mines 55–0, Texas–El Paso 57–13 (1st meeting), New Mexico St. 24–2. *Tied:* Colorado Mines 0–0, New Mexico Military 0–0. *Noteworthy:* resumed competition after 1-year layoff for W.W. I and had 1st unbeaten season since 1-game schedule of 1907.
1924 (5–1) *Won:* Montezuma College 56–0, West Texas St. 12–6, Texas–El Paso 18–0, Arizona 3–0 (1st over Wildcats in 8 games since 1909), Colorado Western 14–0. *Lost:* New Mexico St. 6–0.
1927 (8–0–1) *Won:* New Mexico Mines 35–0, Montezuma College 47–0, New Mexico Military 26–0, Arizona 7–6, Northern Arizona 24–7 (1st

meeting since 1916), New Mexico St. 26–9, Colorado Western 32–0, New Mexico Highlands 12–0. *Tied:* Texas–El Paso 6–6. *Noteworthy:* 1st unbeaten season since 1919.

1934 (8–1) *Won:* New Mexico Highlands 76–7, Northern Arizona 33–6, Texas–El Paso 21–15, Arizona St. 18–12, New Mexico Military 26–7, New Mexico Western 26–0, New Mexico St. 12–6, Colorado St. College 33–6. *Lost:* Arizona 14–6. *Stars:* HB Abdon Paiz, E Ralph Bowyer, C Robert Walker. *Noteworthy:* won 1st Border Conference title in 1st year under Gwinn Henry.

1938 (8–3) *Won:* New Mexico Western 40–0, Arizona St. 21–0, Colorado College 45–0, Northern Arizona 20–0, Arizona 20–7 (1st over Wildcats since 1933), Denver 7–6, New Mexico St. 6–2, Colorado St. 27–7. *Lost:* Texas–El Paso 7–6, unbeaten Texas Tech 17–7. *Stars:* HB William Dwyer, G John Martel. *Noteworthy:* made 1st postseason appearance, losing to Utah 26–0 (1st meeting) in Sun Bowl.

1939 (8–2) *Won:* New Mexico Western 29–7, Wyoming 34–7 (1st meeting since 1931), Denver 7–6, Texas–El Paso 14–0, Northern Arizona 33–0, New Mexico St. 9–6, Arizona 7–6, Colorado St. 21–19. *Lost:* Texas Tech 19–7, Arizona St. 28–6. *Star:* E Jack Henley.

1945 (6–1–1) *Won:* Eastern New Mexico 78–0, Lubbock Air Force Base 39–0, West Texas St. 13–0, Colorado College 6–4, Colorado 12–6. *Lost:* Utah 21–20. *Tied:* Texas Tech 6–6. *Noteworthy:* Won 2nd Border Conference title. Beat Denver 34–24 in Sun Bowl.

1952 (7–2) *Won:* New Mexico St. 23–0, Wyoming 7–0, Texas–El Paso 14–13 (1st over Miners since 1946), Denver 15–0, Colorado St. 3–0, Montana 12–6, Utah St. 28–0. *Lost:* Brigham Young (BYU) 14–10, Arizona 13–7. *Stars:* E Dick Brett (15 pass rec for 205 yds), soph HB Larry White, DT Jack Barger, DL Don Papini. *Noteworthy:* last year under Dud DeGroot.

1958 (7–3) *Won:* New Mexico St. 16–7, Montana 44–16, Utah St. 34–14, Arizona 33–13, Wyoming 13–12, Denver 21–15, Colorado St. 17–12. *Lost:* Texas–El Paso 15–6, BYU 36–19, unbeaten Air Force 45–7. *Stars:* HB Don Perkins (621 yds rush), E Don Black (14 pass rec for 303 yds and 9 TDs). *Noteworthy:* had 1st winning season since 1953 in 1st year under Marv Levy.

1959 (7–3) *Won:* Texas–El Paso 17–7 (1st over

Miners in 5 games since 1952), Utah St. 28–6, Arizona 28–7, Montana 55–14, Denver 42–0, BYU 21–6, Air Force 28–27. *Lost:* New Mexico St. 29–12 (1st to Aggies in 19 games since 1937), Colorado St. 14–9, Wyoming 25–20. *Stars:* Perkins (12 TDs, nation's kickoff return leader with 34.7-yd avg), Black, HB Billy Brown (740 yds rush), C Ron Beaird, Chuck Roberts (6 int). *Noteworthy:* Levy's last team.

1962 (7–2–1) *Won:* New Mexico St. 28–17, Wyoming 25–21, Arizona 35–25, Utah St. 14–13, San Jose St. 25–13, Colorado St. 21–8, Montana 41–12. *Lost:* Texas–El Paso 16–14, BYU 27–0. *Tied:* Utah 7–7. *Stars:* HB Bobby Santiago (806 yds rush, 11 TDs), FB Bucky Stallings, E Larry Jasper, C Eddie Stokes, P Dick Fitzsimmons (40.9-yd avg). *Noteworthy:* led nation in pass defense and won inaugural WAC title.

1964 (9–2) *Won:* Montana 20–0, BYU 26–14, Arizona 10–7, New Mexico St. 18–14, Wyoming 17–6, Texas–El Paso 20–12, Colorado St. 42–0, Hawaii 20–0 (1st meeting), Kansas St. 9–7. *Lost:* Utah 16–0, Utah St. 14–3. *Stars:* G Jack Abendschan, QB Stan Quintana (1,249 yds total off), E Gary Plumlee (19 pass rec for 316 yds), TB Joe Harris (582 yds rush), RB Claude Ward (7 TDs). *Noteworthy:* got share of 3rd straight WAC title.

1970 (7–3) *Won:* Utah 34–28 (1st over Utes since 1965), San Jose St. 48–25, New Mexico St. 24–17, Wyoming 17–7, Texas–El Paso 35–16 (1st over Miners since 1964), Arizona 35–7, BYU 51–8 (1st over Cougars since 1964). *Lost:* Iowa St. 32–3, Kansas 49–23, unbeaten Arizona St. 33–21 (10th straight to Sun Devils). *Stars:* FB Sam Scarber (961 yds rush, 13 TDs), QB Rocky Long (1,323 yds total off), soph HB Fred Henry, LB Houston Ross, DB Jay Morrison (6 int). *Noteworthy:* 1st winning season since 1964.

1982 (10–1) *Won:* Wyoming 41–20, Texas Tech 14–0 (1st over Red Raiders since 1971), Nevada–Las Vegas 49–21, Air Force 49–37, San Diego St. 22–17 (1st over Aztecs in 6 games since 1956), New Mexico St. 66–14, North Texas St. 20–17, Texas–El Paso 31–18, Colorado St. 29–24, Hawaii 41–17 (1st over Rainbow Warriors since 1977). *Lost:* BYU 40–12. *Stars:* DE Jimmie Carter, soph LB Johnny Jackson, soph DB Ray Hornfeck, QB David Osborn (1,609 yds and 15 TDs pass, 539 yds and 7 TDs rush), TB Mike Carter (722 yds rush), WR Keith Magee (39 pass rec for 641 yds and 5 TDs), K Pete

Parks, P Bobby Ferguson (42.3-yd avg). *Noteworthy:* had one of nation's most-improved teams in last year under Joe Morrison.

BOWL SUMMARY

Aviation 1–0; Harbor 0–0–1; Sun 1–2.

BOWL RECORD (2–2–1)

Regular Season	Bowl	Score	Opponent	Record
1938 (8–2)	Sun	0–26	Utah	(7–1–2)
1943 (3–1)	Sun	0–7	Southwestern (Texas)	(9–1–1)
1945 (5–1–1)	Sun	34–24	Denver	(4–4–1)
1946 (5–5–1)	Harbor	13–13	Montana State	(5–3–1)
1961 (6–4)	Aviation	28–12	Western Michigan	(5–3–1)

CONFERENCE TITLES

Border—1934, 1945. **Western Athletic**—1962, 1963, 1964*.

TOP 20 AP AND UPI RANKING

1964	U-16

MAJOR RIVALS

New Mexico has played at least 10 games with Air Force 5–9, Albuquerque High 4–5–1, Albuquerque Indian School 14–4–1, Arizona 18–42–3, Arizona St. 5–22–1, Brigham Young 11–30–1, Colorado College 5–5–1, Colorado St. 19–23, Denver 9–9, Hawaii 3–14, Montana 10–4, New Mexico Military 11–7–3, New Mexico St. 53–25–5, Northern Arizona 19–3, San Diego St. 5–14, San Jose St. 4–9–1, Texas–El Paso 36–25–3, Texas Tech 5–27–2, Utah 10–22–2, Utah St. 8–7, West Texas St. 5–9, Wyoming 21–28. Record against new WAC member Fresno St.: 3–5.

COACHES

Dean of New Mexico coaches is Roy W. Johnson with record of 41–32–6 for 1920–30, including 1 unbeaten team. Other top records for at least 3 years were by R.F. Hutchinson, 13–13–2 for 1911–16; Gwinn Henry, 16–12 for 1934–36 with 1 Border Conference title; Ted Shipkey, 30–17–2 for 1937–41 with 1 bowl team; Willis Barnes, 19–20–5 for 1942–46 with 1 Border Conference title and 2 Sun Bowl teams; Bill Weeks, 40–41–1 for 1960–67 with 3 WAC titles and 1 bowl champion; and Joe Morrison, 18–15–1 for 1980–82.

MISCELLANEA

First game was loss to Albuquerque H.S. 5–0 in 1892 . . . 1st win was over Albuquerque H.S. 4–0 in 1893 . . . 1st win over college foe was over New Mexico A&M (New Mexico St.) 25–5 in 1893 . . . highest score was over Flagstaff St. (Northern Arizona) 108–0 in 1916 . . . highest since W.W. II was over Northern Arizona 78–0 in 1950 . . . worst defeat was by New Mexico A&M (New Mexico St.) 110–3 in 1917 . . . worst since W.W. II was by Fresno St. 94–17 in 1991 . . . longest unbeaten string of 13 in 1926–28 ended by New Mexico Military 7–6 . . . longest losing string of 21 in 1967–69 broken with win over Kansas 16–7 . . . consensus All-American was Terance Mathis, WR, 1989 . . . Academic All-Americans were Bob Johnson, S, 1975; and Robert Rumbaugh, DT, 1977–78.

SAN DIEGO STATE *(Aztecs; Scarlet and Black)*

NOTABLE TEAMS

1923 (8–2) *Won:* USS Melville 10–3, San Diego Marines 14–3, 34–7, Riverside J.C. 39–3, Santa Barbara St. 38–13 (1st meeting), Santa Ana J.C. 26–6, LaVerne 27–0 (1st meeting), Fresno St. 12–2 (1st meeting). *Lost:* Occidental 33–7, UCLA 12–0 in consecutive early games. *Noteworthy:* won 2nd straight Southern California Junior College Conference title.

1924 (7–1–2) *Won:* San Diego Marines 30–0, California Christian (Chapman College) 54–6, Redlands 13–0 (1st meeting), Riverside J.C. 6–0, El Centro J.C. 58–0, Santa Barbara St. 42–6, Santa Ana J.C. 26–14. *Lost:* Fresno St. 7–0 in finale. *Tied:* LaVerne 7–7, UCLA 13–13. *Noteworthy:* won 3rd straight Junior College Conference title.

1936 (6–1–1) *Won:* Occidental 7–0, LaVerne 35–6, Redlands 27–7, San Jose St. 14–6, Santa Barbara St. 9–8, Whittier 19–14. *Lost:* San Diego Marines 14–0. *Tied:* New Mexico St. 7–7. *Star:* G Herb Ward. *Noteworthy:* won 1st Southern California Intercollegiate Athletic Conference title.

1937 (7–1) *Won:* Occidental 3–0, Whittier 6–0, LaVerne 26–0, New Mexico St. 20–0, San Diego Marines 6–0, Santa Barbara St. 13–0, San Jose St. 7–6. *Lost:* Redlands 10–9. *Stars:* T Ward, G Abbie Vanoni, FB Max Glass. *Noteworthy:* repeated as Southern California Conference champ.

1947 (7–3–1) *Won:* Utah St. 24–19 (1st meeting), Cal Poly 56–13, Occidental 14–0, Loyola (Calif.) 13–12, Whittier 19–0, Brigham Young (BYU) 32–7 (1st meeting), Santa Barbara College 19–0. *Lost:* Pacific 13–0, San Jose St. 32–7. *Tied:* Fresno St. 7–7. *Stars:* John Simcox (7 TDs), Jack Kaiser (12 pass rec for 216 yds and 5 TDs), OG George Brown. *Noteworthy:* 1st year under Bill Schutte. Made 1st postseason appearance, losing to Hardin-Simmons 53–0 in Harbor Bowl at San Diego after dropping behind 27–0 by halftime.

1951 (10–0–1) *Won:* San Francisco St. 32–14, Submarines Pacific 37–21, Cal Poly–San Luis Obispo (SLO) 32–13, San Diego Marines 34–18, Los Angeles St. 64–0, Fresno St. 13–7, Redlands 46–14, Pepperdine 27–6, Santa Barbara 40–0, Hawaii 34–13 (Pineapple Bowl). *Tied:* Arizona St. 27–27. *Stars:* QB Jesse Thompson (1,304 yds and 13 TDs

pass), B Art Preston (588 yds rush, 14 TDs), E Chet Nicholson (30 pass rec for 510 yds and 6 TDs), OT-DL Jim Erkenbeck, DL Hugh Lathman and Ferman McPhatter, DBs Ed Ricketts (12 int) and George Leja. *Noteworthy:* had 1st unbeaten season and won 2nd straight California Collegiate Athletic Association title.

1961 (7–2–1) *Won:* Cal Poly–SLO 9–6, Redlands 32–20, UC–Santa Barbara 21–6, Pepperdine 21–6, Cal Western 54–34, San Diego U. 42–12, San Diego Marines 18–13. *Lost:* Long Beach St. 17–15, unbeaten Fresno St. 27–6. *Tied:* Los Angeles St. 13–13 in opener. *Stars:* soph RB Kern Carson (560 yds and 5 TDs rush), Wayne Sevier (8 TDs, 59 pts), soph WR Neal Petties (19 pass rec for 428 yds). *Noteworthy:* had 1st winning season since 1956 in 1st year under Don Coryell.

1962 (8–2) *Won:* Los Angeles St. 26–14, Cal Poly–SLO 35–14, Long Beach St. 36–8, Redlands 39–0, UC–Santa Barbara 46–8, Fresno St. 29–26 (1st over Bulldogs since 1951), San Fernando Valley St. 39–0,

Coach Don Coryell, 1961–72: Had record of 104–19–2 with 7 conference champs and 3 bowl teams

Pacific 32–18 (1st over Tigers in 7 games since 1941). *Lost:* Cal Poly–Pomona 13–6 (opener), San Diego Marines 34–6 (finale). *Stars:* Carson (796 yds rush, 12 TDs), Petties (22 pass rec for 384 yds), OT David Lay, Larry Korsmeier (5 int). *Noteworthy:* won 3rd California Collegiate title.

1963 (7–2) *Won:* Cal Poly–Pomona 42–7, Cal Poly–SLO 69–0, Long Beach St. 33–8, UC–Santa Barbara 42–14, Fresno St. 34–6, Pacific 34–18, San Fernando Valley St. 21–6. *Lost:* Cal St.–L.A. 43–30, San Diego Marines 16–12. *Stars:* Carson (555 yds rush, 12 TDs), Petties (22 pass rec for 465 yds and 5 TDs), QB Rod Dowhower (1,136 yds and 11 TDs pass), Jim Allison (5 int), P Eddie Mendez (40.1-yd avg). *Noteworthy:* got share of 4th California Collegiate title.

1964 (8–2) *Won:* Cal Poly–Pomona 53–8, San Francisco St. 54–0, Cal Poly–SLO 59–7, Long Beach St. 45–8, UC–Santa Barbara 50–9, Fresno St. 44–6, San Fernando Valley St. 53–0, Cal Western 50–6. *Lost:* Cal St.–L.A. 7–0, San Jose St. 20–15 (1st meeting since 1957). *Stars:* Dowhower (1,728 yds and 22 TDs pass), WR Gary Garrison (78 pass rec for 1,272 yds and 15 TDs), Allison (1,186 yds and 16 TDs rush), OT John Farris, David Lawson (6 int).

1965 (8–2) *Won:* Pacific 46–6, Akron 41–0, Cal Poly–SLO 41–0, Cal Poly–Pomona 41–13, Fresno St. 26–7, San Fernando Valley St. 50–0, Northern Arizona 20–0, Cal Western 44–0. *Lost:* Long Beach St. 35–32, Cal St.–L.A. 26–12 in consecutive mid-season games. *Stars:* Garrison (70 pass rec for 916 yds and 11 TDs, 14 TDs total), QB Don Horn (1,688 yds and 21 TDs pass), B Nate Johns (921 yds and 9 TDs rush), E Ken Madison, OG Ralph Wenzel, MG Larry Martin, LB/P Cliff Kinney (41-yd punting avg).

1966 (11–0) *Won:* Mexico Polytechnic 45–0, Weber St. 38–34, Cal Poly–SLO 14–13, Long Beach St. 21–18, San Jose St. 25–0, Fresno St. 34–13, North Dakota St. 36–0, San Fernando Valley St. 21–0, Northern Arizona 16–8, Cal St.–L.A. 39–12. *Stars:* Horn (2,234 yds and 18 TDs pass), WR/K Craig Scoggins (81 pass rec for 1,212 yds and 8 TDs, 73 pts), WR Haven Moses (1,145 yds pass rec), E Don Fisher, B Teddy Washington (591 yds and 6 TDs rush), OG Larry Schakel, OT Steve Duich, DE Leo Carroll, LBs Jon Wittler and Jeff Staggs, John Williams (5 int), DBs Bob Howard and Bob Jones, P John Beck (41.9-yd avg). *Noteworthy:* Won 5th California Collegiate title in 1st unbeaten season

since 1951. Beat Montana St. 28–7 in Camelia Bowl, jumping to 21–0 halftime lead.

1967 (10–1) *Won:* Tennessee St. 16–8, Weber St. 58–12, Cal Poly–SLO 26–20, Long Beach St. 20–7, Cal St.–L.A. 28–0, Northern Illinois 47–6, Fresno St. 28–21, San Fernando Valley St. 30–21, Montana St. 14–3. *Lost:* Utah St. 31–25 in finale. *Stars:* Moses (54 pass rec for 958 yds and 7 TDs), Washington (608 yds and 7 TDs rush), B Lloyd Edwards, Duich, OG Paul Daniels, C Curt Hansen, MG Jim Hight, DT Dick Weber, DE Cliff Hancock, DBs Beck (6 int) and Jim Crossley. *Noteworthy:* Won 6th and last California Collegiate title. Beat San Francisco St. 27–6 in Camelia Bowl after taking 14–0 halftime lead.

1968 (9–0–1) *Won:* Texas-Arlington 23–18, Northern Illinois 40–21, Montana St. 34–22, Texas Southern 42–23, Cal St.–L.A. 37–14, San Jose St. 48–6, Fresno St. 42–12, Southern Mississippi 68–7, Utah St. 30–19. *Tied:* Tennessee St. 13–13. *Stars:* QB Dennis Shaw (2,139 yds and 19 TDs pass), Tom Nettles (62 pass rec for 1,227 yds and 14 TDs), Edwards (809 yds and 7 TDs rush), DE Fred Dryer, Nate Wright (5 int).

FL Haven Moses, 1966–67

1969 (11–0)   *Won:* Cal St.–L.A. 49–0, San Jose St. 55–21, West Texas St. 24–14, Texas-Arlington 27–10, UC–Santa Barbara 55–13, Fresno St. 48–20, Pacific 58–32, New Mexico St. 70–21, North Texas St. 42–24, Long Beach St. 36–32. *Stars:* Shaw (nation's passing efficiency leader with 3,185 yds and 39 TDs, nation's leader with 3,197 yds total off), TE Tim Delaney (85 pass rec for 1,259 yds and 14 TDs), soph WR Tom Reynolds (18 TDs), George Brown (558 yds and 5 TDs rush), OTs Tom Shellabarger and Lee Felice, C Bill Pierson, K Al Limahelu, Tom Deckert (8 int). *Noteworthy:* Coryell's 3rd unbeaten team led nation in total off, pass, and scoring (46.4-pt avg) and won PCAA title in 1st year in league. Beat Boston University 28–7 in Pasadena Bowl after trailing 7–0 going into 2nd quarter.

1970 (9–2)   *Won:* Northern Illinois 35–3, North Texas St. 23–0, Cal St.–L.A. 35–0, BYU 31–11 (1st meeting since 1948), Southern Mississippi 41–14, San Jose St. 32–6, Fresno St. 56–14, Pacific 14–13,

UC–Santa Barbara 64–7. *Lost:* Long Beach St. 27–11, Iowa St. 28–22 in last 2 games.   *Stars:* QB Brian Sipe (2,618 yds and 23 TDs pass), Delaney (62 pass rec for 794 yds and 6 TDs), WR Ken Burrow (12 TDs), Eddie Steward (580 yds rush), Shellabarger, OG Henry Allison, Limahelu, DE Leon Van Gorkum, DB Tom Hayes.   *Noteworthy:* got share of 2nd PCAA title.

1972 (10–1)   *Won:* Oregon St. 17–8, North Texas St. 25–0, Kent St. 14–0, San Jose St. 23–12, Bowling Green 35–19, Fresno St. 21–14, West Texas St. 37–6, Pacific 20–7, Long Beach St. 33–14, Iowa St. 27–14.

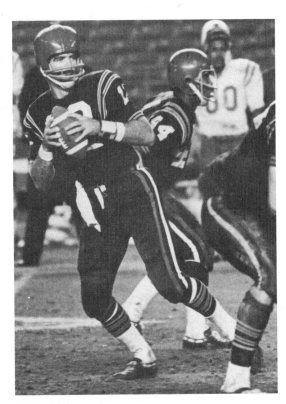

QB Dennis Shaw, 1968–69

QB Brian Sipe, 1969–71

Lost: Houston 49–14. *Stars:* QBs Bill Donckers (1,325 yds pass, 223 yds rush) and Jesse Freitas (1,200 yds pass), WR Isaac Curtis (44 pass rec for 832 yds and 7 TDs), DL Randy Bixler, LB Bill Ferguson, DB Joe Lavender. *Noteworthy:* Coryell's last team won 3rd PCAA title.

1973 (9–1–1) *Won:* Utah St. 35–7, Kent St. 17–9, New Mexico St. 27–0, Pacific 13–10, Florida St. 38–17, Long Beach St. 17–2, Fresno St. 41–6, North Texas St. 56–9, Iowa St. 41–28. *Lost:* Houston 14–9. *Tied:* San Jose St. 27–27. *Stars:* Freitas (nation's leader with 2,993 yds and 21 TDs pass and with 2,901 yds total off), TE Darold Nogle (59 pass rec for 945 yds and 6 TDs), WR Keith Denson (11 TDs), OG Tony Bachmann, C Dave Limebrook, OT Claudie Minor, K Benny Ricardo, DL Bill Van Leeuwan and Lon Woodard, LB Carl Weathers, DB Billie Hayes, Bobby Henderson (5 int). *Noteworthy:* led nation in pass and won 4th PCAA title in 1st year under Claude Gilbert.

1974 (8–2–1) *Won:* Tampa 28–25, Texas–El Paso 26–12 (1st meeting), Fresno St. 24–21, San Jose St. 40–14, Long Beach St. 27–17, Pacific 37–9, New Mexico St. 35–14, Utah St. 34–6. *Lost:* Arizona 17–10, North Texas St. 14–9 (1st in 6-game series begun in 1969). *Tied:* Bowling Green 21–21. *Stars:* Dwight McDonald (nation's leader with 86 pass rec for 1,157 yds and 7 TDs), QB Craig Penrose (1,683 yds and 10 TDs pass), RB Bill Kramer (905 yds rush), Bachmann, Ricardo (10 FGs), DL Mike Gilbert and Rick Ash, LB Burt Blackwell, Henderson, DB Monte Jackson (6 int). *Noteworthy:* won 3rd straight PCAA title (5th overall).

1975 (8–3) *Won:* Texas–El Paso 31–10, Oregon St. 25–0, North Texas St. 30–12, Utah St. 19–10, Cal St.–Fullerton 59–14, Fresno St. 29–0, New Mexico St. 48–3, Pacific 31–13. *Lost:* Arizona 31–24, San Jose St. 31–7, Long Beach St. 21–17 in last 3 games. *Stars:* Penrose (nation's leader with 2,660 yds and 15 TDs pass), WR Duke Fergerson (57 pass rec for 886 yds), Monty Reedy (617 yds and 9 TDs rush), OG Charlie Wortiska, K Steve La Plant (13 FGs, 74 pts), DE Reggie Lewis, Gilbert, DL Ed Imo, LB Travis Hitt, Ed Kertel (5 int). *Noteworthy:* led nation in pass.

1976 (10–1) *Won:* Arkansas St. 24–14, Fresno St. 7–3, Bowling Green 27–15, Pacific 21–15, Cal St.–Fullerton 27–14, Texas–El Paso 27–16, San Jose St.

30–17, Utah St. 7–6, Long Beach St. 10–3, New Mexico 17–14 (1st meeting since 1956). *Lost:* BYU 8–0 (1st meeting since 1970). *Stars:* RB David Turner (982 yds and 7 TDs rush), Ronnie Smith (27 pass rec for 416 yds), La Plant (12 FGs), Imo, Hitt, DB Herman Edwards.

1977 (10–1) *Won:* Cal St.–Fullerton 34–17, Arizona 21–14, Utah St. 19–0, Texas–El Paso 49–7, Nevada–Las Vegas 31–7, Tulsa 41–7, Pacific 29–7, Long Beach St. 33–22, Florida St. 41–16, San Jose St. 37–34. *Lost:* Fresno St. 34–14 (1st to Bulldogs since 1971). *Stars:* Turner (1,252 yds and 13 TDs rush), QB Joe Davis (2,360 yds and 24 TDs pass), Dennis Pearson (49 pass rec for 864 yds and 5 TDs), Smith (14 TDs), soph OG Pete Inge, Terry Jackson (6 int).

1979 (8–3) *Won:* Fresno St. 32–23, Wisconsin 24–17, New Mexico 35–7, Miami (Fla.) 31–20, Utah 17–13, Wyoming 31–21, Arizona 42–10, Texas–El Paso 42–20. *Lost:* Missouri 45–15, Colorado St. 37–3, unbeaten BYU 63–14. *Stars:* RB Tony Allen (1,094 yds and 10 TDs rush), QB Mark Halda (1,684 yds and 10 TDs pass), WR Steve Stapler (37 pass rec for 794 yds and 5 TDs), Inge, DB Terrell Ward, P Pat Mulholland (41.7-yd avg).

1986 (8–4) *Won:* Long Beach St. 27–24, Utah 37–30, New Mexico 38–34, Texas–El Paso 15–10, Colorado St. 27–26, Wyoming 31–24, Hawaii 35–5, BYU 10–3 (1st over Cougars in 10 games since 1970). *Lost:* UCLA 45–14, Stanford 17–10, Air Force 22–10. *Stars:* QB Todd Santos (2,553 yds and 14 TDs pass), Corey Gilmore (48 pass rec for 325 yds), RB Chris Hardy (947 yds and 12 TDs rush), TE Bob Awalt, OG Doug Aronson, K Kevin Rahill, DT Levi Esene, DBs Steve Lauter and soph Mario Mitchell, P Wayne Ross (40.3-yd avg). *Noteworthy:* Won 1st WAC title in 1st year under Denny Stolz. Lost to Iowa 39–38 in Holiday Bowl on 21-yd FG with 47 seconds left; Santos passed for 298 yds and 3 TDs, Hardy ran for 83 yds and a TD and caught a TD pass, and Gilmore ran for a TD and caught 9 passes for 70 yds.

1991 (8–4–1) *Won:* Long Beach St. 49–13, Pacific 55–34 (15th straight over Tigers), Hawaii 47–21, New Mexico 38–24, Texas–El Paso 28–21, Utah 24–21, Wyoming 24–22, Colorado St. 42–32. *Lost:* Air Force 21–20, UCLA 37–12, unbeaten national cochamp Miami (Fla.) 39–12. *Tied:* BYU 52–52. *Stars:* frosh RBs Marshall Faulk (nation's leader with 1,429 yds rush and in scoring with 140 pts, including 23 TDs) and Wayne Pittman (606 yds rush), soph QB David Lowery (2,575 yds and 19 TDs pass), Patrick Rowe (57 pass rec for 822 yds), frosh WR Darnay Scott (35 pass rec for 727 yds and 6 TDs), WR Merton Harris (33 pass rec for 526 yds), TE Ray Rowe (27 pass rec for 301 yds), Larry Maxey (22 pass rec for 314 yds), OG Jim Jennings, DL Eric Duncan, LBs Lou Foster and Andy Cov-

iello, DBs Damon Pieri and Gary Taylor. *Note-worthy:* lost to Tulsa 28–17 in Freedom Bowl; Faulk ran for 157 yds and a TD.

Bowl Summary

Freedom 0–1; Harbor 0–1; Holiday 0–1; Pasadena 1–0.

Bowl Record (1–3)

Regular Season	Bowl	Score	Opponent	Record
1947 (7–2–1)	Harbor	0–53	Hardin-Simmons	(7–3)
1969 (10–1)	Pasadena	28–7	Boston U.	(9–1)
1986 (8–3)	Holiday	38–39	Iowa	(8–3)
1991 (8–3–1)	Freedom	17–28	Tulsa	(9–2)

Conference Titles

Southern California Junior College—1922, 1923, 1924. **Southern California Intercollegiate Athletic**—1936, 1937. **California Collegiate Athletic Association**—1950, 1951, 1962, 1963*, 1967, 1968. **Pacific Coast Athletic Association**—1969, 1970*, 1972, 1973, 1974. **Western Athletic**—1986.

TOP 20 AP AND UPI RANKING

1969	U–18	1972	U–20	1973	U–19	1977	16–19

Major Rivals

San Diego St. has played at least 10 games with Air Force 3–10, Arizona 5–6, Brigham Young 5–13–1, Cal Poly–San Luis Obispo 13–9, Cal St.–Los Angeles 11–5–1, Cal Tech 4–6, Colorado St. 9–4, Fresno St. 22–17–4, Hawaii 9–7–2, LaVerne 10–2–3, Long Beach St. 19–10, New Mexico 14–5, Occidental 11–7–1, Pacific 16–7, Pepperdine 11–2–1, Pomona 10–7–1, Redlands 17–7–2, San Jose St. 10–16–2, Texas–El Paso 15–3, UCLA 0–15–1, UC–Santa Barbara 26–8–1, Utah 8–5–1, Utah St. 9–1, Whittier 10–11–2, Wyoming 6–9.

Coaches

Dean of San Diego St. coaches is Don Coryell with record of 104–19–2 for 1961–72, including 7 conference titles, 3 bowl teams (2 minor), and 3 unbeaten teams. Other top records for at least 3 years were by C.E. Peterson, 43–31–4 for 1921–29 with 3 SCJCC titles; Leo Calland, 34–22–4 for 1935–41 with 2 SCIAC titles; Bill Schutte, 48–36–4 for 1947–55 with 2 CCAA titles, 1 bowl team, and 1 unbeaten team; Claude Gilbert, 61–26–2 for 1973–80 with 2 PCAA titles; Denny Stolz, 16–19 for 1986–88 with 1 WAC title and 1 bowl team; and Al Luginbill, 25–19–3 for 1989–92 with 1 bowl team.

MISCELLANEA

First game was win over Army-Navy Academy J.C. 6–0 in 1921 . . . 1st win over 4-year college was over Santa Barbara St. 38–13 in 1923 . . . highest score was over Santa Barbara College 72–0 in 1953 . . . worst defeat was by Fresno St. 66–0 in 1942 and by Arizona St. 66–0 in 1957 . . . highest against was by Pacific 68–17 in 1958 . . . longest unbeaten string of 31 in 1967–70 ended by Long Beach St. 27–11 . . . longest win streak of 25 in 1965–67 ended by Utah St. 31–25 . . . 16-game unbeaten string in 1923–24 ended by Fresno St. 7–0 . . . longest winless string of 10, in 1942–45 (no team in 1943–44) broken with win over Fresno St. 7–0 and in 1959–60 with win over Pepperdine 27–20 . . . consensus All-American was Marshall Faulk, RB, 1992 . . . San Diego St. has had no 1st team Academic All-Americans.

TEXAS–EL PASO (Miners; Orange, White and Blue)

NOTABLE TEAMS

1925 (5–1–1) *Won:* New Mexico 19–2 (1st in 6-game series dating to 1919), New Mexico Military 28–0, El Paso J.C. 12–6, Silver City Normal (New Mexico Western) 21–0, Arizona St. 21–12 (1st meeting). *Lost:* Sul Ross 31–7 in opener. *Tied:* New Mexico A&M 6–6.

1929 (6–1–2) *Won:* New Mexico Mines 46–0, Arizona St. 31–7, Wayland 9–6, New Mexico A&M 8–0 (1st homecoming), New Mexico Military 20–14, Gila College 40–0. *Lost:* Northern Arizona 19–0. *Tied:* Sul Ross 0–0, St. Edwards 0–0. *Noteworthy:* 1st year under Mack Saxon.

1930 (7–1–1) *Won:* Arizona St. 19–6, Gila College 36–6, Texas Tech 31–0 (1st meeting), New Mexico Military 27–0, New Mexico 20–0, Sul Ross 25–7, New Mexico A&M 25–0. *Lost:* Texas 28–0 (1st meeting) in opener. *Tied:* Arizona 0–0 in finale.

1931 (7–1) *Won:* Wayland 10–0, Arizona St. 28–13, Sul Ross 26–0, New Mexico Military 31–6, McMurry 18–7, Texas Tech 14–12, New Mexico A&M 20–0. *Lost:* Hardin-Simmons 45–0 in mid-season.

1932 (7–3) *Won:* Wayland 38–7, Howard Payne 19–7, Hardin-Simmons 13–2, New Mexico Military 14–12, New Mexico A&M 31–6, Army All-Stars 44–0, St. Edwards 27–13. *Lost:* Arizona St. 15–14

(1st to Bulldogs since 1927), Oklahoma A&M 20–7. *Noteworthy:* lost to Southern Methodist (SMU) 26–8 in postseason charity game in El Paso.

1937 (7–1–2) *Won:* New Mexico Military 19–3, West Texas St. 16–14, Greeley St. 10–0, Arizona St. 19–0, Northern Arizona 53–13, Sul Ross 34–0, St. Edwards 34–7. *Lost:* New Mexico A&M 14–0 in opener. *Tied:* New Mexico 7–7, Santa Barbara 13–13. *Star:* soph QB Kenneth Heineman.

1948 (8–2–1) *Won:* McMurry 33–14, Houston 35–7, West Texas St. 21–7, Brigham Young (BYU) 34–20, New Mexico 27–13, Arizona 25–14 (1st over Wildcats in 6 games since 1939), New Mexico A&M 92–7, Hawaii 49–6 (1st meeting). *Lost:* Texas Tech 46–6. *Tied:* Hardin-Simmons 27–27. *Stars:* Fred Wendt (nation's leader with 1,570 yds rush and with 152 pts on 20 TDs and 32 extra pts), T Raymond Evans, G Ernest Keily. *Noteworthy:* Led nation in rush. Lost to West Virginia 21–12 in Sun Bowl, scoring on 1-yd run by soph Pug Gabriel and 60-yd run by Wendt.

1949 (8–2–1) *Won:* BYU 47–6, John Carroll 33–7, Hawaii 14–7, West Texas St. 34–7, Arizona 28–0, New Mexico 7–0, New Mexico A&M 69–13. *Lost:* Hardin-Simmons 33–14, Texas Tech 13–0 in consecutive late games. *Tied:* West Virginia 13–13. *Stars:* Gabriel (886 yds and 11 TDs rush), Keily, T James DeGroat, C Wayne Hansen. *Noteworthy:* Jack Curtice's last team again led nation in rush in school's 1st year as Texas Western. Beat Georgetown 33–20 in Sun Bowl; Gabriel scored 2 TDs, Danny Fraser ran 32 yds for a TD, Hansen scored on 51-yd run, and Bill Chesak scored on 1-yd run.

1950 (7–3) *Won:* New Mexico A&M 40–32, Idaho 43–33, Arizona 14–13, New Mexico 48–13, Hardin-Simmons 21–20, West Virginia 48–7, Hawaii 46–13. *Lost:* Cincinnati 32–0, Texas Tech 61–7, West Texas St. 40–12. *Stars:* Lee Cargile (573 yds rush), Tom Steel (8 TDs), E J.D. Partridge. *Noteworthy:* 1st year under Mike Brumbelow.

1953 (8–2) *Won:* Sul Ross 26–7, Arizona St. 28–27, New Mexico A&M 39–0, North Texas St. 26–21, Midwestern 27–7, Arizona 28–20, West Texas St. 27–7. *Lost:* Texas Tech 27–6, Hardin-Simmons 14–13. *Stars:* Clovis Riley (548 yds and 5 TDs rush), Gene Odell (25 pass rec for 391 yds), soph Jesse Whittenton (5 TDs), G Harris Cantrell. *Noteworthy:* beat Southern Mississippi 37–14 in Sun Bowl, jumping to 30–7 lead by halftime; QB Dick Shinaut passed for 2 TDs (25 yds to Whittenton and 44 yds to soph E John Howle) and kicked 25-yd FG and 4 ex pts, and Riley scored on 43-yd run.

1954 (8–3) **Won:** Sul Ross 35–14, McMurry 27–6, North Texas St. 6–0, New Mexico A&M 12–7, Hardin-Simmons 20–7, Arizona 41–21, West Texas St. 33–13. **Lost:** Arizona St. 34–27, Texas Tech 55–28, unbeaten Trinity (Texas) 20–14 (1st meeting) in successive early games. **Stars:** QB/K Whittenton (6 TDs rush, 61 pts), Howle (27 pass rec for 339 yds), Reve Tevis (676 yds and 7 TDs rush). **Noteworthy:** beat Florida St. 47–20 in Sun Bowl, jumping to 34–7 lead by halftime; Whittenton passed for 3 TDs (56 yds and 16 yds to frosh Rany Rutledge and 19 yds to frosh Bob Forrest), ran for 2 TDs, and kicked 6 ex pts.

1956 (9–2) **Won:** Texas Tech 17–13, Abilene Christian 20–0, New Mexico 34–0, Arizona 28–6, New Mexico A&M 51–7, Hardin-Simmons 51–13, Arizona St. 28–0, West Texas St. 16–13, Trinity (Texas) 54–0. **Lost:** North Texas St. 13–6. **Stars:** soph QB Bob Laraba, HB Don Maynard, Jimmy Bevers (606 yds and 9 TDs rush), Forrest, T Keith Wharton, G Ken George. **Noteworthy:** Won only Border Conference title in Brumbelow's last year. Lost to George Washington 13–0 in Sun Bowl.

1965 (8–3) **Won:** North Texas St. 61–15, New Mexico 35–14, New Mexico St. 21–6, Colorado St. 35–10, Utah 20–19, Xavier (Ohio) 57–33, West Texas St. 38–21. **Lost:** Wyoming 38–14, Arizona St. 28–20, Arizona 10–3 in successive mid-season games. **Stars:** soph QB Billy Stevens (3,032 yds and 21 TDs pass), Chuck Hughes (80 pass rec for 1,519 yds and 12 TDs, 13 TDs total), Dick Weeks (5 TDs rush), Ron Bostwick (7 int). **Noteworthy:** Had nation's most-improved team in 1st year under Bobby Dobbs. Beat Texas Christian (TCU) 13–12 in Sun Bowl after trailing 10–0 at half; scored on 35-yd pass from Stevens to Hughes, and ex pt and 2 FGs by Joe Cook.

1967 (7–2–1) **Won:** UC–Santa Barbara 50–14, BYU 47–17, New Mexico 75–12, New Mexico St. 46–24, Colorado St. 17–0, Utah 28–8. **Lost:** Arizona St. 33–32, unbeaten Wyoming 21–19. **Tied:** Arizona 9–9. **Stars:** Stevens (1,365 yds and 11 TDs pass), Volly Murphy (40 pass rec for 747 yds and 5 TDs, 12 TDs total), Tom Galloway (42.8-yd punting avg). **Noteworthy:** Led nation in pass and scoring (35.9-pt avg) in 1st year as Texas–El Paso. Beat Mississippi 14–7 in Sun Bowl on 2 last quarter TDs (5-yd pass from Stevens to David Karns and 4-yd run by Larry McHenry).

1988 (10–3) **Won:** Mankato St. 37–3, Weber St. 48–21, Tulsa 27–24, Utah 38–28, Hawaii 42–25, Colorado St. 34–14, New Mexico 37–0, New Mexico St. 42–9, San Diego St. 58–7, Air Force 31–24 (1st in 8-game series dating to 1978). **Lost:** BYU 31–27, Wyoming 51–6. **Stars:** QB Pat Hegarty (2,529 yds and 17 TDs pass), soph WR Reggie Barrett (50 pass rec for 781 yds and 6 TDs), Arnie Adkison (25 pass rec for 339 yds), Rob Housler (16 pass rec for 288 yds), TBs John Harvey (751 yds rush, 12 TDs) and soph Scooter Menifee (516 yds rush, 7 TDs), Willie Fuller (590 yds rush, 6 TDs), Eddie Dixon (6 TDs rush), C James Spady, K Chris Jacke (25 FGs, 123 pts), DE Tony Tolbert, LB Ken Sale, Richie Wright (5 int, 2 returned for TDs), DB Terry Walker, soph P Lance Brownlee (41.9-yd avg). **Noteworthy:** Last year under Bob Stull. Lost to Southern Mississippi 38–18 in Independence Bowl after trailing only 10–7 at halftime; scored on 30-yd pass from Hegarty to Barrett, 2-yd pass and 2-pt conversion pass from David Flores to Fuller, and 37-yd FG by Jacke.

BOWL SUMMARY

Independence 0–1; Sun 5–3.

BOWL RECORD (5–4)

Regular Season	Bowl	Score	Opponent	Record
1936 (5–2–1)	Sun	6–34	Hardin-Simmons	(8–2)
1948 (8–1–1)	Sun	12–21	West Virginia	(8–3)
1949 (7–2–1)	Sun	33–20	Georgetown	(5–4)
1953 (7–2)	Sun	37–14	Southern Miss.	(9–1)

(continued)

Regular Season	Bowl	Score	Opponent	Record
1954 (7–3)	Sun	47–20	Florida State	(8–3)
1956 (9–1)	Sun	0–13	George Washington	(7–1–1)
1965 (7–3)	Sun	13–12	TCU	(6–4)
1967 (6–2–1)	Sun	14–7	Mississippi	(6–3–1)
1988 (10–2)	Independence	18–38	Southern Miss.	(9–2)

Conference Titles

Border—1956. **Western Athletic**—None.

TOP 20 AP AND UPI RANKING

None.

Major Rivals

Texas–El Paso has played at least 10 games with Air Force 1–11, Arizona 11–34–2, Arizona St. 13–31–3, Brigham Young 6–24–1, Colorado St. 9–20, Hardin-Simmons 10–18–1, Hawaii 9–12, New Mexico 25–36–3, New Mexico Military 12–7–1, New Mexico St. 42–28–2, North Texas St. 5–13–3, San Diego St. 3–15, Sul Ross 10–5–1, Texas Tech 6–11–1, Trinity (Texas) 6–4, Utah 8–19, West Texas St. 17–10, Wyoming 6–23–1. Record against new WAC member Fresno St.: 1–3.

Coaches

Dean of Texas–El Paso coaches is Mack Saxon with record of 66–44–8 for 1929–41 with 1 bowl team. Other top records for at least 3 years were by George B. Powell, 11–6–3 for 1924–26; Jack Curtice, 24–13–3 for 1946–49 with 2 bowl teams; Mike Brumbelow, 45–24–4 for 1950–56 with 1 Border Conference title and 3 bowl teams; Bobby Dobbs, 41–35–2 for 1965–72 with 2 Sun Bowl champions; and Bob Stull, 21–15 for 1986–88 with 1 bowl team.

Miscellanea

First game was win over YMCA 7–6 in 1914 . . . 1st win over 4-year college foe was over Daniel Baker 3–0 in 1922 . . . highest score was over New Mexico St. 92–7 in 1948 . . . worst defeat was by New Mexico Military 79–0 in 1916 . . . worst since W.W. II was by BYU 83–7 (highest ever against Miners) in 1980 and by Utah 82–6 in 1973 . . . longest unbeaten string of 12 in 1937–38 ended by Texas Tech 14–7 . . . longest losing string of 14 in 1976–77 broken with win over New Mexico St. 23–21 . . . Texas–El Paso has had no consensus All-Americans and no 1st team Academic All-Americans.

UTAH (Utes; Crimson and White)

Notable Teams

1904 (6–1) **Won:** Montana 17–0 (1st meeting), Denver 12–0, Wyoming 23–0 (1st meeting), Fort Douglas 107–0, Utah St. 43–0, Colorado College 43–0 (1st meeting). **Lost:** Colorado 32–6 in opener. **Noteworthy:** 1st year under Joseph Maddock.
1905 (6–2) **Won:** Wyoming 31–0, Montana 42–0, Fort Douglas 129–0, Denver 24–6, Utah St. 5–0, Colorado A.C. 24–0. **Lost:** Colorado 46–5, Colorado Mines 22–0 (1st meeting) in successive late games.
1906 (4–1) **Won:** Denver 24–0, Montana 42–0, Colorado 10–0 (1st in 4-game series begun in 1903), Utah St. 35–0. **Lost:** Colorado College 6–0 in opener.
1909 (5–1) **Won:** Ogden H.S. 37–0, Utah St. 28–0, 22–0, Fort Douglas 21–5, Montana St. 46–0 (1st meeting). **Lost:** Colorado Mines 14–8. **Noteworthy:** Maddock's last team.

1911 (6–1–1) *Won:* Ogden H.S. 12–0, Colorado A&M 51–0 (1st meeting since 1903), Montana St. 97–0, Colorado Mines 15–0, Colorado College 18–0, Idaho 19–0. *Lost:* unbeaten Colorado 9–0. *Tied:* Denver 0–0.

1912 (5–1–1) *Won:* Denver 66–0, Colorado Mines 18–3, Montana St. 10–3, Colorado College 42–0, Wyoming 9–0. *Lost:* Colorado 3–0. *Tied:* Utah St. 7–7.

1915 (6–2) *Won:* Alumni 13–0, Wyoming 70–7, Colorado Mines 7–0, Southern California (USC) 20–13, Utah St. 14–0, Colorado 35–3. *Lost:* unbeaten Colorado A&M 21–9, Colorado College 27–7.

1922 (7–1) *Won:* Idaho College 16–12, Brigham Young (BYU) 49–0 (1st meeting), Colorado 3–0, Wyoming 27–0, Colorado College 20–6, Whitman 24–0, Utah St. 14–0. *Lost:* Idaho 16–0. *Noteworthy:* won 1st Rocky Mountain Conference title.

1925 (6–2) *Won:* Arizona 9–0, Colorado 12–7, Denver 27–0 (1st meeting since 1912), BYU 27–0, Colorado College 20–0, Wyoming 7–6. *Lost:* USC 28–2 in opener, Utah St. 10–6 in finale. *Noteworthy:* 1st year under Ike Armstrong.

1926 (7–0) *Won:* South Dakota 13–0, Colorado 37–3, Colorado A&M 10–6, Denver 13–0, BYU 40–7, Utah St. 34–0, Hawaii 17–7 (1st meeting). *Noteworthy:* won 2nd Rocky Mountain title in 1st undefeated season since 4-game schedule of 1899.

1928 (5–0–2) *Won:* Nevada-Reno 32–7, Colorado A&M 6–0, Colorado 25–6, Colorado College 27–21, Utah St. 20–0. *Tied:* Creighton 7–7, BYU 0–0. *Star:* T Alton Carman. *Noteworthy:* won 3rd Rocky Mountain crown.

1929 (7–0) *Won:* Nevada-Reno 31–0, Colorado 40–0, Colorado A&M 21–0, BYU 45–13, Colorado College 12–3, Wyoming 44–0, Utah St. 26–7. *Stars:* QB Bob Davis, FB Earl Pomeroy, C Marwin Jonas. *Noteworthy:* repeated as Rocky Mountain champ.

1930 (8–0) *Won:* Nevada-Reno 20–7, Wyoming 72–0, BYU 34–7, Denver 59–0, Colorado A&M 39–0, Colorado College 41–6, Colorado 34–0, Utah St. 41–0. *Stars:* Jonas, E George Watkins, HB Ray Price, soph FB Frank Christensen. *Noteworthy:* won 3rd straight Rocky Mountain title.

1931 (7–2) *Won:* Idaho College 52–0, BYU 43–0, Denver 46–0, Colorado A&M 60–6, Colorado College 28–6, Colorado 32–0, Utah St. 34–0. *Lost:* Washington 7–6 in opener (ending 24-game unbeaten string), Oregon St. 12–0 (1st meeting) in finale. *Star:* Christensen. *Noteworthy:* won 6th Rocky Mountain title.

1932 (5–1–1) *Won:* BYU 29–0, Utah St. 16–0, Colorado 14–0, Denver 27–0, Colorado A&M 16–0. *Lost:* unbeaten national cochamp USC 35–0. *Tied:* Nevada-Reno 6–6. *Stars:* Christensen, T Jack Johnson. *Noteworthy:* won 5th straight Rocky Mountain title.

1938 (7–1–2) *Won:* Montana St. 34–0, Utah St. 33–0, Denver 21–0, Colorado A&M 13–0, Wyoming 39–0 (1st meeting since 1930), Hawaii 14–13. *Lost:* Idaho 16–6. *Tied:* BYU 7–7, Colorado 0–0. *Star:* T Bernard McGarry. *Noteworthy:* won 1st Mountain States Conference title. Made 1st postseason appearance, beating New Mexico 26–0 (1st meeting) in Sun Bowl.

1939 (6–1–2) *Won:* Wyoming 60–0, BYU 35–13, Idaho 35–0, Hawaii 34–18, Colorado A&M 42–7, Utah St. 27–0. *Lost:* Colorado 21–14. *Tied:* Santa Clara 7–7, Denver 7–7. *Noteworthy:* led nation in scoring (28.4-pt avg).

1940 (7–2) *Won:* BYU 12–6, Arizona 24–0, Denver 25–14, Colorado 21–13, Wyoming 34–7 (10th straight over Cowboys), Colorado A&M 27–0, Idaho 13–6. *Lost:* Santa Clara 34–13, Utah St. 7–0. *Noteworthy:* won 2nd Mountain States title.

1941 (6–0–2) *Won:* Idaho Southern 26–7, Wyoming 60–6, Colorado 46–0, Colorado A&M 26–13, Utah St. 33–21, Arizona 12–6. *Tied:* BYU 6–6, Denver 0–0 in successive early games. *Star:* T Floyd Spendlove. *Noteworthy:* repeated as Mountain States champ in 1st unbeaten season since 1930.

1946 (8–3) *Won:* New Mexico 56–14, Arizona 14–7, BYU 35–6, Wyoming 27–7, Colorado 7–0, Colorado A&M 13–0 (10th straight over Rams), San Francisco 21–13, Honolulu All-Stars 40–6. *Lost:* Denver 20–14, Utah St. 22–14 (1st to Aggies in 5 games since 1940), Hawaii 19–16 (1st meeting since 1939).

1947 (8–1–1) *Won:* Oregon St. 7–6 (1st meeting since 1931), Hawaii 35–0, BYU 28–6, Denver 13–7, Wyoming 26–6, Colorado 13–7, Colorado A&M 19–0, Utah St. 40–14. *Lost:* Idaho 13–6. *Tied:* Arizona 20–20. *Star:* B Frank Nelson (1,109 yds total off). *Noteworthy:* won 5th Mountain States title.

1948 (8–1–1) *Won:* Idaho 21–6, Arizona 47–14, BYU 30–0, Wyoming 19–7 (15th straight over

Cowboys), Denver 17–0, Colorado 14–12, Colorado A&M 12–3, Utah St. 41–7. *Lost:* USC 27–0 in opener. *Tied:* Oregon St. 20–20. *Noteworthy:* won 7th and last Mountain States title.

1953 (8–2) *Won:* Arizona 28–7, Idaho 21–0, Hawaii 47–24, Utah St. 33–13, Denver 40–6, Wyoming 13–12, Colorado A&M 35–14, BYU 33–32. *Lost:* Washington 21–14, Colorado 21–0. *Stars:* QB Don Rydalch (1,059 yds total off), Don Petersen (720 yds rush, 9 TDs). *Noteworthy:* won 3rd straight Skyline 8 title.

1960 (7–3) *Won:* Hawaii 33–6, Arizona 13–3, BYU 17–0, Denver 49–16, Colorado St. 27–6, Montana 16–6, Utah St. 6–0. *Lost:* Oregon 20–17, Wyoming 17–7, UCLA 16–9.

1964 (9–2) *Won:* New Mexico 16–0, Idaho 22–0, Colorado St. 13–3, Arizona St. 16–3, Texas Western (Texas–El Paso) 41–0 (1st meeting), BYU 47–13, California 14–0, Utah St. 14–6. *Lost:* Missouri 23–6, Wyoming 14–13 in early games. *Stars:* SE Roy Jefferson, HB Ron Coleman, FB Allen Jacobs, OT Mel Carpenter, C.D. Lowery (8 int). *Noteworthy:* Got share of 1st WAC title. Beat West Virginia 32–6 in Liberty Bowl (indoors at Atlantic City), jumping to 19–0 halftime lead; Jefferson kicked 2 FGs and Ute TDs included 53-yd run by Coleman, 47-yd run by Andy Ireland, and 33-yd pass from Richard Groth to William Morley.

1969 (8–2) *Won:* San Jose St. 42–7, Texas–El Paso 24–6, Arizona St. 24–23, New Mexico 24–0, Oregon St. 7–3, Utah St. 27–7, Wyoming 34–10, BYU 16–6. *Lost:* Oregon 28–17, Arizona 17–16. *Stars:* TE Dale Nosworthy, K Marv Bateman (11 FGs), LB Larry Stone, DB Norm Thompson (5 int, 3 returned for TDs), DB/P Craig Smith.

1978 (8–3) *Won:* Idaho St. 56–0, Colorado St. 30–6, Iowa 13–9, Weber St. 30–7, Texas–El Paso 38–0, BYU 23–22 (1st over Cougars since 1971), Utah St. 23–20, San Diego St. 20–18 (1st meeting).

Lost: Houston 42–25, Wyoming 34–21, New Mexico 24–12. *Stars:* QB Randy Gomez (2,027 yds and 19 TDs pass), Frank Henry (44 pass rec for 711 yds and 6 TDs), OG Tom Krebs, DE Jeff Lyall, P Rick Partridge (44-yd avg). *Noteworthy:* 1st winning season since 1973.

1981 (8–2–1) *Won:* Utah St. 10–0, Portland St. 46–0, Northwestern 42–0, Texas–El Paso 38–10, Colorado St. 25–13, Nevada–Las Vegas 69–26, San Diego St. 17–14, Wyoming 30–27. *Lost:* Arizona St. 52–10, BYU 56–28. *Tied:* New Mexico 7–7. *Stars:* Del Rodgers (1,127 yds rush, 14 TDs, 88 pts), TB Carl Monroe (522 yds and 5 TDs rush), Robbie Richeson (516 yds rush), QB Tyce Ferguson (1,235 yds pass), WRs Tony Graham (29 pass rec for 476 yds) and soph Roderick Wise (14 pass rec for 297 yds), TE Ray Elgaard (18 pass rec for 265 yds), Jim Teahan (15 pass rec for 338 yds), OT Jack Campbell, OG Wayne Jones, K Gilbert Alvarez (14 FGs, 79 pts), DT Steve Clark, LB Bill Gompf, DB Tony Reed. *Noteworthy:* last year under Wayne Howard.

1985 (8–4) *Won:* Boise St. 20–17, Hawaii 29–27, Washington St. 44–37, Texas–El Paso 55–19 (10th straight over Miners), Wyoming 37–20, San Diego St. 39–37, Utah St. 34–7, New Mexico 58–49. *Lost:* Arizona St. 34–27, Air Force 37–15, Colorado St. 21–19, BYU 38–28. *Stars:* DB Erroll Tucker (6 int, nation's punt return leader with 24.3-yd avg and 2 TDs, and kickoff return leader with 29.1-yd avg and 2 TDs), QB Larry Egger (2,988 yds pass), Loren Richey (73 pass rec for 971 yds and 7 TDs), OG Kevin Reach, K Andre Guardi (18 FGs, 94 pts). *Noteworthy:* 1st year under Jim Fassel.

BOWL SUMMARY

Copper 0–1; Liberty 1–0; Sun 1–0.

BOWL RECORD (2–1)

Regular Season	Bowl	Score	Opponent	Record
1938 (7–1–2)	Sun	26–0	New Mexico	(8–2)
1964 (8–2)	Liberty	32–6	West Virginia	(7–3)
1992 (6–5)	Copper	28–31	Washington St.	(8–3)

CONFERENCE TITLES

Rocky Mountain—1922, 1926, 1928, 1929, 1930, 1931, 1932, 1933*. **Mountain States**—1938, 1940, 1941, 1942*, 1947, 1948. **Skyline 8**—1951, 1952, 1953, 1957. **Western Athletic**—1964*.

TOP 20 AP AND UPI RANKING

1964	U–14

MAJOR RIVALS

Utah has played at least 10 games with Air Force 3–9, Arizona 16–13–2, Arizona St. 6–15, Brigham Young 40–24–4, Colorado 24–30–3, Colorado College 14–11, Colorado Mines 7–3, Colorado St. 45–16–2, Denver 28–9–5, Hawaii 13–11, Idaho 14–11–2, Montana 10–0, New Mexico 22–10–2, Oregon 6–14, Oregon St. 4–8–1, San Diego St. 5–8–1, Texas–El Paso 19–8, Utah St. 59–27–4, Wyoming 39–27–1. Record against new WAC member Fresno St.: 1–3.

COACHES

Dean of Utah coaches is Ike Armstrong with record of 140–57–13 for 1925–49, including 13 conference titles, 1 Sun Bowl champion, and 5 unbeaten teams. Other top records for at least 3 years were by Harvey R. Holmes, 11–10–1 for 1900–03; Joseph H. Maddock, 31–10–1 for 1904–09; Fred Bennion, 16–7–3 for 1910–13; Nelson H. Norgren, 14–11 for 1914–17; Thomas Fitzpatrick, 23–17–3 for 1919–24 with 1 Rocky Mountain Conference title; Jack Curtice, 45–32–4 for 1950–57 with 4 Skyline 8 titles; Ray Nagel, 42–39–1 for 1958–65 with 1 WAC title and 1 Liberty Bowl champion; Bill Meek, 33–31 for 1968–73; and Wayne Howard, 30–24–2 for 1977–81.

MISCELLANEA

First game was loss to Utah St. 12–0 in 1892 . . . 1st win was over YMCA 4–0 in 1892 . . . 1st win over college foe was over Utah St. 21–0 in 1900 . . . highest score was over Fort Douglas 129–0 in 1905 . . . highest over college foe was over Montana St. 97–0 in 1911 . . . highest since W.W. II was over Texas–El Paso 82–6 in 1973 . . . worst defeat was by Colorado College 64–0 in 1943 . . . worst since W.W. II was by Ohio St. 64–6 in 1986 . . . highest ever against was by BYU 70–31 in 1989 . . . longest unbeaten string of 24 in 1927–30 ended by Washington 7–6 in 1931 opener . . . longest losing string of 9, in 1973–74 broken with win over New Mexico 21–10 and in 1985–86 with win over Colorado St. 38–28 . . . Utah has had no consensus All-Americans . . . Academic All-Americans were Mel Carpenter, T, 1964; Scott Robbins, DB, 1971; Steve Odom, RB, 1973; and Dick Graham, E, 1976.

WYOMING (Cowboys; Brown and Yellow)

NOTABLE TEAMS

1904 (4–1–1) *Won:* Cheyenne H.S. 56–0, 12–6, Wyoming Faculty 11–0, Ft. Russell 12–0. *Lost:* Utah 23–0 (1st meeting). *Tied:* Colorado St. 6–6.
1949 (9–1) *Won:* Idaho St. 58–13, New Mexico 41–14 (1st meeting since 1941), Colorado St. 8–0 (1st over Rams in 8 games since 1937), Montana St. 48–0, Utah St. 27–0, Utah 13–0 (1st in 24-game series dating to 1904), Brigham Young (BYU) 45–0, Northern Colorado 103–0, Denver 25–6 (1st over Pioneers in 22 games since 1920). *Lost:* Baylor 32–7. *Star:* Sonny Jones (817 yds rush). *Noteworthy:* 1st winning season since 1931.
1950 (10–0) *Won:* Montana St. 61–13, Baylor 7–0, Colorado St. 34–0, Utah St. 40–7, Utah 53–13, New Mexico 44–0, Idaho 14–7, BYU 48–0, Denver 42–13.

TB Eddie Talboom, 1948–50

Stars: TB Eddie Talboom (130 pts on 15 TDs and 40 extra pts, 920 yds and 8 TDs pass), Harry Geldien (10 TDs). *Noteworthy:* Won Skyline 6 title in 1st unbeaten season since 1-game schedule of 1902. Made 1st postseason appearance, beating Washington & Lee 20–7 in Gator Bowl on TDs by Dick Campbell, Talboom (who also kicked 2 ex pts), and John Melton.
1951 (7–2–1) *Won:* Idaho 28–0, Denver 20–14, Utah St. 37–0, Utah 13–0, Montana 34–7 (1st meeting), New Mexico 41–7, Arizona St. 20–7 (1st meeting). *Lost:* Florida 13–0, Colorado St. 14–7. *Tied:* BYU 20–20. *Stars:* Geldien (11 TDs), E Dewey McConnell (nation's leader with 47 pass rec for 725 yds and 9 TDs), Chuck Spaulding (8 TDs, nation's leader with 43.5-yd punting avg).
1955 (8–3) *Won:* Kansas St. 38–20, Montana 35–6, Utah St. 21–13, Tulsa 23–19, Utah 23–13, BYU 14–6, New Mexico 20–0. *Lost:* Colorado St. 14–13, Denver 6–3 (1st to Pioneers since 1948), Houston 26–14. *Stars:* Bs Joe Mastrogiovanni, and Jerry Jester (696 yds rush). *Noteworthy:* beat Texas Tech 21–14 in Sun Bowl on TDs by John Watts, Hank Marshall, and Ova Stapleton.

1956 (10–0) *Won:* Western St. 40–13, Arizona 26–20, Denver 27–0, Colorado St. 20–12, New Mexico 20–13, Utah 30–20, Kansas St. 27–15, Utah St. 21–0, Montana 34–13, BYU 7–6. *Star:* HB Jim Crawford (14 TDs, 96 pts, nation's leader with 1,104 yds rush). *Noteworthy:* won Skyline 8 title in last year under Phil Dickens.
1958 (8–3) *Won:* Montana 21–14, Denver 15–12, Oregon St. 28–0, Colorado St. 7–6, Utah 25–20, Utah St. 41–13, BYU 22–14. *Lost:* Kansas St. 17–14, New Mexico 13–12, unbeaten Air Force 21–6. *Noteworthy:* won 2nd Skyline 8 title (3rd Skyline crown). Beat Hardin-Simmons 14–6 in Sun Bowl on 2nd quarter TDs by sophs Mark Smolinski and Clifford Snyder.
1959 (9–1) *Won:* Montana 58–0, Utah St. 27–2, Colorado St. 29–0, BYU 21–6, Utah 21–7, N.C. State 26–0, San Jose St. 28–7, New Mexico 25–20, Denver 45–0. *Lost:* Air Force 20–7 in 2nd game. *Star:* Gerald Hill (8 TDs, 50 pts). *Noteworthy:* repeated as Skyline 8 champ.
1960 (8–2) *Won:* Montana 14–0, New Mexico 13–3, Denver 41–2, Colorado St. 40–8, Air Force 15–0, Utah 17–7, Texas Tech 10–7, BYU 30–6. *Lost:* Arizona 21–19, Utah St. 17–13 (1st to Aggies since 1948). *Star:* Hill (636 yds rush). *Noteworthy:* led nation in total defense and rush defense, and got share of 3rd straight Skyline 8 title.
1961 (6–1–2) *Won:* Montana 29–0 (10th straight over Grizzlies), N.C. State 15–14, Colorado St. 18–7, BYU 36–8, Utah 13–6, New Mexico 33–7. *Lost:* Arizona 20–15. *Tied:* Kansas 6–6, unbeaten Utah St. 6–6. *Noteworthy:* Bob Devaney's last team got share of 6th Skyline title (4th straight).
1964 (6–2–2) *Won:* Colorado St. 31–7, Washington St. 28–7, Kansas 17–14, Utah 14–13, Texas–El Paso 20–6, BYU 31–11. *Lost:* Arizona 15–7, New Mexico 17–6 in consecutive mid-season games. *Tied:* Utah St. 20–20, Air Force 7–7. *Stars:* G Bill Levine, T Herm Memmelaar, E Darryl Alleman.
1966 (10–1) *Won:* Air Force 13–0, Arizona St. 23–6, Arizona 36–6, Utah 40–7, New Mexico 37–7, Utah St. 35–10, Wichita St. 55–0, Texas–El Paso 31–7, BYU 47–14. *Lost:* Colorado St. 12–10 (1st to Rams since 1955). *Stars:* QB Rick Egloff (13 TDs pass), TB Jim Kiick, HB Vic Washington (nation's punt return leader with 13-yd avg), Es Jerry Marion (33 pass rec for 612 yds and 7 TDs) and Tom Frazier, Ts Mike LaHood and Ron Billingsley,

Gs Jerry Durling and Dave Rupp, DBs Dick Speights (6 pass int) and Paul Toscano (6 pass int), K/P Jerry DePoyster (71 pts, nation's leader with 13 FGs). *Noteworthy:* Won 1st WAC title while leading nation in rush defense. Beat Florida St. 28–20 in Sun Bowl after trailing 14–7 at half; Kiick scored 2 TDs, Marion scored on 39-yd pass from Egloff (who scored other Cowboy TD), and De-Poyster kicked 4 ex pts.

1967 (10–1) *Won:* Arizona 36–17, Air Force 37–10, Colorado St. 13–10, BYU 26–10, Utah 28–0, Wichita St. 30–7, Arizona St. 15–13, San Jose St. 28–7, New Mexico 42–6, Texas–El Paso 21–19. *Stars:* Kiick, Washington, Speights, QB Toscano (1,791 yds and 18 TDs pass), FL Gene Huey (53 pass rec for 868 yds and 5 TDs), E Tim Gottberg, LaHood, T Mike Dirks, DePoyster (15 FGs, 66 pts, 41.7-yd punting avg), LB Jim House. *Noteworthy:* Repeated as WAC champ and again led nation in rush defense in 1st unbeaten season since 1956. Lost to Louisiana St. (LSU) 20–13 in rainy, chilly Sugar Bowl (1st loss in 5 bowls) after leading 13–0 at halftime; scored on TD by Kiick and 2 FGs and ex pt by DePoyster.

1968 (7–3) *Won:* Utah St. 48–3, Arizona St. 27–13, BYU 20–17, Utah 20–9, New Mexico 35–6, Colorado St. 46–14, Texas–El Paso 26–19. *Lost:* Nebraska 13–10, Air Force 10–3 (1st to Falcons in 5 games since 1962), Arizona 14–7. *Stars:* K/P Bob Jacobs (42.1-yd punting avg, 68 pts, nation's leader with 14 FGs), Huey (43 pass rec for 626 yds and 9 TDs), Ts Byra Kite and Larry Nels, G Tommy Tucker, House. *Noteworthy:* led nation in total defense and won 3rd straight WAC title.

1976 (8–4) *Won:* South Dakota 48–7, Utah St. 20–3, Arizona St. 13–10, BYU 34–29, New Mexico 24–23, Utah 45–22, Arizona 26–24, Texas–El Paso 14–10. *Lost:* Michigan St. 21–10, Colorado St. 19–16, Air Force 41–21. *Stars:* Robbie Wright (718 yds rush), TE Walter Howard, Ts Dennis Baker and Ray Stawowy, LB Paul Nunu, DB Kevin McClain. *Noteworthy:* Got share of 4th WAC title in 1st winning season since 1969. Lost to Oklahoma 41–7 in Fiesta Bowl; scored on TD by soph Latraia Jones in last quarter.

1981 (8–3) *Won:* Cal St.–Fullerton 38–13, Air Force 17–10, Nevada–Las Vegas 45–21, Texas–El Paso 63–12, BYU 33–20 (1st over Cougars since 1976), Colorado St. 55–21, San Diego St. 24–13, New Mexico 13–12. *Lost:* Oklahoma 37–20, Ha-

waii 14–9, Utah 30–27. *Stars:* QB Phil Davis (1,173 yds and 9 TDs pass, 575 yds and 10 TDs rush), SE Steve Martinez (37 pass rec for 629 yds), TE James Williams (27 pass rec for 421 yds and 6 TDs), soph FB Walter Goffigan (6 TDs rush), RB Peter Ruel (5 TDs), C Joe DiGiorgio, OL Gary Crüm, LB Jim Eliopulos, Lee Mitchell (5 int), soph P Jack Weil (41.4-yd avg). *Noteworthy:* 1st year under Al Kincaid.

1987 (10–3) *Won:* Air Force 27–13, Iowa St. 34–17, San Diego St. 52–10, BYU 29–27 (1st over Cougars since 1981), Houston 37–35, Colorado St. 20–15, New Mexico 59–16, Utah 31–7, Texas–El Paso 37–13, Hawaii 24–20. *Lost:* Washington St. 43–28, Oklahoma St. 35–29 in consecutive early games. *Stars:* QB Craig Burnett (2,799 yds and 21 TDs pass), WR Anthony Sargent (68 pass rec for 929 yds and 11 TDs), TE Bill Hoffman (68 pass rec for 786 yds), James Loving (42 pass rec for 772 yds), RB Gerald Abraham (1,305 yds and 13 TDs rush), OT Tony Kapushion, DT Jeff Knapton, LB Garland Thaxton, P Tom Kilpatrick (42.9-yd avg). *Noteworthy:* Won 5th WAC title in 1st year under Paul Roach. Lost to Iowa 20–19 in Holiday Bowl after leading 19–7 at halftime; scored on 15-yd pass from Burnett to Loving, 3-yd run by Abraham, and 2 FGs and ex pt by Greg Worker.

1988 (11–2) *Won:* BYU 24–14, Louisville 44–9, Louisiana Tech 38–6, Air Force 48–45, Cal St.–Fullerton 35–16, San Diego St. 55–27, New Mexico 55–7, Utah 61–8, Colorado St. 48–14, Texas–El Paso 51–6, Hawaii 28–22. *Lost:* Houston 34–10. *Stars:* QB Randy Welniak (2,791 yds and 21 TDs pass, 415 yds and 16 TDs rush), Freddie Dussett (42 pass rec for 583 yds and 6 TDs), WR Ted Gilmore (40 pass rec for 594 yds), Kilpatrick (30 pass rec for 416 yds and 7 TDs, 42.1-yd punting avg), TE Gordy Wood (24 pass rec for 321 yds), RB Dabby Dawson (1,119 yds rush, 21 pass rec for 249 yds, 10 TDs), Peter Gunn (9 TDs, 1,179 all-purpose yds), C Grant Salisbury, frosh K Sean Fleming (17 FGs, 110 pts), DT Pat Rabold, DEs David Edeen and soph Mitch Donahue, LB Mike Schenbeck, DB Eric Coleman. *Noteworthy:* Repeated as WAC champ. Lost to Oklahoma St. 62–14 in Holiday Bowl after trailing only 17–7 at halftime; scored on 2 short runs by Welniak.

1990 (9–4) *Won:* Temple 38–23, Washington St. 34–13, Arkansas St. 34–27, Air Force 24–12, Utah 28–10, San Diego St. 52–51, New Mexico 25–22,

Weber St. 21–12, Texas–El Paso 17–10. *Lost:* Colorado St. 17–8, BYU 45–14, Hawaii 38–17 in last 3 games. *Stars:* QB Tom Corontzos (2,730 yds and 15 TDs pass), WRs Shawn Wiggins (51 pass rec for 899 yds and 6 TDs), Robert Rivers (23 pass rec for 517 yds, 1,001 all-purpose yds, 5 TDs) and frosh Ryan Yarborough (23 pass rec for 413 yds), Wood (55 pass rec for 527 yds, 5 TDs), RBs Dwight Driver (684 yds and 5 TDs rush) and Jay Daffer (7 TDs rush), OL Tyrone Fittje, Fleming (16 FGs, 79 pts), Donahue, LB Willie Wright, soph DB Paul

Wallace (5 int). *Noteworthy:* Roach's last team. Lost to California 17–15 in Copper Bowl; Corontzos passed for 226 yds, Wiggins had 7 pass rec for 119 yds, and Rivers scored on 70-yd punt return.

BOWL SUMMARY

Copper 0–1; Fiesta 0–1; Gator 1–0; Holiday 0–2; Sugar 0–1; Sun 3–0.

BOWL RECORD (4–5)

Regular Season	Bowl	Score	Opponent	Record
1950 (9–0)	Gator	20–7	Washington & Lee	(8–2)
1955 (7–3)	Sun	21–14	Texas Tech	(7–2–1)
1958 (7–3)	Sun	14–6	Hardin-Simmons	(6–4)
1966 (9–1)	Sun	28–20	Florida State	(6–4)
1967 (10–0)	Sugar	13–20	LSU	(6–3–1)
1976 (8–3)	Fiesta	7–41	Oklahoma	(8–2–1)
1987 (10–2)	Holiday	19–20	Iowa	(9–3)
1988 (11–1)	Holiday	14–62	Oklahoma State	(9–2)
1990 (9–3)	Copper	15–17	California	(6–4–1)

CONFERENCE TITLES

Skyline 6—1950. **Skyline 8**—1956, 1958, 1959, 1960*, 1961*. **Western Athletic**—1966, 1967, 1968, 1976*, 1987, 1988.

TOP 20 AP AND UPI RANKING

1950	12–14	1959	16–18	1966	U–15	1988	U–20
1956	U–16	1961	U–17	1967	6–5		

MAJOR RIVALS

Wyoming has played at least 10 games with Air Force 14–14–3, Arizona 10–12, Arizona St. 6–9, Brigham Young 28–32–3, Colorado 2–22–1, Colorado College 1–16–1, Colorado Mines 9–16–2, Colorado St. College 17–5–3, Colorado St. 36–43–5, Denver 11–32–2, Ft. Russell 12–1, Hawaii 7–8, Montana 12–0, Montana St. 11–6, New Mexico 28–21, Northern Colorado 17–5–3, San Diego St. 9–6, Texas–El Paso 23–6–1, Utah 27–39–1, Utah St.

20–34–4. Record against new WAC member Fresno St.: 0–1.

COACHES

Dean of Wyoming coaches is Lloyd W. Eaton with record of 57–33–2 for 1962–70, including 3 WAC titles, 2 bowl teams, and 1 team unbeaten in regular season. Other top records for at least 3 years were by William McMurray, 15–11–1 for

1900–06 with 2 unbeaten teams; Bowden Wyatt, 39–17–1 for 1947–52 with 1 Skyline 6 title and 1 unbeaten Gator Bowl champion; Phil Dickens, 29–11–1 for 1953–56 with 1 Skyline 8 title, 1 Sun Bowl champion, and 1 unbeaten team; Robert S. "Bob" Devaney, 35–10–5 for 1957–61 with 4 Skyline 8 titles and 1 Sun Bowl champion; Al Kincaid, 29–29 for 1981–85; and Paul Roach, 35–15 for 1987–90 with 2 WAC titles and 3 bowl teams.

MISCELLANEA

First game was win over Cheyenne H.S. 14–0 in 1893 . . . 1st win over college foe was over Colorado A&M (Colorado St.) 34–0 in 1895 . . . highest score was over Northern Colorado 103–0 in 1949 . . . worst defeat was by Utah 79–0 in 1923 . . . worst defeats since W.W. II were by LSU 66–7 in 1977 and BYU 59–0 in 1985 . . . highest against Cowboys since W.W. II was by Utah 69–14 in 1983 . . . longest unbeaten string of 16 in 1956–57 ended by Utah 23–15 . . . longest win string of 14 in 1966–67 ended by LSU 20–13 in 1968 Sugar Bowl . . . longest winless string of 12 in 1929–30 broken with win over Colorado St. 21–6 . . . 10-game winless string in 1946–47 broken with win over BYU 12–7 . . . consensus All-Americans were Jack Weil, P, 1983; and Jay Novacek, TE, 1984 . . . Academic All-Americans were Bob Dinges, DE, 1965; George Mills, OG, 1967; Mike Lopiccolo, OT, 1973; Bob Gustafson, OT, 1984; and Patrick Arndt, OG, 1987.

APPENDIX A
Individual Awards

HEISMAN TROPHY WINNERS

(Nation's outstanding college player, awarded
by Downtown Athletic Club of New York)

1935	Jay Berwanger, HB, Chicago	1964	John Huarte, QB, Notre Dame
1936	Larry Kelley, E, Yale	1965	Mike Garrett, HB, USC
1937	Clint Frank, HB, Yale	1966	Steve Spurrier, QB, Florida
1938	Davey O'Brien, QB, TCU	1967	Gary Beban, QB, UCLA
1939	Nile Kinnick, HB, Iowa	1968	O.J. Simpson, HB, USC
1940	Tom Harmon, HB, Michigan	1969	Steve Owens, HB, Oklahoma
1941	Bruce Smith, HB, Minnesota	1970	Jim Plunkett, QB, Stanford
1942	Frank Sinkwich, HB, Georgia	1971	Pat Sullivan, QB, Auburn
1943	Angelo Bertelli, QB, Notre Dame	1972	Johnny Rodgers, FL, Nebraska
1944	Les Horvath, QB, Ohio State	1973	John Cappelletti, HB, Penn State
1945	Felix "Doc" Blanchard, FB, Army	1974	Archie Griffin, HB, Ohio State
1946	Glenn Davis, HB, Army	1975	Archie Griffin, HB, Ohio State
1947	John Lujack, QB, Notre Dame	1976	Tony Dorsett, HB, Pittsburgh
1948	Doak Walker, HB, SMU	1977	Earl Campbell, HB, Texas
1949	Leon Hart, E, Notre Dame	1978	Billy Sims, HB, Oklahoma
1950	Vic Janowicz, HB, Ohio State	1979	Charles White, HB, USC
1951	Dick Kazmaier, HB, Princeton	1980	George Rogers, HB, South Carolina
1952	Billy Vessels, HB, Oklahoma	1981	Marcus Allen, HB, USC
1953	John Lattner, HB, Notre Dame	1982	Herschel Walker, HB, Georgia
1954	Alan Ameche, FB, Wisconsin	1983	Mike Rozier, HB, Nebraska
1955	Howard Cassady, HB, Ohio State	1984	Doug Flutie, QB, Boston College
1956	Paul Hornung, QB, Notre Dame	1985	Bo Jackson, HB, Auburn
1957	John David Crow, HB, Texas A&M	1986	Vinny Testaverde, QB, Miami (Fla.)
1958	Pete Dawkins, HB, Army	1987	Tim Brown, FL, Notre Dame
1959	Billy Cannon, HB, LSU	1988	Barry Sanders, HB, Oklahoma State
1960	Joe Bellino, HB, Navy	1989	Andre Ware, QB, Houston
1961	Ernie Davis, HB, Syracuse	1990	Ty Detmer, QB, BYU
1962	Terry Baker, QB, Oregon State	1991	Desmond Howard, WR, Michigan
1963	Roger Staubach, QB, Navy	1992	Gino Torretta, QB, Miami (Fla.)

MAXWELL AWARD WINNERS

(Nation's outstanding college player, awarded by
Maxwell Memorial Football Club of Philadelphia)

1937	Clint Frank, HB, Yale	1965	Tommy Nobis, LB, Texas
1938	Davey O'Brien, QB, TCU	1966	Jim Lynch, LB, Notre Dame
1939	Nile Kinnick, HB, Iowa	1967	Gary Beban, QB, UCLA
1940	Tom Harmon, HB, Michigan	1968	O.J. Simpson, RB, USC
1941	Bill Dudley, HB, Virginia	1969	Mike Reid, DT, Penn State
1942	Paul Governali, QB, Columbia	1970	Jim Plunkett, QB, Stanford
1943	Bob Odell, HB, Pennsylvania	1971	Ed Marinaro, RB, Cornell
1944	Glenn Davis, HB, Army	1972	Brad VanPelt, DB, Michigan State
1945	Felix "Doc" Blanchard, FB, Army	1973	John Cappelletti, RB, Penn State
1946	Charley Trippi, HB, Georgia	1974	Steve Joachim, QB, Temple
1947	Doak Walker, HB, SMU	1975	Archie Griffin, RB, Ohio State
1948	Chuck Bednarik, C, Pennsylvania	1976	Tony Dorsett, RB, Pittsburgh
1949	Leon Hart, E, Notre Dame	1977	Ross Browner, DE, Notre Dame
1950	Reds Bagnell, HB, Pennsylvania	1978	Chuck Fusina, QB, Penn State
1951	Dick Kazmaier, HB, Princeton	1979	Charles White, RB, USC
1952	John Lattner, HB, Notre Dame	1980	Hugh Green, DE, Pittsburgh
1953	John Lattner, HB, Notre Dame	1981	Marcus Allen, RB, USC
1954	Ron Beagle, E, Navy	1982	Herschel Walker, RB, Georgia
1955	Howard Cassady, HB, Ohio State	1983	Mike Rozier, RB, Nebraska
1956	Tommy McDonald, HB, Oklahoma	1984	Doug Flutie, QB, Boston College
1957	Bob Reifsnyder, T, Navy	1985	Chuck Long, QB, Iowa
1958	Pete Dawkins, HB, Army	1986	Vinny Testaverde, QB, Miami (Fla.)
1959	Rich Lucas, QB, Penn State	1987	Don McPherson, QB, Syracuse
1960	Joe Bellino, HB, Navy	1988	Barry Sanders, HB, Oklahoma State
1961	Bob Ferguson, FB, Ohio State	1989	Anthony Thompson, RB, Indiana
1962	Terry Baker, QB, Oregon State	1990	Ty Detmer, QB, BYU
1963	Roger Staubach, QB, Navy	1991	Desmond Howard, WR, Michigan
1964	Glenn Ressler, C, Penn State	1992	Gino Torretta, QB, Miami (Fla.)

OUTLAND TROPHY WINNERS

(Nation's outstanding college interior lineman)

1946	George Connor, T, Notre Dame	1957	Alex Karras, T, Iowa
1947	Joe Steffy, G, Army	1958	Zeke Smith, G, Auburn
1948	Bill Fischer, G, Notre Dame	1959	Mike McGee, T, Duke
1949	Ed Bagdon, G, Michigan State	1960	Tom Brown, G, Minnesota
1950	Bob Gain, T, Kentucky	1961	Merlin Olsen, T, Utah State
1951	Jim Weatherall, T, Oklahoma	1962	Bobby Bell, T, Minnesota
1952	Dick Modzelewski, T, Maryland	1963	Scott Appleton, T, Texas
1953	J.D. Roberts, G, Oklahoma	1964	Steve DeLong, T, Tennessee
1954	Bill Brooks, G, Arkansas	1965	Tommy Nobis, G, Texas
1955	Calvin Jones, G, Iowa	1966	Loyd Phillips, T, Arkansas
1956	Jim Parker, G, Ohio State	1967	Ron Yary, T, USC

(continued)

OUTLAND TROPHY WINNERS *(continued)*

1968	Bill Stanfill, T, Georgia	1981	Dave Rimington, C, Nebraska
1969	Mike Reid, DT, Penn State	1982	Dave Rimington, C, Nebraska
1970	Jim Stillwagon, MG, Ohio State	1983	Dean Steinkuhler, G, Nebraska
1971	Larry Jacobson, DT, Nebraska	1984	Bruce Smith, DT, Virginia Tech
1972	Rich Glover, MG, Nebraska	1985	Mike Ruth, NG, Boston College
1973	John Hicks, OT, Ohio State	1986	Jason Buck, DT, Brigham Young
1974	Randy White, DE, Maryland	1987	Chad Hennings, DT, Air Force
1975	Lee Roy Selmon, DT, Oklahoma	1988	Tracy Rocker, DT, Auburn
1976	Ross Browner, DE, Notre Dame	1989	Mohammed Elewonibi, OG, BYU
1977	Brad Shearer, DT, Texas	1990	Russell Maryland, DT, Miami (Fla.)
1978	Greg Roberts, G, Oklahoma	1991	Steve Emtman, DT, Washington
1979	Jim Ritcher, C, N.C. State	1992	Will Shields, OG, Nebraska
1980	Mark May, OT, Pittsburgh		

LOMBARDI AWARD WINNERS

(Nation's outstanding college lineman)

1970	Jim Stillwagon, MG, Ohio State	1982	Dave Rimington, C, Nebraska
1971	Walt Patulski, DE, Notre Dame	1983	Dean Steinkuhler, G, Nebraska
1972	Rich Glover, MG, Nebraska	1984	Tony Degrate, DT, Texas
1973	John Hicks, OT, Ohio State	1985	Tony Casillas, NG, Oklahoma
1974	Randy White, DT, Maryland	1986	Cornelius Bennett, LB, Alabama
1975	Lee Roy Selmon, DT, Oklahoma	1987	Chris Spielman, LB, Ohio State
1976	Wilson Whitley, DT, Houston	1988	Tracy Rocker, DT, Auburn
1977	Ross Browner, DE, Notre Dame	1989	Percy Snow, LB, Michigan State
1978	Bruce Clark, DT, Penn State	1990	Chris Zorich, DT, Notre Dame
1979	Brad Budde, G, USC	1991	Steve Emtman, DT, Washington
1980	Hugh Green, DE, Pittsburgh	1992	Marvin Jones, LB, Florida State
1981	Kenneth Sims, DT, Texas		

COACH OF THE YEAR WINNERS

(The American Football Coaches Association award was first given in 1935; the
Football Writers Association of America award was first given in 1957)

AFCA   *FWAA*

1935	Lynn Waldorf, Northwestern
1936	Dick Harlow, Harvard
1937	Edward Mylin, Lafayette
1938	Bill Kern, Carnegie Tech
1939	Eddie Anderson, Iowa
1940	Clark Shaughnessy, Stanford
1941	Frank Leahy, Notre Dame
1942	Bill Alexander, Georgia Tech

(continued)

COACH OF THE YEAR WINNERS *(continued)*

AFCA	FWAA
1943 Amos Alonzo Stagg, Pacific	
1944 Carroll Widdoes, Ohio State	
1945 A.N. "Bo" McMillin, Indiana	
1946 Earl "Red" Blaik, Army	
1947 Fritz Crisler, Michigan	
1948 Bennie Oosterbaan, Michigan	
1949 "Bud" Wilkinson, Oklahoma	
1950 Charlie Caldwell, Princeton	
1951 Chuck Taylor, Stanford	
1952 "Biggie" Munn, Michigan State	
1953 Jim Tatum, Maryland	
1954 Henry "Red" Sanders, UCLA	
1955 "Duffy" Daugherty, Michigan State	
1956 Bowden Wyatt, Tennessee	
1957 Woody Hayes, Ohio State	Hayes
1958 Paul Dietzel, LSU	Dietzel
1959 "Ben" Schwartzwalder, Syracuse	Schwartzwalder
1960 Murray Warmath, Minnesota	Warmath
1961 Paul "Bear" Bryant, Alabama	Darrell Royal, Texas
1962 John McKay, USC	McKay
1963 Darrell Royal, Texas	Royal
1964 Frank Broyles, Arkansas	Parseghian
Ara Parseghian, Notre Dame	
1965 Tommy Prothro, UCLA	"Duffy" Daugherty, Michigan State
1966 Tom Cahill, Army	Cahill
1967 John Pont, Indiana	Pont
1968 Joe Paterno, Penn State	Woody Hayes, Ohio State
1969 "Bo" Schembechler, Michigan	Schembechler
1970 Charles McClendon, LSU	Alex Agase, Northwestern
Darrell Royal, Texas	
1971 Paul "Bear" Bryant, Alabama	Bob Devaney, Nebraska
1972 John McKay, USC	McKay
1973 Paul "Bear" Bryant, Alabama	Johnny Majors, Pittsburgh
1974 Grant Teaff, Baylor	Teaff
1975 Frank Kush, Arizona State	Woody Hayes, Ohio State
1976 Johnny Majors, Pittsburgh	Majors
1977 Don James, Washington	Lou Holtz, Arkansas
1978 Joe Paterno, Penn State	Paterno
1979 Earle Bruce, Ohio State	Bruce
1980 Vince Dooley, Georgia	Dooley
1981 Danny Ford, Clemson	Ford
1982 Joe Paterno, Penn State	Paterno
1983 Ken Hatfield, Air Force	Howard Schnellenberger, Miami (Fla.)
1984 LaVell Edwards, BYU	Edwards
1985 Fisher DeBerry, Air Force	DeBerry
1986 Joe Paterno, Penn State	Paterno

(continued)

COACH OF THE YEAR WINNERS *(continued)*

AFCA	*FWAA*
1987 Dick MacPherson, Syracuse	MacPherson
1988 Don Nehlen, West Virginia	Lou Holtz, Notre Dame
1989 Bill McCartney, Colorado	McCartney
1990 Bobby Ross, Georgia Tech	Ross
1991 Don James, Washington	James
1992 Gene Stallings, Alabama	Stallings

APPENDIX B

TEAM NATIONAL CHAMPIONS

The Associated Press (Sportswriters' Poll)[a]		United Press International (Coaches' Poll) USA Today/CNN (since 1991)[a]
1936	Minnesota	
1937	Pittsburgh	
1938	Texas Christian	
1939	Texas A&M	
1940	Minnesota	
1941	Minnesota	
1942	Ohio State	
1943	Notre Dame	
1944	Army	
1945	Army	
1946	Notre Dame	
1947	Notre Dame	
1948	Michigan	
1949	Notre Dame	
1950	Oklahoma	Oklahoma
1951	Tennessee	Tennessee
1952	Michigan State	Michigan State
1953	Maryland	Maryland
1954	Ohio State	UCLA
1955	Oklahoma	Oklahoma
1956	Oklahoma	Oklahoma
1957	Auburn	Ohio State
1958	Louisiana State	Louisiana State
1959	Syracuse	Syracuse
1960	Minnesota	Minnesota
1961	Alabama	Alabama
1962	Southern California	Southern California
1963	Texas	Texas

[a]AP selected only the top ten teams in 1962–1967; in other years, AP and UPI (USA Today/CNN since 1991) selected at least twenty top teams.

(continued)

TEAM NATIONAL CHAMPIONS *(continued)*

The Associated Press (Sportswriters' Poll)[a]	United Press International (Coaches' Poll) USA Today/CNN (since 1991)[a]
1964 Alabama	Alabama
1965 Alabama	Michigan State
1966 Notre Dame	Notre Dame
1967 Southern California	Southern California
1968 Ohio State	Ohio State
1969 Texas	Texas
1970 Nebraska	Texas
1971 Nebraska	Nebraska
1972 Southern California	Southern California
1973 Notre Dame	Alabama
1974 Oklahoma	Southern California
1975 Oklahoma	Oklahoma
1976 Pittsburgh	Pittsburgh
1977 Notre Dame	Notre Dame
1978 Alabama	Southern California
1979 Alabama	Alabama
1980 Georgia	Georgia
1981 Clemson	Clemson
1982 Penn State	Penn State
1983 Miami (Fla.)	Miami (Fla.)
1984 Brigham Young	Brigham Young
1985 Oklahoma	Oklahoma
1986 Penn State	Penn State
1987 Miami (Fla.)	Miami (Fla.)
1988 Notre Dame	Notre Dame
1989 Miami (Fla.)	Miami (Fla.)
1990 Colorado	Georgia Tech
1991 Miami (Fla.)	Washington
1992 Alabama	Alabama

[a]AP selected only the top ten teams in 1962–1967; in other years, AP and UPI (USA Today/CNN since 1991) selected at least twenty top teams.

APPENDIX C

ALL-TIME COACHING RECORDS

Listed are coaches with at least 200 career victories
won mostly at Division I-A (or equivalent) schools:

Record	Coach	Schools Coached
323–85–17	Paul "Bear" Bryant	Maryland (1945) 6–2–1 Kentucky (1946–53) 60–23–5 Texas A&M (1954–57) 25–14–2 Alabama (1958–82) 232–46–9
314–199–35	Amos Alonzo Stagg	Springfield (1890–91) 10–11–1 Chicago (1892–1932) 244–111–27 Pacific (1933–46) 60–77–7
313–106–32	Glenn "Pop" Warner	Georgia (1895–96) 7–4 Cornell (1897–98, 1904–06) 36–13–3 Carlisle (1899–1903, 1907–13) 109–42–8 Pittsburgh (1915–23) 59–12–4 Stanford (1924–32) 71–17–8 Temple (1933–38) 31–18–9
247–67–3	Joe Paterno	Penn State (1966–92) 247–67–3
238–72–10	"Woody" Hayes	Denison (1946–48) 19–6 Miami (Ohio) (1949–50) 14–5 Ohio State (1951–78) 205–61–10
234–65–8	"Bo" Schembechler	Miami (Ohio) (1963–68) 40–17–3 Michigan (1969–89) 194–48–5
227–77–3	Bobby Bowden	Samford (1959–62) 31–6 West Virginia (1970–75) 42–26 Florida State (1976–92) 154–45–3
207–176–19	Jess Neely	Rhodes (1924–27) 20–17–2 Clemson (1931–39) 43–35–7 Rice (1940–66) 144–124–10
203–95–14	Warren Woodson	Central Arkansas (1935–39) 40–8–3 Hardin-Simmons (1941–42, 1946–51) 58–24–6 Arizona (1952–56) 26–22–2 New Mexico St. (1958–67) 63–36–3 Trinity (Texas) (1972–73) 16–5

(continued)

ALL-TIME COACHING RECORDS *(continued)*

Record	Coach	Schools Coached
201–77–10	Vince Dooley	Georgia (1964–88) 201–77–10
201–128–15	Eddie Anderson	Loras (1922–24) 16–6–2
		DePaul (1925–31) 21–22–3
		Holy Cross (1933–38, 1950–64) 129–67–8
		Iowa (1939–42, 1946–49) 35–33–2

APPENDIX D

TOP-10 TEAM AND INDIVIDUAL STATISTICS, AND MISCELLANEOUS RECORDS

Top 10 Total All-Time Victories (Current Division I-A Teams)

Team	Wins
Michigan	731
Notre Dame	712
Alabama	682
Texas	682
Penn State	664
Nebraska	662
Oklahoma	650
Ohio State	649
Tennessee	627
Southern California	622

Top 10 All-Time Winning Percentages (Current Division I-A Teams)

Team	Years	Won–Lost–Tied	Percentage
Notre Dame	104	712–210–41	.761
Michigan	113	731–238–36	.745
Alabama	98	682–234–43	.733
Oklahoma	98	650–237–52	.720
Texas	100	682–268–31	.711
Southern California	100	622–249–52	.702
Ohio State	103	649–264–52	.699
Penn State	106	664–289–41	.689
Nebraska	103	662–289–40	.688
Tennessee	96	627–274–52	.685

Top Winning Percentages for Former Major Teams

Team	Total Years	Span	Won–Lost–Tied	Percentage
Carlisle Indian School	25	1893–1917	167–88–13	.647
Detroit	64	1896–1964	305–200–25	.599

(continued)

TOP-10 TEAM AND INDIVIDUAL STATISTICS, AND MISCELLANEOUS RECORDS (continued)

Top Winning Percentages for Former Major Teams (continued)

Team	Total Years	Span	Won–Lost–Tied	Percentage
Centenary	36	1894–1947	148–100–21	.589
Xavier (Ohio)	61	1900–1973	302–223–21	.572
St. Louis	49	1899–1949	235–179–33	.563
Creighton	43	1900–1942	183–139–27	.563
Gonzaga	39	1892–1941	130–99–20	.562
Marquette	68	1892–1960	273–220–38	.550
Haskell Institute	43	1896–1938	199–166–18	.543
Denver	73	1885–1960	273–262–40	.510

Top-10 Total Bowl Victories

Team	Wins	Won–Lost–Tied	Percentage
Alabama	25	25–17–3	.589
Southern California	22	22–13	.628
Oklahoma	19	19–10–1	.650
Tennessee	18	18–15	.545
Georgia Tech	17	17–8	.680
Penn State	17	17–10–2	.621
Texas	16	16–16–2	.500
Georgia	15	15–13–3	.532
Mississippi	14	14–11	.560
Nebraska	14	14–17	.452

Top-10 Bowl-Winning Percentages (Minimum of 10 Appearances)

Team	Won–Lost–Tied	Percentage
Oklahoma State	9–3	.750
Georgia Tech	17–8	.680
Notre Dame	12–6	.667
Oklahoma	19–10–1	.650
Arizona State	9–5–1	.633
Southern California	22–13	.628
Penn State	17–10–2	.621
Florida State	12–7–2	.619
Clemson	11–7	.611
Washington	12–8–1	.595

Teams with 20 or More Bowl Appearances

Team	Appearances	Won–Lost–Tied
Alabama	45	25–17–3
Southern California	35	22–13

(continued)

TOP-10 TEAM AND INDIVIDUAL STATISTICS, AND MISCELLANEOUS RECORDS (continued)

Teams with 20 or More Bowl Appearances (continued)

Team	Appearances	Won–Lost–Tied
Texas	34	16–16–2
Tennessee	33	18–15
Georgia	31	15–13–3
Nebraska	31	14–17
Oklahoma	30	19–10–1
Penn State	29	17–10–2
Louisiana State	28	11–16–1
Arkansas	26	9–14–3
Georgia Tech	25	17–8
Mississippi	25	14–11
Ohio State	25	11–14
Michigan	24	11–13
Auburn	23	12–9–2
Florida State	21	12–7–2
Washington	21	12–8–1
Texas A&M	20	11–9
Florida	20	9–11

Ten Longest Winning Streaks

Wins	Team	Years	Ended By	Score
47	Oklahoma	1953–57	Notre Dame	0–7
39	Washington	1908–14	Oregon State	0–0
37	Yale	1890–93	Princeton	0–6
37	Yale	1887–89	Princeton	0–10
35	Toledo	1969–71	Tampa	0–21
34	Pennsylvania	1894–96	Lafayette	4–6
31	Oklahoma	1948–50	Kentucky	7–13[a]
31	Pittsburgh	1914–18	Service Team[b]	9–10
31	Pennsylvania	1896–98	Harvard	0–10
30	Texas	1968–70	Notre Dame	11–24[a]

[a]Streak ended in bowl game.
[b]Cleveland Naval Reserve

Ten Longest Unbeaten Strings

Games	Ties	Team	Years	Ended By	Score
63	4	Washington	1907–17	California	0–27
56	1	Michigan	1901–05	Chicago	0–2
50	4	California	1920–25	Olympic Club	0–15
48	1	Oklahoma	1953–57	Notre Dame	0–7
48	1	Yale	1885–89	Princeton	0–10
47	5	Yale	1879–85	Princeton	5–6

(continued)

TOP-10 TEAM AND INDIVIDUAL STATISTICS, AND MISCELLANEOUS RECORDS (continued)

Ten Longest Unbeaten Strings (continued)

Games	Ties	Team	Years	Ended By	Score
44	2	Yale	1894–96	Princeton	6–24
42	3	Yale	1904–08	Harvard	0–4
39	2	Notre Dame	1946–50	Purdue	14–28
37	1	Oklahoma	1972–75	Kansas	3–23

The Ten Teams with the Most Consensus All-Americans (Current Division I-A)

Team	Selections	Individuals	First Year	Last Year
Notre Dame	90	75	1913	1992
Michigan	65	53	1898	1991
Southern California	57	50	1926	1989
Ohio State	53	38	1916	1987
Oklahoma	52	43	1938	1988
Pittsburgh	46	39	1915	1990
Nebraska	39	32	1915	1992
Army	37	28	1898	1959
Alabama	34	33	1930	1992
Texas	32	28	1945	1984

The Ten Teams with the Most Academic All-Americans (Current Division I-A)

Team	Selections	Individuals	First Year	Last Year
Nebraska	42	35	1962	1992
Notre Dame	34	29	1952	1992
Ohio State	26	22	1952	1992
Texas	20	14	1959	1992
Oklahoma	19	16	1952	1988
Penn State	19	16	1952	1986
Southern California	19	15	1965	1986
Michigan	18	16	1952	1989
Stanford	18	15	1970	1991
Air Force	17	14	1958	1992

Top 10 Single-Season Team Total Offense Averages (Per Game)[a]

Team	Year	Yards per Game
Houston	1989	624.9
Houston	1990	586.8
Brigham Young	1983	584.2
Oklahoma	1971	566.5
Arizona State	1973	565.5

[a]Since 1937, national leaders only.

(continued)

TOP-10 TEAM AND INDIVIDUAL STATISTICS, AND MISCELLANEOUS RECORDS *(continued)*

Top 10 Single-Season Team Total Offense Averages (Per Game)[a] *(continued)*

Team	Year	Yards per Game
Houston	1968	562.0
Fresno State	1991	541.9
Brigham Young	1980	535.0
San Diego State	1969	532.2
Utah	1988	526.8

Top 10 Single-Season Team Passing Averages (Per Game)[a]

Team	Year	Yards per Game
Houston	1989	511.3
Houston	1990	473.9
Brigham Young	1980	409.8
Houston	1992	407.1
Utah	1988	395.9
Brigham Young	1983	381.2
San Diego State	1969	374.2
Houston	1991	372.8
Brigham Young	1979	368.3
Brigham Young	1981	356.9

Top 10 Single-Season Team Rushing Averages (Per Game)[a]

Team	Year	Yards per Game
Oklahoma	1971	472.4
Oklahoma	1974	438.8
Oklahoma	1987	428.8
Oklahoma	1978	427.5
Oklahoma	1986	404.7
Nebraska	1983	401.7
UCLA	1973	400.3
Nebraska	1982	394.3
Oklahoma	1956	391.0
Nebraska	1988	382.3

Top 10 Single-Season Team Scoring Averages (Per Game)[a]

Team	Year	Points per Game
Army	1944	56.0
Houston	1989	53.5
Nebraska	1983	52.0
Oklahoma State	1988	47.5

[a]Since 1937, national leaders only.

(continued)

TOP-10 TEAM AND INDIVIDUAL STATISTICS, AND MISCELLANEOUS RECORDS *(continued)*

Top 10 Single-Season Team Scoring Averages (Per Game)[a] *(continued)*

Team	Year	Points per Game
Brigham Young	1980	46.7
Arizona State	1972	46.6
Oklahoma	1956	46.6
Houston	1990	46.5
San Diego State	1969	46.4
Army	1945	45.8

Top 10 Single-Season Total Defense Averages (Per Game)[a]

Team	Year	Yards per Game
Santa Clara	1937	69.9
Texas A&M	1939	76.3
Penn State	1947	76.8
Alabama	1938	77.9
Navy	1940	96.0
Syracuse	1959	96.2
Virginia	1944	96.8
Alabama	1945	109.9
Duquesne	1941	110.6
Texas	1942	117.3

Top 10 Single-Season Team Rushing Defense Averages (Per Game)[a]

Team	Year	Yards per Game
Penn State	1947	17.0
Syracuse	1959	19.3
Santa Clara	1937	25.3
Alabama	1945	33.9
Wyoming	1966	38.5
Louisiana State	1969	38.9
Duke	1943	39.4
Texas A&M	1939	41.5
Wyoming	1967	42.3
Oklahoma	1938	43.3

Top 10 Single-Season Team Pass Defense Averages (Per Game)[a]

Team	Year	Yards per Game
Penn State	1938	13.1
Michigan State	1944	26.7

[a]Since 1937, national leaders only.

(continued)

TOP-10 TEAM AND INDIVIDUAL STATISTICS, AND MISCELLANEOUS RECORDS (continued)

Top 10 Single-Season Team Pass Defense Averages (Per Game)[a] (continued)

Team	Year	Yards per Game
Purdue	1941	27.1
Iowa State	1960	30.2
Harvard	1937	31.0
Harvard	1940	33.3
Georgia Tech	1957	33.4
Kansas	1939	34.1
North Carolina	1943	36.5
Holy Cross	1945	37.7

Top 10 Single-Season Team Scoring Defense Averages (Per Game)[a]

Team	Year	Points per Game
Tennessee	1939	0.0
Duke	1938	0.0
Santa Clara	1937	1.1
Mississippi	1959	2.1
Alabama	1961	2.2
Tennessee	1940	2.6
Notre Dame	1946	2.7
Auburn	1957	2.8
Duquesne	1941	2.9
Penn State	1947	3.0

[a]Since 1937, national leaders only.

Ten Most-Played Rivalries (Current Division I-A)[a]

Games	Teams	Began	Won–Lost–Tied
102	Minnesota–Wisconsin	1890	55–39–8
101	Missouri–Kansas	1891	48–44–9
99	Baylor–Texas Christian	1899	46–46–7
99	Nebraska–Kansas	1892	75–21–3
99	Texas–Texas A&M	1894	64–30–5
97	Miami (Ohio)–Cincinnati	1888	53–38–6
97	North Carolina–Virginia	1892	53–40–4[b]
96	Auburn–Georgia	1892	45–44–7
96	Oregon–Oregon State	1894	47–39–10
95	Purdue–Indiana	1891	58–31–6
95	Stanford–California	1892	47–37–11

[a]Teams with most wins are listed first.
[b]Virginia claims 52–41–4 by 1956 forfeit.

TOP-10 TEAM AND INDIVIDUAL STATISTICS, AND MISCELLANEOUS RECORDS *(continued)*

Ten Largest Stadiums (Division I-A Teams)

Team	Stadium	Capacity
Michigan	Michigan	102,000+
UCLA	Rose Bowl[a]	99,563
Penn State	Beaver	93,000
Southern California	Los Angeles Coliseum[a]	92,516
Tennessee	Neyland	91,902
Ohio State	Ohio	91,470
Stanford	Stanford	85,500
Georgia	Sanford	85,434
Auburn	Jordan-Hare	85,214
Florida	Florida Field	83,000

[a]Located off-campus.

Top 10 Coaches' Career-Winning Percentages (Minimum of 10 Years)

Coach	Years	Span	Won–Lost–Tied	Percentage
Knute Rockne	13	1918–30	105–12–5	.881
Frank W. Leahy	13	1939–53	107–13–9	.864
George W. Woodruff	12	1892–1905	142–25–2	.846
Barry Switzer	16	1973–88	157–29–4	.837
Percy D. Haughton	13	1899–1924	96–17–6	.832
Robert R. Neyland	21	1926–52	173–31–12	.829
Fielding H. Yost	29	1897–1926	196–36–12	.828
Bud Wilkinson	17	1947–63	145–29–4	.826
Jock Sutherland	20	1919–38	144–28–14	.812
Robert S. Devaney	16	1957–72	136–30–7	.806

Top 10 Coaches' Total Bowl Victories

Coach	Wins	Won–Lost–Tied in Bowls
Paul "Bear" Bryant	15	15–12–2
Joe Paterno	14	14–8–1
Bobby Bowden	12	12–3–1
Don James	10	10–5
John Vaught	10	10–8
Bobby Dodd	9	9–4
Lou Holtz	9	9–6–2
Johnny Majors	9	9–7
Terry Donahue	8	8–2–1
Barry Switzer	8	8–5
Darrell Royal	8	8–7–1
Vince Dooley	8	8–10–2
Tom Osborne	8	8–12

TOP-10 TEAM AND INDIVIDUAL STATISTICS, AND MISCELLANEOUS RECORDS *(continued)*

Top 10 Coaches' Total Bowl Appearances

Coach	Bowls	Won–Lost–Tied
Paul "Bear" Bryant	29	15–12–2
Joe Paterno	23	14–8–1
Vince Dooley	20	8–10–2
Tom Osborne	20	8–12
John Vaught	18	10–8
Lou Holtz	17	9–6–2
LaVell Edwards	17	5–11–1
Glenn "Bo" Schembechler	17	5–12
Johnny Majors	16	9–7
Darrell Royal	16	8–7–1

Top 10 Single-Season Individual Total Offense (Yards per Game)

Player and Team	Year	Games	Total Yards	Average per Game
David Klingler, Houston	1990	11	5,221[a]	474.6
Andre Ware, Houston	1989	11	4,661	423.7
Ty Detmer, BYU	1990	12	5,022	418.5
Steve Young, BYU	1983	11	4,346	395.1
Scott Mitchell, Utah	1988	11	4,299	390.8
Jim McMahon, BYU	1980	12	4,627	385.6
Ty Detmer, BYU	1989	12	4,433	369.4
Troy Kopp, Pacific	1990	9	3,276	364.0
Jim McMahon, BYU	1981	10	3,458	345.8
Jimmy Klingler, Houston	1992	11	3,768	342.5

[a]All-time record.

Top 10 Single-Season Individual Total Offense (Total Yardage)

Player and Team	Year	Rush	Pass	Total Yards
David Klingler, Houston	1990	81	5,140	5,221
Ty Detmer, BYU	1990	−106	5,188	5,022
Andre Ware, Houston	1989	−38	4,699	4,661
Jim McMahon, BYU	1980	56	4,571	4,627
Ty Detmer, BYU	1989	−127	4,560	4,433
Steve Young, BYU	1983	444	3,902	4,346
Scott Mitchell, Utah	1988	−23	4,322	4,299
Robbie Bosco, BYU	1985	−132	4,273	4,141
Ty Detmer, BYU	1991	−30	4,031	4,001
Robbie Bosco, BYU	1984	57	3,875	3,932

TOP-10 TEAM AND INDIVIDUAL STATISTICS, AND MISCELLANEOUS RECORDS (continued)

Top 10 Single-Season Individual Passing (Yards per Game)

Player and Team	Year	Games	Yards	Yards per Game
David Klingler, Houston	1990	11	5,140	467.3
Ty Detmer, BYU	1990	12	5,188[a]	432.3
Andre Ware, Houston	1989	11	4,699	427.2
Scott Mitchell, Utah	1988	11	4,322	392.9
Jim McMahon, BYU	1980	12	4,571	380.9
Ty Detmer, BYU	1989	12	4,560	380.0
Troy Kopp, Pacific	1990	9	3,311	367.9
Jim McMahon, BYU	1981	10	3,555	355.5
Steve Young, BYU	1983	11	3,902	354.7
Dan McGwire, San Diego St.	1990	11	3,833	348.5

Top 10 Single-Season Individual Passing (Total Yardage)

Player and Team	Year	Games	TDs	Yards
Ty Detmer, BYU	1990	12	41	5,188
David Klingler, Houston	1990	11	54[a]	5,140
Andre Ware, Houston	1989	11	46	4,699
Jim McMahon, BYU	1980	12	47	4,571
Ty Detmer, BYU	1989	12	32	4,560
Scott Mitchell, Utah	1988	11	29	4,322
Robbie Bosco, BYU	1985	13	30	4,273
Ty Detmer, BYU	1991	12	35	4,031
Todd Santos, San Diego St.	1987	12	26	3,932
Steve Young, BYU	1983	11	33	3,902

[a] All-time record.

Top 10 Single-Season Individual Passing Efficiency

Points, Player, Team	Year	Attempts	Completions	Int	Pct	Yards	TDs
176.9 Jim McMahon, BYU	1980	445	284	18	.638	4,571	47
175.6 Ty Detmer, BYU	1989	412	265	15	.643	4,560	32
172.6 Jerry Rhome, Tulsa	1964	326	224	4	.687	2,870	32
169.0 Elvis Grbac, Michigan	1991	228	152	5	.667	1,955	24
168.5 Ty Detmer, BYU	1991	403	249	12	.618	4,031	35
168.5 Steve Young, BYU	1983	429	306	10	.713	3,902	33
165.8 Vinny Testaverde, Miami	1986	276	175	9	.634	2,557	26
165.8 Brian Dowling, Yale	1968	160	92	10	.575	1,554	19
164.3 D. McPherson, Syracuse	1987	229	129	11	.563	2,341	22
164.2 Dave Wilson, Ball St.	1977	177	115	7	.650	1,589	17

TOP-10 TEAM AND INDIVIDUAL STATISTICS, AND MISCELLANEOUS RECORDS (*continued*)

Top 10 Single-Season Individual Pass Receptions (Catches per Game)

Player and Team	Year	Games	Total Receptions	Per Game
Howard Twilley, Tulsa	1965	10	134	13.4
Manny Hazard, Houston	1989	11	142[a]	12.9
Jason Phillips, Houston	1988	11	108	9.8
Fred Gilbert, Houston	1991	11	106	9.6
Jerry Hendren, Idaho	1969	10	95	9.5
Howard Twilley, Tulsa	1964	10	95	9.5
Sherman Smith, Houston	1992	11	103	9.4
James Dixon, Houston	1988	11	102	9.3
David Williams, Illinois	1984	11	101	9.2
Jay Miller, BYU	1973	11	100	9.1

Top 10 Single-Season Individual Pass Receptions (Total Catches)

Player and Team	Year	Games	Yards	TDs	Catches
Manny Hazard, Houston	1989	11	1,689	22[a]	142
Howard Twilley, Tulsa	1965	10	1,779[a]	16	134
Jason Phillips, Houston	1988	11	1,444	15	108
Fred Gilbert, Houston	1991	11	957	7	106
Sherman Smith, Houston	1992	11	923	6	103
James Dixon, Houston	1988	11	1,103	11	102
David Williams, Illinois	1984	11	1,278	8	101
Jay Miller, BYU	1973	11	1,181	8	100
Jason Phillips, Houston	1987	11	875	3	99
Mark Templeton, Long Beach	1986	11	688	2	99

Top 10 Single-Season Individual Rushing (Yards per Game)

Player and Team	Year	Games	Total Yards	Per Game
Barry Sanders, Oklahoma St.	1988	11	2,628[a]	232.1
Marcus Allen, USC	1981	11	2,342	212.9
Ed Marinaro, Cornell	1971	9	1,881	209.0
Charles White, USC	1979	10	1,803	180.3
Mike Rozier, Nebraska	1983	12	2,148	179.0
Tony Dorsett, Pittsburgh	1976	11	1,948	177.1
Ollie Matson, San Francisco	1951	9	1,566	174.0
Lorenzo White, Michigan St.	1985	11	1,908	173.5
Herschel Walker, Georgia	1981	11	1,891	171.9
O.J. Simpson, USC	1968	10	1,709	170.9

[a]All-time record.

TOP-10 TEAM AND INDIVIDUAL STATISTICS, AND MISCELLANEOUS RECORDS *(continued)*

Top 10 Single-Season Individual Rushing (Total Yardage)

Player and Team	Year	Games	TDs	Yards
Barry Sanders, Oklahoma St.	1988	11	37[a]	2,628
Marcus Allen, USC	1981	11	22	2,342
Mike Rozier, Nebraska	1983	12	29	2,148
Tony Dorsett, Pittsburgh	1976	11	21	1,948
Lorenzo White, Michigan St.	1985	11	17	1,908
Herschel Walker, Georgia	1981	11	18	1,891
Ed Marinaro, Cornell	1971	9	20	1,881
Ernest Anderson, Oklahoma St.	1982	11	8	1,877
Ricky Bell, USC	1975	11	13	1,875
Paul Palmer, Temple	1986	11	15	1,866

Top 10 Single-Season Individual All-Purpose Total Yardage

Player and Team	Year	Rush	Receptions	Punt Returns	Kickoff Returns	Yards
Barry Sanders, Oklahoma St.	1988	2,628	106	95	421	3,250
Ryan Benjamin, Pacific	1991	1,581	612	4	798	2,995
Mike Pringle, Fullerton St.	1989	1,727	249	0	714	2,690
Paul Palmer, Temple	1986	1,866	110	0	657	2,633
Ryan Benjamin, Pacific	1992	1,441	434	96	626	2,597
Marcus Allen, USC	1981	2,342	217	0	0	2,559
Sheldon Canley, San Jose St.	1989	1,201	353	0	959	2,513
Mike Rozier, Nebraska	1983	2,148	106	0	232	2,486
Chuck Weatherspoon, Houston	1989	1,146	735	415	95	2,391
Anthony Thompson, Indiana	1989	1,793	201	0	394	2,388

Top 10 Single-Season Individual All-Purpose Yards per Game

Player and Team	Year	Games	Total Yards	Per Game
Barry Sanders, Oklahoma St.	1988	11	3,250[a]	295.5
Ryan Benjamin, Pacific	1991	12	2,995	249.6
Byron White, Colorado	1937	8	1,970	246.3
Mike Pringle, Fullerton St.	1989	11	2,690	244.6
Paul Palmer, Temple	1986	11	2,633	239.4
Ryan Benjamin, Pacific	1992	11	2,597	236.1
Marcus Allen, USC	1981	11	2,559	232.6
Sheldon Canley, San Jose St.	1989	11	2,513	228.5
Ollie Matson, San Francisco	1951	9	2,037	226.3
Art Luppino, Arizona	1954	10	2,193	219.3

[a]All-time record.

TOP-10 TEAM AND INDIVIDUAL STATISTICS, AND MISCELLANEOUS RECORDS (*continued*)

Top 8 Single-Season Individual Scoring Totals

Player and Team	Year	TDs	Extra Points	Total Points
Barry Sanders, Oklahoma St.	1988	39[a]	0	234
Mike Rozier, Nebraska	1983	29	0	174
Lydell Mitchell, Penn St.	1971	29	0	174
Art Luppino, Arizona	1954	24	22	166
Bobby Reynolds, Nebraska	1950	22	25	157
Anthony Thompson, Indiana	1989	25	4	154
Fred Wendt, Texas–El Paso	1948	20	32	152
Pete Johnson, Ohio State	1975	25	0	150

Top 10 Single-Season Individual Field Goal Totals

Player and Team	Year	Percentage	Total/Attempts
John Lee, UCLA	1984	.879	29/33
Paul Woodside, West Virginia	1982	.903	28/31
Luis Zendejas, Arizona State	1983	.757	28/37
Fuad Reveiz, Tennessee	1982	.871	27/31
Chuck Nelson, Washington	1982	.962[a]	25/26
Chris Jacke, Texas–El Paso	1988	.926	25/27
John Diettrich, Ball State	1985	.862	25/29
Kendall Trainor, Arkansas	1988	.889	24/27
Carlos Reveiz, Tennessee	1985	.857	24/28
Chris White, Illinois	1984	.857	24/28

Top 10 Single-Season Individual Pass Interception Totals

Player and Team	Year	Yards Returned	Pass Interceptions
Al Worley, Washington	1968	130	14
George Shaw, Oregon	1951	136	13
Terrell Buckley, Florida St.	1991	238	12
Cornelius Price, Houston	1989	187	12
Bob Navarro, Eastern Michigan	1989	73	12
Tony Thurman, Boston College	1984	99	12
Terry Hoage, Georgia	1982	51	12
Frank Polito, Villanova	1971	261	12
Bill Albrecht, Washington	1951	140	12
Hank Rich, Arizona State	1950	135	12

Top 6 Single-Season Individual Punt Return Averages

Player and Team	Year	Number	Yards	Average
Bill Blackstock, Tennessee	1951	12	311	25.9
George Sims, Baylor	1948	15	375	25.0

[a]All-time record.

(*continued*)

TOP-10 TEAM AND INDIVIDUAL STATISTICS, AND MISCELLANEOUS RECORDS *(continued)*

Top 6 Single-Season Individual Punt Return Averages *(continued)*

Player and Team	Year	Number	Yards	Average
Gene Derricotte, Michigan	1947	14	347	24.8
Erroll Tucker, Utah	1985	16	389	24.3
George Hoey, Michigan	1967	12	291	24.3
Floyd Little, Syracuse	1965	18	423	23.5

Top 5 Single-Season Individual Kickoff Return Averages

Player and Team	Year	Number	Yards	Average
Paul Allen, BYU	1961	12	481	40.1
Forrest Hall, San Francisco	1946	15	573	38.2
Tony Ball, UT-Chattanooga	1977	13	473	36.4
George Marinkov, N.C. State	1954	13	465	35.8
Bob Baker, Cornell	1964	11	386	35.1

Top 10 Single-Season Individual Punting Averages

Player and Team	Year	Punts	Average
Reggie Roby, Iowa	1981	44	49.8
Kirk Wilson, UCLA	1956	30	49.3
Ricky Anderson, Vanderbilt	1984	58	48.2
Zack Jordan, Colorado	1950	38	48.2
Reggie Roby, Iowa	1982	52	48.1
Marv Bateman, Utah	1971	68	48.1
Owen Price, Texas–El Paso	1940	30	48.0
Jack Jacobs, Oklahoma	1940	31	47.8
Bill Smith, Mississippi	1984	44	47.7
Ed Bunn, Texas–El Paso	1992	41	47.7

PHOTO CREDITS